A TEXT-BOOK OF ROMAN LAW FROM AUGUSTUS TO JUSTINIAN

A TEXT-BOOK OF ROMAN LAW FROM AUGUSTUS TO JUSTINIAN

BY

the late W. W. BUCKLAND, LL.D., F.B.A.

sometime Regius Professor of Civil Law in the University of Cambridge

THIRD EDITION

revised by

PETER STEIN

Professor of Jurisprudence in the University of Aberdeen

CAMBRIDGE

AT THE UNIVERSITY PRESS

1963

CAMBRIDGE UNIVERSITY PRESS
Cambridge, New York, Melbourne, Madrid, Cape Town, Singapore, São Paulo

Cambridge University Press
The Edinburgh Building, Cambridge CB2 8RU, UK

Published in the United States of America by Cambridge University Press, New York

www.cambridge.org
Information on this title: www.cambridge.org/9780521043601

First published 1921
Second edition 1932
Third edition 1963
This digitally printed version 2007

A catalogue record for this publication is available from the British Library

ISBN 978-0-521-04360-1 hardback
ISBN 978-0-521-04368-7 paperback

FOREWORD TO THIRD EDITION

Professor Buckland died in 1946. The Text-book was published in 1921, the second edition in 1932; and from then till his death he went on writing articles (listed in the Bibliography on page xxvii) and annotating an interleaved copy of the Text-book. It was thus possible to discover Buckland's latest opinion on all matters, and the present edition is intended in the main to represent Buckland's own views.

When the book went out of print a few years ago, without being replaced by any work of comparable scope and authority, the Syndics of the Press considered whether to re-print it without change, to let it die, or to have it thoroughly revised so as to be essentially a new book. In the end they decided to re-publish it with the 1932 pagination unchanged and with only such revision as seemed strictly necessary; and Professor Stein accepted their invitation to undertake that task. He has incorporated Buckland's later views partly by changes in the text and footnotes and partly by writing the longer notes which have replaced blank spaces on pages 232, 364, 404, 526 (in text), 673 and 718. Section CCX on pages 616–18, dealing with *iudicis postulatio* and *condictio*, has been completely rewritten, but at exactly the same length. He has also written the two Notes on pages xvii and xxiii to indicate the main developments in the study of Roman Law since the publication of the second edition. I have read what he has written and made some suggestions, but the revision is his.

P. W. DUFF
Regius Professor of Civil Law
in the University of Cambridge

CONTENTS

PREFACE TO FIRST EDITION

THE following pages contain an attempt to state the main rules of the Private Law of the Roman Empire for the use of students, and the chief purpose of the writer has been to set out the established or accepted doctrines. This consideration may be held to justify the arrangement of the book. Much criticism, often well founded, has been directed at the arrangement adopted by Gaius and followed by Justinian in his *Institutes*, and many modern treatises adopt arrangements differing from it in important respects. But these arrangements differ so widely among themselves that it may fairly be assumed that none of them has such overwhelming advantages as to make it desirable for the present purpose to adopt it, in view of the fact that the texts to which the student is directed adopt a different order. The general plan of the book therefore follows the Institutional arrangement, though with no hesitation in abandoning it where this course seems to tend to lucidity of exposition. In truth no order of treatment can be quite satisfactory. The study of any branch of the law calls for some knowledge of ideas which are to be looked for in other branches. The law of Persons suffers least from this source of difficulty and can therefore conveniently be studied first. But it is not quite free from it: in particular, ideas connected with civil procedure are frequently involved. This is the case throughout the law: in all systems, the remedy is the root of the matter. Rules of Law do not enforce themselves, and a general idea of the system of remedies, of the steps to be taken if a right is infringed, of the broad distinctions between the different remedies for infringement of different kinds of right, and of the nature of the relief which can be obtained, will be found greatly to facilitate the study of the substantive law. A very brief account of these matters has been prefixed[1] to the detailed account of the law of procedure, and the student is advised to familiarise himself with this, before beginning his systematic study of the book.

The subject treated is the law of the Empire—what is called the classical law—with later developments, including the legislation of Justinian. But the system elaborated by Labeo and his successors has its roots in the past and is scarcely intelligible without some knowledge

1 *Post* §§ CCVI, CCVII.

of the earlier institutions on which it is based. These earlier institutions are therefore taken into account, but are dealt with only in outline and only in so far as knowledge of them seems to be essential to the main purpose of the book.

The great constitutional changes which marked the foundation of the Empire would not of themselves justify the adoption of that event as the starting-point for a statement of the Private Law, but there are other reasons for choosing this or perhaps the slightly earlier age of Cicero. His writings give us the earliest contemporary account, from a more or less legal point of view, of the system of Private Law. The conquest of Greece was somewhat older, but the influence of Greek ideas on Roman institutions was only now becoming important. The first idea which this allusion brings to mind is the *Ius Naturale.* It is borrowed from Greek philosophy, but it does not appear that the expression was in use among the lawyers till the time of Augustus. The expression *ius civile* was in use, but in republican times it meant merely the unwritten part of the law, the "common law" as opposed to that which had been expressly enacted. The expression *ius gentium* is as old as Cicero, but we do not know that it is older, and there is no evidence that it was as yet used by lawyers to mark a sharp contrast with another system known as the *ius civile.* The contrast of *ius civile, ius gentium, ius naturale* belongs to the Empire. There is no trace of the conception of *obligatio naturalis* among the lawyers of the Republic. But this new traffic in ideas is only one indication of the rapid evolution of legal notions which was now beginning. The complex law of manumission described by Gaius is a very different matter from the simple system of the Republic. Most of the family law is indeed more ancient, but while the main framework of the Law of Property, even Equitable Ownership, is republican, many parts of it (some of which seem to us indispensable) were unknown to the Republic. Praedial servitudes were few in number, and the personal servitudes, though some of them were extant, were not thought of as servitudes: it is not quite clear how they were thought of, or indeed whether they were "servitudes" till a much later date. There was no such thing as acquisition of property by agent. In the law of succession the praetorian changes had as yet gone a very little way towards rationalisation of the system except so far as actual descendants of a man were concerned. It was the early Imperial law which gave something like due weight to the claims of a mother and invested the praetorian will with real efficiency. The early history of the "real" and "consensual" contracts is not certainly known, but it is not probable that any of them were recognised very long before Cicero. The use of *stipulatio* as a general form into which any undertaking might be cast may perhaps be little older than the Empire, and it is at least possible that *mutuum*, unsupported by either *nexum* or *stipulatio*, is unknown as a contract to the earlier law. Most of the elaborate classification of actions which plays so large a part in the later juristic writings was the work of lawyers of the Empire.

These are changes in the broad institutions of the law, but still more important is the new scientific spirit. Constructive activity on the part of the lawyers was no new thing. Gallus Aquilius, who added so much to the law in the time of Cicero, had no doubt predecessors who inspired a great part of the Edict, but there is no mistaking the new creative impulse which appears with him and Quintus Mucius, and Servius Sulpicius, perhaps the most important of the three, all contemporaries of Cicero. Nearly all the subtle distinctions and refinements of the law, corresponding to the "case law" of our system, are the work of the classical jurists, the earliest of whom were trained by these men. That these refinements were introduced was not a misfortune: it was a necessity. That the introduction occurred then was not an accident: it was inevitable. Rome was now the capital of the civilised world, the chief market for all commodities, including brains. Her conquests and the peace she had imposed on the world led to a great increase of commerce of which she was the centre. The infinitely varying relations of trade created innumerable questions which demanded solutions, and the demand created the supply. From every quarter of the State men of ability gravitated to Rome, and the legal profession, then, as always, an avenue to political life, and having the additional advantage that it was the only career which still preserved its independence, naturally attracted a large proportion of them, many of them, perhaps the majority of the most famous, coming from the remoter parts of the Empire. The system elaborated by these men and modified by their successors is the primary subject of the book.

The subject is the Law, not the history of the Law. But between Labeo and Tribonian there elapsed more than 500 years, and throughout this long period the law was changing, sometimes rapidly, sometimes slowly, but always changing. Any attempt to state the law as a complete single system without reference to its changes would give a misleading result, and if this were remedied by historical footnotes there is some danger that the book would be unreadable. The method adopted therefore is that of a narrative treatment, in which, while the system, as a system, is kept in view and forms the main framework of the book, the historical development is also kept in view and the perspective distorted as little as possible. Further, the subject is the Private Law and little is said of such institutions as the Colonate and the privileged and

State-controlled trade corporations of later law[1], of which, important as they were in practice, the chief interest is social and political.

There are certain fundamental notions which find their application in nearly all branches of the law, and which, for this reason, it is frequently found convenient to treat once for all at the beginning of the discussion. The field of these notions is indeed differently conceived by different writers, but among typical matters may be mentioned the effect of mistake, fraud, duress or impossibility on legal transactions, the law of conditions, and of representation, the basis of legal obligation and so forth. But, apart from the fact that many of these notions cannot well be understood without some knowledge of the institutions to which they can be applied, there is in Roman Law the further serious difficulty that they are not handled in a uniform manner in different branches of the law. The treatment of conditions is not the same in the Law of Contract and in that of Wills. Even in the same branch of the Law there are often two systems to be considered. The effect of mistake or fraud is not the same in relation to Formal Transfers of Property and in transfer by delivery, *traditio*. It is not the same in *iure civili* contracts and in those *iure gentium*. The attempt to treat the law of representation once for all is likely to lead to a cumbersome result, partly because there was much change and partly because the change proceeded at different speeds, by different methods, and to different lengths in different branches of the law. The general result is that brevity, which is the main advantage to be derived from this mode of treatment, is not really attained in the discussion of classical law, though it may be in treatises on "Pandektenrecht," from which the formal and *iure civili* elements of the Roman Law have disappeared, and the various evolutions are more or less complete. There is therefore no attempt at this mode of treatment in the following pages.

On many points in the law, especially on its historical development, there is much controversy. It has seemed undesirable, on the one hand, to confuse the student by over much insistence on these doubtful points, or, on the other, to leave him in the belief that matters are clear and settled which are in fact obscure or disputed. There will therefore be found many references to controverted questions, but discussion of them is brief and, for the most part, relegated to the footnotes.

The question of the proper amount of detail has been found difficult. To a writer on a subject of which the principles are well known and settled, such as the English Law of Contract, the matter is easily dealt

1 An excellent account of both these matters can be seen in Cornil, *Droit Romain, Aperçu historique*, pp. 506–519, a work which was not available till the greater part of this book was in print.

with. Such details are selected as seem to the writer to illustrate the principle under discussion, and the reader is sent, for further information, to the Law Reports and the practitioners' textbooks. But the principles of the classical Roman Law are not known in the same way. Much, no doubt, is known, but scarcely a year passes without some new elucidation of principle, some new point which compels reconsideration of a hitherto accepted notion, and the starting-point in such cases is not unfrequently some point of detail which had been regarded as quite insignificant. In stating the common law for the student we start from the principle and illustrate by detail, while there are many parts of the Roman Law in which it is not too much to say that we have not really passed the stage of arriving at the principle by the study of detail. There is always a danger of imposing on the reader for Roman Law what is really a modern conception and for classical law what is Byzantine. It is difficult to say beforehand what detail may prove illuminating, and the state of the study seems to justify a rather freer use of detail than would be necessary or convenient in a treatise on English Law. But here too it has been possible to rely to a considerable extent on footnotes.

Propositions of private law will be found to be, in general, supported by references to the original texts, but in the Chapter on the "Sources of the Law," since many of the rules stated are inferences from a large number of documents, this was hardly practicable and thus reference is frequently made only to authoritative modern writers. But the rest of the book also is, as such a book must be, largely indebted to earlier writers. Due acknowledgement is made in the footnotes, but more than this is necessary in the case of the well-known "Manuel" of M. Girard. It is impossible to estimate what the writer owes to this book, which he has kept within reach for twenty years.

The book is also indebted to many friends of the writer, in particular to Professor F. de Zulueta, of Oxford, who has read most of the proofs, and to the Master of Trinity Hall, who has seen several parts of the book in manuscript, for countless hints and necessary corrections. Of the helpfulness and care of the Secretary and Staff of the Cambridge University Press, it is hardly necessary to speak: this is so much a matter of course.

W. W. B.

18 *July* 1921

PREFACE TO SECOND EDITION

No change has been made in the plan of the book. Errors and false references have been corrected where observed, and in some cases the new text reflects a change of opinion. Many paragraphs have been added and the attention of the student has been here and there directed to the literature on some historical and theoretical questions not dealt with in the first edition[1]. But there is still no "General Part." The plain fact is that the Roman Law had no such thing, not merely in the sense that the jurists never formulated it but in the sense that, as was noted in the preface to the first edition, the treatment of fundamental points differed in different branches of the law and was not the same in praetorian and civil law. If, indeed, we force a "general part" on Roman Law, we must, for the period covered by this book, provide at least three. The theoretical outlook of the Institutes of Gaius, which seems to be that of the first century, is very different from that of Paul or Ulpian, which differs profoundly from that of Tribonian. It is at least doubtful whether the theoretical matters which must be the chief element in a "general part" can be understood until the reader knows something about the law. In Bonfante's monumental *Corso*, the "general part" is to come at the end of the volumes on substantive law, a fact from which it seems that certain relevant inferences can be drawn. Is the writer a solitary heretic in believing that for the pedestrian purpose of understanding the Roman Law, the "Allgemeiner Teil" with its all-pervading "Willenstheorie" is the least serviceable part of Windscheid's great work? A "general part" almost inevitably contains a legal philosophy. So far as it does not, the rules which it states are, for Roman Law, most conveniently handled in the body of the work. So far as it does contain such a philosophy, it is not too much to say that this is not usually Roman. If it is not Roman, it is, for the purpose of explaining the Roman Law, worse than useless. The purpose of a legal theory is, apart from considerations *de lege ferenda*, to enable one to draw inferences from a recorded rule for analogous cases. To apply non-Roman theory is, inevitably, to draw false inferences: it does not fertilise the text—it sterilises it. This is not

1 The *chief* changes and additions will be found on the following pages of this edition: pp. 44, 55, 98, 102 *sqq.*, 169, 173, 180, 197, 201, 204, 207, 209, 229 *sq.*, 266, 268, 282, 295 *sq.*, 307, 319, 339, 341, 350, 406 *sq.*, 409, 412, 421, 424, 436, 451, 481, 492 *sqq.*, 528 *sq.*, 532, 537, 554 *sq.*, 564, 596, 600, 628 *sq.*, 643, 653 *sq.*, 665 *sqq.*, 674 *sq.*, 697 *sq.*, 706 *sq.*, 716 *sq.*

to say that modern analysis is not of the greatest value or to deny that Roman texts provide material to which it can usefully be applied: it means only that it seems out of place in a book which seeks to state the Roman Law as the Romans saw it.

It is perhaps less easy to defend the continued absence of Comparative Law from the book. It seemed however to the writer that any adequate treatment of Hellenistic and remoter material would call for more space than was available and that little purpose would be served by mere references to papyrological literature. But this consideration does not stand alone. When we find an institution in Greek Law, and, a little later, in Roman Law, it is easy to infer borrowing. But, to take an example, hypothec, proclaimed 50 years ago to be borrowed from Greece, is now held to be indigenous, and it is the writer's belief that a similar fate awaits some borrowings more recently proclaimed. And even where the borrowing may be held certain, it is very difficult to say when it occurred. The fashionable view seems to be (though protests are not wanting) that what is Greek either in rule or in grammar is Byzantine, though there was the closest intercourse with Greek and Hellenised communities from long before the Empire, and the lay literature of the age in which the great jurists wrote is full of graecisms. Comparative Law has shed much light on Roman legal history, and, here and there, some darkness. To have discussed these matters would have given the book a controversial character, out of keeping with its main purpose.

The first edition was published at a time when foreign books were, and had long been, hard to come by. Some references have therefore been added to books which were not then available, owing to the conditions, and many references have been added to more recent works. But there is no attempt at a bibliography. The aim has been to put the reader on the track of the literature, not to specify it in detail. Even this modest aim has certainly not been wholly achieved: for such gaps as exist the writer can only apologise.

W. W. B.

March 1931

SOME RECENT TRENDS IN ROMAN LAW STUDIES

In the last 25 years much new light has been thrown on the actual practice of the law, which has been shewn to differ considerably from the theoretical law found in the writings of the jurists. Through the business documents and court records evidenced by the Egyptian papyri a new and better understanding has been obtained of the law in action[1]. Sometimes, however, it is difficult to decide whether a document relates to Roman Law or to local Egyptian or Greek Law. Leopold Wenger has popularised the notion of a general legal history of the Ancient World (*antike Rechtsgeschichte*), according to which the development of Roman Law is better understood in the context of the history of the legal systems of the Mediterranean basin than in isolation. Papyrologists who follow Wenger have accordingly studied not only the Greek and Latin papyri but also the Coptic, Demotic (native Egyptian), and Aramaic documents. It is not suggested that one system influenced another but rather that similar problems tend to be tackled in similar ways even in systems which are independent of each other. Helpful analogies for Roman Law can frequently be derived from the course of development taken by other legal systems where the community in question had reached a similar stage of development to the Roman. The comparative approach is more valuable for early Roman Law than for classical law, and particularly in such matters as family law[2].

The papyri have been of more particular assistance in furthering our understanding of the *Corpus Iuris* itself[3]. Sometimes they furnish a text from a classical writer which is also reproduced in an interpolated form in the Digest. When this happens it is possible to fix the extent of the interpolation with considerable certainty. These discoveries have provided a valuable control against some of the excesses of the hunt for interpolations. Thus the discovery of the Oxyrhynchus and Antinoite fragments of

1 R. Taubenschlag, *The Law of Greco-Roman Egypt in the Light of the Papyri*, 2nd ed., 1955. 2 For a recent example of the technique, R. Yaron, Minutiae on Roman Divorce, *Tijdschrift*, 1960, 1. 3 E. Seidl, Papyrologie und Interpolationenkritik an den Digesten, *Annales Universitatis Saraviensis, Phil-let.* 1959, 21, from which the examples in the text are taken.

Gaius, as Buckland[1] pointed out with some satisfaction, went some way to vindicating the authority of the Veronese MS. of Gaius which had recently been strongly attacked.

A recent example is PSI 1449, actually a small fragment of parchment containing an entirely new text of D. 19. 2. 13. 4. This fragment shows that some of the previous assumptions of interpolations in the Digest text were quite unjustified[2].

The mere discovery of a fragment dating from the fourth or fifth century containing a text in the same terms as the corresponding Digest text is, however, no proof that the text gives us the classical jurist's original words. It may have been subjected to pre-Justinianian interpolation. In the last two decades the interest of Romanists has shifted from the discovery of interpolations attributable to Justinian's compilers to the observation of pre-Justinianian interpolations made by unknown scholars of the middle period from the latter part of the third century to the beginning of the sixth. D. 12. 1. 1. 1 was generally considered to have been interpolated by the compilers. A papyrus fragment[3] from the fourth century, P. Ryl. III. 474, reproduced the text in substantially the same words as it appeared in the Digest. It could not therefore have been interpolated by the compilers. Instead of the text being attributed to Ulpian, responsibility for the interpolation was attributed to early post-classical commentators[4]. Buckland[5] pointed out that for these pre-Justinianian glosses to have been incorporated into the text they must have been written in Latin, and therefore probably have had a Western origin. He considered that they were less numerous than is currently supposed. "Many passages which are taken for glosses by reason of their doctrine or their Latinity or their structure may well be badly executed shortenings by the compilers."

Even where there is no direct comparison of texts, the papyri can confirm or contradict the validity of a hypothetical interpolation. Thus a contract may be drafted or a decision may be given in a way that is compatible only with a particular state of the law. For example, one of the recently published Apokrimata[6], decisions of the Emperor Septimius Severus, given in answer to petitions submitted to him by private individuals during his visit to Egypt in the winter of A.D. 199–200, throws

1 Reflections suggested by the new fragments of Gaius, *Juridical Rev.*, 1936, 339. The fragments are P. Oxy. xvii, 2103 (ed. A. S. Hunt) and PSI, xi, 1182 (reed. V. Arangio-Ruiz in *B.I.D.R.* 1935, 571).

2 Arangio-Ruiz, *Arch. Giur.* 1957, 140.

3 Identified by Buckland, de Zulueta, *Studi Besta*, 1. 139.

4 F. Schulz, *Z.S.S.* 1951, 1. *contra* Stroux in *Miscellanea Academica Berolinensia*, II, 1950, 1.

5 *Juridical Rev.*, 1936, 344.

6 P. Col. 123, edd. W. Westermann and A. A. Schiller, 1954, rev. Stein, *Am. Jo. Comp. Law*, 1956, 686–90.

considerable doubt[1] on the suggested interpolation of D. 16. 1. 28. 1, while another of these decisions suggests that the notion of *diligentia quam in suis rebus*, which had been attacked as post-classical, was known to Septimius[2]. The collection of Apokrimata contains the imperial rescripts but not the original petitions to which they refer, and there is much dispute as to the purpose of the collection. The absence of the facts of the cases decided suggests that this particular collection was not a form of law report, but other papyri do provide evidence that it was the practice in Egypt to cite decided cases as authority in the courts, and that judgements were sometimes based on such authority[3]. This practice was made possible by the use of collections of decisions. There was no rigid system of precedent, but case law had its place as an independent source of law. Although the evidence is confined to Egypt, it does not appear that the practice of citing decided cases was confined to that province.

The papyri throw light mainly on the law of the Eastern Empire. In recent years much attention has been given to the post-classical law of the Western Empire, for which E. Levy has popularised the term "Vulgar Law", an expression invented by H. Brunner in 1880. In a series of studies[4] Levy pointed out that between Diocletian and Justinian the Western Empire suffered not only political changes but also economic, social, cultural and religious changes, which would all require considerable modification of the law in practice if it was to fit the new conditions. Vulgar Law is essentially the law of practice[5]. Its rules were not introduced by imperial legislation. They were not the fruit of jurisprudence, for there was no longer any juristic activity worthy of the name. Nor again were they peregrine law received from a non-Roman source. Vulgar Law was "degenerate Roman law". The standard of legal scholarship was so low that the ordinary practitioner could not understand the abstract concepts and subtle distinctions of classical law, and in practice he abandoned them in favour of simpler and less technical rules more adapted to the conditions of the times. Levy himself conceives of Vulgar Law as a complex of rules with a particular character. But many critics who accept his detailed results regard this concept as too rigid and abstract; they prefer to talk of vulgar tendencies. Vulgar elements become law by being incorporated into other sources. The main sources for the study of Vulgar Law have been the *Interpretationes* to the Gregorian, Hermogenian and Theodosian Codes and of Paul's Sentences, which

1 Pringsheim, *EOS* (Symbolae Taubenschlag I), 1956, 243. 2 Seidl, *op. cit.* 26.
3 H. F. Jolowicz, Case Law in Ancient Egypt, *J. Soc. Pub. Teach. Law*, 1937. 4 *West Roman Vulgar Law, The Law of Property*, 1951; rev. A. H. Campbell, *J.R.S.* 1953, 179–81. *Weströmisches Vulgarrecht, Das Obligationenrecht*, 1956; rev. D. Daube, *J.R.S.* 1958, 196–7.
5 M. Kaser, *Das römische Privatrecht*, II, 1959, 13–18 and *passim*.

were incorporated into the Breviary of Alaric and the Roman portions of the other Barbarian Codes. Certain Imperial Constitutions reject rules of Vulgar Law which had found their way into practice, but sometimes the Constitutions themselves use the terminology of Vulgar Law and betray its influence, so that to a limited extent they may be used as sources. The Digest is of little use for the study of Vulgar Law: its compilation was the fruit of a revival in the academic study of law in the East which had no parallel in the West. It represents a deliberate classicising policy on the part of Justinian, who sought to restore the classical law to its pristine beauty. In any case, the Digest was scarcely applied at all in the West except during Justinian's temporary reoccupation of Italy in the middle of the sixth century.

Both in the field of property and of obligations, substantial differences have been observed between classical law and Vulgar Law. For example, the clear classical notion of *dominium*, as a positive mastery over the thing quite distinct from possession and having its own remedy, disappeared in the post-classical period. Various kinds of limited *dominium* unknown in classical law were recognised. Usufruct was treated as a form of *dominium* which was eventually regarded as the best right to possession. There was no longer any distinction between the owner's and the possessor's remedies.

The distinction between contract and conveyance also disappeared[1]; sale became a cash transaction in which payment of the price was essential, and *traditio* of the object sold normally accompanied payment. As sale gradually took on the characteristics of barter, the buyer lost some of his protection against defects. Aedilician remedies seem to have been retained only in so far as they related to slaves, in contrast with their extension in the Eastern Empire.

In classical law obligation and action were very closely associated; the classical lawyer regarded a legal situation from the point of view of the form of action available. When the formulary procedure was abandoned and replaced by the *cognitio* procedure, matters were viewed more from the standpoint of substantive law alone. The secondary distinction between various forms of action also disappeared.

Although it retained little of the subtlety and juristic interest of the classical law, the Vulgar Law was not entirely lacking in originality and progressive ideas. Forms were simpler; there was general enforceability of undertakings; oral contracts were replaced by written contracts; representation was admitted where authorisation had been given or could be presumed, and assignment of obligation was easier.

1 F. Gallo, *Il principio Emptione Dominium Transfertur nel diritto pregiustinianeo*, 1960.

Buckland discussed the sources of Vulgar Law in two articles[1] towards the end of his life in which he anticipated some of Levy's detailed conclusions. He concludes that the interpreter of Paul's Sentences "was a very ignorant man, and since he must have been well thought of, or his work would hardly have been preserved, we must suppose that he was one of the best men available. That means a tremendous decline in the level of knowledge and skill, and such decline postulates a great gap in time—*nemo repente stultissimus.*" Thus where the text shows that a *mandator credendae pecuniae* is not released by an action brought against the principal debtor, the interpreter confused this with the rule that if a *procurator litis* is condemned, the *actio iudicati* goes against the principal. He also betrays his ignorance of the nature of *bonae fidei iudicium.* He does not know what *custodia* and *diligentia* mean and therefore omits the reference to them. Buckland asks what those who contend that *diligentia* as a measure of liability is a post-classical notion make of this fact.

1 The *Interpretationes* to *Pauli Sententiae* and the *Codex Theodosianus*, *L.Q.R.* 1944, 361–5. *Pauli Sententiae* and the Compilers of the Digest *L.Q.R.* 1945, 34–48.

BIBLIOGRAPHICAL NOTE

It has not been practicable to bring up to date the bibliographical references in the footnotes of this book. Since 1932, however, a number of important works, both general treatises and monographs on specific topics, have been published and the number of periodicals wholly or partly devoted to Roman Law has increased. Furthermore, some useful guides to this mass of literature have been provided, as well as several aids to the study of the Roman legal texts themselves. Mention of the main items, especially those in English, may indicate the richness of the material and how it may be found.

Adolf Berger's *Encyclopedic Dictionary of Roman Law,* Transactions of the American Philosophical Society, 1953, provides explanations of most technical terms, as well as accurate short articles on the sources and main institutions of the substantive law, each furnished with bibliographical lists. A general work of a totally different kind is Fritz Schulz's *Principles of Roman Law,* Oxford, 1936, a discussion not of the rules themselves but of the views of law and justice held by the Romans. The notions which characterise the activity of the jurists are delineated with great skill.

Among works devoted to the history of the law, H. F. Jolowicz's *Historical Introduction to the Study of Roman Law,* Cambridge, 2nd ed. 1952, is especially valuable as it was specifically designed to supplement Buckland's *Text-book,* with a historical discussion of the sources of law, constitutional developments and legal procedure. For even more detailed information about sources, Leopold Wenger's monumental *Die Quellen des Römischen Rechts,* Österreichische Akademie der Wissenschaften, 1953, should be consulted. The activities of the legal profession and the different kinds of legal literature which it produced are treated by Fritz Schulz in his fundamental *History of Roman Legal Science,* Oxford, 1946, rep. 1954, while the careers and social background of the individual jurists are described by Wolfgang Kunkel in *Herkunft und Soziale Stellung der Römischen Juristen,* Weimar, 1952. Earlier general works on Roman legal history have not, however, been superseded and much useful information can still be found in H. J. Roby's *Introduction to the Study of Justinian's Digest,* Cambridge, 1886, and in Paul Krüger's *Geschichte der Quellen und Litteratur des Römischen Rechts,* 2nd ed. 1912. The Danish scholar, C. W. Westrup, has published an interesting series of sociological studies of the Patriarchal Joint Family under the title *Introduction to Early Roman Law*, Copenhagen–London, 5 vols., 1934–1954. The earlier volumes of this uncompleted work are devoted to the house community with its common cult and property and the notion of *patria potestas*, while the later volumes deal with sources and methods. In a short study, *Forms of Roman Legislation*, Oxford, 1956, David Daube applies the technique of form criticism, developed mainly by biblical scholars, to certain characteristic forms in which rules are expressed, seeking the original setting in life of each.

Among systematic accounts of the substantive law, the most substantial work in English in the last 30 years has been Fritz Schulz's *Classical Roman Law*, Oxford, 1951. This is a lively statement of the private law during the period from Augustus to Diocletian, written with authority by an author who held strong personal views. Each section is followed by an extremely full bibliography. A good recent treatment in French is R. Monier's *Manuel élémentaire de Droit Romain* in two volumes, (I) History, Persons, Real Rights, Succession, 6th ed. 1947; (II) Obligations, 4th ed. 1948. The most up-to-date general treatise is Max Kaser's *Das Römische Privatrecht*, (I) Early, Preclassical and Classical Law, 1955; (II) Post-classical developments, 1959 (Handbuch der Altertumswissenschaft, x. iii. 3). For the law of procedure, an English translation of L. Wenger's *Institutionen*, to which frequent reference is made in the *Text-book*, has been published as *Institutes of the Roman Law of Civil Procedure*, New York, 1940. It contains the author's latest views and references to the more recent literature.

Such dogmatic statements of the law as a whole must be based on detailed studies of particular parts, many of which appear in periodicals published in different countries. The most important of these are the following:

Belgium. *Revue internationale des droits de l'antiquité*, 3rd ser. 1954–

France. *Revue historique de droit français et étranger*, 4th ser. 1922–

Germany. *Zeitschrift der Savigny Stiftung für Rechtsgeschichte, Romanistische Abteilung* (General Index to vols. 1–50, 1932), 1880–

Italy. *Archivio Giuridico*, 1868–

Bullettino dell'istituto di diritto romano, 1888–

IURA—Rivista internazionale di diritto romano e antico, 1950–

Labeo—Rassegna di diritto romano, 1955–

Studia et Documenta Historiae et Juris, 1935–

Netherlands. *Tijdschrift voor Rechtsgeschiedenis* (*Revue d'Histoire du droit*) (General Index to vols. 1–25, 1957), 1918–

United States. *Seminar* (Annual extraordinary number of *The Jurist*), 1943–1956.

A comprehensive index to the mass of periodical literature is now provided by the *Collectio Bibliographica operum ad jus romanum pertinentium* of L. Caes and R. Henrion, Brussels, which covers work published from 1800 to the present day and is divided into three series: (I) *Opera edita in periodicis Miscellaneis Encyclopaediisque*, 12 vols. (1949–1962); (II) *Theses* (1. *Theses Galliae* (1959); 2. *Theses Germaniae* (1885–1958) (1960)); (III) *Opera praeter theses separatim vel etiam conjunctim edita* (no volumes yet published). Works are arranged alphabetically according to the name of the author, and at the end of each volume is a subject-index giving the names of authors who have dealt with particular topics.

The annual volumes of *IURA* from 1950 onwards contain a large bibliography of all books, articles and reviews on ancient law which have appeared in the previous year. This is divided into sections, each devoted to a particular branch of law, e.g. family relations, real rights, obligations, studies of sources, papyrology, etc. Within each section the various works are cited alphabetically according to the name of the author, and each item, apart from reviews, has a short summary of the main contents together with a list of the texts discussed. Each volume has both an index of authors and an index of texts. The scholar may thus obtain a panoramic view of all the work appearing on a given topic in a certain year, or see whether a particular author has dealt with it, or find where and by whom a certain text has been recently discussed. The review *Labeo*, which appears three times a year, also contains bibliographical references arranged systematically according to subject-matter, but without any indication of contents or texts cited.

All serious study of Roman Law must ultimately be based on the texts themselves and various aids are available. Thus the *Palingenesia Iuris Civilis* of Otto Lenel, 2 vols., Leipzig, 1889, sets out the surviving fragments of the writings of the classical jurists in the order in which they appeared in the original work. It is thus possible to see the context in which a text first appeared, and how the compilers of the Digest changed its meaning by placing it in a different context, as well as to judge the total surviving work of a particular jurist. Detailed exegesis requires precise information about the uses of individual words and to that end the Savigny Stiftung began the *Vocabularium Jurisprudentiae Romanae*, Berlin, 1903– which cites under each word all the juristic texts in which it appears, arranged according to its different uses. The Digest texts are cited according to page and line in Mommsen's two-volume edition of the Digest, Berlin, 1880. The work, which is still proceeding, so far covers the letters A to G and R to Z inclusive (vols. I, II and V), as well as certain parts between H and N. For words which have not yet been covered by the *Vocabularium*, Heumann–Seckel, *Handlexicon zu den Quellen des römischen Rechts*, 9th ed. Jena, 1907, should be used. The *Thesaurus Linguae Latinae*, itself incomplete, also includes juristic texts. Words appearing in Gaius' Institutes are listed in P. Zanzucchi's *Vocabolario delle Istituzioni di Gaio*, Milan, 1910. The words used in the imperial constitutions contained in Justinian's Code are set out in Robert Mayr's *Vocabularium Codicis Justiniani*, Prague, part I (Latin words), 1923, part II (Greek words), 1925, with references to the constitution in which they appear. The language of Justinian's Institutes is covered by the *Vocabularium Institutionum Iustiniani Augusti*, of Rodolfo Ambrosino, Milan, 1942, who distinguishes between terms derived from Gaius and those introduced by the compilers. Finally, Ernst Levy's *Ergänzungsindex zu Ius und Leges*, Weimar, 1930, provides a guide to the vocabulary and proper names found in the miscellaneous and fragmentary post-classical works which have survived apart from the *Corpus Iuris*, such as the *Collatio legum mosaicarum et romanarum*, the *Interpretationes* to Paul's Sentences and to the Theodosian Code, The Edict of Theoderic etc.

In the last half century much of the textual study of juristic texts has been devoted to the discovery and identification of interpolations in the classical writings. In this respect, the *Index Interpolationum quae in Iustiniani Digestis inesse dicuntur*, edited by E. Levy and E. Rabel (vol. I and Supplement (books 1–20), 1929; vol. II (books 21–35), 1931; vol. III (books 36–50), 1935) is invaluable. This work lists, text by text in the order of the Digest, the various passages which had been declared to be interpolated up to the publication of each volume. The index is uncritical and many of the passages condemned as non-classical in the early enthusiasm for interpolation-hunting have since had their classical character vindicated. One of the main criteria for recognising interpolations is philological and certain words and phrases have been held to be signs of interpolations. A guide to such words is the *Indice delle Parole, Frasi e construtti ritenuti indizio di interpolazione nei testi giuridici romani*, by A. Guarneri Citati, Milan, 1927, Supplementum I in *Studi Riccobono*, I (1934), 701 *sqq.*, Supplementum II in *Festschrift Koschaker*, I (1939), 117 *sqq.* For the pre-Justinian sources, E. Volterra's "Indice delle glosse, delle interpolazioni...nelle fonti pregiustinianee occidentali", in *Rivista di storia del diritto italiano*, 8, 1935, 9, 1936, provides a useful guide.

The extreme interpolationist argument that the Digest expresses a modernised oriental law quite different in its guiding notions from classical law is best stated by E. Albertario in his *Introduzione Storica allo Studio del Diritto Romano Giustinianeo*, Milan, 1935. Buckland replied in detail to this work, with an evaluation of the various criteria by which the existence of interpolation is proved, in "Interpolations in the Digest: A criticism of criticism", *Harvard Law Rev.*, 54, 1941, 1273–1310.

The best translation of the Digest into English is *The Digest of Justinian* by C. H. Munro, 2 vols., Cambridge, 1909, but this only covers books 1–15 (the last two books were completed by Buckland after Monro's death). There is an English version of the whole Corpus Juris by S. P. Scott, *The Civil Law*, Cincinnati, 1932. This work contains a number of mistakes which make it unreliable but is useful if used with caution. Certain titles of the Digest have been given separate editions with translations. Recent examples include: H. J. Jolowicz, D. 47. 2. *De Furtis*, Cambridge, 1940; F. H. Lawson, *Negligence in the Civil Law* (D. 9. 2. De Lege Aquilia), Oxford, 1950. F. de Zulueta's *Roman Law of Sale*, Oxford, 1945, is a useful selection of texts with translation and commentary. *The Theodosian Code and Novels and the Sirmondian Constitutions* have been translated with Commentary, Glossary and Bibliography, by Clyde Pharr, Princeton, 1952. The *Institutes of Gaius* have been given a most useful students' edition by F. de Zulueta (Oxford, (I) Text and Translation, 1946; (II) Commentary, 1953), who takes full account of the Antinoite fragments, published in 1933, which are the main new source of Roman Law to be discovered since the second edition of this Text-book and which have required the main alterations to the text.

Many *leges*, senatorial decrees, magisterial edicts and imperial enactments, taken partly from the collections of legal sources of Bruns, of Girard (see *List of Books cited*) and of Riccobono (*Fontes Iuris Romani Anteiustiniani*, 3 vols., Florence, 1940–1943) and partly from general collections of inscriptions and papyri and quotations from classical authors, have been translated with Commentary, Glossary and Index by A. C. Johnson, P. R. Coleman-Norton and F. C. Bourne under the title *Ancient Roman Statutes*, Austin, Texas, 1961.

Finally it may be useful to give a list of Buckland's own writings on Roman Law published since 1932:

(1) *Aestimatum*, *L.Q.R.* 1932, 495–505.

(2) *Culpa* and *bona fides* in the *actio ex empto*, *L.Q.R.* 1932, 217–29.

(3) *Exceptio rei residuae* (G. 4. 112), *R.H.* 1932, 301–3.

(4) Marcian, *Studi Riccobono*, I, 1934 (offprint, 1932), 275–83.

(5) Les limites de l'obligation du *fideiussor*, *R.H.* 1933, 116–29.

(6) *Casus* and Frustration in Roman and Common Law, *Harvard Law Rev.* 46, 1933, 1281–1300.

(7) Review of S. P. Scott, The Civil Law, in *Tulane Law Rev.* 1933, 627–32.

(8) L'*Edictum Provinciale*, *R.H.* 1934, 81–96.

(9) The duty to take care, *L.Q.R.* 1935, 637–49.

(10) *Finium Regundorum*, *R.H.* 1936, 741–51.

(11) Reflections suggested by the new fragments of Gaius, *Juridical Rev.* 1936, 339–64.

(12) Classical Roman Law, *Cambridge Ancient History*, XI, 1936, 806–44.

(13) Gaius and the *Liber Singularis* again, *L.Q.R.* 1937, 508–18.

(14) Civil proceedings against Ex-Magistrates in the Republic, *J.R.S.* 1937, 37–47.

(15) Note on the vocabulary of Gaius, *L.Q.R.* 1938, 182–3.

(16) Les sources du droit romain et du common law, *Recueil Lambert*, II, 1938, 18–31.

(17) D. 12. 4. 16, *Tijdschrift*, 1938, 359–71.

(18) *Superficies* et *lex contractus*, *R.H.* 1938, 666–71.

(19) Praetor and Chancellor, *Tulane Law Rev.* 1939, 163–77.

(20) Ritual acts and words in Roman law, *Festschrift Koschaker I*, 1939, 16–26.

(21) *Per liberam personam nihil adquiri posse*, *Bull. Acad. roy. de Belgique*, *Cl. Lett.* 1939, 188–210.

(22) Cumulation in the *Actio Doli*, *L.Q.R.* 1939, 222–9.

(23) Interpolations in the Digest, *Harvard Law Rev.* 54, 1941, 1273–1310.

(24) Principal and *Fideiussor*. *Consumptio litis*, *Juridical Rev.* 1941, 1–17.

(25) *Contrectatio*, *L.Q.R.* 1941, 467–74.

(26) Alienation and Manumission by one of *Consortes* (Gaius, 3. 154a), *L.Q.R.* 1942, 483–6.

(27) Cause of Action: English and Roman. *Seminar*, 1943, 3–10.

(28) Gaius 1. 166, "*Tutela parentis manumissoris*", *J.R.S.* 1943, 11–14.

(29) The *Interpretationes* to *Pauli Sententiae* and the *Codex Theodosianus*, *L.Q.R.* 1944, 361–5.

(30) The nature of contractual obligation, *Cambridge Law J.* 1944, 247–51.

(31) *Pauli Sententiae* and the Compilers of the Digest, *L.Q.R.* 1945, 34–48.

LIST OF BOOKS AND PERIODICALS CITED BY A MUCH ABBREVIATED TITLE OR REQUIRING AN INDICATION OF THE EDITION USED

Accarias, *Précis*: Précis de Droit Romain, C. Accarias, 4me Éd.

Affolter, *Inst.*: Das Römische Institutionensystem, F. X. Affolter.

Arangio-Ruiz, *Ist.*: Istituzioni di Diritto Romano, 2da Ed.

Arch. f. c. Pr.: Archiv für civilistische Praxis.

Bertolini, *Obblig.*: Le Obbligazioni, Parte Speciale, G. Bertolini.

Beseler, *Beitr.*: Beiträge zur Kritik der Römischen Rechtsquellen, Gerh. Beseler.

Bethmann-Hollweg, *C.P.*: Der Römische Civilprozess, M. A. von Bethmann-Hollweg

Betti, *Ist.*: Corso di Istituzione di Diritto Romano, 1, E. Betti.

Bonfante, *Corso*: Corso di Diritto Romano, P. Bonfante.

—— *Scr. Giur.*: Scritti Giuridici Varii, P. Bonfante.

Brugi, *Ist.*: Istituzioni di Diritto Romano, P. Brugi, 3za Ed.

Bruns: Fontes Iuris Romani, ed. C. Bruns, Ed. 7a, ed. O. Gradenwitz.

Buckland, *Slavery*: Roman Law of Slavery, W. W. Buckland.

Bull.: Bullettino dell' Istituto di Diritto Romano.

Clark, *R.P.L.*: Roman Private Law, E. C. Clark.

Collinet, *Études Hist.*: Études historiques sur le droit de Justinien, P. Collinet.

Collinet-Giffard, *Précis*: Précis de Droit Romain, P. Collinet et A. Giffard, 2me Éd.

Cornil, *A.D.R.*: Ancien Droit Romain, G. Cornil.

—— *Dr.R.*: Droit Romain: Aperçu historique sommaire, G. Cornil.

Costa, *Profilo Storico*: Profilo storico del Processo Civile Romano, E. Costa.

—— *Le Acque*: Le Acque nel Diritto Romano, E. Costa.

—— *Storia*: Storia del Diritto Romano Privato, E. Costa, 2da Ed.

Cuq, *Man.*: Manuel des Institutions juridiques des Romains, E. Cuq, 2me Éd.

Daremberg et Saglio: Dictionnaire des Antiquités grecques et romaines, sous la direction de Ch. Daremberg et E. Saglio.

D.P.R.: Le Droit Public Romain, par Th. Mommsen, traduit par P. F. Girard.

Esmein, *Mél.*: Mélanges d'histoire de droit, A. Esmein.

Ét. Girard: Études d'histoire juridique, offertes à P. F. Girard, par ses Élèves.

Fitting, *Alter und Folge*: Alter und Folge der Schriften Römischer Juristen, von Hadrian bis Alexander, H. Fitting, 2te Bearbeitung.

Gibbon (Bury): Decline and Fall of the Roman Empire, E. Gibbon, ed. J. B. Bury.

Girard, *Man.*: Manuel élémentaire de Droit Romain, P. F. Girard, 8me Éd., ed. F. Senn.

—— *Mélanges*: Mélanges de Droit Romain, P. F. Girard.

—— *Org. Jud.*: L'Organisation judiciaire des Romains, P. F. Girard.

—— *Textes*: Textes de Droit Romain, P. F. Girard, 5me Éd.

Gött. Gel. Anzeigen: Göttingische gelehrte Anzeigen.

Heumann-Seckel: Heumanns Handlexicon zu den Quellen des Römischen Rechts, 9te Aufl., bearbeitet von E. Seckel.

Huschke: Jurisprudentia Anteiustiniana, P. E. Huschke, Ed. 5a.

Huvelin, *Furtum*: Études sur le Furtum, 1, P. Huvelin.

Ihering, *Geist*: Geist des Römischen Rechts, R. von Ihering.

Jobbé-Duval, *Proc. Civ.*: Études sur l'histoire de la Procédure, E. Jobbé-Duval.

Jörs, *Röm. Rechtsw.*: Römische Rechtswissenschaft der Republik, P. Jörs.

—— *R.R.*: Römisches Recht, P. Jörs.

J.R.S.: Journal of Roman Studies.

Karlowa, *C.P.*: Der Römische Civilprozess, O. Karlowa.

—— *R.Rg.*: Römische Rechtsgeschichte, O. Karlowa.

Keller-Wach, *C.P.*: Der Römische Civilprozess, F. L. von Keller, 6te Aufl., ed. A. Wach.

Kipp: Geschichte der Quellen: Th. Kipp, 4te Aufl.
Krueger, *R.Rq.*: Geschichte der Quellen und Litteratur des Römischen Rechts, P. Krueger, 2te Aufl.
Krv.: Kritische Vierteljahresschrift.
Kuebler: Geschichte des Römischen Rechts, P. Kuebler.
Lenel, *E.P.*: Das Edictum Perpetuum, O. Lenel, 3te Aufl.
—— *Paling.*: Palingenesia Iuris Civilis, O. Lenel.
L.Q.R.: Law Quarterly Review.
Marquardt, *Privatl.*: Privatleben der Römer, J. Marquardt, 2te Aufl.
Mélanges Appleton, Cornil, Fournier, Gérardin, Girard, etc.: Collections of Essays published in honour of the writers named.
Mitteis, *R.Pr.*: Römisches Privatrecht bis auf die Zeit Diocletians, L. Mitteis.
—— *Reichsr. und Volksr.*: Reichsrecht und Volksrecht in den Östlichen Provinzen, L. Mitteis.
Mommsen, *Ges. Schr.*: Gesammelte Schriften, Th. Mommsen.
—— *Staatsr.*: Römisches Staatsrecht, Th. Mommsen, 3te Aufl.
—— *Strafr.*: Römisches Strafrecht, Th. Mommsen.
Moyle, *Instt. Iust.*: Imperatoris Iustiniani Institutionum Libri Quattuor, with commentary, J. B. Moyle, 5th Ed.
—— *Sale*: Contract of Sale in the Civil Law, J. B. Moyle.
N.R.H.: Nouvelle Revue Historique de Droit Français et Étranger.
Partsch, *Neg. Gest.*: Studien zur Negotiorum Gestio, 1, J. Partsch.
—— *Schriftformel*: Die Schriftformel im Römischen Provinzialprozesse, J. Partsch.
Perozzi, *Ist.*: Istituzioni di Diritto Romano, S. Perozzi, 2da Ed.
Puchta, *Inst.*: Cursus der Institutionen, G. F. Puchta, 5te Aufl.
P.W.: Paulys Real-Encyclopädie der Classischen Altertumswissenschaft, Neue Bearbeitung, ed. G. Wissowa.
Revue Gén.: Revue générale du droit, de la législation et de la jurisprudence.
R.H.: Continuation of *N.R.H.*, from 1922.
Riccobono, *Dal Dir. Rom.*: Dal Diritto Romano Classico al Diritto Moderno (Annali del Seminario Giuridico della R. Università di Palermo, iv), S. Riccobono.
Riv. It. p. l. Sc. Giu.: Rivista Italiana per le Scienze Giuridiche.
Roby, *Introd.*: Introduction to the study of Justinian's Digest, H. J. Roby.
—— *R.P.L.*: Roman Private Law in the Times of Cicero and of the Antonines, H. J. Roby.
Savigny, *System*: System des heutigen Römischen Rechts, F. K. von Savigny.
Schulz, *Einführung*: Einführung in das Studium der Digesten, F. Schulz.
Siber, *R.R.*: Römisches Recht, H. Siber.
S.M.W.: Institutionen des Römischen Rechts, R. Sohm, 17te Aufl., bearbeitet von L. Mitteis, herausgegeben von L. Wenger.
Studi, Bonfante, Brugi, Fadda, Perozzi: Collections of Essays published in honour of the writers named.
Vangerow, *Pand.*: Lehrbuch der Pandekten, K. A. von Vangerow, 7te Aufl.
de Visscher, *Ét.*: Études de Droit Romain, F. de Visscher.
Wenger, *Zpr.*: Institutionen des Römischen Zivilprozessrechts, I. Wenger.
van Wetter, *Pand.*: Pandectes, P. van Wetter.
Willems, *D.P.*: Droit Public Romain, P. Willems, 7me Éd.
Windscheid, *Lehrb.*: Lehrbuch des Pandektenrechts, B. Windscheid, 9te Aufl.
Z.S.S.: Zeitschrift der Savigny-Stiftung, Romanistisches Abteilung.

(References for Roman Juristic Sources are to the Berlin Stereotype edition of the Corpus Iuris Civilis, to Mommsen's edition of the Codex Theodosianus and to Girard's Textes. Any exceptions are noted at the reference.)

CHAPTER I

THE SOURCES OF THE LAW IN THE EMPIRE

I. Though the history of the modes of formation of Law[1] in earlier Rome is outside the scope of this book, it is convenient to have an outline of the facts before us in order the better to understand the material with which Augustus had to deal in his reconstruction. The story may be said to begin with the XII Tables. There are indeed traditions of legislation by more or less legendary kings[2], of a collection of these *leges regiae* issued by one Papirius about the time of the foundation of the Republic[3] and of a commentary on the *Ius Papirianum* by Granius Flaccus[4], near the end of the Republic, and there are what purport to be citations from these *leges regiae* by later writers, mostly non-legal[5]. It is probable that the *leges regiae* are merely declarations of ancient custom: they are largely sacral, and play no important part in later law. The XII Tables are of vastly greater importance. They were a comprehensive collection of rules framed by officers called *Decemviri*, specially appointed for the purpose, perhaps in two successive years, and superseding for the time being the ordinary magistrates of the Republic. They were enacted about 450 B.C.[6] by the *Comitia Centuriata*, perhaps the first express legislation, in the Roman State, affecting Private Law. They consisted mainly of ancient Latin custom, but there was some

1 Krueger, *Röm. Rechtsquell.* 3–82; Kipp, §§ 5–10; Clark, R. P. L., *Regal Period*; Hirschfeld, *Kleine Schriften*, 239, 264; Cornil, *A.D.R. Liv.* 1. 2 Krueger, *op. cit.* 3 *sqq.* 3 1. 2. 2. 36. *Praenomen* variously stated. 4 50. 16. 144. 5 Girard, *Textes*, 3 *sqq.*; Bruns, 1. 1 *sqq.* Most are attributed to the earlier and certainly mythical kings. 6 On the sceptical views sometimes expressed as to the story of the *Decemviri* generally, Girard, *Mélanges*, 1 *sqq.*; Greenidge, *Engl. Hist. Rev.* 1905, 1; de Francisci (*Storia*, 1. 193 *sqq.*), who accepts the main story, though not all the attributions to the XII Tables.

innovation and apparently some incorporation of rules of Greek Law[1]. They have not survived in their original form, but have been partially reconstructed from the numerous references to them in later legal and lay writings, some of which purport to give the actual wording of particular rules, though in all cases this is in a much modernised form[2]. Though they were in great part superseded by later legislation long before the end of the Republic, they continued to be held in great reverence. Livy describes them as the "*fons omnis publici privatique iuris*[3]," and citations and allusions are found even in Justinian's compilations. But the XII Tables did not contain the whole law. They stated general rules: the countless details, especially of form, were left to be elucidated by officials. In early Rome, as in other nascent civilisations, there was no great difference between religious and legal rules and thus those to whom it fell to expound the laws and advise thereon, and this not merely informally, but by virtue of their official position, were priestly officers, the Pontiffs[4]. In this age it does not appear that any authority was thought of as capable of altering the provisions of the XII Tables: these were a fundamental law. But while civilisation is advancing, the law cannot stand still, and the power of *interpretatio* and formulation placed in the hands of the Pontiffs[5] was in effect a power to alter the law, by ingenious and useful, though not very logical, interpretations, some of which we shall meet with later on[6].

Of express legislation there was, to the middle of the Republic, but little, and what did occur was mainly on constitutional matters[7]. Of the various popular assemblies the oldest was the *Comitia Curiata*. This was an assembly of the whole people, or perhaps of all heads of families, grouped in 30 *curiae*, the *curia* being the voting unit. Each *curia* consisted of a number of *gentes*, or clans, the members of which were connected by a real or assumed relationship[8]. This body probably never exercised legislative power in the ordinary sense. Important as its functions[9] were, they belong, in the main, to an age before legislation was thought of as an ordinary method of law reform. The *Comitia Centuriata* was, in historical times, a much more important body. The centuriate organisation, existing, at the latest, soon after the foundation of the Republic,

1 Bonfante, *Scr. Giur.* 1. 337, rejects any close relation between early Roman and Greek Law. 2 For the most usually accepted reconstruction, see Girard, *Textes*, 9 *sqq.*, who states the evidence on which the somewhat speculative attribution of individual provisions to their proper *Tabula* is based. 3 Livy, 3. 34. 4 Krueger, *cit.* 27; Mommsen, *Staatsr.* 2. 18 *sqq.*; *D.P.R.* 3. 19 *sqq.* 5 See D. 1. 2. 2. 6 as to the relation of the pontiffs to the public. 6 E.g. *post*, §§ XLIV, LXXXVII. 7 See Karlowa, *Röm. Rg.* 1. 116 *sqq.*; Rotondi, *Scr. Giur.* 1. 1 *sqq.* 8 See Mommsen, *Staatsr.* 3. 9, 30, 90; *D.P.R.* 6. 1. 8, 32, 98, as to the conception of a *Gens*, the introduction and position of *minores gentes*, the extension of the notion to plebeians and the vote of these in the *Comitia Curiata*. But see also de Francisci, *Storia cit.* 1. 106 *sqq.* 9 Willems, *D.P.* 36.

was a grouping of the whole people, patrician and plebeian[1], as a military force, on a plan attributed to Servius Tullius. The grouping was into *classes*, subdivided into *centuriae*, and, when the body acted as a political assembly, the voting unit was the *centuria*. The *classes* consisted of one *classis* of *Equites* and five *classes* of *Pedites*[2]. The *centuriae* within each class were divided into an equal number of Senior and Junior, but the number of *centuriae* assigned to the *Equites* and the *prima classis* amounted to more than half of the total number[3]. As the Senior centuries were chiefly employed in home defence, this arrangement put the practical voting power, in this assembly, into the hands of the older and the well-to-do, a result not seriously affected by the fact that the very poor, not subject to regular military service at all, were constituted into one *centuria* for voting purposes[4]. As the total number was 193, this gave them no power, but it served to secure an odd number of voters. Such a body was necessarily conservative, and it must be remembered that it could vote only on propositions submitted by the presiding magistrate, in the earlier part of the Republic always a patrician, that it was usual, if not legally necessary, to submit the proposal for the previous approval of the Senate[5], and that a *lex* of the *centuriae* also required *auctoritas patrum*, commonly supposed to mean approval of the patrician members of the Senate[6]. This approval, which had followed enactment by the *Comitia*, was made to precede the vote by a *lex Publilia Philonis*[7], traditionally dated 339 B.C., and soon became unimportant. A considerable amount of legislation seems to have been effected by the *Comitia Centuriata*, the *Comitia Maxima*[8]. A third assembly of the whole people was the *Comitia Tributa*. Its voting unit was the *tribus*, a subdivision, essentially local, of the whole territory of the State. Tradition assigns the establishment of these local tribes to Servius Tullius, the number increasing as the State grew, till it reached the maximum, 35, about 240 B.C.[9] This body seems to have had the power of legislation soon after the enactment of the XII Tables[10], but there were few *leges tributae* in

1 Nature of the *plebs*, de Francisci, *Storia cit.* 1. 172; Rose, *Journal of Rom. Studies*, 1922, 106 *sqq.*, denies any racial distinction. 2 Originally only the highest group was a *classis*, the others were *infra classem*, but in historic times the organisation was as stated. Mommsen, *Staatsr.* 3. 262; *D.P.R.* 6. 1. 297. 3 Mommsen, *Staatsr.* 3. 254, 267; *D.P.R.* 6. 1. 288, 302. 4 *Proletarii, capite censi.* Chief authorities, Livy, 1. 43, and Dion. Halic. 4. 20 *sqq.* The accounts do not agree in detail, and historical evolution is obscured. The provision for an odd number of votes seems to have been observed in the gradual extensions of the Tributal system (below). 5 Mommsen, *op. cit.* 3. 1037; *D.P.R.* 7. 236. 6 *Ibid.* 7 Livy, 8. 12. 8 Cic. *de legg.* 3. 4. 12; Girard, *Textes*, 20; Kuebler, 69. All clearly "private" laws seem to be plebiscites, Rotondi, *Scr. Giur.* 1. 1 *sqq.* 9 Mommsen, *op. cit.* 3. 161 *sqq.*; *D.P.R.* 6. 1. 180 *sqq.* 10 As to the confused story of the validation of *leges tributae* and plebiscites by the *l. Valeria Horatia* (449 B.C.), *l. Publilia Philonis* (339 B.C.) and *l. Hortensia* (about 287 B.C.), Mommsen, *Staatsr.* 3. 1037 *sqq.*; *D.P.R.* 7. 236 *sqq.*; Kipp, § 6; Brini, *Mem. Acc. Bologna*, 1930 (*Sc.M.*), 67.

the earlier part of the Republic. As in the *Comitia Centuriata*, the proposal by the presiding magistrate was usually submitted for previous approval of the Senate, and *auctoritas patrum* was required[1].

II. In the later Republic the law had become secularised. The Pontificate having been thrown open to plebeians[2], the control of the Pontiffs over law lost its old value to the patricians as a weapon against plebeian aggression, and with the gradual passing of power into the hands of the plebeians the pontiffs disappeared as factors in the development of the ordinary law. Their place as advisers and expounders was taken by professed jurists who were quite unofficial, but, as advisers to magistrates, as well as to private persons, exercised great influence and became very prominent in the later centuries of the Republic[3]. Little of the writings of these *veteres* remains[4], but it was the beginning of a rich literature to which we owe most of our knowledge of the law.

Legislation by the *Comitia* now covered a wider field but still remained a relatively unimportant source of private law. The *Comitia Centuriata* legislated little[5]: its chief influence on law was exercised by its appointment of the higher magistrates. Legislation was carried on to some extent by the *Comitia Tributa* and in an increasing degree by the assembly of the *plebs* alone, *concilium plebis*[6], which, in historical times, was also based on the tributal organisation. This assembly, presided over by a tribune of the *plebs*, was active from early times and there was early legislation on constitutional questions, enacted by that body and approved by the Senate, which was regarded as binding on the whole community[7]. Its enactments, *plebiscita*, were often called, as binding the whole community, *leges*, though in strictness this name does not cover any *rogationes* except those in a *Comitia*, i.e. of the *populus*. They never needed *auctoritas patrum*, but they did not bind any but plebeians unless previously approved by the Senate. This requirement seems[8], however, to have been abolished by the *l. Hortensia*, itself a plebiscite, about 287 B.C.[9] It is probable that most of the later legislation was by this body, though the recorded story does not clearly distinguish its acts from those of the *Comitia Tributa*.

1 Mommsen, *op. cit.* 3. 1040; *D.P.R.* 7. 240. 2 According to Livy, 10. 6, by a *l. Ogulnia*, 300 B.C. Tiberius Coruncanius, the first plebeian *Pontifex Maximus*, was also the first public teacher of law, D. 1. 2. 2. 38. 3 Jörs, *Röm. Rechtsw. der Rep.*, 1. ch. 2. §§ 18–25, especially 24. 4 Bremer, *Jurisprudentia Antehadriana*, vol. 1. 5 Thus difficulties from concurrent powers were avoided. In any case they would be lessened by the reference to the Senate, and by the reorganisation of the *C. Centuriata* which to an extent not fully known assimilated it to the *Com. Tributa*, Mommsen, *op. cit.* 3. 270; *D.P.R.* 6. 1. 305 *sqq.*; Rotondi, *Leges publicae populi Romani*, a history of comitial legislation and a chronological account of all known *leges*, with reff. to literature. *Addenda, Scr. Giur.* 1. 411 *sqq.* 6 Mommsen, *op. cit.* 3. 150 *sqq.*; *D.P.R.* 6. 1. 166 *sqq.* 7 E.g., *lex Icilia*, 492 B.C.; *lex Canuleia*, 445 B.C. 8 Mommsen, *op. cit.* 3. 159; *D.P.R.* 6. 1. 178. 9 Further details on influence of Senate on legislation, *post*, § v.

The chief new factor in the late Republic remains to be stated. Roman magistrates had the right to issue Edicts, *ius edicendi*[1], but while the Edicts of the Curule Aediles were of importance in some branches of law[2], those of the Urban and Peregrine Praetors and the Provincial Governors, who administered justice respectively between *cives* in Italy, in cases in Italy[3] in which those without *commercium* were concerned (*peregrini*[4]) and in the Provinces, were far more significant in legal history. The Edict of the *Praetor Urbanus* was much the most potent instrument of law reform in the last century of the Republic[5].

The control of litigation, *iurisdictio*, was transferred from the Consuls to the newly created Praetor by one of the Licinian Rogations in 367 B.C.[6] So long as litigation was conducted by the *legis actio*, this may have meant little but formal and almost ministerial co-operation[7]. But the *l. Aebutia* of about 140 B.C., authorising the use, instead of *legis actio*, of the more elastic *formulae* framed by the Praetor himself and variable as need arose, resulted in a great change in the position of the magistrate. He was now found refusing actions where civil law gave them, giving them where it did not, creating new defences and so forth. By these means he introduced, side by side with civil law rights and duties, another system, technically, and in some cases practically, less effective than civil law rights and duties, but in the end completely transforming the working of the law[8]. How far this change resulted directly from the *lex*, the exact provisions of which are not recorded[9], is not clear. But as the Praetor's Edict remained in force only for his year of office, and could be changed by his successor, so that a rule which worked badly could be stopped and one which worked well carried on[10], it is likely that it was in great part an aggression accepted by Senate and people as being a convenient form of experimental legislation: the *Comitia*, nominally an assembly of the whole people, could not adequately represent a population scattered

1 Not Quaestors, except in praetorian provinces, Mommsen, *op. cit.* 1. 203; *D.P.R.* 1. 234. Account of the magistracies, their significance, collegiality, etc., Kuebler, 70 *sqq.* 2 *Post*, §§ CLXXII, CCV. 3 Both Praetors sat at Rome, but both had jurisdiction over all cases except so far as local jurisdictions were created or recognised. Of these the most prominent was that of the provincial governors. But in the cities of various kinds in Italy there were many local jurisdictions which more or less excluded the Court at Rome. As to these, Girard, *Org. Jud.* 1. 272 *sqq.* 4 *Post*, § XXXVI. 5 The Praetor is not necessarily a lawyer. What we call praetorian law is often the Praetor's only in form. The ideas come from the lawyers, both as his *consilium*, and as advising suitors before him. De Francisci, *Storia*, 2. 1. 190. 6 Livy, 6. 42; Mommsen, *op. cit.* 2. 193; *D.P.R.* 3. 221. 7 His powers under this régime are much disputed, *post*, §§ CCVII, CCXIV. 8 Jörs, *op. cit.* 158 *sqq.* A *l. Cornelia* (67 B.C.) required the Praetors to abide by their own Edict, Krueger, *R.Rq.* 34. Buckland, *Tulane L.R.* 1939, 163 *sqq.* 9 *Post*, § CCXIV. 10 His Edict for his year is *E. perpetuum*; special Edicts for temporary purposes are *E. repentina* (Cicero, *Verr.* 2. 3. 14. 36, not official). A provision carried on from the last Praetor is *E. praelatum* as opposed to *E. novum*. That part habitually carried on is *E. tralatitium*.

over all Western Europe, and was in fact little more than the Roman mob.

When, after a long period of exhausting civil war, Augustus became undisputed master of Rome it was clear to him that the first need of the State was reorganisation and good administration. It was clear also that the old republican methods, already in decay, could not really be revived. The State had outgrown them, and their inefficiency under existing conditions had rendered possible the domination of one man after another, which culminated in the Dictatorship of Caesar. But though the institutions could not be restored, the pious reverence for them which still existed made them convenient instruments in his reconstruction. The history of the previous 150 years had shewn that avowed despotism, however well meant, gave no promise of stability. Thus his course was marked out. He was a conservative wherever conservatism was possible[1]. One of his earliest acts was one of the most significant. The Triumvirate (of which he had been a member), whose régime had ended in civil war, had received full legislative power. This Augustus renounced and restored to the popular assembly in which it was traditionally vested[2]. On the other hand he claimed and received the fullest magisterial authority. He had *tribunicia potestas*[3] in Rome and proconsular power through the Empire. And, since power for a year only was of little use to the founder of a new political system, and had shewn its unsuitability to existing conditions, he had these powers conferred on him for life, though this was hardly more consistent with republican notions than supreme legislative power would have been.

III. We have now to consider the different Sources of Law in the Empire, beginning with those which survived from the Republic.

Leges. Enactments of the popular assembly[4]. Surviving records tell us of many *leges*, but these, spread over 500 years, are too few to suggest that they were ever a main source of private law[5]. This view is confirmed

1 Heitland, *Short Hist. of the Rom. Repub.* 508. For a study of the policy of Augustus, see id., *Hist. of Rom. Repub.* 3. 509 *sqq.*, and de Francisci, *La Costituzione Augustea*, and *Storia*, 2. 1. 233. 2 See on all these matters, Mommsen, *op. cit.* 2. 745; *D.P.R.* 5. 1; Wenger, *Hausgewalt und Staatsgewalt*, 46. 3 He is not Tribune, though he has the powers. The ordinary tribunes continue with dwindling powers. 4 *Ll. latae*, as opposed to *ll. datae*, imposed by a magistrate duly authorised on a community under his charge, and *ll. dictae*, a name applied to laws laid down for private domains of the Emperor. 5 As to mode of promulgation of *ll.* and *scc.*, Mommsen, *Ges. Schrift.* (*Jur.*) 3. 290. The *liber singularis regularum*, 1, classifies *ll.* under three heads: A *l. perfecta* annuls the act; most of the later *leges* are of this type. A *l. minus quam perfecta* inflicts a penalty but leaves the act valid, e.g. the *l. Furia Testamentaria* (G. 4. 23; *post*, § CXIX) and the *l. Marcia* (G. *ib.*). A *l. imperfecta* merely forbids the act, e.g. *l. Cincia* (*Fr. Vat.* 260 *sqq.*; *post*, § XCI), the prohibition in this case being made effective by an *exceptio*. It is suggested that earlier legislation takes this form because it is by way of plebiscite, and thus cannot alter the civil law, the fact that it is later than the *l. Hortensia* being explained as meaning only

by a study of their subject-matter. Apart from the XII Tables the earlier republican *leges* are constitutional[1], and though in the later Republic their field is wider, still most of them deal with matters closely connected with public order[2], and the same is true of those enacted after the accession of Augustus[3]. There are many in his reign, several under Tiberius, one or two under Claudius and there is one under Nerva[4]. After this we hear only of the *lex de imperio*, conferring various powers on a new emperor; the part of the *Comitia* being merely formal[5].

The legislation of this period was in no real sense legislation by a popular legislative body. The Emperor restored the legislative power not because he wished the people to make their own laws, but because he desired to use what reverence existed for the ancient institution in order to give effect to his own wishes, along the line of least resistance. No one knew better than Augustus that the *Comitia* were unfit to exercise legislative power. It must however be remembered that these bodies had never at any time had a right to initiate legislation. They voted only on a proposal submitted by the presiding magistrate, on whom therefore all depended. By virtue of his permanent *tribunicia potestas* the Emperor could convoke the plebeian assembly and submit proposals to them, and there is no doubt that all important *leges* of this time were so voted. When, as was sometimes the case, he held the Consulship, he could do the same with the centuries, but the people in their centurial organisation do not seem to have legislated in this age. When he restored legislative power to the *Comitia*, he restored also the power of choosing the magistrates, which, also, had been conferred on the Triumvirate. This was not a question of submitting a nominee to the vote, so that the worst that could happen would be his rejection: the *Comitia* could choose whom they would. That would not have suited Augustus, and accordingly, in his

that an old form has survived its purpose. This would be more weighty if we had *ll. centuriatae perfectae* on private law between the XII Tables and the *l. Hortensia*. Another view suggested by a text of Ulpian (24. 2. 11. pr.) is that legislation could not directly affect an act formally valid in the civil law, to which Mitteis objects (*R.Pr.* 1. 248) that it is little more than giving the rule as a reason for itself. Rotondi, *Scr. Giur.* 1. 36 *sqq.*; Senn, *Ll. perfectae, minus quam perfectae et imperfectae*; Baviera, *St. Fadda*, 2. 205 *sqq.* All these defective laws seem to run counter to provisions of the XII Tables, and are evasions of it. *S.M.W.* 54. The *l. Canuleia*, however, is an early direct contradiction of the XII Tables (11. 1). But it is really constitutional.

1 Even *l. Canuleia* (445 B.C., *post*, § XLI). 2 E.g. the numerous statutes establishing procedure in criminal law (Mommsen, *Strafr.* 202 *sqq.*), those regulating remedies against debtors, the old order having caused grave public danger, those regulating civil procedure (*post*, § CCXIV), in effect a successful revolt against the old patrician order of things. The few which deal with private law are plebiscites. 3 E.g. laws on manumission (*post*, § XXVIII), and laws dealing with the encouragement of marriage (*post*, §§ CIII, CXI, CXXXIV). 4 A *l. agraria* (47. 21. 3. 1). 5 Bruns, 1. 202; Girard, *Textes*, 107. It may have been a senatusconsult confirmed by a *lex*. Mommsen, *Staatsrecht*, 2. 878 *sqq.*; *D.P.R.* 5. 154.

reconstruction, when he abandoned the power of election, he provided that he should have the right of deciding whether a candidate was eligible and of commending particular candidates, which was equivalent to a direction to choose them, and was so understood. Thus he controlled the magistracy and thereby the submission of proposals of law to the Assembly[1]. The security was soon carried further. Tiberius transferred the selection of magistrates to the Senate[2], which by this time consisted entirely of the Emperor's nominees. Unreal as was the positive part of the people in legislation, if they could not choose what they would consider, they could at least choose what they would refuse, and this power they exercised. We know that they refused, for many successive years[3], to pass the comprehensive legislation on marriage which ultimately took effect in the *l. Iulia de maritandis ordinibus* and the *l. Papia Poppaea*[4].

These *leges* seem to have all been Tributal[5] and to have been submitted by or for the Emperor by virtue of his *tribunicia potestas*: there is no trace of legislative proposals by the actual *Tribuni plebis*. Though the centuries still met in the *Comitia Centuriata* their power was confined to the election of magistrates, and even this, as we have seen, they lost under Tiberius. They still continued to issue a formal *renuntiatio* of the name of the person elected till the third century, when the *Comitia* disappeared altogether[6].

IV. *Edicta* of the Magistrates[7]. Among the attributes of the Emperor was of course a *ius edicendi*, to be considered later: we are now concerned with the Edicts of the republican magistrates.

The re-establishment, in form, of republican institutions, which was, as we have seen, part of the scheme of Augustus, meant that the *ius edicendi* of magistrates continued unaltered: the Edicts of the Urban and of the Peregrine Praetor, that of the Aediles and the Provincial Edicts continued to appear for some centuries[8]. As to the Provincial Edicts it is to be remembered that Augustus divided the provinces into

1 Mommsen, *Staatsr.* 2. 916; *D.P.R.* 5. 198. 2 Tacitus, *Ann.* 1. 15. 3 Karlowa, *R.Rg.* 1. 617. 4 *Post*, §§ CIII, CXI, CXXXIV. 5 Machinery of voting, Mommsen, *Staatsr.* 3. 380 *sqq.*; *D.P.R.* 6. 1. 437 *sqq.* 6 *Ib.* p. 348; *D.P.R.* 6. 1. 397. In other matters the power of the *Comitia* was much cut down by Augustus. He took into his own hands foreign relations, the making of war and treaties (Willems, *D.P.* 429 *sqq.*, and the *lex curiata de imperio Vespasiani*, Girard, *Textes*, 107; Bruns, 1. 202). He removed the little that was left of criminal jurisdiction in the *Comitia* and transferred it to *Quaestiones perpetuae*, though the Senatorial jurisdiction which soon came into existence overshadowed this. Mommsen, *Staatsr.* 2. 958; *D.P.R.* 5. 246. 7 Gai. 1. 6. 8 Wilcken, *Z.S.S.* 1921, 137, holds that in Egypt and possibly in the provinces generally, the Edict of the *praeses* was of permanent validity. On the view that the Edict of the Emperor was permanent (*post*, 18) this might well be true of those of his officials in the Imperial appanage of Egypt but is hardly proved by citation in later years under the name of their introducer. In Rome the name of the introducer clings to the Edict. If in the provinces generally the Edict was so much more durable, the *amplissimum ius* of G. 1. 6 is misleading.

two groups. One group, the Senatorial provinces, were governed by republican magistrates and ex-magistrates in the old way, but all provinces of military importance, and all those newly acquired[1], were kept under the direct control of the *Princeps*, and put in charge of new imperial officers called *Legati Caesaris*, with the powers of Praetor (*pro praetore*), who held office at the will of the Emperor and often for many years, being regarded as representatives of the Emperor rather than as independent magistrates[2]. They issued Edicts in the ordinary way, except that it appears that in these provinces the Edict of the Aediles was not issued; it is not clear that its principles were not applied[3].

But the Edicts were now of less importance as sources of new law. Already in the Republic the pace of reform by this method had begun to slacken. The new Praetor tended simply to carry on the old Edict. New clauses were few, so that the Edict tended to be wholly *praelatum*, carried on from the former Praetor, and indeed, as many clauses had long been, *tralatitium*, traditional, regularly carried forward[4]. This tendency is accentuated under the new régime. Such changes as occur seem to be of three types. First, obsolete clauses drop out. Secondly, existing clauses are modified as occasion requires. We can trace this process, e.g., in the case of the interdict *unde vi*[5], and in the Edict of the Aediles as to defects in things sold[6]. Thirdly, new clauses are added. It is in relation to these that the change in legislative method is most obvious; there is little sign of any new clause added on the initiative of the Praetor himself.[7] The change made is normally merely provision in the Edict of machinery for giving effect to changes in the law made by other agencies[8]. Thus the *lex Papia Poppaea*, regulating the law of succession for the encouragement of marriage, gave in certain cases *bonorum possessio*[9], the praetorian right of succession, instead of the civil law *hereditas*. Whatever the reason for this, it resulted in a new clause in the Edict, promising *bonorum possessio* where a statute required it[10]. When *fideicommissa*, bequests in trust, were recognised, the ordinary Praetor did not deal with them: they were administered by a new officer, the *Praetor fideicommissarius*[11]. But when the *sc. Trebellianum* enacted that where a *hereditas* had been handed over under a trust, all actions that lay at civil law to and against the *heres* should lie to and against the *fideicommissarius*, this brought the matter into the Praetor's

1 As to areas governed by *Procurator* and *Praefectus* (Egypt), Marquardt, *Staatsverw.* 1. 90 *sqq.* esp. p. 337.
2 Mommsen, *Staatsr.* 2. 1087 *sqq.*; *D.P.R.* 5. 395 *sqq.* See, however, *post*, § XIX.
3 Gai. *ib.* The Quaestors issued Edicts there.
4 The Edict does not lose its importance: the latest jurists speak of the *ius honorarium* as the "*viva vox iuris civilis*," 1. 1. 8.
5 See Lenel, *E.P.* 462 and *post*, § CCXLIX.
6 Lenel, *op. cit.* 555.
7 See, however, as to Cassius, 4. 6. 26. 7; 29. 2. 99; 42. 8. 11; 44. 4. 4. 33.
8 Karlowa, *R.Rg.* 1. 629.
9 E.g., Gai. 3. 50.
10 D. 38. 14.
11 Inst. 2. 23. 1.

sphere: *formulae* were provided, in the Edict, of *actiones fictitiae* for this case[1], but there was no Edict about them. The *sc. Macedonianum* forbidding loans to *filiifamilias*, and the *sc. Velleianum*, forbidding surety by women, were made effective by suitable provisions in the Edict[2].

It should be added that new magistrates with special functions created by the Emperor for various purposes, with the name of Praetor, e.g., *Praetor fideicommissarius* just mentioned, *tutelaris*[3] and *de liberalibus causis*[4], never acquired the right of issuing Edicts: it was no part of the imperial scheme to extend praetorian institutions.

The next step in the history of the Edict is Julian's revision. Soon after A.D. 125 Hadrian ordered him to put the Edict into permanent form, a death-blow, as was intended, to all further praetorian initiative. All we know of his instructions is what Justinian tells us 400 years later[5], for Pomponius' account stops short of this event. The new Edict was confirmed by Senatusconsult[6], and that Julian's work on the Edict was traditionally regarded as of great importance appears from the fact that he is repeatedly spoken of as *compositor, conditor, ordinator* of the Edict[7]. We have now to consider what is known as to what he actually did.

(*a*) *The Urban Edict.* He seems to have added little. Only one new clause is known and it is called *nova clausula* of Julian[8]. This need not necessarily be "the" new clause, but the language suggests that Julian was not active in this direction. It has been made clear, further, by Lenel, that he did not alter materially the general order of the Edict[9]. There was a good deal of restating of individual rules, but that leaves little trace. It is in relation to the *formulae* of actions that Julian seems to have done most. In the Edict before his time all the various *formulae* may have been in an appendix at the end. There were other appendixes, i.e. the interdicts, the *exceptiones* and the *stipulationes praetoriae*, which he left where they were. But he dealt differently with the *formulae*. Under each edict, or group of edicts, he put the appropriate *formulae*, and, following these, usually, the *formulae* for civil actions connected with the same matter. Thus the Publician Edict was followed by the

1 Gai. 2. 253. The various ancillary protections which the Edict provided for legatees were gradually extended to *fideicommissa*, but it is likely (Lenel, *op. cit.* 372) that this was done by juristic practice and not by Edict. 2 14. 6. 11; 16. 1. 6; Karlowa, *loc. cit.*, thinks that when the *l. Aelia Sentia* prevented slaves freed under 30 from being citizens, there must have been an alteration in the Edict bringing them under the clause protecting those informally freed (*post*, § XXVII). But we do not know the form of that clause, and it may well have been wide enough to cover them. The date of the *l. Iunia*, which gave such persons the legal status of Latins, is not certain (*post*, § XXVIII), so that the clause in the Edict may have been already obsolete. 3 Vat. Fr. 232, *post*, § LIII. 4 C. 4. 56. 1. 5 *Const.* "*Tanta*," 18. 6 *Ibid.* 7 See reff. in Krueger, *R.Rq.* 94; Girard, *Mélanges*, 1. 200. 8 37. 8. 3. 9 Lenel, *E.P.* 18; Girard, *Mélanges*, 1. 177 *sqq.*

formula for the *actio Publiciana*[1] and this by the *formulae* for claims of civil ownership and the like. There was no Edict relative to these or any other civil remedy[2].

The Edict was divided into titles with separate rubrics under which there was an edict or group of edicts. There is no trace of any express division into parts, and the question what was the principle of its arrangement is too controversial to be considered in detail. Lenel holds[3] that it was essentially in four parts with the three appendixes. The first part dealt with the initiation of litigation to the issue of the *formula*, the fourth with matters after judgement. The three appendixes were in the order in which they would come into question in litigation. As to the second and third parts, he considers that the second part was concerned with litigation in the ordinary form before a single *iudex*, while the third was concerned with other forms, especially the recuperatory procedure[4]. Each contained matters which will not fit into this scheme. These he explains as cases of attraction: matters of which the chief aspects concerned, e.g., the third section, appeared there, even though subsidiary parts of them belonged to the second.

(*b*) *The other Edicts.* Julian's task covered them all, but it is clear that he did not incorporate them all in one document, for there is evidence of their continued existence in a separate form. Even the Edict of the Aediles, though the jurists commented on it as a sort of appendix to the Praetor's Edict, does not seem to have been such in fact[5]. For Gaius it is still a separate document[6]. So too the Peregrine Edict still existed. Gaius wrote a commentary on the Urban Edict which seems to shew that there were still two[7], though they would be much alike. Little indeed is heard of the Peregrine Edict afterwards, a result no doubt of Caracalla's edict on *civitas*[8]. Similarly the Provincial Edict continued: Gaius wrote a commentary on it[9]. But it seems that, after Julian, there was one general *Edictum Provinciale*, applicable in all Provinces, with such special clauses as local circumstances might require, issued, however, as a separate edict for each Province[10].

The effect of the revision or codification was to put an end to the Edict as a source of new law, for Hadrian provided that if experience shewed a need for further changes, these were to be made not by the magistrate but by *imperialis sanctio*[11], i.e. not merely by authority of the Emperor but by imperial enactment, so that the Edict was fixed for ever. Even if the text were taken in the other sense it would remain

1 *Post*, § LXX. 2 Girard, *Mélanges*, 1. 300 *sqq.* 3 *Op. cit.* 31 *sqq.* 4 *Post*, § CCXVII.
5 Karlowa *contra* (*R.Rg.* 1. 631), but the remark of Justinian on which he relies (*Const.* "*Omnem*," 4) is more usually held to refer merely to its inclusion in the commentaries.
6 Gai. 1. 6. 7 See, e.g., 28. 5. 32. 8 *Post*, § XXXVII. 9 See, e.g., 28. 5. 31.
10 Lenel, *E.P.* 4; Buckland, *R.H.* 1934, 81 *sqq.* 11 *Const.* "*Tanta*," 18.

true that the Edict would not in future initiate changes, but only register them. In fact, though there have been attempts to find new clauses added after Julian's time, none of them has resisted criticism[1]. The Edict so settled was confirmed by a Senatusconsult which bound the magistrates to follow it[2], and may be said to have given it the force of law[3]. The Edicts were still issued by the magistrates on entry on office, though they had now no control over the content. They may have lasted as long as the offices did, i.e. for the Peregrine Praetor till the third century, and for Urban Praetors and Provincial Governors till the fourth.

V. *SENATUSCONSULTA.* The Senate of the Republic had no legislative authority, but the course of events early in the Empire cannot be understood without some knowledge of the part played by the Senate in earlier days in this sphere. Throughout the later Republic the Senate became more and more the real governing body of the State[4]. The *l. Ovinia*[5], which filled it with ex-magistrates, greatly increased its weight, and few magistrates cared to enter on a struggle with such a body. In the bad days which preceded the Empire it was the only body which had any real stability. The starting-point of its legislative power was the fact that it had long been its function to direct the magistrates. There are indeed many *senatusconsulta* of republican times[6], some of which look like laws, but, if carefully looked at, are seen to be merely directions to magistrates to act in particular ways and in particular to lay down certain rules in Edicts. At first they are merely requests in form, and we must not forget that the name *Senatusconsulta* is best suited to orders which had of themselves no binding force. The later ones are obviously directions, but it is still true that it is the magistrate, the officer of the Senate, who actually lays down the rule[7].

Another point to note is that in early times all projects of law were first approved by the Senate and had, after enactment, to be approved

1 Many *utiles actiones* and the like were invented by the lawyers, after this time, so that much of what would have been edictal law in earlier days came in without express legislative authority at all. Whether the *formulae* were added to the Edict we do not know.
2 *Const.* "*Tanta,*" 18.
3 Girard (*Man.* 58) thinks it inaccurate to say that it had "force de *loi*" since this would have ended the distinction between *ius honorarium* and *civile*, which remained till Justinian. But the proposition expresses the fact that the rules were now binding on all persons until repealed, like any other law, which was not true of the old Edict, which lapsed in a year. The fact that the machinery was distinct is immaterial: it was equally true for another century of rules enforced by *cognitio extraordinaria.* It was still a distinct branch of the law, established by *sc.* which by that time had the force of law. The *l. Papia Poppaea* was not less a statute because it created *bonorum possessio* for certain cases and this was enforced by praetorian machinery. It was by giving civil remedies where there were praetorian rights that Justinian fused the systems and this only imperfectly.
4 Mommsen, *Staatsr.* 3. 1024 *sq.*; *D.P.R.* 7. 219; Kuebler, 100; de Francisci, *Storia*, 2. 1. 73.
5 Festus, s.v. *Praeteriti* (*senatores*). See Willems, *D.P.* 187 *sqq.*
6 Girard, *Textes*, 129 *sqq.*; Bruns, 1. 164 *sqq.*
7 See Kipp, 60.

by the *patres* (*auctoritas patrum*) before they became law. We need not discuss the confused story of the disappearance of these requirements as matter of law[1]: the important point is that there is evidence that this consultation of the Senate continually occurred in the later Republic[2]. Further, the Senate could declare a law invalid for defect of formality or disregard of auspices[3]. It had also the power of dispensing from or suspending laws in urgent cases, i.e. of directing a magistrate not to apply a given law in a certain case or for a time. This required confirmation by the *Comitia* as soon as possible, but by 150 B.C. it seems to have been freely done without this confirmation. In the last half-century of the Republic the restriction of urgency disappeared in practice. An attempt was made to get rid of the power, but it led only to a *lex Cornelia* which confirmed it, requiring, however, the presence of at least 200 senators and a subsequent vote of the assembly[4]. It could issue orders in relation to branches of administration under its care, notably in foreign relations, the distribution of *provinciae* among magistrates, and the supervision of religious organisations so far as their functions concerned the State. In the late Republic it could relax the rules of procedure for the *Comitia* or for itself: it could give exemptions from foreign service, and authorise triumphs[5]. All this shews a good foundation for the acquisition of legislative power which occurred soon after the founding of the Empire.

We saw that Augustus sought to galvanise the *Comitia*, for his own purposes: he did the same for the Senate, an easier task since that body had not so utterly decayed. It was not his plan that the Senate should have real power. As a part of his reorganisation he fixed its number at 600. The membership was to be revised annually and, when he held the office of Censor, the Emperor nominated to all vacancies[6]: indeed, from Domitian's time, he nominated always[7]. As *Princeps Senatus* he had the right to preside, and the Senate, like other bodies, could consider only what was submitted to it by its president. It could be no more than a mouthpiece of the Emperor. The power of making general *senatusconsulta* with the force of laws was never actually conferred on it. Texts which have been cited as attributing the conferment to various persons do not for the most part deal with the point at all[8]. Theophilus, writing in the sixth century, attributes the change to the *l. Hortensia*[9], but no weight attaches to this. The true account is to be found in the jurists. Pom-

1 Mommsen, *Staatsr*. 3. 1037 *sqq.*; *D.P.R.* 7. 236 *sqq.* 2 Mommsen, *Staatsr*. 3. 1045; *D.P.R.* 7. 243. 3 Willems, *D.P.* 182. 212. 4 67 B.C.; Willems, *Sénat Romain*, 2. 118. 5 Willems, *D.P.* 212. 6 Suetonius, *Augustus*, 35; Willems, *D.P.* 449. 7 Willems, *D.P.* 450. 8 Suetonius says of Julius Caesar (*Jul.* 41): "*comitia cum populo partitus est.*" Tacitus says of Tiberius (*Ann.* 1. 15): "*tum primum e campo comitia ad patres translata sunt.*" In each case the context shews that these obscure expressions have to do with appointments of magistrates. 9 Theoph. *ad* Inst. 1. 2. 5.

ponius treats it as an inevitable outcome of the decay of the *Comitia*[1]. Gaius shews that there had been disputes as to the existence of the power[2], which indicates a gradual growth. It was an usurpation encouraged by the Emperor for obvious reasons: the starting-point was the old directions to magistrates. Nearly all *senatusconsulta* of the first century of the Empire were really directions to magistrates. Thus the well-known *scc. Velleianum* and *Macedonianum*[3] operated as directions to the Praetor to insert *exceptiones* in his Edict. Others were extensions and interpretations of existing laws, e.g. those under the *l. Fufia Caninia*[4]. It is possible that the right was not fully recognised until the *Comitia* had quite ceased to legislate, and Girard finds no clear case till the *sc. Tertullianum* of Hadrian's time[5]. Krueger points out that *senatusconsulta* have no official name: many have none. It was customary to give them the name of the Consul at the time of their enactment in a lengthened adjectival form, but that this was not official appears from the fact that it was sometimes his *nomen*, sometimes a *cognomen*, and in one well-known case—the *Macedonianum*—the enactment is named after the man whose misconduct produced it[6].

The Senate soon lost any independence in legislation. Very early the practice grew of submitting to the Senate proposals already drafted by a committee or *consilium*, the Senate merely voting. The committee was intermittent and its constitution varied. Its relation to the *Consilium Principis*, found in full operation after Hadrian, is not clear: opinions differ on the question whether they were independent developments, or the latter grew out of the former[7]. The Emperor himself proposed the most important *scc.*, and it is noted by Mommsen[8] that no one else is ever in the Empire described as *auctor senatusconsulti*. He acted sometimes personally, sometimes by a representative who read his *Oratio*, and before long there was always a written *oratio*, whether the Emperor was present or not. The vote was a matter of course, so that the *oratio* came to be regarded even by the lawyers as the real source of law: they cited it rather than the formal vote which made it effective. Karlowa points out traces in the language of surviving *orationes* of a transition from language of request to that of command[9]. The seven witnesses, so common in the later Roman Law, appear here: the formal record of the senatusconsult was accompanied by the *signatio* of seven senators, who took part in the vote[10].

1 1. 2. 2. 9. 2 Gai. 1. 4. 3 The language of 16. 1. 2. 1 is very significant. 4 The *sc. Silanianum* (A.D. 10) which orders that the will of a murdered man is not to be opened till his slaves have been put to the torture is sometimes treated as a direct alteration of the civil law, but it was a direction to the magistrate embodied in the Edict. Lenel, *E.P.* 364. 5 *Man.* 62. 6 14. 6. 1. pr. 7 Krueger, *R.Rq.* 116. 8 *Staatsr.* 2. 899; *D.P.R.* 5. 178. 9 *R.Rg.* 1. 644. 10 Karlowa, *op. cit.* 1. 646.

In the later days of *senatusconsulta* the jurists habitually speak of them as laid down by the Emperor. How long they continued to be issued is uncertain, but the last of which anything is known is spoken of in the life of Probus (A.D. 276–282), and the language is instructive. The writer, after recording the *oratio* and the resulting senatusconsult, adds that the Emperor, by a second *oratio*, "*permisit patribus*" certain things, amongst others "*leges quas Probus ederet senatusconsultis propriis consecrare*[1]." They were allowed to go through the form of registering imperial enactments. It was time for them to cease[2].

VI. *PRINCIPUM PLACITA.* We saw that when Augustus became sole ruler he renounced and restored to the popular assembly the legislative power held by the triumvirate, and also that this was in no way designed to restore power to the people: it merely provided him with a means of making his will effective in an indirect way. The language of the *lex de imperio*, by which power was conferred on him, might be understood to give him legislative power[3], but it is fairly clear that it merely gave him absolute discretionary power in administrative matters. The Emperors were at first subject to the laws, being simply chief magistrates. Some texts speak of them as *legibus soluti*[4], but these are in the Digest and torn from their context. When their source is looked into it becomes clear that they originally referred to specific statutes and express the undoubted fact that the Emperor could dispense himself from, and could be, and often was, excluded from, the operation of particular statutes. But from some time in the third century the Emperor began to be regarded as above the law[5].

From the beginning however he exercised a certain legislative power. Late in the Republic it had been usual to authorise magistrates to make laws for communities which had become part of the State, laws so made being called *leges datae*[6]. The Emperor seems to have been regarded as authorised to do this, but these *leges datae* are of small importance for us[7]. The same may be said of *ll. dictae*, statutes imposed by the Emperor on regions regarded as in his private ownership, i.e. not the imperial provinces but the Emperor's private domains[8]. More important for our purpose was the gradual transfer to the Emperor of the power to

1 *Vita Probi*, 13. 1.

2 Account of the most important *scc.*, Kuebler, 246.

3 Girard, *Textes*, 107; Bruns, 1. 202. Di Marzo, *St. Perozzi*, 129 *sqq.*, holds that military *imperium* was conferred by the Senate, administrative powers by a *lex tributa*, the *lex de imperio*. But as to the merely formal character of this and the real importance of the Senate in the matter, Schulz, *Das Wesen des Röm. Kaisertums*, and de Francisci, *Storia*, 2. 1. 255.

4 E.g. 1. 3. 31.

5 Karlowa, *op. cit.* 1. 826.

6 Specimens, Bruns, 1. 120 *sqq.*

7 Some of them shew, however, that institutions and ideas had already appeared in Roman Law of which we have no other equally early trace.

8 The best known instance is the *lex metalli Vipacensis*, Girard, *Textes*, 119; Bruns, 1. 289.

dispense from, and to suspend, to interpret and even to extend, *leges*, a transfer which was already beginning in the time of Augustus.

Actual legislation was thus very early and it was fully recognised by the time of Hadrian that the Emperor could make what were in effect laws. Theoretically there was however a certain inferiority, and the progress is shewn in three well-known texts. Gaius says that the Emperor's enactments "*legis vicem obtinent.*" Ulpian a little later says that "*legis vigorem habent*" and, immediately after, he says, or is made to say, "*leges esse*[1]." This is very different from the attitude of Augustus. *Fideicommissa* were really his work, but he did not enact that they should be valid. He directed the consuls to enforce them in a few individual cases, "*semel iterumque gratia personarum motus,*" rather, apparently, as a matter of *mores* than as a legal system, and they only gradually became a settled institution, "*paulatim conversum est in adsiduam jurisdictionem*[2]." The permanent officers to deal with them were no doubt appointed by the Senate.

In his legislative as in other work the Emperor was assisted by a *Consilium*, older than Hadrian, but first put on an organised footing by him[3]. It was a large body containing a number of jurists, the chief member being the *Praefectus Praetorio*, often a lawyer. In the later Empire this body came to be called the *Consistorium* and its principal member was the *Quaestor Sacri Palatii*, also usually a lawyer[4]. The *Consilium* was merely advisory: its members had no vote and the Emperor decided all questions himself. Several cases are recorded in which he decided against the sense of the great lawyers on the *Consilium*[5].

By the end of the third century the Emperor was sole legislator. The jurists had difficulty in finding a basis for his right, but they settled on the *lex regia*[6], though this was not intended to give the power: it was in fact a gradual encroachment.

When, early in the fourth century, the Empire was divided into two parts, Eastern and Western, these two halves, retaining their character as parts of the same Empire, were governed by two Emperors with co-ordinate authority. The law of one was the law of the other, and thus any law promulgated in either region was at once law in the other[7]. This could not work well, and Theodosius the Great, when, in A.D. 439, he put his codification into force, provided that future legislation by the Emperor of one part should not be law in the other till it had been

1 G. 1. 5; D. 1. 4. 1. pr. and 1. 2 Inst. 2. 23. 1. 3 *Vita Hadriani*, 18, where the special reference is to judicial action; *ante*, 15, n. 3. 4 This office was held by Justinian's great adviser, Tribonian; Inst. *Proem.* 3. 5 4. 4. 38. pr.; 14. 5. 8. On this *consilium*, Mommsen, *Staatsr.* 2. 988; *D.P.R.* 5. 279. 6 1. 4. 1; Gai. 1. 5, whose language, basing it on *imperium*, shews the unreality of this explanation. 7 Krueger, *R.Rq.* 310.

promulgated by the Emperor of that part[1]. This too might have led to difficulties, but not long after, the Western Empire ceased to exist[2].

There is some difficulty about the nomenclature of imperial enactments. The word *placitum* covers them all, but is not technical and it would include decisions which are not legislation. The most common term is *Constitutio*, but there is confusion as to what that term covers. Gaius includes under it *Edicta, Decreta* and *Epistolae* or *Rescripta*. No jurist includes *Mandata*. In one text *Constitutiones* are opposed to *Rescripta*[3], and a rubric distinguishes them from *Edicta*[4]. Ulpian gives much the same account as Gaius, but says the name is not technical—"*quas volgo constitutiones appellamus*[5]." The point is not important: all might make law; none always did. Of those with which we are concerned, the great majority are rescripts, till late in the empire. Each form of enactment has its own history and they must be considered separately[6].

VII. *Edicta.* The Emperor, as chief magistrate, had the *ius edicendi*, and imperial *Edicta* are found from the time of Augustus. The earlier *Edicta* follow the republican pattern: they do not usually embody any actually new developments, but are mainly concerned with extensions and corrections of existing legislation. As the power of the Emperor grew this was disregarded, and in Hadrian's time and thereafter law was freely made by Edict. These continued throughout the Empire. Many of Justinian's are in existence: the edicts of later law are however of little importance for us: they are concerned with public matters. But many rules of classical law are based on imperial Edict[7].

The republican magistrate had power only for a year, and in a determined area, and the force of his Edict was similarly limited. But the Emperor had magisterial authority over the whole empire for life, and his Edict had force everywhere, and for his life. It may have failed at his death, in the first two centuries, for though a text speaks of an Edict of Augustus as having been abolished after his time[8], this is not conclusive: Edicts were frequently renewed by the successor, and this may have been so renewed and afterwards withdrawn. This frequent renewal would tend to become tacit, a process helped by the develop-

1 Krueger, *op. cit.* 331. 2 At the time of Justinian's codification Italy was not part of his empire, and the essentially eastern character of his legislation is brought out by Collinet, *Études historiques*, 1. So long as both Empires existed laws bore the names of both Emperors. It is usually easy, from internal evidence, to tell in which Empire the law was enacted. 3 C. 2. 42. 3. pr. 4 C. Th. 1. 1. 5 1. 4. 1. 1. 6 Mode of promulgation of imperial enactments, Mommsen, *Ges. Schr.* (*Jur.*), 2. 178 *sqq.* 7 E.g. C. 7. 6. 1. 3; Inst. 2. 6. 14; 3. 7. 4. Mommsen, *Staatsr.* 2. 906; *D.P.R.* 5. 186. 8 28. 2. 26.

ment of the notion that the Emperor's orders "*legis vicem obtinent*[1]." In later law they were certainly permanent.

The Emperor issued Edicts not by virtue of any particular magistracy, but under his general imperial authority. They were not published through an official, but directly by the Emperor.

Decreta[2]. These were judicial decisions of the Emperor, either on hearings in first instance, where the Emperor was sitting in his capacity as magistrate, or on appeals which had reached the imperial *auditorium*, or, brought about by *supplicatio* of some private person, operating as a sort of overriding equity[3]. We are told that they might be *interlocutiones*, i.e. the Emperor might intervene at any stage in a legal process and issue a *Decretum* which would tie the hands of the official in charge of the case. In one recorded case it is not clear that there had been any litigation, but the Emperor was in some way informed of an apparent injustice which was being done in accord with law, and at once issued a *Decretum* deciding the matter in a way certainly inconsistent with the existing law[4]. The great majority of *Decreta* made no new law: they were merely decisions on the existing law. But Gaius and Ulpian tell us[5] that where they did make new law or settle doubts they had the force of law. It was not necessary that the *Decretum* should purport to lay down a new rule: if it actually did so, the rule was law. It seems that those which did this were published while others were not, at any rate till the third century. By this time *Decreta* had become less important. Most of them had been decisions on appeal, and a practice developed of taking appeals by method of Rescript. Instead of appeal by the parties, there was a submission of the case by the magistrate or judge, somewhat like the English practice of "stating a case," and the Emperor's decision would be by Rescript. When it is remembered that the primary purpose of a *Decretum* was not to make new law, it becomes clear that its history as a source of law is not a long one. Recorded *decreta* in private law are few, and mostly on small points[6].

VIII. *Rescripta, Epistolae, Subscriptiones*[7]. These were in principle answers to enquiries. *Epistolae* were answers to officials, embodied in a separate document, issuing from the office *ab epistulis* and addressed to the enquiring official. *Subscriptiones* were answers to enquiries or petitions from private persons, applying personally or by

1 Karlowa, *R.Rg.* 1. 647. Wilcken, *Z.S.S.* 1921, 133; Wenger, *Abh. d. Bay. Akad.* 1928, *Abh.* 2, p. 70 give reason for believing that they were always permanent. 2 Karlowa, *op. cit.* 649; Krueger, *R.Rq.* 103; Kipp, 70. 3 *Post*, § CCXXVII. 4 40. 5. 38. 5 G. 1. 5; D. 1. 4. 1. 1, 2. 6 40. 5. 38; 48. 7. 7. Paul made a collection of imperial *decreta*; see Lenel, *Palingenesia*, 1. 959. On procedure by rescript, *post*, § CCXXVII. 7 Karlowa, *op. cit.* 1. 650; Kipp, 71; Krueger, *op. cit.* 304; Wilcken, *Hermes*, 1920, 1.

representative[1], endorsed on the application itself, issuing from the office *a libellis*[2] and returned to the applicant[3]. The name Rescript was applied to both, though more commonly to *Epistolae*. There were also *Rescripta* issued to an official without previous application, though here the name seems to be misplaced[4]. It seems from the evidence that law or etiquette prevented any but high officials from applying for a Rescript.

Rescripts were not primarily intended to change the law, but to explain it to the applicant, and at first they merely did this. *Epistolae* are found as early as Trajan and *Subscriptiones* at any rate under Hadrian[5]. From that time both were common: they are supposed to have owed their increasing importance as sources of law to the cessation of legislation by the Praetor's Edict, changes now being made by *imperialis sanctio*[6]. The increase in frequency and importance of Rescripts[7] is also in part due to the fact already noted that in later law the method of appeal by statement of the case by the magistrate largely superseded ordinary appeal by the parties. As in the case of *Decreta*, Rescripts not intended to alter the law do not seem to have been published, at any rate till the third century. It should be added that though Rescripts which were in effect decisions on appeal were common, so also were Rescripts on application before the decision: these were remitted to the Court and bound it. If the application contained allegations of fact the Emperor did not enquire into these: his Rescript was sometimes expressly conditional on their truth, and even if this was omitted the principle held good, and the Court must look into the facts before deciding[8].

There remained one great practical difficulty in the use of Rescripts. As we have seen, their primary purpose was not law reform: it was only gradually and incidentally that they gained this function. There were thus four classes: (*a*) those which merely stated the law, (*b*) those which laid down a new rule but were *privilegia*, not intended for general application[9], (*c*) those which embodied a change for general application, (*d*) those which laid down a new rule, but were in fact errors and were not intended to do so. How was the Court to determine to which of these classes a Rescript brought to its notice belonged? In some cases the Rescript expressly said that it was or was not to be taken as a precedent. But in many cases, and especially where the Rescript embodied

1 Wilcken, *cit.* § 2. 2 Willems, *D.P.* 436. Form, Wilcken, *cit.* § 4. 3 Wilcken, *cit.* § 3, shews that *subscriptiones* were posted up in the second century (*propositae*) while *epistolae* were registered (*insinuatae*) though they might be *propositae* by the officials to whom they were addressed. 4 Kipp, *loc. cit.* 5 Krueger, *op. cit.* 104. 6 *Ante*, § IV. The power of legislation by rescript is, as usual, based on the *l. regia*. 1. 4. 1. 7 Appleton, *N.R.H.* 1910, 777, as to lack of authority in the early Empire. 8 49. 1. 1. 1; C. 1. 21. 1. 9 1. 4. 1. 2. A poor authority says that Macrinus deprived all rescripts of his predecessors of any authority as having been very likely given by favour. *Vita Opilii Macrini*, 13.

an error, this would not appear. The difficulty was felt and in the later Empire there was legislation to deal with it. Constantine enacted that Rescripts *contra ius* were not to be binding in future cases, while those which laid down *publica iura* were[1], but this left the Court still to determine which were which. Arcadius provided that Rescripts were not to be binding in future cases[2] (which suggests that Constantine's law had in fact deprived *subscriptiones* of all authority). Valentinian III limited this by providing that they were to be binding if expressed to be binding in future cases[3]. Justinian provided that even where there was no such declaration, if the Rescript, or other form of imperial pronouncement, in its terms, laid down a general rule, this was to apply in future cases, though not so expressed[4].

Mandata[5]. These are unimportant in private law. Usually administrative directions to provincial officials, they occasionally laid down rules of law. They operated only for the life of the issuing emperor and only in the region to which they were addressed, but in fact they were renewed and often addressed to many districts. And as the Emperor could make law in any form he chose, he could do it by Mandate. They are occasionally quoted by jurists[6].

When, by the third century, the Emperor's right to make law was fully recognised, with the corollary that its form was his own affair, any utterance of his being binding, and when, in addition to this, he became sole legislator, at latest by the fourth century, it is plain that any distinction between modes was of secondary importance. Much confusion of terminology arose. The name Edict was applied to provisions for special districts: nearly all Justinian's Edicts are more like *mandata.* It became usual to call imperial enactments *leges.* Many of the important enactments of later emperors in the Code of Justinian are what are called *leges generales* or, somewhat confusingly, *leges edictales,* and hardly conform to the classification above stated. Some appear in the form of *Orationes ad Senatum,* a reminiscence of the earliest form of imperial enactment, but of a different character. The Senate had changed: it was now little more than a town council. The enactment was addressed to it as a convenient mode of publication which would also be gratifying to the Senate and population of the city. There was no question of cooperation by the Senate: there was no senatusconsult[7].

IX. The Jurists. As has been observed, the jurists of the classical age are the real builders of the great fabric of Roman Law which we

1 C. Th. 1. 2. 2. 2 C. Th. 1. 2. 11. 3 C. 1. 14. 3. 4 C. 1. 14. 12. 7 Krueger, *op. cit.* 109. 6 Heumann-Seckel, *Handlex.* s.v. *Mandare.* 7 Krueger, *op. cit.* 301 *sqq.*; another late method is *Pragmaticae Sanctiones* or *Pragmaticae Formae.* Most of these resemble *leges datae* or *mandata,* but a few contain new general rules of private law. Sometimes they are declared to be *leges generales.* Some are called *Pragmatica Rescripta.*

study. Space does not admit of more than a brief statement of the main points of interest in their history.

THE FUNCTIONS OF THE JURISTS[1]. The account which Cicero gives[2] of the early jurists as constantly consulted on every kind of affair, juristic or not, had ceased to be true of his own time. But the picture which he draws here and there of the jurists remains true for the age of classical jurisprudence. He states their *interpretatio* as a source of law side by side with laws and edicts[3]. He tells us in passages which make no pretence of scientific exactness, but which no doubt give a true enough account, that the business of the jurist is three (or four) fold[4]:

(*a*) *Respondere.* This was giving advice on consultation, not merely to private persons, but to *iudices* and magistrates, and not necessarily formally, as in the case of privileged *responsa* shortly to be considered, but in any form and place, even in a walk across the Forum[5].

(*b*) *Agere.* This was guiding the conduct of lawsuits. The jurists did not act as advocates: this was the business of the *oratores*, the class of which Cicero was the ornament. What the jurist did was to instruct the advocate on the points of law involved and help him with advice.

(*c*) *Cavere.* This was assistance in the performance of legal transactions and might well include what Cicero calls *scribere*, the preparation of legal documents.

He also mentions as a duty of the good jurist, instruction. This is not the ordinary elementary teaching in law: that was presumably then, as later, in the hands of professional teachers. The great men may have acted as chiefs of legal schools[6], but for the most part their teaching consisted in permitting younger men to be present at consultations, with, no doubt, informal talk on points which had arisen.

Responsa were usually written, and, where they were in connexion with litigation, either sent direct to the *iudex* or put in by the *orator*. Apart from the privilege of the *ius respondendi* they were in no way binding on the *iudex*[7]: they owed their weight to the personal reputation of the jurist, but unlearned *iudices*, who were mere private persons, would tend to follow them, and thus they exercised a great influence on the law. The jurist held no official position and took no fees. It was not directly as a means of living that this career was entered on, but as one of the surest roads to popularity[8] and eminence in public life, and to the rewards of public office. The careers of soldier, orator and jurist are

1 Jörs, *Röm. Rechtswissensch. der Rep.* §§ xx–xxiv; de Francisci, *Storia*, 2. 1. 186.
2 *De Orat.* 3. 33. 133–135.
3 *Topica*, 5. 28.
4 *De Orat.* 1. 48. 212; *Pro Murena*, 9. 19.
5 *De Orat.* 3. 33. 133.
6 *Post*, §§ IX–XI.
7 Cicero tells us of a decision in direct opposition to the view of Q. M. Scaevola, one of the greatest jurists of his time. *Pro Caec.* 24. 67–69.
8 See D. 1. 2. 2. 37 for the story of C. Scipio Nasica who was given a house on the *Via Sacra* by the State "*quo facilius consuli posset.*"

repeatedly spoken of as the most honourable open to a citizen[1], and of these, under imperial conditions, the last was by far the most independent.

These activities do not exhaust their modes of exercising influence in the law. They sometimes acted as assessors to *iudices* and practically dictated the judgements. Often they were assessors or *comites* to the magistrates, who were not always lawyers, guiding them in legal questions[2]. Much of the Praetor's Edict was due only nominally to him, but was the work of his more learned councillors. Further, they were active in producing juristic literature[3]: for the purposes of legal development it was their most important work.

THE *IUS RESPONDENDI*. It is recorded that at an early date in the empire certain jurists were given the right *publice respondendi*, i.e. of giving *responsa* under seal, authorised by the Emperor, which were binding in the case in connexion with which they were issued. Pomponius tells us in a rather corrupt passage[4] that, before Augustus, lawyers gave *responsa* in any form or conditions they liked, but that Augustus, to increase their authority, gave certain jurists the right *publice respondere*, or, as he also puts it, to give *responsa ex auctoritate principis*, such *responsa* being under seal, and so sent to the *iudex*. The Institutes[5] tell us that *Caesar*, i.e. the Emperor, had anciently given the *ius respondendi* to certain of the jurists who were to interpret the law "*publice*" and that their *responsa*, if submitted to a *iudex*, bound him, but not if the opinions submitted disagreed. Till a century ago this was substantially all the evidence and the text of the Institutes was naturally coupled with that of the Digest, which said nothing about binding effect, and the result arrived at that Augustus made the opinions of privileged jurists binding on the *iudex*. Early in the last century Gaius became available and a passage was found which was plainly the source of the text in the Institutes. But Gaius says that Hadrian made *responsa* bind the *iudex* if they were in agreement[6]. It was thus no longer obvious that Augustus made them binding and different opinions began to appear. The majority of writers however still hold that it was Augustus who gave *responsa* binding force, and they explain the text of Gaius as meaning that Hadrian settled a difficulty which had arisen where conflicting opinions were given by equally privileged jurists. Apart from the foregoing texts this rests partly on a text of Seneca, written before Hadrian's time, which says incidentally that *responsa* of jurists *valent*[7] though no reasons are assigned, and partly on such considerations as the consistency of the device with the general

1 Jörs, *op. cit.* 255. 2 Cicero, *Topica*, 17. 65; Lévy-Bruhl, *Prudent et Préteur*. 3 *Post*, § XI. 4 1. 2. 2. 49. 5 Inst. 1. 2. 8. 6 Gai. 1. 7. 7 Seneca, *Epist.* 94. 27.

policy of Augustus. But in fact it would not be like his method elsewhere. His changes were made by utilising the republican machinery, worked by him in the strong position of chief magistrate. Within the system he framed he could not himself have bound the *iudex* to any particular judgement[1]. It is difficult to see how he could have authorised anybody else to do so. On the other hand the method of attaching the jurists to himself and making their power appear an emanation from his own, by giving the chief among them a sort of patent of precedence, which would inevitably in the long run mean *de facto* authority, was exactly on his lines.

No juristic text suggests that Augustus made *responsa* binding. Gaius, whose text is corrupt but explicit on this point, says that Hadrian made them binding if they agreed, and does not mention Augustus. It is said indeed that Augustus laid down a general rule and Hadrian a necessary corrective. So obvious a point could not have been open for more than a century, and Gaius could hardly have ignored the real source of the rule.

Pomponius in his long discussion shews that in his time there had been no fundamental change[2]. He states the sources in historical order, and in his list the *interpretatio prudentium* appears as a synonym for *ius civile* in the old sense. It is mentioned after *lex* and before *plebiscitum* and is clearly the *interpretatio* of the old jurists. Then come the later sources, but there is no reference to *responsa*, from which the inference is that they were no more sources of law than they had been for centuries. He was writing before Hadrian's changes, at any rate he does not mention the revision of the Edict. Gaius, in a scheme which is apparently historical, puts *edicta* after *principum placita*, which shews that he is referring to Julian's revision, and *responsa* after *edicta*[3]. This suggests that the authoritative *responsa* as he knew them were due to Hadrian. If Pomponius really meant to tell us of such an important change he was unfortunate in omitting the main point[4].

1 Different view, de Francisci, *Storia*, 2. 1. 2 1. 2. 2. 5, 6, 35 *sqq*. *Contra*, Bonfante, *Storia*, 1. 159. 3 Gai. 1. 2. 4 Pomponius (1. 2. 2. 49 *in f.*) mentions another rescript of Hadrian which has been supposed to create difficulties. After stating Augustus' enactment he adds: "*et ideo Hadrianus cum ab eo viri praetorii peterent ut sibi liceret respondere rescripsit eis hoc non peti sed praestari solere, et ideo si quis fiduciam sui haberet delectari se ad respondendum se praepararet.*" This corrupt text has been amended so as to support various hypotheses. It has however nothing to do with his legislation. Pomponius cites it as a commentary on the enactment of Augustus, and especially on the words "*ex auctoritate eius.*" The applicants omitted the important part, and Hadrian says no authority is wanted for what they ask for. It is a little jest: he was partial to jests (*Vita Hadriani*, 20. 8). The only significance of the text is the further evidence it provides for the view that the *auctoritas* Augustus provided had not so far affected the position of the jurists, but that error as to its purport was possible, and that he did not prevent unauthorised jurists from giving *responsa*.

It is clear that a change in the position of the jurists did occur under Hadrian[1]. They began freely to hold imperial magistracies, *praefecturae*, etc.[2] The only jurists not alive under or after Hadrian who are known to have issued *responsa* are Labeo[3], who probably never had the *ius respondendi*, and Sabinus, who received it from Tiberius[4]. Collections of them were very usual forms of literature after the time of Hadrian[5].

The remark of Seneca implies no more than *de facto* authority: one accepts an expert's opinion whether he gives his reasons or not. Cicero might have said it[6]. So too Caligula is reported to have said that he would destroy the jurisconsults: "*se mehercule effecturum ne quid respondere possint praeter eum*[7]." This too implies no more than practical weight and neither Seneca nor he distinguishes between one class of lawyers and another.

There seems no real evidence for the view that Augustus made *responsa* binding for the actual case and Hadrian for future cases as well. The better opinion is that Augustus did not change the legal position of *responsa*, but that a license from the Emperor could not fail, before long, to give these privileged *responsa* an overriding influence on the mind of the judge, that this is the régime to which the texts of Seneca and Suetonius refer, and that Hadrian set the matter on a regular footing, using the legislative power which he undoubtedly had and Augustus had not[8]. It seems clear that whatever the nature of Augustus' change it did not bar unprivileged jurists from giving *responsa*[9]. Augustus is not likely to have given his opponent Labeo the *ius respondendi*, but he issued a volume of *responsa*. It is probable that in later times only the privileged jurists issued such books[10].

The question remains: what were the limits of Hadrian's authorisation? The most probable answer is that his authorisation extended only to the case for which the *responsum* was obtained[11]. But this is

1 Gaius in enumerating the sources of law does not mention custom and treats *responsa* as sources like *leges*. Thus it may be said that for him they are *ius scriptum*. The distinction, *scriptum, non scriptum*, is found in no classical juristic text. For Perozzi (*Ist.* 1. 42) it is borrowed in Byzantine times from Greek law in which it was familiar. This requires wholesale rejection of the texts in D. 1. 3. 2 Cassius and Pegasus however had held imperial magistracies. Roby, *Introd. to Dig.* cxlv, cli. 3 Coll. 12. 7. 3 (cf. D. 9. 2. 27. 8 where the ref. to Labeo is omitted. The work is not in the Florentine index). 4 1. 2. 2. 48. 5 See the Florentine index. 6 Cicero, *Topica*, 5. 28. 7 Suetonius, *Caligula*, 34. The words being corrupt have been amended by reading *rem* for *eum*. This is inconsistent with the rest of Suetonius' language, and it is unlikely that Suetonius meant to charge the emperor with such an innocent remark as this. 8 Opinion is much divided. For binding force under Augustus, e.g., Karlowa, *R.Rg.* 1. 660; Krueger, *R.Rq.* 121; Girard, *Man.* 76; Jörs, *R.R.* 20; Bonfante, *Storia*, 1. 158; de Francisci, *Storia*, 2. 345. *Contra*, Kipp, 108; Cuq, *Man.* 53; Siber, *R.R.* 1. 51. 9 Karlowa, *op. cit.* 1. 659, holds that others might give *responsa* but these might not be cited in court. 10 *Responsa* were not binding on magistrates, Wenger, *Praetor und Formel*, § 6, citing contrary views. 11 See

difficult to reconcile with the language of Gaius, who speaks of *sententiae et opiniones* of those to whom it has been allowed *iura condere*. Justinian says much the same except that he does not expressly mention Hadrian. This language suggests a wider authorisation, and many views are held. The words *iura condere* have led some to hold that *responsa* were binding in future cases. The words *sententiae et opiniones* have led to the improbable view that all writings of privileged jurists were binding. But literary work is a different matter from advice to clients: it would be impossible to give binding force to the speculative opinions of any living man however distinguished. The other view has more to be said for it, but it is unlike the Emperors to set up an authority so little under their control. The text is corrupt[1]: opinions differ as to the degree of corruption, but the only part that can be really relied on is the reference to Hadrian. Ancient works which have existed for generations in manuscript, repeatedly recopied, undergo a steady process of corruption largely by the incorporation into the text of marginal comments. Something of this sort has happened here; how much is uncertain, but enough to disentitle us to draw inferences from the wording. Later in the empire there was legislation giving authority to the writings of deceased jurists[2], a very different matter. It is easy to see how in view of this legislation such glosses would creep into the text.

Whatever be the scope of *ius respondendi* it would seem important enough to have been recorded in the information we have as to any jurist. But, though we may assume that it was not granted to many at the same time, it was probably granted to all who were in the Emperor's *consilium*, and yet we do not know that this was so. Only of two jurists do we know that they had this privilege. One is Sabinus at the beginning, who received it from Tiberius[3], the other is an otherwise unknown man, Innocentius, who received it from Diocletian[4], so that the grant of the privilege survived the age of the great jurists[5].

X. THE CONFLICTS OF THE SCHOOLS[6]. The jurists of the Empire up to the time of Hadrian appear as divided into two opposing groups (*scholae*

lit. cit. p. 24, n. 8 and Glasson, *Ét. sur Gaius*, 54. They could be cited in later cases, but that is a different matter, de Francisci, *Storia*, 2. 1. 346 and reff.

1 For wholesale rejection Kniep, *Gai. Comm. Primus*, 3 and 105. 2 *Post*, § XII. 3 1. 2. 2. 48. 4 Krueger, *op. cit.* 296. 5 In case of conflict was the *iudex* absolutely free or must he follow one of the opinions expressed? Does the *omnium* of Gaius mean all who are cited or all the patented jurists of the time? If the latter view is correct, *responsa*, as decisive, would not play a prominent part in legislation. Neither the *liber singularis regularum* nor Paul (*Sententiae*) ever cites a *responsum*. Gaius cites one (3. 198), but it is clear from the corresponding text in the Inst. of Justinian that the point was still open (4. 1. 8). They are a little more freely cited in collections made before Justinian, but after legislation giving some sort of authority to writings. 6 Roby, *Introd. to Dig.* cxxvii *sqq.*; Krueger, *op. cit.* 160 *sqq.*

or *sectae*). The two *sectae* are said by Pomponius to have been founded by Labeo and Capito and may have originated in the personal rivalry and political opposition between Antistius Labeo, the republican, a man of independent mind and prone to innovation, and Ateius Capito, the adherent of the empire, inclined to follow tradition and to rest upon authority. Divergent tendencies, however, are to be found earlier between Quintus Mucius on the one hand and Servius Sulpicius on the other, and the schools may be remotely descended from them[1]. The growth into distinct schools may have been gradual, for the schools derive their names from later leaders, that resting on Labeo from Proculus, a follower of Labeo's follower, Nerva, and the other from Masurius Sabinus, a follower of Capito, or sometimes from Cassius[2], who followed Sabinus. The schools had recognised leaders whom Pomponius speaks of[3] as "succeeding[4]" the one the other, a form which he never uses of the republican lawyers. He gives lists, perhaps not complete, down to his own time, Julian, the Sabinian, being the last. Of no jurist later than Julian is it certainly known that he was attached to either school, except that Gaius speaks of the schools as still existing and of himself as a Sabinian. It is sometimes said that the schools lasted to the time of Papinian, whose greatness united all. But there is no evidence of their endurance to his time, and if any individual jurist ended the schools by his ascendency it is far more likely to have been Julian[5]. From the fact that in the lists given by Pomponius there are sometimes, towards the end, two leaders on each side at the same time, it has been conjectured that the schools may have perished from internal dissensions, and that, even in the time of Gaius, the schools as organisations were dead, though some jurists still attached themselves to the doctrines propounded by the one or the other.

The Sources, especially Gaius, record many disputes between the schools and others which probably are such, though they are stated as disputes between individual jurists. Many attempts have been made to determine what, if any, was the difference of principle which divided

1 Karlowa, *R.Rg.* 1. 483; Arnò, *Scuola Muciana e scuola Serviana*; Vernay, *Servius et son école, conclusion*; Huvelin, *Furtum*, 1. ch. XII. But for Vernay, *op. cit.* 303, Servius is the forerunner of the Proculians. For Arnò and Huvelin, *op. cit.* 681, he is the forerunner of the Sabinians. This seems the better view. Arnò has illustrated it in a number of studies.

2 For Baviera, *St. Scialoja*, 2. 759, the names are late: *Cassiani* is the primary name, and any text before Severus using a collective school name is interpolated. The name *Sabiniani* may have been originally based on Caelius Sabinus (Arnò, *St. Perozzi*, 264). See, for a study of Cassius and his importance, Arnò, *Nuovi Studi su Cassio*.

3 No work of Sabinus or of Cassius seems to have survived to Justinian's age, for though they are very frequently cited by other jurists, there is in the Digest no direct quotation from them. Earlier jurists are directly represented, e.g. Aelius Gallus, Quintus Mucius and Alfenus.

4 1. 2. 2. 48.

5 Kipp, § 18.

the schools. It is not necessary to go into them, for none has any wide acceptance[1] or stands the test of submission to the actually recorded opinions, but two conclusions emerge from the discussion. There is no evidence that the characteristics of Labeo and Capito were reflected in their respective schools: it is clear that they were not. And many of the disputes were on small points in which it is difficult to see any principle at stake: those who do find such principles find different and conflicting ones in the same text.

The exact meaning of the terms *schola* and *secta*, which are applied to these groups[2], is not quite clear. *Secta* suggests "party," groups of jurists attached to particular views and leaders, analogous to the "High" and "Low" parties in the Church of England, and perhaps this is all that it practically meant in the time of Gaius. But there is evidence of a more elaborate organisation, such as is suggested by the name *schola*. For though we speak of "schools" of opinion without necessarily implying an organisation, it is not clear that this word was so used in classical or silver Latin. When we remember how great a part in juristic activity was played by instruction, and how Pomponius speaks of the leaders as "succeeding[3]" one the other, the suggestion is obvious that these were real schools, of which the jurists named as leaders were the heads. It has therefore been suggested that they were modelled on the Greek schools of philosophy, definite organisations controlled by leaders sometimes nominated by the retiring chief, sometimes elected. The schools were held at definite places, and we learn from Aulus Gellius[4] that in the second century there were such *stationes docendi* for lawyers at Rome. It may be that there was no necessary opposition of principle at all, but that the Proculian doctrine is only that taught at a *statio* founded by Proculus[5].

XI. THE JURISTIC LITERATURE. Literary production is active among the classical lawyers. An attempt to classify its forms is not very helpful, but they may be grouped under five heads. (1) Books for elementary instruction, e.g. *Institutiones*, *Regulae*, etc. (2) More advanced, unsystematic treatises, e.g. *Quaestiones*, *Disputationes*, etc. (3) Collections of *Responsa* for practitioners which appear to vary in the degree of systematisation thought needful. (4) Systematic general treatises on the civil law, e.g. Sabini *Libri iuris civilis*, or on the *ius honorarium*, e.g. Ulpiani *Libri ad edictum*, or on the whole, e.g. Juliani *Digesta*[6], and

1 Kipp, *ib.*; Krueger, *cit.* 161; Chénon, *Proculéiens et Sabiniens*. Huvelin, *cit.* 1. 764, holds that the Sabinians rested on authority (*Anomalisten*) and the Proculians aimed at making the law logical (*Analogisten*). (Varro, *de l.l.* 8. 23.)
2 1. 2. 2. 47; Gai. 1. 196.
3 1. 2. 2. 48 *sqq.*
4 *Noctt. Att.* 13. 13. Bremer, *Die Rechtslehrer und Rechtsschulen*.
5 For another conjecture, Ebrard, *Z.S.S.* 1925, 134.
6 As to nature of a jurist's "*Digesta*," Mommsen, *Ges. Schr.* (*Jur.*) 2. 90 *sqq.*, and H. Krueger, *Z.S.S.* 1916, 311 *sqq.*

(5) Monographs on particular laws or senatusconsults, or on earlier writers or on special topics[1]. The treatment is in general more systematic than that which appears to have marked earlier writings, a change which is the natural result of the increased systematisation of the law itself which has already been noted.

It is impossible in the available space to discuss the characteristics of the jurists individually[2], but something must be said of those who made the greatest mark on the course of the law.

Gaius[3]. He is the most mysterious person who plays a large part in the law. He seems to have been born under Hadrian and to have done most of his work in the following reigns[4]. He was evidently a teacher and the Law of Citations[5] implies that he never had the *ius respondendi*. He does not seem to have been of eminence in his own day, for he is never mentioned by any classical lawyer, the few allusions to a jurist by the name of Gaius being supposed to refer to Gaius Cassius Longinus[6]. Only his *praenomen* is known. His reputation grew after his death, and his book seems to have been used in the work known as *liber singularis*[7] *regularum*. The Law of Citations includes him in the list of five jurists who may be cited, though he is much earlier than any of the others. He wrote commentaries on the Edicts but they are little used in the Digest of Justinian, while much use is made of his elementary books, and they are expressly made the basis of the Institutes. He has been credited with the invention of the division of the law into *Ius personarum, rerum, actionum*, but it is more probable that it was already traditional[8]. He was a Sabinian, the last known partisan of a school, but he did not always accept the Sabinian view[9]. There has been much controversy as to his origin and place of work. The weighty view of Mommsen is that he was a Greek provincial, but there are not wanting dissident opinions. The evidence is really insufficient to justify a confident opinion, and much of the argument is flimsy[10].

1 Of this class of book Paul produced a great number. See the Florentine index.
2 Roby, *Introd.* xci *sqq.*; Kipp, § 18; Kuebler, 256 *sqq.* Fitting, *Alter und Folge*, is an enquiry into the dates of the various writings of jurists from Hadrian's time onwards.
3 Roby, *Introd.* clxxiv; Glasson, *Étude sur Gaius*; Kniep, *Der Rechtsgelehrte Gaius*. 4 As to dates of his various writings, Fitting, *Alter und Folge*, 49; Balog, *Alter der Edictskommentare des Gaius*; Kuebler, 270. 5 *Post*, § XII. 6 Roby, *loc. cit.* 7 Fitting, *Alter und Folge*, 52; Grupe, *Z.S.S.* 1899, 90 *sqq.*; Buckland, *L.Q.R.* 1922, 38. *Contra*, Krueger, *R.Rq.* 248; Girard, *Mélanges*, 1. 325 *sq.* This view ignores the close, almost servile, following of the earlier book. See also *post*, § XI *fin.* 8 *Post*, § XXI. 9 E.g. Gai. 3. 98.
10 See Roby, *loc. cit.* and Kniep, *op. cit.* 9 *sqq.* One writer, observing that he names three Eastern cities in a certain context (D. 50. 15. 7), assumes that he puts Troas first because he was born there and Berytus second because he taught there, an argument adequately dealt with by Dernburg who suggests that he no doubt put Dyrrachium last because he died there. See Glasson, *Étude sur Gaius*, 35. Kroll, *Zur Gaiusfrage* (revised by Erman and H. Krueger), makes him of oriental extraction but of Roman origin and Latin speech. For

Julian[1]. Salvius Julianus is a much greater figure. We have already noticed his *ordinatio* of the Edict carried out perhaps while he was *Quaestor Augusti*[2], and, as we are told, received twice the usual stipend on account of the great learning he displayed[3]. An honorific inscription which has been found[4] shews that he held all the important senatorial offices from Quaestor to Consul, and many imperial offices as well, and that he was in the *Consilium* of Hadrian and of Antoninus Pius. He seems to have died in the reign of M. Aurelius and Verus, who describe him in a rescript as *amicus noster*. His fame did not lessen as time went on, for later Emperors speak of him in the most laudatory terms[5]. That he is not one of the five singled out for citation in the Law of Citations is no doubt due to his early date, and it is to be noted that the clause authorising citation of jurists, approved by any of the five, instances Julian among others. The last recorded chief of the Sabinians, he was too strong to be bound by the traditions of any school. It seems to be truer of him than it is of Papinian that his greatness united all schools, for though we hear of one Sabinian after him (Gaius) we hear of no more Proculians, and it may fairly be presumed that the predominance of Sabinian doctrine in the later classical law was in great part due to the ascendency of Julian. No other jurist exercised so great an influence on the destinies of the law. He issued many *responsa*, and though no collection of them is known, they are so often discussed by Africanus that much of his work may be regarded as a commentary on the *responsa* of Julian. His principal work was his *Digesta*, which mainly followed the order of the Edict, but was a comprehensive treatise on both civil and praetorian law[6]. It has been thought that Justinian's compilers used this book as the basis of their scheme: in any case nearly 500 passages are quoted from it. The publication of this comprehensive work explains the absence of any volume of *responsa*: what would have been its content is embodied therein[7]. The principal characteristics of Julian's work seem to be a very lucid style and a clear recognition of the fact that legal conceptions must move with the times. He seems to have played some-

Seckel-Kuebler (*Pref. to* Huschke, *Jurisprudentia antejustiniana* (6)) he probably learnt and worked at Rome.

1 Buhl, *Salvius Iulianus*; Appleton, *La date des Digesta de Julien.* 2 But see, e.g., Appleton, *N.R.H.* 1911, 623. 3 See the inscription mentioned in the next note. 4 Quoted by Krueger, *op. cit.* 183; see also Mommsen, *Ges. Schr.* (*Jur.*) 2. 1 *sqq.* 5 In the *Constitutio* Δέδωκεν, 18, Justinian speaks of him as the most illustrious of the jurists. The parallel text in "*Tanta*" uses somewhat less strong expressions. 6 Mommsen (*Ges. Schr.* (*Jur.*) 2. 8 *sqq.*) considers it to have had a theoretical aim. The answers to enquiries which it contains he thinks, on internal evidence, to have been in the main replies to students, not formal *Responsa* to litigants. 7 At least ten jurists published *Responsa*, and at least seven *Digesta*. Only two are known to have published both, Marcellus and Scaevola, both late.

what the part which Lord Mansfield did in English Law. He did a great work of co-ordination and generalisation, sweeping away unreal and pedantic distinctions. Karlowa justly observes that the appearance of Julian was epoch-making[1].

Papinian. Aemilius Papinianus[2] was *Praefectus Praetorio* under Severus with whom he is said to have been connected by marriage. Under Caracalla he declined to make a public declaration approving the Emperor's murder of his brother Geta. The result was the immediate murder of Papinian. It is interesting to note that he was Prefect at York, where he may have had as assessors, Paul and Ulpian, who certainly at one time acted in that capacity. It would be difficult to form a stronger court[3]. He was evidently regarded by those who came after as the greatest of the jurists: he was given a special preponderance by the Law of Citations[4], and though Justinian forbade the irrational method of assessing opinion directed in that law, he speaks repeatedly of Papinian in such terms as to shew that his ascendency had not diminished. Moderns usually rate him less highly. Most put Julian before him and some Ulpian. He was certainly a very great lawyer, one of whose signal merits it was that he was never captious, as Paul was. His criticism is sure but moderate in tone, and he speaks always from a lofty ethical point of view. No chicanery appealed to him, and doubtless part of his fame is due to this. But his work shews other merits. As Bruns says[5], his concise mode of statement, which brings out the essential point and only that, is an indication of the way in which his mind proceeded to fix the true relation of the facts to the general legal principle which was to govern them. But he wrote no comprehensive systematic treatise and his chief works, *Quaestiones* and *Responsa*, which cover much ground, shew a judicial and critical mind rather than intellectual fertility. In any case he was a very great figure.

Paul[6]. Julius Paulus was a contemporary of Ulpian and a younger contemporary of Papinian. He held the highest imperial offices and was long a member of the imperial council. He was a voluminous writer: extracts from him fill one-sixth of the Digest, being almost as numerous as, though much less bulky than, those from Ulpian. He enjoyed a high reputation and was one of the favoured five in the Law of Citations. He is one of the very few of whom we possess a book unhandled by Justinian, the *Sententiae*, and this we owe to the fact that his popularity led to the insertion of his work in the Code of the Visigoths for Roman subjects—the *Breviarium Alaricianum*, and to the adoption of extracts

1 *R.Rg.* 1. 709. 2 Roby, *Introd.* cxci; Fitting, *Alter und Folge*, 71; Krueger, *op. cit.* 220; Costa, *Papiniano*, 1. 3 *sqq.* 3 Roby, *Introd.* cxciii; *Vita Alexandri*, 26. 6; *Vita Pescennii*, 7. 4. 4 *Post*, § XII. 5 Cited, Karlowa, *op. cit.* 1. 736. 6 Roby, *Introd.* cci; Krueger, *op. cit.* 227; Fitting, *op. cit.* 81.

from it in other works older than Justinian. But, as the sources of our knowledge would suggest, we have it only in an imperfect form[1].

There is no other jurist about whom modern opinions differ so widely as they do about Paul. It is difficult to understand these divergences in view of the fact that we have a great mass of material on which to form a judgement. But he is described in turn as a profound thinker and original jurist, as an unoriginal but clear-sighted critic, as a mere compiler and populariser, and as a fanciful person of whom we sometimes doubt whether he is in his right mind. Equally remarkable are the differences of opinion on his style. For some he is lucid, for others obscure, but only from compression, for others, simply obscure, and there is disagreement whether this is his own fault or that of Justinian's compilers[2]. Whatever his capacities, much of his work is critical. He wrote much comment on earlier writers: some of it extremely useful, some of it captious. Constantine rejects his notes on Papinian because, though able, they aim rather at *depravare* than *corrigere* and this seems from what is left not too severe a judgement[3]. He delights in sharp contradiction, and in general his criticism does not give an impression of urbanity[4].

Ulpian[5]. Domitius Ulpianus[6], like Paul, held all the highest offices. He was for a time exiled under Elagabalus. He was a member of the *Consilium* of Severus Alexander, to whom he was related[7], and of Caracalla. He was murdered by his own praetorians when he was *Praefectus Praetorio*[8]. His works fill nearly a third of the Digest and he and Paul account for nearly a half. He was one of the favoured five in the Law of Citations, and later writers and Emperors speak of him in the most laudatory terms[9]. Part of the praise, and the great use made in the Digest of his work, are not due wholly to his personal merits. He and Paul are the latest of the great systematic writers, and, other things being equal, the later a lawbook is the better it is. The writer has the advantage of his predecessors' work, and an intelligent writer can produce a great book without contributing much of his own. This seems

1 It is probable (Beseler, *Beitr.* 3. 6) that the *Sententiae* are a "*florilegium*" by a later hand from Paul's works. Levy, *Z.S.S.* 1930, 272, attributes the work to a time soon after the end of the line of classical jurists. For Lauria, *Ricerche su Pauli Sententiarum libri*, it is an anthology from many writers and constitutions, put together at the end of the third century. It is scarcely credible that such a work should so soon as 327 (C. Th. 1. 4. 2) have been thought by the Emperor's council to be the work of Paul.

2 See Buckland, *Equity in Roman Law*, 120.

3 C. Th. 1. 4. 1. Ulpian shares the condemnation, with, so far as appears, less reason.

4 See, e.g., 41. 1. 65; 49. 15. 28; 50. 16. 244. It is specially Labeo with whom he deals in this way.

5 Roby, *op. cit.* cxcvi; Krueger, *cit.* 239; Fitting, *Alter und Folge*, 99.

6 Jörs, P.-W., *s.v.* Domitius.

7 C. 4. 65. 4.

8 Exhaustive discussion of the dates of tenure of this office by Paul and Ulpian, Balog, *Ét. Girard*, 2. 339.

9 Roby, *cit.* cxcix.

to be what Ulpian did. The age of progress in legal thinking was ending: it fell to Ulpian to set forth the splendid result. This view is however modern: in the middle ages Ulpian seems to have been almost another name for Roman Law.

We possess a book attributed to him, the *liber singularis regularum*, in an imperfect abridgement[1], made, probably, early in the fourth century, to which have been added a few fragments found in other sources. He does not seem to have written books specially devoted to criticism of earlier writers, except notes on Papinian, which may not have been an independent book. He wrote indeed *Ad Sabinum*, but that was a recognised title for a comprehensive work on the *ius civile*, and it is rather an honour to Sabinus than anything else.

XII. The line of classical jurists ends somewhat suddenly. After Ulpian there are only Marcian and Modestinus, of whom the latter is one of the five. Two of almost a century later appear in the Digest, Arcadius and Hermogenianus, but their contribution is small.

As to the causes of the decay it is not enough to say that the principles were worked out and had yielded all they could: this misconceives the nature of legal evolution, which consists in expansion of the law to fit changing conditions, and also ignores the fact that just when this decline occurred Rome was getting into touch with Christian ethic, and was acquiring new ideas from increased contact with oriental thought. Change of law was still rapid: lawyers were still plentiful, but the law ceased to attract the best equipped minds. There were several reasons for this. The *pax Romana* was ending. That the growth of law proceeds best in an age of order and good government is illustrated by the history of the empire in the first and second centuries. But the State was now entering on a period of disorder and bad government. Able men will not devote themselves to the severe study of the law if their labours are to be stultified by disorder and corrupt courts. No doubt there are men who will, but that sort does not produce Papinians. Kipp[2] assigns as a cause the increasing absolutism of the Emperor, who no longer gives *ius respondendi*, but seeks to make himself the source of equitable reform. He adds as an instance the Law of Citations, but this is effect rather than cause, and we have seen that *ius respondendi* outlived the great jurists. Krueger

1 The abridgement is probably post-classical. Schulz, in the introduction to his admirable edition, contends that what we have is an abridgement of an abridgement, the latter itself post-classical. The original writer seems to have relied largely on Gaius (*ante*, p. 28). Arangio Ruiz (*Bull.* 1921, 178; *Ist.* 11) holds that it is a second edition of Gaius. For Albertario (*Bull.* 1922, 73) what we have is a *florilegium* from the works of Ulpian. Neither view seems acceptable. Buckland, *L.Q.R.* 1922, 38; 1924, 185. It is by no means clear that the original author is Ulpian. The abridgement seems to have been done by omissions, not in general by abbreviation of statements. The MS., as we have it, does not extend to obligations and actions.

2 p. 127.

notes the introduction of Christianity, which caused many struggles physical and intellectual, and diverted men's minds to a new channel[1]. Theology at any rate was actively studied. Karlowa[2], besides these, associates it with a general sinking of the intellectual level, which is only another name for decay of the State.

The lack of living great jurists increases the importance of the dead. In A.D. 321 Constantine enacted that certain notes of Ulpian and Paul on Papinian were not to be of authority[3], language which implies either that the works of the great jurists had acquired *de facto* authority, or that there had been earlier legislation giving authority to some books[4]. Some notes of Marcian were excluded in the same way[5]. In 327[6] a statute confirmed all the writings of Paul, specially mentioning the *Sententiae*: it is supposed that this did not cover these notes. In the next century there is no sign of legislation of this sort. The development of the law by the settlement of points of detail, which had hitherto been the work of jurists, was now done by imperial enactment, but rests on the old literature as a basis. In 426 came the famous *lex de responsis prudentium*—the Law of Citations[7]. Its provisions may be shortly stated as follows:

(*a*) All writings of Papinian, Paul, Gaius, Ulpian and Modestinus are confirmed and may be cited, except notes of Paul and Ulpian on Papinian. Gaius is to have the same authority as the others.

(*b*) Any writers quoted and approved by any of these may be cited, such as Scaevola, Sabinus, Julian and Marcellus, provided by reason of the doubt due to their antiquity their books are confirmed by comparison of manuscripts.

(*c*) If those cited disagree the majority is to be followed: if numbers are equal, Papinian. If he is silent, the *iudex* may please himself.

This law lessened the difficulties of the courts in dealing with juristic literature. It excluded a huge mass of conflicting doctrine, the relative value of which had not been determined, and which yet had to be used by the judges as a source of principle on which to base their decisions. It was even more important than it seems, for it is evident that by this time even the old *leges* were in effect looked for and applied only as they were represented in juristic writings. But the enactment is not clear and calls for remark on other grounds. It is the earliest certain

1 *Op. cit.* 297. As to the effect of Christianity on the law itself, Riccobono, *Riv. di diritto civile*, 1911, 37; *Nichilismo critico-storico*, 14 *sqq.*; *contra*, Baviera, *Mél. Girard*, 1. 67.
2 *Op. cit.* 1. 932.
3 C. Th. 1. 4. 1; cf. C. Th. 9. 43. 1 = C. 9. 51. 13. See on these "*notae*," H. Krueger, *St. Bonfante*, 2. 303.
4 As the *Codex Theodosianus* begins with Constantine, earlier legislation would not appear in it, and it was obsolete under Justinian.
5 *Const.* "*Deo auctore*," 6 = C. 1. 17. 1. 6.
6 C. Th. 1. 4. 2.
7 C. Th. 1. 4. 3, issued in the West but operative in both empires.

reference to Gaius, who must have lived 250 years before. From the fact that his admissibility is emphasised and that no *responsa* of his are known it is conjectured that he never had the *ius respondendi*.

The rule as to the jurists approved by the five is obscure. Presumably, but not certainly, the admissibility extends to all their writings and not merely the work quoted. What is meant by comparison of manuscripts? It is probable that in some cases manuscripts of the more ancient works were rare or non-existent. It is difficult to construe the words except to mean comparison of the extract with the original, or of different copies of the original, but it is sometimes held to mean examination of different manuscripts of the quoting authority[1]. It may be added that, in view of the wide range of admissible writers, little important classical matter was excluded. It may be the mass of post-classical writings that the legislator had in mind.

The provisions for conflict are ridiculous: opinions should be estimated by weight, not number[2]. Equally absurd is the rule that Papinian is to be better than any one but not than two. These provisions mark probably the lowest point reached by Roman jurisprudence. A century later, Justinian, in his instructions for the compilation of the Digest, directed his ministers not to select any view merely because it had a majority in its favour, and not to take any notice of the rule that notes by Paul, Ulpian and Marcian on Papinian were to be rejected[3].

Theodosius, named with Valentinian as propounder of this law, planned a great scheme of codification[4]. In view of the low quality of the men who were at his service, it is hardly to be regretted that only the earlier and simpler part of his codification was carried out. The standard of knowledge under Justinian, though low, was not quite so low, a state of things brought about by the labours of the professors, especially of Beyrout. The influence of that school can be traced for centuries[5].

XIII. REMAINS OF THE JURISTIC LITERATURE[6]. Besides the three well-known books of Ulpian, Paul and Gaius[7], we have not much from the classical age directly. Apart from a number of small fragments we

1 Krueger, *op. cit.* 300. 2 A plural tribunal must decide by majority, but this is precisely because it is they themselves who decide. On appeal, no attention is paid to the question which was the majority view in the lower court. 3 There is however in C. 9. 51. 13=C. Th. 9. 43. 1. (321) a passage excluding the authority of the notes of Ulpian and Paul on Papinian in a certain question of validity of a will, apparently an enactment a fortnight earlier than the general reprobation of these notes (C. Th. 1. 4. 1). The point at issue is made the subject of an express enactment. 4 C. Th. 1. 1. 5. 5 Collinet, *Hist. de l'École de Droit de Beyrouth.* 6 *Collectio librorum iuris anteiustiniani*; Girard, *Textes*; Riccobono, Baviera, Ferrini, *Fontes Iuris Romani anteiust.*; Huschke, *Iurisprudentia Anteiustiniana*, ed. Seckel and Kuebler. 7 Besides the text of Gaius discovered a century ago, we have a very poor abridgement in the *Breviarium Alaricianum*, which has long been known, and the recently discovered *Autun* Gaius which looks like notes of lectures on Gaius, which is not very useful, but has added something to our know-

have an account by Volusius Maecianus of the abbreviations which were usual in describing the subdivision of a *hereditas* and for other purposes of weight and measure, and a list by Valerius Probus of *notae iuris*, consisting of the initial letters of common forms with their expansions. We have only a part, and that partly through medieval sources, but it has been made to give us a good deal of information about the edict before Julian's revision[1]. We have also a fragment on manumissions, part of a larger work, usually called the *Fragmentum Dositheanum* or *Dositheum*.

Of original Latin juristic literature after the decline and before Justinian we have practically nothing, and it may be presumed that there was not much of value. We have however works put together in the later Empire which contain juristic texts not otherwise extant. The most important is the so-called Vatican Fragments, which though fragmentary is fairly bulky. It deals with several topics in separate titles and consists of extracts from Papinian, Paul and Ulpian, interwoven with imperial constitutions ranging from A.D. 295 to 378, mainly from Diocletian. As it knows nothing of the *Codex Theodosianus* it must date from the confines between the fourth and fifth centuries. It looks like a practitioner's commonplace book: it is possible that it was of earlier date, added to from time to time. There is also the *Collatio legum Romanarum et Mosaicarum*, dealing mainly with criminal law, probably of the beginning of the fourth century and of no great value for Roman Law, though it has given us passages from Paul's *Sententiae*, not otherwise known[2]. There remains the *Consultatio Veteris jurisconsulti*. It consists of ten legal problems submitted to an unknown lawyer and answered by him by citations from Paul's *Sententiae* and *constitutiones* from the Gregorian, Hermogenian and Theodosian Codes. The nature of the authorities quoted suggests that it dates from late in the fifth century[3]. In addition to these more or less continuous works there are a few fragments of which the most important are some Greek *scholia* to Ulpian, *ad Sabinum*, called the *Scholia Sinaitica*[4].

Apart from private juristic writings we have barbarian codes containing Roman material. As the various parts of the Western Empire were overrun by barbarian chiefs, these established codes of law designed in whole or part for their Roman subjects[5].

ledge. It is supposed to be of the fourth century, but may be earlier. It is contained in the collections cited in the previous note.

1 Girard, *Mélanges*, 1. 177 *sqq.* 2 Volterra, *Collatio Legum Mosaicarum et Romanarum* (*Mem. Acc. dei Lincei*, 1930, 3) and review by Levy, *Z.S.S.* 1930, 698 *sqq.*, who notes that the Roman texts are probably not interpolated. But the MSS. have many corruptions. 3 Krueger, *op. cit.* 347. No MS. is extant, but one was known to Cujas. 4 The *Scholia* to the *Basilica* (*post*, § XVIII) contain some matter written before Justinian. 5 Krueger, *op. cit.* 350 *sqq.*

(*a*) The *Lex Romana Visigothorum*[1], or *Breviarium Alaricianum* established in A.D. 506 by Alaric II. It was declared to be intended to amend the errors and obscurities of the Roman lawyers, but the men of that age did not understand the profound Roman lawyers: what they did was to pick out what they more or less understood. The result has little scientific value, but has been of the utmost service in re-establishing the text of the Theodosian Code. It contains selections from the three codes above mentioned and shortly to be considered and some later enactments, with *interpretationes* attached, a very bad abridgement of Gaius, an abridgement of Paul's *Sententiae*, and a scrap of Papinian. It is doubtful whether the *interpretationes* and abridgements were new or not: the latter seems the most general opinion[2].

(*b*) The *Edictum Theoderici*[3]. This was published a few years later by Theoderic for the East Goths. It uses the same sources, but has much less in it. It is of little use as it does not usually even purport to give the original text, but a brief statement of the gist of it. It differs from the foregoing also in that it was applied to both Romans and Goths.

(*c*) The *Lex Romana Burgundionum*[4], of about the same time, uses the same sources. It is similar but here and there follows more closely the wording of the *lex* recited. It acquired in the middle ages the name of the *Papianum*, the result it seems of a curious blunder[5].

Much has been learnt, in recent years, especially as to the Eastern Empire and Egypt, from the study of numbers of private documents. Even in relation to classical law private documents have been of use but for the later period they are our chief source. They are mostly on papyrus and in Greek[6]. They cover all kinds of transactions and they have in general two striking characteristics. They testify to an immense infiltration of oriental ideas which had not found their way into earlier law, which indeed Diocletian is shewn by his enactments to have taken some trouble to keep out[7]. They shew also a very low standard of legal skill. They are longwinded, as every document of that age was, and they are very unintelligently drawn. They use old Roman forms in transactions with which they have no concern[8], and the same absurdities

1 Ed. Haenel; systematic exposition, Conrat, *Breviarium Alaricianum*. 2 Conrat ("*Die Westgothische Paulus*," *Abh. der K.A.d.W.* (Amsterdam), *Letterkunde* 1907) gives reason for thinking the *interpretationes* to be the work of the compilers of the *Breviarium*. See also P.W. *s.v.* Gaius. But as to use of pre-existing *interpretationes*, Krueger, *op. cit.* 353. 3 Baviera, *Fontes Iuris R. anteius.* 2. 571 *sqq.* 4 *Ib.* 2. 600 *sqq.* 5 The word *Papiniani* stood at the beginning of an extract from him at the end of the *L. R. Visigothorum*. Some MSS. contained the Burgundian Code at the end of that, and a scribe misread the word and thought it was the title of the Burgundian Code. 6 Many collections have been and are being published. A list of the chief will be found at the beginning of Mitteis, *Röm. Privatrecht*. See also *Grundzüge und Chrestomathie der Papyruskunde, Juristischer Teil*, Mitteis, and Kuebler, 287 *sqq.* 7 See, e.g., C. 8. 46. 6. 8 Krueger, *op. cit.* 349, mentions a will with a stipulation clause.

recur so frequently as to make it clear that the offenders are practitioners and not private persons who do their own law.

XIV. Late Imperial Legislation before Justinian. The Codes. One great piece of work in Roman Law remained to be done. The best lawyers of the fourth and fifth centuries seem to have turned their attention to codification, to setting forth the law in a systematic form. The first steps were not ambitious and, as might be expected, were taken by private persons. The first attempt at anything like a Code was the *Codex Gregorianus*[1], a collection of imperial enactments, arranged in books and titles, following fairly closely the order of Julian's *Digesta*, and, within the title, chronological. It was apparently published about A.D. 300. It is not extant: we have only citations in the late literature and the barbarian codes. We have about seventy constitutions, but these are from only a few of its books and titles, which are numerous. As Justinian directed his compilers, in making his Code, to compile it from the pre-existing codes eliminating their prolixity and repetitions[2], it has been inferred that all the constitutions he gives of a date earlier than Constantine, with whom Theodosius begins, are from one or other of the two earlier[3]. But this is unsafe: it does not follow that omissions were not to be corrected[4].

The *Codex Hermogenianus*[5], a collection of somewhat similar type, is not divided into books but only into titles, arranged in much the same order. Still less of it is left, preserved in the same way. It appears to be later than the other, but it is said that it cannot have been much later, for some constitutions in Justinian's code are referred to Constantine and Licinius[6]. Licinius was ejected in 323, and in the Theodosian his name is struck out. It is inferred that these came from the Hermogenian, and the failure to make the erasure would indicate that it was put together before 323. There is the further difficulty that this Code is credited with constitutions of about 365[7]. This is explained away as a mistake: the reference should have been to the Theodosian. But this is a guess and another explanation is that the Hermogenian was re-edited from time to time, and this was in a later issue. We are in fact told that Hermogenianus edited his book three times[8]. But Hermogenianus, the same or another, wrote another book, cited in the Digest, to which this remark may refer[9]. The Hermogenian must have been fairly bulky, since

1 *Collectio libror. juris anteiust.* 3. 224 and Baviera, *Fontes, cit.* 2. 547. There were earlier less comprehensive collections. Papirius Iustus published a collection of the rescripts of M. Aurelius and Verus (Lenel, *Paling.* 1. 947) and Paul published a collection (or two, Lenel, *Paling.* 1. 959) of judicial decisions with notes, apparently of cases in which he had been on the *consilium* at the hearing.

2 *Const.* "*Haec quae necessario,*" pr.; *Const.* "*Summa,*" 1.

3 Krueger, *op. cit.* 317.

4 See, however, Rotondi, *Scr. giur.* 1. 128 *sqq.*

5 *Ib.* 316 *sqq.*

6 C. 3. 1. 8; 7. 16. 41; 7. 22. 3.

7 *Consultatio,* 9

8 Krueger, *op. cit.* 321.

9 *Iuris Epitomae,* Lenel, *Paling.* 1. 265.

we possess the 120th constitution of the 69th title. It is sometimes said to be merely a supplement to the Gregorian, but there is the difficulty that some constitutions appear in both[1].

These codes or collections were private enterprises, but they soon became authoritative and were so regarded till Justinian's time. They were not superseded by the Theodosian, since that did not go behind Constantine, while the Gregorian went back to Hadrian.

The *Codex Theodosianus*[2] is much more important. Theodosius was perturbed at the low state of legal skill in his empire of the East. He founded or refounded a law school at Constantinople[3]. We saw that, by the Law of Citations, an attempt was made to systematise the citation of jurists. We have now to note a greater undertaking. In 429[4] he appointed a commission to make a collection of imperial general constitutions from the time of Constantine. It was to be in books and titles, giving the actual words, except that immaterial matter might be omitted, and constitutions which dealt with several matters were to be split up and the parts set in their appropriate places. With a view to education, he directed that all constitutions were to be set out, even though no longer law, to which direction we owe much of our knowledge of the course of change in the later Empire. He added that another code was to be prepared containing only operative enactments, with additional matter from juristic sources. This work was evidently to have served as a general statement of the whole law, but it was never prepared, though no doubt the plan gave a hint to Justinian. After some years a fresh commission was appointed, mostly of other men, with new instructions, but this was a continuance, not a supersession, for in 438, when the Code was completed and adopted also for the Western Empire by Valentinian III, the proceedings at its reception recite the instructions to the first commission[5]. Our knowledge of it is derived from a number of manuscripts, which give various parts—none is even approximately complete—and thé Breviary of Alaric[6], which embodied a great part of it. It is far from complete. Critics tell us that the compilers altered much, and omitted much which has been found in other sources and which under their instructions should have been included, and that in distributing constitutions which dealt with more than one matter they shewed more zeal than skill[7]. The work is arranged in sixteen books with several titles in each, and follows roughly the order of the classical writers of *Digesta*. Most of the defective part is in the first five or six

1 E.g. Coll. 6. 5. 1. 2 Ed. Mommsen, 1905. Incomplete ed., Krueger, 1923, 1926. Of earlier editions that by J. Gothofredus (ed. Ritter, 1736–45) still remains valuable by reason of the exhaustive commentary. 3 C. Th. 14. 9. 3. 4 C. Th. 1. 1. 5; 1. 1. 6. 5 *Gesta Senatus de Theodosiano publicando*, Mommsen, *Theodosianus*, 1. 2. 6 *Ante*, § XIII. 7 Krueger, *op. cit.* 326 *sqq.* See, e.g., Gradenwitz, *Bull.* 1929, 231.

books, of which we have, it is said, only about a third. It was superseded by Justinian's codification in the East, but remained authoritative for a considerable time under the barbarians in Western Europe[1].

Theodosius and succeeding Emperors continued to legislate, and collections exist of their *Novellae constitutiones*, usually edited with the Theodosian[2]. They come from the East and the West, the latest being one of Leo and Anthemius in A.D. 468. Those later than Majorian (A.D. 460) are known only from their inclusion in manuscripts of the *Lex Romana Visigothorum*. All the manuscripts are from the West[3]. We know little of the legislation of later Emperors of the East except as contained in the Code of Justinian.

XV. THE LEGISLATION OF JUSTINIAN. He seems to have framed a plan for going down to posterity as a great legislator. From the fact that Tribonian appears prominently in all parts of the work, and that Justinian's legislative activity lessens and almost stops on the death of Tribonian, it seems that he was the inspirer, as he certainly was the chief instrument, of the whole undertaking. Justinian's greatest legal work was his codification, of which the following are the principal steps.

(*a*) The *First Code*. In 528 commissioners were appointed to prepare a code of imperial enactments. It was to be a consolidation of the existing codes, omitting what was out of date, correcting where necessary, and restating in clear language where the old words were obscure. Constitutions were to be divided where they dealt with distinct matters, so that rules might be in their right place, and, conversely, to be combined where this seemed convenient[4]. The code was published in A.D. 529[5], but, for reasons shortly to be stated, it had but a short life[6].

(*b*) The *Digest* or *Pandects*[7]. This was the well-known codification of the juristic writings. It was begun in 530 and published in 533, a time so short for such a work[8] that the view has been maintained that there was in existence a compilation of the same sort used for instruction—a predigest, and that the compilers of the Digest were really only editing this and modifying it in accordance with Justinian's instructions. But though there did no doubt exist comprehensive collections of texts—the

1 The MSS. are all from the West. De Wretschke, in Mommsen's ed., cccvii *sqq.* There is another small group of constitutions of the fourth and (early) fifth centuries, mainly on church law. Mommsen, *Theodosianus*, 1. 907 *sqq.*

2 See Mommsen's edition, vol. 2.

3 Mommsen, 1. xxxviii.

4 *Const.* "*Haec quae necessario.*"

5 *Const.* "*Summa.*"

6 A fragment containing an index of constitutions in some titles of Book 1 has recently been discovered (*Pap. Oxyrh.* xv, 21. 709; Bonfante, *Bull.* 1922, 277 *sqq.*). It shews that the Code contained the law of citations, which suggests that when this Code was published there was as yet no plan for codifying the whole law. More than 18 months elapsed between the publication of the Code and the instructions for the Digest.

7 Ed., Mommsen, 2 vols., with *Prolegomena*. Stereotype edit. (Krueger); pocket edit. in 2 vols. (Bonfante *et al.*), repr. in 1 vol., Milan, 1960.

8 Much less than was expected, *Const.* "*Tanta,*" 12.

so-called Vatican Fragments may be part of one—nothing is known which justifies the view that anything existed which could be considered as a sort of first edition of the Digest which reduced the task of the compilers in the manner suggested[1].

Justinian appointed a committee of sixteen, with Tribonian (who was to select the other members) at the head, to make the compilation[2]. They were to study and abridge the writings of all those *prudentes* to whom the Emperors at any time had given *auctoritas conscribendarum interpretandarumque legum.* This would confine them to those with *ius respondendi*, but he says further that they are not to use books of writers whose works had not been received and *usitatae* by the *auctores.* This widens the field and implies that any, even posthumous, authorisation would suffice: the words recall the language of the Law of Citations as to those cited and approved by any of the five. This would bring in lawyers of any age, and the Digest contains direct quotations from three republican jurists, Q. M. Scaevola, Alfenus and Aelius Gallus. They were to embody the result in fifty *libri* subdivided into titles, the order to be based on that of the Edict of Julian and Justinian's own Code. In case of conflict they were to eliminate contradictions and choose what seemed the best view, not being guided by the number who held any view, or giving any writer a preference over others. And though certain notes of Ulpian, Paul and Marcian on Papinian had been barred by legislation, they were not on that account to neglect them. They were to correct and bring the matter up to date where this was necessary, but not to deal with matters already handled in the Code, except where they called for fuller treatment. For the sake of accuracy there were to be no abbreviations. The work was to be the sole authority for the *leges* and the jurisprudential writings, and no one was to raise objections on the ground of differences from the originals, which were superseded. There were to be no commentaries written upon it. The book was to be called *Digesta* or *Pandectae*[3].

The work was published in 533 and confirmed by a *constitutio*[4] which describes the arrangement and its division into seven parts[5] (chiefly for educational purposes), and emphasises the rule that the codification was

1 Notwithstanding Justinian's statement that nothing of the kind had been attempted before ("*Deo auctore*," 2), this has been maintained by H. Peters (*Die Oströmische Digestencommentare und die Entstehung der Digesten*). But the case set up has been destroyed by various critics. See Lenel, *Z.S.S.* 1913, 373 *sqq.*; Mitteis, *ib.* 402 *sqq.* Mitteis points out, however, that the compilers may have been much aided by existing compilations for instructional purposes. Rotondi, *Scr. giur.* 1. 87 *sqq.*; Arangio Ruiz, *Di alcune fonte postclassiche del Digesto.* 2 *Const.* "*Tanta.*" 9. 3 These instructions are in *Const.* "*Deo auctore.*" 4 *Const.* "*Tanta,*" Greek parallel text, *Δέδωκεν.* 5 On the mediaeval division into *Digestum vetus*, *Infortiatum* and *Digestum novum*, Roby, *Introd.* ccxxxix; Kantorowicz, *Z.S.S.* 1910, 40.

to be the sole authority for old law. It explains that there may be accidental repetitions but that many are intentional, by reason of the importance of the rule, and adds (the statement is very far from true) that any contradictions are only apparent if the text is properly looked at. The prohibition of commentaries is repeated[1] (literal translations into Greek being allowed) and all future copies are to be written in full with no abbreviations.

The great mass of the material is from few writers, Ulpian and Paul make up nearly a half and Papinian and Julian are the others most used. Of the thirty-nine writers whose works are used, only three are from the republic and only about the same number after A.D. 250. The compilers did not keep out contradictions and there are many repetitions; but this was inevitable, in a work of such magnitude, carried out at such speed. The title is the real unit: the division into books is determined partly by considerations of symmetry and partly by the requirements of education. The order is in the main that of Julian's Edict, but there are divergencies, into the reasons for which it is not necessary to go[2].

In each title the quotations are in separate extracts bearing the author's name, the title of the book and usually the section or *liber* of the book. To these extracts, and in all but the shortest, to paragraphs within the extract, numbers have been prefixed by editors, for ease of reference. The order of fragments within the title is at first sight puzzling. The same topic may be discussed at two or three points in a title with no obvious reason for the separation: occasionally the matter seems utterly disorderly. About a century ago Bluhme published an essay[3], the conclusions of which are generally accepted, accounting for the arrangement in the following way[4]. The commissioners, to hasten the work of dealing with the great number of works, divided into three committees, probably after the order of titles had been settled. The books were divided into three masses, one of which was entrusted to each committee[5]. One committee had Ulpian on Sabinus and the works dealing with the same topics: this is called the Sabinian mass. Another had those parts of Ulpian on the Edict which dealt with the purely praetorian part of the Edict, as opposed to civil law matters which Julian incorporated with it, and other books dealing with the same matters: the Edictal mass. The other had the works of Papinian and other books dealing with the same topics:

1 *Indices* and *paratitla* (citations of parallel texts) were allowed. 2 Roby, *Introduction*, ch. 3. In one case a single title fills three books, 30–32. 3 Bluhme, *Zeits. f. Gesch. Rechtswissenschaft*, iv. 257 *sqq.* 4 Some apparent returns to the same topic are explained in respect of many passages, by the fact that the jurist after commenting on the Edict proceeds to discuss the *formula* of the action based on it. 5 There is evidence that the committees worked by sub-committees, to each of which a section of the principal work in the Mass was entrusted. H. Krueger, *Herstellung der Digesten*.

the Papinianian mass. There is a small group of books which do not seem to belong to any of the three. It comes frequently at the end of a title and as the Papinianian mass is often the last to be inserted, this group is called the Appendix or the Post-Papinianian mass. It usually follows the Papinianian mass even where this is not the last. It is supposed that a few books, overlooked, were, on their appearance, handed to the Papinianian committee as having the smallest mass, and perhaps having finished their work.

The three committees met and incorporated the whole in the pre-arranged titles, striking out repetitions and contradictions as they had within their own masses. That mass came first in a title which from its bulk or other considerations was the most important in relation to it. The most common order is SEPA, but almost every possible order is found[1]. In some titles only two masses occur[2], in the short titles often only one[3], and in some, where the committee fused two or more intended titles, the masses occur more than once[4]. An examination of the books assigned to each mass[5] will shew that subject matter does not explain the distribution, which may have been done hastily. When the principle is applied to the different titles it is seen to work correctly, except that short extracts from one mass are occasionally found interspersed in another. This is sometimes to complete a defective account but perhaps more often to get, early in the title, some general definition or the like, which the mass which was to come first does not provide, or to contrive an easy transition from one mass to another[6].

XVI. The Digest is of course our chief authority for the Law of Justinian, but it is also our chief authority for much of the earlier law. For the purpose, however, of arriving at the classical law, it must be used with caution. The compilers were to alter the original texts so as to make them state current law. It follows that, in determining from a text of Julian in the Digest, what was the law of his time, we have several difficulties to contend with. The literature was already old and no doubt many corruptions and glosses had crept into it. Even the main manuscript which we have of the Digest, though it was written not long after the time of Justinian[7], has corruptions of its own. These difficulties present themselves with all manuscripts. The intentional alterations of the text are a more serious matter. Much legal history has been concealed

1 E.g. 3. 1–3, EPS; 3. 4, ESP; 4. 3, EPAS; 13. 5, SPEA, etc. 2 Illustrations, Krueger, *R.Rq.* 381. 3 1. 2 is fairly long, but consists only of two fragments, from the Papinianian mass. 4 The composition of each title and the distribution of the masses is indicated for each title in the Berlin stereotype edition. 5 See Roby, *Introd.* ch. 4. 6 Bluhme's theory though almost universally accepted was attacked by Schmidt in 1855, by Hofmann in 1900 and by Peters in 1913 (*ante*, 41) who holds that they merely revised an existing work. It is generally agreed that the criticisms are ineffective. Girard, *Man.* 89. 7 Mommsen, *Ed. maior*, 1. xxxx.

by the compilers and is to be found, if at all, by reading between the lines of the Digest. In the last fifty years a great deal of study has been devoted to these alterations, which have acquired the name of "interpolations[1]," a word used in a loose sense to cover elisions, misplacements and alterations as well as actual additions[2]. Very striking results have been obtained. The best known is the case of *fiducia*, of which not much was known until Rudorff observed that a text dealing with *pignus* incidentally used a feminine pronoun, *eam* instead of *id*[3]. He inferred that the text spoke originally of *fiducia*, and, consequently, the same would be true of other texts from the same part of the original work. Lenel carried the matter on by ingenious work with other texts[4] with the result that this trifling slip of the compilers was the starting point of a brilliant series of researches into the history of the Roman Law of Pledge[5].

The methods of detection of these interpolations are numerous and fresh devices are constantly being found. The simplest is comparison with the original text, but new original texts are not discovered very frequently. Apart from this, the methods may be grouped under two heads: those based on style, grammar and language, and those based on the nature of the argument. Both have their dangers. Sixth century words and grammar suggest alteration, but we do not always know what was possible to writers many of whom were of foreign extraction. Greek idioms suggest Byzantine work, but many of the great lawyers were provincials. Florid language suggests Justinian, but classical lawyers could[6] be guilty of it. Involved sentences with many parentheses and hypotheses are characteristic of Justinian, but Gaius has some specimens[7]. Barbarous Latin does not prove material alteration: the scribe, intending to write what was before him, may have slipped into the grammar of his own time. Intentional alteration need not mean material change: in many cases comparison has shewn that small alterations in wording were made without any intention to affect the meaning of the text[8]. The same is true of some of those tests which turn on matter. Where a text writes nonsense, it may be a word mis-written which has made the passage absurd: even the compilers did not intentionally write nonsense. Even where one text plainly contradicts another, interpolation is not certain: classical disagreements were sometimes retained by over-

1 General account, H. Appleton, *Des Interpolations et des méthodes propres à les découvrir*. For the present state of the question, Schulz, *Einführung in d. stud. d. Digesten*. 2 Formerly called *Emblemata* Triboniani. 3 13. 7. 8. 3; h. t. 34. See Lenel, *Z.S.S.*, 1882, 104. 4 Lenel, *ib.* 5 The history of innominate contracts, of *dotis dictio*, of remedies in sale for defect of title, of security in litigation, etc., have been illuminated in the same way. 6 15. 1. 32 pr. Lenel, *Z.S.S.* 1904, 369. 7 H. Appleton, *op. cit.* p. 47. 8 Roby, *Introd.* lxiii *sqq.*; Buckland, *Yale Law Journal*, 1924, 345.

sight[1]. No doubt where a text plainly contradicts itself it is probably altered[2]. When an obviously poor reason is given interpolation is likely, but even here the rule may be classical, the reason due to the compilers. Even bad reasons may be classical[3]. A sure indication of interpolation is an allusion by a jurist to an institution which did not exist in his day. Thus Paul is made to apply the rule, introduced by Justinian, that a tutor must be 25[4]. Ulpian is made to say that legacies and *fideicommissa* are completely assimilated, a step not taken till Justinian[5].

The problem would be easier if we were sure of Justinian's standpoint. Was he, as his prefaces suggest, seeking to restore classical doctrine, so far as possible, taking account of legislation, or was his language misleading, and his aim to state new doctrine under cover of ancient authority? On the latter view, we should expect the texts to be full of new matter. On the first, which is the most probable view[6], there would still be many interpolations and adoptions of older alterations[7], both Western and Eastern. There had been long practice under oriental conditions and the compilers, some professors, the rest advocates, were all orientals, accustomed to local notions. Such men, with the traditions of the schools of Beyrout and Constantinople behind them, would certainly adopt and introduce Greek notions, often without knowing that they were doing so[8].

The systematic search for interpolations has been carried on now for more than half a century. In some hands it has given excellent results[9]. In others it has been done with more zeal than discretion. It is easy to throw suspicion on a text, and those who had theories which the texts did not suit were provided with a handy instrument. But when some indications relied on had been shewn to be untrustworthy[10], and a text held to be interpolated proved on discovery of the original

1 The disagreements as to possession by a *hereditas* are clearly classical, *post*, § CVII. 2 13. 6. 22. On the point itself, Buckland, *Law of Slavery*, p. 126. 3 Paul says that loss of a tooth is not a redhibitory defect under the Edict of the Aediles. The real reason is that it is not a serious defect. But he gives as the reason that, if this were a defect, all babies must be defective as they have no teeth at all. This looks so absurd (for it would be equally true of inability to walk) that it seems impossible that a jurist could have said it. In fact it seems that Labeo said it in the course of a discussion with Servius which Aulus Gellius has preserved, D. 21. 1. 11; *Noctes Att.* 4. 2. 12. 4 26. 2. 32. 2; see C. 5. 30. 5. 5 D. 30. 1. *Post*, § CXXV. 6 *Const.* "*Deo auctore,*" 4. 5. 7 On the questions whether the main source of the new ideas was the East or the West, and whether it was the school or the Courts (doctrine or practice) see, e.g., Riccobono, *Mél. Cornil*, 2. 237 *sqq.*; *Ann. del. Sem. Giur. Palermo*, 1928, 479 *sqq.*; Collinet, articles in *R.H.* 1928, 1930. 8 Various views; Krueger, *R.Rq.* 391; *S.M.W.* 125 *sqq.*; Brugi, *Ist.* 5; Collinet, *Ét. Hist.* 1. xxv *sqq.* 9 Instances, Gradenwitz, *Interpolationen*, and *Z.S.S.* 1885 (two articles), and Eisele, *Z.S.S.* 1886, 15; 1890, 1; and 1892, 118, and *Beiträge* 225 *sqq.* 10 Service has been rendered by Kalb in a series of works, *Juristenlatein*, *Roms Juristen*, *Jagd nach Interpolationem*, *Wegweiser in die Römische Rechtssprache.*

to be essentially genuine[1], a more careful method began to prevail, and it seemed to be an accepted canon that no text was to be regarded as materially interpolated on linguistic grounds alone. But the undoubted alterations in the Digest may be reckoned, perhaps, by thousands, and there are a vast number more of doubtful cases[2]. Some parts have suffered more than others. Procedure and transfer of property have been drastically handled, but the titles dealing with *bonae fidei* transactions are apparently not so much affected[3].

Thus this enormous book is in effect a palimpsest. Concealed in its propositions are other propositions written by greater men, difficult to find but of supreme interest to the student of legal history when found.

It must be added that the work done in such haste was not well done. Obsolete doctrines are retained side by side with the new. Conflicts which should have been eliminated are left standing—many supposed interpolations are really cases of this kind. In some cases the growth of doctrine can be traced in the passages which are supposed to present existing law[4], a result convenient for the historian, but not for the practising lawyer.

There are of course a large number of rules in the Digest which do not represent civil law and the question has been much discussed where we are to look for the source of these ideas, East or West. On one view, which accords (but is by no means bound up) with the view that the work represents a remodelling of the law for eastern conditions, the main source is the East, and, so far as doctrine is concerned, the school of Beyrout[5]. On another view the West is the main source, some of the doctrines being post-classical, others merely a triumph of rules of praetorian law[6]. On another view the private law views are mainly western, the publicistic notions mainly eastern[7]. But the matter is still very controversial[8].

1 Lenel, *Z.S.S.* 1904, 369. 2 Recent editions of the Berlin stereotype edition of the Digest indicate at the text and in Appendixes a great number of supposed interpolations with the name of the writer who points them out, but not all all are universally accepted. (An index has been published in Germany (*ante*, p. xxvi) indicating with exact reference all alleged interpolations noted in any published work, without critical matter.) In recent years there has been marked renewal of activity in the pursuit of these interpolations, but while some of the results may be accepted as certain there has been a great deal published which, to say the least, is still *sub iudice*. In many cases the material objection is only the author's thesis, and reliance is placed on the uncertain test of form. On these apparent excesses, Lenel, *Z.S.S*, 1925, 17; 1930, 1; Buckland, *Yale Law Journal*, 1924, 345 *sqq.* 3 They provide however one possible important case. It is widely held that the passages dealing with *custodia* are largely interpolated. See *post*, § CXCI. 4 See Buckland, *Tijdschr.*, 1930, 117 *sqq.* on D. 47. 2; C. Appleton, *Tijdschr.* 1931, 19. 5 See, e.g., Collinet, *Ét. Hist.* 1 and 2. 6 See, e.g., Riccobono, *Ann. Palermo*, 1928, 500 *sqq.*; 1929, 3 *sqq.*; *Tijdschr.* 1929, 1 *sqq.* 7 Wenger, *Krit. Vierteljsch.* 1929, 126. 8 Judicious review of the matter, Levy, *Z.S.S.* 1929, 230 *sqq.*

XVII. (*c*) THE INSTITUTES, compiled in the last year of the preparation of the Digest and published almost with it. It was to be, and still is, a first book for students. The compilers (three were appointed) were directed[1] to utilise the old institutional writers, especially Gaius, and they modelled the plan on that of Gaius. The difference in the dividing line between books 3 and 4 is merely a matter of symmetry, but the book has a wider scope than the Institutes of Gaius, since it has titles on *officium judicis* and on criminal law, for which he has no counterpart and has indeed a somewhat different aim[2]. A great part of the matter comes from his Institutes and *Res cottidianae*, but internal evidence shews that the compilers also used the Institutes of Florentinus, Ulpian and Marcian, and they probably used those of Paul[3]. The book was to have the force of law[4], an unusual thing for a textbook, and inconvenient, since it does not always agree with the Digest[5]. It is a dogmatic exposition of the main rules with little historical matter or argument, a rather mechanical production, much less interesting than Gaius himself.

(*d*) The *Quinquaginta Decisiones*. Imperial legislation of the ordinary kind was still going on, and the Code, as we have it, contains a great number of Constitutions of Justinian. Many of these are directly aimed at settling old disputes[6]. A collection of these was published under the above title, but the book went out of use as soon as the new Code was in force. As there are many more than fifty enactments of this type, while there are few of which there is direct evidence that they were in this book, much controversy has arisen as to what it did contain, but it is little more than conjecture. It has been suggested[7] that as there are about fifty dated before the Digest was begun in 530, the collection was issued then. The difficulty that there are two from 531 which are known to have been in the book is pointed out but not met.

(*e*) The *CODEX REPETITAE PRAELECTIONIS*[8]. The mass of new legislation had made the first edition of the Code obsolete. Accordingly instructions were issued for a new edition[9], which is that we have. A commission of five of the Digest commissioners with Tribonian at the head were to do the work. The new Code was to be the sole authority for imperial constitutions up to its publication. There was a reservation for future enactments if any should be required[10], and presumably the

1 *Const.* "*Imperatoriam*" (Preface to Instit.); *Const.* "*Tanta,*" 11. 2 *Post,* § XXI. 3 Whether they used more advanced books, and if so whether they used the originals or the Digest is uncertain. See Ebrard, *Z.S.S.* 1917, 327 *sqq.* 4 *Const.* "*Imperatoriam,*" 6. 5 E.g., Inst. 2. 1. 21; D. 41. 1. 7. 2, and Inst. 3. 15. 3; D. 4. 6. 43. 6 Perhaps to assist the compilers of the Digest, but more probably, as nearly all are before the publication of the first code, to simplify the working of the old law (see *ante*, 39, n. 5); Bonfante, *Scr. giur.* 4. 132; Rotondi, *Scr. giur.* 1. 230. 7 Krueger, *op. cit.* 369. 8 Ed. P. Krueger, 1877 (smaller edition in the Berlin stereotype edition of the *Corpus Iuris Civilis*). 9 *Const.* "*Cordi.*" 10 *Const.* "*Cordi,*" 4.

reservation of validity for certain *privilegia* and regulations for officials, not in the Code, but not in conflict with it, which was stated for the earlier Code[1], applied equally to the new. There were to be no repetitions or contradictions, a direction which was imperfectly carried out, and only operative law was to be retained. The book was published in 534, in twelve *libri*, subdivided into titles. The order is roughly, Church Law, Sources, Functions of high Officials, Private Law, Criminal Law and Details of Administrative Law[2]. The Digest and the Code were to be read together and thus what was in one was not to be in the other, a practice which so far as it was carried out was rather inconvenient, since what looks like a complete account in the Digest is often much affected by what is in the Code[3].

(*f*) The *Novellae Constitutiones*[4]. It is evident that on the completion of the codification Justinian thought the system adequate and supposed that new legislation would not be a very important factor. But, in fact, new and important legislation began almost at once, and the new enactments acquired the name of *Novellae Constitutiones*, which had been applied to imperial enactments after the publication of the *C. Theodosianus*. They were to have been officially collected from time to time[5], but they never were, and what we know of them is due to private collections. They are mostly in Greek. The majority are concerned with public matters, but some of those which deal with private law are of the greatest importance. Thus the law of succession on intestacy was not only reformed, but absolutely changed in principle[6]. The rapid flow of novels slackens shortly before the death of Tribonian in 546 and thereafter there are few[7]. In Justinian's time an epitome of about 120 *Novellae*, ending in 555, was published, the Greek novels mostly in a Latin translation and all the novels abridged. Another translated collection without abridgement commonly called the *Authenticum* appeared late in the sixth century. It contains more *leges*, but goes no later. A fuller collection[8] in the original languages made about the same time contains 165 novels and a few other matters. From these and a few minor collections the modern editions are made up.

XVIII. Justinian's Codes were to be the law for the whole empire, but he was to find, like other legislators, that custom was too strong for

1 *Const.* "*Summa*," 4. 2 Krueger, *R.Rq.* 388. 3 Thus the law of theft from a borrower as stated in the Digest is much altered by an enactment of Justinian in the Code, C. 6. 2. 22. 4 Ed., Schoell and Kroll, see the Berlin stereotype edition of the *Corpus Iuris Civilis*. It gives the original *lex*, the *Authenticum*, and a new Latin translation. 5 "*Cordi*," 4 *in fin.* 6 *Novv.* 118, 127. Great changes in the law of the *Q. inofficiosi testamenti* (*post*, § CXIV), surety, marriage, procedure, etc. 7 About 135 to A.D. 540, about 30 after. 8 As to these collections Krueger, *op. cit.* 401. Summaries of the *Novellae* (*authenticae communes*) are found, at appropriate points, in old editions of the Code.

him. Even in the East, for which his legislation was specially designed, it was far from universal in application: the remoter parts of the empire were little affected by it. The Syro-Roman Lawbook[1], said to have been in circulation before Justinian and containing besides old Roman Law some rules not Roman Law at all, was in use in the provinces long after his codification[2]. Indeed there is reason to think his legislation fell into neglect in the seventh century. It was revived by the publication in 740, under Leo the Isaurian, of the *Ecloga*, a sort of collection from all the Codes, and again about the beginning of the tenth century by the *Basilica*[3], a Greek paraphrase of the books of Justinian, to which were soon appended a number of *scholia*, consisting mainly of extracts from the commentaries of writers of the sixth and later centuries.

Further light is thrown on the Justinianian system by the surviving juristic writings of the period, and by the steadily increasing number of private documents made available in the various collections of papyri[4]. Of the former the most important are the Greek commentary on the Institutes attributed to Theophilus[5], shewing knowledge of Gaius, the *Consultatio veteris iurisconsulti*, the Syro-Roman Lawbook and the glosses to the Basilica. But there is a good deal more[6]. The papyri must be used cautiously: they testify to the persistence of non-Roman practices and doctrines—most of them are from outlying parts of the Empire, especially Egypt[7].

Even the partial success of Justinian's legislation is largely due to the fact that Justinian was himself an oriental, served by orientals, and thus the work was much influenced by local conditions. A recent work maintains the thesis[8] that Justinian must be regarded not as seeking to revive the classical jurisprudence, but as one who, governing an oriental State, seeks to make the classical law available for an oriental people by a steady remoulding of it under the guidance of eastern traditions. The introduction of eastern principles, mainly late Greek, is, on this view, the keynote of his work, and this is supported by analysis

1 Ed., Bruns and Sachau. See also Sachau, *Syrische Rechtsbücher*, containing more recently discovered versions. A Latin translation from the Syriac version by Ferrini, *Fontes iuris R. antei.* (ed. Riccobono, Baviera, Ferrini), pt. 2. pp. 641 *sqq.* But as to origin, purpose and history of this enigmatic book see now Nallino, *St. Bonfante*, I. 203.
2 Krueger, *op. cit.* 363.
3 Ed. Heimbach, with supplements by later editors, but far from complete. Krueger, *op. cit.* 415 *sq.* Transln. of *Ecloga*, Freshfield, 1926.
4 Mitteis, *Grundz. der Papyrusforschung* and articles by various authors especially in "*Aegyptus*" and *Zeits. f. vergl. Rechtsw.*
5 Ed. Ferrini.
6 Cornil, *D.R.* 446 *sqq.*; Conrat, *Gesch. der Qu. und Litt. des R.R.* 107 *sqq.*
7 See, for striking illustrations, Arangio Ruiz, *Persone e familia nel dir. dei papyri.*
8 Collinet, *Ét. Hist.* I. He points out that at the time of the compilation Justinian had only a shadowy suzerainty over Italy, in virtue of which he repeatedly names Rome as part of his territory, e.g. there is to be a law school at Rome ("*Omnem,*" 7 "*urbes regias*"). No doubt he had already formed the idea of expelling the Goths. There was no western jurist in his councils.

of his various reforms. Whether we accept this or not, it must be agreed that to get a real understanding of Justinian's influence on the law we must see him as a Byzantine potentate, and not a Roman.

So far as the Digest is concerned there is little evidence of more than unconscious orientalising, but much, on the other hand, of preservation and some unintended restoration of ancient doctrine[1].

There is another interesting question, the answer to which depends somewhat on that to the problem just stated. There are in the Digest and Code many texts stating pure classical doctrine and others on the same points giving other solutions. These are sometimes survivals of conflict, but often of oriental post-classical origin. Which of the conflicting solutions is really Justinian's law? It is held by Riccobono that the texts expressing the older rule are mere survivals; the effective law is the later rule (whatever its origin), which is certainly in general that adopted, some centuries later, by the medieval glossators[2]. But it is equally possible, as has also been said[3], that the texts of Justinian represent a system in transition, a "*regime in divenire*." In the end the new ideas triumphed: it is not so certain that Justinian meant this.

Justinian was a reformer not only of law, but of legal education. There had been a law school at Constantinople at any rate from the time of Theodosius[4] and there was a famous one at Berytus. These he preserved, but he suppressed the schools at Athens, Alexandria and Caesarea[5]. In the same Constitution, he tells us all we know of the existing system of study, which he thought defective in plan and badly carried out, and states his reformed scheme. The old scheme was a four-year course to be completed before the age of 25. The student attended lectures for three years and gave the fourth to private study of Paul's *Responsa*. Freshmen were called *Dupondii*[6], second year men, *Edictales*; third year men, *Papinianistae*, because they mainly studied Papinian, and fourth year men, Λύται, which may mean released from attendance at lectures[7]. He prescribes a five-year course. Freshmen were no longer to be called by the frivolous name of "Twopennies," but *Novi Justiniani*; fifth year men were *Prolytae*, and the other names remained[8]. Freshmen were to be lectured on the Institutes and on the first part of the Digest (Books

1 Pringsheim, *Die archaistiche Tendenz Justinians* (*St. Bonfante*, 1. 55 *sqq.*); Appleton, *R.H.* 1930; Buckland, *D.* XLVII. 2 *and the methods of the compilers*, *Tijdsch.* 1930, 117; Riccobono, *La verità sulle pretese tendenze arcaiche di Giustiniano.* 2 Riccobono, *Dal. dir. Rom. class. al. dir. mod. Ann. Palermo*, 4. 165 *sqq.*; *Stipulatio ed Instrumentum*, *Z.S.S.* 1922, 262 *sqq.* and elsewhere. 3 Arangio Ruiz, *Ist.* 79. 4 *Ante*, § XIV. Legal education in Empire, P.-W. *s.v. Rechtsunterricht.* 5 "*Omnem*," 7; Krueger, *op. cit.* 393. 6 Name perhaps (H. Pernice) first applied to pupils in gladiatorial schools (allusion to small pay), then to soldiers, then to law students. See, however, Krueger, *op. cit.* 398; Kretschmar, *Z.S.S.* 1928, 559. 7 The form of the word, if this is its meaning, gives trouble to philologists. 8 "*Omnem*," 2–5; Roby, *Introd.* xxvii.

1–4, "*Prota*"), second year men on the second part (Books 5–11, *de iudiciis*) or the third (Books 12–19, *de rebus*) and Books 23, 26, 28 and 30. Third year men had the third or the second part, and Books 20–22. In the fourth year there were no lectures, but men studied all the rest up to Book 36. In the fifth year the Code was read. The way in which Justinian kept the needs of education in mind is illustrated by the fact that in Book 20, the first of those specially reserved to third year men, nearly all the titles begin with an extract from Papinian, so as to justify the retention of the old name, *Papinianistae*, for these students[1]. Every student had to receive a certificate of diligence and competence from his professor before he could practise[2]. The alternative in the second and third years was probably designed to economise teaching, so that two years could attend the same lectures. There were only four professors in each school, and apparently the students were distributed amongst them so that each man studied continuously under the same professor.

XIX. Some general account of the administrative organisation of the Empire[3] is necessary to the proper understanding of the legal texts.

We speak of the empire till the time of Diocletian as a Dyarchy, in which Senate and Emperor divided the administration. Formally this was so: the Senate had a field nominally reserved to it, e.g., the control of the Senatorial provinces. But the reorganisation under Diocletian was the formal registration of a change which had in fact long since taken effect, so far as this point is concerned. The Emperor had had, from the beginning, a great power over the Senate[4]: it would be more in accord with fact to say that the real monarchy began with Hadrian, when the Emperor's power of legislation was fully recognised, the praetors lost the power of legislation[5], and there remained no republican magistracy with any real power. The specially imperial officials were at first mere representatives of the Emperor. Those who governed the imperial provinces, though they had pro-praetorian power, were officially *Legati Caesaris*[6]. The great magnates, the *Praefectus Urbi* and *Praetorio*, were mere delegates, as were the subordinate *praefecti, annonae* and *vigilum*. But their functions tended to increase at the expense of those of republican magistrates and they came to be regarded as great officers of State rather than of the Emperor. The *Praefectus Urbi* and his subordinates ousted the aediles and praetors from their functions in Rome[7],

1 "*Omnem*," 4. So does Book 22. In the first 19 books only 3 titles begin with an extract from Papinian. 2 Krueger, *op. cit.* 394, n. 9. 3 Republican organisation, De Francisci, *Storia*, 2. 1. 1–3. 4 *Ante*, § v. A recently discovered *stele* of Augustus, at Cyrene, shews him issuing what are practically laws in a Senatorial province, by virtue of his *imperium*, with no reference to the Senate, Premerstein, *Z.S.S.* 1928, 419. 5 *Ante*, § IV. 6 Mommsen, *Staatsr.* 2. 244; *D.P.R.* 3. 280. 7 Willems, *D.P.* 470, 502, etc.

and the *Praefectus Praetorio* gained control of all military forces[1]. The rapid development of *cognitio extraordinaria* brought with it a system of appeals culminating in the Emperor. At first, if he did not hear the case himself, he delegated it to the Urban Praetor, but by the third century it was in the hands of the *Praefectus Urbi*, who also exercised the imperial criminal jurisdiction[2]. Appeals to the Emperor from criminal judgements of the provincial magistrates were referred by him to the *Praefectus Praetorio*[3], and similar developments went on steadily in all departments of administration.

The office of *Princeps*[4] was not hereditary. The Emperor nominated his successor, frequently from his family. But the successor had, at least nominally, to be approved by the Senate, and conflicts arose, since the Senate might adopt one candidate, the army, growing steadily more aggressive in politics, might set up another, and yet others might claim to have the Emperor's nomination. Diocletian tried to systematise matters, and avoid conflict, by associating with himself another *Augustus*, Maximian, of equal authority, and with each a subordinate emperor, with the title of *Caesar*, who was to succeed as *Augustus*[5]. Laws were issued in the names of the two *Augusti*, but in administrative matters they governed distinct regions of the Empire. The name *Caesar* had been in use before as an honorific title to a destined successor, but the new *Caesares* were administrative chiefs who acted for the Emperors in many fields. There was no guarantee of permanence (Constantine governed the whole Empire), and the fourth century gives a story of constantly renewed civil wars. In 364 Valentinian became undisputed *Augustus*. He associated with himself his brother Valens, and handed over to him the administration of the East[6]. But Valens could not hold his own and, after the death of Valentinian, Gratian became in effect Emperor of the whole. In 395 a more permanent division was made. Arcadius became Emperor of the East and Honorius of the West in succession to their father, Theodosius I, who had governed the whole[7]. From that time the distinction was maintained: the two Emperors were colleagues governing distinct sections of one great State. We have already considered the changes in the rules as to the validity in one empire of laws made in the other[8].

The notion of a province underwent a change. In the earlier Empire a *provincia* had meant an outlying part of the Empire, a dependency, the inhabitants of which, though subjects of Rome, were not in general

1 Willems, *D.P.* 430 *sqq.* 2 *Ib.* 502. 3 *Ib.* 4 Mommsen, *Staatsr.* 2. 1132 *sqq.*; *D.P.R.* 5. 444 *sqq.* 5 Gibbon (Bury), i. 352, 353. 6 Gibbon (Bury), iii. 10. 7 Mommsen, *Staatsr.* 2. 1145 *sqq.*; *D.P.R.* 5. 459 *sqq.* 8 *Ante*, § VI. On the divinity claimed by the later emperors, Kuebler, 308 *sqq.*

Roman citizens. The extension of *civitas* under Caracalla[1] made the distinction rather unreal and paved the way for a complete reorganisation. Under Diocletian[2] the whole Empire, except the capitals, was divided into four *praefecturae*, two in the West, and two in the East, each under a *Praefectus Praetorio*. Each *praefectura* was divided into a small number of *dioceses*, each under a *Vicarius Praefecti*, appointed by the Emperor[3]. Each diocese consisted of a number of provinces governed by an officer, usually called *Rector*, but differing in rank and title in different cases[4]. The Diocese of Italy had two *Vicarii*, for North and South respectively, the latter being called *Vicarius Urbis Romae*, and having, though the capitals were excluded from the provinces, a certain concurrent jurisdiction in civil and criminal matters with the *Praefectus Urbi*, the chief magistrate of Rome[5]. A province was now a small territory, or might be (Italy contained seventeen provinces), and the name province did not now connote any sort of inferiority: it was merely the name of the administrative unit[6].

XX. CUSTOM. *IUS CIVILE, GENTIUM, NATURALE.* The sources of law which have been considered are those of what came to be called[7] *ius scriptum*, the means by which new rules were expressly introduced into the system. But many old institutions originated in custom[8], as did many of the rules expressed in the XII Tables. Long continued usage was recognised in the Republic[9] and throughout the classical age[10] as a kind of tacit consent, equivalent to legislation and thus capable not only of creating new rules and institutions, but of modifying, and even in effect repealing, statutes[11]. Constantine indeed provided that long continued usage was of no force against a statute[12], but the Digest states the contrary rule as from Julian[13]. It may be that Constantine is dealing with purely local usages as against *leges generales*[14].

In historical times, apart from adoption by express legislation, cus-

1 *Post*, § XXXVII. 2 Karlowa, *R.Rg.* 1. 850, a gradual reform begun before, and completed after, Diocletian. 3 In one or two eastern dioceses, these officers have special names; see for these and other exceptional cases, Willems, *D.P.* 602. 4 Asia, Achaia and Africa, ancient and privileged provinces, continued to be governed by proconsuls in the old way and were thus excluded from the general scheme. Willems, *cit.* 605. 5 Mommsen, *Staatsr.* 2. 968, 985; *D.P.R.* 5. 257, 276. 6 Rules in which distinctions had been drawn between Italy and the provinces still appear as survivals under Justinian. See, e.g., Inst. 1. 25. pr.; D. 47. 18. 1. 2; 47. 22. 1, pr., etc. 7 *Ante*, p. 25. 8 See, e.g., G. 3. 82; 4. 27; D. 24. 1. 1, etc. 9 Cicero, *de legg.* 2. 10. 23; *de inv.* 2. 22. 67; 2. 54. 162; Appian, *Bell. C.* 1. 54. 10 Ulp. 1. 4.; D. 1. 3. 32 *sqq.* 11 Appian, *cit.*; Aul. Gell. 2. 24. 3–11; D. 1. 3. 32. 1 in f. 12 C. 8. 52. 2. 13 D. 1. 3. 32. 1 in f. Solazzi, *La desuetudine della legge* shews that for early law disuse is not regarded as amounting to repeal. For classical law the evidence from Pliny (*Ep. Plini et Traiani*, 114, 115) is not conclusive: the abuse may have been only recent. Steinwenter (*St. Bonfante*, 2. 437) rejects the last clause of 1. 3. 32. 1 as a fifth century notion, inconsistent with both classical law and Justinian's ideas. 14 On the conflict, Kipp, 23.

tom commonly achieved recognition by the activity of the jurists[1], and was hardly to be distinguished from the *interpretatio prudentium*, the *disputatio fori*[2], to which, as we have seen, the name *ius civile* was applied in the Republic. But for classical lawyers the expression *ius civile* had a wider meaning: it was used sometimes to mark off the rest of the law from that made by the magistrates, *ius honorarium*, and sometimes to mark off the essentially Roman part of the law from that available also to peregrines, *ius gentium*, an expression often found associated with another, *ius naturale*[3]. This last notion originated in Greek philosophy it was a system of moral rules implanted in man, not necessarily in other living things, by nature—an intuitionist morality. The notion of *ius gentium* is a more controverted matter. The expression appears first in Cicero, but in a phrase which implies that it is older[4]. How old the thing itself is we do not know. Originally it meant the rules applied in dealings with aliens, whether originally imported from alien usage[5] or of internal origin[6], the simpler parts of the Roman Law applied to aliens, we need not consider. But we must say a word on the significance of these terms, and especially *ius gentium*, among the classical lawyers. The jurists do not tell a clear story. For Gaius *ius gentium* and *ius naturale* are the same thing: the law which nature has instilled into all nations[7]. But the other jurists who mention the matter, who are later, commonly distinguish, pointing out that slavery is *iuris gentium*, contrary to *ius naturale*. Ulpian goes further and identifies *ius naturale* with instinct[8], and Justinian adopts the views of Gaius and Ulpian as if they were the same. Accordingly it has been maintained[9] that, for the age of Hadrian and before, there was no difference, but that in the late classical age the two ideas began to be distinguished, and the distinction became a standing part of medieval political thought. It is said that it is a mistake to regard the jurists as Stoic philosophers, governed by the notion of life according to nature[10]. But, though not philosophers, they were educated men. Greek philosophy played a large part in Roman education, and this view of the course of thought seems a little too simple. It is true that Gaius identifies *ius gentium* and *ius naturale*, or, what is the same thing[11], *naturalis*

1 *Ante*, § IX. 2 See Jörs, *Röm. Rechtsw. d. Rep.* 80 *sqq.* 3 Krueger, *R.Rq.* 43 *sqq.*; Mitteis, *R.Pr.* 1. 62 *sqq.*, and as to influence of local usage, *Reichsr. und Volksr.*, *Einleitung.* 4 *De off.* 3. 17. 69. 5 A view held with differences, see Jörs, *op. cit.* 1. 114 *sqq.* 6 Clark, *Pract. Jurisp.* 353, for the principal views and criticism. A Roman origin for most of it is probable if we accept the view (*post*, § CCXIV) that the *formula* was in use for some transactions before the *l. Aebutia.* 7 G. 1. 1. *Frag. Dos.* 1. 1., as in MS., distinguishes them, but it is corrupt and as ordinarily edited it identifies them. 8 D. 1. 1. 1. 3, 4; cf. Inst. 1. 2. pr., an old rhetorical Greek notion, Castelli, *St. Perozzi*, 55. 9 Carlyle, A. J., and R. W., *Hist. of Med. Pol. Thought*, 1. 36 *sqq.* 10 Nettleship, *Journ. of Phil.* 13. 169 *sqq.* 11 As to *naturalis ratio*, Koschembar-Lyskowski, *St. Bonfante*, 3. 469.

ratio[1], but no other jurist of his age or earlier has left us his views on the matter. The current notions on the relation of these two conceptions were doubtless derived from the philosophers, and Cicero, who expresses their views, uses the term *ius gentium* in several senses. His best-known utterance speaks of it as a branch of the law, a part of the law distinguished from the strictly Roman part by *maiores*[2]. Elsewhere he treats it as a code of rules supposed to exist everywhere[3]. Again, he infers from this universality that it is "natural[4]," and elsewhere he speaks of it as *iuris naturalis*[5]. Of these various significations Gaius adopts the last, but it is clear that the philosophic view was not the only one, or itself absolutely settled. We find, of course, many later texts in which *ius gentium* is spoken of as a branch of existing law to which various institutions are referred[6]. But we also find the more speculative aspect of it considered[7]. Commonly the later jurists treating *ius gentium* as universal, nevertheless distinguish between it and *ius naturale*, on the ground that slavery is *iuris gentium*, but *contra naturam*[8]. But elsewhere Ulpian seems to identify them[9]. The general conclusion is that *ius gentium*, in the only sense in which it is of value in legal discussion, means certain rules which, whatever their origin, were a part of the law and had been applied in dealings with peregrines, and that the more speculative conception of it as universal was borrowed from the philosophers, and, being for legal purposes no more than ornament to discussion, was not very exactly formulated. The difficulty of slavery was sometimes considered and sometimes neglected. It seems to be never mentioned as the basis of distinction except in texts dealing *ex professo* with slaves.

The expression *ius naturale* is also used in more than one sense. Sometimes it is an ideal to which law ought to conform[10], sometimes it is the basis of all law and is thus not to be set aside by the law of the State[11]. The notion is of small importance in legal discussion, for though various institutions are referred to it, they are all equally referable, and referred, to *ius gentium*, and it was as *ius gentium* that they were law. But while the *ius gentium* steadily superseded the old *ius civile*, it must

1 G. 1. 1.; 2. 65–69; 3. 154 *a*; D. 41. 1. 3, 9. 3. 2 *De off.* 3. 17. 69. 3 *Part. or.* 37. 130. 4 *De off.* 3. 5. 23; *de rep.* 3. 22. 33; *Tusc.* 1. 13. 30. 5 *De harusp. R.* 14. 32. 6 E.g. 46. 4. 8. 4; 48. 19. 17. 1; 48. 22. 15, etc. 7 Pomponius applies it to the rules for State intercourse, the nearest Roman equivalent to Public International Law, 50. 7. 18. 8 Inst. 1. 2. 2; 1. 3. 2; Flor., D. 1. 5. 4. 1; Tryph. 12. 6. 64; Ulp. 1. 1. 4. pr. His confusion with instinct may be neglected (1. 1. 1. 3); Mitteis, *loc. cit.*, and others, attribute it to Justinian. 9 Ulp. 1. 1. 6. pr., where "*ei*" is sometimes read "*eis*" which alters the sense. Interpolations are assumed to avoid the differences. Perozzi, *Ist.* 66, 73, holds the differentiation due to Justinian; *Contra*, Longo, *Rendic. Lomb.* XL (ii) 632; Scialoja, *Ist.* 95; Beseler, *Tijdsch.* 8. 319. 10 Krueger, *op. cit.* p. 133. 11 Cicero, *de rep.* 3. 22. 33; *de invent.* 2. 22. 65 *sqq.*; *de leg.* 2. 5. 11 *sqq.*; G. 1. 158; Inst. 1. 2. 11; D. 4. 5. 8.

not be forgotten that its supposed universality was a great force to this end, and this was its point of contact with *ius naturale*. This name, *ius naturale*, expresses a tendency in the trend of legal thought, a ferment operating all over the law. The notion of *obligatio naturalis* was a direct result of the conception of *ius naturale*. But the fact that *ius naturale* was not law is brought out by the gradual and incomplete development of this idea: it seems to be generally agreed that a pact did not necessarily create a *naturalis obligatio*[1].

It is a mistake to treat the Edict as originating in the *ius gentium*[2]. Many ideas in the Edict no doubt were due to this idea, but many had no direct connexion with it. The Publician action is not *iuris gentium*: it is confined to things capable of *usucapio* and to persons with *commercium*. The traffic of everyday life and the *disputatio fori* no doubt produced many new ideas, and many rules may have come to be thought of as *iuris gentium*, though they owed their appearance in the edict to other influences. Conversely, much of *ius gentium* had nothing to do with the Edict. *Traditio* and the other *iure gentium* (*naturali*) modes of acquisition were not established by the Edict, nor were *stipulatio* or *acceptilatio*, both of which were *iuris gentium*[3].

The word *aequitas* figures in juristic texts, in so many senses that it is of no great use[4]. Its basic meaning for classical law is "fairness[5]" but in post-classical texts it is used to mean *benignitas*, *indulgentia* and the like and is used to justify modifications of law in favour of the weaker party in a way which has little relation to the old conception of "fairness" and often ushers in a rule the implications of which must have made the application of the law very uncertain. That the strict law at times worked unfairly (*summum ius, summa iniuria*) was recognised in the Edictal reforms and the juristic "*interpretatio*." It has recently been shewn with a wealth of illustration[6] that the modification of law in the direction of *aequitas*, inspired by Greek philosophy, through the rhetoricians, was strongly operative among the lawyers from Cicero's time. It tends to interpretation according to intent, rather than literal (*voluntas* as against *verba*) and to such interpretation as gives a fair result, which is not quite the same thing. The changes are only gradually realised, but their prominence in republican times is a serious difficulty in the way of those writers who are inclined to see in allusions to "*voluntas*" and the like signs of Byzantine interpolation.

1 *Post*, § CLXXXIX. 2 16. 3. 31. pr. 3 G. 3. 93; D. 46. 4. 8. 4. 4 Cicero gives it many senses, as the basis of all law, or of the civil law or as contrasted with this. Krueger, *R.Rq.* 135. 5 Clark, *Pract. Jurisp.* 365 *sqq.*; *Hist. R. L.* 2. 1. 106. Paul says *aequitas* is a characteristic of *ius naturale* (1. 1. 11), and the expression *naturalis aequitas* is not uncommon. Reff. Krueger, *cit.* 138. 6 Stroux, *Summum ius summa iniuria*; see studies by Levy, *Z.S.S.* 1928, 668; Riccobono, *Gnomon*, 1929, 65.

CHAPTER II

THE LAW OF PERSONS. LIBERTY AND CITIZENSHIP

XXI. The arrangement of the private law adopted by Justinian is expressed in a famous text in the words: "*Omne ius quo utimur vel ad personas pertinet vel ad res vel ad actiones*[1]," borrowed from the Institutes of Gaius and expressly quoted from that work in the Digest[2]. It has naturally been inferred that the classification is due to Gaius, but this is not inevitable and there are circumstances which tend to throw doubt on it. The Institutes of Gaius is the only classical manual which has come down to us in such a form as to shew clearly the plan on which it is designed, and in view of the respect in which Gaius was held by Justinian the fact that the text is cited from him does not prove that he invented the scheme. Of other elementary books a considerable part has come down to us, and there are others of which the general order can be made out from the passages preserved in the Digest. The majority of these have an arrangement similar to that of Gaius and are probably based on the same scheme. Nearly all of them, however, are as late as Gaius or later, and may have copied him[3], but there is one case of special interest. We have a few fragments of the *Regulae* of Neratius[4], too little indeed to enable us to say with confidence what his order was, but such as to suggest that it was that of Gaius. Neratius must have

1 Inst. 1. 2. 12. 2 G. 1. 8; D. 1. 5. 1. 3 The works which seem to have adopted this order (Lenel, *Paling.*) are the Institutes of Callistratus, Ulpian and Marcian (so far as they go), the *Regulae* of Scaevola, Ulpian and Paul (but in all these cases with variations, and they do not cover the whole ground) and probably Neratius and to some extent the *Res cottidianae* of Gaius. 4 Lenel, *Paling.* 1. 774.

died at latest when Gaius was young. On the whole the most acceptable view is that Gaius adopted a traditional order[1]. He may have popularised it, though even this is hardly probable, since it is used by contemporary or almost contemporary writers who, so far as is known, never refer to him, though his works may have been[2] used by the great writers of the age of Severus and Caracalla[3].

The important question remains: what do the terms of the classification mean, or, more exactly, what did they mean to Gaius? They are so general as to be ambiguous, and examination of the various topics discussed under the different heads has created differences of opinion as to the nature of the distinctions intended. The difficulty of the question is increased by the fact that the loose logic of the Roman lawyers in matter of arrangement makes it likely that, whatever the scheme was, part of the resulting disposition of matters will be inconsistent with it. Of the interpretations which the threefold scheme has received two have been so widely accepted that it is desirable to state them with some fulness and to give some of the reasons which have been urged in favour of them.

According to one, which may be called the orthodox, and is certainly the most obvious, view, it is the object of the scheme to divide the law into three branches, the Law of Persons, the Law of *Res*, the Law of Actions. This is supported by the occurrence of such expressions as *Ius Personarum*[4] and gives a neat result acceptable to modern readers. But this explanation leaves open the question what is intended to come under each head. No doubt the law of actions is in the main the law of procedure, a description of the steps to be taken in the enforcement of a right, but the law of *res* and of persons is a more difficult matter. There are many opinions as to what is intended to be discussed in the law of persons. According to some[5], now few, it is the law of the rights and duties of persons in specific exceptional positions. In fact, the rights

1 Girard, *Textes*, 222. Kniep, *Der Rechtsgelehrte Gaius*, 95, thinks the phrase comes from an original dating back to the Republic. 2 Fitting, *Alter und Folge* (1908), 52, 116; see also however Krueger, *R.Rq.* 211, and *ante*, p. 33. 3 *Ante*, § XI. Maine (*Early Law and Custom*, 367) thinks there is no reason to suppose that the Romans set much store by this classification: it is confined to institutional books and has but little legal importance. This is no doubt substantially true, though D. 1. 5–8, and the Rubrics of D. 44. 7 and C. 4. 10 may be inspired by it. But this rather adds to its importance. It is in such books that scientific arrangements first appear, and the remark is a reflection rather on Tribonian than on Gaius. It is in works for students that we find the most logical arrangements of the English Law, and modern Codes which have adopted a scientific order derive it from books written by teachers. The real question is of its value to us. Nothing is more helpful to an understanding of a system of law than expositions of it from different points of view. This we have in the Institutes as contrasted with the Digest and Code. 4 E.g. G. 1. 9, 48. 5 Austin, *Jurisp.* 2. 709; "Law of Unequal Rights," and Poste's *Gaius* (ed. Whittuck), 15.

and duties of such persons are not considered under that head, though for convenience modern writers usually treat them there, and they are so dealt with, to some extent, in this book. For others it is the Family Law[1], but this is open to the same objection and to the opposite objection that matters are discussed by Gaius under this head, such as the ways in which a member of a Latin community can acquire *civitas*, which can hardly be brought under the notion of the family. If we treat it as the law of personal rights as opposed to property rights we have the difficulty that Gaius says not a word about the content of *patria potestas*, except, quite incidentally, as to consent to marriage. Other explanations starting from the same point of view are to be found[2], but they all fail to take account of what seems the most striking characteristic of Book I of Gaius, i.e. that it contains scarcely anything about rights and duties, except as concerning changes of *status*.

On another view, Gaius does not contemplate a division of the law into three branches: his proposition means that every rule of law has three aspects. It may be regarded from the point of view of the persons it affects, or from that of the subject matter concerned, or from that of the remedies[3]. This is the view taken in the paraphrase attributed to Theophilus, in the sixth century, where the words are taken to mean that every rule of law has three objects[4]. It has been said[5] that if Gaius had intended to divide the law into three branches he would have used the word *aut* and not *vel*, but it appears to be the better opinion that the practice of Latin writers in the second century is not such as to justify us in attaching decisive weight to this consideration. It has been objected that this interpretation is too abstract[6], but it is not too abstract for Theophilus, and it seems possible to reply that the other view is too abstract for the Romans. The conception of a right is so familiar to us as to seem obvious. But it represents a feat of abstraction which the Romans never thoroughly achieved. Maine goes so far as to say[7]: "On the whole, the Romans must be considered to have constructed their memorable system without the help of the conception of legal right." Though this may be an overstatement, the usually accepted view which makes right and duty the basis of the classification would scarcely have been possible for Gaius and still less for a republican author of the scheme. It is in favour of the view of Theophilus that Justinian follows our text with the remark that as all law is made for persons we must therefore know what these are[8]. This language suggests that what is under

1 Savigny, *System*, 1. 400. 2 See discussion, Moyle, *Inst. Just.* 90. 3 Moyle, *cit.* 92; Girard, *Man.* 8. 4 Paraphr. *ad.* In. 1. 3. pr. 5 Emerton, *The Threefold Division of Roman Law.* 6 E.g., Moyle, *loc. cit.* 7 *Early Law and Custom*, 365. 8 Inst. 1. 2. 12. For various meanings of the word *ius*, Heumann-Seckel, *s.v.*

discussion is persons, not the law of persons, and though we find the expression *ius personarum*[1] the word *ius* is never used in the passages which mark the transition from one of these topics to another[2].

In connexion with the law of persons this view is illuminating. The topics which one would expect to find therein are scattered all over the Institutes. Book I tells us little or nothing about the differences of right, duty or capacity which result from differences of *status*[3]. If we desire to learn the effect of a conveyance or acquisition, a contract or a delict, by a slave or *filius*, we do not find it in the law of persons but in different sections of the law of *res* or of actions. What Gaius gives us in Book I is an account of the more important variations in *status* which are legally material: we get a description of the *status*, and an account of the ways in which it is acquired or lost, and, practically no more. In very few passages does Gaius depart from this standpoint. In discussing *tutela* of women, he notes the marked difference which exists between the powers of a woman's *tutor* and those of *tutor pupilli*[4], an interjected remark which in a modern book would have been in a footnote. Justinian, by introducing a title on the *auctoritas* of tutors[5], suggested by this remark, has in fact obscured the whole plan of the book. There are similar remarks to distinguish the two classes of Latins and *dediticii*[6], and there is a phrase or two on the position of slaves[7]. That seems to be the whole contribution of Gaius at this point to the law of persons in the modern sense. His subject is quite unlike Austin's Law of Persons or Bentham's Special Codes. It is in fact hardly possible to mark it off as a branch of law having as its subject matter any set or sets of rights and duties. The writer is giving an account of the principal differences of *status* which the student will meet.

This characteristic of Book I is that of the whole of the Institutes of Gaius. We are told nothing of the rights and duties involved in ownership or usufruct or in servitudes. In the law of contract all that we get is a word or two as to the nature of the relation, and this not always, and an account of the way in which it is created and how it is dissolved. Nothing is said of the duties of the parties. The treatment of delict looks at first sight different: in the case of theft, for instance, we get the law of the matter treated in detail. In fact the principle is the same.

1 G. 1. 9; Inst. 1. 3. pr. 2 "*Videamus de rebus*," G. 2. 1; Inst. 2. 1. pr.; "*superest ut de actionibus loquamur*," Inst. 4. 6. pr. 3 The word *status* has no very precise meaning. In regard to persons, the Romans commonly use it much as we do to denote rank or position, but in general only where legal rights are concerned. More precisely used it seems to be equivalent to *caput* (*post*, § XLIX), i.e., the elements which make up a man's position as a *civis*, so that *status mutatio* would mean much the same as *capitis deminutio* (P. 1. 7. 2), but *status mutatio* sometimes means loss of *civitas*, so that here *status* means the elements involved in *civitas* itself (38. 17. 1. 8, *salvo statu*), the original meaning of *caput*.
4 G. 1. 190 *sqq*. 5 Inst. 1. 21. 6 G. 1. 22–27. 7 G. 1. 53.

Gaius is shewing how the obligation arises, and for this purpose it is essential to state the facts which give rise to an *obligatio ex delicto* for theft. An elementary account of the law of sale which says nothing of the duties of the parties is absurd, but Gaius is not giving an elementary account of the law. He is stating the main legal relations, their sources and modes of determination. As in the law of persons, so noticeably in the law of obligation, Justinian takes a different line. He repeatedly discusses the duties created by the relation[1].

Not every legally material difference of *status* is considered: we hear little of vestal virgins, *decuriones*, *auctorati*, or so forth, though these have many special capacities and incapacities. Gaius gives us no indication of his plan of selection, but it is clear that only those of legal significance come into account, and in an elementary book only those of importance. Very few classes are in fact considered: the slave, the *filiusfamilias*, the person *in manu* or *in mancipio*, the *paterfamilias* with full capacity or under control, the *tutor* and the *curator*. Wife and husband are considered not as part of the subject matter, but incidentally, in explaining the "investitive facts" of the *status* of *filiusfamilias*. So-called *personae fictae* are not considered. *Peregrini* are not discussed, perhaps because there was nothing to say[2]. But, in fact, Gaius is concerned only with the everyday *civis*: the important points of whose *status* are *libertas*, *civitas* and *familia*. He is not concerned with *peregrini* as such: all we hear of them is in connexion with access to *civitas*[3]. Slaves and Latins are discussed, partly because of their importance in everyday life, but also because they are sources from which the class of *cives* is constantly being recruited. Manumission is a common investitive fact of citizenship; it is therefore necessary to consider when it does and when it does not confer that *status*. Thus it is that in discussing those grades of freemen who are not *cives* Gaius appears to confine himself almost entirely to those who are *libertini*. The only topic in connexion with *Latini* in which Gaius shews interest is that of their means of access to *civitas*, and these he treats at length[4]. Of *dediticii* he notes that they cannot attain *civitas* or Latinity[5]. In support of this view of the scheme of Gaius it may be noted that in the *Regulae* attributed to Ulpian, a work the plan of which is unmistakably based on that adopted by Gaius, there is a title on *Latini* which deals exclusively with the ways

1 E.g., Inst. 3. 14. 2 (*commodatum*); 3. 17. (*stipulatio*); 3. 23. 3 (sale); 3. 24. 5 (*locatio*); 3. 25. 9 (*societas*), with brief statements of the effects of the relation, having no counterpart in Gaius. He dealt with these matters in his *Res cottidianae* (see 44. 7. 1; 18. 6. 2, 16; 17. 2. 72, etc.). 2 Moyle, *cit.* 88. 3 G. 1. 14, 15. The remarks in 1. 25–27 refer to freed slaves *in numero dediticiorum*, 1. 27 in f. We shall see that *civitas* itself is not treated distinctly. 4 G. 1. 28 *sqq.* 5 We have already noted, p. 59, that here G. goes a little further.

in which a Latin can acquire *civitas*[1]. Soo too in the part of the *Regulae* which corresponds to Book I of Gaius, we hear nothing of the position of slaves or of *filiifamilias* or of Latins, and in relation to *tutela* the departure from the plan supposed is the same, roughly, as that of Gaius[2]. As the language and to some extent the matter are different from those of Gaius, the fact that here too the law of rights and duties is not handled seems not without significance. The few cases in which resulting rights and duties are discussed cannot be explained logically on this view, but they are few and in every case have the air of illustrative matter[3]. Justinian departs from this point of view, and repeatedly, but not always, gives some account of the rights and duties resulting from the condition he is discussing[4].

XXII. It is convenient to base the treatment of the law of persons on the threefold classification of *capitis deminutiones* given by Gaius, i.e., *maxima*, involving loss of liberty, *media* or *minor*, involving loss of *civitas*, and *minima*, involving only loss of family rights[5]. This would naturally result in the treatment of it under the three heads: Liberty, Citizenship and Family, but that is not what Gaius does. He treats it from the points of view of liberty and family. This does not mean that the difference between *civis* and peregrine is negligible in private law: on the contrary it recurs over and over again in his treatment, but it is considered only incidentally. This is probably due to the treatment of the matter in his source, which no doubt ignored the triple division of *deminutiones*, a notion which in all probability was of no great antiquity in the time of Gaius[6]. The unfortunate result is that *civitas* is inadequately treated. It is not surprising that the same arrangement recurs in Justinian's Institutes: he follows Gaius very closely, and indeed in his day the question of *civitas* is not important, as practically every freeman who need be considered is a *civis*[7].

SLAVERY. Roman legal definitions are not usually good. Liberty is defined as the power of doing what one will, except so far as prevented by law or force[8]. Everyone is free under this definition, even slaves. We may, indeed, credit the framer with a refined conception of liberty, making it depend on the subject's internal freedom from the restrictions of his lower nature; the words may be derived from a source in philosophy in which they bear this meaning[9]. But, so understood, they are useless

1 Ulp. *Reg.* 3. 2 Ulp. *Reg.* Titt. 1–15. 3 On the notions of *ius rerum* and *ius actionum*, *post*, §§ LXVI, CCVI. 4 There has been much study of the institutional scheme, e.g., Affolter's *Das röm. Institutionensystem*. Justinian's main classification is from Gaius but his treatment, the matter being drawn from various sources, is different. The method of Gaius is that expressed in "Theophilus." That of Justinian tends, incompletely, to what is above described as the orthodox scheme. 5 G. 1. 159 *sqq*. 6 *Post*, § XLIX. 7 *Post*, § XXXVII. 8 Inst. 1. 3. 1; D. 1. 5. 4. pr. Florentinus. 9 Cicero, *Paradoxa*, 5.

as a definition of legal liberty, and it seems more likely that they are an attempt to state what liberty means in law, as unsuccessful as most such attempts.

All men, we are told, were either slaves or free; there was no intermediate position[1]. Slavery is defined by Justinian, after Florentinus, as an institution of *ius gentium* by which one man is subjected to the dominion of another contrary to nature[2], a view made to rest on the propositions that slavery originates in war and that war is contrary to nature[3]. It has been objected that this is inaccurate, as some slaves (*servi poenae, hereditarii, sub usufructu manumissi*[4]) had no owners, and that it is unscientific since it makes slavery a relative *status*[5]. A definition is therefore substituted which makes it a condition of rightlessness (it is to a great extent dutilessness also[6]), an absolute *status* not depending on relation to others. But Roman definitions, however imperfect, usually bring out the material point, and their own seems preferable. In the age of Florentinus and later, a slave was not rightless; he could in some cases appeal to the courts for protection[7], and enemies under arms seem to have been more rightless though they were not slaves. A graver objection is that the definition looks at the matter from a non-Roman point of view. It is not easy to translate "a rightless man" in language which Gaius would have understood. Further, the Roman definition does not make slavery a relative *status*. It does not mean that every slave must at every moment be owned, but that a slave is a human being capable of being owned—the one human chattel. Like other chattels he might be at a given moment a *res nullius*. This seems to be correct and vivid[8].

XXIII. Slaves were both things and men or persons. As *res*, they were *res mancipi*[9], of such importance that they figure largely in the texts and were the subject of much legislation, most of the special rules being due to their character, as having mental and moral qualities. Like other *res*, they might be productive. There might be earnings,

1 G. 1. 9; Inst. 1. 3. pr.; D. 1. 5. 3. *Servus* is a slave. *Mancipium* is a slave as a chattel, D. 21. 1. 51. pr. *Homo* is common, *famulus* rare in legal texts. *Ancilla* is a female slave, *serva*, rarer. *Puer*, for adults, more used in literary than in legal texts. *Puella* seems always to mean a girl; terminology, Desserteaux, *Capitis Deminutio*, 1. 372 *sqq*. *Coloni adscriptitii* (*post*, § XXXIII) are technically free, though practically serfs. 2 G. 1. 52; Inst. 1. 3. 2; D. 1. 5. 4. 1; 12. 6. 64. The only case of conflict between rules of *ius gentium* and *ius naturale*. 3 Justified by the view that a captor may kill prisoners, and benefits them by giving them their lives: *servi ut servati* (1. 5. 4; 50. 16. 239. 1). 4 *Post*, §§ XXV, XXIX, CVII. 5 Moyle, *Inst. Just. ad* 1. 3. 2. 6 50. 17. 22. pr. Judgement against a slave is void, 5. 1. 44. 1. Slavery is akin to death, 50. 17. 209. If a man is enslaved his debts cease and do not revive on manumission, 44. 7. 30. As to liabilities on delict, *post*, § CCV. 7 *Post*, § XXIII. 8 Buckland, *Slavery*, 1 *sqq*. The element of truth in the modern definition is that in a freeman capacities are presumed, not in a slave. On the question whether a slave was a person, *post*, § LXIII. 9 *Post*, § LXXXVI.

profits on their transactions, gifts to them, and so forth, which are not exactly *fructus*, but *loco fructuum*. It was settled in classical law that the only *fructus* a slave could produce, i.e. issue, were not legally *fructus*[1], as were those of lower animals[2], a concession to human dignity, of some practical importance. The usufructuary of an *ancilla* had no right to her child[3], nor was such a child an "accessory[4]." Wrongs were possible in respect of slaves which were not in respect of other things, e.g. insult[5]. Having mental and moral qualities, a slave could be damaged in ways not possible with other things[6]. Theft of slaves might be abduction, *plagium*[7]. For most chattels death or destruction is the only way of ceasing to exist, but, for a slave, there was also manumission. If freed he ceased to exist as a slave so completely that no rights in him revived on re-enslavement, and, in general, manumission released from any liability in respect of the slave to the same extent as did his death.

The special character of the slave appears most clearly in sale. As in other cases the vendor must hand over all acquisitions through the *res* since the contract, which covered earnings, gifts, etc.[8] Slave dealers having an evil reputation, provision was made against dishonesty. Thus, for defects, any member of a firm of *venaliciarii*, if his share was not less than any other, could be sued on a sale by any of them[9]. The liabilities themselves were greater. On sales of live stock the vendor was bound by the Edict of the Aediles to disclose defects, *morbus* or *vitium*, affecting the animal, and was liable even if ignorant of their existence. This applied to slaves[10], and, owing to their human character, other types of defect were put on the same level[11].

It was possible on sale of anything to impose restrictions on its use, but these had in general only contractual force: if the forbidden thing was done, an action lay against the other party, but the restriction had no force against third parties. If slaves, however, were sold to be kept

1 Inst. 2. 1. 37; D. 5. 3. 27. pr., disputed in republic, Cicero, *de fin.* 1. 12. 2 Inst. 2. 1. 37. 3 P. 3. 6. 19; D. 7. 1. 68. 4 The rule that, in a legacy of a thing and its accessories, the gift failed if the principal thing ceased to exist did not apply to a legacy of an *ancilla* and child, 30. 62, 63. The fact that it is not an accessory is important in the law of *usucapio*. If the child was born after possession of the mother had begun, there was dispute whether it was acquired under the same "*causa*," whether good faith was required at the moment of its birth, whether it was a *res furtiva* if the mother was, and so forth, Buckland, *Slavery*, 24 *sqq*. 5 G. 3. 222; D. 47. 10. 15. 44 *sqq*. 6 *Actio servi corrupti* for harming a slave, which covered demoralising him, D. 11. 3, *post*, § CCIII. 7 48. 15. 6. Killing a slave, while it gave an action for damages (*actio e lege Aquilia*, *post*, § CC), was also the crime of homicide, G. 3. 213; Inst. 4. 3. 11. 8 P. 2. 17. 7. Perhaps disputes as to damages recovered for theft of the slave after the sale, 18. 4. 21; 47. 2. 14. pr. 9 21. 1. 44. 1. 10 21. 1. 1. 1. *Post*, § CLXXII. 11 E.g., that he was given to running away, or had attempted suicide, or was under a liability for wrongdoing, or was from any cause incapable of manumission. His nationality must be stated, as this affected his suitability for certain employments, 21. 1. 31. 21.

away from Rome, or to be freed after a certain time, or not to be freed, there were means of enforcing the direction even if the slave had passed into other hands[1].

We are told that while, *iure naturali*, a slave was a man, like any other, he was *pro nullo* at civil and praetorian law[2]. But this gives a false picture of the law of the Empire. In the Republic a slave had no protection against his master, supreme in his household, but the Empire brought restrictions. Criminal slaves were to be tried by public courts[3]. A *l. Petronia* forbade masters to punish slaves by making them fight with beasts, except by a magistrate's authority[4]. Claudius provided that if a master abandoned a sick slave the slave should be free and a Latin[5]. Hadrian, besides dealing with specific cases, by *privilegium*, laid down many restrictions: in particular, he forbade masters to kill even criminal slaves without magisterial sanction[6]. These provisions are analogous to modern laws against cruelty to animals, but Pius took a great step forward. He allowed slaves cruelly treated to take sanctuary at a temple or the statue of the Emperor and required the magistrate to investigate the case, and, if he found cruelty proved, to sell the slave on the terms that he was not to return to his old master[7], a rule which gives the slave power to move the law in his own protection. To the close of the classical age it was not homicide in a master to kill a slave by excessive punishment, unless wilfully, though the same text says that the punishment must be reasonable[8]. There was later legislation[9]: under Justinian the master might not exceed reasonable castigation[10].

Although, from burial inscriptions and other evidence, we know that slaves lived habitually in a relation similar to marriage, permanent and monogamous, and that family relations were recognised among them[11], they were incapable of lawful marriage and the law in general ignored these relationships[12]. But they were not nullities. Servile relationship was a bar to marriage after freedom[13], and there were other rules, mostly of a negative or restrictive character[14]. Under Justinian a

1 On sale to be kept away it was usual to agree for a power of seizure, and, apart from other effects, this right existed against third party owners, 18. 7. 7 *sq.* As to sale to be freed at a certain time, *post*, § XXXI. If sold not to be freed at all, manumission by a later owner was void, 18. 7. 6. pr. 2 28. 1. 20. 7; 28. 8. 1; 50. 17. 32. Partial recognition of servile cognation, *post*, § CXXXII. 3 48. 2. 12. 3. 4 48. 8. 11. 2. Older than the destruction of Pompeii (A.D. 79)—a record of it was found there. 5 40. 8. 2; C. 7. 6. 3. 6 Coll. 3; D. 1. 6. 2; 48. 8. 4, 5. 7 G. 1. 53. 8 Coll. 3. 2. 9 C. Th. 9. 12. 1. 2. 10 Inst. 1. 8. 2. 11 Buckland, *Slavery*, 76 and reff. 12 Ulp. 5. 5; P. 2. 19. 6. 13 23. 2. 14. 2. 14 After freedom children could not bring proceedings against their parents, 2. 4. 4. 3. Sales and legacies were construed, so far as possible, so as not to involve separation of families, P. 3. 6. 38; D. 33. 7. 12. 7. If brothers were sold the sale could not be in part set aside for defects: all or none must be returned, 21. 1. 35, 39. C. Th. 2. 25. 1, provides that in dividing a *hereditas* slaves related were to

further logical and important step was taken, by the provision of rights of succession on intestacy, after freedom[1].

Slaves were liable for crimes and delicts. In the last case the personal liability meant little so long as they were slaves, but it was reinforced by a liability in the master to surrender the slave to the injured person —*noxae deditio*—unless he was prepared to pay the damages[2].

In commerce slaves were important. In the classical age free hired service was not common: most of the work now done by clerks and servants was done by slaves. Though they could have no property, it was customary from early times to entrust them with a fund, called *peculium*, sometimes large, in connexion with which slaves appear, in the Empire, almost as independent business men, contracting with their owners and others as if free[3]. As they could neither sue nor be sued, the master intervened if any question of enforcement arose. As a slave's acquisitions were his master's[4], the latter could bring any necessary actions, but obligations contracted by a slave did not bind his owner[5], at civil law, and a man would not readily contract with a slave, if he had to rely on his *naturalis obligatio*, useless while he was a slave, and having little effect if he was freed. The praetor therefore facilitated the employment of slaves in trade by giving actions against the master imposing a liability, varying with the circumstances, of which the *actio de peculio* was the most important[6]. But capacity to acquire for the master and to bind him within limits does not suffice; to be an effective instrument in commerce the slave must have a power of alienation. He could be authorised to alienate anything. In practice it was usual to give slaves, who traded with their *peculium*, *administratio peculii*[7], which might vary in extent, but usually meant the right to alienate in the way of business, to sell or pledge, to pay debts, but not to make gifts[8].

be kept together. Relationship was recognised for the purposes of the law of *parricidium*, 48. 2. 12. 4. See also, 28. 8. 11. Other rules, Cuq, *Man.* 133.

1 *Post*, § CXXXII. Slaves shared to some extent in the domestic cults, and there were cults peculiar to them. Wallon, *Histoire de l'Esclavage* (2) 2. 231 *sqq.*; Warde Fowler, *Roman Essays*, 56 *sqq.* It was the duty of the master to give them proper burial, and with his consent they might be members of *Collegia tenuiorum*, burial clubs, 11. 7. 31. 1; 47. 22. 3. 2. 2 *Post*, § CCV; as to crimes, Buckland, *Slavery*, 91. 3 2. 13. 4. 3; 17. 2. 18, 63. 2. A partnership of a slave might in practice survive sale of him, h. t. 58. 3. 4 G. 2. 86, 87; Inst. 2. 9. 3; D. 41. 1. 10. 1. Where lesser rights in him exist, the holder may acquire to some extent through him, *post*, § XCIX. Bonitary ownership, *post*, § LXX. 5 Liability of the master would not follow from the principle under which he acquired and the traditional untrustworthiness of slaves (*quot servi, tot hostes*) made it inadmissible. 6 The master liable so far as the *peculium* will go, *post*, § CLXXXIV for this and the other actions. 7 12. 6. 13; 13. 7. 18. 4; 20. 6. 8. 5; 46. 4. 22. 8 Power perhaps implied in gift of *peculium*, express grant of *administratio* being needed only in late law, Albertario, *Rend. Ist. Lomb.* 1928, pp. 833 *sqq.* Thus the rich Roman could safely invest in trade without engaging in it. There were no limited companies, and State contracts which admitted

Slaves were freely employed in the public service, of the State and the municipalities, those in the State service (*servi publici populi Romani*) enjoying special privileges, and often reaching high rank in the civil service[1]. But they were gradually excluded from one post after another, till under Arcadius it was enacted that *administratio*, which had been essentially servile, should be wholly closed to slaves[2]. The *servus publicus* to whom security was given in some cases, e.g. *adrogatio* of an *impubes*, was replaced in the later empire by a *publica persona* who was free[3]. There were many activities in which slaves had no share. Not being *cives*, they could not serve in the legions. They could be parties to a formal civil law transfer, *mancipatio*, having a derivative capacity from their owner[4], but they could not be witnesses in it[5]. They could not be parties to judicial proceeding[6], or to *cessio in iure*, a transfer which was in form a feigned lawsuit[7]. In general they could not be witnesses in civil suits, but convenience dictated relaxation of this rule[8]. Where their evidence was admissible it was normally by torture, as in criminal cases, the torture being allowed only where there was some evidence, but not enough[9]. An old rule excluded their evidence against their master: in classical law this was extended to evidence on his behalf[10].

Justinian describes all slaves as of one condition: *in conditione servorum nulla differentia est*[11]. There were of course wide differences *de facto*[12], but there were also differences in law. *Servi publici populi Romani* had rights of testation of some of their *peculium*[13], and there were other cases. But the cases were few and the differences in law slight.

XXIV. Enslavement. Justinian groups the causes of enslavement under two heads: they are *iure gentium* or *iure civili*[14]. The former,

of "sleeping partners" would not cover the ground. There were risks in appointing free *institores* to manage businesses (*post*, § CLXXXIV) and in sleeping partnerships in private concerns. The *actio de peculio* created limited liability which could be cut short at any time by mere expression of intent, subject only to rights of existing creditors.

1 Buckland, *Slavery*, 320. 2 C. 10. 71. 3; 11. 37. 1. 3 Inst. 1. 11. 3; D. 1. 7. 18. The increasing use of the free agent in private life is another indication of the same tendency: in the bad times freemen who found it hard to make a living objected to the competition of slaves. 4 G. 2. 87. 5 G. 1. 119. So they could take for their master under a will, but could not make or witness one, *post*, § CIII. 6 Or formal acts and undertakings connected therewith, 2. 8. 8. 2; 2. 11. 9. 7 *Post*, § LXXXIV. 8 They could be witnesses in a transaction with which they were concerned, if there was no other evidence, P. 5. 16. 1, 2. Other exceptions, Buckland, *Slavery*, 86. 9 P. 5. 16. 2; D. 48. 18. 1. 1, 9. pr. 9. 1, 18, etc. 10 Cicero, *pro Milone*, 22. 59; P. 1. 12. 3; D. 1. 12. 1. 8, etc., P. 2. 17. 12; C. 9. 41. 6, etc. Tendency to extend the exclusion: slaves of near relatives were excluded and a slave could not give evidence against his *bona fide possessor*, 48. 18. 1. 3, 1. 8, 10. 2. There were crimes to which the rule did not apply, C. 9. 41. 1; D. 48. 18. 10. 1, etc. 11 Inst. 1. 3. 4. 12 Some had *peculia*, some not. A labourer on a country estate is in a very different position from a banker at Rome. 13 *Post*, § CII. Some slaves could never be freed, *post*, § XXIX. Slaves unowned had no derivative capacities. Special rules for *captivi*, *post*, § XXIV. 14 Inst. 1. 3. 4.

birth and capture, are the more important, and birth is the most important of all[1]. It is however only as to general principle that these are *iure gentium*: in each case there were many specially Roman rules.

Capture in War. Prisoners of foreign war became slaves, the property of the State, commonly sold to private owners. The same principle was applied to Romans captured by the enemy. During his slavery a captive did not differ from other slaves. But difficult questions arose as to the fate of his acts and rights before enslavement, further complicated by the law of *postliminium*[2], by virtue of which one who returned might be more or less restored to his old position[3].

The effect of events during captivity was in suspense, differently determined according as the captive returned with *postliminium* or died in captivity. Acquisitions by a son would belong to the captive or the son, according as he returned with *postliminium* or did not[4]. All property was lost, subject to revival[5]. But possession was a question of fact; it did not revive by return, but only by retaking, when it was a new possession[6]. The position of those who had been in his *potestas* was in suspense[7], but any guardianship he held, or was under, was ended but might be restored, for the future, by *postliminium*[8]. In classical law his marriage ended and did not revive, except by consent; under Justinian[9] it continued so long as he was certainly alive. If this was not certain the wife could not remarry for five years[10].

If he died a captive the suspense was ended and on the view which

1 Justinian does not call it *i. gentium*, but see G. 1. 82; D. 1. 5. 5. 1. 2 The rules are such that it is sometimes said that he was not a slave, but *servi loco*. Mommsen, *Ges. schrift.* (*Jur.*), 3. 3; Mitteis, *R.Pr.* 1. 128. It is held by Desserteaux (*Capitis Deminutio*, 1. 82, 135 *sqq.*, 2. 79, etc.) that it was *de facto* slavery in classical law, but true slavery later. (See G. *Ep.* 2. 3. 5.) Views difficult to reconcile with the texts. Livy, 22. 60; G. 1. 129; Festus, *s.v. Deminutus*; Inst. 1. 3. 4; D. 49. 15. 19. 2, 21. 1, etc. Nor is it easy to see why *de facto* slavery should deprive him of his property (see 3. 5. 18. 5; 9. 2. 43; but see also 41. 2. 23. 1) or why *postliminium* was needed. A man *in servitute* did not need *postliminium*. Ratti, *Riv. It. p. l. Sc. Giur.* 1, 175 reverses the doctrine of Desserteaux; Sertoris, *Z.S.S.* 1929, 666 holds it true slavery. 3 G. 1. 129; P. 2. 25. 1; D. 49. 15. 4. 4 9. 2. 43; 45. 1. 73. 1; 49. 15. 12. 1, 22. 1. 5 Early protection by *l. Hostilia*, later by *curator bonorum* who gives security to *servus publicus*. Inst. 4. 10. pr.; C. 8. 50. 3; D. 4. 6. 15. pr., etc. 6 If held for him, view finally reached that of a *res peculiaris* held by son or slave possession was retained, notwithstanding the capture, that *dominium* might be acquired in the meantime by lapse of time, for whose benefit would depend on events; 41. 3. 15. pr.; 49. 15. 22. 3, etc. So, in general, time is running for or against him, though the machinery of *restitutio in integrum* (*post*, § CCXLIII) makes this rather unreal; 4. 6. 1. 1, 15. pr. On return, as his *possessio* is a new one, there will not be *accessio possessionum* (*post*, § LXXXVII). 7 G. 1. 129; Ulp. 104. 8 G. 1. 129, 187; Inst. 1. 12. 5; D. 26. 1. 14. 2; 38. 16. 15. 9 Possible exception where he was patron of his wife, 24. 2. 1, 6; 23. 2. 45. 6; 49. 15. 8, 12. 4, 14. 1; *Nov.* 22. 7. Some texts interp. The rule last stated, due to a *Nov.* of Justinian is credited in D. 24. 2. 6 (i.e. before the enactment) to Julian. The puzzle thus created is explained in many ways. 10 On the difficult historical points in connexion with these rules, Ratti, *Bull.* 1927, 105 *sqq.*

prevailed he was regarded as having died when captured[1]. Strictly, his will was void, and he could make none while a captive. But under a provision of a *l. Cornelia*, the *fictio legis Corneliae*[2], his will took effect as if he had not been captured, but had died at the moment of capture[3].

Postliminium was practically restoration of the *captivus* to his rights on return[4]. For this to arise there must have been nothing discreditable about his capture[5]; he must have returned at the first opportunity[6], and according to some modern writers, this must have been during the war[7]. If he was redeemed by payment his ransomer had a lien on him for the money and there was no *postliminium* till this was in some way discharged[8].

Where a slave was captured, the rules were different. One who voluntarily went over to the enemy, a *transfuga*, had no *postliminium*, nor had one who returned without intending to stay, but a slave reverted to his owner in both cases[9]. A *civis* had *postliminium* as soon as he reached Roman territory: a slave reverted only when possessed by someone[10].

Birth[11]. In general, the child of an *ancilla* was a slave, even if the father was free, in accordance with the *ius gentium*, which traced descent from the mother, while in Roman marriage it was traced from the father[12]. So, by the *ius gentium*, the child took her status at the time of the birth, and belonged to her owner at that time[13]. To these principles Roman Law recognised two groups of exceptions.

In a few cases the child of a freewoman might be a slave. The *sc. Claudianum* provided that if a freewoman lived with a slave, his owner consenting, issue might, by agreement between the master and the woman, be born his slave. Hadrian abolished this rule[14]. In the fifth

1 Succession determined as if he had died at capture, G. 1. 129; D. 49. 15. 12. 1.
2 Identity of this *lex*, and nature of the provision, disputed. *Post*, § CII; Balogh, *St. Bonfante*, 4. 679.
3 Ulp. 23. 5; P. 3. 4a. 8; D. 35. 2. 18. pr.; 49. 15. 22. 1, etc. Codicils made during captivity, Vassali, *Misc. crit.* 2. 26; Ratti, *Riv. It. p. l. sc. Giur.* 2. 10, holds their validity on return due to Justinian. He also discusses *institutio* as *heres*; 28. 5. 32. 1, *post*, § CIII.
4 Beseler, *Z.S.S.* 1925, 192, holds that it was not retrospective in classical law, but see Ratti, *Riv. cit.* 2. 5 *sqq.*
5 49. 15. 17.
6 49. 15. 12. pr.
7 Texts hardly bear this out. Reff., Buckland, *Slavery*, 305.
8 38. 16. 1. 4; 49. 15. 12. 14. Difficulties as to position in meantime, Buckland, *Slavery*, 312. Taubenschlag, *Röm. Prr. zur Z. Diocletians*, 152. 267. 276 and Albertoni, *Redemptio ab hostibus*, hold that in classical law he was in *mancipii causa* and needed manumission, not in later law. For H. Krueger, *Z.S.S.* 1931, 203, redeemer was owner in classical law, pledgee under Justinian. We know practically nothing about one who returns without *postliminium*. (He may be a traitor, 48. 19. 38. 1; 49. 15. 12. 17, 19. 4.) His rights not being restored, his liabilities cannot be.
9 41. 1. 51. pr.; 49. 15. 12. 9, 19. 4.
10 49. 15. 30. In later law he belongs to a ransomer, but can be claimed by old owner on payment, 29. 2. 71. pr.; 49. 15. 12. 7, 8, obscure. Buckland, *Slavery*, 315.
11 Messa, *Ingenuitas*.
12 G. 1. 56, 82.
13 Ulp. 5. 9, 10; P. 2. 24. 1; D. 13. 7. 18. 2.
14 G. 1. 84; P. 4. 10. 2. Messa, *cit.* 19. "*Inelegantia*": freewoman's child a slave. Normally pact cannot vary *status*, 40. 12. 37.

century it was enacted that a woman who married her *libertus* was liable to deportation, and her children were slaves of the Fisc[1]. The rule was gone under Justinian. In more numerous cases the child of an *ancilla* might be born free. In classical law, and later, a child was free if the mother was free at any time from the conception to the birth[2]. In some cases in which the mother would normally have been free at the birth but circumstances had barred this, the child was born free, e.g. where the mother was conditionally freed, and the child was born after the condition occurred, but owing to her captivity or *condemnatio* she never became free[3], or her holder was under a trust to free her, and, though freedom was demanded, delayed wilfully to do it, and a child was born in the meantime[4], or there had similarly been wilful delay in entering under a will by which the woman was freed[5].

XXV. *Jure Civili* modes of enslavement. By the Twelve Tables a thief caught in the act was enslaved, if a freeman. Those who evaded the *Census* (thus escaping, *inter alia*, military service) might be sold by the State, but this disappeared with the *Census*. Similar rules applied to other attempts to evade military service[6]. One who failed to satisfy a judgement might, in early law, be sold into foreign slavery.

Of modes of enslavement abolished by Justinian[7] two are important.

Servitus poenae. Those sentenced in certain ways for crime became slaves[8]. Not every capital sentence (i.e. involving destruction of *caput*, civil capacity) involved slavery. A *deportatus* lost *civitas*, but was not a slave. No temporary punishment involved slavery, nor did all perpetual punishments[9]. It resulted from condemnation *in metallum*, labour in mines or quarries, and a death sentence made the condemned a *servus poenae* till it was carried out[10].

The convict's marriage was dissolved; his family rights were destroyed[11], and his property was forfeited subject to concessions, frequently

1 *Nov. Anthemii*, 1. The case in G. 1. 85, 86 is probably not Roman Law at all. Huschke *ad loc.* 2 P. 2. 24. 2, 3. Set down to *favor libertatis*, but ultimately applied to cases not concerned with liberty; 1. 5. 7, 26; see 1. 5. 18. Possible exception, G. 1. 91, but rule perhaps not fully developed. Brini, *Mem. d. R. Accad. di Bologna, Sc. Mor.* 1923, 175 *sqq.* 3 40. 7. 6. pr. 1. 4 P. 2. 24. 4; D. 1. 5. 22. He might be a *suus heres*, 38. 16. 1. 1. 5 40. 5. 55. 1. So too under *sc. Silanianum* (*post*, § CIX), C. 6. 35. 11, and in delayed manumission for cause approved by *consilium*, 40. 2. 19. Many cases; texts are confused as the result. Montel, *St. Bonfante*, 3. 633 *sqq.* 6 Mommsen, *Strafr.* 561. 7 *Dediticii* returning to Rome, *post*, § XXXVI; *Liberi expositi*, C. Th. 5. 9. 1, 2; *post*, § XXXI; *Coloni fugitivi*, C. Th. 5. 17. 1, *post*, § XXXIII, etc. 8 48. 19. 2. pr. 9 E.g., *opus publicum*, road-making and the like, 48. 19. 10. pr., 17; C. 9. 47. 1. 10 So also certain forms of condemnation to the arena, not involving death, 48. 19. 8. 11, 29, 36. The punishment was more freely inflicted on slaves than on freemen, and, apart from death sentence, could not in general be inflicted on the higher orders at all, 48. 19. 9. 11, etc. 11 48. 19. 2. 1, 29.

varied, in favour of children, and, at one time, some other relatives[1]. Finally the whole was given to the children[2]. A *servus poenae* belonged to no one: he did not vest in the State[3]. Thus he had none of the derivative capacities of a slave. A gift to him was a nullity[4]. He could not be freed, but pardon was possible and would restore freedom, but not family or property rights[5] and a pardoned slave did not revert to his owner, the ownership being destroyed[6]. But a freeman on pardon did not apparently become a *libertinus*: he reverted to *ingenuitas*. The pardon might, however, be accompanied by a restoration of rights, more or less full, according to the terms of the decree, such a *restitutio* being an administrative, not a judicial, act[7]. A man condemned and subsequently found innocent was not pardoned: he was *restitutus*. But this idea was not applicable to one who before condemnation was a slave. Here there was *revocatio* of the sentence, and the old ownership was restored[8]. In 536 Justinian abolished the rule that a convict became a slave[9].

The *sc. Claudianum*. This enactment (A.D. 52) provided, *inter alia*, that if a freewoman cohabited with a *servus alienus*, after notice that the owner forbade it, she and the issue should be his slaves, a magistrate's decree being necessary[10]. If she was a *filiafamilias*, whose father had not consented, the rule did not apply, as it would deprive him of a daughter[11], and if a *libertina*, she became, unless the patron had consented, the slave of her patron[12]. If the man was a *servus fisci*, she became, not a slave, but a *liberta Caesaris*, subject here too to the rights of father and patron[13]. Justinian abolished the rule of the *sc.* retaining a punishment for the slave concerned[14].

1 48. 20. 1, 7. pr., 8; C. Th. 9. 42. 2. Not applicable in *maiestas* or magic, C. Th. 9. 42. 2, 6, etc. 2 *Nov.* 17. 12. Only a fortnight before penal slavery was abolished. A convict woman's children took nothing, the right being primarily based on civil law rights of succession, non-existent in their case, *arg.* C. 9. 49. 6; D. 48. 20. 7. pr. Buckland, *Slavery*, 409. 3 34. 8. 3 (*et ita divus Pius rescripsit*); 49. 14. 12. In later classical law a slave convicted and pardoned vested in the fisc (40. 5. 24. 5). This fact and the fact that the child of a *serva poenae* belongs to the fisc (h. l. 6) have led to the view that in principle a *servus poenae* vested in the fisc; the rule that the fisc acquired nothing through them was an arbitrary self-denying rule. Mommsen, *Strafr.* 948, n. 1; Desserteaux, *Capitis Deminutio*, 2. 430 *sqq.*; Affolter, *Persönlichk. d. herrenlosen Sklaven.* 11. 4 29. 2. 25. 3. 5 C. 9. 49. 4; 9. 51. 9, or liabilities, h. t. 4. 6 48. 19. 8. 12. 7 If it gave back his property there was legislation to deal with the obvious complications, e.g. P. 4. 8. 22; C. 9. 51. 3, 4, 9. 8 If he had been made *heres* by his old master before *condemnatio*, this was good, 40. 4. 46. 9 *Nov.* 22. 8, dealing primarily with alterations in the law of marriage. 10 G. 1. 91, 160; Ulp. 11. 11; P. 2. 21a; C. Th. 4. 12. 1–5. Rule, varied from time to time, requiring notice three times as evidence of persistence, and as to who might denounce. Position of children already conceived not clear. 11 P. 2. 21a. 9, 10. 12 *Ib.* 6, 7. 13 C. Th. 4. 12. 3; *Fr. de iure Fisci*, 12; details, P. 2. 21a. 11–18, Buckland, *Slavery*, 416. 14 Inst. 3. 12. 1; C. 7. 24.

There remained in Justinian's law several grounds for enslavement, three of which need mention[1].

Young children sold under pressure of poverty. From the third century onwards[2] sale of new-born children was allowed, with a right of redemption, and in the fourth and fifth centuries this seems to have been, for a time, allowed with older children[3]. As to new-born children it continued under Justinian[4]. On redemption the child was *ingenuus*, but the intermediate *status* was true slavery.

Libertus ingratus. There was much legislation dealing with this case. The punishment varied with the degree of misconduct[5], but from the time of Claudius enslavement might be imposed in serious cases and Justinian retained this, though it seems to have been rarely inflicted[6]. It needed a decree of the chief magistrate[7], and was allowed only where the manumission was voluntary, e.g. not where it was under a trust[8].

Fraudulent sale of freeman. The general rule was that a free person over 20, who knowingly allowed him, or her, self to be sold as a slave in order to share the price, was enslaved, or, as it is put, forbidden *proclamare in libertatem*, i.e. to bring a claim of liberty[9]. It was a *capitis deminutio maxima*. If manumitted he became a *libertinus*, The child of a woman so dealt with, born during her slavery, was a slave[10]. To be liable he must have received part of the price and the buyer must have been deceived[11]. There was no *restitutio in integrum*, but Hadrian allowed *proclamatio* in some cases if the whole price was restored. This was a general rule of later law, so that the effect might be undone without manumission[12].

1 Other cases, Buckland, *op. cit.* 419. 2 Not in classical law, P. 5. 1. 1. 3 Vat. Fr. 34; C. Th. 3. 3. 1; 5. 10. 1. 4 C. 4. 43. 2. 5 For lesser cases, fine, whipping, or even loss of citizenship, 37. 14. 7. 1; C. Th. 2. 22. 1. 6 25. 3. 6. 1; 37. 14. 5; C. 6. 7. 2. 7 1. 16. 9. 3; C. 6. 7. 1 in classical law imperial decree, De Francisci, *Mél. Cornil*, 1. 297 *sqq.* 8 C. 6. 7. 1. Patron's children might accuse, and in later law any *heres*, though, possibly, between 417 and Justinian, other *heredes* and perhaps children too were barred, C. Th. 4. 10. 2; *Nov.* Val. 25. 1; C. 6. 7. 3; D. 50. 16. 70. It seems that in later law children of *liberti* could similarly be accused. C. Th. 4. 10. 3 = C. 6. 7. 4. 9 Inst. 1. 3. 4; D. 1. 5. 5. 1; 40. 13. 3; 40. 14. 2. pr. 10 Inst. 1. 3. 4; 1. 16. 1; D. 1. 5. 21; 40. 12. 40; 40. 13. 3. Thus it was actual slavery, not as is sometimes said a mere procedural rule. *Contra*, Perozzi, *Ist.* 1. 236. 11 40. 12. 7. 2; 40. 13. 1. pr. 12 40. 14. 2. pr. No classical text refers to this institution, and Justinian's texts give a confused account of its origin. Probably it rests on *scc.* It is sometimes called edictal, but this seems unevidenced. Marcian calls it *iure civili* (1. 5. 5. 1), but his language is explained away (Karlowa, *R.Rg.* 2. 1116). There was a praetorian action *in factum* for damages wherever a freeman allowed himself to be sold in fraud (40. 12. 14–22), no doubt the oldest remedy. The *scc.* strengthen it for specific cases. The rule that he must have shared in the price cannot be traced earlier than Hadrian and may be later (40. 14. 2. pr. ? interp.). But sale in order to be qualified for duties appropriate to slaves seems to have been dealt with in classical law in the same way (28. 3. 6. 5). And Paul tells us that gift

Effect of enslavement. We are told that it was like death[1]. Like death it ended all public and private relations, but it did more, for wills and *donationes mortis causa*, made operative by death, were avoided by slavery[2]. It destroyed cognation, which was not revived by manumission[3]. Property went, not to the *heres*, but to the person who acquired the slave, subject to debts[4], and probably debts to him were due to his owner[5]. Liability *ex delicto*, however, exceptionally, survived. His owner might be sued noxally, and if this was not done, he might himself be sued if he was freed[6]. There could be no noxal action in the case of a *servus poenae*[7].

XXVI. Determination of slavery. There was no temporary slavery. If it was to end otherwise than by death this must be by a juristic act. For *servi poenae* the only such acts were pardon and *revocatio*, but in other cases it might end in many ways. Omitting *postliminium*, reversion on refund of price, and redemption of a child sold, the slavery of a living man might end by manumission, an act of the owner, voluntary at least in form, or by some act or event wholly or partly independent of his intention, of which groups the first is much the most important.

MANUMISSION, release from slavery by the owner, was originally thought of as the creation of a *civis*[8]. It was not a transfer of ownership: a man does not own himself. It was not merely release from ownership; that was abandonment, *derelictio*, which did not make the man free[9] and destroyed all rights in the former master, which manumission did not. It was the transfer of a man from the class of things which can be owned into the class of persons who are members of the civil body. At the beginning of the Empire the law of manumission was simple. There were three modes, all actually or in origin subject to State control, in view of their effect in making the slave a Roman citizen. These were Entry on the Census Roll, *Vindicta*, a fictitious claim of liberty, and Will.

Census. The *Census*, taken normally every fifth year[10], was a list of citizens made for fiscal and military purposes. It was prepared before the Censors at Rome, and it was still doubted when the institution fell into decay whether manumission operated at once or only at the final formal act of closing the *Census* (*lustrum condere*), which brought the

in dowry or *donatio* or pledge is on the same footing as sale (40. 12. 23). Thus the rule probably was at one time wider than in Justinian's law. Buckland, *Slavery*, 427 *sqq.*

1 50. 17. 209. 2 G. 2. 147; Inst. 2. 17. 4; D. 24. 1. 32. 6. 3 38. 8. 7, i.e. as to rights. 4 4. 5. 2. pr., 7. 2. Owner not personally liable, but the property is. 5 *Arg.* from *adrogatio* (*post*, § CXLI). As to *servi poenae*, *ante*, p. 70. 6 Inst. 4. 8. 5; D. 9. 4. 24. 7 *Ante*, p. 69. Noxal actions, with the alternative of paying the damages or surrendering the wrongdoer might have operated so as to allow the man to pass from severe punishment into ordinary ownership. 8 Ulp. 1. 6; D. 38. 2. 1. pr. 9 41. 7. 8, till *Nov.* 22. 12. 10 Fr. Dos. 17; Mommsen, *Staatsr.* 2. 343; *D.P.R.* 4. 15.

new lists into operation[1]. The process involved three steps: the slave presented himself for entry like an ordinary *civis*, the master's consent was shewn and the name was entered[2], the Censor probably having the right to refuse the name for unworthiness. The manumitter must have full civil law ownership and there could be no conditions. Gaius speaks of it in the present tense[3], but there does not seem to have been a real *Census* for a long time[4]: it is doubtful whether manumission by this mode survived the Republic.

Vindicta. In form a fictitious claim of liberty, a formal application of the machinery by which a man who alleged that he was wrongly held in slavery claimed his freedom (*causa liberalis*), modelled on the ancient process for recovery of property (*vindicatio*), by *sacramentum*. Some person seems to have claimed on his behalf (*adsertor libertatis*[5]), he being present. The formal words were modelled on those in *sacramentum*[6]. The *adsertor* touched the slave with a rod (*festuca, vindicta*) as he would if the claim was a real one, from which act the process draws its name. The master did the same, but otherwise made no reply[7]. The magistrate declared the man free. It was in form a litigation, and, as such, could be carried out only before a magistrate with the right to preside in a *legis actio*[8]. Its forms were gradually relaxed and in later classical law its litigious character was recognised as a mere pretence[9]. There could not be condition or *dies*, for it was in form a judgement, which did not admit of these[10].

The manumitter must be full civil law owner, and, the process being a *legis actio*, it must be done personally: no representative could act[11]. As in all essentially "formal" acts form was more important than consent. One who had done the act was bound by it, whatever his state of

1 Fr. D. 17; Cicero, *de Or.* 1. 40. 183. 2 Cicero, *loc. cit.*; Ulp. 1. 8. 3 G. 1. 17, 44. 4 Mommsen, *op. cit.* 2. 336 *sqq.*; *D.P.R.* 4. 7 *sqq.* The last is in A.D. 74, and they had long been irregular. For the *liber singularis regularum* (Ulp. 1. 8) it is an antiquity. 5 G. 4. 14. 6 *Arg.* G. 2. 24. 7 Silence being a sign of assent, a *mutus* or *surdus* could not free in this way; P. 4. 12. 2. No longer true in later law, 40. 2. 23. Literary texts speak of the master as slapping the slave's cheek and turning him round (reff., Roby, *R.P.L.* 1. 26). Meaning of these symbolic acts disputed, Roby, *loc. cit.*; Karlowa, *R.Rg.* 2. 133. Probably not legally required but made clear the fictitious nature of the transaction. 8 P. 2. 25. 4; Ulp. 1. 7. D. 1. 7. 4. 9 It might be done in the street, without lictors, and on days not available for legal process, G. 1. 20; D. 40. 2. 7, 8, 23. 10 49. 4. 1. 5 (but see *post*, § CCXXVII for later law). There might be tacit conditions in the sense that it might be in suspense, as the owner's right might be. It would operate only if he proved to have been then owner. Whether the magistrate could refuse is disputed. Wlassak, *Z.S.S.* 1907, 106, citing Livy, 41. 9, holds the more probable view that he could. *Contra*, Girard, *Mél.* 1. 140. 11 *Post*, § CCXXXIX, Texts frequently state an exception: a son, duly authorised, could so free for his father. This is clearly law for Justinian. Mitteis holds that the numerous texts are interpolated, and that it was not so in classical law, *Z.S.S.* 1900, 199; 1904, 379. *Rom. Pr.* 1. 211. *Contra*, Buckland, *N.R.H.* 27. 737; *Slavery*, App. 5.

mind, e.g. where he did not think he was owner, but in fact was. Most of the "formal" acts were gone by Justinian's time, but this remained[1].

XXVII. Will, *Testamento*[2]. This is much the most important case. The Will of early Rome was made before the public assembly, convoked periodically for the purpose, and thus the element of control is traditionally present, though, the will of historical times being in an entirely different form, the control had disappeared. The full civil owner could free his slave so that the gift took effect, *ipso facto*, by the acceptance of the inheritance by the *heres*, provided that the testator had owned the slave both when the will was made and when it operated[3]. The gift must be in express imperative words, e.g. *liber esto, liberum esse iubeo*[4], and *nominatim*, i.e. he must be so described or named that his identity was clear[5]. Thus there could not strictly be an implied gift, but we are told, *in obscura voluntate favendum est libertati*[6]. Two such cases were much discussed, that in which a man made his slave *heres*, with no gift of freedom, to be dealt with later[7], and that in which he simply appointed him *tutor*. Justinian declared this good, the needful gift of freedom being implied. The dominant view in later classical law seems to be that it was not directly good or void, but was a *fideicommissum*, a direction to *heres* to free, shortly to be considered, but some jurists seem to have held it directly good[8].

Manumission, like a legacy, might be adeemed, i.e. revoked, by express further provisions of the will[9], or acts inconsistent with the gift, alienation of the slave or legacy of him, but in these cases, if he was again acquired or the legacy was adeemed, the gift revived[10].

It might be conditional or deferred (*ex die*[11]). *Dies* might be *certus* or *incertus*. The former is a time so fixed that it is clear, when the will operates, when it will be, e.g. ten days after my death. The latter is a day sure to come, but uncertain as to date, e.g. when *X* dies (*certus an*,

1 40. 2. 4. 1. The *peculium* passed unless reserved, 15. 1. 53. For Levy-Bruhl *M. per vind.* is not fictitious litigation and there is no *adsertor*: it is a formal act of release confirmed by the magistrate. *R.H.* 1930, p. 609. 2 Based on XII Tables, but probably older, as the Tables contain a rule about conditions. Girard, *Textes*, 17; Bruns, 1. 28. Manumission by will does not carry *peculium*, 33. 8. 8. 7. 3 G. 2. 267; Ulp. 1. 23; D. 40. 4. 35. Harsh result, 28. 5. 50. pr. The gift is indestructible when it has taken effect: though the entry of *heres* be set aside the gift of liberty stands; C. 7. 2. 3. 4 G. 2. 267; D. 40. 5. 41. pr. Might not precede the *institutio heredis* in classical law, G. 2. 230; Ulp. 1. 20. Greek equivalents served in later law; C. 7. 2. 14. Rules follow those of legacy with differences, e.g. G. 2. 236, *post*, § CXIX. 5 *L. Fufia Caninia*, G. 2. 239; Ulp. 1. 25; P. 4. 14. 1. 6 50. 17. 179. 7 *Post*, § CVIII. 8 26. 2. 10. 4, 32. 2; C. 6. 27. 5. 1b; 7. 4. 10. Donatuti, *Le Praesumptiones iuris*, 90. 9 Ulp. 2. 12; D. 28. 5. 6. 4; 40. 4. 10. 10 34. 4. 27; 40. 4. 58; 40. 5. 50. Difficulties where the conflicting dispositions were in the same document, Buckland, *Slavery*, 468; Desserteaux, *Capitis Deminutio*, 2. p. 126, nn. 2, 3. 11 35. 1. 49; not, in classical law, *post mortem heredis*, Ulp. 1. 20, *post*, § CXIX.

incertus quando). But, in wills, *dies incertus pro condicione habetur*[1]: it operated as condition, though it did not in contracts. *Condicio* is an event both future and uncertain (*incertus an*, whether *incertus quando* or not). "To be free if I die this year," or "To be free if he was born at Rome," are not conditions. The gifts are good or bad. There is no uncertainty or futurity about them when the will operates[2]. An impossible condition, "contrary to the nature of things," e.g. if he touch the sky with his finger, was struck out, the gift being absolute, and the same is no doubt true of illegal and immoral conditions[3]. Impossibility merely to the person concerned was not so treated, and would bar the gift[4].

Negative conditions, e.g. "if he does not do so and so," were not treated as in legacy. There the gift was effective at once, with some restrictions, but security was taken for return if the condition was broken[5]. But a manumission which has taken effect cannot be undone. The method adopted, since the gift would be a farce, unless some relief was given, was to allow the testator to impose a condition of taking an oath, remitted in other cases[6], not to do the forbidden thing—a poor security, as there was no way of compelling obedience to the oath.

Till the condition was satisfied the slave was still a slave (*statuliber*[7]), and the child of a *statulibera* was thus a slave[8]. But no act of the *heres* could destroy the prospect of liberty, and thus though the *statuliber* could be commercially dealt with in ordinary ways any rights in him created by the *heres* were destroyed when the condition was satisfied[9]. *Statuliberi* were better off than ordinary slaves in other respects. They could be sold, but not under harsh conditions which made their position worse[10]. They might not ordinarily be tortured as witnesses[11]. Where slaves and freemen were differently punished they had the right to be treated as freemen[12]. On satisfaction of the condition the gift took effect[13]. If the condition was to do an act to or for the *heres* and before perfor-

1 Ulp. 24. 31; D. 35. 1. 75, *post*, § CXIX. 2 If testator did not so die, if donee was not so born, the gift was void. This is certain at the death, though it might not be known. When it is known he is shewn to have been free (or not free at all) from the operation of the will; 40. 4. 7; 40. 5. 18. Gifts, "*pridie mortis heredis*," "*post mortem heredis*," were treated as in legacy, G. 2. 233, *post*, § CXIX. 3 Inst. 2. 14. 10; 3. 19. 11; G. 3. 98. Rule the same in *institutio heredis*, *post*, § CIV. 4 This refers to initial impossibility: supervening impossibility (*casus*) below and *post*, § CIV. 5 *Cautio Muciana*, *post*, § CXIX. 6 40. 4. 12. pr. In some cases the gift was treated as derisory and void, 40. 4. 61. pr. In cases other than manumission a *condicio iurisiurandi* was released by the praetor, security being required, at least in later classical law, that the thing should be done, or not done. *Post*, § CIV. 7 Ulp. 2. 1–6. 8 40. 5. 45. 2; 40. 7. 16. 9 Ulp. 2. 3; D. 20. 1. 13. 1; 30. 81. 9; 40. 7. 6. 3. Fraud was easy: much law as to sales of this kind, Buckland, *Slavery*, 288. 10 40. 7. 25, 33. 11 48. 18. 8. 1, 9. 3. 12 48. 18. 14; 48. 19. 9. 16. 13 If it is that he shall promise to do an act, the promise frees him, though a slave's promise cannot be enforced after he is free, 40. 7. 13. 3, 24, 41. 1.

mance the *heres* sold him, it must be done to or for the acquirer, unless it was plainly a personal service[1]. Supervening impossibility was more favourably treated than in legacy. A gift of liberty "when *X* is 20" was good, though *X* died younger[2], as was a gift on the condition of rendering a service to *X*, who died before it could be done[3]. This is *favore libertatis*; a legacy would fail[4]. The rule of later law seems to be that the condition was satisfied where it was to be done by the donee, if it was not his fault that it was not done. Thus if he was prevented by anyone from fulfilling the condition, it was satisfied[5]. But these relaxations applied only if the condition was one to be fulfilled by him: if any other condition failed, the gift failed[6].

Fideicommissary gifts. Under Augustus some rules of the law of wills were relieved against by the institution of *fideicommissa*, trusts imposed on a beneficiary under the will, not subject to all the restrictive rules[7]. *Fideicommissa* of liberty were a common case; directions to a beneficiary by a will or codicil to free a slave, his own, or one coming to him by the will, or one to be bought and freed[8]. No particular form was needed; it might be implied, and in many cases a gift not imperative enough to constitute a direct gift was construed as a direction to the *heres* to free, an interpretation more readily adopted under Justinian than earlier[9]. A direction to the *heres* to free a man *si volueris* was void, but little more was needed to make it mean "if he deserves it," a conditional *fideicommissum*[10]. The gift failed if the will or codicil failed[11].

The gift having been accepted, the trust must be carried out, even though the amount was less than the value of the slave, except that, if

1 Payment of money must be made to alienee, 40. 7. 6. 5; Ulp. 2. 4; condition to teach the *heres* to read must be satisfied in his person, 40. 7. 6. 7. (See, on some difficulties, Grosso, *Sull' applicazione della regola: heredi* 10 *dare iussus*, etc.)
2 40. 4. 16 etc.
3 40. 7. 20. 3.
4 40. 7. 19, 20. 3.
5 40. 5. 55; 40. 7. 3. pr.; Ulp. 2. 5, 6. In legacy, only if the prevention is by one interested in failure of the condition, 28. 7. 3, 11; 30. 92. 1. Grosso, *Contributo allo studio dell' adempimento della condizione.*
6 40. 7. 4. 7. A slave made *heres* might not refuse. Rules were applied where there were conditions, to secure that the gift should be valid and that he should not get the liberty and then refuse the *hereditas*. Both under the same condition gave no difficulty. If only liberty was conditional, this was, strictly, bad—not free till *heres*, or *heres* till free. Condition read into both, 28. 5. 3. 1. So in converse case, lest he be free by entry of another *heres* and then refuse the *hereditas*. Modifications, *favore libertatis*, if the condition failed or if under different conditions, 28. 5. 21, 22; 40. 4. 14; 40. 7. 2. 3. Buckland, *Slavery*, 511.
7 *Post*, § CXXIV.
8 Ulp. 2. 9; 25. 18; G. 2. 263.
9 Ulp. 2. 7; D. 26. 2. 10. 4; 40. 5. 24. 7. Where there was doubt whether a gift was direct or fideicommissary, there was a leaning to direct construction, 40. 4. 9. pr., 15, 19, 56.
10 40. 5. 46. 3. *Post*, § CIV.
11 40. 5. 24. 11; C. 7. 2. 12. Buckland, *Slavery*, 609, for reliefs against collusion, etc. In classical law liberty could be given to an unborn person by will, but only by *fc.* (P. 4. 14. 1) and some jurists doubted (C. 7. 4. 14). If the slave is regarded as the donee, it should be void, for in Paul's time *fcc.* to *incertae personae* and *postumi alieni* were void (G. 2. 238 *sqq.*). If he is the subject-matter, no difficulty. Future things could be given. Justinian allows it even direct, so that the child will be born free (C. 7. 4. 14).

the trust was to buy and free a slave, no more than the gift need be spent in buying him[1]. If the owner refused to sell, the trust was void in the time of Gaius, but in later law it was still valid if the owner afterwards changed his mind[2].

Till the trust was carried out, the slave was still a slave. Thus, subject to what has been said[3], the child of an *ancilla* in this position was a slave not affected by the trust[4]. But the subject of the trust was treated like one conditionally freed—he was a quasi *statuliber*[5]. The manumission not being voluntary, it might not be made subject to a promise of services, and the manumitter, though actually patron, had less rights than an ordinary patron[6], the object being often that the man should be the freedman of the person directed to free, and not, as he would be under a direct gift[7], of the maker of the gift (*libertus orcinus*).

These were the only normal modes of manumission in the Republic, and were available only to the full civil law owner. But cases occurred of informal manumission and of manumission by one whose ownership, though effective, was not civil law ownership (*qui habet in bonis*[8], bonitary owner). Here, though the manumission was void at law, the praetor intervened to protect the man[9], where in his judgement it was a proper case for protection[10], and only where the master was of full age and competence and acted quite freely[11]. Not every informal declaration was accepted: we are told of only two cases: *per epistolam*, a letter of enfranchisement, and *inter amicos*, declaration before witnesses[12]. Late in the empire we hear of a mode *in convivio*, declaration before guests at a feast[13], but this seems to be only a variant of the last. It was immaterial that the ownership was only bonitary, and conversely a bonitary owner could produce no better effect even if he freed by will[14]; he could not do it at all by *vindicta*.

One so freed was still a slave: his *peculium* and his acquisitions were his master's[15]. A child of an *ancilla* so freed was an ordinary slave for all purposes[16]. The only effect was that if the master sought to make slaves, so freed, work for him, the Praetor intervened[17]. The act was not revocable and no doubt bound successors in title. The persons affected

1 40. 5. 24. 12–16. 2 G. 2. 265; Ulp. 2. 11; Inst. 2. 24. 2; C. 7. 4. 6; perhaps as early as A.D. 220. If the *fc.* was only one of liberty he need not take the gift, as he must in some other cases (36. 1. 54. 1; *post*, § CXXIV). If it was his own slave he need not, though there was a *fc.* of the *hereditas*, *contra* if the slave were the testator's. 36. 1. 23. 1. 3 *Ante*, p. 68. 4 35. 2. 24. 1; 40. 5. 45. 2. 5 40. 5. 15, 24. 21, 30. 16. 6 38. 1. 13. 1. 7 G. 2. 266, 267; Ulp. 2. 8. 8 G. 1. 54; *post*, § LXX. 9 G. 3. 56; Ulp. 1. 16. 10 Fr. D. 8. 11 Fr. D. 7. It must be clear that a real gift of *libertas* was meant, not merely to let the man do as he liked, to be *in libertate* (Wlassak, *Z.S.S.* 1905, 367). 12 G. 1. 44. *Amici* is a common term for witnesses, Wlassak, *loc. cit.*; Girard, *Textes*, 854; Jörs, *R.R.* 49. 13 G. *Ep.* 1. 1. 2. 14 G. 1. 16, 167; Fr. Dos. 9; Ulp. 1. 16, 22. 8. 15 Fr. Dos. 4, 5. 16 *Ib.*, *arg.* 17 G. 3. 56; Fr. D. 5.

were said *in libertate auxilio* (or *tuitione*) *praetoris esse, in libertate morari*, etc.[1]

XXVIII. The law was profoundly modified by Statutes of the early empire which must now be considered.

Lex Fufia Caninia, 2 B.C. Slaves were now so numerous and manumissions so frequent that the large number of *libertini* were a menace to the stability of society. This statute imposed a limit on manumissions by will, the commonest case, as it cost nothing and provided a procession of grateful *liberti* for the funeral cortège. It enacted that an owner of not more than two slaves might so free all, of from 2 to 10 half, of from 10 to 30 one-third, of from 30 to 100 one-fourth, of from 100 to 500 one-fifth, and never more than 100[2]. An increase in the number of slaves was not to involve diminution in the number who could be freed[3]. The slaves must be named or clearly described[4]. If more than the lawful number were freed only the earliest named were free[5]. A gift to "all my slaves" was void[6]. The law did not, as stated, refer in terms to fideicommissary gifts, but it must have applied to them, or it would not have been worth while to resort to evasions.

Lex Iunia (*Norbana*). This statute, of uncertain date[7], put an end to the equivocal position of those *in libertate tuitione praetoris*. It provided that they should be really free, but not *cives*, and invented for them the *status* of *Latini Iuniani*, i.e. they were to have the same *status* as existing *Latini*, subject to serious restrictions[8]. The nature of this *status* and these restrictions will be considered later[9].

Lex Aelia Sentia, A.D. 4. This was a comprehensive enactment, containing, *inter alia*, the following important provisions.

1. The manumitter must be 20, otherwise the manumission was void[10].

1 G. 3. 56; Fr. D. 5. Other exceptional forms were (*a*) manumission *sacrorum causa* (Festus, *s.vv. Manumitti, Puri*), Mommsen, *Staatsr*. 3. 421; *D.P.R.* 6. 2. 2; Wlassak, *Z.S.S.* 1907, 22. It may be only manumission *vindicta*; (*b*) giving a slave in adoption (Aul. Gell. 5. 19. 13, 14, *post*, § XLV), also may be only a case of *vindicta* in effect. As to adoption of slave by master, *post*, § XLV. 2 G. 1. 42, 43; Ulp. 1. 24; P. 4. 14. 4. The total included *fugitivi*, P. 4. 14. 3. 3 G. 1. 45; Ulp. 1. 24. Thus one with 12 could free 5. 4 Ulp. 1. 25; P. 4. 14. 1. The *sc. Orfitianum* makes clear description suffice. 5 G. *Ep*. 1. 2. 2. There were other provisions against fraud on the law (there was no general theory in *R.L.* on "*fraus legi*," Perozzi, *Ist*. 1. 147), e.g. if they were set in a circle so that it could not be said which were first, all were void, G. 1. 46, who speaks of *scc.* on the matter. A *sc.* provided that manumissions *inter vivos*, but on the point of death, might be treated as frauds on the *lex*. 6 G. *Ep*. 1. 2. 2. 7 There is confusion as to what was in this *lex* and what in the *l. Aelia Sentia* (G. 1. 29; Ulp. 3. 3). The name *Iunia Norbana* fits only A.D. 19, but only Justinian calls it *Norbana*. It deals with those freed under 30 as well as the informally freed, but they were *cives* till the *l. Aelia*. These points would make the *l. Iunia* the later. But Gaius makes the *l. Aelia* refer to Junian Latins which would make the *l. Iunia* the earlier. 8 G. 1. 16, 22, 23; 3. 56; Ulp. 1. 10, 16. 9 *Post*, § XXXIV. 10 G. 1. 38, 40; Ulp. 1. 13; C. 2. 30. 3. pr.

Evasions, e.g. by transferring the man to one over 20 to be freed, were stopped by a *sc.* which seems to have nullified transactions tending to such a result, and thus to have been applicable to new devices as they appeared[1]. There was an important limitation. If the manumission was approved by the *Consilium* (which sat periodically for such cases), and was afterwards completed *vindicta*, the rule did not apply and the man became a *civis*[2]. If it were completed informally he became a *Latinus*[3]. To obtain this approval *causa* must be shewn[4]. There was no rule as to what was a sufficient *causa*: it might be merit or a service rendered, or something to be done in the future which a slave could not do[5]. It must be a *honesta causa*, and if it was with a view to marriage there were special restrictions and rules[6].

2. The slave must be over 30, or he did not become a *civis*, unless it was done *vindicta*, on cause approved by the *Consilium*[7]. Where no *causa* was shewn the result is uncertain. If it was informal, or by will (where there is no question of *causa*), he seems to have become *in libertate tuitione praetoris*, or, after the *l. Iunia*, a Latin[8]. No classical text mentions Latinity as resulting from manumission *vindicta*, and a corrupt text suggests that it was simply void, but it may be that as it could in any case, on such facts, give no more than Latinity, there was no purpose in the form, and the case therefore did not occur[9].

3. Manumission in fraud of creditors or patron of the manumitter was void[10]. Of the case of fraud on the patron we know little and it is not mentioned by Justinian[11]. Fraud on creditors was committed if the manumission was with intent to injure them, i.e. with knowledge that it would do so, and did in fact harm them, i.e. when the owner was insolvent or the manumission would make him so[12]. If it was on death, as no doubt it usually was, and the *heres* was solvent, the creditors

1 18. 7. 4; 40. 9. 7. 1; C. 7. 11. 4. Rule did not apply where he was bound to free from any cause, 40. 1. 20. pr., etc. 2 G. 1. 38; Fr. D. 13. At Rome the *consilium* was five senators and five *equites*, elsewhere, twenty *recuperatores cives*, who met on the last day of the *Conventus*, the judicial assize. 3 G. 1. 41; Fr. D. 13, or *in libertate praetoris tuitione*, according to the view taken of the date of *l. Iunia*. 4 Whether he was to be freed formally or informally. 5 G. 1. 19, 39; D. 40. 2. 9. pr., 15. 1. 6 40. 2. 13, 16. pr. "To be *heres* if he frees *X*" gave a good *causa*, 40. 2. 15. pr. 7 G. 1. 18; Fr. D. 17; Ulp. 1. 12. 8 *Ib.* and G. 1. 17. 9 Ulp. 1. 12. 10 G. 1. 37; Ulp. 1. 15; Inst. 1. 6. pr. Schulz, *Z.S.S.* 1928, 197 *sqq.* 11 Presumably where a dying *libertinus* freed his slaves, who, if he was a Latin, would go to his patron, and if he was a *civis*, would do so if he had no children, *post*, § CXXXIV. 12 D. 40. 9. 16. 2; Inst. 1. 6. 3; D. 40. 9. 10. Guarneri-Citati (*Mél. Cornil*, 1. 427 *sqq.*) shews, *inter alia*, the need of "*animus*" in both classical and later law, 42. 8. 10. 1 says that if there was intent to defraud creditors, but these were paid off, later creditors could revoke if the payment was with their money. This he, with others, holds interpolated, on insufficient grounds. The citations of Marcellus and the imperial rescript look perfectly genuine. It is very like *successio in locum* (*post*, § CLXVIII).

would not suffer, for, till very late[1], he was fully liable on the ancestor's debts. Some jurists thought, logically, that this saved the gift, but the view prevailed that it was immaterial[2], possibly because any other view rendered refusal and intestacy likely, and this was avoided as far as possible. But there are difficulties[3].

The rule applied where the manumitter was a *peregrinus*, though the other provisions did not[4], and whether it was done *inter vivos* or by will, directly or by *fideicommissum*, but in this last case *eventus* sufficed —intent was not material[5]. But it did not apply where the manumitter was bound to free, either under a trust or otherwise[6].

Where the gift was bad it was void *ab initio*, not revoked: there was no revocation of a manumission[7]. Some time might elapse before the point was clear, and for this time the man's position was in suspense: he was a quasi *statuliber*[8]. It was not void unless steps were taken, and there were provisions, to be stated later, protecting apparent liberty after a certain lapse of time[9].

4. Certain degraded slaves, on manumission, however effected[10], did not become *cives* or Latins, but were put *in numero dediticiorum*[11]. They were those who had been punished by branding or chains or imprisonment by their masters, or condemned to fight with beasts or tortured and convicted of crime. Their disabilities were severe[12]: *inter alia*, they could never become citizens.

None of these four restrictions applied if the manumission was by will, and the testator, being insolvent, instituted and freed a single slave so as to have a *necessarius heres* (to avoid the stigma of intestacy and posthumous insolvency[13]), provided no other *heres* entered under the will. This had no bearing on other restrictions on manumission[14].

XXIX. Such restrictions were numerous and some of them need mention.

(*a*) A slave specially pledged could not be freed unless the creditor

1 *Post*, § CX. 2 40. 4. 57; C. 7. 2. 5. 3 *Heres* could not attack it, 40. 12. 31; C. 7. 8. 5; C. 7. 16. 7, and if he was solvent creditors had no interest. Perhaps he refused to enter unless the creditors undertook to proceed. Where the liberty was conditional on payment of money which a third party provided, so that the estate suffered no loss, this did not save it (40. 9. 18. 1) but a gift "if my debts are paid" was held valid (40. 4. 57, see, however, Schulz, *Z.S.S.* 1928, 232, who thinks the end interp.). 4 G. 1. 47. 5 40. 5. 4. 19; C. 7. 11. 7. 6 *Fr. d. i. fisci*, 19; D. 28. 5. 56; 40. 1. 10; C. 7. 11. 5. 7 G. 1. 37; Fr. D. 16; Ulp. 1. 15. 8 40. 7. 1. 1. 9 *Post*, § XXXI. 10 Ulp. 1. 5, 11; G. 1. 13, 15; details P. 4. 12. 3–8. Not where tortured but not convicted, P. 4. 12. 3. If *vindicta*, possibly void. If informal, gives the odd result that if the *l. Iunia* is later than the *l. Aelia Sentia* he would be better off than an honest man: he would be free; the other would be, technically, a slave. 11 "*In numero dediticiorum*" means the same as "*dediticii*": in fact G. 1. 12 calls these men *dediticii*. It is not clear why Schulz, *Liber singularis regularum* (*ad* 1. 14), considers this usage post-classical. 12 *Post*, § XXXVI. 13 G. 1. 21; Ulp. 1. 14; D. 40. 4. 27; Inst. 1. 6. 1. 14 28. 5. 84. pr.

consented, though the owner was solvent[1]. But in late classical law such a manumission seems to be regarded, if *inter vivos*, as informal manumission, conditional on release of the pledge, so that if the debt is paid, the slave becomes a Latin[2]. If by will, it was void as a direct gift, but came to be construed as a *fideicommissary* gift on the same condition[3].

(*b*) Except in the case of the old *consortium* of joint heirs, a slave owned by two or more could not be freed by one, till Justinian[4].

(*c*) A slave in whom someone held a life interest (usufruct) could be freed by the owner's will, the gift being construed as conditional on the expiry of the usufruct[5]. But there could be no condition on manumission *vindicta*, and the texts leave the classical law uncertain[6]. Justinian confirmed the old rule that if both owner and usufructuary agreed the man was free, and made manumission by the owner alone give freedom, without releasing the man from his duty of service to the usufructuary[7].

There were a number of other restrictions[8].

Slaves of corporate bodies and public authorities were freed in special ways: those of a municipality by *decretum* of the local senate[9]. We do not know the form for those of other corporate bodies[10]. *Servi populi Romani* seem to have been freed by declaration of the magistrate, authorised by the Senate, or later, the Emperor[11].

When the State became Christian, a new mode of manumission was introduced. So soon as the church was recognised, it became a common practice for masters to free slaves before the congregation, a form of manumission *inter amicos*, giving Latinity. Constantine regulated this, requiring a writing signed by the master, and providing, a little later,

1 40. 1. 3; 40. 8. 6; C. 7. 8. 4. Nothing to do with the *l. Aelia Sentia*. 2 Fr. D. 16; D. 40. 9. 26. Schulz, *Z.S.S.* 1928, 263 *sqq.*, denies any distinction in classical law between general and special pledge, for this purpose. 3 40. 5. 24. 10. 4 *Post*, pp. 252, 404. Rotondi, *Scr. Giur.* 3. 78 *sqq.*, discusses the various possibilities in joint manumission of a *servus communis*. 5 28. 5. 9. 20. 6 Fr. D. 11; Ulp. 1. 19. Such a manumission, *vindicta*, made the slave a *servus sine domino*, *ib.* As to informal manumission, *quaere*, void or suspended? 7 C. 7. 15. 1. He allowed manumission by fructuary, strictly a nullity, to protect him from seizure by owner till usufruct would have ended. 8 Sale with prohibition of manumission, *ante*, § XXIII. Prohibition to sell is prohibition to free, C. 4. 51. 7; legacy of slave, slave freed by *heres*, Buckland, *Slavery*, 581; manumission under threats or popular clamour, or, under M. Aurelius, at public games, Fr. D. 7; D. 40. 9. 9. pr., 17. pr.; *Dediticius* enslaved for living in prohibited area, *post*, § XXXVI; bonitary owner, *ante*, § XXVII; Latin or peregrine cannot give slave a better *status* than his own, Fr. D. 12; *sc. Silanianum*, under Augustus, on suspicion that a man had been killed by his slaves, will not to be opened, and thus no manumission operative, till slaves who might have been concerned examined by torture, to ascertain who was guilty and who, being able to render help, had failed to do so. Penalties for breach of the rule, P. 3. 5. 1–12; D. 29. 5. Other restrictions on manumission, Buckland, *Slavery*, 591 *sqq.* 9 C. 7. 9. 10 40. 3. 1. 11 *C.I.L.* 6. 2340; as to these and *servi Caesaris* and *Fiscales*, see Buckland, *Slavery*, 590 and reff., and *post*, § LXIV.

that it should give *civitas*. The rule that the slave must be 30 does not seem to have applied, an accidental result of the mode of development, as Latinity never required this. The method survives in Justinian's law but is not prominent[1].

XXX. The law of manumission was simplified by Justinian. Much was made obsolete by other changes, e.g. abolition of bonitary ownership[2], and of the inferior grades, Latins and *dediticii*[3]. As to manumission itself he repealed the *sc. Claudianum*[4] and the *l. Fufia Caninia*[5], and legislated sweepingly on the forms.

Manumission *vindicta* remained, in the relaxed form it had taken in the later classical law, as did the mode *in ecclesiis*. Will remained much the most important form. Place in the will was immaterial[6], and it might be *post mortem heredis*[7]. Implied gifts were allowed, and appointment of one whom the testator knew to be his slave, as *heres* or *tutor*, implied a gift of liberty[8], but, in all cases of implication, the intent must be clear[9]. Fideicommissary and direct gifts of liberty might be made to unborn persons, who would be born free[10]. There was legislation settling doubts in the law and on the informal modes[11]. Those that were valid were to be *legitimi modi* having the same effect as manumission *vindicta*. The modes *per epistolam* and *inter amicos* now required writing and five witnesses. Some other informal modes were recognised[12].

The main rules of manumission under Justinian are the following:

1. All manumission if valid makes the slave a *civis*, whatever is intended[13].

2. The master must be 20, unless (*a*) it is *vindicta* for cause approved by the *consilium*, or (*b*) the slave was received, under a trust to free, from one competent to free, or (*c*) it is by will, when it is allowed under the Institutes at 14, to provide a *necessarius heres*, as in earlier law, otherwise at 17[14]. Later it is allowed at 14, in any case, the earliest age for testation[15].

3. It must be *nominatim*: description is enough but the donee must

1 C. Th. 4. 7. 1; C. 1. 13. 1, 2. Priests may free without witnesses in any form they like. 2 *Post*, § LXX. 3 *Post*, § XXXVI. Repealing the rule of the *l. Aelia Sentia* requiring the slave to be 30 and also its provisions as to criminal slaves. 4 Inst. 3. 12. 1; C. 7. 24. 1. 5 Inst. 1. 7; C. 7. 3. 6 Inst. 2. 20. 34. 7 Inst. 2. 20. 35. 8 26. 2. 32. 2; Inst. 1. 6. 2. 9 Soldier's will more favourably construed, 40. 4. 49. 10 C. 7. 4. 14. 11 C. 7. 6. 12 *Ib*. Giving to the slave, or destroying, evidences of slavery, before five witnesses; recording the slave as a son on *acta* of court, which seems to have given Latinity in post-classical times; giving an *ancilla* in marriage to a freeman with a *dos*; order of testator or *heres* to wear the *pileus*, cap of liberty, in the funeral procession. It also provided that in many cases in which Latinity had resulted from facts other than manumission, *civitas* should result. 13 C. 7. 6. 6. 14 Inst. 1. 6. 7. 15 *Nov*. 119. 2.

be certainly identifiable[1]. It may be to an unborn person: *qui ex ea ancilla nascetur*[2].

4. The slave need not consent, except in fideicommissary gifts where the intent was only a benefit to him: *beneficium invito non datur*[3].

5. It must be by the owner. One whose ownership is determinable on some event may free: the gift is good, though he may be liable to someone for it[4]. It cannot be done by representative, except that a *filiusfamilias* duly authorised can free on the father's behalf by *vindicta*. This is clear for Justinian's law, whatever the law was before[5].

6. If in fraud of creditors it is void. Justinian does not deal with fraud on the patron: the abolition of Latinity had removed the chief case of this[6].

7. It must be in perpetuity and is irrevocable[7]. Thus it is good even if induced by fraud or effected under a trust, or to satisfy a condition, afterwards shewn to be a *falsum*, or not binding[8].

8. It may be conditional or *ex die* (except *vindicta*)[9].

XXXI. The cases of liberty without manumission break into two groups:

(A) Independent of voluntary manumission. Freedom was given as a reward, e.g. for giving information against certain criminals[10]; or, in the Byzantine empire, on becoming a monk[11]. It might also be given as a penalty on the master. A slave abandoned for sickness became a Latin in classical law, a *civis* under Justinian[12]. A woman prostituted in violation of a contract of sale was free[13]. In both these groups of cases there is some obscurity as to the way in which liberty was conferred. In some cases the master was compelled to free, in others the public authority declared the man free, in others he became free by the event.

Besides *postliminium*, pardon, and sale of new-born children[14], there were exceptional cases. Under Justinian, a slave noxally surrendered

1 40. 4. 24. 2 "Whichever the *heres* shall choose" is enough, C. 7. 4. 14, 16. pr. 3 40. 5. 32. 1; 50. 17. 69. 4 36. 1. 26. 2. 5 *Ante*, § XXVI. Messengers (*nuntii*) might be employed of course in informal manumission. 6 The title on revocation of acts done in fraud of patron contains no ref. to manumission (D. 38. 5), and the act is revocable, not void. 7 40. 4. 33. 34. 8 4. 3. 7. pr.; 40. 4. 47. So too where a minor entered and liberties took effect and he was *restitutus in integrum*, C. 7. 2. 3. The omnipotent Emperor could set aside even a manumission, 4. 4. 10. Provisions for compensation in some of these cases. 9 *Ante*, p. 73; 40. 7. 1. 10 47. 10. 5. 11; C. 7. 13. One given to the Emperor's household was free and *ingenuus* whether the donor so intended or not, C. 12. 5. 4. 11 C. 1. 3. 37; *Nov.* 5. 2. He is free, but reverts to slavery if he leaves the monastery, a breach with principle. *Nov.* 123. 17 lays down the same rule on his becoming a priest *non contradicente domino*. 12 40. 8. 2. 13 40. 8. 6. Numerous later cases, e.g. heresy and judaic proselytising (C. Th. 16. 9. 4, etc.), fraudulently marrying an *ancilla* to a freeman, C. 7. 6. 1. 9; finally, any abandonment of a slave, *Nov.* 22. 12. No reason to confine this to sick slaves (n. 13). Perozzi, *Ist.* 1. 263. 14 *Ante*, p. 71.

for a wrong was freed, *auxilio praetoris*, when his service had recouped the injured person[1]. Constantine allowed one who reared an exposed child to bring him up as slave or free whatever he was by birth. Under Justinian the child was free and *ingenuus* in all cases[2].

No pact or acknowledgement or lapse of time in apparent slavery made a freeman a slave[3]. No pact or acknowledgement made a slave a freeman[4]. Lapse of time was in later law on a different footing: apparent liberty begun in good faith was confirmed by a lapse of time which Justinian fixed at 20 years[5]. A *heres* could not attack his ancestor's manumission on technical or formal grounds, but this did not bar third parties. Here too a certain lapse of time, perhaps five years from manumission, protected the *manumissus*[6]. And the *status* of a man who died apparently free could not be attacked after five years from his death, by those claiming property or that his children were slaves[7].

(B) Inchoate manumission, which has failed to take effect.

1. Abortive gift of liberty. Where an *institutio heredis* failed from causes other than invalidity of the will and injustice was done, relief was given in some cases, e.g. the *heres*, also entitled on intestacy, took in that way so as to defeat the gifts in the will[8].

2. Fideicommissary liberty overdue. By the operation of three *Scc.*[9] it was provided that where the fiduciary had failed to carry out the trust, the Praetor would declare the man free as from the time when he should have been freed. If the fiduciary was in fault and the slave belonged to the *hereditas* he lost his patronal rights[10], the freedman being the *libertus* of the deceased (*orcinus*).

3. *Bonorum addictio libertatium conservandarum causa.* M. Aurelius provided that if no *heres* entered and *bonorum venditio* was likely, so that gifts of liberty would fail, the estate might be assigned to one of the slaves freed, who gave security for payment of debts, and gifts of

1 Inst. 4. 8. 3. 2 C. Th. 5. 9. 1, 2; C. 8. 51. 3. 3 40. 12. 37; C. 7. 14; C. 7. 16. 5. 1; C. 7. 22. 3. 4 C. 7. 14. 8. 5 C. 7. 22. 2; perhaps 16 before, C. Th. 4. 8. 7, where *iustum initium* seems to mean no more than *bona fides*. 6 Buckland, *Slavery*, 650. 7 40. 15. Litigation on a man's liberty decided in his favour did not bar others from disputing his *status* (40. 12. 42). The same would appear to be true on decision the other way. Literary texts allude to a rule that such cases should be tried twice or even thrice, Buckland, *Slavery*, 668 *sqq*. 8 29. 4. 6. 10; 40. 4. 23. pr. Or is bribed not to enter, C. 7. 4. 1. 1; or will upset by collusion, etc., 49. 1. 14. 1. A *heres* directed to choose and free one of the children of an *ancilla* wilfully refuses, Justinian makes them all free, C. 7. 4. 16. Many other cases. 9 *Rubrianum*, A.D. 103, *Dasumianum*, A.D. 119 (Besnier *R.H.* 1930, 836), *Iuncianum*, A.D. 137; others on special points, H. Krueger, *Z.S.S.* 1928, 170 *sqq*. 10 40. 5. 26. 7 *sqq*., 28. 4, 36. pr., 51. 4, 8, 10; 31. 84. Much discussion, where slave has been alienated, as to who is liable and what are the patronal rights, and also where several are bound to free. Buckland, *Slavery*, 613. In *Nov*. 1. 1, Justinian enacted that beneficiaries under the will might claim what was given to the defaulter, in a certain order, giving security that they would carry out the gift.

liberty would operate as if the *heres* had accepted[1]. This was soon extended to gifts of liberty by codicil without a will[2], and to application by an *extraneus*[3]. The slaves need not consent. The addictee was liable and entitled like a praetorian successor[4]. A gift in fraud of creditors was good, as they did not suffer[5]. Justinian allowed assignment to a slave not freed, who thus got freedom; and also within a year after the goods were sold, and, if the creditors agreed, on security for less than full payment, and so that only some of the gifts should operate[6].

4. Inheritances passing to the Fisc. Where this occurred liberties took effect as if a *heres* had entered, at least under Justinian[7], so that gifts in fraud of creditors failed[8].

5. Transfer *ut manumittatur*. M. Aurelius provided that one sold or given to be freed at once or later and not so freed, should be free, *ipso facto* without decree, on the failure[9]. The case of gift may be an extension: here there was a right to withdraw, before it was effective[10].

6. *Servus suis nummis emptus*[11]. M. Aurelius and Verus provided that a slave *suis nummis emptus*, which, as a slave has none, means with money not provided by the buyer, could claim immediate manumission. The case was dealt with like an overdue *fideicommissum*[12]. The purpose must have been declared at the outset[13], and the money might have come from the slave's *peculium*, if the master consented[14].

7. The slave whose master has taken money to free him. Here the ownership was an existing one, not as in the last two cases, created *ad hoc*. It was enforcing a bargain between slave and master. The texts disagree on the effect. Some make it operate *ipso facto* as in case 5, others require a decree, as in cases 2 and 6[15]. The rule appears to come

1 Inst. 3. 11. 1. 2 40. 5. 2. 3 40. 4. 50. 4 40. 5. 4. 21. 5 40. 5. 4. 19. 6 Inst. 3. 11. 7; C. 7. 2. 15. 7 Suman, *Favor Testamenti*, 222, holds that where *bona vacantia* (not *caduca*) passed to the fisc, everything in the will failed in classical law. As to his remarks on 40. 4. 50 etc., Buckland, *Slavery*, 626 *sq*. 8 40. 5. 4. 19, 51. pr. Many such cases. Controversy as to gifts in fraud of creditors, Buckland, *Slavery*, 626. 9 18. 7. 10; 38. 1. 13. pr.; 40. 1. 20. 2; 40. 8. 1, 9; C. 4. 57. 1, 2, 6. The purpose might be to make the actual manumitter patron or to avoid the difficulty that the owner, as he was physically incapable (*mutus*, *surdus*), could himself have freed only informally, so that the man would not be a *civis*. P. 4. 12. 2. Lotmar, *Marc Aurels Erlass über die Freilassungsauflage*. 10 Such gifts were sometimes by *mancipatio cum fiducia* (*post*, § CLI; Grosso, *Fiducia allo Scopo di Manumissio*), which gave a right of revocation before completion. If the gift were revoked before the freedom took effect the constitution would not apply and the man could be recovered. Though this characteristic is due to *fiducia*, it was generalised in later law, and there was a *condictio ex poenitentia*, whether it had been done with *fiducia* or not; Buckland, *Slavery*, 633; *post*, § XCI, as to *donatio sub modo*. 11 Seuffert, *Loskauf von Sklaven mit ihrem Geld*. 12 5. 1. 67; 40. 1. 4. pr., 5. pr., i.e. by decree. 13 40. 1. 4. 2, 4, 6. 14 C. 4. 49. 7. There may be a *ius poenitendi* before the actual transfer and even after (12. 4. 5. 1, 2) but it is not clear that the text covers this type of case, where the slave initiates the business. 15 40. 1. 19; 40. 12. 38. 1; C 4. 6. 9; C. 4. 57. 4; C. 7. 16. 8.

from Greek law[1], and to be post-classical. The agreement might be that he was to be a Latin[2]. There was a *ius poenitentiae* in the payer, till the man was free, which seems to be due to Justinian[3].

Some points as to the effect of supervening freedom on transactions must be noted. Liabilities for crime or delict remained; *noxa caput sequitur*[4]. Rights arising from them remained with the master; a slave could have no rights[5]. A slave who had committed a wrong against his master could not be sued after freedom any more than he could before[6]. Inheritances left to a slave would go to him personally if he was free before acceptance[7]. There might be *naturalis obligatio* between owner and slave, but the latter had no right after manumission, except that if he took his *peculium* the claim was reckoned in it[8]: conversely it was only against the *peculium* that the master had a right[9]. On contract with *extranei*, the right remained with the master[10], and though the contract might impose a *naturalis obligatio*, the slave could not be sued after he was free[11]. But if he took his *peculium* he was liable to an action, *de peculio*, for one year[12], as the master would have been, had he kept it[13].

XXXII. CIVITAS. From this point of view the main classification is into *Cives*, *Latini* and *Peregrini*, a classification more convenient than exact since Latins are a class of privileged Peregrines. But their privileges are so marked as to bring them closer to *cives* than to *peregrini*[14].

Cives. Of *cives* in general little need be said[15], but there were on the one hand specially privileged classes, and, on the other, classes whose

1 Dareste, *Recueil des inscr. jurid. grecques*, 2. 252 *sqq.*, 273 *sqq.* 2 Girard, *Textes*, 854. 3 12. 4. 3. 2, 3. 4 G. 4. 77; P. 2. 31. 8; D. 9. 4. 24. In minor wrongs command by *dominus* was a defence after manumission, 9. 4. 2. 1; 25. 2. 21. 1. 5 An action might lie for an insult to a slave. Even this remained with the master, 47. 10. 30. pr.; 47. 2. 46. pr.; 9. 2. 15. 1. 6 47. 2. 17. 1; C. 3. 41. 1. 7 G. 2. 189; Ulp. 22. 12, 13. As to legacies, *post*, § CXX. 8 33. 8. 6. 4. 9 Of retention merely; Buckland, *Slavery*, 690. C. 4. 14. 3, Alexander (interp.) gives *A. in factum* where a slave promises money for manumission and fails to pay it when free. 10 44. 7. 56, even conditional, 45. 3. 40; 50. 17. 18. 11 P. 2. 13. 9; C. 4. 14. 2. 12 *Post*, § CLXXXIV. Disputed. 13 15. 2. 1. 7. 14 The existence in the same community of persons of similar race and speech with widely different civil rights caused difficulties (see *Vita Alexandri*, 27. 1) and mistakes, resulting in prominence of rules remedying resulting evils. Thus sale of a freeman as a slave is a valid contract, *quia difficile dignosci potest liber homo a servo* (18. 1. 5) though it cannot be carried out. See also fraudulent sale of freeman (*ante*, p. 71), *erroris causae probatio* (*post*, § XXXV), attestation by slave supposed free (*post*, § CIII), *institutio* in same conditions (*post*, § CVIII), acquisition through *liber homo b. f. serviens* (*post*, § XCIX), position of child of *ancilla* supposed free (G. 1. 85), persons *de statu suo incerti* (*post*, § CII), etc. A slave could not be *arbiter* but if one thought free was so appointed his decision was good (C. 7. 45. 2). A fugitive slave got himself appointed Praetor: his official acts were valid (1. 14. 3). 15 As to double *civitas* of Rome and another city, Brugi, *Ist.*, 68; Stroux-Wenger, *Abh. Bayer. Ak. der Wissensch.* 1928, *Abh.* 2. 57 *sqq.*

rights were more or less restricted. The only privileged classes that need mention are:

1. *Ordo Senatorius.* A nobility founded by Augustus, based on descent from a Senator[1], a title which itself gradually became more a rank than an office. Membership of the *ordo* passed to agnatic descendants, but only to the grandchildren of an actual senator, not *in perpetuum.* The privileges belong mainly to public law, but these *clarissimi* could not take the lucrative government contracts[2] and a marriage between one of this class and a *libertinus* (*a*) was void[3].

2. *Ordo Equester*[4]. This descends from the equestrian centuries of Servius Tullius, but in the Empire its character had altered. It was an aristocracy of wealth, not in the sense that all the rich belonged to it, for membership was conferred by the Emperor, but in the sense that wealth was essential, though birth and character played a part. The position was held for life, subject to removal or promotion to the Senate, but was apparently not inherited[5]. Members of this *ordo* formed the chief element in the *album iudicum*[6]. They held the chief financial administrative posts, and provided most of the officers in the army. They tended to increase in wealth, as the business of State contracts was mainly in their hands, but most of their various privileges had small importance in private law.

Classes with specially restricted rights are more important[7]. Leaving out of account the distinctions of the Republic, and omitting for the present *addicti* under a judgement[8], and persons *in mancipio*[9], who will call for consideration in other connexions, there were four classes who appeared in the Empire.

1. Freedmen, *Cives Liberti, Libertini Cives*[10]. Many of the disabilities of *libertini* belong to public law and need not be considered[11], but some relate to private law. A *libertinus* could not marry a person of the *ordo senatorius*[12]: he was barred from taking State contracts, at any rate until,

1 Mommsen, *Staatsr.* 3. 458 *sqq.*; *D.P.R.* 6. 2. 47 *sqq.* 2 Mommsen, *op. cit.* 3. 509; *D.P.R.* 6. 2. 109. 3 23. 2. 44. pr. 4 Mommsen, *op. cit.* 3. 476; *D.P.R.* 6. 2. 68. 5 Mommsen, *op. cit.* 500; *D.P.R.* 6. 2. 98; *Contra*, Kuebler, *Z.S.S.* 1928, 652. 6 *Post*, § CCXVII. 7 Perozzi, *Ist.* 1. 550 *sqq.* 8 *Post*, §§ CCXI, CCXIX. 9 *Post*, § XLVIII. *Auctorati*, P.-W. *s.v. auctoratus.* 10 *Libertinus* denotes the freedman in relation to the rest of the community, *libertus* his relation to his patron. See G. 1. 10, 11. A *libertinus* freed by T. is the *libertus* of T. The name *libertinus* is applied to all grades of freedmen, the name *libertus*, at least in legal texts, in the time of Gaius, only to *cives*. Cp. G. 1. 12, with G. *Ep.* 1. 1. pr. Perozzi, *Ist.* 1. 274, holds the word *libertini* to have been similarly confined to *cives*. But see, e.g., G. 1. 12; 3. 55; G. 3. 56, *liberti latini hominis*, is under suspicion, see, e.g., Krueger und Stud. *ad h.* 1. The true reading seems to be "*neque, ut liberti, latini hominis*" etc., Buckland, *N.R.H.* 1923, 293 *sqq.* 11 E.g. inability to hold Roman magistracies or vote in *comitia*, under the Empire. Mommsen, *op. cit.* 3. 440; *D.P.R.* 6. 2. 25. 12 See n. 3. In the Republic he could not marry any free-born person.

in the second century, he became admissible to equestrian rank[1]. But more important practically than these points were the rules affecting his relation with his *patronus*. The main rules in this matter are the following:

The patron had a right of succession—*iura in bonis*[2]. This right, stated in the XII Tables, carried with it the right of guardianship over the *libertus impubes* or *liberta*—*tutela legitima*[3]. It was protected by rules annulling alienations which in intent and effect were frauds on the patron's right[4]. It was regarded as in some sort compensation for loss of services, rendered by the *libertus*, for if the *heres* instituted by the will of the freedman undertook to continue these, and the patron accepted this, he could not afterwards attack the will[5].

The patron was entitled to *obsequium*. This is not easily defined, but the duty of respectful conduct is expressed in many specific rules. *Obsequium* was due though the liberty was the result of a bargain[6], and, to some extent, to parents and children of the patron[7]. The *libertus* might not bring any action involving discredit against the patron or these relatives, or, without leave of a magistrate, any action at all[8]. He could not be accuser, or give evidence, in a criminal case against the patron[9]. Gifts by the patron were revocable without proof of ingratitude[10] and gifts to the patron were not limited by the *l. Cincia*[11]. A woman freed for the purpose of marriage could not refuse it[12]. Apart from any special obligation to *operae* and *munera* undertaken, a *libertus* was bound to support his patron in need, according to his means[13]. The obligations were not all one way. The *libertus* must not be treated as a slave[14]. In classical law the patron could not give evidence against him in criminal matters, and in later law he could not be compelled to do so[15]. He must provide for him in need[16], and there were other protections[17].

1 Mommsen, *op. cit.* 3. 518; *D.P.R.* 6. 2. 118. Most of these rules applied in the Republic *de facto*, though not in law, to the child of a *libertus*—it took two generations to wipe out the stain of slavery. There is evidence that at one time the name *libertinus* had been applied only to the children of *liberti*, Suetonius, *Claudius*, 24; Isidorus, 9. 4. 47. Bruns, 2. 83. 2 *Post*, § CXXXIV. 3 *Post*, § LII. 4 Enforced by *a. Calvisiana* where the *libertus* was intestate (38. 5. 3. 3) and *a. Fabiana* where he had made a will (P. 3. 3; D. 38. 5, *passim*), thus only after death (*post*, § CCIII). 5 37. 14. 20; 38. 2. 1. 2; 38. 2. 37. 6 37. 15. 3. 7 37. 15. 5, 6. Machinery for dealing with ingratitude, *ante*, p. 71. 8 G. 4. 46; C. 6. 6. 1; D. 37. 15. 2, 6, 7. 9 Coll. 4. 4. 2; 9. 2. 2; 9. 3. 3; D. 48. 2. 8; C. Th. 9. 6. 4 (=C. 4. 20. 12). Or in some cases children, parents or patron of the patron. 10 Vat. Fr. 272. 11 Vat. Fr. 308, 309. 12 *Post*, § XLI. 13 P. 2. 32. 1; C. 6. 3. 1. *Libertus* punishable for seeking to marry *patrona* or patron's wife or daughter (P. 2. 19. 9), must accept *tutela* of patron's child in circumstances which excuse him from others (P. 2. 29. 1; Vat. Fr. 152, 224). A woman's power to change *tutor* did not apply to *patronus* except temporarily, in case of urgency, G. 1. 174. 14 C. 6. 6. 6. 15 Coll. 9. 3. 3; P. 5. 15. 3; D. 22. 5. 4. 16 37. 14. 5. 1. 17 Patron cannot prevent *libertus* from trading in competition, but Justinian allows him to stop this in case of actual damage; 37. 14. 2, 18; 37. 15. 11; 38. 1. 45. *Libertus* cannot be compelled to live with patron, C. 6. 3. 12.

If the manumission was voluntary and gratuitous in other respects it was allowed, and usual, for the patron to require services, *operae*, and gifts, *munera*[1]. *Munera* were gifts on special occasions of no great importance, as it was forbidden to exact money *onerandae libertatis causa*[2], though it was allowed to agree for money in lieu of promised services, the choice being with the *libertus*[3]. *Operae* were more serious. They might not be excessive and must be suitable to the age, *status* and training of the *libertus*[4]. Sickness excused without compensation[5]. The right to *operae* of a *liberta* was lost by marriage or concubinage with her, by her marriage, with patron's consent[6], and by her reaching the age of 50 or a rank which made the services unreasonable[7]. The right to those of a *libertus* was lost by his having two children (but not by mere marriage[8], or, it seems, dignity) and by redemption for money, which ended the patron's rights altogether[9]. An *opera* is a day's work, conceived of as a definite unit of value, a *dandum*, not a *faciendum*[10].

Other facts might destroy the right to *bona*, i.e. in effect, to the patron's rights generally. Such were: reclaiming him as a slave[11]; exacting an oath not to marry or have children[12]; having freed a woman under a *fideicommissum*, excusing himself from *tutela* of her[13]; and breaches of various duties above enumerated and others[14]. The rights were destroyed by *capitis deminutio maxima* or *media* on either side, but of course the condemnation of the patron did not destroy the independent right of his children to the *bona*[15]. *Adrogatio* of the patron merely transferred the rights: that of the *libertus*, not usually allowed, did not affect the patron's rights[16].

Not all patrons had these rights. We have seen when a right to *operae* arose. Sometimes, where a slave was freed for misconduct of the master the latter was patron in name without the patronal rights[17]. One who

1 38. 1. 7. 4; C. 6. 3. 3, 5. 2 38. 1. 32, 36, 39. 3 37. 14. 6. 1; 38. 1. 39. 4 38. 1. 2, 16. 1, 50. 5 38. 1. 15. pr. 6 38. 1. 13. 4, 30. 1, 46; C. 6. 3. 9. Marriage of *liberta* did not destroy right of *patrona*, 38. 1. 48. 2. 7 38. 1. 34, 35. 8 C. 6. 3. 7. 1. (*lege Iulia*); 38. 1. 13. 3. 9 38. 2. 37, expressing the fact that succession replaces right to services. Right to support in need remained, P. 2. 32. 10 Thélohan, *Ét. Girard*, 1. 355 *sqq.*; *post*, §§ XCVI, CLX. *Operae* other than personal services were assignable, 38. 1. 9. 1; h. t. 23. pr. (interp., Desserteaux, *Capitis Deminutio*, 2. 290, and reff.). Services the render of which had already been claimed, *operae indictae*, were debts to the patron and so the claim passed to his *heres*. Whether future services were due to *liberi* or *heredes* depended on terms of undertaking, 38. 1. 5, 22. 1. *Iudicium operarum*, *post*, § CLX. As to succession to *operae*, *post*, § CX and Bonfante, *Corso*, 6. 112 *sqq.* 11 38. 2. 9. 12 37. 14. 6. 13 37. 14. 3. 14 Failure to support in need (*l. Aelia Sentia*, 38. 2. 33), exacting money, *libertatis onerandae causa* (38. 1. 32), wrongly bringing or supporting a capital charge against him, with some exceptions. If rightly, the goods are *publicata*, 37. 14. 9–11; 38. 2. 3, 9, 14. 5. In some of these cases the same effect is produced if a child of the patron does the act, 38. 1. 48. 15 *Post*, § CXXXIV. 16 *Post*, § XLV. Effect of *cap. dem.* of patron on *iusiurandum operarum*, *post*, § CLX. 17 C. 7. 6. 1. 4.

freed under a trust had *iura in bona* and *tutela*, and could not be sued but the other rules of *obsequium* did not apply[1]. We have seen that for default in carrying out the trust he might lose the *libertus* altogether[2]. The transferee, *ut manumittatur*, was in the position of one who freed under a trust[3]. Where a slave was *suis nummis emptus*, the manumitter could not be sued[4], but the other rules of *obsequium* did not apply, and though he succeeded on intestacy like any other patron, he could not attack the freedman's will[5]. A *libertinus* could be put in the same legal position as if he had been born free, *ingenuus*[6]. Augustus gave a certain freedman the rights of *ingenuitas*, allowing a collusive claim that he was *ingenuus*, known to be a fiction, in order to introduce him to the equestrian class[7], and soon there were direct gifts of the *ius anuli aurei*, the mark of this class[8]. From the second century this right marked only an *ingenuus*, and from Commodus onwards, grants of it to freedmen were common[9]. The grant made the man an *ingenuus* for general legal purposes but did not affect the patron's rights[10]. A little later a further step was taken. By decree of the Emperor a freedman might get *restitutio natalium*[11], which made him *ingenuus* for all purposes, but the consent of patron and his children was usually required, as their rights were destroyed[12]. In a late novel, Justinian gave all *libertini*, existing or future, the *ius regenerationis* and *anuli aurei*. This left the patron's rights unaffected, but he provided that these were destroyed if the patron at any time expressly waived them[13]. The practical result was that the general disabilities of a *libertinus* disappeared.

XXXIII. 2. *Coloni Adscriptitii, Adscripti Glebae*[14]. This is a class of serfs who appeared in the Empire, not certainly traceable before Constantine, but probably older, evidently a very large class in the Byzantine empire, and the subject of much legislation[15]. They were the rustic cultivating class. The *colonus* was free and a citizen[16]. He could marry and engage in ordinary transactions[17] and he did not owe servile *obsequium*[18]. But he could not leave the land or sell it, or his other property.

1 2. 4. 9; 27. 1. 24; 38. 1. 7. 4; Vat. Fr. 225. 2 *Ante*, p. 84. 3 2. 4. 10. pr.; 37. 15. 3; 38. 2. 3. 3; C. 6. 3. 2, etc. 4 2. 4. 10. pr. 5 C. 6. 4. 1. 6 Messa, *Ingenuitas*, 41 *sqq.* 7 Suetonius, *Augustus*, 74. 8 Mommsen, *Staatsr.* 2. 893; *D.P.R.* 5. 172. 9 *Ib.*; Vat. Fr. 226. 10 Commodus required the patron's knowledge and non-prohibition, 40. 10. 3. 11 Marcian tells us that the *natalia* restored are not of course their own but those originally the common right of all men, 40. 11. 2. 12 P. 4. 14 a. 13 C. 6. 4. 3. *Nov.* 78. 14 Heitland, *Agricola*, chh. 50, 51; Seeck, Pauly-Wissowa, *s.v. colonatus*; Girard, *Man.*; Cornil, *D.R.*, 506 *sqq.*; Brissaud, *Régime de la terre.* 15 For the legislation affecting them, Gothofredus ad C. Th. 5. 9. The *papyri* give much information and raise new problems. Evidence of gradual extension and local variations. As to the modified position of certain *coloni liberi* in the fifth century, Brissaud, *cit.*, 121 *sqq.* 16 C. 11. 50. 2; 11. 52. 1. 17 C. 11. 48. 8. 2, 24. 18 C. 11. 50. 2; 11. 55. 1.

If he deserted he could be reclaimed and those who detained him were liable[1]. His lord could not remove him from the land or sell it away from him or raise his rent, which was paid in kind[2]. The position was hereditary[3]. There was no enfranchisement, and though in 419 it was provided that 30 years apparent liberty from it should release, this had disappeared under Justinian[4]. But the *colonus* could be released by an agreement under which he was to hold the land free of the burdens[5], and under Justinian was released by becoming a bishop[6]. The *status* arose by birth, by voluntary acceptance, e.g. in distress[7], by lapse of time[8], and by *denunciatio* (sturdy vagrants were assigned to landowners who denounced them[9]) and by marriage[10]. *Coloni* could not sue their lord except as to his title or on an increase of rent[11]. Most of the rules belong to the fifth century when the institution was becoming more important in the growing distress; an expression of the tendency to secure the due functioning of matters important to the State by making many *status* hereditary, thus holding the people to the work and *status* to which they had been born[12].

3. *Infames*[13]. These appear in Justinian's law[14] as a sharply defined group who, by reason of wrongful or unseemly conduct, are subjected to serious disabilities. Shameful trades, condemnation in certain actions and criminal charges, dismissal in disgrace from the army, and misconduct in family relations are the chief cases[15]. The rule is essentially praetorian[16], but some of the Praetor's cases have disappeared from the list in the Digest[17], and the Praetor does not speak of *infamia*, but only of prohibition to appear as advocate for any one (*postulare*[18]) or to represent or be represented in litigation (*cognitores dare, dari*[19]). This last rule, applying also to the less formally appointed *procuratores*, was no longer expressly stated under Justinian[20], but that of *postulatio* remained[21].

1 C. Th. 5. 17. 1–3; 5. 19. 1, 2; C. 11. 48. 6, 12; 11. 50. 2. 2 C. 11. 48. 2, 5, 7, 15. A similar class called *Inquilini*, of whom little is known, apparently somewhat earlier, seem to have been barbarians settled on Roman territory, 30. 112. pr.; C. 11. 48. 12, 13. 3 C. 11. 48. 13, 16. 4 20 years, if a woman, C. Th. 5. 18. 1; C. 11. 48. 22. 5 C. 11. 48. 21. 6 *Nov.* 123. 4. Not by any other privilege, C. 11. 48. 11; can hold no *militia*, h. t. 18. 7 C. Th. 5. 6. 3; Salvianus, *de gubernatione dei*, 5. 8. 8 C. 11. 48. 19, 20. 9 C. Th. 14. 18. 1. 10 Brissaud, *cit.* 106 *sqq.* 11 C. 11. 48. 20; 11. 50. 1, 2. 12 Cornil, *D.R.*, 514 *sqq.*; vivid *résumé*, Declareuil, *Rome et l'évolution du droit*, Liv. 2, ch. 1. These classes were very numerous in the fifth century and their powers were so restricted that the ordinary commercial law can have had little application to them. 13 Greenidge, *Infamia in Roman Law.* 14 Chief texts, Vat. Fr. 320–324; D. 3. 1. 1. 5–8; 3. 2. *passim*; C. 2. 11. 15 Greenidge gives a list of about 40 sources of *infamia.* 16 It originated with the *Censor*, but this aspect of it disappears with the *census.* 17 E.g., *auctorati*, Coll. 9. 2. 2, persons condemned in the *actio fiduciae*, obsolete, *post*, § CLI. 18 Lenel, *E.P.* 76 *sqq.*; D. 3. 1. 1. 5. 19 G. 4. 82; Lenel, *op. cit.* 86 *sqq.* One who could not *postulare* could not be *cognitor*, P. 1. 2. 1. 20 Inst. 4. 13. 11; *post*, § CCXXXIX. 21 3. 1. 1. 5.

Certain *condemnati* could not *postulare* for anyone[1]. *Infames* in general could act only for connected persons and could not appoint persons to act for them[2]. They could not *accusare* in criminal cases[3], or hold offices or dignities[4]. They were not necessarily *intestabiles*, though the provision which made them *infames* might also provide this[5]. We are better informed as to the cases of *infamia* than as to its effects. Most of the disabilities of *infamia* had no bearing on women, and the original censorian conception of *infamia* did not apply to them. They appear, however, in the law of the Empire: probably the chief result was that they could not appoint representatives[6].

4. *Intestabiles*[7]. Certain persons might not be witnesses, i.e., might not give evidence in litigation[8], or act as witnesses in formal transactions, e.g., *mancipatio* and will[9]. Gaius tells us that some jurists excluded them from having witnesses[10], which bars them from conveying property in civil form and from making wills, and is applied to this last case by Ulpian[11]. In addition to these persons who are declared *intestabiles*, generally, there are others who are excluded by specific statutes from giving evidence in cases with which they deal[12].

XXXIV. Free subjects other than *Cives* are *Latini* or *Peregrini*, and each of these groups has subdivisions.

(*a*) *Latini Veteres*, *Prisci* (*nomen Latinum*). These, i.e. the Italian communities of Latin race, had been endowed with *civitas* long before the Empire and do not therefore directly concern us[13]. But the name of Latin had been applied to

(*b*) *Latini Colonarii*. These were communities on which, at or after their incorporation into the State, an inferior *status* modelled on that of the old Latins had been conferred, in some cases on the old inhabitants of the region, in others on emigrants sent out from Rome to occupy the territory or town[14]. Such colonies continued to be founded[15] till the middle of the second century, but, owing to the progressive extensions of *civitas*, the later ones were in the remoter parts of the Empire, and the class disappeared under Caracalla[16]. Latin colonies were of two main types, those with *minus* and those with *maius Latium*, the difference being that in the first, the superior officials acquired Roman *civitas* for themselves and their children, while, in the other, *decuriones*, i.e. mem-

1 3. 1. 1. 6. 2 h. t. 1. 8. 3 Coll. 4. 4. 4 48. 7. 1. pr.; or to be *iudices*, Greenidge, 155. 5 28. 1. 18. 6 Greenidge, ch. VII. 7 Notion as old as the XII Tables, 8. 22. 8 Coll. 9. 2; D. 22. 5. 20. 9 22. 5. 15; 28. 1. 18. 1. 10 28. 1. 26. 11 28. 1. 18. 1. 12 Greenidge, 166. 13 The name *Latini* was applied to the inhabitants of the earliest colonies, before the name *Latini Colonarii* was invented, Girard, *Man.* 120. 14 Mommsen, *Staatsr.* 3. 620 *sqq.*; *D.P.R.* 6. 2. 241 *sqq.* 15 By Senate or Emperor, G. 1. 95; *Vita Hadriani*, 21. 16 *Post*, § XXXVII.

bers of the local *curia* or town council, shared the privilege[1]. The general position of such Latins was as follows[2]. They might not serve in the Roman legions. They could not hold a Roman magistracy (*ius honorum*) and, apart from special provisions[3], a marriage between a Latin and a Roman had not the effects of a Roman marriage (*ius conubii*). But in the ordinary relations of private law they were on a level with Romans (*ius commercii*)[4], and thus might be parties to *legis actio*[5].

(*c*) *Latini Iuniani.* These are the inferior class of manumitted slaves already considered[6]. Just as, by "economy of juristic conceptions," the *nomen Latinum* was extended to communities which had nothing to do with Latium, so was it here extended to a class which had no local or racial significance at all. Their position was that of colonary Latins, except so far as restricted by the patron's rights, or by legislation, or by the fact that they were not members of a Latin community. The limitations were serious. They could not acquire *civitas* by holding office in their community for they were not members of a Latin community[7]. They owed *obsequium* to their patron, with the liabilities already considered[8]. They were said to become slaves at their death: their property reverted to their patron, as *peculium*, not as inheritance, and their children had no claim[9]. They had no capacity for civil marriage[10]. They had *commercium*, with the important exception that by a rule of the *l. Iunia*, they could not make a will or take an inheritance or legacy under one, or be made *tutores* by will[11]. As this resulted from express enactment and was not an inherent disability, they could act, like other Latins, as witnesses in wills and other formal acts[12]. Having *commercium* they had access to the law courts[13]. After an enactment of Caracalla shortly to be considered[14] the name *iuniani* went out of use: there were no longer any colonary Latins. There was a gradual development of new ways of becoming a Latin. Some of them were merely new modes of informal or imperfect manumission[15], but some clearly were not, e.g. Latinity given by law to a slave who detected certain criminals[16]. Many of the

1 G. 1. 96. At expiry of office? Hirschfeld, *Kl. Schr.* 294, but see Autun G. 7.
2 Each had its own statute (e.g., *l. Salpensana*, Bruns, 1. 142; Girard, *Textes*, 108), not uniform but the differences were mainly in details of local administration.
3 G. 1. 56; Ulp. 5. 4.
4 Ulp. 19. 4, 5. A Latin could give his child in adoption to a Roman (Livy, 41. 8) and by a survival of the notions of the old Latin league Latins resident at Rome could vote, at any rate in the Tribes (Livy, 25. 3; Mommsen, *op. cit.* 3. 643; *D.P.R.* 6. 2. 267). No evidence of this in the Empire and that for the late Republic not good.
5 Girard, *Man.* 116.
6 *Ante*, § XXVIII.
7 They might be, if freed by a member of the community.
8 *Ante*, pp. 71, 88.
9 Inst. 3. 7. 4; *post*, § CXXXIV.
10 Ulp. 5. 9. Special provisions of *l. Aelia Sentia*, *post*, § XLI.
11 G. 1. 23, 24; 2. 110, 275; Ulp. 11. 16. They could take *fideicommissa.*
12 They had *testamenti factio*, but not *ius capiendi*. Ulp. 20. 8; 22. 3.
13 Ulp. 5. 4; 19. 4.
14 *Post*, § XXXVII.
15 E.g., pledged slave freed, 40. 5. 24. 10; Fr. Dos. 16; *ancilla* married to freeman with *dos*, C. 7. 6. 9.
16 C. Th. 9. 24. 1. Numerous cases, Buckland, *Slavery*, 548 *sqq.*

cases are late: it is impossible to say how far the beneficiaries were subject to the disabilities of junian Latins. The same is true of the children of junian Latins, but for reasons now to be stated the class affected would not be numerous.

XXXV. Access to citizenship was made easy by the legislation of the Empire[1]. Gaius and Ulpian state many ways, open apparently to all Latins, but, in the case of *Iuniani*, not affecting the patron's rights. Office in a Latin colony has been mentioned[2]. Claudius gave *civitas* to Latins who built a ship of a certain size and carried grain to Rome for six years[3]. A *lex Visellia* (apparently A.D. 25) gave it to those who served in the *Vigiles* for six years[4]. Nero gave it to any Latin of a certain wealth, who should build a house in Rome at the cost of half his patrimony[5], Trajan to any Latin who should work a mill of a certain capacity at Rome for three years[6]. A senatusconsult gave it to *Latinae* who had three children, even *volgo concepti*[7]. It was frequently given by special decree of the Emperor, and though in general the patron's rights were unaffected there is reason to think that if the patron consented, the man became a *civis libertus* for all purposes[8].

There is another group of cases of more importance in which the Latin became a *civis* for all purposes.

Iteratio[9]. A slave who on manumission became a Latin could become a *civis* by a repetition of the manumission without the defect, and by a senatusconsult this would affect his children also[10]. The cases recorded seem to be: the man informally freed, or freed under 30, or by a bonitary owner[11]. We are told that he became the *libertus* of the one who iterated. Where this was the original manumitter or his successor in title there was no difficulty. If the bonitary owner freed and the quiritary owner iterated, the *bona*, i.e. right to the goods, remained with the late bonitary owner[12], no doubt because the quiritary owner could not acquire anything through him while he was a slave or Latin. And by a rescript of M. Aurelius rights to *munera* and *operae* remained with the bonitary owner[13]. It might have been thought that *tutela* would also have been with the bonitary owner, but his right is not *hereditas*[14], and the quiritary

1 G. 1. 28. 2 *Ante*, p. 92. 3 G. 1. 32; Ulp. 3. 6. 4 Shortened by *sc.* to three, G. 1. 32; Ulp. 3. 5. 5 G. 1. 33. 6 G. 1. 34; Ulp. 3. 1. 7 Ulp. 3. 1. If of marriage with Latin, another rule applied, *post*, p. 95. If of marriage with peregrine, to apply this rule would put them in a better position than *Latini*. It was not desirable to encourage marriage between *cives* and *Latinae*, who were usually *libertinae*. 8 *Ante*, p. 90. 9 As to problems connected with *iteratio* involving the fundamental conception of manumission, Buckland, *Slavery*, Appendix 4. 10 G. 1. 35; Fr. D. 14; Ulp. 3. 4; Vat. Fr. 221. Probable that children would be in his *potestas*. The whole rule is to exclude the doubt whether as he was not now a slave any act of manumission might not be a nullity. 11 Pliny, *Ep.* 7. 16. 12 G. 1. 167. The rights are those he had in the goods, as those of a Latin. 13 Vat. Fr. 221. 14 *Post*, § CXXXIV.

owner became *tutor*[1]. No doubt the ordinary rules of *obsequium* applied to both[2]. It is thus only in a very restricted sense that the *libertus* was the *libertus* of the former quiritary owner[3].

Anniculi Probatio. The *l. Aelia Sentia*[4] or the *l. Iunia*[5] provided that a *Latinus iunianus*, freed under 30, could, on marrying a *Latina colonaria* or *iunia* or a *civis*, before seven witnesses (aware of the purpose of the marriage), and having a child one year old, go before a magistrate and prove these facts. He thus acquired *civitas* for himself, his wife and child, unless indeed the wife was a *civis* already, in which case the child would be a *civis* on general principle[6], and *patria potestas* over the child. If the man died before acting the mother could do it to get *civitas* for herself and child. A defective text of Gaius seems to say that, if both were dead, then, if the child were a *civis*, through his mother, he himself could proceed, so as to become *heres* to the father[7]. The limitation to those under 30 is not reasonable, and a *sc. Pusio-Pegasianum* (A.D. 72) gave the right to all junian Latins[8].

The position thus obtained was better than that gained by the methods of the first group, but it applied in terms only to Latins, and Trajan held that one who, having obtained *civitas* in some way, had ceased to be a Latin could not afterwards utilise *anniculi probatio*, so that his *bona* must go to his patron and his children would have no claim. Hadrian however[9], observing the unfairness of this, allowed those who had gained *civitas* with the inferior result to proceed nevertheless afterwards under the rules of *anniculi probatio*, as if still Latins.

Erroris Causae Probatio. This is one of the provisions, so prominent in Roman Law, to deal with the results of error in *status*. Gaius, in mutilated texts[10], deals with cases in which, a marriage having been contracted under mistake of *status*, so that the *status* of issue was not what was expected, the effects of the error, if it was not grossly negligent, might be set aside by decree so soon as there was issue. The cases, all resting on senatusconsult, fall into three groups.

1 G. 167; Ulp. 11. 19. The point is that the civil law right of succession is not divested, though emptied of content by the praetorian right, *post*, § CXXXV. 2 Ulp. (Vat. Fr. 221) not clear whether he is bound to accept *tutela* of children of both or only of the bonitary. 3 Where he acquires *civitas* by one of the first group of methods, he becomes the *libertus* of his former quiritary owner, but the *bona* are still with the bonitary owner, G. 1. 35. 4 G. 1. 29. 5 Ulp. 3. 3. The restriction to those under 30 indicates the *l. Aelia Sentia*, these being the *Latini* specially created by that *lex*. To give them this special privilege does not add to the class of *cives* those who would not have been such in earlier law. 6 *Post*, § XXXVII, and under a *sc.* of Hadrian which seems to have dealt comprehensively with questions of *status* on birth, not always making new law. Ulp. 3. 3. See G. 1. 30, 77, etc. 7 G. 1. 32; Coll. 16. 3. 7, 15. 8 G. 1. 31. A change of principle, see n. 5. As extended it widens the class. 9 G. 3. 72, 73. 10 G. 1. 67–75; G. 1. 87, 2. 142; Ulp. 7. 4.

(*a*) One party intended to satisfy the rules of *anniculi probatio*, but, owing to mistake of *status*, did not, e.g. a Roman woman married a peregrine thinking him a Latin, or a *latina* married a peregrine under a similar error. As soon as a child was a year old, *erroris causa* could be shewn and proceedings taken under the *lex*[1].

(*b*) There was no reference to *anniculi probatio*, but the marriage was not civil because one party, supposed to be a *civis*, was not, and had not *conubium*. It was enough that a child was born[2].

(*c*) One who had *conubium*, mistaking his own *status*, married one who had not. The age of the child was immaterial[3].

The general result was to give *civitas* to the parties not *cives*, and *potestas* to the father[4]. The primary matter in view being *civitas*, the rules were not applied except where the effect was to give someone *civitas*, and the benefits of the rule were not extended to any party to the marriage who, being a *dediticius*, was incapable of *civitas*[5].

Both parties need not have been in error, but only the one who was could avail himself of the rules[6]. The man could always do so, if in error, but the woman only if she was the superior, i.e. a *civis* or *latina* who had married a peregrine[7]. But a peregrine who shewed cause under these rules did not get *potestas* over existing issue except by special decree, though he did if the wife shewed cause[8].

XXXVI. Of the third class, *peregrini*, there were two types.

Peregrini (*socii*). With the earlier meaning of this name we are not concerned: in classical law it denotes the denizens of those outlying parts of the Empire which had never been incorporated as Roman, or endowed with Latin rights—the provinces. Apart from municipalities and the like which here and there received civil or Latin rights, and thus constituted civil enclaves[9], the provinces were governed by their own private law, little altered by Rome. What we have to consider is the relations between these peregrines and Romans in civil life. They had in general no *ius honorum*, *suffragii*, *conubii* or *commercii*[10]. The exclusion from *commercium* does not mean exclusion from commerce, but only from the specially Roman part of the law. They could not have civil *dominium* or transfer property by civil law methods, e.g. *mancipatio* or *cessio in iure*[11]. The land, unless it had received, by *privilegium*, the *ius italicum*, was not regarded as owned; the *dominium* was in the *populus*

1 G. 1. 68–70, 73; 3. 5; Ulp. 7. 4; Coll. 16. 2. 5. 2 G. 1. 67, 68; Ulp. 7. 4. 3 G. 1. 71. 4 G. 1. 67. Sex of child immaterial, G. 1. 72. 5 G. 1. 68. 6 No text mentions the other case. 7 G. 1. 74. 8 G. 1. 93; 1. 68. 9 Mommsen, *Staatsr.* 3. 645 *sqq.*; *D.P.R.* 6. 2. 269 *sqq.* 10 G. 1. 25, 56, 92, etc. By *privilegium*, some had *conubium* (G. 1. 56, 57, 76, etc.) and *commercium*, with access to Roman courts (Ulp. 19. 4). Thus some could proceed by *legis actio* (Girard, *Org. Jud.* 1. 104, 213 *sqq.*). 11 G. 1. 119.

or the Emperor[1], and it paid tribute; methods being devised by which transfers, creation of servitudes, and litigation affecting the land were carried out effectively[2]. The *ius gentium* was open to them, and this, in the Empire, was the most important part of the law. Thus they could transfer property by *traditio*, and since *stipulatio* was *iuris gentium*[3], the law of contract was in practice as free to peregrines as to *cives*[4]. And though, in principle, civil procedure was closed to them, "fictitious" actions were devised by which in the principal cases of dispute between them and *cives*, the matter might come before the courts with the fiction, "*si civis esset*[5]." There were moreover special tribunals (*recuperatoria iudicia*) for cases, at Rome, in which peregrines were concerned, controlled by the *praetor peregrinus*[6], but these grew less important as the above machinery developed[7].

Except so far as they might benefit by the rules of *erroris causae probatio*, there was no standing rule by which peregrines could attain *civitas*. But, apart from grants to communities, or in mass, the emperors often gave it as a reward for service in the irregular and auxiliary forces, and as a qualification for service in the legions, which was confined to *cives*[8]. A peregrine who obtained *civitas* for himself and his wife and children did not get *patria potestas* over children already born, unless he expressly petitioned and benefit of the children was shewn[9].

Dediticii. These were primarily members of nations which had submitted to Rome, but had, as yet, no constitution conferred on them, and those who by reason of treachery or other discreditable dealings were permanently placed in the position[10]. There is little trace of these

1 G. 2. 7. The *populus* as a property owner disappears soon after Gaius. 2 *Post*, §§ LXIX, XCIV. 3 G. 3. 93, not in the form "*Spondes-ne, spondeo.*" 4 Except perhaps for the decaying contract *literis*, G. 3. 132–134. 5 G. 4. 37. 6 Girard, *Org. Jud.* 1. 211 *sqq.* 7 The machinery would apply to some extent to those who suffered *deportatio*, a punishment introduced by Augustus, and gradually superseding exile (*aquae et ignis interdictio*). It could be inflicted only by the Emperor or *Praefectus Urbi* (1. 12. 1. 3; 48. 19. 2; 48. 22. 6. 1), must be perpetual (48. 22. 17. 2) and involved residence in a fixed place (Theoph. *ad* Inst. 1. 12. 1). *Deportati* lost their citizenship without acquiring another—they were "ἀπόλιδες," and did not become citizens of the place to which they were sent, or share the special law of that place. But they had the power of ordinary dealings involved in the *ius gentium* (48. 19. 17. 1; 48. 22. 15). Their goods were usually forfeited (P. 5. 23. 11, 13, etc.), but if they retained some (not otherwise, 4. 5. 7. 3) they could be sued, *pro parte*, on their old debts, but only by *utiles actiones* as they had suffered *capitis deminutio* (48. 22. 14. 3). They could not manumit slaves and they could neither take under a will nor make one and their cognatic position was destroyed, G. 2. 110; Inst. 1. 16. 6; D. 38. 10. 4. 11; the *Fiscus* succeeded to them (48. 22. 2, 15, 16); they had in no case any rights against former debtors to them. Mommsen (*Staatsr.* 3. 140; *D.P.R.* 6. 1. 156) considers them to be *dediticii*. As to their marriage, *post*, § XXXIX; surviving *obligatio* and the position of sureties, *post*, §§ CLVI, CLXXXIX; position generally, Desserteaux, *Capitis Deminutio*, 3. 33 *sqq.* 8 Girard, *Man.* 126. 9 G. 1. 93, 94; 2. 135 a. 10 G. 1. 14.

in the Empire, and the name is applied mainly to those freed slaves who, by reason of their personal degradation, were placed by the *l. Aelia* "*in numero dediticiorum*[1]." They were free but could not become *cives*[2]. If they attempted to live within 100 miles of Rome, they were sold into slavery, with their goods, to one who undertook to keep them beyond that limit. If freed they became the property of the State[3]. They had the ordinary *iure gentium* powers, but could not make wills even by peregrine law, as they were not members of any community[4].

XXXVII. The law was profoundly affected by an enactment of Caracalla[5]. We are told by several writers, in almost identical language, that in A.D. 212 he gave *civitas* to all (*omnes*, πάντας) in the Roman world[6]. It is stated to have been for fiscal reasons[7]. The taxes on manumissions and successions were doubled and as the latter fell only on *cives*, there was profit in increasing the class. It is clear that there were after this enactment, in various parts of the Empire, free subjects who were not *cives*. The enactment did not destroy the different *status*, but only gave *civitas* to existing persons. *Latini* would recur, as there were many ways in which a man might become a Latin[8], even if, which is far from clear[9], the provision applied to existing junian Latins. A recently found papyrus was supposed to be a Greek translation of the enactment. It is imperfect[10], but it seemed to shew that besides the fiscal aim there was the desire to avoid causes of litigation and to further the cult of the Roman gods, and, further, that *dediticii* were expressly excluded. But there is much controversy as to the reading of the critical words, as to the context to which they belong, and even as to the nature of the document itself, so that the papyrus has not yet really helped us much[11]. The questions who were excluded, and whether this exclusion is due to anything expressed in the enactment, are still obscure. All that can be said here is that, besides the various Latins, the *deportati* (who are said to have been called *dediticii*[12]), barbarians settled on the frontiers and freed slaves *in numero dediticiorum*, there were in Egypt, and probably elsewhere, large numbers of the rural population who paid poll tax and were excluded, though it is not clear that all who paid were excluded[13] or that exclusion depended on this liability.

1 *Ante*, § XXVIII. 2 A rule applied in *erroris causae probatio*, *ante*, p. 95; or Latins, G. 1. 15. 3 G. 1. 27, *l. Aelia Sentia*. Not "*servi publici*." 4 G. 3. 75; Ulp. 20. 14. 5 See Bry, *Études Girard*, 1. 1 *sqq.* Segrè, *St. Perozzi*, 137 *sqq.* 6 Dio Cassius, 77. 9; D. 1. 5. 17; *Vita Severi*, 1 and others cited, Bry, p. 4. 7 Dio Cassius, *cit.* 8 *Ante*, § XXXV. 9 See, e.g., *S.M.W.* 181. 10 Pap. Giessen, 2. 25, 3. 164 (Meyer), printed and discussed, Bry, *cit.* 11 Discussion of various views, Meyer, *Z.S.S.* 1926, 264 and 314, and 1928, 595. 12 Mommsen, *Ges. Schr.* (*Jur.*) 2, 68. But it is uncertain: the allusion may be to those *in numero dediticiorum* under the *l. Aelia Sentia*. 13 Girard, *Man.* 128, n. 4. As to *dediticii* in the fifth century, Gai. *Ep.* 1. 1. 3. A class of *Homologoi* is frequently mentioned and variously explained, de Zulueta, *de patrociniis*

Under Justinian a decisive step was taken. In a comprehensive enactment[1], noting that Latins were now few (which indicates that some of the rules of the *l. Aelia* were disused[2]) he reviewed the sources of Latinity still existing, and either nullified them or made them give *civitas*. Noting that *dediticii* had become *vanum nomen* he abolished the class for the future[3]. He did not abolish the class of *peregrini*, nor was this needed. The gift of Caracalla had made all the inhabitants (subject to what has been said) and their descendants, *cives*, and this seems in later times to have been understood as a gift to the community, covering even immigrants. In the result the only peregrines left were foreigners and the *deportati* and barbarians, already mentioned, who were in effect still *dediticii*, though not so called[4].

The chief rules as to the inheritance of civic *status* were these:

1. The general rule of *ius gentium* was that a child took the *status* of its mother[5], but, for Romans, the exceptions ate away most of the rule[6].

2. A child born in Roman civil marriage took the *status* of its father[7]. In general this would be *civitas*, for civil marriage was usually confined to *cives*, but there were privileged peregrines who had *conubium*, and if a Roman woman married such a person, the issue would be peregrines[8].

3. A *l. Minicia* provided that the issue of a marriage between a *civis* and a *peregrinus* or *peregrina* was always a peregrine, a rule operating where, as was usual, there was no *conubium* between them, and the father was the peregrine; in the other case the result followed from rules already stated[9].

4. Marriage under the *l. Aelia Sentia*, though regulated by statute, was not civil marriage, as some thought. Hadrian settled the matter by senatusconsult; any child was born a *civis* if the mother was one[10].

5. Apart from a doubt for junian Latins, as an artificial creation, Latins were, strictly, peregrines. Thus it might be said that in marriage between a Latin and a peregrine, either way, issue would be peregrine by the *l. Minicia*. Hadrian applied the general rule of *ius gentium*: the child took the *status* of the mother[11].

6. The *iure gentium* rule applied where the mother was a slave[12], and we have noted the cases in which the child of an *ancilla* was free[13].

7. Those conceived *legitime*, i.e. in civil marriage (*ex iustis nuptiis*), took their status from conception; others from the time of birth[14]. This

vicorum; Wilcken, *Grundzüge*, 1. 59; Pap. Rylands, ed. Hunt, 2. 286. The word may be used in more than one sense, Segrè, *St. Perozzi*, 159 *sqq.*, 196 *sqq.*

1 C. 7. 6. 1. 2 Perhaps never operated in the East. 3 C. 7. 5. 1. 4 Justinian avoids the word *peregrinus*. Compare C. Th. 4. 6. 3 with its reproduction in C. 5. 27. 1. 5 G. 1. 78, 82; Ulp. 5. 8, 9. 6 G. 1. 83. 7 G. 1. 56, 76; Ulp. 5. 8. 8 G. 1. 77. 9 G. 1. 77, 78; Ulp. 5. 8. 10 G. 1. 80. 11 G. 1. 30, 80. 12 *Ante*, § XXIV. 13 *Ib.* 14 G. 1. 89; Ulp. 5. 10.

in practice meant that where they took the father's *status*, except *e lege Minicia*, they took his *status* at the time of conception. We have already noted that in later classical law this rule was modified in the case of slave mothers by the principle that the issue was entitled to the best *status* the mother had had at any time during the pregnancy[1]. It is not unlikely that the same principle came to be applied in other cases, for we are told twice in the Digest that a child in the womb was regarded as already born, so far as this was to his benefit[2].

1 *Ante*, § XXIV. 2 1. 5. 7, 26. Gaius in 1. 90, 91 discusses the case of a woman *civis* who during pregnancy loses citizenship or liberty, and gives as a probable opinion the rule that if the conception was in *iustae nuptiae* the child is a *civis*, but otherwise takes the inferior *status*. In 92 he considers the case of a *peregrina* who gets *civitas* during pregnancy. If the child was *volgo conceptus* he says it is a *civis* (which is general principle): if of a peregrine marriage it is a *civis* if the father also got *civitas*. This he attributes to the *sc.* of Hadrian. On the whole matter, Brini, *Mem. d. R. Ac. de Bologna* (*Sc. mor.*), 1920, 195 *sqq.*

CHAPTER III

THE LAW OF PERSONS (*cont.*). THE LAW OF THE FAMILY

XXXVIII. The Law of Family Relations is the most important branch of the law of *status*[1]. The word *Familia* has many meanings[2]: in its strict sense it denotes a group consisting of a *paterfamilias* and those under his control, i.e. children, adoptive or natural and remoter issue through males, who have not passed out of the family by emancipation or the like, the wife, if the marriage was one with *manus*, in which case she was *loco filiae*, civil bondsmen and slaves. If, as was usual from the beginning of the Empire, and universal in later law, the marriage was not with *manus*, the wife was not a member of the *familia*, but remained in that to which she had belonged. Conversely, a daughter who married without *manus*, was still in the family, but her children never were. If her marriage was a fully valid civil marriage they were in her husband's family[3]. If she had married a *peregrinus* not capable of civil marriage, or if she was not married at all, any child would be *sui iuris*, i.e. in no family but his own[4]. Every male *civis* not under a *paterfamilias* was himself a *paterfamilias*, whatever his age: conversely, parental control was not ended by maturity of the son, but lasted, unless artificially determined, till the death of the father. Where the *paterfamilias* was the grandfather, his death would cause the grandson to lapse into the *potestas* of the father, if he was still in the family[5]. A *paterfamilias* was *sui iuris*—a subordinate member of a family was *alieni iuris*[6]. A woman

1 Wenger, *Hausgewalt und Staatsgewalt*; Moriaud, *La simple famille paternelle* (review, Partsch, *Z.S.S.* 1911, 440).
2 Heumann-Seckel, *s.v.*; Collinet-Giffard, *Précis*, 1. 173; Cornil, *A.D.R.* 31. Its original basis, accounting for the immense power of the *paterfam.*, is variously conceived. Principal views, Betti, *Ist.* 1. 126. For him (the view is that of Bonfante) the *fam.* is a primitive political group, the function of the organisation being the preservation from dangers, within and without, of the group itself.
3 G.1. 55.
4 G. 1. 64; Ulp. 4. 1, 2. If with *conubium*, a *peregrinus*, *ante*, § XXXVII.
5 G. 1. 127; D. 50. 16. 195. 2.
6 G. 1. 48. The distinction is important outside family relations, e.g. as to power to be party to a suit, *post*, p. 102, and § L.

could be *sui iuris* but could not have *patria potestas*, and thus was *caput et finis familiae suae*[1]. The control of a woman married *in manu* to a *filiusfamilias* was in the *paterfamilias*, to whom she was *loco neptis*[2]. It was possible in classical law (the institution was in decay) to sell a son into a position, in another family, analogous to slavery, and those so sold were said to be *in mancipio, in mancipii causa*[3]. Thus we have to consider three classes of *cives alieni iuris*, those in *potestas, manus*, and civil bondage.

FILIIFAMILIAS and FILIAEFAMILIAS. In early law this relation arose only if the father accepted the child—*ius tollendi, suscipiendi*, but this crude form of judgement on legitimacy, difficult to reconcile with the rights accorded to *postumi*, was apparently obsolete in the Empire and, in law, was ended by a praetorian procedure earlier than Julian, which required fathers to recognise their children[4]. Exposure and sale are different: they both imply a right to dispose of the child.

In classical law, though probably not in primitive law, a *filiusfamilias* was capable of contractual obligation, but *filiae* and those "*in mancipio*" were not[5]. As he has no rights, he can have in principle no actions, but convenience dictated some exceptions[6]. A few actions, thought of as affecting personality, rather than property, were open to him[7], and a few others in cases of urgency where the *pater* for some reason was unable to act, might be brought by him, but only as it seems as actions *in factum*[8]. It is doubtful whether the rule that he could be sued personally on delict is classical[9].

Patria potestas was essentially Roman: both in content, so great that it could be called *patria maiestas*[10], and in its lifelong duration, it had an intensity unknown to the paternal power in any of the systems with which Rome came into contact. It does not rest on presumed paternity: beginning when all marriage involved *manus*, it results from the power over the wife, just as acquisitions by the wife *in manu* belong to the *paterfamilias*[11]. In early Rome the State interfered little within the family; the *paterfamilias*, as domestic judge, normally with a *consilium*,

1 50. 16. 195. 5; some texts (Ulp. 4. 1; D. 1. 6. 4; 24. 3. 24) call such a woman *materfamilias*. The more usual meaning is *uxor iusta*, primarily, wife *in manu*. Aul. Gell. 18. 6. 4 *sqq.* makes *matrona* mean any wife and gives other views; Boethius, in *Top.* 3. 14; Nonius, 442. 2 Coll. 16. 2. 3. 3 G. 1. 49, *post*, § XLVIII. 4 C. 8. 46. 9. There were other proceedings, Lenel, *E.P.* 311. Declareuil, *Mél. Girard*, 1. 326, 333. It may be doubted if in private life it lasted as he suggests into the second century: arbitrary acts in imperial households prove little. The practical effect of the legislation seems to be that the alleged father must satisfy the *iudex* that the child is not his, if it is born at a time consistent with conception *ex iustis nuptiis*. 5 G. 3. 104. 6 44. 7. 9. 7 *Injuria*, 44. 7. 9. See also 2. 4. 12; 5. 2. 8. pr. 8 44. 7. 9; 44. 7. 13. 9 5. 1. 57. See Cuq, *Man.* 141. Clear, undocumented account, Arangio Ruiz, *Ist.* 439. 10 Livy, 8. 7. 11 Wenger, *Hausgewalt*.

exercised supreme power[1] and any restraint was indirect, through the *Censor*. In the Empire, the powers, though still great, were constantly diminishing. The chief elements of *potestas* were:

1. Power of life and death and minor violence[2]. Exposure of infants was not forbidden in classical law: there was later legislation as to the rights of one who rescued the *expositus*. Forbidden in A.D. 374, it still continued[3]. Classical law regarded the killing of a son, except under a formal domestic judgement, as criminal. Ulpian held it so in any case: the son should be handed over to the courts[4]. Constantine seems to have made it parricide to kill a son[5]. In later law the father's right was limited to reasonable castigation[6].

2. Power of Sale. The power to sell into real slavery, *trans Tiberim*, was obsolete long before the Empire, and the power to sell into civil bondage, except for formal sales in emancipation and adoption[7], and for noxal surrender for wrongs[8], was obsolete in the time of Gaius. In that age some parents did indeed sell children into slavery, but Paul denied the validity of such sale or even of pledge[9], and, later, the emperors repeatedly laid down prohibitions[10]. By the time of Constantine the case of new-born children was a permitted exception, and enactments regulating such sales and even sales of older children are frequent in later times[11]. There was in all cases a right of redemption, and, for new-born children, the rule still existed under Justinian[12].

3. Right to veto marriage and control divorce[13].

4. Right of action for recovery of a child from a detainer. There was a *vindicatio, adiecta causa*, and an *actio furti*, but no *condictio furtiva*, the right not being ownership[14]. There were also two interdicts, *de liberis exhibendis et ducendis*, against one who detained a *filius* against his will[15]. There was also a *praeiudicium* on the question whether he was a *filius*, as a preliminary to some other issue[16], and a *notio* or *cognitio praetoris*, perhaps where the *filius* himself raised the question and ordinary litigation was impossible[17].

1 Cuq, *Inst. Jurid.* 1. 154. 2 Coll. 4. 8. 3 C. 8. 51. 2. Justinian legislated on the matter, C. 8. 51. 3. 4 48. 8. 2. Hadrian had punished by deportation a father who had killed his son who had wronged him, 48. 9. 5. 5 C. 9. 17. 1. But see Bonfante, *Corso*, 1. 81. Meaning of "*parricidium*" much controverted. De Visscher, "*Paricidas esto*" (1927); Meylan, *L'étymologie du mot* "*parricide*" (1928); Lenel, *St. Bonfante*, 2. 1 *sqq.* 6 C. 9. 15. 1 = C. Th. 9. 13. 1. In the Empire there was no such right over the wife *in manu*. 7 *Post*, §§ XLIV, XLVII. 8 *Post*, § CCV. He might transfer the son to a Latin colony, G. 1. 131. 9 P. 5. 1. 1. A creditor taking such a pledge was deported. 10 E.g. C. 7. 16. 1; h. t. 37. 11 E.g. C. Th. 3. 3. 1. 12 C. 4. 43. 2. Exposition did not, in classical law, forfeit *potestas*: as to its effects and relation to the obligation of providing *alimenta*, Taubenschlag, *Röm. Prr. z. Z. Diocl.* 271. Later law, Buckland, *Slavery*, 402. 13 *Post*, §§ XLI *sqq.* 14 6. 1. 1. 2; G. 3. 199; D. 47. 2. 38. 1. 15 6. 1. 1. 2; 43. 30; C. 8. 8; *post*, § CCXLVIII. 16 6. 1. 1. 2; *post*, § CCXXII. 17 6. 1. 1. 2; Bonfante, *Corso*, 1. 88; citing 22. 3. 8.

5. Right to all acquisitions, either property rights or obligations, resulting from transactions by the *filiusfamilias*[1]. But the rule that all such acquisitions vested in the *paterfamilias* was greatly cut down in the Empire, the limitations having begun under Augustus[2].

6. Right to hand the child over instead of paying the penalty for a wrong by him, originally a right to ransom him from the consequences of his wrongdoing[3]. Obsolete for females long before the Empire, it was abolished as to males, by Justinian[4]. It probably never applied to wife *in manu*.

7. Power to appoint guardians (*tutores*) to young children, by will[5].

8. Power to appoint a *heres* to take the property if the child, surviving the father, died too young to make a will—pupillary substitution[6].

9. Wrongs to the son, or to property in his hands, were wrongs to the father[7]. In the Empire, when the son began to have separate proprietary interests, he had the same remedies in respect of these as a *paterfamilias*[8].

The restrictions on the father's power were accompanied by recognition of rights of the son against him[9]. As to the funds independent of the father the son seems to have been dealt with much as a *libertus* was with regard to the patron. And conversely, while the praetorian liabilities on his contracts were substantially the same as on those of a slave, they did not arise on dealings in connexion with those funds[10].

XXXIX. We have now to consider how *patria potestas* was acquired. *Anniculi probatio*, *erroris causa probatio*, and imperial decree accompanying gifts of *civitas* have already been considered[11]. There remain the more important cases of Birth *ex iustis nuptiis*[12], the normal case, Adoption, and, in later law, Legitimation.

Birth *ex iustis nuptiis*[13]. *Iustae nuptiae* meant valid marriage between two persons who had *conubium*, the capacity of Roman marriage[14]. If this was not present, but there was no such obstacle as prevented marriage altogether, it was indeed *nuptiae*, but *matrimonium non*

1 G. 2. 86; 3. 163. The right on transactions *inter vivos* vests in the *paterfamilias* at once. Thus if a *filius* takes a promise for payment after he is emancipated, the right nevertheless vests in the *pater*, 45. 3. 40. So too on a conditional promise, though the condition is not satisfied till after the emancipation, 45. 1. 78; 50. 17. 144. 1. Special rules affecting *dos*, *post*, § XL.
2 *Post*, § XCIX. It was usual to give a *de facto peculium* and to this were attributed legacies to the son, *dos* of his marriage, etc. Arangio Ruiz, *Ist.* 437. As to mutual claim to *alimenta* (D. 25. 3; C. 5. 25. 4) and extensions Albertario, *Diritto agli alimenti* (with, however, excessive allegations of interpolation); Bonfante, *Corso*, 1. 279 *sqq.*
3 *Post*, § CCV.
4 G. 4. 75 *sqq.*; Inst. 4. 8.
5 *Post*, § LI.
6 *Post*, § CV.
7 9. 2. 7, etc.
8 49. 17. 4. 1, *post*, § XCIX. As to his own capacity for litigation, *ante*, p. 102.
9 *Inter alia*, a right to *alimenta* in later classical law, D. 25. 3; C. 5. 25. 4. On the history of obligation to *alimenta*, Bonfante, *Corso*, 1. 279; Perozzi, *Ist.* 2. 167.
10 49. 17. 18. 5.
11 *Ante*, §§ XXXV, XXXVI.
12 Corbett, *Roman Law of Marriage*.
13 Exceptional cases, *ante*, pp. 69, n. 4, 95 *sq.*
14 Ulp. 5. 2; G. 1. 56, etc.

iustum, producing no specifically civil effects. There could be no *manus*; children were not in *potestas*[1]. They were related to each other and to their parents' relatives cognatically, not by the Roman tie of agnation[2]. This tie between two persons existed only if they traced connexion by civil descents, from a common male ancestor, through males, unbroken by *capitis minutio*; the connexion being sometimes artificial, e.g. created by *adoptio*[3]. Brothers and sisters by a civil marriage were agnates. The brother's child was an agnate of the sister, but her child was not, either of her or her brother or the paternal relatives. If a member passed out of the family by any step involving *capitis deminutio*[4], the tie was destroyed, though adoption would confer similar rights in the new family. *Cognatio* was any blood relationship, and agnates, even by adoption so long as the artificial tie existed, ranked as cognates also[5].

It must be noted that there is no question of choice between alternative modes of marriage; if the parties had *conubium* it was *iustae nuptiae* or no marriage at all. It was only where either (or both) had no *conubium* that *matrimonium non iustum* could occur[6]: the difference was not so much between the marriages as between the parties[7].

1 G. 1. 55, 65, 66. 2 Inst. 1. 15. 1. Those born out of wedlock are *volgo concepti* or *spurii* (fanciful derivations, "σποράδην," "sine patre," G. 1. 64) and have for most purposes no certain father (Ulp. 4. 2). (Those of a forbidden marriage, and, for classical law, those of concubines, are on the same footing, Ulp. 5. 7, *post*, § XLVI.) They are not related to the father. They do not excuse him from *tutelae* (27. 1. 2. 3; Vat. Fr. 194, where *iniusti* means born of *nuptiae non iustae*). They do not count for the *praemia patrum* (*post*, § CXI). But, where traceable, the relationship is reckoned for the purpose of prohibited degrees (23. 2. 14. 2), and the child, like a legitimate child, cannot initiate proceedings against the father (2. 4. 6). The child is a cognate of the mother (Inst. 3. 5. 4), takes her *status* at birth, and is her child for the purpose of succession both ways (P. 4. 10. 1; Inst. 3. 4. 3; D. 38. 17. 2. 1; *post*, § CXXXI), and counts towards the *ius liberorum* (*post*, § LX). He may not initiate proceedings against her (2. 4. 4. 3). In classical law no rights of such children arise if born in slavery (P. 4. 10. 2). Servile *cognatio*, *post*, § CXXXII. 3 Or, as it may be put, those who would sacrifice to the same set of ancestors, or who would be in the same *potestas* if the common ancestor were alive. 4 *Post*, § XLIX. 5 G. 1. 61; D. 38. 10. 10. 4. 6 A marriage between two *cives* of classes forbidden to intermarry was a nullity, not *nuptiae non iustae*. (*Contra*, Corbett, *Roman Law of Marriage*, 35 *sqq*., and earlier writers cited by him.) The expression *matrimonium iuris gentium* is unjustified. Corbett, *cit.*; Perozzi, *Ist.* 1. 99. 7 Marriage between persons who have not *conubium* becomes civil marriage if they acquire capacity of civil marriage while their marriage is still subsisting (G. 1. 95). A *deportatus* loses *civitas* and with it his capacity for civil marriage, but his marriage is not ended though it loses its civil character and effects for the future. *Dos* and *potestas* are destroyed (G. 1. 128; Ulp. 10. 3; Inst. 1. 12. 1; D. 24. 1. 13. 1; 24. 3. 56; 48. 20. 5. 1; C. 5. 16. 24. 2; C. 5. 17. 1). Arangio Ruiz, *Ist.* 411; *contra*, Bonfante, *Corso*, 1. 243; Desserteaux, *Cap. Dim.* 3. 56. One case goes further. Where two slaves "married" and one was allowed by the master to give to the other a fund as a *dos*, out of the *peculium*, this was no marriage, as slaves were incapable of any marriage. But the intent was clear, and when the *dominus* freed them both, *inter vivos*, not taking away the *peculium*, the union automatically became *iustae nuptiae*, and the fund a *dos* (23. 3. 39). As to two slaves "married," fideicommissary liberty given to them, and its completion wrongly delayed, see *ante*, p. 69, n. 4. Marriage is a question of fact, as possession is, which does not however mean that all the

The chief effects of civil marriage may be shortly stated. The children were *liberi iusti*[1], in the *potestas* of the *paterfamilias*, and agnates of his agnates. Apart from *manus*[2], rare in the early Empire and obsolete in the later, the wife did not enter the *familia*. The husband's home was hers, and they owed each other protection and respect[3]. Apart from *manus* she was not concerned with the cult of the *manes*[4]. The wife did not necessarily take her husband's name, though in the Empire she often did[5]. She shared the honorific titles of her husband[6]. Their properties remained distinct, and gifts between them were void[7].

Thus, apart from issue, the effects of marriage were few, in law, a result of the Roman conception of *liberum matrimonium*. It is discussed, e.g. by Gaius, not as a separate institution but as a step in the most important way of acquiring *patria potestas*. Whether parties to a union were married or not was important if there were issue, and thus full rules appear as to the essentials of a valid marriage. The possibility of issue was its main legal interest. Thus relief against error of *status* was given only if there was issue[8]—if there was not, no relief was necessary; the parties could end the relation at any time. The main titles on marriage say little about its effects[9]. The definition given by Modestinus[10]: "*nuptiae sunt coniunctio maris et feminae et consortium omnis vitae, divini et humani iuris communicatio,*" is, literally understood, so far from exact, that it is plain the legal aspect is not the one primarily in view[11]. Freedom from legal regulation is evidenced by many texts[12] and collateral rules[13].

rules of possession apply to it. It requires *animus maritalis* and the joint life and possibility of joint life involved in this. Thus, in classical law, it was ended by *captivitas* of a party (and not *ipso facto* restored by *postliminium*) and by long disappearance of a party without trace. Levy, *Gedächtnissschr. für Seckel*, 147 *sqq*.

1 G. 1. 55, 77; Vat. Fr. 168. 2 *Post*, § XLIII. 3 Inst. 1. 9. 1; D. 23. 2. 1; 24. 3. 14. 1; 47. 10. 2. No action involving *infamia* lay between them, 25. 2. 1, 2. Limits and meaning of this rule in classical law, Bonfante, *Corso*, 1. 208 and reff. 4 See Wissowa, *Religion und Cultus der Römer*, §§ 26, 27. 5 Marquardt, *Privatleben der Römer*, 18. 6 Vat. Fr. 104, D. 1. 9. 8. 7 *Post*, § XL. 8 *Ante*, § XXXV. 9 D. 23. 2; C. 5. 4. 10 23. 2. 1. 11 Survival from *manus* or Christian interpolation? Bonfante, *Corso*, 1. 193. 12 45. 1. 134; C. 8. 38. 2; C. 5. 4. 14. 13 Marriage is not primarily a legal relation. The question whether two persons are married is often material in law, as is the question whether a person is over 14. But if the *vir* did not support his wife, or she failed in *reverentia*, it is not easy to see in the time of Gaius any direct remedy. Divorce is not the remedy: this was free whether there was misconduct or not, indeed annulment alone is no remedy for breach of contract. Forfeitures of *dos* (*post*, p. 109) formed an indirect check, and, if the wife was *alieni iuris*, the authority of the *paterfamilias* was a real resource. (The *a. de moribus*, *post*, p. 109, seems the only remedy and covers only a narrow field.) The need of appeal to these shews how far we are from contract. As conveyance, it is difficult to see what civil rights against third parties either has lost or gained, apart from *manus*. There was no civil remedy for adultery. There was no *actio utilis e lege Aquilia* to the *vir* for bodily harm to the wife. There was an *actio*

XL. The independence of property[1], consistent as it was with the notion of *liberum matrimonium*, was inconvenient in relation to the maintenance of the household. This was lessened by the institution of *dos*, a contribution by or on behalf of the wife on which the wife's maintenance had a claim, in the sense, at least, that maintenance of her and her household out of it was not *donatio*. In Justinian's time there are signs that this was coming to be regarded as its only purpose[2]. *Dos*, though very ancient, and a usual accompaniment of marriages with *manus*[3], was much increased in importance when *manus* decayed. It was technically the husband's property but his dealings with it were restricted by law, and it had usually to be accounted for at the end of the marriage. Hence we are told that "*quamvis in bonis mariti dos sit, tamen mulieris est*[4]."

Dos was not legally necessary, but, in the absence of legal requirements of form, the existence of *dos* was the best evidence that marriage was intended and not mere concubinage. Thus fathers at times insisted on giving a *dos*, while on the other hand there was legislation under which fathers were required to give *dos*[5]. But *dos* might come from various sources. If provided by the father or other paternal ancestor, or by an *extraneus* by way of gift to the father, it was called *profectitia*[6], if by the wife herself, if *sui iuris*, or from any other source, it was *adventitia*[7], and if, when given by an *extraneus* (and perhaps in other cases), there was an express agreement for its return, it was *receptitia*, and went back wholly to the donor at the end of the marriage[8].

The provision of *dos*, which might be after marriage[9], was not

iniuriarum for insult to her, but that is because it was an insult to the husband. The only serious exception to this absence of remedy is a rule, apparently of later law, that if her father or any other person detained her, the *vir* had an interdict for her production, so that she could return if she wished (43. 30. 2; C. 5. 4. 11; C. 5. 17. 5. 1). Remote analogies can be made out, but marriage has few useful affinities with the *ius rerum*.

1 On wife's independent property (*parapherna*), often managed by the *vir*, juristic texts say little. Castelli, *Parapherna*; Cornil, *Dr.R.* 133, 587; Brugi, *Ist.* 482. On the obscure *stipulatio tribunicia* affecting it, Kuebler, *Festschr. für O. Hirschfeld*, 52. 2 Koschaker, *St. Bonfante*, 4. 3 *sqq.* 3 G. 3. 83; Cicero, *Top.* 4. 23. What a woman *sui iuris* brought in is *dos*. 4 23. 3. 75, modes of creation of *dos*, *post*, § CLX. 5 In 23. 2. 19 such a rule is attributed to the *l. Iulia*, and to Severus and Caracalla. Other texts are supposed to refer to such a duty bearing not only on *patresfamilias* but on other relatives and even on the woman herself (12. 6. 33. 2; 37. 6. 6; C. 1. 5. 12. 20; C. 1. 5. 19. 3; C. 5. 12. 14). Some of these do not express a legal duty and there has certainly been interpolation. C. 1. 5. 19. 3 is a very special case. Probably, apart from this there was no general obligation till Justinian and then only on *patres* (perhaps to *emancipatae*). See, for this view, Landucci, *St. Bonfante*, 4. 601. See also Castelli, *Obbligo di dotare*; Bonfante, *Corso*, 1. 298. Moriaud, *Mél. Girard*, 2. 296, thinks the obligation on *patres* classical. It is an obligation, not an essential of marriage. P. 2. 21 b. 1; C. 5. 17. 11. pr.; *Nov.* 22. 3; *Nov.* 74. 4. 6 Ulp. 6. 3; D. 23. 3. 5. pr. Justinian seems to confine it to the *pater* with *potestas*, C. 5. 12. 31. 3; 5. 13. 1. 13. Bonfante, *Corso*, 1. 305. 7 Ulp. 6. 3. Name probably late, Albertario, '*Adventicius*.' 8 Ulp. 6. 5. 9 P. 2. 21 b. 1.

necessarily an immediate transfer of property; it might be a promise to pay or a transfer of a claim against a third party. The husband administered the *dos*, and had the right to use the fruits[1]. As owner, he could alienate, except that the *l. Iulia de adulteriis* prevented him from alienating Italic land in the *dos* without the wife's consent, or from hypothecating it even with her consent, the latter rule being, perhaps, a juristic extension[2]. Justinian extended the rule to all land, and made the wife's consent ineffective in both cases[3]. The prohibition extended to the releasing of any praedial servitudes attaching to a *fundus dotalis*[4]. But valid transactions might be a breach of his obligations. He was bound to administer the *dos* like a *bonus paterfamilias*[5] and careless disposals of property must be paid for, like other negligent damage, when the *dos* came to be returned. Thus he could free a dotal slave, but if the wife did not consent he might have to account for his value[6].

These rules might be varied by agreement—*pacta dotalia*, which were frequent, and usually dealt with return, but sometimes with duties during the marriage: e.g. so as to vary the rules as to the incidence of risks[7]. They were altered if the *dos* was *aestimata*, i.e. taken by the husband at a valuation. Here there was no question of liability for negligence; the husband must account for the value at the end of the marriage, no matter what happened in the meantime. It was like a sale, and the risks were entirely on him, though in ordinary cases they would be on the wife[8]. *Aestimatio* released the *vir* from the restrictions of the *l. Iulia*, unless the terms were that the wife might choose between the *dos* and its agreed value[9]. But the *aestimatio* would not affect later independent additions to the *dos*[10].

The ultimate destiny of the *dos*[11] depended on the way in which the marriage ended, and on the nature of the *dos*. In early law *dos* was

1 P. 2. 22. 1. 2 G. 2. 63; P. 2. 21 b. 2; Inst. 2. 8. pr.; D. 23. 5. 4; C. 5. 13. 1. 15. 3 Inst. 2. 8. pr. The alienation is not void *ab initio*: it is set aside if at end of marriage the wife has a claim to the *dos* (23. 5. 3. 1) so that the wife can ratify it (24. 3. 50). Effect of Justinian's reform (including *Nov.* 61), Noailles, *L'inaliénabilité du fonds dotal* and review, Pringsheim, *Z.S.S.* 1924, 551. 4 23. 5. 6, or creating servitudes on it, 23. 5. 5. It did not prevent such a transfer of property *per universitatem* as would result from adrogation of the *vir* (23. 5. 1. 1), in which case it retained its inalienability, or bar any person who acquired rights by the operation of rules of law, e.g. *damnum infectum* (23. 5. 1. pr.; *post*, § CCXLV). 5 Perhaps in later law needing to shew only the care he did in his own affairs, *post*, § CXC. 6 24. 3. 24. 4, 62–64. On relation to *dos* of acquisitions by dotal slaves, Berger, *Streifzüge d. Röm. Sklavenrecht, Philologus*, 1914. 96. 7 23. 4. 6; in classical law formal *stipulatio* needed, P. 2. 22. 2; but, in later law, *actio pr. verbis* on pact, C. 5. 13. 1. 13; 5. 14. 7. 8 20. 4. 9. 3; C. 5. 12. 5, 10. See, on *aestimatio* and kindred agreements, Corbett, *cit.*, 172 *sqq.* 9 23. 5. 11. 10 *Dos* might be made or increased after marriage, P. 2. 21 b. 1. 11 On exceptional circumstances in which *dos* could be recovered, *durante matrimonio* (23. 3. 73. 1; 24. 3. 20), Perozzi, *Ist.* 1. 390.

simply the husband's property: there was no obligation to restore it, and classical law differed from that of Justinian[1]. *Dos receptitia* may be neglected, for this went to the donor in any event. If the marriage ended by the husband's death, the wife took the *dos*. So too if by divorce[2], except that if this was caused by the wife or her father, without justification, the husband kept one-sixth for each child up to three. There were other deductions in respect of expenses connected with *dos*, of *res donatae*, of *res amotae* and of misconduct, *mores*, while, if the husband had misbehaved, the periods within which the *dos* must be returned were shortened. These deductions, enforceable in the action for recovery of *dos*, *actio rei uxoriae*[3], were regulated and defined by the *l. Iulia de maritandis ordinibus*, but they were certainly recognised before[4]. There were alternative remedies in some cases, *actio rerum amotarum*[5] where property had been made away with, *actio de moribus*[6], in case of the wife's misconduct, and, it seems, a *condictio* for *res donatae* and *impensae necessariae*[7]. Justinian suppressed the *retentiones*, in A.D. 530[8], leaving the alternative remedies, but a little later he abolished the *actio de moribus*[9]. On the other hand he gave an action for recovery of *impensae utiles*[10]. There were provisions where the wife was *alieni iuris* to secure that the father should not receive the *dos* without her consent, the fund being in a sense their common property[11]. Where the marriage ended by the

1 Ulp. 6. 6 *sqq.* 2 Her *heres* could claim if she died after the *vir* was *in mora.* 3 Ulp. 6. 6. The remedy for recovery was modified by Justinian, *post*, p. 110 and § CCXXIX. 4 See, e.g., Val. Max. 8. 2. 3; Aul. Gell. 10. 23. 4. 5 *Post*, § CLXXXVII. 6 Of this action little is known. Not cumulative with criminal proceedings for adultery (C. Th. 9. 20. 1) or confined to adultery (C. Th. 3. 13. 1, *interpret.*). Not available to or against *heres* (C. Th. 3. 13. 1; D. 24. 3. 15. 1). Not a *praeiudicium*, for security might be required (G. 4. 102). It is praetorian, commonly held to have been limited to the *dos*, and it is most commonly stated in connexion with *dos*. But this involves the same limit for *actio rerum amotarum*, which also corresponds to a *retentio*, and Justinian in the abolishing enactment is dealing with *feminae indotatae* (C. 5. 17. 11). There could be no pact against liability under this head (23. 4. 5. pr.). The passage is struck out by the corrector of the Florentine MS. It was really obsolete, but the abolishing enactment is dated only a few weeks before that confirming the Digest. Literary texts on this action are (see also n. 4): Plut. *Marius*, 38; Pliny, *H.N.* 14. 13 (90). Esmein, *Mél.* 78 *sqq.*; 150 *sqq.*; *N.R.H.* 1893, 145 *sqq.*; Czyhlarz, *Dotalrecht*, 337 *sqq.*; De Francisci, *Azioni penali*, 52. 7 On the rule: *impensae necessariae dotem ipso iure minuunt*, Schulz, *Z.S.S.* 1913, 57, but see reply by Riccobono, *Dal dir. Rom. al. dir. mod.* 370. See also, Bonfante, *Corso*, 1. 364. In classical law the maxim is literally true only so far as *dos* consists of money. Under Justinian *res dotales* cease, proportionately, to be dotal. 8 C. 5. 13. 1. 5. This abolished claims in respect of children, and, on the abolition, three years after, of the *actio de moribus*, claims on *mores*. 9 C. 5. 17. 11. 2 b. 10 Schulz, *cit.* 71. Right of retention for these in classical law, which Paul limits to cases where the wife assented to the expenditure. Both rules are in the Digest (25. 1. 8; 23. 5. 18. pr.). See Riccobono, *Bull.* 1896, 230 *sqq.*; Bonfante, *Corso*, 1. 365 *sqq.* 11 24. 3. 2. 1. This and following *leges* bring out the exceptional character of the claim to restoration of *dos*. Apart from express promise, the wife's right to recover was not lost by *capitis deminutio*. If, when

wife's death *dos profectitia* went to the donor if alive[1], if he was not, the husband took it in classical law, as he did *dos adventitia*, on the wife's death[2]. Where *dos profectitia* returned to the donor the husband kept a fifth for each child[3]. Under Justinian the wife's heirs replaced the husband, who thus, apart from agreement, took nothing in any *dos* of his deceased wife[4].

As the *dos* was the husband's it did not revert *ipso facto* on the end of the marriage; it must be restored. An express agreement for return (*dos receptitia*) gave an action *ex stipulatu*; in other cases there was an *actio rei uxoriae*. The agreement could be enforced at once, but in the other case there were delays. Apart from the reduction of time already mentioned where the husband was in fault, he must, in classical law, restore *res fungibiles* (money and the like) in three annual instalments, other things at once[5]. Security could be taken for the return, and the limitation in amount under the *l. Cornelia* did not apply here[6]. This was later forbidden, apparently on the poor ground that one who could be trusted with a daughter could be trusted with money. Justinian maintained the prohibition[7] and remodelled the system. The *actio rei uxoriae* was abolished and an implied agreement substituted[8], so that the *actio ex stipulatu*, somewhat modified in its results[9], was the general remedy. Further, land had to be returned at once and moveables within a year[10].

In insolvency the wife claiming *dos* had priority over other unsecured creditors, though not over those who had taken a valid security[11]. Justinian went further, and gave her a tacit hypothec over *dos* still in the hands of the husband or his successors[12], a privileged hypothec, taking priority over others of earlier date[13]. But he also gave her an alternative real action, *vindicatio* of the property, a remedy which, as it implies that it is her own, is inconsistent with hypothec[14], and also constitutes an *ipso iure* reversion of the ownership, contrary to classical principle[15].

the marriage ended, she was *alieni iuris*, the claim did not vest simply in the *paterfamilias*, as did other rights acquired through a *filiafamilias*. It passed to her if she became *sui iuris*, and if she was still in the family, neither she nor the *pater* could properly receive or recover it without consent of the other. If this was in fact done, the other still had the action for recovery, which would however be barred if the situation was subsequently regularised. See 4. 5. 9; 24. 3. 2–4, 22. 1–4, 42; C. 5. 18. 2, etc. But if the father, having duly received it, suffers forfeiture, the *dos* is included, 48. 20. 10.

1 Justinian may have confined the right to a father with *potestas* at time of action. Bonfante, *Corso*, 1. 352. 2 Ulp. 6. 5. 3 Ulp. 6. 4. 4 C. 5. 13. 1. 6, 13. A change of principle; the rules shew that return of *dos* could be claimed only by the giver, not by successors. 5 Ulp. 6. 8. 6 G. 3. 125, *post*, § CLVI. 7 C. Th. 3. 15. 1; C. 5. 20. 8 C. 5. 13. 1; Inst. 4. 6. 29. 9 *Post*, § CCXXIX. 10 C. 5. 13. 1. 7 a. 11 C. 8. 17. 12. 1. 12 C. 5. 13. 1. 1 b. 13 Apparently extended, two years later, to all property of the *vir*, C. 8. 17. 12. 5, 6. 14 He gives a laborious explanation of the anomaly which only carries on the involved conception of the ownership which had been current in classical law. C. 5. 12. 30. 1. 15 *Post*, § LXVIII. If it was land

In the Byzantine Empire a new institution appeared called *Donatio ante nuptias*, a converse of *dos*, given by the husband to the wife, whose property it was, but administered by the husband. It originated in ordinary gifts by the man to his betrothed, much influenced by oriental notions[1], but assumed a special character. Its history and the conceptions underlying it are controverted. There was legislation in the West differentiating such gifts from ordinary *donationes*, which became absolutely the property of the donee[2], but as Mitteis shews, this did not create a real new institution; that appeared in the East. Theodosius provided that *donatio ante nuptias* should go to the survivor and on divorce to the divorced party[3]. Leo enacted that on causeless divorce the divorcer lost all right in *dos* or *donatio*, and in case of death the husband surviving took all the *donatio* and half the *dos*, the wife surviving, all the *dos* and half the *donatio*, a rule which makes *donatio* a counterpart of *dos*[4]. He also provided that if there were agreements giving either a greater share, they must apply equally in proportion on both sides[5]. Justin allowed increase of such gifts after marriage if *dos* had been increased, and even creation where there had been none, if there had been such increase in *dos*[6]. Justinian allowed creation of it in any case after marriage and therefore changed the name to *donatio propter nuptias*[7]. He applied most of the rules of *dos* to it (e.g. as to inalienability) with the parts interchanged, and laid it down, following in part earlier legislation, that it was to be of the same amount as the *dos*, and that special agreements to vary the legal rules as to its ultimate disposal must apply to both[8].

These funds, *dos* and *donatio propter nuptias*, were the chief exceptions to a rule that gifts between husband and wife were void[9]. It was a customary rule based by jurists on the considerations which led to a somewhat analogous rule in English law, "lest they be kissed or cursed out of their money[10]." Other exceptions were gifts not to operate till the marriage ended[11], reasonable gifts on festal occasions[12], and gifts not

alienated in violation of the *l. Iulia*, the alienation being void, the action would be available there too. Before Justinian she had in such case a *vindicatio* but only on cession of the action (31. 77. 5). Girard, *Man.* 1020.

1 Mitteis, *Reichsr. und Volksr.* 256 *sqq.* and Collinet, *Ét. Hist.* 1. 145 *sqq.* 2 C. Th. 8. 12. 1; C. 5. 3. 1–5, 15, 16. 3 Bruns-Sachau, *Syr.-Röm. Rb.* 265. 4 *Ibid.* 5 C. 5. 14. 9. 6 C. 5. 3. 19. 7 C. 5. 3. 20. 8 Further legislation in *Nov.* 97. On the whole matter, Cornil, *Dr.R.* 594 *sqq.*; Bonfante, *Corso*, 1. 379; Scherillo, *St. sulla Don. nuziale.* 9 Dumont, *Donations entre Époux*; Thayer, *On gifts between husband and wife*; Corbett, *R. L. of Marriage*, 114 *sqq.* Masked gifts, *sub specie venditionis*, Partsch, *Z.S.S.* 1921, 264. 10 24. 1. 1, 2, 3. pr. Origin disputed. Later than the *l. Cincia* (Vat. Fr. 302). Commonly held customary but also held to be a provision of the *l. Iulia de mar. ordin.*; Alibrandi, *Opere*, 1. 593; Bonfante, *Corso*, 1. 212; Siber, *R.R.* 65; *contra*, Dumont, *cit.* 14. 11 24. 1. 9. 2, 10, etc.; P. 2. 23. 6. 12 Ulp. 7. 1; D. 24. 1. 31. 8, 40, 42.

involving profit to the receiver, e.g. gift of a slave *ut manumittatur*[1]. Forbidden gifts were simply void[2], but might be confirmed by will[3], and in the third century it was provided that they were good if the donor died without having changed his mind[4].

XLI. The requirements of a valid Roman marriage are:[5]

Form. The only form required was the placing of the wife in the husband's control[6], analogous to *traditio*, and, like it, effected in many ways. The normal method was for the husband to receive the wife at his domicile, but it might be in his absence with his consent[7]. There might indeed be no change of domicile; he might go to live at her house or they might have been occupying the same house. An elaborate ceremonial was however usual[8], in which the nature of marriage as "*consortium omnis vitae, divini et humani iuris communicatio*" was expressed. There were a bridal procession, *epithalamia*, feasting, and when the bride reached the house she was lifted over the threshold and offered fire and water, the symbols of life, she uttering the declaration "*ubi tu Gaius ego Gaia*[9]." All this, like the presence of *dos*, shewed that marriage and not concubinage was intended. Just as *traditio* did not transfer ownership unless there was evidence of intent that it should, so here there was no marriage without evidence of intent to marry, *affectio maritalis*[10]. This was presumed, *prima facie*, between parties of equal

1 24. 1. 5. 16; P. 2. 23. 2. 2 24. 1. 3. 10, 36. Dumont, *cit.*, 69; *contra*, De Medio, *Riv. It. p. l. Sci. Giur.* 1902, 378. 3 32. 33. 1. 4 24. 1. 32. pr.–4. Did this cover all gifts (e.g. promises) or only gifts at least in part executed? Texts conflict (24. 1. 23, 33). The better view seems to be that the wider view prevailed, Thayer, *cit.*, *ad ll. Contra*, Bonfante, *Corso*, 1. 22, who holds it due to Justinian. 5 Marriage was usually preceded by betrothal, *Sponsalia* (D. 23. 1), which might be made in absence or by ratification without special form (originally by *sponsio*), but needed the same consents as marriage and so could not be made by *tutor* (*post*, § LVI). As capacity to contract was needed the parties must not be insane or *infantes* (23. 1. 2, 8). Those who could not intermarry could not be betrothed, but, possibly, in classical law a betrothal in view of expiry of a temporary obstruction was allowed (23. 1. 15, 16 interp.). It could be renounced by notice by the parties or the *paterfamilias*, and if the intended husband failed to complete the marriage within two years, without good reason, the other party was discharged (23. 1. 17; C. 5. 1. 1, 2). It gave in classical and later law, no action for breach of promise, but it was important to have rules as to what were valid *sponsalia*. Relationship by marriage might be a bar to marriage and this to some extent applied to those only betrothed. And the bar to alienation of dotal land applied while the parties were yet only betrothed (23. 5. 4). To be betrothed to two at once involved infamy (3. 2. 1). In late law it was usual to give *arra* on one side or both, and there was legislation involving forfeiture, sometimes of a multiple, for causeless renunciation (C. 5. 1. 5; C. 5. 3. 15; C. Th. 3. 6. 1). History of this legislation, Riccobono, *Arra sponsalicia, secondo la C.J.* 5. 1. 5. Cornil, *Dr.R.* 592; Volterra, *Riv. It. p. l. Sc. Giur.* 1927, 581; 4. 3. 6 23. 2. 5; C. 5. 4. 9. 7 23. 2. 5; P. 2. 19. 8. Not in her absence, *ib.* It is control which is needed, not actual *deductio in domum*, though this would be the usual evidence, Perozzi, *Ist.* 1. 317. 8 Marquardt, *Privatleben*, 42 *sqq.* 9 Probably appropriate to *manus.* 10 24. 1. 3. 1, 32. 13.

rank, and, under Justinian, in all cases[1], though circumstances might rebut the presumption, apart from proof, e.g. if the woman was of notoriously bad character[2].

Consent. The consent of the parties was needed, though for those in *potestas* probably not in early law. But if a man freed an *ancilla*, specially for the purpose of marriage (not otherwise), and the manumission was in all respects voluntary, she could not refuse[3]. The parties must be capable of consent, and thus a lunatic could not marry[4]. Neither fraud nor error, however fundamental, vitiated the marriage, in view of the ease of divorce[5].

Other consents might be needed. Since the issue of the marriage would be in *potestas* of the father's *paterfamilias*, adding to his family, his consent was needed[6], as also was that of the father if the *vir* was a grandson whose father was in the same *potestas*[7]. The consent of the wife's *paterfamilias* was needed[8], not for that reason, but under his *patria potestas*, so that the consent of any intervening link was not required. The rule was subject to many limitations. The *l. Iulia* is said to have forbidden causeless refusal[9]; the basis of a rule of Severus and Caracalla, requiring the father to take steps to secure a suitable marriage for his child, on appeal to the chief magistrate[10]. Though in terms this deals with general prohibition, or refusal to seek a marriage, it seems to imply that he must assent to a suitable marriage if he had no other to propose. The consent could sometimes be dispensed with. The child of a *captivus* could marry[11], but Justinian limited this to the case in which the captivity had lasted three years[12]. If the father was absent and it was not known whether he was alive or, if alive, where he was, the child could marry; here too Justinian required a delay of three years[13]. Where the father was insane there were disputes of which Justinian gives an account[14]. There was no difficulty for daughters; the principle that here non-prohibition sufficed gives a sophistical justification of a rational rule. But for sons the leave of the Emperor was needed till M. Aurelius allowed marriage generally to children of *mente capti*[15]. Whether this

1 23. 2. 24; 39. 5. 31. pr. 2 C. 5. 4. 23. 7; D. 23. 2. 24. 3 23. 2. 29. 4 P. 2. 19. 7; D. 23. 2. 16. 2. No words or ceremonial being needed, deaf, dumb or blind folk could marry. 5 *Erroris causae probatio*, *ante*, p. 95. 6 Inst. 1. 10. pr.; P. 2. 19. 2; D. 23. 2. 2; C. 5. 4. 12. 7 23. 2. 9, 16. 1. 8 23. 2. 16. It was enough that he did not forbid. C. 5. 4. 25; D. 23. 1. 7. 1. The same may be true in the other case, but C. 5. 4. 5 does not quite say so. 9 23. 2. 19. Text corrupt, probably interp. Castelli, *Obbligo di dotare*, 7 *sqq.*; Moriaud, *Mél. Girard*, 2. 291, who thinks the *l.* applied only to females, and that Just. made it general by altering *filias vel neptes* into *liberos*. 10 23. 2. 19. 11 Classical disputes, Ratti, *Bull.* 1927, 125. 12 23. 2. 9. 1, 11; 49. 15. 12. 3. 13 23. 2. 11. The requirement attributed to Julian that the marriage must be such as the *pater* would have approved is no doubt due to Justinian. 14 Inst. 1. 10. pr. 15 C. 5. 4. 25.

covered *furiosi*, capable of lucid intervals, was doubted, till Justinian enacted that it should, and provided machinery enabling the *curator* and relatives, with approval of the magistrates, to arrange for *dos* and *donatio*[1].

Where consent was needed and given only after cohabitation began, this was not ratification; marriage dated only from the consent[2].

Age. The male must be 14, the female 12[3], the normal age at which the necessary physical faculties are developed. Thus one who could not have them, e.g. a *castratus*, could not marry[4], and, in classical law, those whose development was retarded could not marry till it was complete[5]. Those who cohabited before attaining the necessary age were not married till they reached it, still living together as man and wife[6].

Conubium. Capacity of civil marriage[7]. A modern terminology distinguishes absolute and relative *conubium*. Absolute *conubium* is capacity to contract civil marriage. This was possessed in general only by *cives* and those *Latini* and *peregrini* to whom, as a community, or personally, it had been granted[8]. *Veterani* who received *civitas* were sometimes (not always) allowed by their diploma of *civitas* to contract civil marriage with any woman they first chose after their discharge[9], so that they could marry in their own tribe without loss of rights, and give the woman chosen a limited *conubium*. But, unless it was expressly so provided, this did not give her *civitas*. The children would be *cives* and in *potestas* as issue of civil marriage whose father was a *civis*[10].

Relative *Conubium*. Those capable of civil marriage might not be capable of intermarriage. The restrictions were numerous and rested on various principles.

(*a*) Rank. In early law freeborn and freed might not intermarry[11], but in the Empire the prohibition to marry freed persons applied only to

1 C. 5. 4. 25. 2 1. 5. 11; Vat. Fr. 102. Other special cases. *Liberta* who had been married to patron could never marry another person without his leave (23. 2. 45, 51; C. 5. 5. 1). *Tutor* and relatives of a girl *sui iuris* had some control over her marriage, and in A.D. 199 it was provided that if they could not agree on a choice, it should go to the *praeses* (C. 5. 4. 1). Precise rules laid down in 408 as to consent of relatives in this case (C. 5. 4. 20). In 371 marriage of widow *sui iuris* was made subject to consent of father (h. t. 18). Non-prohibition sufficed in later law, Bonfante, *Scr. Giur.* 3. 153. On the relation between *consentire* and *non prohibere*, *velle* and *non nolle*, *velle* and *pati*, etc., Donatuti, *St. Bonfante*, 4. 460. 3 Inst. 1. 10. pr.; C. 5. 4. 24. 4 23. 3. 39. 1; 40. 2. 14. 1. 5 Arg. G. 1. 196; Ulp. 11. 28. School dispute, Proculians decided by age, Sabinians by maturity. 6 23. 2. 4. 7 G. 1. 58 *sqq.* 8 Ulp. 5. 4. *Ante*, §§ XXXIV *sqq.* 9 Girard, *Textes*, 125 *sqq.*; Bruns, 1. 274 *sqq.* 10 There were of course *cives* who could not marry, *castrati*, *mente capti*, divorced women accused of adultery, etc. (P. 2. 19. 7; D. 23. 2. 26), soldiers on service, Dio Cass. 60. 24. Meyer, *Das Konkubinat*, 100 *sqq.* 11 Perozzi, *Ist.* 1. 340. Till the *l. Canuleia*, about 444 B.C., patrician and plebeian could not intermarry, Livy, 4. 6.

those of senatorial rank. The *l. Papia* forbade those of this rank to marry actors, actresses and some others without the Emperor's leave[1], and the Christian Emperors legislated further on the matter[2]. Justin, to allow his nephew Justinian to marry Theodora, allowed marriage with retired actresses[3], and Justinian abolished the rule altogether[4].

(*b*) Moral, religious and political considerations. There might be no marriage between adulteress and paramour[5], or between Christian and Jew[6]. A high provincial magistrate or his son might not marry a woman of the province unless betrothed before he held the office[7]. For obvious reasons a *tutor* or *curator* might not marry one who was or had been his ward. The reason for the rule (of the second century) accounts for exceptions. It did not apply if they were betrothed before the office began, or by her father, or she was 26, or the Emperor's leave was obtained[8]. The rule extended to sons and grandsons, even adoptive, provided here that the tie still existed, and whether legitimate or illegitimate, and seems to have been extended in later law to *liberti* and *extranei heredes*[9].

In all these cases the marriage was void, not merely at civil law; it was no marriage at all[10]. In some of the cases, e.g. *tutores* and Jews, it was punishable[11]. In some, e.g. provincial magistrates, the marriage was validated for the future if when the prohibition ceased to apply the parties were still living together[12].

(*c*) Relationship and connexion by marriage.

1. Blood relationship. The rule in the Empire is simple. Ascendant and descendant could not intermarry[13]. Other relatives could not, whether of the whole or half blood, if either was only one degree from the common ancestor[14]. Uncle and niece, great-uncle and great-niece could not intermarry, but cousins could[15]. The rule applied whether the relation was civil or not, and though one or both had been born in slavery[16]. Claudius, desiring to marry his niece Agrippina, allowed marriage with a brother's daughter, though not with a sister's. The sons

1 Ulp. 13. 16. 2; D. 23. 2. 23, 31, 44. pr.; other similar restrictions, Costa, *Storia*, 46. 2 C. 5. 5. 7; C. 5. 27. 1. 3 C. 5. 4. 23 4 *Nov.* 117. 6. 5 48. 5. 41. pr. 6 C. 1. 9. 6. 7 23. 2. 57, 63. Not his daughter, 23. 2. 38. 2. To prevent abuse of power, and relations which would weaken his devotion to Rome of which he was the representative. 8 23. 2. 36, 59, 60, 66. 9 23. 2. 59, 60. 6, 64, 66. 1; C. 5. 6. 4. Not to daughter marrying *pupillus*, 23. 2. 64. 2. 10 The prohibitions of *l. Iulia* and *l. Papia*, at first perhaps mere prohibitions, were interpreted by *scc.* as nullifying, 23. 1. 16; 23. 2. 16. pr. Corbett, *R. L. of Marriage*, 36 *sqq.* No text states any right as arising from a marriage so forbidden. 11 *Tutor*, 23. 2. 64, 66. pr.; C. 5. 6. 7 (infamy as well); Jew, C. 1. 9. 6. 12 23. 2. 65. 1; C. 5. 4. 6. 13 G. 1. 59; Ulp. 5. 6; Inst. 1. 10. 1. 14 G. 1. 60, 61; Coll. 6. 3. 1; Inst. 1. 10. 2. 15 Ulp. 5. 6. 16 *Ante*, p. 64. Justinian says, too widely (Inst. 1. 10. 3), that one who could not marry a woman could not marry her daughter. This would bar relatives however remote.

of Constantine declared such marriage incestuous and restored the old rule[1].

2. Adoptive relationship. As between ascendant and descendant the rule was the same[2]. Between collaterals the bar ceased if the adoptive tie ceased. Thus, while a man might not marry his adoptive daughter or sister, the adoptive father was still barred even though she passed out of the family, while the brother could then marry her, and so also if it was he who was emancipated[3]. The tie being purely artificial, the bar ceased when that ceased, and the adoptive tie and resulting bar applied only to the person adopted. Thus one could marry his adoptive sister's daughter, there being no tie of any kind, and, for the same reason, his adoptive father's half-sister by the same mother[4]. But so long as he was in the family he could not marry his adoptive father's aunt on the mother's side, a rule which, as there is no blood or agnatic tie, seems to jar with the others[5]. Justinian changed the rules of adoption so that an *adoptatus* usually stayed in the old agnatic group[6], but these prohibitions were not modified.

3. Relationship by marriage. *Affinitas.* Marriage was forbidden in classical law between a party to a marriage and an ascendant or descendant of the other, e.g. mother-in-law, step-mother, daughter-in-law, step-daughter and remoter degrees[7]. In the later Empire this was extended to brothers and sisters-in-law[8], but there was no bar to marriage with step-brother or sister. The bar extended, however, to some who cannot be called relatives by marriage. It was forbidden to marry one betrothed to a parent or child[9], though this did not extend to brother and sister. There might be no marriage with a child of a divorced wife by a later husband[10].

In these cases of relationship, of all three types, the marriage was not only void; it was incestuous and penalised. In particular, any *dos* given was forfeited to the State[11].

XLII. Death or slavery of either party ended marriage[12].

Divorce[13] ended marriage, and in the relaxed morality of the Empire this became common[14]. In the Republic and in earlier classical law the

1 Tac. *Ann.* 12. 6; Ulp. 5. 6; G. 1. 62; Inst. 1. 10. 3; C. Th. 3. 12. 1. For the temporary revival of the Republican rule forbidding marriage between first cousins, see C. 5. 4. 19; C. 5. 8. 1. In early Rome prohibition much wider. Exceptional *privilegium,* 23. 2. 57 a.
2 G. 1. 59; Coll. 6. 3. 2; Inst. 1. 10. 1.
3 G. 1. 60, 61; Coll. 6. 3. 2; Inst. 1. 10. 2.
4 23. 2. 12. 4.
5 23. 2. 55.
6 *Post,* § XLIV.
7 G. 1. 63; Coll. 6. 3. 3; Inst. 1. 10. 6.
8 C. Th. 3. 12. 2; C. 5. 5. 5, 6.
9 23. 2. 12. 1, 2.
10 23. 2. 12. 3. If my divorced wife married and I afterwards adrogated her husband, the marriage remained good. 23. 2. 12. pr. In h. t. 67. 3, however, where T. married my former ward and I afterwards adopted him Tryphoninus says the marriage is annulled. Signs of dispute.
11 Ulp. 5. 7; C. 5. 5. 4, 6. Remarriage of widows, *post,* p. 118.
12 Effect of captivity, *ante,* p. 67; of *deportatio, ante,* p. 105.
13 Cornil, *Dr.R.* 601.
14 The *Laudatio Turiae* of the time of Aug. records as rare the fact of a long marriage not interrupted by divorce. Girard, *Textes,* 817.

paterfamilias had power to end by divorce the marriage of his child. A text of Paul which says that Pius forbade the separation of a *bene concordans matrimonium* by the father[1] probably refers to divorce (though it may merely mean that, though the divorce was valid, he could not compel actual separation[2]). M. Aurelius confirmed it in the fuller sense. The power to divorce a son or daughter for *magna causa* survived to Justinian[3].

Divorce by the parties themselves is more important. The conception of *liberum matrimonium*, predominant in the Empire, involved the right to end a marriage at any time by agreement[4], but the facility went much further. It was open to either party to end the marriage by *repudium*, involving a notification before seven witnesses[5], but a *liberta* married to her patron, though she could divorce him, did not thereby acquire the liberty which ordinarily results from divorce. She could not marry another or reclaim her *dos*. The marriage was, apparently, ended[6], and presumably a child born after the period of gestation would not be born *ex iustis nuptiis*. Absolute freedom remained the law, till Justinian forbade divorce by mutual consent except for certain religious objects, a rule immediately repealed by his successor[7]. But divorce, though free, might involve penalties. In the Republic a causeless divorce would involve a *nota censoria*, and we have seen that it also involved loss in respect of *dos*[8]. When the Empire became Christian there was much legislation on the matter. Constantine enacted that for *repudium* apart from certain specified causes, over and above the penalties in matter of *dos*, the woman might be deported and the man might not marry again; if he did, the divorced wife might seize the second wife's *dos*[9]. Ninety years later the extreme penalty was restricted to cases where there was no reason at all; if the reason was insufficient the wife might not remarry and the husband not for two years[10]. These rules do not appear under Justinian[11], but he kept analogous provisions of A.D. 449[12] and set up

1 P. 5. 6. 15. 2 Vat. Fr. 116; Arangio Ruiz, *Persone e Familia nel dir. d. papyri*, 78. 3 P. 2. 19. 2; C. 5. 17. 5. Corbett, *R. L. of Marriage*, 123. 4 Justinian retains an enactment of Alexander (C. 8. 38. 2) which says that, in view of the traditional liberty of marriage, pacts not to divorce or for a penalty in case of divorce are void. It does not appear that the consent of the *paterfamilias* of the husband was essential to divorce. As to the wife, 24. 2. 5 suggests the opposite. Justinian required their consent if they had provided *dos* or *d. propter nuptias*, C. 5. 17. 12. 5 24. 1. 35; 24. 2. 9. Introduced by *l. Iulia*. The view of Levy, *Hergang d. Röm. Ehescheidung*, that this formality applied to marriage with *manus* and is only in later law applied to all marriage, does not seem acceptable. For Bonfante, *Corso*, 1. 248, it was not needed in divorce by consent till Justinian who generalised the rule by interpolations. On the question whether a sealed document was necessary, and on the whole matter, Corbett, *R. L. of Marriage*, 228 *sqq*. 6 23. 2. 45; 24. 2. 11. 7 *Nov.* 117. 10; *Nov.* 140. 8 *Ante*, § XL. 9 C. Th. 3. 16. 1. 10 C. Th. 3. 16. 2. 11 See, however, C. 9. 9. 34. 12 C. 5. 17. 8.

many other legitimate causes of divorce[1]. And he provided that, for divorce not for a recognised cause, the wife should be confined in a nunnery for life, her property being forfeited to various uses including the nunnery; the husband was subject only to money penalties[2]. In all this it must be noted that the divorce was valid.

There was also legislation aimed at preserving for the children of the first marriage the *dos* and *donatio* connected with it, in the event of any remarriage of the parties[3].

XLIII. *Manus*. At a sacrifice of order, it is convenient to consider now the very different relations set up by marriage with *manus*[4]. No doubt at one time all Roman marriage was with *manus*, but so early as the XII Tables there were devices for evading it[5]. In the time of Augustus it was in decay and it seems to have died out altogether not long after Gaius. The *liber singularis regularum*, Paul and Papinian indeed all mention *manus*[6], but most of the allusions are not such as to suggest that it was still real.

Manus placed the wife *filiae loco* and made her the sister of her own children. Her acquisitions vested in the *paterfamilias*, and she had the same right of succession[7] as a daughter. But the traditions of the *ll. regiae* suggest that in practice there were more restrictions on the right of the husband than on those of the father[8]. There is no sign of surrender for *noxa*, or of giving in adoption, or of the right of transferring her by *mancipatio*, like a son. In *coemptio fiduciae causa* the factitious husband sold the woman into civil bondage[9], but this shews only that a real sale was not expressly forbidden by law, not that it was ever practised[10]. According to tradition divorce from *manus* apart from certain justifications was penalised by Romulus.

Three ways of acquiring *manus* are recorded.

1. *Confarreatio*. A religious ceremony at the altar of *Iupiter Farreus* before the *Pontifex Maximus* and the *Flamen Dialis*. As in all early

1 C. 5. 17. 10, 11. 2 *Nov.* 117. 3 C. 5. 9 and 10. There are obvious reasons for penalising immediate remarriage of widows. The marriage was not void, and in classical law the woman incurred no penalty, but her father, if he authorised it, and the husband and his father, became *infames* (Greenidge, *Infamia*, p. 127) if the remarriage was within the year of mourning (3. 2. 1; Vat. Fr. 320). As a corollary a widow was for a time after the husband's death free from the penalties of celibacy. Ulpian, 14, gives the periods. In later law the woman became *infamis*, which was not a notion applicable to women in earlier law (*ante*, p. 92). She forfeited benefits from her husband's estate and any honorific rank which she held. C. Th. 3. 8. 1; C. 5. 9. 1, 2. As to divorce with the same risk of *turbatio sanguinis* Cornil, *Dr.R.* 606. 4 G. 1. 108 *sqq.* 5 G. 1. 111. At that time the idea of Roman marriage and *manus* were probably inseparable and the effect of the *trinoctium abesse* was to prevent the relation from being a marriage at all. 6 Ulp. 24. 23; Vat. Fr. 115; Coll. 4. 7. 1. 7 G. 2. 96, 139; Coll. 16. 2. 3. 8 Bruns, 1. 6; Girard, *Textes*, 6. 9 *Post*, § XLVIII. 10 Such a relatively late and artificial device hardly proves anything for early law.

ritual acts there must be witnesses, here ten, perhaps representing the ten *curiae*. There was a sacrifice and the consumption of a cake of *far*, and what Gaius describes as *complura* ritual acts of which we have indications[1]. It was essentially patrician. It was a necessary qualification for the post of *rex sacrorum*, or the three major flaminates, to be party to, and issue of, confarreate marriage[2]. As, by the end of the Republic, *manus* was unpopular, it was difficult to find persons so qualified, and Tiberius therefore provided that one who married a *flamen Dialis* should pass into *manus* only *quoad sacra*, and in other matters should be as if not in *manus*[3]. An imperfect text of Gaius may mean that it covered all cases of *confarreatio*[4]. Indeed the story suggests that this had gone out of use except for these cases, the office of *flamen* thus tending to become hereditary. Nothing is heard of *confarreatio* after Ulpian[5].

2. *Coemptio*. Essentially a modified form of bride purchase. As described by Gaius it was a sale of the wife to the husband *per aes et libram*[6], i.e. by the formal method used for the transfer of property in civil law, *mancipatio*[7]. But it was not quite *mancipatio*: the words used were so framed as not to treat her as a thing sold[8]. Further, she was not sold, but sold herself with the consent of her father or *tutor*, according as she was or was not *alieni iuris*[9]. *Coemptio* must have been the usual mode of creation of *manus* in the time of Gaius, if real *manus* still existed, but it was by this time more important in certain fictitious applications of the process, called *coemptio fiduciae causa*. Cicero, attacking the lawyers, says they had perverted *coemptio* and used it to destroy *sacra*[10]. This may be no more than collusive marriage with a childless old man who would acquire the woman's property, which she regained at his death, the *sacra* being destroyed by the marriage. But it may have been more complex, the first application of a system fully developed later and applied in two other cases[11]. A woman *sui iuris*, of any age, was normally under *tutela*. She could do no important act tending to diminish her property without leave of her *tutor*, and an *ingenua* could not make a will at all, even with his leave, unless she had passed out of her original

1 G. 1. 112; Ulp. 9; Boethius *in Top.* 3. 14; Warde Fowler, *J.R.S.* 1916, 185. 2 G. 1. 112. 3 Tac. *Ann.* 4. 16. Little is known of the other major flaminates, Daremberg et Saglio, *Dict. des Ant.*, *s.v. Flamen*. 4 G. 1. 136. The enactment there referred to is of 11 B.C., in which year the *flamen Dialis* was re-established (Suet. Aug. 31), i.e. earlier than that mentioned by Tacitus who refers also to this earlier legislation. The *sc.* of 11 B.C. was probably a *privilegium*, Brassloff, *St. Bonfante*, 2. 365. 5 Ulp. 9. 6 G. 1. 113. 7 *Post*, § LXXXV. 8 G. 1. 123. 9 Coll. 4. 2. 2; 4. 7. 1. In primitive Rome she may have been actually sold. Late traditions (Bruns, 2. 74, 76) suggest that the sale was mutual (*coemptio*), not a necessary implication of the word and in itself improbable. 10 *Pro Murena*, 12. 27. 11 G. 1. 115. He does not speak of the *sacra*. The passage in Cicero shews that the powerless tutor was already in existence.

family by *coemptio* and *remancipatio*[1]. These rules spring from the original conception of *tutela*. The *tutor* would take the property if the ward died, and the *tutela* was in the interest of the *tutores*, or, rather, for the protection of the family property. The present device was a means of transferring the woman to a *tutor* whose control was unreal, as his *auctoritas* could be compelled. Gaius tells us that she gave herself by *coemptio* to anyone, with consent of her original *tutor*, for the purpose of the change. The *coemptio* was purely formal, *dicis gratia*, unless she chose her husband for the purpose; if she did she would be *loco filiae*[2]. The *coemptionator* must at her request hand her over by *remancipatio* to a person of her choice, on trust to manumit her. On manumission she passed under the *tutela* of the manumitter, who could be compelled to authorise her acts, and by whose authorisation she could make a will. The *fiducia* or trust was not applied to the purely formal *coemptio*, but to the *remancipatio*. Hence it was not called *coemptio cum fiducia*, but *coemptio fiduciae causa* or *coemptio fiduciaria*[3]. When Hadrian allowed women to make wills with the consent of the *tutor* this process ceased to be necessary for testation[4], but Gaius speaks of it as still applied for the purpose of change of *tutores*. In his time the agnatic *tutela* of women was gone, and the only *tutor* of an *ingenua* who had real power was an emancipating father. But Gaius speaks of her getting rid of her *tutores* and in his time there could be no plurality of *tutores* of an *ingenua* with this oppressive power[5]. Thus as to *ingenuae*, it was now merely one of the many devices by which in classical law a woman could change her tutors, not because of their oppressive power, but precisely because they had none at all. The *liber singularis regularum* still mentions it[6].

3. *Usus*. This was probably in origin a rule that one year's cohabitation turned an unrecognised union into a marriage[7]. As recorded,

1 *Tutela mulierum*, *post*, § LX. The rule was a survival from the original will before the *comitia*, which a woman could not have made, not inevitable under the later forms. Its limited survival aimed at the preservation of the family property. The original *tutores* were those who would take her property if she died, the agnates being the chief and most usual case. The rule that even with their consent she could not make a will may be due to the fact that the present agnates might not be those alive at her death, so that they would be depriving other successors.

2 G. 1. 115 b. The *tutor* might be willing to consent as the right of succession might not compensate for the trouble of supervision. But the practice may possibly be later than the abolition of agnatic *tutela* over women, which disappeared a century before Gaius wrote. The testamentary *tutores* then usual had, as such, no interest in her property. Emancipation, which left the former *paterfamilias* as *legitimus tutor*, presumably made it possible for him to authorise a will.

3 G. 1. 114, 115 a. We are not told how the *coemptionator* was compelled to remancipate. For the later steps it is not likely that the *actio fiduciae* was the remedy (*post*, § CLI). See Coll. 2. 3. 1, and Jacquelin, *De la Fiducie*, 103 *sqq.*

4 G. 1. 115 a.

5 Perhaps referring to *libertina in tutela* of *liberi patroni* or joint patrons, whose power was real, *post*, § LX.

6 Ulp. 11. 5.

7 For various views as to origin, Collinet-Giffard, *Précis*, 1. 206.

it was a rule that *manus* was added to marriage by one year's cohabitation. But as early as the XII Tables[1] this could be avoided by *trinoctium abesse*, i.e. the wife's absenting herself from the husband's house for three nights in each year[2], for this express purpose. This was the earliest mode of creation of *manus* to disappear. It existed in the last century of the Republic[3], but Gaius tells us that in his time it was gone, partly by enactments (unknown), and partly by desuetude[4].

Where there was *manus*, divorce would not necessarily be simple. There could be no divorce for actual *flamines diales*, married by *confarreatio*[5], but in other cases there was a process called *diffarreatio*, a reversal of the union carried out by corresponding religious observances[6]. The language of Gaius makes it probable that after the change made by Tiberius in *confarreatio* the wife could, here too, divorce or be divorced by mere *repudium*[7]. In the other cases, divorce was effected by what was substantially the process for emancipating a daughter[8]. On the question whether the wife could compel this in real marriage-*manus* Gaius, in a defective text, seems to contradict himself. The passage has been explained as meaning that she could destroy the marriage aspect of the *manus* by a *libellus repudii*, and then compel *remancipatio* as if she had not been a wife at all[9].

XLIV. The next mode of acquisition of *patria potestas* is by Adoption, i.e. the acquiring, by voluntary process, of *potestas* over persons not born into the family[10]. Adoption of a person previously *sui iuris*, was *adrogatio*; transfer of a person *alieni iuris* from one family to another was *adoptio*[11], though this name was also used in a wide sense to cover both. They differed greatly in their character and forms.

Adoptio, of a person *alieni iuris*. The elaborate form is derived from a rule of the XII Tables (aimed at checking the cruelty and avarice of some fathers), which provided that if a father sold a son three times the son should be free from *potestas*[12]. The *potestas* being in principle indestructible, the rule was seized on as a means of ending it at will. The process, in classical law, was as follows: The father, *A*, sold[13] *X*, the son, to *B*. *B* freed him and he reverted to *A*'s *potestas*. This was repeated. There was then a third sale which destroyed the *potestas* and left the son in bondage to *B*. *C*, the intending adoptor, now brought a collusive

1 G. 1. 111; Aul. Gell. 3. 2. 13 *sq.* 2 *Ibid.* 3 Aul. Gell. mentions Q. M. Scaevola as treating it. From the expression "*trinoctium*" it has been inferred that the nights must be successive. 4 G. 1. 110, 111. 5 Aul. Gell. *N.A.* 10. 15, 23. Imperial dispensation needed, Plutarch, *Quaest. Rom.* 50. 6 Festus, *vo. Diffarreatio*; Brassloff, *St. Bonfante*, 2. 368. 7 G. 1. 118, 136. 8 G. 1. 137. 9 G. 1. 137 a. 10 This covers legitimation (*post*, § XLVI) which may be thought of as a kind of adoption confined to a man's own children by a *concubina*. 11 G. 1. 98, 99; Ulp. 8. 12 G. 1. 132; Ulp. 10. 1. 13 I.e. transferred by *mancipatio*.

action against *B* claiming *X* as his son. There was no defence and judgement went accordingly. *B* and *C* might be the same person, but in that case *X* would be sold back to *A* after the third sale, and the claim made against *A*, a method often adopted apart from this consideration[1]. As the Tables speak of selling *filium* three times, the pontifical lawyers held, quite illogically, that one sale sufficed for a daughter or grandchild[2]. The sale was by formal *mancipatio*. The transaction had two parts, a preliminary sale or sales to destroy the *potestas*, and the act of adoption, the claim and declaration in court[3]. The vendee could be compelled to carry out the necessary releases by the magistrate, the *mancipatio* being fiduciary[4].

In classical times it was recognised that the sales were empty forms, any defect being remediable by the Emperor[5], the appearance before the magistrate being the essential. Justinian, recognising the uselessness of the sales, dispensed with them; the parties had merely to go before the magistrate and have the transaction entered on the *acta* of the court[6]. There was no fictitious action, but the essence was preserved[7].

The effect of *adoptio* in classical law was to remove the *adoptatus* from one *potestas* (and ordinarily from one agnatic group[8]) to another. The cognatic tie was unaffected[9]. The *adoptatus* acquired the rights of a natural son, but they depended on the agnatic tie, and ceased if he passed out of his new family by emancipation[10]: he became an *emancipatus* of his real father[11]. The adoption affected only himself; if he already had children they remained in the old family, and, on principles already stated, so did any child conceived while the *potestas* was undestroyed, i.e. before the third sale[12]. Those conceived later were in the new family. But the father did not get all the advantages of a natural son. The possession of a certain number of children gave advantages in the law of succession and exemption from irksome duties, but after Nero[13] adoptive children did not, neither did the natural father lose them[14].

It was possible to adopt one's own child, not in one's *potestas*, even though he had been given in adoption to another[15], but a son so readopted was a new person. He did not again become the father of any children he had left in the family. A grandson so readopted would not again be-

1 G. 1. 132–134. Mancipations need not be on same day or with same witnesses, P. 2. 25. 2. 2 G. 1. 134. 3 Essentially *cessio in iure*, a form of conveyance, *post*, § LXXXIV. 4 *Post*, § CLI. 5 1. 7. 38. It might be on a *dies feriata*, P. 2. 25. 3. 6 Inst. 1. 12. 8; C. 8. 47. 11, following, it seems, existing practice, *S.M.W.* 530. 7 Gaius, the *liber singularis regularum* and Justinian all describe it as done essentially by the magistrate. G. 1. 98; Ulp. 8. 2; Inst. 1. 11. 1. 8 Adoption by paternal uncle leaves him in the same agnatic group. 9 *Post*, § CXXX. 10 1. 7. 13. 11 G. 2. 137. 12 G. 1. 135; Inst. 1. 12. 9. 13 Tac. *Ann.* 15. 19. 14 G. 3. 41, 49; D. 31. 51. 1; Inst. 1. 25. pr., etc. *Senatorius* adopted by a *plebeius* was still *senatorius*, but an *adoptatus* got the benefit of any improvement. 1. 7. 35. 15 1. 7. 12.

come the son of his father or his *suus heres* on the death of the grandfather[1]. And though an adoptive child might be emancipated or given in adoption, he could not be readopted[2].

A person might be adopted not as son but as grandson, even if there were no son, and might be attached as a son to any son, with his consent[3]; here he would be a *suus heres* of the son, not of the adoptor.

Justinian profoundly changed the effect of adoption. Remarking upon doubts among classical lawyers as to the rights a child, given in adoption, retained in the estate of his natural father, and observing that adoption lightly undertaken might be lightly ended, so that the child would be in neither family, he provided that in future the adoptive child should retain his rights of succession in his old family and acquire only a right of succession on intestacy in the new, with no right of complaint if passed over in the will, and conversely, such acquisitions of the child as under his law went to the father for life (*bona adventitia*[4]) should go to the natural father. And the child did not pass into the *potestas* of the adoptive father[5]. To such cases Justinian gave the name *adoptio minus plena*, but there were exceptions. In one case he allowed the old law still to apply and this he called *adoptio plena*. This was where the adoptor was a natural ascendant, in which case there was not the same risk of caprice[6]. Where a grandchild was given in adoption while his father was alive he was not a *suus heres*, and as he had no right in his old family Justinian gave him full rights of succession in the new. But it is not shewn that *potestas* passed[7], and if events so turned out that he acquired rights in the old family it became simple *adoptio minus plena*[8].

The principle *adoptio naturam imitatur* bases several rules. Though an adoptor need not be married, a *castratus* could not adopt[9], at least in later law. The adoptor must be old enough to be the father, and Justinian fixed the difference at 18 years[10], *plena pubertas*, the latest age at which maturity might be expected, with presumably proportionate increase if the adoption was in a remoter degree.

Women, being incapable of *patria potestas*, could not adopt in classical law[11]. In an interpolated constitution dated A.D. 291 Diocletian is said to have allowed adoption as a consolation to a woman who had lost her children, and Justinian accepted this as the rule, with the permission of the Emperor[12]. In the constitution the woman was apparently *sui iuris*,

1 1. 7. 41. 2 1. 7. 37. 1. 3 Ulp. 8. 7; Inst. 1. 11. 5; D. 1. 7. 6, 10, 11. 4 *Post*, § XCIX. 5 Inst. 1. 11. 2; C. 8. 47. 10. 6 Inst. 1. 11. 2; C. 8. 47. 10. 1 a. 7 C. 8. 47. 10. 4. 8 C. 8. 47. 10. 4. Monier, *R.H.*, 1927, 596. 9 Inst. 1. 11. 9; D. 1. 7. 16; G. 1. 103 and the Inst. allow it to *spadones*. 10 G. 1. 106; Inst. 1. 11. 4; D. 1. 7. 40. 1, interp. 11 G. 1. 104; Ulp. 8. 8 a. 12 Inst. 1. 11. 10; C. 8. 47. 5. Albertario, *La donna adottante*, 18.

but Justinian's rule was not so limited. The effect of the adoption would be to give the ordinary right of succession, but, of course, no *potestas*.

Adoption, being in form a *legis actio*, could not be subject to *condicio* or *dies*; such a thing no doubt made it void[1].

The question whether the consent of the *adoptatus* was necessary for classical law is obscure. We may be certain that it was not needed in early law. Justinian says, once as a rule of old law, and once as a rule of his own, not necessarily new, that *contradictio* by the *adoptatus* prevented the adoption[2]. Celsus definitely says that his state of mind was not material, but he is made to follow this with words which say that he must consent or not *contradicere*, words probably added, as they follow very closely Justinian's own language[3].

XLV. *Adrogatio*. Adoption of a person *sui iuris*. This is the more ancient institution and the more important in its effects, since it destroyed a family and merged it in another. Though it underwent certain changes, it retained its essential character unaltered throughout the development of the law. Its original form is an expression of its importance. There was a preliminary enquiry by the pontiffs to decide whether in the actual case it was admissible[4]; they considered the question whether it satisfied legal requirements, but it is hardly possible to set limits to the further factors which they took into account. It seems that they gradually created the standing restrictions as we know them, and considered also the material aspects of the individual case. If they approved, the matter went before the *comitia curiata*, called in this case *c. calata*, summoned in a special way, meeting on special days for this and other purposes affecting *sacra*, and presided over by the *Pontifex Maximus*[5]. The parties were *rogati* whether they assented, and there was a third *rogatio* of the *populus*[6], the vote being probably followed by *detestatio sacrorum*, renunciation by the *adrogatus* of the *sacra* of the old family[7]. Nominally this was the form up to the time of Diocletian, but the *comitia curiata* fell early into decay, and the really important element was the inquisition by the pontiffs, the *comitia* being represented by 30 lictors[8], as it already

1 See l. 7. 34. In 50. 17. 77 this is said of *emancipatio*, of which the form is essentially the same but it is probable that Papinian said *mancipatio*.

2 C. 8. 47. 10. pr., 11.

3 1. 7. 5. *Infantes* could be adopted, the fact that the requirement was "*non contradicere*" will save the rule for *infantes*, but if consent of the *impubes* was given we should expect to see cases of *restitutio in integrum*, but we do not, except in *adrogatio*, where his consent was needed. Bonfante, *Scr. Giur.* 3. 154. As to consent where an adoptive child was given in adoption, Bonfante, *Corso*, 1. 62.

4 1. 7. 15. 2, 17; Cicero, *de domo*, 13, 14 (34–38); Aul. Gell. 5. 19.

5 Aul. Gell. 5. 19; Mommsen, *Staatsr.* 2. 27; *D.P.R.* 3. 41.

6 G. 1. 99.

7 Mommsen, *Staatsr.* 3. 38, 318; *D.P.R.* 6. 1. 41, 362. *Rogationes* submitted by the presiding *pontifex*. It is like the Comitial Will and is sometimes said to be a differentiation from it. *Detestatio* sometimes differently explained.

8 Corresponding to the 30 *curiae*. As it is "*auspicatum*," Cicero, *de l. agr.* 2. 12. 31, the augurs are present.

was in the time of Cicero[1]. Diocletian abolished the old system, providing that it might be done by imperial rescript, in effect no change of principle, the existing legislative authority being substituted for the original[2].

Adrogatio brought the *adrogatus* completely into the family. Like *adoptatus* he became a *filiusfamilias* therein, but he brought with him all those in his *potestas*[3]. The *adrogator* acquired, in principle, all his property, while, as the *adrogatus* was *capite minutus*, his obligations *ex contractu* and *quasi ex contractu* ceased, at civil law, to exist, an injustice remedied by the Praetor[4]. And the acquisition by the father was cut down in the Empire in the same way as in the case of other *filiifamilias*[5]. The principle that the adopted person got the advantage of improvement in status, but did not decline, held good, with two exceptions. A *libertinus* who was adrogated[6] did not become an *ingenuus*[7], and a patrician adrogated by a plebeian did become a plebeian[8].

The restrictions stated in connexion with *adoptio* applied also here, but there were many more. *Adrogatio* destroyed a family and thus was allowed only to save another, i.e. to provide a *heres*. Hence the very careful investigation into the circumstances, the character of the *adrogator*, his motives, etc.[9], and hence also the fact that it needed the consent of the legislature. Nearly all the special restrictions are due to these characteristics. The chief are the following:

So long as it was done before the *comitia* it was necessarily at Rome, where the *comitia* sat[10]. When it was by imperial rescript it might be anywhere. A woman having no standing before the *comitia* could not be adrogated[11]; there was no difficulty when it was done by rescript[12], but there was small advantage, for though she continued the family for a generation, it must then fail, as she, the sole successor, could have no *sui heredes*. An *impubes* could not be adrogated in early law[13], perhaps

1 Cicero, *loc. cit.* 2 C. 8. 47. 2, 6. The college of pontiffs being obsolete, the enquiry was conducted by imperial officials. D. 1. 7. 20, 21 (Gaius) speak of *adrogatio* of females by rescript, no doubt by interpolation, Bonfante, *Corso*, 1. 24. 3 G. 1. 107; Inst. 1. 11. 11; D. 1. 7. 15. pr. Though primarily a way of adopting the son of another, it might be, and frequently was, applied to the adoption of a man's own children not in the *potestas*, e.g. emancipated or born out of wedlock. A freedman not infrequently bought, freed and adrogated his children born in slavery. But in later law a man might not adrogate his child by a concubine, C. 5. 27. 7. 3. 4 *Post*, § CXLI. 5 *Post*, § XCIX. 6 *Post*, p. 127. 7 1. 5. 27; 1. 7. 46; 23. 2. 32; 38. 2. 49. Aul. Gell. *N.A.* 5. 19. 10, 11. 8 Cicero, *de domo*, 14 (34–38). Clodius was thus adrogated so as to be eligible for the tribunate of the *plebs*. Cicero attacks the proceedings, but never makes the point that it would not make him a plebeian. But by this time plebeians were rather a different than a lower order. 9 Cicero, *de domo*, 14. 36; D. 1. 7. 15. 2, 17. 10 G. 1. 100; Ulp. 8. 4. 11 G. 1. 101, *magis placuit*. There had been doubts. 12 1. 7. 20, 21. 13 G. 1. 102. His language implies that it was occasionally allowed before the change made by Pius.

for the same reason, but there was also the practical reason that to allow it was to put an easily abused power into the hands of his *tutores*[1]. Antoninus Pius, however, allowed it[2], subject to special rules. There must be careful enquiry as to advantage to the child[3]. The *auctoritas* of *tutores* was required[4], and the *adrogator* gave security that, on the death of the *adrogatus* still *impubes*, his property should be restored to those who would have taken it if he had not been adrogated[5]. There was difficulty as to the person to whom this security had to be given, for, though it preceded the adrogation, the rights, if it were to the child himself, would vest in the *adrogator*, the person liable. The solution found was to give the security to a public slave, perhaps with an idea that those entitled were part owners of the slave, as members of the public[6], the persons concerned having *utiles actiones*[7], a rule which recognises that there was no real ownership. It is the public rather than the "common" quality of the slave which accounts for his use, since in a parallel case we are told that the security could be given to a municipal magistrate[8], and it is certainly the decisive point under Justinian when it could be given to a *tabularius*, a public official[9], not a slave. If the *adrogator* emancipated the *adrogatus*, *impubes*, he had to restore his property at once. If he disinherited him, the *adrogatus* could claim it at the death, and here, and where he had emancipated without shewing cause to a court, the *adrogatus* might claim a quarter of the estate of the dead man (*quarta antonina*), i.e. what an only child was entitled to claim against a will, unless justly disinherited[10]. It is probable that these latter liabilities were covered by the security[11]. If the *adrogatus* reached puberty these securities and liabilities were ended, and he was an ordinary *adrogatus*, except that he could have the *adrogatio* set aside by a forced *emancipatio*, if he could shew good cause[12].

It was allowed only as a last resort, to save a family, and no one might adrogate more than one, or any, if he had a child already[13]. He must be 60 or from some cause unlikely to have children[14]. The question

1 Aul. Gell. 5. 19. 10. 2 G. 1. 102; Ulp. 8. 5. 3 1. 7. 17. 1, 2. 4 1. 7. 17. 1. Not enough in itself: the text notes that it would enable the *tutor* to end a pupillary substitution. 5 Inst. 1. 11. 3. 6 1. 7. 18 (*Utilis actio* if security not given, h. t. 19. 1). Saleilles puts it down (*Personnalité juridique*, 89 *sqq.*) to a more subtle notion. The personality of the *universitas*, though distinct, subsumed those of the members, not as titularies but as beneficiaries, like our *cestui que* trust, which is of course consistent with the *utiles actiones*. But the notion of *utiles actiones* to third parties really interested is a late one and cannot date back to the origin of this method in *tutela*. And the notion will not explain the fact that in *tutela* it could be given to municipal magistrates (27. 8. 1. 15, 16). 7 28. 6. 40. 8 27. 8. 1. 15, 16. 9 Inst. 1. 11. 3. 10 Inst. 1. 11. 3; 37. 6. 1. 21; *post*, § CXIV. 11 1. 7. 20. 12 H. t. 32. pr., 33. He recovers *pristinum ius* which presumably covers property. 13 1. 7. 15. 3, 17. 3; C. 8. 47. 3. 14 1. 7. 15. 2.

whether there were others to attend to the ancestral *sacra* of the *adrogatus* was also material[1]. One under 25 could not be adrogated by one who had been his *tutor* or *curator*[2], and consent of his *curator* was necessary[3]. These restrictions might be overridden for sufficient cause; it was in the discretion of the controlling authorities, and an *adrogatio* which broke these rules was valid if actually carried out[4]. It does not appear that an *adrogator* need be married[5].

In classical law a *libertinus* must not be adopted by any one but his patron[6]. But, here too, if the *adrogatio* was carried through *per obreptionem*, it was valid[7]; *non debet fieri sed factum valet*. But his patron's rights were not affected.

As *adrogatus* was party to the process, he must assent[8], and thus, if insane, he could not be adrogated for lack of assent[9], or if deaf or dumb, as he could not take part in the act. This would not be the case in *adoptio*[10].

There were some exceptional forms of adoption.

Adoption by will. Late in the Republic and early in the Empire there are recorded in literary, but not in legal, texts many cases of adoption by will[11]. The nature of the proceeding is not clear. According to Mommsen, it was *institutio* as *heres* with a direction that the *institutus* was to enter the family of the testator and was followed by *rogationes in c. calatis*, being in effect an *adrogatio* in a modified form. On another view it was never more than an *institutio* with a direction to take the name of the testator (common in the Empire), and did not affect the family relations of the *heres*, though in a few exceptional cases, for political reasons, the *institutus* did subsequently procure a transfer to the testator's family by *rogationes*[12].

Adoption of slaves. Justinian records a dictum of Cato[13] that owners could adopt their slaves, whether by collusive conveyance, followed by *cessio in iure*, i.e. *adoptio*, or by *adrogatio*, is not clear; the latter is the most accepted view[14]. There is no trace of it in classical law. The rule to which Justinian refers in the same text (and regulates elsewhere[15]) is that if a master formally declares that he regards a certain slave as his son (which he might in fact be), this, though void as an adoption, might be a manumission[16].

1 Cicero, *de domo*, 14. 2 1. 7. 17, lest he evade the responsibility of accounting, cf. 1. 7. 32. 1. 3 1. 7. 8. 4 *Arg.* 1. 7. 17; cf. 38. 2. 49. 5 No evidence to the contrary in classical law; Ulp. 8. 6 and D. 1. 7. 30 are not confined to *adoptio* in the narrow sense. 6 1. 7. 15. 3. 7 2. 4. 10. 2; 38. 2. 49. 8 1. 7. 24. 9 *Arg.* 1. 7. 5, 42. 10 Effects of *adrogatio* on property, *post*, § CXLI. 11 Much more important in Greek law where it was the only way of appointing specially a *heres*. Daremberg et Saglio, *Dict. des Antiq.*, *s.v. Testament.* 12 List of the cases and discussion, Michel, *Droit de Cité Romaine*, 240 *sqq.* 13 Inst. 1. 11. 12. 14 The fact that a slave has no standing *in comitiis* is more or less met by the fact that the proceeding makes him *capax*. 15 C. 7. 6. 1. 10. 16 *Ante*, § XXVII.

Aulus Gellius speaks of masters giving slaves in adoption[1] and says that ancient lawyers had held this lawful, though it clearly no longer existed. This was *adoptio*: it was done *apud praetorem*. It would consist of the claim (*cessio in iure*) only: the triple sale would not be needed as there was no *patria potestas* to destroy. In later law the result would be reached by manumission followed by adrogation. There would be no difficulty if, as often, the *adrogator* was a *libertinus*, father of the slave. And if, though an *ingenuus*, he was actually the father, it would no doubt be permitted, the son remaining a *libertinus*.

XLVI. LEGITIMATION. *Patria potestas* could also be acquired by legitimation. *Concubinatus* was a recognised connexion short of marriage[2], which seems to owe its legal recognition to the restrictive legislation of the early Empire on marriage, in particular the rules forbidding soldiers on service to marry and restricting the marriage of provincial officials[3]. It was encouraged by the immorality of Roman women of high rank; men preferred to contract this union with women of lower class but higher character. It was a permanent relation, free from the stigma of *stuprum*, but ordinarily involving loss of caste in the woman[4], so that while it did occur between those of equal rank[5], and even rarely between women of high rank and men of lower[6], there was usually a marked difference of rank the other way[7]. It might be with any woman capable of Roman marriage, and, after Severus, with a peregrine. It might always have been with a man's own slave[8]. Constantine, however, forbade it between persons of senatorian rank and *libertinae* and the abject persons grouped with them[9]. It was subject to restrictions similar to those of marriage. Thus a man might not have a wife and a concubine or two *concubinae*[10]. The parties must not be so near akin that marriage would be barred[11]. Like marriage, it could not exist between *tutor* and ward[12]. There must be marriageable age and consent[13]. Thus it was not always easy to tell concubinage from marriage. *Dos* was the best evidence: there was no *dos* in concubinage, and there was a presumption in favour of marriage. In classical law it produced little legal effect. It was not *stuprum*, but the woman did not take the man's rank[14] and gifts between them were not void. The children were not related to the

1 Aul. Gell. 5. 19. 13. 2 Meyer, *Der Römische Konkubinat*; Castelli, *Il concubinato e la legislazione Augustea*. 3 25. 7. 5. 4 23. 2. 41. 1; 25. 7. 3. 1, 5. 5 25. 7. 3. pr.; Meyer, *op. cit.* 46. 6 Meyer, 47 c, 65. 7 Between *liberta* and her patron or his son, it was honourable and she was still entitled to the name *matrona* (25. 7. 1. pr.; 48. 5. 14. pr.). As in marriage, she could not end it of her own will, at any rate if the manumission was voluntary (*ibid.*). 8 Meyer, 63 *sqq.*, 47 b, 74. 9 C. Th. 4. 6. 3; C. 5. 27. 1. On pain of loss of *civitas*. Modified in *Nov.* 89. 15. Some high officials were here ranked with *senatorii*. 10 P. 2. 20. 1; C. 5. 26. 1. 11 23. 2. 56; 25. 7. 1. 3. 12 Meyer, 61. Not the rule as to provincial governors, 25. 7. 5. 13 25. 7. 1. 4. Not, of course, *affectio maritalis*. 14 32. 49. 4.

father but he could give or leave property to them, subject to the claims of *legitimi*[1], and if he did leave them anything, he could in effect appoint *tutores* to them[2]. They did not count for the *praemia patrum* under the *leges caducariae*[3]. They were, however, cognates of the mother with cognatic succession to her and to her relatives and they counted towards the *ius liberorum*[4]. Towards the end of the classical period we get a rule, applied earlier in the case of *nuptiae non iustae*, which is the germ of the later legitimation. The issue of *concubinae* of soldiers on service acquired, by entering the army, rights of succession to the father, and *civitas* if they were not *cives* already[5]. The Christian Empire was hostile to concubinage. The right to give or leave property to the concubine or the child was destroyed by Constantine, but restored, with limitations, soon after[6], and the rules were varied by a bewildering mass of enactments till post-Roman times[7]. Legitimation might be effected in various ways.

Subsequent Marriage. Constantine enacted that, for existing, but not for future cases, marriage of the *concubina* should legitimate children already born, provided she was *ingenua* and not of one of the abject classes, the children consented, and there was no wife or legitimate child. Zeno seems to have repeated this[8]. Anastasius, in A.D. 517[9], laid down a rule for future cases as well, and for all concubines, capable of marriage, if the children assented, there was no legitimate child, and the marriage was attested by writing and *dos*. Two years later, this was repealed[10]. Justinian by a series of enactments regulated the matter anew, allowing legitimation by subsequent marriage even where the *concubina* was a *libertina*, provided the marriage was attested by *instrumentum dotis* or other writing, the woman was capable of marriage at the conception or birth, and the children consented. And he allowed it even if there were legitimate children[11].

Oblatio Curiae. The office of *decurio* (member of the local *curia*) was avoided in later law, since a *decurio* was personally liable for many charges. As part of a scheme to keep the lists full it was provided in A.D. 443 that if a man had no legitimate child, and made his son by a *concubina* a *decurio*, or married his daughter to one, they might receive all his property and succeed on intestacy like legitimate children[12]. This was not legitimation; it did not make them agnates or cognates of the father's relatives or give *potestas*. Justinian allowed it where there were legitimate children, provided no more was taken than by any legitimate

1 *Post*, § CXIV. The children were *liberi naturales* (as opposed to *iusti* or *legitimi*), a name also used for actual children as opposed to *liberi adoptivi*. 2 *Post*, § LI. 3 Meyer, 56 *sqq.* 4 38. 8. 4; Inst. 3. 5. 4. 5 Meyer, 112. 6 C. Th. 4. 6. 2, 4. 7 Meyer, 134 *sqq.*; Cornil, *Dr.R.* 567. 8 C. 5. 27. 5. 9 C. 5. 27. 6. 10 C. 5. 27. 7. 11 C. 5. 27. 8, 10, 11; *Novv.* 12. 4, 18. 11, 78. 4. 12 C. 5. 27. 3.

child. Finally he gave *potestas*, making it true legitimation, so far as the father was concerned, but not with regard to his relatives[1].

Rescriptum principis. Justinian also provided that on petition by a father or request in his will, in which they were instituted, a rescript of legitimation might issue. The petition must shew that he had *liberi naturales*, but no *legitimi*, and that the mother was dead or not worthy of marriage[2].

Revocatio in patriam potestatem. Constantine lays down, and later emperors confirm, a rule that an emancipated son could be recalled to *potestas* for ingratitude, being bound to restore also any gifts he had received[3]. This is therefore another way of acquiring *patria potestas*. It was not exactly a revocation, since the gifts did not revert *ipso facto*. The machinery is not recorded. It was presumably a *capitis deminutio*, and the father's liability on the son's debts was probably as in *adrogatio*[4].

XLVII. We have now to consider how *patria potestas* would end.

It ended in many cases by transfer, e.g. by *adoptio* or entry into *manus*, or adrogation of a *paterfamilias* who had children in *potestas* (in all which cases there was a rupture of agnatic ties), or by death, deportation or enslavement of a grandfather where the father was alive and in the family (where there was no such rupture)[5].

It was destroyed by sale of a daughter or grandchild into civil bondage, involving rupture of agnatic ties, and by three such sales of a son[6]. It was destroyed by death, loss of *civitas* or loss of liberty by the *pater* or the *filius*[7], with rupture of the agnatic ties in the cases other than death, so far as the person deported or enslaved was concerned.

It was destroyed without effect on agnation by the acquisition by the *filiusfamilias* of certain dignities. A man who became a *flamen dialis* or a woman who became a vestal virgin[8] passed out of *potestas* without *capitis deminutio*. We do not know the machinery, but from the fact that there was no *capitis deminutio*, and the language of Aulus Gellius[9], it seems likely that there was no act by the *paterfamilias*. But vestal virgins hardly became *sui iuris*. They passed under the control of the *populus*, administered by the pontiffs[10]. They acquired the right of testation[11], which did not attach to other *ingenuae* who had not suffered *capitis deminutio*, till long after these had it, so that they were thought of as having property. But their agnates did not succeed to

1 C. 5. 27. 9, 11; Inst. 1. 10. 13. Position of *decuriones* under Justinian, Brugi, *Ist.* 65.
2 *Nov.* 74. 1, 2. Bonfante, *St. Perozzi*, 283, shews that Justinian makes *concubinatus* practically an inferior marriage.
3 Vat. Fr. 248; C. Th. 8. 14. 1; C. 8. 49. 1; D. 1. 7. 12.
4 *Post*, § CXLI.
5 G. 1. 127; Ulp. 10. 2.
6 The earlier sales merely suspend it.
7 Subject to possible *postliminium* or *restitutio*, *ante*, §§ XXIV, XXV; D. 48. 23.
8 G. 1. 130; Ulp. 10. 5.
9 G. 3. 114; Aul. Gell. 1. 12.
10 Aul. Gell. 1. 12. 9; Mommsen, *Staatsr.* 2. 54 *sqq.*; *D.P.R.* 3. 60 *sqq.*
11 Aul. Gell. 1. 12. 9.

them on intestacy: their goods went to the *populus*[1]. And they could not inherit from anyone[2], so that the continuance of the agnatic tie was rather unreal. In later law a few other dignities released from *potestas*[3].

EMANCIPATION. Voluntary release[4]. As in adoption, there were three sales (or one as the case might be)[5] to end the *potestas*. This left the child in bondage to the vendee. The next step might be manumission from bondage in the same form as one from slavery, by the vendee, which would make the manumitter a quasi patron, with rights of succession and *tutela*. But it was usual to remancipate to the father, who in turn would free, and acquire these rights[6]. The sales were fiduciary with the same modes of enforcement as in *adoptio*[7].

Anastasius provided that where the *filius* was absent the *emancipatio* could be effected by petition to the Emperor, a favourable reply completing the *emancipatio*[8]. Justinian abolished the old forms: emancipation was effected by attendance of all parties before a court, the transaction being entered on the *acta*, as in *adoptio*[9].

The consent of the father was not needed to *emancipatio* by the grandfather[10], and in a few exceptional cases[11] a child could compel *emancipatio*. One of these was that of *adrogatus impubes*, for cause[12]. Where a man had a gift by will on condition of emancipating his son he could not claim without doing it. This is no exception[13], but some texts seem to mean that where there was such a gift with a *fideicommissum* to emancipate, and the gift was accepted[14], the *emancipatio* could be enforced, though the machinery for enforcing *fideicommissa* of liberty did not apply here. Another text, of Diocletian, but apparently modified by Justinian, may mean that if a mother instituted her child with a condition of *emancipatio*, the father could be compelled to emancipate him[15].

1 *Ibid.* 1. 12. 18. 2 *Ibid.*, i.e. at civil law: it does not follow that they were excluded under praetorian law. But no one succeeded to them under either law: "*sed bona eius in publicum redigi aiunt. Id quo iure fiat, quaeritur*," Labeo, quoted Aul. Gell. *loc. cit.* 3 Inst. 1. 12. 4; C. 12. 3. 5; *Nov.* 81. Also ended in later law by certain forms of misconduct of the *pater*; Girard, *Man.* 205. 4 G. 1. 132 *sqq.*; Inst. 1. 12. 6 *sqq.* 5 Where a son was noxally surrendered, Gaius tells us (4. 79) that the Proculians held three sales necessary to transfer him, the Sabinians only one, the requirement in the XII Tables referring only to voluntary transfers. 6 G. 1. 132; Ulp. 10. 1. He took his *peculium* if it was not expressly taken away (39. 5. 31. 2; Vat. Fr. 260), as in *manumissio servi inter vivos* (*ante*, p. 74). 7 Inst. 3. 2. 8. In a recorded case, there is an express *fiducia* to remancipate. Oddly, though it is a daughter, there are three sales, Girard, *Textes*, 828. 8 C. 8. 48. 5. In C. 6. 58. 11 he enacts that, by a provision in the *acta*, the *emancipatus* may keep his family rights, i.e. only *potestas* ceases. 9 Inst. 1. 12. 6. Old form mentioned in Digest, 38. 17. 2. 15. 10 1. 7. 28; Inst. 1. 12. 7. 11 1. 7. 31; C. 8. 48. 4. 12 *Ante*, p. 126. 13 P. 4. 13. 1. This is all the text seems to mean. 14 P. 4. 13. 1; 35. 1. 92, 93, *cognitio extraordinaria*, an inference of Paul from a piece of rough justice by Severus, contrary to principle, 35. 1. 92. 15 C. 3. 28. 25. The words "*restituere debet*" at the end have no grammatical connexion with the rest. If more than a

The consent of the person emancipated seems to have been needed. Paul is clear[1], and Justinian adopts a *lex* of Anastasius in the same sense[2], but, dealing with *adoptio*, says what might mean the opposite[3]. The rule no doubt was that, as he must be present, he must not *contradicere*[4], and Anastasius dispensed with consent in the case of an *infans*[5]. No doubt in the Republic it was not needed. But compulsory powers were not needed: a bad son could be dealt with by disinherison[6].

We have seen that emancipation of an adoptive child ended all connexion between him and his adoptive family: he was regarded as having been directly emancipated from his original family[7]. Apart from this, the primary legal effect of *emancipatio* was to destroy *potestas*, and with it the agnatic tie[8]: these effects it always retained. But its practical effect underwent great changes. In early law, as it destroyed all civil connexion between the *emancipatus* and his old family, he lost all right of maintenance and all right of succession to his father and his agnates. Rights of succession the other way were not wholly destroyed, since the emancipating *paterfamilias* was "quasi patron," and had from very early times the same rights of succession to the *emancipatus* as the *patronus* had, under the XII Tables, to a freedman[9]. But before the end of the Republic an *emancipatus* had acquired at praetorian law a certain right of succession, and this right was progressively improved[10] until in the time of Justinian the *suus* had little practical advantage. The ancestral *sacra*, from which he was presumably excluded, were obsolete long before Justinian. Where it was an amicable transaction it was often accompanied by a gift of money and the *emancipatus* usually took his *peculium*[11]. It might be a punishment: the rule that he must not *contradicere* means often submission rather than consent. There probably came to be rights of maintenance against the quasi patron, like those of *libertus* against his patron. An *emancipatus impubes*, or a woman, was under the *tutela* of the quasi patron[12]. In late law an *emancipatus* might have

mere corruption they may mean this. Another case, 27. 10. 16. 2, 3. All probably post-classical, Bonfante, *Corso*, 1. 65; Lauria, *Ann. Macerata*, 6. 75. See 30. 114. 8. The forfeitures of *potestas* for misconduct do not seem to require *emancipatio*, and a text dealing with cruelty by the father (37. 12. 5) does not seem to mean that there was a right to compel *emancipatio* in such a case by established machinery, but that if the Emperor did by his overriding authority order *emancipatio* in such a case, this involved forfeiture of any rights of succession.

1 P. 2. 25. 5. Text suspected of alteration; rule may be post-classical, Beseler, *Beitr.* 4. 116. 2 C. 8. 48. 5. 3 C. 8. 47. 10. pr. *Ante*, p. 124. 4 C. 8. 47. 11. Bonfante, *Scr. Giur.* 3. 153. 5 C. 8. 48. 5. 6 *Abdicatio*, repudiation of a son, an institution of Greek law, is declared by Diocletian to have no place in Roman law, though it was practised then and later, C. 8. 46. 6; Mitteis, *Reichsr. und Volksr.* 212. 7 *Ante*, p. 122; G. 2. 136, 137. 8 G. 1. 163, children of son, already conceived, not affected, *arg.* G. 1. 135. 9 *Post*, § CXXXIV. 10 *Post*, § CXXX. 11 Vat. Fr. 255, 260; D. 39. 5. 31. 2. 12 *Post*, §§ LII, LX.

the *tutela* of his unemancipated younger brothers, though this went in principle only to agnates[1].

Thus in Justinian's time there was little disadvantage in *emancipatio*. What evils had he in view when he changed the law of *adoptio*, owing to the possibility of capricious adoption followed by capricious emancipation? He explains the risk as arising in exceptional cases. Where *A* gives his son *B* in adoption, and dies, *B*, being in another family, has no claim. Some years later the adoptor emancipates him. He is now an *emancipatus* of his original father, but this does not operate retrospectively, and he is thus excluded from either estate. Even if it were retrospective, the estate may long since have been dissipated[2].

XLVIII. CIVIL BONDAGE[3]. A relation set up by transfer by the *paterfamilias* to another by sale, in the form of *mancipatio*, i.e. *per aes et libram*. One so sold was not a *mancipium*, which means a slave, but was in an analogous position and was thus said to be *in mancipio* or *in mancipii causa*[4]. Except for noxal surrender for delict, and the formal sales in *adoptio* and *emancipatio*, the institution was practically obsolete in classical law and it is not clear how far the recorded rules applied to it in earlier times. The bondsman was still a *civis*. His marriage was not affected[5]. His children conceived after the sale were, in the time of Gaius, in his *potestas* (in abeyance while he was *in mancipio*) or in that of his *paterfamilias*, though it is possible that before the Empire they too were *in mancipio*[6]. How his political rights were affected we do not certainly know. But, though free, he was *servi loco*. He acquired for his holder as a slave did[7]. He could take nothing by the will of his holder unless freed by it[8]. If instituted by him he was a *necessarius heres*, with however a *ius abstinendi*, like a *suus heres*[9]. For wrongful treatment of one *in mancipio* an *actio iniuriarum* would lie[10].

The relation might be ended by manumission, like that of a slave, except that the *l. Aelia Sentia* and *l. Fufia Caninia* had no application[11], and the *manumissus* became *ingenuus*, not *libertinus*[12]. Where the bondage resulted from noxal surrender by the *paterfamilias* for a wrong

1 *Post*, § LII. 2 C. 8. 47. 10. pr. 3 Desserteaux, *Capitis Deminutio*, 1. 233 *sqq.*, for a full but conjectural account of this institution. 4 He is not a slave but in an analogous position. Cp. "*in libertate*," for one not really free but in actual liberty; "*in possessione*," for one who holds a thing but has not technical possession (6. 1. 9); "*in servitute*," for one wrongly held in apparent slavery (4. 6. 1. 1). Desserteaux (1. 245) considers that "*in mancipio*" is used where it is real, as in noxal surrender of a *filius*, and "*in mancipii causa*" where it is formal, as in adoption. But see, e.g., G. 1. 135. 5 G. 1. 135. 6 Labeo held that they were, if conceived after *potestas* destroyed (G. 1. 135). But this, which was indeed rejected, proves nothing for the other case. 7 G. 2. 86; Ulp. 24. 23, 24. 8 G. 1. 123. 9 G. 2. 160. 10 G. 1. 141. As to actions on his contracts (G. 4. 80), *post*, § CXLI. 11 G. 1. 138, 139. 12 Follows from the applications in *adoptio*, etc.

by the *filius*, the bondsman, at least in later classical law, could demand manumission as soon as, by his labour, he had repaid the damage[1]. Further, Gaius tells us that at the *Census* a bondsman could free himself, without consent of the holder, by entering his name on the *Census* roll[2]. Whether this is ancient or not we cannot tell: it did not apply in the formal cases or in noxal surrender, and these were the only surviving cases in his time[3], while the *Census* also was obsolete.

These rules no doubt represent different stages in the history of the institution: we cannot discuss their various sources. Other questions will arise in connexion with *capitis deminutio*, but some can be taken here. Could a bondsman be assigned by his holder? We know that he usually was assigned back to his father in the process of *emancipatio*[4], and though this is an artificial proceeding, there seems no reason to doubt that he could be transferred in the ordinary ways of business. Could a man sell himself into bondage? There is nothing inherently improbable in this; if he could not, Roman law was exceptional, for such a right has existed in Jewish, Germanic, Greek, and many other systems[5]. What is known of *nexum* seems to shew that a man could, *per aes et libram*, submit himself to the power of another, but a *nexus* is not *in mancipio*[6]. A woman could sell herself into *manus* by a modified form of *mancipatio*, but it was not actual *mancipatio* and she did not go into bondage[7]. But there is no direct evidence of the possibility.

The subject of persons *alieni iuris* involves the consideration of their power to bind themselves by contract. We have not considered from this point of view the *filiafamilias*, the woman *in manu* and the bondsman. Gaius tells us that they could not so bind themselves[8]: it is not clear how long this state of things lasted. As *manus* and bondage disappeared soon after, the question arises practically only for the *filiafamilias*. The better view seems to be, in view of the incapacity of a woman *sui iuris* to bind herself without the *auctoritas* of her tutor, that the disability of a woman *alieni iuris* lasted throughout the classical age but only so long as the *tutela* of adult women lasted[9].

XLIX. *Capitis Deminutio*[10]. Before passing to persons *sui iuris* we have to consider the principles of *capitis deminutio*. In dealing with the law of persons we have adopted the method indicated by this con-

1 Coll. 2. 3. 2 G. 1. 140. 3 A five-year period is common in Roman Law, e.g. in tax-farming contracts and in hiring of land. See also 5. 2. 9; 40. 12. 29. 1; 40. 15. 1. pr.; C. Th. 5. 7. 2, etc. 4 *Ante*, p. 131. 5 Leviticus, 25. 47; Pollock and Maitland, *Hist. of Eng. Law*, 1. 12; Daremberg et Saglio, *s.v. Servi*. 6 *Post*, § CL. Such a possibility might account for the strange rule in G. 4. 80, *post*, § CXLI. 7 *Ante*, p. 119. 8 G. 3. 104. 9 Girard, *Man.* 497, who cites the material texts, and for later law compares Inst. 4. 7. 7, and D. 14. 6. 9. 2. 10 Desserteaux, *Capitis Deminutio*; *S.M.W.* 185; earlier lit. Girard, *Man.* 208, n. 5.

ception. *Caput* is civil capacity. *Capitis deminutio* is defined by Gaius as *prioris status permutatio*[1]. It has in classical and later law three degrees: *maxima*, loss of liberty, i.e. enslavement, involving loss of *civitas* and family rights; *media* or *minor*, loss of *civitas* without loss of liberty, as by *deportatio*, or (perhaps) joining a Latin colony[2], involving also loss of family rights; and *minima*, change of family position (*status hominis commutatur*), of which the most salient characteristic, or requirement, is that it involves rupture of agnatic ties, leaving liberty and *civitas* unaffected. Such cases are *adoptio*, *adrogatio*, entry into *manus*, emancipation and entry into or manumission from civil bondage[3].

This account of the institution, from Gaius, does not tell us the meaning of the term or the history of the notion, both of which (for the conception of *capitis deminutio* underwent evolution) have been the subject of controversy. The threefold scheme is relatively late: Cicero knows only of *capitis deminutio*, and applies the name only to cases of what were later *capitis deminutio minima*[4], but his language elsewhere might be taken to indicate that he would have put on one and the same level some cases of what were later *maxima* and *media*[5]. Even in the Digest we get in some texts a distinction into two classes, *maior* and *minor*, the latter being what was usually called *minima*[6]. Early law probably knew of only one *capitis deminutio*, but whether that covered all the three types of later law, or whether it applied only to cases involving loss of *civitas* or only to such as left *civitas* intact, i.e. the later *minima*, is disputed. Not all cases thought of as *capitis deminutio minima* in classical law may have been so regarded in earlier law, for the conception of the institution no doubt changed. *Status permutatio* as a definition is certainly not primitive. The only institution, recorded as a case of *capitis deminutio minima*, which is certainly very ancient, is *adrogatio*[7], and it is not clear that this was early thought of as *capitis deminutio*[8].

There is the same obscurity about the notion underlying *capitis deminutio*. On one view its essential is destruction of the personality, a view suggested by texts which speak of it as a sort of civil death[9], but

1 G. 1. 159. 2 G. 1. 131, "*iussu parentis*." It is not clear that it was *c. d.* A Latin coming to Rome had a vote in the *Comitia*, *ante*, p. 93. 3 G. 1. 162, 163; Ulp. 11. 13; Inst. 1. 16. 3. The scheme in classical law is not symmetrical, *Familia* and *Civitas* are linked. No one can have either without both and liberty too. But a man may have liberty without the others. In early times, none but *cives* were thought of as free for Roman Law. 4 *Topica*, 4. 18, 6. 29. 5 *Pro Caecina*, 33. 96; *De Domo*, 29, 30 (77–79). 6 38. 16. 1. 4; 38. 17. 1. 8; Cuq, *Man.* 111. See also Desserteaux, *cit.* 2. 1. 7 Antiquity vouched for by its religious character. 8 Desserteaux (*cit.* 1. 47) thinks *adrogatio* not to have been a *c. d.* till the Empire; Cohn (cited, Desserteaux, *ib.*) thinks it one of the oldest. 9 G. 3. 101, 153, etc. It is shewn by Levy, *Die Röm. Kapitalstrafe*, that the association of *caput* with *civitas* and the notion of capital punishment as covering loss of Citizenship comes in only near the end of the Republic where exile, hitherto a way

this does not fit the facts[1]. On the other hand, the conception of it as annihilation is consistent with the view[2] that death is mentioned as a mere loose comparison. On another view, which suits the name better (especially in the form *capitis minutio*[3]), it is essentially a diminution of capacity[4]. It would follow that it occurred only where the resulting position was worse, as in *adrogatio*, or where in the process the subject was sold into quasi slavery. This would account for the passage of vestal virgins from *potestas* without *capitis deminutio*[5], but it conflicts with rules of classical law, e.g. that the children of *adrogatus* suffer *capitis deminutio*[6], though they undergo no process and take no worse position, which Savigny explains as an error of Paul due to a false conception of *capitis deminutio*[7], and the rule that a woman going into *manus* suffers *capitis deminutio*, though the process does not reduce her to quasi slavery, a rule which Savigny restricts to women *sui iuris*[8]. It conflicts also with the rule that enfranchisement from civil bondage was a *capitis deminutio*[9], a rule not known when Savigny wrote. But these difficulties and others which present themselves in connexion with the various opinions may be met by the view that development, actually traceable in the scheme of *capitis deminutiones* (for whether there existed originally one or two degrees, there clearly were not three) also occurred in the fundamental conception of it. It may be that at first[10] it meant extinction of gentile and therefore of civil right, and that, so far as what came to be called *cap. dem. minima* was concerned, this conception was replaced by the notion of *familiae mutatio*. The distinction between *maxima* and *media*, apparently of the beginning of the Empire, though the immediate effects of the two are the same, may be accounted for by the tendency to threefold arrangements[11], aided by the separation of the notion of *libertas* from that of *civitas*, and the obvious fact that the man

of escaping punishment, came to be regarded as a punishment. The article pursues the history of "*capitis*," "*capitalis*," in association with crime.

1 It destroys a will: death brings it into operation, G. 2. 145, 146; Ulp. 23. 4; Inst. 2. 17. 4. Death destroys criminal and delictal liabilities which *c. d.* leaves unaffected (*post*, § CXCVI). 2 Eisele, *Beiträge*, 167 *sqq.*; Desserteaux, *cit.* 2. 1. 129 *sqq.* Eisele holds *c. d.* essentially diminution, Desserteaux essentially a destruction: both reject the idea of death as more than an analogy. 3 4. 5. 1, 2; Ulp. 27. 5, etc. 4 Savigny, *System*, 2. §§ 68 *sqq.*; Eisele, *Beiträge*, 160 *sqq.* See D. 4. 5. 3, Paul. 5 Aul. Gell. 1. 12. 9. 6 4. 5. 3. pr.; it may indeed be said that the children lose the position of *sui heredes*. 7 *System*, 2. 479. He thinks it an expression of a later, not generally accepted, view of *c. d.* as "*familiae mutatio*." Eisele, *Beiträge*, 215, adopting in general Savigny's view, understands "*placet*" to express a personal "*Belieben*" of the jurist, hardly possible. 8 *System*, 2. 65. Eisele, *op. cit.* 200, leaves open the question whether it applies to women, *sui iuris*. G. 1. 162 and Ulp. 11. 13 express no limitation. 9 G. 1. 162, 163. 10 Beseler, *Beitr.* 4. 92, holds that originally it was the group which was *deminutus*, lessened by a *caput* by expulsion of a member, so that so far as he is concerned it means annihilation. 11 Goudy, *Trichotomy in Roman Law*, 50 *sqq.*

enslaved is really extinct, while the other may still exist, as a Latin or peregrine, and be a factor in commercial relations[1].

These considerations may explain the peculiarities of the *capitis deminutio* resulting from the first or second sale of a *filiusfamilias*. It is a *deminutio*[2], but its character is exceptional. On manumission the subject reverts to *potestas*: the *minutio* and its effects are wiped out. Thus it is provisional. Again we learn that each sale and each manumission is a *capitis deminutio*[3], but also that the whole process is a *capitis deminutio*[4]. Again, children conceived during the bondage are in the *potestas* of the old *paterfamilias*[5] and yet all *capitis deminutio* destroys the agnatic tie[6]. Either this is incorrect for that case, in connexion with which, however, the statement is made, or children may be born into an agnatic group to which the father did not belong at any time between the conception and the birth. If the bondsman was freed after the third sale, the manumitter succeeded at civil law to the exclusion of the father[7], whose rights were destroyed. If, after the first sale, the father died, and the holder then freed him, he succeeded, as a *postumus*, to his own father[8]. The manumitter having no right to succeed him, the rights of the quasi patron were thus non-existent[9]. These conflicting rules do not represent any coherent conception; they seem to represent a state of things in which the old conception of *capitis deminutio*, whatever it was, is breaking down but some resulting rules are retained side by side with others which belong to the conception of it as (at least in the case of *minima*) *familiae mutatio* simply, a conception not fully reached till the later classical age[10].

The obscurity of the early conceptions raises the question whether a Latin suffered *capitis deminutio* on attaining Roman citizenship. The only evidence seems to be a passage quoted by Girard[11] from the *l. Salpensana*, which provides that those who became Roman *cives* in the

1 Eisele (*cit.*, pp. 163 *sqq.*), regarding *c. d.* as essentially diminution also accepts in general the notion of incompatibility (Cohn, *Zur Lehre von der C. D.*), i.e. the effects of *c. d.* are in general due to the incompatibility of the old right or liability with the new position (*op. cit.* 185 *sqq.*). 2 G. 1. 162. 3 *Ibid.* 4 *Ibid.* "*quod accidit in his qui adoptantur.*" 5 G. 1. 135. 6 G. 1. 163. 7 G. *Ep.* 1. 6. 3; Inst. 3. 9. 3. 8 G. 3. 6; Ulp. 23. 3; Coll. 16. 3. 7. 9 Even the view of Kniep (*Der Rechtsgelehrte Gaius*, 48; *Gai. Comm. Prim.* 270) that the statement of Gaius (1. 162) that each sale and *manumissio* is a *c. d.* is a later addition, that the sale and manumission together constitute a *c. d.*, and that in the case of a son Gaius does not mean each sale but only the third, does not mend the matter. The son released would not be, in effect, a *postumus* as he was (n. 8), but would have been a *suus* all the time. And one sold a third time but not yet released would not have suffered *c. d.* at all, though *potestas* was destroyed. 10 So Desserteaux, *cit.* 1. 37, 239, etc., but his argument, in attempting to shew that with his view of the evolution the doctrines can be made coherent, seems to require that Gaius shall have laid down rules which had ceased to be true a century earlier. 11 *Manuel*, 210, n. 1.

colony, e.g. through magistracy, should remain in the *manus*, *potestas* or bondage in which they were, if their holder also acquired *civitas*, and should not lose any rights as patrons or *patroni liberi*[1]. These are provisions to avoid results exactly those of a *capitis deminutio*. One of them seems to be corrupt, but they testify to a close similarity between the institutions of the colony and those of Rome[2] (apart from express adoption of Roman rules, also evidenced). The accounts of *capitis deminutio* do not mention this case[3], nor do the full accounts of attainment of *civitas* by Latins[4] say anything about *capitis deminutio*[5]. In any case certain results of *capitis deminutio* did not occur[6].

L. In considering the effects of *capitis deminutio* it is necessary to distinguish between those which are really the effect of the *deminutio*, however conceived, and those which are merely accompaniments, but result not from the *deminutio* but from the juristic event of which it also is a result. It may be doubted indeed whether the distinction can be clearly made out[7]. The following however are indicated in the texts as results of the *capitis deminutio* itself.

(i) Destruction of agnatic ties and *potestas*[8]. This is the most striking result, and might, in classical law, almost serve for a definition, but for the fact that vestal virgins and *flamines diales* passed out of the *potestas* without *capitis deminutio*[9]. Cognatic ties were not affected. In practice this affected only *capitis deminutio minima*, for enslavement, being *iuris gentium*, destroyed cognation, and a *deportatus*, being a peregrine *sine civitate certa*, could not take under a will or on intestacy[10]. Though *potestas* and *manus* were destroyed, marriage was not ended except by *maxima capitis deminutio*, though *media* converted it to *nuptiae non iustae*[11]. Marriage was not affected by *capitis deminutio minima*, but, if the wife was *in manu*, adrogation would transfer the *manus* to the new *paterfamilias*, while emancipation and *adoptio* would apparently leave the wife in the old *familia*.

(ii) Destruction of life interests (*ususfructus*, *usus*)[12]. The effect of

1 *Lex Salpensana*, XXII, XXIII; Girard, *Textes*, 109, 110. 2 The text seems to attribute *tutoris optio* to males—if this is so it is an error or a rule different from that of Rome. 3 G. 1. 158–163; Ulp. 11. 9–13. 4 G. 1. 28–35; 1. 67 *sqq.*; Ulp. 3. 1–6. 5 The magistrate cannot have dropped his assets and liabilities. The same question arises for a *civis* voluntarily joining a Latin colony, *post*, p. 139. 6 Messa, *Ingenuitas*, 36, for possible cases of *c. d.* other than those recorded. 7 It is indeed maintained by Desserteaux (*cit.*) that the effects are never those of *c. d.* but of the juristic act concerned. The *c. d.* is a mere descriptive term (*op. cit.*, 2. 1. 60, 93, 97, etc.), but when in the Empire certain juristic acts lost characteristics which had produced these effects, while the effects remained, these effects were attributed to the *c. d.* (*ib.* 98, 301, etc.). This is the main thesis of both parts of vol. 2. 8 G. 1. 163; 3. 21, etc.; Inst. 3. 5. 1, etc. It may create new ones, e.g., in adoption. 9 *Ante*, p. 130. 10 *Ante*, p. 97, n. 7. 11 *Ante*, p. 105. See G. 1. 128. 12 7. 4. 1. pr. Not the later developed *habitatio* and *operae servorum*, *post*, § XCVI.

this, for *capitis deminutio minima*, was evaded in classical law by devices for renewal of the right so destroyed, and in Justinian's law the rule no longer applied to this case[1].

(iii) Avoidance of a will previously made. This is laid down generally[2], but the existence of *peculium castrense*, in regard to which a *filius* was treated as a *paterfamilias* and had power of testation, caused some difficulty. In later classical law his will dealing with this remained valid[3]. The effect of the general rule was modified by the Praetor who gave *bonorum possessio* notwithstanding the *capitis deminutio*, if the testator was *capax* when he made the will and at death, provided the *deminutio* was not the effect of his voluntary act[4].

(iv) Transfer of assets of the *minutus*. All passed from him, but the ultimate destination of those not destroyed depended on the rules of each case, which have nothing to do with the *minutio*[5]. There were however exceptions. A *civis* passing to a Latin colony may have suffered *capitis deminutio*. If this was *iussu patris* he had indeed no assets to lose[6], but a *paterfamilias* who so passed over did not lose them: he sometimes did it to avoid a fine[7]. Where a *filius* was emancipated or adopted, his *peculium castrense* and *quasi castrense* went with him: the *capitis deminutio* did not affect them[8]. The right of an *adstipulator*, by reason of its intensely personal nature[9], was extinguished by *capitis deminutio*, as were rights under a pending *iudicium legitimum*[10]. On the dominant classical view *societas* was ordinarily ended by *capitis deminutio minima*, but at some time, probably before Justinian, it was treated as continuing and not a new partnership[11]. Patronal rights were in general ended. In *maxima* or *media* the rights of *liberi patroni* appear to have taken their place[12]: these rights being independent, this is extinction, not transfer. On adrogation they passed to the new *paterfamilias*, except that any *operae*, due under *iusiurandum liberti*, ceased, and *reverentia* was still due to the *adrogatus*[13]. If a *libertus* suffered *capitis*

1 Inst. 2. 4. 3; C. 3. 33. 16. 2. 2 G. 2. 145, 146; Ulp. 23. 4; Inst. 2. 17. 4. 3 28. 3. 6. 13; 37. 11. 1. 8. Eisele, however, *Beiträge*, 195 *sqq.*, attributes this to Justinian. No difficulty as to actual *miles*: his will needs no form (*post*, § CXXVI), and is therefore valid *ex nova voluntate*, 29. 1. 22; Inst. 2. 11. 5. 4 37. 11. 11. 2. Testator was adrogated and later again became *sui iuris*. (Other reliefs in case of *c. d. maior*, *post*, § CII.) In the time of Gaius the *b. p.* was *sine re*, later *cum re*, *post*, § CXXXIX. 5 As to *adrogatio*, *post*, § CXLI; enslavement, *ante*, §§ XXIV *sq.*; *deportatio*, *ante*, p. 97, n. 7. 6 G. 1. 131. 7 Cicero, *Pro Caec.* 33. 98. He had lost *civitas* but still had a vote in the tribes (*ante*, p. 93). Apparently a *tutela* over him still persisted (*Sch. Sin.* 16. 42) but it may have been expressly preserved, *ante*, p. 138. 8 *Post*, § XCIX. *Bona adventicia* of late law were regulated by legislation which gave no operation to *capitis deminutio* as such. 9 G. 3. 114, *post*, § CLV. 10 G. 3. 83. Nature of *iudicia legitima*, *post*, § CCXXXII. They descend from *l. actio*. Rights under them could not be acquired through a representative, Bonfante, *Corso*, 6. 30. 11 G. 3. 153; D. 17. 2. 58. 2; h. t. 65. 11, 12. Eisele, *Beiträge*, 171, 190 *sqq.*; Desserteaux, *op. cit.* 2. 169. 12 37. 14. 4, 21. 13 G. 3. 83; D. 2. 4. 10. 2.

deminutio maxima or *media* the patronal relation was destroyed, if *minima*, the patron's right was not affected, subject to *restitutio natalium*[1]. *Tutela* was ended if the ward suffered *capitis deminutio*, but was not affected by *capitis deminutio minima* of the tutor[2] except in two cases. *Tutela legitima* was ended as it rested on a right of succession, itself destroyed[3], and *tutela cessicia* was also destroyed[4]. Against destruction of rights of succession by *capitis deminutio maxima* or *media* there might be relief on restoration[5], and *minima* had little effect in the praetorian scheme of succession, except where the *minutus* was transferred to, and was still in, another family[6]. The rule did not apply to the reciprocal rights of succession between mother and child introduced in the Empire[7]. Further, a woman's claim for recovery of *dos* was not affected by her *capitis deminutio*, e.g. if she was emancipated by her *paterfamilias*[8].

(v) Destruction of liabilities, other than criminal or delictal[9]. This exception, retained as being necessary, arises from the fact that the remedies are substitutes for revenge[10], the desire for which is not affected by the *minutio*. The extinction of other liabilities, whatever its origin[11], obviously produced unfair results and was relieved against in many ways. On penal slavery or forfeiture the *fiscus* took only the nett balance: it was liable to creditors and could sue debtors[12]. The Praetor applied similar rules, giving *utiles actiones* against the holder where on *capitis deminutio maxima* or *media*, the property passed into private hands[13].

On *adrogatio* and *manus* there were remedies which can best be

1 *Ante*, p. 90. 2 *Tutela*, a *publicum munus*, like other such is not affected, 4. 5. 6, 7. 3 G. 1. 158, 163; later law, *post*, § LII. 4 G. 1. 170. 5 Restoration from slavery, Buckland, *Slavery*, 410. 6 *Post*, § CXXX. 7 4. 5. 7. pr.; 38. 17. 1. 8. A wife emancipated did not lose her claim for *dos*, 4. 5. 8, 9. 8 *Ib.*; *ante*, p. 109. 9 4. 5. 2. 3. The discharge from other obligations apparently left a *naturalis obligatio*, *post*, § CLXXXIX. Senn (*N.R.H.* 1913, 191) suggests a further exception. In a group of actions, all *bonae fidei* and all infaming (*pro socio, depositi, mandati, tutelae*) the claim survived *c. d. minima*. The texts (17. 1. 61; 17. 2. 58. 2; 16. 3. 21. pr.; 27. 3. 4. 1, 11) do not establish the proposition. All are cases in which the *minutus* continues performance of the contract, etc., after the *minutio*, and they shew merely that in such a case the thing must be treated as a whole. They are closely analogous to the case of continued administration by a manumitted slave in which a similar rule is laid down by some jurists (3. 5. 16–17), though a slave cannot be sued after freedom on transactions during slavery (3. 5. 16; C. 4. 14, *passim*). See 16. 3. 21 where the cases of the slave and son are treated side by side. In deposit it is simply for return of the thing, which the depositee still holds. So in 17. 1. 61, what the suggested doctrine requires is that if performance under the mandate is not continued the *mandatarius* can be sued for what was done before the *minutio*; but this is not shewn. 10 *Post*, § CXCVI. 11 Though commonly attributed to the *c. d.* this result may be a survival from old law in which no one not *sui iuris* was capable of *obligatio*. 12 48. 20. 4, 10. pr.; 49. 14. 6, 21. 13 4. 5. 2. pr. If a man enslaved was afterwards released by the State he did not revert to his old rights and liabilities, apart from express *restitutio*, which might be more or less complete, 44. 7. 30; C. 9. 51. 4, 5. In the case of *deportatio*, if the estate was insufficient the creditors had *utiles actiones* against the *deportatus* by which later acquired property could be made available, *ante*, § XXXVI.

considered in dealing with succession[1]. On *emancipatio*, liabilities in respect of *peculium castrense* and *quasi castrense* were not affected. Apart from these there was a difficulty. A *filiusfamilias* of full age was capable of civil *obligatio*, but this was extinguished by the *capitis deminutio*. The Praetor gave an action, but as the transaction may have concerned the father's affairs only, and, in any case, the assets in connexion with which it was gone through did not ordinarily pass, it was given only *causa cognita*[2], and subject to *beneficium competentiae*. If he passed from *potestas* without *capitis deminutio*, but did not inherit, he was civilly liable, but the Praetor allowed an action against him only *causa cognita*[3].

1 *Post*, § CXLI. 2 14. 5. 2. 3 14. 5. 2. pr. See Lenel, *E.P.* 278. If the son had inherited, the action was *in solidum*, and the creditor might choose between this action and an action against him for his share of the debt as *heres*, 14. 5. 4. pr. Against the *heres* of the *minutus* it was always *in solidum*, h. t. 4. 3. But in both these cases it would seem to be still only *causa cognita*. These actions lay only where the transaction was with an *extraneus*. See, as to *causae cognitio*, *post*, p. 723.

CHAPTER IV

THE LAW OF PERSONS (*cont.*). THE LAW OF THE FAMILY (*cont.*). PERSONS *SUI IURIS*

LI. We have to consider persons *sui iuris* only so far as they were under disabilities. Owing to defects of various kinds they might be under guardianship, either *tutela* or *cura* (*curatio*). *Tutela*, the more important, might be over males or females on account of youth, or, in classical law, over women of any age on account of sex[1].

TUTELA of *IMPUBERES*. The governing principle was that every one *sui iuris* under puberty must have a *tutor*, at least if he had property or expectations[2]. Guardianship is no doubt universal, but had in Rome characteristics not found elsewhere, and as it was provided for in the XII Tables it was treated as *iuris civilis*[3]. It seems to have been originally conceived of as an artificial extension of the *potestas* till the child was capable of founding a *potestas* for himself, a notion involving perpetual *tutela* for women, since they could never have *potestas* or *sui heredes*. There was a practical reason for this way of regulating the matter. Originally *tutela* was less in the interest of the child than in that of the guardian. The *tutor* was the person who would take the property if the child died *impubes*: *ubi emolumentum successionis ibi onus tutelae*[4], in which expression the word *onus* would have been represented in early law by *ius*. So soon as a child reached puberty he might have children: the interest of his relatives in the property would cease, and accordingly

1 G. 1. 142–144; Inst. 1. 13. pr. 2 C. 5. 31. 2. 3 Inst. 1. 13. 1; D. 26. 1. 1. pr. The institution existed in Latin colonies. *L. Salpensana*, c. XXIX (Bruns, 1. 146; Girard, *Textes*, 112), contains provisions as to appointment by local magistrates to Latin members of the community; c. XXII contains provisions as to *tutoris optio* (*post*, § LX). *Schol. Sin.* 16 (Girard, *Textes*, 618) speaks of a brother as *tutor* of an *impubes* who has become a member of a Latin colony. 4 Inst. 1. 17. pr.; C. 5. 30. 5. 3. The functions of *heres* and *tutor* may have gone together before the XII Tables, de Visscher, *Ét.* 82; Solazzi, *La legge delle XII Tavole sulla tutela.* Arangio Ruiz, *Erede e tutore*, supposes a kind of fiduciary inheritance in the *tutor*. See Rabel, *Z.S.S.* 1930, 316, for criticism.

the *tutela* ceased. Before the Empire this view had been superseded by the more modern conception of guardianship[1], but the old view is reflected in the fundamental rules of the institution. The rule (out of harmony with the new conception), that *tutela* of children ended at puberty, was retained but supplemented by such devices as *restitutio in integrum* and *curatio*[2], which gave similar but less effective protection. The perpetual *tutela* of women was not abolished when its absurdity became apparent, but types of *tutor* were invented who could not refuse *auctoritas*[3].

Gaius and Justinian classify *tutores* according to the mode of appointment: *testamentarii, legitimi, fiduciarii, a magistratu dativi*. The order is not historical: *legitimi* were the oldest, but *tutela* by will is given priority as being the most usual and important[4].

TUTELA TESTAMENTARIA. The XII Tables authorised a *paterfamilias* to appoint tutors by will to *sui heredes impuberes*, i.e. those *impuberes* who became *sui iuris* by his death[5]. The jurists extended this to *postumi*, i.e. those not *sui heredes* when the will was made but becoming such afterwards, e.g. a child born after the will was made, or even after the testator's death, or grandchildren who became *sui heredes* by the death of the father after the grandfather's will was made[6]. Justinian defines them as those who are in such a position that if they were born in the lifetime of the testator they would be *sui heredes*[7]. This is, as the text says, only one of the many cases in which *postumi* are treated as already born. When, under Augustus, codicils were admitted, the rule arose that a *tutor* could be appointed by codicil if it was confirmed, actually or by anticipation, by a will[8]. Classical law required formal words, e.g. *Titium tutorem do*, or *T. tutor esto*[9]. In later law the appointment might

1 "*Ad tuendum eum*," Inst. 1. 13. 1. As old as Servius, D. 26. 1. 1. pr. 2 *Post*, § LXII. 3 *Post*, § LX. 4 *Fiduciarii* (for whom the Digest has no separate title) seem to have been, for some jurists, a mere variety of *legitimi*. G. classifies *tutores* by the immediate appointing authority. The *Liber singularis regularum* (Ulp. 11. 2) classifies logically but inconveniently by the ultimate legislative authority on which the appointment rests: *legitimi, senatusconsultis constituti, moribus introducti*. The first group covers all the ordinary types, all of which rest ultimately on *lex*. The second consists of special cases provided by *sc.* e.g. substitute tutor for a woman in case of emergency. The third deals with special *tutores praetorii* appointed where litigation arose between tutor and ward, a practice which seems to have grown up without legislative sanction: it does not appear in the Edict. For Schulz, *ad l.* (see also Lenel, *Z.S.S.* 1927, 32), this is post-classical. But G. 1. 188 shews that there were various classifications. This is probably that attributed by him to Servius. 5 Ulp. 11. 14, 15. 6 G. 1. 146. They can upset the will unless instituted or disinherited. 7 Inst. 1. 13. 4; G. 1. 146. This mode of statement is better than that of Gaius in 1. 147 (26. 2. 1. 1), and Q. Mucius (50. 17. 73. 1). These would validate appointment by *avus* where *pater* survived him. They are stating cases in which the appointment may be effective. The Inst. state the case in which it will be effective 8 26. 2. 3. pr.; *post*, § CXXVI. 9 G. 1. 149; Vat. Fr. 229.

be in Greek and under Justinian there were no rules of form[1]. The *tutor* must be a *persona certa*[2], and it must be clear to which child or children he was appointed[3]. The appointment might be conditional or from or to a certain time[4], and even to a disinherited child[5]. Any one might be appointed with whom there was *testamenti factio*, except that the *l. Junia* expressly excluded Junian Latins[6]. Thus a man might appoint his slave, and, at least in later law, this implied a gift of freedom[7]. He might appoint another man's slave, *cum liber erit*, and if these words were omitted they would be implied[8].

In these cases the appointment was valid at civil law: in others, though the appointment was in some way defective, it would be confirmed by the Praetor as a matter of course and the *tutor* considered as a testamentary tutor, the so-called *tutela testamentaria imperfecta*, e.g. where the appointment was in an unconfirmed codicil or informal writing[9], or in a will which failed[10], or informal words were used, or he was called *curator*[11], or where the appointment was to a son not *in potestas* (emancipated or by a *concubina*)[12], provided in these last cases that property was left to him. If the Praetor was satisfied that the father had died without changing his mind the confirmation went with no enquiry as to fitness[13]. In other cases the appointment might be confirmed after enquiry, provided that the *impubes* was instituted and had no other provision, e.g. where an *extraneus* appointed, or a patron to his *libertus*[14]. But these were really appointments by the magistrate[15].

LII. *Tutela legitima*. Though this was said to be based on the XII Tables[16], and therefore called *legitima*, it was probably much older: it represented the primitive notion of *tutela*, as a right in potential successors to look after the estate. The cases of *legitima tutela* were:

Agnates. The XII Tables expressly provided that *impuberes sui*

1 C. 5. 28. 8. Doubted in cl. law if it could be "*post mortem heredis*" or before the *institutio heredis*, G. 2. 234, *post*, § CIV. 2 26. 2. 20; G. 2. 240. 3 Vat. Fr. 229; D. 26. 2. 23, 30. 4 26. 2. 8. 2. 5 26. 2. 4. 6 26. 2. 21; Ulp. 11. 16. 7 *Ante*, p. 74. 8 It might imply a fideicommissary gift, C. 7. 4. 10; see 26. 2. 10. 4, 32. 2. Justinian? Eisele, *Z.S.S.* 1890. 27. Appointment of a *servus alienus* "*cum liber erit*" may have needed magisterial confirmation, as did appointment of one freed by *fc.* 26. 2. 28. 1. Similar rules probably applied as to other temporary disabilities, 26. 2. 10. 3; *captivus*, G. 1. 187. 9 26. 3. 1. 1, 10. 10 h. t. 3. 11 h. t. 1. 1, 6. 12 C. 5. 29. 4. Justinian? In 26. 3. 7 the words "*cui nihil relictum est*" are interp. Bonfante, *Corso*, 1. 418. He holds the same of "*sine inquisitione*," but that is less clear. 13 26. 3. 8. No doubt a praetorian will was in the same position. 14 26. 2. 28. 2; 26. 3. 5. 15 Thus there might be need for security (*post*, § LV). Texts on appointment by mother not clear (see 26. 2. 4; 26. 3. 2; 31. 69. 2; C. 5. 28. 4; C. 5. 29. 1). There was an enquiry as to fitness. If this was clear and the mother had instituted the child the *tutela* was in effect *testamentary*. But if there was no institution of the child, it was in effect an appointment by the magistrate. Bonfante, *cit.* 417 as to interp. of C. 5. 28. 4, making it absolutely valid if the child was instituted. 16 26. 4. 1. pr., 5. pr.; G. 1. 155.

iuris were in the *tutela* of their agnates if there was no testamentary tutor, and, as this was in view of the right of succession, the *proximi*[1]. In historic times this means intestate as to *tutela*: it may be that under the XII Tables agnates came in only on absolute intestacy[2]. If however the nearest agnate was a woman, e.g. a sister, the *tutela* was in the next[3], who would normally be the *tutor* of the woman also. If the nearest died, or was *capite minutus*, the *tutela* passed to the next[4]. If there were several qualified agnates in the same degree, e.g. brothers, or even an uncle and nephew, of the ward, they shared the *tutela*[5]. Changes in the law of succession led, in the later Empire, to corresponding extensions of *legitima tutela*. In A.D. 498 emancipated brothers shared in the *tutela*, though no longer agnates[6]. Justinian in a novel[7] gave the *tutela* to the next of kin whether agnatic or cognatic. It should be added that in default of agnates there was a gentile *tutela* in early law, but it cannot be traced beyond the beginning of the Empire, when gentile succession had already disappeared[8].

Legitima tutela arose only if there was no testamentary *tutor*[9], a rule construed with a tendency to exclusion of the *legitimus*. He was not admitted if there was a possibility of a testamentary *tutor*, e.g. one was appointed conditionally or *ex die*[10], or by a will not yet certain to operate[11], or the *tutor* appointed was under age, or captive or insane or deaf or dumb[12], or was excused, or removed for misconduct[13]. But if the testamentary *tutor* died or lost citizenship, this admitted the *legitimus*[14].

Patronus. The patron had *legitima tutela* not by express provision of the XII Tables, but by juristic inference from the right of succession given to him by the statute[15]. There could be no testamentary *tutor* to exclude him. Here too the *tutela* in general followed the succession. Of several patrons, as all succeeded, all were *tutores*[16], and if some were dead or *capite minuti* the others as they took the whole succession took the *tutela*[17]. If there had been manumission by bonitary owner, and *iteratio* by quiritary owner the latter was *tutor*, though the former took

1 26. 4. 1. 9; G. 1. 164; Inst. 1. 16. 7. 2 Solazzi, *Scr. C. Arno*, 46; De Visscher, *Mél. Cornil*, 2. 607, for a somewhat similar view. 3 26. 4. 1. 1, and no doubt if for any other reason the nearest agnate is incapable of *tutela*. Inst. 3. 2. 7. 4 26. 4. 2, 3. 9. 5 26. 4. 8, 9. 6 C. 5. 30. 4. 7 *Nov.* 118. 5. The *tutela* of mothers in certain cases in later law (*post*, § LIV) does not seem to have been *legitima* till very late. 8 *Laudatio Turiae*, Girard, *Textes*, 818. 9 G. 1. 155; Inst. 1. 15. pr. 10 26. 2. 10. pr., 11. pr. 11 Inst. 1. 20. 1. 12 26. 1. 17; Inst. 1. 20. 2. 13 26. 2. 11. 1, 2. Where a woman frees there is no *legitima tutela*; *patrona* cannot act and *liberi patronae* are not *l. patroni*. G. 1. 195. In 26. 4. 1. 1 the woman was a joint patron. 14 All, if there were several, not if merely some did, 26. 2. 11. 4. 15 G. 1. 165; D. 26. 4. 3. pr.; Inst. 1. 17. pr. 16 26. 4. 3. 4. 17 H. t. 3. 5. If one is a woman the others are the tutors, h. t. 3. 4.

the *bona*[1]. A patron was *tutor* though the manumission was under a trust, for he had the succession[2], but not if deprived of the *libertus* for wrongly impeding the freedom[3].

Liberi patroni. Here too the *tutela* was a juristic construction from the independent right of succession. The principles are as in the last case[4]. Thus the children shared it[5] and survivors held it to the exclusion of the children of deceased *liberi*[6].

Parens manumissor. Where an emancipating father received back the son in bondage, and freed him, he was like a patron: he was quasi-patron, with the same right of succession. Thus Justinian mentions him in stating the different cases of *legitima tutela*[7]. But neither Gaius nor the *liber singularis regularum* does so in the enumeration[8], though the former calls him *legitimus* in one passage[9] and in another says that he is a fiduciary *tutor* who "*et legitimus habeatur*[10]," and Ulpian in the Digest says that he "*vicem legitimi tutoris obtinet*[11]." He was essentially fiduciary, since he derived his right from the *pater fiduciarius* to whom the son was sold and from whom he was reacquired for the purpose of manumission. But, as Gaius says, he was like a patron and was to be honoured in the same way[12]. Thus the classical lawyers gave him honorary rank as a *legitimus tutor* distinct from patron, so that he did not necessarily give security[13]. There could be no joint *tutor*.

TUTELA FIDUCIARIA. As the name shews this was *tutela* arising from a trust. There were two types.

Extraneus manumissor. If, in an emancipation, the purchaser in the third sale freed the son, instead of, as was usual, selling him back to the *parens* to free[14], the manumitter became quasi-patron and had at civil law the same right of succession as the *parens* (though the Praetor postponed him to near relatives[15]). Accordingly he had *tutela*, but he was always regarded as fiduciary *tutor*, not *legitimus*[16]. Justinian's change in the form of emancipation abolished this case[17].

Children of *parens manumissor.* This case would not arise where the

1 One freed by bonitary owner was a Latin. The right to *bona* was with the manumitter, but not at civil law. By an express provision of the *l. Iunia*, the *tutela* was in any case with the quiritary owner, G. 1. 167; Ulp. 11. 19. 2 26. 4. 3. 1, 2. 3 26. 4. 3. 3, *ante*, p. 84. 4 *Arg.* 26. 4. 3. pr. 5 H. t. 3. 6. 6 H. t. 3. 7. A woman was excluded: if the only living child was a daughter, the *tutela* went to *nepotes*, 26. 4. 1. 1. If the patron had "assigned" the *libertus* to a daughter (*post*, § CXLI), though she took the whole succession, her brothers who took nothing were *tutores*, 26. 4. 1. 3. 7 Inst. 1. 18. 8 Ulp. 11. 3; G. 1. 166. Modern editors unjustifiably insert a long passage making Gaius mention him, Buckland, *J.R.S.* 1943, 11. 9 G. 1. 175. 10 G. 1. 172, cf. 1. 168. 11 26. 4. 3. 10. 12 G. 1. 172. 13 *Post*, § LV. 14 *Ante*, § XLVII. 15 Coll. 16. 9. 2; *post*, § CXXXV. 16 G. 1. 166 a, Inst. 1. 19. It was of course possible to employ a woman or two persons for the purpose of the sale but it is unlikely that this would happen. 17 *Ante*, p. 131.

final manumission was not by the father. It is always called fiduciary[1]. Justinian, noticing that the *tutela* of patron and *pater* is *legitima* and that of *liberi patroni* also is, while that of *liberi patris manumissoris* is not, explains this by the proposition that whereas in the case of *liberi patroni* the slave, if the manumission had not occurred, would have been in the control of the *liberi* and therefore falls into their *tutela*, the brother if he had not been emancipated would not have passed into the control of his brothers and thus not into their *tutela*, which is thus not *legitima* but fiduciary. The reasoning is defective, and the premises are not correct. A grandson would have fallen into the son's *potestas* and yet the *tutela* was fiduciary. A slave would not have fallen into the control of a son who had been disinherited, but did fall into his *legitima tutela*, as the disherison did not affect his potential right of succession to the *libertus*, which was independently provided for by the XII Tables and not simply inherited from the father[2]. The *tutela* does not rest on control, but on right of succession. Agnates could never have had control, but they were *legitimi tutores*. The argument does not shew why it was fiduciary: there is no *fiducia*, and the *liberi* do not take it voluntarily as Gaius says fiduciary tutors do[3]. The true explanation seems to lie in the equivocal nature of the *tutela* of the *parens*: this was primarily fiduciary and is in some sort inherited by his children. We do not indeed know that disinherited children were excluded. The case is rarely mentioned and was probably not common[4]. It was confined to males, and from the language of Justinian it is likely that surviving children held it to the exclusion of grandchildren, as in the case of *liberi patroni*[5], though the analogy may be a false one, as there seems to be no evidence of any civil right of succession[6].

LIII. *Tutela a magistratu dativa.* If there was no *tutor* under any of these provisions, one was appointed by the magistrate[7]. Such an appointment was, however, not an exercise of *imperium* or of *jurisdictio*: it was not a normal magisterial function, and existed only so far as expressly created by legislation[8]. It involved the recognition of a change in the conception of *tutela*, and it appeared early. A *lex Atilia*, of unknown but early date[9], provided for the appointment of *tutores* in Rome by the Praetor and the majority of the tribunes[10], and a *lex Iulia et*

1 G. 1. 175; Inst. 1. 19. 2 *Post*, § CXXXIV. 3 G. 1. 172. 4 A text attributed to Gaius (26. 1. 16. 1) says that *tutela* never passes by inheritance to another and adds, "*sed ad liberos virilis sexus perfectae aetatis descendunt legitimae, ceterae non descendunt.*" The words *perfectae aetatis* are due to Justinian and the whole clause may be. 5 Inst. 1. 19; see also G. 1. 175. 6 The name *fiduciaria* survives in Justinian's law though there is now no *fiducia*, even inherited. 7 G. 1. 185; Ulp. 11. 18; Inst. 1. 20. pr. 8 26. 1. 6. 2. 9 See Girard, *Man.* 224. 10 Shewing that it was originally designed for plebeians who had no access to the *comitia*.

Titia, perhaps two laws[1], of the end of the Republic, provided for the appointment in the provinces by the *praeses*. Gaius and Ulpian[2] both speak of this as the existing system[3], but literary evidence shews that Claudius[4] allowed it to be done by the *Consul*, *extra ordinem*, and this became the usual method[5]. M. Aurelius and Verus transferred it to a new official, the *praetor tutelaris*[6]. There was other change and there is some obscurity, especially as to Italy outside Rome[7]. In later law it was the duty of the *praefectus urbis* or the *praetor tutelaris*, at Rome, *secundum suam jurisdictionem*[8]: presumably the former dealt with cases from the higher classes. In the provinces, now all the territory but the capitals, appointments were by the *praeses*[9], or, in small estates (under Justinian, not more than 500 *solidi*), by local magistrates, needing however, till Justinian, authorisation by the *praeses*[10]. In all these cases except that of appointment by local authorities there was an enquiry as to fitness, replaced in the last case by the taking of security[11].

The cases of application of this *tutela* follow from what has been said. There might be none of the other *tutores*, or those that existed might be disqualified or excused or removed[12]. A testamentary *tutor* might be appointed conditionally or *ex die* or might at the moment be a *captivus*[13]. In the case of temporary excuse a *tutor* might be appointed, but in later law it was usual to appoint a *curator* in such cases, and a *tutor* only if actual *auctoritas* to some formal act was wanted. Many texts in the Digest have been altered to express the new system[14].

Ulpian tells us that such an appointment could not be conditional[15], and Papinian that it could not be *in diem*[16], restrictions due to the fact that it was done in court, *pro tribunali*, and not *de plano*[17].

Any relative or friend could take steps to have a *tutor* appointed[18], and if none did, creditors and others interested might give them notice

1 *Contra*, Zocco-Rosa, *Ann. Ist. Catania*, 1914, 31. 2 G. 1. 183, 185, 195; Ulp. 11. 18. 3 Kuebler, *Festschr. f. O. Hirschfeld*, 51, citing *Sch. Sin.* 45 and 54. 4 Suetonius, *Claudius*, 23. 5 The others dropped out. Inst. 1. 20. 3. 6 *Vita M. Aurelii*, 10. 7 Usually held that the *l. Atilia* applied to Italy as well as Rome, and the language of Ulpian (11. 18) seems to imply that though "*Romae tantum locum habet*" it left only the provinces to be provided for. But see Karlowa, *R.Rg.* 2. 285 *sqq.* As to the rules in the early Empire, for Italy, see Girard, *Man.* 225. 8 Inst. 1. 20. 4. 9 Those interested might nominate fit persons to be appointed and the *praeses* might receive names from the municipal magistrates in cases where these could not themselves appoint (27. 7. rub.; 27. 8. 1. 3, 10). 10 Inst. 1. 20. 4, 5. 11 *Post*, § LV. 12 G. 1. 182; Ulp. 11. 23. 13 G. 1. 186; D. 26. 1. 17; Inst. 1. 20. 2. 14 E.g., 26. 5. 7, 15; 27. 1. 28. 2; where litigation arose, by *legis actio*, between ward and *tutor*, a special *tutor* was appointed, called *tutor praetorius*; when *legis actio* disappeared the same rule was applied in all *legitima iudicia* (*post*, § CCXXXII), the *tutor* being appointed by the urban *praetor*, not the *praetor tutelaris*. Under Justinian it is a *curator*, G. 1. 184; Inst. 1. 21. 3. But see *post*, p. 164, n. 4 and § LXII. 15 26. 1. 6. 1; 50. 17. 77. 16 50. 17. 77. 17 26. 3. 7. 1. 18 26. 6. 2. pr.; C. 5. 31. 5.

to apply and, in default, themselves apply to the magistrate[1]. In some cases there was a duty to apply. *Liberti*, if they did not apply for a *tutor* to be appointed to their patron's child, were guilty of failure in *obsequium*[2]. Mothers were bound to apply if necessary, and to take pains to offer suitable *tutores* on penalty of being struck out of the list of successors on intestacy, unless they had grounds of excuse[3].

LIV. *Tutela* was a *publicum munus*[4], thus anyone duly appointed must serve unless disqualified or excused. To this there were two exceptions which had disappeared under Justinian. Ulpian says that a testamentary *tutor* who "abdicates," which he explains as meaning "*dicere nolle se tutorem esse*," ceases to hold office[5]. But there are texts of Ulpian himself, in the Vatican Fragments[6], and thus not altered by Justinian, which shew the testamentary *tutor* as bound, subject to excuse like others, and the same rule appears in the Digest[7]. In Ulpian's time it may have applied only to *tutela* of adult women: it is mentioned in close connexion with *cessio tutelae* which applied only there[8]. The other exception is that of *potioris nominatio*, applying only to those appointed by the magistrate. This was the right to name a person more nearly connected and therefore more appropriate[9]. This might not be done by one himself closely connected[10], but a *libertus* could so act in the case of his patron's child[11]. The namer must shew in detail the grounds of the *nominatio*[12], and the person nominated might himself nominate over[13]. There were elaborate rules as to forms and the time within which the *nominatio* must be made. This might be regarded as *excusatio*[14] but it is clearly distinguished in the texts. There is no trace of it under Justinian.

The law on exemptions or excuses is a mass of detail[15]. Modestinus applies the rules in general words to all *tutores*[16], but it does not appear

1 26. 6. 2. 3. 2 26. 6. 2. 1; C. 5. 31. 2. 3 26. 6. 2. 1; C. 5. 31. 6 *sqq.*; Inst. 3. 3. 6. D. 38. 17. 2. 28 (interp.) applies the same rule to grandmothers and an enactment of A.D. 357 (C. Th. 3. 18. 1), not in Justinian's Code, applies it to all grandparents. 4 4. 5. 6, 7; Inst. 1. 25. pr. 5 Ulp. 11. 17. Cicero (*ad Att.* 6. 1. 4) seems to refer to the same rule. An Egyptian papyrus (Mitteis, *Grundzüge*, 2. 2. 180) shews a testamentary tutor to a male abdicating in 14 B.C. But at that time there was no liability in any case for failure to act (*post*, § LIX) When this was imposed probably the right of *abdicatio* ceased in *tutela impuberum*. 6 Vat. Fr. 156, 173 a, 202. 7 27. 1. 6. 17, 13. pr., etc. 8 *Post*, § LX. It occurs in the same connexion in *Sch. Sin.* 18. 9 P. 2. 28; Vat. Fr. 157–167; 206–220. 10 A fellow-*decurio*, or member of same gild, or one of the excepted *personae* under the *l. Papia Poppaea*, Vat. Fr. 158, 210–214. Relative wealth might come into account, P. 2. 28. 2; Vat. Fr. 157, 166. 11 Vat. Fr. 160, 211. 12 P. 2. 28. 1; Vat. Fr. 166, 210. 13 Vat. Fr. 206. See also *ib.* 164, 208. It is an admission that he is *potior*, and has no excuse. 14 See Vat. Fr. 157. The time allowed is the same, Vat. Fr. 164, 207. But one who has pleaded an excuse and failed can plead another, or nominate a *potior*, but *potioris nominatio* bars excuse, though there may be further nominations if one fails, Vat. Fr. 164. 15 Vat. Fr. 123–247; D. 27. 1. Fully organised under M. Aurelius, 27. 1. 13. 2. 16 27. 1. 2. 5.

that in classical law they applied to *legitimi* or *fiduciarii*[1]. The excuse must be pleaded before the officer charged with the appointment of *tutores*[2] and within limits of time dependent on distance from the place of the court[3]. The grounds of excuse were numerous and various, some available against any *tutela*, some of only special application, some permanent, some temporary. Among general grounds were age, permanent ill-health, ignorance, poverty, exile, high office[4], a certain number of natural born children[5], holding already three substantially independent guardianships[6], etc. Of special application were, e.g., litigation or hostility between the parties, remoteness of residence, etc.[7] Some might be temporary, e.g. absence on public affairs, illness, etc.[8]

Certain cases of partial exemption will recur in the discussion of restrictions on the appointment of *tutor*.

One who had promised the father that he would serve could not excuse himself[9], nor could a *libertus* who was appointed by a magistrate to his patron's child, though, if appointed by the patron's will to a *collibertus*, he could plead excuse to prevent the confirmation of the appointment by the magistrate[10]. Any person appointed by the father, whether subject to confirmation or not, if he claimed excuse, lost any benefit under the father's will, apart from evidence of the testator's intent to the contrary[11].

RESTRICTIONS ON APPOINTMENT OF *TUTORES*. As *tutela* was a *publicum munus* a *filiusfamilias* could serve[12], his disabilities being essentially of private law. But there were many persons who could not be *tutores*, e.g. slaves, peregrines and Junian Latins[13], this last being an express provision of the *l. Iunia*: colonary Latins could serve.

Sex. A woman could not be *tutor*[14]. In classical law there was no

1 27. 1. 13. pr. See Solazzi, *Minore Età*, 272; Perozzi, *Mem. Acc. Bologna*, 1917, 75.
2 E.g., Vat. Fr. 166. 3 Vat. Fr. 154–156; D. 27. 1. 13. 1 *sqq*. In general the excuse must exist at the time of appointment, but supervening matters might sometimes be pleaded after *tutela* had begun. Inst. 1. 25. 3; Vat. Fr. 184, 238, etc.; D. 27. 1. 12. 1, 40.
4 27. 1. 2. pr., 6. 1 *sqq*., 6. 19, 7, 40, etc.; Vat. Fr. 128 *sqq*.; 151, 182–184, 223, 238–243, etc.
5 3 in Rome, 4 in Italy, 5 in a province, those given in adoption or killed in battle counting, Inst. 1. 25. pr.; D. 27. 1. 2. 3 *sqq*., 18; Vat. Fr. 168, 169, 191 *sqq*. 6 Inst. 1. 25. 5; D. 27. 1. 2. 9 *sqq*., 15. 15, 31; Vat. Fr. 125 *sqq*., 186 *sqq*. Held by himself or his *paterfamilias* or *filiusfamilias*, but not such as he could have refused. 7 P. 2. 27. 1; Vat. Fr. 203, 241; Inst. 1. 25. 4, 9–12; D. 27. 1. 21. pr., 46. 2. 8 27. 1. 10. 2, 3, 22. 1, 41; C. 5. 62. 10. In some cases the exemption lasted a year after. Exemptions, though of the general type, might not always be pleaded; *veterani* could not plead them in the case of children of *veterani* of the same legion, members of certain trade gilds in the case of children of other members. Vat. Fr. 142, 175–180; D. 27. 1. 8, etc. Inhabitants of the historic region of Ilium were excused from *tutela* of any but *Ilienses*, h. t. 17. 1. 9 Vat. Fr. 153. 10 P. 2. 29; Vat. Fr. 152, 160; D. 27. 1. 14, 24, 30. 3. Must be a patron with full right. 11 27. 1. 28. 1, 32. 12 Inst. 1. 14. pr. 13 Ulp. 11. 16; Inst. 1. 14. 1. 14 26. 1. 16. pr., 26. 2. 26. pr.; C. 5. 35. 1. See 26. 1. 18 (interp.).

exception, but in A.D. 390, following provincial practice[1], it was provided that if there was no *legitimus* or *testamentarius tutor*, a mother, so desiring, the father being dead, might be appointed by the magistrate, on her undertaking (by oath, under Justinian) not to marry again. If she did, the *tutela* ended and the husband might be sued on liabilities already accrued[2]. In 530 Justinian extended this to mothers of natural children, on their renouncing the privilege of the *Sc. Velleianum*[3]. By a novel the oath was remitted and the renunciation required in both cases[4]. By another novel mothers and grandmothers were *legitimi tutores* if they made the above renunciation[5].

Age. To be under 25 was an excuse in classical law, a disqualification under Justinian[6]. The fact of being *impubes* was always a disqualification except in *legitimae tutelae*, and Justinian made it one for all cases[7]. We are told of the classical rule for *legitima tutela* only in the case of women, and, after the abolition of agnatic *tutela* of women early in the Empire[8], these must be *libertinae*: the texts deal with the only probable case, that of *patroni filii*[9]. Such a *tutor* could not give *auctoritas*: a *tutor praetorius* was appointed where this became necessary[10].

Defect, physical or mental. Deaf or dumb persons could not be *tutores*, except *legitimi* in classical law, and Justinian excluded them altogether[11]. Here too we learn of their capacity only in *tutela* of women[12]: a text of Hermogenianus, probably altered, denies it for *legitima tutela*[13]. Lunacy (*furor*) seems to have been always regarded as curable, and thus was not a disqualification but a ground of temporary excuse[14]. In classical law it was no bar at all in *legitima tutela*[15].

Privilege. Some persons by reason of station or function were excluded from *tutela*. Thus *milites* and certain officials might not be *tutores* even if willing to serve[16], and there were cases in which a person of one class might not be appointed *tutor* to one of another[17].

Misconduct. This was not an absolute disqualification, but would·

1 Wenger, *Z.S.S.* 1905, 449. Cp. *P. Oxyrh.* 10. 1274. 2 C. Th. 3. 17. 4; C. 5. 35. 2. 3 C. 5. 35. 3. *Post*, § CLVI. 4 *Nov.* 94. 5 *Nov.* 118. 5. 6 Inst. 1. 25. 13. 7 *Ib.*; C. 5. 30. 5 shews the absurd effect of the old rule which gave the result that of two brothers, each might be the other's tutor. Perozzi (*Archiv. Giur.* 1921, 86) holds it probable that by the classical age it was a disqualification in all *tutela impuberum*. G. 1. 157. 8 *Post*, § LX. 9 G. 1. 177–179; Ulp. 11. 20.·22. 10 Ulp., *ib.* 11 26. 1. 1. 2, 3. 12 G. 1. 180; Ulp. 11. 21. 13 26. 4. 10. 1. In Vat. Fr. 238 it is said to be a ground of excuse. 14 27. 1. 10. 8, 12; Vat. Fr. 184 (in Vat. Fr. 238 it is perpetual). A *curator* is appointed meanwhile, Vat. Fr. 184. In D. 26. 1. 17 a tutor is appointed. 15 G. 1. 180. 16 26. 5. 21. 3; Inst. 1. 25. 14; *Nov.* 123. 5. The excused "*castris merentes*" of 27. 1. 23. 1, are *veterani*. In *Nov.* 72 Justinian forbids debtors or creditors to be *tutores*, and requires such persons appointed to declare the fact at once, under heavy penalties. 17 E.g., *ingenui* to *libertini* (by magistrates) if *libertini* were available, 27. 1. 1. 4.

have its effect in the magistrates' enquiry before appointment. If a *paterfamilias* appointed an unworthy person, this would apparently be valid, and as *legitima tutela*, in basis, was to safeguard the property rights of the *tutor*, here too misconduct would be immaterial.

Appointment *ad certam rem*. The *tutor* was appointed to the *persona* of the pupil rather than to his *res*, and the rule "*tutor ad certam rem dari non potest*" is a natural corollary. So Justinian treats the matter. He appears to regard the rule as absolute[1], as indeed it seems to have been, so far as testamentary *tutores* were concerned. Ulpian and others express it very strongly[2], and though Ulpian adds that in practice the appointment by will of one *tutor* to the African property and another to the Asiatic, is good[3], the meaning no doubt is that each is in strictness appointed to the whole *tutela*, the words being a direction as to the distribution of actual administration according to the usual plan, shortly to be considered. But where this interpretation was impossible, e.g. where one *tutor* was appointed alone, and there was a limitation to specific properties, the whole appointment was bad[4]. It was equally absolute in all normal appointments to *impuberes* by a magistrate, but there were a few exceptions where a *tutor* was temporarily replaced[5]. There was the *tutor praetorius* (in classical law, under Justinian a *curator*), to act for the ward in litigation (in classical law a *iudicium legitimum*) between him and the *tutor*[6]. So too as an *impubes legitimus tutor* could not give *auctoritas*, he was replaced by another[7], e.g. to authorise entry on a *hereditas*, as was a *furiosus tutor* or the like[8]. There was also a rule that a *tutor* could not be compelled to administer property in a region remote from his residence[9], the difficulty being met by the appointment of a *tutor* to manage those properties, and we are told that he was appointed only to those, so that it is no mere question of distribution of administration[10].

LV. FUNCTIONS AND DUTIES OF THE TUTOR. His first duty, in some cases, was to give security *rem salvam pupillo fore*[11]. This was not required of a testamentary *tutor*[12], or of one confirmed or appointed by the superior magistrates after enquiry[13], but was in all other cases, i.e.

1 Inst. 1. 14. 4. 2 26. 2. 12–14. 3 H. t. 15. 4 26. 2. 13. 5 The temporary substitute for a *tutor* absent or excused is not an instance: he is *tutor* over all affairs. 6 G. 1. 184; Inst. 1. 21. 3; Ulp. 11. 24; *post*, p. 164, n. 4. 7 G. 1. 178, 179. Could not occur under Justinian. 8 Ulp. 11. 21, 22; G. 1. 180. 9 27. 1. 19. 10 27. 1. 21. 2, 4. 11 G. 1. 199; Inst. 1. 24. pr.; D. 26. 4. 5. 1. Whether expressly provided in the Edict is disputed. Texts point in different directions; none is conclusive. The security dates from Trajan at latest, C. 5. 75. 5. See Cuq, *Man.* 214, n. 2; Taubenschlag, *Vormundsr. Stud.* 1. No doubt applied at first only to *dativi* but extended to the others by the time of Hadrian. 12 G. 1. 200; Inst. 1. 24. pr.; D. 26. 2. 17. 13 *Ib.*; 26. 3. 2, 3.

legitimi[1], *fiduciarii*[2] and those appointed by the local magistrates[3]. We are however told that if the *tutor* was a patron or *patroni filius*, the estate small, and the *tutor* a man of substance and probity, the security might be remitted[4]. It was for the local magistrates to see that proper security was given[5]. We are not told how they were informed of the matter, but as, where security was required, the acts of the *tutor* did not bind the pupil until this had been provided[6], those who wished to have dealings would apply the necessary pressure. The security was by personal surety to the ward, or, if he was *infans*, to a slave of his, or if he had none, to a *servus publicus*, or even to the magistrate or a third party nominated by him[7]. In the latter cases, as in *adrogatio*, the ward had only *utiles actiones*[8]. Ulpian in the Digest says that the actual verbal contract need not have been made[9]: the sureties were liable if in their presence and without contradiction their names were submitted by the *tutores* and entered on the *acta*.

The first step in the actual administration was to make an inventory of the estate, unless, under Justinian, the *tutor* was expressly released from this obligation by the testator from whom the property came[10]. It was done with the co-operation of *publicae personae*, and failure to do it involved heavy liabilities[11].

Though the *tutor* was appointed to the *persona*, he was not in classical or later law the custodian of the child. If there was difficulty as to the care of him the magistrate decided[12] and was not necessarily bound by any directions in the will[13]. The *tutor* must however provide out of the estate an appropriate sum for the maintenance of the child[14]: here, too, the magistrate might determine what might be so spent, and the *tutor* would not get credit, in accounting, for more than this, or, in any case, for more than in the circumstances was a reasonable amount[15].

The real business of the *tutor* was with the *patrimonium*, and his functions were twofold: *administratio*, *negotiorum gestio*, management of the pupil's affairs, and *auctoritatis interpositio*, authorisation of "acts in the law" by the *pupillus*. While the child was *infans* he could do no

1 20. 4. 5. 1. 2 If the language of G. and J. (p. 152, n. 11) is to be accepted. But as the fiduciary was chosen by the father the rule may not have been applied here. 3 26. 3. 5; 27. 8. 1. 4 It was exacted only if, *causa cognita*, it seemed to be desirable (26. 4. 5. 1): it may be presumed that it was not required of *parens manumissor*. 5 27. 8. 1. 11. 6 C. 5. 42. 1 *sqq.*; C. 2. 40. 4. There was machinery, imperfectly known, for compelling the giving of security by seizure of pledges, probably only in later law, Inst. 1. 24. 3. 7 27. 8. 1. 15, 16; 46. 6. 2, 3. In h. t. 6 we are told that, *propter utilitatem*, the pupil may stipulate if he can speak, though he has not *intellectus*. *Tabularius* not mentioned in this connexion. 8 27. 8. 1. 16; 46. 6. 4. pr. 9 27. 7. 4. 3. 10 26. 7. 7. pr.; C. Th. 3. 30. 6; C. 5. 37. 24; 5. 51. 13. 2, where it seems to be implied that a fresh inventory must be made of each new succession. 11 *Ib.*, etc. 12 27. 2. 1. 13 27. 2. 1. 1. The mother is the natural person, C. 5. 49. 1. 14 27. 2. 3. 15 27. 2. 2, 3.

legal acts, and there was no room for authorisation[1], but as he grew older this became more and more important[2]. Except in form the distinction is not of primary importance: the responsibility of the *tutor* was the same in both cases, and to some extent the rights and liabilities created by the *tutor* took effect in the ward[3]. What would be an improper act of administration it would be equally improper to authorise.

Administratio. In general he must do the business in a businesslike way, but in some respects he was bound to act as a man acting carefully in his own interest would not necessarily act. In A.D. 195 Severus forbade *tutores* to sell lands, rustic or suburban (i.e. unbuilt but in an urban area), except under directions in the will, or, in case of urgency, by authorisation of the magistrate[4]. Even this authority would not save the *tutor* from liability if, as events shewed, he did not properly inform the magistrate as to the facts[5]. By an enactment of unknown date a contrary direction was given as to unproductive or perishable moveables, urban property (i.e. houses) and urban slaves[6]. Here, even though alienation was forbidden by the will, the *tutor* was still entitled to sell, though not bound, unless the interests of the ward required it[7]. The system did not work well: Constantine[8] forbade the *tutor* to sell urban or suburban property or valuable moveables except in circumstances which would justify the sale of *rustica praedia*.

The *tutor* must take steps to recover debts due to the ward at once[9]. He could bring and defend actions on behalf of the pupil[10], or (if the pupil was old enough and the proceedings were in his name, as, in that case, and if he was available, they should be) represent him in the litigation[11]. He must invest money within a certain time, being liable for interest if he delayed without good reason, at the maximum rate if he used it for his own purposes[12]. These rules, and others similar[13], express the change in the conception of *tutela*: the interests of the *pupillus* were in the foreground and were safeguarded to an almost unreasonable extent.

1 *Infantia*, and exceptional rules, *post*, § LVI. 2 See 36. 1. 38. 1. 3 *Post*, p. 156. 4 An *Oratio*, 27. 9. 1. *Transactio*, compromise of a dispute (*post*, § CLXXXI), was conveyance for this purpose, C. 5. 71. 4. A pupil could not repudiate a legacy of land without authorisation by the magistrate, for as it had vested in him (*post*, § CXVII) this was an alienation, 27. 9. 5. 8. The prohibition was extended in practice to *curatores*. 5 27. 9. 1; C. 5. 71. 5. 6 See C. 5. 37. 22. pr., possibly in the *Oratio* of Severus. 7 26. 7. 5. 9. May have been written before the enactment. See also 26. 7. 7. 1; 50. 16. 198; C. 5. 38. 3. 8 C. 5. 37. 22. 1 *sqq*. Under Justinian, as to *praedia rustica* or *suburbana*, though the conveyance was void, it was validated by lapse of five years from full age, C. 5. 74. 3. Constantine had allowed one year to suffice. C. Th. 3. 32. 1. 9 He must not allow time, even though this be to the advantage of both sides, 26. 7. 15. 10 12. 2. 17. 2; 26. 7. 1. 2, 2, 15, 22, 23, etc. 11 26. 7. 1. 2, 2. As to one of active *contutores* suing another, *pupilli nomine* (26. 7. 12. pr.), *post*, p. 164, n. 4. 12 26. 7. 7. 3, 4. 13 E.g. 26. 7. 5. 8, 7. 1, 7. 8, 7. 14, etc. As to the liability for *culpa*, see *post*, p. 558.

The *tutor* could not always act alone: shortly, it may be said that he could act on the ward's behalf in all acts *iuris gentium*, but not in acts *iuris civilis*. He could not alienate or acquire for him by *mancipatio*[1]: whether he could by *cessio in iure* depends on the interpretation of the rule allowing representation in the *legis actio* "*pro tutela*[2]." He could acquire *bonorum possessio*, i.e. praetorian succession, for the child[3], but not civil law succession till the later Empire, when this was allowed for an *infans*[4]. He could acquire and alienate by *traditio* in the second century[5]. Some of the restrictions could be evaded by using a slave of the ward (even bought for the purpose[6]) who could acquire and probably alienate for him by *mancipatio*[7], and accept a civil succession for him[8].

Contract was a more personal matter. In early classical law the tutor's contract was his own: the ward took no right and incurred no liability, though of course the matter would come into account. But, here too, a remedy was found before the close of the classical age. The texts are much interpolated, and there has been much discussion[9]. The course of evolution may have been as follows. Where the *tutor* had defended an action for the ward, or had sued on his behalf, the pupil being absent or *infans*, so that it was reasonable for the *tutor* to act personally instead of giving *auctoritas*, the *actio iudicati* lay directly against or to the pupil, from, at latest, the time of Antoninus Pius. The action was not *utilis*, or postponed to the end of the *tutela*[10]. It was as if he had been a *cognitor*[11]. By the time of Justinian the limitation to cases of absence, etc., had disappeared[12]. But contract was a personal matter, in which there was no representation, and thus a contract by the *tutor* was enforceable only by or against him[13]. But as early as Aristo the ward was liable to the extent of his enrichment for any fraud of the *tutor* in his affairs, in a special action described as *tributoria*[14]. When the *tutela* ended the *tutor* was no longer concerned, and a rule appeared that where he had himself reasonably contracted on behalf of the ward, he

1 Mitteis, *R.Pr.* 1. 208. But the matter is not wholly clear. 2 Inst. 4. 10. pr. The power under *l. Hostilia* applies only to *furtum*. From the fact that special machinery was devised to enable an *infans* to free *vindicta* (40. 5. 30) it seems that *tutor* could not *lege agere* for the ward. There is however another reason for this. *Manumissio* is not administration, 40. 1. 13; 40. 9. 22. Cuq, *Man.* 215. 3 37. 1. 7. 2, but not repudiate it, h. t. 8; 38. 9. 1. 4. 4 C. Th. 8. 18. 8; C. 6. 30. 18. 5 Shewn by the above limitations. It may be older. 6 Though, if he was *infans*, civil ownership could not be acquired, bonitary could, and a slave acquired for his bonitary owner, G. 2. 88. 7 *Post*, § LXXXV; G. 2. 87. 8 *Post*, § CIX. On tendency in later law to restrict power of administration, Bonfante, *Corso*, 1. 442. 9 See, e.g., Wenger, *Actio Iudicati*, 193 *sqq.*; Solazzi, four articles, *Bull.* 1910–12. 10 26. 7. 2. pr. (interp.); 26. 9. 5 (ref. to *tutor* interp.); 26. 9. 6; 26. 9. 7; 42. 1. 4. 1. D. 26. 7. 39. 12 deals with *cognitio extraordinaria* and the facts are not clear. 11 *Post*, § CCXXXIX. 12 It has thus disappeared from some of the texts in n. 10. 13 26. 7. 39. 4; C. 2. 24. 4. 14 26. 9. 3. In h. t. 1 the extension to *culpa* is due to Justinian.

could not then be sued on the contract and an *actio utilis* lay against the ward[1]. Some such rule was needed: he could not assign his liabilities to the ward so as to bind creditors from proceeding against him, and the rule seems to be quite general under Justinian, i.e. not limited to cases of *infantia*[2], etc. But the same difficulty did not arise the other way: the *tutor* could transfer his rights of action (*procuratio in rem suam*) to the ward[3], and cease to be concerned in the matter; and the view, generally held, that the same rule applied and the ward could bring a *utilis actio*[4], is doubtful[5]. The texts, laying down the general rule, deal only with the other case. Ulpian says that obligations are not acquired for the pupil by the *tutor*, but remain with him[6], and Diocletian says that the ward cannot acquire an action through the *tutor*, "*nisi ex certis causis*[7]." Two such cases are recorded. If *A* lent *B*'s money, *B* acquired a *condictio*, though not any subsidiary obligations which might have been created[8]. This was equally true if *A* was *B*'s *tutor*, and there was nothing *utilis* about it[9]. But if, as was usual, the loan was accompanied by a *stipulatio*, this superseded the *mutuum*, and thus barred the *condictio*[10]. Relief was given against this technical obstacle, by an *actio utilis*, where the tutor's act was reasonable. This limit, and the *utilis* character of the action, were gone under Justinian, and there was never any question of postponement to the end of the *tutela*[11]. Again, if a *tutor* made a *constitutum* for payment to the ward, the ward could sue *utilitatis gratia*. But this rule, which applies to other cases[12], was an exception to the rule that there could not be a valid promise of payment to a third person[13]: there was no question of the end of *tutela*.

The degree of care which a *tutor* must shew in his administration seems to have varied historically. Here, as in all infaming actions, it is probable that the liability was originally only for *dolus*[14], a restriction consistent with the original conception of *tutela*. This would in practice cover liability for gross negligence[15], difficult as a matter of evidence to

1 2. 11. 15; 26. 9. 5. 1; h. t. 8=36. 3. 18. 2; C. 5. 37. 26. 3 (Bas. 38. 9. 39); C. 5. 39. 1. See also, 21. 2. 4. 1; 19. 1. 13. 7 (? interp.). 2 C. 5. 39. 3 does not speak of the action as *utilis*, and the expression *actio personalis* suggests Justinian. 3 *Post*, § CCXXXIX. 4 Girard, *Man.* 231; Mitteis, *R.Pr.* 1. 222; Duquesne, *Translatio Iudicii*, 47. 5 A feeling for symmetry prompts the view. But such adjustments are not always symmetrical. Pius gave *a. utilis* to vendee of *hereditas* (2. 14. 16) but not against him, a converse but equally rational solution. He knows who the debtors are: the creditors may know nothing of him. 6 13. 7. 11. 6. 7 C. 5. 39. 5. 8 C. 4. 27. 3. 9 26. 7. 47. 5. 10 See the discussion in 26. 7. 16; 45. 1. 126. 2, and *post*, §§ CLXII, CXCIV. 11 12. 1. 26; 26. 7. 9. pr.; 26. 9. 2; C. 5. 39. 2. Similar concession where the lender was *procurator* of a *miles*. 12. 1. 26. 12 13. 5. 5. 9. *Curator furiosi* or *minoris*, *actor municipii*. As to this rule, *post*, § CXLIX. 13 *Post*, §§ CXLIX, CLIV. 14 Mitteis, *R.Pr.* 1. 324 *sqq.* 15 *Culpa lata.* See 26. 7. 7. 2, "*lata neglegentia*." See also 26. 10. 7. 1; C. 2. 18. 20; C. 5. 51. 2; C. 5. 55. 2.

disentangle from *dolus*. But, at some time, possibly as early as Celsus, an increased liability appeared: the *tutor* must shew the same care that he did in his own affairs[1], a notion also perhaps influenced by the conception of *dolus*. Some texts make him liable for all negligence, *culpa levis*[2]. But there were disputes among the lawyers, and the whole story of *culpa* is much disputed[3].

It must be noted that all this was *administratio* and governed by that notion. A *tutor* could not, by act or authorisation, make gifts of the property[4]. Acts of spoliation were not *administratio*, and thus not merely gave an action for damages but were void[5].

LVI. *Auctoritatis interpositio*. This means co-operation of the tutor with the ward: the act was done by the ward with the *auctoritas* of the *tutor*. This *auctoritas* involved presence: it must be by oral declaration[6], not by letter or ratification[7]. There is evidence that it was commonly in answer to interrogation by the other party[8], but no ritual words were used[8a]. In later law actual presence of the other party was not necessary[9]. *Auctoritas* could not be conditional[10].

The possibility of *auctoritatis interpositio* did not in strictness arise till the child had reached a certain development. He could not be authorised to act till he was capable of conscious action. He must have *intellectus*: what the *tutor* provided was judgement whether it was wise to do the act or not. But the logical rule, that there could be no *auctoritas* while he was *infans* or *infantiae proximus*[11], was departed from and the terms used need explanation. Till the fifth century *infantia* meant, simply, incapacity to speak[12]. But about A.D. 407 the limit of *infantia* was fixed at seven years[13]. Though texts link *infantia* and lack of *intellectus*[14], these are not the same. A child too young to speak cannot well have *intellectus*, but he is also barred from many transactions, those in which speech is needed, by his inability to speak[15]. And a child may be

1 16. 3. 32, written of *tutela*, Mitteis, *op. cit.* 326; 27. 3. 1. pr., "*diligentia quam suis rebus*" called by moderns "*culpa levis in concreto.*" 2 Coll. 10. 2. 3; D. 26. 7. 10, etc. *Dolus* only, 26. 7. 7. pr. etc. Mitteis, *op. cit.* 327. M.'s explanation of C. 5. 54. 1 (p. 329) seems forced, but the text has probably been altered. It is hard to reconcile p. 334, n. 68 with p. 326, n. 10 which seems to ignore 26. 7. 7. 2; C. 2. 18. 20; C. 5. 51. 7, etc. 3 *Post*, § CXC. 4 26. 7. 22; C. 5. 37. 16. So, a slave with *administratio peculii* cannot make gifts out of it, 20. 3. 1. 1; 20. 6. 8. 5. 5 41. 4. 7. 3. For similar reasons a *tutor* could not act in matters between himself and the ward. Inst. 1. 21. 3; G. 1. 184. 6 26. 8. 3, 9. 5. 7 26. 8. 9. 5, 10; Inst. 1. 21. 2. 8 26. 8. 3. 8*a* See *post*, p. 673. 9 26. 8. 9. 6. 10 26. 8. 8. 11 G. 3. 109. Refutation of the view that the distinction between *infantiae prox.* and *pubertati prox.* corresponded to some definite age limit. Dirksen, *Verm. Schriften*, 1. 180 *sqq.* 12 Varro, *L.L.* 6. 52; D. 27. 8. 1. 15; 40. 5. 30. 1, 2; 45. 1. 70, etc. See also Inst. 3. 19. 10 and Theophilus thereon. 13 C. Th. 8. 18. 8; C. 6. 30. 18. D. 23. 1. 14; 26. 7. 1. 2 are interp. Girard, *Man.* 217, n. 3. 14 41. 2. 32. 2; 47. 2. 23; 50. 17. 5, etc. 15 26. 7. 9. pr., etc. Cf. 45. 1. 1. pr. Dumb man excluded for same reason though of perfectly sound mind.

able to speak and yet not have *intellectus*[1]. Such a child was said to be *infantiae proximus* and when past that stage *pubertati proximus*, but there was no fixed age in this matter. On grounds of utility however, in view of the fact that the *tutor* could really supply the necessary mental element, those *infantiae proximi* were allowed to contract with *auctoritas tutoris* as early as the time of Gaius[2], and the same was allowed, then or a little later, to *infantes*, in matters which did not involve speech, though it is clear that such children could have no real understanding of the matter[3].

As the judgement of the *tutor* was the essential point, *auctoritas* could not be compelled, though there were remedies for improper refusal[4].

The *tutor* could not validly authorise acts in which he himself had an interest. Thus a loan to the pupil by him with his *auctoritas* was invalid and created only a *naturalis obligatio* to the extent of enrichment[5]. If he was sole *tutor* no such transaction was possible, unless a *tutor praetorius* was appointed for the purpose of authorising it[6]. If there were other *tutores* one of these could authorise it, if the *tutela* was such, and the transaction such, that the *auctoritas* of one *tutor* sufficed[7].

Not all transactions needed *auctoritas*: the ward could carry through those which could only benefit him, not bind him, without *auctoritas*[8]. Informal acts of acquisition could be done for an *infans* by the *tutor*, and by the *impubes* capable of acting at all, and the formal acts which had created difficulty during *infantia* could now be done by him, or, if they involved liability, by co-operation, though the *tutor* could not perform them for the ward[9]. Thus in unilateral transactions the matter was simple: if it was one which bound the other party it was valid; if it purported to bind the *pupillus* it was void unless there was *auctoritas*. But the most common transactions are bilateral; and here the matter was not so simple. To treat the other party as bound and the ward as not bound would be unjust, and the matter was otherwise dealt with. If a pupil had purported to go through such a transaction he could not

1 29. 2. 9; 44. 7. 1. 13. 2 G. 3. 109; Theoph. *ad* Inst. 3. 19. 10; D. 29. 2. 9. 3 36. 1. 67. 3; C. 7. 32. 3. In 41. 2. 32. 2, where it is a question of acquiring possession, double illogicality: *auctoritas* not in principle needed for acts involving no liability or possible loss, like *possessio*, 41. 2. 1. 3. The point of *intellectus* was however still material in respect of liability for wrongdoing. See, e.g., G. 3. 208; Inst. 4. 1. 18; D. 4. 3. 13. 1; 9. 2. 5. 2; C. 9. 47. 7, etc. 4 26. 8. 17. 5 Inst. 1. 21. 3; D. 26. 8. 1. pr. 6 The method where litigation arose between ward and sole tutor, G. 1. 184 (see *post*, p. 164, n. 4): a *curator* under Justinian. A *tutor* not acting, under the decree of the *praetor* (*post*, § LVIII), might have dealings with the ward, 26. 8. 6. 7 *Post*, § LVIII. 8 G. 2. 83; 3. 107; Inst. 1. 21. pr.; D. 26. 8. 9. Collinet-Giffard, *Précis*, 1. 232. 9 Formal acceptance of *hereditas*, *cretio* (*post*, § CIX), formal conveyance, *mancipatio*; formal manumission, *vindicta*; *acceptilatio*; formal surrender of rights, *cessio in iure*. G. 2. 80; D. 40. 5. 30. 1–4.

cry off without returning any benefits received, and he could not enforce the contract without doing his part[1]. If he had done his part he could recover what he had handed over or sue on the contract[2]. If the transaction had been carried out on both sides without *auctoritas* the pupil could, e.g. in sale, recover his property but must refund to the extent of enrichment, or conversely, could recover the price on returning the goods[3]. Payment to a pupil was specially dealt with. A receipt by him was not valid, but if he sued again for the money he must account for what he still had or had advantageously expended[4]. A receipt by the *tutor* was not safe, as the pupil might get *restitutio in integrum*[5] and fraud of the *tutor* would suffice for this[6]. The safe way was to pay it to the ward with presence and *auctoritas* of the *tutor*. This created difficulties, as the ward was not in the charge of the *tutor*, and might be far away. Justinian therefore provided that payment might be safely made to the *tutor* under sanction of a *iudex*[7].

LVII. CLOSE OF *TUTELA*. The *tutela* might end in many ways, e.g. by death or *capitis deminutio*[8], or puberty, of the ward, by occurrence of the date or event till which the *tutor* had been appointed[9], completion of the purpose for which a temporary *tutor* had been appointed, death or *capitis deminutio maxima* or *media* of the *tutor*, or supervening ground of exemption. In several of these cases there was only a transfer of *tutela*, and, apart from this, which does not need discussion, the only thing that need be said is that in later law puberty was fixed at 14 for males, 12 for females, while in the time of Gaius it was still disputed whether in the case of males it was determined by age or by actual physical development[10]. There are two cases of more importance.

Capitis deminutio minima of the *tutor*[11]. Operated only in the case of *tutores legitimi*. Here the *tutela* was ended and passed to the person with the next civil law right of succession. *Capitis deminutio minima* of one of two patrons left the *tutela* wholly with the other[12]. That of a sole

1 If he had agreed to sell he could not sue for the price without delivering the goods (and conversely he could not claim the goods without payment), 18. 5. 7. 1. 2 G. 2. 82. 3 26. 8. 5. pr., 1. As he had only to restore enrichment, there might be loss to the other side, who thus bore the risk. Inst. 2. 8. 2. 4 G. 2. 84; Inst. 2. 8. 2. Rule applies only to voluntarily undertaken obligations. Those resulting incidentally from ownership of property (quasi-contract, *post*, § CLXXXVI) bind a *pupillus* like anybody else, 44. 7. 46. 5 See, however, *post*, § CCXLIV. 6 Payment could be validly made to a *tutor*, even one *tutor* of several, if he was an acting *tutor* (*post*, § LVIII), 46. 3. 14, 100. 7 C. 5. 37. 25, 27. Applies to capital payments and rents, interest and the like above a certain limit. Below this limit they can be paid to the *tutor*, as before. 8 *Sch. Sin.* XVI (42) shews a man *tutor* to his *impubes* brother who has been sent to a Latin colony, *ante*, p. 138. 9 Inst. 1. 14. 3. 10 G. 1. 196, the latter the Proculian view. Javolenus required both, Ulp. 11. 28. 11 Ulp. 11. 9, 17. As to disputes and effect of *c. d.* on previous rights, etc., 26. 7. 37. 2; 27. 3. 11; Cuq, *Man.* 140. 12 G. 1. 165; 3. 60.

patron would normally transfer it to his *adrogator*[1], and the same is presumably true in the case of *parens manumissor*[2].

Removal for misconduct. If a *tutor* wronged the pupil this must be accounted for when the *tutela* ended[3]. If he committed an actual delict an ordinary delictal action lay, and there were special remedies for certain cases[4]. Apart from this there was a machinery for removing him in case of misconduct, called the *Crimen Suspecti Tutoris*[5]. This was a petition for his removal, based on the XII Tables[6] and tried before the chief magistrate of the district[7]. *Tutela* being a *publicum munus*, any one might proceed (*postulatio*) except the *impubes* himself, e.g. a fellow *tutor*, or even a woman if a near relative, or the magistrate was satisfied of the purity of her motives[8]. Immediately on the accusation the *tutor* was suspended from acting[9]. It was available against any *tutor*, even a patron[10]. There was no definite list of grounds of removal: it was at the discretion of the Court. It might be for fraud or incompetence or gross negligence[11], but mere poverty was not sufficient[12]. The effect was not always the same. If the evidence shewed *dolus* the *tutor* became *infamis*, but not for mere incompetence or negligence[13]. The purpose being removal, the proceeding ended if the *tutor* died or the *tutela* ended otherwise[14]. The misconduct must have been during the *tutela*, though, at least in later law, it might be before actual administration[15]. Although a patron could be removed, there were special rules in his case. The grounds of removal were not stated, so that he never became *famosus*[16]. His own *libertus* might not accuse him[17], and it was usual, as it was in the case of *patres* and other relatives, not to remove him but to appoint a *curator* to act with him[18]. This was also usual in case of poverty[19].

The foregoing is the institution as presented by the Sources. But many of the texts shew signs of interpolation and there are divergent views as to its history. The view is maintained that besides this *postulatio suspecti* there was also a power of *remotio* by the magistrate *mero motu*, later in origin and applicable where the *crimen* was not. This, it is said,

1 *Post*, § CXLI. 2 Children pass with them. 3 *Post*, § LIX. 4 Inst. 1. 26. 11; D. 26. 10. 1. 8, 2. 5 Inst. 1. 26; D. 26. 10; C. 5. 43. 6 Inst. 1. 26. pr.; D. 26. 10. 1. 2. 7 Inst. 1. 26. 1; D. 26. 10. 1. 3. 8 Inst. 1. 26. 3; D. 26. 10. 1. 7. 9 Inst. 1. 26. 7; C. 5. 43. 7. 10 Inst. 1. 26. 2; D. 26. 10. 1. 5; C. 5. 43. 4. Probably it applied originally only to testamentary *tutores*, was extended to *dativi* (*Atiliani*, *Titiani*) when they appeared, its application to *legitimi* being Byzantine. Solazzi, *Bull.* 1915, 131 *sqq.*; *Curatio impuberis*, 50. 11 Failure to provide maintenance, evil life, etc., 26. 10. 3. 5 *sqq.*, 5, 6, 7. 1, 7. 2, 8; Inst. 1. 26. 5, 9–13; C. 5. 43. 1–3, 5, 9. 12 26. 10. 8; Inst. 1. 26. 13; C. 5. 43. 6. 2. Probably failure to act was a ground before *gestio* could be compelled, *post*, p. 163. 13 Inst. 1. 26. 6; D. 26. 10. 3. 18; C. 5. 43. 9. 14 Inst. 1. 26. 8; D. 26. 10. 11. 15 26. 10. 3. 5, 4. 4; C. 5. 43. 2; Inst. 1. 26. 5. Thus if a man was excused and afterwards reappointed, no *crimen* lay under the second *tutela* for wrong during the first, 26. 10. 3. 7. 16 26. 10. 1. 5, 4. 2. 17 26. 10. 3. 1. 18 26. 10. 9. 19 C. 5. 43. 6.

applied only in case of *dolus* and only to *tutores testamentarii* and *dativi*. The power of *remotio* was applied to cases of neglect to act or negligent administration and to *legitimi tutores*. It is only by the compilers that the two institutions were fused. Thus Ulpian seems to hold that all removal by the *crimen* involves *infamia*[1]. On the other hand neither Gaius nor Ulpian[2] seems to know of any mode of removal except as *suspectus*[3].

LVIII. Plurality of *tutores*[4]. Where there were several *tutores* it was possible, though not usually convenient, for them to administer in common. In this case any one of them was competent to administer in any matter, but the question arises how far the *auctoritas* of one would suffice. The classical rule seems to have been that of testamentary *tutores* the *auctoritas* of one sufficed, except, no doubt, for a matter which would end the *tutela*, such as *adrogatio*, and thus if a question arose between a *tutor* and the ward, no temporary *tutor* was needed—another could act[5]. Some jurists held that the same was true of *dativi* appointed after enquiry, but in all other cases all must authorise[6]. Justinian provided however that in all cases of undivided *tutela* the *auctoritas* of one would suffice, except in a matter which would end the *tutela*[7].

It was possible for the *tutores* to arrange to distribute the administration[8], or one or more might give the other or others a mandate to act, or simply permit him to act, taking security. All this made no difference to their capacity in law or to their ultimate responsibility *in solidum* for breaches of duty[9]. But the effect was different if these arrangements were made under the provisions of an Edict dealing with this matter[10], but in its terms only with testamentary *tutores*. The Praetor summoned the *tutores* to arrange how the work was to be done[11]. It might be all assigned to one named in the will, or if there was none or the Praetor did not approve him, to one whom the Praetor allowed them to elect[12]. Or one might offer security and it might be assigned to him unless

1 Vat. Fr. 340 b; D. 26. 10. 4. 4. 2 G. 1. 182; Ulp. 11. 23. 3 Taubenschlag, *Vormundschaftsrechtl. Studien*, 27 *sqq.* (who holds that the field of *remotio* was gradually widened in cl. law); Solazzi, *Minore Età*, 259 *sqq.*; *Bull.* 1915, 131 *sqq.*, *contra*, Berger, *Z.S.S.* 1914, 39 *sqq.*; Perozzi, *Ist.* 1. 499 *sqq.*, who holds that cl. law applied the *crimen* to *culpa* and to *legitimi*; Laprat, *Le crimen suspecti tutoris*, who limits it to *dolus* for cl. law. 4 The texts dealing with *contutores* have been much altered: there is acute controversy on the evolution of the rules, *post*, § LIX, *fin.* 5 26. 2. 24. Apparent conflict, 26. 8. 4; 29. 2. 49. Bonfante, *Corso*, 1. 446. As to limitations on the rule that actions against one *tutor* could be brought by or with the *auctoritas* of another, Peters, *Z.S.S.* 1911, 218 *sqq.* 6 Ulp. 11. 26. 7 C. 5. 59. 5. Here he says all must authorise: "*ut quod omnes similiter tangit ab omnibus comprobetur*," a proposition destined to a much wider application. Figgis, *From Gerson to Grotius*, 12. 8 C. 5. 52. 2. 3. 9 26. 7. 55. 2; C. 5. 52. 2. 3, 3. 10 Lenel, *E.P.* 316. 11 26. 7. 3. 7; Inst. 1. 24. 1 suggests an order of preference among possible courses, but all was in the discretion of the Praetor, 26. 2. 17. pr.; 26. 7. 3. 3, 6. 12 26. 2. 19; 26. 7. 3. 7.

another offered equal security, when he might be preferred, or the Praetor might choose the *idoneor*, which seems to mean the most substantial man, otherwise desirable[1]. Or it might be given to all who offered security, in common, or with divided administration[2]. If none of these plans was adopted it might be distributed either as directed by the will, or by the Praetor[3] at the wish of the *tutores*, either *in partes* or *in regiones*, i.e. according to the nature or place of the property[4]. But if the *tutores* insisted on acting in common; this must be allowed[5]. A rescript of M. Aurelius and Verus applied the same system to those appointed *ex inquisitione*[6], of whom in the opinion of some jurists the *auctoritas* of one sufficed, and later still, probably not till Justinian, it was applied to *legitimi*, though not to *patroni* or probably *liberi patroni*[7].

Thus, on the texts, the *tutores* might administer in common, or they might privately arrange a distribution, in which case those not acting[8], or not acting in the particular field, were liable only in the last resort. Or they might do so under the Edict, in which case those not acting, or not acting in the particular field, were liable only in the last resort, and only for failure in supervision, e.g. for not getting the acting *tutor* removed if necessary, or leaving large sums of money in his hands uninvested[9]. It seems to have been possible to appoint *tutores*, either by the will or *ex inquisitione*[10], with a general duty of supervision, but the same responsibility as if they were *gerentes*; and the appointee would usually be a *libertus* chosen for his knowledge of the business[11]. But it is uncertain how far this is classical law[12].

As this scheme of distribution was praetorian it might seem that it did not affect civil law rights and some texts suggest that action or authorisation by a non-acting *tutor* was met by praetorian defences[13]. But it seems that, in *iure gentium* matters, his intervention was void, if the other party knew the facts. Thus in such a case ownership did not pass[14]. If a pupil accepted a *hereditas* with the *auctoritas* of a *tutor* who was not acting, he was bound (written no doubt of formal acceptance, *cretio*), and the same may have been true of *mancipatio* or *cessio in iure*[15]. We are told that payment might be made to a non-acting *tutor*. Justinian

1 26. 2. 17. pr.; h. t. 18. 2 26. 2. 17. pr. 3 26. 7. 3. 9. 4 26. 7. 4. 5 26. 7. 3. 8. 6 26. 2. 19. 7 26. 4. 5. 2. As security was always needed in case of agnates, the edictal proceedings must have been to some extent modified. 8 Sometimes called *honorarii*, but this seems to be late and to confuse them with *tutores* expressly appointed by will *honoris causa* with no duties and no liabilities, 23. 2. 60. 2; 46. 3. 14. 1; Levy, *Z.S.S.* 1916, 71 *sqq.* 9 26. 7. 3. 2, 14; C. 5. 52. 2. 1. 10 26. 2. 32. 1; 27. 3. 1. 7; 46. 3. 14. 1, 14. 6. 11 C. 5. 38. 1. Here an allowance might be made to the *tutor*, at any rate under Justinian, 26. 7. 33. 3, interp.? 12 *Post*, p. 164, n. 11. 13 26. 7. 4, "*exceptione summovebitur*"; 26. 8. 4, "*id ratum a praetore haberi non debet.*" 14 26. 8. 4. 15 29. 2. 49. See however Peters, *Z.S.S.* 1911, 232, and reff. Levy, *Z.S.S.* 1916, 73, gives many instances of the invalidity of the action of such a *tutor*; Bonfante, *cit.*

has so mutilated the text[1] that it is not clear: it probably applies only to a *de facto* arrangement: it adds that this is not so if the Praetor has forbidden the *tutor* to administer.

LIX. Removal is not a remedy but a preventive of future damage; we have now to consider the remedies against a *tutor* who fails in his duty.

The two primary remedies are:

Actio de rationibus distrahendis. This action lay against any *tutor* when the *tutela* ended[2]. It lay only for actual embezzlement of the ward's property[3]. It was essentially delictal, giving double damages[4], and available to, but not against, *heredes*[5]. It dates from the XII Tables[6] and was by itself a crude and insufficient remedy. Its original application was no doubt to *legitimi tutores*[7].

Actio tutelae. This action, later in origin, but dating from the Republic[8], gave a remedy for any breach of duty by a *tutor*[9]. It was available only at the end of the *tutela*[10], and condemnation involved infamy[11]. It originally lay only for maladministration and thus was not available where a *tutor* refused to act at all, however detrimental to the ward his inaction was. But from the first century of the Empire[12] the rule was that if, on application, the magistrate ordered him to act, he at once became responsible, and in the second century, without any such steps, inaction was put practically on a level with maladministration[13]. The ward's claim was privileged: it took precedence of other unsecured debts of the *tutor*[14], and in later law there was a tacit hypothec[15], with priority, dating presumably from the time when the liability first accrued. The action, being quasicontractual, was available to and against *heredes*[16]. As it was for settlement of accounts the *tutor* could deduct what had been properly expended out of his own funds[17]. This right was all he had

1 46. 3. 14. 1. 2 27. 3. 1. 19, 24. 3 27. 3. 2. pr. 4 P. 2. 30; D. 26. 7. 55. 1. 5 27. 3. 1. 23. 6 26. 7. 55. 1. 7 Arangio Ruiz, *Ist.* 455, accepting the view of Solazzi (*Rend. Ist. Lomb.* 1917, 178) that it lay (perhaps only) during impuberty. See also Peters, *Z.S.S.* 1911, 218. 8 Cicero, *de Off.* 3. 17. 70. 9 Perhaps not available against *tutores legitimi* in cl. law. Solazzi, *Rend. Ist. Lomb.* 1917, 178. 10 27. 3. 1. 24. It is a *bonae fidei iudicium*, Cicero, *loc. cit.* G. 4. 62. 11 G. 4. 182. 12 Inst. 1. 20. 3; D. 46. 6. 4. 3. As to the evolution, Girard, *Man.* 236. 13 Vat. Fr. 155; D. 26. 7. 1. The action is here *utilis*, 46. 6. 4. 3. 14 26. 7. 42, 44. 1; 27. 3. 22. All claims of ward against *tutor* could be dealt with by this action instead of the action appropriate to them, with the advantage of giving this privilege, and also, of perpetuating them where the action was *temporaria*, since *a. tutelae* was *perpetua*. The principle was that it was his duty as *tutor* to collect these debts from himself—*a semetipso exigere*. 27. 3. 5; 26. 7. 9. 2–5; 46. 1. 69, etc. Peters, *Z.S.S.* 1911, 190 *sqq.* 15 C. 5. 37. 20; C. Th. 3. 30. 1. 16 27. 3. 1. 16, 17. *Heres* liable only where there was *dolus* or gross negligence, 27. 7. 4. Rotondi, *Scr. Giur.* 2. 290, holds that the rule limiting the liability of *heres* to *dolus* of *tutor* is a reintroduction by Justinian, for the *heres*, of what had once been the rule for the *tutor* himself. 17 27. 3. 1. 4–9; 27. 4. 1. 4.

at first: to give him a right of action was to bind the *pupillus*. But as the funds in his hands might be less than was due to him the Praetor introduced an *actio contraria tutelae*[1] by which he could claim reimbursement, *perpetua* and available to and against the *heres*[2].

Besides these primary remedies there were others. For delict by the *tutor* the ordinary action lay, when the *tutela* ended[3]. So, where security had been given, actions lay on this, on the promise of the *tutor* and those of his sureties but not till the end of the *tutela*, when the account was due[4]. Further, there was an action (*actio subsidiaria*) against the inferior magistrates who were required to exact security, if they had not adequately done this, or, in cases where they did not appoint but nominated for appointment by the superior magistrates, had nominated carelessly[5]. They were liable only in the last resort when all other resources had failed[6]. They were not absolutely liable for any deficit, but only if they did not take such security and precaution as were reasonably adequate at the time, not, e.g., if a surety afterwards lost his money[7]. If they had been guilty of *dolus* in the matter, their heirs were equally liable[8].

Of several *tutores* each was liable in the *actio de rationibus distrahendis* only for his own malversation[9]. In the *actio tutelae*, if they acted in common, all were liable. If they made a private division those not acting were liable last[10]. If the administration had been formally divided, or wholly vested in one, none was liable beyond his own sphere, unless, at least in later law, he had failed in the duty of supervision[11], and the persons directly liable had proved insufficient[12].

1 27. 4. 1. See however Partsch, *Neg. Gestio*, 40 *sqq.*, who holds that till Justinian he had only *n. g. utilis*. The *a. tutelae* being *bonae fidei* the tutor's counter-claims would come in, and it is at least possible (Partsch, *cit.* 55 *sqq.*) that the *formula* was so expressed as to permit of judgement against the pupil for them where they exceeded what was due to him. As to *contraria iudicia* of this type, *post*, §§ CCXVIII, CCXXXIV. Lenel, *E.P.* 319.
2 27. 4. 3. 9. It may lie even where expense greater than estate (h. t. 3. pr.), but only lies at end of *tutela*, h. t. 1. 3.
3 27. 3. 1. 22, 2. 1; 47. 2. 33.
4 As to difficulties and changes in the rules on the availability during *tutela* of actions between *tutor* and ward, Peters, *Z.S.S.* 1911, 218. Cosureties of *tutor* had no *ben. divisionis*, 46. 6. 12.
5 *Sc.* under Trajan, C. 5. 75. 5; cf. D. 27. 8. 1.
6 C. 5. 75. 3.
7 27. 8. 1. 11, 12.
8 27. 8. 4. Further, in later classical law, a pupil, like a minor, could probably get *r. in integrum*, though the *tutor* had authorised, but only exceptionally, *causa cognita*, *post*, § CCXLIV.
9 27. 3. 2. pr.
10 26. 7. 38; h. t. 55. 2; C. 5. 52. 2. 3, *ante*, § LVIII. A surety for one is liable like his principal, and other *tutores* are treated like sureties for the one in fault, have *b. divisionis* (*post*, § CLVII), 27. 3. 1. 11; C. 5. 52. 1, and can claim to have the creditor's action transferred, in fact, buying the debt, 27. 3. 1. 18, 21; C. 5. 52. 2. If one *tutor* paid a debt this transfer implied after Pius, 27. 1. 13.
11 C. 5. 52. 2. 1.
12 46. 6. 12. See 27. 3. 1. 15; 26. 7. 3. 2, 39. 11; 27. 3. 1. 15 (corrupt); C. 5. 52. 3; C. 5. 55. 1. Much difficulty as to the rules in joint *tutelae* and no doubt much change, Levy, *Z.S.S.* 1916, 14 *sqq.*, suggests the following evolution. No non-acting *tutor* is liable to the *actio tutelae*. One freed from *gestio* by the Praetor or the will, or limited to a particular field, is not liable at all outside any field assigned to him. One merely not acting or not

There was other machinery which needs mention. There was an *actio protutelae* where a person acted as *tutor*, but was not validly in that position[1], and similarly there were remedies to third persons who had suffered loss owing to the intervention of such a person or of one not qualified to give *auctoritas* in that particular matter[2]. A *tutor* who continued to act after the *tutela* had expired was liable as a *negotiorum gestor*[3].

LX. *TUTELA PERPETUA MULIERUM*[4]. This institution was plainly in the interest of the *tutor*. Gaius indeed says that it was due to the light-mindedness of women, but elsewhere observes that this is "*magis speciosa quam vera*[5]." Its real origin was in the fact that a woman could have no *sui heredes* to exclude the agnates or the patron: the expectation of succession being lifelong, so was the *tutela*. Discredited in classical law, it lasted at any rate to Diocletian[6]. It will suffice to state the main differences between the rules and those of *tutela impuberum*.

Tutores testamentarii. The chief difference was that the husband of a woman *in manu*, as *paterfamilias*, could not only appoint a *tutor*, but could give the wife a choice of *tutores*, inconsistent with the principle that the *tutor* must be a *certa persona*[7]. One so chosen was called *tutor optivus*[8]. The choice allowed might be general or limited. *Optio tutoris*

acting by agreement with the others is at first not liable at all (Vat. Fr. 228), later by *utilis actio*. But the conception of *gestio* is wide: one who gets another to act for him is acting. *Tutela* is thought of as a whole: it is not a question of individual transactions. No man can be both *gerens* and *cessans*. All *gerentes* are equally liable for the acts of any. All *cessantes* are equally liable for damage from inaction of other *cessantes*. *Cessantes* are liable only subsidiarily, if *gerentes* cannot satisfy, but before the magistrates. All much changed by the Byzantines. They hold that a man can be *gerens* as to one transaction and *cessans* as to another, apart from exclusion, so that he may be primarily liable on one transaction and secondarily on another. This leads to a general duty of supervision in *cessantes*, even in those excluded from *gestio*. All *tutores* are now primarily responsible for their own acts and negligences and subsidiarily for all others. Hence the joint liability of all is limited to what they have done or neglected in common, and this is subject finally to *b. divisionis*. The author makes the fact of change clear (see also Beseler, *Beiträge*, 1. 92, 2. 50, 3. 37, 3. 168), but his main thesis requires a great number of uncertain interpolations.

1 *Post*, § CLXXXVII. 2 D. 27. 6. Edictal, h. t. 1. pr. 3 P. 1. 4. 2; D. 27. 3. 13. Transfer of actions on puberty, *ante*, § LV. 4 History, Bonfante, *Scr. Giur.* 2. 184. 5 G. 1. 144, 190; Ulp. 11. 1 says: "*infirmitas sexus et ignorantia rerum forensium.*" 6 Vat. Fr. 325. An Egyptian case of A.D. 350 or later (Mitteis, *Grundzüge*, 2. 2. 116) shews women with *tutores*. One has none and says nothing about release. One is in *tutela* of her husband, an application of Greek notions. See G. 1. 193. It may be under the enactment of Constantine abolished in 362 (C. Th. 3. 1. 3) by which a minor wife was in *tutela* of the *vir*, with more power than an ordinary *tutor*: he could sell her *praedia* without a *decretum*, *ante*, p. 154. One of the women is stated to have the *ius liberorum*. Girard notes that, as *ius liberorum* releases, the system cannot have lasted after 410 when all women received this right (*Man.* 241); C. Th. 8. 17. 3. See, however, Cuq, *Man.* 222. Taubenschlag, *Vormundschaft. Untersuch.* 83. 7 G. 1. 148, 150 *sqq.*, *ante*, § LI. 8 G. 1. 154.

in general terms gave the right to change as often as she chose—*tutoris optio plena*, but it might be *tutoris optio duntaxat semel, bis*, etc.[1]

Legitimi tutores. A *lex Claudia* abolished agnatic *tutela* of women, apparently even if under age[2]. Constantine restored it for young girls[3], the perpetual *tutela* being practically obsolete. One result of the *l. Claudia* was that *tutela legitima*, the only serious one, could not arise for an *ingenua*, except in her *paterfamilias* who emancipated her[4].

Tutores fiduciarii. There was a case of this which could not occur with males, i.e. the *tutor* obtained by *coemptio fiduciae causa* for the purpose of change of *tutor*[5]. He was like the *extraneus manumissor* of an *impubes*: the only difference is that here he was produced by the activity of the woman herself, with the consent of her existing *tutor*.

Tutores a magistratu dati. Here the only thing to note is that in the absence of agnatic *tutela* there was more occasion for these[6].

Tutores cessicii. These existed only for women. *Legitimi tutores*, in the strict sense[7], might make formal *cessio* or surrender of the *tutela* to another[8]. It is in connexion with this that Gaius tells us that *parens manumissor* is treated as a *legitimus tutor*[9]. The reason he gives for the privilege is that the *tutela* is burdensome[10], but this would apply to other cases than *legitima*: the real reason is that the *tutela* was in the interest of the *tutor* who was thus merely allowed to waive his rights. *Tutor cessicius* was a sort of representative. If he died or was *capite minutus*, or purported to cede it again, the *tutela* reverted to *cedens* and if *cedens* died or was *capite minutus* the *tutela cessicia* ended[11].

The unreality of the *tutela* of adult women in classical law is shewn by the number of devices for change of *tutor*. Besides *tutoris optio*, *tutela cessicia* and *coemptio fiduciae causa*, involving consent of someone else, there was a rule that a woman inconvenienced by absence (however short) of her *tutor* might apply to a magistrate to have another appointed, which done, the former ceased to serve[12]. Where he was a *legitimus tutor*, the only one with real control, this was not allowed, but, if the *tutor* was away and there was temporary urgency, e.g. need to arrange for *dos*, or an inheritance to be accepted, a *tutor praetorius* was appointed who ceased to serve as soon as the urgency was over[13]. There was similar

1 G. 1. 152, 153. *Abdicatio, ante*, p. 149. She might even choose a *tutor* for specific things, G. 1. 150. The *l. Salpensana*, XXII (Girard, *Textes*, 109) seems to refer to *optio tutoris* in males. 2 G. 1. 157, 171; Ulp. 11. 8. 3 C. Th. 3. 17. 2; C. 5. 30. 3. Taubenschlag, *cit.* 84. 4 Thus Ulpian, speaking of *cessio tutelae*, treats *tutela libertae* as the typical case, Ulp. 19. 11. 5 *Ante*, p. 119; G. 1. 115. 6 See G. 1. 195. 7 G. 1. 168–172; Ulp. 11. 6–8. Doubts as to *parens manumissor* and *extraneus manumissor*. 8 Not to another *legitimus*, *Sch. Sin.* 51. 9 G. 1. 172. 10 G. 1. 168. 11 G. 1. 170; Ulp. 11. 7. It would probably be most frequent in the case of a *liberta*. See Ulp. 19. 11. 12 G. 1. 173. 13 G. 1. 174–178, 181; Ulp. 11. 20–22.

relief where a *legitimus tutor* was deaf or dumb or mad or a *pupillus*: apparently the *tutor* so appointed was not permanent but created for each occurrence of the need[1]. Thus the rule *tutor ad certam rem dari non potest* has its application much cut down in this case.

There were great differences in function. The *tutor* of an adult woman did not administer: his only function was *auctoritatis interpositio*[2]. Further, a woman could do, without *auctoritas*, many things which a *pupillus* could not. She could alienate less important property, *res nec mancipi*[3]. She could give a valid receipt[4]. She could be party to the less formal modes of litigation, *iudicia imperio continentia*[5], and appoint a *procurator* to act for her in others[6]. But, without *auctoritas*, she could not contract an obligation or take part in a *iure civili* transaction[7], including testation, formal manumission, formal conveyance of property, creation of servitudes, creation of *dos* (except by *datio* where the *dos* contained no *res mancipi*[8]), acceptance of a *hereditas* or giving a fictitious release (*acceptilatio*[9]). But though *auctoritas* was often needed, it was usually unreal: all *tutores* except *legitimi* could be compelled to give it[10], the *tutela* being in such cases no protection but merely a nuisance. But *legitimi tutores* could not be compelled to authorise the making of a will or a contract to bind the ward, or alienation of *res mancipi*, for which Gaius gives the honest reason that it might be against their interests[11]. No doubt the same rule applied to her passing into *manus*. It meant more than it did in the case of *impuberes*, for there the *tutor* might eventually have to pay damages for refusal, but that was not so here. Thus there was an exception: if the case was urgent and clear, the Praetor would compel even these to authorise[12].

The *tutela* was *perpetua*: maturity did not end it[13]. All the other modes of ending applied and there was from the beginning of the Empire a mode peculiar to this case. A woman with the *ius liberorum* (three children, or four if a *liberta* in the patron's *tutela*) was free of *tutela*, a right sometimes given without actual satisfaction of the requirement[14].

As the *tutor* did not administer he had no accounts to render and gave no security: there was no *actio tutelae* against him[15], or any other of the remedies for maladministration.

1 G. 1. 179, 180; Ulp. 11. 21. 2 G. 1. 190, 191; Ulp. 11. 25. 3 G. 2. 80, and so make a valid loan by *mutuum*, G. 2. 81. 4 G. 2. 85, as early as Cicero, *Top.* 11. 46. 5 Ulp. 11. 27. 6 Vat. Fr. 325, 327. 7 G. 1. 192; Ulp. 11. 27. *Obligatio*, for Gaius, meant civil obligation and perhaps so here. 8 G. 1. 178, 2. 118, 3. 176; Fr. D. 15; Ulp. 1. 17; Vat. Fr. 45. 9 G. 1. 176; Ulp. 11. 27. 10 G. 1. 190. 11 G. 1. 192. 12 G. 1. 191, 192. 13 G. 1. 190; Ulp. 11. 1. 14 G. 1. 145, 194, 3. 44; Ulp. 29. 3; P. 4. 9. Vestal virgins were free from *tutela*. G. 1. 145. 15 G. 1. 191. *Tutor* of a girl under 12 had the same responsibility as *tutor* of a male *impubes*. Thus at 12 *actio tutelae* lay for an account though *tutela* was not ended.

LXI. *Cura, curatio.* This name is applied to several cases with little in common except that they cannot, like *tutela*, be regarded as a substitute for, or artificial extension of, *potestas* till the subject is able to found one. Even in the oldest cases, in which the interest of the guardian is certainly in view, the *curatio* may supervene after the subject of it has been in enjoyment of full rights as a *civis sui iuris*[1].

Cura furiosi. By the XII Tables, *furiosi*, lunatics conceived of as capable of lucid intervals, were placed in the *cura* of their agnates, or, failing these, *gentiles*[2]. The Praetors extended similar protection to all cases of mental incapacitation (*insani, mente capti*) and even permanently incapacitating disease[3]. In cases clearly not within the XII Tables the magistrate appointed the *curator*, accepting and confirming a testamentary nomination by the *paterfamilias*[4]. In cases within the XII Tables the better view is that, strictly, the Praetor appointed only if there were no agnates[5], but that there was a tendency to depart from this, notably to the exclusion of unworthy relatives[6] and more generally in later law[7]. The *curator* had the care of the person of the *furiosus*[8]: apart from this his functions were similar to those of *tutor infantis*. The XII Tables gave him the power of alienation for administrative purposes[9] of the lunatic's property, presumably even by formal modes[10]. The *furiosus* regained capacity in a lucid interval and the *curator* ceased to act, but, though there had been doubts, in later law he needed no reappointment on relapse[11]. The law as to removal, excuses and security[12] was similar to that in *tutela*. The remedy for maladministration was an *actio negotiorum gestorum*, available at any time and privileged like the similar claims under *tutela*[13].

Cura prodigi. The XII Tables placed under *cura*, of agnates or *gentiles*, *prodigi* who wasted goods received on intestacy. The Praetor[14], after a decree of interdiction, placed other *prodigi* under *curatores dati*[15], the

1 On the publicistic character of these *curationes*, De Visscher, *Ét.* 7. 2 Bruns, 1. 23; Girard, *Textes*, 14. "*ast ei custos non escit*" i.e. not if *alieni iuris* or *in tutela*, Perozzi, *Ist.* 1. 524. 3 26. 5. 8. 3, 12. pr.; Inst. 1. 23. 4. Not *caeci*, P. 4. 12. 9. 4 27. 10. 16. pr.; Inst. 1. 23. 2. Those appointed under the XII Tables are *legitimi*, those by the Praetor, *honorarii*; Ulp. 12. 1. 5 C. 5. 70. 5. 6 27. 10. 1. 1; h. t. 13; C. 5. 70. 7. 6. 7 De Francisci, *Bull.* 1921, 154, shews that agnatic was still the primary form in cl. law, and survived under Justinian. Appointment by will, confirmed by magistrate, appears in late law, 27. 10. 16. pr.; C. 5. 70. 7. 6. 8 27. 10. 7. pr.; *contra*, Perozzi, *Ist.* 1. 524. 9 27. 10. 17. 10 G. 2. 64. As to formal modes, see the texts cited, Mitteis, *R.Pr.* 1. 210, and Girard, *Man.* 243. Siber, *R.R.* 322, calls attention to Cicero, *Tusc.* 3. 5. 11, and concludes that *res mancipi* were originally inalienable. The texts tell us nothing as to power of acquisition by formal modes *inter vivos*, and we learn that *curator* could not accept a *hereditas* (*post*, § CIX) for the *furiosus* (C. 5. 70. 7. 3) till Justinian. 11 27. 10. 1. pr.; C. 5. 70. 6. 12 27. 10. 7. 1, 2; C. 5. 70. 7. 4 *sqq.* 13 27. 10. 15. 1; 27. 3. 4. 3. 14 Ulp. 12. 2; D. 27. 10. 1 pr. 15 Ulp. 12. 3; P. 3. 4a. 7. The form of *interdictio* given by Paul is traditional but too narrow for the rules as we know them.

interdictio being sometimes said to be based on *mores*[1]. So far all is clear, but there is much dispute on the reason of the limitation in the XII Tables, on the question of the real origin of the *interdictio* and on the question whether the XII Tables expressly provided for it. The state of the texts makes the questions extremely obscure and we shall not discuss them[2]. The person interdicted might be a woman[3]. The evolution as to modes of appointment, security, excuses and remedies seems to have been as in the last case[4], but the *cura* was presumably continuous till the interdiction was removed[5]. The functions were different. The *prodigus* was much in the position of a *pupillus pubertati proximus*. He could do acts which could not harm the estate[6]. We have little information as to the powers of the *curator*. According to one view the rules were as in the last case, except that the *prodigus* could enter on a *hereditas*[7]. According to another, suggested by this last rule, which involved the possibility of loss, the *prodigus* could go through ordinary transactions with the consent of the *curator*, though he could make no will[8]. But no sufficient evidence is available. The restrictions on alienation imposed in *tutela* apply here as in *cura furiosi*[9]. The action is *negotiorum gestorum*.

LXII. *Cura minoris*. This is the guardianship of persons *sui iuris* between 12 and 25. It is much later: as a system it is almost post-classical. The development seems to begin with a *l. Plaetoria*, dating probably from late in the third century B.C. The machinery set up by this *lex*, which is mentioned in many literary texts, but little in legal sources, is imperfectly known[10]. A noxal action based on fraud on minors seems to have been set up by it, and another, based on acts contrary to the *lex*, may have been introduced not much later[11]. One of these is described by Cicero as a *iudicium publicum rei privatae*[12]. There was

1 P. 3. 4a. 7; D. 27. 10. 1. pr. 2 For various views, Collinet, *Mél. Cornil*, 1. 149 *sqq.*; De Visscher, *Ét.* 23.; Solazzi, *St. Bonfante*, 1. 47 *sqq.* 3 P. 3. 4a. 6; D. 27. 10. 15. 4 27. 10. 1. pr., 13, 15. 1, 16. 1; 27. 3. 4. 3; C. 5. 70. 1. If the father nominated in a clear case of prodigality, the Praetor must usually appoint the nominee, 27. 10. 16. 1. The following passages, no doubt due to Justinian, consider how the father could have avoided the need of a *curator*. 5 Two texts seem to contradict this. In P. 3. 4a. 12 the reversing decree is probably assumed. D. 27. 10. 1. pr., is more difficult—it does not seem to be here interpolated: in any case it does not say what evidence is needed of return to *boni mores*. 6 D. 12. 1. 9. 7; 27. 10. 10. pr.; 45. 1. 6. 7 29. 2. 5. 1; Girard, *Man.* 246. 8 Ulp. 20. 13; P. 3. 4a. 12. 9 C. 5. 70. 2 and rubric. 10 The chief texts are Plautus, *Pseud.* 1. 3. 69; *Rudens*, 5. 3. 24; Cicero, *de nat. deor.* 3. 30. 74; *de off.* 3. 15. 61; *Vita Marci*, 10; Suetonius, *ap.* Priscian, 8. 4. 21; 18. 19. 149; *Tab. Heracl.* 1. 112 (Bruns, 1. 108; Girard, *Textes*, 87); *Fr. de form. Fab.* 4; C. Th. 8. 12. 2; *Berl. Gr. Urk.* no. 611. 1. 6. It appears to be referred to in 4. 4. 24. 3; 44. 1. 7. 1; 46. 2. 19; sometimes called *Laetoria*, Suetonius, *cit.*, *Vita Marci*, *cit.*; C. Th. 8. 12. 2. *Pap. Oxyrh.* 10, 1274. 11 Probably only one action, a *privatum iudicium populare* for a penalty. Duquesne, *Mél. Cornil*, 1. 217. 12 *De nat. deor.* 3. 30. 74.

also, no doubt of later development, an *exceptio legis Plaetoriae*, a defence to an action brought to enforce the impeached transaction. Further a non-legal writer of the fourth century says that *curatores* were appointed *e lege Plaetoria* for specific causes. This seems to mean not that the *lex* provided for these, but that persons dealing with minors took the precaution of seeing that the minor had an adviser, as it seems a mere *de facto* guarantee of good faith. The *curator* probably acted only in the specific transaction: it may be doubted if he had any legal *status*[1].

The Praetor carried the matter further, supplementing the provisions of the *lex* by machinery for setting the transaction aside—*restitutio in integrum*[2]. Not every unprofitable transaction could be set aside but only one in which either the minor was tricked or he made a bad bargain owing to inexperience, what Ulpian calls *inconsulta facilitas*[3]. It was in the hands of the Praetor, decided *causa cognita* and on the merits of each case[4]. Here too the presence of an adviser was a protection, *prima facie* evidence that the transaction was fair, but not conclusive: there might still be *restitutio* if the adviser was careless or fraudulent[5], but if competent persons acting carefully and honestly thought it a fair bargain there was no *restitutio* however it turned out.

The first appearance of anything like an official *curator* of minors was the right of those who had certain dealings with a minor to require that he should have a *curator* for the transaction, e.g. for settlement of the accounts of a *tutor* at the end of *tutela*[6], for payment of a debt[7], and where action was to be brought against the minor[8]. These were temporary. But in the second century a change occurred, attributed to M. Aurelius[9]. Any minor might apply for a *curator*, who, once appointed, acted for the whole minority[10]. An appointment by the father's will was confirmed without enquiry, but, in general, the magistrate appointed[11]. The function of *curator* differed somewhat from that of *tutor*, and the remedy against him was the *actio negotiorum gestorum*[12], but the rules as to the magistrate who appointed, security, excuses, removal, restrictions on alienation, termination, etc., were, in later law, in the main

1 See for various views, Girard, *Man.* 249; Cuq, *Man.* 227; Debray, *Mél. Girard*, 1. 265 *sqq.*; Roby, *R.P.L.* 1. 123.
2 P. 1. 7. 2; D. 4. 4.
3 4. 4. 1, 7. 1, 7. 5, 7. 7, 9. 2, 11. 3–5, 24. 1, 24. 2, 44; C. 2. 21. 5; *post*, § CCXLIV.
4 4. 4. 11. 3, 16. pr.; no *restitutio* where the act of the *minor* was a delict or offence, P. 1. 9. 1; D. 4. 4. 9. 2, 37.
5 4. 4. 39. 1; C. 2. 24. 2–5.
6 C. 5. 31. 7.
7 4. 4. 7. 2.
8 Inst. 1. 23. 2; C. 5. 31. 1.
9 *Vita Marci*, 10. Gaius' account of *cura minorum* is only partly preserved, 1. 197 *sqq.* (older than M. Aurelius; Fitting, *Alter und Folge*, 56). Thus it is only in certain cases, "*ex iisdem causis*," but law before M. Aurelius not clear. Collinet-Giffard, *Précis*, 1. 258.
10 4. 4. 1. 3.
11 26. 3. 6. A *furiosus minor* had a *curator*, *qua minor*, 26. 1. 3. 1.
12 Lenel, *E.P.* 319. Available during *cura*, 26. 7. 26; 27. 3. 16. *Post*, § CLXXXV. Whether originally *utilis*, as not based on purely voluntary intervention, is disputed. Arangio-Ruiz, *Ist.* 464; Lenel, *E.P. cit*

the same[1]. The age of termination was 25, subject to *venia aetatis*, i.e. Severus and Caracalla allowed the privilege of full age in exceptional cases, by imperial decree, before it was actually attained[2]. Constantine provided that this might be applied for only by a man of 20 or a woman of 18[3].

As to function and capacity two periods must be distinguished, in both of which the rule seems to have been that no one need have a *curator* unless he so wished, though it was usual, and, under Justinian, almost a matter of course. One with no *curator* was under the régime of *restitutio in integrum*. One with a *curator* was not in classical law deprived of powers: he could act independently and was then under the old régime[4]. But it was safer to act with the *consensus* of the *curator*, which unlike the *auctoritas* of the *tutor* was quite informal[5]. It was not indeed a complete protection against *restitutio*[6], but made it much less likely. It is indeed disputed that the *curator minoris* had, under the scheme of Aurelius, any power of acting alone, any *administratio*. The texts which give him this power shew some signs of interpolation. As the minor was capable of acting, *consensus* would be all that was ordinarily required and the rarity of occasions where independent action was needed may account for the absence of allusions to the matter in the texts in their original form[7]. One text in Paul's *Sententiae*[8] speaks of a *curator* as bringing an action in the minor's concerns, but this text, like others in that work may have received post-classical retouching. Even if (and

1 Differences in detail. No one need be *curator* to one whose *tutor* he had been, C. 5. 62. 20; Inst. 1. 25. 18; P. 2. 27. 2; Vat. Fr. 200 (except *libertus* to patron's child, C. 5. 62. 5); or to his wife or *sponsa* or daughter-in-law, 27. 1. 1. 5; C. 5. 34. 2; C. 5. 62. 17; Vat. Fr. 201. Many texts on *curator* are interpolated and refer to the system established about the time of Diocletian (*post*, p. 172). Thus *curator* often appears in texts which originally dealt only with *tutor*, (see, e.g., Albertario, *Z.S.S.* 1912, 240). The rules were not necessarily new: the Vat. Frr. shew the assimilation with *tutela* in progress. 2 4. 4. 3. pr.; C. 2. 44. 1. 3 C. 2. 44. 2. As to the machinery of the application, C. 2. 44. 2; D. 4. 4. 3. pr. Justinian holds such persons still bound by the restrictions on alienation. C. 2. 44. 3, *ante*, p. 154. 4 He could litigate on his own behalf. It may be that the powers of the *curator* did not extend in classical law to representation in litigation. Lenel, *Z.S.S.* 1914, 197 *sqq.* 5 There is no authority for the view that consent could be given by letter or ratification. No text speaks of consent in absence, and most texts emphasise the need of presence (Vat. Fr. 110; D. 4. 4. 7. 2; 42. 2. 6. 3; C. 2. 24. 2; C. 2. 26. 4; C. 5. 59. 1; C. 8. 37. 7). In 4. 8. 49. pr. and 26. 7. 25 the wards are *furiosus* and *pupillus*. The *consensus* of *curator* is distinguished from *auctoritas* of *tutor* in the rubric of D. 26. 8, and *consensus* occurs in C. 3. 6. 2 and D. 23. 3. 60. *Auctoritas* is more common (1. 7. 8; 23. 3. 61. pr.; 49. 1. 17. 1; C. 5. 4. 8; C. 5. 59. rubr.). Some of the texts are interp.: it is not evident that all are. *Consensus* is used of a *tutor* (26. 7. 1. 4). 6 C. 2. 24. 2, *ante*, p. 170. 7 Against any classical *administratio*, Solazzi, *Minore Età*, 33; *Curator impuberis* (in which, in various passages, a reply is made to Lenel); Albertario, in various publications, e.g. *Rend. Ist. Lomb.* 1929; Partsch, *Neg. Gest.* 1. 66; Bonfante, *Corso*, 1. 491 (with full reff. to literature), see also Beseler, *Beitr.* 4. 88. In favour, Lenel, *Z.S.S.* 1914, 129; Perozzi, *Ist.* 1. 536. 8 P. 1. 4. 2, see Solazzi, *Minore Età*, 213.

when, as he certainly did in later law) he administered, there might still be *restitutio*[1]. In any case there occurred, before Diocletian, a change[2], the nature of which is disputed, but which seems to mean that, while it was still possible to act without a *curator*[3], a minor who had one lost his power of independent action and was almost in the same position as a *pupillus*: he could do no act which would make his position worse without the consent of his *curator*[4], so that a minor *sui iuris* had less civil capacity than one *alieni iuris*[5].

There were in later law two tendencies, first, to an assimilation of *tutor* and *curator minoris* and thus to the practice of giving a *curator* as a matter of course[6], and secondly to independent action of these guardians[7] as opposed to giving *auctoritas* or *consensus*. Only a small proportion of the texts which deal with *cura* speak of co-operation[8]. Of these many spoke originally of *tutor* or of *cura pupilli*[9], and most of the rest are about litigation[10]. The rubric of the relevant title of the Digest[11] speaks of *consensus curatoris*, but the title gives no instance. It seems plain that in later law the *curator* usually carried on the business himself, and that *consensus* was subordinate: it would be needed where the *curator* could not do the act, e.g. *aditio hereditatis*[12], or where the minor had been made a party to litigation.

Cura pupilli. There were several cases in which a person normally under *tutela* might have a *curator*.

(*a*) Where in temporary absence or excuse a *tutor* had been appointed in classical law a *curator* was appointed in later times[13]. In view of the similarity of powers at this time the change means little but recognition of the fact that *tutor ad certam rem* is an anomaly.

(*b*) Where any *tutor* was incapable from ill-health or poverty, or estates were far apart, or a patron or *parens manumissor* was unworthy,

1 C. 2. 24. 3, 5. 2 C. 2. 21. 3. Known to Dio Cassius; Partsch, *Neg. Gest.* 87. 3 For the view that a minor always had a *curator* after this change see Cuq, *Man.* 230, but the texts cited hardly bear out the contention. There seems no reason to think the change a direct result of legislation. 4 The D. still contains an expression of the old view, 45. 1. 101. 5 Accarias, *Précis*, 1. 451 *sqq.* 6 Rotondi, *Scr. Giur.* 3. 483; Albertario, *Z.S.S.* 1912, 240. 7 Thus the legislation and comment on restrictions on sales of property speak of the act as done by the *tutor* (27. 9 *passim*), and the same is true of the more concrete cases discussed in C. 5. 71. The short title on *auctoritas tutoris* suggests that this was mainly used in formal transactions "*quae sollennitatem iuris desiderant*," 26. 8. 19. 8 See the expressive language in 4. 4. 1. 3 and h. t. 2 and C. 2. 21. 3. 9 Inst. 1. 21. 3; D. 1. 7. 8 (?); 23. 3. 60, 61. pr.; 26. 1. 3. 2; 26. 7. 25, 43. 1; 49. 1. 17. 1. Solazzi, *Curator impuberis, passim.* 10 4. 4. 7. 2; 26. 7. 1. 4; 42. 2. 6. 3; C. 2. 26. 4; 3. 6. 2; 5. 59. 4. One at least deals with *stipulatio*, C. 5. 59. 1=C. 8. 37. 7, and Justinian lays down a general rule, C. 5. 59. 5. 3. 11 D. 26. 8. 12 29. 2. 90. 13 26. 5. 7, 15; Inst. 1. 21. 3; Ulp. 11. 20; G. 1. 178; *ante*, pp. 148, 151 *sq.* Evolution of *cura pupilli*, Taubenschlag, *Vormundschaftsr. Studien*, § 3. 47 *sqq.*, and for a quite different view, Solazzi, *Curator impuberis.*

and in some other cases, it was usual not to remove him, but to appoint a *curator* to act with him[1]. This is not an *adiutor tutoris*. If a tutor was for some temporary reason unable to act in some business he might if the pupil was absent or *infans* or *infantiae proximus* either appoint with leave of the Praetor, or ask the Praetor to appoint, an *adiutor* who was merely an agent and acted at the risk of the *tutor*[2]. An older pupil could appoint a *procurator*[3].

(*c*) Where legal proceedings arose between a *tutor* and his ward a *curator* was appointed in later law[4].

(*d*) A girl over 12, still a child, could not manage her affairs and her *tutor* had no *administratio*. A *curator* was appointed to act for her[5].

Other forms of *cura*, such as *cura ventris*[6], have some relation to the law of persons; others, e.g. the various *curationes bonorum*[7], have hardly any.

LXIII. Personality. Juristic Persons.

The word *persona* has not always meant the same thing. Primarily signifying a mask it comes to mean the part played in life by a man and hence the man who plays it. It is in this untechnical sense that the Roman lawyers seem to use the word *persona*. Every man, slave or free, is a person, and has a *persona*[8]; and nothing else, no group or other conception, has the name. The first sign of a more technical meaning appears in texts which speak of a more or less complete *persona*, where the word means something like *caput*. Slaves and young persons incapable of taking part in legal proceedings are regarded as having an imperfect *persona*[9]. In the Byzantine age, but not represented in the *Corpus Iuris*, there appears a technical sense for the word in which it has come to mean a being capable of legal rights and duties[10]. We can indeed frame two meanings for the expression, besides that of "man": the "legal," i.e. that which is capable of rights and liabilities in law, and the "philosophical," any unity possessed of self-consciousness and will[11].

1 26. 1. 13. pr.; Inst. 1. 23. 5; P. 2. 29. 2 26. 1. 13. 1; 26. 7. 24; Inst. 1. 23. 6. For Solazzi, *cit.* 16, a *curator* in cl. law. 3 26. 7. 24; C. 2. 12. 11. Solazzi, *cit.* 19, holds that all these cases except that of "insufficiency" of *tutor* are due to Justinian. Cl. law gave a *tutor*. The cases are enumerated by Bonfante, *Corso*, 1. 488. 4 Inst. 1. 21. 3; cf. G. 1. 184; Ulp. 11. 24. *Ante*, p. 152. 5 See G. 1. 190; Vat. Fr. 201; Inst. 1. 23. pr.; C. 5. 37. 12, 5. 60. 1. 6 D. 37. 9, *post*, § ccxlv. *Crimen suspecti* applies, 26. 10. 3. 3. 7 Lenel, *E.P.* 434. 8 G. 1. 120; 3. 189; Vat. Fr. 82; Inst. 3. 17, 2, etc. Desserteaux, *Capitis Deminutio*, 2. 99, etc., holding that a slave is a *persona*, thinks that this is due to his being "doué d'une fonction juridique." This half-way house between the view that he was not a *persona* and the language of the texts implies that a *servus sine domino* not held by anyone would not be a *persona*. It is difficult to reconcile with Gaius 1. 120, 121, where the *servilis persona* is being mancipated as a chattel, or with 30. 86. 2. The expression would hardly have been used in these texts if any such distinction had been in the writer's mind. Affolter, *Persönlichk. d. herrenlosen Sklaven*, § i. 9 Autun Gaius, 89, 90; C. Th. 3. 17. 1=C. 5. 34. 11. 10 *Nov.* Theod. 17. 1. 2. 11 Kuhlenbeck, *Entwicklungsgeschichte des R. Rechts*, 2. 10 *sqq.*

Units other than individual men can be thought of as capable of rights and liabilities, and, possibly, even of acts and volitions. This is true of corporate bodies and, so far as rights and duties are concerned, of such a notion as the *hereditas iacens*, an inheritance on which the *heres* has not yet entered. For such groups and conceptions the name juristic persons is convenient, though neither this nor the medieval name, *persona ficta*[1], was used by the Romans.

It is important to grasp the distinction between common and corporate rights. If several men agree to carry out a business undertaking together or to buy, e.g., a yacht for their common use, they become in the ordinary way common owners of the assets of the business or of the yacht in undivided shares. Each owns his proper proportion. There is nothing corporate about this, no artificial person to whom the property belongs. But the position is different in the case of a corporate body, a municipality or a railway company. Here the property belongs to the corporate body and not to the individuals. A shareholder who walks on the railway is just as much a trespasser as any other person. The inhabitants of the town do not own undivided shares in the guildhall[2]. In Roman law this group personality could not arise of itself: it was always the creation of the State[3]. Hence arose the question, put in the middle ages and still debated, whether it is real or fictitious. It always had been created by the State, and when it was once conceived of as fictitious it followed that it must be so created[4]. But into these questions we cannot go[5].

If we accept the "legal" definition, capacity for rights and duties[6], it is clear that personality can attach to groups, and possible to regard it as attached to conceptions other than groups, e.g. the *hereditas iacens*. German law has gone far: it recognises, as juristic persons, Foundations (*Stiftungen*), i.e. Funds consisting of property earmarked for certain purposes, usually charitable, the ownership being vested, not in the administrators, who are mere agents, but in the Fund itself[7].

1 Maitland, *Coll. Pap.* 3. 304 *sqq.* 2 The recognition of this distinction does not come by nature; Maitland, *Township and Borough*, 12 *sqq.* 3 3. 4. 1. pr. 4 Maitland, *Political Theories of the Middle Age*, xviii; *Coll. Papers*, 3. 314. The fiction theory involves the concession theory. The converse is not true. The State could confer "legal" personality on a slave; in early Rome all manumission was controlled by the State, but there was nothing fictitious about a freedman's personality. 5 The matter has attracted more attention on the Continent, where it has been of more political and practical importance. Exhaustive discussion and statement of many shades of opinion, Saleilles, *La Personnalité Juridique*. See also Hallis, *Corporate Personality*. 6 Girard, *Man.* p. 101. 7 The ultimate beneficiaries are a quite unknown quantity. For the *Stiftung*, Windscheid, *Lehrbuch*, 1. § 57; Schuster, *Princ. of Germ. Civ. Law*, 37. But the conception, though in the *Bürg. Gesetzb.*, seems to be ignored in practice.

Roman law recognised right-holding units other than individual[1] men, though it did not apply the word *persona* (or even *caput*, which corresponds with *persona* in its modern legal sense) to them. Ulpian indeed speaks of individuals as *personae singulares*[2], which suggests the extension, and these group persons were said to have *corpus*[3].

LXIV. In the Republic there were three types of corporate body: the State (*populus Romanus*), the municipality, and private corporations of various kinds. The *populus* is the most important of all corporations[4], but it makes little appearance in private law, its rights and obligations being regulated not by the ordinary courts but by administrative machinery: it was essentially a "publicistic" entity. As the Emperor waxed the *populus* waned. In the third century the popular treasury, the *aerarium*, almost disappeared, and the Imperial treasury (*Fiscus*) took its place. The right conception of fiscal property, i.e. of the juristic nature of the *Fiscus*, has been much discussed[5]. It is bound up with other obscure questions, e.g. with the relation of the *privata res Caesaris* with the *patrimonium*, and of both these to the *Fiscus*. The first two need not here be considered, but the *Fiscus* is prominent in the *Corpus Juris*. It acquired property under private law in many circumstances, e.g. *bona vacantia*. It sued and could be sued before the ordinary courts in relation to transactions of its officials[6]. Its property is described sometimes as that of the *Fiscus*[7], but often as that of Caesar[8]. But there was nothing corporate about the Emperor[9]. His really private property he could dispose of, e.g. by his will, like any other citizen[10], but he commonly made his successor his *heres*. But fiscal property of all types went to his successor. It was thought of in the early Empire as the property of the Emperor, while as yet the imperial officials were mere agents of his, and the *populus*, represented by the Senate, shared the sovereignty with him. There is no difficulty in the fact that he was a private man: this property was dealt with under special "publicistic"

1 Mitteis, *R.Pr.* 1. 339; Saleilles, *La Personnalité Juridique*, 45; *S.M.W.* 165, where it is noted that the property of juristic persons, in Roman law is not applicable to individualistic purposes. 2 4. 2. 9. 1; 50. 16. 195. 1. *Hereditas sustinet personam*, but it is that of deceased or *heres*. *Post*, § CVII. See 46. 1. 22 where similar language is applied to "*municipium, decuria, societas.*" 3 3. 4. 1. pr. 4 Attribution of property to *populus* does not connote common ownership, any more than does our word Commonwealth. 5 Mommsen, *Staatsr.* 2. 998; *D.P.R.* 5. 290; Mitteis, *op. cit.* 350; Koschaker, *Z.S.S.* 32. 407; Jones, *L.Q.R.* 1927, 499. 6 Bethmann-Hollweg, *R. Civilpr.* 3. 78. There were for the most part special tribunals in later law, Mitteis, *op. cit.* 364. 7 E.g. 49. 14 *passim*. 8 E.g. *Fr. de iure Fisci, passim.* 9 The Romans approach this notion here and there. By a rescript of Pius a legacy to the Emperor takes effect in his successor if a change occurs before the will operates, even though it is a question of his really private property, and the same rule is not extended to the Empress, 31. 56, 57. 10 Mommsen, *Staatsr.* 2. 999, n. 1; *D.P.R.* 5. 292, n. 1; cp. Mitteis, *R.Pr.* 1. 354.

rules[1]. But when *populus* and *aerarium* had lost all importance and the imperial officials were the real State officers, though the attribution to Caesar still persisted, the property was in fact contemplated as that of the State, the attribution meaning no more than does the appearance of *Rex* as plaintiff in our courts when claims of the State are in question. Mitteis[2] goes further, and holds that the *Fiscus* itself, as an independent *Anstalt*, was really the owner of the property. Whether the ownership is here contemplated as in the group of officials, or the case is one of a true *Stiftung* and the ownership in the Fund or *Zweck* itself, is not clear. But the author cited recognises that for practical purposes it was the property of the State[3].

Municipalities[4] were of many types. During the Republic they were mainly the subjugated, incorporated, communities which received, or were not deprived of, corporate character, but early in the Empire similar rights were conferred on local communities of all kinds[5], the foundation of such a community being always an act of State. Their power of acting as legal persons was restricted in various ways. Nerva authorised *civitates* to receive legacies and Hadrian regulated this[6], but they could not in general be instituted *heredes* till the later Empire[7]. Italian communities could free their slaves from early times, but the right was not extended to the provinces till A.D. 129[8]. As a community could not act for itself, persons were appointed to act for it, *ad hoc* in classical law[9], permanently in later law.

Of private associations[10] Rome knew many kinds. There were the *sodalitates*, devoted to particular cults, some very ancient, others expressly founded by the State. There were numerous gilds or societies with diverse objects, trade gilds, burial clubs, etc. Many had corporate character, many had not, and it is not easy for early law to distinguish.

1 The Prince of Wales is a private man, but his Duchy of Cornwall passes under rules unknown in other cases. 2 *Op. cit.* 350. 3 The *Stiftung* idea would have been unintelligible to the Romans, and if the conception of ownership in the *Anstalt* had given any practical result differing from that of State ownership, it would have been repudiated by the Emperor. 4 Mitteis, *op. cit.* 376. Kuebler, 228; *S.M.W.* 194. 5 46. 1. 22. Mitteis, *loc. cit.* 6 Ulp. 24. 28. Earlier instances cited by Mitteis, *loc. cit.*, may be *privilegia*. See 30. 73. 1. 7 C. 6. 24. 12. *Post*, § CIII. 8 C. 7. 9. 3. Manumission was by vote of the *curia*, C. 7. 9. 1–3; C. 11. 37. 1. 9 Liebenam, *Städteverwaltung*, 301. Mitteis, *op. cit.* 342, observes that in the Republic there are still traces in corporate municipalities, of common ownership, as opposed to corporate, but that it all disappears under the organising hand of the Emperor. The rules as to the giving of security to public slaves suggest the same thing, *ante*, pp. 126, 154. Bonfante, *Scr. Giur.* 1. 309 and Albertario, *Actio de universitate*, 12, deny any cl. recognition of artificial personality of a corporation. They do not really dispose of G. 2. 11 where the word "*ipsius*" can mean only the corporation as opposed to its members. So understood the contradiction in terms, which B. sees, does not exist. To translate it as he does: "It is not the property of any of them because it is the property of all of them," is surely to create one. 10 Mitteis, *op. cit.* 390.

The *sodalitia* had, but with "publicistic" remedies. Many gilds had. Nothing can be inferred from the name *collegium*. The College of Pontiffs was merely a group of officials and the same is true of the other old official "colleges." Whether private *collegia* needed authorisation under the Republic is uncertain, but it does not appear that they had corporate character. They had certainly no power of litigation under the *legis actio* system, since they could not themselves appear and there was no representation. In the Empire no *collegium* could be founded without authority of the State, either express or by general enactment, e.g. the *sc.* of uncertain date which gave a general authority to found *collegia tenuiorum*, in essence, burial clubs[1]. The change dates from a certain *l. Iulia*, probably of 7 B.C., which while confirming many existing *collegia* required State authority for new ones[2]. It is widely held, on the authority of an obscure text, attributed to Gaius[3], that every *collegium* founded on authority had corporate capacity. But the text does not say this, and Mitteis remarks that while we know that *collegia* were very numerous in the Empire the same text says that the power to have a *corpus* was given very sparingly, and he points out that it was not till M. Aurelius that all *collegia* acquired such normal attributes of personality as the right to free slaves and receive legacies. He concludes that the right to form a *collegium* and grant of corporate capacity were distinct and given separately till the time of M. Aurelius[4]. When corporate they could be instituted by their *liberti*[5], but so far as is known not by other people[6]. And they had the patron's right of succession[7].

LXV. In the early Empire, certain deities, but not all[8], could be instituted *heredes*, but it is far from clear who was thought of as the actual owner of the property. Probably[9] it was the State, for even the administration was by the magistrates and not by the temple priests. Soon after the adoption of Christianity by the State, Constantine authorised gifts by will to Christian churches[10]. All church property was contemplated as, in a sense, that of the church as a whole, but this is a sort of eminent domain, and it is fairly clear that in each community the church property was regarded as a separate patrimony. It was administered by the bishop and the *Oeconomus*, but the ownership seems to have been thought of as in the religious group as a body, either in the clergy or the whole of the members, the latter being the more probable. Administration was not free: there were elaborate rules regulating the

1 47. 22. 1. pr., 1. 2 Mitteis, *op. cit.* 395. 3 3. 4. 1. pr. 4 Mitteis, *op. cit.* 399; D. 40. 3. 1; 34. 5. 20. Jörs, *R.R.* 52, holds that *corpus* has no reference to juristic personality which he regards as taken, not granted, a view more Germanic than Roman. 5 37. 1. 3, 4; 40. 3. 2. 6 Mitteis, *op. cit.* 402, who notes exceptions resting on *privilegia*. 7 40. 3. 2. *Societates publicanorum*, *post*, § CLXXVIII. 8 *Post*, § CIII. 9 Mommsen, *Staatsr.* 2. 59 *sqq.*; *D.P.R.* 3. 67. 10 C. 1. 2. 1.

application of the various parts of the revenues, and restricting alienations[1]. This notion of funds earmarked for certain purposes was utilised by those desirous of founding charities, a thing difficult to do with any guarantee of permanence in the classical law[2]. Property was given or left to a church to be applied to the charitable purpose[3], and if it was permanent the bishop set up an establishment managed by his nominee and staffed by clergy. There were many kinds, hospitals, almshouses for the old, poorhouses, orphanages, etc.[4] Probably (the matter is disputed)[5] the church of the place was the owner of the property. A further step was taken when men began to found such charities without express reference to the church. Gifts for these purposes to the church or to existing institutions raised no new questions, and if the founder did not specify the mode of execution it was in practice treated as one of these[6]. Thus the institution of *pauperes* or *captivos* generally, as *heredes*, was not to be objected to on account of the rules as to *incertae personae*, but was interpreted as institution of the local establishment for such purposes (or, if there was none, the bishop, who would set up the necessary *domus*) with directions as to application[7]. If the founder gave full directions as to the establishment, the person charged must set it up; only if he failed had the church any part. Even then the bishop must appoint to the control any person nominated by the founder[8]. These might still be called ecclesiastical because they were usually staffed by priests and there was a general right of supervision in the bishop, as a State commissioner. There were two classes of these establishments, those directly under the bishop and those of which the administration was independent[9]. Indeed some founders sought to exclude the church from any interference with the charity, and Justinian enacted that such a direction should not exclude the bishop's general right of supervision[10]. These relatively independent *domus* seem to belong to the age of Justinian.

This state of the texts raises three questions. Are these establishments juristic persons or merely church departments? The language of

1 E.g. C. 1. 2. 12. 2; h. t. 17; 1. 3. 41. 3, 45. 9, etc.

2 To give it to a *civitas* was the safest plan. For the various experiments, Pernice, *Labeo*, 3. 1. 56. The gift would be *sub modo* and there might be a gift over to another *civitas* if the purpose was not observed. Betti, *Ist.* 1. 2. 230, supposes stipulations between *actores* of the two communities. But in view of the temporary nature of such appointments and the long time which might elapse, there are obvious practical difficulties. Administrative methods seem more probable.

3 E.g. C. 1. 2. 19. They are called *Piae causae*. The expression or its Greek equivalent is common in the sources but seems to mean merely the purpose, not the foundation, Duff, *Personality in R. pr. law*, 203. Later it is the general name for such "foundations."

4 Enumerations, C. 1. 2. 15, 19, 23, etc.

5 Saleilles, *Mél. Gérardin*, 513, with many reff. to earlier literature; Duff, *Camb. Legal Essays*, 83; Bonfante, *Corso*, 6. 323.

6 C. 1. 3. 28, 48; *Nov.* 131. 11.

7 C. 1. 2. 15; 1. 3. 28, 48. The texts treat it as a gift to an establishment (C. 1. 3. 48).

8 C. 1. 3. 45. 3.

9 *Nov.* 120. 6. 1.

10 *Nov.* 131. 11; C. 1. 3. 45. pr.

the texts from which any conclusion must be drawn, which are mostly in Greek, is so diffuse and lacking in juristic precision that no inference from exact wording is justifiable. But the texts so constantly treat them as on the same footing as churches, monasteries and *civitates*[1] that it is hardly possible not to credit them with personality, and this is in fact almost universally accepted. The question arises how this comes to be attributed to them, since *corpus habere* required a state concession. It might be said that by reason of their ecclesiastical character they were thought of as covered by the concession to churches[2], but this hardly seems sufficient for those specially independent *domus*, in which the church had so little official part. Or it may be said that the authorisation of gifts to them was in itself an implicit gift of personality. It may well be that it is merely a gradual tacit extension from the recognition of those which were essentially under the bishop. The question remains: who or what constituted the person? According to one view it is the foundation itself; the Fund earmarked for certain purposes owns itself[3]. But this is not the Roman view: it is a description in terms of the rules of certain modern systems which give a similar practical result: it is no explanation for an English lawyer who recognises no such conception. The texts shew that the property is attributed to men. When we ask what men, there are two alternatives. For M. Saleilles[4], they are the indeterminate ultimate beneficiaries, all corporate idea being really gone, surviving only in a few descriptions of them as *corpora* and the like[5]. The other alternative, and it seems more in accord with the texts, is to regard them as true corporations[6]. It is possible that where the purpose was the dispensation of funds or temporary relief the ownership was in the administrators, the trustees of the charity as we should say, and where it was a permanent asylum, in the residents therein[7].

1 C. 1. 2. 13, 15, 19, 22, etc., esp. C. 1. 2. 23. 3. 2 Saleilles, *Mél. Gérardin*, p. 547. 3 Girard, *Man.* 257, holds that some were *Stiftungen*, but it is difficult to identify the type he has in mind. The obvious illustration of "masses de biens affectés à un office déterminé sans établissement grevé quelconque" would be funds for redemption of captives. But, apart from *legatum* or the like, *sub modo* (C. 1. 3. 28. 1), texts usually attribute this to the bishop, precisely because there is no establishment (C. 1. 3. 28. 2, 48. 2; *Nov.* 131. 11); it seems an improbable refinement to separate this from the rest of the property the bishop held for the church. 4 *Mél. Gérardin*, 538. 5 *Ib.* 541. 6 The allusions to them as *corpora, domus, consortia, collegia* or Greek equivalents are too frequent to be looked on as mere survivals of a terminology that was never appropriate to them. The frequent assimilation to bodies certainly corporate makes in the same direction (see n. 1). 7 See Duff, *cit.* 92, who regards the administrators as the owners. Laum, *Stiftungen in der gr. und röm. Antike*, refuses to see any independent *Stiftungen*. San Nicolò (*Krv.* 1919, 297) holds that there were such but formulates the point wrongly. He asks: "Was the holder owner, or administrator of an independent fund?" The right question is: "Would a contemporary lawyer have thought of him as owner?"

CHAPTER V

THE LAW OF THINGS. *RES*. PROPERTY. POSSESSION. *IURE GENTIUM* MODES OF ACQUISITION OF PROPERTY

LXVI. The second and largest of the three divisions of the Private Law is concerned with *Res*[1]. It differs essentially from Austin's Law of Things since the classification itself starts from a different point of view. The special effects of transactions by persons in exceptional positions, e.g. slaves, are considered under this head, so far as they create assets

1 As to the threefold scheme, *ante*, p. 56. On the notion "*res*" and property in general, Bonfante, *Corso*, 2. 1. chh. 1 and 10 and Scialoja, *Proprietà* (chh. 1 and 15). The various rights with which we are concerned spring commonly from "acts in the law," *negotia*, transactions, though not invariably, since death, lapse of time, accident and wrongful act can create and destroy rights. The Romans had no precise term for "act in the law." *Actus legitimus* (the expression occurs only once, 50. 17. 77) is not defined, but seems to mean only ancient formal acts, perhaps once the only acts in the law, but in historic times a narrow class. *Negotium* almost covers the ground, but does not seem to be applied to such acts as testation and usually, but not always, seems to exclude *donatio*—what a man with "*administratio*" can do (e.g. *ante*, pp. 65, 154) is a *negotium*. The Romans never reached any synthesis of acts in the law, but dealt with each group of institutions separately and not always on the same lines. Moderns have elaborated such a theory, with classifications of the different kinds of transaction (e.g. Mitteis, *R.Pr.* ch. 3; *S.M.W.*, §§ 39–45; Cuq, *Man.* 122). It seems more economical of space and less misleading to treat of the requirements of a transaction in connexion with the transaction itself, since they are differently handled. A few words may be said, however, on the topics (apart from classification) dealt with in most of these discussions. There is the question of capacity: it must be noted that capacity for acts is not the same as capacity for rights: a lunatic has rights, but he cannot contract or transfer property. There is also, since any dealing is, or purports to be, an expression of the will, the question what circumstances make this expression ineffective or unreal, the law of *dolus*, *metus* and *error*, and here the Romans seem to have reached something near a general principle, though with differences of mechanism in different fields (*post*, §§ LXXXIII, CIV, CIX, CXLVI). There is a distinction between acts which are simply void. e.g. *institutio* of a peregrine as *heres*, and those which can be set aside by

for the *paterfamilias*[1], while, for Austin, these are matter for the Law of Persons[2]. The *Ius Rerum* is not the general law as opposed to that which can best be discussed in detached provisions: it is the law of patrimonial rights, all those rights known to the law which are looked on as capable of being estimated in money[3]. The rights incidentally mentioned under the law of persons do not constitute a difficulty: in general they do not admit of valuation. A man may bring an action claiming liberty, a father may "vindicate" a son[4], but there is no question of damages in either case. Liberty, we are told, is inestimable[5]. The rights which may be held in a slave are *dominium*, usufruct, etc., and form part of the *ius rerum*.

There is more difficulty with respect to the rights incidentally discussed in the *ius actionum*. Besides pure procedure this branch of law contains discussion of some obligations, of some rights of action, as well as rules of procedure. Most of these are introduced merely incidentally as illustrating the form of action under discussion. This is plainly so with those mentioned in the course of the explanation by Gaius of *actiones fictitiae*[6] and of the praetorian actions against an owner on the contracts of his slave[7], as to which Gaius expressly says[8] that he is compelled to discuss them as he has just spoken of the *actio de peculio*[9]. The discussion of this type of accessory actions suggests that of the others, the noxal actions. But they are considered systematically, not merely allusively. The question why it seemed more appropriate to discuss them there than in the *ius rerum* will be considered later[10].

restitutio in integrum or otherwise (*restitutio, post,* § CCXLIII, *querela inofficiosi testamenti, post,* § CXIV). There is also the question how far there can be modalities, *dies, condicio* and what came in late law to be called *modus*: here there are great differences in treatment and field of application (e.g. *post,* §§ LXXXIII *sq.*, CIV, CXLVIII). Finally there is the question of representation, where no sort of synthesis is possible (*ante,* pp. 73, 83; *post,* §§ XCIX, CIX, CLXXXIV, CCXXXIX). As to *actus legitimi*, it is clear that they could not be subject to express *dies* or *condicio* (50. 17. 77; Vat. Fr. 329), though there were exceptions in the Empire, for *institutio heredis* must have been an *actus legitimus* and it then admitted of *condicio* (*post,* § CIV). Nor did they admit of representation, for though a son or slave could act in some of them for the *paterfamilias* (*ante,* p. 73; *post,* § LXXXV), this rests not on representation but on the unity of the family.

1 G. 2. 86 *sqq.*; 3. 163 *sqq.*; Inst. 2. 9; 3. 28. 2 *Jurisprudence*, 2. 708 *sqq.* 3 Anything by which one is "actually or prospectively better off," Moyle, *Inst. Just.* 187. The word "property" is similarly used in the expression—a man of property. A man with a million in government securities would be called a man of property, though he had nothing else, but a mere claim on the State. 4 6. 1. 1. 2. 5 50. 17. 106. Ulpian, 19. 11, makes *tutela legitima libertae* a *res incorporalis*. This might be justified by the fact that the patron has an indefeasible right of succession to such a woman and he loses the certainty of this if he transfers the control. (*Ante,* p. 166; G. 3. 43 *sqq.*) The word *res* is not always used in the technical sense, p. 182. 6 G. 4. 34 *sqq.* 7 G. 4. 69 *sqq.* 8 *Ib.* 9 Earlier mention may have been in the two preceding illegible pages. 10 *Post,* § CCVI.

In the institutional scheme a *res* is an element in wealth, an asset, an economic conception, essentially different from the Austinian thing, a permanent external object of sensation[1], which is a physical conception. Austin is really thinking of objects over which there may be ownership, a notion useless for our present purpose[2]. We shall shortly see that the sea and air were *res*, but *res communes*: they had a potential value, but it could not be appropriated to any individual. The important point is that what was present to the mind of the author of the Roman classification was legally guaranteeable value.

The subject of *res* (or *ius rerum*) is treated under two heads, i.e. what are now called *iura in rem* (including *universitates iuris*), rights available generally, and *iura in personam*, *obligationes*, available only against specific persons, the names being derived from the Roman *actio in rem*, *in personam*, which express the same distinction[3]. But such a division cannot be quite exact. *Hereditas* included rights both *in rem* and *in personam*[4], and so, in a less complex way, did a pledge of property[5] (though pledge is not expressly treated as a *ius in rem*). When we remember that even an ordinary contract, essentially a relation *in personam*, might nevertheless, in some cases, give rights against third parties, and so operate *in rem*[6], it is clear that no exact division of the law under these two rubrics can be expected.

LXVII. Justinian's main classification[7] of *res* groups them according to the rights existing over them, a matter in some cases affected by the nature of the thing. *Res* were *in patrimonio*[8], i.e. belonging to some one, or *extra patrimonium*. These last were of various kinds.

(*a*) *Res communes*[9]. Open to every one: the air, running water, the

1 *Jurisprudence*, 1. 368. 2 *Res* has as many meanings as "thing," but, used technically, always connotes a right, though not necessarily all rights, or in early law all rights having a money value, came within the notion. In the famous "*Uti legassit...suae rei*" (XII T. 5. 3) it probably means nothing but physical things the subject of ownership, and the primitive rustic servitudes. 3 Klingmüller, *Z.S.S.* 1924, 211, who also discusses the expression *ius ad rem*. 4 In the XII Tables such debts as existed were not treated as part of the *hereditas* and were specially dealt with (see C. 2. 3. 26; 3. 36. 6). So Karlowa, *R.Rg.* 2. 907, though his reasons are not conclusive. But claims were included, in classical law: *hereditatis petitio* lay against one who held no part of the property but owed money to the estate and refused to pay, claiming to be *heres* (5. 3. 13. 15). Normal debtors must be sued by separate actions for the debts. 5 But to some pledges, such as pledges of a debt, the notion of *ius in rem* cannot be applied. *Post*, § CLXVII. 6 Apart from pledge. Thus *actio doli* lay against a third party who wilfully made performance impossible and so released a party, 4. 3. 18. 5. 7 Inst. 2. 1. pr. *sqq.* 8 *Patrimonium* means properly the same thing as "property" in the wide sense, or *res*. Paul, saying (50. 16. 5) that *res* includes what is not in the *patrimonium*, is not discussing this classification, but perhaps limitation of jurisdiction in certain cases to *res* not above a certain value, and means that all assets are included whether heritable or not, *patrimonium* being used in a narrow sense. Lenel, *Z.S.S.* 1881, 43. 9 The conception of *res communis omnium* is late. It may be due to Marcian, but is sometimes held to be Byzantine. Perozzi, *Ist.* 596.

sea, and, in later law, the seashore to the highest winter floods[1]. Access to the shore was open to all, but no one might build on it: it was not *iuris gentium* like the sea itself. Its use was, and therefore one might build shelters and the like, under licence[2], for purposes connected with the use of the sea. These shelters seem to have been owned, but as shelters only, giving no right to the soil, and thus, if the shelter fell or was taken down, the shore was again common[3].

(*b*) ***Res publicae.*** Property of the State. Such were highways, rivers[4] and harbours, so that all might navigate and fish and make fast at the ports, etc., the use of the banks being public for this purpose[5].

(*c*) ***Res universitatis.*** Property of a corporation. Justinian takes the *civitas* as the type, mentioning *theatra, stadia* and the like[6], but the property of *collegia* would come under the same class.

(*d*) ***Res nullius.*** Property of no one. Such things might be either *divini* or *humani iuris. Divini iuris* were *res sacrae, religiosae* and *sanctae. Res sacrae* were those formally accepted and consecrated by the priests, with statutory authorisation[7], as well as dedication, e.g. churches, and their contents, and sites[8]. They could not be commercially dealt with, except that Justinian allowed them to be sold for redemption of captives, and like purposes[9]. *Res religiosae* were tombs and burial grounds. Like *res sacrae* they could not be commercially dealt with. The rules under which land became *religiosum* were precise. The burial must be in all respects lawful[10]. The corpse must be one the buryer was entitled to bury[11], and the land such that he had a right to bury in it. If another had any proprietary right in the land it was not *religiosum*

1 *Post*, p. 184. 2 43. 8. 3. 4; 41. 1. 50 Perhaps needed only under J.; Bonfante, *Corso*, 2, ch. 3; perhaps no general requirement even under J. Grosso, *Atti Acc. Torino*, 1931, 388; *Res publicae* generally, Karadje-Iskrow, *Les Choses Publiques.* 3 By a sort of *postliminium*, 1. 8. 6. pr.; 43. 8. 3. 1, etc. 4 Rivulets were private (*rivi*), 43. 12. 1. See Brugi, *St. Bonfante*, 1, 361, who shews that some actual rivers were private at least in earlier cl. law. See 43. 12. 1. 4. 5 See *post*, p. 185. 6 Property of the State and *universitates* is of two types. The things above mentioned are not only the property of the body but are open to the use of its members, but public slaves or land, or money in the treasury, differ from the same things in private hands only in having a different kind of owner. They are *in patrimonio universitatis.* No classical text calls public slaves *res publicae.* See 1. 8. 6. 1; 18. 1. 72. 1. 7 G. 2. 5; D. 1. 8. 9. 1, requirement confined to land under Justinian. Brassloff, *St. zur Röm. Rechtsgesch.* § I. 8 Soil *sacrum* though the church be pulled down. As the contents belong to no one there can be no *furtum* of them: it is treated as sacrilege, Ps. Quintil, *Dec.* 252; Mommsen, *Strafr.* 762. They cannot be usucapted (*post*, § LXXXVII), but as they belong to none there is a difficulty in reclaim. Justinian allows administrators of the church to "vindicate" (C. 1. 2. 21): in classical law probably administrative machinery as in charities, Pernice, *Labeo*, 3. 1. 150. As to *res sacrae* and lands constituting endowments of temples, Scialoja, *Proprietà*, 144. 9 Inst. 2. 1. 8; C. 1. 2. 21. 10 G. 2. 6; Inst. 2. 1. 9. Burial *in urbe* where it is forbidden does not suffice, P. 1. 21. 2; D. 47. 12. 3. 5. Reinach, *Gnomon de l'Idéologue*, 40; Bonfante, *Corso*, 2. 1, ch. 2. Historical account of the various connected ideas. 11 G. 2. 6.

unless he consented[1], but with consent another's land might be made *religiosum*. Only the space occupied by the body was *religiosum*, except that the character affected in practice a whole space set apart as a sepulchre[2].

Res sanctae, the gates and walls of a city, but that conception is of little importance in private law. It was a capital offence to commit any outrage on them, e.g. scaling them[3].

Res nullius, humani iuris, which belonged to no one. They are not mentioned here, but appear later under modes of acquisition, where acquisition of these *res nullius* is the first point considered. Wild animals and abandoned property were the most important examples[4].

The classification differs from that of Gaius[5] in arrangement rather than in principle. After stating the distinction between *res in patrimonio* and *extra patrimonium*, Gaius gives a main division into *res divini* and *humani iuris*. The former were *res sacrae, religiosae* and *sanctae*. Speaking from the pagan point of view he makes *res sacrae* devoted to the *di superi* and *religiosae* to *di inferi, manes*. He tells us that as no *civis* really owned provincial land it could not be made *religiosum*, but might be treated as *pro religioso*, and he makes a corresponding remark for things made *pro sacris* in the provinces by authority, probably, of the *praeses*. He divides *res humani iuris* into public and private (the subject of private ownership), the former covering *res publicae* and *res universitatis*. He does not here expressly mention either *res communes* or things wholly unowned, such as wild animals.

Some of the distinctions involved in this classification were rather fluid in classical law. Gaius seems to include under the class *res nullius* everything which had not an individual owner or owners. For him the property of a *universitas* is *nullius in bonis*, but he at once adds that it belongs to the corporation[6]: he could admit that a corporation could have rights but was not quite able to contemplate it as a person, an owner like a man. So too Marcian and Justinian made the seashore common[7], but Celsus makes it public, at any rate where the land behind is Roman[8]. Paul[9] avoids either expression and says: "*nullius sunt, sed iure gentium*

1 Or ratified, D. 1. 8. 6. 4. Relaxations under Justinian, 7. 1. 17. pr.; 11. 7. 2. 7–9, 41. Perozzi, *Ist.* 1. 593. 2 Inst. 2. 1. 9; D. 1. 8. 6. 4. As incapable of being commercially dealt with, a tomb included in land sold was *ipso facto* excluded from the sale, P. 1. 21. 7. Claim for reduction of price, if buyer in good faith. 18. 1. 22–24. Costa, *Sopra un inscrizione sepolchrale* (1926). Half a *jugerum* is devoted to a tomb. It does not follow that the whole area was in law *religiosum*, 18. 1. 73. 1. 3 The city walls cannot well be carried off and there was adequate protection without appealing to the law of property. See D. 1. 8. 8, 9. 4 There are things unowned but not susceptible of *occupatio*, apart from *res s. r.* and *s.* See *post*, §§ CVII, CXVII. 5 G. 2. 1 *sqq.* 6 G. 2. 11, *ante*, p. 176, n. 9. 7 Inst. 2. 1. 1; D. 1. 8. 2. 8 43. 8. 3. 9 18. 1. 51.

omnibus vacant." Neratius[1] also treates it as a sort of *res nullius*, though he admits that if a building erected thereon falls the acquisition is at an end. For Marcian, the *litus* is common, but not *iuris gentium* like the sea[2]. The better view is perhaps that also stated in the Institutes, i.e. that only the use was public, as is clearly the case with the banks of rivers[3]. As to rivers themselves the texts contain differences of opinion as to the sense in which they are public[4]. According to one view they are public, soil and all, but this can hardly be reconciled with the rules of *alluvio*, *insula nata*[5], etc. Accordingly it has been held that what was public was the river as such, not the water, which was common, or the soil of the bed which belonged to the riparians[6]. Others have held that the river was public only *quoad usum*. Probably the earlier lawyers merely held that a river was public, without refinements[7]. As early as Cicero[8] rules arose giving riparian owners rights, and there was a tendency among classical lawyers to regard them as owners of the soil, the public rights being merely of use[9].

We have from Justinian another classification from a different point of view. *Res* were either *corporales* or *incorporales*[10], the former *quae tangi possunt*, the latter, *quae tangi non possunt*. So stated the distinction is simple. Physical objects are given as illustrations of *res corporales*. *Res incorporales* were abstract conceptions, notional things, and, as *res* meant assets, *res incorporales* were rights. The illustrations given are rights of various kinds[11]. When these are examined the fact

1 41. 1. 14. Costa, *Le Acque nel dir. Rom.* 93, notes that only Inst. 2. 1. 1, D. 1. 8. 2, and the interpolated 47. 10. 13. 7 make *litus* "*commune*" while many make it public, and infers that it is a later notion, the classics making it public, Cic. *Top.* 7. 32; D. 41. 1. 14; h. t. 50, 65. 1; 43. 8. 3; 50. 16. 112. But Marcian is very late and may be the author of the doctrine. So Bonfante, *Corso*, 2. 1, ch. 3; *contra*, Biondi, *St. Perozzi*, 269, who thinks the classics oscillated; reply by Costa, *Rend. Acc. Bologna*, 1925 (*Sc. m.*), 1 *sqq.* Costa also holds that the State claimed ownership over the adjacent seas, arguing from 1. 8. 10 and leases of fishing rights, 47. 10. 13. 7, and the fact that buildings in the sea were on the same footing as those on the *litus*. But no text calls the sea public and many make it *commune* with no reservation. The rule as to fisheries may be construed as matter of pure jurisdiction. Debray, *Rev. Gén.* 1921, 1, seeks to explain away 43. 8. 3 (Celsus).

2 1. 8. 4. pr.

3 1. 8. 5; Inst. 2. 1. 4.

4 See, e.g., 1. 8. 4, 5; 43. 12. 1. 3; Inst. 2. 1. 2.

5 *Post*, § LXXVII.

6 See Pernice, *Labeo*, 1. 273. Costa, *cit.*, and Longo, *Riv. Ital. p. l. Sc. Giur.* 1928, 243, generally, on the distinction between public and private waters, *rivi*, *lacus*, *stagna*, etc., and of the various rights which could be created in them. See also Sokolowski, *Philosophie in R. Pr.* 2, ch. 1, § 4.

7 Scialoja, *Proprietà*, 216, takes a different view of the history.

8 *De or.* 1. 38. 173.

9 41. 1. 65. 2. In view of the water rights which existed, it has been said that the main importance of the fact that rivers were public is that there could be no theft of the water. Paul, alone, treats river banks as public, 41. 1. 65. 1; 43. 12. 3. pr.

10 G. 2. 12, 13; Inst. 2. 2. pr., 1. The words are post-Augustan, and though Cicero uses the idea (Affolter, *Inst. Syst.* § VIII b), he is philosophising, merely restating Greek notions, not talking law. There is no evidence that notional things were dealt with in law as such for a century after.

11 G. 2. 14; Inst. 2. 2. 2. As to *r. corporales* in the sense of *r. non fungibiles* (12. 1. 46, etc.), Arangio Ruiz, *Ist.* 148.

emerges that the most important of all rights in the *ius rerum* is not there. *Dominium* was not a *res incorporalis*. It was treated as a *res corporalis*, indeed the only *res corporalis*. The thing was spoken of when ownership was meant, as in ordinary speech and indeed in our Real Property Law in the distinction between Corporeal and Incorporeal hereditaments[1]. Throughout the treatment of acquisition of *dominium* both Gaius and Justinian speak of acquisition of *res corporales*.

Res incorporales, being *res*, did not include matters belonging to the law of persons: liberty, *patria potestas*, etc., were intangible, but not *res*[2]. We know that the *ius rerum* distinguished between *iura in rem* available against all, and *iura in personam*, *obligationes*, available only against a specific person or group. Both Gaius and Justinian, after him, speak of obligations as *res incorporales*[3], but elsewhere they sharply distinguish them[4], and in fact most texts do not so include them[5]. Obligations were more commonly coupled with actions[6].

The distinction between land and moveables[7] was of only subordinate interest in Roman Law. It was, however, material in the law of *usucapio*[8], *mancipatio*[9], *possessio*[10], *dos*[11], *tutela*[12], theft[13], and to some extent in procedure[14]. In classical law, land itself was of two varieties, the distinction being of great importance, *solum italicum* and *solum provinciale*[15]. But this distinction had disappeared under Justinian, as had the important distinction between *res mancipi* and *nec mancipi*[16].

LXVIII. *Dominium*. Before entering on the *ius rerum* something must be said of the order in which it is treated by Justinian (and, in the main, in this book). *Jura in rem* are treated first, beginning with modes of acquisition of *dominium, iure gentium*. Then follow modes of acquisition of *res incorporales* which are *iura in rem*, i.e. practically servitudes. Then comes the discussion of such civil law methods as existed in his day. It is however more convenient to consider all modes of acquisition of *domi-*

1 With an oddly different result. Where property is given by will to *A* with a life estate reserved to *B*, *B* has the corporeal hereditament in English law, *A* has the *res corporalis* in Roman law. 2 *Tutela, ante*, p. 181. A more notable omission is Possession. Reasons for this, *post*, § LXXIV. 3 G. 2. 14=D. 1. 8. 1. 1; Inst. 2. 2. 2. 4 G. 3. 83; Inst. 3. 10. 1. 5 See Ulp. 19. 11; 8. 1. 14. pr.; C. 7. 33. 12. 4. A few texts speak of *iura incorporalia*, which are all *iura in rem*, C. 7. 33. 12; C. 7. 37. 3. 1d; D. 41. 3. 4. 26. But these are of little significance since the name *ius* is ordinarily confined to *iura in rem*. 6 *Post*, § CXLIII. Kniep, *Gai. Inst. Comm.* 2, ad 2. 14 (p. 121), holds that the passage including obligations is Gaian, and indeed from an original which he dates back into the Republic, and the text which excludes them an addition. That the republican lawyers used the expression *res incorporalis* at all seems improbable. A post-classical evolution in the opposite direction is far more likely. As to the position of the inferior modes of ownership in the scheme of things corporeal and incorporeal, *post*, § LXXI. 7 Scialoja, *Proprietà*, 62. 8 *Post*, § LXXXVII. 9 *Post*, § LXXXV. 10 *Post*, §§ LXXIV, CCXLIX. 11 *Ante*, p. 108. 12 *Ante*, p. 154. 13 *Post*, § CXCVI. 14 *Post*, §§ CCVIII, CCXL, CCXLIX. 15 *Post*, § LXIX. 16 *Post*, §§ LXX, LXXXVI.

nium before passing to servitudes. Justinian's order, suggested by that of Gaius, is due to the fact that the discussion is, in form, a commentary on the proposition that all things are either corporeal or incorporeal. Then follows agency in acquisition and alienation, and then acquisition of *res, per universitatem, hereditas* being the chief case. He then proceeds to obligation. It is in the main the order of Gaius except that Gaius treats the *iure civili* methods before the *iure gentium*. They were the most important in his day, but *mancipatio* and *cessio in iure* have disappeared under Justinian. A text from another work of Gaius declares that it is desirable to treat the *iure gentium* methods first, as the most ancient[1]. But this may be due to the compilers: the order suggested is not that of the Institutes of Gaius.

We have now to consider what is meant by *dominium*, which the existence of inferior modes of ownership makes it impossible to define as Ownership[2]. Moderns describe ownership as *ius utendi fruendi abutendi*. But whether the right concerned is *dominium* or one of the inferior modes it is practically never so unrestricted as this. All civilisations lay down restrictions on what a man may do with his own. An owner might not cruelly treat his slaves. The law might forbid him to build above a certain height, or within a certain distance of his boundary[3]. He might not, for purpose of profit, pull down his house[4]. Thus the principle is subject to such restrictions as the State may impose[5]. And the owner can restrict his right by conferring rights on others, e.g. a right of way, without ceasing to be owner.

All this is true of every form of ownership: it does not help to establish the essential characteristic of *dominium*. To reach this we must abandon the conception of *ius utendi fruendi abutendi*. If, in the time of Gaius, a *dominus* of land sold and delivered it, i.e. transferred it informally, he lost all practical interest in it, but as he had not formally transferred *dominium* he remained *dominus*, till, by lapse of time, the *dominium* had passed to the purchaser. Conversely, the buyer had all practical rights in the land but was not *dominus*: he had not the *ius Quiritium*. Our early land law provided a close analogy to this in the right of a lord of the fee who had granted the land to a freehold tenant, except that there the relation was permanent: in Roman law it was, in the case stated,

1 41. 1. 1. pr. (see Berlin stereotype edition); Inst. 2. 1. 11. 2 Evolution of conception of property, Cornil, *A.D.R.* 57. 3 C. 8. 10. 12. 2; C. h. t. 3; D. 8. 2. 14. 4 18. 1. 52; 39. 2. 48; Bruns, 200; for an exorbitant rule of Justinian, C. 3. 34. 14. 1. 5 Girard, *Man.* 277; Cuq, *Man.* 246; Scialoja, *Proprietà*, 1. 317. Bonfante, *Corso*, 2. 1. chh. 13 *sqq.*, shews that there was no right of expropriation for public utility but only for necessity. With Scialoja he rejects any doctrine of abuse of rights, though it appears as an ethical make-weight in relation to vicinal water rights. As to "social necessity" as a limitation, Stoll, reviewing M. Rotondi, *Z.S.S.* 1927, 425. *Prospectus montium*, Riccobono, *St. Fadda*, 1. 289; Jones, *Expropriation in R.L.*, *L.Q.R.* 1929, 512.

temporary[1]. *Dominium* is the ultimate right, that which has no right behind it. It may be a mere *nudum ius* with no practical content, but it is still *dominium ex iure Quiritium*[2]. It is a "signoria[3]."

The question arises whether it was possible to attach incidents to the ownership of a transferee, not servitudes, but binding on future holders. It was possible to contract for such restrictions but this would bind only the other party and his heirs. This is the meaning of a text attributed to Gaius[4]: "*in traditionibus rerum quodcumque pactum sit id valere manifestissimum est.*" As this is from a treatise on the XII Tables it no doubt referred originally to *mancipatio* and the allusion is to such things as a *fiducia*[5]. If the restriction were disregarded by the other party, this would be a breach of contract but no more: if by a subsequent holder there would be in general no remedy against him. There were however certain cases in which such an incident attached to a conveyance had an effect *in rem*, and not merely against the other party, especially in the law of slavery[6]. There are some signs of a similar tendency in the case of *pacta adiecta* in ordinary sales[7]. They do not go far: there is no rule that restrictive covenants bind future holders if they had notice of them. The cases seem to be sporadic and to express no general principle.

There was nothing to prevent the creation of an ownership to begin in the future or on a certain event, but this possibility was cut down, for classical law, by the fact that the most important forms of conveyance of property were *actus legitimi* which did not admit of express suspension or condition[8]. It could be done by *traditio*[9]. But a determinable ownership could not be expressly created in classical law[10]; it might indeed arise by operation of law, e.g. where a *heres* created rights in a thing left to someone else conditionally. The right of the *heres* was determined by the occurrence of the condition, and rights created by him then failed also[11]. Apart from such cases a man could not be made owner for a time.

1 Ownership of provincial lands gives a similar analogy, *post*, § LXIX. 2 If a thing which can be the subject of *dominium* is abandoned by the holder, and no one has now a claim to it, the late holder was *dominus*. 3 De Francisci, *Trasferimento della proprietà*. As to his inferences, *post*, § LXXV. 4 2. 14. 48. 5 *Post*, § CLI. 6 Conditions that the slave should not be sold or prostituted or freed, or should be freed. They differed in their effect *in rem*: the most straightforward case is that of a slave sold not to be freed. Manumission by any later holder was void. 18. 7. 6. Buckland, *Slavery*, 68. 7 Where a man bought part of an estate under restrictions which could not be servitudes the rights and liabilities extended to subsequent assignees if they had notice. But the facts were very like a servitude, 8. 4. 13. pr. Where a man acquired a usufruct by will and knew the testator had been under restrictions, he was bound, since a fructuary must act as a *bonus paterfamilias*, to respect them, 7. 1. 27. 5. 8 *Mancipatio* and *Cessio in iure*, *post*, §§ LXXXIV, LXXXV. 9 41. 2. 38. 1. As to nature of a conditional right, Vassali, *Bull.* 27. 192 *sqq.* 10 Girard, *Man.* 359. 11 Girard, *loc. cit.*, adverts to *postliminium*.

An agreement to that effect might impose an obligation to retransfer the property, but it did not revert *ipso iure*[1]. *Dos* was no exception: the husband is spoken of as owner during the marriage, but he was owner in perpetuity like any other owner, though under a duty to reconvey the property in certain events[2].

Under Justinian the rule is relaxed: it is possible in some cases to convey *dominium* on the terms that it should revert *ipso facto* on a certain event. *Donatio mortis causa* is a well-known instance[3].

It was impossible in classical law to convey property with a restriction against alienation, operative *in rem*: an alienation, though a breach of contract, would be valid. This rule may have disappeared under Justinian. Texts conflict: whether there was a clear doctrine under Justinian may be doubted[4].

The desire to keep property in the family, a main cause of such restrictions, was not encouraged in Roman law, at least as to conveyance *inter vivos*. Beyond creating a usufruct, a life interest, essentially inalienable, there was little that a settlor could do[5]. In the classical age it was a common thing to establish a fund for charitable or other public purposes, and it is clear that some of these had considerable permanence. But the devices employed were precarious and usually depended on the voluntary conduct of the holder for the time being[6]. The most effective way was to give the property to a *civitas* with directions as to the disposal of the income, and in some cases a gift over to some other body if these were not obeyed. Neither gifts over nor directions were binding in law, but the taking of security might give some protection. It seems, however, that, on appeal to the public authorities, administrative machinery would be set at work to enforce the proper application of the funds. So far as such public trusts were concerned the difficulty disappeared when these received legal personality[7].

LXIX. Apart from the *dominium ex iure Quiritium* which we have considered, there were in classical law inferior modes of holding which may be called Ownership[8]. Such are:

1 Slave law provides as usual an exception. A slave sold on condition that he was kept abroad vested in the *Fiscus* if this was broken, unless the vendor had reserved a right of seizure in such event: in that case his ownership revived, Vat. Fr. 6. 2 *Ante*, p. 109. *Revocatio* of a *donatio inter vivos*, *post*, § XCI. 3 *Post*, § XCI. The new principle can be seen by comparing Vat. Fr. 283 with its revision, C. 8. 54. 2. *Dos* gives another case under Justinian, *ante*, p. 110. See in connexion with *vindicatio utilis*, *post*, §§ XCI and CCXXVIII. 4 20. 5. 7. 2; C. 4. 51. 7; 18. 1. 75; 45. 1. 135. 3, etc. As to "real" effect of restrictive and resolutive conditions, Senn, *Études Girard*, 1. 283, who thinks the classical rule still held good under Justinian. *Post*, § CLXXIII. Under Justinian a thing left by legacy or *fc.* was not alienable by the *heres*, *post*, § CXXV. 5 Family settlements in wills, *post*, § CXXVII. 6 Pernice, *Labeo*, 3. 1. 150 *sqq.* 7 *Ante*, p. 179. 8 Of *ager publicus*, property of the State, large tracts were occupied by private persons, without

1. Ownership of provincial land[1]. The *dominium* of this was in Caesar or the *populus* according as it was in an imperial or a senatorial province[2]. The exploitation was largely in private hands under arrangements with the authority concerned, of which the most important is the system of *agri tributarii*, in imperial provinces, and *stipendiarii*, in others, both permanent holdings at a fixed rent. The holders were practically owners, but as they were not *domini* formal methods of transfer were not applicable. The holdings were however transferable informally[3]. A holder who lost possession could not recover by the action appropriate to the recovery of Italic land, *vindicatio*, since this involved an assertion of *dominium*. We are not fully informed as to the nature of his remedy. We know that he had a modified *vindicatio* as early as Trajan[4], but can only guess at its form. Probably his action instead of *dominium* asserted a right "*habere frui possidere licere*," which is found as the technical description of his right[5]. The case disappeared when Justinian abolished the distinction between Italic and provincial land[6]. Not all land in the provinces was *solum provinciale*: many provincial communities were given *ius italicum*, the chief result being that the land was in the *dominium* of the holder and not of the State, so that it could be transferred and claimed at law by civil law methods[7].

2. Ownership by peregrines. In general they had not *commercium*[8], were incapable of *dominium*, and could not transfer, acquire or claim by civil law methods. Informal methods of transfer were open to them, but we have no real knowledge of their proprietary remedies. They may have had an *actio fictitia*, such as we find in some branches of the law[9], or more probably one alleging "*habere frui possidere licere.*" The case disappears under Justinian, and any difficulty as to remedies probably ceased[10] with the generalisation of *cognitio extraordinaria*[11].

definite legal title (*possessores*) but in practice not disturbed, see, e.g., Heitland, *Agricola*, 174. Its importance is of the Republic. Questions of title were quieted by enactment of Domitian who "*donavit atque concessit*" all land so occupied in Italy to the *possessores* (*ut usucapta*, Suetonius, *Dom.* 9). The enactment is frequently cited by the *agrimensores*, Scialoja, *Proprietà*, 209.

1 Mommsen, *Staatsrecht*, 3. 730 *sqq.*; *D.P.R.* 6. 2. 366. 2 Tenny Frank, *Journ. of Rn. St.* 1927, 141, shews ground for thinking that the doctrine that provincial land belongs to the State was not accepted till the time of Claudius. 3 G. 2. 21. 4 Frontinus, *de controv.* (ed. Lachmann), p. 36, cited Lenel, *E.P.* 188. 5 *Lex agraria*, 50, 81, etc., Girard, *Textes*, 46 *sqq.* He may have had a *vindicatio* with a fiction that the land was Italic, but it is not evidenced. Partsch, *Schriftformel*, 105 *sqq.*, holds it impossible to reconstruct the *formula*. 6 Inst. 2. 1. 40; C. 7. 31. 7 Mommsen, *Staatsr.* 3. 807; *D.P.R.* 6. 2. 456. 8 *Ante*, p. 96. 9 G. 4. 37. 10 Girard, *Man.* 286. 11 For an alleged *vindicatio*, "*meum esse aio*," with no reference to *ius Quiritium* there seems to be no evidence. A few texts use the word *dominus* for others than a civil law owner. So Gaius (1. 54; 2. 40), but he does not call the holder *in bonis*, *dominus*. He says that peregrines have one kind of *dominium* (2. 40, 41) but it is straining his meaning to

LXX. 3. Bonitary ownership. This is for our purposes much the most important of the inferior modes. It arose where a person received a *res mancipi* from the *dominus* by mere *traditio*, without the *mancipatio* (or *cessio in iure*) needed for the transfer of *dominium* in such things. The Romans had no substantive name for the holder or the right: the *res* was said to be *in bonis*[1], from which early commentators formed the name *dominium bonitarium*[2]. It is a commonplace that the holder was as well protected as *dominus*, and that a main part of his protection was the *actio Publiciana*, but we are not told in any surviving classical text that this was available to him, and, the case being obsolete under Justinian, we could not learn it from him. But there are texts from which this application of the action may be inferred, and there is now almost complete unanimity in favour of the view that the holder *in bonis* could use this action, though opinions differ as to the identity of the *formula* with that used by the *bona fide possessor*[3].

The statement that the bonitary owner was protected involves two main points. If the *dominus* attempted to recover the thing he would be met by the *exceptio rei venditae et traditae*. If the holder lost possession he could recover by the *actio Publiciana*[4].

Exceptio rei venditae et traditae[5]. A bonitary owner in actual enjoyment could not be effectively attacked by anyone but the *dominus*, these expressions covering persons holding or claiming under the original bonitary owner or *dominus* respectively[6]. If there were an outstanding usufruct or pledge, created by vendor or a previous owner, this could be enforced against a bonitary owner[7], but neither more nor less than it could even if the conveyance had been formal. The old owner being still technically *dominus* could prove what the plaintiff in a *vindicatio rei* had to prove, i.e. that the thing was his *ex iure quiritium*. This would be conclusive at civil law, but the Praetor's Edict came to the relief of the bonitary owner and gave him the above *exceptio*. That is, he was allowed to plead that the plaintiff, or one through whom he claimed, sold and

imply that inferior holdings in Rome were *dominium*. Diocletian applies the name *dominus* to holders of provincial lands (Vat. Fr. 315, 316) and Justinian speaks of *differentiae inter dominos* (C. 7. 25). These texts are few and do not indicate that the name *dominium* was applied technically to inferior modes of ownership. Gaius also speaks of *possessio* and *ususfructus* (G. 2. 7).

1 E.g., G. 1. 54. It is the substantial ownership: a slave acquired for his bonitary owner, not the quiritary. G. 2. 88; Ulp. 19. 20; other cases of "*in bonis*," *post*, p. 195.

2 No authority for the name *possessio in bonis*. Greek original of *bonitarium dominium*, Theophilus, *ad* Inst. 1. 5. 3.

3 Lenel, *E.P.* 169; Appleton, *Propriété Prét.* 1. 54.

4 Other protection is necessary and exists, e.g. the various remedies for interferences not amounting to ousting, and the possessory interdicts.

5 Bonfante, *Scr. Giur.* 2. 450.

6 If an owner sells, delivers and dies, and the buyer resells and delivers, the *heres* replaces the vendor, the second buyer the first buyer.

7 See D. 21. 3.

delivered the thing to the defendant, or one through whom he claimed, and proof of this was a complete defence[1]. The exact form of the *exceptio* is not known, but the name probably followed it closely[2]. This was complete defensive protection, but it was plainly of no effect against one who did not claim under the vendor[3]. It was useless to a mere *bona fide possessor*, for it was not good against the true owner, who was not the person from whom he acquired[4], and it was not necessary against any other person, since a claimant must prove his title.

Actio Publiciana[5]. It might happen that, from some cause, the holder lost actual possession. Some other person might, during his absence, enter on the property, and refuse to give up possession. How was the bonitary owner to recover it? One or other of the possessory interdicts by which peaceful possession was protected, apart from title, might serve his turn[6], but many cases of adverse possession would not be within the terms of these interdicts. Not being *dominus* he could not claim that the thing was his, *ex iure quiritium*, and thus he could not vindicate. The Praetor provided an action, called the *actio Publiciana*[7], based on the fact that the bonitary owner would in the ordinary way become *dominus* in course of time by what was called *usucapio*[8], of which he satisfied all the requirements, as he held the thing *bona fide* and *ex iusta causa*. The action was a *vindicatio* modified in form so that its *formula* directed the *iudex* to give judgement in favour of the plaintiff, if he would have been *dominus* had he held the thing for the period of *usucapio*. It was thus presumed in his favour only that the period of *usucapio* had run: he must still shew that he was *in via usucapiendi*. This he could, on the facts, readily do if the thing was free from any *vitium* which made it incapable of usucapion[9]. Technically it was an *actio fictitia*, in which the plaintiff was feigned *anno* or *biennio possedisse*[10]. Lapse of time was conclusively

1 At first probably applicable only to sale, in classical law, *mutatis mutandis*, to any case of transfer *ex iusta causa*, e.g. gift, 44. 4. 4. 31. 2 21. 3. 3. 3 Except where a selling non-owner, after the sale and delivery, acquired the *dominium* and sued the holder under his new right, 21. 3. 1. 4 If the right alleged by the claimant is not ownership, but, e.g., usufruct, the action will not be *vindicatio rei*, but the appropriate action, in this case *v. ususfructus*. If the usufruct was created after the delivery, as it might be, the *exceptio* was available in an appropriate form. 5 Form of the Edict much disputed, Lenel, *E.P.* 169; Bonfante, *Scr. Giur.* 2. 389 (account of various views); Appleton, *Propriété Prétorienne*, ch. 4. 6. *Post*, § LXXII, CCXLIX. 7 G. 4. 36; Inst. 4. 6. 4; D. 6. 2. Introduced presumably by an urban Praetor, Publicius, probably not long before Augustus. 8 *Post*, § LXXXVII. It did not apply to *res incorporales*, 6. 2. 11. 1 is interp., Lenel, *E.P.* 172, following Perozzi. Did it lie in early law for such praedial servitudes as were then usucaptible? 9 I.e. was a *res habilis* and not privileged against *usucapio*, or *res furtiva*, etc., *post*, § LXXXVII. 10 This is not a presumption that he has acquired by *usucapio*. G. does indeed say "*fingitur usucepisse*" (G. 4. 36; see also Inst. 4. 6. 4) but the *formula* which he gives at the same point is more exact. A fiction that he had acquired would leave the *iudex* nothing to try: if in a real action we begin by presuming that the thing belongs to the plaintiff, all that is left is to give judgement in his favour.

presumed, and *bona fides* was always presumed, though this presumption could be rebutted. In the case we are supposing there is no question of this, since good faith is clear on the facts. The other requirements of *usucapio* were subject to the ordinary rules of proof. It is clear that bonitary owner was well protected by the *exceptio* and the *actio*.

The *actio Publiciana* was also available, perhaps primarily available, to an ordinary *b. f. possessor*, one who has received the property in good faith from one whom he supposed to be capable of transferring ownership to him, but who, in fact, was not so capable, e.g. a non-owner. His protection must be less complete: it was not the object of the Praetor to destroy the law of *usucapio*, or bar an owner from recovering his property[1]. Such a *possessor* was not protected against the true owner, but only against third parties. Thus the *exceptio rei venditae et traditae* had in general, for reasons already stated, no application here[2]. The *b. f. possessor* had the *actio Publiciana* against all but the *dominus*; in a sense even against him. The facts alleged in his claim were true in that case also, but the owner was allowed to plead in reply the *exceptio iusti dominii*, an allegation that he was the true owner[3]. In strictness a *b. f. possessor* cannot know that he is one; he thinks he is really entitled: as used here, however, the expression means one whose possession began in good faith, one who is *in via usucapiendi*. It was immaterial that he had discovered his mistake[4].

When the parties came into court the Praetor, who might never have heard of them before, could not know, though he had to issue the *formula*, whether the claimant was bonitary owner or *b. f. possessor*, or whether the defendant was owner or not. To settle these points would be to try the case, which was not his business[5]. He could not take their words for it, unless they were agreed: the parties themselves might not know the real state of affairs till the matter was thrashed out. Some facts might be admitted, e.g. that the holder was only a *b. f. possessor* in the above sense, while the plaintiff's claim that he was owner might be disputed. The essential elements of the formula would then run somewhat as follows: "If it appears that *A* would be owner of this thing which has been sold and delivered to him if he had held it for a year, then, unless *N* (defendant) is *dominus*, condemn him, unless at your discretion he restores; if it does not so appear, absolve him." We are told that the *exceptio iusti dominii* was allowed only after enquiry (*causa*

1 6. 2. 16, 17. 2 Though praetorian ownership and, with it, the normal application of this *exceptio*, is gone under Justinian, it survives for exceptional cases, *ante*, p. 192, n. 3. Bonfante, *Scr. Giur.* 2. 457. 3 6. 2. 16, 17. 4 While he thought he was *dominus* he would not bring the Publician but a *vindicatio*. 5 In cl. and earlier law the magistrate does not normally try cases: he approves a "*formula*," in which the issue is stated, to be submitted to a *iudex* to decide; *post*, § CCVII.

cognita[1]), and thus the Praetor would refuse it if it was clear that the defendant had sold and delivered the thing.

If all material facts were disputed the formula would run somewhat as follows: "If *A* would be owner of the thing, which was sold and delivered to him, if he had held it for a year (or two years, for land) then, unless it appears that *N* is owner, and even then if it appears that *N* or his predecessor in title sold and delivered to *A*, condemn *N* to pay the value unless he restores at your direction. If it does not so appear, absolve *N*[2]." This submits the whole issue to the *iudex*, and if he decides correctly the result will be what is laid down above[3].

LXXI. One or two possible complications must be considered.

It might happen that a bonitary owner or *bona fide possessor* lost possession and the new possessor acquired the *res* by lapse of time, *usucapio*. Was the *actio Publiciana* still available? On the *formula* stated above it might be, for it would still be true that if the dispossessed holder had possessed the thing for a year (or two) he would be *dominus*. But to allow it on such facts would be contrary to the purpose of the law of *usucapio* and even to that of the Publician itself. There is little authority, and much diversity of opinion[4], not so much on the practical outcome, for it is usually held that the Publician was barred, but on the way in which this result was arrived at. On one view it was barred because even if he had possessed for the necessary time he would not be owner, as there had been a transfer to someone else. On another the action was available in principle, but was barred by the *exceptio iusti dominii*[5]. On another this *exceptio* was not available where the alienation was by operation of law, e.g. *usucapio*, or *accessio*[6], so that here the Publician would still be available.

A point material to the decision of these questions is whether the possession feigned for the purpose of the action is to be dated forward from the *traditio*, or backward from the date of the action. This is material also on another point. If a bonitary owner brought his action successfully and again lost possession before *usucapio* was completed, there was nothing to bar him from bringing his action again if he needed it. But how if it was a *bona fide possessor*? If his feigned possession dated back from the time of the action it was a new possession. But if when he brought the first action he knew that he was not owner it might be argued that his possession, a new possession, did not begin in good faith, so that he was not *in via usucapiendi*: a second possession

1 17. 1. 57. 2 See G. 4. 36. 3 Details doubtful: it is not clear, e.g., that all texts dealing with *exceptio iusti dominii* are in accord—it may be that there were different views as to formulation. Appleton, *Propriété Prétorienne*, ch. XVI; Lenel, *E.P.* 169. It does not seem that the price need have been paid, 6. 2. 8. 4 Girard, *Man.* 376, n. 5; another view, Appleton, *cit.* chh. XX, XXI. 5 See 17. 1. 57. 6 Appleton, *cit.* ch. XX.

begun in bad faith cannot be added to the earlier for the purpose of *usucapio*[1]. But the better view appears to be that it is a continuation of the actual possession[2].

Two persons might each be entitled to the Publician, e.g. a bonitary owner lent the thing to the *dominus*, who died and whose *heres* sold and delivered the thing in good faith to a third person. Which of these was entitled against the other? If one was a bonitary owner and the other a mere *b. f. possessor* the law is clear, the former would win as defendant or plaintiff, though the form of his defence is not known. If both were *bona fide possessores* the texts are not clear, but it seems that if they had received the *res* from the same non-owner, the first deliveree would prevail, if from different, the actual possessor[3].

The formula contained nothing to prevent its use by the actual *dominus*, and it has been said that in the later Empire it practically superseded *vindicatio*[4]. But in all the texts which apply it the time of *usucapio* has not run, and the absence of reference to it in the Code, the prominence of *vindicatio*, and the language of the texts, suggest that it was used only where *usucapio* was not complete, and thus only in a small percentage of cases[5]. Its chief advantages would be that there was no need to prove that time had run, and that evidence that a conveyance relied on was not by the true owner would not be fatal, as it would in *vindicatio*, apart from *usucapio*. This would not often be material, and thus the jurists say little of the action[6].

There are cases other than that of *traditio* of a *res mancipi* in which a holder under praetorian title will become *dominus* by *usucapio*. The formula of the Publician would be applicable at least with slight modifications in many such cases, and is actually recorded in the cases of *adiudicatio* in a *iudicium non legitimum*[7], a slave noxally liable seized *iussu praetoris* for lack of defence[8], a plaintiff in whose favour judgement was given under *iusiurandi delatio*[9], a *missio in possessionem* in *damnum infectum*[10], and *iura in re aliena* created by informal methods[11].

1 41. 3. 15. 2; 41. 4. 7. 4. 2 Girard, *loc. cit.* See however Appleton, *cit.* ch. XV, § XIV. 3 6. 2. 9. 4; 19. 1. 31. 2. Appleton, *cit.* ch. XVII. In the case given above both are bonitary owners: the *heres*, being *dominus*, could make a good conveyance. Here the first vendee could recover from the other. 4 Appleton, *ib.* But see Girard, *Man.* 379, n. 1. 5 I.e. only where the disturbance complained of had occurred within a relatively short time after the possession had begun. 6 The words "*et nondum usucaptum*" which appear in the Edict (6. 2. 1) would negative the view, but they are not conclusive as, according to Lenel, *E.P.* § 60, there is no trace of them in the *formula*. 7 6. 2. 7. pr.; *post*, §§ XC, CCXXXII. 8 6. 2. 6; *post*, § CCV. 9 6. 2. 7. 7; *post*, § CCXV. But here, owing to the purely relative effect of a judgement, only against the other party. 10 39. 2. 18. 15; *post*, § CCXLV. 11 6. 2. 11. 1; see, however, *post*, § XCIV. Other cases: *bonorum possessor* (*post*, § CXXXVIII), *bonorum emptor* (*post*, § CXLII), etc. Appleton, *cit.* 1. 4 (full list); Bonfante, *Scr. Giur.* 2. 370; Arangio Ruiz, *Ist.* 169. Possible extension to *longi*

LXXII. *Possessio.* Before considering acquisition of *dominium* it is necessary to examine the notion of possession. No other topic in the Roman law has been so much discussed[1]. It is easy to describe possession roughly. A man "possesses" a thing if he has control of it—if he "has" it, with title or not. A man possesses his watch in his pocket, but if he drops it, and someone else picks it up and keeps it, it is he who now possesses it, though it is still the property of the loser—it still "belongs" to him. Rough description is not definition[2]: before attempting this, it seems best to consider the legal importance of possession. The main point is that one who had possession, whether he had a legal title or not, and subject to reservations for the case of one whose possession was tainted by certain forms of wrongdoing, had the protection of what are called Possessory Interdicts.

Apart from these reservations, the general principle of these remedies was that one who had actual possession was not to be disturbed therein, whether he had a title or not, except by legal process. If the owner wished to recover it, he must bring an action—a *vindicatio*. If, instead, he ejected the occupier, a possessory interdict would compel him to restore possession, and he might not plead his ownership in reply to the claim of the possessor[3]. He could however now do what he should have done at first, i.e. bring his *vindicatio*, and, if he proved his title, the wrongful possessor would be compelled to give up possession.

Not all whose position agreed with the rough description above set out had possession for these purposes. It is easy to see that my guest at my table and my servants at their work have not possession of the implements they are using. But the law went much further. A borrower for use, a depositee, a tradesman working on the thing, none of these had possession. And as there could be no possession of a *res incorporalis*[4], and interests less than ownership (*ususfructus*, etc.) were incorporeal, persons holding such rights did not possess. This last re-

temporis praescriptio, *post*, § LXXXIX. The texts do not consider the question whether these inferior modes of ownership were *res corporales* or *incorporales*. We may suppose that in cases such as the Publician, protected by fictitious actions, the answer would be that whether the right was or was not a *res corporalis* it was treated by the help of fictions as if it was. As to ownership of provincial land, the *dominium* of which was in *Caesar* or the *populus*, the answer depends on the form of the remedy, which is not certainly known (*ante*, p. 190). As to peregrine ownership so far as this was protected by fictitious actions, the answer would be as in the first case. But it may be held that the classification was part of the Roman law and had nothing to do with relations outside the *commercium*.

1 Indication of the wealth of literature, Windscheid, *Lehrbuch*, § 148, n.*. Rotondi, *Scr. Giur.* 3. 94. On the difficulty with which the distinction between possession and ownership is reached in experience, Kuebler, 155.

2 Thus possession of a house or other complex thing is not possession of the materials, 41. 2. 30. pr.; 41. 3. 23. pr. *Post*, § LXXVIII.

3 As to reasons, *post*, § CCLII.

4 43. 3. 1. 8, etc.

striction is rather unreal: though they had not *possessio*[1], they had interdictal protection, in a modified form[2].

The terminology of the texts is confusing. We find *possessio, possessio naturalis*, and *possessio civilis*, and the exact meaning of the distinctions is disputed. The better view seems to be that *possessio* means, properly, interdict possession, *possessio civilis* that which gives a civil right, a basis for *usucapio*[3], and *possessio naturalis* mere detention, e.g. the holding by a borrower. But there is both looseness in the use of the terms[4] and a probability of alteration by the compilers, who use *possessio civilis* to mean interdict possession[5].

The definition of *possessio* to give the results here outlined is a matter of great difficulty. No perfectly correct solution may be possible. Among the jurists, in whose writings, if anywhere, the answer is to be found, there were differences of opinion on many fundamental points, and there is none on which such differences are more easily conceivable than on this of the exact definition of possession. The texts suggest that, apart from interpolation, the same man does not always speak with the same voice on this matter, a thing readily understood when we remember that lawyers do not in every case go back to first principles and that it is more important to have a good practical set of rules than one logically impeccable. Many attempts have been made to answer the question[6], and of these two have received so much more attention than any others that some account of them must be given[7].

Of these opinions that of Savigny[8] was the earlier, long accepted almost universally, indeed still the most widely accepted. On his view, resting mainly on texts of Paul who alludes to, and argues from, *animus possidentis*[9], possession consists of physical control (*corpus*) with the intention to hold as one's own—detention with *animus habendi* or *domini*. This last is lacking in the cases mentioned of *possessio naturalis* and in usufruct. If we find nevertheless that possession is attributed to *emphyteuta* and pledgee who do not hold the thing as their own, this, says Savigny[10], is a case of derivative possession. Later writers seek to avoid

1 Many texts speak of him as having "*quasi possessio*" or "*possessio iuris*." It is, however, widely held that this terminology is post-classical, on which view "*aut quasi possessione*" in G. 4. 139 is a gloss. Albertario, *Bull.* 1912, 1 *sqq.* and 1914, 275, developing Perozzi, who lays down this proposition as to the analogous case of praedial servitudes. See Vat. Fr. 90–93. 2 Vat. Fr. 90; D. 43. 16. 3. 13, 17; 43. 17. 4. 3 *Post*, § LXXXVII. 4 E.g. 41. 2. 1. 1; 43. 16. 1. 9, 10. 5 Bonfante, *Scr. Giur.* 3. 534; Riccobono, *Z.S.S.* 1910, 321. Various opinions, Albertario, *Bull.* 1914, 275; Beseler, *Z.S.S.* 1924, 374; Fitting, *St. Brugi*, 231; Rotondi, *Scr. Giur.* 3. 229. *Detentio* and its congeners are rare in the sense of "holding" or "having" and when so used may mean any kind of *possessio*, Radin, *St. Bonfante*, 3. 153. See *post*, p. 232. 6 Riccobono, *Arch. Giur*, 1893, 46. 7 Windscheid, *Lehrb.* §§ 148 *sqq.*; Girard, *Man.* 288 *sqq.*; Vermond, *Possession en Droit Romain.* 8 *Recht des Besitzes*, tr. Perry. 9 13. 7. 37; 41. 2. 1. 20. 10 *Op. cit.* § 25.

this expedient, by adhering to the expression *animus possidendi*, and speaking of intention to hold the thing to the exclusion of anyone else, a way of putting the matter which enables them to retain Savigny's doctrine in essentials. The fact that a depositee did not possess even where he determined to keep the thing, is explained on textual authority as resting on the principle: *nemo potest causam possessionis mutare*[1]. The original *animus* was decisive.

These views were strongly attacked by Ihering[2]. Without going into detail of his criticism, it may be said that while he draws attention to the fact that the theory does not explain some cases, e.g. the continued possession of a fugitive slave, and derivative possession, his main attack is on the conception of *animus domini*. He considers that the texts of Paul on which this rests present an opinion peculiar to him, and maintains that no other jurist supports this "subjective" theory which makes possession or non-possession depend on the intent of the holder. He shews the unpractical nature of the idea, and the impossibility of proof, and points out that this impossibility, coupled with the rule that a man cannot change his *causa possessionis*, has led later supporters of the theory to look at the *causa* for proof of the intention[3], so as to give a result similar to that arrived at by those who find the test in external circumstances. But their false theory leads them, he holds, to false conclusions on points of detail.

Ihering's own theory[4], treating *animus domini* as an error based on a view peculiar to Paul (given to subjective tests), but not justified by his language, defines possession as the externals of ownership. A man possesses who is, in relation to the thing, in the position in which an owner of such things ordinarily is, *animus* being merely an intelligent consciousness of the fact[5], so that a *furiosus* cannot acquire possession: he has not *intellectus* (or *affectio*) *possidentis*[6]. This is in effect an external fact, for this *animus* proves itself. The physical relation is not decisive: possession or no possession may depend on the nature of the thing[7]. A slave who has run away is in the same position to an observer as one sent on an errand. A man at his home possesses the things at his office, and *vice versa*, though it is easy to state cases in which it is hard to say whether possession continues or not. Every conscious holder, whether

1 E.g. 41. 2. 3. 19. 2 *Besitzwille* (French tr. by Meulenaere). 3 *Op. cit.* §§ II, XII. 4 *Op. cit.* and *Grund des Besitzesschutzes*, also tr. Meulenaere. Lightwood, *L.Q.R.* 1887, 32 *sqq.*; Bond, *L.Q.R.* 1890, 259 *sqq.* 5 Rotondi, *Scr. Giur.* 3. 94, holds that *animus* and *corpus* were not in early law distinct but interpenetrative, that from Paul onwards the former grows in importance and becomes the main factor. 6 41. 2. 1. 3; h. t. 1. 9, 10. As to possession of *tignum iniunctum*, *post*, § LXXVIII. 7 I possess my carriage in the roadway in front of my house: I should not possess my watch lying in the same place.

for himself or another, satisfies the requirements of possession. Every case of detention, *possessio naturalis*, not giving interdicts, is one in which the law, for reasons differing in the different cases, has expressly taken away possession from persons, who, apart from this express provision, satisfy its requirements.

It is widely held that Ihering's criticism is sound, and, less widely, that his constructive doctrine is also sound. It has however some difficulties, and the texts are held to shew that *animus* played a more important part, according to some jurists, than Ihering's theory allows[1]. The difficulties are almost entirely in connexion with acquisition or loss of possession through the act of third parties, in connexion with which we shall meet them again. The theory of the Romans was probably not completely coherent[2].

The question why possession without title was protected has had much attention. Savigny maintained[3] that it was to protect those who had no title, not in their private interest, but for the preservation of the public peace. It would not make for order if even one without title could be ejected by one who, perhaps, had no more. Ihering's view, now more widely accepted, is that possession is protected as an outwork of ownership[4]. The law assumes that a peaceful possessor is more often than not the person entitled, and that to enable him to recover his possession, as such, without proof of right, is, in most cases, to restore an owner without requiring him to prove his title. It is only accidentally, and in a minority of cases, that it works to protect a wrongful holder, not, as Savigny holds, as the intended result of the system[5].

LXXIII. Acquisition of possession by one's own act is a fairly simple matter. It involves *animus* and *corpus*[6]. The thing must be placed in our control, not necessarily about our person: effective control will vary with the nature of the thing. The *animus* is no more than consciousness and willingness. Thus, where a thing has been placed by our direction in a certain place for us, we possess without knowing that the act has been completed: previous authorisation is as good as knowledge[7]. But, as *animus* is necessary, the acquirer must be *capax*—a *furiosus* cannot acquire possession[8]. And in things *extra commercium* there can be no *possessio* any more than there can be ownership.

1 Windscheid, *Lehrb.* Sect. 148, n. 4a, gives a number of objections of varying weight. Girard, *Man.* 295, n. 6, cites one. But see *post*, pp. 202, 203. 2 Girard, *Man.* 291. 3 *Recht des Bes.* §§ II, VI. 4 *Besitzesschutzes*, § VI. 5 It has been said (Holmes, *Common Law*, 208, from Bruns) that the view that the possessor is more likely to be entitled than the ejector is not necessarily true. Even though this be an objection to the theory, as a philosophic truth, it is no answer to the view that it was the Roman doctrine. 6 41. 2. 3. 1. A *pupillus* if he has *intellectus* can acquire *possessio* without his tutor's *auctoritas*, 41. 2. 1. 3, 32. 2. 7 41. 2. 18. 2. 8 41. 2. 1. 3.

Acquisition through an *extraneus* presents more difficulty[1]. One group of cases may be excluded. If I buy a thing and at my direction it is given to you, my *procurator*, for me, I possess, but I am not technically acquiring possession through you, any more than, if it is put in my house at my orders, I acquire possession through my house[2]. Omitting this case, the rules shew a gradual change. For Gaius it was uncertain if possession could be acquired through free persons not possessed[3]. Neratius had already held that it could be acquired through a *procurator* —a general agent[4]. Severus and Caracalla declared it settled law that it might be acquired *per liberam personam*[5], and Ulpian cites this[6] as meaning any *libera persona*. This text may be interpolated[7], but since by his time the name *procurator* was applied to a *mandatarius* employed for a single transaction, and in mandate ratification sufficed, and Paul, who tells us of the extended meaning of *procurator* tells us also that possession can be acquired through a *procurator, utilitatis causa*[8], interpolation is doubtful[9]. In any case the wider rule was that of later law[10]. But this refers to the *corpus*. As to *animus*, previous authorisation sufficed, even general[11], but apart from this there must be knowledge by the principal[12]. For *usucapio*, indeed, knowledge was required in any case, not from principle, but because of the danger of the other rule, "*quia contra statui captiosum erit*[13]."

For slave (and *filiusfamilias*, apart from *peculium castrense*, etc.) the main rules were simple. A slave could acquire the *corpus*, but the master's possession was not complete till he assented[14]. But on this there are some remarks to be made.

(i) The *peculium* was the master's and acquisition for it was acquisition for him, but its purpose would be defeated if the master had to intervene in its dealings. Hence an illogical rule, based on convenience, that the master need not know; the slave could supply *animus* here[15].

1 The question whether possession could be acquired through *tutor, curator*, or *actor reipublicae* in cl. law is disputed. 41. 1. 13. 1; 41. 2. 1. 20. *Contra*, Alibrandi (*Opere*, 275, *cit.* Siber), followed by most, but not all, Italian scholars; for, Solazzi, *Bull.* 1911, 143; Mitteis, *R.R.* 213; Girard, *Man.* 294; Siber, *R.R.* 2. 142, etc. 2 41. 2. 18. 2. In 41. 2. 42. 1 the *procurator* is the negotiating party. 3 G. 2. 95, probably the word is *procurator*. 4 41. 1. 13; 41. 3. 41. 5 C. 7. 32. 1. 6 13. 7. 11. 6. 7 Mitteis, *R.Pr.* 1. 212. For him every text declaring for acquisition "*per liberam personam*" is interpolated; he cites 41. 1. 20. 2, 53; 13. 7. 11. 6; 47. 2. 14, 17; C. 7. 32. 1. He regards P. 5. 2. 2, with its distinction between *libera persona* and *procurator*, as decisive, but in view of the wide meaning the word *procurator* had acquired by this time (*ib.* 1. 3. 2) it seems more probable that the text is not comparing procurators and others, but *possessio* and other rights. Buckland, *Bull. Acad. R. Belg. cl. lett.* 1939, 188 *sqq.* 8 P. 1. 3. 2; 5. 2. 2. The *procurator unius rei* seems to be classical. 9 Peters, *Z.S.S.* 1911, 205 *sqq.*, for other suggested emendations. 10 Inst. 2. 9. 5. 11 41. 2. 1. 13; 41. 2. 42. 1; 41. 3. 41. 12 P. 5. 2. 2. 13 41. 3. 41; C. 7. 32. 1. 14 G. 2. 89; P. 5. 2. 1; D. 41. 2. 1. 5, 48. 15 41. 2. 44. 1. See, however, Beseler, *Beitr.* 4. 61.

(ii) If the master was a lunatic or *infans*, and so incapable of *animus*, there was logically no acquisition of possession. One text gets over the difficulty in the case of *infans* by saying that he could assent by *auctoritas* of his *tutor*[1]. But in general it was not till *infantia* was over that there was any question of *auctoritas*[2], and then it would not be needed for possession, which does not impose an obligation[3]. Pomponius lays down the more reasonable rule, no doubt on grounds of convenience, that a slave can acquire possession for a lunatic or infant master[4].

(iii) A *hereditas* had no *animus*: there were difficulties as to acquisition of possession. A *servus hereditarius* could complete *usucapio* already begun[5]. Probably in classical, certainly in later, law such a slave could acquire possession for his *peculium*[6]. It is not clear that even under Justinian he could acquire it apart from *peculium*[7].

(iv) Although the *animus* came from the master, the slave contributed something to it. A man without consciousness cannot have control: thus possession could not be acquired through an insane slave[8].

(v) The slave's intent ought not, it might seem, to be material, but Paul says that if he takes not intending to acquire for his master, the latter does not acquire[9]. But this has really nothing to do with *animus possidendi*. It is a question of *corpus*. I cannot be said to have obtained control where the thing is taken by one who makes it clear that he is not taking for me. I cease to possess a fugitive slave so soon as he asserts himself as a freeman[10].

(vi) As to fugitive slaves there was dispute. Some texts deny[11], others admit[12], continuance of possession. Some allow it, *utilitatis causa* for *usucapio* alone[13]. There are similar differences of opinion as to acquisition of possession through a *fugitivus*[14]. There was no doubt movement of thought. Whether it went the whole way in classical law is disputed[15].

1 41. 2. 32. 2. See also Papinian, C. 7. 32. 3, *in fin.* As to "*per*" *tutorem*, Peters, *Z.S.S.* 1911, 205. As to acquisition by the *tutor* acting by himself, see the general discussion, Lewald, *Z.S.S.* 1913, 452. 2 *Ante*, § LVI. 3 41. 2. 32. 2. The contradiction in h. t. l. 3 is no doubt due to interpolation, as also in h. t. l. 11, l. 13; 41. 3. 4. 2, etc. See Lewald, *Z.S.S.* 1913, 450, reviewing Solazzi. 4 41. 3. 28. 5 41. 3. 20, 31. 5, 40. 6 6. 2. 9. 6, 10; 41. 2. 1. 5; 44. 7. 16. 7 6. 2. 9. 6, 10; 41. 3. 44. 3, 45. 1. 8 41. 2. 1. 9, 10. 9 41. 2. 1. 19. 10 41. 3. 15. 1. There are several texts in which the intent of slave or *procurator*, when he takes possession, is treated as material, e.g. 39. 5. 13 and 41. 1. 37. 4, with some conflict. The real question seems to be of *corpus* in all these cases. For statement of this view and discussion of the texts, Buckland, *R.H.* 1925, 355. C. Arnò, *Fictio brevis manus*, traces the conflict to opposition between the followers of Servius and those of Q. Mucius. 11 E.g. 41. 1. 54. 4. 12 E.g. P. 2. 31. 37; 4. 14. 3. 13 E.g. 47. 2. 17. 3. 14 E.g. 41. 2. 1. 14, 50. 1; 6. 2. 15. 15 Other texts are 7. 1. 12. 3; 40. 12. 25. 2; 41. 2. 13. pr.; 15, 47; 44. 3. 8. Most of these texts are interp. for Albertario, *I Problemi possessori, relativi al serv. fugitivus*. For him, anything beyond admission of *usucapio utilitatis causa* is post-classical. But, *inter alia*, the texts in n. 12 with their "*animus*" look very Pauline. Other views, Arnò, *St. Perozzi*, 263; Rotondi, *Scr. Giur.* 3. 143.

(vii) There was an old notion that a man could not acquire possession through one he did not possess[1]. Accordingly some jurists doubted whether a usufructuary of a slave could acquire possession through him, but the difficulty was disregarded in classical law[2]. Similarly Gaius records a doubt whether possession could be acquired through women *in manu* and persons *in mancipio*[3]. As these soon became obsolete, we have no later information, but Gaius sees no difficulty in the case of a *filiusfamilias*[4] though he was not possessed in classical law[5], whatever may have been the original state of things.

LXXIV. In general, *possessio* continued normally, *animo et corpore.* If it needs both elements it ought to cease if either ceases, but this is obviously not so, as a general principle. A man does not lose possession if he goes mad or asleep[6]. But there were cases in which possession was retained *animo solo*, e.g. *saltus hiberni, aestivi*[7], which were abandoned for half the year. During this period possession was lost by mere intent not to possess[8]. There are, however, texts which seem to say that what was possessed in both ways could be lost *animo solo*. Two of these give facts which shew them to mean only that a delivery which, on the face of it, was consistent with retaining actual *possessio* would be a transfer of possession if the necessary *animus* was present[9]. Paul however says: "*si in fundo sis et tamen nolis eum possidere, protinus amittes possessionem*[10]." But this may be merely *constitutum possessorium*[11]. If a vendor of land arranged to hold it as tenant, the full process would involve handing it over and taking it back as tenant, and a tenant had only *possessio naturalis*. For simplicity, the process was taken for granted, and possession shifted without actual transfer[12].

Death ended possession, and the fiction by which the *hereditas* was considered as continuing possession did not benefit the *heres*, who,

1 G. 2. 94. 2 G. 2. 94; D. 7. 1. 21; 41. 2. 1. 8, etc. In general, *b. f. possessor* was, as to acquisition, in the same position as fructuary, but here this difficulty did not arise. G. 2. 94; D. 41. 2. 1. 6. 3 G. 2. 90. 4 G. 2. 89. 5 Thus the ordinary possessory interdicts were not available: special ones were needed, Lenel, *E.P.* 488. 6 41. 3. 31. 3. 7 41. 2. 3. 11; C. 7. 32. 4. 8 41. 2. 25. 2. A *furiosus* cannot lose *possessio, animo solo*, h. t. 27. Paul says that as *animus* and *corpus* are both essential to acquisition of *possessio*, this cannot be lost till both cease, 50. 17. 153; see also 41. 2. 8. So stated this is absurd. One who has dropped a shilling in the street has lost possession even though he knows nothing about it. It is sometimes explained by taking "*utrumque*" distributively, hard to reconcile with the comparison in the text. De Zulueta, D. 41. 1, 2 *ad* 41. 2. 8. Papinian (41. 2. 46) lays down the similar but more rational rule that what is held *animo solo* can be lost *animo solo*. On the question how soon possession of what was held *animo solo* was lost by adverse holding, Rotondi, *Scr. Giur.* 3. 129. 9 41. 2. 17. 1, 44. 2. 10 41. 2. 3. 6. 11 To this explanation De Zulueta, *Cambridge L. J.* 1922, 172, objects 41. 2. 30. 4. This may be the same case. It speaks however only of moveables. 12 41. 2. 18. pr. Possession is lost if the thing is handed to one who cannot possess, e.g. a *furiosus*, 41. 2. 18. 1. See, however, as to possible conflict, Arnò, *Fictio brevis manus*, 52, citing h. t. 1. 4, 1. 20, 30. pr.; 43. 16. 18. pr.

at least if there was no holding by a slave or *colonus*, did not possess until he had actually taken possession, this being a matter of fact[1]. If at the time of the owner's death, a *colonus* was in occupation, Cicero tells us that the *heres* had possession by the *colonus* with no act of his, but this is in an advocate's speech[2] and is in plain contradiction with a text of Paul which no doubt states classical law[3], and says that the *heres* did not possess in such a case, till he had actually taken possession.

There is difficulty as to loss of possession by an act of the subordinate. It might be said that, as a slave could not make his master's position worse, he could not deprive him of possession. But when once *possessio* was acquired the slave's personality was immaterial: he was a mere receptacle. If a thing fell from the slave's hand, it was much as if it had fallen from the master's pocket. And *possessio* was a question of fact. But if my slave refuses to let me have the thing, I still possess[4]. If a slave or *colonus* wilfully abandoned land the classics disagreed as to loss of possession till a third party had taken it[5], on which event they held it lost[6]. Justinian in an obscure and much discussed enactment seems to have provided that it was not lost in either case[7].

The question whether *possessio* was or was not a right is somewhat empty. Whether it existed or not was regarded as a question of fact[8], but if it existed, it conferred rights[9]. It was not called a *res*, nor was it thought of as a *ius in rem* analogous to ownership or usufruct. This seems to rest on the fact that it had no assignable money value. A pledge creditor had more than possession, since he had an action and could resist *vindicatio*, but was rarely spoken of as having a *ius*[10]. And acquisition of a *nomen* carried with it the securities by way of pledge[11] with no thought of the principle that *iura in rem* are not transferred by mere agreement. The wealth of pledgee is not increased by a pledge, though his security is[12]. The distinction is brought

1 41. 2. 23. pr. 2 *Pro Caecina*, 32. 94. 3 41. 2. 30. 5. A transfer may involve loss of *possessio* without acquisition by the transferee, e.g. transfer to a *furiosus*, h. t. 1. 10. 4 41. 2. 15, 40. pr. 5 41. 2. 3. 8, 31, 40. 1, 44. 2. 6 41. 2. 40. 1, 44. 2. Not of *saltus hiberni* or *aestivi*, which are possessed *animo solo*, till the owner knows, h. t. 3. 7, 25. 2, 46. 7 C. 7. 32. 12. Rotondi, *Scr. Giur.* 3. 186. 8 *Animus* and *corpus* are both facts. But on the neo-Savignian view (*ante*, p. 198) we must say that the facts are presumed from certain dealings, and on that of Ihering that in some cases the law deprives the facts of their normal legal effect. 9 *S.M.W.* 276. 10 E.g. 9. 4. 30=39. 2. 19. pr., where the decisive words look like a gloss. 11 C. 4. 10. 6, 7. 12 A text tells us that a usufruct, the claim for which is barred by certain facts, still exists till it is lost by non-user, while a *pignus* is simply destroyed by such facts: *nullum enim est pignus cuius persecutio denegatur* (9. 4. 27. pr.). This turns on the fact that pledge has no content but its enforceability: it is matter for the law of actions. This is not to say that it has no value: it is of the utmost importance from a procedural point of view and many texts shew that lawyers were alive to its economic importance (e.g. 13. 5. 14. 1; 18. 4. 6; 50. 17. 72, etc.). What it means is that notwithstanding its economic importance the considerations mentioned prevented lawyers from regarding it as a *res*.

out in a text which says that a captive retains his *iura* but loses his *possessio*[1].

It is the notion of possession as a right which leads to its treatment in modern books in close connexion with *dominium.* The Roman institutional writers did not so treat this merely provisional and procedural right: it was dealt with under interdictal procedure. *Bona fide possessio* was mentioned, because it gave a right to fruits. This explains what looks like a sharp contrast in the method of the Digest. The title on acquisition of *dominium* is followed by one on that of possession[2]. But the succeeding titles shew that this is because possession is an important factor in the law of acquisition of *dominium* by *usucapio*: it is discussed as an introduction to that subject.

LXXV. ACQUISITION OF *DOMINIUM*. Modes of acquisition of *res corporales*, i.e. of *dominium*, can be classified in various ways. They were Formal or Informal, a distinction turning not on the degree of ceremonial but on the point that in formal transactions, e.g. *mancipatio*, the form sufficed apart from intent or *causa*, while in such cases as *traditio* intent and *causa* were material. They were Original, e.g. *occupatio*, or Derivative, e.g. *traditio*[3]. This distinction is not found in the texts. Indeed the conception of *dominium* as a Seignory or Sovereignty, a personal relation between the owner and the *res*, has led to the view that the notion of transfer of *dominium* is alien to the classical law, that though the *res* is transferred, the ownership created is a new one[4]. It is clear that the expression "*translatio dominii*" has been interpolated into many texts and that late lawyers said "*dominium transferre*" where the earlier usually said "*rem transferre*," but this may well be no more than a preference among earlier lawyers for concrete, and among later for abstract, terms[5]. But the institutional treatment, which will be fol-

1 41. 2. 23. 1. Release of pledge from husband to wife was not *donatio* (42. 8. 18; cf. D. 24. 1. 5. 16). We are however told that there could not be a *donatio* of possession between them (24. 1. 46). Rotondi, *cit.* shews the tendency in Justinian's law to regard it as a right and thus (p. 200) explains the extravagant rule in C. 7. 32. 12 (above, p. 203, n. 7). See also Vassali, *Misc. Crit.* 2. 40. A *possessor* as such can draw no advantage from the thing: all he has is a right to resist if his possession is interfered with except by legal process. But those inferior modes of ownership, of provincial lands, and by peregrines, which if they have a substantial name at all must be called *possessiones* are substantive rights giving enjoyment of the property and not defeasible by legal process.

2 41. 1; 41. 2.

3 A distinction different from that between bilateral and unilateral, though all original methods are unilateral.

4 De Francisci, *Il trasferimento della Proprietà.*

5 The author recognises that classics occasionally spoke of transfer of the right where the word "*res*" would be obscure, e.g. "*transferre proprietatem*" where there was a usufruct (p. 21). But this shews them acquainted with the notion of transfer of the right. *Translatum dominium* does not seem more unlikely than *translatum imperium* (*Sc.* Claudianum, Bruns, 1. 196). The change seems in any case earlier than the author holds, for he does not really dispose of Vat. Fr. 263, 267, 283 or *Fr. de Form. Fab.* 1. 5 (Lenel, *Z.S.S.* 1925, 30). He shews that the classics had no such notion as "singular succession" but that is a different matter.

lowed, classifies them as *iuris civilis* or *iuris naturalis* (or *gentium*[1]), by which Gaius seems to mean that some were thought of as peculiar to Rome, while others were universal. The concrete cases shew what look like inconsistencies. Acquisition by long possession (*usucapio*) and treasure trove are both known to other systems and in both the details were regulated by statute. But *usucapio* was *iuris civilis* and *inventio* was *iuris gentium*. *Usucapio* is treated in the XII Tables: no doubt the civil law methods are so called as belonging to the early formal law.

Acquisition from the State. This "publicistic" matter is not expressly treated in the Institutes. There were many cases: distribution of booty, allocation of public lands, *bonorum sectio*, and, generally, sales by the *Fiscus*[2]. The State was not bound by rules of form. All that seems to have been needed was a declaration by the official charged with the business, sometimes called *addictio*[3]. This ignores the principle that transfer of property *inter vivos* required, not necessarily delivery, but some act or circumstance shewing an assertion of control of the thing acquired: *traditionibus et usucapionibus dominia rerum, non nudis pactis, transferuntur*[4]. There were exceptions, e.g. the rule in *societas omnium bonorum*, that the mere agreement vested in the partners in common the ownership of what had belonged to each[5], the creation of servitudes by pact and stipulation[6], and, in later law, some rules of *donatio* and *dos*[7]. The vesting of the owner's share in treasure is difficult to reconcile with it[8]. *Traditio brevi manu* and *constitutum possessorium* were only apparent exceptions[9], and the creditor's right in hypothec was not thought of as a *ius in rem*[10]. With the exception of *traditio*, for practical purposes the most important of all modes of acquisition, and the special cases of acquisition of *fructus*, the *iure naturali* methods are of secondary importance in actual life. *Occupatio*, as being original and not derivative, is treated as the primary mode, and, as we shall see, most of the others have a close affinity with it.

LXXVI. *Occupatio*[11]. This was acquisition by taking. It was not of great significance, its chief importance being in relation to wild animals captured for food or other purposes. These were acquired only when effectively seized, which was true of all *occupatio*[12], but there was in their case the further rule that the ownership lasted only while they were effectively held, subject to the modification that of certain things, e.g. bees and pigeons, the ownership lasted so long as they retained the habit

1 G. 2. 65; Inst. 2. 1. 11. See also 41. 1. 1. pr. where the "*gentium*" is probably due to the compilers, not to Gaius. 2 Cuq, *Man.* 258. 3 See Girard, *Man.* 305. 4 C. 2. 3. 20. 5 *Post*, § CLXXVIII. 6 *Post*, § XCIV. 7 *Post*, § XCI; *ante*, p. 110. 8 *Post*, § LXXX. 9 *Ante*, p. 202; *post*, § LXXXIII. 10 *Ante*, p. 203; *post*, § CLXVI. Does not apply to acquisition by legacy. 11 G. 2. 66–69; Inst. 2. 1. 12 *sqq.*, as to this and other *iure naturali* modes of acquisition, De Zulueta, D. 41. 1 and 2. 12 Inst. *ib.*

of returning to their quarters—*animus revertendi*[1]. The question what amounted to such capture as gave effect to the intent to acquire is, in effect, what amounts to gaining possession. It was agreed after disputes that a wounded animal was not "occupied" till seized[2]. We are nowhere told whether killing was itself enough and, as to trapping, the matter seems to have depended somewhat on the position of the trap[3].

What amounted to loss of control is again a question of fact[4]: clearly it was not lost while the old owner was in close pursuit: perhaps the true account is that the beast ceased to be owned when the chance of recovering him was not materially greater than that of capturing any other wild animal[5]. To the question why ownership was, in this case, limited by possession[6], the answer may be that the whole institution antedates law: it comes from a time when the strong man armed, and he alone, held his goods in peace. The rule had a curious result. If the beast escaped, and, when free from control, did damage, the old owner was not responsible: it was not his beast. He need not therefore keep it securely however dangerous it was[7]. The aediles met the case by a provision that one who kept wild beasts of certain kinds near a highway was responsible for any damage they did. In later law this was extended to any wild animal[8]. And the Institutes[9] allow *actio de pauperie* in respect of wild animals[10].

Occupatio is also said to be applicable to *res derelictae*[11], abandoned property. If a thing was intentionally abandoned by its owner, without the desire of recovery (such as existed where things were thrown overboard to lighten a ship[12]), it could be "occupied" by anyone. But there are difficulties. If I picked up what had been abandoned but I supposed to have been accidentally dropped, and decided to keep it, had I acquired it? The difficulty is that I could hardly be said to intend to acquire what I did not think to be susceptible of acquisition. The only text requires knowledge on the part of the *occupans*[13].

An owner not in actual possession could not make *derelictio*, if it required a cesser of possession[14], but it would seem that any declaration by the owner that he had done with the thing would suffice in this case. The Proculians held that a thing was not derelict till some other person actually possessed it, but Julian's contrary view prevailed[15]. The Pro-

1 41. 1. 3, 4; Inst. 2. 1. 14, 15. 2 Inst. 2. 1. 13; D. 41. 1. 5. 1. 3 41. 1. 55. Texts do not shew clearly whether there was property in the game or fish in land or *stagna* reserved for sport. 4 41. 1. 5. 4. 5 Czyhlarz, *Eigentumserwerbsarten*, 46. 6 Analogy with ownership of shelters on seashore, *ante*, p. 183. 7 Inst. 4. 9. pr. 8 21. 1. 40–42; Inst. 4. 9. 1. 9 Inst. 4. 9. 1. 10 But as to history of these remedies, *post*, § ccv. 11 Berger, *In tema di derelizione*; Bonfante, *Scr. Giur.* 2. 327. *Post*, p. 232. 12 Inst. 2. 1. 48. 13 41. 7. 2. pr. Texts on *usucapio* are not here in point. 14 Czyhlarz, *cit.* 90. 15 41. 7. 2. 1.

culian doctrine has been explained as meaning that *derelictio* was not complete till it was too late for change of mind[1], and this is in accord with the fact that the Proculians do not say that the adverse taking must have been with a view to acquisition: any possession would, it seems, suffice. But there is a different explanation. Many modern writers, treating the Proculian view as the logical doctrine, hold that *occupatio* had nothing to do with the matter, and regard the case as one of *traditio incertae personae*[2]. Neither Gaius nor Justinian mentions this in connexion with *occupatio*, and there is no text in the Digest which clearly does so, while some texts put this case side by side with others, treated as *traditio*[3]. The difficulty is however that, when the view prevailed that *derelictio* was complete by mere abandonment, it followed that it became a *res nullius*, and there could be no *traditio* of such a *res*.

This point apart, *derelictio* of moveables was completed by throwing them away. In land, this was impossible: the owner must, so to speak, remove himself from the land. But people leave their land for long periods for many reasons other than intention not to own it[4], and as land usually has some value, it does not seem that *derelictio* of land was common[5].

We are told in a much discussed text that there may be dereliction of an undivided share, but only where that is all the *derelinquens* had[6]: one cannot abandon a part and keep the rest. The question arises: What becomes of the abandoned share? Can it be "occupied" or does it accrue to the others? The answer may turn on the view taken of the nature of common ownership. If each has the whole ownership, limited only *concursu*, accrual follows, but if each owns only a *pars*, it does not, and there are many ways of "constructing" common ownership[7]. A text in the Vatican Fragments seems to deny accrual[8], and no text asserts it, but it is generally held that there was accrual, the analogy of *hereditas* and legacy, joint usufruct and manumission of common slaves being followed[9].

1 See Czyhlarz, *cit.* 114. 2 *Post*, § LXXXIII. 3 Inst. 2. 1. 46, 47 directly associate it with a case of *traditio incertae personae*, using the word "*occupare*," but in a context which shews that it means no more than seizing and does not imply a particular juristic construction of the facts. D. 41. 7, on *usucapio* "*pro derelicto*" uses the word "*occupantis*" in l. 1. But here too the word is not technical. Even P. 2. 31. 27 is not conclusive. 4 E.g. *saltus hiberni, aestivi*. 5 *Derelictio* of land is often mentioned in the sources (reff., Czyhlarz, *cit.* 93) but usually in the sense of leaving it uncared for, without necessary implication of intent to abandon. Arrears of tax might make it dangerous to "occupy." 6 41. 7. 3. 7 *Post*, § CLXXXVI. 8 Vat. Fr. 77, *med.* 9 For various opinions and discussion, Riccobono, *Essays in Legal History*, Oxford, 1913, 52; Bonfante, *Corso*, 2. 2. 18; Scialoja, *Proprietà*, 441. Brini (*Rend. Accad. Bologna*, 1923 (*Sc.M.*), 43), denies that it can be, strictly, *derelictio*, which can apply only to a physical thing, and thus accounts for the "*relinquere*" of the text. See also Perozzi, *Ist.* 1. 744 *sq.*

We are told that among things capable of *occupatio* were those captured from the enemy[1], but, in general, *praeda* did not go to the captor, but to the State. It was at the disposal of the general, who might give or sell it[2], but this was acquisition from the State. What is here referred to is enemy property in State territory in time of war, and property of members of a State with which Rome had no friendly relations[3].

Occupatio was a *iure gentium* mode of acquisition, and it has been contended that it therefore gave only *iure gentium* ownership. But the name refers to origin, not to effect[4]. The suggestion has also been made that in classical law it gave only *iure gentium* ownership of *res mancipi*[5]. This is true of the most important *iure gentium* mode, *traditio*, and is probable here also. Otherwise it would be an easy way of evading *mancipatio*. *A* could abandon the slave and *B* then "occupy" him, and it would be easy to create by agreement the obligations which would have resulted from *mancipatio*. The case is, as we have seen, closely associated with *traditio incertae personae*, and, if so interpreted, it could not give more than *iure gentium* ownership[6]. Classical texts give no hint of anything of the kind, but there are few and doubtful references to *occupatio* of *res derelictae* and *res hostis*, the only cases in which the point could arise[7].

LXXVII. *Accessio*[8]. Acquisition of property by its incorporation in what already belonged to the acquirer. The rules are complex and there are several distinct cases. The question whether it created civil or merely bonitary ownership in classical law cannot arise here, for what was acquired merged in the old thing and was necessarily held as that was held[9].

The simplest case of *accessio*, that of moveables to moveables, was of rather rare occurrence. If two things of different owners were so mixed, not by consent, as to be readily separable (*commixtio*), they were merely

1 In G. 2. 69 the acquisition contemplated is no doubt to the State. 2 Mommsen, *Strafr.* 765. 3 41. 1. 51. 1. Girard, *Man.* 340, limits this to "expédition de partisans," no doubt the usual case. 4 Cf. the case of *traditio*. 5 Girard, *Man.* 339. 6 Bonfante, *Corso*, 2. 2. 192, treats *derelictio* as an act of alienation analogous to *traditio* and thus requiring *usucapio* where it was a *res mancipi*. For Berger, *op. cit.* 36, taking after *derelictio* is an "original" mode of acquisition giving civil ownership even of *res mancipi*. See also S. Romano, *L' occupazione delle res derelictae*. 7 Not all *res nullius* could be "occupied," e.g. *divini iuris*. See, too, G. 2. 200 as to the Proculian view of property subject to a conditional legacy *per vindicationem*. Things in a *hereditas iacens* were *res nullius*. None of these could be occupied and the interests of those really concerned were provided for, as we have seen for *res divini iuris* and shall see later for other cases, by a variety of expedients. 8 *Accessio* is not a technical term: it is not clear that all topics commonly treated under this head can be referred to one principle. Bonfante, *Corso*, 2. 2. 70. 9 Collinet-Giffard, *Précis*, 1. 312.

separated again: there was no change of ownership[1]. If it was by consent, ownership was presumably common: in neither case was there any *accessio*[2]. If they were so joined as not to be readily separable (*confusio*), whether by consent or not, ownership was common: there was no *accessio*[3]. These rules seem to exclude *accessio* altogether, but there was an important exception. If, of the two things so united by *confusio*, one was merely an accessory to the other, its identity was merged in that other: there was *accessio* and the whole belonged to the owner of the principal thing[4]. Whether it was or was not an accessory was a question of fact, not always easy. In some cases it seems obvious, as where *A*'s wool was woven into *B*'s coat[5], but in some cases there were disagreements, not only whether, in a given case, the thing was an accessory, but on the tests to be applied in determining the point. No doubt philosophy had its share in the settlement of the rules[6].

The test sometimes applied, and, as it seems, the best, is whether the total thing would retain its identity as the same thing, if the added element were removed, whether this is the thing which gives the object its essence and its name[7]. Another test applied was that of relative

1 41. 1. 12. 1. *A. ad exhibendum*, 6. 1. 23. 5; 10. 4. 6. The better view seems to be that during the union the ownership of the accessory is dormant (Guarneri-Citati, *App. crit. in mat. di accessione* and *La cosidetta accessione separabile*). For Pernice (*Labeo*, 2. 1. 31) it is extinct, but capable of reviving. For Ratti (*St. Bonfante*, 1. 265) there was a school dispute. In one sense there is *accessio* wherever the thing added becomes in fact part of the *maior species*, whether separable or not (41. 1. 26. pr.). But, apart from buildings, the rules of which are affected by another rule, it is convenient to confine the term to cases of definitive acquisition, i.e. excluding cases for the *a. ad exhibendum*. On a Sabinian tendency to be satisfied with relative value and importance of the two elements, while the Proculians considered what was essentially the economic thing (41. 1. 27. 2), Bonfante, *cit.* 78.

2 It is possible that the cl. law applied the notion only to metals and fluids. See Perozzi, *Ist.* 1. 6. 88, on *specificatio*. In the case of grain the Inst. (2. 1. 28) say that where grain is indistinguishably mixed not by consent the ownership is unchanged. In money, the ownership appears to vest in the one who mixes them, subject to liabilities (46. 3. 78). But the text has been so shortened as to leave it obscure.

3 Inst. 2. 1. 27. Simple soldering is *commixtio*, for it can be melted off (*plumbatura*), but welding (*ferruminatio*) is *confusio*. 6. 1. 23. 5. A mixture of "*aes*" and silver was thought of as separable, *commixtio*, 41. 1. 12. 1, one of gold and silver was not so thought of, *confusio*, h. t. 7. 8; more subtle explanation of the difference, Bonfante, *Corso*, 2. 2. 79.

4 Inst. 2. 1. 26.

5 Arnò (*Mél. Girard*, 1. 27) argues that *textura* is not a true case of *accessio*, but is on an equality with *plumbatura*. He cites 10. 4. 7. 2 and contrasts G. 2. 79 and Inst. 2. 1. 25, 26.

6 According to Sokolowski, *Philosophie in Privatr.*, Labeo, a peripatetic, held that, if the thing began to form part of a new or other εἶδος, it merged in that. Cassius with the Stoics of his time does not attribute primacy to the εἶδος: the old thing no longer exists and both old ownerships are gone. Thus it cedes to the ownership of the more important part of the material. This holds only for *ferruminatio* and the like. Later, the ἕξεις, thought of as material, is the determining factor, the *maior species*. Thus from a Stoic materialistic point of view we get something like the peripatetic point of view, a *media sententia*. But see Bonfante, *Corso*, 2. 2. 74.

7 See Girard, *Man.* 352, who cites 34. 2. 29. 1; 41. 1. 26. pr.; Inst. 2. 1. 33. A diamond ring may, it should seem, be regarded as

value[1], but this was ignored in the case of writing on parchment, which ceded to the parchment though the lettering were of gold. Here the test applied was that the writing could not exist without the parchment, while the converse is not true[2]. In the case of painting on a tablet, there were disputes. On the view which prevailed the tablet ceded to the picture, since, says Justinian, the picture has the greater value. This is not always true, and is not alleged by Gaius (from whom Justinian adopts the opinion), who observes that there is no good reason for it[3]. Paul adverts to this reason but rejects both it and the rule[4] and makes the painting cede to the tablet as not capable of existing without it[5].

It was indifferent whether the absorption was *bona fide* or not, by whom it was done, or whether there was consent, though all these points were material on the question of compensation, on which the chief rules were these[6]:

(i) If the loser effected the fusion voluntarily in knowledge of the facts, he was regarded as having made a gift and had no claim[7], unless he did it as a reasonable act of administration on behalf of the other party, when he would have an *actio negotiorum gestorum contraria*[8].

(ii) If he did it thinking the thing was his, then, if still in possession, he could resist *vindicatio* by *exceptio doli* unless he received compensation for his loss, not the added value[9]. If the other party had acquired possession of the thing, he had, it seems, no remedy at all[10].

(iii) If it was done in bad faith by the acquirer and he had possession, the loser could proceed for theft[11]. If on such facts the loser was still in possession, the owner could no doubt vindicate subject to payment for the added value, but would still be liable to the *actio furti*.

(iv) If it was done in good faith by the acquirer, he was liable, in later law, if in possession, to an *actio in factum* for the loss[12]. If the other had possession he could vindicate, paying for the added value[13].

(v) In the picture case compensation was dealt with on peculiar lines. The three texts are all substantially the same and due to Gaius[14].

a jewel in its setting rather than a ring with its ornament. But at least in legacy, the ring was the principal, the gem accessory (34. 2. 19. 16), which may be mere interpretation of intent. Ehrlich, *St. Scialoja*, 2. 731.

1 Inst. 2. 1. 34. Another test (41. 1. 27. 1), unhelpful, is, on whose account the addition was made. 2 G. 2. 77; Inst. 2. 1. 33; D. 6. 1. 23. 3. Rather like *specificatio, post,* § LXXIX. 3 G. 2. 78; Inst. 2. 1. 34; D. 41. 1. 9. 2. 4 6. 1. 23. 3. 5 Bonfante, *Corso*, 2. 2. 83, holds that there was a school dispute, the view which prevailed being based on *specificatio*. See also Arnò, *Sculptura e Pictura*. 6 This is matter for the law of obligations, but is discussed here in the Institutes. 7 *Arg. Greg. Wis.* 6. 2; D. 41. 1. 7. 12. 8 3. 5. 44. pr. 9 G. 2. 77; Inst. 2. 1. 33. 10 12. 6. 33; 41. 1. 7. 12, 9. pr. 11 Inst. 2. 1. 26. 12 6. 1. 23. 5, interp. 13 6. 1. 23. 4. It is said (*arg.* 6. 1. 23. 5) that there was an *actio ad exhibendum* in some of these cases. 14 G. 2. 78; Inst. 2. 1. 34; D. 41. 1. 9. 2.

They tell us that, the tablet being still in the possession of the old owner, the painter could vindicate, subject to *exceptio doli* if he did not pay the value of the tablet, presumably only if he was in good faith. If the painter possessed, the old owner had an *actio utilis* for the tablet subject to paying *impensam* (or *pretium*) *picturae* if the maker was in good faith. If not he had *actio furti*. This *actio utilis* whether *vindicatio utilis* or *in personam* was odd enough. If *impensa* means the value of the picture he had no remedy except on purchase of the picture which he might not want. If it means merely the cost of materials, he got what might be a valuable picture for practically nothing. And, on the rules as stated, each could recover it from the other[1].

The next form of *accessio* to consider is to land apart from buildings. Imperceptible deposit of soil on a man's boundaries by the action, e.g., of a river, belonged to him[2]. An island arising in the middle of a river belonged to the owners on each side, to the middle line[3]. Apart from temporary inundation, if a river changed its bed, the old bed belonged to the owners on each side and the new bed became public, reverting if the river reverted[4]. If a solid identifiable piece of land was carried on to *A*'s borders by the force of the river, the ownership was unchanged, until trees rooted in it struck root in *A*'s land, when it became his[5]. Similarly anything sown or planted in a man's land was his[6].

In *alluvio* we hear nothing of compensation, for obvious reasons. As to plants rooted in land, the little we are told[7] suggests that, as we should expect, the rules were as for moveables.

The rules of *alluvio*, etc., harmonise with the doctrine that the owners of land on the banks owned the soil to the middle line, and this is strengthened by the fact that they did not apply if the land concerned was *ager limitatus*, i.e. defined by straight lines, having no necessary relation to natural features, as was usual in grants by the State[8]. So too of *insula nata*, which was on the same level as *alluvio* (while an island in the sea, the bottom of which certainly belonged to no one, was *res*

1 Bortolucci, *Scr. ded. a C. Arnò*, 14. These rules do not deal with the case of fusion effected by one who owned neither principal thing nor accessory. It might be very complicated. 2 G. 2. 70; Inst. 2. 1. 20; D. 41. 1. 7. 1. 3 G. 2. 72; Inst. 2. 1. 22; D. 41. 1. 7. 3, 4. 4 41. 1. 7. 5; Inst. 2. 1. 23. The unfair result is that if the new bed coincides with a whole *fundus* and the river again removes itself, the old owner does not regain his property (41. 1. 7. 5). The text adds: "*sed vix est ut id obtineat,*" no doubt Justinian (Riccobono, *St. Schupfer*, 1. 220; Guarneri-Citati, *Il ripristino della proprietà*). On the puzzling 41. 1. 38 (the Attius case) De Zulueta, D. 41. 1. and 2, *ad text.* and *ad h. t.* 30. 3. 5 G. 2. 71; Inst. 2. 1. 21; D. 41. 1. 7. 1, 2. The Institutes speak of the *tree* only. See also 6. 1. 5. 3. 6 When rooted. Common, if rooted in two estates, G. 2. 74, 75; Inst. 2. 1. 31, 32; D. 41. 1. 7. 13. 7 G. 2. 76; *Greg. Wis.* 6. 1; Inst. 2. 1. 32. 8 41. 1. 16. Practical difficulties and temporary departure from principle, Cuq, *Man.* 261, and reff.; Costa, *Le Acque*, 4 *sqq.*

nullius[1]) and cannot be thought of as accessory to the land or ceding to it, unless the right extended to the middle line. Celsus held that the soil belonged to owners on each side and was public only *quoad usum*[2]. But some texts make the bed public[3], and even so late as Labeo there were controversies as to riparian owners' rights to islands[4]. There are, as we have seen, other traces of differences of opinion on many of these points[5]. The better opinion seems to be that the classical lawyers were reaching the doctrine that the bed belonged to the riparians[6].

LXXVIII. As to buildings, the texts discuss two cases:

(*a*) *A* built on his own land with *B*'s materials. The house was *A*'s: *superficies solo cedit*[7]. But the Romans were capable of a rather metaphysical distinction. Though the house was *A*'s, *B*'s materials were still *B*'s[8], with the limitation, based on the XII Tables, that so long as they were part of the house, even though separable, he could not reclaim them[9]. His ownership was dormant, but capable of reviving. If, however, they had been used in bad faith, the old owner had an *actio de tigno iniuncto*, also based on the XII Tables, for double value[10], and after bringing this action he could still recover the materials when the house came down[11]. The act seems to be *furtum*, but if the *actio furti* were brought, no doubt that *de tigno iniuncto* was barred. If, though the builder was in good faith, the materials had been stolen by someone, the old owner could either bring the *actio de tigno iniuncto* or reclaim the materials when the house came down, but not both[12]. If there was no theft, and all was in good faith, he could reclaim the materials when the house was pulled down. The Institutes, and an interpolated text in the Digest[13], give him the alternative of *de tigno iniuncto*, but most of the texts, the nature of the action, and the language of the relevant title in the Digest leave little doubt that, for classical and earlier law[14], this action never lay unless the materials had been stolen by someone. This leaves no remedy, in case of good faith, beyond the very poor one of eventual reclaim[15]. It has therefore been suggested, on the authority

1 Inst. 2. 1. 22. 2 41. 1. 30. 1. 3 *Ante*, p. 211, n. 4. 4 Girard, *Man.* 350; D. 41. 1. 65. 4. 5 41. 1. 7. 5; in 7. 1. 9. 4 Ulp. gives usufructuary the usufruct of *alluvio*, but denies him any right in *insula nata*, though he agrees that it belonged to the owner of the land. He rests his view on Pegasus but seems to give his own reason, which is that such a thing is not within the intention of the original grant. 6 The rule stated by Paul (41. 1. 65. 3) is somewhat adverse. 7 G. 2. 73; Inst. 2. 1. 30. 8 *Usucapio* of the house was not *usucapio* of the materials, 6. 1. 23. 7; 41. 1. 7. 11. De Zulueta, D. 41. 1 and 2 *ad* h. l. 9 41. 1. 7. 10; Inst. 2. 1. 29. 10 47. 3; 24. 1. 63. 11 41. 1. 7. 10. 12 24. 1. 63; 47. 3. 1. pr., 2. 13 Inst. 2. 1. 29; D. 6. 1. 23. 6. 14 It may be doubted, in view of the other texts, whether the two texts (see n. 13) which can be so interpreted really intend to extend the *actio de tigno iniuncto* to cases of good faith throughout. In 46. 3. 98. 8 Paul says (there is nothing about theft) that the *pretium* can be recovered. 15 Did the *actio de tigno iniuncto* lie against one who was not

of a text probably interpolated[1], that, as in the corresponding case in moveables, there was an *actio in factum* for the value of the materials[2].

Where the building passed into the possession of the owner of the materials before any of these proceedings were taken, the builder (owner of the land) could presumably recover only on paying for the materials, without prejudice to his liability for theft if in bad faith.

(*b*) *B* built with his own materials on *A*'s land. There are here many difficulties. There are several possible cases, but no analysis of them will provide a coherent story from the texts. There was evidently evolution and difference of opinion among the jurists themselves.

(i) *B* still in possession was in good faith, i.e. reasonable error, all through. If the owner vindicated, *B* could, by *exceptio doli*, get reimbursement of expenses[3]. If the place came down while still in *B*'s possession the materials reverted[4]. Here difficulties begin. Celsus says that if the work was what the owner would have done, he must refund either cost or value, whichever was the less[5]. This is rather favourable to him, though stated as a concession to the builder. Celsus adds that if he was too poor to do this, he might let the builder take away the material, so far as this could be done without damage. To this is added a clause, certainly of Justinian, that he might instead pay what it would be worth to the builder when removed, so that the latter might not destroy for mere malice, e.g. by erasing frescoes. Words added seem to mean that these alternatives did not apply if the owner had a customer for the house: here he must pay the added value. This *ius tollendi* has caused much difficulty. Three other texts mention it, but they look interpolated[6]. It is in conflict with the principle so often laid down that it was forbidden to pull down houses. It looks genuine here and it occurs in other branches of the law[7]. It was clearly law under Justinian[8].

himself the *iunctor*? The better view seems to be that no text need be so understood, Lenel, *E.P.* 330; Monier, *Tignum iunctum*, 166. See however De Francisci, *Azioni penali*, 48. Was the *iunctor* liable after he ceased to possess?

1 *Arg*. 6. 1. 23. 5. 2 Under Justinian the owner of the materials seems to have been allowed to bring *ad exhibendum* and *vindicatio* at once. Texts conflict (47. 3. 1. 2, 2; 6. 1. 23. 6; 41. 1. 7. 10; Inst. 2. 1. 29) and the rule, which conflicts with the XII Tables, can hardly be classical. 3 41. 1. 7. 12; 44. 4. 14; Inst. 2. 1. 30; *ius retentionis*. 4 C. 3. 32. 2. 5 6. 1. 38. 6 6. 1. 27. 5, 37; C. 3. 32. 5. 7 Pernice, *Labeo*, 2. 1. 384. 8 Celsus tells us, or is made to tell us, that "without damage" means that the premises are left no worse than they were before the matter was added. Some writers harmonise the texts by holding that, in classical law, the *ius tollendi* applied only to additions to a house, not to complete buildings; see Pernice, *cit*. 386; 3. 132. Riccobono, *Dal dir. cl. al dir. mod*. 445, holds that the Proculians gave a *ius tollendi* and *a. ad exhibendum* for what retained its identity (doors, tables, etc.) on the principles of *accessio*, that later classics denied this and Justinian gave *ius tollendi* in all cases, where no loss of value would result. It is sometimes held that the whole notion of *ius tollendi* is Byzantine. See Beseler, *Beitr*. 2. 39; 3. 132 and reff. One text says that any fruits received while the builder was *in bona*

(ii) *B*, still in possession, was in bad faith. It is not *furtum*: there is no *furtum* of land. We are told that he had no *ius retentionis*, for which the reason is assigned that he was construed as having given it[1]. And he had no *ius tollendi* in classical law, though two interpolated texts give this right[2]. The same principle would exclude any right in him if the place fell down. Presumably though he built knowingly on another's land, if he did it as an act of *gestio* for the owner, reasonably, this would be a case of *negotiorum gestio*[3].

(iii) The owner of the land has recovered possession. Here, apart from *negotiorum gestio*, the builder had no action, a rule set down to the fact that there had been no *negotium*[4]. On this point good or bad faith was immaterial, but if he had bought the land in good faith these expenses would come into account in his claim on eviction[5]. Nor had he, it seems, any *ius tollendi*, even under Justinian. If he was in good faith, since he clearly did not intend a gift, the materials reverted when the house came down[6]. If he built knowing that the land was not his, the Institutes and Digest say that it was construed as a gift and he had no such claim[7]. But the Code modifies this by saying that, whether he was in good or in bad faith, the materials reverted if the house came down, unless it appeared that the erection was *donandi animo*[8]. That is a very different proposition: in general he did not intend a gift, and the rule about *donandi animus* was a legal fiction to penalise a wrongdoer. The language of the Code suggests interpolation[9].

The texts do not consider the possible case of a building by *A* on *B*'s land with *C*'s materials[10]. If the house was still in the builder's possession it was, as between him and the owner of the materials, as if it were his own land, and, as between him and the owner of the land, as if they were his own materials. If the land was in its owner's posses-

fide are set off against the *ius retentionis*, 6. 1. 48. Justinian gives even a buyer from the *b. f. p.* a *ius retentionis* for these expenses, 10. 3. 14. 1, interp. He also gives *b. f. p.* a *condictio* if the retention has not been made, 30. 60; cp. 6. 1. 48; 12. 6. 33. Riccobono, *cit.*, 170 *sqq.*, 180.

1 *Greg. Wis.* 6. 2; Inst. 2. 1. 30; C. 8. 10. 5. 2 C. 3. 32. 5, for *impensae utiles.* Another text of Ulpian (6. 1. 37), probably interp., gives him *ius tollendi* if he acquired possession in good faith, but built after he knew the truth. 3 *Post*, § CLXXXV. 4 12. 6. 33. 5 C. 8. 44. 9. But 19. 1. 45. 1 says that as he need not have given up possession without receiving "*impensam aedificiorum*" he has no claim against his vendor. 6 C. 3. 32. 2. 7 41. 1. 7. 12; Inst. 2. 1. 30. 8 C. 3. 32. 2. 9 *Contra*, Monier, *Tignum iunctum*, 104. 10 The case occurs. The squatters in Epping Forest built huts on land not their own out of materials taken from the forest, the property of the Lord of the Manor. A builder erecting a stable in his yard built the back wall by accident or design beyond his proper boundary. In taking materials from his yard he used some which were the property of a customer. Such facts as these might give rise to difficulty in applying the rules. If the owner of the land on which the back wall is built uses it to support a roof, or attaches fruit trees to it, which of the parties is in possession of the wall?

sion, the owner of the materials was not affected by the good or bad faith of the builder, but was bound by the rule that the house might not be pulled down. His only right against the landowner was, apparently, to vindicate if the house came down. If the builder had used them in bad faith there would be *de tigno iniuncto* against him if possession is not necessary[1], as an alternative to *actio furti* and *condictio furtiva* if there had been no *vindicatio*. If the builder had used them innocently, there was no remedy against him, any more than in the case of any other *bona fide possessor* who had ceased to possess, *sine dolo malo*. But if, on handing over, he exercised his *ius retentionis* there are indications that *negotiorum gestorum utilis* would lie, for in claiming the *ius retentionis* he managed the owner's affair thinking it his[2]. If he did not claim it, and was in good faith, there was no claim against him.

LXXIX. SPECIFICATIO. Acquisition of a new thing by making it of materials wholly or partly another's. The name is medieval, and the institution had close affinities with *accessio*, with which it is entangled in the Sources[3]. The general notion is simple. Where *A* made a new thing out of material of *B*'s the Sabinians denied any change of ownership: the ownership of the materials was decisive. The Proculians held that a new thing, having come into existence, had a distinct identity and belonged to the maker[4]. But Justinian tells us that there had been many opinions and that he adopts the *media sententia* of those who had held that the *nova species* (specific thing) should belong to the maker if not reducible to its original form, but, otherwise, should still belong to the owner of the materials. This *media sententia* is not due to the compilers themselves, but it is not known to Gaius[5].

The first question is: what is a *nova species*? This is independent of the question whether it can be restored: a statuette cast out of another's bronze was a *nova species*, but being reducible, did not go to the maker[6]. A *nova species* is not defined, but from instances given modern definitions have been framed. The Romans had difficulties in some cases. Some imported the idea of irreducibility. Ears of corn, they said, could not be restored after threshing, and thus grain was a *nova species*. But the rational view prevailed, according to the Digest, though the Institutes give the other, that it was the same thing taken out of its wrappings[7]. Grapes plucked were not new things, but wine was. To kill a pig, and even to cut him into joints, does not make a *nova species*. But sausage is a *nova species*. So is an omelette: a broken egg is not. What then is

1 Not clear. 2 3. 5. 48, *post*, § CLXXXV. 3 Differentiation, *S.M.W.* 307.
4 G. 2. 79. As to influence of doctrines of conflicting philosophical schools, Sokolowski, *Philosophie in Prr.* 1. 69; résumés, Cornil, *Dr.R.* 201; De Zulueta, D. 41. 1 and 2 *ad* 41. 1. 7. 7. 5 Inst. 2. 1. 25; D. 41. 1. 7. 7. 6 *Ibid.* 7 Inst. 2. 1. 25; D. 41. 1. 7. 7 in f.

the test? The matter is discussed by Czyhlarz[1] and Windscheid[2], who cite various opinions[3]. Perhaps it is best to accept Windscheid's view that there is no juristic answer: it would rarely give difficulty in practice.

The Institutes say that if part of the material belonged to the maker of the *nova species*, this belonged to the maker[4]. If this adds anything, it must mean that here it need not be irreducible, but the distinction seems unreasonable, and the illustrations are of irreducibles. The form "*praestavit*" shews the remark to be due to the compilers.

There is difference of opinion on another requirement. Was it essential that the act of manufacture be done in good faith? No text in the *sedes materiae* suggests this. In *accessio* good faith was material only on the question of compensation. *Specificatio* has close affinity with *accessio*. Where the maker used his own and another's materials it might be difficult to say which it was. If, as some hold, it was essentially a case of *occupatio* (a point discussed below), good faith ought to have been immaterial, since it was none the less a *res nullius*. And though no text says that good faith was not necessary, the concluding words of the principal text in Gaius[5] allow of *specificatio*, where the matter was stolen, but are not conclusive, as it is not said that the maker was the thief. What the view of Gaius himself was does not appear. On the whole the better view seems to be that *bona fides* was not needed[6].

1 *Op. cit.* 248 *sqq.* 2 *Lehrbuch*, § 187. 3 Fitting (*Archiv f. c. Pr.* 48, 6) holds that the question is whether the product is of a new kind, comes under a new "*Begriff.*" C. rightly rejects this, as, if I take your vase and melt it and cast it into a new one exactly similar, it is yet a *nova species*. He, himself, holds that the test is whether the work has resulted in a new creation which did not before exist, but this seems to say only that a new thing is a new thing. Fischer says (*Bresl. Festg. für Ihering*, 2. 70, cited Windscheid, *loc. cit.*) that the labour expended on it must be economically more important than the material since the whole rule is intended as a reward for labour. Platinum worked from the form of a dipping rod to a *spatula* is unquestionably a new thing but the material is worth tenfold the labour. This view confuses *nova species* and acquisition, which are distinct points. A *nova species* is not necessarily the reward of labour. Vinegar from wine is a *nova species* and the acetic fermentation often occurs without any labour. 4 Inst. 2. 1. 25. 5 G. 2. 79. 6 The chief texts cited in favour of the view that *bona fides* was needed are the following: 13. 1. 13 (but there is no acquisition on the *media sententia*, the *condictio furtiva* would be available in any case, and the inclusion of the added value is only the usual rule against a thief. The position of Paul and his authority Fulcinius on the subject of *specificatio* is not clear); 13. 1. 14. 3 (no *nova species*, and the author is a Sabinian): 47. 2. 52. 14 (same case, the old owner has *condictio furtiva*, as he has in any case. No doubt "*soli domino competit*," but that is the old ownership. He would still have it if the thing had ceased to exist): 10. 4. 12. 3 (Paul, who may be a Sabinian on the matter. Text suspected of interpolation, Bonfante, *Corso*, 2. 2. 121 and apart from this the language shews disputes and is too wide. Windscheid, a supporter of this view, says (*Lehrb.* § 187, n. 3) that it gives no certain result); 41. 3. 4. 20 (Paul again, and it really makes against this view, for in order to give *condictio furtiva* where the thing has been made into a new *species*, he says: *verius est ut substantiam spectemus et ideo vestis furtiva erit*). For *S.M.W.* 304, *bona fides* was needed under Justinian.

What was the basis of this right of acquisition? According to a view widely held, it was *occupatio*[1]. A new thing which had no owner was "occupied" by the maker. This is supported by the language of the Digest in expressing the Proculian view: "*quia quod factum est antea nullius fuit*[2]." Further, both in the Digest and the Institutes, the case of *occupatio* is followed by the cases of *alluvio* and the like and then by this topic. Czyhlarz[3], with others, rejects this view. He says that, though the Proculian view speaks of *res nullius*, it says nothing of *occupatio*, but as the fact is given as the reason of the acquisition, the inference to *occupatio* is inevitable[4]. On any other basis it would be not the reason but the occasion. He adds that, if it were open to *occupatio*, some one else could so acquire it and the maker would not get it, and that is not so. But creation and *occupatio* occur at the same moment. There was no measurable time in which it was a *res nullius*: if the maker was not on the spot at the moment of completion, he was in possession and became owner. If he waived his right shortly before completion, no doubt, anyone could "occupy." The competing view is that the act of making sufficed: the acquisition was by *creatio*. This is held by most of those who require good faith. The distinction is not unimportant. If the acquisition rested on the fact that it was a *res nullius*, this must be equally true even if the material was the maker's. But *creatio* is an arbitrary notion on which it is possible to set limits, as Czyhlarz does, and to say that acquisition by *creatio* did not apply if the material was the maker's[5].

As to compensation we are ill informed. Gaius says that if the thing had been stolen, there was *condictio furtiva* against the thief and some others[6]. As this could not lie against an innocent maker it has been suggested without textual support that in this case there was *condictio sine causa*[7]. Another text gives *vindicatio utilis*, like that in the case of the picture, where a woman made clothes out of wool which her husband had given her[8]. But gifts between husband and wife being void, this, even if genuine, may be no more than a means of enforcing that special rule[9]. That the old owner should have no remedy seems so unfair that many writers appeal to the general notion of enrichment and *condictio*. But there is no evidence for this application. In a case of bad faith there were the *actio furti* and *condictio furtiva*, but it may be that in

1 See Czyhlarz, *cit.* 315. 2 41. 1. 7. 7. 3 *Cit.* 314 *sqq.* 4 Express reference to *occupatio* as such is unusual. We get "*occupantis fit*" and the like sometimes (41. 1. 3. pr.; 43. 12. 1. 6, etc.). Most of the texts dealing with *occupatio* do not use this word, or *occupare.* 5 Fitting, *cit.* Windscheid, *Lehrb.* § 187, n. 2, holds the singular view that it was *occupatio* in classical law but *creatio* under Justinian. It is difficult to see in *creatio,* which cannot be extended to other cases, anything but a label. 6 G. 2. 79. Perhaps only the *heredes.* 7 Witte, *Bereicherungsklage*, 329, cited Czyhlarz, *op. cit.* 380. 8 24. 1. 30; probably interpolated. 9 Girard, *Man.* 343.

cases of good faith there was no more remedy than where a *bona fide possessor* had ceased to possess, *sine dolo malo*.

Ownership of the new thing in a new person must be a new ownership. How far was it affected by rights in third persons which affected the material in the hands of the old owner? Clearly a usufruct or a pledge of the material was destroyed[1]: we have no evidence as to the position of the usufructuary in matter of compensation. He had no *condictio furtiva*, though he could sue for the theft[2]. A legacy of the material was not a legacy of the thing, but this turns not on the rules of *specificatio*, but on construction of the probable intent of the testator[3].

LXXX. *Thesauri Inventio.* This is a principle under which treasure found by anyone goes to him in whole or part under a number of conditions. Treasure means valuables that have been deposited for so long that all trace of their present ownership is lost. As to what are valuables, Paul speaks merely of *pecunia*[4]. The *C. Theodosianus* calls them *monilia*, which seems to mean precious metals and stones and the like[5]. Justinian calls them *mobilia*[6], either a mere slip or intended to widen the class: in any case it means things of very special value. Deposited seems to mean intentionally placed there, which would exclude an ornament accidentally dropped and dug up long after[7]. The purpose of the deposit is immaterial. Concealment was a common case, but a pious offering may have been on the same footing. How ancient it must be cannot be said: what was needed was that there should be no means of finding any owner[8]. It was none the less treasure because, in the deposit, the name of the depositor was found, if it could not be said who represented him to-day. Most texts speak of it as found in land[9], and none suggests a right, as treasure, to what was found in a moveable[10].

There is much controversy as to the juristic ground of the acquisition. A thing which has no traceable owner is much like one which has none, and this suggests *occupatio*. It was certainly acquisition by taking, and it can hardly be doubted that the notion of *occupatio* played some part in it. But if it is *occupatio* it is *occupatio* with special characteristics. It is confined to one person (the finder) like *specificatio*. The share that the landowner took was not acquired by *occupatio*: he acquired though he knew nothing about it. His share vested in him at once: it was not a case of

1 7. 4. 10. 5, 6; 13. 7. 18. 3. 2 47. 2. 46. 1, etc.; 13. 1. 1. 3 32. 88. pr.; many other questions arising out of *specificatio*, especially where the material was that of the maker. Czyhlarz, *cit.* 266 *sqq.* 4 41. 1. 31. 1. 5 C. Th. 10. 18. 2. 6 C. 10. 15. 1. 7 The whole point was elaborately discussed from the point of view of modern law in *Attorney General* v. *British Museum Trustees* (1903), 2 Ch. 598. 8 Bonfante, *Corso*, 2. 2. 108, notes that 41. 1. 31. 1 speaks of it as having no owner. This makes it possible to regard the rule as a specially regulated *occupatio*. But C. Th. 10. 18. 2 and C. 10. 15. 1 speak of deposit *ab ignotis dominis*. 9 Reff., Czyhlarz, *cit.* 212. 10 Some writers hold that the rule applied there.

obligatio to hand over a share to the owner[1]. It rested entirely on imperial enactment, based we are told on natural equity[2], and it seems that *occupatio* must have been present to the mind of the legislator. It seems needless to look behind that, but Czyhlarz holds that as to the finder's half it rested on *inventio*, just as in *specificatio* he makes the acquisition rest on *creatio*[3]. The landowner's half was acquired, he holds, by *accessio*[4], but as he was regarded as acquiring only at the moment of finding, it was a strange kind of *accessio*. *Accessio* rests on addition of something to a unit of property: its basis is merger or absorption. But this acquisition occurred at, and by the act of, separation. As to what is finding, the general effect of the texts is that the acquirer was not the person who first saw it, but he who first got effective control[5], which recalls *occupatio*. It does not seem necessary that he should intend to acquire it, which differs from the rule in that case[6].

Justinian's history begins with Hadrian, and the earlier story is uncertain[7]. One text in the Digest[8] suggests that in the Republic treasure belonged to the owner of the land, not as treasure, but as part of the land, and a passage in Plautus[9] makes in the same direction, but other views are held. A story about Nero is supposed to shew that in principle all treasure belonged to the *Fiscus*, but it proves nothing[10], though such a rule would be quite in accordance with the financial policy of the time. Finally, we are told that the Emperor Nerva decreed that treasure should in all cases go to the owner of the land[11].

Hadrian legislated comprehensively. He provided[12] that if a man found treasure on his own land it was his. So too if he found it, by chance, on *solum sacrum* or *religiosum*. If he found it on another's land, by chance, he shared with the owner, with Caesar if the land were Caesar's. Justinian continues that it is consistent with this that if he found it on land of a city or the *fiscus*, half should go to these. We learn elsewhere that if the finding was the result of search the finder had no right, but the owner of the land took all[13]; what happened if the land had no owner

1 41. 1. 63. pr., Inst. 2. 1. 39. Czyhlarz, *cit.* 221. 2 Inst. 2. 1. 39. 3 These may be reasons which led to the introduction of the rule, but there seems little purpose in erecting them into juristic bases apart from evidence (which is lacking) that the Romans so conceived the matter, and that they can be utilised to explain any other institution. 4 *Loc. cit.* 5 Czyhlarz, *cit.* 229. 6 The placing of this method under those *iure naturali*, though it rests on enactment, is justified by the repeated allusion to *naturalis aequitas* (C. Th. 10. 18. 2. 1; Inst. 2. 1. 39) coupled with the fact that it is not part of the ancient formal law. 7 Rotondi, *Scr. Giur.* 3. 344. 8 41. 2. 3. 3. 9 Plautus, *Trin.* 150 (Goetz and Schoell), Girard, *Man.* 341. 10 Sueton. *Nero*, 31; Tacit. *Ann.* 16. 1. The story involves assignment of the treasure to a known past owner, whose rights had vested in the Roman State. The present owner was therefore known. Bonfante shews (*Mél. Girard*, 1. 123) that the claim of the *fiscus* is not due to Nero, but is older, and suggests that the finder's half is a bribe to informers. 11 Zonaras, 440, cited Gothofredus *ad* C. Th. 10. 18. 1. 12 Inst. 2. 1. 39. 13 C. 10. 15. 1. 3.

is not clear[1]. M. Aurelius and Verus provided that where treasure was found on public or religious or Caesar's land, or *in monumentis*, half should go to the *fiscus*, half to the finder, provided he duly reported it, otherwise all to the *fiscus*. But there was no duty to report where the *fiscus* would not have any claim[2].

Constantine[3] lays down a rule like that of M. Aurelius and Verus, but does not say anything about the place of discovery. Presumably he means any land in respect of discovery on which the *fiscus* had a claim under existing legislation. Late in the fourth century there was further legislation apparently lessening the rights both of the *fiscus* and of the landowner, but Justinian does not preserve this[4].

A constitution of A.D. 480[5] (Leo), dealing only with private lands, allows a finder to keep all he finds on his own lands, even on search, provided he used no sacrifices or forbidden arts, and a half of what he finds, by chance, on another's land. What he finds there on search goes wholly to the landowner. This agrees with Hadrian's rule, stated in the Institutes, so that, as to private lands, Justinian's rule is that of Hadrian. But as to what may be loosely called public land, he preserves both Hadrian's rule and that of M. Aurelius and Verus[6], and they do not agree. Where the discovery is on land which has no owner, Hadrian gives all to the finder, while the other rule gives half to the *fiscus*, and where it is on land belonging to cities (*publica loca*) Hadrian gives half to the city, as to other owners, while the other rule suppresses the right of the city and gives half to the *fiscus*[7].

A usufructuary was not owner, and thus if he found treasure on the land he got only the finder's half and had not even a usufruct in the other half[8]. A pledgee in possession had only the finder's half. But where he had, before the finding, taken the proceedings established by Severus

1 As to *casus fortuitus*, Guarneri-Citati, *Misc. Eseg.* 8. 2 49. 14. 3. 11. An enactment of Alexander Severus (*vita Alexandri*, 46), hardly intelligible as reported, seems to have benefited the finder at the expense of the *fisc*. At some time in the third century this was reversed and towards the end of the century it was restored: the finder kept the treasure (*Arg.* C. Th. 10. 18. 1, Gothof.). These vague literary allusions do not tell us whether he took it all, or whether the rights of private landowners were affected. 3 C. Th. 10. 18. 1. Not preserved by Justinian. 4 C. Th. 10. 18. 2, 3. The owner has only a quarter, and apparently the *fiscus* has no claim where treasure is found by chance on fiscal lands. 5 C. 10. 15. 1. 6 49. 14. 3. 10; Inst. 2. 1. 39. 7 One account of Hadrian's legislation in a non-legal work (*Vita Hadriani*, 18) says that if treasure is found in any public place (which seems by the context to mean any place not privately owned) half goes to the *Fiscus*, i.e. the owner's half, agreeing on this point with the rule of M. Aurelius and Verus, but not with the Institutes. But the account is inaccurate: it speaks of a duty in the finder to give a share to the landowner, but the share vests in the landowner by the finding. In systems of law which have had to apply these rules in practice, it seems to have been generally held that the rule of M. Aurelius and Verus, being the later, must be applied. 8 *Arg.* 41. 1. 63. 3.

for having the property declared his (foreclosure)[1], the rule was that if the property had been assigned to him, and the time within which the debtor could get the foreclosure set aside had elapsed, he was owner and took the whole. If it was after he had begun to hold as owner, but while the debtor might still redeem, he would have the finder's half if the debtor ultimately did redeem, otherwise the whole[2].

LXXXI. Acquisition of fruits by one not owner of the thing. These cases fall into two groups. In one, acquisition was by gaining actual control of the fruits, *fructuum perceptio*. In the other it was by separation of them from the fruit-bearing thing, no matter by whom effected, *fructuum separatio*. The probable explanation of the distinction is that in the cases of *perceptio* (*conductor* and usufructuary) the person who was to acquire had not *possessio* of the thing itself, as he had in the cases of *separatio* (*emphyteuta* and *bona fide possessor*). We are not informed as to *precario tenens*.

Fructuum perceptio. The *conductor*. The moment at which fruits were "gathered" was a question of fact: reaping without stacking was enough[3]. The principle was that acquisition rested on assent of the *dominus*[4]. By their separation, which first gave them a separate existence, they vested in the owner of the soil. He allowed the tenant to take them—in effect *traditio brevi manu*[5]. As assent was the essence of the matter, if the landlord revoked his assent, the property would not vest in the tenant[6], though the revocation might be a breach of contract, e.g. where the land was let for a certain time. It was the consent of the person entitled which was material, so that, if the land was sold, the new owner must assent, either tacitly or by an express *relocatio*[7]. The assent must have existed at the time of the *perceptio*, which leads to the conclusion that if the *locator* became insane, or died, there could be no such acquisition[8]. The texts do not say or deny this: convenience seems to require that, where the tenancy continued, the assent should be held to continue till there was someone who could give or revoke it[9].

As to what are fruits for this purpose, there is no great difficulty in the case of land: they would be the ordinary agricultural produce[10]. If the tenant sublet the land the rent was his: there was no question of *perceptio*[11]. Where slaves were hired there would usually be no question. Their children were not *fructus*[12]. If the hirer sublet, any money he

1 *Post*, § CLXVII. 2 41. 1. 63. 4. 3 7. 4. 13. 4 47. 2. 62. 8. 5 *Post*, § LXXXIII. 6 39. 5. 6. 7 *Arg*. 19. 2. 32. 8 So Czyhlarz, *cit*. 462. 9 Other cases in which the principle of continuance of assent is applied, and acquisition based on a sort of *traditio brevi manu*, e.g. digging from a chalkpit, 39. 5. 6. 10 There may be variations, a question of fact in each case. There may be agreement that the tenant will not remove straw, or some of the crop may be reserved as rent, 47. 2. 83. 1; 19. 2. 19. 3. 11 19. 2. 7 Ownership will depend on delivery. 12 6. 1. 16. pr.; 7. 1. 68. Disputes.

received was his, but was not *fructus*, and if the slave sublet himself and received the wage, it may be that a kind of *fructuum perceptio* would apply[1].

Usufructuary. He too acquired only by *perceptio*[2], but the principle is different. Here the right rested on his *ius*, not on the assent of the owner, and there was no question of *traditio brevi manu*. If some one else separated and carried off the fruits, the fructuary, not being owner, could not vindicate or bring *condictio furtiva*[3].

What amounted to *perceptio* was a question of fact: it was some act amounting to exercise of the right of ownership. Gathering them is the typical case[4]. It is a disputed question whether any such act was needed in the case of young of animals[5].

As to what were fruits, this is matter for the law of usufruct: a few words here will suffice. The young of animals were fruits: the children of *ancillae* were not[6]. One ordinarily thinks of fruits as taken in kind, and if the fructuary sold the crops, in the land, these still were the fruits and would or would not be available for the buyer according as they were or were not *percepti* when the usufruct ended. But if he leased the usufruct, we get what are sometimes called *fructus civiles*, the rent, and there were rules, which have nothing to do with *fructuum perceptio*. If all the crops of the year had been gathered, the fructuary took all the rent, though the year might not have ended. If none, then he got nothing: if part, then proportionately[7]. If it was a slave whom he had let out on hire, he was entitled to the hire for so many days as had expired when the usufruct ended[8]. This has nothing to do with acquisition of ownership. The money was due under contract, and if he

1 If subletting was forbidden in the original agreement the crops would not go to the subtenant, and any *fructus civiles* through the slave would go to his owner, *Arg.* C. 4. 65. 6.

2 7. 4. 13; Inst. 2. 1. 36. Buckland, *L.Q.R.* 1927, 335, on the view of Pampaloni, *Bull.* 1910, 135, that in classical law usufructuary acquired by *separatio*.

3 7. 1. 12. 5; 13. 1. 1. He had *actio furti* (7. 1. 12. 5): what was stolen was part of the thing in usufruct. Why *perceptio* is needed is disputed. What the rule expresses is a need for reduction into possession, as fructuary does not possess, but this does not seem to be logically required, as there is no question of assent or *traditio*. Girard (*Man.* 345) treats it as a sort of *occupatio*, but as, from *separatio* to *perceptio*, it is the property of the *dominus* (7. 1. 12. 5), not a *res nullius*, it is not easy to apply this notion. Czyhlarz (*op. cit.* 423) holds that as the right rests on his *ius*, it accrues only by an exercise of it, but this would be equally true of *emphyteuta* or of owner himself. The point does not seem to be proved by shewing that *ususfructus in fruendo consistit* (7. 3. 1. pr.). It is not a usufruct that he is acquiring.

4 Reaping is enough, 7. 4. 13.

5 The material texts seem to be Inst. 2. 1. 37 and the slightly different rendering in 22. 1. 28 which puts *bona fide possessor* and usufructuary together as acquiring "*statim.*" Czyhlarz holds that no act is necessary (p. 425); *contra*, Girard, *Man.* 345.

6 7. 1. 68; P. 3. 6. 19.

7 7. 1. 58. pr.

8 7. 1. 25. 2, 26; 45. 3. 18. 3. The slave made the contract: it was acquired *pro rata* by fructuary and *dominus*. If fructuary had made it, the right, so far as he was concerned, would be the same. Apart from *relocatio*, nothing would vest in the *dominus*.

or his *heres* received more than he ought, it was none the less acquired, by *traditio*, not by *perceptio*, and the rights of those to whom it ought to go must be enforced by *actio in personam*.

The rule that young were fruits and went to the fructuary was modified in a common case. Where a usufruct was of a *universitas*, e.g. a flock, the fructuary must keep up its numbers, so as to be able to hand over the flock undiminished at the expiry of the usufruct. He must replace those which died, from the young or otherwise—the usual course was to do it from the young[1]. This duty, *summittere*, might be construed in either of two ways. It might be looked at as matter of obligation: the young were his: if he did not use them to replace the missing, this was merely a breach of his duty as a usufructuary, against which the owner normally held security[2]. This view is taken in one text, which says that if there was a case for *summissio*, the lambs from which the substitutes were to be taken were the fructuary's, but when he had effected the *summissio*, the lambs concerned ceased to be his and vested in the *dominus*[3]. This may be seen as a *traditio*, the *summissio* being some act of incorporation into the flock. But according to another rule elsewhere declared to be correct, if there was a shortage, and there were lambs, the ownership of these lambs was in suspense till it was certain which were *summissi*. The act would determine retrospectively the ownership of these and of the others[4]. The rule, which does not look convenient, gives the duty of *summissio* a real and not merely obligatory effect. There was however a limitation. A lamb born before the vacancy occurred was not subject to the rule: it was only those born after of which the ownership was in suspense[5].

If the fructuary gathered fruits before they ought to be gathered (some fruits ought to be gathered unripe) they were none the less fruits and were his[6]. But this was not acting like a *bonus paterfamilias*: presumably, if the usufruct ended before the proper time of plucking, the owner would have a claim, though no text says this[7].

LXXXII. *Fructuum separatio. Emphyteuta.* Of this case we are merely told that a holder of *agri vectigales*, which in Justinian's time is understood to cover *emphyteusis*[8], acquired fruits by *separatio*[9]. The acquisition rested on his *ius*, but here he had possession, and was much like an owner, since he commonly held in perpetuity[10].

1 P. 3. 6. 20; D. 7. 1. 68. 2, 69. Those which die are thus at the risk of the fructuary and become his property, though of course they are not fruits, *ib.* 7. 1. 18. 2 *Post*, § xcv. 3 7. 1. 69. 4 7. 1. 70. 1. 5 7. 1. 70. 4. If none are born afterwards the gaps will of course have to be filled up either from earlier lambs or from outside sources. 6 7. 1. 48. 1. Roby, *De Usufructu*, 216. 7 See 7. 1. 62. 8 Czyhlarz, *cit.* 613. *Emphyteusis, post*, § xcvii. 9 22. 1. 25. 1 *fin.* 10 And thus, like owner, acquires fruits as soon as they come into existence separately. Though possession and no possession

Bona fide possessor. This is the most important and most discussed case. The rule is simple: a *bona fide possessor* of property became entitled to fruits, by *separatio*, by whomsoever effected[1]. Apart from theory, a good reason why, if he was to have the fruits, he should have them by *separatio*, is that, the owner not being known, any other rule would benefit a malefactor who knew that the *possessor* was not owner. It is not obvious why he should have them at all, and it was formerly held that he acquired not *dominium* but usucapion possession, the same "right" in fact that he had in the thing itself. But the texts are clear[2], and it has been sought to make this a legal consequence, on the view that he was a kind of bonitary owner and took the fruits accordingly[3]. No text so states the matter or equalises him with bonitary owner. His right to fruits was of a different kind[4]; he acquired in certain events, but he could not complain if the owner prevented him from having them. And he might have them where he could not usucapt, and thus would not have the *actio Publiciana*, e.g. where the *res* was incapable of being usucapted[5]. According to the Institutes[6]: the fruits went to him because they were the result of his labour. This is true in general, though not of those which were maturing when his possession began or of those, *fructus naturales*, grass as opposed to corn, which need little cultivation, and there is indeed a text of Pomponius which limits the acquisition to those fruits which were the result of labour[7]. That view did not prevail, but its existence is confirmation of this opinion, as to the origin of the rule[8].

is probably the deciding point in the distinction, this is not logically pushed home. The *dominus* owns the fruits, even though at the moment not in possession, unless there is some adverse claim such as that of a *bona fide possessor*.

1 41. 1. 48. One who receives a *res mancipi* from a woman without tutor's *auctoritas* is a *b. f. p.* as she can alienate possession without *auctoritas*. Vat. Fr. 1. 2 E.g. Inst. 2. 1. 35, etc. 3 Brinz, *B. F. Possessio*, 1. 548, *cit.* Czyhlarz, *op. cit.* 506. 4 Czyhlarz, *ib.* 5 *Post*, § LXXXVII; 41. 1. 48. 1. 6 Inst. 2. 1. 35. 7 22. 1. 45; narrower interpretation, Pernice, *Labeo*, 2. 1. 358, n. 2; Bonfante, *Corso*, 2. 2. 130. 8 Ferrini (*Bull.* 1889, 218) *cit.* Girard, *Man.* 346, who adds another possible explanation. The possessor has naturally been living as if these things were among his resources, and it would be a hardship to make him account for them. This is robbing Peter to pay Paul, and where a similar point arose in connexion with *b. f. possessio* of a *hereditas*, this view was expressly rejected. 5. 3. 25. 12. Czyhlarz (*loc. cit.*) cites other utilitarian explanations. For Ihering (*Jahrb.* 12. 320) it is with a view to trade: men can buy fruits with the same confidence that their title will not be disturbed as they feel when they buy manufactured goods. It is pointed out by Czyhlarz that this is inconsistent with the emphasis laid on good faith. From the point of view of the purchaser, whom, on this view, the rule is to protect, the vendor's state of mind is immaterial. In modern systems, specially protected market purchases do not depend in general on the good faith of the vendor. It has also been said that it is to protect the possessor who has sold the fruits in good faith, and there are texts which limit his acquisition to *fructus consumpti*. But classical law gave him all, and it is objected by Czyhlarz that such a rule is too wide for the purpose. But a rule making his ownership begin only at the moment when it also ceased is artificial;

Fructus properly so called are the natural, and, usually, periodic products of the thing. But property can give other profits, sometimes described as *fructus civiles*, already mentioned in connexion with usufruct. The same questions arise here. If the *bona fide possessor* let the land, or e.g. a horse, and received hire, there was no question of *fructuum separatio*: if he received the rents it was by way of *traditio*. They were his, and he was under no obligation to account for them: the owner was entitled, in general, to what he would have had if the thing had been handed over at the moment of joinder of issue[1]. These points and others of a similar type arose especially in the case of *bona fide possessio* of a slave and will be considered later[2].

One who took possession in good faith would commonly acquire the thing by *usucapio*, even though he learnt that he was not entitled[3]. The question arises whether he still acquired the *fructus* received after he knew that he was not entitled. Julian held that he did, not only *fructus* properly so called, but also acquisitions *ex re et operis* of a slave so possessed[4]. Ulpian denied this, with special reference to the latter case[5], and Paul, citing Pomponius, denied it for *fructus*[6]. This was therefore, presumably, the doctrine of later law[7].

The acquisition of fruits is complicated by another point. Some texts speak of the acquisition to the *bona fide possessor* as definitive: they were his and there the matter ended[8]. Others say that though they were his he must account for them to the *dominus*, so far as they were unconsumed, or, what means the same thing, that "*fructus consumptos suos facit*[9]." Strictly it is absurd to say they became his by ceasing to exist: the meaning is that the economic advantage was his only on consumption, as, till then, he might be called on to account for them. This did not create an exception to the rule of acquisition, but an obligation to restore those still existing. Some of the texts which mention this duty of restoration have clearly been altered, and thus it has long been held that the rule was not classical, but it was still supposed to be

indeed the whole conception is artificial and there is no textual evidence in its favour, for classical law, in which the principle of the rule must be sought. As to a later view of Ihoring, Cuyhlarz, *cit.* 509.

1 6. 1. 20. 2 *Post*, § XCIX. On *fructus* generally, Bonfante, *Corso*, 2. 1. ch. 7; Herzen, *Mél. Girard*, 1. 523 (casual profits). 3 *Post*, § LXXXVII. 4 22. 1. 25. 2. He speaks only of "*emptor.*" 5 41. 1. 23. 1. 6 41. 1. 48. 1. 7 It gives however a strange result. If the knowledge supervened soon after the taking, and the period of *usucapio* elapsed, the old owner has no claim to the property but is entitled to compensation in respect of fruits accrued after the date at which the possessor knew he was not entitled. This does not look practical. It would presumably be a *condictio*, and the plaintiff would have to prove the date of supervening knowledge. 8 22. 1. 25; 22. 1. 28, etc. 9 41. 1. 40; 41. 3. 4. 19, etc. These are the texts which led to the old view, already mentioned, according to which there was no real acquisition of *fructus*, but only *bona fide possessio* with a resulting right of *usucapio*.

not much later, since an enactment of Diocletian[1], in the Code, which has no sign of alteration, states it as settled law. But it has been shewn[2] that an enactment of 369, in the Theodosian Code, explicitly gives *bona fide possessor* all fruits received before *litis contestatio*, in the *vindicatio* by the owner[3], and that a text in the Digest states the same doctrine[4]. Thus the rule requiring restoration of unconsumed fruits was very late, possibly as late as Justinian[5]. It may be that it was an extension to *rei vindicatio* of a rule already existing in the *hereditatis petitio*[6].

The question then arises: what is *consumptio*? If the corn was eaten, that was of course *consumptio*. But, if it was sold, was the price the fruits in a new form or was sale *consumptio*? The question is not answered[7]. The little evidence is in favour of the view that sale was *consumptio*, and that even under Justinian the owner could not claim the proceeds[8]. Any other view leads indeed to inextricable difficulties, since the fate of the price would have to be investigated[9]. If the possessor had ceased to possess in such a way that he was no longer liable for the thing[10], could he be sued under Justinian for fruits still in his possession? The texts usually contemplate restitution as enforced in the *vindicatio rei*[11], but there would probably be a *condictio sine causa*.

LXXXIII. *Traditio*. The only *iure naturali* mode, clearly derivative and voluntary. It is described as the proper method of transfer for *res nec mancipi*[12], but as it is assigned to the *ius naturale* or *gentium* by the texts[13], it is sometimes said that it did not give civil ownership, even in *res nec mancipi*, till the recognition of *ius gentium*. On the question how, if at all, civil ownership was acquired in such things in early days various answers are given[14].

1 C. 3. 32. 22. 2 Alibrandi, *cit.* Herzen, *Mél. Girard*, 1. 523; see also Czyhlarz, *cit.* 559 *sqq.* 3 C. Th. 4. 18. 1. 4 6. 1. 48. 5 Albertario (*Bull.* 1913, 250 *sqq.*) treats the new rule as an expression of Justinian's tendency to legislate against causeless enrichment. 6 *Post*, § cx. It is generally held that under the *sc. Iuventianum* the *bona fide possessor* of a *hereditas* had to restore all existing fruits. It has however recently been maintained by Albertario (*cit.* p. 275) that in this case also the *possessor* was not bound in classical law to restore fruits received before *litis contestatio*. See also Bonfante, *Corso*, 2. 2. 131. 7 This itself is evidence that the rule of restitution did not exist in classical law. 8 Czyhlarz, *cit.* 565. 9 Texts on *hereditatis petitio* face a similar difficulty, but do not surmount it satisfactorily, 5. 3. 23 and 25. See, however, Bonfante, *Corso*, 2. 2. 129. 10 *Post*, § xci. 11 E.g., C. 3. 32. 22; Inst. 2. 1. 35. 12 G. 2. 19; Ulp. 19. 7. 13 G. 2. 65; Inst. 2. 1. 40; D. 41. 1. 9. 3. 14 *Cessio in iure* has been suggested (so Poste, *Gaius*, ed. 2). But this, more formal than *mancipatio*, cannot have been applied to small matters. Nor is there evidence of its extreme antiquity as a mode of conveyance. It is also said that there was no civil ownership, but such things were vindicated in a form without the words: "*ex iure Quiritium.*" This is not evidenced. On another view the only protection was the law of theft, this being then wide enough to cover the case of one who refused to return a thing when it was shewn that he had no right to it (Poste, *Gaius*, ed. Whittuck, 137; Muirhead, *Roman Law*, § 10). This is the primitive state of things in many systems, but it belongs to a stage earlier than any possible date for the recognition of *ius gentium* in Rome. Clark, *Hist. of Rom. Law*, iii. p. 547.

Traditio was transfer of ownership by transfer of the thing itself[1]. In general it was transfer of possession, but there were cases in which the ownership passed though the transferee had not yet technically acquired possession. Thus a man acquired ownership of a thing given to his slave for him, at once, though he did not possess till he knew the fact[2]. Where, in later law, the acquisition was through an *extraneus*[3], the texts presuppose either authorisation or knowledge[4].

Since *traditio* was, in effect, the giving of control, it might take other forms than that of simple delivery, e.g. putting the thing in the transferee's house or a place indicated by him, or handing it to his nominee[5]. *Traditio longa manu* was pointing out the thing to the transferee, and authorising him to take it, in such conditions that it was in his immediate power to do so[6]. *Traditio brevi manu* was effected by a declaration allowing the transferee to hold as his own a thing which was already in his control[7]. *Constitutum possessorium* was the converse of this. Where the vendor was, as part of the bargain, to retain the thing, e.g. as a hirer, it might be agreed that in future he was to hold it as a mere *detentor*, avoiding the absurdity of handing the thing over and taking it back again[8]. When, in the fourth century, rules were set up requiring publicity in transfer of land[9] and actual *traditio* in all donations of land whether there was *mancipatio* or not[10], this was evaded by use of a similar device. A document was prepared declaring the conveyance and reserving for the transferor a brief usufruct. At the expiry of this, unrestricted ownership had passed with no actual delivery. A prohibition of this in 415 was repealed two years later[11] and this statute appears in Justinian's Code with its authorisation extended to sales[12], and *mancipatio* being now gone this meant that *traditio* could be effected by a document containing such a reservation. Approximate delivery was giving the transferee the means of control, e.g. the key of the place where the thing was. This has been called symbolic delivery, but the key was more than a symbol: it was the actual means of control. It was not a real means of control, if the act was in one place and the store in another, and some texts say that it must be on the spot[13]. The common element in all these cases was the actual putting of the transferee in control of the thing.

Mere delivery may mean many things: there was no transfer of *dominium* unless there was on both sides the intent that it should have

1 Delivery of the thing by one who had only an undivided share was delivery of his share, 21. 2. 64. 4. 2 Inst. 2. 9. 3; *ante*, § LXXIII. 3 *Post*, § XCIX. 4 *Ib.* 5 41. 2. 1. 21. 6 *Ib.* 7 41. 1. 9. 5; *Post*, § CLXII. 8 41. 2. 18. pr. Schulz, *Einführung*, 73 holds that the institution is not classical. See, however, Buckland, *R.H.* 1925, 355. 9 *Post*, p. 232. 10 *Post*, § LXXXVI. 11 C. Th. 8. 12. 8 and 9. 12 C. 8. 53. 28; Collinet, *Ét. Hist.* 1. 242. 13 18. 1. 74; 41. 1. 9. 6; Inst. 2. 1. 45; *post*, p. 232, n. 1.

that effect[1]. This might arise at a different time from that of delivery, as in the case of *traditio brevi manu*. Intent being a mental matter, a *furiosus* could neither make nor take *traditio*[2], and there could be no acquisition by *traditio* either by or to an insane slave[3].

There must be *iusta causa*[4]. This however is not a requirement independent of intent: it is the motive or evidence which accounts for the intent. It is the external fact shewing the existence of the intent. To describe *iusta causa* as the primary notion, and as covering the conception of intent is to reverse the order of significance. What was material was intent: the *causa* was the only evidence of it which was wanted or indeed could ordinarily be had. Hence a putative or imaginary *iusta causa* was enough. If the parties thought the thing was due on a sale, and so made *traditio*, this was valid: ownership passed, though there was no sale and the value could be recovered by *condictio indebiti*[5]. The belief accounted for, and indicated, intent to transfer ownership. So too if one handed over the thing as a gift, the other taking it under the impression that he was to give something in return, the *traditio* was valid, though there was no real transaction at all[6]. Ulpian indeed expresses a contrary view where the parties had different *causae* in view[7]. He regards it as material that the *iusta causa*, considered as the basis, should really exist, whereas, on the view which prevailed, it was just as good evidence of intent, whether it really existed or not[8].

Intent to transfer ownership being enough, the question arises what happened if, while *A* did in fact intend to transfer ownership to *C*, and was acting as representative of *B*, the state of facts was such that the alienation if valid would transfer the ownership of *A* and not of *B*.

1 For Bonfante, *Corso*, 2. 2. 174, what is required is intent to give and receive legal *possessio*, the actual control. This avoids the difficulties of 22. 6. 9. 4. But pledge transfers possession. Full discussion of the necessary intent, G. Segrè, *Scr. Giur.* 1. 222 *sqq.*, who regards it as directed to the practical, not the juridical, effect. (So Betti, *Ist.* 1. 287.) It may be doubted whether the jurists would have been unanimous in any precise analysis.
2 G. 3. 106.
3 41. 2. 1. 9, 10. No doubt if the slave were merely a messenger his insanity would be immaterial.
4 G. 2. 20; Ulp. 19. 7. Fitting, *Sciens indebitum accipere*, 51.
5 41. 1. 36.
6 *Ib.* If *A* hands *B* a book and a guinea, intending a gift and *B* takes them as a loan, the ownership of the guinea passes, since in loan of money the property passes, and thus *B* intended to acquire. But that in the book does not, for in such loans ownership does not pass, and thus *B* did not intend to acquire. So if the error was the other way, but there would be a *condictio* for the money.
7 12. 1. 18. pr.; 41. 1. 36. Recent writers, holding that *traditio*, as a "causal" transaction, depends for its validity on the concurrent acceptance by both parties of a certain *causa* as its basis, consider Ulpian's view classical, the other interpolated. Beseler, *Beitr.* 3. 56; Siber, *R.R.* 2. 74; Betti, *St. Bonfante*, 1. 305; De Francisci, *Trasferim.* 202; Monier, *St. Bonfante*, 3. 219; Ehrhardt, *Iusta causa traditionis*. There are wide differences in the reconstructions and the reasonings.
8 Even if the transaction were not merely void or non-existent, but for an illegal purpose. If *A* gives *B* money to commit a crime, the ownership passes. D. 12. 5 *passim*. Not if the act of transfer itself is forbidden. 24. 1. 3. 10.

For instance, *B* authorised *A* to transfer a thing for him: *A* delivered it: it was in fact *A*'s. Did ownership pass? A *tutor* delivered, thinking it the ward's, what was really his own. It is said by Ulpian and Paul, citing Pomponius, that on such facts the ownership did not pass[1]. The contradiction in a text attributed to Marcellus may be only apparent[2], but Africanus seems to declare such an alienation valid[3].

There must be intent to transfer ownership in the actual thing handed over. If our respective agents had agreed for the sale of a certain thing, and we met and I handed over to you a thing which we wrongly supposed to be what was sold, the ownership passed: it was a case of putative *causa*. But it is different if there was error as to the identity of what was delivered. Where *A* agreed to sell Stichus to *B* and by mistake delivered Eros, if this was in the wrong belief that he had sold Eros, the *traditio* was good. But if *A* thought Eros was Stichus, it would appear to be bad. But on these questions the texts are not clear[4]. There might be *traditio* to an *incerta persona*, e.g. coins thrown to a mob[5].

A question arises on the effect of error as to the person to whom the *traditio* is made[6], and we have a difficult series of texts. Some say that knowingly to receive an *indebitum* is theft[7]: presumably the *traditio* is void. Others say that if money is paid to a *falsus creditor* or *procurator*, by way of *solutio*, *donatio* or loan, this is theft, nothing being said to shew that the fraud must amount to personation[8]. Others say that this is so only if the *procurator* (etc.) pretends to be a specific person who is a *procurator*[9]. In other cases the ownership passes and the remedies are different. If I, in good faith, pay to one who knows that his authority is withdrawn, this is *furtum*, but for Ulpian I am released, and the theft is against the employer, while Africanus says I am not released and the

1 41. 1. 35; 18. 1. 15. 2; cf. 12. 4. 3. 8. 2 17. 1. 49. If acting as *procurator* for *A*, *B* sells and delivers what is in fact his own, he cannot afterwards vindicate. The most generally accepted view is that the rule is as stated by Paul and Ulpian. It turns, not on error, but on the fact that a person, acting under authority to transfer the property of *A*, cannot transfer the property of *B* and that this is not less true if he himself is *B*. If he knew the facts, he would not be acting under the authority and ownership would pass. Marcellus does not say that ownership passes, but that the selling *procurator*, whose property it in fact was, cannot vindicate it. The point is that in contract there was no agency. In conveyance one could act for another, but his contract was his own, and therefore bound him personally. He cannot recover the thing in defiance of his own obligation to deliver it under his contract of sale, and therefore the *vindicatio* will be refused, no doubt by an *exceptio rei venditae et traditae*. If in handing it over he had not been under any such contractual liability he could have recovered it by *vindicatio*. But the text has been altered. Schulz, *Z.S.S.* 1917, 137 *sqq.* 3 12. 1. 41 *med.* See Ulp., D. 12. 4. 3. 8 *fin.*, perhaps interp. Cf. 22. 6. 8. 4 See 41. 2. 34. pr. 5 41. 1. 9. 7; Inst. 2. 1. 46. We have seen that *derelictio* was sometimes explained in the same way. 6 For the case of a thing handed to *procurator* for principal and taken for himself and similar cases, *ante*, p. 201. 7 13. 1. 18; 47. 2. 43. 2. 8 12. 4. 14; 47. 2. 43. pr., 44. pr., 76. 9 47. 2. 43. 1, 43. 3, 52. 11, 52. 21, 67. 4, 81. 6.

theft is against me[1]. If I give you money to pay or donate in my name and you do it in your own, this is theft against me and ownership does not pass[2]. Some of the conflict is only apparent and reflects differences in the facts, suppressed in the text. Some is due to differing conceptions of *furtum* and of the effect of error. That between Ulpian and Africanus may reflect growing definiteness on both points, and this appears in the doctrine of most of the texts that if the fraud did not amount to personation, there was no *furtum* in the taking (though there might be in the ultimate disposal) and the ownership passed[3]. These texts deal only with cases of bad faith—most of them are in connexion with *furtum*. And as, in *traditio*, the only point in which bad faith could be material would be *causa*, it is usual to refer these texts to *causa*[4]. But when we remember that error of identity in subject matter vitiated a transaction[5], it is a fair assumption that material error in the person has the same effect, which would be the same if the *falsus procurator* was in good faith, and that the texts are not concerned with *causa*, but lay down, for later classical law, a rule that material error as to the identity of the other party vitiates a *traditio*.

As *traditio* was informal, not an *actus legitimus*, it might be subject to condition and *dies*[6], and the ownership would not pass till the condition was satisfied, or the day arrived. Under Justinian the death of the transferor *pendente condicione* did not affect the transaction, but it may be that in classical law the transfer was void[7].

If the *traditio* was on a sale, ownership did not, at least in later law, pass on delivery, unless the price was paid or credit agreed on, or security given[8].

1 46. 3. 18, 38. 1. 2 39. 5. 25; 46. 3. 17; 47. 2. 56. 16. 3 See on these texts Buckland, *Tijdschr.* 1930, 132 *sqq.* 4 Bonfante, *Corso*, 2. 2. 182, who accepts the view that any bad faith vitiated the *causa* and rejects the texts restricting this to personation but also treats the matter as arising only in *solutio*, while the texts shew it as arising also in *donatio* and loan, where the *causa* is not so easy to handle. F. Fitting, *Sciens indebitum accipere*, applies it to *causa* and holds the conflicts to mean that for some jurists *voluntas* was sufficient *causa*, but does not consider what is meant by *causa*, or the relevance of error. 5 Inst. 3. 19. 23; D. 45. 1. 137. 1. 6 41. 2. 38. 1. Not, in cl. law, what are called resolutive conditions, under which the *dominium* was to revert in certain events, *ante*, p. 188. 7 23. 3. 9. 1; 39. 5. 2. 5, both interp. Bonfante, *Corso*, 6. 153. The same rule would not necessarily apply to obligations, *post*, § CXLVIII. 8 Inst. 2. 1. 41; D. 18. 1. 19, 53; C. 4. 54. 3. It does not seem that part payment passed ownership *pro rata*. For Pringsheim, *Kauf mit fremdem Geld*; *Z.S.S.* 1914, 328, and *Z.S.S.* 1930, 333, reply to critics, payment was made a condition in post-classical times under Greek influence. It is irreconcilable with G. 2. 19, 20. Justinian put surety and credit on a level with payment. The D. has inconsistent texts: those asserting the rule he thinks interpolated. (It is found in the *Interpretatio* of P. Sent. 2. 17. 14.) This view is accepted by Mitteis (*ib.* 1916, 369); Jörs, *R.R.* 87 (who calls it Byzantine); Perozzi, *Ist.* 1. 675; Bonfante, *Scr. Giur.* 2. 600; *Corso*, 2. 2. 144; Siber, *R.R.* 2. 76. Rejected by Appleton, *R.H.* 1928, 14 *sqq.*, 173 *sqq.*; Boyer, *Rech. hist. sur la résolution des contrats*; Cuq, *Man.* 275; Collinet-Giffard, 328. Not adopted by Girard, *Man.* 319; Cornil, *Dr.R.* 198. In view

This rule is declared to rest on the XII Tables[1], but if so it must have originally referred only to *mancipatio*, its wider application being a juristic extension, a view suggested by the fact that Justinian, after stating the origin of the rule in the XII Tables, adds that it is a rule of the *ius gentium*[2].

If the thing sold was a *res mancipi*, *traditio* did not pass *dominium* in classical law, but only bonitary ownership[3]. Although in general this was effective, there were disadvantages. The bonitary owner of a slave could not free him so as to make him a *civis* or be his *tutor*[4], till *usucapio* had ripened his ownership. It was only if there was *mancipatio* that the *actio auctoritatis* lay for a defect in title[5]. It was not possible to attach a *fiducia* to a conveyance by *traditio*[6]. It was not in classical law possible to create a usufruct by *deductio* in a conveyance by *traditio*[7].

Traditio, being informal, could be effected by representative. Possession could be acquired through authorised persons in classical law, and the inference that if possession could be so acquired, ownership would pass also, if the necessary intents were present, was soon drawn[8].

When *traditio* superseded *mancipatio* in sale of lands, the absence of requirement of witnesses may have led to frauds. Constantine required public announcement to the neighbours, and later there appears, whether legally necessary or not, an *introductio*, a solemn *perambulatio* of the bounds in the presence of witnesses, all this and the fact of delivery being recorded in the *acta*[9]. This last is preserved in later times[10].

These written evidences of transactions served another purpose. A sale of land is not usually quite a simple matter. Besides the well-known warranties, it would often be necessary to embody all sorts of subsidiary arrangements, restrictions on user, reservation of servitudes and so forth, which it would not be safe to trust to memory.

It must, finally, be noted that in the Byzantine Empire the use of written documents led to a further development. Delivery of the docu-

of Appleton's objections, not fully met by P.'s reply, the case is not quite made out, but the language of P. Sent. 1. 13. 4; 2. 17. 14, compared with that of the *interpretationes*, is strongly in favour of the thesis. For Albertario, *Momento del trasferimento della proprietà*, the rule did not apply to *traditio* even under Justinian. For Meylan, *St. Bonfante*, 1. 443, the XII Tables knew the rule but applied it only to *traditio*, and it never applied to praetorian ownership. Both these opinions seem improbable. *Post*, p. 240.

1 Inst. 2. 1. 41. 2 The Digest does not apply the rule to cases under the Publician, 6. 2. 8. 3 G. 2. 41; Ulp. 1. 16; 19. 7; *ante*, § LXX. 4 G. 1. 17, 167. 5 Girard, *Man.* 591; *post*, § CLXXI. 6 G. 2. 59. 7 Vat. Fr. 47. Some of these points could not arise under Justinian. The *actio auctoritatis* and *fiducia* were obsolete, *post*, §§ CLXXI, CLI. The rule excluding *deductio* in *traditio* was gone, 8. 4. 3. 8 *Post*, § XCIX. 9 Vat. Fr. 35; C. Th. 3. 1. 2; Costa, *Storia del Dir. priv. Rom.* 226. Special rules in cases of *donatio*, *post*, §§ LXXXVI, XCI. 10 Registration under Justinian, C. 8. 53. 31. pr. Cornil, *Dr.R.* 614. Bonfante, *Corso*, 2. 1. 187, discusses these rules of late law and their local variations.

ment tended to replace physical transfer of the property, and we get conveyance by *epistola traditionis, traditio cartae,* etc. How far it proceeded is not clear but it seems to have applied to *donatio*[1]. An ingenious application of *constitutum possessorium* aiding in the supersession of physical transfer has already been noted[2].

Note on the terminology of *possessio*

The view in the text, p. 197, is Riccobono's. Kunkel (*Symbolae Frib. in hon. O. Lenel,* 40 *sqq.*) agrees that *possessio civilis* means possession with civil effects but holds that when the jurists are contrasting other *possessio* with this they use *possessio naturalis* to mean both *detentio* and interdictal possession. As the notion of interdictal possession rested on the words of the edicts they did not systematically analyse it. The texts which create difficulties are due to post-classical attempts to systematise the matter, which were mainly ineffective.

Note on *derelictio*[3]

Derelictio is not a declaration of will but conduct showing intent not to have the thing. There can only be *derelictio* of ownership, not of lesser rights. In classical law it involved immediate loss of ownership in both *res mancipi* and *nec mancipi.* The dispute in 41. 7. 2. 1 was on the question whether ownership was lost in both cases before the thing was occupied by another. *Traditio incertae personae* (Inst. 2. 1. 46), although closely analogous to *derelictio,* was not its source, so that *derelictio* was not a form of *traditio. Iactus in mare* was for some early jurists a *derelictio,* and possibly also *iactus missilium* and abandonment of property to avoid liability for *damnum infectum.* The notion has no particular relationship with *donatio,* notwithstanding 45. 3. 36.

1 Riccobono, *Z.S.S.* 1912, 259; 1913, 159. The history of the limitation may be that *mancipatio* was compulsory for *donatio* of land, after A.D. 355 (*post,* § LXXXVI), that *mancipatio* degenerated to a written form and that thus there was no great change in the new rule. Riccobono's thesis is that in Justinian's Law, but not before, tacit or fictitious *traditio* replaces the actual *traditio* of the older law in many cases. Besides delivery of title-deeds he cites, e.g., *traditio clavium,* not on the spot, *instrumentum dotis,* the transfer of the property of the *socii* in *societas omn. bon.,* etc., and he adverts to other cases such as *appositio custodis* (41. 2. 51) in which though the rule is classical the point of view is altered, and it is valid not because it is in effect taking control, but as a symbol of delivery—*traditio ficta.* Bonfante, *Corso,* 2. 2. 172, holds that the suppression of the reff. to actual delivery in texts dealing with *donatio* has nothing to do with passing of ownership but only with validity of the transaction and is due to disappearance of the rule of *l. Cincia,* requiring delivery for "perfection" of the gift. *Post,* § XCI. But C. 8. 53. 1 cannot be so explained.

2 *Ante,* p. 227.

3 This account is based on Romano, *Studi sulla derelizione nel dir. rom.,* with whom Buckland expresses agreement.

CHAPTER VI

THE LAW OF PROPERTY (*cont.*). *IURE CIVILI* MODES OF ACQUISITION. SERVITUDES. AGENCY

LXXXIV. The *iure civili* modes of acquisition, as stated by Gaius, were all ancient, and are, indeed, more or less directly referred to the XII Tables[1]. The two most important voluntary modes were intensely formal, not only in the sense that their ceremonial was elaborate, but in the sense that form was the essential element: consent (and therefore error) was in strictness not material, a principle of which, as might be expected, praetorian law destroyed most of the significance[2].

Cessio in iure. The form of this transaction was based on that of a "real action" (*vindicatio*) under the system of *legis actio*, i.e. *sacramentum*. The intended transferee claimed the thing, using the words employed in an actual *vindicatio*: "I declare this thing to be mine by Quiritian Law." In an actual claim the other party now made a *contravindicatio*, but, here, on the Praetor's enquiry whether he made a claim, he said, "No," or was silent. If he did this in a *vindicatio*, there was no judgement: the plaintiff took the thing, but there would be no *res iudicata* to bar a later claim by the defendant: it was essential to an effective *legis actio* that both parties should claim. In *cessio in iure* a step now occurred which was not found in a *vindicatio*[3]. The Praetor "addicted" the thing to the claimant[4]. We are not told that there was an actual touching of the thing with a wand[5] (*festuca, vindicta*) as there was in an actual claim. Thus there are essential differences, and though we speak of the proceeding as fictitious litigation, it has been contended[6] with some force that these variations have precisely the purpose of

1 *Donatio*, *post*, § XCI. 2 P. 1. 7. 6–9. The essence of a "formal" transaction is (Leist, *Mancipatio*, 25) that it operates without reference to *causa*. 3 See, however, *post*, § CCIX. 4 G. 2. 24; Ulp. 19. 9–11. 5 It appeared in manumission *vindicta*. 6 Wlassak, *Z.S.S.* 1904, 102.

shewing that it is not litigation, so that it may be construed as conveyance by State authority, using court machinery, or possibly as confirmation by the court of a conveyance by the parties, the *addictio* being an official confirmation, not itself the operative act[1]. But the rules of *cessio in iure* cannot be harmonised with any single conception of the nature of the transaction. Manumission *vindicta*[2] was *cessio in iure*, but not conveyance: what the owner had was *dominium*, what the slave acquired was *civitas*. The forfeiture of *tutela cessicia*[3], from an attempt to cede it again, gave the attempted *cessio* an effect different from that of a void conveyance. *Cessio in iure* had effects which a judgement would not have. If an agnate ceded the inheritance, after acceptance, he lost, *inter alia*, his rights against debtors to the estate[4], but these were not parties to the judgement and a judgement had no force with regard to third parties[5]. It was not abandonment, for manumission *vindicta* left rights in the manumitter, and the Proculians, who held that rights were lost in some cases of *cessio* to which the Sabinians did not apply the rule[6], held that *derelictio* was not complete till a third person had taken possession[7]. These and other differences of view as to the effect of *cessio in iure* indicate differences (and probably changes) of view, as to the nature of the transaction, with a tendency to treat the matter more and more as one of conveyance. But, especially in the matter of capacity, the fact that it was done before the court led to the retention of rules belonging to the conception of it as litigation. Thus it was open to those who could be parties to a *legis actio*, not, e.g., to slaves or *filiifamilias*[8].

As to its antiquity we know little. We are told that it is confirmed by the XII Tables, but this need mean no more than that the *legis actio* is there dealt with[9]. Apart from this, we hear of it directly only in the last century of the Republic[10], but it must be much older. Manumission *vindicta*, a case of *cessio in iure*, is a very ancient institution[11].

Ulpian tells us that it could be used for both *res mancipi* and *res nec mancipi*[12], but except for this general proposition there is little indication of its use for single things. Gaius tells us that it was rarely used for *res mancipi*[13], in view of the more convenient *mancipatio*, and this applies with still more force to *res nec mancipi*, in view of *traditio*. Its field of usefulness was clearly for transfers which could not be effected directly,

1 Naber, *St. Perozzi*, 343, shews that its effect of passing ownership is consistent with some of the texts on the effect of a false judgement. 2 *Ante*, p. 73. 3 *Ante*, p. 166. 4 G. 2. 35. *Post*, § CXLI. 5 44. 1. 10; C. 7. 60. 1. This, however, may not always have been so, Esmein, *Mél. Gerardin*, 229. 6 *Post*, § CXLI. 7 *Ante*, p. 206; D. 41. 7. 2. 1. 8 G. 2. 96; *Schol. Sin.* XVIII (49). 9 Vat. Fr. 50. Late and corrupt. 10 Varro, *R.R.* 2. 10. 4, which may refer to *cessio in iure hereditatis*, and does not prove its use for single things so early. 11 Livy, 2. 5, traces it to the beginning of the Republic. 12 Ulp. 19. 9. 13 G. 2. 24, 25.

of *res incorporales*[1], of *hereditates*[2], of *tutelae*[3], of children in adoption[4], etc. The form of the *cessio* cannot have been the same in all cases: the words of the claimant would be modelled on those used in the claim which was simulated.

Cessio in iure could not be conditional, since it was an *actus legitimus*, and, further, a *vindicatio* necessarily asserted a present right[5]. It might contain a *deductio*[6]. Since it was possible to vindicate ownership without usufruct it was possible to make this fictitious claim, *deducto usufructu*: the effect being a transfer of *proprietas* leaving a usufruct to the other party. Whether the *deductio* itself could be conditional was debated[7]. There might be a *fiducia*[8], but this was a separate agreement, not part of the transaction[9]. It does not seem that special terms (*leges*) could be embodied in the transfer[10].

Like *vindicatio per sacramentum*, *cessio in iure* of ownership required presence of the thing[11], but probably here too it became sufficient in the case of land to have a symbolic turf instead of going to the spot. There was probably some of the progressive simplification which we find in *manumissio vindicta*. We do not know how *tutela* was represented.

We are not told of the effect of error; no doubt the form was everything, and, so far as the transfer of the right was concerned, error was immaterial[12].

Cessio in iure seems to have been obsolete as a mode of transfer of *res* under Justinian: it was not abolished, but ignored, and it cannot be surely traced later than the end of the third century[13]. The fate of some of its applications in the law of persons is different. Manumission *vindicta* continued in a much simplified form[14]. In *adoptio* and *emancipatio* the old form was only abolished by Justinian[15], but the *constitutio* in which he abolishes the old form, while speaking contemptuously of the sales, etc., does not mention the final *cessio in iure*[16].

LXXXV. *Mancipatio.* The most important of the direct modes of

1 G. 2. 29; Ulp. 19. 11. 2 G. 2. 34. *Post*, § CXLI. 3 *Ante*, p. 166. 4 *Ante*, p. 122. 5 It might be *ad tempus*, Vat. Fr. 48. We are told in 50. 17. 77 that there might be implicit conditions. It might be suggested that *cessio in iure* by a non owner would be operative if he became owner. But a number of texts originally written of *mancipatio* deny this for that case. 6. 1. 72; 21. 3. 2; 44. 4. 4. 32 (see also 21. 2. 17). Bonitary ownership would pass if the *res* had been delivered but no more. Mere *c. i. i.* must have been on such facts a nullity. But as in *acceptilatio* (50. 17. 77) it may have been operative if the transferor had received a conveyance under a still pending condition. 6 Vat. Fr. 47. 7 Vat. Fr. 50. 8 G. 2. 59. 9 *Post*, § CLI. 10 Even if the *uti lingua nuncupassit* clause of the XII Tables had this effect in *mancipatio*, which is unlikely, there is no ground for extending the notion to *c. i. i.* Girard, *Man.* 311. 11 G. 4. 16. 12 40. 2. 4. 1. 13 Cons. 6. 10. 14 *Ante*, p. 73. 15 *Ante*, pp. 122, 131. 16 C. 8. 47. 11. This had probably long since taken the form which he prescribes for the whole process, entry on the *acta*.

transfer of property in classical law. It is older than the XII Tables[1], and was the appropriate mode of transfer for just those things which are the chief belongings of a pastoral and agricultural people such as were the early Romans. The form is described by Gaius[2]. There were present not less than five adult *cives* as witnesses[3], and a sixth, a *libripens* carrying a balance. The transferee, e.g. of a slave, holding a piece of metal (*aes*), said: "*Hunc ego hominem ex iure Quiritium meum esse aio, isque mihi emptus esto hoc aere aeneaque libra.*" Then he struck the *aes* on the balance and gave it to the transferor by way of price. The declaration was thus in two separable parts, an assertion of ownership, and then one of purchase by copper and scales, the assertion of ownership being identical in form with that used in *vindicatio* and *cessio in iure*. The form was not quite the same in all cases. It was varied for the purpose of *coemptio*, and, in the *familiae emptio* for the purpose of testation, it did not, as recorded by Gaius, contain the first member[4].

So far as Gaius tells us the transferor said nothing, but there is literary evidence that he did say something[5]. We know, however, that a *mancipatio* was formally valid even though effected by force[6], which suggests that the transferor took only a passive part. In a release of debt *per aes et libram*, it does not appear that the creditor said anything[7]. In fact in all formal transactions of secular law, it was the person benefiting who took the prominent part[8]. From the recorded instances of *mancipatio*, it seems that the actual price was mentioned (no doubt in view of the *actio auctoritatis* in case of sale)[9], though Gaius does not mention it[10].

The form looks illogical: first the transferee asserts that he is owner, which is not true and may never be true, if the price is not paid[11]. Then he says, "let it be bought to me". One view[12] is that the essential part was the first, a man's right to a thing being based on his own unilateral assertion of ownership, rather than on transfer from another. The second phrase would be a later accretion, perhaps added to comply with the rule that

1 Bruns, 1. 25; Girard, *Textes*, 15. 2 G. 1. 119; see G. 2. 22, 23; Ulp. 19. 3. 3 The *antestatus* occasionally mentioned is merely the first witness (Will of Longinus Castor, Girard, *Textes*, 805). See Mitteis, *R.Pr.* 1. 295. He figures however as a separate person in some late texts in which the practice of using seven witnesses is illustrated. Gai. Ep. 1. 6. 3. 4 Most modern editors however reconstruct the text so as to introduce such a clause. 5 Varro, *L.L.* 5. 163, and Festus *s.v. Rodus* attribute to the vendor the words "*Rauduscculo libram ferito.*" Some legal texts dealing with *deductio* say that the vendor "*dicit*" the *deductio*, e.g. 19. 1. 7. In the *emptio familiae* he makes a *nuncupatio*, but this is no part of the *mancipatio*, Ulp. 20. 9. See, however, Pernice, *Labeo*, 3. 97 *sqq.* 6 P. 1. 7. 6, 8. 7 G. 3. 174. 8 *Post*, p. 673. 9 *Post*, p. 489. 10 Girard, *Textes*, 849 *sqq.*; Bruns, 1. 329 *sqq.*; Vat. Fr. 50. 11 But see *post*, p. 240. 12 Lévy-Bruhl, *R.H.* 1932, 205, *Nouv. Études*, 7; for reff. to different views, Jolowicz, *Hist. Int. Rom. Law*, 2nd Ed., 145 *sqq.*, 544 *sqq.*

the price must be paid before ownership passes. But the first phrase occurs neither in the account of *mancipatio* given in the Vatican Fragments,[1] which put *deductio* of a usufruct in the *emptio* clause, or in *emptio familiae* as described by Gaius[2]. Another view is that the assertion of ownership was added to make it clear that the transferor was liable for double damages under the *actio auctoritatis* if his title turned out to be defective[3]. There is late authority for reading *emptus est* instead of *esto*[4], suggesting that the thing was already bought. But this is contradicted by Gaius and the fact that the striking of the balance follows the words. The form as recorded[5] calls for the presence of the *res*, but there might be *mancipatio* of land not on the spot and even, it seems, of land not in the possession of the *mancipio dans*[6].

It has been suggested[7] that even in classical law the *mancipatio* had ceased to be real, and was practically replaced by the written document of which we have instances[8]. It is said that by the time of Gaius the mancipatory will was merely a written instrument, and the case of the written stipulation is cited in support. But for stipulation we have an express text and an express enactment[9]. Gaius tells us the form of the mancipatory will[10] and sharply differentiates the praetorian will as less effective[11]: it is unlikely that if so great effect resulted from a mere difference of wording praetorian wills would have been important in practice. It seems the better view that throughout the classical age *mancipatio* retained its ceremonial, though this may have been at times neglected: people were content not to go behind the written document[12].

Of the words in the XII Tables: "*cum nexum faciet mancipiumque, uti lingua nuncupasset, ita ius esto*[13]," it has been generally held that they authorise the insertion of subordinate clauses in the *mancipatio*, to which the name *leges mancipii* was given. Thus Gaius, speaking of civil bondage, says: "*quem pater ea lege mancipio dedit ut sibi remancipetur*[14]." But this agreement was not part of the *mancipatio*: it was an agreement under which the *mancipatio* was made. There is no sign of subordinate clauses except such as define what is conveyed, e.g. the *deductio*[15]. The *pactum fiduciae* affords a strong argument against this view: it is an agreement

1 Vat. Fr. 50. 2 G. 2. 104 (editors, observing corruption in the text, insert it). 3 *Post*, p. 489. The precaution of selling *nummo uno*, when the sale was fictitious or gratuitous (and so the guarantee would not be needed) would not have been required if this clause could be omitted. But forms become stereotyped and the simple precaution would be very natural. 4 Boethius, *ad Top.* 5. 28. 5 G. 1. 121; Ulp. 19. 6 (whether in 1. 119 G. says *aes tenens* or *rem tenens*). 6 *Ib.*; *arg.* G. 4. 117a, where the action must be an *actio in rem.* 7 Collinet, *Ét. Hist.* 1. 257. 8 Bruns, 1. 329 *sqq.*; Girard, *Textes*, 849 *sqq.* 9 P. 5. 7. 2; C. 8. 37. 1, *post*, § CLII. 10 G. 2. 104. 11 G. 2. 119. 12 The ritual in a copyhold admission is probably sometimes neglected, though legally necessary. 13 Bruns, 1. 25; Girard, *Textes*, 15. 14 G. 1. 140. 15 Girard, *Man.* 311.

as to what is to be done with the *res* in certain events, an exact parallel to the *lex* in Gaius, and the *fiducia* was not a part of the *mancipatio*, but a separate transaction[1]. We know that there could be no express conditions or *dies* in *mancipatio*[2]. The words of the XII Tables probably mean no more than that servitudes, etc., could be validly created for and over the land sold, by inclusion in the statement[3].

The witnesses (whom, in the mancipatory will, the testator's *nuncupatio* describes as *Quirites*)[4] no doubt in some sense represent the people. The number 5 has been held to shew that they represent the five Servian classes, since the *mancipatio*, altering the wealth of the parties, might affect their class. But there is little evidence for or against this view[5]. In later law, in the decay of *mancipatio*, there seem to have been sometimes seven witnesses[6], this being the number required in many transactions. The additional two were the *libripens* and an extra person to whom the name *antestator* was transferred[7]. But there is no reason to suppose that seven were legally required.

Mancipatio was open only to those who shared in *commercium*. *Filiifamilias* and slave could thus acquire for the *paterfamilias*[8], and, with authority, a *filiusfamilias* could so alienate. On what seems the better view a slave could also, but this is disputed[9].

LXXXVI. *Mancipatio* was the appropriate mode of conveyance for the most important elements of wealth in early Rome—*res mancipi*[10]. If moveable they must be on the spot and only so much could be man-

1 Bruns, 1. 332; Girard, *Textes*, 825. 2 Vat. Fr. 329; D. 50. 17. 77. Error, *ante*, p. 233; Wlassak, *Z.S.S.* 1905, 403. 3 Girard, *Man.* 310, suggests that they recognise *mancipatio* in the fictitious form in which alone we know it, i.e. with a pretended weighing. But, apart from procedure, the XII Tables do not deal with forms. 4 G. 2. 104. 5 Apart from the above "*Quirites*" the only evidence for it is that Festus calls them *classici testes* (*s.v.*) in the mancipatory will. Girard suggests (*ib.*) that the unit would have been the century, the voting unit. But that is derivative: the *census* is not primarily concerned with voting, but with wealth, the *classes*. He also says that it would have been a fixed number, not a minimum, "*non minus quam quinque.*" So G. elsewhere describes it (e.g. 2. 104). The other form means that surplusage is no error. The objection would indeed apply to any basis. The source of the seven *testes* of the praetorian will is clear. Gaius (2. 119) speaks of them as seven, the *lib. sing. regg.* as "*non minus quam septem*" (U. 28. 6). Girard also suggests that it was known to communities with Latin right who had not this division of the people (*l. Salpensana* XXII). But a *lex* in the time of Domitian no doubt contained many long since borrowed notions. The *lex* is, moreover, far from shewing that the civil bondage was in fact created in the same way, and we do not really know how widespread was the notion of classification by wealth. For Sinaiski, *La cité Quiritaire*, 27, they represent the 5 *campi* of the city. 6 Ep. Gai. 1. 6. 3. 7 Kniep, *Gai. Inst.* 1. p. 207. 8 Ulp. 19. 4, 18. 9 Discussion and reff. Buckland, *L.Q.R.* 1918, 372; Mitteis, *R.Pr.* 1. 208, who holds that a slave could not mancipate even with authority, but he does not appear to lay this down for a *filiusfamilias*. 10 G. 2. 14a, 22; Ulp. 19. 1, 3. Bonfante, *Scr. Giur.* 2. 1. On the suggested equations, *R.M.* = *Familia*, *R.N.M.* = *Pecunia*, Jörs, *R.R.* 44.

cipated at once as could be held or grasped[1]. It is generally held on the authority of Cicero[2] that it could not be applied to *res nec mancipi*. Literary texts shew it so employed, but it is likely that there was delivery as well and the form was mere surplusage[3]. It was used for transfer of the *familia* in the mancipatory will, and a *hereditas* would ordinarily include *res nec mancipi*, and is not itself given under the list of *res mancipi*[4], but this is an exceptional institution from which it is not possible to argue. It could be used for transfer of rights other than ownership, e.g. for transfers of persons in *potestas*, but they were *servorum loco*, and slaves were *res mancipi*. Rustic praedial servitudes could be so created but these are expressly stated to be *res mancipi*[5], and urban servitudes could not be so created[6]. A woman *sui iuris* is not a *res*, but *coemptio*, in which she sold herself, was a much modified form, and throws no light on the question. On the whole the better view seems to be that *res nec mancipi* could not be mancipated[7].

Res mancipi, as we know them, were *solum italicum*, slaves, beasts of draught and burden and rustic servitudes[8]. This did not cover elephants and camels, which were not in use when this list was first drawn up[9]. But the list is not as it stood at first. There was no separate property in land in early Rome except for the *heredium*, or houseplace, which was not alienable[10]. And it is probable that, till the Empire, only the four primitive rustic servitudes were *res mancipi*, i.e. *iter*, *actus*, *via* and *aquaeductus*[11]. There was dispute between the schools on the question when a farm beast became a *res mancipi*, the Proculians holding that it became such only when trained or in training, the Sabinians holding that it was such from birth[12]. As to the reason why these things and no others were included, it is generally held[13] that they were the things essential to the maintenance of the household in a régime passing from the pastoral to the agricultural stage[14].

1 G. 1. 121; Ulp. 19. 6. Of land, several pieces in different places could be mancipated at once. 2 *Top.* 10. 45; Ulp. 19. 3 is hardly conclusive. 3 *Mancipatio* of pearls (Pliny, *H.N.* 69. 9. 35). The case in Bruns, 1. 335; Girard, *Textes*, 829, seems rather to be a gift of right of access to, and use of, what is contemplated as part of the land. 4 In transfer of *hereditas* to *fideicommissarius* G. says nothing of *mancipatio*, though the Autun Gaius does (67). Consult. 6. 11 shews that in the time of Diocletian there was no way of transferring a mass as a unit. 5 G. 2. 17. 6 G. 2. 29. 7 Bonfante, *Scr. Giur.* 2. 139. On the question whether in early law there was *dominium* of *res n. m.*, *ib.* 180. The primary meaning of *mancipium* is ownership. 8 G. 2. 14a, 17; Ulp. 19. 1. 9 G. 2. 16; Ulp. 19. 9. 10 See Girard, *Man.* 308, n. 1. 11 *Post*, § CXIII. 12 See n. 9. 13 Karlowa, *R.Rg.* 2. 354; Maine, *Anc. Law*, 277, etc. 14 The fact that a *peregrinus* can have only one kind of ownership raises difficulties where a *res mancipi* is delivered to him. If, after holding it some years, he alienates to a *civis*, is the latter *dominus* or is the old owner? If *accessio possessionum* applies (*post*, § LXXXVII) the new owner is at once *dominus*. Apart from *usucapio* an acquirer of a *res mancipi* from a peregrine could not become *dominus*. This kind of difficulty has suggested

The rule that, on sale, ownership passed only when the price was paid or security taken or credit given, which is stated by Justinian, no doubt with accretions, as a rule of the XII Tables[1], is applied in later law to *traditio*, but is commonly thought to have applied primarily to *mancipatio*; a tacit condition such as can exist in *actus legitimi*[2].

Though the fact is not stated the form makes *mancipatio* of a part possible, whether it is or is not all the *mancipans* has[3]. Presumably also error was immaterial, at civil law, if the form was gone through[4]. In early times *mancipatio* was no doubt accompanied by *traditio*, but this seems to have disappeared from classical law[5].

The later history of *mancipatio* is obscure. The distinction between *res mancipi* and *nec mancipi* was formally abolished by Justinian[6], but, for moveables, *mancipatio* seems to have been out of use in the fourth century[7]. The texts deal with *donatio*, and may require delivery without implying that it is always enough, but the most obvious interpretation is that *traditio* is as good as *mancipatio*. The survival of *mancipatio* for adoption and emancipation, till Justinian, means nothing for the *ius rerum—cessio in iure* continued even under Justinian for manumission

the view that a *res mancipi* loses its special character in the hands of a peregrine. Two texts suggest this (Ulp. 1. 16; Vat. Fr. 47a), but are not conclusive; the rule would give the odd result that the forms of *mancipatio* could be evaded by using a peregrine as *interposita persona*. It would be easy to arrange, by *stipulatio*, for the obligations which would have arisen automatically if there had been *mancipatio*.

1 Inst. 2. 1. 41; D. 18. 1. 19, 53. 2 It is reasonable to accept so much of Justinian's statement as indicates that there was a rule about payment in the XII Tables: its content is a different thing. As the process involves a (fictitious) payment, it has been said that the rule has no real operation and this is why Gaius does not mention it. It is difficult to reconcile this with P. 2. 17. 1, dealing with *mancipatio*, though it is said by Pringsheim (*ante*, p. 230, n. 8) that "*pretio accepto*" is inserted by a later hand. The rule of the XII Tables was perhaps that the *actio auctoritatis* did not lie unless the price was paid, and this came to be understood to mean that ownership did not pass. That the rule existed in cl. law is suggested by the *mancipationes* of the second century in which payment of price is stated. Appleton, *R. Gén.* 1920, 225 *sqq.*; Naber, *Mnemosyne*, 1890, 151; Cornil, *A.D.R.* 65. See also, in favour of its application to *mancipatio*, Perozzi, *Ist.* 643. Against, Bonfante, *Corso*, 2. 2. 144 and Meylan, *St. Bonfante*, 1. 443. See also *ante*, p. 230, n. 8. 3 The case in Bruns, 1. 331 is of a divided part. 4 Wlassak, *Z.S.S.* 1905, 403. 5 *Contra*, Riccobono, *Z.S.S.* 1913, 178, but neither G. nor the *liber sing. regg.* speaks of a requirement of delivery (G. 1. 119; 2. 22 *sqq.*; U. 19. 3). Vat. Fr. 310, 311 shew that under the *l. Cincia* mere *mancipatio* completed the gift for *exceptae personae*, while for non-excepted persons *traditio* also was needed (Vat. Fr. 263, 266a, 285, 313 etc.). G. tells us that *praedia absentia* could be mancipated (1. 121). G. 2. 204, on which R. relies, shews only that the *heres* was, as is natural, bound to hand over. If understood as R. takes it, it would imply need of *traditio* in *c. in iure*. Cicero (*Top.* 10. 45) asks whether, if a *r. n. mancipi* is mancipated, ownership passes, a question which could not arise if there had been *traditio*. See also Bonfante, *Corso*, 2. 2. 153 citing Vat. Fr. 268. 6 C. 7. 31. 1. 5. 7 Vat. Fr. 263; C. Th. 8. 12. 1; C. 8. 53. 25. Naber, *Mnem.* 1889, 394 *sqq.*, shews that *mancipatio* was still the proper form of conveyance for *res mancipi* in the time of Diocletian.

vindicta[1]. But the Epitome of Gaius says of *emancipatio*: "*mancipat—hoc est manu tradit*[2]." For Italic land *mancipatio* had the advantage that it need not be on the spot. It existed in A.D. 355[3], but it probably was not usual even then. The provisions of Constantine, for *traditio*, seem designed to meet the fact that land was commonly conveyed by this method[4]. *Fiducia* is mentioned later and as this involved *cessio in iure* or *mancipatio*, this seems to imply the survival of one, probably the latter. But in most, if not in all, of these texts, *fiducia* means no more than pledge[5], and it is not certain that it remained impossible to attach a *fiducia* to *traditio*[6]. Thus *mancipatio* seems to have practically disappeared from commercial dealings even before 355[7].

But in the West the law of 355 seems to have been treated as creating a need of *mancipatio* in *donatio* of land, and the documents collected by Marini[8], even from the sixth and seventh centuries, shew a simulacrum of *mancipatio*, but in general only in *donatio*[9]. But there is no real *mancipatio*: the word is in the present tense, *mancipo*, *mancipamus*, not as in genuine forms "*mancipio accepit*[10]."

LXXXVII. *Usucapio*. *Usucapio* was acquisition of *dominium* by possession for a certain time[11]. As we know it, it was based on a rule of the XII Tables: "*usus auctoritas fundi biennium est...ceterarum rerum omnium...annuus est usus*[12]," in which expression *usus* means acquisition by use, and *auctoritas* means liability to the *actio auctoritatis* on eviction

1 *Ante*, §§ XXVI, XXX. 2 Ep. Gai. 1. 6. 3. 3 C. Th. 8. 12. 7. 4 Vat. Fr. 35; C. Th. 3. 1. 2. 5 Reff., Girard, *Man.* 558, n. 2. 6 Girard holds (*cit.* 553, n. 3) that, if it had been possible in *traditio*, *fiducia* would have been retained by Justinian. But it had long been used only in mortgage and perhaps in gifts *ut manumittatur*. In his desire for simplicity and solicitude for debtors he would hardly retain what, so far as it differed from pledge, was severer, and the other institution is provided for by the *actio praescriptis verbis* and the *condictio ex poenitentia* (*post*, § CLXXXVII). See besides the above texts (n. 5) C. Th. 2. 29. 2; C. 4. 3. 1; see Collinet, *Ét. Hist.* 1. 225 and Girard, *Man.* 314. 7 C. Th. 8. 12. 7. The enactment of 394 (C. Th. 2. 29. 2) has nothing to do with *mancipatio*. In saying that delivery is essential it is adding to its rule that in a gift of the kind it mentions, *suffragium* (Dirksen, *Manuale*, *s.v.*), *traditio* does for moveables, but a writing is necessary for land, a warning that writing alone will not do. Justinian's *lex*, cited by Collinet (C. 8. 53. 37) to shew the survival of *mancipatio*, shews only, as indeed it says, that old forms of words were still in use in documents in which they had no meaning. 8 Collinet, 254, 255. 9 Marini's collection contains many conveyances on sale in sixth and seventh centuries, always by *traditio* or *epistola traditionis* (*ante*, p. 232). Two mention *mancipatio* (120, 123?) but only in the traditional clause against *dolus*, a survival of common form. Thus two of the sales (114, 118) record the payment of "*nummus unus*," quite out of place in a sale. 10 Collinet (255) cites a later Lombard sale with the old words, "*emit, mancipio accepit*." It is the word, not the thing: it must be read in view of G. Ep. 1. 6. 3, *mancipat, hoc est manu tradit*. 11 This is not merely the barring of action: it is a mode of acquisition. The acquirer becomes *dominus*: his right may in some cases be set aside, but there is no question of his having become owner against *A* and not against *B*. 12 Cicero, *Top.* 4. 23, only an approximation to the original.

in case of sale, a liability which ends at the moment of *usucapio*[1]. The rules were no doubt gradually evolved on the basis of this general proposition. It was a civil law mode of acquisition and gave *dominium*[2]. The acquisition rested on mere lapse of time, not on the fiction which appears in some systems, under which time is evidence of a lost grant[3]. Gaius tells us that its purpose was to enable us to acquire what had been transferred by a non-owner[4], but it had other applications, e.g. where a *res mancipi* had been transferred by mere *traditio*[5], and in some cases of *missio in possessionem* under praetorian law[6].

The first requirement was uninterrupted possession for two years of land, one year of moveables[7]. The brevity of the time is explained by the fact that when it was introduced the State was very small, and control of property much closer than it would be in modern conditions[8]. The possession required is in general the technical *possessio* needed for interdictal protection[9]. The meaning of *usus*, the word here employed in the XII Tables, was probably much the same. As acquisition depended on possession, and not on mere non-possession by the owner, it must have continued through the whole period[10], and must be one uninterrupted continuous possession. Thus if a man lost possession and regained it later he could not add the two durations together: he must begin afresh[11]. This is illustrated by the rules of *accessio possessionum.* If one *in via usucapiendi* died, and his *heres* entered in the ordinary way, he stepped into the legal shoes of the deceased and could complete *usucapio*[12]. It was regarded as one continuous possession. There was no new *initium* and thus the *bona fides* of the *heres* was immaterial. But if one *in via usucapiendi* sold or gave the *res*, the receiver did not represent the old holder as a *heres* did: the possession was a new one. But there had been no interruption (*usurpatio*) or interference with possession, and the two possessions could be added together, if the new holder himself satisfied the conditions of *usucapio*[13]. But if the new holder came into possession without consent of the first, by ejecting him, or taking possession without his consent, then there had been interruption: even if the new holder could usucapt, he could not count the earlier time[14]. This *accessio pos-*

1 *Post*, § CLXXI. 2 Not identical: *iure gentium* modes may do this. 3 Faint suggestion of lost grant in 39. 3. 1. 23, concerned with *l. temp. praescriptio*. 4 G. 2. 43. 5 *Ante*, p. 197. 6 *Post*, § CCXLV. 7 G. 2. 42; Ulp. 19. 8. Land in the XII Tables, buildings by interpretation. *Possessio* of buildings not *possessio* of materials for *usucapio*, *ante*, p. 212, n. 8. 8 G. 2. 44. 9 Thus if I rent land, I do not possess and can not usucapt though I think that it is my own. We have seen that if a *procurator* has taken possession the principal may have interdict possession before he has usucapion possession (*ante*, § LXXIII). Conversely, the *heres* will be usucapting before he has interdict possession (see n. 12). 10 41. 3. 3, 25. 11 41. 3. 15. 2, not conclusive. The second *possessio* was *vitiosa*. 12 4. 6. 30. pr.; 41. 2. 23. pr.; 41. 3. 40; 41. 4. 2. 19. 13 41. 3. 14; 41. 4. 2. 17. 14 41. 3. 5; 44. 3. 14, 15.

sessionum, for buyers and the like, is not found till late in the classical age. It applied at first to *praescriptio*[1], was perhaps extended to *usucapio* by a buyer by Severus and Caracalla[2], but not generalised till Justinian[3].

Usurpatio might be natural, mere loss of possession, or civil, a claim at law. It is not always easy to say what is loss of possession, e.g. where physical possession was held by a subordinate holder[4], e.g. a *colonus*, and where a holder in good faith leased the *res* to the true owner. In this last case it was held that the possession was lost, on the ground that the contract was a nullity[5]. In *usurpatio civilis*, the difficulty is to say when the *usurpatio* occurred. Apparently in the Republic any formal claim, even short of litigation, was *usurpatio*[6]. In classical law, even joinder of issue (*litis contestatio*) was not, for *usucapio* might be completed between this and judgement[7]. But this meant little: the *iudex* decided by the state of things at *litis contestatio*[8]. He would therefore give judgement for the plaintiff, and the defendant must transfer or pay the value[9]. Civil *usurpatio* did not need actual disturbance. If a possessor was sued and judgement given against him, but his *de facto* possession was undisturbed, he could not now usucapt, for it was a new possession, and did not begin in good faith[10].

The next requirement is *bona fides*[11], difficult to define. It did not consist in thinking one was *dominus*, for one who received a *res mancipi* by *traditio* knew he was not this. It was not enough to think he was in rightful possession: a pledge creditor thought that. It was not necessarily a belief that no one had a right to take it from him: a *missus in possessionem* for *damnum infectum* could usucapt though he knew the owner could redeem on putting matters right[12]. Many cases are disposed of by the maxim: "*qui auctore Praetore possidet, iuste possidet*[13]."

1 C. 7. 31. 1. 3; see P. 5. 2. 5. Many texts on this point originally written of the interdict *utrubi*, *post*, § CCXLIX. De Zulueta, D. 41. 1 and 2, *ad* 41. 2. 13; Bonfante, *Corso*, 2. 2. 226 (inconsistencies due to hasty transfer). 2 Inst. 2. 6. 13. Mitteis, *R.Pr.* 113. But the history is disputed. It may be that Severus and Caracalla first applied it to *l. t. p.* and did no more. Perozzi, *Ist.* 1. 657. 3 In one way the buyer is better off than *heres*, who is barred by defect in the *possessio* of ancestor, immaterial to buyer. 44. 3. 11; C. 3. 32. 4. Lit., Siber, *R.R.* 84. On Inst. 2. 6. 12 which seems to say that Justinian introduced the rule for *heres*, Bonfante, *Corso*, 2. 2. 221. 4 *Ante*, p. 203. 5 41. 3. 21, 33. 5. 6 Cicero, *de Or.* 3. 28. 110. 7 6. 1. 17–21. 8 The rule *omnia iudicia absolutoria* (G. 4. 114; *post*, § CCXVII) does not apply. 9 6. 1. 18. The rule may have been otherwise in *l. t. praescriptio*, *post*, § LXXXIX. 10 *Arg.* C. 7. 33. 1. 1. As to Justinian, *post*, § LXXXIX. 11 G. 2. 43, 93; Inst. 2. 6. pr. *Bona fides* and *iusta causa* are not part of the original scheme but a juristic creation probably late in the Republic (Stintzing, *Das Wesen des bona fides*) when the narrowing of the notion of *furtum* had made the rule excluding *res furtivae* less effective. They are a corrective of the short period. It has been said (Appleton, *Le Trésor et la iusta causa usucapionis*) that the notion exists in germ in the primitive rule: one holding my property and refusing to say how he got it is apt to be treated as a thief. It is, however, only a germ, for the burden of proof is reversed. 12 39. 2. 5. pr. 13 41. 2. 11; 50. 17. 137.

Subject to this, *bona fides* may be described as belief that the holder had a right to hold it as his[1]. Usually, but not always (e.g. *missio*, bonitary owner and some noxal cases), it rests on mistake. The error must be reasonable and of fact[2]. Indeed, where there was an error of law, the transaction was often void, and *usucapio* excluded for lack of *iusta causa*, e.g. where one bought from a *pupillus* thinking that *auctoritas* was not necessary, or could be by ratification. Here, the transaction being void, there was only a putative *causa*, which fact barred *usucapio*[3].

Where the acquisition was through a slave (or *procurator*[4]), apart from *peculium*[5], both must have been in good faith, the slave when he took, the master when he knew. Pomponius indeed says that, where the acquisition was *domini nomine*, the master's state of mind was the material one[6]. This may refer to acquisition under express instructions, for the other rule is laid down for sons[7], and *bona fide servientes*[8].

In classical law *bona fides* need exist only at the *initium*, the moment when possession began[8a], but there were some exceptional cases.

(i) In sale, *bona fides* was needed at the time of the contract and at that of delivery[9]. This probably dates from the time when the two were contemporaneous and was carried over to the new state of things owing to the double meaning of the word *emere*, which means both to buy and to acquire. The Digest, purporting to give the Edict on the Publician, says: "*qui bona fide emit*[10]." The rule remained in Justinian's law.

(ii) In *usucapio lucrativa*, resulting from gift of a *res aliena*, texts shew that here *bona fides* must persist throughout the possession, and that Justinian abolished this rule[11].

Gaius mentions cases in which *bona fides* was not needed. That of *usucapio lucrativa pro herede* is ancient, no doubt older than the rule requiring *bona fides*[12]. Where a *hereditas* was, or had been, *iacens* (there being no *heres suus* or *necessarius*, who was in without acceptance), anyone might, by taking the property or part of it not yet possessed by the *heres*, even after acceptance, become owner by holding it (even land) for one year without good faith[13]. The rule that one year sufficed for land

1 Some texts shew a wider conception. Where a man in collusion with an authorised *procurator* buys at an absurdly low price he is not a buyer in good faith. 41. 4. 7. 6, 8; C. 7. 33. 6 (*praescriptio*). It is not necessarily bad faith to buy through a nominee. See *Greg. Wis.* 7. Bonfante, *Scr. Giur.* 2. 709. *B. f.* is an ethical, not a psychological point, though it arises in the form of knowing or not knowing. As to the scope of *b. f.* and *i. c.* in earlier law, Collinet, *Mél. Fournier*, 71. 2 22. 6. 4, 6; 41. 3. 31. pr. 3 41. 4. 2. 15, 16. 4 *Arg.* 41. 4. 7. 2. 5 Here, *utilitatis causa*, the slave can usucapt without the master's knowledge, 41. 2. 1. 5, 44. 1; 6. 2. 7. 10. 6 41. 4. 2. 11, 12. 7 41. 3. 43. 8 41. 4. 7. 8. 8*a* G. 2. 43; D. 41. 3. 4. 18; 41. 1. 48. 1. 9 41. 4. 2. pr. 41. 3. 10. pr. Bonfante, *cit.* 580, holds that in cl. law it was disputed which time should be taken. Only Just. makes both material. See also Siber, *R.R.* 2. 91. The view seems improbable. 10 6. 2. 7. 11. 11 6. 2. 11. 3; C. 7. 31. 1. 3; Bas. 15. 2. 11 (Heimbach, 2. 171). 12 *Ante*, p. 243. 13 G. 2. 52 *sqq*.

was a perversion of the rule of the XII Tables that for "*ceterae res*" one year sufficed. A *hereditas* was *cetera res*, and therefore, said the Pontiffs, a part of it was, even if it were land. According to Gaius the reason for this "*tam improba usucapio*" was that it caused the *heres* to enter promptly so that debts and *sacra* might be attended to. He says that originally the *usucapio* was of the *hereditas* itself, though, in historic times, only of the specific things[1]. But the real reason and early history of the institution are obscure[2]. A *Sc.* under Hadrian destroyed the importance of the rule by providing that the *heres* could set aside the *usucapio*[3]. It was treated as extinct in the time of Caracalla, and probably earlier[4].

Another case was *usureceptio ex fiducia*[5]. A *res* conveyed subject to *fiducia* could be reacquired by getting possession without good faith and holding for a year. Where it was *cum amico*, e.g. a *res* was handed over to be looked after, or where it was *cum creditore*, by way of mortgage[6], and the debt had been paid, this is reasonable. Where it had not, the rule applied only if it was not held by hiring or *precarium* from the creditor[6a]. It is difficult to see why it was allowed at all, or rather, as no doubt it antedates the rule of *bona fides*, why it was allowed to survive in a time when, unlike *usucapio pro herede*, it served no useful purpose, but was a mere injustice. Presumably the rule was originally general and the limitation in mortgage is an equitable restriction.

There is the same difficulty about *usureceptio ex praediatura*[7]. Where property had been lawfully seized and sold by the State to a *praediator*, the old owner could reacquire, without good faith, but here the ordinary times of *usucapio* must have expired. Unless the *praediator* must have been recouped, which is not said, the rule seems a gross injustice[8].

Another case, *usucapio ex Rutiliana constitutione*[9], where a man bought *res mancipi* of a woman without *auctoritas tutoris* (to which the ordinary times applied), did no injustice, for he had paid, and the usucapion could be prevented by repayment.

Bona fides was presumed, i.e. need not be proved[10], but could of course be disproved[11]. The rule means less than it seems to, for *iusta causa* must be proved, and a valid form of conveyance is all that could

1 Cicero, *ad. Att.* 1. 5. 6, probably does not mean *hereditas* in a strict sense, but *res hereditariae*. The allowance of seizure after entry but before possession is probably not ancient; in an analogous case 47. 4. 1. 8 and rubric say that the moment the *heres* entered and the slave was free there was a civil action against him, ignoring possession. Huvelin, *Furtum*, 677; Buckland, *L.Q.R.* 1927, 338; *Contra*, Bonfante, *Corso*, 6, 230. 2 *S.M.W.* 565; Bonfante, *Corso*, 6. 226. 3 ? *Rest. in integrum*, Berger, *Z.S.S.* 1925, 229. Hypothesis in which the old *u. p. h.* might occur after Hadrian, Appleton, *R.H.* 1930, 624. 4 C. 7. 29, 1. 5 G. 2. 59, 60. 6 *Post*, § CLXVI. 6a *Arg.* 44. 7. 16. 7 G. 2. 61. 8 Perhaps merely to compel the buyer to take possession promptly, Poste, *ad G.* 2. 61. 9 Vat. Fr. 1. G. 2. 47 for the older law. 10 C. 8. 44. 30. *Mala fides* never presumed. 11 *Ib.*

ordinarily be given as proof of *bona fides*. To prove *bona fides* is to prove that certain facts were not known, and a negative can hardly be proved[1].

LXXXVIII. *Iusta causa*[2]. The taking must have been based on some fact which is ordinarily a basis of acquisition[3]. In general this is a fact having legal effect, e.g. legacy or sale, but it need not be—a pact to give sufficed[4]. The *iussum* of the Praetor was enough. *Iusta causa* (*iustus titulus*) must be proved. The chief rule, often laid down, is that the *causa* must be real[5]: a putative *causa* did not serve. This distinguishes it from the *iusta causa* of *traditio*. If a thing was handed to me who thought there was a legacy to me, but there was none, the property passed if it belonged to the transferor[6], but if it did not, I did not usucapt, for there was no *iusta causa*[7]. There are however signs of differences of opinion. Neratius is quoted as saying that putative *causa* should suffice, because it did in *traditio*, and Pomponius approves[8], thus identifying them. No other text goes so far, and many are inconsistent with it. Each *causa* may have had its own rules, but it is probable that these writers are here expressing a personal view, based on a false analogy, and that, in general, a real *causa* was needed, but that in sale, on grounds of commercial convenience, some held that putative *causa* served, and that the ultimate rule was that, in sale, it sufficed if there were reasonable grounds for the belief[9]. It is not quite easy to say what is a putative *causa*. There might have been a sale, but it did not cover this thing. There might have been a legacy, revoked by a codicil unknown at the time[10].

Justinian discusses some of the *causae* under separate titles: his list is not complete, but on some of them there is something to be said.

1 Buyer from *pupillus* without *auctoritas*, in knowledge of the facts, is not a *b.f. emptor* (18. 1. 27). But in what may be the original of this text we learn that, if it was a woman, he is a *b. f. emptor* even though it is a *res mancipi*, as a woman can alienate possession without *auctoritas*, and if he has paid he will usucapt (Vat. Fr. 1). This raises the question whether good faith required payment. If *traditio* was conditional on payment before a certain day, and this was not made, there was no sale and thus no *iusta causa*, but if credit was agreed on, *usucapio* might proceed: this was not a conditional sale, though it might be a resoluble one (41. 4. 2. 3. *Post*, § CLXXIII). But this says nothing about *bona fides*, or about a sale in which nothing was said about credit, but the price was simply unpaid. The Praetor did not name payment of the price as a requirement of the *actio Publiciana* (6. 2. 7. 16, 8). Vat. Fr. 12 clearly contemplates *usucapio* though the price is due, making it not essential. Other views are held. Karlowa, *R.Rg.* 2. 396.

2 Bonfante, *Scr. Giur.* 2. 469, holds *i. c.* the primary requirement, *b. f.* tending to supersede it in importance. Hence the notion of putative *causa*.

3 Bonfante, *Corso*, 2. 2. 243, defines it as such a relation as indicates that the taking is not a lesion of another's right, which gives a theoretical, and not purely dogmatic explanation of praetorian *missiones*.

4 41. 6. 1.

5 41. 3. 27; Inst. 2. 6. 11.

6 12. 6. 3, 46.

7 41. 8. 2.

8 41. 10. 3. Esmein (*Mélanges*, 204) adds 41. 3. 48, and 41. 4. 2. pr., in both of which there may have been a *causa*, not referable to that *res*. His other text, 41. 3. 46, is not in point.

9 41. 3. 33. 1; 41. 4. 11; 41. 10. 5. 1. Beseler, *Z.S.S.* 1925, 225. A purchase from a *furiosus* was void, but *usucapio* was allowed, *utilitatis causa*, 41. 3. 13. 1; 41. 4. 2. 16.

10 41. 2. 34. pr.; 41. 4. 2. 6; 41. 5. 3; 41. 8. 2–4; 41. 10. 4. 2; 41. 3. 27.

U. pro derelicto, where a thing was abandoned, but by one not in fact owner. If only supposed to be abandoned there was no *usucapio* for lack of *causa*[1]. Here there is no mutual act[2].

U. pro empto was subject to special rules as to *bona fides* and *iusta causa*. It included one case which was not sale: payment of damages in an action for the thing[3]. There was difference of opinion whether it covered anything but what was actually bought, e.g. the child of an *ancilla* born after the sale[4]. It does not seem that the price need have been paid[5].

U. pro donato had special rules as to *bona fides* till Justinian[6]. There must have been a real *donatio*. A gift to one's son in *potestas* could not be usucapted: if after the father's death the *heredes* assented, time would then run[7]. A gift to the donor's wife was null: there was no *usucapio*, unless on the facts the donor was not impoverished[8].

U. pro herede is not important in later law. The *heres* cannot usucapt what is not of the *hereditas*, as there is no *causa*. One text, however, attributed to Pomponius, allows it[9]. Others deny it[10]. Several texts treat of *usucapio* of *res hereditatis* by apparent *heres*: some are mere survivals: others may represent an effort by Justinian to bring the old institution, limited to cases of good faith, within the ordinary scheme, notwithstanding lack of *causa*[11].

U. pro soluto does not mean merely what was handed over in discharge of an *obligatio*, which would be, e.g., *pro empto*. It would apply where a thing was handed over in lieu of the price, or under a *stipulatio*[12]. But in fact it overlaps the other *causae*[13].

U. pro suo has two senses. In one sense it covered nearly all[14], but it had a narrower sense. If *dos* was handed over before the marriage there was no *usucapio pro dote*, till the marriage, but there could be *usucapio* in the meantime, *pro suo*[15]. If an *ancilla furtiva* had a child, *apud bona fide possessorem*, some texts make this *pro empto*, others *pro suo*[16]. If the father divided his property *inter vivos*, and on his death the heirs agreed to abide by this any *usucapio* would be *pro suo*[17].

1 41. 7. 2. pr., 6. 2 Regarded as *traditio* to an *incerta persona*, it would be *pro donato*. There is no *pro occupato*; that is not the *titulus*, but the act of acquisition. 3 41. 4. 3. 4 Buckland, *Slavery*, 25. 5 *Arg.* 41. 4. 2. 3. *Ante*, p. 246, n. 1. Opinions differ, according to the views of the writer as to requirement of payment of price for passing of ownership in *mancipatio* and *traditio*. See Perozzi, *Ist.* 1. 662. 6 *Ante*, p. 244. 7 41. 6. 1. 1; h. t. 4. 8 41. 6. 1. 2, 3. 9 41. 5. 3; 41. 10. 2, *fin.* 10 C. 7. 29. 4; 7. 33. 4. 11 See for this and the other *causae* Bonfante, *Corso*, 2. 2. 250. Different view, Siber, *R.R.* 85. Perozzi, *Ist.* 2. 486, holds both cases "*pro herede*" for Justinian. 12 41. 3. 46. Not expressly included in Justinian's series, 41. 4–10. But in early editions of the Digest the last four *leges* of 41. 3 are a separate title *pro soluto*. 13 Bonfante, *Scr. Giur.* 2. 555, putative *causa* admitted. 14 41. 10. 1. pr. It would not cover Praetorian *missio in possessionem*. 15 41. 9. 1. 2; cf. h. t. 2, "*aestimata res*." 16 6. 2. 11. 4; 41. 3. 33. pr.; 41. 10. 2, 4. 17 41. 10. 4. 1. Texts not in accord. Fitting, *Sciens indebitum accipere*, 54.

As *usucapio* was a civil institution, it did not exist in favour of peregrines, or over provincial land, or things not capable of private ownership (*res sacrae, sanctae, religiosae*[1]). But it applied to everything else, unless it had a *vitium* or defect which barred *usucapio*, or was specially protected by law. The *vitia* were few. The most important was that *res furtivae* or *vi possessae* could not be usucapted till they had returned to the owner[2]. The XII Tables and an early *l. Atinia* forbid it in the case of *res furtivae*[3], and the *l. Iulia et Plautia* in that of *res vi possessae*[4], there being, in classical law, no theft of land. The return which purged the *vitium*, was complete if the owner knew where the thing was and there was no obstacle to his vindication of it[5]. But he must know. To put it secretly in his house was not enough, unless he had never known of the theft[6]. It must be to the *dominus*, who is not necessarily the person from whom it was stolen[7], though there were complications if it was stolen from a slave or a *conductor* or a pledgee[8]. Restoration to vendee of the *dominus*, or payment of value would equally purge the *vitium*[9]. The child of an *ancilla furtiva* was *furtivus* if conceived *apud furem*[10], and, notwithstanding the rules of *specificatio*, it seems that not only wool of a stolen sheep was *furtiva*, but also a garment made of it[11].

As to young of stolen animals (*fetus*), the texts disagree: the better view seems to be that here as elsewhere they were treated as fruits and if born *apud b. f. possessorem* were his no matter where conceived[12]. As land could not be *furtiva*, *usucapio* of land was more common than that of moveables, for if moveables are in the wrong hands there will

1 G. 2. 46, 48. 2 G. 2. 45, 49; D. 41. 3. 41. 3 *Ib.*; Inst. 2. 6. 2. Hence doubts as to origin of the rule. Various views, Huvelin, *Furtum*, ch. 6; Bonfante, *Corso*, 2. 2. 228; Cornil, *A.D.R.* 69. 4 Inst. 2. 6. 2. *Vis*, not fraud, G. 2. 51. 5 41. 3. 4. 6, 33. 2; 47. 2. 57. 4; 50. 16. 215. Or his *tutor* unless the *tutor* was the thief, 41. 4. 7. 3. It is not enough that it gets back to a *procurator*, 41. 3. 41. 6 41. 3. 4. 7 *sqq.* 7 41. 3. 4. 6. 8 If my slave steals and replaces my article, I knowing nothing of the matter, the *vitium* is purged (41. 3. 4. 7), but it is not enough if he holds it as *peculium*, unless it was before, or I assent (h. l. 9). Paul seems to add that *vitium* is purged even if I knew of the theft, if the *res* was *peculiaris* with my consent, but the text is confused (h. l. 7. See also Julian, 47. 2. 57. 2). Where depositee sells and gets it back, whether owner knew or not the *vitium* is purged (41. 3. 4. 10). Where stolen from pledgee or *commodatarius*, it must return to *dominus* if thief a third party (41. 3. 4. 6). In theft by debtor from pledgee the texts record doubts. The rule reached is, probably because the rule is statutory, and the statute speaks of return to *dominus*, that where a *res* is stolen by the owner from a *bona fide* buyer or usufructuary, or a pledge creditor, it does not become *furtiva* (41. 4. 5; 47. 2. 20. 1, Paul). But 41. 3. 49, also Paul, says that it is a *res furtiva* and the *vitium* is purged by return to creditor. Vangerow holds (*Pand.* 1. 587) that here the debtor was a non-owner: in the others owner. This does not shew why return to creditor purges the *vitium*, nor is it indicated. In C. 7. 26. 6 the debtor sells a *res hypothecata*: this is *furtiva*. 9 41. 3. 32, 4. 13, 14; 47. 2. 85. 10 41. 3. 10. 2; 47. 2. 48. 5. Buckland, *Slavery*, 26. 11 41. 3. 4. 20. 12 Bonfante, *Corso*, 2. 2. 230: chief texts 41. 3. 10. 2; 47. 2. 48. 5; 41. 1. 48. 2; 41. 3. 4. 19.

frequently be a theft in the background. But Gaius instances, in moveables, the *heres* dealing with things he wrongly believes to be part of the estate, or sale by a man who by error of law thinks a thing is his[1]. Another case of *vitium* is that of a gift to a Praetor or Proconsul, these being forbidden. There was no *usucapio* till the gift returned to the donor[2].

The chief cases of specially protected property were:

(*a*) The property of the fisc or the Emperor, but this did not apply to the property of a vacant *hereditas* not yet reported to the authorities[3].

(*b*) *Res mancipi* of a woman in agnatic *tutela*, subject to the Rutilian rule[4].

(*c*) Land of a pupil (as being inalienable) or (later) one under *cura*: perhaps in later law any property of a *pupillus*[5].

(*d*) Dotal land, a result of the *l. Iulia* which made it inalienable[6].

(*e*) In late law, land devoted to religious or charitable purposes[7].

(*f*) In early law, the five feet of land bordering *fundi*[8].

(*g*) *Bona adventitia*, sold by the *pater*, could not be usucapted by the vendee[9], and apparently such things could not be usucapted at all[10]. Probably anything inalienable was so protected[11].

A completed *usucapio* could, in certain circumstances, be rescinded, by a rescissory action brought within one year of the time when it was first possible, i.e. where the *usucapio* had run against one who, from absence on State service, imprisonment or the like, could not sue, or in favour of one who, from some similar cause, could not be sued[12].

LXXXIX. *Longi temporis praescriptio*[13]. *Usucapio* was *iuris civilis*. *Longi temporis praescriptio* was based, not on the Edict, but on imperial enactments, to protect where *usucapio* did not apply, especially, at first no doubt exclusively, the holding of provincial lands[14]. The principles were in part the same, but there are differences.

(*a*) The protection was different, and less effective. *Usucapio* was a mode of acquisition: it was not merely a bar, but made the usucaptor

1 G. 2. 50, 51; Inst. 2. 6. 3–6. 2 48. 11. 8. 3 41. 3. 18. 4 G. 2. 47.
5 *Usucapio* of *res mobiles pupilli*, 27. 5. 2; no *usucapio* of *res pupilli* (? *immobiles*), 41. 1. 48. pr., probably interp. De Zulueta, D. 41. 1 and 2 *ad l.* A minor could get *restitutio in integrum* till Justinian enacted that time should not run against them. C. 7. 35. 3. C. 2. 40. 5. 1. Restrictions on alienation of *res pupilli* (*ante*, p. 154). 6 23. 5. 16; see 50. 16. 28. pr. 7 *Nov.* 111. 1; 131. 6; Girard, *Man.* 331. 8 Cic. *de legg.* 1. 21. 55. 9 C. 5. 12. 30. 2; 6. 61. 4. 10 C. 7. 40. 1. 2; Bonfante, *Corso*, 2. 2. 238.
11 See 50. 16. 28. pr. 12 Inst. 4. 6. 5; D. 4. 6. 21 *sqq.* The edictal grounds seem to have been (Lenel, *E.P.* 120) absence compelled by *metus*, or in good faith on public service, *vincula*, including imprisonment, lawful or unlawful (4. 6. 9), apparent slavery and captivity (4. 6. 1) and such absence of defendant as made action against him impossible.
13 Partsch, *Longi Temporis praescriptio*. 14 Introduced late in second century. C. 7. 33. 1, and rescript in Girard, *Textes*, 201, 906. Partsch, *cit.* 105 *sqq.*

owner. It was positive or acquisitive. *Praescriptio* was in principle merely negative or extinctive[1]. It gave the holder a defence if sued for the *res*, but did not make him owner, and there was, besides the defence, the protection of the possessory interdicts[2]. Before Justinian, however, and probably long before, it became acquisitive[3].

(*b*) The time was much longer: ten years if the parties were "present" in the same district, twenty if they were not[4]. Present is explained by Justinian to mean domiciled in the same province: he does not discuss the effect of change of domicile. In the longer period there was of course more likelihood of the thing being temporarily incapable of such acquisition, e.g. belonging to a *pupillus*[5].

(*c*) Its field was different: it applied primarily to things capable of *iure gentium*, but not of *iure civili*, ownership, though the rules as to *vitium*, etc., seem to have been the same[6]. As its effects were not quite the same as those of *usucapio*, it might be useful in *iure civili* cases, and there is evidence of its application before Justinian to Italic land[7], and to moveables from the time of Caracalla[8], though most of these latter texts may have applied originally to peregrines and *res mancipi*.

(*d*) The better view seems to be, though the matter is disputed, that *litis contestatio* interrupted *praescriptio*[9].

(*e*) The rules of *accessio possessionum* for buyers, etc., were applied first to *praescriptio*, and gradually extended to *usucapio*[10].

(*f*) *Usucapio* did not destroy servitudes on the land, except so far as they expired from non-use, or hypothecs[11]. *Praescriptio* had the same rule for servitudes, but a hypothec might be destroyed by lapse of time, if, when possession began, the possessor did not know of its existence[12].

1 Partsch, *cit.* 100, considers it not a mere bar, but positive evidence of title, though available only in defence (see 39. 3. 1. 23, "*veluti iure imposita*"), based on Greek practice in which such facts were persuasive but not conclusive evidence. 2 *Ante*, p. 196; *post*, § CCXLIX. 3 Justinian says (C. 7. 39. 8) that "*veteres leges*" if properly looked into gave a *vindicatio*, which looks like a juristic perversion of a *lex*, perhaps an *actio fictitia*. We are told that there was a modified Publician (6. 2. 12. 2), but the text is probably interpolated. On the face of it this refers to interim protection, indicating, *a fortiori*, protection after the time had expired. No difficulty under Justinian: all ownership is alike. 4 P. 5. 2. 3; C. 7. 33. 9, 12, settling other points: domicile is matter of province, not of town: the position of the property is not material. For presence, the document cited p. 249, n. 14, uses the indefinite word "διατρείβοντας." 5 Suspended *praescriptio*, *post*, § CXCII. *Res* becoming *dotales*, 23. 5. 16. 6 C. 7. 33. 2. 4. 7 Partsch, *cit.* 151. 8 44. 3. 3, 9. 9 P. 5. 2. 4, 5; C. 3. 19. 2; C. 7. 33. 10. Partsch, *cit.* 32 *sqq.* Cuq, *Man.* 288, holds that it was interrupted by mere protest, citing C. 7. 33. 2; C. 7. 35. 4. Under Justinian, protest to the *praeses* or certain other public authorities sufficed. C. 7. 40. 2. This does not mean that such a protest by *X* interrupted my *possessio* as against *Y*, but only that time ceases to run as against *X*. 10 Krueger, *Z.S.S.* 1905, 144. 11 41. 3. 44. 5; 7. 4. 19. 12 44. 3. 5. 1.

(*g*) *Bona fides* (as opposed to *iusta causa*) is not mentioned in the earliest evidence we have, but seems soon to have been required[1].

Under Justinian the two systems were more or less fused, a result of the abolition of differences in ownership and civil status. The new system appears to have followed the rules of *praescriptio*, but the period for moveables was fixed at three years, it was directly acquisitive[2], and probably it was interrupted by *litis contestatio*[3].

Apart from this regular system there appeared in the later Empire a system called *longissimi temporis praescriptio*. Two unsatisfactory texts[4] tell us that under Constantine, or his sons, it was enacted that 40 years' possession should give extinctive protection, whatever the origin of the possession. The enactment of Theodosius[5], which cut down *actiones perpetuae* to 30 years, gave an extinctive protection after 30 years, and expressly said that there was no further protection for women or *absentes*, but only for *impuberes*. There was no question of *fides* or *causa* or *vitium*. It is clear that in some cases[6] 40 years were required, but not what these were. Justinian further provided that if the possession had been *bona fide* the protection was acquisitive and gave a *vindicatio*, whatever defects or *vitia* there might be[7].

In A.D. 544 Justinian enacted that if a *bona fide* buyer from a *mala fide* holder held a *res* for 10 (or 20) years, and the person who thought he was entitled took no steps, it was acquired by *usucapio*[8]. This is hardly new, for if he knew and could vindicate, this would purge the furtivity in older law[9]. He adds that if the old owner did not know, it would be acquired only by 30 years, which was existing law for moveables, but new for land, which could not be *res furtiva*[10].

There were special rules for sales by the *fiscus*[11]. Where it lawfully sold an estate, but wrongly included property not part of it, M. Aurelius enacted that a buyer who held for five years should have an *exceptio*

1 The rescript of Severus and Caracalla, *ante*, p. 249, n. 14, speaks only of *iustum initium*, but a document of a few years later uses words which, though obscure, are supposed to require *bona fides* (Girard, *Textes*, 906), as does a slightly later rescript, C. 5. 73. 1. See also 44. 3. 11. 2 Inst. 2. 6. pr.; C. 7. 31. 1. 3 Less probable for the earlier scheme. Inst. 4. 17. 3. In the fusing enactment he retains the name *usucapio* for moveables, and does not say that the rules are to be the same (C. 7. 33. 1). In the Inst. (4. 17. 3) his language suggests that in *usucapio*, *litis contestatio* was still not a *usurpatio*. This may be a survival, but may indicate a difference between moveables and land. C. 7. 40. 2 puts both cases on the same footing. 4 C. Th. 4. 11. 2; C. 7. 39. 2. 5 C. Th. 4. 14. 1; C. 7. 39. 3. 6 C. 7. 39, Rubr.; 5, 6, 7. 7, etc. 7 C. 7. 39. 8. Little known of details of these schemes. There were exceptions which may have been numerous. Texts speak of possession by the defendant, but the principle is bar by non-enjoyment of the plaintiff, rather than adverse possession. It does not appear that the fact that defendant had been out of possession for a time was material: cp., for *usucapio*, 41. 3. 3. 8 *Nov.* 119. 7. 9 *Ante*, p. 248. 10 It might mean that, now, mere knowledge where the thing was, purged the *vitium*, but this is unlikely. 11 Inst. 2. 6. 14; C. 7. 37. 2, 3.

against the owner's claim. This is longer than the period of *usucapio*, and thus applies only where there was *vitium*, or bad faith. It left the fisc still liable for five years to claims for defect in title. Zeno provided that any acquirer, by any title from the fisc, should have a good title at once, free of charges, but owners or pledgees who suffered might claim from the fisc for four years. Justinian applied this to alienations by officials of his, or the Empress's, household.

XC. *ADIUDICATIO*[1]. In three "divisory" actions, *communi dividundo*, for dividing common property, *familiae erciscundae*, for dividing a *hereditas*: and *finium regundorum*, for regulating boundaries[2], the *iudex* had a function beyond giving a judgement. He had to make an *adiudicatio*. In the first two he had to distribute what the claimants held in common, in proportion to their rights, so that each would now own a part separately, instead of an undivided share. His decree vested property and was thus a mode of acquisition. It might be necessary to create easements, e.g. rights of way over one part, in favour of another, or to give one a life interest over a part and another the *dominium* subject to it, but he could not create such rights except over the property submitted to him[3]. Where a fair adjustment by division was impossible, he might have to order equalising payments. This was no part of the *adiudicatio*: it was a *condemnatio* and created only obligations[4]. In the third case he might have to shift boundaries, where the object was to make them more convenient, giving here and taking there, with the same need of *adiudicatio*[5]. As an *adiudicatio* affected only those who were parties to it, if one of the owners had given a pledge of his undivided share, this would still burden every part of the property[6]. If the action was a *iudicium legitimum*[7], the *adiudicatio* created civil ownership[8], otherwise only praetorian ownership which would ripen by *usucapio*[9].

LITIS AESTIMATIO. The payment of damages in lieu of restitution in a *vindicatio* vested the property in the defendant[10], as also in a claim under deposit, loan etc.[11] Presumably, if it was not a *iudicium legitimum*[12], the ownership was praetorian[13].

IUS ACCRESCENDI. This expression, found in many connexions, here refers to a rule, obsolete under Justinian, that where a slave was owned in common by two or more, an act of formal manumission, by one, merely destroyed his right and increased that of his co-owners, without making the man free[14].

1 Inst. 4. 17. 6, 7; Ulp. 19. 16. 2 Buckland, *R.H.* 1936, 741; *post*, p. 544. 3 10. 3. 7. 1, 18. 4 *Post*, § CLXXXVI. 5 10. 1. 2. 1. 6 10. 3. 6. 8. 7 *Post*, § CCXXXII. 8 Vat. Fr. 47 a. 9 See 10. 2. 44. 1. 10 6. 1. 46. 11 13. 6. 5. 1; 16. 3. 30. 12 *Post*, § CCXXXII. 13 Arangio-Ruiz, *Ist.* 178, and *post*, § CLXIV. 14 *Fr. Dos.* 10; Ulp. 1. 18; P. 4. 12. 1. If a common owner makes a *fc.* of liberty to the slave, the co-owner is compelled to sell his share to the fiduciary. C. 7. 7. 1. 1 a; D. 40. 5. 47. 1. Difficulties where it is a direct gift, Buckland, *Slavery*, 575 *sqq.* In the ancient *consortium*, any *consors* could effectively manumit and the man would be *libertus* of all, *post*, p. 404.

If it was done informally the act was void on the view which prevailed[1], perhaps because the accrual was a civil law mode of acquisition and thus did not occur unless all the civil law requirements of manumission were satisfied.

Lex. A general term used by commentators to group together certain cases in the sources, not expressly classed. We even find *accessio* placed here, though it is certainly not the creation of express enactment. More reasonably the conception is applied to a number of cases in which a statute has regulated the matter[2]. Even this is not the language of the Sources[3], in which *lex* as an express mode of acquisition plays a very small part. Ulpian mentions legacy, as based on the XII Tables, and "*caducum vel ereptorium*" under the *l. Papia Poppaea*[4]. He is dealing with acquisition of single things, and seems to be finding a basis for such cases of acquisition of single things as are illogically but conveniently treated under acquisition *per universitatem*: there seems no purpose in giving it a wider scope. In the Digest he carries, or is made to carry, the matter a little further, but in the same field, where he says that *hereditas* itself may be said "*non improprie*" to be acquired *lege*[5].

XCI. *Donatio.* This is in general not a mode of acquisition but a *iusta causa*[6]. If *A* gives *B* a book it becomes his by *traditio*: if he promises a book, there may be a "right" to it, but ownership will not pass without delivery[7]. It may be that Justinian treats it as a mode of acquisition[8] because in later law property did sometimes pass, as we shall see, without delivery, but he may have had no logical reason, but found it a convenient way of grouping the special rules on gratuitous transfers[9]. But a *donatio* was not necessarily transfer of a *ius in rem.* It might be a promise, or a release (*acceptilatio*)[10], or a *delegatio*, i.e. acceptance by the donor, by formal agreement between all parties, of a liability of donee to a third party, or a similar undertaking by a third party to pay to donee instead of donor[11].

Donatio inter vivos[12]. The first point to notice is revocation. Where a gift was made *sub modo*, i.e. to be applied in certain ways, and the application was, or became, impossible or it was not so applied, it could

1 *Fr. Dos.* 10. Maqueron, *R.H.* 1930, 580, discusses the dispute, for him a school controversy. 2 Girard, *Man.* 328; Cuq, *Man.* 279. 3 Cuq includes *Thesauri inventio*, a statutory creation. But this makes it a civil mode of acquisition; Inst., 2. 1. 39, treats it as *iure gentium.* 4 Ulp. 19. 17. 5 50. 16. 130. 6 On the nature of *donatio* and of *animus donandi*, Perozzi, *Ist.* 2. 270 *sqq.* 7 Not under the same obligations as one delivering under sale. He need not warrant against eviction. If he does, Paul says it is not binding (P. 5. 11. 5); C. 8. 44. 2 says it is. Some correct P.; some limit the *lex.* 8 Inst. 2. 7. pr. 9 Not treated with modes of acquisition in the Code. But Sabinus seems so to have handled it; Lenel, *Sabinussystem*, 87. 10 *Post,* § CXCV. 11 *Post,* § CXCIV. 12 Special rules on gifts between husband and wife, Ulp. 7; P. 2. 23, and *ante*, p. 111.

be recovered by *condictio*, on ordinary principles[1], but in the third century it seems to become possible to recover it by a *vindicatio utilis*, which looks very like a revocable ownership but does not go quite so far[2]. There is much legislation on revocation for ingratitude, limited, till Justinian, to gifts to children or grandchildren or *liberti*[3]. Revocation was allowed to the donor, but not to successors, or against successors of the donee[4]. There was a judicial enquiry into the allegation of ingratitude[5], and the effect may have been to revoke the gift *in rem* or to give a remedy *in personam*. The former is perhaps more probable, but this is forfeiture, not *ipso iure* termination. Under Justinian the rules applied to gifts to anyone[6]. An enactment of A.D. 355 introduces the remarkable rule that if a patron having no child made gifts to *liberti*, and afterwards had a child, these gifts were *ipso facto* revoked, and apparently, though the words are vague, the revocation directly restored *dominium*[7].

Restrictions on amount of *donationes* were imposed by the *l. Cincia* of about 200 B.C.[8], gifts above a certain amount (unknown) being unenforceable, as to the whole gift, certain near relatives being exempted from its operation[9]. The rules under it, created by the jurists, gave a complicated result. There was a general overriding rule, perhaps a later growth, not in the *lex*, that only the donor, not successors, could take advantage of the statute, *Cincia morte removetur*[10]. The governing

1 39. 5. 2. 7. In a promise, revocation would be made effective by *exceptio doli*; presumably *replicatio* from an informal release, and *condictio* for payment or release where there had been acceptance of liability to a third person. Duquesne, *Mél. Cornil*, 1. 228. Similar machinery, Inst. 2. 20. 13; D. 17. 1. 45. 2; C. 8. 55. 7. Where it was *sub modo*, and the application stipulated for, there was no need for revocation: it could be enforced. If not, there was a *condictio*, C. 4. 6. 3, 8 (classicality disputed), and if the ultimate purpose was in any way for the benefit of the donor it was, in later law, an innominate contract (C. 8. 53. 9, 22. 1; 39. 5. 28). De Francisci, *Synallagma*, 1, ch. VIII. 2 In the case the purpose was *alimenta* to donor (C. 8. 54. 1) and the rule is declared to have been laid down by earlier Emperors. See Pringsheim, *Kauf mit fremdem Geld*. 123 *sqq*., who holds all *vindicatio utilis* to be Byzantine. See Von Mayr, *Vindicatio utilis*; Collinet, *Ét. Hist*. 1. 176; Lenel, *E.P.* 186. They are certainly often post-classical. Did they lie against third persons or only against the same defendant? Even under J. there was an advantage in an *a. in rem* even so limited, e.g. in insolvency, though the advantage in matter of security is gone. De Francisci, *cit*. 1. 254. Innominate contracts, *post*, § CLXXXI. 3 Vat. Fr. 272; C. Th. 8. 13 and C. 8. 55 *pass*.; the Vat. text speaks of ingratitude but does not make this essential, in terms, but its reproduction in C. 8. 55. 1 does and so does the later legislation. 4 C. 8. 55. 1. 3, 7. 3. 5 In the action for revocation. 6 C. 8. 55. 10. 7 C. 8. 55. 8: as to revocation of excessive gifts in fraud of *querela inoff. testam*., *post*, § CXV. 8 Girard, *Man*. 989. Sanction before *l. Aebutia* obscure. G. supposes an action, but does not explain its disappearance. Suggestions as to amount, Kuebler, 181. 9 Cognates to second cousins, any female cognate for *dos*, *affines*, and acting *tutores*, Vat. Fr. 298–305, 310; other cases Vat. Fr. 307–9; it did not apply to rewards for service gratuitously rendered in emergency, P. 5. 11. 6. It is aimed at corruption, rather than at prodigality. 10 Vat. Fr. 259. Perhaps Caracalla, Vat. Fr. 266.

principle was that the *lex* could be enforced only by way of defence. This was an *exceptio legis Cinciae*[1]. Broadly it was only where the claimant must come into court, if he wanted his gift, that the law was effective. If it was a gift of land and it had been mancipated and handed over, there was no more to be said, but if, though mancipated, it was still in the donor's hands, and the donee vindicated, he could be met by the *exceptio*[2]. If land had been handed over without *mancipatio*, as the ownership had not passed, the donor could vindicate, and if met with *exceptio rei donatae et traditae* would have *replicatio legis Cinciae*[3]. The donee having to come into court to protect his interest the *lex* was available. If it was a gift of land, *deducto usufructu*, then, if there had been a *mancipatio* or *cessio in iure*, the conveyance was complete and no question arose. If there was even a valid contract this could be enforced against the *heres*, for he had not the *exceptio*[4]. If the thing given were a *res mobilis*, duly conveyed and handed over, the possibility of the *exceptio* was not extinct. For, by the interdict *utrubi*[5], a possessor could get the thing back if he had held it for a greater part of the last year than that for which the donee had held it. In such a case the donor could regain possession by the interdict, and meet a *vindicatio* by the *exceptio legis Cinciae*[6].

These rules were replaced in the later Empire[7] by a system of registration (*insinuatio*) for all gifts. Under Justinian a gift above a certain amount, ultimately fixed at 500 *solidi*, was void, if unregistered, as to

1 Vat. Fr. 266. 2 Vat. Fr. 311. 3 Vat. Fr. 313. C. Th. 8. 12. 7.
4 Vat. Fr. 313, complicated by the fact that donee is a *libertus*. 5 *Post*, § CCXLIX.
6 G. 4. 160; Vat. Fr. 293, 311. If the gift is perfect the *l. Cincia* does not affect it, and thus the fact that it has got back to the donor does not entitle him to use the *exceptio l. Cinciae* (*arg*. P. 5. 11. 2, 4). Presumably if it was a usufruct which was given and duly conveyed, and the donor then vindicated the thing, he could not reply to the defence of usufruct by pleading the *l. Cincia*. If the gift was a promise (39. 5. 22) the *exceptio* was available. A gift by way of *acceptilatio* (39. 6. 24) is perfect, and the *exceptio* is barred (C. 8. 43. 2). But a mere informal release, enforceable only by an *exceptio*, could be met by a *replicatio l. Cinciae* (20. 6. 1. 1. interp.). Formal taking over of debt is a completed gift (*delegatio*, 39. 5. 21. pr.). So too if a debt to donor is transferred to donee (h. t. 33. 3). But cases of this type create a difficulty. In 11. 1. 5. 5 a donor whose gift was the taking over of a liability has a *condictio* for return or release according as he has paid or not. In 39. 5. 21. 1 a similar right is given where the gift was transfer of a claim against a third person. These texts are variously explained as survivals (on the assumption that the original remedy under the *lex* was an action), as interpolated, and as a special remedy for these cases, necessary because, though the gift is still in the stage of promise and therefore the *lex* ought to be applicable, it is in fact barred, as in each case the promise by the *delegatus* is one of an existing debt (Gide, adopted by Duquesne, *Mél. Girard*, 1. 389, who discusses the various views). Vat. Fr. 266 which gives *condictio* where the promise has been fulfilled is dealing with *C. indebiti*, which presupposes error, so that it is not in point, Girard, *Man*. 997. 7 The *lex* may have been in force in 355; C. Th. 8. 12. 7. But see Radin, *R.H.* 1928, 249.

the excess[1], apart from some excepted cases[2]. If the thing was transferred the ownership passed only *pro parte*, the larger interest, whichever it was, having the right to buy out the other. If the gift was indirect (*delegatio*) there was *condictio* for the excess[3].

Donatio commonly contemplates transfer of property. As there could be no temporary ownership, this excludes, for classical law, any *donatio* for a time or to be returnable on any event. The alienation accompanied by this proviso was void. But, under Justinian, such gifts were allowed[4], and it seems that the ownership reverted on arrival of the time or condition[5]. But security could be exacted for return[6].

Donatio inter vivos afforded exceptions to the rule that ownership passed only by *traditio* or formal conveyance. A gift by *paterfamilias* to one in his *potestas* was void[7] whether delivered or not. But if he died in the same mind, without revoking the gift, it was confirmed, operating as *donatio mortis causa*[8]. Some texts from Diocletian onwards require express confirmation on the will[9]. Justinian allowed non-revocation to suffice if the gift was below the amount requiring *insinuatio*, or was duly registered, in other cases he required express confirmation, with some further distinctions[10].

Gifts between parent and child not in *potestas* were in earlier classical law like other gifts. But there was confusing legislation of which the story may be as follows. From the time of Pius they were valid and enforceable however informally expressed[11], though mere declaration did not transfer ownership[12]. This remained the law even under Justinian. He, perhaps following predecessors, made such informal *pacta donationis* binding even between *extranei*[13]. In both cases *traditio* remained necessary[14]. But by an evolution which may have begun under Diocletian or Constantine[15] for gifts between parents and children not in *potestas*, but was not generalised till Justinian, the delivery of *instrumenta* came to be regarded, in *donatio*, as a valid *traditio* of the thing[16].

1 Much legislation requiring registration, with variations as to conditions and effect; Vat. Fr. 249; C. Th. 8. 12. 1 *sqq.*; C. Th. 3. 5. 1; C. 8. 53. 34, 35; *Nov.* 162. 1; etc. 2 Excepted cases under Justinian, *piae causae* up to a specially high limit, *donationes ante nuptias*, or for *dos*, gift by the Emperor (C. 8. 53. 34, 36), and some others. 3 See p. 255, n. 6. 4 Vat. Fr. 283. Cp. reproduction, C. 8. 54. 2. 5 At least to the extent of *vindicatio utilis*; *ante*, p. 254, n. 2. 6 *Arg.* C. 6. 37. 26. 7 Vat. Fr. 295, 6; *Greg. Wis.* 8. 2, not a basis of *usucapio* (41. 5. 2. 2; 41. 6. 1. 1). Confirmed by *emancipatio* without ademption of *peculium*. 39. 5. 31. 2; C. 8. 53. 17. 8 P. 5. 11. 3; *Greg. Wis.* 8; Vat. Fr. 274, 277, 278, 281, etc., subject to *l. Falcidia* and *querela* (*post*, §§ CXIV, CXIX). 9 Vat. Fr. 292–296. One of Pap. requires confirmation (Vat. Fr. 294; but see Vat. Fr. 250), one of 315 (Vat. Fr. 274) treats non-revocation as enough. 10 C. 5. 16. 25. Conflict in texts, Bonfante, *Corso*, 1. 118. 11 P. 4. 1. 11; cf. C. Th. 8. 12. 4. 12 Vat. Fr. 263, 266a, etc.; cf. Vat. Fr. 265. 13 *Post*, § CLXXXIII. 14 C. 8. 53. 6. 15 C. Th. 8. 12. 4, 5. 16 Riccobono, *Z.S.S.* 1912, 259; 1913, 159; *Mél. Girard*, 2. 415; Lauria, *Ann. Macerata*, 6. 93. C. 3. 29. 2 is in part Justinian Develop-

Gifts for charity (*piae causae*) and to the church were specially provided for under Justinian[1]. In one enactment[2] he laid down a rule which may mean that the mere promise to give gave a real action, indeed this is its most obvious meaning. But the *lex* does not say anything of the formalities needed, and its main purpose was the extension of the period of limitation. Its meaning has been disputed for centuries[3].

Donatio mortis causa. A gift made in expectation of death, either general or on a certain event[4], to be absolute only if and when the expected death occurred. It might be a gift of property, a promise, a release or a *delegatio*[5]. It was essentially revocable, and was revoked *ipso facto* by insolvency of donor, or predecease of donee[6]. This revocation would operate differently in the two types of such gift, which are:

(i) Under suspensive condition. Here in a gift of property the *res* was handed over but the ownership was not to pass unless and until the expected death occurred[7]. Whether the revocation was express or by insolvency, death of donee, or non-occurrence of the expected death, the ownership not having passed, the thing could be vindicated.

(ii) Under a resolutive condition. Ownership passed on delivery but on failure of the condition it was to be restored[8]. The ownership did not revert *ipso facto*, in classical law, but there was an obligation to restore. Under Justinian it did so revert[9] and the thing could presumably be vindicated[10]. It is not clear that this was new, though it is post-classical[11].

The *l. Cincia* did not affect these gifts[11a] and, operating only on death, they were free from some of the restrictions on gifts *inter vivos*. They could be made by father to son, between *vir et uxor*, indeed to anyone who could take a legacy[12]. As to form we are not informed for classical law, but a *lex* of Constantine suggests that, then and later, the rules

ment probably connected with the fact that *mancipatio* was necessary for *donatio* of land and gradually degenerated into a mere memorandum. *Ante*, pp. 232, 241.

1 *Ante*, p. 178. 2 C. 1. 2. 23; cf. C. 8. 53. 36. 3 Riccobono, *Z.S.S.* 1913, 195; Bonfante, *Corso*, 2. 2. 169. 4 39. 6. 1–6; Senn, *Don. à cause de mort*; Biondi, *Donatio mortis causa*. They probably originated in *mancipatio cum fiducia*. Senn, *cit.* ch. 2. He draws from this origin and from a distinction between gifts to be returned if the expected death does not occur, and gifts not to be returned unless the donee dies before the donor, some conjectural conclusions as to the evolution of the institution. 5 Indirect forms, 39. 6. 18. 2, 24, 28, 34. 6 It has been suggested that the texts making it revocable at will are interpolated; see Biondi, *cit.* 35; Cuq, *Man.* 800; *contra*, Suman, *Favor testamenti*, 204. There could be no difficulty in gifts of the first class. P. 3. 7. 1, 2; Inst. 2. 7. 1; D. 39. 6. 7, 13, 16, 17. 7 39. 6. 2. 8 On the question of revocability in this case, Senn, *cit.* ch. 2, who shews that the right of revocation was a generalisation from the principles of *fiducia*, a common mode of such gifts. 9 39. 6. 18. 1, 37; C. 6. 37. 26. 1. 10 The point did not arise in "indirect" gifts, by *acceptilatio* or *delegatio*. The special remedy here was *condictio*. 39. 6. 18. 1, 24, etc. 11 Girard, *Man.* 1006. 11a As they were perfected by the death, Siber, *Z.S.S.* 1933, 139. 12 39. 6. 9.

were the same as for gifts *inter vivos*[1]. Justinian laid down a new rule. He prescribed a certain form, with five witnesses, the form he required for codicils[2], and provided that where the gift was so made it should have the same effect as legacy, so that it would transfer property on the death, but not till then, without transfer of possession[3], transfer by mere agreement. Such gifts were not necessarily void unless made in this form: if the thing was actually handed over or the right created in the appropriate way the old rules presumably applied.

This was a part of his general policy of bringing together legacy and *donatio mortis causa*, of which we are frequently told that it is similar to legacy[4]. The assimilation was progressive. A *sc.* made such gifts subject to the *ll. caducariae*[5]. *Fideicommissa* could be imposed on donee[6]. Severus made them subject to the *l. Falcidia*[7]. But even under Justinian they differed from legacy in many ways. Thus they did not depend on a will[8], a *filiusfamilias* could make them, *consentiente patre*[9], the *regula Catoniana* did not bear on them[10], and they were not lost by unsuccessfully[11] attacking the will[12].

1 Vat. Fr. 249. 2–4. 2 C. 8. 56. 4. 3 D. 6. 2. 2 puts *donatio* on a level with legacy in this respect. 4 Inst. 2. 7. 1; D. 39. 6. 17, 37, etc. 5 39. 6. 35. pr. 6 31. 77. 1. 7 C. 6. 50. 5. 8 39. 6. 25, and thus did not await entry of *heres*. 9 39. 6. 25. 1. 10 *Arg.* 39. 6. 22; *post*, § CXXI. 11 34. 9. 5. 17, *post*, § CXXI. 12 The action for the enforcement of the right of ownership is the *vindicatio*. Hist. account, *S.M.W.* 308. The forms and main characteristics of this action will be considered under the law of procedure (*post*, § CCXXVIII): some points may be mentioned here. The plaintiff's claim is that he is the *dominus*, Quiritarian owner, and in early law the defendant made a similar claim. This last point leaves a trace in early classical law: the action did not lie against a mere *detentor* unless he claimed to be *dominus*, Siber, *Passivlegitimation*, 26 *sqq.*, who also holds (*R.R.* 2. 97) that some jurists allowed it if the *detentor* held of a third party. It should be brought against the person under whom he holds—the *possessor*, and if this is the plaintiff himself an action *in personam* based on the *negotium* between them is the proper remedy. Ulpian allows vindication (6. 1. 9). The *detentor* of land could avoid liability under Constantine, by declaring of whom he held (C. 3. 19. 2). In later law, but perhaps not till Justinian (Girard, *Man.* 366, but see also, Siber, *Passivleg.* § III, and Jörs, *R.R.* 95 who credit the rule to the latest cl. law), it lay against one who had fraudulently parted with possession (an extension from *hereditatis petitio*), and against one who falsely alleged that he possessed. 5. 3. 45, much altered. How far it lay in cl. law against one claiming usufruct (there is an *a. negatoria*, *post*, § CCXXVIII) is disputed, Siber, *Passivleg.* 88. *Bona fide possessor* who has ceased to possess, *post*, § CLXXXVII. Texts under J. which give it where possession has been lost, *culpa*, e.g. 6. 1. 15. 3, 16, 21, cited by Siber, *R.R.* 2. 101, refer to loss after *litis contestatio*, when, in cl. law, liability existed only for *dolus*. See also Kaser, *Z.S.S.* 1931, 92. As to one who *liti se offert*, *post*, § CCXL. The defendant, if defeated, must restore the thing, its accessories (*causa*) and the fruits received since *litis contestatio*: his further liabilities varied according as he was in good or bad faith and historically. A *b. f. possessor*, in cl. law, did not restore earlier fruits: under J. he must restore *fructus extantes*. A *m. f. possessor* must account for all fruits, in cl. law, by special actions, under J. in the *vindicatio* itself. Bonfante, *Corso*, 2. 2. 306 and *post*, § CCXXXVI. As to *vindicatio utilis*, or *actio in rem utilis*, an extension to cases in which a change of ownership which has taken effect is rescinded. (Inst. 4. 6. 6; D. 6. 1. 5. 3; 24. 1. 30, 55; 26. 9. 2; 39. 6. 30; 41. 1. 9. 2; C. 3. 32. 8; C. 8. 54. 1, etc.), *ante*, p. 254.

XCII. *Iura in re*[1], i.e. rights *in rem* less than ownership. Of these by far the most important class were servitudes.

A servitude[1a] was essentially a right or group of rights vested in some person other than the *dominus* of land subject to it. It may be thought of as a burden on the *res*, a *ius in rem* in another person, to which the owner must submit. Thus praedial servitudes are rights over a piece of land vested in one, not owner of that land, but of adjacent land to which, rather than to him, it is attached, so that if he alienates the land the servitude goes with it[2]. The conception is reflected in the terminology. The land under servitude is spoken of as *praedium quod servit*[3]: hence the expressions *praedium dominans* and *serviens*. It is indeed a burden rather on the land than on the ownership, for a servitude might exist over land which had no owner. If a *praedium* was abandoned by its owner, a right of way attached to or over it did not cease to exist[4]. But there could be no servitude on *res sacrae* or *religiosae*—that was inconsistent with religion[5].

The chief general principles of servitudes are these:

(i) *Servitus in faciendo consistere non potest.* It could not impose an active duty[6]. It was a right *in rem* and such rights are negative: there cannot be a right that everyone shall do something, but only that everyone shall abstain from doing something. It might be a right to prevent anyone from doing something—*ius prohibendi*[7]—a negative servitude, e.g. a right to ancient lights, or a right to do something without being interfered with—*ius faciendi*—a positive servitude, e.g. a right of way[8]. There was however one remarkable exception. The servitude *oneris ferendi*, a right to have one's wall supported by a neighbour's, imposed on him the duty of keeping the support in repair[9], an active duty[10]. But it can hardly have been a part of the servitude, for it was not available against all: a third party could not be made to repair the wall. It is therefore sometimes explained as having originated in an agreement, at first express, and later implied[11]. This agreement would bind only the

1 An expression not used by the jurists: cf. Justinian's definition of usufruct in Inst. 2. 4. pr.; cp. D. 7. 1. 1 (Paul). 1 *a* This name is probably not very ancient: Gaius uses it (2. 14, 17) as a secondary name. Cicero uses it in this sense (*Ad Quint. fr.* 3. 1. 2 (3)). Primarily it is a *ius*. For early lawyers it is a right existing independently of ownership, with its own remedies. This old view led to the rule that it could be acquired by *usucapio*, and the *l. Scribonia* (*post*, § XCIV) which abolished this may mark the change of view. Buckland, *L.Q.R.* 1928, 426. 2 8. 4. 12. 3 8. 2. 30, 32. 4 *Arg.* Ulp. 1. 19. A *servus sine domino* may be subject to usufruct. *Fr. Dos.* 11. Fadda, *Studi*, 1. 211. Disputed, Pampaloni, *Bull.* 1910, 119. Buckland, *L.Q.R.* 1928, 426. 5 A *res* cannot be *religiosa* without consent of all having *iura in rem*; difficulties in *res sacrae*, as to which we are not informed; see 8. 1. 14. 2. 6 8. 1. 15. 1. *Contra*, Bonfante, *La Regola: Servitus in faciendo consistere nequit.* 7 8. 2. 15. 8 Active duties could of course be imposed on a transferee, but this is contract and would not bind third parties. 9 8. 5. 6. 2. 10 8. 5. 8. 2. 11 Elvers, *Servitutenlehre*, 56. Beseler, *Z.S.S.* 1925, 231.

promisor and his *heres*, while this duty lay on any owner for the time being, and was enforced like a servitude[1]. And Labeo says that the servient owner could avoid the liability by abandoning the wall, as it was a duty on the land rather than on him[2]. It is an anomaly, of which the explanation may be historical. It may have been an old customary institution, the lines of which were settled before the conception of servitude was fixed[3], but its existence was still matter of doubt at the end of the Republic[4]. It may have been recognised on grounds of convenience: it was better that the owner should do it than that he should have to submit to entry of an outsider to do it[5].

(ii) *Nulli res sua servit*[6]—a man cannot have a servitude on his own land: servitude is essentially a right in a non-owner. Thus if the two ownerships came together, the servitude was merged and did not, in general, revive if the ownerships again became separate[7]. There were apparent exceptions. If having adjoining properties *A* gave *B* a usufruct over one, reserving a right of way, this was not a servitude over *A*'s own property: it was part of his ownership, and the usufruct he had given was less than the normal to the extent of that right[8].

(iii) *Servitus servitutis esse non potest.* There could be no servitude on a servitude. There might be two servitudes over the same land[9], and there was the same apparent exception as in the last case.

(iv) *Servitus civiliter exercenda est*—it must be so used as to cause as little inconvenience as possible[10]. Hence there was no servitude unless it was advantageous to the property, not one merely to annoy a neighbour, or for a personal advantage not affecting the land[11].

(v) A *servitus* was a *res incorporalis* and thus could not be possessed. This means less than it seems to, for enjoyment was much the same as possession and was protected by similar interdicts[12]. In later law and perhaps in classical it was "quasi-possessed." The fact that some servitudes could originally be acquired by *usucapio* is not an application of the notion of quasi-possession. It is a rule framed on the notion of use, before the theory of possession had been evolved, and it disappeared

1 8. 5. 6. 3. 2 8. 5. 6. 2. 3 Girard, *Man.* 383. 4 8. 5. 6. 2. 5 Elvers, *op. cit.* 62. 6 8. 2. 26; 8. 6. 1. 7 8. 6. 1. Exceptions in practice to this rule, Elvers, *op. cit.* 126; Windscheid, *Lehrb.* § 215, n. 10; D. 8. 1. 18, etc. 8 Distinction not meaningless. It could not, e.g., be lost by non-use unless the land itself was lost by *usucapio.* 9 We are told that there cannot be a usufruct of a right of way, for the reason, probably due to Justinian, that there cannot be a servitude on a servitude. The text adds that effect can be given to it by Praetorian remedies (33. 2. 1). *Post,* § XCVI. 10 8. 1. 9; 8. 5. 8. 6; 8. 1. 15. pr. The servitude in 8. 1. 19 (Labeo) may be a survival, or may be allowed as being of potential value to the land though useless for the time being. 11 8. 1. 8. pr.; h. t. 9; h. t. 15, etc. Enjoyment may be limited to certain times, 8. 1. 5. 1. 12 E.g. 43. 19. *Possessio iuris, ante,* p. 197.

before the classical age. And the references to quasi-possession of praedial servitudes may be all interpolations[1].

Servitudes were divided in later law into two classes: Praedial and Personal, so different that they scarcely seem to belong to the same branch of the law. Praedial servitudes applied only to land, were perpetual, were almost innumerable and gave only limited definite rights. Personal applied also to moveables, were limited in duration, were few, and gave indefinite rights including physical possession of the property concerned. But the characteristic difference was that praedial servitudes belonged to a man, only as owner of a *praedium* to which they attached, so that they were spoken of as belonging to the *praedium*: personal servitudes attached to a man personally.

XCIII. PRAEDIAL SERVITUDES. These were rights vested in a person as owner of one *praedium* over another, effective not only against its owner, but against all: they were *iura in rem*. Land subject to such a servitude was said *servire*, a terminology which treats them as burdens. But in speaking of the servitudes themselves the other aspect was commonly looked at: they were *iura praediorum*[2]. Their nature, coupled with the general principles of servitudes, accounts for most of their special rules. They were perpetual and could thus exist only over what was capable of perpetuity[3], but it seems that if a thing was practically such, but not technically, the classical law admitted the servitude[4]. The principle of perpetuity had one modification. If the ownership was liable to resolution by law, a servitude imposed by the interim owner ceased when the ownership ended. A recorded case is that of a *heres* where property had been left by a conditional legacy. If the condition occurred any servitude created by him was destroyed[5]. But there were in this case doubts as to the interim ownership[6]. *Dos* affords a contrast. We are told that where a husband sought to create a servitude on dotal land, this was void, as, under the *l. Iulia*, he could alienate no interest in it[7]. If a vendor before delivery created a servitude it was good, but he was liable to his buyer[8]. A servitude could not be created conditionally or *ex die*[9], nor was it possible to create one, *ab initio*, to end at a certain time or in a certain event. But if such an agreement were made, effect could be given to it, in praetorian law, by an *exceptio doli* or

1 Albertario, *Bull.* 1914, 275 *sqq.* who supposes the quasi-possession of G. 4. 139 to be a gloss. 2 G. 2. 29. 3 8. 2. 28. Perozzi, *Riv. It. p. l. Sc. Giur.* 14. 175. 4 8. 2. 28; 8. 3. 9; 8. 4. 2. 5 8. 6. 11. 1. 6 G. 2. 200; *post*, § CXVII. 7 23. 5. 5; C. 4. 51. 7; *ante*, p. 108. 8 He must deliver it as it was at the time of the contract. 18. 1. 59. 9 *Cessio in iure* and *mancipatio*, the ordinary civil methods, could not be suspended, nor could *adiudicatio*, Vat. Fr. 49. There might be *modus* in the sense of any limitation on the right. 8. 1. 4. 2, etc. As to creation by pact and stipulation, and *quasi traditio*, *post*, § XCIV.

pacti conventi. Even in Justinian's law the principle was so far preserved that the servitude was not *ipso facto* ended by the arrival of the time or occurrence of the condition, but only by way of equitable defence[1].

From the principle that servitudes were allowed only so far as advantageous to the tenement came the rules that the *praedia* must be near together, though not necessarily adjoining[2], and that they must be used only with that tenement[3]. Thus water drawn under a *ius aquaehaustus* might not be sold[4].

Praedial servitudes were indivisible. The chief results of this arose in connexion with loss of servitudes by *confusio*[5], but there were others. If it extended over two *fundi* it was not lost by non-use over one, if it had been used over the other[6]. If one, of several persons entitled, sued in respect of it, he claimed the whole[7]. If, having a *fundus*, *A* assigned an undivided part, he could not reserve a servitude[8]. Of common owners of a *fundus* all must assent, to produce any change in acquisition, abandonment, imposition or release of a servitude[9].

These servitudes were numerous. The oldest are *iter*, *via*, *actus* and *aquaeductus*, which go back to the XII Tables[10]. Others were added from time to time, till in later law they were almost innumerable.

Praedial servitudes were of two kinds, Rustic and Urban[11], the exact principle of distinction being uncertain. But as in Roman usage the epithet was attached to the *praedium dominans* and not to the servitude (*ius rustici praedii*[12]) the distinction must have turned on a characteristic of the dominant tenement. It is usually held that urban servitudes were those which primarily contemplated a building on the dominant land, while the others were rustic. But there are texts which raise difficulties. *Aquaeductus*, usually called rustic, is once called urban[13]. *Ius altius tollendi*, usually called urban, is called rustic by Neratius[14]. This has led to the view that a servitude, irrespective of its nature, was urban if it

1 8. 1. 4. pr. 2 There must not be intervening a piece of land over which there could not be such a servitude, 8. 1. 14. 2; 39. 3. 17. 4; h. l. 3; a right of way blocked by an intervening *praedium* is null, 8. 3. 7. 1. 3 8. 3. 5. 1, 24. 4 *Ib.* 5 *Post*, § xciv. 6 8. 3. 18; 8. 5. 9. 1. 7 8. 1. 17; 8. 5. 4. 3, 4. 8 8. 4. 5, 6. 1. 9 8. 2. 30. 1; 8. 3. 34. 10 See Bruns, 1. 27; Girard, *Textes*, 16, 17; D. 8. 3. 1. pr.; cf. h. t. 1. 1. *Aquaeductus* originally only from the source, but later from any point in the stream. 43. 20. 1. 7, 8, 38; 8. 3. 9. Arangio Ruiz (St. Brugi, 245; *Ist.* 216) holds that *iter* is a right to walk or ride, *actus* a right to drive cattle; on the dominant cl. view the *via* of the XII Tables is *iter* and *actus*; the view of it as something more is due to Justinian and it is not clear what more it includes. Inst. 2. 3. pr.; D. 8. 3. 8. 11 Inst. 2. 2. 3. 12 *Ib.*, Inst. 2. 3. pr.; D. 8. 2. 2. 13 6. 2. 11. 1; cf. 8. 2. 18. 14 8. 3. 2, with others that look urban.

was in connexion with a building, and rustic if it was not[1]. But the general language of the texts is against this[2].

The distinction already noted between positive and negative servitudes agrees nearly with that between rustic and urban: to some jurists the distinctions were apparently identical[3]. Servitudes have also been classed as continuous and discontinuous, those which do not, and those which do, require an act for their enjoyment, a distinction which also agrees somewhat nearly with those just mentioned.

The many rustic servitudes apart from the original four, e.g. the right to draw water, to burn lime, to dig sand, to pasture cattle, to take cattle to water, were later additions[4], differing fundamentally in character. The original four were easements: they gave mere use of the land for specific purposes. The others were "commons" or "profits": they involved taking some of the produce of the land. Since a usufruct might be limited in extent it is easy to see that such a right as *pecoris pascendi* was very like usufruct, a point to which we shall recur[5]. All rustic servitudes seem to have been positive. They were *res mancipi*[6], which, as they could not be alienated, means that they could be created by *mancipatio*. Possibly only the original four were *res mancipi*: indeed there is reason to think that, for the Sabinians, only the original four were rustic servitudes at all[7]. They could be pledged[8], which no doubt originally meant that they could be mancipated *cum fiducia*[9] with the land to which they were attached. In classical law it meant more: it was possible to give a rustic servitude to a creditor who had a near *praedium*, on the terms that he was to enjoy it till the money was paid, and if it was not, might sell it to some other neighbouring owner[10]. Thus it ceased when the debt was paid, and was transferable, both, as Paul notes, anomalies. The text has been the subject of much discussion[11]: its express limitation to the four old rights is confirmation of the view that only these four were *res mancipi*, for some jurists.

1 Girard, *Man.* 387; Cuq, *Man.* 329. It is difficult so to understand such texts as 8. 2. 2 and 8. 3. 1. If I acquire a right of way to land, and then build a house, does the servitude cease to be rustic and become urban? If I had previously pledged it, would the pledge cease to exist? 8. 3. 2 (Neratius), the main stumbling-block, does not suggest this view, nor apparently does any other text. For if 43. 19. 1 is so interpreted it conflicts with the rubric and leaves no interdictal protection to a right of way leading to a house. And Ulpian, twice in the title, refers to use of the easement by a "*hospes*" (43. 19. 1. 7, 3. 4). Indeed the explanation does not account for the text of Neratius, who gives, as other instances of rustic servitudes, *protectum habere*, and *cloacam habere*, which seem to assume buildings on the dominant tenement. His list is much more like a list of urban servitudes. 2 As to texts raising a similar suggestion as between praedial and personal servitudes, *post*, § XCVI. 3 *Post*, § XCIV. 4 8. 3. 1. pr., 1. 5 *Post*, § XCVI. 6 G. 2. 17. 7 8. 3. 1. pr.; Inst. 2. 3. pr., 2; Karlowa, *R.Rg.* 2. 357. 8 20. 1. 12. Only the original four are mentioned. Urban could not. 9 *Post*, § CLI. 10 20. 1. 12. 11 *Post*, § CLXVII.

The urban servitudes were also numerous. Most of them were negative but a few look positive: all were apparently continuous. Some of them were much alike[1], and there is uncertainty in the texts, in some cases, as to their exact definitions and distinctions, into which we need not go[2]. It does not appear that they could be pledged. Some of them present peculiarities. *Oneris ferendi* has been considered[3]. *Altius non tollendi*, obligation not to build higher, *ne luminibus officiatur*, not to obstruct your neighbour's light, and *stillicidium*, to receive your neighbour's drip, are all simple, but each of them had a peculiar looking counterservitude, *altius tollendi*[4], *luminibus officiendi*[5], and *stillicidii non recipiendi*[6]. All these seem to be rights which would exist apart from servitude. They have been explained in many ways. On one view they were modes of release from an existing servitude, but they were unnecessary for that[7]. Another is that they were releases from local laws concerning constructions[8], but that a private person should have a right to release from a law is unusual. There were such laws as to *altius tollendi*[9], and such agreements. But they are mostly late and *altius tollendi* was known to Gaius[10]. Another view is that they were a partial release, e.g. a counterservitude to build five feet higher. For this too there is some evidence[11]. As servitudes were indivisible it is not easy to see how they could be partially released, except by counterservitude[12], but it seems to be a servitude on one's own property.

XCIV. Acquisition of servitudes. Rustic, or some of them, could be created by *mancipatio*[13], and all praedial servitudes by *cessio in iure*[14], both gone under Justinian, by *adiudicatio*[15], by legacy or the like[16], and they were acquired by acquisition of the *praedium* to which they attached. On alienation of the land, the servitudes pass, or they would be extinct[17]. To this extent urban servitudes could be acquired by *mancipatio*. Servitudes could also be acquired by reservation in *mancipatio* or *cessio in iure* of the land to be servient[18], and, in Justinian's time, in *traditio*[19].

1 *Lumen* and *ne luminibus officiatur* (8. 2. 4). Elvers, *Servitutenlehre*, 444. *Tigni immittendi* and *oneris ferendi*. 2 See 8. 2. 2 *sqq*. 3 *Ante*, p. 259. 4 G. 2. 31; 4. 3; D. 8. 3. 2. 5 8. 2. 2. 6 *Ib*. 7 Release by *cessio in iure* is as simple as creation of a counterservitude in the same way. 8 Girard, *Man*. 386. 9 C. 8. 10. 12. Accarias, *Précis*, 1. 676. 10 See n. 4. 11 44. 2. 26; 8. 2. 11. 1. Vat. Fr. 53; D. 8. 6. 8. 12 Cuq, *Man*. 330, citing 8. 2. 11. pr. and C. 3. 34. 1, thinks them releases by way of counterservitude from the rule requiring new buildings to conform to the old state of things, as to lights, etc. But the first text has been held to be due to Justinian and the other merely says that a servitude of light may be acquired by lapse of time, is unique in that, and also suspected. 13 G. 2. 29. 14 G. 2. 29, 31. Statement that they could not be created under condition (8. 1. 4. pr.), not true of legacy (33. 3. 3), means only that the modes of creation *inter vivos* (*c. i. iure* and *mancipatio*) could not themselves be conditional. 15 *Ante*, p. 252. 16 8. 2. 31. 17 41. 1. 20. 1. 18 8. 4. 3, 6. pr. Not called *deductio*. 19 8. 4. 3. Even earlier, *deductio* of a usufruct might effect a *traditio* of the land. C. Th. 8. 12. 9 = C. 8. 53. 28; *ante*, p. 227.

They could be usucapted till a *l. Scribonia*, probably late in the Republic, which forbade this[1]. There were under Justinian certain other methods of the history of which something must be said.

Some servitudes or quasi-servitudes, not admitted at civil law, yet existed. Such were the rights to water not from the *caput aquae*, but from an intermediate point[2], and also similar rights in public lands and rivers[3]: these may be the only cases. Clearly they could not be created by civil law methods, and the question arises how they were created, and how far and with what effect these methods were applied to other servitudes in classical law. The relevant texts are much altered, and there is a "chaos of opinions[4]" on the matter. It must suffice to indicate the modes recorded in the Sources and to state what seem the more probable conclusions.

Quasi Traditio. We are not told that a *lex* could be attached to a *traditio*, for the creation of a servitude over other land of the vendor, with praetorian remedies[5], but several texts, taken at their face value, suggest that *traditio* and *patientia* of, e.g., a right of way, did in fact give rise to praetorian protection. In classical law *res incorporales* were incapable of *traditio*[6] and the texts all shew signs of interpolation or have to do, not with creation, but with the question of enjoyment necessary to the interdicts[7]. But it is not impossible, and it is in the line of natural evolution, that, as apparently in usufruct[8], the Praetor did give a remedy in such cases, perhaps an *actio in factum*[9].

Pact and *stipulatio*. From Gaius[10], it appears that this method (presumably the Greek method of agreement, reinforced for Roman practice by *stipulatio*[11]) was applied only in provincial land, in his time. It does not follow that no change occurred in the classical age, and though texts which mention this method are treated as either interpolated or referring to provincial land, this is hardly proved of all[12]. It

1 Some texts suggest (P. 1. 17. 2; D. 8. 1. 14. pr.; 41. 3. 4. 28) that only the four original were usucaptible and that the *lex* did not destroy this for water rights. But P. 1. 17. 2 does not shew that such a right could be so acquired *de novo*. 2 8. 3. 9 (interp.); 43. 20. 1. 7. 3 43. 13. 1. 1; h. 1. 9; Costa, *Le Acque*, 24 *sqq*. Elvers, *Servitutenlehre*, 267. 4 Rabel, *Mél. Girard*, 2. 387 *sqq*.; Peters, *Z.S.S.* 1912, 595. 5 See, however, Collinet, *Mél. Girard*, 1. 185. 6 G. 2. 28. 7 Chief texts: 6. 2. 11. 1; 7. 1. 3, 25. 7; 7. 6. 3; 8. 1. 20; 8. 3. 1. 2; 8. 4. 2; 39. 5. 27; 43. 19. 3. 8. Interdictal protection of the original rustic servitudes is complete. There seems no evidence of special interdicts for any others, or for *uti possidetis* in negative servitudes. 8 *Post*, § XCVI. 9 Girard, *Man.* 401. In Vat. Fr. 61 "*tuitione praetoris*" can hardly apply, as Rabel holds, to provincial lands. 10 G. 2. 31. 11 Bonfante, *Scr. Giur.* 3. 146. Perhaps originally a *stipulatio* for a penalty. 12 The texts are 7. 1. 25. 7, 27. 4; 8. 3. 33. D. 7. 1. 27. 4 is not discussed by Rabel or by Collinet (*Ét. Hist.* 1. 161) and is said by Peters to refer to provincial land. He gives no reason. It seems to give the *stip.* an effect *in rem*. But it is not conclusive: it may turn, like the text which follows it, on the duties of fructuary.

may be that it did not give a *ius in rem*, even praetorian, in classical law, since, on the view suggested above, *quasi traditio* sufficed. In the normal case the two would be combined, in positive servitudes. But it is difficult to apply the notion of *traditio* to negative servitudes, and nothing in the texts excludes the possibility that here the *stipulatio* operated *in rem*. Pact and *stipulatio* was recognised by Zeno in terms which imply an institution known before the time of his predecessor Leo[1].

Long enjoyment. Texts speak of this as a root of title to a servitude[2]. Under Justinian it is a case of *l. t. praescriptio*, with the normal periods, but apparently, instead of a requirement of *bona fides* and *iusta causa*, it had the rule that enjoyment must not have been *vi clam aut precario*[3]. The earlier law is obscure. Perhaps the most probable view is that in the later part of the second century, possibly in connexion with water rights, a practice grew of treating very long enjoyment (the term being left to the *iudex*, probably with guidance in the *formula*) as raising a presumption that the right had been duly created, in absence of proof that it had been *clam vi aut precario*. This would seem to create a civil right but the action is called *utilis*[4], which, if the word is genuine, need mean no more than a specialised *formula*, but it cannot properly be called praetorian, as it is almost certainly later than the consolidation of the Edict. The idea is said to be borrowed from Greek ideas of prescription[5].

All these methods gave full title under Justinian and probably before[6].

A servitude could cease to exist in many ways. *Cessio in iure* extinguished it in classical law[7], renunciation, either express or by authorising acts inconsistent with it, under Justinian[8].

It ended by *confusio*, but there are distinctions to be drawn. If the *confusio* was set aside, by operation of law, the servitude might revive, e.g. where the *heres* conveyed the dominant property to the owner of the servient, in the belief that there was a *fideicommissum* of it, or the transaction which caused the *confusio* was set aside by *restitutio in*

1 C. 8. 10. 12. 1, 4. 2 Discussion and reff. Bonfante, *Scr. Giur.* 2. 956; chief texts, 8. 5. 10; 39. 3. 1. 23; h. t. 26; 43. 19. 5. 3; C. 3. 34. 1, 2, 7. There has been interpolation: it is doubtful if it applied to anything but way and water before Justinian. 3 8. 5. 10. pr.; C. 3. 34. 1. 4 8. 5. 10. pr. 5 Partsch, *Longi Temp. praescr.* 96, 118. 6 Remedies, *post*, §§ CCXXVIII, CCXLVIII. 7 *Arg.* G. 2. 30. Perozzi, *Ist.* 1. 774, noting that the texts apply only to usufruct, is inclined to doubt whether servitudes could be released by *i. i. c.* There seems no reason for the limitation: they could certainly be so created (G. 2. 29, 31). The method he suggests (transfer of the dominant land with a pact for retransfer) seems highly improbable and inconvenient. Servitudes are things and when G. says (2. 29) that *cedi possunt*, his statement applies both ways. A rustic servitude might no doubt be released by *remancipatio*. 8 8. 2. 21; 8. 3. 20. Before him it would have given an *exceptio pacti conventi*.

integrum[1]. But voluntary reconveyance did not revive it. As the servitude attached to the whole *praedium*, the acquisition of a defined part of the dominant by the owner of the servient did not affect it[2]. Where the dominant owner acquired part of the servient, if it was a defined right of way, the effect would depend on the question whether the whole way was included or not[3]. The acquisition of an undivided share in either, by the owner of the other, did not affect the servitude[4].

It ended by destruction of either *praedium*, or by such an alteration of the conditions of the servient that there could be no servitude on it, or by disappearance of the subject of the servitude[5]. Thus *aquaehaustus* ceased if the stream permanently dried up[6]. But in this case, if the original state of things was restored before expiry of the period of non-use, the right revived[7].

It was lost by non-use for two years before Justinian, ten or twenty under him[8]. For rustic servitudes, mere abstention from enjoyment was enough, but for urban there must have been something done (by the servient owner[9]) inconsistent with the servitude[10]. In negative servitudes there was in fact no non-use till something inconsistent was done. A right to light was not lost by not looking out of the window. This is the main illustration of the point that for some purposes, and for some jurists, negative and urban meant the same thing, difficult to reconcile with the view that any servitude might, in appropriate circumstances, be rustic or urban[11]. The distinction was expressed by the proposition that rustic were lost by non-use, urban by *usucapio libertatis*. This last name looks at the matter from the point of view of the servient tenement: a right detached had returned, a burden been released[12]. As it was *usucapio*, it had the characteristics of *usucapio*. Thus if the owner of the servient land ceased to possess it, time ceased to run in his favour[13]. *Bona fides* was not needed, not having been an original element in *usucapio*[14], but, if the adverse act was done *precario*, time did not run against the holder of the servitude[15]. The rule as to possession had no application to the case of non-use. It is a singular result of the rules as stated that a *ius tigni immittendi* was not lost by removing the beam. Time did not

1 8. 1. 18; 8. 4. 9; 21. 1. 31. 3; 23. 5. 7. 1; 30. 116. 4. 2 8. 2. 30. 1; 8. 6. 15, or the acquisition of a usufruct. 3 See 8. 6. 6. 4 *Ib.* and 8. 3. 31. 5 E.g. 7. 4. 24; 8. 2. 20. 2. 6 8. 3. 35. 7 8. 6. 14. 8. 2. 20. 2; *Restitutio* if too late, 8. 3. 35. This seems to be the practical effect of the texts. The rule may be due to Justinian, Guarneri-Citati, *Real. Ist. Lombard.* LIX. 147. 8 P. 1. 17. 1; C. 3. 34. 13. If the right was only to intermittent enjoyment, e.g. every other year, the time was proportionally lengthened, but not where it might be enjoyed every day, but only for part of it, or even on alternate days, 8. 6. 7. 9 So the texts say, but if done by a third party the effect would presumably be the same. If by the dominant it would presumably be abandonment. 10 8. 2. 6. 32. 11 *Ante*, p. 262. 12 P. 1. 17. 1; D. 8. 2. 6; 8. 6. 18. 2, etc. 13 8. 2. 32. 1. 14 *Ante*, p. 243. 15 8. 2. 32. pr.

run till the servient owner plugged the hole in which it rested[1]. The same was no doubt true of the other similar servitudes.

The effect on the servitudes of abandonment of one or both of the *praedia* is disputed. The only directly relevant text seems to imply that it was unaffected by abandonment of the *praedium serviens*[2] and the same is probably true of abandonment of the *praedium dominans*. This is difficult to reconcile with the conception of them as *iura in re aliena*, but no Roman text so describes them. A servitude is a burden on the land rather than on the ownership. It is an independent *ius* which must be thought of rather as parallel to ownership than as a burden on it. If we reflect on the fact that the earliest servitudes were *res mancipi*, capable of *usucapio* and pledge, the idea that they were thought of as physical things, actual visible tracks and channels, will account for those rules which may look anomalous in classical law[3].

XCV. Personal servitudes. These were servitudes belonging to a man personally, not as owner of anything else, applying to moveables as well as land, limited in duration, few in number (usufruct and two or three others derived from it), and giving indefinite rights, including physical possession of the property subject to them. They did not originate in the needs of agricultural life, but in the much more advanced idea of provision for dependents, and the introduction of usufruct, the earliest, was probably associated with prevalence of marriage without *manus*. It was recognised in the time of Cicero[4] and earlier[5], but is not in Plautus[6]: the others seem to be later. Much later than the introduction of these rights was their recognition as a class of servitudes. No legal text independent of Justinian calls them servitudes. Gaius sharply distinguishes them[7], as does Justinian in the Institutes, following him[8]. So do the rubrics in the Digest[9]. The expression "personal servitude" is rare[10]: usufruct is called a servitude only about six times[11], and most of these texts are suspected of interpolation. The conception of usufruct as a servitude may thus be due to Justinian[12]. But the texts which use the notion seem to be all from late jurists and it may be that the idea appeared late in the classical age. In earlier classical law it was thought of as a *ius* attached to a person, having no juristic relation to the physical thing, a conception still reflected in some of the texts[13].

1 8. 2. 6. 2 8. 5. 6. 2, *fin.* 3 Buckland, *L.Q.R.* 1928, 426; *contra*, Desserteaux, *R.H.* 1929, 291. 4 *Top.* 3. 15; *pro Caec.* 7. 19, etc. 5 Cicero, *de fin.* 1. 4. 12. 6 For opinions as to its antiquity, Costa, *Storia*, 264. 7 G. 2. 14; G. Ep. 2. 1. 3. 8 Inst. 2. 2. 3. 9 D. 7 and 8. 10 8. 1. 1; 34. 3. 8. 3. See also, 8. 1. 15. pr. 11 Longo, *Bull.* 1899, 281. The fragment supposed to be of the *Regulae* of Pomponius (*Coll. Lib. iur.* 2. 148; Girard, *Textes*, 220) uses *servitus* in a way which clearly excludes usufruct. The usage may be due to Marcian, Buckland, *St. Riccobono*, I. 275 *sqq.* 12 Girard, *Man.* 381. 13 Riccobono, *Ist.* 377; Buckland, *L.Q.R.* 1927, 326, on an early view of usufruct as consisting in the fact of enjoyment.

It is clear that there were doubts, conflicts and changes of opinion as to the conception of usufruct. The transition from the view of it as an absolute *ius* to that of it as a right in a physical thing, culminating in the view of it as a servitude, is reflected in changes in subsidiary rules. Late law allows the fructuary to proceed for *damnum infectum* and the like and to vindicate servitudes attached to the land, which he could not in earlier law[1]. The remedies for usufruct were the same as those for servitudes. It was a *ius*, claimed by real action, the *actio confessoria* of Justinian[2].

Ususfructus was the right to enjoy the property of another and to take the fruits, but not to destroy it[3], or fundamentally alter its character[4]. It was usually for life, never more, but sometimes for a fixed term[5]. Where it was given to a corporation its limit under Justinian was 100 years[6]. Even if a term was fixed, death of the holder ended it[7].

The fruits were the ordinary produce of the thing and did not include accidental acquisitions through it. The young of animals were fruits but, by an exception set down to respect for human dignity, children of *ancillae* were not[8]. An *insula nata* was not *fructus*: the fructuary had not even a usufruct in it[9]. As to what were fruits, something depended on the nature of the estate. Trees were not ordinarily fruits, but they were in a "timber estate", where timber was the normal source of profit. The same was true of minerals, but new mines might be opened up, if this did not alter the character of the property[10]. The fructuary's right to rents, etc., the so-called *fructus civiles*, has already been considered[11]. He had the use of tools, accessories, etc.[12] He might improve the property, provided he did not alter its character[13], but he might not remove what he had erected[14]. He must keep the premises in repair[15], cultivate the land and keep it in proper heart and condition[16]. As he took the profits he must pay the outgoings[17]. All this expresses a rule that he must behave as a *bonus paterfamilias*, but in classical law the rule was stricter: he must use the property only as the donor had, not, e.g., sell produce, where the donor had not[18]. The Edict required him to

1 7. 6. 5. 1, 43. 25. 1. 4, 39. 2. 13. 8. It is probable that there was gradual movement as to the admissibility of these remedies. 2 *Post*, § CCXXVIII. D. 7. 6. 5. 6. Vat. Fr. 47, 55, 56, etc., shew that at least the affinity with servitudes was recognised. 3 7. 1. 1. 4 P. 3. 6. 21. 5 7. 4. 3. pr., 3. 6 7. 1. 56. 7 *Arg*. 7. 4. 3. pr., 3; 7. 1. 51. 8 5. 3. 27. pr.; P. 3. 6. 19; D. 22. 1. 28. 9 7. 1. 9. 4. *Alluvio* is not *fructus*, but the usufruct applies to it. P. 3. 6. 22. It is a question of probable intent. Acquisitions through slaves, *post*, § XCIX. Lambs in a flock, *summissio*, *ante*, p. 223. He must maintain woods and nursery gardens, 7. 1. 9. 6, 10. 10 7. 1. 9. 2, 13. 5, 13. 6. 11 *Ante*, p. 222. 12 7. 1. 9. 7, 15. 6. 13 7. 1. 13. 7. 14 7. 1. 15. pr. 15 7. 1. 7. 2. But need not rebuild old buildings which fall. For repairs he may use materials from the estate, 7. 1. 12. pr. 16 7. 1. 13. 2. As to his right to punish slaves, Vat. Fr. 72. 17 7. 1. 7. 2. 18 Riccobono, *St. Brugi*, 173, comparing Vat. Fr. 70. 1 and D. 7. 1. 9. 6, 7.

give security for this and for return on expiration of the right[1], a rule first established for the case of legacy, always the commonest type, but later applied to all cases[2]. It is disputed whether the obligations as specific duties of a fructuary were themselves created by the Praetor, or existed at civil law and were merely better protected by him[3].

Usufruct was inalienable: the effect of an attempted *cessio in iure* by the fructuary to a third party was disputed. On one view it was an admission that he had no right: it worked a forfeiture and the right lapsed to the *dominus*. On the other it was a nullity[4]. But though the right itself could not be transferred, there was no objection, in classical or later law, to letting or selling the enjoyment, the position and responsibilities of the usufructuary being, however, retained[5].

As we have seen there was room for differences of theory as to the true conception of its relation to *dominium*. Was it a separate right, contrasted with ownership, or a fraction of ownership—a *pars dominii*? The point, of practical importance, was not always decided in the same way. A pact not to sue for an estate gave a defence to a claim for the usufruct, as usufruct was *pars dominii*[6]. If an estate was due to me on contract and I released a claim to the usufruct this was a nullity as usufruct was not a part[7]. To some extent the divergence merely shews that words are being used in different senses. To say that it is *pars dominii* is to say that it is a group of rights which, with others, make up the bundle of rights constituting *dominium*. To say that it is not a *pars dominii* means that *dominium* is none the less *dominium* because rights are cut out of it. But there are real conflicts. Julian says that one who stipulated for land and then for a usufruct in it, or *vice versa*, was like one who stipulated for a whole and then for a part or *vice versa*, and holds the *stipulatio* for the usufruct to be void[8]. Ulpian says that one who, having stipulated for land, gave a release of the claim to usufruct produced no effect since the usufruct was not a part[9]. Julian could hardly have so held. If the stipulation for the usufruct was void because usufruct was a part, the release must have been good for the same reason[10].

Usufruct being incorporeal could not be possessed, but the notion of quasi-possession was applied to it[11]. There was no special interdict

1 P. 3. 6. 27; D. 7. 9. 1. pr. 2 7. 9. 1. 2. 3 Praetorian origin, Girard, *Man.* 394; civil origin, Karlowa, *R.Rg.* 2. 539. See also De Ruggiero, *St. Scialoja*, 1. 71. The distinction is less important than it might appear. Doing what he was not entitled to do with the property would usually be a delict. Girard, *loc. cit.* 4 G. 2. 30; Inst. 2. 4. 3; D. 23. 3. 66. 5 7. 1. 12. 2; Vat. Fr. 41. 6 2. 14. 27. 8. 7 46. 4. 13. 2. Principal texts, Roby, *De usufructu*, 42. 8 45. 1. 58. 9 46. 4. 13. 2. 10 Paul says a pact not to sue for land bars action for usufruct, and his comparisons shew that for him it is a part. 2. 14. 27. 8. 11 In classical law fructuary was "*in possessione*," cf. 41. 2. 12. pr.

for protection of enjoyment as in rights of way and water, but *uti possidetis* was available with the necessary modifications[1].

Unlike praedial servitudes, usufruct was divisible[2] (though the other personal servitudes were not), a rule with important results. There could be common ownership of a usufruct. A usufruct might be granted in an undivided share of property[3]. It might fail *pro parte*[4]. Where several held it in common there might be *ius accrescendi*, but not where two held each a usufruct of half by independent gifts[5]. This *ius accrescendi* was subject to special rules based on the proposition that in usufruct accrual was to the person, not to the *portio*[6].

As the usufructuary was bound to return the thing in good condition, there was no usufruct of perishables[7]. The earliest usufructs were commonly over all a man's goods, which would usually include perishables, but as to these the gift seems to have been void[8] till early in the Empire, when a senatusconsult[9] provided that, if a usufruct created by will covered such things, they should belong to the legatee, who must give security for return of their value at the expiry of the usufruct[10]. Usufruct of money could be so left and by the end of the first century there might be quasi-usufruct even in a *ius in personam*. It was possible to leave a life interest in a debt due to the testator, to the debtor or to a third person, in effect, a loan for life of the money without interest[11].

XCVI. Originally usufruct was always by legacy, and this remained much the most usual mode, but, subject to limitations, the methods for urban servitude were applicable[12]. It could not be acquired by acquisition of the *praedium* to which it was attached, for it was not so attached. *Longi temporis praescriptio* was applicable to it under Justinian[13], and he is clearly regulating an existing institution. We have no earlier evidence[14], and we do not know whether, like *praescriptio* for ownership, it required *bona fides* and *iusta causa*, or, like praedial servitudes, did not[15]. There were cases in which usufruct arose by law without express creation, e.g. the usufruct of the *paterfamilias*, in later

1 43. 17. 4; Vat. Fr. 90, 91; G. 4. 139. 2 7. 1. 50. 3 Ulp. 24. 26. 4 7. 1. 49, 50; 7. 4. 14; Elvers, *Servitutenlehre*, 542. 5 For accrual there must be a joint gift. Legacy of usufruct had special rules, *post*, § CXXIII. 6 7. 2. *passim*, 7. 3. 1; 7. 4. 18; 33. 2. 13; 45. 3. 26; Vat. Fr. 75 *sqq.*, and *post*, § CXXIII. 7 Ulp. 24. 26. 8 *Arg.* Cicero, *Top.* 3. 17. The text is consistent with a right in the legatee to detain, e.g. a cellar of wine, though not to consume it. 9 Ulp. 24. 27. 10 Inst. 2. 4. 2; D. 7. 5 *passim*. 11 7. 5. 3. In the first case it is a defence: in the second the *heres* must authorise the legatee to claim the debt or interest; *procuratio in rem suam*. It is only because these are in wills that they are thought of as quasi-usufruct. If I make a pact not to sue my debtor for interest or till his death, no one would call this a quasi-usufruct, though the effect is the same. There is of course no question of *actio confessoria*, or care of *bonus paterfamilias*. 12 *Deductio* in alienation by *mancipatio* or *c. i. i.*, or, under J. by *traditio*, *ante*, pp. 235, 264. 13 C. 7. 33. 12. 4. 14 History probably as in praedial servitudes. 15 *Ante*, p. 266. Did *usucapio* apply to it in classical law? Beseler, *Beiträge*, 3. 171, 4. 78.

law, in *bona adventitia*[1], the usufruct of the emancipating father under Justinian[2], and cases in late law in connexion with second marriages[3].

It ended by *cessio in iure* to the owner[4]. In later law any voluntary release sufficed. It ended if the two interests came together in the same hands, here called *consolidatio*[5], not as in praedial servitudes, *confusio*. It ended by death or *capitis deminutio* of the holder, limited by Justinian to *maxima* or *media*[6], and, if for a term, by the expiry of time[7]. It was lost by non-use for the period of *usucapio*[8]. It was lost if the title of the owner who created it was invalidated in any way[9]. And it ended if the property was fundamentally altered[10]. It is sometimes said that for loss by non-use the owner must have been in possession, at least under Justinian, but the evidence is on the whole against this[11]. Non-use is not here quite a simple idea. If a third party had taken profit or done any act in relation to the thing, in the fructuary's name, this was use even though not authorised by him[12]. If the enjoyment of the right had been sold for cash it could not now be lost by non-use[13]. Destruction by *capitis deminutio*, especially *minima*, caused inconvenience, and the lawyers found ways of evading it. One method was to give the usufruct with a gift of another usufruct to take effect if the first failed by *capitis deminutio*, and so on whenever it should happen[14]. Another was, since usufruct could be for a term, to give it "*in singulos annos*," i.e. a new one for each year, so that the *deminutio* would affect only the current year[15]. Traces of these safeguards appear in the Digest[16], but *capitis deminutio minima* no longer affected usufruct.

Usufruct could be acquired through a slave or a *filiusfamilias*: if this was by legacy, though it was acquired by the *paterfamilias* and failed on his death, it failed also on the death, sale or manumission of the slave, death or *capitis minutio* of the *filius*[17]. This rule is laid down only for *legatum per vindicationem*[18]: it would not cover *l. per damnationem* or *fideicommissum*, as these were completed *inter vivos*. The rule was gone

1 C. Th. 8. 18. 1=C. 6. 60. 1, *post*, § XCIX. 2 Inst. 2. 9. 2; *post*, § XCIX. 3 E.g. C. 6. 61. 4. 4 P. 3. 6. 28 *sqq.*; *ante*, p. 270, n. 4. 5 P. 3. 6. 28; Vat. Fr. 83; D. 7. 2. 3. 2, 6. pr. (In 7. 4. 27 the word *confusa* is used.) When the terminology was framed, usufruct was not thought of as a servitude. 6 Vat. Fr. 61, 62; C. 3. 33. 16. 2. 7 7. 4. 3; Vat. Fr. 52, lapse of 100 years if to a corporate body, 7. 1. 56. 8 P. 3. 6. 30; under Justinian only by such lapse of time as would bar a claim to *dominium*; C. 3. 33. 16. 1. Use of part saved the whole, 7. 1. 53. 9 35. 1. 105. 10 P. 3. 6. 28 *sqq.* Where land was in usufruct and the *dominus* built a house on it, the usufruct ended, but he was liable to the fructuary, 7. 4. 5. 3, 10. Alteration of an accessory part did not affect the right even in that part, 7. 1. 34. 2, 53; 7. 4. 8. 11 The term of two years suggests *usucapio libertatis*, but that notion is not applied: it is always non-use. See n. 8 and D. 7. 4. 25; C. 3. 34. 13; Inst. 2. 4. 3. But C. 3. 33. 16. 1 suggests the other view. 12 7. 1. 12. 2 *sqq.*; 7. 4. 29. 13 7. 1. 12. 2. 14 Vat. Fr. 64. 15 Vat. Fr. 63. Hence puzzling questions of accrual where there were joint fructuaries. *Post*, § CXXIII. 16 7. 4. 1. 3, 3. pr. (=Vat. Fr. 63); 33. 2. 23. 17 Vat. Fr. 57. 18 *Post*, § CXVII.

under Justinian, but he provided that a usufruct so acquired through a *filius* who survived the father, should go to the son till his death[1]. These rules apply the principle of which there are many other traces, that, in gifts by will to a subordinate, his personality was primarily considered though the gift went to the *paterfamilias*[2].

Usus, of recent introduction in the time of Labeo[3], was a fraction of usufruct. The rules as to acquisition, destruction, security and remedies were the same, but the rights were less. It was usufruct without *fructus*. There could be no right of *fructus* without *usus*, so that, if *usus* was left to one and *fructus* to another, the latter shared the *usus* and had the *fructus*[4]. It was indivisible, so that it could not be created in undivided shares, or fail *pro parte*[5]. Its main rules express the principle that the right was to use, but not to take fruits, relaxed in various ways, starting from the fact that of some things there is no use but by taking fruits. The usuary of a house might live in it, with his household and guests, but might not sell or let it, as this was in the nature of taking fruits, but from early times he might take paying guests, provided he did not himself vacate the house[6]. Of the produce he might sell nothing. At first he could take nothing, but this was gradually relaxed[7], and the rule of the Digest was that he could take produce for the needs of his household but no more[8]. *Usus* seems commonly to have been created by legacy[9].

The rights of usufructuary or usuary were not necessarily so wide as those stated: they might be limited by the instrument of creation[10]. If the right were very limited it might not be easy to say whether it was a personal servitude, extinguished by the death of the holder, or, if given to the owner of an adjoining *praedium*, a praedial servitude, essentially perpetual, extinguishable only *ope exceptionis* (*doli*)[11]. There are texts all dealing with gifts by will, which contemplate rights of this kind[12]. Paul says there cannot be *usus* or usufruct of a praedial servitude, and adds that such a legacy will give an action to the legatee to compel the *heres* either to allow the enjoyment, which makes it a mere *ius in personam*,

1 C. 3. 33. 17. At this time the *paterfamilias* had a usufruct in what the son acquired from outside, *post*, § xcix. 2 31. 82. 2. In all legacy of usufruct, whether to a *paterfamilias* or subordinate, *dies cedit* only on entry of the *heres* (*post*, § cxx), so that if the actual donee is then dead the gift fails. 3 Its content was still controverted. See 7. 8. 2, 4. 1. Q. Mucius is mentioned: he "*primus admisit*" a certain rule. 4 P. 3. 6. 24, 25; D. 7. 8. 14. 2. But see as to *fructus* without *usus*, Accarias, *Précis*, 1. 693. 5 7. 8. 19. It is difficult to reconcile the rule with that stated in the texts cited in n. 4. 6 7. 8. 2 *sqq.*, 8; 10. 3. 10. 1. 7 7. 8. 12. 2. 8 7. 8. 12, 15. An interpolated text (7. 8. 12. 1) says that one could take the fruits of a *villa* of which he had *usus* for supply of his house in town. For Riccobono, *St. Scialoja*, 1. 581, all rights to fruits are due to Justinian. 9 All the instances are, but it need not be. 7. 8. 1. 10 7. 1. 15. 6. 11 *Ante*, p. 261. 12 Riccobono, *Tydschr.* 1922, 350.

or to create the servitude, with security for surrender at death, making it a praedial servitude[1]. The first method seems to be contemplated in another text of his, which says that where a man left the use of water to his brother, by name, this was personal and would not go to his heir[2]. Papinian says that rights of pasture and watering are *prima facie* praedial, but if the beneficiary is named personally, they do not go to a *heres* or buyer[3]. If Paul is correct, Papinian cannot mean that it was *usus* of pasture or watering, nor is it easy to regard it as a very limited *usus* of the land. It was presumably a mere *ius in personam*. Pomponius cites Proculus as saying that a building may be left in usufruct with a *servitus ne altius tollatur* imposed on it, for the benefit of another property in the *hereditas*[4]. Elvers so interprets this[5], but the text makes it an actual servitude, and, apparently, over *res sua*[6]. Ulpian carries the matter further in a self-contradictory text usually understood to mean that a *fideicommissum* may be made of a right to water, to one who has no *praedium dominans*, and that this will be a servitude[7], which must therefore be *usus* of a right of water. But the latter part of the text is supposed to be a gloss: if that is so, Ulpian makes it only a *ius in personam*[8].

Habitatio was a modification of *usus* of a house or lodging, probably only temporary at first, and given with no intention to create a *ius in rem*, e.g. *habitatio* given to a *libertus* by his patron's will. It dates from the Republic. It was gradually differentiated from *usus*: its recognition as a distinct servitude (with, originally, only praetorian remedies[9]) may be due to Justinian. It could apparently be created only by will or codicil[10], and had more liberal rules, based on presumed intent. It was for life[11]. It was not lost by non-use or *capitis minutio*[12]. Justinian provided that the right might be let, but not sold or given away[13]. All this seems to be inferred, as the testator's intention, from his saying *habitatio* rather than *usus*[14].

Operae servorum vel animalium had the same relation to *usus* of these as *habitatio* had to *usus* of a house. There was a special reason why the right was not lost by *capitis deminutio*, or non-use[15]. An *opera* is a "daywork," and such a legacy can be regarded as a series of legacies

1 33. 2. 1. 2 8. 3. 37. 3 8. 3. 4. 4 7. 1. 19. pr. 5 *Servitutenlehre*, 704. 6 Roby, *de usufructu*, 144, is inclined to accept Elvers' view. The transaction is plain and rational: it is only the word *servitus* which makes difficulty. 7 34. 1. 14. 3. 8 In 43. 20. 1. 43, Ulpian discusses a grant, by the Emperor, of right of water. It may be, he says, to a *praedium* or a person: in the latter case it dies with him. But such a grant is not a servitude. 9 *S.M.W.* 327. 10 Justinian says (Inst. 2. 5. 5): "*si habitatio legata sive aliquo alio modo constituta est*," which may refer to *fideicommissum* or the divisory actions. 11 Vat. Fr. 43; D. 7. 8. 10. 3 mentions an old view limiting it to a year. 12 7. 8. 10. pr. 13 Inst. 2. 5. 5; D. 7. 8. 10. pr. 14 The classics were doubtful about these distinctions; Inst. 2. 5. 5; D. 7. 8. 10; C. 3. 33. 13. 15 33. 2. 2.

of dayworks[1]. Thus these events would affect only the current day. It did not fail by death of legatee, as it was not usufruct, the later legacies being thus *ex die*[2]. The whole interpretation is one of intent. The text adds[3] that it was destroyed by *usucapio* of the slave (or animal[4]).

XCVII. Of three rights usually treated as an appendix to the law of servitudes, *pignus* will be considered under contract. It was a *ius in rem*, as it gave possessory rights, but the Romans did not so treat possession and the texts point out the importance of keeping distinct the notions of possession and property[5]. The others are *emphyteusis* and *superficies*. They resembled servitudes, being rights *in rem* over property of another, analogous to personal servitudes, but though of unlimited duration, like praedial servitudes, they gave indefinite rights, like personal servitudes. The real reason why they were not treated as servitudes is that they belong to late law: they were not known to the civil law.

Emphyteusis originated in *ager vectigalis*, which, in the early Empire, meant land of the State or a city granted either in perpetuity or for a long term at a rent fixed in kind. It was thought of as *locatio*, but, before Hadrian, its long duration caused it to acquire the characteristics of a praetorian *ius in rem*, very like ownership, transferable by *traditio*, and protected by interdicts and *actiones fictitiae*. In the fourth century the name *emphyteusis* was applied to grants of imperial domains for long terms on like conditions. In the fifth, these institutions were fused and by its end the method was adopted by private owners. Zeno found it necessary to settle a dispute by deciding that it was not *locatio* or *emptio* but a contract *sui generis*[6]. Justinian settled its rules, largely by interpolations. It could be created by any form of agreement (followed by entry), or by will. The holder (*emphyteuta*) might deal freely with the land provided it could be returned unimpaired if the interest ended. An existing *emphyteusis* could be left by will or sold, subject in Justinian's time to a right of pre-emption in the *dominus*, and a fine of 2 per cent. on the price, if the option was not exercised[7]. It ended by agreement, lapse of term, destruction of the land, death of holder without successors, and forfeiture for irretrievable damage or non-payment of rent or taxes for (usually) three years[8].

1 *Ante*, p. 89; *post*, § CLX. 2 33. 2. 2. Girard, *Man.* 397. Text obscure. The ref. is presumably to death after the gift has taken effect. It can hardly mean (though the language suggests it) that it cedes on death, for 33. 2. 7 says that it cedes only on actual claim. 3 Probably applies, *mutatis mutandis*, to *habitatio* of a house. 4 As to the remedies in connexion with servitudes, by action and interdict, *post*, §§ CCXXVIII, CCXLVIII. 5 41. 2. 12. 1, "*nihil commune habet proprietas cum possessione*"; 41. 2. 52. pr., "*nec possessio ac proprietas misceri debent*"; 43. 17. 1. 2, "*separata esse debet possessio a proprietate.*" Ihering (*Grund d. Besitzesch.* § VI) discusses these texts from the point of view of his theory of possession. *Post*, § CLXVI. 6 C. 4. 66. 1. 7 H. t. 3. 8 Chief legal sources, C. 4. 66; C. 11. 63. 1; C. Th. 5. 15; D. 6. 3; 27. 9. 3. 4; Inst. 3. 24. 3. Girard, *Man.* 413 *sqq.*; Costa, *Storia*, 273.

Superficies originated in building leases by the State and cities. In the Empire it was not always *locatio*: it might arise by *emptio* or even *donatio mortis causa*. Before Hadrian it had come to be granted by private persons[1] and there were edictal remedies, *in rem*. Besides giving an interdict *de superficiebus*[2], the Edict is said to have provided that the Praetor would give any action which might be necessary[3], if the right was perpetual[4]. Elsewhere we hear of *actiones utiles, hypothecaria, confessoria, communi dividundo*[5]: interpolation being alleged, though hardly proved[6]. No surviving classical text refers to a case between private parties[7].

XCVIII. The Institutes close the discussion of *dominium* and servitudes with a statement of cases in which the maxim "*dat qui habet*" did not hold, cases in which an owner could not alienate and cases in which a non-owner could. The chief cases in which an owner could not alienate were the following:

(*a*) A husband, though *dominus*, could not alienate dotal land[8].

(*b*) *Pupilli*, women in *tutela*, as to *res mancipi*, *furiosi* and *prodigi* under interdict, could not alienate[9].

(*c*) Owners for the time being, but in such circumstances that their right might determine by operation of law (e.g. a *heres* where there was a conditional legacy, or the owner of a *statuliber*), could alienate only subject to the rule that any right created by them would end by the legal determination of their ownership[10]. But a mere *restitutio in integrum* would not end an ownership which had become vested in persons not parties to it[11].

(*d*) *Res litigiosae*. Property the subject of litigation was under special rules to be considered in connexion with the law of actions[12].

(*e*) Property could not in general be conveyed on the terms that it should not be alienable: this would be mere contract and would not nullify an alienation[13]. But in the Empire there was legislation, affecting *fideicommissa*, associated with family settlements by will, which will be considered later[14]. And Justinian seems to have made prohibition on alienation in a will or by agreement operative to annul transfers[15].

The chief cases in which a non-owner could alienate were these[16]:

1 The Edict shews this. 2 Lenel, *E.P.* 476; D. 43. 18. 3 43. 18. 1. pr. Lenel thinks this an *actio in factum*. 4 43. 18. 1. 3. 5 Lenel, *op. cit.* 478. 6 E.g., Beseler (*Beitr.* 1. 100; 2. 99; 3. 169) doubts the classicality of other than purely contractual effects: *contra*, Buckland, *R.H.* 1938, 666. 7 Vat. Fr. 61 is apparently a public case. 8 *Ante*, p. 108. 9 *Ante*, pp. 158, 167, 169. 10 *Ante*, pp. 75, 189. 11 *Post*, § CCXLIV. 12 *Post*, § CCXLIV. 13 Exception (*ante*, p. 188) in case of slavery. 14 *Post*, §§ CXXV, CXXVII. 15 C. 4. 51. 7. The text aequiparates prohibition by law and by party, but it is commonly explained otherwise. Windscheid, *Lehrb.* § 172a, n. 5. The *Basilica* (XIX. 8. 75; Heimb. 2. 299) make it prevent alienation; the Gloss makes it prevent only in wills. 16 Sales by Fisc, *ante*, p. 251.

(*a*) Guardians of various types had powers of alienation, differing in different cases, already considered[1]. In general this must be by *iure gentium* modes, but *curator furiosi* could alienate by *mancipatio*[2].

(*b*) *Filiifamilias* could alienate for the *paterfamilias* if authorised[3], but not by *cessio in iure*, as they could not take part in a *legis actio*[4].

(*c*) Slaves, duly authorised, could alienate for their owners, but not by *cessio in iure* or *adiudicatio*, as they could take no part in legal proceedings[5]. Similarly a slave in usufruct could alienate for his holder[6].

(*d*) A pledgee could alienate the *res* if the debt was not paid, when due, at first only where an express agreement to that effect had been made (but even where the debtor revoked his authority[7]), but later as an implied incident of the transaction[8]. It could not be by a civil law method. The agreed power of sale appeared early[9], the implied power may be a transfer from *mancipatio cum fiducia*, in which the creditor was owner.

(*e*) Alienation by a third party agent. Possession was lost even if a third party handed over the thing. It is therefore sometimes said that even in the Republic, if the necessary intents existed, a third party could alienate for the owner[10]. This is logical, but means little. If the owner intended to transfer ownership to *X* and told me to deliver it, the ownership would pass, but I was a mere *nuntius*[11]. The difficult case would be where the authorisation was, e.g., to sell to whom the agent liked, on what terms he liked, subject to liability for a careless bargain. It does not seem likely that if there had been such a possibility as is supposed, Gaius would have spoken of alienation by *procurator* (i.e. general agent) as one of the few cases[12]. It may be that in classical law a man with general authority could alienate, and sale[13] and delivery within a mandate transferred ownership[14]. But there is little evidence of an earlier development than in case of acquisition, and the Byzantines seem to require special authorisation, except for perishables and the like[15].

1 *Ante*, p. 276, n. 9. 2 Mitteis, *R.Pr.* 1. 208, considers also other guardians. 3 See e.g. 6. 1. 41. 1. 4 *Schol. Sin.* XVIII (49); see G. 2. 96. 5 50. 17. 107. 6 7. 1. 25. 1; 24. 1. 3. 8. Mitteis holds that a slave could not alienate by *mancipatio*. *Ante*, § LXXXV. 7 G. 2. 64. 8 20. 5. 4. Details, *post*, § CLXVI. 9 20. 1. 35. 10 E.g. Mitteis, *R.Pr.* 1. 213. 11 Our case is that in which the representative is the actual negotiating party. Difference from a *nuntius*, *S.M.W.* 243. 12 G. 2. 64. 13 41. 1. 9. 4; Inst. 2. 1. 42. 14 17. 1. 5. 3, Paul, who in Sent. 2. 15. 3 appears as saying that, even though the mandate is not followed, the alienation is good. Though it is the earlier authority it can hardly be correct. As our MS. is only the *l. Romana Wisigothorum*, it is likely that this is a fourth or fifth century addition. If I send a man to sell articles in the street at a certain price with no power to give undertakings, and he so sells, the alienation is not, properly speaking, by an agent, any more than it would be if the thing were done, as it constantly now is, by a slot machine. 15 *Post*, § CLXXIX.

XCIX. The cases in which a man acquired through the *negotium* of another were these[1]:

(*a*) Free persons not in his possession. The development of the rule that possession could be acquired by the act of an *extraneus* has been considered[2], and it seems that, in later classical law, ownership would be acquired if the necessary intents were present[2a]. Classical texts speak only of possession[3], but Diocletian regards acquisition of ownership as an existing institution[4], and it is clear for later law[5]. Delivery at the buyer's request to a third person is not however acquisition through him. It is not clear how far, under general authorisation to acquire, there would be acquisition through a *procurator*[6], by *occupatio* or the analogous *iure naturali* modes. Servitudes could not be acquired through a *procurator* in classical law, since the modes of acquisition were primarily civil. As to the informal methods, *quasi traditio* and *praescriptio* would presumably be possible, but even if pact and stipulation gave the right[7], it would not serve, for there was no agency in contract[8].

In acquisition by representative, if knowledge is material, the question would arise whether the agent's or the principal's must be considered. The contradictory texts are to some extent interpolated. The most probable view is that in classical law, if the property passed directly, even in general mandate the *scientia*, etc. of the principal only was material, but the compilers tend, incompletely, to make the state of mind of principal and agent material[9]. But the matter is obscure.

(*b*) Slaves possessed by their *domini*. What they acquired went to the owner, but a slave, as he was incapable of taking part in a judicial process, could not acquire by *cessio in iure* or *adiudicatio*[10]. He acquired for the bonitary, not for a merely quiritary owner[11]. If owned in common he acquired *pro rata* though it were in the affairs of one owner[12], but if expressly in the name of one owner this barred acquisition by any other[13]. This was not representation, for it operated *invito domino*[14].

(*c*) Slaves in usufruct, the rules being in general the same for persons *bona fide* possessed. They could acquire possession and ownership for the fructuary[15] subject to the limitation that it must be *ex operis* or *ex re*

1 De Zulueta, D. 41. 1 and 2, pp. 22 *sqq.* 2 *Ante*, p. 200. 2a *Mancipatio* to a representative who was not a member of the family did not transfer ownership. 3 G. 2. 95; P. 5. 2. 2. 4 C. 7. 32. 8, "*utilitatis causa.*" 5 Inst. 2. 9. 5. 6 Conception of *procuratio, post*, § CLXXIX. 7 *Ante*, p. 265. 8 Mitteis, *R.Pr.* 1. 213. 9 Schulz, *Z.S.S.* 1912, 37; see also Debray, *N.R.H.* 1914, 396, reviewing Solazzi, *Errore e Rappresentanza*, and Siber, *R.R.* 2. 413. 10 G. 2. 96. 11 G. 2. 88. 12 G. 3. 167. Adjustment in *communi dividundo.* 13 41. 1. 37. 3; Inst. 3. 28. 3. Gifts to slave by one owner vest in the other *pro parte* (45. 3. 7. 1) apart from *nominatio.* If one of common owners leaves the slave a legacy, it is wholly valid for the other (33. 5. 11; 35. 2. 49. pr. Buckland, *Slavery*, 380). The rule applies equally in classical law whether there is a manumission or not, for that is void, P. 3. 6. 4. *Ante*, p. 252. 14 41. 1. 32. 15 G. 2. 86; Vat. Fr. 51.

fructuarii, and that what the holder did not acquire went to the owner[1]. "*Ex operis*" covers only the case of a slave hiring out his services to a third person[2]. The hire was acquired by the fructuary, *ex operis*. "*Ex re*" is more important. It covers all property received in the affairs of the holder, buying with his money, borrowing for a purpose of his estate[3], etc. Inheritances and legacies given to the slave did not concern the fructuary. They were clearly not *ex operis*[4], and though some texts suggest that intent to benefit the holder caused him to acquire[5], this view, though suggested by Labeo, did not prevail in classical law[6]. Many texts say also that the fructuary could not acquire a *donatio*[7], but several say that intention to benefit the holder made it go to him[8].

These rules were much modified where there was *nominatio* or *iussum*. If there was *nominatio* of anyone, no other could acquire. If it was *ex re fructuarii*, but *nominatim domino*, the owner acquired: he could acquire anything[9]. If it was *ex re domini, nominatim fructuario*, it was void: *nominatio* excluded the *dominus*, and it was not *ex re fructuarii* or *ex operis*[10]. If it was *iussu domini, ex re fructuarii*, the *dominus* acquired[11]. If it was *iussu fructuarii ex re domini*, the *dominus* acquired, since it was not *ex re fructuarii* or *ex operis* and *iussum* had not the privative effect of *nominatio*[12]. The Sabinians held that *iussum* had the same effect as *nominatio*[13], where it stood alone, to the extent of making one acquire where otherwise there would have been division, and later classical law accepted this. But *nominatio* of one limited acquisition to him though there was *iussum* of another. Later law equated the two in all respects, with confusing results[14].

(*d*) For persons in *manus* or bondage the rule was as in case of slaves[15].

1 G. 2. 91, 92; Ulp. 19. 21; P. 5. 7. 3; Vat. Fr. 71b; Inst. 2. 9. 4. 2 Salkowski, *Sklavenerwerb*, 118. Nothing to do with results of labour on property of the holder. This belongs to holder but is not acquired through the slave. It does not cover earnings where the fructuary made the contract. 3 E.g. 41. 1. 23. 3; 2. 14. 19; 46. 4. 11. pr. 4 41. 1. 19; 29. 2. 45. pr. 5 7. 1. 21; 29. 2. 45. 4; 41. 1. 19 (interp.). 6 G. 2. 92; Inst. 2. 9. 4; C. Th. 4. 8. 6. 6; D. 6. 1. 20; 28. 5. 60. pr.; 41. 1. 10. 3, 4, 19, 54, etc. For Berger, *Philol.* 1914, 61, Vat. Fr. 71b (his restoration on this point following Lenel's) compared with 7. 1. 21 shews that Tribonian adopts Labeo's view. The other appears in so many texts that this seems bold. Other views, Herzen, *Mél. Girard*, 1. 523; Partsch, *Neg. gestio*, 1. 95; Mommsen *ad* Vat. Fr. 71b. Transactions by *liber homo b. f. serviens*, not within the *causae*, Riccobono, *Ann. Palermo*, 1917, 679. 7 41. 1. 10. 3, 4. 8 41. 1. 19 (interp.); 7. 1. 22, 25. pr.; 41. 1. 49. The interpolations shew that this rule was the rule of later law. Textual case stronger than in *hereditas*. 9 41. 1. 37. 5. 10 45. 3. 1. 1; h. t. 22. 11 7. 1. 25. 3. 12 45. 3. 31. As to *condictio* for adjustment, 45. 3. 39. Details, Buckland, *Slavery*, 349, 363. Where the slave bought, ownership might be in suspense till it was clear out of whose money it was paid for. Buckland, *cit.* for this and analogous cases of suspense. 13 G. 3. 167a. 14 Schulz, *Z.S.S.* 1930, 230; Buckland, *Slavery*, 380. 15 G. 2. 86, 90; Ulp. 19. 18.

(*e*) It is commonly held, though the evidence is defective, that guardians could acquire by *traditio* for their wards, from early times.

(*f*) As to *filiusfamilias*[1] there is a long history. In the Republic the position of a son in this matter was the same as that of a slave. He could have a *peculium*, like a slave, but under Augustus a new kind of *peculium* appeared, from which this old *peculium* may be distinguished as *peculium profectitium*. The new institution was *peculium castrense*[2], consisting of what was given to the man for the purpose of military service or acquired by him as a result of it[3]. While the son lived, the father had no interest in it[4]. The son could alienate it freely even by will (though, till Hadrian, he must, for this, be still on service[5], in which case a military will sufficed[6]). For the protection of it he had the rights of action of a *paterfamilias*[7]. If he survived the father, he kept it. If emancipated or adopted, he took it with him[8]. If he made a will of it, it was an inheritance, but if he did not, and died in the family, it reverted to the father as *peculium*[9]. Under Justinian, even if the son died intestate, his issue and his brothers and sisters were preferred to the father[10], and this was real succession, the property being *bona adventitia* in their hands. If it went to the father, it is not clear whether he took it as *hereditas* or as *peculium*, a point of some practical importance[11].

Peculium quasi castrense was an extension of the same idea, beginning under Constantine[12], applied to earnings in certain public services, and extended from time to time to new posts and professions: the rules may not have been in all cases identical, as the legislation is imperfectly known[13]. The two funds were clearly similar and the only known difference between these rules and those of *peculium castrense* is that in general no will could be made of *peculium quasi castrense*. In the privileged cases in which it was devisable the will must be in ordinary form[14]. Under Justinian it was freely devisable in this form[15].

Bona materna. Bona adventitia. Constantine provided that what a child inherited from his mother should be his, not merged in the father's estate, though he had a kind of usufruct[16] of it. This was gradually

1 Special rules in *dos* of a *filiafamilias*, *ante*, p. 109. 2 Rules a gradual development. Fitting, *Das peculium castrense*. C. Appleton, *Pouvoir du fils de famille sur son pécule castrans*. Albertario, *Bull.* 1931, 5. 3 49. 17. 11. 4 14. 6. 2. 5 Inst. 2. 12. pr., or make *don. m. c.*, 39. 6. 15. 6 Inst. 2. 11. 3. 7 49. 17. 4. 8 49. 17. 12. 9 49. 17. 2. 10 Inst. 2. 12. pr. and *don. m. c.*, 39. 6. 15. 11 *Post*, § CXXXIII. 12 C. 12. 30. 1=C. Th. 6. 35. 15. Name not found till Justinian; full account Fitting, *cit.* 388 *sqq.* 13 Principal texts, Accarias, *Précis*, 1. 772. 14 Inst. 2. 11. 6. Consuls, *praefecti legionum, praesides provinciarum*, etc. C. 3. 28. 37. 1 a. Under Justinian this, like the soldier's will, was not subject to *querela inofficiosi testamenti*, h. t. 37. 1 f. 15 Inst. 2. 11. 6. Father not liable *de peculio* on contracts connected with these funds, 49. 17. 18. 5. *Post*, § CLXXXIV. 16 C. 6. 60. 1=C. Th. 8. 18. 1. Constantine's law makes the *pater dominus* with rights limited to enjoyment. Justinian's reproduction makes the *filius* the *dominus*, cp. C. Th. 8. 18. 2 and C. 6. 60. 2.

extended[1], and under Justinian all acquisitions of a child, not from the father, or under the preceding heads, belonged to this class of *bona adventitia*[2]. While the son was in the family the father had the usufruct with no power of alienation[3], and the son had no special capacities in regard to it as he had in *castrense* and *quasi castrense*[4]. He could make no will of it: on his death it went to his father, at first no doubt as *peculium*, but, later, in some cases at least, as *hereditas*[5]. There was much legislation late in the fifth century on succession to *filiifamilias* in regard to these *bona adventitia*. Justinian provided that it should be an inheritance for his issue and brothers and sisters (subject to the father's usufruct), and, failing these, for his paternal ancestors[6]. If he was emancipated (and probably if adopted) Constantine gave him two-thirds, the father keeping the rest. Justinian gave the father the usufruct of half, all going ultimately to the son[7], and further provided that the father should have no right where the donor expressed this intent.

1 See C. Th. 8. 18 *passim*. 2 C. 6. 61. 6. In a few cases, the so-called *bona adventitia irregularia*, it was provided that the father had no rights of enjoyment. See Windscheid, *Lehrb*. § 517, nn. 17 *sqq*. 3 C. 6. 61. 4. pr., 6. 2. In many ways more favourably treated than a usufructuary, Cornil, *Dr.R.* 551. 4 Nor the father any exemption from *actio de peculio*. 5 Inst. 2. 12. pr.; *Nov*. Theod. 14. 1. 8; C. 6. 61. 3, 4, 7; elaborate rules as to what is to be done in case of inheritance and legacy where one wishes to take it and the other does not. 6 C. 6. 61. 6. 1c. 7 C. 6. 61. 6. 3; *post*, § CXXXIII.

CHAPTER VII

ACQUISITION *PER UNIVERSITATEM*. SUCCESSION BY WILL

C[1]. The will of Roman Law had for its primary purpose in historical times the appointment of a *heres*[2] or *heredes*, a successor or successors in whom the rights and liabilities of the deceased should vest as a whole. No doubt it might and usually did contain a number of other matters, appointment of *tutores*, legacies, *fideicommissa*, manumissions, directions as to the application of particular funds, but its essence was the appointment of a *heres*: *testamenta vim ex institutione heredis accipiunt, et ob id velut caput et fundamentum intellegitur totius testamenti heredis institutio*[3]. Two further propositions almost equally fundamental are (i) *semel heres, semper heres*: a person who has once assumed or been invested with the position of *heres* cannot divest himself of it, a rule which, e.g., greatly affected the construction of an *institutio ad tempus*, and (ii) *nemo pro parte testatus*: a will must cover the whole estate: a man cannot deal with part of his property, leaving the rest to pass on intestacy. These principles were in full force at the beginning of the Empire though there has been controversy as to their actual antiquity[4]. The simplest explanation of the rule: *nemo pro parte testatus*, is given by the hypothesis that the will is originally nomination of a successor in the chieftaincy

1 On the conceptions of "singular" and "universal" succession, *post*, § CVII.
2 Notwithstanding Festus, *s.v. heres*, this word seems to have nothing to do with *herus*. See, e.g., Perozzi, *Ist.* 2. 443.
3 G. 2. 229.
4 Divergent views, Lenel, *Essays in Legal History*, ed. Vinogradoff, 120; Ehrlich, *Zeits. f. verg. Rechtsw.* 1904, p. 99; Appleton, *Le testament Romain*, p. 57, n. 5; Suman, *Favor testamenti*, ch. 1.

of the group, a doctrine involving (1) priority of testation over intestacy, the system being older than the notion of hereditary sovereignty, (2) priority of *institutio* of *sui* to that of *extranei* and (3) exclusion of *institutio* of women in early law[1]. This speculative question is beyond the scope of this book. It should be added that to both of these principles practical needs led to the admission at various times of real or apparent exceptions[2], but they are in no case such as to create any doubt whatever about the principles themselves[3].

FORMS OF WILL. Gaius[4] gives us a brief account of two ancient forms of will obsolete long before the beginning of the Empire, and therefore needing for present purposes no full discussion[5].

Testamentum in comitiis calatis[6]. The close connexion of the *familia* with religious law made transfer of the rights and duties to a successor matter of public interest. Thus variation of the established order of succession was supervised by public authority. The *comitia curiata*, the assembly of the people, *curiatim*, met twice a year for this purpose, after a summons by a *lictor* and apparently under the presidency of a pontiff. When meeting in this way, for purposes affecting religion (also *inauguratio* of *rex* or *flamen*, *adrogatio*, *detestatio sacrorum*), it was called *comitia calata*[7]. The will was presumably approved by the pontiffs before its submission to the *comitia*. Whether the *comitia* voted on the will or merely gave its solemn attestation is disputed[8]. The will was not extant in historic times[9].

Testamentum in procinctu[10]. A will made before his comrades by a

1 This view is set out by Bonfante in various works (e.g. *Corso*, 6. 70 *sqq.*). Maine, *Anc. Law*, 182, had expounded a kindred doctrine with a different view of the relation between State and Family. Most of the results of the hypothesis could be reached on the view that what was transmitted was the care of the *sacra*. B.'s view is widely accepted in Italy (Scialoja, *Diritto Ereditario*, 45; De Francisci, *Storia*, 1. 118, 335; Fadda, *Dir. Ered.* 27) but not universally, see Arangio Ruiz, *Ist.* 469, and Perozzi, *Ist.* 2. 478. See also Lévy-Bruhl, *Le très ancien testament Romain*, who accepts the original limitation to *sui*, but not, it seems, the theory on which B. rests it. Critical appreciation of the doctrine, Rabel, *Z.S.S.* 1930, 295. See also Siber, *Geschichtliches und rechtsvergleichendes, über die Haftung für Nachlassschulden.* On the early relation between *hereditas* and *tutela* see lit. cited *ante*, p. 142, n. 4.

2 *Post*, § cxv. The rule that *sui*, other than sons, omitted, can come in and claim by *ius accrescendi* (§ cxii) is sometimes regarded as an exception, Scialoja, *Dir. Ered.* 55.

3 Relief against acceptance, *post*, § cix; will operating only on part of the estate, *post*, §§ cxv, cxxxiv; will in which all *institutiones* are invalid but the other provisions remain, in the latest law, *post*, § cxv.

4 G. 2. 101.

5 Girard, *Man.* 849 and reff.

6 G. *loc. cit.*; Aul. Gell. 15. 27. 1–5; Ulp. 20. 2.

7 Aul. Gell. *loc. cit.*

8 All sorts of views are held: that the *comitia* voted the will, that they merely witnessed it, that the XII Tables substituted witnessing for voting, that it did this and also destroyed the control of the pontiffs, and so forth. See Appleton, *Testament Romain*; Greiff, *Origine du testament Romain*; Jörs, *R.R.* 224; Girard, *Man.* 849 *sqq.*

9 It has been doubted whether it dealt with the inheritance at all (Lenel, *Essays in Legal History*, ed. Vinogradoff, 120 *sqq.*). Reply Girard, *loc. cit.* and lit., there cited. See also Buckland, *L.Q.R.* 1916, 97 *sqq.*

10 G. 2. 101; Aul. Gell. 15. 27. 3.

soldier, when a campaign was under way and no sitting of the *comitia* was imminent. Whether this was an assembly, the *centuriata*, analogous to the *comitia* (*curiata*) *calata*, as is suggested by the language of Aulus Gellius, or was a mere declaration before his immediate comrades is uncertain, the former being more probable, as auspices were necessary[1]. It seems to have lasted into the seventh century[2], but Cicero describes it as obsolete[3], though having coexisted with the mancipatory will[4].

Testamentum per aes et libram. Of these earlier forms of will, one could be made only on two days in the year, perhaps only by patricians, the other only in war-time. The inconvenience was met by the device of *mancipatio familiae*: the whole property was mancipated to a *familiae emptor* who, according to Gaius, was *loco heredis*[5]. Whether he took the property, subject to any instructions, not at first binding, or whether he was never more than a sort of trustee, is much disputed[6]. Such a transaction was not much like a will. It was oral, made only at the point of death, open, irrevocable, perhaps taking effect at once. But its character gradually changed. It became usual to write down the instructions, thus securing secrecy; they became enforceable, and variable. The final stage is that which Gaius speaks of as existing in his day[7], though it was much older[8]. The *familiae emptor* was now a mere formality. The contents of the document were the true will: no longer directions to be carried out by the *familiae emptor*, the gifts took effect of their own force[9]. This was the important will of the classical law, the *testamentum per aes et libram*. Gaius tells us that[10] there were present testator, *familiae emptor*, *libripens* and not less than five witnesses (as for an ordinary *mancipatio*). The actual document had been previously prepared. The *familiae emptor* took a formal *mancipatio* in words which may be thus translated: "Let your *familia* and *pecunia*[11] be bought into my mandate and custody by this copper" ("and scale" according to some, says Gaius) "in order that you may be able to make a will in accordance with the public statute." He struck the scale with the copper and handed it over by way of price. The testator holding the written will said: "As these provisions are written in these tablets so do I give and bequeath and make my will, and so do you, Quirites, bear me witness."

1 Cicero, *de nat. deor.* 2. 3. 9. 2 Vell. Paterc. 2. 5. 3. 3 Cicero, *loc. cit.* 4 Cicero, *de or.* 1. 53. 228. 5 G. 2. 103, "*heredis locum obtinebat.*" 6 Lenel, *Essays, cit.*, and Ehrlich, *cit.* 7 G. 2. 103 *sqq.* 8 It is the usual will in the time of Cicero, *de or.* (*cit.*). 9 It is impossible to fix dates. The most diverse views are held. For Lambert, *Fonction du droit civil comparé*, 1. 496, the true mancipatory will dates from about 150 B.C. For Mommsen it seems to be much older (*Staatsr.* 3. 319, n. 2; *D.P.R.* 6. 1. 364, n. 1). See Girard, *Man.* 856 *sqq.*; Lenel, *cit.* 134; Grieff, *cit.*, 101 *sqq.*; Appleton, *Testament Romain*, 103 *sqq.*; Cuq, *Recherches historiques sur le testament per aes et libram.* 10 G. 2. 104. As to corruptions, Weiss, *Z.S.S.* 1921, 105. 11 As to these terms, Bonfante, *Scr. Giur.* 2. 206; Girard, *Man.* 272.

The *mancipatio*, as thus stated, differs from the ordinary form. It does not contain the first member declaring the right, though editors, observing corruptions in the text, emend it so as to introduce such a clause[1]. Again, what is said to be bought or acquired is not the property but the guardianship of it, and the declaration of the purpose "in order that you may make your will" is unlike anything in the ordinary form. The words "*secundum legem publicam*" are obscure but may mean that the power of testation was regarded as based on the XII Tables. The *nuncupatio* by the testator was not regarded as a part of the *mancipatio*[2]. This was a true will, not necessarily open, ambulatory, i.e. not operating in any way till the death, and capable, if not of revocation, of variation in any degree.

In practice it seems to have been usually in writing, but it does not appear that this was legally necessary, though the various praetorian remedies seem not to have been available in classical law except where the will was written, a fact which would ensure the use of writing[3]. It has been contended that if there was a writing in due form the actual *mancipatio* was no longer in use in the time of Gaius[4], and it is probable that, in a somewhat later age, the parties were content not to go behind the formal document alleging the *mancipatio*: it is another thing to say that they were compelled by law to accept this.

Like other formal acts the will must be in Latin[5], till A.D. 439 when it was provided that it might be in Greek[6].

CI. The praetorian will, spoken of by Gaius as a *testamentum*[7], though hardly entitled to that name. The Praetor, recognising that the formality of the mancipatory will was useless, provided by his Edict that a will sealed by seven witnesses (i.e. having the substantial safeguard of the mancipatory will) should be operative to entitle the *heres* under it to obtain *bonorum possessio secundum tabulas*, if the testator died a *civis sui iuris*[8]. It did not make a *heres*, for, even though the testator used this form, the beneficiary did not get *hereditas* but *bonorum possessio*. Moreover it was not till the second century that this became *cum re*, i.e. effective against the civil *heres*[9]. And a will might do many things other than the appointment of a *heres*, which, so far as we know, this instrument could not. There is no evidence that a *tutor* could be

1 Krueger, *ad* G. 2. 104 in *Coll. librorum jurisp. antei.* Surviving mancipatory wills, Girard, *Textes*, 801 and Meyer, *Zeitschr. f. verg. Rechtsw.* 1918, 81. 2 Ulp. 20. 9. 3 C. 6. 11. 2 (A.D. 242) says that *b. p.* can be claimed under a *nuncupatio*. This, even if genuine (see p. 286, n. 10), is post-classical. 4 Collinet, *Ét. Hist.* 1. 257 *sqq.* The *mancipatio* is treated as necessary in the *liber singularis regularum* (Ulp. 20. 9), *ante*, pp. 237 *sq.* 5 Except for *miles*, *post*, § CXXVI. 6 C. 6. 23. 21. 6. 7 G. 2. 119, 147, and, according to Lenel, in the Edict (*E.P.* 342). 8 G. 2. 147; Ulp. 23. 6; 28. 5, 6. Simplification not great; only ritual acts dispensed with. 9 *Post*, § CXXXIX; G. 2. 120.

appointed by it, though one so appointed would probably be confirmed by the Praetor. There is no trace of manumission by it[1]. It operated under certain edicts which, so far as appears, dealt only with giving possession to persons who could shew gifts to them in a document authenticated by seven witnesses. It was not only as to defect of form that the Praetor's intervention was important. Where the consent of *tutor* to a woman's will had not been obtained *bonorum possessio* was given. It could be obtained where a *suus omissus* died before the testator, where the will was *irritum* by *capitis deminutio* or non-entry, or *ruptum* by *agnatio* of a *postumus* or by the making of a valid second will which failed to take effect or was revoked with intent to revive the first[2], and other cases[3]. The circumstances in which this was *cum re* will be considered later[4]. The *bonorum possessor* must carry out the provisions of the will[5], and if, being also entitled on intestacy, he neglected the will, he would come within the provisions of the Edict, "*si qui omissa causa testamenti*[6]." It will be observed that this *bonorum possessio*, at least so far as it was *cum re*, prevented the application of the *ll. caducariae*. But the *bonorum possessio* could not be claimed if the testator had not *testamenti factio*[7] or, it seems, if the words of the *institutio* were looser than those necessary for a true *heres*[8].

Later forms of will. In A.D. 413 two public forms were provided, one *apud acta*, i.e. entered on the rolls of a court, the other deposited in the State archives[9], with no need of further attestation. Soon after there was obscure legislation authorising a civil will without *mancipatio familiae*, but with seven, sometimes five, witnesses[10]. An enactment of 439 settled the law by introducing the tripartite will[11], so called as deriving its rules from three sources. It must be made in one operation, *uno contextu*[12], with seven witnesses, both civil law requirements[13]. The

1 It probably would not make the slave *tuitione praetoris liber* (*ante*, p. 78). It is not clear that a testator could despoil his *heres* and not himself without full form. Cf. 15. 1. 53; 33. 8. 8. 7. The *Fr. Dos.* mentions no case in a will. D. 29. 4. 6. 10, 12, 17, 28 prove nothing for the praetorian will. 2 G. 2. 118 *sqq.*; 2. 147 *sqq.*; Inst. 2. 17. 6 *sqq.*; 3. 9. pr.; D. 28. 3. 12. pr.; 37. 11. 2, 3; Ulp. 23. 6. 3 If testator lost and regained capacity before death, G. 2. 147. Practical restriction, 37. 11. 11. 2. *Post*, § CXXXIX. It could not be given under any will of a woman in *legitima tutela*, before Hadrian, Cic. *Top.* 4. 18, or, if *tutor legitimus* had not consented, after, G. 2. 121, 122. 4 *Post*, § CXXXIX. 5 28. 3. 12. pr., legacies and *fideicommissa*. 6 29. 4. 1. 7; *post*, § CXXI. 7 G. 2. 147; Cicero, *Ad fam.* 7. 21; *Top.* 4. 18. 8 37. 11. 6; *post*, § CIV. *B. p. secundum tabulas* exists in the time of Cicero (*Verr.* 2. 1. 45. 117). Its original aim seems to have been to give possession to the person entitled at civil law, its reforming effect being a later product, Girard, *Man.* 844. 9 C. 6. 23. 19. 10 C. Th. 4. 4. 3, 7; *Lex Rom. Burg.* 45. 2. There is an enactment of A.D. 242 which speaks of a will with seven witnesses as fully valid without *mancipatio familiae*, but it has in all probability been altered. C. 6. 11. 2. 11 C. 6. 23. 21. 12 The documents may be prepared before, but the witnesses must do their part on one day, *nullo actu interveniente*. 13 Seven becomes the normal number of witnesses for most transactions; *repudium* in divorce, 24. 2. 9;

witnesses must seal, which was praetorian. They and the testator must "*subscribere*[1]," a new imperial requirement. This is the important will of later law: after its introduction we hear little of the praetorian will[2].

There were under Justinian less important forms of general application. The public wills survived, and there was an oral will with seven witnesses[3]. It existed in and before the time of Theodosius, and survived under Justinian, but was probably used only in cases of extreme urgency[4].

There were a number of special forms of will. In time of pestilence the witnesses need not be in the same room with a testator suffering from contagious disease[5]. In remote districts, where *cives* were rare, five, or even fewer, witnesses would suffice[6]. Blind men could dictate their wills before seven witnesses and a *tabularius* or, having had it written out before, have it read to them before the witnesses by a *tabularius* (an eighth witness being used if no *tabularius* was procurable), acknowledge it and have it duly sealed by the witnesses and the *tabularius*[7]. There were also special provisions for deaf mutes and other cases[8], and a great number of special rules for soldiers' wills[9].

There was a general holograph will the history of which is bound up with that of informal wills in favour of issue. Constantine provided in A.D. 321 that males could devise their estate among *liberi* by an unattested will, and in A.D. 327 that a mother's informal division among her issue should be valid[10]. In 439 Theodosius II provided that such an imperfect will was to be good only among *liberi*, which suggests that it had been used in a wider field[11]. Justinian recites these provisions, treating the extension to women as being due to Theodosius, Constantine having dealt with arrangements *inter vivos*, to be binding on the death[12]. In 446 Valentinian provided that a holograph will, i.e. written entirely by the testator, was to be valid for all purposes without witnesses[13]. Justinian adopted the enactment of Theodosius with some corrections in statement[14], but not that of Valentinian. In a novel[15] he

grants of *civitas* to soldiers, *ante* p. 97; Girard, *Textes*, 124; Bruns, 1. 275; in many cases even in *mancipatio* itself, *ante*, p. 238. Further illustrations, Lévy-Bruhl, *Le Témoignage instrumentaire*, 148 *sqq*. In our case the seven are the five witnesses, the *libripens* and the *familiae emptor* of the mancipatory will.

1 *Subscriptio* is an acknowledgement of the document by the seal, with (usually) the name and word "*subscripsi*," but often more full, Kroell, *Rôle de l'Écrit*, 100. If the will was in the testator's own hand and so stated, he need not *subscribere*. Justinian added, and afterwards removed, other formalities, C. 6. 23. 29; *Nov*. 119. 9.

2 C. Th. 4. 4. 7. 2 (see also the *interpretatio* of C. Th. 4. 4. 3) is earlier than the tripartite will, but the praetorian will is mentioned in C. 6. 11. 2.

3 C. 6. 11. 2. *Ante*, p. 286, n. 10.

4 Recorded cases of oral mancipatory will are cases of urgency, Girard, *Man*. 860, n. 1.

5 C. 6. 23. 8. Diocl.

6 C. 6. 23. 31, *ruri conditum*.

7 C. 6. 22. 8; P. 3. 4a. 4.

8 C. 6. 22. 10.

9 *Post*, § CXXVI.

10 C. Th. 2. 24. 1, 2.

11 *Nov*. Theod. 16. 5.

12 *Nov*. 107. pr.

13 *Nov*. Val. 21. 2. 1.

14 C. 6. 23. 21. 3.

15 *Nov*. 107.

regulated divisions among children, providing that the essential parts must be in the testator's writing and in full. Provision for others could be made, if declared before witnesses (number not stated), without other formality, and an arrangement *inter vivos* between father and children for division among them, subscribed by all parties, was valid. A will not satisfying the rules of form is *imperfectum*[1].

CII. CAPACITY. *Testamenti factio.* We are told that "*testamenti factio publici iuris est*[2]," which may mean that the rules of wills, as to form, capacity and effect, were governed by law and not variable by the testator. The first question is of capacity of testation (active *testamenti factio*). In general any *civis sui iuris* over puberty could make a will[3], but there were several exceptions, the chief being:

(*a*) Those declared *intestabiles* as a punishment[4].

(*b*) Deaf mutes from birth. This is Justinian's rule[5]. No deaf mute could have made a mancipatory will, and probably before Justinian no such person could make a will without imperial permission[6].

(*c*) Those *de statu suo incerti*, e.g. a slave freed by will, or a *filius*, not aware that the *paterfamilias* was dead, and the rule applies to those *dubitantes vel errantes* as to their *status*[7]. It rests on a rescript of Pius. The principle seems to be that, as testation is an act involving intent as to *patrimonium*, one who is not certain that he has a *patrimonium* cannot have this intent: he "*certam legem testamento dicere non potest*[8]."

(*d*) In early law a woman could not make a will: she could not appear before the *comitia*[9]. *Libertinae* could make mancipatory wills with consent of the patron as *tutor*[10], but *ingenuae*, except vestal virgins[11], could not, unless they had suffered *capitis deminutio* and so passed under a *tutor fiduciarius*[12]. The practical reason probably is that the *tutor* whose consent was needed might not be the relative who would suffer by the will. Though he were the nearest agnate at the time of testation, he might be dead and those in another line the nearest at her death. And he might be a testamentary *tutor*. The rule disappeared under Hadrian, who allowed women to devise, with consent of their *tutores*[13].

1 Inst. 2. 17. 7. 2 28. 1. 3. For de Visscher (*Mél. Cornil*, 2. 560, *Ét.* 44) "*publicum*" means having political significance. From this to incapacity to contract out of it (which he thinks a modern notion) is a short step. 11. 7. 20. pr.; 2. 14. 27. 4; 35. 2. 15. 1; 38. 1. 42. Heumann-Seckel, *s.v.* 3 G. 2. 113; Ulp. 20. 12; P. 3. 4a. 1. Even though under minor punishment for crime, P. 3. 4a. 9. 4 28. 1. 18. 1; 28. 1. 26, which however had when written probably no application to this matter. *Intestabiles*, *ante*, p. 92. 5 C. 6. 22. 10; cf. D. 28. 1. 7; Inst. 2. 12. 3. 6 Ulp. 20. 13. 7 Ulp. 20. 11; D. 28. 1. 14 and 15. 8 28. 1. 14. 9 Perozzi, *Ist.* 2. 507, seeing in the original will a testamentary adoption explains the exclusion as due to the fact that women could not adopt. 10 G. 3. 43. 11 Aul. Gell. 1. 12. 9. 12 G. 1. 115a; *ante*, p. 286. 13 G. 2. 112, 113, so that they could make wills at twelve while males must be fourteen, P. 3. 4a. 1; Ulp. 20. 15; G. 2. 118. It may be that, since the process

(*e*) A man's will might be valid, though he was at the moment incapable of making one. A lunatic could not "test" except in a lucid interval, but a will made before he was insane was good[1]. A similar rule applied to an interdicted *prodigus*. The mancipatory will was barred as being an act in the *commercium*, and the rule remained in later law, for practical reasons[2]. A *captivus*, as a slave, could not make a will[3], but one previously made was good provided he returned with *postliminium*, and, if he died in captivity, it was good as the result of a *l. Cornelia*, of Sulla[4]. It seems to have been an express provision, but there is controversy as to what this *fictio legis Corneliae* was[5]. Probably the *lex* did not declare the will good, but provided that his estate was to be dealt with as if he had never been captured, and on this the lawyers built the further rule that the case was to be handled as if he had died at capture.

Some persons not *cives sui iuris* could make wills. On principle it would seem that colonary Latins, having *commercium*, could do so, and this is confirmed by the way in which the exclusion of Junian Latins is stated[6], and, at least for some *coloniae*, by Cicero[7]. As each *colonia* had its separate statute, it is possible that in some the power did not exist, and the express exclusion of Junian Latins may be to exclude them from the rights of peregrines in their locality, for these could of course make wills (though not Roman wills), if their local laws allowed this[8]. *Servi publici populi Romani* could make wills of half their *peculium*[9]. *Filiifamilias milites* could devise freely their *peculium castrense*, as, after Hadrian, could those who had been *milites*[10].

The capacity must have existed when the will was made[11], and capacity to have a will, at the death[12]. If, in the meantime, the power was lost and regained, the will was in general destroyed at civil law. The *furiosus* was no exception, for he had not lost the capacity to have a will, but the *captivus* was. If a criminal was afterwards pardoned and completely restored, his will was revalidated[13], but not if, as was usual, he was merely pardoned[14]. But where capacity was reacquired the Praetor gave *bonorum possessio, sine re* in classical law[15]. Justinian seems to have required confirmation[16].

of emancipation involved sale and manumission from bondage this was treated as making them, *pro tanto, libertae*. Cuq, *Man.* 690.

1 P. 3. 4a. 5, 11; Ulp. 20. 13; Inst. 2. 12. 1. 2 Ulp. 20. 13; Inst. 2. 12. 2; P. 3. 4a. 12. 3 P. 3. 4a. 8; Inst. 2. 12. 5; D. 49. 15. 12. 5. 4 Ulp. 23. 5; Inst. 2. 12. 5; D. 28. 1. 12. 5 Various opinions, Buckland, *Slavery*, 299, 308. See Balog, *St. Bonfante*, 4. 625. 6 G. 2. 110; Ulp. 20. 14. 7 *Pro Caecina*, 35. 102. 8 Ulp. 20. 14. 9 Ulp. 20. 16. Does not seem to have extended to *servi publici* of municipalities. 10 G. 2. 109; Ulp. 20. 10; P. 3. 4a. 3. *Ante*, p. 280 for this and *pec. qu. castr.* 11 28. 1. 2, 4. 12 28. 1. 6. 1, 8. 1, 18. 13 28. 3. 6. 12. 14 C. 9. 49. 4. 15 G. 2. 147–149; Ulp. 23. 6; D. 28. 3. 12. pr. 16 37. 11. 11. 2; Bonfante, *Corso*, 6. 276.

CIII. Capacity to take under a will (passive *testamenti factio*). The class of those who can take is wider, since it covers children and so forth. In general anyone may be instituted who has *commercium*, but there are so many special cases that it is simpler to enumerate the chief classes who were at various times and for various reasons excluded.

The capacity must exist at testation (*postumi* give an exception), at the time of *delatio*, which is normally the death, but, in conditional institutions, the arrival of the condition, and all the time from *delatio* to entry. Loss and regaining of capacity between the first two dates was immaterial—*media tempora non nocent*[1]. There is much controversy on the question why loss and regaining of capacity in the first interval was indifferent and on what is really the fundamental question, why capacity was required at testation as the document operated only on death[2].

(*a*) *Peregrini* not having *commercium*[3]. Unimportant under Justinian.

(*b*) The Gods, in general. Exceptions were made from time to time; it is not clear why particular gods were favoured[4]. It is probable that, so far as Roman Law is concerned, none of these exceptions much preceded the Empire: *cretio* could hardly have been gone through. The practical question in whom the *hereditas* vested is answered by Mommsen[5] in favour of the State, by whose officers it was administered, though it was paid into the Temple treasury: the Temple priests were not corporate. Constantine allowed the institution of the Catholic Church[6], and later we get institutions of particular churches[7]. Under Justinian an *institutio* of Christ went to the church of the district[8].

(*c*) Women. As incapable of appearance in the *Comitia* they may have been excluded in early law, but not under the mancipatory will. By the *l. Voconia*, of 168 B.C., however, they could not be made *heredes* by a testator in the first class of the *census* by wealth[9]. This rule died out early in the Empire, probably because the *census* was out of use and the *lex* applied only to those actually *censi*[10]. The rule did not apply on intestacy: it seems that the point was not to bar women from being rich, but from being rich and independent[11]. Succeeding on intestacy they

1 28. 5. 6. 2, 50. 1, 60. 4. 2 Bonfante, *Corso*, 6. 276, who also discusses the oscillation between *duo* and *tria tempora* in 28. 5. 50. 1. 3 Ulp. 22. 2. 4 Ulp. 22. 6. Girard observes (*Man.* 872) that they are nearly all peregrine deities, and supposes this to mean merely that the national gods were provided for. Perhaps it is merely the recognition for Roman Law of an existing practice. Various opinions, Bonfante, *Corso*, 6. 325. 5 *Staatsr.* 2. 60; *D.P.R.* 3. 68. 6 C. 1. 2. 1. 7 C. 1. 2. 14. 8 C. 1. 2. 25. 9 G. 2. 274. 10 Perhaps not originally confined to *classici*. Cicero applies it to all on the *census* in any class, excluding only the poor and women testators. *Verr.* 2. 1. 41–44 (104–114). There may have been a further rule in the *lex*, forbidding women in any case to receive more than half the estate, as *heredes* or legatees; Ps. Quintilian, *Decl.* 264. Rotondi, *Leges publicae*, 284. 11 Gide, *Condition de la femme*, (2) 148.

would be in agnatic *tutela* but if instituted there is some evidence that even if no *tutor* was appointed they were free from agnatic *tutela*[1]. It may be that women could not be instituted in the law of the XII Tables and, *a fortiori*, were not *necessarii*, the practice of instituting them being later and the *l. Voconia* a check on this[2].

(*d*) Natural children and their mother. Legislation, beginning with Constantine, prohibited, or restricted, the institution of such children, if not legitimated, or their mother, the rules differing according as there were or were not legitimate children. Justinian provided that if there were, the *naturales* and their mother might not take more than one-twelfth, or a *concubina* without children more than half this. Otherwise they might take all[3], subject to *querela inofficiosi testamenti*[4].

(*e*) *Incertae personae*. This expression would cover persons ambiguously described, but its important application seems to have been, so far as the illustrations shew, to those of whose identity the testator could have formed no certain idea[5], persons so defined that anyone might chance to come within the terms, e.g. "whoever shall be first at my funeral." The fact that the individual person who might benefit was uncertain was no objection if he was of a class clearly defined, e.g. "whoever of my present cognates shall be first at my funeral[6]." Justinian allowed *institutio* of *incertae personae* already conceived[7].

(*f*) *Postumi*. These are described by Gaius as *incertae personae*[8], but are sometimes treated as a distinct class[9], as in fact they are. There is nothing uncertain about "the next child of such and such parents." The real objection was that they were persons not existing when the will was made, so that they could not then be *capaces*[10]. *Postumi sui* were dealt with by jurisprudence and legislation, to be considered later[11]. *Postumi extranei* could not be validly instituted before Justinian, though the Praetor would give *bonorum possessio secundum tabulas*[12].

(*g*) Corporate bodies. These seem to be excluded as *incertae personae*, no distinction being drawn between the corporation and its

1 De Visscher, *Mél. Cornil*, 2. 592 *sqq*. (*Ét*. 83). 2 Brasloff, *St. zur Röm. Rechtsgesch*. 1. 66. 3 C. 5. 27, *passim*; *Nov*. 89. 12 *sqq*. 4 *Post*, § CXIV. 5 Cf. 28. 1. 14. 6 G. 2. 238; Ulp. 22. 4; Inst. 2. 20. 25. 7 C. 6. 48. It seems to have been in the first Code, Inst. 2. 20. 27. 8 G. 2. 242. 9 G. 2. 241, 287. Inst. 2. 20. 26 *sqq*. 10 Even if already conceived, the rule, perhaps rather late, that one conceived was treated as already born, would not cover the case, for that rule applies only so far as it benefits him alone, and this would benefit the testator by validating his will, 1. 5. 7; 50. 16. 231. 11 *Post*, § CXII. 12 Inst. 3. 9. pr. In another text (Inst. 2. 20, 28) he says that they could be instituted in earlier law, and this is commonly explained as a reference to *bonorum possessio*. But the closing words of the two texts suggest an entirely different explanation. The *institutio* of a *postumus extraneus* though it could not take effect, as such, might nevertheless be so far valid as to revoke an earlier will, though it did not itself take effect. See *post*, § CVIII, and Buckland, *N.R.H*. 1920, 560.

members. Other reasons are assigned from the same point of view. Ulpian, who says that *universi* cannot "cern" or *pro herede gerere*[1], must have been familiar with acts of administration of property conceived of as binding the whole body though everybody had not joined in them[2]. And legacies to *municipia* are found from the beginning of the Empire[3]. From whatever cause, *municipia* could not be instituted, apart from *privilegia*[4], in classical law, except that *scc.* allowed them to be instituted by their *liberti*[5]. In 469 it was provided that all "*civitates*" could be instituted, and this is Justinian's law[6]. No doubt for similar reasons other corporate bodies could not be instituted, except under *privilegia* or by their *liberti*[7] (though they could receive legacies[8]). It does not appear that there was a general power till the time of Justinian[9]. The State, essentially a magnified *municipium*, could not be instituted[10] and, by the time *municipia* could be, the State as an owner of property was superseded by the Emperor, who was an individual man and could of course be instituted. As to the case of *piae causae*, the way in which these were treated in later law has already been considered[11].

Other less important exclusions were introduced at various times. Such are those of *intestabiles*[12], heretics, children of traitors, women remarrying within the year, etc.[13] But a captive or his slave could be instituted, the gift taking effect if he returned with *postliminium*[14].

Some persons could be validly instituted, but were disqualified from taking unless they satisfied certain requirements before it was too late to claim. They had *testamenti factio* (passive), but not *ius capiendi*.

(*a*) Junian Latins. The *l. Iunia* expressly barred them from taking anything under an inheritance unless they had qualified by becoming *cives* before the time for *cretio* had expired: in that case they could enter[15]. This rule lasted till Justinian abolished the class[16].

(*b*) *Coelibes, orbi*, etc. These rules are a creation of the *l. Iulia* and the *l. Papia Poppaea*, designed to encourage marriage and improve the birth-rate: it is not possible to distinguish, in this connexion, what was done by each statute. A *coelebs* was an unmarried person, male over 25, female

1 Ulp. 22. 5. 2 Mitteis attributes it to a difficulty in admitting vote of the body for private law, though it was familiar in public (*R.Pr.* 1. 379). Ulpian's difficulty in *cretio* seems to be the practical one that "*universi*" could not do it—there would be some who could not and in any case it would not be practicable. But it might have been done by a slave. 3 Reff. in Mitteis, *op. cit.* 377, n. 7; Ulp. 24. 28. 4 See Accarias, *Précis*, 1. 890. 5 Ulp. 22. 5; cf. D. 36. 1. 27. 6 C. 6. 24. 12. ? all *municipia*. 7 C. 6. 24. 8; D. 37. 1. 3; *heredes ab intestato*, 40. 3. 2. Mitteis, *op. cit.* 402. 8 34. 5. 20. 9 C. 6. 48. 1. 10. 10 Such texts as Livy, *Epit.* Bk. 58; Aul. Gell. 7. 7. 6; Cicero, *de l. agr.* 2. 16. 41, prove nothing for Roman Law. 11 *Ante*, § LXV. 12 Possibly, but see *ante*, p. 92. 13 C. 1. 5. 4. 2; C. 5. 9. 1; C. 9. 8. 5. 1, etc. Cuq, *Man.* 691. 14 28. 5. 32. 1. Ratti, *Riv. It. p. l. Sc. Giur.* 1927, 12, holds this interp., but parallels on his p. 17 throw doubt on this. 15 G. 2. 110; Ulp. 22. 3. 16 *Ante*, p. 99.

over 20[1]. Such persons could claim nothing under a will[2]. *Orbi* were childless married persons. These could take only half of any gift to them[3]. *Pater solitarius* seems to mean a widower with children[4]: he was penalised to an extent which is unknown[5]. Here too, those concerned could avoid the prohibition and gain *ius capiendi* by satisfying the *leges* before it was too late to claim[6]. There were exceptions. Ascendants and descendants to three degrees were said to have *ius antiquum*, and, though *coelibes* or *orbi*, could take anything left to them, and their share of lapsed gifts[7]. Relatives to six degrees could take anything expressly left to them: they had *solidi capacitas*[8]. Some relatives by marriage were similarly exempted[9], as were women who had been married, for a certain time after the marriage ended[10]. The destination of gifts which thus failed will be considered later[11]. There is controversy on details: a comparison of Gaius and Ulpian[12] suggests that the rules were changed from time to time. The adoption of Christianity, which from early times regarded celibacy as a chief virtue, made it impossible to retain these rules. It is clear from the devices for evasion that they were always unpopular, and, under Constantine all disabilities attaching to celibacy or *orbitas* were abolished, at any rate as far as express gifts were concerned[13].

Capacity to witness a will. Texts say that anyone might witness with whom there was *testamenti factio*[14], but, as there were many exceptions not reducible to any one principle, it is more exact to say that no one could witness unless he had *testamenti factio*. Gaius limits the right to *cives*[15], but Latins, even Junian, could be witnesses[16]. Women were excluded[17]: they could probably not be instituted in early law[18] and apparently could not be witnesses to *mancipatio*. For this reason deaf or dumb people were excluded, the rule surviving, as often, the reason for it[19]. Interdicted *prodigi* were excluded, apparently as an inference from their incapacity to make a will[20]. Slaves, though there was *testamenti factio*

1 Ulp. 16. 1. Not applicable to men over 60 or women over 50 unless they were not satisfying the law when they reached that age. Ulp. 16. 3. 2 G. 2. 111. 3 G. 2. 286a. The rest governed by *ll. caducariae*. A text of Ulpian rather suggests that women must satisfy the requirement of *ius liberorum* to avoid this penalty; Ulp. 16. 1a. But see G. 2. 111, 286a, and D. 50. 16. 148. 4 Ulp. 16. rubr. 5 *Vir et uxor inter se* are under special disadvantage. They can take from each other only one-tenth if they have no children—relaxations in respect of children of an earlier marriage or deceased children of the present marriage, Ulp. 15. 16; restriction abolished only A.D. 410 (C. 8. 57. 2). 6 Ulp. 17. 1, the ordinary time of *cretio* (Ulp. 17. 1; 22. 3); for widows and those divorced longer terms fixed by legislation (Ulp. 14). 7 Ulp. 1. 21; 18. 8 Vat. Fr. 216, 217. 9 *Ib.* 218, 219. 10 Ulp. 14. 11 *Post*, § CXI. 12 Ulp. 13–18; G. 2. 111, 144, 286a; see also Vat. Fr. *cit.* 13 The expression *ius capiendi* occurs under Justinian (e.g. 49. 14. 2. 2) but it now meant only *testamenti factio*, C. 8. 57. 1; 8. 58. 1. 14 Ulp. 20. 2; Inst. 2. 10. 6. 15 G. 2. 104. 16 Ulp. 20. 2. There was *testamenti factio* with them. 17 Inst. 2. 10. 6. 18 They could not have appeared in the *comitia*. 19 Ulp. 20. 7; Inst. 2. 10. 6. 20 Inst. 2. 10. 6; D. 28. 1. 18. pr.

with them, were excluded[1], but if at the time supposed by all parties to be qualified their attestation was good—*error communis facit ius*[2]. Lunatics and *impuberes* were excluded for obvious reasons[3] as also were *intestabiles*[4]. Apart from general exclusions, a person might be excluded because of his relation to the particular will. No one could witness a will who was in the same family group as the testator or the *familiae emptor*[5]. The exclusion of various witnesses in classical law rested on grounds not of prudence, but of form. The *familiae emptor* and his family were excluded because they could not have been witnesses in a *mancipatio*. The *heres*, who is most interested in setting up a false will, or one in his family group, could be a witness, though Gaius suggests the prudential point by advising against this[6], and in Justinian's time the exclusion became law[7]. But legatees could still witness[8], and all the witnesses might be of one family[9].

If the witness was capable when the will was made, the fact that he afterwards became disqualified was immaterial[10]. His function must be noticed. With us he witnesses the signature: he need not know that the document is a will. In Rome he witnessed the transaction: he must know it was a will though he need not know its contents[11]. The surviving witnesses would be wanted at the formal opening of the will, done before an official as soon as possible after the death. Each witness acknowledged his seal and said, "*in hoc testamento interfui*," shewing that he attested not merely the sealing but the transaction[12].

A will which broke the rules of *testamenti factio* or did not appoint a *heres* was said to be *iniustum* or *non iure factum*[13].

CIV. *Institutio heredis*. The principal, perhaps at one time the only, function of the will[14]; there could be no will without an effective *institutio heredis*[15]. The will must cover the whole property: *nemo pro parte testatus*[16]. We shall see that there were exceptions to this rule[17]. Where the Praetor upset a will by giving *bonorum possessio contra tabulas*, the *institutiones*

1 Inst. 2. 10. 6; D. 28. 1. 20. 7. 2 Inst. 2. 10. 7; C. 6. 23. 1. Probably of wider application. 3 Inst. 2. 10. 6; D. 28. 1. 20. pr. and 4, except *furiosus* in a lucid interval. 4 Inst. 2. 10. 6; D. 28. 1. 18. 1, 26. 5 G. 2. 105, 106; Inst. 2. 10. 9. Or be *libripens*, G. 2. 107; Ulp. 20. 3–5: *domestici testes adhibendi non sunt*. 6 G. 2. 108. 7 Inst. 2. 10. 10. 8 Inst. 2. 10. 11. 9 Ulp. 20. 6; Inst. 2. 10. 8. 10 28. 1. 22. 1. 11 P. 3. 4a. 13; D. 28. 1. 20. 9. Descends from *mancipatio*. The whole system is coloured by reminiscence of *mancipatio*. The principle is shewn by the exclusion even in late law of *surdi* and *muti*. *Nov*. Theod. 16. 1 in laying down that witnesses need not know the content of the will is enacting nothing new, but it states that a contrary practice had grown up. 12 Girard, *Textes*, 815; Bruns, 1. 317. P. 4. 6 describes the process, designed to facilitate collection of duties. 13 29. 2. 22; 28. 3. 1. 14 G. 2. 116. 15 G. 2. 229, 248. But some things ordinarily in a will could be done by codicil without a will; *post*, § CXXVI. The rule remains in principle in later law. 16 Inst. 2. 14. 5. 17 *Post*, §§ CXV.

failed, but some other provisions remained good. This is not a real exception: the will was still valid at civil law[1].

In classical law the *institutio* must be at the beginning, not in the sense that otherwise it was void—the desire to avoid intestacy led to a different interpretation of this and other rules. The principle is that nothing could come before the *institutio* which could lessen what was taken by the *heres*: any provision so placed was void. Disherisons[2], but not legacies or manumissions[3], might precede the *institutiones*. The Proculians held that appointments of *tutores* might precede as they took nothing from the *heres*, the Sabinians taking the other view, though their reason is not recorded[4]. The whole rule is a reminiscence of *mancipatio familiae*, in which the transaction necessarily began with the *mancipatio* of the *familia*, and, more remotely, of the comitial will. Under Justinian the place of the provisions was immaterial[5].

In classical law imperative words were needed: "*T. heres esto*" or "*T. heredem esse iubeo*" or the like. Even "*T. heredem facio*" or "*heredem instituo*" was not enough or, *a fortiori*, precative forms such as "*T. heredem esse volo*[6]." In 339 it was provided that any form sufficed if intent was clear[7]. A century later, it was provided that a will might be made in Greek[8]. The *institutio* must make it clear who was to be *heres*, but even in classical law any description sufficient for identification sufficed[9].

Institutio heredis, being a legal transaction, might be affected by fraud or error. Where one by violence or *dolus* prevented a man from making or altering a will, or induced him to make a will, *bonorum possessio* was refused. In Justinian's law the result was apparently that in both cases the property was forfeited to the *fiscus* for *indignitas*, but it is possible that for classical law this was true only of the first case. In the second, *bonorum possessio* may have been granted to those entitled in default of the incriminated will[10]. The case of *filius suppositus* seems to be on the same footing: the *institutio* is void and the estate may have been forfeited for *indignitas*, though the *institutus* need not have been a

1 *Post*, § CXIII. 2 28. 5. 1 (Trajan); 28. 3. 3. 2. 3 G. 2. 229, 230; Ulp. 1. 20; 24. 15. The rule did not apply to *fideicommissa*, Ulp. 25. 8. 4 G. 2. 231. Perhaps because *tutela* originally conceived of as a right, of which *heres* is thus deprived. 5 Inst. 2. 20. 34; C. 6. 23. 24. 6 G. 2. 117; Ulp. 21. 7 C. 6. 23. 15. Even in (later) classical law defective words were sometimes treated as mere error of scribe, 28. 5. 1. 5, 6. 8 C. 6. 23. 21 (*Nov.* Theod. 16); as to *miles*, *post*, § CXXVI. Reinach, *Gnom. de l'Idios Logos*, 54, cites an enactment of Alexander allowing wills in Greek (*Pap. Rayneri*, 1502), commonly held to apply only to Egypt, which he thinks general. He refers to C. 6. 23. 21 "*quoniam graece iam testari concessum est.*" But *concessum* suggests a special rule and the words are accounted for by the rule in Egypt and for soldiers. Cp. C. 5. 28. 8; 7. 2. 14. 9 P. 3. 4b. 3. 10 D. 29. 6; 34. 9. 19; Lenel, *E.P.* 360; Fadda, *Dir. Ered.* 1. 251, elaborate analysis of error, Betti, *Ist.* 1. ch. 13.

party to the fraud[1]. Ordinary error of motive was in general disregarded, but in several cases the Emperor set aside the *institutio* and even gave effect in some of them, at least partially, to what the testator may be supposed to have intended. No principle is deducible from these cases[2]. The chief are: the enactment of Tiberius[3] dealing with a slave supposed free and a substitute, one of Hadrian dealing with a woman's son omitted as he was thought dead[4], two of Severus and Caracalla, one dealing with a *postumus* omitted by a woman and the other with a will made, and stated to be made, because the *heres* under a first will was (wrongly) thought dead[5], and the above mentioned case of the supposititious child. Of other forms of error we hear little. There is a general rule that if a mistake is made in identity and the wrong name inserted, neither the man named nor the man meant is *heres*. And where a testator naming several *heredes* added one which he did not intend this was void[6]. Subject to this, the rule *falsa demonstratio non nocet* applied to *institutiones*[7].

As the *heres* was universal successor an *institutio ex certa re* was inadmissible. It was not void, but, to preserve the will, the limitation was ignored if he was sole *heres*[8]. The case might be more complicated and the main rules appear to have been the following.

Where there were two *heredes* each instituted to specific things only, so expressed as to cover the whole, Ulpian says that nominally they shared equally so that each was liable for half the debts, but the *iudex* in the action for division, *familiae erciscundae*, confined each *heres* to what was expressly given to him, so that, if debts were heavy, one might get nothing at all. This was to give them each a half subject to a *praelegatum* to each of what is expressly left to him: we may suppose the same rule to apply where the things stated were not the whole[9].

Where one was instituted for a certain fraction of a *fundus* and the other for a fraction of the same or another *fundus*, the *fundus* and the shares were ignored and the case was dealt with on the lines of Ulpian's rule above stated[10]. Where some were appointed *ex certa re*, and others to shares in the *hereditas*, Justinian declares the former mere legatees[11]. The language indicates that the rule was not essentially new, though in

1 C. 6. 24. 4; D. 34. 9. 16. pr.; 37. 10. 1. 11; 49. 14. 46. pr. Fadda, *cit.*, 255; Schulz, *Gedenks. f. Seckel*, 100.
2 Full study of these texts, Schulz, *cit.*, 88. *Post*, § CXIX.
3 28. 5. 41; Inst. 2. 15. 4.
4 5. 2. 28.
5 C. 3. 28. 3; D. 28. 5. 93.
6 28. 5. 9. pr., 7.
7 *Post*, § CXIX.
8 28. 5. 1. 4. Exceptional rule of Severus, *post*, § CXVI.
9 28. 5. 35. As these gifts are *praelegata*, they will however be subject, so the text seems to say, to the *l. Falcidia*. The text is corrupt and probably largely due to Justinian.
10 28. 5. 9. 13, 10. The texts may not wholly represent cl. law. Suman, *Favor testamenti*, shews a gradual evolution from *favor testamenti*, i.e., maintenance of the will, to *favor voluntatis*, effectuating the wish of the testator, not complete till Just. See also Siber, *R.R.* 2. 348. David, *Institutio ex re certa*, was not available.
11 C. 6. 24. 13.

classical law they may have taken shares, being under a *fideicommissum* to hand over to the others all but the specific things[1].

A *heres* might not be instituted from a certain day—the day was struck out[2]. It may have been too definite a breach of the continuity between deceased and *heres*. It could have served little purpose—it was a mere wanton postponement of other claims under the will[3]. A *heres* could not be appointed till a certain day—the limit was struck out as an infringement of the rule: *semel heres semper heres*[4].

Dies incertus, i.e. a time certain to come but uncertain as to date (*certus an, incertus quando*) had in *institutiones* the effect of a condition. This does not involve a necessary breach of continuity: the ordinary illustration taken, *cum T. moreretur*, might happen at once[5].

A *heres* might be appointed conditionally, i.e. subject to an event both future and uncertain[6]. A gift to *X* "if St Paul's is 400 feet high" was not conditional: it was valid or not according to the facts. A gift "if *X* becomes Consul" was conditional and there could be no acceptance of it, *aditio*, till *X* was consul, which he might never be. Conditional institutions were subject to restrictions. An impossible condition was struck out, the *institutio* being treated as absolute, on the principle of maintaining *institutiones*[7]. An impossible condition is one not in the nature of things, not an exact idea, but shifting with the advance of knowledge: many modern achievements of science would have been set down as not in the nature of things by the Romans[8]. Impossibility to the person concerned was immaterial if the thing could conceivably happen. "If he becomes Consul" was not an impossible condition, though it might in the given case be most unlikely. Impossibility is initial impossibility[9]. Supervening impossibility (*casus*) was on a different footing, and was treated in *institutiones* as failure of the condition[10]. Immoral or illegal conditions also were struck out[11], a strong illustration

1 Cf. Inst. 2. 17. 3, *post*, § CXVI. 2 28. 5. 34. 3 Windscheid, *Lehrb.* § 555, n. 3. 4 28. 5. 89; h. t. 34; Inst. 2. 14. 9. 5 35. 1. 75; C. 6. 24. 9. *Dies certus quando incertus an*, e.g. if or when he shall reach the age of fourteen, is a condition, 28. 6. 33. pr. But see *post*, § CXIX. As to *institutio* "cum ipse morietur," Brunetti, *Dies incertus*, 130, with special reference to C. 6. 24. 9. He holds that this was not treated as condition, but, exceptionally, allowed to be valid as *dies*, otherwise it must fail in the case of an *extraneus* as he could not possibly enter. 6 Inst. 2. 14. 9; D. 28. 7 *passim*. Conditional *institutiones* are relatively late. Such as can be satisfied at once appear not long before the end of the Republic; those involving suspension not till the Empire. Buckland, *Tydschr.* 1922, 239. 7 28. 7. 1; Inst. 2. 14. 10; in contract a different rule is applied: there the impossible condition vitiates the transaction, *post*, § CXLVIII. 8 The common instance is "to touch the sky with one's finger." In one case it is said, after hesitation, that a condition "if he build a tomb within three days" must be treated as impossible, 28. 7. 6. 9 Difficulties where the *condicio* assumes a non-existing state of facts, 28. 5. 46; 40. 7. 28. pr., Buckland, *Slavery*, 490; Vernay, *Servius et son école*, 184. 10 9. 2. 23. 2. 11 28. 7. 14; P. 3. 4b. 2. Suman, *cit.* 114, holds that they were struck out by the Praetor.

of the desire to save *institutiones*: a testator who imposed such a condition deserved that his will should fail[1].

To the rule that impossibility to the person concerned left the condition valid, there was an important exception. If a *paterfamilias* instituted a son whom he wished to exclude, on a condition not technically impossible, but one that in practice the son could not satisfy, e.g. "if he is Praetor at the earliest possible age," this was not an *omissio* (which would upset the will[2]) or an *exheredatio* (which, if unjust, gave the *querela*[3]), but the son would be excluded. The rule was established that a son in *potestas* could be instituted conditionally only on a condition in his power. Other conditions were treated as omissions, and even one in his power was so treated if it outraged natural affection. If it was in his power and he neglected it, he was excluded[4].

A resolutive condition or *dies* on an *institutio* was struck out, as conflicting with the rule: *semel heres semper heres*[5]. This applied whether it was an event or some act to be done by him, but, in late law, a way was found by which the testator in this last case could achieve much the same result. A *heres* instituted "if he does not do so and so" took the estate at once, giving security that he would return it if he did the act barred. He would not cease to be *heres*. No doubt, what he had to restore was the net assets, as he was liable for the debts[6]. This *cautio Muciana*, probably due to Q. M. Scaevola of Cicero's time[7], was, it seems, originally applicable only to legacies and extended to *institutiones* only under Justinian, or at any rate in post-classical times[8]. There are difficulties as to the limitation of its application, but these will be considered under legacy[9].

Some conditions vitiated the *institutio*. Such were *institutiones captatoriae*, institution of *A* on condition that he instituted the testator, or likely so to operate[10], and *conditiones perplexae*, self-contradictory, e.g. "Let *T* be *heres* if *X* is and let *X* be *heres* if *T* is[11]." Technically this is impossible, for neither can take till the other has, and they cannot

1 It was suggested that such a thing was evidence of insanity which would upset the will. 28. 7. 27. 2 *Post*, § CXII. 3 *Post*, § CXIV. 4 Not applied to other *sui heredes*. It was permissible in classical law to impose any condition, such that it must be determined in his life, with an *exheredatio* in the contrary event, 28. 2. 28. pr. The rule in the text may have applied to all *postumi* who, in classical law, upset the will if not provided for. *Post*, § CXII. 5 Inst. 2. 14. 9; D. 28. 5. 34. 6 35. 1. 7. pr. 7 Girard, *Man.* 877. It serves little purpose in *institutiones*; one conditionally instituted could get *b. p.* in any case on giving security, 37. 11. 6. *Post*, § CXXXV. 2. 8. 12; 28. 5. 23. pr. Possible difference in effect, Girard, *Man. cit.* 8 H. Krueger, *Mél. Girard*, 2. 1, shews that most of the texts applying it to *institutiones* were written of legacy (35. 1. 7. pr., 1, 18), and shew signs of interpolation. 28. 7. 4. 1 does not seem to have been so written, but may not refer to *c. Muciana*. See 35. 1. 7. 1. 9 *Post*, § CXIX. 10 28. 5. 72. 11 28. 7. 16.

accept together, for *aditio* cannot be made while a condition is outstanding[1]. Why it was so harshly treated is not clear[2].

The condition, "*heres esto, si volet,*" is null; it adds nothing[3]. An *institutio* in the terms "*quos T. volet*" or "*si T. volet*" is void; an *institutio* may not be at the absolute discretion of a third party. But the result might be reached by making the *institutio* depend on a trifling act of a third party, e.g. *si T. capitolium ascenderit,* which was quite valid[4].

The condition must be satisfied before entry. It was usually indifferent how or when, but if it was an act to be done, of such a nature that it could be done many times, it was inferred to be the testator's intent that it be done after the death[5]. Circumstances might release the *heres* from the obligation to satisfy the condition. Where a man was instituted under a condition of swearing to do something, the Praetor remitted the condition, but, in Ulpian's time, refused the hereditary actions till the thing had been done[6], nearly the same as substituting the act for the oath[7]. If a condition required the co-operation of a third party and he would not act, the condition was regarded as satisfied[8]. And if the *heres* was prevented from satisfying it by one who had an interest in his not doing so, the condition was treated as satisfied[9]. But there was no relief where the act was to be done by some third party independently of him[10].

Conditions in *institutiones* are, as we have seen, relatively late. It is not clear how they came to be allowed at all in what must have been a typical *actus legitimus*[11]. The fact that the Praetor's remission produced civil effects[12] suggests that the Praetor may have been the first agent in introducing them.

A man might institute as many *heredes* as he liked, and vary the shares as he would, subject to claims of *sui heredes*. It was the usual practice, borrowed from the system of weights, to regard the whole as an *as*, of which one or more *unciae* (twelfths), called *uncia, sextans* (2 *unciae*), *quadrans* (3), *triens* (4), *quincunx* (5), *semis* (6), *septunx* (7),

1 28. 7. 13, 14; 29. 2. 10, 21. 2, 22. 1; as to *b. p.*, *post*, § CXXXV. 2 Bufnoir, *Conditions*, 31, says it is as not seriously meant, but there seems no ground for this. 3 28. 7. 12. But see *post*, p. 339. More prominent in legacy, *post*, § CXIX. 4 28. 5. 32; h. t. 69. In 28. 5. 83 the condition "*si legitimus heres vindicare nolit*" was held valid. Cp. 28. 5. 87. pr., *post*, p. 339. 5 35. 1. 2, 11. 6 28. 7. 8. pr. Remission operates *ipso iure* (h. l. 8). It produces full civil law effect, Pernice, *Labeo*, 3. 1. 54. 7 Not identical: he is *heres* at once and can enter before doing the act. 8 28. 7. 3, 11; 35. 1. 14. Must be distinguished from supervening impossibility, *ante*, p. 297. 9 50. 17. 161. It must have been intended to prevent. See 40. 7. 38. Prevention is essentially interference with the action of donee. 10 40. 7. 4. 7. See n. 4. As to evolution in the conception of conditional gifts, Vassali, *Bull.* 1914, 192. 11 50. 17. 77. 12 See n. 6, and for other possible cases Suman, *cit.*, 114; *ante*, p. 297, n. 11.

bes (8) (two-thirds[1]), *dodrans* (9), *dextans* (10), *deunx* (11), *as* (12)[2], were assigned to each *heres*. They might be subdivided, the smallest name recorded being *scriptula*, the twenty-fourth part of an *uncia*[3].

The division need not be into 12: the testator might make his testamentary *as* of as many *unciae* as he pleased. As he could not be partly testate, if he gave only nine shares there would be nine *unciae*. If 12 were allotted and a *heres* to one *uncia* refused or was disqualified, there would be only 11 *unciae* covering the whole, or, what is the same thing, his *uncia* would accrue to the others[4].

If nothing was said of shares, the *heredes* took equally. If some had shares allotted and others had not, those to whom no share was named took all unallotted out of 12, but here if 12 or more were allotted, the *as* was doubled and assumed to have 24 *unciae* (*dupondius*), and they took all unallotted out of 24[5]. This gave an odd result: if five were allotted to *A*, six to *B* and *C* was merely instituted, *C* took one *uncia*, but if six had been given to *A*, *C* would have taken 12, i.e. a half.

CV. *Substitutio* (*subinstitutio*). One of the safeguards against intestacy was the rule that a testator might appoint others to take if the *institutio* did not take effect. This was the purpose of the most usual, possibly not the oldest, form of *substitutio*, *substitutio vulgaris*. In its simplest form this ran "*T. heres esto, si heres non erit, C. heres esto*[6]." Technically, *T.* was said to be *heres* in the first grade, and *C. heres* in the second[7]. It might be more complex, e.g. there might be a further *substitutio, tertius gradus*[8]. *Heredes* might be reciprocally substituted, the purpose being to avoid, not intestacy, which this would not do, but the operation of the *ll. caducariae*[9]. The substitute might have a different share, or two might be substituted to one[10]. In general, as the form shews, if the *institutus* took, the substitute was excluded. But there were exceptions. If a man instituted a slave thinking him free, and substituted *X* to him, Tiberius decided in the case of his own slave, Parthenius, that the slave's owner and the substitute divided[11]. Where an insolvent instituted a *heres necessarius*, a slave, and substituted to him, the sub-

1 *Duae* (*partes*) *assis*, but see Varro, *L.L.* 5. 172. 2 The names for 9, 10 and 11 are derived from *dempto*(*a*) *quadrante, sextante, uncia*. 3 *Semuncia* ($\frac{1}{2}$), *binae sextulae* ($\frac{1}{3}$), *sicilicus* ($\frac{1}{4}$), *sextula* ($\frac{1}{6}$), *dimidia sextula* ($\frac{1}{12}$), *sescunx* ($1\frac{1}{2}$ *unciae* $=\frac{1}{8}$ *as*), *uncia duae sextulae* ($\frac{1}{9}$ *as*). Symbols for these, Volusius Maecianus (Seckel-Kuebler, *Jurisp. Anteiust.* 1. 409). 4 Inst. 2. 14. 5, 7. 5 Inst. 2. 14. 6. 6 Inst. 2. 15. pr. *Institutio* in the first grade would often be conditional. As to security which *substitutus* could claim where such a *heres* had obtained *b. p.* (*post*, § cxxxv), P. 5. 9. 1. 7 G. 2. 154; P. 3. 4b. 4. 8 G. 2. 174; Ulp. 22. 33; D. 28. 5. 54; 28. 6. 1. 9 *Post*, § cxi. 10 Inst. 2. 15. 1, 2. Difficult questions on the point whether if a *suus* is disinherited in an *institutio*, this must be repeated in the *substitutio*, 28. 2. 8. Text corrupt; *post*, § cxii. In later cl. law the substitute took over the burdens of legacies, etc. (30. 74; 31. 61. 1) unless the contary intent appeared (31. 29. 1). 11 Inst. 2. 15. 4; 28. 5. 42, where a theoretical justification is attempted. Error, generally, *ante*, p. 295.

stitute was preferred if he was willing to take, for it was only where no other *heres* would take that an insolvent might free a slave by will to the detriment of his creditors[1]. If a common slave was instituted and one owner refused, that share would go to a substitute if there was one[2], so that the slave and he would both take. But another text denies this; there is difficulty on the question whether the *institutio* of a common slave is one *institutio* or two[3].

The chief rules of *substitutio vulgaris* were these:

(i) The testator, in substituting, might vary shares, conditions and charges, but in general the substitute took the share with its burdens[4].

(ii) It was in effect a conditional *institutio*; thus the *hereditas* was *delata* to the substitute only when the condition was satisfied by failure of the *institutio*, so that the *substitutio* would fail if the *substitutus* was not then alive and *capax*[5].

(iii) The two gifts are distinct *institutiones*. The question arose whether an *institutus*, also substituted to another *heres*, could accept one share and refuse the other. Just as one instituted for two separate shares accepted both by accepting one[6], so here[7], though one text, corrupt[8], seems to deny it. One who had entered under an *institutio* could not refuse a share to which he was substituted and the one entry sufficed. So if he entered under the *substitutio* first[9].

(iv) *Substitutus substituti instituto substituitur*[10]. If *B* was substituted to *A* and *C* to *B*, *C* was also substituted to *A* if *B* failed, whether they were also *coheredes* or not. If *B* was dead, or refused before *A*'s share fell in, *C* would not get this, apart from the present rule, though he would if the events happened in the other order[11].

(v) *Coheredes* might be substituted to each other[12]. The effect of this was that if one refused, his share passed to the other. This was much what would have happened in early law even if they were not reciprocally substituted. But the *substitutio* was material in several ways.

(*a*) The testator could vary the shares, conditions and charges.

(*b*) Substitution, being express *institutio*, was subject to all its rules. Thus, as *delatio* did not occur till the *institutio* had failed, the substitute must still be alive and *capax*, or he could not take it; *institutio* failed if *heres* died before *delatio*. The benefit was personal. If, having entered

1 Ulp. 1. 14. 2 28. 6. 48. pr. 3 29. 2. 65. Buckland, *Slavery*, 384. The law of *cretio imperfecta* provides a further apparent exception, but it really illustrates a different principle, *post*, § CIX. 4 31. 61. 1. 5 29. 2. 69; 38. 16. 9. 6 29. 2. 80. 7 29. 2. 35, 76. 8 29. 2. 80. 1: "*si tamen delatae sint.*" 9 29. 2. 76. The difficulty which would result in this case if the *spatium deliberandi* of the *institutio* had expired is not discussed. 10 Inst. 2. 15. 3. Rule here attributed to Severus and Caracalla, but elsewhere laid down by Julian, 28. 6. 27. Based on presumed intent of the testator: hence a limitation mentioned and rejected by Papinian, h. t. 41. pr. 11 Papinian, *loc. cit.* 12 Inst. 2. 15. 3, etc.

for his own share he died before the other *institutio* failed, the *substitutio* failed and the share would be divided among the other *heredes*[1]. If there had been no *substitutio* his representatives would take the part of the lapsed share which would have come to him had he still been alive[2].

(*c*) The *ll. caducariae*, excluding *coelibes*, etc., exempted relatives[3] so that they could take *in solidum*, but, except as to ascendants and descendants, this applied only to what was expressly given to them. Thus if *heredes* were reciprocally substituted, and one was a bachelor brother, he would take his share of a gift which fell in, as there was an express gift of it. But if there were no substitution, and a share fell in, the *ll. caducariae* excluded him from any share in it[4].

Substitutio pupillaris. Of narrower application and different purpose. Where a man had a *suus heres*, born or unborn, he might provide for the case in which this *suus* survived him, and so inherited, but died under puberty, and thus unable to make a will. The father might, in his will, substitute a person to take the inheritance of the child in that event[5], in effect, making a will for the child[6], but the original view seems to have been rather that it was another will of the father. Both views appear[7]. This ancient institution may at first have required that the child should have been instituted, and have covered only what came from the father, but in the Empire it covered the child's whole estate, and was allowed though the child was disinherited[8]. It had a practical purpose, besides avoidance of the child's intestacy. If a father had disinherited a *suus* for misconduct, and an instituted son survived him, and died *impubes*, the property might, but for this provision, go to that disinherited *suus*. It was often coupled with a *substitutio vulgaris* of the same person, either or neither operating according to the event[9]. The *substitutio vulgaris* was usually in the will, but the *pupillaris* was preferably put in a separate document, not to be opened unless the child died *impubes*, to avoid the risk that, for what might be many years, someone would have an interest in making away with the child[10]. But it was so usual to make both institutions in favour of the same person that, from M. Aurelius

1 28. 6. 23. 2 Subject to the *ll. caducariae*, *post*, § CXI. 3 *Ante*, p. 292; *post*, § CXI. 4 They had not the *ius antiquum* or *praemia patrum*. G. 2. 206; Ulp. 17. 2.
5 G. 2. 179; Ulp. 23. 7; Inst. 2. 16. Not possible in any other case, G. 2. 184.
6 Cicero, *de inv.* 2. 21. 62; G. 2. 180. 7 28. 6. 1. 1; h. t. 3. Arangio Ruiz (*Erede e tutore*) gets rid of the conflict with the rule: *semel heres semper heres*, by the view that *s. pup.* began, very early, as a power in the *pater* to appoint someone *heres* and *tutor*, to hand over everything when the child reached puberty (*ante*, p. 142, n. 4). Similar thesis, La Pira, *St. Bonfante*, 3. 273. But if the *impubes* does not die there is the same difficulty: the *hereditas* passes from the *tutor heres*. 8 Cicero, *loc. cit.*; G. 2. 182; Ulp. 23. 8; Inst. 2. 16. 4. But here no legacy could be charged on the substitute. 30. 126. pr.
9 See Inst. 2. 16. pr.; G. 2. 179. 10 G. 2. 181; Inst. 2. 16. 3. Safer still to put both in the separate document.

onwards, one kind of *substitutio* implied the other unless the contrary appeared[1].

The person so substituted might also be an *institutus* in the father's will. Hence the question arose whether, as the *substitutio* might cover property not in the father's *hereditas*, the case was to be treated as two wills or one, i.e. whether one who had accepted the *institutio* was bound to accept the *substitutio* as no more than a further share, which he could not refuse, or whether it was a distinct will under which he might refuse if he liked. The view which prevailed, a survival on this point of the original notion, was that it was one will, so that having accepted the *institutio* he could not refuse the *substitutio*[2]. Ulpian laid it down that a slave made *heres necessarius* of the father and substituted to the *impubes* was *heres necessarius* of the latter also[3]. The older lawyers held indeed that even if the *institutus*, also *substitutus*, died before the pupil, but after accepting the *institutio*, his representatives took under the *substitutio*[4], but Ulpian held that it was a distinct *institutio*, in so far that it failed if he was not alive when the *impubes* died[5]. Other difficulties of the same kind resulted from the notion that it was one will and two *hereditates*: the language of Justinian shews the confusion[6]. Finally he decides that acceptance or repudiation as to one binds as to the other[7].

The chief rules of *substitutio pupillaris* were these:

(i) Its validity depended on that of the father's will. If that failed the *substitutio* failed[8]. But if any validity was left to any *institutio*, this saved the pupillary substitution, e.g. if the will was partially upset by the *querela*[9], or was upset by *bonorum possessio contra tabulas*, which left it valid at civil law[10]. An inference drawn from its dependence was that, if in a separate document, it must be made after the will[11].

(ii) It must be in favour of a *certa persona*, except that it might be "whoever shall be my *heres*," which was understood to mean *heres* under the will, entering and surviving the *impubes*[12].

(iii) It might be to a disinherited *suus*, but not to an *emancipatus*. Thus it failed if the child was emancipated or given in adoption, or predeceased the testator[13].

1 28. 6. 4. pr. The case of Curius seems to have raised the question: it is frequently discussed by Cicero and others. Texts, Meyer, *Orat. Rom. Fragg*. 304, 318. 2 29. 2. 59; 28. 6. 10. 3. 3 28. 6. 2. 4 *in f.*, 10. 1. 4 29. 2. 59. 5 28. 6. 8. 1. The same illogicality in *s. vulgaris*. No new entry was needed for the *substitutio*, for it was no more than another share. But if the *substitutus* was dead when the *substitutio* was *delata* his representatives had no claim, 28. 6. 23. 6 Inst. 2. 16. 2. La Pira, *cit.* ch. 3, regards the dominant cl. view as making it one will and one *hereditas* and the substitute *heres* to the father, the *impubes* not being *heres* at all. 7 C. 6. 30. 20. 8 Ulp. 23. 9; D. 28. 6. 1. 3, 2. 1. 9 28. 6. 31. pr. 10 28. 6. 34. 2. Other cases, h. t. 2. 1, 2. 3, 38. 3 (corrupt). 11 28. 6. 16. 1. 12 Inst. 2. 16. 7. 13 28. 6. 41. 2. So if he was adrogated after the death of the father, though here there would be the Antonine

(iv) It could not last beyond puberty, but it might be for less, and different substitutes might be appointed according to the age at which the child died[1].

(v) It might be under condition, like any other *institutio*[2].

(vi) If the substitute, knowing his position, neglected for a year to get a *tutor* appointed, the *substitutio* failed, at least in later law[3].

(vii) If the *substitutio* operated it was treated for most purposes as if it had been in the original will, and the *pupillus* was ignored[4]. Thus, e.g., legacies charged on pupil and substitute were treated together for the *l. Falcidia*, not as charged on different *heredes*[5].

Substitutio exemplaris or *quasi pupillaris*. An extension of the foregoing, for insane descendants, not necessarily *sui* or *impuberes*. The Emperors allowed testators, on petition, to substitute *heredes* for descendants incapable of testation from insanity or other defect. If the *incapax* died, still afflicted, the substitute took: if he recovered, the *substitutio* was void and did not revive on relapse[6]. Justinian, leaving other cases unaffected, allowed it without special petition in the case of the insane. Any ascendant might appoint such a substitute for anything to which he instituted the defective. He must be a *certa persona*, a sane descendant of the *furiosus*, if any; if none, some other sane issue of the testator. Failing these, anyone. If several were so appointed it seems that each took what came from his appointor, but it is not clear what happened to what came from none of them. As in earlier practice, the defect must be *perpetuum*, and the *substitutio* is void altogether on recovery[7].

CVI. CLASSIFICATION OF *HEREDES*. These are in three classes[8]:

Necessarii heredes. These are slaves of the testator freed and instituted by his will, *heredes* with no power of refusal[9]. The name applied to all such slaves freed and instituted, but its most important application was in insolvency. An insolvent might name a slave as one of his *heredes*, so that, if the others refused, the slave would be *heres*, and the disgrace of insolvency would fall on him and not on the deceased[10]. The slave had indeed a certain protection. The Edict allowed him to apply for *bonorum*

security for restoration to the substitute, as in all *adrogatio* of an *impubes*, *ante*, p. 126, and the *substitutus* had *actiones utiles*, 28. 6. 40.

1 28. 6. 14, 38. 1, 2. 2 28. 6. 8. 3 C. 6. 58. 10, extracted from *Nov*. Theod. 11 (A.D. 439). 4 La Pira, *cit*. 286 for evidence and limitations. 5 36. 2. 7. 4. 6 28. 6. 43. 7 Inst. 2. 16. 1; C. 6. 26. 9. 8 G. 2. 152 *sqq*.; Ulp. 22. 24, 25. 9 G. 2. 153; Ulp. 22. 24; Inst. 2. 19. 1. Those *in mancipio* were also *necessarii* (G. 2. 160). One of whom testator had only bonitary ownership could not be so utilised; he could not be *heres* as he would be only a Latin. Ulp. 22. 8. Where a testator instituted a *servus alienus* with a gift of liberty and afterwards acquired the slave the two gifts were void, liberty to a *servus alienus* being a nullity, 28. 5. 50. pr. Was the *heres* under the comitial will originally *necessarius*? Cornil, *A.D.R.* 112. 10 Inst. 2. 19. 1.

separatio, so long as he had not meddled with the estate, so that anything acquired by him, either before or after the sale of the estate by the creditors, would not be liable to the creditors[1], who thus took no more than if there had been no *heres*. As the creditors suffered to the extent of his value, no more than one could be so freed; only the first named was free. The rules under the *l. Aelia Sentia* did not apply[2], but if the slave was incapable of freedom under any other rule he could not be so utilised[3]. It must be a voluntary manumission. If, e.g., the *dominus* held a slave under a *fideicommissum* to free him, the slave was not *necessarius* and could be free without taking the inheritance[4].

Sui et necessarii heredes. These were those in the *potestas* of the deceased who became *sui iuris* at his death, and *postumi* who would have been in that position if born soon enough[5]. They were *sui* as, in a sense, *heredes* to themselves, and *necessarii* as being *heredes* without any power to refuse[6]. But this civil law unfairly disgraced them for their father's insolvency, and the Edict allowed them the *ius abstinendi*, if they stood aloof, did not intermeddle, and shewed that they did not mean to be *heredes*[7]. The *bonorum venditio* would then proceed in the name of the deceased, and though the will was technically valid the Praetor refused any action against the *suus*[8]. Pupillary substitutions and manumissions were good[9], and, if the estate proved solvent, legacies must be paid. Any surplus belonged to the *heres*, not to the creditors[10]. In classical law the *suus* could alter his mind and take the *hereditas* at any time before the goods were sold, but Justinian limited this to three years, even though the estate had not yet been realised[11]. If the attitude of the *heres* was obscure, a creditor could sue him, when he would have

1 42. 6. 1. 18; G. 2. 155. Another case of *bonorum separatio*, *post*, § CX. 2 G. 1. 21; Ulp. 1. 14. 3 28. 5. 84. pr. If alienated or freed, *post testamentum factum*, he is not *necessarius*, but acquires for his new master or himself. Ulp. 22. 11, 12; G. 2. 188; Inst. 2. 14. 1. 4 28. 5. 3. 3. 5 G. 2. 156 *sqq.*, 183; Inst. 2. 19. 2. Ulp. 22. 14 and G. 1, 159 include *nurus in manu filii*, but she will be a *sua* only if the son dies *vivo patre*. 6 28. 2. 11; 38. 16. 14; G. *loc. cit.*; Inst. 2. 19. 2. It is objected (Strachan-Davidson, *Problems in Rom. Crim. Law*, 1. 86 *sqq.*) that this idea of *condominium* cannot be ancient. The absolute *dominium* of the *paterf.* over his family is inconsistent with *condominium* of these in the property. He adopts the view that it is a late piece of idealism. But it is implied in the language of the XII Tables (5. 4) and in the ancient inalienability of the *heredium*. Cuq, *Inst. Jurid.* 1. 287, n. 3, and *post*, § CXXIX. In 28. 5. 87. pr., it is said that a *suus* can be instituted "*si volet*" and anyone substituted to him. This seems to make him no longer *necessarius*. The text is corrupt. Beseler, *Beitr.* 3. 153. Perozzi, *Ist.* 2. 622. 7 29. 2. 71. 9; G. 2. 158; Inst. 2. 19. 2. G. gives *ius abstinendi* also to one *in mancipio*, though he is not a *suus* but merely a *necessarius* (G. 2. 160). The right being lost if the *heres* intermeddles (G. 2. 163), it was provided that one who did acts of piety or urgent necessity might guard himself by declaring that he did not do them as *heres*. 29. 2. 20. pr. 8 29. 2. 57. pr. 9 29. 2. 42. pr.; 40. 4. 32, if not in fraud of creditors. And *fcc. hereditatis*, 36. 1. 28. 3. 10 36. 1. 69. 2. 11 28. 8. 8; C. 6. 31. 6.

to take one position or the other. In later classical law the *beneficium deliberandi* seems to have been extended to him, i.e. he could, like an *extraneus*, apply to have a time fixed within which to make up his mind[1].

CVII. *Extranei heredes.* All other *heredes* could refuse. Some time would elapse before they decided, and in that time the *hereditas* was said to be *iacens*[2], and to be offered to them (*delata*). Rules were evolved to deal with difficulties resulting from the fact that in the meantime the goods belonged to none, and yet must be protected, and business must be carried on. The impunity with which they could be stolen or damaged would strike the imagination sooner than commercial inconvenience, and was provided against in many ways, usually independent of any notion of personality or ownership in the *hereditas* itself. There could be no theft of *res hereditariae*, but a special machinery was invented, the *crimen expilatae hereditatis*[3]. On the other hand for damage to the *hereditas* the *heres* could use the Aquilian action, on the ground, not elsewhere supported, that the word "owner" does not necessarily mean owner at the time of the wrong[4]. There was machinery for dealing with freed slaves who pillaged the *hereditas* before their liberty took effect[5]. These proceedings shew no coherence among themselves, and fall short of vesting rights in the *hereditas*. One case is specially striking. Under the interdict *quod vi aut clam*, the question whether the *heres* could proceed in respect of acts done before acceptance is discussed in a long text[6]. Early jurists are cited, and the rule arrived at is that he could. The reasons assigned are independent of the personification of the *hereditas*; it was admitted that *hereditas* could not be owner. Then comes the remark that, besides all this, the *hereditas* could be considered as the owner, no doubt an addition.

The conception of *hereditas iacens* thus reached was of great importance in private law. It was an incomplete personification of the *hereditas*, arising only where there was no *heres necessarius*, and thus there would be an interval between the death and the entry of the *heres*[7].

1 28. 8. 8. One not within either definition may be a *necessarius*, i.e. a grandchild instituted by a grandfather who disinherited the father. He cannot refuse, but he is not a *suus*, and has no ground of complaint if omitted (28. 3. 6. pr.) and he is not a slave. The cause of the defective terminology is no doubt that the idea of disherison is not primitive, but is superimposed on the existing classification. In classical law such an institution would simply benefit the father, but under Justinian the property would be *bona adventitia*, *ante*, p. 280.

2 43. 24. 13. 5.

3 47. 19; C. 9. 32. After the disappearance of *usucapio lucrativa*.

4 9. 2. 43.

5 47. 4. 1. pr. Existed while the law of *usucapio lucrativa* still allowed other people to seize the goods. Other illustrations, Pernice, *Labeo*, 1. 360 *sqq*.

6 43. 24. 13. 5.

7 Where a *suus* is yet unborn, or a *necessarius* is instituted conditionally, the position is much the same, and no doubt the rules were the same, but no text applies the theory of *hereditas iacens* to this case. We have little discussion, but on the texts *hereditas iacens* and *heres extraneus* are inseparable ideas. See, e.g., 43. 24. 13. 5.

During this interval the *hereditas* was offered to the person entitled, *hereditatis delatio*. If he decided to accept, his acceptance was *aditio*, and, as we shall see, was sometimes declared in a formal manner, called *cretio*[1].

The jurists did not go so far as to call the *hereditas* "*persona ficta*"; that expression is medieval. They said that the *hereditas* "*personae vicem sustinet*" or the like. The compilers of the Digest were not particular on this point: the modern technical meaning of *persona* was developing in their age. There are at least two texts in which the *hereditas* is spoken of as *dominus* of *res hereditariae*[2]. These texts shew signs of alteration, and there is none that goes the length of calling the *hereditas* a person. Justinian in the Institutes makes it clear that it is not[3]. The obviously altered state of some texts has led to the suggestion that any quasi-personification of the *hereditas* is due to Justinian[4]. But the texts to which the compilers have added the notion of personification[5] shew that the jurists themselves had gone some way on the road. The notion that it "*sustinet personam* (*heredis, defuncti*)" expresses the tentative feeling for a personality which is as far as the jurists went[6]. This point is connected with the notion of "singular and universal" succession. "Singular" succession is not classical, nor therefore is the contrast, and it is a natural step to say that universal succession is not classical. It is maintained[7] that in classical writers "*universitas*" means only "in the lump" with no suggestion of an ideal unit. Gaius speaks of *hereditas* as acquisition *per universitatem*[8], which means only acquisition in mass, but he also speaks of *hereditas* and *ius successionis* as convertible terms[9]. The *Corpus iuris* speaks often of *successio in universum ius*, which expresses the more abstract idea. Gaius calls *hereditas* a *res incorporalis*, which is as far as he goes. *Pauli Sententiae* and the *liber singularis regularum* go no further. The Autun Gaius however calls *hereditas* "*universitas iuris*[10]." When we remember the uncertainty of Gaius as to the inclusion of obligations under *res*, it seems doubtful whether he, or the earlier writer he is following, thought of rights of obligation as intrinsic parts of the *hereditas* or, definitely, of such a notion as *successio in universum ius*. The two ideas are not the same. One may think of *universum ius* and still not think of obligations as part of it. There seems no good reason for holding the notion "*universum ius*" post-classical. It appears in many texts not excepted to on linguistic[11] grounds. "*Hereditas est*

1 See G. 2. 162 *sqq.*, and *post*, § CIX. 2 9. 2. 13. 2; 28. 5. 31. 1. 3 Inst. 3. 17. pr. General conception of personality in Roman Law, *ante*, § LXIII. 4 E.g. Marchi, *St. Scialoja*, 2. 51; Bonfante, *Corso*, 6. 46. 5 See n. 2. 6 Saleilles, *Festschr. f. Gierke*, 1015. Seneca, *De Benef.* 6. 5. 3 shews that lawyers were already familiar with the idea that *hereditas* was distinct from its content. 7 Bonfante, *Scr. Giur.* 1. 250; Albertario, *Actio de universitate*. See *post*, p. 364. 8 G. 2. 97. 9 G. 2. 14. 10 *Aut.* Gai. 62. 11 29. 2. 37 (Pomp.); 50. 17. 62 (Julian); 50. 16. 24 (Gaius); 50. 16. 208 (Africanus).

successio in universum ius" is a brocard, but a classical brocard. To reject it on the ground of late development of the abstract idea is to beg the question. The better view seems to be that the notion of *hereditas* as an ideal unit was developing in classical law, though much of the terminology (e.g. *actio de universitate*) is post-classical. But the ideal *universitas* does not necessarily include the debts, nor is this inclusion implied by the expression *hereditas damnosa*[1]. The language of the Code and Digest is consistent with their being regarded as burdens, not as parts. A novel indeed speaks of testator and *heres* as having "one *persona* by our laws[2]" and the gloss specifically makes the *heres*, by a fiction of law, the same person as the testator[3]. It has been objected[4] that to speak of *universum ius* is to ignore the possible plurality of *heredes*, but this is to ignore that each is potentially entitled to the whole—*concursu partes fiunt*.

The *hereditas* represented a *persona*, but whose? On this point there was disagreement. It is laid down by some jurists, not exclusively representing either school, that it represented the person of the future *heres*, and thus that the entry of the *heres* was retrospective so as to date from the opening of the succession. The view which prevailed, however, was that the *hereditas* represented the *persona* of the deceased. Though this view is dominant in the Digest[5], there are texts which express the opposite view. Thus, on the question whether a *servus hereditarius* could stipulate in the name of the future *heres*, both opinions are several times expressed[6], and it may be that for most purposes the later jurists accepted the view that entry was retrospective[7], on grounds of convenience, however difficult it might be to reconcile this with the view, also dominant, that the *hereditas* represented the person of the deceased.

The *hereditas* did not represent the *persona* of the deceased for all purposes. The Institutes express a limitation in the words: *in plerisque personam defuncti sustinet*[8]. This might merely mean that the *hereditas* did not take up the political, social and family rights of the dead man, but the restriction is more significant. Its practical application was mainly in limitations on the activity of *servi hereditarii*, who were the only people capable of acting on behalf of the *hereditas* (and were so capable only through the principle we are considering), since ordinary

1 G. 2. 163; P. 3. 4b. 11. But claims were included in *hereditatis petitio*, *ante*, p. 182; *post*, p. 318. 2 *Nov.* 48. pr. 3 Gloss "*heredem*" ad 50. 17. 59. For Jörs, *R.R.* 217, the classics had reached the point of including in the ideal *universitas* all assets and liabilities; *S.M.W.* 554 regards universal succession as ancient. 4 Bonfante, *Corso*, *cit.* 5 41. 1. 33. 2, 34. 6 2. 14. 27. 10; 45. 3. 16, 18. 2, 28. 4, 35. 7 46. 2. 24; 50. 17. 138. But the texts allowing *stip.* in the name of the *heres* may be interp. 8 Inst. 3. 17. pr.

mandates were ended by death[1]. These limitations express the fact that the representation was not complete, but there is usually a good reason for them, apart from any theoretical one. A *servus hereditarius* could not acquire, for the *hereditas* to which he belonged, another to which he had been instituted, as there could be no authorisation[2]. If he was allowed to accept without authorisation the *heres* to whom he would ultimately go might find himself saddled with a *hereditas damnosa*[3]. He could not stipulate for a usufruct for the *hereditas*; there was no life to which it could attach[4]. He could not stipulate in the name of his late master, as he no longer existed[5], or as most jurists thought, but not all, in that of the future *heres*, who was, as yet, an *extranea persona*[6]. But he could stipulate in the name of himself or a fellow slave, or in no name at all[7]. He could be examined as a witness in litigation affecting the *hereditas*, though a slave could not ordinarily be heard where his master was concerned; the *hereditas* was not his master, it only represented him[8]. In all these matters there was no strict adherence to a theory. The rules were based on considerations of convenience; logical justification is little more than excuse.

To the endowment of a *hereditas* with the attributes of personality, there were inevitable limits. It could do nothing involving a conscious act. It could not commit or be privy to delict or crime. It could not authorise a contract, appoint an *institor*, or grant a *peculium*. Strictly an *institor* would cease to serve and a *peculium* to exist, but in practice this was not so: *peculia* continued, and a contract with *institor*, even by one who knew of his principal's death, bound the *heres*[9]. The continuance of *peculium* is important in the story of the changes of the law as to acquisition of *possessio*. A *hereditas*, having no *animus*, could not possess[10], and could not acquire *possessio* through a slave, for even where a slave took *possessio* for a living owner, the owner had not ordinarily *possessio* unless he knew the fact[11] or had authorised.

These rules, however logical, were too inconvenient to stand. The first inroad was in the field of *peculium* as it had been in the case of a living owner. There were disputes and changes of rule[12]. It is clear that *servus hereditarius* could, in classical law, continue an existing possession, and even complete it for the purpose of *usucapio*. But as to beginning

1 See, however, 14. 3. 17. 3 and *post*, § CLXXIX. 2 41. 1. 61. pr. 3 A legacy to a *servus hereditarius* would vest in the *hereditas* if any *heres* could and did take (31. 55. 1; 30. 116. 3) but the slave could not accept it, so as to bar repudiation by the person in whom it would ultimately vest under the gift, since this would bar him from attacking the will under which the legacy was made, as having accepted a benefit under it. 4 Vat. Fr. 55; D. 45. 3. 26. 5 12. 1. 41; 45. 3. 18. 2. 6 See p. 308, n. 6. 7 Inst. 3. 17. 1. 8 1. 8. 1. pr.; 48. 18. 2. 9 14. 3. 17. 3 (but the words referring to knowledge may be corrupt); 15. 1. 3. pr. 10 *Ante*, § LXXII. 11 *Ante*, p. 201. 12 41. 2. 1. 5; 41. 3. 45. 1; 44. 7. 16.

possessio, the law is not clear even in the case of *peculium*. Papinian is made to express conflicting views on the question whether *servus hereditarius* could acquire usucapion possession, even *in re peculiari*. The view commonly held, supported by emendations, is that classical law allowed him to begin usucapion possession for *peculium*, but that Justinian first allowed it in a wider field[1]. Apart from *peculium*, he could not acquire interdict possession before Justinian, and perhaps not even then[2].

Although *servus hereditarius* played for the moment an important economic part, the facts did not alter his character, or increase his faculties. His powers were still dependent and derivative, which was important if the *hereditas* was not accepted. If no *heres* entered under a will or on intestacy, all that the slave had done was void, and the *fiscus*, which took the property, subject to rights of creditors, ignored obligations incurred since the death[3]. And, since such a slave could not bring actions, any remedies that there were in the region of civil, as opposed to criminal, law, must stand over till a *heres* entered. Thus the discussions in the Digest take the form of enquiry how far the *heres* could sue or be sued for what was done when the *hereditas* was *iacens*.

CVIII. In relation to *heredes extranei* the question of *testamenti factio* arose. The *institutus* must have been capable of being instituted at the time when the will was made, at the death (or in conditional institutions, when the condition was satisfied), and thenceforward till actual entry[4]. Loss of *testamenti factio* between these last dates was fatal even though it was regained; if *delatio* became impossible while it was running, the *delatio* was destroyed. But it was immaterial between the two earlier dates, if regained before the later of them—*media tempora non nocent*[5], the rule as to capacity at the time of testation being merely a survival from the *mancipatio familiae*.

The cases in which *testamenti factio* did not exist have been considered[6], but some remarks are needed as to *postumi*. At strict civil law no *postumi* could be instituted. The relaxations for *postumi sui* will be considered later[7]. A *postumus suus* was a person who would be a *suus heres* if born before the death of the testator[8]. But as he need not be even conceived when the will was made, it was impossible to tell who might or might not be a *suus heres*. It was therefore allowed to institute

1 Chief texts 6. 2. 9. 6; 41. 3. 20, 31. 5, 40, 44. 3, 45. 1. 2 No texts on possessory interdicts discuss dispossessed *servi hereditarii*, or cases in which they began possession. In 43. 24. 13. 5 it is said that the *heres* has "*quod vi aut clam*" for acts done while the *hereditas* was *iacens*, but the text does not handle the case in which a *s. hereditarius* had taken possession. Pernice, *Labeo*, 1. 360 *sqq*. 3 45. 1. 73. 1. 4 28. 5. 50. 1; Inst. 2. 19. 4, etc. See however Schulz, *Z.S.S.* 1914, 112 *sqq*. 5 28. 5. 60. 4, 6. 2, etc. 6 *Ante*, p. 290. 7 *Exheredatio*, *post*, § CXII. 8 G. 1. 147; Inst. 1. 13. 4; cf. D. 50. 17. 73. 1. These statements differ in form. Justinian defines one who is a *suus*; Gaius and Q. Mucius define one who can be such.

a future child of any woman, not at present married to anyone else, who could afterwards lawfully be the testator's wife. Such an institution was in any case so far valid as to make the document a will which would revoke one previously made[1], but it did not operate positively if, in the event, the child born was not such as to satisfy the definition of a *suus heres*, e.g. the child of another marriage altogether. In that case he was a *postumus extraneus*; the *institutio* was not valid, but as we have said, he could get *bonorum possessio secundum tabulas*[2]. Here, as in all cases, he must be actually conceived at the time of death[3]. Under Justinian[4] any such *postumus* could be effectively instituted.

Slaves had derivative *testamenti factio* for this purpose[5]. A slave instituted heir by his owner was *heres necessarius*. In the classical law, notwithstanding the general favour both of *institutiones* and gifts of liberty, the dominant view was that the *institutio* was void unless accompanied by an express gift of liberty[6]. Some jurists, however, held a different opinion[7], and Justinian enacted that *institutio* should imply *manumissio*[8]. If sold or freed before the will operated, he was not a *necessarius*, but might acquire *iussu* (*novi*) *domini* or for himself, as the case might be[9]. We have seen that in classical law, if an owner freed a man in whom another had a usufruct, he became *servus sine domino*, at least for a time, and the *institutio* may have been void. Under Justinian he became free and no doubt, if instituted, took the *hereditas*[10]. The case of a *servus communis* presents difficulties. If simply freed, in classical law he vested wholly in the other owner[11], but under Justinian was free[12]. If instituted with no gift of liberty, this was said to be "*ut alienus*," and the right to take vested in the other owner[13], who might even be made *coheres*[14]. If there was also a gift of liberty, this was "*ut proprius*," but we are not told what happened in classical law. It is generally held that the slave entered for, and at the command of, the other owner. There are logical difficulties[15]: the upshot seems to be that the *institutio* took effect, and the manumission did not, but it is not clear why the text should

1 28. 2. 9, 4, 28. 3. 2 D. 37. 11. 3. 3 *Ib.* 4 C. 6. 48. 1; Inst. 3. 9. pr. On apparent conflict between Inst. 2. 20. 28 and Inst. 3. 9. pr., Buckland, *N.R.H.* 1920, 560.
5 Cuq, *Man.* 702, notes that, while *c. d. med.* of *institutus* avoided the *institutio*, *c. d. max.* did not, apart from *servitus poenae*.
6 G. 1. 21; 2. 186. If I institute my slave with no gift of liberty and later free or sell him, he cannot take for himself or his master. G. 2. 187; Ulp. 22. 12.
7 See C. 6. 27. 5. 1; Inst. 2. 14. pr.
8 C. 6. 27. 5. 1b. *sqq.*
9 G. 2. 188; Ulp. 22. 12; D. 28. 5. 7. 1, 9. 16.
10 *Ante*, p. 81; Ulp. 1. 19; C. 7. 15. 1. pr. Esmein holds (*Mél. Gérardin*, 233 *sqq.*) that this originally applied only to *vindicta*, depending on the (supposed) absolute effect of a judgement in early law. Elaborate rules for the case where a master frees and institutes, but one or both of the gifts is or are conditional: they were in general so interpreted as to secure that the slave should not get liberty without the *hereditas*, Buckland, *Slavery*, 510 *sqq.*
11 P. 4. 12. 1; Ulp. 1. 18.
12 *Ante*, pp. 81, 252.
13 Ulp. 22. 7, 10.
14 28. 5. 90.
15 Salkowski, *Sklavenerwerb*, 18 *sqq.*

distinguish the two cases, if their effect was the same. Justinian provided that the slave was free and took the *hereditas*, the other master being compensated[1].

Servi alieni could be instituted. There is no evidence that this was ancient, though it is sometimes so held. It serves a practical purpose, since the slave, if alienated, takes the right of entry with him, thus providing the master, in effect, with a means of alienating the *hereditas* before entry, putting him in fact on a level with *heres legitimus*[2]. The *institutio* was, in general, *institutio* of the master, with whom there must be *testamenti factio*[3]. The owner took, not one with lesser rights, at least in classical law, whatever the testator's intent[4]. If the slave changed hands before entry, his new master acquired[5]. He must then have *testamenti factio*, but it is not clear that he must have had it when the will was made, if he acquired the slave later. Of several owners each acquired *pro rata*, and there might be several entries, or, if all approved, one entry for all[6]. But though in general the *institutio* was equivalent to that of the master, this was true only in relation to *testamenti factio* and other broad principles; the personality of the slave counted in many ways. Thus the time allowed for claim (under *cretio vulgaris*) ran from that of the slave's knowledge. And the slave himself must enter[7].

CIX. *Aditio*. Entry[8]. As entry could not be made by representative[9], it follows that if the *heres* was *infans* or *furiosus* the *hereditas* was lost at civil law, unless the *infans* attained *intellectus* or the *furiosus* became sane. The difficulty was lessened by the fact that in classical law curator of *furiosus* could get *bonorum possessio decretalis*[10] and *tutor*

1 C. 7. 7. 1. 1. As to one supposed to be free, *ante*, p. 300. 2 *Post*, § CXLI.
3 *Fideicommissa* can be imposed on him. Ulp. 22. 9; D. 28. 5. 31; 36. 1. 26. 1. A gift of liberty accompanying an *institutio* of a *servus alienus* was ignored. P. 3. 4b. 7. If testator afterwards acquires the slave, the gift of liberty being a nullity the whole gift is void. Justinian states the rule from Florentinus (28. 5. 50. pr.), but it seems an anachronism.
4 29. 2. 45. 3, etc. Doubts and conflicts, 7. 1. 21; see *ante*, p. 279. 5 Inst. 2. 14. 1; D. 37. 11. 2. 9. Or himself if freed, G. 2. 189; Ulp. 22. 13. 6 29. 2. 68; Inst. 2. 14. 3.
7 G. 2. 190; D. 29. 2. 26, 30. 7, 36; 31. 82. 2, etc. 8 In general the will may be opened and entry made at once. But, under Augustus, a *sc. Silanianum* provided that, if there was suspicion that the deceased had been killed by his slaves, there might be no opening or acceptance until there had been enquiry and torture of slaves who might have been concerned—pain of forfeiture. P. 3. 5; D. 29. 5. The *ll. caducariae* did not allow rights to vest till the will was opened. Thus there could be no entry till then and the gift might fail by death of *institutus* between death of testator and opening of the will. Ulp. 17. 1.
9 29. 2. 36. An *actus legitimus*. But a slave or son could enter if authorised, h. t. 26. *Procurator Caesaris* could enter for him (1. 19. 1. 2), and where a *ff.* was instituted two texts say that long enjoyment of the *hereditas* by son or father vests the *hereditas* in the father. 29. 2. 6. 3; C. 3. 31. 10. 10 *Post*, § CXL. Some allowed *curator* to claim ordinary *b. p.* De Francisci, *Bull.* 1921, 154. Under Just. *curator* can claim *b. p.* but it is still provisional and fails if *furiosus* dies still insane or, on recovery, refuses. C. 5. 70. 7. 8.

(or father) could, it seems, obtain actual *bonorum possessio secundum tabulas*[1].

Acceptance is called *aditio*. Gaius tells us that this might be by a formal act of acceptance called *cretio* (*cernere*), by acting as *heres*, *pro herede gestio*, or by mere expression of intent, *nuda voluntas*[2]. In the Empire *cretio* was not necessary unless expressly required by the will, but it probably was in the time of Cicero[3]. No jurist but Gaius mentions *nuda voluntas*[4]. The formal declaration, *cretio*, was made in a traditional form of words of which the essential part appears to be "*adeo cernoque*[5]." It was usual to have witnesses: there is no evidence that they were required by law[6]. Like all formal declarations it must be in Latin[7].

The name *cretio* is also applied to the clause, sometimes inserted in the will, by which the *heres* was required to accept in this manner. The primary purpose of this was not to secure unequivocal acceptance, but to make good a defect in the civil law, which set no time within which a *heres* must accept[8]. Thus it invariably set a limit of time within which the *cretio* must be made[9], and it might of course impose other directions as well[10]. The time was commonly 100 days, though others might be fixed[11]. The days ordinarily ran from the time when the *heres* had notice and was able to enter; this was *cretio vulgaris*. But the days were sometimes made to run from the opening of the will; here it was called *cretio continua*[12]. The form must be carefully looked at. It did not make *cretio* a condition, but directed the *heres* to make *cretio*. As it stands this would be empty in classical law, for if he did not "cern" there was nothing to prevent informal acceptance. Thus it was reinforced by such words as "*si non ita creveris, exheres esto*[13]," so as to exclude him altogether if he did not "cern." The *exheredatio* negatives the *institutio* altogether in that event, and we may gather, from the language of Gaius, that these words were a matter of course. But, if there was a *substitutio*, there were two forms of *cretio*, *perfecta* and *imperfecta*[14]. In the perfect form the words were, after the direction: "*si non ita creveris exheres esto et C. heres esto.*" Here even if the *institutus* (*T.*) acted as *heres*, he was

1 37. 1. 7. 2, perhaps only *decretalis*. In A.D. 426 it was allowed to *pf.* to enter on a *hereditas* falling to *infans ff.* C. 6. 30. 18. pr. Buckland, *Tijdschr.* 1922, 275. 2 G. 2. 167; Ulp. 22. 25. 3 Cicero never mentions *pro herede gestio*. D. 29. 2. 62 shews that *nuda voluntas* was not known to Javolenus, but *pro herede gestio* was to Labeo. 4 It is copied into the Institutes, 2. 19. 7, and it appears in C. Th. 5. 1. 1. 5 G. 2. 164–66; Ulp. 22. 28. The forms differ only in the omission in U. of the useless words, "*testamento suo.*" 6 *Autun* Gaius, 42. 7 Cp. *Cretiones* of Sarapias; Girard, *Textes*, 810. 8 G. 2. 164, 167. 9 G. 2. 170. 10 See Cicero, *ad Att.* 11. 12. 11 G. 2. 170. Example of 60 days, Cic. *ad Att.* 13. 46. 3. If too much time was given the Praetor might shorten it, G. 2. 170. 12 In *vulgaris*, "*quibus scieris poterisque,*" in the other these words do not appear. G. 2. 165, 171–73; Ulp. 22. 31, 32. 13 G. 2. 165; Ulp. 22. 27. 14 G. 2. 174 *sqq.*; Ulp. 22. 32–34.

excluded, unless he made *cretio*, and the substitute took. If the words "*exheres esto*" were omitted, there was nothing to exclude him even if he did not "cern." But this was the condition on which *C*. was to be *heres*. If *T*. made *cretio* he was sole *heres*; if he did not, but accepted informally, he and *C*. shared. This was the logical rule of earlier classical law[1], but M. Aurelius provided that even if, in *cretio imperfecta*, *T*. did not "cern," he would exclude *C*., however *T*. accepted[2]. He seems to mean, within the fixed time, his point being that the aim of the testator, to secure acceptance within a certain time, has been realised.

Gaius notes a dispute on another point. Some had held that, in the imperfect form, if *T*., while the time was running, acted as *heres* without formal *cretio*, he admitted *C*. to a share and could not afterwards fall back on *cretio* and exclude him[3]. The logic of this seems to be that the words "*si non ita creveris*" are understood to mean "if you do not become *heres* by *cretio*," and he had made this impossible by becoming *heres* otherwise, so that the condition on *C*.'s institution was satisfied. But this is not the *prima facie* meaning of the words, and the view of Sabinus, probably the accepted one, was that at any time before the time limit had expired he could fall back on *cretio* and exclude *C*. The point was rendered obsolete by the rule of Marcus Aurelius.

How late *cretio* existed it is hard to say. A law of A.D. 339 perhaps allows in its stead any declaration before certain officials[4]. An enactment of 407 abolished it altogether, in terms, and is so stated in Justinian's Code[5]. But in its original form it was part of an enactment which dealt with inheritances coming to a child in *potestas*, and did not necessarily apply to any other case[6]. It is likely that at this date *cretio* was not in use except in cases of this kind, in which there is evidence of a special requirement of it[7]. On any view it was gone under Justinian.

If the will contained no *cretio* clause, any recognised form of entry sufficed. *Pro herede gestio* means doing an act as *heres*, a conception perhaps not at first clearly defined[8], but, in classical law, meaning some act of administration. It was however permissible to carry out an act of piety or urgency without being bound, by making it clear that it was not done *animo heredis*[9]. But since, apart from the *cretio* clause, there was no limit of time, the *heres* might delay as he would, with

1 G. 2. 177. 2 Ulp. 22. 34. 3 G. 2. 178. 4 C. 6. 9. 9. Justinian refers it to *B.P.*, cf. C. 5. 70. 7. 3a *in f.*, but for earlier law its language seems to exclude this, especially when compared with C. Th. 8. 18. 8, where closely similar language is used to denote entry as distinguished from claim of *B.P.* In its present form it can refer only to *B.P.* Originally it may have dealt with both. 5 C. Th. 8. 18. 8; C. 6. 30. 17. 6 Or even probably, Girard, *Man.* 924. 7 See C. Th. 4. 1. 1 and C. Th. 8. 18. 1–8. Buckland, *Tijdschr.* 1922, 274. 8 *Aut.* Gaius 44 makes *p. h. g.* cover any declaration of intent. See also 29. 2. 62. 9 29. 2. 20. pr.

resulting inconvenience to creditors and substitutes. The remedy was found in the *spatium deliberandi*. The *heres* might apply to have a time fixed, which might not be less than 100 days, extensible for cause, or, under Justinian, apart from imperial sanction, more than nine months[1]. If he did not apply, a creditor might sue him and, in court, submit an *interrogatio* "*an heres sit.*" If the *heres* was silent, this was a refusal. If he asked for a *spatium*, this was given to him. If at the end of the time he had not accepted, this was refusal. If he accepted, the matter was clear[2]. Exclusion if he did not answer, or allowed the time to pass, is praetorian, not civil. But it would mean denial of the *actiones hereditariae*, which comes, practically, to much the same[3].

If at any time within the *spatium*, if one was fixed, the *heres* expressly repudiated the *hereditas*, not having intermeddled, he was at once excluded[4]. But if there was a *cretio* clause, mere repudiation within the time did not bar; he could still fall back on the *cretio*[5]. As the substitute was admitted only "*si T. non creverit*," his admission was not effective till this was impossible.

Acceptance was in general irrevocable, but there were exceptions. A *minor* could get *restitutio*[6]. Hadrian, by *privilegium*, relieved one who had accepted in ignorance of heavy debt which afterwards came to light, and this was made a ground of relief for *milites*, but not for others[7]. And if a man was compelled by threats to accept or refuse a *hereditas*, the Praetor gave him *restitutio in integrum*[8]. In the case of *dolus* the remedy in both cases was the *actio doli*; the acceptance or repudiation was not undone[9].

Error raises difficult questions. The act of acceptance must be done as *heres*: it is not an *aditio* if acts of administration by *institutus* or *legitimus* are done in the belief that deceased was his slave[10], or if he was not certain that testator was dead or the will valid[11]. But error as to the share taken is immaterial: acceptance is good for the actual share, and, potentially, for all[12]. And, where a man is entitled actually or potentially to more than one share, acceptance of one is acceptance of all: there can be no *scissio*[13]. But there can be no *aditio* while the *institutio* is still conditional: there is as yet no *delatio*[14]. Similar rules apply to repudiation[15].

1 28. 8. 1 *sqq.*; G. 2. 167; C. 6. 30. 22. 13a. 2 C. 6. 30. 9; D. 29. 2. 69. 3 It does not appear that a substitute has the same means of putting pressure. 4 P. 4. 4. 1; G. 2. 169; Ulp. 22. 29. 5 G. 2. 168; Ulp. 22. 30. 6 G. 2. 163; Inst. 2. 19. 5. 7 G. 2. 163; Inst. 2. 19. 6. Justinian points out that the *beneficium inventarii* (p. 316) makes this unnecessary. 8 4. 2. 21. 5, 6. But Celsus quoted by Ulp. in a corrupt text says that acceptance under *metus* is void, 29. 2. 6. 7. 9 4. 3. 9. 1; h. t. 40. 10 29. 2. 22. 11 29. 2. 19, 51. 12 29. 2. 21. 3. But h. t. 75 says that if, instituted for half, he accepts for a quarter, this is void. It seems to be a conditional *aditio* which is impossible, 29. 2. 50. 2. 13 29. 2. 1. 14 29. 2. 3, 21. 2. 15 29. 2. 18, 21. 2. As to mistake of *status* as affecting *aditio*, Beseler, *Z.S.S.* 1924, 391.

CX. LEGAL POSITION OF THE *HERES*. The *heres* stepped, roughly speaking, into the shoes of the deceased, so far as what may be called property rights were concerned. There were of course many limitations. Some rights were extinguished, e.g. usufruct, *adstipulatio*, the right of succession to *liberti* (replaced by a right in the *liberi*, not necessarily *heredes*[1]), the *iudicium operarum* as to future services[2] and, in classical law, the widow's claim for *dos*[3]. Some rights of action were destroyed, e.g. *actio iniuriarum*, if it had not reached *litis contestatio*[4]. A few contractual liabilities were ended, e.g. those of *sponsor* or *fidepromissor*[5] and those involving personal service[6]. The *heres* of a person under a mandate did not succeed him, though he would be liable for any breaches of contract committed before the death[7]. Delictal obligations did not pass at all, except so far as the *heres* had benefited by the proceeds[8]. The *exceptio legis Cinciae* was not available to the *heres*[9]. And, conversely, he had, or might have, obligations that the testator had not; the legacies and so forth were clearly not binding on the testator. These he must carry out, subject to the *l. Falcidia*, etc., so far as the estate would go. But debts he must pay in full, whatever the state of the finances[10]. Hence the power of refusal.

The situation was profoundly altered by an innovation of Justinian, the *beneficium inventarii*. He provided that the *heres* must make an inventory of the estate, to be begun within 30 days of his knowing of his right and finished within 90. If he did, he was not liable beyond the assets[11]. The *spatium deliberandi* was not abolished, but the *heres* who

1 *Post*, § CXXXIV. 2 *Ante*, p. 89, n. 10. Claims of service already overdue passed to *heres*. As to confusion created by the compilers who have substituted for the distinction between past and future, one between *officiales* and *fabriles*, Biondi, *Iudicium operarum*, 16. 3 *Post*, § CCXXXIII. 4 *Post*, § CCII. *Actio injuriarum, nomine filii* passed to *filius* as such, not to *heres*, 47. 10. 17. 22. 5 *Post*, § CLVI. 6 *Post*, §§ CLIV, CLXXVI. As to conditional obligations, *post*, § CXLVIII. 7 17. 1. 27. 3. 8 G. 4. 112; D. 50. 17. 38. *Post*, § CCXXXIII. Things left *per vindicationem* belong to legatee on acceptance of *hereditas*; as to this and the case of conditional legacy, *post*, § CXVII. The action for interference with the family sepulchre is available not only to a *heres* who has accepted, but to *sui* who abstain, who are not *heredes* except in form, i.e. not for any other practical purpose. Damages recovered by such a person were not part of deceased's estate, 47. 12. 6, 10. 9 *Ante*, p. 254. Justinian tends to make *heres* represent deceased in all respects. Thus, if *A* becomes *heres* to *B*, who had sold *A*'s property, Justinian makes the conveyance good against *A* by *exc. rei vend. et trad.*, or *doli*. Cl. law did not, but he would inherit the liability for eviction, 21. 2. 73; 21. 3. 1. Bonfante, *Corso*, 6. 146. At pp. 129 *sqq.* he collects the various cases in which rights did not pass to the *heres*. 10 29. 2. 8. pr. Agreements with a majority of creditors, binding the rest to accept less than full payment (2. 14. 7. 19, 10. pr.), Wenger, *Zivilprocessr.* 305; Solazzi, *Estinz. della Obbl.*, ch. 12. Entry under compulsion, where from any cause the *fc.* fails, *post*, § CXXIV. 11 The mode of administration seems crude. Apparently the *heres* pays creditors on the principle, "first come, first served." When no more creditors appear he may realise what is left and pay legacies. If a belated creditor now appears he has no claim against *heres* or a vendee, but can enforce hypothecs against legatees, and even bring *condictio indebiti* against them. C. 6. 30. 22. 5.

preferred this was penalised; he was liable for all debts, and had to pay legacies in full without the benefit of the *l. Falcidia*. If he let the time elapse, he was regarded as accepting[1]. It would be only in a minority of cases that this would be material: most testators were solvent, and few left away more than three-quarters of the estate in legacies.

As the *heres* replaced the deceased, it might be supposed that each *heres* was liable for the whole. But a rule attributed to the XII Tables provided that each *heres* could sue and be sued only in proportion to his share[2]. It was possible for the testator to vary this by charging specific debts or any fraction of the debts on any particular *heres* to the benefit of the others, but Papinian notes that this must not be done to the practical exclusion of that *heres*[3]. A restriction was reached by treating the charge as a kind of legacy. It must be found what would be the share of that *heres* in the net estate, if debts were distributed proportionally: the total amount of debt imposed on him must not bring his actual benefit below one quarter of that. Thus, *A*, *B* and *C* being *heredes* in equal shares and all debts charged on *A*, the assets being 1000, the debts 400, the net value being 600, each share would be 200. Not more than 150 could be charged on *A* so that he would get 50 and the others 275 each[4].

The debts due to or by the deceased were now due, to the extent stated, to or by the *heredes* personally. There was no fiction, and the name of the dead man would not ordinarily appear in the action at all. If the *heres* was insolvent[5], the confusion of the two estates might injure the creditors of the deceased, but the Praetor gave relief by *bonorum separatio*[6], *causa cognita*. The creditors, or any of them (even conditional)[7], might apply to have the estates kept distinct till the debts were paid. This must be within a reasonable time, before mingling of the estates. The Digest, probably by interpolation, fixes a limit of five years and before the *heres*, has, in good faith, sold the *hereditas*[8]. No creditor who had in any way accepted the personal liability of the *heres*, could claim *separatio*[9], but if it was validly claimed, no pledge created by the *heres*

1 C. 6. 30. 22. 12, 14b, 14c. In earlier law one who let the time pass was treated as refusing. G. 2. 167.

2 Debts, 10. 2. 25. 13 (Paul); C. 2. 3. 26 (Diocl.); C. 4. 16. 7 (Diocl.). Claims, D. 10. 2. 25. 9 (Paul); C. 3. 36. 6 (Gord.). In C. 4. 2. 1 Caracalla describes the rule as to debts as "*explorati iuris.*" In C. 8. 35. 1 he bases the rule as to claims on "*antiqua lex.*"

3 10. 2. 20. 5.

4 Same result in a different way. Each share of gross is 333½. Each normal share of debt 133⅓. Net for each, 200. But *A* being charged with all debts must pay the others so much as the *l. Falcidia* allows, as if it were a legacy. This is 150, making 75 each. Thus *A* gets 50, the others 275 each. The case might be much more complicated.

5 Probably in cl. law only if proceedings for *b. venditio* had begun; Bonfante, *Corso*, 6. 367.

6 Perhaps applicable only under wills in cl. law, intestacy being dealt with under the provisions for *heres suspectus* (*post*, § CCXLV), Lenel, *E.P.* 433; Perozzi, *Ist.* 2. 636.

7 Perhaps only under Just.

8 42. 6. 1. 12, 13.

9 H. t. 1. 10, 11.

was good against creditors[1]. The *heres* might claim any surplus, as he did not claim the *separatio*[2]. On the question whether the creditors who had claimed it could come on the *heres* for any deficit, the texts disagree. Paul and Ulpian exclude them, as they have made their election[3]. Papinian allows them to come in, but only after the creditors of the *heres* are satisfied[4].

The *heredes* owned the property in common and might go on doing so, but this "*consortium*[5]" would occur only if the *heredes* were close relatives, and was almost out of use in classical law. In default of division by arrangement[6], the machinery was the *iudicium familiae erciscundae*[7]. Its main purpose was distribution of *iura in rem*; it was not concerned with debts. But the *iudex* in adjudicating the properties and issuing, if necessary, condemnations for equalising payments, took into account payments made or undertaken by one of the *heredes* by agreement, and might assign particular claims and liabilities to particular *heredes*[8]. This did not bind the creditors, who, if they liked, could still sue the *heredes* separately. But one action is more convenient than many, and it was usual for the *heredes* under such an arrangement, of their own or the judge's making, to give the *heres* to whom a claim of debt was assigned authority to act as *procurator* (*in rem suam*[9]).

Apart from claims against coheirs, the primary remedy of the *heres* was *hereditatis petitio*[10], a real action for the recovery of all or any part of the *hereditas* held by one who claimed in good faith, adversely, to be *heres* (a holder *pro herede*), or, setting up no honest title at all, held merely "*pro possessore*." It was extended (*actio utilis*) against one who had bought the *hereditas* or a share of it from a holder *pro herede*[11], but apart from this it did not lie against those claiming to hold under another title[12]. It was available for recovery of debts, where these were due from one who claimed to be *heres*, and it covered things in the *hereditas*, but not of it, e.g. things lent to the deceased, in which there could be no question of a *ius in rem*[13]. Apart from this, the *heres* had the ordinary actions. *Hereditatis petitio* thus differed from an ordinary real action in scope. It differed also in its rules as to damages[14]. Before Hadrian the

1 H. t. 1. 3. Sale of the *hereditas, bona fide,* before the claim, was not affected, h. t. 2. As to *missio in possessionem* where a *heres suspectus* does not give security, *post,* § CCXLV. Another case of *bonorum separatio* of a different type, *ante,* p. 305; special case, 42. 6. 6.1.
2 H. t. 1. 17.
3 *Ib.*; h. t. 5.
4 H. t. 3. 2. If a *heres,* to damage his creditors, accepted an insolvent estate, there was no corresponding right, but, under Justinian, there might in an extreme case be *r. in int.*, h. t. 1. 2, 5.
5 17. 2. 52. 8; *post,* p. 513.
6 See e.g. Cicero, *ad Att.* 11. 13. 3; 11. 15. 4; 12. 38 a. 2; 13. 12. 4; 13. 13. 4; 13. 46. 3.
7 D. 10. 2. *Ante,* p. 252.
8 10. 2. 2. 5–4.
9 10. 2. 2. 5, *post,* § CLXXXIX.
10 D. 5. 3. Tried before the *centumviri* in the late Republic and early Empire. Longo, *Riv. It. p. l. Sc. Giur.* 1929, 171.
11 5. 3. 13. 4, 5.
12 One liable must restore what he holds under any other title, Lenel, *Z.S.S.* 1926, 1; *E.P.* 176.
13 5. 3. 19
14 C. 3. 31. 7.

possessor was treated as administering for the *heres*, bound to account for profits, and damage due to bad administration, and entitled to claim reasonable expenses. A *sc. Iuventianum*, under Hadrian, dealing with a fiscal claim to a *caducum*, distinguished between *bonae* and *malae fidei possessores*; the former must restore only his enrichment at the time of judgement, the latter all loss to the *heres* caused by his intervention. And it allowed the action against one who had *dolo malo* ceased to possess[1]. The same rules were applied *inter privatos* in claims of *caduca* and, under Justinian, but probably not till post-classical times, to ordinary *hereditatis petitio*[2]. Under Justinian it lay against one who "*liti se obtulit*," who in classical law would simply have been liable to *actio doli*[3] or under the *clausula doli* of his *satisdatio*.

CXI. LAPSED SHARES. If an *institutio* was void *ab initio*, e.g., a peregrine was instituted, the will was simply construed without it[4], a rule never altered. But where a valid *institutio* lapsed from any cause, there were great changes. In early law the will was construed without it; the shares of the other *heredes* were increased, and they could not refuse this. Legacies specially charged on that *institutio* fell with it[5], till Severus made the lapse carry its burdens with it, as a *substitutio* then did[6]. But the *ll. caducariae*, the *l. Iulia* and the *l. Papia Poppaea* had made a profound change. It will be remembered that they introduced some cases of complete or partial incapacity, and that the *l. Iunia* at about the same time introduced another. The *ll.* went further; they set up a new destination for lapsed gifts, whether the lapse was due to their provisions or not. Lapsed gifts were classed as *caduca*, those which failed after the death, and gifts *in causa caduci*, which failed before the death[7], though both classes seem to have been treated alike. They went to other *heredes* with children, failing these to *legatarii* with children, and failing these to the *Aerarium*, the popular treasury[8]. Ascendants and descendants to three generations were however entitled to *ius*

1 5. 3. 20. 6 *sqq.* 2 Beseler, *Beitr.* 4. 4; Wlassak, *Anklage*, 153; Desnoyers, *Le Sc. Juventien*; (rev. Lewald, *Z.S.S.* 1928, 638; Fliniaux, *R.H.* 1930, 110); C. Appleton, *R.H.*, 1930, 1, 621, who holds that for ordinary *h. p.* the rules were established not by the Juventian, but by the *sc.* which did away with *u. luc. p. h.*, and did not distinguish between *b. f.* and *m. f. possessores*: the compilers confuse the two by a misunderstanding of certain texts. The case for the distinction is strong, but the texts are very confused and it seems by no means clear that this rational extension is very late. But the last word has not yet been said on this enigmatic legislation. 3 Beseler, *Beitr.* 1. 28; 4. 6; Cuq, *Man.* 299. But see also, Girard, *Man.* 367. *Post*, § CCXL. 4 *Pro non scripto*, not a case of lapse, C. 6. 24. 1. 5 31. 29. 1, 2. 6 31. 61. 1. 7 C. 6. 51. 2 a, 4. Not easy to see why they are distinguished, for though all lapses caused by the *ll.* are in the first class, so are others. The *liber regularum* does not distinguish. Bonfante, *Corso*, 6. 262, says that gifts *in causa caduci* were like those *pro non scriptis* and not subject to the *ll. cad.*; the old law of *ius accrescendi* continued to apply to them. But C. 6. 51. 2 a, 4 expressly distinguishes them. The latter did not carry their burdens (Ulp. 17. 1). 8 G. 2. 150, 207.

antiquum, and could take these lapses whether they had children or not[1]. Accrual, where it occurred, was not necessarily to all qualified *heredes*. If some of them were grouped for a share, other shares being assigned to other *heredes*, and one of the group failed, the lapse was to the others of the group, as also if, though not instituted together for the share in one phrase, it was clear that the second *institutio* did in fact refer to the same share (*re et verbis* or *re coniuncti*[2]). The principles applied were as in legacy[3].

At some time, not later than Caracalla and probably earlier, the *Aerarium* was replaced by the imperial treasury, the *Fiscus*. The *liber singularis regularum* says that Caracalla suppressed the rights of *heredes* and legatees in such windfalls, reserving those of persons with *ius antiquum*. Failing these all went to the Fisc[4]. But this is doubtful, since elsewhere the same book speaks of "*praemia patrum*" as still existing[5]. *Caduca*, etc., took their burdens with them; he who benefited by them must carry out the legacies and manumissions charged on them, and thus they might be refused[6]. It seems that, for these laws to apply, the will must retain some validity; if all *institutiones* failed there was intestacy[7]. There were various modes of evasion. Adoptive children sufficed till Nero[8]. The restrictions did not apply to *fideicommissa* till the *sc. Pegasianum*, A.D. 71[9]. A little later tacit trusts not expressed in the will were forbidden and penalised[10]. It was always possible to avoid the *leges* by substitutions, and by making the *institutio* of a *coelebs* conditional on his having qualified.

When the State adopted Christianity, for which celibacy was a virtue, it was impossible to maintain these penalties. Constantine abolished the incapacitation of *coelibes* and *orbi* so far as direct gifts were concerned[11]. But he left the *praemia patrum* in the case of lapse[12], and the special rules between husband and wife. These last were abolished in 410[13], and Justinian swept away the *praemia patrum*[14]. Under him the old *ius accrescendi* was restored, but the rule was maintained that such a lapse carried its burdens[15].

1 Ulp. 17. 2, 18; uncertain whether equally or in proportion to their benefits. 2 Jörs, *R.R.* 240. 3 *Post*, § CXVIII. 4 Ulp. 17. 2. 5 Ulp. 25. 17; 1. 21; Fr. *de iure fisci*, 3 cited Accarias, *Précis*, 1. 1012. Girard suggests (*Man.* 936; *Textes*, 499) that the *praemia patrum* were soon after reintroduced by Macrinus. Dio Cassius (78. 12) says that he abolished the laws of Caracalla on inheritances and manumissions (cited, Girard). The legislation mentioned by Dio would seem to be that on taxes, and the *Regulae* appear to have been written before the time of Macrinus (Fitting, *Alter und Folge*, 116). 6 Ulp. 17. 3. They are claimed, "*caduci vindicatio*," and do not accrue *ipso iure*. G. 2. 207; Vat. Fr. 195; Ulp. 25. 17. 7 *Arg.* G. 2. 144; Accarias, *Précis*, 1. 1013. 8 Tac. *Ann.* 15. 19. 9 G. 2. 286. 10 Ulp. 25. 17. 11 C. 8. 57. 1. 12 See e.g. C. Th. 13. 5. 7. 13 C. 8. 57. 2. 14 C. 6. 51. 1. 4. 15 H. 1. 4. The enactment is very complex and verbose.

There were however two sets of circumstances which would prevent the operation of these rules: *indignitas* and *transmissio hereditatis*.

In some cases the law deprived a beneficiary of the gift, on the ground of *indignitas*. It was not treated as void, giving rise to lapse or *caducum*, but as effective but forfeited. A *tutor* by will who excused himself lost any benefit under the will[1], as did anyone who attacked the will unsuccessfully[2], and one who accepted a legacy under a secret trust in favour of one who could not take[3]. There are many other cases[4]. These forfeits were not all dealt with alike. Thus in the case of the *tutor* the gift went to the child concerned, but usually it went to the Fisc[5].

Where the person entitled died without claiming, his rights sometimes passed to a successor. Most of the cases were late, but even in classical law if a minor failed to accept and died, his *heres* was sometimes allowed to claim[6]. Pius applied a similar rule where a father, whose son was instituted, had been entitled to *restitutio in integrum* for absence[7], the son having died meanwhile[8]. Later law went further. In 426 it was provided that where a *hereditas* was *delata* to a child under seven, from his mother, and he died before the *paterfamilias* could enter for him, the latter could still claim the *hereditas*[9]. In 450 it was provided that if issue were instituted and died before the will was opened, their rights passed to their issue, so that there was no lapse[10]. In 529 Justinian laid down a general rule. If anyone to whom a *hereditas* was *delata* died within one year, not having made up his mind, his own successors could come in and claim provided they did so before the expiration of that year[11].

CXII. Restrictions on the power of devise. There were rules requiring the testator, if he wished to exclude his issue, to do so in express terms, the law of *exheredatio*, of formal restriction. There were other rules, less ancient, aimed at preventing exclusions which satisfied the forms, but were essentially unjust. These may be called material restrictions, and the most important was the *querela inofficiosi testamenti*.

EXHEREDATIO. The original principle was that *sui heredes* were so closely connected with the *hereditas* that any exclusion must be express; it was an outcome of the omnipotence of the *paterfamilias* that he could

1 34. 9. 5. 2. 2 34. 9. 5. 1, 3 *sqq*. 3 34. 9. 10. 4 Bonfante, *Corso*, 6. 329. 5 See D. 34. 9; C. 6. 35. Donee loses the property and is not liable for debts. The other effects of *aditio*, however detrimental, remain. There is no *restitutio* against a *confusio* created by the *aditio*. *Filius suppositus* is not mentioned in these titles. Texts conflict. 49. 14. 46. pr.; 34. 9. 16. pr.; 37. 10. 1. 11; C. 6. 24. 4. Fadda, *Dir. Eredit*. 1. § 204; Schulz, *Gedächtnisschr. für Seckel*, 88. 6 4. 4. 18. 5. 7 29. 2. 30. pr. 8 Other cases, where, e.g., the delay was caused by *sc. Silanianum* (*ante*, p. 312), 29. 5. 3. 30, or incertitude as to *status*, or absence on public service. Cuq, *Man*. 735, n. 4, for a list of cases. 9 C. 6. 30. 18. 1. 10 C. 6. 52. 1. 11 C. 6. 30. 19. 1. He says that Paul had laid down this doctrine.

do this. It was not always practical exclusion from benefit. Fathers disinherited young children and provided for them by *fideicommissum* "*ut eis consulant*[1]." The rules changed greatly under the influence of the tendency to diminish the importance of agnation. A will breaking the rules is *nullius momenti*[2].

Civil law rules[3]. Sons in *potestas*, if not instituted, must be disinherited *nominatim*, otherwise the will was void. *Nominatim* does not necessarily mean "by name"; "my wife's son, born in adultery" was enough if there was only one[4]. The form was "*exheres esto*," but under Justinian any clear words sufficed[5]. If this *exheredatio* was before any *institutio* there was no need to repeat it in other *institutiones* and substitutions, nor was it necessary, if the son was instituted in the first place, to disinherit him for the case of his abstention. And the will did not fail if the son was not duly disinherited in each successive class of institutions and substitutions, but those in respect of which he was not disinherited were void[6]. *Exheredatio* of a son might not be conditional, unless he was instituted on the contrary condition[7]. Other existing *sui heredes* might be disinherited by a general clause, "*ceteri exheredes sunto*": if this was not inserted the will was not void, but the *omissi* came in by *ius accrescendi*[8], increasing the number of the *heredes*[9]. The share they took is oddly stated. If the *instituti* were *sui*, the *omissi* took equally with them (*pars virilis*); if *extranei*, the *omissi* took half the *hereditas*. If there were both, the *omissi* took *pars virilis* as against *sui* and half as against *extranei*[10]. This would sometimes give an *omissus* more than the share of the instituted *suus* and more than he would have obtained on intestacy[11]. The effect where a *suus filius omissus* died before the testator

1 28. 2. 18. 2 28. 2. 13. 2. 3 Antiquity doubtful. The case of *miles* omitted in false belief that he was dead gave rise to litigation in the late Republic (Cicero, *de or.* 1. 38. 175; 57) which looks as if the rule existed, but was not settled. Girard points out that the question may have been whether the *ceteri* clause was enough for a son, and the *centumviri* ruled that it must be *nominatim*; *Man.* 905, citing Hölder and C. 6. 28. 4. 2. 4 The language of the principal texts (28. 2. 3. pr., 14. 2, 15; 37. 10. 1. 9) coupled with the rules of *falsa causa* in legacy (*post*, § CXIX) and *institutio* (*ante*, p. 295) have led to the probable view that for cl. law an *exheredatio*, expressly on the ground that the person was not a *filius*, was void if he was a *filius*, as he was not *ut filius exheredatus*, and idle if he was not a *filius*. Schulz, *Einführung*, 30; Debray, *N.R.H.* 1919, 93; *Ann. Ist. Catania*, XVI, 115. 5 G. 2. 127; C. 6. 28. 3. 6 28. 2. 3. 3 *sqq.*, 8, 14. Some texts corrupt. 7 28. 2. 3. 1. A *postumus*, even a son, may be disinherited conditionally, 37. 9. 1. 5. 8 G. 2. 124, 128; Ulp. 22. 17; P. 3. 4 b. 8. Not *pro parte testatus*: they were subject, e.g. to legacies. 9 *Fr. de iure fisci*, 11. 10 G. 2. 124; Ulp. 22. 17. 11 Two sons and an *extraneus* instituted equally, a daughter omitted. Sharing with her brothers she gets two-ninths with them and one-half the third of the *extraneus*. This gives her seven-eighteenths, more than either brother gets and more than she would get on intestacy. If there were several *omissi*, Karlowa, *R.Rg.* 2. 890, holds that they took only a *pars virilis* between them as against *sui instituti*. But C. 6. 28. 4, which emphasises the point that under this system legacies were wholly valid, while under the praetorian scheme (*post*, § CXIII)

was disputed. The Proculians held that the will was saved; the Sabinians that it was void, and this view prevailed[1].

Difficulty arose if, after the will was made, persons came into existence of the class requiring *exheredatio* or *institutio*[2]. This would upset the will, since, as *incapaces*, they could not be instituted or disinherited by anticipation[3]. It seems that whether the *postumus* was male or female, child or grandchild, the will was void[4], except that the rule early developed that, if such a person died before the will operated, he was ignored at praetorian law[5].

Relief from these rules was given partly by juristic interpretation and partly by legislation. These *postumi* were those who would have been *sui heredes* if they had existed when the will was made. The same difficulty arose with those who became *sui* of their grandfather by the death of their father between testation and the grandfather's death. The first class provided for, late in the Republic, were *postumi legitimi*. These were children and grandchildren born after the testator's death, if, in the latter case, the father was dead when the will was made. They might be instituted or disinherited by anticipation[6]. To be safe there should be express disherison of "what issue may be born of my wife (etc.[7])," but, if it proved to be a girl or a *nepos*, the *ceteri* clause sufficed, provided, says Ulpian, something was left to them to shew they were not forgotten[8]. The next class were *postumi Aquiliani*. Aquilius Gallus devised a form for instituting or disinheriting grandchildren born after the grandfather's death, whose father died after the will but before the grandfather, and this was gradually extended to all remoter issue born after the death who would have been *sui* if then alive[9], e.g. great-grandchildren or grandchildren whose father had been exiled or emancipated[10].

The next step was the *l. Iunia Velleia*, probably of A.D. 26[11]. It dealt with two cases: first, anyone born a *suus* between the testation and the death (*postumi Velleiani, primi capitis*), and, secondly, grandchildren born before the testation, becoming *sui* later, their father passing from the family, in the grandfather's life, by death or *capitis deminutio* (*secundi capitis*[12]), sometimes called *quasi postumi*. They were not *incerti*, and could be instituted, but previous institution would not, apart from

some failed, and treats this as the main distinction between the two systems as against *sui*, is against the view that there was this other great difference. It is difficult to reconcile with *L. R. Burg*, 45, which says that they took "*in aequalem*" with *sui*.

1 G. 2. 123; Inst. 2. 13. pr.; D. 28. 2. 7.
2 G. 2. 130–134 (defective); Ulp. 22. 18 *sqq.*; P. 3. 4 b. 10.
3 *Ante*, p. 291.
4 Ulp. 22. 18; Inst. 2. 13. 1. This harsh rule may not be ancient. Cicero applies it only to sons, *de or.* 1. 57. 241; *pro Caec.* 25. 72. It is not an application of the praetorian rule; Ulp. 22. 18 uses the word "*ruptum*." The fact that they are likely to have been forgotten hardly accounts for it.
5 28. 3. 12. pr.
6 Ulp. 22. 19.
7 Ulp. 22. 22; D. 28. 2. 28. 3.
8 Ulp. 22. 21.
9 28. 2. 29. pr.–5.
10 *Ante*, p. 132, n. 8.
11 Girard, *Man.* 909.
12 Ulp. 22. 19; D. 28. 2. 29. 15.

the statute, have saved the will. The next dealt with were the *postumi Iuliani*. Julian held that on the combined effect of the two provisions of the *lex*, it was possible to provide for grandchildren born after the will was made, but before their father's death[1]. This covered most cases. Tryphoninus laid down the general rule that it was possible to provide by anticipatory *institutio* or *exheredatio* for anyone who became a *suus* after the will was made, in the natural course of things so far as he was concerned[2]. If he became a *suus* by his father's *emancipatio*, this was within the rule, there had been no juristic event touching him, but not if he became a *suus* by himself being adopted[3].

Where persons were voluntarily introduced into the family by adoption, *anniculi probatio* or similar act, there was no relief in earlier classical law[4]. Previous *exheredatio* would be a nullity, and it was held, without obvious logical necessity, that previous *institutio* did not save the will[5]. Hadrian, however, in an exceptional case of *erroris causae probatio*, allowed it to do so[6], and the jurists generalised this, so that the rule of later classical law, and after, was that such persons would not upset the will if previously instituted, but that previous *exheredatio*, being a nullity, would not save the will[7]. There was no hardship in requiring a man, who did such an act as adoption, to reconsider his will.

CXIII. Praetorian changes. The Praetor could not affect the civil validity of a will; he could not make or unmake a *heres*[8]. He could, however, give *bonorum possessio* to a person, *heres* or not at civil law[9], which gave him power to take possession of the goods by appropriate steps, *b. p. contra tabulas*, the effects of which will shortly be stated. The tendency of his changes was two-fold, to equalise the rights of women and men, which he did only imperfectly, and to ignore the strict civil conception of the family, by admitting *emancipati*[10] and some others. His rules, which applied only to male testators, were as follows:

1. Male *sui*, sons or remoter issue, must be instituted or disinherited *nominatim*—the *ceteri* clause still sufficed for women[11].

2. In either case, if this was not done, the will was upset. The omitted person could get *b. p. contra tabulas*[12].

3. Persons other than *sui* admitted to the right included those who would be *sui* but for a *capitis deminutio* and were not in another family, with some others. Such were *emancipati*, children left in the grandfather's

1 28. 2. 29. 15. 2 28. 2. 28. 1. It was important so to frame the *institutio*, etc. as to cover all cases, P. 3. 4 b. 9; 28. 2. 28. 2; Accarias, *Précis*, 1. 907. 3 Inst. 2. 17. 1; as to *missio in possessionem* in the interest of unborn heirs—*missio ventris* (D. 37. 9), and where legitimacy is doubted (*ed. Carbonianum*, D. 37. 10), *post*, § CCXLV. 4 See the instances in G. 2. 138 *sqq.*; Ulp. 23. 3. 5 G. 2. 142. 6 G. 2. 143. 7 28. 2. 23. 1; G. 2. 140. 8 Inst. 3. 9. 2. 9 Inst. 2. 13. 3. 10 Ulp. 22. 23. 11 *Ib.*; G. 2. 129. 12 G. 2. 125; Inst. 2. 13. 3; D. 37. 4. 3. 10.

family by the deceased when he was emancipated, his children emancipated by the grandfather while the deceased was in *potestas*[1], or after, those not put under *potestas* when the father obtained *civitas*[2], and perhaps vestal virgins and *flamines*, who passed out of *potestas* without *capitis deminutio*[3]. If a father with an emancipated son was adrogated, the son could claim in later classical law[4]. Adoptive children, emancipated, had no claim, being now in their original group[5], but a child given in adoption to his father by the grandfather could claim in the grandfather's estate, as not in another family[6] from the Praetor's point of view. *Liberi* instituted, even a child given in adoption into another family, could claim if there was some other person with a claim, who brought the Edict into operation[7], the point being that they might thus increase their share.

The rules of *collatio bonorum* created an important restriction of this right. Any of these persons who were *sui iuris* might have received property when emancipated[8], and had had means of acquiring property since then, such as a *filiusfamilias* had not. The unfairness was met by a rule that if such persons claimed to share with *sui*[9], they must bring in for division what they possessed, subject to the provision, indicated by the purpose of the rule, that the *collatio* was due only if the *institutus* was a *suus*, and the coming in of the *emancipatus* benefited him and injured the *suus*[10]. If a *suus* was instituted for a quarter and an *extraneus* for three quarters, an *emancipatus* who upset the will benefited the *suus*, who now got half[11]. There would be no *collatio*, but there would, if the figures were reversed. If an *emancipatus* upset a will and lost legacies as large as his share there was no *collatio*: he had gained nothing[12]. *Collatio* might be due in favour of one *suus* and not another. Where a son in *potestas* was given half, and two children of an *emancipatus*, left in the family, the other half, and the *emancipatus* upset the will, the son had no claim as he took the same amount, but as the *emancipatus* took half of what his children would have taken, they could claim *collatio*[13].

There was another case—*collatio dotis*. A daughter who had received *dos* might, if it was to revert to her, have to make *collatio* of it if she in any way claimed to succeed[14]. If the *dos* was not directly available as

1 Ulp. 22. 23; G. 2. 135; Inst. 2. 13. 3; D. 37. 4. 3. 9, 6, 7, 17. 2 *Ante*, pp. 96, 97; G. 3. 20, 25, 26; Coll. 16. 7. 2. 3 *Arg.* 37. 4. 1. 6. 4 37. 4. 17. 5 G. 2. 136, 137. 6 37. 4. 21. 1. 7 37. 4. 3. 11, 8. 11, 10. 6. The title contains other analogous cases. 8 39. 5. 31. 2. 9 C. 6. 20. 9; D. 37. 6. 1. 5. 10 37. 6. 1. 4 *sqq.* Security required, P. 5. 9. 4, and *b. p.* was not *ex edicto* till it was given or the property brought in, Ulp. 28. 4. 11 37. 4. 8. 14. 12 37. 6. 1. 4–7. 13 37. 6. 3. 6; 37. 8. 1. 17. Probably (texts not conclusive) he need bring in no more than would balance the loss, 37. 6. 1. 3, 8. Where a child given in adoption came in, the adoptive father, who acquired, must make *collatio*, 37. 6. 1. 14. 14 37. 7. 1. Difference in later law between *profectitia* and *adventitia*, C. 6. 20. 4.

the marriage still existed it was allowed for in arriving at her share[1]. The principles seem to have been much the same, but the rule applied essentially to a daughter in *potestas*, since in any other case the *dos* would come in under the other rule.

Collatio did not apply to what a *filiusfamilias* could acquire, e.g. *peculium castrense*. The change in the economic position of *filiifamilias* lessened the importance of this form of *collatio*, which had indeed almost disappeared in the time of Justinian[2].

4. *Bonorum possessio contra tabulas* did not completely upset the will; this was still valid at civil law, but that meant little, as the *bonorum possessio* became *cum re* soon after its introduction[3]. But some provisions were unaffected; *exheredationes*, pupillary *substitutiones* and legacies to parents, children, wife and son's wife[4]. Manumissions failed, apart from some exceptional cases[5]. As to *tutelae* it appears that the appointments needed confirmation[6].

Before Justinian, the chief changes were two; Pius provided that women *sui heredes* were not to have more under the Praetor's rules than they would have had under *ius accrescendi*, which still existed. One entitled at civil law could proceed under those rules, if he or she preferred. The rule was understood to apply to *emancipatae*, in whose case it meant that they were not to get more than they would, had they been entitled to claim *ius accrescendi*[7]. The change was important. All legacies were due: some failed under the praetorian rule[8]. And an *extraneus* might have been instituted alone, who was extruded under the praetorian rule. The other change is in the law of *collatio*[9].

The rules of *exheredatio*, under Justinian, may be shortly stated as follows:

All *exheredatio*, of existing *liberi* or *postumi*, must be *nominatim*, i.e. express; the *ceteri* clause being abolished. If this was not duly done the will failed, in the case of a *suus omissus*, altogether, in other cases except as to certain provisions already mentioned[10].

CXIV. Material restrictions. The power of *exheredatio* was not unlimited. The general provisions for unjust exclusion will be stated shortly, but some minor provisions must first be dealt with[11].

1 C. 6. 20. 5. 2 *Collatio* under Justinian, *post*, § CXXVIII. 3 *Post*, § CXXXIX. 4 37. 5 *passim*. 5 40. 4. 29. 6 26. 3. 3. 7 G. 2. 126. C. 6. 28. 4. 1 puts it down to Caracalla. Kniep (*Gaius*, *ad* 2. 126, p. 211) accepts this, holding the passage in G. a later addition, and P. and U. know nothing of it. But Pius did legislate on legacies in *b. p. c. t.* 37. 5. 5. 6, 23. 8 Gaius does not say what becomes of what she cannot take, accrual?, *caducum*? He does not tell us whether of two *emancipatae*, one omitted and the other instituted, the *instituta* ranks as a *sua* or an *extranea* for the purpose of applying the rules of *ius accrescendi*. 9 *Post*, § CXXVIII. 10 Inst. 2. 13. 5; C. 6. 28. 4. 6–8. 11 Restrictions on testation by *curiales* in late law, Brugi, *Ist.* 597.

A *sc. Afinianum* (date unknown)[1] provided that one who adopted one of three brothers must leave him a quarter in any event, i.e. probably, a quarter of what he would get on intestacy, though Theophilus makes it a quarter of the estate[2]. Failure in this did not upset the will (unless some other rule was broken, e.g. he was omitted), but he had an action against the *heres* for the quarter. The purpose of the rule is controverted[3]. Justinian abolished it in recasting the law of *adoptio*[4].

The *adrogatus impubes* had a right to the *quarta Antonina*[5].

The patron had indefeasible rights, to be discussed under the law of intestacy[6], and the *parens manumissor* seems to have been in the same position. A widow without *dos* was entitled, under a novel of A.D. 537[7], to one-fourth of the husband's estate, however many children there were, subject to diminution if she had other means, with a maximum limit of 100 *aurei* and a converse rule for husbands without *donatio*. In 542 it was provided that the share should be a *pars virilis* if there were more than three children, but only for life[8].

The remaining rule is much more important.

QUERELA INOFFICIOSI TESTAMENTI[9]. However formally done, *exheredatio* might be unjust, and there were other cases in which the law recognised a moral duty to make provision unless there was plain reason for exclusion. The remedy devised was this *querela*, a complaint that the will was *inofficiosum*, rested nominally on the notion that the testator must have been insane[10]. This would involve complete nullity of the will, but the notion was not logically applied, for in some cases the will was left partly effective. In classical law the proceedings were before the *centumviri*[11]. The burden of proof that exclusion was unjust was on the claimant[12]. The exact nature of the proceeding is controverted. It was probably a basis for *hereditatis petitio* rather than an independent procedure, but it involved a special preliminary enquiry, so that it can be treated as a separate matter. Whether there was a separate judgement or judgement in the *hereditatis petitio* followed directly on the enquiry, is not clear: the better view seems to be that there was a separate judgement[13]. As it involved some reflection on the testator no one might use

1 Inst. 3. 1. 14. 2 *Ad* Inst. 3. 1. 14. 3 For various opinions, Girard, *Man.* 195; Cuq, *Man.* 201. 4 C. 8. 47. 10. 3. 5 *Ante*, p. 126. 6 *Post*, § CXXXIV. 7 *Nov.* 53. 6. 8 *Nov.* 117. 5. 9 P. 4. 5; Inst. 2. 18; D. 5. 2. Neither Gaius in the Institutes nor the *liber singularis regularum* mentions the *querela*: much from Ulpian in D. 5. 2. 10 Inst. 2. 18. pr.; D. 5. 2. 2; h. t. 5. Only "*color insaniae*." 11 5. 2. 17. pr. An alternative method by *cognitio* is referred by Eisele (*Z.S.S.* 1894, 256) to *b. possessores* (the original centumviral process for civil claims having, if successful, avoided the whole will), by v. Woess (*Das R.R. und die Erbanwarter*, 178) to simpler cases, the magistrate deciding before which it should go. According to 5. 2. 4 it was usually second marriages which led to unjust exclusions; Kuebler, 193. Various views, Costa, *Storia*, 512. 12 See 5. 2. 3. Not excluded by pact *inter vivos*, P. 4. 5. 8. 13 Girard, *Man.* 915; Jobbé-Duval, *Mél. Gérardin*, 355 and *Mél. Fitting*, 1. 437. In the sixth century

it if he had any other remedy. Thus a *suus omissus*, as he could proceed under the rules of *exheredatio*, could not bring the *querela*[1].

The *querela* might be brought by various persons, subject to the rule (resulting from its relation to *hereditatis petitio*) that no one might bring it who was not entitled on intestacy[2]. If one not entitled brought it, and got judgement, through judicial error or because the defendant made no defence (e.g. knowing that though this case was unfounded, there were others which would succeed), the successful litigant benefited not himself, but the person really entitled[3]. There were however exceptional cases in which one not *heres* on intestacy could bring it for his own benefit: if the nearest *heres* failed, being justly excluded, the next could bring it, if within the classes to whom it applied. The same was true if the nearer person refused to claim[4]. The rules determining the classes who could claim, not all recognised at the same time[5], express two distinct ideas, the old idea of common property in the family estate and the later one of duty to consider claims of near relatives.

The classes are:

1. Descendants, i.e. *liberi*, of a man, unjustly disinherited[6], and descendants of a woman, unjustly omitted, including *postumi*[7].

2. Ascendants unjustly omitted[8].

3. Brothers and sisters unjustly omitted, if a base person was instituted[9]. This is an early case, confined till Justinian to those having both parents in common and still agnatically connected. Under him it covered all consanguineous brothers and sisters (i.e. of the same father) whether the agnatic tie existed or not. But uterines (i.e. having only the same mother) were always excluded. *Turpes personae* are defined in the *Codex Theodosianus* in vague terms; they included *infames* and all who earned their livings in disreputable ways[10]. Justinian is more precise: in particular, he adds *liberti*[11].

The classical rule was that the persons entitled might bring the *querela* not merely if wholly neglected, but if they took less than a fourth of what they would have on intestacy, *pars legitima*. It is sometimes called the *quarta Falcidia*[12], which has led to the view that the rule itself

it is clearly not an independent proceeding but a ground for *hereditatis petitio*, Collinet, *Ét. Hist.* 1. 204. Evidence for cl. law is scanty. P. 4. 5. 8–10 seems to treat it as independent. But "*querela*" is unique for the name of an action. It cannot be very ancient. The equitable idea is not primitive, nor are the *centumviri*. Even if it was distinct at any time it probably began in the admission of unfairness in reply to, or support of, *hereditatis petitio*. The definite quota was probably not fixed till A.D. 176 (Alibrandi, *St. Giur. p. l' VIII cent. della Univ. di Bologna*).

1 5. 2. 23. pr.; Inst. 2. 18. 2. 2 5. 2. 6. But even against the Emperor *heres*. P. 4. 5. 3. 3 5. 2. 6. 1. 4 5. 2. 14, 31, perhaps post-classical. 5 Jörs, *R.R.* 231. 6 Express *exheredatio* of *emancipati*, 5. 2. 23. pr. 7 Inst. 2. 18. pr.–2; P. 4. 5. 2; D. 5. 2. 1, 5, etc. Even *spurii*, h. t. 29. 1. 8 H. t. 15. pr. 9 C. Th. 2. 19. 1, 3; C. 3. 28. 27. Restriction probably post-classical. 10 C. Th. 2. 19. 1, *interpretatio*. 11 C. 3. 28. 27. 12 C. 3. 28. 31.

rests on the *l. Falcidia*[1]. If the will, containing an insufficient gift, contained also a direction that the amount was to be made up, there was, at least from the fourth century, no *querela*, but an action lay against the *heres* to have the due amount made up—*actio ad supplendam legitimam*[2]. There was much law as to what sort of gift counted for the exclusion of the *querela*. All gifts under the will and all *donationes mortis causae* counted[3], but not, in general, *donationes inter vivos*. Ulpian held that such a *donatio* would count if it had been expressly given with that aim, but this view was not accepted, and was negatived by Justinian[4]. Zeno allowed *dos* and *donatio ante nuptias* to count[5], and Justinian added gifts to defray the expense of obtaining a *militia*[6].

Apart from the reorganisation in the Novels Justinian made several changes in detail. He provided that any benefit under the will excluded the *querela*, the aggrieved person being confined to the *actio ad supplendam legitimam*, which did not affect the will; in fact implying the direction to make up the amount wherever it was needed[7]. In A.D. 536 he established a fresh minimum in the case of children. They were to be entitled to one-third if there were four or less, and one-half if more[8].

CXV. If the court held the exclusion just, the *querela* failed[9], and other circumstances would exclude it. The chief were:

(i) At first two years delay, later five, to run, not, as Modestinus held, from the death, but, as Ulpian held, and Justinian enacted, from entry of the *heres*[10]. The Emperor might extend it for good reason; if he did, manumissions which had taken effect were good, the *libertus* being bound to pay 20 *aurei* to the successful claimant[11].

(ii) Recognition of the validity of the will, e.g. accepting a benefit under it[12]. A *tutor* was not personally barred by accepting for his ward, nor did he bar the ward by accepting for himself[13]. But one who volunteered to act as *procurator* to accept for another was barred[14].

(iii) *Transactio*. If a valid compromise with the *scriptus heres* was carried out, the *querela* was barred, and the will valid[15].

(iv) Death of claimant without taking steps. But in later law, if he

1 *Ante*, p. 327, n. 9. As in the *Falcidia*, debts, funeral expenses and value of freed slaves are deducted in arriving at the value of the estate, P. 4. 5. 6. 2 C. Th. 2. 19. 4; C. 3. 28. 36. pr. The *lex* does not seem to lay down a new rule. P. *Sent.* 4. 5. 7 seems to imply it. Indeed, as expressed, P. states Justinian's rule. 3 Inst. 2. 18. 6. 4 5. 2. 25. pr.; 38. 16. 16; C. 3. 28. 35. Pacts between father and son accepting this in substitution, Mancaleone, *St. Scialoja*, 2. 611. 5 C. 3. 28. 29; cf. *Greg. Wis.* 4. 2. 6 C. 3. 28. 30. 2. In later law, *militia* includes certain heritable and transferable offices about the court. Brissonius, *de verb. signif. s.v.* 7 Inst. 2. 18. 3. 8 *Nov.* 18. 1. Hasty: if there were four their legitim was one-twelfth each: if five, one-tenth. 9 C. 3. 28. 11. 10 C. 3. 28. 36. 2. Pliny, *Ep.* 5. 1. His language suggests that the two years were based on the period of *usucapio*. 11 5. 2. 8. 17. 12 5. 2. 12. pr. 13 Inst. 2. 18. 4; D. 5. 2. 22. 1, 3. 14 5. 2. 32. pr. 15 5. 2. 27. pr.

had taken steps shewing intent to bring the *querela*, and died without evidence of changed intentions, the claim survived to his *heres*[1]. In classical law he must no doubt have begun the action[2].

(v) Abandoning the *querela* after beginning it, i.e. after definite joinder of issue, but not where the withdrawal was due to fraud of the *scriptus heres*[3].

The question remains: What was the effect of the *querela*? This varied with the facts, and only a few typical cases can be dealt with.

Where there was one claimant who succeeded against all the *instituti*, the will was void; manumissions and other gifts failed and legacies paid could be recovered as *indebita*, unless the *scriptus heres*, when he paid, knew of the *querela*: here he was liable to the successful claimant[4]. If however the decision was reached by default, then, as in case of collusion, legacies and manumissions were valid[5]. If he failed he lost all benefits, and they went, not to the *heres*, but, in general, for *indignitas*, to the fisc[6]. But he did not suffer this penalty unless the matter went to judgement. Death or withdrawal or compromise saved the gift[7]. Nor did he if he was not acting on his own behalf. Thus, where a *tutor* was acting on his ward's behalf, neither he nor the ward suffered[8].

Where a claimant succeeded against one *heres* and failed against another, the fact is brought out that the *querela* was not necessarily an arraignment of the whole will, but litigation *inter partes*[9], and a decision against one did not affect others. This might happen in several ways. A brother might bring it against two *heredes* of whom only one was a base person[10]. A claimant might bring it against different *heredes* in different actions and the *iudices* decide differently (or one of the *instituti* might have by the will only what he would have on intestacy). Or he might withdraw it against one. The result would be that the will stood partly good, so that, in effect, a man was *pro parte testatus*[11]. Except so far as they were charged solely on the *institutio* which was upset, legacies were good *pro rata*, and manumissions, which of course could not be reduced, altogether[12]. Similarly, if he brought it only against one of several *heredes*, the will was valid *pro parte*[13].

The texts, on the case in which there were two or more *prima facie*

1 5. 2. 6. 2, 7 (interp.). 2 P. *Sent.* 1. 13 b. 4. 3 5. 2. 8. 1, 21. pr. 4 5. 2. 8. 16. 5 5. 2. 17. 1, 29. pr. 6 5. 2. 8. 14. *Fideicommissa* charged on him are unaffected, P. 4. 5. 9; D. 5. 2. 8. 14, and, in classical law, a substitute of an *institutus* who failed in the *querela* was preferred to the *fiscus*, P. 4. 5. 10. As this involved his *institutio* the case could hardly arise under Justinian. 7 5. 2. 8. 14. 8 5. 2. 30. 1; 34. 9. 5. 9, 22. 9 Pliny, *Ep.* 5. 1. 6, where a *querela* is brought only against some of the *heredes*. 10 5. 2. 15. 2, 24. 11 *Ib.* He did not die intestate; his will was not *pro parte* void, it was set aside *pro parte*. 12 31. 76. pr.; C. 3. 28. 13. 13 5. 2. 25; h. t. 19, one of the famous *leges damnatae*: almost any conclusion can be drawn from one or other of the propositions in it.

entitled, but only one acted, are obscure and opinions conflict[1]. If the one who did not act was justly excluded or renounced his claim or withdrew, the will seems to have been valid *pro parte*, as in the last case. What happened if one had simply not acted is not clear. According to one view the will was void; on another it was *pro parte* valid. In any case if the claimant failed he alone lost his benefit; the other was unaffected. If two claimed and one succeeded while the other failed, there is the same modern conflict in opinion[2].

In 542[3] Justinian made sweeping changes. In estimating the *pars* nothing was to count unless the claimant was *institutus* for a share, but if he was, all *mortis causa capiones* counted. The exclusion of children would be treated as unjust, and the will as *inofficiosum*, unless it was on one of fourteen grounds, set out in the Novel, and the ground was stated. If the will was broken, the *institutiones* were void, but the minor provisions stood good, so that there would be a will with no *heres*. There were similar provisions for ascendants, eight grounds being stated, but brothers and sisters were left under the old law.

The rule requiring exclusion to be express clearly tends to assimilate omission and *exheredatio*, and there is doubt as to the effect of the change. Some writers hold that the rules of *querela* and *exheredatio* were fused, the new system superseding them both. But those who hold this are not agreed as to the proper way in which to state the result. On one opinion the real result was the survival of a system based on the principles of *querela*, and substantial disappearance of the law of *exheredatio*. Another opinion reverses this. The new rules supersede the *querela*, and are a remodelled set of rules of *exheredatio*. The main practical difference would be that, if the rules are those of *querela*, the proceedings would have to be brought ordinarily within five years, while on the other view the claim would be barred only by the ordinary period of limitations, then 30 years. The language of the novel itself favours the view that both sets of rules survived, that omission of *suus* or *emancipatus* was still remedied by ordinary *hereditatis petitio* or *bonorum possessio contra tabulas*, the new rules applying only in cases which in earlier days would have given rise to the *querela*[4].

Querela inofficiosae donationis, dotis. As *donatio mortis causa* might be cut down like legacy under the *l. Falcidia*, the amount of such gifts may have been taken into account in arriving at the value of the estate for the purpose of estimating the *pars*. *Donationes inter vivos* were not. But Severus Alexander, in a case in which such gifts had been made on

1 Chief texts, 5. 2. 8. 8, 16, 17, pr., 23. 2, 25. 2 Various views, Windscheid, *Lehrb.* § 584, nn. 24–26; Accarias, *Précis*, 1. 963; Jörs, *R.R.* 233. 3 *Nov.* 115. 3, 4. 4 Windscheid, *Lehrb.* § 591: an old quarrel, Haenel, *Dissensiones dominorum*, 454.

a large scale in order to defeat the claim under the *querela*, ordered the gifts to be cut down by half[1]. Legislation, beginning in A.D. 245, but mainly under Diocletian, laid down general rules for such cases[2]. The effect was that both under wills and in intestacy[3] there was machinery similar to the *querela*[4], by which immoderate *donationes* and *dotes* might be set aside. As it was post-classical, we have no juristic discussion and the texts leave some questions uncertain. Some texts require, as in the *querela*, only *eventus*, i.e. that successors in fact suffer, others require intent as well[5]. It was the gift which was attacked, not the will, and the texts are not in agreement whether the gift was wholly revoked or only *pro tanto*—probably the real rule was the latter. It was presumably under the same time-limit and general conditions as the *querela*[6]. Justinian[7] established a system, applicable only where the donee was a *filius*, of which the effect was to cut down the gift, but it is expressed as a new system and throws little light on the earlier rules.

CXVI. FAILURE OF WILL. A will validly made might nevertheless fail to operate. We have considered one case, that of the *querela*. The expression, *testamentum irritum*, might be used to cover any of the cases, but in practice was confined to two, that of a testator who suffered *capitis deminutio*, and that of a will under which no *heres* entered, also called *testamentum destitutum* or *desertum*[8]. Where a will failed owing to appearance of *postumi*, etc. it was called *testamentum ruptum*, and this name was also applied to a revoked will[9]. This case must be considered[10]. *Mancipatio* was irrevocable, but this did not prevent the testator from altering the written instructions which he had given to the *familiae emptor*. Hence arose the rule of classical law that a will could be revoked at civil law only by making another[11]. Failure of the second, if it was validly made, did not revive the first, except by special imperial relief[12]. If, however, in the second will, the *institutio* was *ad certam rem*[13], the rule that the restriction was ignored was, in this case, set aside, in effect, by Severus, who provided that though the old will was revoked, the *heres* under the second was under a trust, *fideicommissum*, to give to those

1 31. 87. 3. 2 Chief texts: C. 3. 29. 1, 2, 3, 4 (=Vat. Fr. 282), 5, 6, 7 (=Vat. Fr. 280), 8, 9 (=C. Th. 2. 20. 1); C. Th. 2. 21. 1 (=C. 3. 30. 1); Vat. Fr. 270, 271; D. 31. 87. 3; *Nov.* 92. As to revocation by donor where it appeared that legitim would be interfered with, C. 3. 29. 5. 3 C. 3. 29. 3. 4 "*Iuxta*," "*ad instar*," "*ad similitudinem*," "*ad exemplum*," etc. 5 C. 3. 29. 1, 6, 8; Vat. Fr. 270. 6 C. 3. 29. 6. 7 *Nov.* 92. 8 G. 2. 145–147; Ulp. 23. 1, 4; Inst. 3. 1. 7, 8. 9 Ulp. 23. 2. As to possibility of validity for certain purposes of a testamentum *irritum* or *ruptum* (G. 2. 148–150), *ante*, p. 322 and below, n. 12 and p. 333, n. 3. 10 Suman, *Favor testamenti*, 137. 11 G. 2. 144, 151; Ulp. 23. 2. 12 G. 2. 144. Any *institutio* which could possibly take effect would upset the earlier will. Thus the *institutio* of a *postumus*, which failed because in the event he proved to be an *extraneus*, would upset an earlier will, if he could have been a *suus*. See 28. 2. 9. 4. 13 See *ante*, p. 296.

interested under the first will all but the things mentioned, with enough added, if necessary, to make up a quarter of the *hereditas*[1].

The Praetor took a different line. If a will or its material parts had been destroyed by the testator, he would refuse *bonorum possessio* under it[2]: and if a second will had been so revoked, he would give *bonorum possessio* under the earlier will, at least if the revocation was with intent to revive the old will[3]. Where the testator struck out the name of the *heres* M. Aurelius excluded him, the other provisions remaining good. Apparently the *institutio* was still formally valid[4]. In the later Empire there was further change. Honorius laid down the odd rule that a will should be revoked, *ipso facto*, by the lapse of ten years. His reasoning is not clear but apparently he held that a man must have changed his mind by that time[5]. A little later Theodosius provided that a will would be revoked by a second will, even if, in this, the proper formalities were not complied with, provided five witnesses were prepared to attest its genuineness, but only if the *instituti* in the first will were not entitled on intestacy, while those in the second were[6]. It was only a revocation; the new document was not a will but was regarded as expressing the wishes of an intestate, which no doubt means that its main provisions were treated as *fideicommissa*. Justinian adopted this: for the rule of Honorius he substituted the more rational enactment that a will could be revoked after ten years by declaration, in court, or before three witnesses[7]. The praetorian rules were still operative.

1 Inst. 2. 17. 3. *Ante*, p. 295, as to error. 2 G. 2. 151 a; D. 38. 6. 1. 8. A hiatus in the text of G. is supposed to have contained words providing that if under such a will the *scriptus* claimed, and no one was entitled on intestacy, it went to the *fiscus*. 3 37. 11. 11. 2. 4 34. 9. 12. See Bohàček, *St. Bonfante*, 4. 319; Donatuti, *Le praesumptiones iuris*, 71, and D. 28. 4 *passim*. 5 C. Th. 4. 4. 6. 6 *Nov*. Theod. 16. 7; C. 6. 23. 21. 5. 7 C. 6. 23. 27. 2.

CHAPTER VIII

THE LAW OF WILLS (*cont.*). LEGACY, *FIDEICOMMISSUM*. SOLDIER'S WILL. SETTLEMENTS

CXVII. The will was a document (or declaration) by which the *hereditas* of the deceased was transferred to a successor, who stepped into his shoes, but it served other purposes. Some of these, manumissions, and appointments of tutors, have already been dealt with. We have now to consider gifts of property (in the widest sense), not by way of "universal" succession[1], legacies, together with *fideicommissa*, which last however will be found to present in one, indeed the most important, case, the characteristics of universal succession.

A legacy is a gift, chargeable only on a *heres*[2], usually of *res singulae*, having an assignable money value[3]. It must be in Latin, if in the will, as opposed to a confirmed codicil[4], till, in 439, it was allowed to make wills in Greek[5]. Even where it was a gift of a share of the estate, it was not universal succession; the legatee could not sue or be sued in respect of rights and liabilities of the estate. As we have seen, a legacy was void, in classical law, if it preceded the *institutiones*[6].

Forms of Legacy. In the classical law there were four forms[7].

1. *Per vindicationem*. "I give the thing to *X*." The proper words were

1 *Ante*, p. 307. Treating it here is illogical but convenient, avoiding repetition, see G. 2. 191. 2 So that if son or slave is made *heres* it cannot be charged on the *paterfamilias*, as a *fc.* can. Ulp. 24. 21. 3 Thus *manumissio* is not legacy. Pledge may be created or released by will, but no *fc.* can be imposed, 13. 7. 26; 32. 3. 4; 33. 1. 9. The gloss to 32. 3. 4 notes that it is hardly a legacy any more than, *inter vivos*, it would be *donatio* (20. 6. 1. 1; 42. 8. 18; cp. 30. 116; C. 4. 29. 11). 4 *Post*, § cxxvi. 5 C. 6. 23. 21. 6 *Ante*, p. 295. 7 Antiquity disputed: nothing learnt from Cicero. The first two are no doubt much older than the others. The differences of opinion among the classical lawyers as to the effect of the others suggest that they were recent. The *l. Falcidia*, as cited by Paul in D. 35. 2. 1, seems to recognise only the two main forms. Weiss, *K.R.V.* 1919, 13; Wlassak, *Z.S.S.* 1910, 196.

"*Do, lego,*" but Gaius says that in his time it was agreed that "*sumito*" or "*sibi habeto*" or "*capito*" produced the same effect[1], which was to vest the thing in the legatee, so that he could "vindicate" it, to which fact, he says, it owes its name[2]. The legatee could bring a real action against anyone who held the thing, but, conversely, only quiritarian property of the testator could be so left, and, except fungibles, the thing must have been his at the time of testation[3]. There were school dissensions as to this form. For the Proculians the thing was a *res nullius* (not open to *occupatio*), till the legatee accepted or refused. But the Sabinian view prevailed, that it vested in the legatee on the entry of the *heres* and devested if he refused[4]. Thus, at least in the law as finally settled, he was entitled to *fructus* from *dies cedens*[5]. A more important divergence arose in conditional legacy. It could not vest in the legatee till the condition was satisfied. Meanwhile the Proculians held it a *res nullius*, the Sabinians holding that it belonged to the *heres*, who would thus get the fruits[6]. Apparently the Sabinian view prevailed, the acceptance being only so far retrospective as to annul alienations and charges created by the *heres*[7].

2. *Per damnationem.* The strict form was "*heres meus damnas esto dare,*" but in classical law, "*dato,*" "*dare iubeo,*" "*facito,*" "*facere iubeo,*" or probably any explicit command would serve[8]. This is the most important form: anything could be left by it, services, and *res alienae* or *futurae*[9]. It gave only a *ius in personam* against the *heres*[10]. Like most other obligations resting on the words "*damnas esto*[11]," it had given a right, where it was for a *certum*, to *manus iniectio*, with double damages in case of denial, and though in classical law *manus iniectio* was gone, the double liability remained, whether the words "*damnas esto*" were used or not[12].

1 G. 2. 193; Ulp. 24. 3. 2 G. 2. 194; Ulp. 24. 7. 3 G. 2. 196; Ulp. 24. 7. Was a legacy of *peculium* in this form valid if, as would usually be the case, its content had changed? Probably, for this purpose only, it was treated as a *universitas*. 4 G. 2. 195, 200; P. 3. 6. 7; 8. 1. 19. 1; 34. 5. 15. G. 2. 195 (if the text is genuine). Appleton, *R.H.* 1929, 218, considers the proculian view to have prevailed. Wlassak, *Z.S.S.* 1910, 196 *sqq.*, holds that Julian held that ownership was in suspense till legatee accepted or refused. Silence for a certain (unknown) time was acceptance. Acceptance was retrospective. He holds that later jurists adopted this view, but does not dispose of the contrary texts. He rejects for cl. law the texts (30. 84. 13, 95) which give a choice of real or personal action commonly attributed to juristic *interpretatio* after the *sc. Neronianum*, but does not give sufficient weight to the well-established practice of making the gift in both forms (Girard, *Textes*, 798). See however Ciapessoni, *St. Bonfante*, 3. 699, who holds that in such gifts the form *per damn.* was available only if the other, from any cause, failed. 5 Girard, *Man.* 982. 6 G. 2. 200. 7 10. 2. 12. 2; 35. 1. 105; C. 6. 43. 3. 3. Guarneri-Citati, *St. Bonfante*, 3. 439, holds, on theoretical, not always convincing, grounds, that servitudes (not alienations) were absolutely valid. 8 G. 2. 201; Ulp. 24. 4. 9 G. 2. 197, 202, 203; Ulp. 24. 8; 24. 9; P. 3. 6. 10. 10 G. 2. 204; P. 3. 6. 17. 11 *Post*, § CCXII. 12 G. 4. 9. The forms make a difference on the question of position of the gift. If between two *institutiones* which operate, Paul says (P. 3. 6. 2) that it is good if *per damnationem*

3. *Sinendi modo.* "*Heres meus damnas esto Lucium sinere rem capere.*" This too gave only a *ius in personam*[1]. It does not seem to have been important. Anything could be left by it which belonged to testator or *heres* at the death, as its words indicate, but Gaius says that the dominant view was that it could not apply to anything the *heres* acquired after the death[2]. Though the word *damnas* was used, it is not shewn to be ever *in duplum*, perhaps because it was first used in matters for which there could be no *manus iniectio*. Gaius speaks of a doubt, also due to the form, whether the *heres* was bound to make a formal conveyance, or it sufficed, even for a *res mancipi*, to let the legatee take it. The latter view prevailed[3].

4. *Per praeceptionem.* "*Titius rem praecipito*[4]." As the form shews, the legatee was entitled to the legacy before the estate was divided[5]. The schools disagreed about this legacy[6]. The Sabinians, arguing from the name, held that it could only be to a *heres*, so that enforcement would be by the *iudicium familiae erciscundae*. It must therefore be a thing in the *hereditas*, but not necessarily at testation and it might be merely *in bonis*. The Proculians held that *praecipito* meant *capito*: it was a case of *vindicatio* and might be to anyone. Gaius says, doubtfully, that Hadrian confirmed this. On the Proculian view, if it was to the *heres*, and had been quiritary property of the testator, it could be vindicated. If only *in bonis*, *familiae erciscundae* was applicable. If it was to an *extraneus*, only the testator's quiritary property could be so left, and it gave a *ius in rem*. Thus it still differed from the first form: the *res* might have been acquired after testation, and, if to the *heres*, need not have been in quiritarian ownership at all. In later classical law only what could be left by *vindicatio* could be left in this way[7].

These rules were modified by the *sc. Neronianum*[8] (A.D. 64), providing according to the texts that, where a gift was made in a form not suited to it (*minus aptis verbis*), it should be construed, if that would make it valid, as in the most favourable form, i.e. *damnatio*, by which

(it is a direction to the first *institutus*), but if *per vindicationem* only in proportion to the share of the first *heres*. It is effectively charged only *pro parte*. If the first fails, the legacy fails: if the second, the legacy is good. But this seems to express republican law. The *ll. caducariae* provide (*ante*, p. 319; *post*, § CXVIII) that gifts which become *caduca* go to certain beneficiaries as *heredes*. Hence the *liber singularis regularum* says (Ulp. 1. 21), dealing with *manumissio*, which is indivisible, that if the second fails and the lapse goes to the first, the gift is good, but if it goes to *legatarii patres*, they take as *heredes* and it will be as if both had operated. If the first failed the legacy would fail as in old law. He adds that some ignored this and applied the old law. The *ll. caducariae* and the rules of position are gone in later law.

1 G. 2. 209, 213; Ulp. 24. 5. 2 G. 2. 210, 211, 212; Ulp. 24. 10. Not necessarily property. P. 3. 6. 11. 3 G. 2. 214; G. Ep. 2. 5. 6. 4 G. 2. 216; Ulp. 24. 6. 5 The precursor of the *praelegatum* of later law, *post*, § CXXIII. 6 G. 2. 217–223; Ulp. 24. 11; P. 3. 6. 1. 7 Ulp. 24. 11. 8 G. 2. 197; Ulp. 24. 11 a.

anything could be left[1]. There were disagreements as to the scope of the enactment. Some held that it applied only to defects of form and not of capacity[2]. Some of the Sabinians, who held that *praeceptio* could be only to a *heres*, thought the *sc.* would not save such a legacy to an *extraneus*, but the wider interpretation prevailed[3]. The forms did not lose their importance; each had its own rules, e.g. in case of lapse, and these still existed. In A.D. 339 it was enacted[4] that no importance was to attach to the exact use of words, which is understood to mean that, in deciding which type of legacy was meant, the intent was to be followed whatever the words used. Justinian provided that all legacies were to be of one nature and enforceable by the same remedies[5].

CXVIII. Joint Legacies and Lapses. Legacies to two or more may be joint in two ways. They may be:

(i) *Re et verbis coniuncti* (*coniunctim*). "I give Stichus to *X* and *Y*."

(ii) *Re coniuncti* (*disiunctim*). "I give Stichus to *X*. I give Stichus to *Y*." A gift in the form: "I give Stichus to *X* and *Y* in equal shares" is really two distinct gifts and is not here material, though the donees are sometimes said to be "*verbis tantum coniuncti*[6]."

If a legacy to a single legatee failed from any cause the *heres* benefited (apart from the *ll. caducariae*), but in the case of joint gifts there were complications, due to the different rules, in the different forms, as to sharing among joint legatees. Thus the two sets of rules, i.e. as to shares and as to the effect of lapse, must be taken together.

In *vindicatio* and *praeceptio*, *coniunctim* or *disiunctim*, "*concursu partes fiunt.*" Each had a right to all, cut down by the other's right, so that if one failed the other benefited, not the *heres*[7]. Again, if a *res* was left to *A* and *B* *coniunctim*, and to *C* *disiunctim*, if *A* or *B* failed *B* or *A* benefited, not *C*. If *C* failed, *A* and *B* benefited, taking the lapse as *disiunctim*[8]. If *A* and *B* failed, *C* benefited, if all three, the *heres*.

In *damnatio*, *coniunctim*, they shared, on presumed intent, but lapses went to the *heres*, his obligation being treated as separate, not solidary. In *damnatio*, *disiunctim*, each was entitled to all or its value; failure of one made no lapse[9]. In *sinendi modo*, the rules were the

1 For a different view of the scope of the *sc.*, involving many interpolations of texts and glosses in Gaius, Ciapessoni, *St. Bonfante*, 3. 651. 2 G. 2. 218. 3 G. 2. 218. Where a man left a *res*, *per vindicationem*, and sold it, there was no relief under the *sc.*, since if it had been originally left *per damnationem* and alienated there would be an *exceptio doli* against the legatee, G. 2. 198. Alternative actions, *ante*, p. 335, n. 4.
4 C. 6. 37. 21. 5 C. 6. 43. 1. As the forms had different rules in various matters, he had to choose between them. He adopts usually, but not always, the rules of *vindicatio*.
6 32. 89; 50. 16. 142. 7 G. 2. 199, 223; Ulp. 24. 12; P. 3. 6. 26. 8 30. 34. pr.; 33. 2. 26. 1. 9 G. 2. 205; Ulp. 24. 13. It would benefit the *heres*, since he would only have one legacy to pay.

same except that some held that if it were *disiunctim*, the *heres* was released by letting one legatee have the *res*, as his only duty was not to prevent his having it[1]. The point could not arise if the gift was *coniunctim*.

Except as to gifts void *ab initio*, e.g. to a peregrine or person already dead, which were still *pro non scriptis*, the law was profoundly modified by the *ll. caducariae*. All lapsed gifts, *caduca* or *in causa caduci*[2], went to those who would have had them in earlier law, if they had the *ius antiquum*; failing these, to *collegatarii patres coniunctim*; failing these, to *heredes patres*; failing these, to other *legatarii patres*; and failing these to the Treasury[3]. They need not be accepted, but carried their burdens[4]. Apparently a colegatee *disiunctim* was not a colegatee for this purpose[5]. The form was immaterial, so far as the *leges* applied. But if there were joint legacies *disiunctim* by *damnatio*, as each was entitled to all, there was no *caducum*. The changes made about the time of Caracalla, and when the Empire adopted Christianity, have already been considered[6]. Under Justinian the forms and the *leges* were gone. He restored the old *ius accrescendi* with modifications[7]. Apart from joint gifts, a lapsed legacy went to the *heredes*, carrying its burdens, but if the legacy had been solely charged on a particular *heres*, the lapse went to him. All joint legatees took in shares. Lapses went, in first instance, to colegatees. If the gift was *coniunctim* they might refuse, but if they accepted they took also the burdens. If *disiunctim*, they must take, but the burdens failed. This odd distinction is rested on the view that the testator by making them *disiunctim* meant that no one was to be liable for more than his own burden[8]. In the case of *pro non scriptis* the old law remained; accrual was compulsory but, in general, burdens failed[9].

CXIX. PRINCIPAL RULES OF LEGACY. In Justinian's law there was no need of formal words (*legis modo*[10]); so long as it was unambiguous the form and the place in the will were immaterial[11]. The law of conditions was much as in *institutiones*, and the preference for maintaining the gift and annulling the offending modality existed here also, though without the justification that failure of the gift would imperil the will. The principle may be that[12] it is reasonable to apply the same canons of

1 G. 2. 215. 2 *Ante*, p. 319. A conditional legacy was a *caducum* if the condition failed after testator's death. 35. 1. 31, altered. 3 G. 2. 206–208; Ulp. 24. 12, 13. As we have seen the windfall is treated as *hereditas*. 4 Ulp. 17. 3. 5 Opinions differ. This seems to be what Gaius means, 2. 207, 208. Paul, D. 32. 89, says the same. 6 *Ante*, p. 320. 7 C. 6. 51. 1. 8 H. t. 1. 11 g. 9 H. t. 1. 3, 3 a. As to merely *verbis coniuncti*, the express statement of Paul (D. 32. 89) and the language of G. 2. 207 suggest that, under the *ll. caducariae*, they were treated as *coniunctim*. 10 Ulp. 24. 1; G. 2. 193. 11 P. 3. 6. 13; Inst. 2. 20. 34. 12 Neither the rule nor its extension is ancient. Rationalistic explanations of purely juristic developments are more probable than those of ancient rules.

interpretation to different parts of the same instrument[1]. But though in general any condition which would avoid an *institutio* would avoid a legacy, the rule that a son could not be instituted on a condition not in his own power did not apply here. And though by Ulpian's time it was clear that impossible conditions and those grouped with them were struck out[2], the Proculians had held that they ought to vitiate the gift as in contract, and Gaius, a Sabinian, admits the distinction to be unreasonable[3]. *Causa* is not condition; a gift to a man for a stated reason which was not true would not avoid the gift, unless the court thought that it was intended as a condition; *falsa causa non nocet*[4]. Misdescription did not avoid the gift if it was clear from the will who was to have it and what it was—*falsa demonstratio non nocet*[5]. The law as to what was fulfilment, and what prevention excused non-fulfilment, was as in *institutiones*, but gifts of liberty were more favourably construed. In legacy if impossibility supervened after *aditio*, the gift failed; a manumission took effect[6]. In legacy prevention excused fulfilment only if by one interested in non-fulfilment. In manumission, prevention by anyone excused[7].

Many texts deal with legacy, etc., more or less at the discretion of the *heres* or a third party, "*si volueris,*" "*si tibi videbitur,*" "*si dignum putaveris,*" "*si te non offenderit,*" "*si meruerit*[8]," etc. The first form is void. Many texts say that forms like the last two are good if the beneficiary has behaved well, which the court will decide. Others make the middle forms valid, the gift not being at absolute discretion: the *heres* must exercise the *arbitrium* of a *bonus vir*. If it is left at the absolute discretion of a third party some texts make it good; others make it necessary to disguise it[9]. Many of the texts shew signs of interpolation and there is

1 As to reasons for extending the "*favor testamenti*" to legacies, see Hoffmann, *Krit. St.* 158. Conditions existed in legacies before they did in *institutiones*, but it is difficult to see why this rule should have developed for legacy. The language of Gaius shews that its application to them was still disputed (G. 3. 98). From D. 28. 7. 1 (where, though the passage is from Ulpian, it is probably Sabinus who is speaking) it seems to have been long settled in the case of *institutiones*. 2 28. 7. 14; 35. 1. 3. 3 G. 3. 98. Manenti, *St. Scialoja*, 1. 393. 4 Ulp. 24. 19; Inst. 2. 20. 31; D. 35. 1. 72. 6 (interp.). 5 Ulp. 24. 19; Inst. 2. 20. 29, 30. Grosso, *St. Bonfante*, 2. 187, shews *falsa demonstratio* to be an objectively false description of what is otherwise identifiable. He discusses the evolution of the rule and Justinian's confused handling of it. Donatuti, *St. Perozzi*, 311, shews a tendency under Justinian to aid interpretation by evidence outside the will. On the general question of interpretation, Betti (*Ist.* 1. 400) remarks that, while in contract interpretation of obscurity is against the framer of the agreement, in wills the rule is that of possible interpretations that is to be adopted which the testator meant, but if what he meant is inconsistent with the meaning of the words neither what he meant nor what he said is effective. See *ante*, p. 296. 6 35. 1. 94. pr.; 40. 7. 20. 3. 7 28. 7. 3, 11; 40. 7. 3. pr. Sporadic texts in the D., modified by Just., make it suffice "*si per eum non stet.*" Grosso, *Contributo allo studio dell' adempimento della cond.* 8 30. 43. 3; 30. 75; 32. 11. 6–8; 40. 5. 46. 3, etc. 9 31. 1; 28. 5. 32, etc.

much controversy as to classical law[1]. The better view on a doubtful matter seems to be, as to discretion in a third party, that there was disagreement among the jurists[2]. As to the other case there seems no sufficient reason to doubt that if the words were: "if he deserves it" or the like, this was a normal condition, on the fulfilment of which the court would adjudicate. As to the middle forms there is room for doubt: perhaps the better view is that in *fideicommissa* and manumissions the *arbitrium* measured on that of a *bonus vir* was accepted, but not for legacies, till Justinian[3]. In Roman law, as in our own, the interpretation of words in wills gave much trouble. The evasion by such words as "*si in Capitolium non ascenderit*" applied here as in *institutiones*[4].

A negative condition, dependent on the act of the beneficiary, might if strictly construed make the gift nugatory, for it might not be certain till he died that he would not do the act. The *cautio Muciana*, introduced probably by Q. Mucius Scaevola, gave some relief. The legatee took the gift at once, giving security for return if he broke the condition[5]. It applied in classical law only in legacy, only to such negative conditions as were in the power of the legatee, and, probably, among these, only to such as must otherwise remain open for the legatee's life. In the Digest there are texts so confining it, and others applying it to all negative potestative conditions[6]. Whether this represents a variable practice or the wider application is due to Justinian, as is the extension to *institutiones*, is matter of dispute[7]. In gifts of liberty there could be no *cautio Muciana*, for the manumission could not be undone. Where the act was indifferent in itself, there was a forced construction *favore libertatis*; "*si Capitolium non ascenderit*" was understood to mean "*cum primum potuerit*[8]." Where it was not indifferent, there was no relief, for this reason *condicio iurisiurandi*, remitted in other cases, was allowed in manumission[9].

Under Justinian much of the utility of the *cautio Muciana* was gone, in legacy, since he allowed resolutive conditions with somewhat similar security, and covering a wider field[10].

Dies incertus was treated as condition, as in *institutiones*, but the extension of this principle to legacy seems late[11]. *Dies incertus an, certus quando*, properly condition and so treated in *institutio* and legacy, was

1 Albertario, *Arbitrium boni viri del debitore*; *Arbitrium boni viri nel onerato di un fide commisso*; Beseler, *Beitr.* 3. 198; Donatuti, *Verba et voluntas*, *Bull.* 1925, 185; Riccobono, *Mél. Cornil*, 2. 311; Schulz, *Z.S.S.* 1928, 691. 2 40. 5. 46; 31. 1; 35. 1. 52. Riccobono, *cit.* 333. 3 Riccobono, *cit.* 339 *sqq.* 4 31. 3. *Ante*, p. 299. 5 35. 1. 7. 6 35. 1. 7, 72. pr., 72. 2, 106. 7 H. Krueger, *Mél. Girard*, 2. 1. 8 40. 4. 17. pr. Elsewhere the same writer (Julian) says that such gifts are derisory and void. 40. 4. 61. pr.; 40. 7. 4. 1. It is no doubt a question of intent. 9 28. 7. 8. 6, 7; 40. 4. 12. pr. 10 C. 6. 37. 26. 11 Much controversy on this matter. Appleton, *Terme certain et incertain*, 22, shews reason for holding it due to Just. 35. 1. 79.

treated as *dies* in manumission[1]. *Dies certus* was allowed in legacy[2], and an uncertain day (*certus an, incertus quando*), certain to arrive within the lifetime of the donee, was treated here as *dies certus*[3]. Thus a legacy at death of legatee was valid, while one payable after the death of *heres* or legatee was void, "*ne ab heredis herede legari videatur, quod iuris civilis ratio non patitur*[4]." There is not much difference, and Gaius says the distinction is unreasonable. The truth is that the Romans solved the puzzling logical question whether, at the moment of death, a man is alive or dead in the sense that he is alive. A legacy payable so many days before the death was void[5], probably as being "*praepostere conceptum.*" Justinian legalised all these, as he did resolutive conditions and gifts *ad diem*[6].

Modus is not condition. A gift *sub modo* was an absolute gift with a direction as to its application. If the direction was positive, the legatee could not compel delivery till security was given for its application[7]. If negative, it might perhaps under Justinian be dealt with by the *cautio Muciana*.

In classical law (the rule is set down to Pius) *legata poenae causa* were void. They are defined as those intended to compel the *heres* to a certain course of action, rather than to benefit the legatee, e.g. "If he gives his daughter in marriage to *X* let him give 1000 to *Y*." The same rule was applied to penal ademption or transfer of a legacy, to *fideicommissa*, to manumissions (though here there were doubts) and even to *institutio* of a *coheres*. The rule must have created difficulties and Justinian repealed it[8]. The illustration chosen does not express a rule as to restrictions on marriage: as to these the rule is that, while an absolute restraint is bad[9], a legacy "provided he does not marry *X*" or even "*X*, *Y* or *Z*" is good[10]. A limit is found in the rule that anything which substantially bars marriage is a fraud on the *l. Iulia* and is void[11].

The rules of personal capacity were in general as in *institutio*[12], but some types of beneficiary, e.g. municipalities, could receive legacies before they could be instituted[13], and the rule of the *l. Voconia*, forbidding *institutio* of women by *classici*, did not apply to legacies[14]. On legacy to one in the *potestas* of the *heres* there was dispute. As a gift of his own property to a man was void, and a gift to a slave was practically one to his master, the difficulty is plain. Servius, ignoring the *regula Catoniana*[15],

1 40. 4. 16; 40. 7. 19. 2 36. 2. 5. 1. 3 36. 2. 4. 4 G. 2. 232; Ulp. 24. 16; P. 3. 6. 5, 6; Inst. 2. 20. 35; see *post*, § CXLIX. 5 G. 2. 232; cf. Inst. 3. 19. 14. 6 Inst. 2. 20. 35; C. 6. 23. 25; C. 6. 37. 26; C. 8. 37. 11. *Post*, § CLIV. 7 32. 19. 8 G. 2. 235–237; Ulp. 24. 17; 25. 13; Inst. 2. 20. 36; C. 6. 41. 1. 9 35. 1. 72. 5; 36. 1. 67. 1. 10 35. 1. 63, 64. pr. 11 35. 1. 64. 1. An absolute prohibition to one's widow might be good if limited in time, e.g. till the children reached puberty, 35. 1. 62. 2. 12 No legacy to *postumus extraneus*, G. 2. 241, till Justinian, Inst. 2. 20. 26. 13 *Ante*, p. 292. 14 See however, *ante*, p. 290. 15 G. 2. 244; *post*, p. 345.

held that the gift was valid, but that it failed if at the time when it vested the "*honoratus*" was still in the *potestas* of the *heres*. The Sabinians held, on the *regula Catoniana*, that the gift was good if conditional, bad if simple. The Proculians held it bad in both cases, because, says Gaius, we can no more owe to one in our *potestas* conditionally than we can absolutely, which is giving the rule as a reason for itself, and ignores the distinction under the *regula Catoniana*. Justinian adopts the Sabinian view, adding the restriction, attributed to Servius, where the *honoratus* was still in the *potestas* when the right vested, which was probably also part of the Sabinian view[1].

The fact that a slave is not the same person as his master led to some unexpected rules in this connexion. A legacy of the property of *X* to the slave of *X* was absolutely good[2]. And no legacy to a slave was good unless it was of a thing he could take if he was free. Thus a legacy to him of a right of way was void, for the land to which it must attach would not be his if he was freed[3]. The rule stated by Paul that "*cum servo alieno aliquid testamento damus domini persona ad hoc tantum inspicitur ut sit cum eo testamenti factio, ceterum ex persona servi constitit legatum*[4]" had other applications. The rule as to *duae lucrativae causae* did not apply where *A* left a thing to *B*, and *C* made a *donatio* of it to *B*'s slave[5]. A legacy to a slave *post mortem domini* was good[6]. Where a will was upset by *bonorum possessio contra tabulas*, a legacy to a slave failed, though his *dominus* was a person legacies to whom would be saved[7].

Excessive legacies might cause refusal of the *hereditas* and intestacy. After ineffective legislation in the Republic[8], the problem was solved by the *l. Falcidia*, of 40 B.C.[9] Its main rule was that if legacies exceeded three-quarters of the estate they might be cut down *pro rata*[10]. The calculation was made as at the death, debts, funeral expenses, and the value of slaves freed, being deducted[11]. If a legacy was incapable of division, the legatee must refund proportionately[12]. If there were several *heredes*

1 Inst. 2. 20. 32; Ulp. 24. 23. The converse case of legacy to one whose slave was *heres* gave no difficulty: it was valid whether simple or conditional, but failed if at *dies cedens* he was still in *potestas*. G. 2. 245; Inst. 2. 20. 33. The difference is that in the first case the legacy cedes on opening of will and the inheritance is also fixed on the master, so that he is inevitably the person entitled to the legacy. In the second case the identity is not inevitable, as the slave can be alienated before entry. In Ulp. 24. 24 it is supposed that the "*non*" is an error.

2 31. 82. 2. Not affected by the Catonian in any way.

3 *Ib.*; 33. 3. 5. The contradictory 32. 17. 1 is probably corrupt.

4 31. 82. 2.

5 *Post*, § CXCII; 30. 108. 1 (interp.).

6 30. 68. 1.

7 37. 5. 3. 2.

8 *L. Furia*, date uncertain, forbade legacies of more than 1000 *asses*, with some exceptions, with *manus iniectio* (G. 4. 23) and fourfold penalty (Ulp. 1. 2). *L. Voconia* (168 B.C.) forbade any legacy to exceed what the *heredes* took, where the testator was *census*, Cic. *Ver.* 2. 1. 43. 110; sanction unknown, probably nullity; G. 2. 225, 226.

9 35. 2. 1 pr. On school disputes as to the working of the *lex*, Arnò, *Le due grande correnti della giurisp. romana, Appendice.*

10 G. 2. 227; Inst. 2. 22; P. 3. 8; Ulp. 24. 32.

11 P. 4. 3. 3; D. 35. 2. 73.

12 D. 35. 2. 80.1.

and legacies were specially charged on particular *heredes*, the calculation was separately made for each, so that even where some legacies were cut down, more than one-quarter might remain with the *heredes*[1]. Conversely, the testator might direct that any particular legacy should or should not bear the loss, thus relieving or burdening the others[2]. In classical law the testator might not forbid the *heres* to keep this quarter; a private agreement with that aim was void[3]. Apart from the military will, the chief cases free from this reduction were one of legacy of debt to the creditor, not exceeding the debt[4], and one of a slave, with nothing else, with a trust to free[5]. There were controversies as to mode of computation of conditional debts, limited interests and so forth[6], complicated by the various types of legacy[7]. The *heres* was charged, in general, only with what he took as *heres*, not, e.g., with a *praelegatum*[8]. The reduction was *ipso iure*, so that a legatee *per vindicationem*, where a case for the *Falcidia* arose, would be able to vindicate only a proportionate part of the thing[9].

It might be uncertain if, or how far, a deduction would be necessary. In that case the practice was to pay the legacy, taking security from the legatee for refund if the payment proved excessive[10].

The chief changes made by Justinian were that he allowed the testator to forbid the retention of a quarter[11], and excluded it altogether if the *heres* had not made an inventory[12].

CXX. Vesting of Legacies. The expressions *dies cedit* and *dies venit* were used to express two critical points of time in the acquisition of the legacy. The opposition is one of tense. *Dies cedit* means "the day is coming," *dies venit*, "the day has come." The use of different verbs makes a third term possible. The expression *dies cessit, cessisset, cesserit*[13] means that *dies cedens* is past, but not that *dies venit*.

At *dies cedens* the legacy "vested" with three principal effects. The gift became transmissible, so that, if it was of more than a life interest, the representatives of the legatee could claim the gift, though he had not accepted[14]. It might determine the destination of the gift, for if

1 35. 2. 77. 2 35. 2. 64, 88. 2. Attempts to defeat the gift forfeited the right, 35. 2. 59. The rule applied in later cl. law to *d. mortis causa*, C. 6. 50. 5. 3 35. 2. 27. 4 35. 2. 5. 5 35. 2. 33–35. 6 35. 2. 73. 1 speaks of alternative modes of calculation. It might be estimated, market value of the gift as it is, or taken at value of the *res*, security being given for either event by *heres* or legatee. Vassali (*Bull.* 1913, 52 *sqq.*) holds the former system due to Justinian; 35. 2. 45. 1, 66 pr., 73. 2, 88. 3. 7 35. 2. 30. 1, 36–38, 45, 66, 68, 73. 1 *sqq.*, 82, etc. 8 35. 2. 74. Some exceptions. 9 35. 2. 73. 5. Difficulties where a share lapses and its burden is carried over, 35. 2. 1. 13, 14, 78, etc. Vangerow, *Pandekten*, § 535. 10 D. 35. 3. Lenel, *Mél. Girard*, 2. 79. Where the legacy is not immediate, mesne profits are charged against the quarter, 35. 2. 15. 6, 24. 1. 11 *Nov.* 1. 12 *Ante*, p. 316. 13 E.g. 36. 2. 31; 33. 5. 10. 14 Ulp. 24. 30; P. 3. 6. 7. Sommer, *Z.S.S.* 1913, 394, arguing from 31. 45. 1 holds that *dies cedens* did not involve

the legatee was a slave it was his owner at *dies cedens* who could claim[1]. It failed if the legatee was *incapax* on that day[2]. Legatee took the fruits from that day[3]. It determined what was left. If a *universitas rerum* such as a flock was left, the legatee was entitled to it, in general, as it was on that day[4]. If two things were left together, of which one was clearly an accessory to the other, and the principal thing had ceased to exist on that day, the gift failed[5].

When *dies venit*, the legacy was recoverable, unless repudiated, and, at any rate in later law, *dies cedit* and, *a fortiori*, *dies venit* without the knowledge of the legatee[6]. No time was fixed within which to claim. This is because in the view which prevailed, an inchoate right to the legacy was acquired by the legatee at *dies cedens*, though it devested, e.g. on repudiation. But actual acceptance had some importance; it was, e.g., only this which prevented a legatee from attacking the will[7].

There were elaborate rules as to the occurrence of these days. In *legata pura* or *sub modo*, *dies cedit* on the death (or opening of the will), *dies venit* on the entry of the *heres*. In *legata ex die*, *dies cedit* at the death, *dies venit* at entry of *heres* or occurrence of the day, whichever was the later. In conditional legacy, *dies cedit* on occurrence of the condition, *dies venit* then or at entry of the *heres*, whichever was the later[8]. But certain legacies were under special rules. Thus legacy of a *usus* or usufruct, in which there was no question of transmission, ceded only at entry of the *heres*, and if there was *dies* only from the *dies*[9]. The same was true of *legatum*, with liberty, to a slave of the testator[10], as he could not be free, and thus no right could vest in him, till the *heres* had entered. In *usus* and usufruct, the rule had the practical effect that, even under Justinian, if it was to a slave the master could claim nothing if the slave died before *aditio* of the *heres*. In legacy of *operae servorum* it seems not to cede till it is claimed[11].

the existence of the right. His explanation of 7. 3. 1. 4 seems inadmissible. There is no doubt about the rules stated above in the text.

1 30. 91. 6. In *institutio* the slave carries the gift with him to the moment of acceptance (*ante*, p. 312). Both this and the distinction last above mentioned turn on the fact that legacy is acquired without acceptance, while *hereditas*, apart from *necessarii*, is not (37. 11. 2. 9; *ante*, § CIX). 2 Ulp. 24. 30. 3 30. 120. 2. 4 Inst. 2. 20. 20. 5 Inst. 2. 20. 17. But much depends on intent, the governing factor in questions under wills; 33. 7. 5. 6 36. 2 *passim*. "Vesting" does not imply that ownership passes to legatee—this cannot occur till the *heres* has accepted. G. 2. 195. 7 34. 9. 5. pr. 8 Ulp. 24. 31. 9 7. 3. 1. 2; Vat. Fr. 60; D. 36. 2. 2, 3. Hence the unfair result that fruits between death and entry go to *heres*. (36. 2. 3. Ulp.) The non-transmissibility stated as the reason of the rule is hardly adequate for this. Elsewhere he (D. 7. 3. 1. 2) explains it on the ground that usufruct, which consists in use, cannot exist till it can be enjoyed. *Ante*, p. 268. Elvers (*Servitutenl.* 726) explains it on the ground that it is essentially conditional on the giving of security. But *dies cedens* does not await the giving of security. 10 Or if he himself is left *per vind.* 35. 2. 1. 4; 36. 2. 7. 6, 8. 11 33. 2. 7.

By the *ll. caducariae*, *dies cedit* not at the death, but only at the opening of the will[1]. The purpose of the rule, which the *liber singularis regularum* attributes to the *l. Papia*[2], Justinian to *scc.* based thereon, is obscure[3]. As wills must be opened as soon as possible after the death, it had little effect[4]. Justinian restored the old rule[5].

CXXI. Failure of Legacy. The requirements of a valid legacy have already been stated. A point still to be mentioned is the *regula Catoniana*[6]: a gift which would have been *inutile* if the testator had died at the moment of testation could not be validated by subsequent events. This is not a mere application of the wider rule that "*quod ab initio vitiosum est non potest tractu temporis convalescere*[7]," which avoids, e.g., institutions of, or legacies to, a *peregrinus*[8]. Though in one sense wider, since it would avoid gifts which in classical law might in the opinion of some jurists eventually be valid, if they had been *institutiones*[9], it had a very narrow field. It did not apply to fundamental defects, but only to those of a less basic type. Of the few cases in which it is applied, all but one were cases of gift quite valid but for some relation of the parties concerned (legacy to slave of testator or *heres*, legacy to a man of what was his[10]). But one text puts on the same level a legacy of materials of a house, which could not be left[11], so that it is difficult to specify the exact limits of the rule[12]. It did not apply to *institutiones* or to any legacy which "ceded" only on *aditio*, of which conditional legacies were the chief case[13], or to the disabilities created by the *l. Iunia* and the *ll. caducariae*[14].

If a legacy was given *pure* and was such that the *regula* avoided it, an *ademptio* of it under a condition, which had the effect of making it subject to the contrary condition, did not remove it from the operation of the *regula*—an *ademptio*, being designed to lessen the right, was not

1 Ulp. 24. 31. 2 *Ib.* 3 C. 6. 51. 1. 1 c. 4 P. 4. 6. 3. 5 C. 6. 51. 1. 1 c. Postponement under *l. Papia* did not perhaps apply where there was one *heres* only. Pothier, *ad* 22. 6. 1. 4; Sommer, *Z.S.S.* 1913, 394. 6 D. 34. 7. 7 50. 17. 29. 8 Ulp. 22. 2; *ante*, p. 290. For these rules, indifferent whether the gift was simple or conditional. In alternative legacies, where one of the two is in any way conditional, *dies cedit* only on arrival of the condition, or failure of it. 36. 2. 14, 16, 25, etc. 9 G. 2. 123. For this and similar cases, Machelard, *Règle Catonienne*, §§ 25–27. 10 Inst. 2. 20. 32. H. t. 10 says that legacy of legatee's property is bad even though he sells it. D. 34. 7. 1. 2 may be read as contradictory but is supposed to mean that there was a condition of alienation, which would exclude the *regula*. 11 30. 41. 2. 12 Machelard says that the rule applied (*op. cit.* § 33) where "il n'y a qu'une incapacité transitoire de nature à s'évanouir d'un jour à l'autre." But a *peregrinus* is as likely to become a *civis*, *vivo testatore*, as a house is to be pulled down. Sommer (*Z.S.S.* 1913, 396) holds that the rule assumes a gift "objectively and subjectively valid." The proper application of the rule is probably to relative obstructions, due to the relation of the parties, and that the application to *materia aedibus iuncta* is an extension, out of keeping with the original principle. J. Lambert, *Regula Catoniana*, confines it to legacy of property of beneficiary. Other views, Monier, *R.H.* 1927, 525; Kreller, *Z.S.S.* 1927, 436. 13 34. 7. 3, 4. 14 34. 7. 5.

to be so construed as to increase it[1]. But if a legacy originally conditional became *purum* by satisfaction of the condition, *vivo testatore*, the effect would apparently be to bring it within the rule. This gave rise to difficulties. Three cases are put: a legacy "if the legatee marry *X*," who at the testation was under twelve, and he married her, *vivo testatore*; a legacy "if I die after such a date," and the testator did so die; a legacy to *X* of land which was his "if he alienates it in my life," and he did so alienate[2]. In all the cases it had become *purum* and if the testator had died when he made the will the gift could not have operated; there was an obstruction. In each case the gift was valid; we are told that the rule is inaccurately expressed[3], but not how it should have been expressed. To make such gifts void would be to make all gifts under condition void, if the condition could not be satisfied at once, and was in fact satisfied *vivo testatore*[4]. The *regula*, according to the texts, applied under Justinian to *fideicommissa*: it can hardly have done so in classical law[5].

A valid legacy might fail owing to later events:

(*a*) *Ademptio*. An express revocation in the will or a codicil, following the form of the gift, destroyed it *ipso iure*[6]. But other causes adeemed in effect by giving an *exceptio doli*, and the *ademptio* seems usually to have been *ipso iure* under Justinian. Such were extreme hostility between the parties, erasure, informal ademption in the will, alienation, unless, in later law, the circumstances shewed that there was no intent to adeem[7]. But in these tacit cases the revocation was ambulatory; if, e.g., the hostility ceased, the gift revived[8], though mere repurchase would not revive a gift[9]. Giving the value of the thing to the legatee, *inter vivos*, was in general in substitution for the legacy[10], and *ademptio* might be conditional or partial[11].

(*b*) *Translatio*, in effect *ademptio*. This is a change in the thing left, or a transfer to another legatee, expressed to be in substitution. The first gift was destroyed, even though the second gift failed[12]. But if the second gift was conditional, so was the *ademptio*, and if the condition failed the old gift stood, unless a contrary intent appeared[13].

(*c*) Death of legatee before *dies cedit*, or incapacity at that time[14].

1 34. 4. 14. 2 34. 7. 1. 1, 1. 2, 2. 3 H. t. 1. pr. 4 This does not negative the rule that it became subject to the *regula* if it became *purum*. 5 Machelard, *cit.* §§ 81 *sqq.* J. Lambert, *cit.* 185; C. Appleton, *Tijdschr.* 1931, 19, who shews that it could not rationally apply to *fcc.*, and holds that it was obsolete under J., its appearance in the texts being only one of the many evidences of the haste and ineptitude of the compilers. 6 Ulp. 24. 29; D. 34. 4. 2. 7 34. 4. 3. 11, 16, 18; Inst. 2. 20. 12; G. 2. 198; P. 4. 1. 9. Sale of part adeems as to that part, 30. 8. pr. Pledging does not destroy it. P. 3. 6. 16. History of doctrine, Arnò, *Cascellio*, 73. Suman, *Favor testamenti*, 200. 8 34. 4. 4. 9 H. t. 15. In cl. law a *l. per vind.* was avoided by sale of the *res*. G. 2. 196. Riccobono, *Mél. Cornil*, 2. 354. 10 31. 22. 11 34. 4. 2, 11, 32; C. 6. 37. 17. 12 30. 34. pr.; 34. 4. 6, 20. 13 34. 4. 7. 14 *Ante*, p. 343.

(*d*) Debts, subject to the power of the testator to charge particular debts on particular beneficiaries[1].

(*e*) Operation of the *l. Falcidia.*

(*f*) *Ereptio.* The gift might be forfeited for *indignitas.* It went usually to the *fiscus,* but there were exceptions[2].

(*g*) Destruction. If this was not due to the *heres,* the legatee took nothing[3], e.g. a *servus alienus legatus* was freed by his master[4]. If the destruction was by the *heres* the value was due whether he knew of the legacy or not[5]. If several things were left, destruction of one did not bar claim to the rest, unless they were principal and accessory, and the principal thing was destroyed before *dies cedit*[6].

(*h*) Acquisition of the thing *ex lucrativa causa.* A case of a general rule, applicable to all obligations and discussed later[7].

(*i*) Failure of the will. To this there were exceptions. If an *institutus* refused, in order to take on intestacy, or abstained for a price, legacies, etc., were good[8], as also if the will was upset by collusion[9], and apparently wherever the *hereditas* passed to the fisc[10]. In partial failure, gifts specially charged on the *institutio* which failed were destroyed under the old *ius accrescendi,* but preserved under the *ll. caducariae* and Justinian[11], and it seems that, in later classical law, this was applied also in the cases to which *ius accrescendi* still applied, the accrual being regarded as a sort of substitution[12]. This would occur if the lapse went to one with *ius antiquum*[13], and in a legacy of usufruct, since it could not go to anyone but the person named[14]. If the gift which failed was *pro non scripto,* it did not ordinarily carry its burdens at any time[15]. But all this depended on the intent of the testator; it was open to him to use words which shewed that the legacy was not to be payable unless it fell on one particular *heres.*

A second will, validly made, revoked the first even though it never operated[16]. If invalid *ab initio,* it did not, and although legacies could be adeemed informally, a second *testamentum* which was *non iure factum,* though it omitted or altered the earlier gift, did not affect it[17].

1 *Ante,* p. 317. 2 *Ante,* p. 321. 3 30. 47. 4, 5; Inst. 2. 20. 16. 4 30. 35. 5 31. 63. Liability even in ignorance due to Justinian? These rules take no account of the forms. In cl. law there was probably *a. doli* in *l. per vind., a. ex testamento* in *l. per damn.* Krueger, *ad l.* and 4. 3. 7. 5. 6 33. 8. 12. A matter of interpretation; very fine lines are drawn. On a gift of *fundus cum instrumentis,* the *instrumenta* were accessories, not in one of *fundus et instrumenta.* But the child of an *ancilla* was never an accessory. 33. 7. 1, 5; Inst. 2. 20. 17. 7 *Post,* § cxcii. 8 29. 4. 1; C. 6. 39. 1. 9 49. 1. 14. 10 30. 96. 1. 11 *Ante,* p. 320. 12 *Ante,* § cv. 13 *Ante,* p. 319 *sq.* If all entitled to *caduca* refused them, i.e. failed to vindicate them, they went to the fisc, which on general principles would carry out the charges. 14 *Post,* § cxxiii. 15 C. 6. 51. 1. 3, "*nisi perraro.*" 16 *Ante,* p. 332. 17 32. 18. ? interp. Di Marzo, *Mél. Girard,* 2. 145, holds that the original rule was that if it was not in the second will it was adeemed

(*k*) Repudiation by the legatee, which might not be *pro parte* and was irrevocable[1].

CXXII. Remedies of Legatee. Apart from right of action, a legatee could claim, whether the legacy was immediate, deferred or conditional, that the person liable should give him security for performance, unless the testator had prohibited this[2]. If this, which was not mere *cautio*, but *satisdatio*, i.e. personal surety, was refused, the legatee could get *missio in possessionem* of the goods of the *hereditas* for custody[3]. He could not sell property except what must be dealt with at once, or turn out the *heres*; the object, as we are unaffectedly told, was that he might so incommode the *heres* as to force him to give security[4]. If, whether security had been given or not, there was six months' delay in payment, Caracalla provided that a *fideicommissarius* might get *missio in possessionem* of the property of the person liable, and use and enjoy the property till he had satisfied his claim out of the fruits[5]. Justinian extended this to legatees[6]. In A.D. 535 Justinian[7] gave legatees and others a still more drastic remedy. On application a *iudex* would decree fulfilment within a year. On failure the *heres* was excluded, except to the extent of his *pars legitima*, if any, his rights passing to other beneficiaries, who must give security. The order was, generally, first, substitutes, then *coheredes*, then *fideicommissarii hereditatis*, then other legatees, etc., then any freed slaves, then *heredes ab intestato*, not expressly disinherited, and then the fisc.

We saw that in classical law the legatee had an action *in rem* or one *in personam* according to the form of the legacy[8]. The action *in personam* was the *actio ex testamento*, a *strictum iudicium*, for double damages *contra infitiantem*, at least if what was left was a *certum*[9]. If the legacy was charged on the *heredes* generally, the legatee could bring *actio ex testamento* (or *vindicatio*) against each in proportion to his share. If the legacy was charged on some *heredes*, but not all, these were liable in the proportion of their shares *inter se*[10]. But if some of the *heredes* made

"*nuda voluntate,*" but a mere change was ignored, the revocation being conditional on validity of the new gift: this being void the old gift stood.

1 P. 3. 6. 12. No repudiation while the legacy still *conditional* or *sub die*. 31. 45. 1.
2 Or the person liable is the *fiscus*; 36. 3. 1. pr., 1. 18, 12, 14.
3 36. 3. 1. 2; 36. 4 *passim*.
4 36. 4. 5. pr.
5 H. 1. 16, 17.
6 "*Legatarios et*" in 36. 4. 5. 16 is interpolated, Mitteis, *Z.S.S.* 1912, 206.
7 *Nov.* 1. 1.
8 *Ante*, § CXVII.
9 G. 2. 282; 4. 9; 4. 171; P. 1. 19. 1; Inst. 3. 27. 7, perhaps replacing an earlier liability to *manus iniectio*. On change of view as to what was a "*certum*," De Francisci, *St. Perozzi*, 327. Ulpian says (24. 33) that a legacy wrongly paid cannot be recovered. Gaius, more in accordance with principle, confines this to cases in which it is *duplex contra infitiantem* (2. 283). If there was no legacy, owing to ademption, Paul says it could always be recovered, P. 3. 6. 92. Cf. P. 1. 19. 1; Inst. 3. 27. 7. The allusion in Inst. 2. 20. 25 is to J.'s new rules.
10 31. 33; 45. 2. 17.

liable were named personally, it seems that they were liable equally[1], though older lawyers took the view that they were liable *pro rata*[2], and the rule in the real action may have been either this, or that, if charged only on some *heredes*, the gift failed *pro parte*[3].

Justinian, by a sweeping enactment[4], provided that all legacies were to have the same nature, and to be enforceable by the same remedies, of which he established a new scheme. Every legatee was to be entitled to three distinct actions, between which it seems he must elect. These were the *actio in rem* (*vindicatio*, if it was a gift of property, *confessoria*, if it was a servitude), a personal action, *actio ex testamento*, against the person liable, and an *actio hypothecaria*, of which it was a new application. He provided that all the estate should be under a hypothec for each legacy, and that no *heres* should be liable for more than his share[5]. There were of course cases in which no real action was conceivable, e.g. a legacy of a *res aliena*, or of a service to be rendered, or a *legatum nominis* or *liberationis*[6], or of fungibles of which there were none in the *hereditas*.

It should be added that legatees could claim *bonorum separatio* in much the same way as creditors[7], and that Justinian, nominally generalising the double liability on denial, nearly abolished it, for while extending it to all kinds of legacy and *fideicommissum*, he enacted that it was to apply only where the beneficiary was the Church or a charity[8].

CXXIII. Special types of Legacy. Certain types of legacy had special characteristics which need discussion.

Legatum rei alienae. Anyone's property might be left, except the legatee's, and even his, if the legacy was conditional, so that the *regula Catoniana* did not apply, and it had ceased to be his at *dies cedens*[9]. The fact that the testator thought it was the legatee's did not avoid the gift, if it was really his own[10], but in any case if it was a *res aliena*, the legatee must shew that the testator knew it was not his own[11]. In that case the *heres* must buy it or give its value[12]. But a legacy of a thing incapable of ownership, *extra commercium*, was void[13].

L. optionis, generis, of alternative. *L. optionis* is a gift to legatee of free choice among two or three things. Till Justinian this needed personal choice so that it failed if legatee died without choosing. There were

1 30. 54. 3, 124. 2 45. 2. 17. 3 The texts cited to prove this are not conclusive, see, e.g., Pothier, *ad* 30. 81. 4 and Pampaloni, *Mél. Girard*, 2. 348. In this text, if it is so understood, there must be anachronism for Justinian. There is a point of construction involved: some meaning has to be assigned to absurd language of the testator. The words about value are usually omitted by commentators on the text, see Vangerow, § 521. 4 C. 6. 43. 1. As to the possible right of legatee *per vindicationem* to use the personal action; see *ante*, p. 335. 5 C. 6. 43. 1. 5. 6 *Post*, § CXXIII. 7 42. 6. 6. pr. 8 Inst. 3. 27. 7; C. 1. 3. 45. 7. 9 Inst. 2. 20. 4, 10; D. 30. 41. 2. 10 Inst. 2. 20. 11. 11 22. 3. 21; P. 4. 1. 8; Inst. 2. 20. 4 (exception, C. 6. 37. 10). 12 *Ib.* 13 Inst. 2. 20. 4; D. 30. 39. 10.

disputes: it does not seem that it was conditional for all purposes[1]. Justinian allowed successors to choose: if they did not, lot decided[2]. If the choice was to be by a third party, and he did not act, the legatee chose, but, under Justinian, might not choose the best[3]. Such a gift was normally by *vindicatio*: no doubt the same result was reached where the *heres* was directed to give whichever the legatee should choose, otherwise *heres* had the choice[4]. *L. generis* is a gift of a thing of a kind, e.g. a horse, but not a specific horse. Here, under Justinian, express reservation apart, the legatee chose[5]. In classical law this is true of *vindicatio*, but in *damnatio* the *heres* chose[6]. There is a rule (its classicality is doubtful) that *heres* with choice must not choose the worst, or legatee the best[7]. A legacy in this form does not seem to have been thought of as conditional, so that it vested at once[8] and choice could be made by successors[9]. Legacy of an alternative: "I leave to *X* this or that" seems to have been, so far as these rules are concerned, on the same footing. Legatee might choose if it was *per vindicationem*[10], and successors could choose[11].

Gifts "to *A* or *B*" gave difficulty. Justinian says it would take a book to set out all the different opinions[12] and conflicting enactments, as to whether such *institutiones*, legacies, *fideicommissa*, manumissions, appointments of *tutores*, were void, or entitled both or one only and if so which, and whether all the gifts were alike in these matters. He enacts that "*aut*" shall mean "*et*," admitting both, wholly in *tutela* and *manumissio*, dividing in the other cases. Where words giving the *heres* the choice were added, if he made no choice within "*iustum tempus*" all could claim—the gift cedes at once, it seems, for all, but the *heres* if he makes due choice will destroy the legacy for the others[13]. But if he is to make his choice at death, the gift does not vest in any till the death[14]. If it was a fettered discretion, e.g. "*qui meruerunt*," there were further complications[15].

Legatum rei obligatae. A legacy of a thing held by the testator subject

1 33. 5. 8, 19; 35. 1. 69; Inst. 2. 20. 23. The words might differ: disputes may have turned on this. 2 C. 6. 43. 3. 1. Same rule where *l. optionis* was joint. 3 C. 6. 43. 3. 1 b; Ulp. 24. 14. 4 Ulp. *ib.* 5 30. 20; 33. 5. 2. 1. The case in 30. 108. 2 has been altered. As put, the case is not one for such a book as Africani *Quaestiones*: probably A. discussed the common case where the legacy was put in both forms. The compilers adopt the reasoning and apply it to the new state of the law. 6 Ulp. 24. 14; D. 33. 5. 12. 7 30. 37. pr., 110. 8 36. 2. 12. 7. 9 *Ib.* 10 31. 19, 23. 11 33. 5. 19. Modern editors insert a "*non*" reversing the doctrine. This is due to the words "*utrum elegerit legatarius*," making it look like a *l. optionis*. But P.'s point is that these words add nothing to the effect of "*illud aut illud*" and do not change the character of the gift. 12 C. 6. 38. 4. P. 3. 4 b. 3; 3. 6. 13; Vat. Fr. 227 (D. 26. 2. 30); D. 31. 8. 3, 16; 34. 4. 3. 7; 34. 5. 10, 27; 35. 1. 33; 40. 4. 31. 13 31. 16, 24, 25. 14 31. 67. 7, 77. 4; *ante*, p. 339. 15 31. 77. 25. There might be conditions, the satisfaction of which made it clear who was entitled. 30. 108. 3; cp. 34. 5. 10.

to a charge or usufruct, was construed according to his knowledge. If he knew of the charge the *heres* must free it[1]. If he did not, the thing passed subject to the charge, but, in later law, the legatee when sued on the charge could claim cession of actions[2].

Legatum debiti. A legacy of the testator's debt, to the creditor, was void unless it, in some way, increased his right, e.g. was absolute, while the debt was conditional. If valid, it superseded the debt, but questions of intent were material[3]. It was not subject to the *l. Falcidia*, nor could a *fideicommissum* be imposed on it, except as to its excess value[4].

Legatum nominis. Legacy of debt due to the testator. If due from a third person, the legatee could require the *heres* to transfer his rights of action[5]. It failed if there was no debt or it was paid *vivo testatore*[6]. If it was due from the legatee (*legatum liberationis*), it was a defence to any action and entitled the legatee to a formal release[7]. A *legatum liberationis* might also be from a debt of the legatee to a third person; here the legatee could require the *heres* to procure his discharge[8].

Legatum dotis to the wife was valid, though it would usually be hers in any case. The point was that the legacy could be recovered at once, while recovery of *dos* involved delays[9]. A legacy of "*dos*," where there was none, was void, but a legacy of property was not avoided (so decided Severus and Caracalla) merely because it was wrongly described as *dos*[10].

Legacy of a life annuity was treated as a series of annual legacies, the first *purum*, the others conditional on survival into that year. If limitation to life was not expressed, "*si vivat*" was implied[11].

Legatum peculii, to *extraneus*, entitled a legatee to it as it was at the death, apart from the *ll. caducariae*, i.e. *dies cedens*. He took nothing but ordinary accretions after that. If the legatee was the slave, he took all additions of any kind, up to the time of entry, when he was free[12]. This also was *dies cedens*, but the rule did not depend on this, but on presumed intent. It indicates that in Julian's view[13] the *peculium* was an artificial unity, retaining that character if it was left to the slave, but otherwise losing it at the death.

1 P. 3. 6. 8; Inst. 2. 20. 5. After Severus, Schulz, *Gedächtnisssch. für Seckel*, 110. 2 C. 6. 42. 6. This has no application to legacy of a thing subject to usufruct, 31. 66. 6. 3 30. 28. pr.; Inst. 2. 20. 14. 4 32. 7. 2; 35. 2. 1. 10. A legacy to one who is in fact a creditor is not of course necessarily a legacy of the debt. 5 30. 105, and, if this is not done, an *actio utilis* in later law. C. 6. 37. 18. 6 30. 75. 1; 34. 3. 31. pr. Novation of form did not affect it, 31. 76. 3. D. 32. 11. 13 though interp. (Vitrano, *Ann. Palermo*, 3. 28) shews that circumstances might even make it survive payment. 7 Inst. 2. 20. 13. 8 Inst. 2. 20. 21. 9 *Ante*, p. 110. 10 Inst. 2. 20. 15. *Falsa demonstratio non nocet*, *ante*, p. 339. On the Edict "*de alterutro*," abolished under Just., imposing on a widow the choice between a legacy to her and her *dos*, Lenel, *E.P.* 308. 11 33. 1. 4, 5, 8. Death would end it though it was for a term not yet expired. A promise of an annuity was differently handled, *post*, § CLIV. 12 Inst. 2. 20. 20. 13 15. 1. 57. 1.

Legatum usus fructus had many peculiarities. It did not cede before entry[1]. The special causes of failure when it was acquired through a son or slave have been considered[2]. As a gift of land included one of the usufruct, it follows that, if the land was given to *A* and a usufruct to *B*, *A* and *B* shared the usufruct, of which there were in fact two gifts[3]. We have also noted the practice of *repetitio*, to avoid loss by *capitis minutio* or non-use[4]. But the most striking peculiarities were in the law of accrual. It does not seem to have been affected by the *ll. caducariae*[5]; the classical texts treat the old law of accrual as still operating in this case[6], and it was substantially unchanged under Justinian[7]. Further, though in general the rules of lapse applied only where the gift failed altogether, in usufruct (left *per vindicationem*) there was accrual between joint usufructuaries, even where the lapse occurred after enjoyment had begun[8]. And it was said "*personae adcrescere, non portioni*," the chief effect being that, if one of joint fructuaries lost his share by non-use, and another share fell in, he could still claim accrual out of that. This accrual however would not cover any part of what he had lost, though that or some of it would be vested in the man whose share had now fallen in[9]. These rules are no doubt connected. Ulpian's[10] reason for the rule as to lapse is that each is entitled to the whole (*concursu partes fiunt*), so that if one disappeared, the other had all. He notes that the rule would apply in any other case in which "*concursu partes fiunt*" and that there were cases in usufruct in which there was no such accrual, as there were distinct gifts of parts[11]. For the second rule he gives the reason of Celsus and Julian that "*usus fructus cottidie constituitur et legatur, non ut proprietas eo solo tempore quo vindicatur*[12]." This hardly agrees with the rule that, in *legatum usus fructus, dies cedit* once for all, as Ulpian himself seems to note, and it would make unnecessary the precaution of repetition already adverted to[13]. The real explanation is the original conception of usufruct[14], as consisting in enjoyment. The share that had been enjoyed would be lost by non-use[15]. Nothing else would.

Praelegatum was legacy to a *heres*, where there were more than one[16].

1 *Ante*, p. 344. 2 *Ante*, p. 272. 3 33. 2. 19. Similarly as *fructus* cannot exist without *usus*, if there is a legacy of *fructus* to *A* and of *usus* to *B*, *A* shares in the *usus*, of which there are two gifts, P. 3. 6. 24, 25. 4 *Ante*, p. 272. 5 *Ante*, p. 338. 6 Vat. Fr. 75 *sqq.* 7 D. 7. 2. No doubt due to its personal character: a life estate could not vest in any but the named person. 8 7. 2. 1. 3; Vat. Fr. 77. 9 7. 1. 33. 1; 7. 2. 10. etc. 10 Vat. Fr. 78, 79 quoting Neratius and Celsus. 11 Vat. Fr. 78, 82; D. 7. 2. 1. pr. 12 7. 2. 1. 3. 13 *Ante*, p. 272. 14 *Ante*, p. 269. 15 7. 2. 10; 7. 4. 3. 2; Vat. Fr. 75. There was evidently much controversy among the classical lawyers on the application of the rules to a number of complex cases. Effect of a *legatum* of *nuda proprietas*, the usufruct remaining with the *heres*, Pampaloni, *Mél. Girard*, 2. 331 *sqq.* 16 It resembles *l. per precept.* but it may be in any form, Jörs, *R.R.* 246.

As the *res* was in part his, as *heres*, the legacy was void, so far as it fell on his share[1]. Thus where *A* was *heres* to one twelfth and *B* to the rest, and a *praelegatum* was left to them equally, *B* would get only one-twelfth of it and *A* the rest[2]. Where a praelegatee was also under a *fideicommissum hereditatis*, he could keep only that part of the legacy which was not void[3].

Legatum partitionis. Legacy of an aliquot part of the *hereditas*[4]. The legatee was *legatarius partiarius*. It is ancient, but its purpose is not certainly known; it may have been to evade the rule of the *l. Voconia* against *institutio* of women[5]. The legatee was not *heres*. He did not represent the deceased; he could not bring *hereditatis petitio* or *familiae erciscundae*, or sue or be sued as *heres*. But as he was entitled to a part of each claim, and liable to a part of each debt, it was usual to enter into agreements (*stipulationes partis et pro parte*) with the *heres* that the *heres* should hand over *pro rata* what came in, and that the legatee would refund *pro rata* what creditors recovered from the *heres*[6].

CXXIV. *Fideicommissa*. Their primary purpose was to evade restrictions on *institutio*[7]. In the Republic they were not enforceable, but rested on the good faith of the *heres*[8]. Augustus ordered them to be carried out in a few cases, not by the ordinary courts, but by the administrative authority of the consuls, in some cases because the testator had asked the beneficiary to carry them out "*per salutem principis*," in others because of glaring perfidy. They were soon recognised as legal institutions and a special Praetor, *praetor fideicommissarius*, was appointed to deal with them[9]. They are not necessarily connected with codicils, but one Lentulus, having made Augustus his *heres*, with others, imposed *fideicommissa* on him and others, by codicil. Augustus ordered them to be carried out and then asked the opinion of lawyers whether codicils ought to be recognised. Opinion was in favour, and when Labeo made them, they were definitely recognised as legal[10]. *Fideicommissa* thus were not praetorian; they were juristic creations. The relations between *heres* and *fideicommissarius* were handled by the *praetor fideicommissarius*.

1 Ulp. 24. 22. 2 30. 34. 12. 3 36. 1. 19. 3. Where one of two *heredes* has a joint legacy with two others, not *heredes*, he can claim only one-half of his third, so that the two others will share five-sixths. 30. 34. 11, 116. 1. 4 Ulp. 24. 25. 5 Girard, *Man.* 988. 6 G. 2. 254, 257; Ulp. 25. 15. School dispute on the question whether he was entitled to the things themselves or only to their value, 30. 26. 2. When Justinian fused legacy and *fideicommissum* (*post*, § CXXV) it seems that *l. partitionis* would be merged in *fideicommissum hereditatis*. But it is still treated in the Digest as a distinct institution, though the *stipulationes partis et pro parte* do not appear. 7 See the cases in Cicero, *de fin.* 2. 17. 55; 2. 18. 58. 8 The cases enforced, rightly or wrongly, by Verres seem to have been all with public objects with provision for forfeiture on failure to perform. Cicero, *Verr.* 2. 1. 10; 2. 2. 14; 2. 2. 25. Similar provisions for private purposes paved the way for recognition of *fcc.* Cicero, *de fin., cit.* 9 Inst. 2. 23. 1. 10 Inst. 2. 25. pr.

But the case was different as between *fideicommissarius* and debtors and creditors of the estate. He was not *heres*, and here the ordinary *praetor* intervened. At first, *fideicommissa* could be created by codicil, only if there was a will[1], but, before Gaius, the further step was taken of allowing codicils in which they were imposed on the *heres ab intestato*[2]. It was still held that if there was a will, codicils failed, if the will failed[3], but Severus and Caracalla provided that unconfirmed codicils preceding a will could create *fideicommissa*[4]. There were no rules of form, and thus *fideicommissa* might be oral[5].

Restraints, at first few, were gradually imposed. Peregrines, for whom they were introduced, were early excluded: Hadrian forfeited to the fisc anything so given to them[6]. The *sc. Pegasianum* subjected *fcc.* to the *ll. caducariae*[7], and Hadrian forbade them in favour of *postumi extranei* or *personae incertae*[8]. But Gaius gives a long list of distinctions which still existed[9]. They might benefit a wider class, e.g. Junian Latins and women barred by the *l. Voconia*[10]. Freedom could be given to *servi alieni* in this way, and a direction could be given that slaves under 30 should be freed at that age[11]. They might be in Greek[12], in an unconfirmed codicil, at any point in the will[13], and *post mortem heredis*[14]. Where a son or slave was made *heres*, a *fideicommissum* could be charged on the *paterfamilias*, though a legacy could not[15]. No formal words were needed: any direction would suffice—*volo, rogo, te daturum scio*, etc.—but there was no *fideicommissum* if it was clear that the testator meant it to be quite discretionary, e.g. *si volueris*[16]. Such a gift might not, however, be given *poenae causa*, in classical law[17], nor could anyone make a *fideicommissum* who had not *testamenti factio*[18].

It might be charged on any person who took a benefit by will or on intestacy, not merely the *heres*, even on a *fideicommissarius*[19], and, as it might be *post mortem*[20], even on the *heres* of the *heres*, thus providing a means of making successive gifts of the property.

The action was *in simplum*, not as in some cases of legacy, *in duplum*, and if it was not due, *condictio indebiti* lay for recovery[21]. Interest was due from *mora*, though not in legacy, except *sinendi modo*[22]. As the case

1 *Arg.* Inst. 2. 25. pr., 1. 2 G. 2. 270, 273; Ulp. 25. 4; P. 4. 1. 4. 3 29. 7. 3. 2, 7. 16. A *fc.* in a will which did not appoint a *heres* is bad as the document is void. G. 2. 248; Inst. 2. 23. 2. See however, as to *clausula codicillaris*, *post*, § CXXVI. 4 P. 4. 1. 10; Inst. 2. 25. 1. 5 P. 4. 1. 5, 6; Ulp. 25. 3. 6 G. 2. 285. Probably as they had been used to benefit *deportati*, Huschke, *ad l.* 7 G. 2. 286. 8 G. 2. 287; Ulp. 25. 13. 9 G. 2. 268–283; Ulp. 25 *passim*. 10 G. 2. 274, 275. 11 G. 2. 272, 276; Ulp. 2. 10. 12 G. 2. 281; Ulp. 25. 9. 13 G. 2. 269; Ulp. 25. 8. 14 G. 2. 277. 15 Ulp. 25. 10. 16 G. 2. 249; Ulp. 25. 1, 3; P. 4. 1. 5, 6; D. 30. 115; 32. 11. 2. It might be conditional, G. 2. 250. 17 Ulp. 25. 13. 18 Ulp. 25. 4; D. 30. 2. 19 G. 2. 271. 20 *Post*, § CXXVII. 21 G. 2. 282, 283. 22 G. 2. 280.

was tried by *cognitio* before the *praetor fideicommissarius*, an administrative procedure, not by formula[1], it could be heard at any time, even when the ordinary courts were not sitting.

Fideicommissum hereditatis was the most important case. It might be charged on a *heres* (*heres fiduciarius*) or on a prior *fideicommissarius*[2], but not on a mere legatee. It might be of the whole or part[3]. In the first case, the *heres* being still *heres*, and liable for the debts, it was usual for him to make a formal sale of the *hereditas* to the fideicommissary at a nominal price. This was followed by stipulations, *emptae et venditae hereditatis*, the *heres* undertaking to hand over all assets, and to allow the fideicommissary to sue in any actions, as *procurator* (or *cognitor*) *in rem suam*, the *fideicommissarius* undertaking to recoup anything the *heres* was compelled to pay, and to undertake any necessary defence[4]. If the *fideicommissum* was of a part, the stipulations were "*partis et pro parte*" as in *legatum partitionis*, but there was no *procuratio* to sue, or be sued[5]. This system was unsatisfactory: the *heres*, if he was to get no benefit, might abstain, and so destroy the *fideicommissum*, and if either was insolvent, the *stipulationes* would be useless.

A first attempt at a better system was the *sc. Trebellianum*, of probably A.D. 56[6]. It provided that agreements should not be necessary; the handing over of the *hereditas*, effected by any expression of intent, vested the property in the *fideicommissarius*, as praetorian owner, and the actions available at civil law, to or against the *heres*, passed to and against the *fideicommissarius*, the *heres* having an *exceptio restitutae hereditatis* if sued, and being met by one if he sued[7]. If part was transferred, the actions passed *pro rata*[8]. The *fideicommissarius* had also a *hereditatis petitio utilis*[9]. The *sc.* did not affect the civil liability; like many *scc.* it was a direction to the magistrate[10], who was to give the necessary actions and defences. Thus the *heres* was still technically liable and entitled, subject to *exceptio*, and the actions of and against *fideicommissarius* were *utiles*. The *sc.* speaks only of actions available at civil law; those

1 G. 2. 278, 279; Ulp. 25. 12. 2 G. 2. 270, 277. Only an actual beneficiary. Legacy of *dos* to wife could not be subject to *fc.* P. 4. 1. 1. It might be imposed on a *postumus*, P. 4. 1. 2. A man gave all his property to an *emancipatus* by *don. int. viv.* stipulating that the son would restore on demand or at his death to the father if alive or to his nominee. The father, *moriens*, sent an "*epistula fideicommissaria*" to the son telling him to give a sum to *X* and to free *Y*. The son was neither *heres* nor *bonorum possessor*. The *fcc.* are binding, under a rescript of Pius (32. 37. 3). The principle appears in 30. 77. The *fc.* is binding on the *heres*. It is thus *pro tanto* a release of the obligation to restore. The son is thus a beneficiary and *fcc.* can be imposed on any beneficiary on the death, even a donee *mortis causa*, 31. 77. 1. 3 G. 2. 250. 4 G. 2. 251, 252. 5 *Arg.* G. 2. 254 *in fin.* 6 See Girard, *Man.* 989. 7 G. 2. 253. 8 G. 2. 255; P. 4. 2. 9 G. 2. 253; *familiae erciscundae utilis*, 10. 2. 40. 10 See G. 2. 253; D. 36. 1. 1. 2. *Ante*, § v.

conferred by the Praetor he could deal with, without authority: we learn that they too passed, and all obligations, natural and civil[1].

This did not work well. *Heredes* still refused and destroyed the *fideicommissum*; possibly they demanded payment, and a further remedy was found in the *sc. Pegasianum* of about A.D. 73[2]. It provided that *heres rogatus* could keep a quarter, as in legacy, under the *l. Falcidia*. If he refused to enter he could be compelled, taking no benefit and incurring no liability, actions passing as under the Trebellian. Entry was not dispensed with, but compelled, no doubt by magisterial *coercitio*[3]. If he entered voluntarily and there was no case for deduction, the Trebellian applied. If he entered and deducted, the Trebellian did not apply and stipulations *partis et pro parte* were needed[4]. If there was a right to deduct, not exercised, texts conflict on the question whether stipulations were needed or not[5]. The rules applied separately to *heredes pro parte*, as under the *l. Falcidia*[6].

It was usual, perhaps necessary, to declare under which *sc.* the surrender was made[7]. This is the basis of Paul's view, with which others disagreed, that if more than three-quarters were left, but the *heres* did not mean to deduct, he could make his surrender under the Trebellian, so that actions would pass *ipso facto*[8]. The contrary view presumably rests on the proposition of the Pegasian, which can be gathered from Gaius[9], that the Trebellian was to apply only if the *fideicommissa* covered less than three-quarters.

Justinian simplified the system, repealing the Pegasian, and grafting its compulsory *aditio* and right to deduct on to the Trebellian, of which he declares his rules to be a recast[10]. He thus got rid of the notion that the case was to be dealt with as one of legacy, and actions now passed wholly or *pro rata*, with no need for stipulations. In a Novel he allowed the testator to forbid the retention of a quarter[11].

Where the testator, in directing transfer, reserved to the *heres* a thing worth one-fourth or more, instead of a share, the *heres* kept it

1 36. 1. 41. pr.; as to protection against alienations by *heres*, *post*, § CCXLV. 2 G. 2. 254, 256; Ulp. 25. 14 *sqq.*; P. 4. 3; on the lines of the *Falcidia*, P. 4. 3. 3. Apparently it did not apply till Pius to *fcc.* on intestacy, 35. 2. 18. pr. 3 G. 2. 258; Ulp. 25. 16; P. 4. 4. 2, 4. *Missio in possessionem* by decree if *heres* failed to appear, P. 4. 4. 3. If, after such entry, the *fc.* failed to operate, the *heres* was relieved by Pius. The goods were sold as if no *heres* had entered, *r. in integr.*, 42. 6. 1. 6. 4 G. 2. 257; Ulp. 25. 14, 15; P. 4. 3. 2. This rule seems to rest not on a rational basis, but, as Paul and the *Regulae* suggest, on something in the Pegasian. Probably the language of G. is that of the *sc.*, i.e. that *fcc.* should be cut down "as in legacies." There could be no question of actions passing. 5 G. 2. 257. Ulp. 25. 14; P. 4. 3. 2. If he paid when he might have deducted there was no *condictio indebiti*: it could not be said not to be due, P. 4. 3. 4. 6 G. 2. 259. 7 E.g. Ulp. 25. 14. 8 P. 4. 3. 2. 9 *Locc. citt.* 10 Inst. 2. 23. 7, "*exploso sc. Pegasiano*" to get rid of the irrational interpretations of the wording. See n. 4. 11 *Arg. Nov.* 1. 2. 2 *in f.*

and was treated as a legatee, all actions passing. If it was worth less, he could have it made up. Before Justinian this was a case for the Pegasian, and stipulations would be needed. Under him the actions passed in proportion to the necessary supplement[1].

CXXV. *Fideicommissa* of single things could be charged on any beneficiary[2]. If on a *heres* they could be cut down under the Pegasian[3], but not if charged on a legatee, there being no question of avoiding intestacy. There was no compulsion to enter on account of such *fideicommissa*, or any transfer of actions. Anything could be so left which could be left by *damnatio*[4]. Under a *fideicommissum* to buy a *res aliena* and give it, the thing must be bought or its value given, as in *legatum per damnationem*, but Gaius says that some held that, if the owner refused to sell, the gift failed[5]. Freedom might be thus given to a *servus alienus*, by directing the *heres* to buy and free, or by giving the owner something and directing him to free. In the latter case he was bound if he accepted. In the former the gift failed if the owner refused to sell[6], till Justinian provided that it should still operate if it ever became possible to buy the man[7]. Gaius says that a *fideicommissum* imposed on a legacy was void as to any excess over what the legatee took[8], but this was so only where they were commensurable quantities. A man who received a gift of money with a *fideicommissum* to hand over a *fundus* could not, after acceptance, refuse to carry out the trust because the land was worth more[9]. Finally, it is to be noted that in classical law *fideicommissa* of *singulae res* gave only a *ius in personam*[10].

Justinian, by a sweeping enactment[11], declared that for the future there should be no difference between legacies and *fideicommissa* of single things, but each kind of gift was to have all the advantages of the other. This is not easy to interpret. In *legatum per vindicationem* the legatee was entitled to *fructus* from *aditio*, as the thing was then his; in *fideicommissa*, from *mora*; in legacy by *damnatio* only from *litis contestatio*[12]. The first and most favourable of these rules was never applied under Justinian, though ownership passed at once. Again, till Justinian, *fideicommissum* had in the main been construed like legacy by *damnatio*. Thus if it had been made to two, *disiunctim*, each was entitled to the

1 Inst. 2. 23. 9. 2 G. 2. 260; Inst. 2. 24. pr., 1. 3 G. 2. 254; Inst. 2. 23. 5. G.'s language suggests that this was not in the *sc*. It may be due to Pius, who dealt with these matters. 36. 1. 1. 17, 11. 2, 12, etc. 4 Ulp. 25. 5. 5 G. 2. 262. 6 G. 2. 263, 265. In manumission there could be no question of giving the value. 7 Inst. 2. 24. 2. 8 G. 2. 261. 9 D. 31. 70. 1; 35. 2. 36. pr. Just. (C. 6. 49. 7) gave the ultimate beneficiary *actiones utiles* if evasions were attempted or the fiduciary died without successors. 10 P. 4. 1. 18. 11 C. 6. 43. 1, 2; Inst. 2. 20. 3. On a tendency in cl. law to apply to *leg.* some substantive rules of *fcc.* (G. 2. 280), Perozzi, *Ist.* 2. 671. 12 G. 2. 280; C. 6. 47. 4 (interp.). *Damnatio* gives a *strictum iudicium*, G. 2. 204; *post*, § CCXXIX.

whole[1], but under Justinian the rule of *vindicatio* was applied and they shared[2]. In his new system Justinian had a general leaning to the rules of *vindicatio*, but he often departed from them and adopted the rule he thought most rational, whether it tallied or not with the notion of giving both forms the advantages of each. Legacies had some advantages which were extended to *fideicommissa*. Thus ownership now passed at once, apart from modalities. And the rule giving double damages for denial, and refusing *condictio indebiti*, in gifts to the Church and charities, applied both to legacy and to *fideicommissum*[3].

There remained an ineffaceable difference in gifts of freedom. A *servus alienus* could be freed by *fideicommissum* but not by direct gift, and *fideicommissa* of liberty to slaves of the testator were preserved[4], though logically these should have become direct gifts. The point was that one freed directly was *libertus orcinus*, having no living patron—one freed under *fideicommissum* was the *libertus* of the fiduciary[5].

There remain one or two difficult points, postponed for convenience.

If a *fideicommissarius* was himself subject to a *fideicommissum* the question arises: could he deduct the *quarta Pegasiana*? The texts have been so altered that it is difficult to say what the answer is. On the whole the rules seem to be as follows. If the *heres* could not have deducted, the *fideicommissarius* could not. If the *heres* might, but did not, the *fideicommissarius* might, at least if the *heres* refrained in order that he might. If the *heres* had deducted, so could he, unless he was a freedman of the deceased, or there was evidence that the testator did not mean him to have such a right. The principle seems to be that as the right of the *fideicommissarius* was derived from the *heres*, he could have no right which the *heres* had not[6].

If there were legacies and the *heres* had handed over the whole estate, could *fideicommissarius* deduct the Falcidian quarter? The relative titles shew the difficulty of this question[7]. It must first be determined whether the testator meant legacies to be charged on *heres* or on *fideicommissarius*, the presumption being in favour of the latter rule, if the transfer was to be immediate. If they were to be charged on the *heres*, legacies and *fideicommissa* were treated as a whole and, if necessary, cut down *pro rata*, the *heres* keeping a quarter and there being no question of further deduction. If the *heres* entered under compulsion a *fideicommissarius* of the whole might cut down legacies to three-quarters. If they were to be charged on *fideicommissarius*, his *fideicommissum* was regarded as being of the whole, less the legacies. The *heres* kept one-

1 Vat. Fr. 85. 2 C. 6. 51. 1. 11. 3 Inst. 4. 6. 19, 26. Converse extension, *ante*, p. 348, n. 6. 4 Inst. 2. 24. 2. 5 G. 2. 266, 267; Ulp. 2. 8. 6 Chief texts, 35. 1. 43. 3; 35. 2. 25. 1, 32. 4 and 5, 47. 1; 36. 1. 1. 17, 1. 19, 57. 2, 65. 11 and 12, 80. 11. 7 D. 35. 2; 36. 1; C. 6. 49, 50.

quarter—the rest was distributed *pro rata*. Thus if the estate were 4, legacies were 3, and there was a *fideicommissum* of all, the *heres* kept one-quarter and of the rest the legatees took three-quarters, the *fideicommissarius* the rest. If the *heres* entered only under compulsion, the *fideicommissarius* would also get the quarter the *heres* would have had. There was a governing rule that the fact that *heres* entered under compulsion would not entitle legatees to more than they would have had if he had entered voluntarily. If *heres*, entering voluntarily, refused the quarter, the *fideicommissarius* would not benefit at cost of legatees, unless there was evidence that he refrained in order to benefit the *fideicommissarius*[1]. In *fideicommissa* of part there were complex cases.

Paul tells us[2] that in any *fideicommissum*, if the *heres* sold the property, the *fideicommissarius* could get *missio in possessionem* against a buyer who had notice of the trust, and the *possessio* would actually be given to him, *potestate praetoris*[3]. Justinian abolishes this system as ineffective and obscure, substituting a general hypothec in all cases of legacy or *fideicommissum*[4], and, as we have seen, making the *fideicommissum* vest the ownership in the beneficiary so that the *heres* had no right in the thing. If the *fideicommissum* was conditional or *ex die*, satisfaction of the condition or arrival of the *dies* avoided any alienation or charge which the *heres* might have effected.

In the early Empire it was common to leave lands as security for legacies of *alimenta* and the like. Papinian says that this is in effect a *fideicommissum* of the land, entitling the beneficiaries to the above *missio in possessionem*[5]. Modestinus construes in the same way a simple gift of land to provide *alimenta*[6]. But by his time a better security had appeared. Severus and Caracalla recognised, as an existing institution, an actual pledge of property for this purpose, probably confined to this kind of provision[7], valid as against any buyer, with notice or not. If the land was not enough there was a claim against the *heres* to make up the deficit[8], and presumably any surplus went to him[9]. Justinian allowed such a pledge for any legacy, over all or part of the *hereditas*, but it was

1 Discussion and reff. Poste's *Gaius*, ed. Whittuck, 250. Refusal of *heres* to enter even under Justinian's scheme may be rational. If the estate is insolvent and the fact is discovered only after entry, the *fideicommissarius* may refuse the gift and the *heres* will be liable—*semel heres semper heres*. His remedy against fideicommissary, even though the latter had previously agreed to accept, may be illusory. The inventory will protect the *heres*, but if he is to get nothing it is not worth while, as he will have to deal with all the claims.
2 P. 4. 1. 15. For Beseler, *Z.S.S.* 1930, 66, the institution is post-classical.
3 43. 4. 3. pr., giving usucapion possession.
4 C. 6. 43. 3; *Nov.* 39. pr. See, however, Klingmüller, *Z.S.S.* 1924, 216.
5 33. 1. 9. Paul's final remark refers to refusal of *heres* to give security.
6 34. 1. 4.
7 13. 7. 26. pr.; 34. 1. 12.
8 34. 1. 12.
9 *Arg.* 34. 1. 4. pr. *med.* Contrary decision due to the fact that it is construed as a gift of the property.

of little importance, in view of his more general provision in the same enactment[1] in which this is mentioned.

CXXVI. *Codicilli*. In this connexion, these are informal documents dealing with disposal of the estate on death. Their early history has been considered[2]. The main point to notice is the distinction between confirmed and unconfirmed codicils. Even in the latest law the latter could do nothing but create *fideicommissa*, while a codicil confirmed by will, even by anticipation, could do anything that a will could, except dispose of the *hereditas*[3]. Under Justinian confirmation need not be express, but might be implied[4]. A codicil was for most purposes treated as forming one document with the will[5]. It could be made by anyone with *testamenti factio*, and *postliminium* validated one made in captivity[6]. No form was needed, till Constantine required the same number of witnesses as for a will, if it imposed a *fideicommissum* on the *heres ab intestato*[7]. Theodosius extended this to all codicils[8]. Justinian required five[9], but provided that, though there were no, or not enough, witnesses, the *fideicommissarius* having first sworn to the good faith of his claim (*iusiurandum calumniae*) might put the person, supposed to be charged, to his oath that the deceased had never mentioned such a thing to him. If he refused it he must carry out the *fideicommissum*[10].

A will which failed, as such, could not be interpreted as a codicil. A text of Ulpian leaves it uncertain whether this rule could be displaced by evidence of intention[11]: other texts and an enactment of Theodosius suggest that it could be evaded by a direct expression in the will of a wish that if it failed as a will it should be good as a codicil. He provided that if there was such a clause (*clausula codicillaris*), the *institutus* might choose whether to take it as a will or as a codicil, but, unless he was a near relative, he might not change his mind[12].

The difference between a confirmed and an unconfirmed codicil means little under Justinian, legacies and *fideicommissa* being assimilated. Direct gifts of liberty could not be given by unconfirmed codicil, and it is not clear that *tutores* could thus be fully appointed.

MILITARY WILL. The privileges attaching to the will of a soldier or naval seaman[13] date from the first century of the Empire, and were settled by the earlier classical lawyers, building on vague rescripts of

1 C. 6. 43. 1, 2. 2 *Ante*, p. 354. 3 Ulp. 25. 11; D. 29. 7. 3. 2; Inst. 2. 25. 1, 2; Ulp. 25. 8. 4 29. 7. 5. 5 29. 7. 2. 2. 6 49. 15. 12. 5; 29. 7. 6. 3. 7 C. Th. 4. 4. 1. 8 C. Th. 4. 4. 7. 2. 9 C. 6. 36. 8. 3, interp. 10 Inst. 2. 23. 12; C. 6. 42. 32. A man might make more than one codicil, Inst. 2. 25. 3. 11 29. 7. 1. 12 C. Th. 4. 4. 7=C. 6. 36. 8; D. 29. 1. 3; 28. 3. 12. 1; see C. 7. 2. 11. This implies that if there was a *cl. codicillaris* manumissions were good. This is not a confirmed codicil but it seems to be so treated. 13 37. 13. 1. 1. This title specifies the persons to whom the privilege applies: all officially present in the camp, whether soldiers or not.

several emperors[1]. The privilege lasted throughout military or naval service, till Justinian limited it to the time of actual service with the colours[2]. It confirmed, subject to intent, wills made before the service began[3], and a will validly made during service remained valid for a year after discharge unless for misconduct[4]. All privilege then ended, except that the fact that a condition could not be satisfied within the year did not affect the validity of the will[5]. If the man purported to test *iure communi* the will had probably to satisfy the rules in classical law though not under Justinian[6].

No form was needed, but Trajan provided that there must be some evidence other than the word of the claimant[7]. A deaf and dumb *miles* could test[8]. A *miles* could institute from or to a certain day, and the *clausula codicillaris* was implied[9]. He was not bound by the rules of *testamenti factio*[10], *exheredatio*[11], the *querela*[12], *Falcidia*[13], or *Pegasiana*[14], and the restrictions, on *institutio*, of the *ll. caducariae* and the *l. Iunia* did not apply[15]. He could revoke his will, at civil law, by any expression[16]. He could substitute without a will[17], and even make a pupillary *substitutio* to an *emancipatus* or a *pubes*, but here the *substitutio* covered only what came from him[18]. He could be partly testate[19]. *Capitis deminutio minima* did not affect his will (even, in later classical law, if it occurred in the year after service ceased), nor did *media* or *maxima*, where it was a military punishment[20]. But in some respects his will was subject to ordinary law. He could not institute an *incerta persona*, till others could[21]. He was bound by the *ll. Aelia Sentia* and *Fufia Caninia*[22]. An *institutio captatoria* was void[23]. A *captivus miles* could not make a will[24]. Penal gifts were void in classical law[25].

If the *miles* was a *filiusfamilias*, the power applied, even under Justinian, only to *bona castrensia* and *quasicastrensia*, not to *adventitia*[26].

CXXVII. LIMITED INTERESTS AND SETTLEMENTS[27]. The desire to "found a family," to secure that the "family property" should remain in the hands of descendants in perpetuity, existed in Rome as elsewhere. The question thus arises how far a testator could "settle" his property so as to determine its devolution in the future. Apart from

1 29. 1. 1; Inst. 2. 11. 1. 2 G. 2. 106; C. 6. 21. 17. 3 Inst. 2. 11. 4. 4 29. 1. 25, 26; Ulp. 23. 10. 5 29. 1. 38. pr. 6 21. 1. 3, interp. Guarneri-Citati, *Misc. Eseg.* 17. 7 G. 2. 114; Inst. 2. 11. 1. 8 29. 1. 4; Inst. 2. 11. 2. 9 29. 1. 3 (corrupt). 10 G. 2. 109, 114; 29. 1. 13. 2. 11 29. 1. 7, 8, 33. 2; 37. 12. 1. 4. 12 5. 2. 27. 2; C. 3. 28. 37. 13 29. 1. 17. 4. 14 C. 6. 21. 12. 15 G. 2. 110, 111. 16 29. 1. 15. 1, 19. pr. 17 29. 1. 15. 5. 18 29. 1. 5, 41. 4. 19 29. 1. 6. Thus the rules of accrual did not apply, 29. 1. 37. 20 29. 1. 11, 22, 23; 28. 3. 6. 13; Inst. 2. 11. 5. Many other privileges. 21 Inst. 2. 20. 25. 22 29. 1. 29. 1. 23 C. 6. 21. 11. 24 29. 1. 10. 25 Inst. 2. 20. 36. 26 Inst. 2. 11. 6. 27 The practice of requiring the devisee, where he was not a descendant, to take the name of the testator, is ancient. Cicero, *ad Att.* 7. 8. 3.

fideicommissa the power was small in the time of Gaius. No *incerta persona* could be made *heres* or legatee and thus, though a testator could create a series of usufructs, they must all be to existing persons, or at least to persons already conceived, so that property could not be settled in this way for more than existing lives and the period of gestation. The right to institute *postumi* was not a real extension of this power. All *postumi* instituted, whether *sui*, who could be instituted at civil law, or *extranei*, who could get *bonorum possessio*, must have been born or conceived at the time of the testator's death[1]. The power to institute them was not intended to increase the power of testation and settlement, but to prevent the intestacy which would otherwise result from the agnation of a *postumus*. The rule as to *postumi extranei*, an analogous extension, carries the matter no further for the present purpose[2]: the possibility of holding over *delatio* for more than the period of gestation does not seem to have been contemplated.

Fideicommissa however afforded a means of going further. They could at first be made in favour of *incertae personae*, and, as there could be *fideicommissa* on *fideicommissa*, it was possible to burden each successive beneficiary with a trust to hand over the property at his death to his son, and so on in perpetuity[3]. We know that this was done. The will of Dasumius, A.D. 108, is still in existence[4]. It gives lands to *liberti*, with no power to alienate, with a right of accrual or survivorship, and a direction that on the death of the last survivor the lands are to go to *posteri* on the same terms. The last of these may alienate. This is substantially a complete perpetuity. It is not possible to say whether such things were usual or not. The will, or the copy which we possess, is inscribed on marble, a permanent record made perhaps on account of the permanent nature of the relations set up. In any case Hadrian forbade *fideicommissa* in favour of *incertae personae*[5], so that the power ceased.

Thereafter testators inserted in their wills directions not to alienate, usually referring to specific properties[6]. If valid they would produce

1 37. 9. 10; 38. 7. 5. 1.

2 The purpose of this praetorian extension is not quite clear. It may have been to provide for the posthumous children of *emancipati*, or a development from the rule, recognised at civil law, that the slave of a *postumus extraneus* might be instituted, for this is involved in the *institutio* of *servi hereditarii*, and is clearly recognised by Labeo for the similar case of the *institutio* by a third party of a slave forming part of the *hereditas* the person entitled to which is a *suus heres* yet unborn, 28. 5. 65. But, more probably, it rests on the fact that it was not always possible to say whether a child of a certain woman would be a *suus* or an *extraneus* of the testator. See 28. 2. 9.

3 *Fideicommissa* for transference to other than issue at death were usually in absence of issue, and if this limitation was not expressed, it was implied in later classical law. 35. 1. 102; C. 6. 42. 30.

4 Girard, *Textes*, 801; Bruns, 1. 304.

5 *Ante*, p. 354.

6 Declareuil, *Mél. Gérardin*, 135 *sqq.*, a study of the social conditions which produced these trusts. He thinks they began in arrangements for tombs and the like enforced usually by *multae*.

much the same result, but Severus and Caracalla provided that such a direction was void, unless combined with a *fideicommissum*[1]. The *fideicommissum* would usually be for members of the family: the Digest gives[2] many illustrations of such family trusts. They could not be perpetual: they were not, it would seem, binding in classical law except for donees alive at the testator's death and their immediate issue[3]. Such restrictions seem to have had effect *in rem*, i.e. they not merely imposed a duty on the *heres* and his successors, but they vitiated any sale by the fiduciary, at any rate if there was an express prohibition of sale[4]. In the absence of such prohibition there was the *missio in possessionem* against a buyer with notice, already dealt with, abolished by Justinian as ineffective and obscure[5]. Under Justinian, all property subject to a *fideicommissum* was by that fact rendered inalienable[6].

Another change under Justinian was of much greater importance. Gifts of all kinds could now be made to *incertae personae*[7], but as *institutiones* were still confined to persons conceived at the time of the death[8], and *ususfructus sine persona esse non potest*[9], neither of these could establish perpetuities. But, as in the time before Hadrian, *fideicommissa* were available and were used for the purpose. It was possible to direct the *heres* to hand over the property on his death to his son, the latter to do the same and so on for ever. The difficulty, of the quarter which the *heres* might keep, could be met by reservation, and in any case Justinian allowed the testator to override this[10]. In a Novel[11], Justinian states and decides a case of this kind. Hierius had given specific estates, each to a different son, on the terms that he was not to alienate it away from his name and family. Those who had issue were to leave it to them, the shares of those without issue going to the survivors on the same terms. In a codicil[12] he gave land to a grandson, on similar terms, but adding a direction that it was to remain for ever in the family, thus, unlike the will, creating a perpetuity. The grandson obeyed the directions, but his son left the property, under conditions which occurred, to his wife and mother jointly. A surviving *heres* of the original testator claimed the property on the ground that the wife and mother were not

1 30. 114. 14. 2 30. 114. 15; 31. 67. 3, 88. 16; 36. 1. 76, etc.; Buckland, *Equity in R.L.* 83. 3 31. 32. 6. 4 31. 69. 1; 32. 38. 3, etc. But see Beseler, *Beitr.* 2. 77 on 30. 114. 14. Security could be required from anyone taking under such a *fc.*, to carry out its further purpose, 31. 67. 6. 5 *Ante*, p. 359. P. 4. 1. 15; C. 6. 43. 3. 2. This *missio* was not apparently available against devisees, who indeed (Declareuil, p. 142) were subject to the trust. 6 *Ante*, p. 359; C. 6. 43. 3. 2 a. At about the same time he made the testator's prohibition of alienation operative *in rem*, C. 4. 51. 7. 7 C. 6. 48. 1. 8 C. 6. 48. 1. 2. 9 Vat. Fr. 55; D. 45. 3. 26. 10 *Ante*, p. 356. 11 *Nov.* 159. 12 Hierius' will may have been made before the enactment authorising gifts to *incertae personae* and the codicil after.

of the family. The decision was that, for the purpose, they were, so that there had been no breach. Justinian then decided, or rather enacted, that it had been going on long enough, that the present holders might do as they liked with the property, and that for the future no such prohibition was to hold good for more than four generations[1].

Note on the conception of *hereditas*

Several texts speak of *hereditas* as *successio in universum ius defuncti*[2]. It has been shewn[3] that the notion of singular succession is not classical and thus that the expression "universal succession" is unnecessary: there is only one kind of "*successio*". But criticism has not stopped there[4]. It expunges the word *universum* from the texts on the ground that the *hereditas* is not thought of in classical law as an ideal unit consisting of a mass of rights, partly because it also includes duties and partly because it does not include all the rights, so that *universum* is incorrect. Yet it still apparently conceives of *hereditas* as an ideal unit, though in a different sense; it is the succession to the *ius* of the deceased, to his juristic position. But the *heres* does not succeed to the *ius* in this sense any more completely than he does to *universum ius* in the sense of all the rights.

The classical lawyers, starting from the idea of the *hereditas* as a mere assembly of rights, which is probably all that Gaius means by *per universitatem* (his theoretical concepts seem to have been derived from a much earlier writer) are more likely to have reached the idea of an ideal unit comprising all these rights than to have passed without that idea to the highly abstract notion of a man's juristic position as a legal unit.

1 This became the common law of "fideicommissary substitutions" in the countries governed by Roman Law. See Strickland *v.* Strickland [1908] A.C. 551. 2 29. 2. 37; 50. 16. 24, 119, 208; 50. 17. 62, 128, 1. 3 C. Longo, *St. Fadda* I, 125 *sqq.* 4 E.g. by Solazzi, 178. 1, *Dir. ered. rom.* I, 199 *sqq.*

CHAPTER IX

THE LAW OF SUCCESSION. INTESTACY. *BONORUM POSSESSIO.* SUCCESSION NOT ON DEATH

CXXVIII. The subject of Intestacy is, in one sense, or even two, of minor importance. Long before classical times intestacy had become unusual, indeed a misfortune, and as early as Plautus[1] a feeling had developed which has been called, with some exaggeration[2], a horror of intestacy. The artificial state of the law of succession on intestacy is hardly an adequate explanation. There have been many attempts to explain it, but they are little more than conjectures: here as elsewhere it is difficult to be sure of the historical origin of a social sentiment. It may be that, as has been said, the feeling is at bottom religious: a *heres ab intestato* could, by *cessio hereditatis*, shift the *sacra* to the care of another, uninterested person, a *heres ex testamento* could not[3].

A second point of view from which the subject can be regarded as unimportant is that of its juristic value. Apart from a few main principles, it is a mass of detail, throwing little light on other parts of the law, and for this reason it will be treated briefly.

Many of the subsidiary rules of succession applied in intestacy as well as to succession by will, e.g. the rules as to modes of acceptance[4], *beneficium abstinendi*, *spatium deliberandi*, inventory, *fideicommissa*, *here-*

1 *Curculio*, 5. 2. 24. 2 Maine, *Ancient Law*, 223. See Radin, *Roman Law*, 414.
3 See e.g. Accarias, *Précis*, 1. 840. 4 G. 2. 167, 3. 62, 3. 85 shew that *cretio* was the formal mode of entry on intestacy.

ditas iacens, ius accrescendi, sc. Pegasianum, etc.[1] But the *ll. caducariae* did not apply[2]. Even if they had they would have been of less importance, since almost all relatives were so far excepted that they could take their share, and the *heres* on intestacy would be a relative. But they did not: where an agnate refused, accrual existed in favour of the others in the same degree, whether they were married or not[3], while under a will they would have been excluded from sharing in *caduca* or the like. And, in intestacy, there could be no *servus heres necessarius*.

As has been said, while the old *collatio bonorum* applied in intestacy, it had lost most of its importance in later law. But a new kind of *collatio* appeared. The old *collatio* turned on the notion that the *emancipatus* had means of acquiring property, denied to the *filiusfamilias*, but *collatio dotis*, which might be required from a daughter in *potestas*[4], introduced two new ideas: the person making *collatio* might be in the family, and the fund out of which it was made commonly came from the father. Hence the new form of *collatio*. It was a gradual growth: under Justinian it was a rule that any descendant claiming to succeed to any ascendant must bring in for division (*conferre*) anything which had been received from the deceased by way of *dos* or *donatio propter nuptias*, or to set him up in life[5]. Till Justinian it had applied only on intestacy, but in a novel he extended it to wills: the descendant could not claim the gift without bringing in these previous benefits[6].

The succession might not be immediate on the death. The significant date was not the death, but that on which the succession "opened," the date on which it was clear that there would not be any *heres* under any will[7]. This might not be till long after the death. A *heres institutus* might refuse only at the end of the *spatium deliberandi*, or it might be long before it was clear that the condition on an *institutio* would not be fulfilled. The importance of the opening of the succession was that the person entitled at that date took, though he may not have been the nearest at the time of death[8]. If *A*'s brother survived him, but died before the *institutus* had refused, his cousin might be *A*'s nearest agnate, though he was not when *A* died. But the date of death was material: no one could succeed on intestacy unless born or conceived at the time of the death[9]. *Postumi* could claim, as under wills, and one in respect of whom *anniculi probatio* or *erroris causae probatio* was made or com-

1 G. 2. 157, 158; Inst. 3. 2. 7; C. 6. 30. 22. pr., 1 a; Ulp. 26. 5. D. 36. 1. 1. 5 says that the Trebellian applied. This seems to be due to Pius (*ante*, p. 356): the *sc.* spoke of *scriptus heres* (G. 2. 255 *sqq.*). 2 Ulp. 17. 1. 3 P. 4. 8. 22 *sqq.*; Ulp. 26. 5. 4 D. 37. 7; C. 6. 20. 5 C. 6. 20. 17, 20. 1. 6 *Nov.* 18. 6. Unsatisfactory reason for the extension assigned that the testator in haste may have forgotten these gifts. Earlier legislation on this form of *collatio*, C. 6. 20. 17–21. 7 Inst. 3. 1. 7; D. 38. 16. 2. 6. 8 G. 3. 11; Inst. 3. 1. 7. 9 37. 9. 7. pr.; 37. 11. 3.

pleted after the death, had the same right[1]. A child given in adoption might be emancipated and so become an *emancipatus* of the deceased after the opening. It does not appear that he had any claim[2].

The rules of succession on intestacy underwent constant change, nearly always in one direction. A system resting absolutely on agnation was gradually superseded, at first under the Edict, but, at least as early as Hadrian, through express legislation, by one in which natural blood relationship was more and more regarded, till in Justinian's final legislation, in the Novels[3], there was no longer any trace of the old civil law notions. The earliest rules we know are those of the XII Tables, and though in the Empire these were largely superseded, the later changes can scarcely be understood without some knowledge of them. Indeed it was not till Justinian's final legislation that all trace of them disappeared.

In the Institutes the order stated in the XII Tables is taken as the basis of treatment, and an attempt is made to state the development of the law by discussing the changes made in each class in turn, substituting cognatic succession for that of *gentiles*. But for brevity and clearness it seems better to take the law in periods, a method which coincides closely in effect with that of treatment of the changes in relation to the agency by which they were effected, for the progressive praetorian changes were almost over when imperial changes began[4].

CXXIX. SUCCESSION TO *INGENUI* UNDER THE XII TABLES. The order of succession is:

1. *Sui heredes*[5]. These were such persons as, having been in the *potestas* of the deceased, became *sui iuris* by his death. It was immaterial whether they were natural or adoptive[6]. Grandchildren by a son, and remoter issue generally, through males, were *sui heredes* if the intervening links were dead or out of the family, and they took the share that their father would have taken[7]. *Postumi* were included and, as we have seen, there were other similar cases, e.g. children in respect of whom there

1 G. 3. 5; Coll. 16. 2. 5; 16. 3. 7. 2 I.e. under the classical law of *Adoptio*. 3 *Novv*. 118, 127. 4 Where two died in the same catastrophe it was often important, for succession, to determine which died last. Cl. law seems to have had no presumptions in the matter. Where father and son were killed in a battle, Hadrian decided that the father must be held to have died first (34. 5. 9. 1). But several texts in the D. lay down presumptions. A *libertus* and his son die "*simul*"—the father is held to have died last (h. l. 2). Man and wife die "*simul*"—the husband is held to have died last (h. l. 3) A man and his son die together—a *pubes* son is held to have died last, an *impubes* first, (h. l. 4). The same is said as to mother and son (h. t. 22, 23). But certainly in some, and perhaps in all, cases the generality of the rule is due to the compilers. Other texts leave the matter to the ordinary rules of proof, e.g. 34. 5. 9. pr.; 36. 1. 18. 7; Cuq, *Man*. 898; Donatuti, *Le Praesumptiones iuris*, 22. 5 Inst. 3. 1. 1. On the whole matter of early succession, Siber, *cit.*, *ante*, p. 283. 6 G. 3. 2; Coll. 16. 2. 2. 7 G. 3. 8, by *iuris interpretatio*, G. 3. 15.

had been *anniculi* or *erroris causae probatio*, since the death[1]. On the same footing was a son, who having been *in mancipio* to a third person, after a first or second sale, was released from it after the father's death[2]. If it had been after the third sale, the agnatic tie being destroyed, there would be no claim[3]. As we know, *sui heredes* were *necessarii*: they were *heredes* without acceptance, and they could not refuse. For Gaius they were not so much acquiring a new property as succeeding to the administration of what was in a sense theirs already, this being, he says, the import of the name *suus heres*[4]. It is noticeable that the XII Tables do not expressly lay down the right of succession of *sui heredes*: it is assumed in the famous text: "*si intestato moritur cui suus heres nec escit, agnatus proximus familiam habeto*[5]." The fact that they were called *sui heredes* implies other *heredes* not *sui*. These were probably the *heredes scripti* under the Comitial will, though this is controverted[6].

2. *Proximus Agnatus*. This right is expressed in the text above printed. It will be recalled that agnation is the tie connecting those related to each other, naturally or by adoption, by legitimate descents from a male through males, unbroken by *capitis deminutio*[7], including *postumi*. The nearest agnates, if more than one, took equally (*per capita*): there was no representation[8]. Unlike the *sui*, agnates had discretion to accept or refuse[9]. They were not *heredes* till actual acceptance, which was no doubt in early law by formal *cretio*, but in the law of the Empire it is clear that informal *pro herede gestio* did as well, and probable that *cretio* was unusual.

The *agnati* are not described as *heredes*: the words are not "*heres esto*," but "*familiam habeto*." This is usually interpreted to mean that the agnate did not at first become *heres*: he was not personally liable for debts or *sacra*, and when in course of time he did so become liable he came to be considered as *heres*. This view is indeed controverted[10]: in any case *agnatus proximus* was *heres* long before the Empire.

The word "*proximus*" is a limit: only the nearest agnate had any right under the XII Tables. If he refused, the claim did not pass to the next[11]. On the other hand, the nearest took, however remote[12]: there was

1 G. 3. 5; Coll. 16. 2. 5. 2 G. 3. 6; Coll. 16. 2. 6. 3 Other cases, Accarias, *Précis*, 1. 1158. 4 G. 2. 157; Inst. 2. 19. 2. Karlowa, *R.Rg.* 2. 880. It is also said that *suus* here = *eius*—agnates were not, strictly, *heredes* at all under the Tables. 5 XII Tables, 5. 4; Bruns, 1. 23; Girard, *Textes*, 14. 6 *Ante*, p. 283. 7 It may be created by *capitis deminutio*, e.g. *adrogatio*, *adoptio* and even *legitimatio*. For *captivi, restituti*, etc., Accarias, *op. cit.* 1. 1165. 8 G. 3. 15; Inst. 3. 2. 5. 9 Inst. 2. 19. 5; 3. 2. 7; G. 3. 12. 10 Lenel, *Essays in Legal Hist.*, ed. Vinogradoff, 120 *sqq.*, holds that the words *heres esto* were avoided lest they should make the agnate a *necessarius*, that he was a true *heres*, but became so only when he had actually taken possession. See, however, Bonfante, *Bull.* 1914, 97 *sqq.*; Buckland, *L.Q.R.* 1916, 97 *sqq.* 11 Inst. 3. 2. 7. 12 Arangio Ruiz (*Ist.* 393) suggests that the limit which we know for *cognatio* (*post*, § cxxx) applied originally to agnates.

no arbitrary limit of remoteness such as we shall see in the praetorian scheme. But, late in the Republic, a remarkable restriction appeared: no woman could succeed as an agnate except a *consanguinea*, a sister, a rule which kept the property on the male side of the family[1] and was, so far, an expression of the agnatic idea, and an exception to the general tendency of change. The rule was said to be based on "*Voconiana ratio*" and is obviously similar in principle to the rule of the *l. Voconia* (168 B.C.) by which a person in the first class of the *census* was forbidden to institute a woman as his *heres*[2]. It is a civil law rule, but nothing is known as to the date of its appearance. The earliest reference we have is by Gaius, but it was clearly no novelty[3]. The language of Paul[4] suggests, but does not prove, that it was subsequent to the *l. Voconia*[5].

3. *Gentiles.* The XII Tables, after dealing with *proximus agnatus*, said: "*si agnatus nec escit, gentiles familiam habento*[6]." This rule was so early obsolete—there is no trace of it in classical law—that we need not discuss the nature of a *gens*, or the question whether the *gentiles* took in common or as individuals[7]. From the language of the text it seems that it was only in the absence of agnates that the *gentiles* took, not on their refusal, and also it is not quite clear that they were regarded in strictness as *heredes*. There is evidence from Cicero[8] that the case was rather looked at as one of return to a common stock, a conception which also colours some of the texts which deal with agnatic succession[9].

The language of the XII Tables is interesting from another point of view: it expresses a striking principle of the old law of succession. It admits neither *successio graduum* nor *successio ordinum*. If the nearest in a class did not take (the point arose only in connexion with agnates, for there was no question of refusal among *sui heredes*) the text excludes the next: *proximus agnatus familiam habeto*. These words give no right to any but *proximus*, and whether, as some hold[10], agnatic succession was introduced by the XII Tables, or not, that enactment was always regarded as expressing the fundamental law of the matter. Thus there was no *successio graduum*, and, if we are to follow the text, a refusal by the agnates did not let in the *gentiles*: it was only if there were none that

1 The rule might seem to exclude agnates altogether where it applied, for a remoter male would not be *proximus agnatus*. But the point of view is that women agnates are excluded altogether: *consanguinei* are treated as a distinct and prior class (see e.g. 38. 16. 2. pr., 1) so that agnate means male agnate.
2 *Ante*, p. 289.
3 G. 3. 14. See also Inst. 3. 2. 3 a "*media iurisprudentia...imperiali sanctione anterior*."
4 P. 4. 8. 20.
5 Karlowa, *R.Rg.* 2. 883.
6 XII Tables, 5. 5; Girard, *Textes*, 14; Bruns, 1. 23.
7 Karlowa, *R.Rg.* 2. 884; Cuq, *Man.* 718; De Francisci, *Storia*, 1. 106.
8 *De or.* 1. 39. 176.
9 Cuq, *Institutions juridiques*, 1. 290, who besides literary texts cites 31. 69. pr.; 38. 10. 10. pr.
10 E.g. Muirhead, *Roman Law*, § 32; Michon, *N.R.H.* 1921, 119 and reff.

the *gentiles* came in: *si agnatus nec escit*. There was no *successio ordinum*. As we shall see, the methods of later law were different.

CXXX. THE PRAETORIAN SCHEME OF SUCCESSION. It must be borne in mind that the Praetor could not give the *hereditas*. He gave *bonorum possessio*: his Edict declared that in the absence of a will he would give *bonorum possessio* to claimants under certain rules, in a certain order. The nature and effect of this will be considered later[1]. For the present we are concerned only with the order. This is:

1. *Liberi*. These included *sui heredes*, *emancipati*, children of deceased *emancipati*, children left in a family from which the deceased had passed by *emancipatio*[2], substantially, those who could claim *bonorum possessio contra tabulas* if a will failed to provide for them[3]. In the praetorian scheme the distribution among *liberi* was a more complex matter than that among *sui* at civil law. They took, in general, *per stirpes*, the nearer excluding the more remote, but when the Praetor admitted *emancipati*, it is obvious that their claims and those of any children they had left in the family would clash. Logically it would seem that the rule should have been that if the emancipated son claimed, his children should be excluded. But they were *sui*, and a special Edict so far respected their right as to make them share with their father[4]. It is a remarkable fact that this rule was not laid down till the time of Julian: it is the only clause which he is known to have added to the Edict[5]. The rule had the result that, as the coming in of the father injured no *heres* except his own children, since he merely took part of their share, he had no *collatio* to make in respect of other *sui*, but only as against these children[6].

2. *Legitimi*. As its name shews, this class covered those only who had a statutory claim. The main case was the agnate, but there were many others, details of which will be considered later[7]. As in this class only those with a civil claim were admitted, there was no question of *successio graduum*: refusal by the nearest agnate did not let in the next, though, according to Gaius[8], some jurists, inspired no doubt by the Praetor's practice in *cognatio*, took the contrary view. But it was no part of the Praetor's policy to extend the operation of the agnatic idea[9].

3. *Cognati*. Failing claimants under earlier heads the Praetor gave *bonorum possessio* to the nearest cognates[10], ignoring the *gentiles*. Cog-

1 *Post*, §§ cxxxv *sqq*. 2 Ulp. 28. 7, 8; Inst. 3. 1. 9 *sqq*. 3 Not exactly the same class. It did not cover children given in adoption and still in another family, though these under certain conditions could get the benefit of *b. p. contra tabulas*, 37. 4. 8. 11; *ante*, p. 325. 4 37. 8. 1. pr.; h. t. 3. 5 37. 8. 3. 6 37. 8. 1. pr. *in f*. 7 *Post*, § cxxxv. 8 G. 3. 28. 9 As to *b. p. unde decem personae*, *post*, § cxxxv. 10 38. 8. 1. pr. The confusing language of Inst. 3. 6. 11, 12 seems to mean that some who are cognates, but not the nearest, may nevertheless be entitled in preference to the nearest

nation was, broadly, any blood relationship. It covered therefore relatives through females, agnates who had not claimed as such, those who would be agnates, but for an *emancipatio*, children given in adoption[1], female agnates remoter than sisters, and even illegitimate children, in succession to the mother or her cognates, or *vice versa*, or to each other[2]. Although *cognatio* was a natural tie, it covered adoptive relatives so long as the artificial agnatic tie existed, but, if that was broken, e.g. by *emancipatio*, the cognatic tie also was destroyed[3], even where the breach occurred after the death, but before the claim[4].

The nearest was entitled, and if there were more than one they shared *per capita*[5]: there was no representation of deceased *cognati* by their children. But there was an arbitrary limitation of remoteness, similar to, but not the same as, the excepted cases under the *l. Furia testamentaria*[6], and the *l. Cincia*[7]. No one could succeed as a cognate who was beyond the sixth degree of relationship, or, in one case, the seventh, a second cousin once removed, i.e. the child of a second cousin[8]

Here the Praetor allowed full play to *successio graduum* and *ordinum*. If the *legitimi* refused, the cognates might claim, *successio ordinum*[9]. It might well happen that those included in one class might also be covered by another, so that they had two chances to claim. Thus, *sui* who had failed to claim as *liberi* might still be entitled as *legitimi* or *cognati*[10]. As to *successio graduum* he applied in general, apart from the case of *legitimi*, the same principle. If the nearest *cognati* allowed the time to pass, or if they refused, the next *cognati* might claim[11].

4. *Vir et uxor*[12]. In the absence of claims of blood relatives the Praetor gave *bonorum possessio* to husband and wife reciprocally. This applied essentially to civil marriage without *manus*, since a wife *in manu* came under the head of *liberi*. But the law of succession before Justinian went no further. *Dos*, and *donatio ante nuptias*, frequently supplemented or replaced by a legacy of usufruct[13], no doubt did what was necessary. We have already considered Justinian's rules as to widows without *dos*[14].

It must be noted that the foregoing is merely an outline of that part

cognates, e.g. remote descendants, *unde liberi*, cousins, *unde legitimi*. If, however, they fail to claim under these heads within the time allowed, the priorities of *cognatio* will apply.

1 G. 3. 31. 2 38. 8. 2, 5. *Milites* could not marry while on service: if they purported to do so, children had no right of succession to the father. Hadrian allowed them to claim as *cognati*. See the rescript in Girard, *Textes*, 195. 3 38. 8. 1. 4. 4 38. 8. 1. 6, 7, 3. 5 38. 8. 1. 10. 6 G. 2. 225; Vat. Fr. 298 *sqq*. 7 *Ante*, 254. Perozzi, *St. Brugi*, 267, notes that these limits vary in different branches of law and that the variations seem arbitrary. 8 38. 8. 1. 3; Inst. 3. 5. 5. 9 38. 9. 1. pr. 10 38. 9. 1. 11. 11 38. 9. 1. 6, 1. 10. Not where a prior cognate had accepted, and received *restitutio in integrum*, h. t. 2. There was a *caducum*. 12 38. 11. 1. 13 See, e.g., Vat. Fr. 58, 69, 86–88. 14 *Ante*, p. 327.

of the Praetor's scheme which dealt with *ingenui*, and, even so, it is incomplete. The actual order is much more complex[1].

CXXXI. IMPERIAL CHANGES BEFORE JUSTINIAN. Apart from *privilegia*, e.g. that by which Claudius gave a mother who had lost her children their property[2], the legislation on *causae probatio*, etc.[3], creating new classes of *sui*, and that on succession to *liberti*, to be considered later, there was no intervention by legislation till the second century.

The earlier law of succession on intestacy is stated almost entirely from the point of view of the *paterfamilias*, the rules of succession to a woman being, in fact, implicit in what is said. The results arrived at were so unjust that it is not surprising to find that the legislation which now began was largely concerned with claims of, or to the property of, women. The earliest dealt with succession between mother and child.

Sc. Tertullianum. At civil law a mother, if not *in manu* of her husband, had no claim: even at praetorian law she was only a cognate. This enactment, under Hadrian[4], dealing however only with mothers who had the *ius liberorum*, much improved her position. This *ius* rests on her having had three children (for a *libertina*, four) by separate births, their survival being immaterial[5]. The order established by the senatusconsult[6] was (1) *sui heredes*, and those grouped with them, i.e. *liberi*; (2) the father, whether *parens manumissor* or not, provided he was not in another family; (3) consanguineous brothers and sisters, taking together; (4) mother and sisters, the mother taking half. The deceased child need not have been legitimate[7], and the mother did not lose her right by a *capitis deminutio*[8]. These rules were changed from time to time[9]. Constantine improved the mother's position; in particular he gave her a reduced share even if she had not the *ius liberorum*[10], and there was further legislation of similar tendency in A.D. 369 and 426[11].

While the order under the *sc.* differed widely from that under the earlier rules, it left these unaffected. The *sc.* did not supersede the older law, on which the rules, a direct creation of the enactment, in no way depended. There were near relatives who had rights of succession who were not mentioned in the *sc.* What rule was to be applied if, in the given case, there were such persons? The answer is to be found in two governing principles which controlled the operation of the enactment. The first was that it was to be applied only where the claimants were those whom it mentioned, i.e. not if there existed a claimant not mentioned in its order, who would, apart from it, take before any person

1 *Post*, § CXXXV. 2 Inst. 3. 3. 1. 3 *Ante*, pp. 95, 96. 4 Inst. 3. 3. 2. 5 P. 4. 9. 1; 4. 9. 9. 6 Ulp. 26. 8. 7 Inst. 3. 3. 7. 8 Inst. 3. 4. 2. 9 Inst. 3. 3. 3. 10 C. Th. 5. 1. 1. 11 C. Th. 5. 1. 2; h. t. 7. Justinian's changes, *post*, § CXXXII.

entitled under it[1]. The second, even more important, was that the enactment was not to give any person other than the mother any greater rights than he or she had under earlier law[2]. If in the given case there were persons who, on the terms of the *sc.*, would be preferred to the mother, the enactment was not applied: the earlier law governed.

Illustrations in the texts must be handled cautiously: it may be uncertain whether the decision is that of the original author or has been edited by Justinian in view of his changes. A grandfather emancipated a grandson, who died, leaving surviving his father and mother and this grandfather. The grandfather as *parens manumissor* had the prior claim apart from the *sc.*, and even under it the father excluded the mother, so that the common law applied and the grandfather took, as *parens manumissor*—quasi patron[3]. A man died leaving a mother, an agnatic cousin, and a father given in adoption into another family. Agnates are not mentioned in the enactment, as recorded, but the reference to brothers and sisters was understood as amounting to exclusion of remoter agnates[4]. The mother excluded both the agnates and the father, who, being in another family, was not preferred in the *sc.*[5]

Sc. Orphitianum[6]. Children had no civil law right of succession to their mother and were only cognates under praetorian law. This enactment, of A.D. 178[7], gave them the first claim[8] in succession to the mother. They need not be legitimate, provided they were freeborn[9], and the right was not lost by *capitis deminutio*[10].

Where a woman died leaving mother and children there might be difficulties in applying these *scc.* If there was a person whose claim, under the scheme of the Tertullian, was preferred to that of the mother, e.g. a brother, the children took the property as of course, for, as brothers excluded the mother, the Tertullian did not apply and the Orphitian gave the succession to the children. But if there was no other claim than those of mother and child, their rights as cognates were equal under praetorian law, and neither had any right at civil law. The Tertullian, alone, would give the property to the mother (for the children of a woman were not *liberi* in the technical sense): the Orphitian, alone, would give it to the children. Accordingly they shared, until, in the later Empire, it was provided that children should succeed to the mother notwithstanding anything in the *sc. Tertullianum*[11].

It is at first surprising that the rule that children succeed in first instance to the mother comes historically later than the provision for

1 Inst. 3. 3. 3, "*scilicet cum inter eos solos de hereditate agitur*"; unless those with a prior claim renounced, 38. 17. 2. 8, 10. 2 See, e.g., 38. 17. 2. 20. 3 38. 17. 5. 2. 4 See Inst. 3. 3. 5. 5 38. 17. 2. 17. 6 Ulp. 26. 7; Inst. 3. 4. 7 Inst. 3. 4. pr. 8 Excluding the patron. Schulz, *ad* Ulp. 29. 2 in his edition. Cp. C. 6. 57. 6. 9 Inst. 3. 4. 3. 10 Inst. 3. 4. 2. 11 C. 6. 55. 11.

a rarer case, that of the mother succeeding to her children. The explanation is that the two pieces of legislation rest on quite different ideas. The Tertullian is a late part of the legislation for the encouragement of marriage of which the *ll. caducariae* are the best known part. The Orphitian is an early part of that legislation which ultimately superseded the agnatic idea altogether, so far as intestacy was concerned.

The *sc. Orphitianum* gave no rights to remoter issue. This was remedied by legislation of A.D. 389, which provided, on the one hand, for grandchildren of a man through a deceased daughter, and on the other, for grandchildren of a woman through a son or a daughter. In the first case they were to take two-thirds of the share their mother would have taken, as against surviving *sui heredes*, and three-quarters of the estate as against agnates. The rule was similar in the second case, except that it is not clear that there was any deduction for surviving children of the grandmother, though there was for agnates[1].

The law of agnation underwent a change consistent with the course of earlier legislation, though not with the true principle of agnation. Anastasius (A.D. 491–518) allowed emancipated brothers and sisters to succeed as agnates, subject to a deduction if there were unemancipated persons of the same class[2]. The terms in which Theophilus tells us of this deduction are obscure[3], but it seems to have been of one-third. The rule applied of course only to brothers and sisters by the same father, and it did not benefit children of deceased brothers and sisters[4].

CXXXII. THE RULES OF THE INSTITUTES. The changes made by Justinian, before the great reform in the Novels, can hardly be called a system. A number of small changes were made, always in the direction of rationalisation, but they were unsystematic and tentative and may well have rendered the law even more confusing and complicated than it was before. The chief changes were the following:

Grandchildren of or through a woman now took the whole estate as against agnates, and the rule was extended to great-grandchildren. There was still a deduction of one-third in favour of *sui heredes*[5].

The *sc. Tertullianum* was remodelled. The *ius liberorum* was obsolete and the mother shared with the brothers, taking a *pars virilis*, instead of being excluded by them[6].

The exclusion of female agnates beyond sisters was abolished[7], and *successio graduum* was introduced—if the *proximus* refused, the next could take[8]. The deduction where emancipated brothers and sisters claimed with agnates was removed[9] and the right extended to their

1 C. Th. 5. 1. 4. 2 Inst. 3. 5. 1. 3 *Ad* Inst. 3. 5. 1. 4 Inst. *ib.*
5 Inst. 3. 4. 1; C. 6. 55. 12. 6 Inst. 3. 3. 4, 5; C. 8. 58. 2. 7 Inst. 3. 2. 3; C. 6. 58. 14. 8 Inst. 3. 2. 7. 9 C. 6. 58. 15. 1.

children, to brothers and sisters by the same mother, and to their children[1].

The most significant change was the recognition of *cognatio servilis.* Even in classical law, in interpreting wills, the word "*filius*" had been held to cover a son now free but born in slavery, where the facts shewed this to be the meaning[2], but such persons had no claim on intestacy. Justinian however provided that a freedman's children were to exclude the patron, whether they were freed before or after or with the father, or born free, and similar rights of succession were given to them[3] *inter se*, and to the parents to them, but no further.

THE SYSTEM OF THE NOVELS[4]. Ten years after the publication of the Institutes, a new system of rules was introduced, with the aim, as Justinian tells us, of doing away with the old unfair distinctions between male and female. The rules abandon the old notions: there is no word of *sui* or *agnati* or *cognati*. The rules look modern and have indeed found their way, of course much modified, into many modern legislations. The order of succession is, shortly, as follows:

1. Descendants, without distinction of sex, remoter issue taking their deceased parents' share.

2. Ascendants, the nearer excluding the more remote. Of several in the same degree, but in different lines, each line took half, irrespective of number. Brothers and sisters of the whole blood shared with ascendants[5], and it seems that all took equally. Children of deceased brothers and sisters represented their parents if there survived a brother or sister with whom to take, i.e. representation was allowed if there was some existing person to keep the class alive. Thus if *X* left father[6], brother, and nephew by a deceased brother, each took a third. If *X* left a father and a nephew, the father took all. If he left only a number of nephews by different brothers and sisters, all dead, the nephews took equally: if a brother survived, what did not go to him was divided *per stirpes.*

3. Brothers and sisters, with the same rule of representation.

4. Half brothers and sisters, with the same rule. But if there were half brothers or sisters and also children of deceased brothers or sisters, the latter took.

5. The nearest relatives, *per capita*, with no representation.

6. Husband or wife reciprocally[7].

If there was no claim, the property passed to the *Fiscus*[8], subject to the claims of creditors, but this is not a case of succession.

1 H. l. 2. 2 28. 8. 11. The text has been altered. 3 Inst. 3. 6. 10; C. 6. 4. 4. See *Nov.* 18. 5 as to a limited right of succession to children by a *concubina*, not legitimated. 4 *Novv.* 118, 127. 5 The ascendant has no usufruct, *Nov.* 118. 2; *ante*, p. 280. 6 *Nov.* 127. 1. 7 Not stated in the Novel, but dealt with in Bas. 45. 5. 8 Another body sometimes preferred, Brugi, *Ist.* 641.

CXXXIII. It will be convenient to place here, by way of appendix, some account of the rights of succession of the father, or *paterfamilias*, in the various possible circumstances.

1. The father of one who died in *potestas*. Apart from the cases of the *adrogatus impubes*, and the *adoptatus* under Justinian, already sufficiently stated[1], there are only the cases of *peculia castrense* and *quasi-castrense* and *bona adventitia* to be considered. The actual destination of the *peculia castrense* and *quasi* has been considered[2], and the only question here is whether, under Justinian, the father, if he took them, took them as *peculium* or as *hereditas*. Justinian says that it was "*iure communi*." Does this mean as inheritance, which, it is said, had before Justinian's time become the method of treating *bona adventitia*[3], or does it mean that, in absence of preferred claims, they reverted as *peculium*? The main arguments for the former view are the alleged fact, that *bona adventitia* were already so treated, that the words do not suggest that the father was to take in any way different from that in which the children took, and that the beneficiaries are called *parentes*, and not *patresfamilias*. In favour of the other view are the texts in the Digest, which treat it as reversion of *peculium*[4], and the fact that Theophilus in his Paraphrase of the Institutes so regards it[5]. But these may possibly be mere survivals: neither view can be considered certain.

In *bona adventitia* there was no question of succession till the fifth century. If the child died they reverted to the *pater* as *peculium*, and perhaps did so in absence of preferred claims till Justinian. But by the time of Theodosius the fund covered all successions from the mother, all successions and gifts from a maternal ascendant, and gifts from husband and wife of the child[6]. There were provisions reserving to children of any marriage on death of either parent what had come from the other parent by way of *dos*, *donatio*, or other gratuitous acquisition[7]. Theodosius provided that all these were to go to the children of the deceased child as *hereditas* and not to *pater* or *avus* as *peculium*[8]. In 472 brothers and sisters were also preferred, with distinctions as to whole and half blood[9]. Justinian extended the rule to all acquisitions other than those from the *pater*, and it is clear that it was now succession, for he provided that if the father was himself in *potestas*, it was he who took it, and not the *avus*: in the hands of the father it was *bona adventitia*[10].

1 *Ante*, §§ XLIV, XLV. 2 *Ante*, p. 280. 3 Inferred from *Nov*. Theod. 14. 8 = C. 6. 61. 3, which can be more naturally interpreted the other way. C. Th. 8. 18. 4 says that the father takes them *iure patrio* (339). In C. Th. 8. 18. 10 (426) the attitude is the same.
4 30. 44. pr.; 41. 1. 33 pr., 1. Monro, *De furtis*, 65. 5 *Ad* Inst. 2. 12. pr.
6 Gifts from a betrothed put on same level later, C. 6. 61. 5. 7 C. Th. 3. 8. 2; C. 5. 9. 3. In A.D. 339 it was provided (C. Th. 8. 18. 4) that if the child died under 6, the successions were to go back to the line from which they came. 8 *Nov*. Theod. 14. 9 C. 6. 61. 4. 10 C. 6. 60. 3. 1 (interp.).

2. *Emancipatus*. The father, if *parens manumissor*, had the rights of patron (quasi-patron), if there were no children, till Justinian preferred brothers and sisters to him[1], but also provided that all emancipating fathers should have the rights of *parens manumissor*[2]. If there were children but they were disinherited, he had, like the patron, *bonorum possessio* of the whole (or half if there was a will), but this right did not extend to his *liberi*[3]. If there was an *extraneus manumissor*, the father had no civil claim, but in the absence of children he had the first claim, *unde decem personae*[4], at praetorian law.

If the grandfather was *parens manumissor* the quasi-patronal right was with him, so long as he lived. The father's position if the *emancipatus* survived the grandfather is not clear. Analogy suggests that there was no question of the rights of *liberi patroni*. He had not *tutela legitima* as they had, and the right above mentioned to *B.P.* of a half, in certain events, did not apply to him[5]. As an *emancipatus* had no agnates, the father was the nearest cognate, so that, on principle, in the absence of children he shared with the mother, but it seems that the Edict preferred him, as *pater*, to the mother, in this case[6]. This may have been "*unde decem personae*," which on that view applied wherever the father was not *parens manumissor*, and preferred father to mother. This is suggested by the fact that, as, under Justinian, all *emancipatio* by the father was held to be done in such a way as to give civil succession[7], the only case in which, in the absence of children, the father would have *bonorum possessio* as opposed to *hereditas* would be where the grandfather had emancipated[8].

3. The grandfather had emancipated the father, but not the son, his *nepos*. Here the father had only cognatic right and was excluded by agnates. The same seems to be true if he had been given in adoption[9], or both had been emancipated.

4. Either was emancipated by the *avus* and readopted[10]. If the father was emancipated and readopted, the *nepos*, having become a *suus heres* of *avus*, did not lose the position, and thus, on death of *avus*, was not in his father's *potestas*[11]. The father re-entered the family as an adoptive son[12]. The *nepos* was not a *suus* of his father, but if he died after the death of *avus* we are not told the father's right of succession[13]. At the worst he was an agnatic brother[14], and probably, though no longer father for

1 C. 6. 56. 2 (interp.). 2 Inst. 3. 9. 5. 3 37. 12. 1 pr., 1. 5, 3; *post*, § cxxxiv. 4 *Post*, § cxxxv. Literary texts mention a *sc.* of 176 which improved, to an uncertain extent, the father's position, Cuq, *Man.* 722. 5 See n. 3. 6 37. 12. 1. 6; 38. 17. 2. 15 *sqq.*, not an adoptive father, 38. 17. 2. 17. 7 Inst. 3. 9. 5. 8 38. 16. 10; 38. 17. 5. 2. 9 38. 17. 2. 17, 18. 10 Not adoptive children 1. 7. 12, 37. 1. 11 1. 7. 41. 12 38. 6. 1. 7. Not quite for all purposes, h. t. 4. 13 *Nepos* could claim *unde liberi*, *arg.* 38. 6. 4. 14 Unless readopted as a *nepos*, 38. 6. 1. 7.

potestas, was still the nearest agnate[1]. The case of *nepos* emancipated and readopted is not dealt with. If adopted as *nepos*, and son of his father, which needed the father's consent, the civil relation was no doubt re-established for all purposes. If readopted as a son, his successoral relations to his own father are obscure[2].

The readopted father or son might die still in *potestas* of the *avus*. If the son died leaving *p. castrense*, etc., this went to the *avus* as *peculium* before Justinian: under him, its destination depends on the meaning of *iure communi*[3]. As *peculium* the *avus* would take it. As *hereditas* it seems probable that it would go to the father notwithstanding the emancipation and readoption, and would be *bona adventitia* of his, whichever of them had passed out and back[4]. *Bona adventitia*, on the views adopted above, would go to the *avus* before Justinian, apart from prior claims of children; under Justinian to the father[5].

The distinction between reversion as *peculium* and *hereditas* was of considerable importance, in the following, and other, ways:

As *peculium* there was no question of *aditio*: it belonged to the *paterfamilias*, though of course he could abandon it, as he could any property. As *peculium* it would not render him liable for debts, except within the limits of the edicts *de peculio*[6], etc. As *hereditas* it would render him absolutely liable on acceptance. As *peculium* there was no general action for recovery of it from holders without title: the *peculium* was not a *universitas* for this purpose. Each thing must be vindicated specially. As *hereditas* there would be *hereditatis petitio* to recover it as a whole[7]. As *peculium* theft of it after the death would be ordinary *furtum*: as *hereditas*, wrongful taking before acceptance was not *furtum*[8]. If the father was under *potestas*, as *peculium* it would go to the grandfather, as *hereditas* it would go to the father, in whose hands it would be *bona adventitia*, as it did not come from the *paterfamilias*.

CXXXIV. SUCCESSION TO FREEDMEN. *A. Cives Liberti.* As, till Justinian, such persons could have no relatives but children, the early law is simply stated. The order under the XII Tables was (1) *Sui Heredes*, (2) *Patronus*, (3) *Liberi patroni*[9]. A *liberta* could of course have no *sui heredes*. The right of the *liberi patroni* was not exactly inherited from the patron: it was an independent right, expressly created by the Statute, so that the fact that a child was disinherited or had refused his father's

1 *Arg.* 38. 16. 12. 2 They were agnates, probably the nearest, but the son could probably claim, *unde liberi*. 3 *Ante*, p. 376. 4 If the father died the son would presumably take, *unde liberi*. 5 *Nov.* Theod. 14: the word used is *liberi*. If it was the father who died, *lucra nuptialia* went to the *nepos* (with other *liberi*) after 439 and all *bona adventitia* did under Justinian. 6 *Ante*, p. 65; *post*, § CLXXXIV. 7 *Ante*, p. 318. 8 *Post*, § CXCVI. 9 G. 3. 40; Ulp. 29. 1, 4; Inst. 3. 7.

succession did not, in principle, bar him[1]. And thus *extranei heredes* of the patron had no claim[2]. The *libertus* could make any will he liked as against the patron[3], but the will of a *liberta* needed his consent, so that as she could have no *sui*, he could not be excluded save by his own act[4].

The Praetor, giving *bonorum possessio*, somewhat improved the patron's position. Born *sui* and *emancipati* excluded him (unless the *libertus* had disinherited them, when they were wholly excluded), but not *adoptivi*: against these and wife *in manu* the patron was entitled to one-half, as he was against any outside claimant under a will[5]. Sons of patron had the same right, unless disinherited, but not *patrona* or *filia patroni*[6]. Failing these, or *vir*, or *uxor*, he gave a claim to *cognati* of the patron[7].

The *l. Papia Poppaea* (A.D. 9) established, as part of the machinery for encouraging marriage and increasing the birth-rate, an elaborate scheme, details of which need not be stated[8]. The rights varied according as the claimant was a patron, patroness, or son or daughter of a patron. The rights of patron and his son varied with the wealth of the *libertus*, in the other cases according as the *patrona*, etc., were themselves *ingenuae* or *libertinae*, and according to the number of their children, the rights of a *patrona* being greater than those of *patroni filia* with the same number of children. They varied also according as the deceased was a man or a woman with similar subordinate variations. A notable characteristic of this legislation was that it gave what were, in form, praetorian rights. It declared, for instance, that an *ingenua patrona*, mother of two children, was to have the edictal rights of a patron[9]. This surprising method[10] leaves no doubt that *bonorum possessio* on intestacy was ordinarily *cum re*. Notwithstanding the disappearance of other penalties on childlessness, this legislation seems to have survived till Justinian substituted a simpler scheme.

The order laid down by Justinian is[11] (1) *Liberi*, whether *sui* or *emancipati*, but not *adoptivi*; (2) *Patronus* or *patrona*[12]; (3) *Liberi patroni*, not *adoptivi*, but including those emancipated or given in adoption;

1 G. 3. 58; D. 37. 14. 9. pr. Disherison as a punishment seems to have excluded, in late cl. law. 38. 2. 12. 2, 47. pr. Another effect in *Assignatio libertorum*, *post*, § CXLI.
2 G. 3. 58. 3 G. 3. 40, Ulp. 29. 1. 4 G. 3. 43. *Libertae* could make wills with consent of *tutor*, at a time when an *ingenua in legitima tutela* could not. 5 G. 3. 41; Ulp. 29. 1. It is *contra tabulas*, but it upsets the *institutio* only to the extent of the half. 38. 2. 25, 35. 6 G. 3. 46. *B. p. tum quem ex familia patroni*, *post*, § CXXXV. 7 *Post*, p. 385. 8 G. 3. 42–53; Ulp. 29. 3–7; Inst. 3. 7. 2. 9 G. 3. 50; Ulp. 29. 6; see also G. 3. 47, 52. It may have given both *b. p.* and *hereditas* in some cases, 38. 7. 3. 10 There is no trace till after the *l. Papia* of direct legislation modifying the law of succession on intestacy. The *l. Voconia* did not affect intestacy. The rule excluding women agnates (*ante*, p. 369) was not legislation but *interpretatio*: from Inst. 3. 2. 3 it seems to be older than *bonorum possessio unde cognati*. 11 Inst. 3. 7. 3; C. 6. 4. 4, reconstructed from the *Basilica*. 12 The patron's right may be renounced and is subject to the mutual rights of succession of parents and children noted *ante*, p. 375; C. 6. 4. 4. 1, 11.

(4) *Cognati* of the patron to the fifth degree, *per capita*, with *successio graduum*. If the *libertus* had less than 100 *aurei* his will was good against the patron, otherwise, unless he had children, and left the *hereditas* to them, or they could upset the will, the patron could claim a third, free of charges, and his issue, so far as great-grandchildren, had the same right.

It will be remembered that Justinian admitted *servilis cognatio*, so that the *liberi* of the *libertus* would include those born in slavery, if now free[1]. The succession of *liberi patroni* was still independent of the patron's right. Thus if there were two patrons, both dead, leaving children, the children would all take equally, not *per stirpes*[2]. And, if one of the patrons had left only grandchildren, the surviving children of the other would take all[3].

B. Junian Latins. Here there was no question of succession: on death, the Latin became a slave, and his goods, by an express provision of the *l. Iunia*, reverted to the patron[4], or, if he was dead, to his *heredes*. Thus a disinherited child took nothing, and the Latin's children had no claim. It was however so easy for a Latin so to arrange his marriage that he and his family should be *cives* that the case would be rare.

The *sc. Largianum* (A.D. 42) modified this system without benefiting children of the Latin. It provided that, if the patron were dead, any issue of his not disinherited *nominatim* might take to the exclusion of the *extranei heredes*[5], thus giving a claim to those disinherited by the *ceteri* clause and to issue who had refused their share in the patron's estate[6]. The reason of the change is obscure, and as these persons could have had no claim to *peculium*, the case looks rather like inheritance. Gaius rejects this, but shews that there were disputes on some points[7]. *Liberi patroni* took in proportion to their shares in the patron's *hereditas*, under the *l. Iunia*. What they took by virtue of the *sc.* they took equally, and some held that where it came into operation all was divided equally[8]. But the *sc.*, and therefore this distinction, applied only where there were *extranei instituti*[9]. On the view which prevailed, grandchildren through a daughter, and children of a *patrona*, could not claim under the *sc.*[10]

Trajan enacted that if a Latin acquired *civitas* by imperial rescript, without the patron's assent, the latter's rights remained[11]. The man's *civitas* was so far recognised that he might make a will: he must indeed institute the patron for the whole, but might substitute for the case of his refusal[12], but the will was probably not good against *liberi patroni*,

1 C. 6. 4. 4, 11; Inst. 3. 6. 10. 2 C. 6. 4. 4. 19 b. 3 H. l. 19 a. This enactment retains the language of the old system: the case is not handled in any extant Novel. 4 G. 3. 56; Inst. 3. 7. 4. 5 G. 3. 63. 6 G. 3. 65–67. 7 G. 3. 64 *sqq.* 8 G. 3. 70. 9 G. 3. 69. 10 G. 3. 71. The argument is that the *sc.* talks about children not disinherited, which is inappropriate to such cases. 11 G. 3. 72. 12 *Ib. in f.*

if the patron died before the testator. Hadrian excepted the case in which, having so acquired *civitas*, he afterwards underwent a process which would have made him a *civis* for all purposes, e.g. *anniculi probatio*. The rule did not strictly apply to him as he was no longer a Latin, but Hadrian ruled that gaining the inferior status should not bar him from obtaining the better[1]. Under Justinian there were no Latins[2].

C. Persons *in numero dediticiorum*. Their children could have no claim. The property went to the patron, and there was no power of testation[3]. Subject to this there were no special rules. If the manumission would have made him a *civis*, but for the misconduct which caused him to be a *dediticius*, the property went to the patron, as that of a *civis libertus*. If it would otherwise have made him a Latin, the property went to the patron as that of a Latin, i.e. as *peculium* reverting[4]. Presumably claims posterior to those of the patron himself were admitted in this case as in that of an actual Latin.

Some effects of the distinction between succession and reversion of *peculium* have been considered in the case of a son's *peculia*[5]. Of others which could occur only in the case of a freedman, Gaius[6] cites several, of which a few may be mentioned here by way of illustration. The patron's *extranei heredes* had a claim if it was reversion, but not if it was *hereditas*: the patron's *heredes* had, as such, no claim if the freedman outlived the patron. Two patrons taking as *heredes* shared equally, taking it as *peculium* they took in proportion to their shares in the man, which might not be equal. If one of two patrons was dead, the other took all, in *hereditas*: in the other case he shared with representatives of the dead patron. If both were dead, leaving children, all took *per capita*, if it was succession: each patron's share would go to his children in the other case. If one had left children and the other only grandchildren, Justinian says the surviving children would take all if it were succession[7]. This would not be so on reversion of *peculium*. These *dediticii* no longer existed under Justinian.

CXXXV. THE SYSTEM OF *BONORUM POSSESSIO*[8]. The working of an ordinary succession at civil law, the remedies, the steps to be taken, etc., are in the main simple, but the corresponding rules in praetorian succession were of such a special kind that a general account of the system must be given. It is not within the present purpose to consider the origin of *bonorum possessio*[9], and many other controversial topics can only be lightly touched on. The subject of discussion is the ordinary praetorian succession, *b. p. edictalis*, not *b. p. decretalis*[10].

1 G. 3. 73. 2 Inst. 3. 7. 4. 3 G. 3. 75. 4 G. 3. 76. 5 *Ante*, p. 378.
6 G. 3. 57 *sqq.* 7 Inst. 3. 7. 3; G. 3. 60. 8 Leist, Glück's *Erläuterung*, 37, 38.
9 Moyle, *Instt. Just.* 471 *sqq.*; Costa, *Storia*, 468; Girard, *Man.* 844. As to the meaning of the expression itself, Cornil, *Dr.R.* 375. 10 *Post*, § CXL.

The Praetor granted *bonorum possessio* to claimants in an order not that of the civil law. If the receiver of a grant of *bonorum possessio* was also entitled at civil law, his *possessio* would be effective succession—*bonorum possessio cum re*. If, however, he was not entitled at civil law, it might be effective against the *heres* or not, *cum re* or *sine re*: we shall see later in what circumstances.

Where *bonorum possessio* was given to one also entitled at civil law it was said to be given *iuris civilis confirmandi* (or *adiuvandi*) *gratia*. If given to others with the *heres*, it was *supplendi iuris civilis gratia*, e.g. where an *emancipatus* came in with *sui*. If in disregard of a civil claim, it was said to be *corrigendi* (or *emendandi* or *impugnandi*) *iuris civilis gratia*, e.g. given to cognates to the exclusion of the *gentiles*[1].

There was a system of priority of claims, and a time was allowed within which each of these claims might be made. If a person had not claimed within the time, he was excluded, and if there were no others in the class, who could still claim, the next claim could come in; but as we have seen, a person might conceivably have a claim under more than one head, so that though he had failed to claim in the first place he still had an opportunity of coming in. This was governed by the *edictum successorium*, which provided that where one class was barred by time or repudiation, the next could claim, and fixed the time for each class[2]. It might, however, chance that he would have stood alone under the first head, but would now have to share with others, e.g. a *suus* who had not claimed, *unde liberi*, coming in, *unde legitimi*[3].

In administering the estate the first question to be asked was whether there was or was not a will. And if a will was produced, it could not be acted on, under a system which imposed restrictions on testation, unless it was clear that there was no one entitled to object to its provisions. Accordingly the first *bonorum possessio* was

A. Bonorum possessio contra tabulas. We have seen where this was available among *ingenui* in general, and have noted that omission of one of the *liberi* admitted, to share with him, any children given in adoption, and thus not entitled to claim on their own account[4], and that those who had obtained their "legitim" under the will could not complain, but would get their full share under *bonorum possessio contra tabulas*[5] if

1 Inst. 3. 9. pr., 1; G. 3. 41; D. 1. 1. 7. 1; 37. 1. 6. 1. 2 D. 38. 9. See h. t. 1. 11.
3 A grandson would in that case have to share with brothers and sisters. There are difficulties and it is contended by Beseler, *Beitr.* 4. 158, that classical law did not admit this further claim. 4 *Ante*, § CXIII; 37. 4. 8. 11, possibly late law. 5 37. 4. 3. 11. If a child given in adoption is instituted and accepts, *iussu patris adoptivi*, and is afterwards emancipated, he can claim *contra tabulas*, as he has not had the benefit, h. t. 10. 2, 3. Conversely an *emancipatus praeteritus*, who is adrogated before claiming, loses the right, h. t. 3. 6. Cf. 38. 6. 9.

someone else effectively claimed it. It was also available to patron or *liberi patroni* whose rights were disregarded[1]. The resulting state of things was not intestacy. Some parts of the will were good[2], e.g. *exheredationes* and legacies to near relatives[3], so that this *bonorum possessio* is a distinct case and cannot be fused with *unde liberi*. If no one could thus attack the will, there was

B. Bonorum possessio secundum tabulas[4]. This involved the production of a will which satisfied the praetorian requirements whether it satisfied those of civil law or not[5]. Two things must be noted. This *bonorum possessio* could be claimed notwithstanding that there was an outstanding condition on the *institutio* of the claimant (on his giving security to those entitled in his default), who would not be entitled to make *aditio* on the *hereditas*, as such[6]. And at first, *bonorum possessio* required a written and sealed document, while the mancipatory will might conceivably be oral[7]. If there was no such will or none claimed under one, the case was one for:

C. Bonorum possessio ab intestato. Here there was a lengthy list of cases set out in order of priority.

(i) *B. p. unde liberi*. The word "*unde*" here as elsewhere is not part of the Edict. It is used in referring to "that part of the Edict in which" *liberi* (etc.) are entitled to claim[8]. We have considered what persons can succeed under this head[9]. It must further be observed that a child entitled to upset a will, who failed to claim *b. p. contra tabulas*, and thus let in claimants under the will, could not afterwards obtain a valid grant *unde liberi*, and that if no one had claimed under the will, so that he could still come in, *unde liberi*, he must make good all gifts which would have been good if he had claimed *contra tabulas*[10].

(ii) *B. p. unde legitimi*. This applied to all cases of statutory claim, e.g. to agnates and those entitled in later law to claim with them, to the patron and his children, the *parens* or *extraneus manumissor*, and to cases under the Tertullian and Orphitian, and their later extensions[11]. As it covered all who were *heredes* at civil law, it availed to *sui* as well as remoter claimants, so that if a *suus* had not claimed *b. p. unde liberi* and no others had claimed it, he might still be entitled to come in under this head to the exclusion of agnates, if he was nearer in degree[12]. This he would not necessarily be: a son is nearer than a brother, a great-grandson is more remote.

1 37. 14. 10. 2 As to patron, *ante*, p. 378. 3 *Ante*, p. 326. 4 As to the many cases in which this was available, *ante*, p. 286. 5 G. 2. 119 *sqq*. 6 37. 11. 6; *ante*, p. 299; *post*, § cxxxvi. 7 *Ante*, p. 285. 8 Lenel, *E.P.* 375; D. 38. 6. 2. 9 *Ante*, p. 370. 10 29. 4. 6. 9; 38. 6. 2. So where one entitled by will and on intestacy claims only in intestacy, 29. 4. 1. pr. And he must make *collatio* (37. 6. 9), which he would not have had to do if he had taken under the will. 11 38. 7. 2, 3. 12 38. 7. 2. pr.; 38. 16. 12.

(iii) *B. p. unde decem personae*, a special case. Where an *ingenuus*, in emancipation, had been finally manumitted by the *extraneus* without remancipation to the father, the *extraneus* was *heres*, and therefore, *prima facie*, entitled to *b. p. unde legitimi*. But the Praetor by a clause in the Edict preferred certain relatives to him. The list and order, *inter se*, are given twice, not quite identically[1]. They are roughly descendants, ascendants, and brothers and sisters of the whole or half blood. Under Justinian, the institution was extinct[2].

(iv) *B. p. unde cognati*. This was a purely praetorian[3] creation: we have already considered what persons it covered[4]. It need only be noted that those entitled to claim as *legitimi* who had failed to do so might still be, alone or with others, the nearest *cognati*[5].

(v) *B. p. unde familia patroni* (*tum quem ex familia*[6]). The purpose of this is not certain. It seems at first sight to give rights only to persons who might have come in earlier, which is of so little use that it can hardly be the right explanation. Of the various explanations, that of Lenel[7] is supported by some textual authority. It is that the class includes a *patronus* who has been *capite deminutus*, emancipated children of the patron, and perhaps the *parens manumissor* of the patron. The Praetor gave these a right[8] (they had none at civil law), and there is no other obvious place for them. But the fact that such texts as certainly refer to this case do not hint at any but the civil law meaning of "*familia*" has led to the view that it refers to agnates of the patron, who have no civil law claim, and of whom Theophilus says that they come in here[9]. A long text discussing the word "*familia*," from a work commenting on these Edicts, says "*communi iure familiam dicimus omnium agnatorum*[10]." But there is no direct reference to the case of *libertus*: it is not clear why the Praetor should have admitted agnates of the patron, and neither Gaius nor the historical part of Justinian's enactment[11] refers to any such right.

(vi) *B. p. unde patronus patrona liberi et parentes eorum*. There is some evidence that this obscure case refers to manumission by one who is himself a freedman[12], and on that view this clause gives a right of succession to the patron's patron, and the issue and ascendants of the

1 Coll. 16. 9. 2; Inst. 3. 9. 3. 2 This *b. p.* is stated after *unde legitimi*, of which, in the only case in which it could occur, it takes precedence. It is supposed by Lenel, *E.P.* 356, arguing from Ulp. 28. 7, that it was not an independent clause in the Edict giving a definite class of *b. p.* as Justinian states it, but a proviso in *unde legitimi*. 3 38. 8. 1. 4 *Ante*, p. 371. 5 But as agnation was recognised, however remote, and cognation was limited, an agnate might be too remote to claim as a cognate, 38. 8. 9. pr. And where the agnation was adoptive and had ceased there was no *cognatio*. 6 "*tum quam*," "*tamquam*," etc. As to the proper reading Lenel, *E.P.* 357. 7 *E.P.* 357. 8 38. 2. 2. 2, 23. pr. 9 Roby, *Rom. Priv. Law*, 1. 278. 10 50. 16. 195. 2. For this view and some suggestions, Accarias, *Précis*, 1. 1222. 11 C. 6. 4. 4. 12 Coll. 16. 9. 1.

latter. This interpretation is supported by the language of Justinian's reorganising enactment[1], but it is not free from difficulties[2].

(vii) *B. p. unde vir et uxor.* In the absence of relatives the Praetor gave *bonorum possessio* to the husband or wife of the deceased, as the case might be[3]. This applied (like *unde liberi* and *unde legitimi*) to *ingenui* and *libertini* alike[4], but it is strange in view of this that the right of cognates of the patron was postponed to it.

(viii) *B. p. unde cognati manumissoris.* In this last grade the Praetor gave *bonorum possessio* to *cognati* of the patron[5] to the fifth degree.

There was another case of edictal *b. p.* which cannot be placed in this scheme: it was a single provision of the Edict applying to diverse cases. This was *b. p. uti ex legibus*[6]. There were cases in which *b. p.* was given by statute: we have noted this in dealing with succession to freedmen under the *l. Papia Poppaea*[7], the best known case. It was placed in the Edict after the others, but detached, some subsidiary provisions being interposed. Not much is known of it, but we are told that no previous grant of *b. p.* prevented a grant under this head[8].

Under Justinian the order was simplified. *Unde decem personae* was obsolete. *Unde familia patroni, unde patronus patrona,* and *unde cognati manumissoris* were brought under *unde cognati,* so that on intestacy there were left only *unde liberi, unde legitimi, unde cognati* and *unde vir et uxor,* with the exceptional *uti ex legibus*[9]. The new scheme changed the relative positions of *unde vir et uxor* and *unde cognati manumissoris.* Apart from this the placing of several degrees under one head was unimportant. They were still in the same order: the claim of a later, if an earlier refused, was presumably now *successio gradus,* not *ordinis.* Cognates of the patron were still recognised only to five degrees[10].

CXXXVI. Before entering on the actual working of this system it is convenient to recall certain matters already mentioned. Though the Praetor's order was not that of the civil law there were points of agreement. In some cases he admitted only those with a civil law claim (e.g. *legitimi*). In others he admitted those who had no such claim, to share with those who had (e.g. *unde liberi*). In others he excluded those with a civil law claim (e.g. *gentiles*). And it did not follow that a person who had obtained a valid grant of *b. p.* would in the long run be entitled to

1 C. 6. 4. 4. 23. 2 Lenel, *E.P.* 358. 3 D. 38. 11; Inst. 3. 9. 3, 7. 4 As did *unde cognati* under Justinian, Inst. 3. 6. 10; C. 6. 4. 4. 5 Inst. 3. 9. 3, 6; Coll. 16. 9. 1. 6 38. 14; 37. 1. 6. 1, *in f.*; Inst. 3. 9. 8. As to the application of this to *municipia* succeeding to their freedmen, Lenel, *op. cit.* 361. 7 *Ante*, p. 379. 8 38. 14. 1. 1. One who could claim under this head could also claim *unde legitimi*, 38. 7. 3. This was followed by a special Edict for *postumi*, promising *b. p. ventris nomine*, Lenel, *E.P.* 359; *post*, § CCXLV. 9 Inst. 3. 9. 8. 10 C. 6. 4. 4. 14 e, f.

keep the property: *bonorum possessio* might be *sine re*. What this meant and how it came about we shall consider later.

Bonorum possessio was granted by the Praetor to claimants in a certain order, and a fixed number of days was allowed within which the claimant in any class must apply. In general the time allowed was 100 days, but to ascendants and issue, whether claiming under a will or on intestacy, a year was allowed[1]. The days were *dies utiles*[2], and in each *bonorum possessio* the time ran only from the expiration of that allowed for the previous claim[3]. These facts had important results.

(i) Only those days counted on which a demand for *b. p.* could lawfully be made. This means little, for the Praetor heard and granted such applications *de plano*, and without the use of the formal words, *do, dico, addico*, which involved a sitting of the court[4].

(ii) The days ran only from the time when the claimant was *certus* of his right, i.e. on matters of fact[5], and was able to take the necessary steps. If, after time had begun to run, he became *incertus* of his right, in the same sense, or became incapable of acting, the running of the time was suspended[6].

(iii) As a corollary, the times for different members of the same class might expire at very different times[7].

It appears therefore that where there was no will, and there were no near relatives, who claimed, it might be a long time before remoter claims, e.g. *vir et uxor*, could be put in. This might indeed be so; the resulting inconvenience led to the adoption of devices for shortening the time. Thus if a particular class was non-existent, the time for that class was disregarded, so that if, for example, a man had died intestate and unmarried, a *b. p. unde legitimi*, given at once, was valid[8]. Again, if all the members of a class repudiated the right, the time for that class stopped at once, and claims by the next class became admissible, the repudiation being irrevocable[9]. Where persons entitled had an *annus utilis*, the person entitled in the next place could, *urgentibus creditoribus*, ask them in court if they repudiated. They need not answer, but if they did, and repudiated, and there were no others of the class[10], the next in order could claim. So too if a whole class died out while its time was running, or was excluded from any cause[11]. But if any single member of a class died or repudiated, the effect in intestacy, and, apart from the *ll. caducariae*, under wills, was to cause accrual in favour of other mem-

1 Inst. 3. 9. 9; D. 38. 15. 2. 4, 4. 1; 38. 9. 1. 11, under whatever class they are actually claiming. 2 38. 15. 2. pr.; Inst. 3. 9. 11. 3 37. 1. 9; Inst. 3. 9. 10. 4 38. 15. 2. 1. 5 37. 1. 10. As to children and *furiosi*, Accarias, *Précis*, 1. 1259, n. 3. 6 37. 1. 10; 38. 15. 2. pr. Roby, *Rom. Priv. Law*, 1. 265. 7 Inst. 3. 9. 11. 8 38. 7. 2. pr.; 38. 9. 1. 6. 9 38. 9. 1. 6. 10 38. 9. 1. 12. 11 38. 9. 1. 8.

bers of the class[1]. Thus in an ordinary case no very long time would elapse before the claim, however remote, could come in.

It must be remembered that any *bonorum possessio* could in fact be given at any time. The Praetor, who knew nothing of the facts, gave it on application, without serious enquiry, to anyone who set up a *prima facie* claim, on *ex parte* evidence. But such a grant would be a mere nullity unless the person to whom it was made was a person entitled to it at that time, i.e. as the technical expression ran, unless he had it *ex edicto*, in accordance with the terms of the Edict.

The demand for *bonorum possessio* was made to the magistrate and granted by him. It is sometimes spoken of as a judicial proceeding, but in classical law, though there may possibly have been necessary formal words of application[2], there is little judicial about it, whatever may have been the case in earlier days. Even a slave could obtain a grant[3] for his master, though it is a commonplace that he could take no part in judicial proceedings. In later law, though not in classical law, the magistrate might grant it without any express application, any evidence of intent being enough, and the class of magistrates who might grant it extended as time went on[4]. On another point of detail in Justinian's law, there is dispute. He tells us that there was no longer any need to demand *bonorum possessio*; it could be obtained by any expression of wish[5]. The question is whether this means that there was now no need to go before the magistrate. That is the natural meaning and would put the matter on the same footing as *aditio*. But as he says that the rule was laid down by earlier Emperors, and such a rule certainly was not, it is usually held that all he means is that, as was already the law, no special words were needed, and the grant might be made by any magistrate[6]. The truth is that while the grant was essential to further proceedings, it had no other significance. The real question at later stages would not be merely whether there was a grant, but whether the grant was *ex edicto*. Usually there was no enquiry: it sufficed that the claimant shewed a *prima facie* case, or even less. Thus on production of a will, *b. p. secundum tabulas* could be given without opening it[7], though

1 38. 9. 1. 10. 2 The view that there was a form rests on Theoph., *ad* Inst. 3. 9. 10 (which only shews that there must have been express claim), C. 6. 59. 1, 2 (which say the claim was made *sollenniter*) and C. 6. 9. 9 (which, though in its present form it refers to this, may originally have had to do with *cretio*). 3 37. 1. 7, which also says that it may be given without demand. See also the demand by messenger, Girard, *Textes*, 814. It may be that in Justinian's law there was no difference between obtaining *b. p.* and *aditio hereditatis*. See Biondi, *Legittimazione processuale nelle azioni divisorie*, 39 *sqq.* 4 Inst. 3. 9. 10. Accarias, *Précis*, 1. 1258. 5 Inst. 3. 9. 12. 6 37. 1. 7. pr.; C. 6. 9. 8, 9. Various views, Girard, *Man.* 925, Moyle, *Instt. Just.*, *ad* Inst. 3. 9. 3; Leist, Glück's *Erläuterung*, 38. 2. 314; Accarias, *Précis*, 1. 1279. 7 37. 11. 1. 2. A conditionally *institutus* can get *b. p. sec. tab.* This may be valid, *ex edicto*, but it may not be

the claimant might not be entitled under it. It follows that it might often be given to a person not entitled to it and such cases are recorded[1]. Thus it might be given under a forged, or a revoked, will, or on intestacy where there really was a will, the Praetor being told that there was none. *Legitimi* might, innocently or wilfully, allege falsely that there were no *liberi*, or that their time had expired, or that they had repudiated. In all these cases the *bonorum possessio* obtained, not being *ex edicto*, granted, that is, to one not at the time entitled to it under the Edict, was worthless: it did not enable the grantee to go any further. It was merely like the issue of a writ to one who had no sort of claim. The grantee would not succeed in the interdict *quorum bonorum*, or be able to use effectively any of the edictal remedies[2].

Since *bonorum possessio* was granted without serious enquiry, a grant to one not entitled to it, a grant not *ex edicto*, did not bar a grant to one entitled to it, in the same or another class, and, presumably, one who had a grant which was not *ex edicto* was not thereby barred from applying later for a valid one. As these later grants would also be without enquiry, the rule practically was that no grant was a bar to another grant, though we shall see shortly that this meant little. Moreover a grant to one of a class was not a grant to all. Each person who wanted *b. p.* must ask for it[3]. Hence arose cases of accrual. If, e.g., one of the *liberi* had received a grant, and the others allowed the time to expire without taking steps, he would have *b. p.* of the whole[4].

Where *bonorum possessio* had been granted to anyone in accordance with the Edict, *ex edicto*, it could not be validly granted to anyone else, adversely to him (which means, practically, to anyone in a different group), while the grant stood[5]. Such a grant might be made, but it was a nullity: it could not be *ex edicto*. A valid grant *unde liberi* did not bar other *liberi* from getting a grant, but it rendered nugatory any grant *unde legitimi*, unless and until all valid grants *unde liberi* were revoked. Thus it may be said, with truth, but in different senses, that one grant of *bonorum possessio* barred another, and that it did not.

CXXXVII. Claim and grant of *bonorum possessio* operated somewhat like *aditio* at civil law: they entitled the beneficiary to take steps to recover the property, but did not of themselves give him possession of it. This is a question of, *inter alia*, physical control, and the grant

cum re as the condition may fail, and a substitute may require security. P. 5. 9. 1; D. 2. 8. 12; 37. 11. 6; 46. 5. 8.

1 E.g. C. 8. 2. 1. 2 See 37. 5. 5. 3. 3 Application need not be made personally. *Paterf.* can apply for *infans* child (at least in later law), a *tutor* for ward (though he cannot repudiate), and "*actor*" for a municipality, and a representative duly appointed for anyone. 37. 1. 3. 4, 7, 8, 16; 38. 9. 1. 4. 4 37. 1. 3. 9, 5. 5 *Uti ex legibus* is no exception: if this is valid, the other is not.

could not give him this; there was no magic in it. We have now to consider how it was made effective, remembering that there were two kinds of valid *bonorum possessio, cum re* and *sine re.* We deal first with *bonorum possessor cum re*, the true praetorian successor. His remedies and liabilities were as follows:

1. He might use the interdict *quorum bonorum*[1], of which the exact effect must be noted. It was not a universal remedy: it applied only to matters of which possession was possible, or at least, *possessio iuris*, as in usufruct[2], and thus was not a means of recovery of debts. But it has a still more important and less obvious limitation. It was available only against those who held *pro herede*, i.e. who claimed to be *heredes*[3], or who refused to state any title at all[4]. Thus it was useless against one who claimed to have bought the thing[5], and thus to hold it *pro emptore.* But as against a holder *pro herede*, or *pro possessore*, it was available not only as to what he possessed, but as to things which he had fraudulently ceased to possess, and even things he had usucapted[6]. It must be remembered that under Hadrian *usucapio pro herede* was made ineffective against claimants of the *hereditas* whether it had been in good or in bad faith.

To recover under the interdict, the mere issue of which, like a grant of *bonorum possessio*, was made as of course, without real enquiry, the *bonorum possessor* must shew that he was entitled to it, and it was at this point that the validity of the grant of *b. p.* to him would be considered. The wording of the interdict brings this out. It orders that the goods be handed over to the claimant who has a grant of *bonorum possessio ex edicto*[7], i.e. in accordance with the Edict. If, e.g., the grant was *unde liberi*, it must appear that he was one of that class, that the grant was made within the proper limits of time, that there was no previous valid grant to one or more of another group, still in force, that the goods formed part of the estate of the deceased, and that the defendant set up no title except as *heres*.

This interdict, like all possessory interdicts, was merely provisional[8]. If the claimant proved his right to the interdict against the defendant, the goods were, as the result of procedure not here material, handed over to him. No question of title was thereby determined. It did not follow that he would be able to keep the property. The whole legal effect was that anyone who wished to recover the property from him must bring the appropriate action against him and prove his case.

1 43. 2; C. 8. 2; G. 3. 34; 4. 144; Inst. 4. 15. 3. 2 43. 3. 1. 8, which gives *quod legatorum.* 3 *Ante*, p. 318. 4 43. 2. 1. pr. 5 *Ante*, p. 318, *hereditatis petitio* where a similar rule held. 6 43. 2. 1. pr.; C. 8. 2. 2. Not available if the claimant had had *possessio* before, since the grant, G. 4. 144. 7 43. 2. 1. pr. 8 Ubbelohde, *Die erbrechtl. Interdicte*, 8 *sqq.*

Before leaving this interdict another interdict must be mentioned of similar type, but less importance, called *quod legatorum*[1], available to the *bonorum possessor* against one who had taken possession of property, alleging a legacy of it to him, without the consent of the *bonorum possessor*, who must, under this interdict, give security for the restoration of the legacy if it should prove to be due[2].

2. He was, at least in later law, entitled to the *hereditatis petitio possessoria*[3]. This was an extension of the *hereditatis petitio* of the *heres*, available, like the interdict, only against holders *pro herede* or *pro possessore*, and it covered the various *iura in rem* of the estate, of which the defendant had possession (or *possessio iuris*), and, to a limited extent, debts. The action had the same general rules as the *hereditatis petitio*[4]. To recover under it the plaintiff must shew that he had a valid grant of *bonorum possessio*, but he need not shew that it was *cum re*, though, if it was not *cum re*, he would fail if the defendant was the *heres*[5]. The judgement differed in force from that on the interdict. It was not merely provisional; like that on the actual *hereditatis petitio* it was final, dealing not merely with the question of possession, but also with that of substantive hereditary right. As it called for the same proof as the interdict, covered more property (for the interdict dealt only with what could be in some sense possessed) and would cover things other than those held by the defendant *pro herede* or *pro possessore*[6], lay against the same persons, and gave a definitive result, it is not easy to see, at first sight, why a *bonorum possessor cum re* ever preferred the interdict. The following considerations may explain the matter.

(*a*) A *bonorum possessor* might not know whether he was *cum* or *sine re*. The texts speak of *b. p.* as being granted *cum* or *sine re*[7], but it was not so stated in the grant, and the party concerned might not know which it was. As, in *b. p. sine re*, if the opponent was the *heres* the possessor would fail in *hereditatis petitio possessoria*, but win on the interdict, he would, if there was doubt, bring the interdict, leaving the *heres* to proceed against him afterwards by *hereditatis petitio*. If, e.g., an *extraneus* was claiming under a praetorian will, he might know that no one had claimed *b. p. contra tabulas*, but this did not prove that there was no child; there might be one who was content to rest on his civil law

1 Alleged availability of this remedy to *heres*, as such, *post*, § CCXLIX. 2 Lenel, *E.P.* 453. 3 D. 5. 5; classicality denied; Biondi, *Leg. pro. nelle azioni div.* 20; Lenel, *E.P.* 180. Argumentation hardly conclusive—the parallelism at which the Pr. aimed would not be reached if *b. possessor* had no definitive action except for "*singulae res*", and *fam. ercisc.* (*utilis*), 10. 2. 2. 1. 4 *Ante*, p. 318; D. 5. 5. 2, "*tantundem consequitur bonorum possessor quantum superioribus civilibus actionibus heres consequi potest*"; 37. 4. 13. pr. 5 Not expressly stated but inferred from 37. 10. 3. 13. 6 *Ante*, p. 318; *post*, § CCXLIX. 7 E.g. Ulp. 28. 13.

claim. The *bonorum possessio* would be no answer to *hereditatis petitio* brought by such a child, but it would give the *bonorum possessor* the advantage of the position of defendant. So also, he might not know whether the opponent was actually *heres* or not; this was indifferent in the interdict. Similar doubts might arise in a number of ways.

(*b*) Till Hadrian, *hereditatis petitio* was not available against one who had fraudulently ceased to possess. The interdict was. Nor does *hereditatis petitio* seem to have applied to things of which the holder had completed *usucapio*[1].

(*c*) The interdict procedure might involve *sponsiones*[2]. The payments under these were actually enforced; they were not merely formal. Thus success in the interdict might involve a profit.

(*d*) Even in later law, the interdict had the advantage of being subject to restrictions in the matter of appeal[3].

3. If, having obtained the possession, he was now sued by the *heres* by *hereditatis petitio*, he had of course no defence at civil law, but he had an *exceptio doli*[4].

4. He could recover property of the estate held by persons claiming by a title other than inheritance, who were not to be reached by the interdict or the *hereditatis petitio possessoria*. His remedy in this case was an *actio fictitia*, the fiction being that he was *heres*; the *iudex* was directed to condemn, if the plaintiff would be entitled "*si heres esset*[5]."

5. He could sue and be sued on account of debts by actions with a similar fiction[6]. These would cover the cases in which the *heres* himself could sue or be sued in respect of events since the death, so that they formed a complete scheme.

Here there is a difficulty. Gaius states the *intentio* of the actions under this and the last head: it says nothing about the fact that the plaintiff is a *bonorum possessor*. What then was there to prevent anyone from bringing such actions against a debtor, since the question whether the plaintiff was *bonorum possessor* or not was not put in issue? The fact of the grant would be on record, and the *formula* would not be issued except where there was one. But it might not be *ex edicto*, and the fact that the grantee was not really entitled to it would not be brought out till the interdict or the *petitio* had been tried, while there is nothing to shew that these *actiones fictitiae* could not be brought in the first instance. The way in which this material point was raised is not certainly known. Lenel holds[7] that it was by means of an *exceptio bonorum possessionis non*

1 The *heres* might have completed *usucapio* since the death, see 5. 3. 19. 1. 2 Although not necessarily, the interdict being restitutory, *post*, pp. 731, 739. 3 C. Th. 11. 36. 22. 4 G. 2. 120. 5 G. 4. 34. 6 G. 4. 34; 3. 81 (imperfect). 7 *E.P.* 183.

datae, mentioned by Paul, which, though he does not state its application, seems suitable[1].

6. The acquisition of possession under the interdict or the *petitio* did not confer *dominium*, though Ulpian, in the Digest[2], uses language inconsistent with this. The *bonorum possessor* would become *dominus* by *usucapio*; in the meantime he had the protection available to all praetorian owners. Under Justinian, *bonorum possessio* and *hereditas* were almost fused: the two systems of remedies coexisted almost as alternative remedies for the same end. There was no longer any praetorian ownership, so that these distinctions ceased to exist[3].

CXXXVIII. We can now turn to the *bonorum possessor sine re*, one who had a valid grant, i.e. *ex edicto*, but who was not one of those whom the Praetor would, in the long run, protect against the civil law *heres*. His rights and liabilities can be scheduled as in the other case.

1. He had the interdicts *quorum bonorum* and *quod legatorum*, and, so far, he was in the same position as the *bonorum possessor cum re*. The interdicts were effective as against even a true *heres* or legatee[4].

2. He had *hereditatis petitio possessoria*[5] against anyone who held *pro herede* or *pro possessore*, but the true *heres* would meet it by an *exceptio*, probably *doli*[6].

3. If the *heres* sued him by *hereditatis petitio*, he had no reply, and the action would cover what he had recovered by any of his various remedies or without litigation—everything which he held as *bonorum possessor*, and, in some cases, what he had made away with[7].

4. He had the same *actiones fictitiae* against debtors and detainers of property as if his *b. p.* were *cum re*, being of course liable to be called on by the *heres* to restore, as just stated. This situation raises a curious question. If a *bonorum possessor* had thus handed over what he had received, he was still a *bonorum possessor*, *ex edicto*, since the grant was valid and not revoked. Logically he might still sue debtors. There is no authority, but analogy suggests an *exceptio doli*.

5. He might be sued by creditors. If, having paid debts, he was ejected by the *heres* he could deduct, in accounting, the amount of these payments[8]. If sued after the *heres* had recovered from him, he had, presumably, an *exceptio*. Here too a difficulty might arise. If, having

1 44. 1. 20. It is odd that if, e.g., a creditor of the estate brings action against a person entirely unconnected with the matter, his only answer should be an *exceptio*. But the *formula* would be issued only where there had been an apparent grant, and the *exceptio* would raise the question whether the grant was valid. 2 37. 1. 1; 50. 16. 70 (Paul). 3 Thus the Digest gives *Quod legatorum* to the *heres* as such. *Post*, § CCXLIX. As to *b. p. sine re* under Justinian, *post*, § CXXXIX. 4 G. 4. 144. 5 *Ante*, p. 390, n. 3. 6 Accarias, *Précis*, 1. 1269, citing 37. 11. 11. 2, where however it was not a valid *b. p.* 7 *Ante*, p. 318. 8 5. 3. 31.

a grant of *bonorum possessio*, he paid debts out of his own pocket, intending to recoup himself when he got in the estate, his expectation might be disappointed: the *heres* might step in and recover the assets from those who were holding them, so that nothing reached the hands of the *bonorum possessor*. Could he claim an indemnity from the *heres*? It was not *negotiorum gestio*: he was acting on his own account[1]. It may be that as he was still *bonorum possessor*, he could put pressure on the *heres* by recovering the property from him by the interdict, and then, when sued by him by the *hereditatis petitio* or any proprietary action, set off the amount of the debts paid.

6. He could usucapt in the same way as the *bonorum possessor cum re*, but was liable to have his *usucapio* interrupted by the intervention of the *heres*.

CXXXIX. We have now to consider when *bonorum possessio* was *cum re* and when *sine re*. The *heres* and the *bonorum possessor* might of course be the same person. A *suus heres* was entitled to *bonorum possessio unde liberi*. A claimant under a formal mancipatory will was commonly entitled, since sealing was usual, to *b. p. secundum tabulas*. An omitted *suus* could proceed either by *hereditatis petitio* or by *b. p. contra tabulas*[2]. An agnate had *hereditatis petitio* or *b. p. unde legitimi*.

In Justinian's time all *bonorum possessio* was normally *cum re*, which explains the existence of doubts on some points in *b. p. sine re*. The *heres* was usually the person entitled to *bonorum possessio*, and he might proceed either by *aditio* and *hereditatis petitio*, or by demand of *b. p.* and the foregoing remedies. The difference was chiefly of form. The Digest gives titles to *quorum bonorum* and *hereditatis petitio possessoria*, but says, in them[3], only a word or two about each, which indicates that they still existed but had lost their importance. But some cases might give difficulty even under Justinian's law.

(i) For those entitled in both ways it mattered little in which form they claimed. The limits of time were not the same, but if too late for one, they could fall back on the other. But there were still a few cases in which *bonorum possessio* was the only course, and here, if the time had gone by, total exclusion resulted even under Justinian. The praetorian will was obsolete. The enactments extending the class of *legitimi* expressly gave all the rights of agnates, i.e. *hereditas* as well as *b. p.*[4]

1 *Post*, § CLXXXV. Some texts suggest, but do not prove, that he had *condictio indebiti* (12. 6. 2). There is however the difficulty that a *bonorum possessor ex edicto* is liable for debts, so that it is not an *indebitum*. The fact that in the long run he gets no benefit out of it does not make his act a payment in error of what was not due. 2 *Hereditatis petitio* would be better, for *b. p. contra tabulas* left some of the provisions of the will standing, *ante*, p. 326. 3 D. 5. 5; D. 43. 2. 4 See Inst. 3. 2. 4; C. 6. 58. 14. 6, etc.

On the other hand Justinian expressly confined *emancipati* and *emancipatae*, who attacked a will, to *b. p. contra tabulas*[1], and *unde cognati* and *unde vir et uxor* remained, it seems, purely edictal[2].

(ii) If one entitled to *b. p.* let his time pass (at least if he was the whole of a class) it is clear that the person next entitled could come in[3]. On intestacy, the *sui*, relying on their civil law right, might not claim *b. p. unde liberi*. When their time had expired, could the agnates, etc., claim, *unde legitimi*? They could under the old law, though of course it would be *sine re*, and there seems to be nothing in the texts to prevent their still doing so. But if they could there would still be *b. p. sine re*[4], though the Digest expressly says that *bonorum possessio* is the right of getting and retaining the goods[5]. In view of this, and as the *Corpus iuris* nowhere says, even where the statement might have been expected if it was true, that *quorum bonorum* was available against the *heres*, it is generally held that the interdict was now in such a form as to be ineffective against him[6]. It seems more probable that while the interdict, or rather the possessory action which has taken its place[7], was still formally available, it would be paralysed by an *exceptio doli*, so that practically this was not *b. p.* at all. This would explain the fact that Justinian, in discussing the interdict *quorum bonorum*, omits the words "*qui heres est*," which are in Gaius[8], leaving the words "*qui putat se heredem esse*."

In classical law all *bonorum possessio* was *cum re* if the claimant was *heres* or there was no *heres*, and thus any *bonorum possessio* might conceivably be *cum re*. In other cases various *bonorum possessiones* were *cum* or *sine re* according to epoch (for there is much historical change) and circumstances, of which circumstances the Praetor would not, and the parties might not, be informed when the grant was made.

B. p.[9] *contra tabulas* was, no doubt, *cum re* in the time of Gaius though this is not stated: the language of many texts could not have been used if there were normal cases in which it was *sine re*. The system of *collatio bonorum* would be unintelligible if the *bonorum possessio* of *emancipatus omissus* was *sine re*, liable to be defeated by the *institutus*. The restriction laid down by Pius[10] on what a woman might take would not have been necessary, if she did not keep what she took. It must have

1 C. 6. 28. 4. 6; Vangerow, *Pand.* § 515. 2 No alteration in the position of these by any legislation of Justinian, before *Nov.* 118. After this, *cognati* were *heredes*, but *vir et uxor* are not mentioned and presumably remain on the old footing. 3 38. 9. 1; 38. 15. 1. 1. 4 Windscheid, *Lehrb.* § 532, n. 6, cites 37. 4. 14. pr.; 37. 5. 15. 2; 37. 6. 10. 5 37. 1. 3. 2. Ulp., but no doubt altered. Cf. Ulp. 28. 13. 6 Accarias, *Précis*, 1. 1280; he compares Inst. 4. 15. 3 with G. 4. 144 and Inst. 2. 17. 6 with G. 2. 148, 149. 7 *Post*, § CCLII. 8 G. 4. 144; Inst. 4. 15. 3. 9 On all these cases, Girard, *Man.* 941. 10 *Ante*, p. 326.

been *cum re* when Julian revised the Edict, since the *bonorum possessor* was liable for some legacies under that system. *Collatio* is discussed by Cassius, in the first century[1]. There is evidence that it was *cum re* when obtained by a patron or his issue in the time of Cicero, where it was not based on a civil law claim[2]. On the whole it seems that this *bonorum possessio* was *cum re* by the beginning of the Empire.

Of *bonorum possessio secundum tabulas* there were many cases. If the will was valid at civil law the *bonorum possessio* would of course be *cum re*. Under a praetorian will, the *b. p.* would be *cum re* if the *instituti* were the *heredes* or there were no *sui* or *legitimi*[3]. If there were adverse claims of agnates, it seems to have been *sine re* till Pius made it *cum re* against them, though it is possible on the texts[4] that it may have already been *cum re* as against agnates remoter than *frater et patruus*. Hadrian made it *cum re* where the only defect was that there was a *postumus praeteritus* who died before the testator[5]. Where the defect was that it was a woman's will made without consent of her *tutor fiduciarius* Pius made it *cum re* whether it satisfied civil law rules of form or not, but if the *tutor* was *legitimus*, it was still *sine re*[6]. Where a will had been upset by *capitis deminutio*, but the testator died *sui iuris*, there might be *b. p. secundum tabulas*, but under Justinian unless he had in some way confirmed his previous will there was an *exceptio*[7]. Other cases of this *bonorum possessio* are discussed[8], but enough has been said to shew that there were many factors to be considered, of which the Praetor could not be informed when he issued the interdict, and that up to the end of the classical age this *bonorum possessio* was often *sine re*.

Unde legitimi, *unde cognati*, and *unde vir et uxor* were at all times normally *cum re*. They excluded none but the *gentiles*, who were disregarded. If, however, they took effect merely because earlier claimants, entitled at civil law as well, had not troubled to claim *b. p.*, they would be *sine re*, if the other claimants had made, or, having still time, afterwards made, *aditio*. If however these others had renounced or were excluded by lapse of the *spatium deliberandi*, the *b. p.* would be *cum re*[9]. Similar distinctions must be taken in regard to the *b. p.* of the patron and his relatives, in succession to a freedman. We know that the *l. Papia Poppaea*[10] gave statutory basis to some of them, which indicates that they were normally *cum re*.

We are not told that *unde liberi* was *cum re*, but as *contra tabulas* was,

1 37. 6. 2. 5. 2 *In Verr.* 2. 1. 48; Girard, *Man.* 921, n. 2. 3 Ulp. 23. 6; G. 2. 119. 4 G. 2. 120; Coll. 16. 3. 1. Arnò, *Mél. Cornil*, 1. 102. 5 28. 3. 12. pr. 6 G. 2. 122. 7 G. 2. 147; D. 37. 11. 11. 2. *Ante*, p. 289. 8 *Ante*, p. 285. A will was destroyed by the testator but no other made. Pius provided that *bonorum possessio* under it should be *sine re*. 9 G. 3. 37; 2. 149; Ulp. 26. 8; 28. 11. 10 *Ante*, p. 379.

from early times, and this case affects nearly the same persons, is also subject to *collatio*, and is older, it may be assumed that this too was *cum re*. It is, *a priori*, probable that *unde decem personae* was *cum re*, and this view is confirmed by the language of Ulpian, to the effect that the XII Tables gave the *hereditas* to the *extraneus manumissor*, but the Praetor, on grounds of equity, preferred the *decem personae* to him[1].

It was not always the Praetor who made a particular *b. p. cum re*. In the case of the *postumus praeteritus* who was in fact dead, it was Hadrian[2]. In *b. p. secundum tabulas*, against agnates, and where a testatrix had acted without consent of her *tutor fiduciarius*, it was Pius[3]. The cases of the *l. Papia Poppaea* and Justinian's changes speak for themselves. It may be that even in the older cases, before the Empire, the Praetor never of his own authority gave effect *cum re* if there was an adverse civil claim, but no such general statement is warranted; *unde liberi* and *unde decem personae* are probably both republican, and may both owe their efficacy to the Praetor. The language of Cicero[4] implies that the Edict could give an effective right as against civil law claims. It must be remembered that a *b. p.* not *ex edicto* was neither *cum* nor *sine re*; it was a mere nullity, not for practical purposes *bonorum possessio* at all[5].

CXL. The foregoing statement raises two questions:

(i) What was the advantage of obtaining *b. p. sine re*? There are obvious answers. One who was, or thought he was, entitled to *b. p.* might not know, on the facts, whether it would prove to be *cum* or *sine re*, since this depended on circumstances which might not, and in some cases could not, be within his knowledge. And where he knew that it was technically *sine re*, it might yet be effective because the person entitled abstained, from whatever cause, from taking steps against him. And a *bonorum possessor* who had obtained actual possession under the interdict *quorum bonorum*, for which result it was indifferent whether his *b. p.* was *cum* or *sine re*, had the advantage of being defendant if the property was claimed from him by the *heres*, no small matter, as the burden of proof was on the plaintiff.

(ii) Why did the Praetor give *b. p. sine re*, i.e. to one to whom on his own principles the property was not ultimately to belong? The final answer to this is no doubt to be found in the answer to the other question of the origin of *bonorum possessio*. But apart from this there are several answers. So far as the original grant was concerned the Praetor could not know whether the *possessio* would be *cum* or *sine re*; in appropriate

1 Coll. 16. 9. 2. 2 28. 3. 12. pr. 3 G. 2. 120–22. 4 *In Verr.* 2. 1. 48.
5 The *exceptio bonorum possessionis non datae*, 44. 1. 20, *ante*, p. 391, seems to mean "*non ex edicto datae.*"

circumstances any *b. p.* might be *cum re*, and the Praetor had ordinarily never heard of the case till the demand was made. Again, the fact that a *b. p.* was *sine re* is no evidence that the Praetor wished it to be so. No doubt every grant was originally *sine re*, if there was an adverse civil law claim. The first step in the evolution of a new praetorian right of succession would be to grant *b. p.* and no more. Later, the Praetor or some other agency[1] might make it *cum re*, by giving an *exceptio doli* if the *bonorum possessor* was sued by the *heres*, and, in due course, the *hereditatis petitio possessoria* against the *heres*, that is, by excluding his *exceptio doli*. Again when *bonorum possessor* brought the interdict *quorum bonorum*, even if the *b. p.* was *sine re*, the *heres* was not permitted to prove this in the interdictal procedure, but must yield to the *bonorum possessor*, and, if he thought fit, bring *hereditatis petitio* later, though the facts which he must then prove might conceivably have been admitted, under an *exceptio*, in the interdictal procedure itself. The plea of title was not admitted in that procedure, a restriction not peculiar to this case; it runs through all the possessory system. Taking this principle as a starting-point, it is clear that *b. p.* was necessarily granted without reference to the question whether it would ultimately prove to be *cum re*.

If we ask why title might not be pleaded in reply to a possessory claim, we may find ourselves in difficulties. The most fundamental answer will probably have nothing to do with Roman law specially[2], for the same principle is to be found in the ancient system of possessory remedies in English law[3], which do not seem to owe anything to Roman law. It may be suggested, that if *b. p. sine re* was only a first step towards *bonorum possessio cum re*, there was an obvious reason for not facilitating proof of title. But the Praetor's aims in originating the system of *bonorum possessio* we have not considered.

We have seen that demand of *b. p.* was analogous in nature and effect to *aditio*. The time limits, though not the same, are similar. A hundred days, even a year, seems very short as a period of limitation, but one who had let these times pass could not claim either as *heres* or as *bonorum possessor*. But in all cases of *b. p.*, and where the Praetor fixes a *spatium deliberandi*, and, usually, where a will fixes the time, this runs only from the date at which the party has notice of his right, and all he need do is to make a certain formal, or, in some cases (always in later law), informal, declaration or claim. When he has done that his right is an ordinary right of action, subject only to the ordinary rules of limitation or adverse prescription.

1 *Ante*, p. 396. 2 See, however, *post*, § CCLII. 3 The remark of O. W. Holmes (*Common Law*, 210) that "English law has always had the good sense to allow title to be set up in defence to a possessory action" pays the common law an undeserved compliment. See Pollock and Maitland, *Hist. of English Law*, 2. 57 *sqq*.

Bonorum possessio decretalis. The foregoing is an account of what may be called routine *bonorum possessio, bonorum possessio edictalis.* There was another form called *bonorum possessio decretalis.* In a few cases, probably survivals of a much larger number, it was not given as a matter of course, but only by a *decretum* of the magistrate given after investigation. It was given *pro tribunali*, in court, and not *de plano*, as in the other case[1]. The applications of it were, in general, cases in which, for some reason, ordinary *b. p.* could not be given to the person entitled, e.g. a lunatic, whose *curator* could get this *b. p.* for him, but not *edictalis*[2], an unborn person, who would be entitled to *b. p.* if he came into existence[3], and whose mother could claim this for him, and that of a child whose legitimacy was contested[4]. The purpose was to provide for the administration of the estate till the difficulty was out of the way. It was essentially provisional, and did not necessarily put the holder into the position of a praetorian owner, but gave him usually only such rights as were essential to administration, the extent of the rights differing somewhat in the different cases[5], and always ceasing if the definitive claim became impossible.

CXLI. Death created by far the most important case of universal succession, but there were other occasions on which a man's *universitas* was transferred. Each of them had its own special rules, which renders it necessary to consider them separately.

Adrogatio. The forms and restrictions of *adrogatio* have already been considered[6], but only general notions as to its results have been mentioned and these must now be considered. Gaius tells us that all the *res, corporales* and *incorporales*, of the *adrogatus* passed to the *adrogator*, so far as they were not destroyed by the *capitis minutio*[7]. But rights which were not *res* passed also. Persons in his *potestas* and *manus* passed into the *familia* of the *adrogator*[8]. This of itself shews that it is not to be thought of as a case of quasi-inheritance, for such rights as this did not pass to a *heres*. On inheritance the obligations would have passed too but this is not what happened. *Iura in rem* could be vindicated by the *adrogator*, as his own, and all rights of action passed to him without need of any fiction[9], while the obligations were, at civil

1 38. 9. 1. 7; 37. 1. 3. 8. The same number of *dies utiles* covered more time; only days available for judicial proceedings counted. 2 38. 17. 2. 11. Doubts in classical law, C. 5. 70. 7. 3. 3 37. 9. 1. pr., 14. 4 37. 10. 1. pr., 3. pr. *Tutor* or *pater* for an *infans* are other possible cases, *ante*, p. 312. 5 Accarias, *Précis*, 1. 1274. 6 *Ante*, § XLVI. 7 G. 3. 83. He states, as destroyed, usufruct, *operarum obligatio* created by *iusiurandum liberti* and *lis contestata iudicio legitimo*. 8 *Ante*, p. 125. 9 G. 3. 83. The changes in capacity of a *filiusfamilias* to own property make the acquisition somewhat unreal in later law. See Inst. 3. 10. 2. The statement that Justinian reduced the right of the *adrogator* to a usufruct, while it states the practical result, is a little misleading. There is no special rule for *adrogatio*. It is "*ad similitudinem naturalium parentum.*" The ac-

law, extinct[1]. The principle applied at civil law was that the *adrogatus* was regarded as always having been under the *potestas*, and such praetorian modifications as were applied were correctives. Contractual and quasi-contractual obligations did not bind the *adrogator*[2]; they would not have bound him as *paterfamilias* at civil law. Delicts of *adrogatus* continued to bind him; they would have bound him had he been a *filiusfamilias*, and the obligation was not destroyed by *capitis deminutio*[3]. They bound the *adrogator*, noxally: they would have bound him as *paterfamilias*, when they were committed[4]. Contractual obligations which *adrogatus* had inherited bound the *adrogator* fully at civil law, not as being *heres* to the *adrogatus*, but as having acquired the *hereditas* through him, being *heres* to the person from whom he had inherited, as a *paterfamilias* acquires inheritances through his son[5]. Acquisition of the *hereditas* involved acquisition of the liabilities.

As to contractual debts this civil system was unfair: the *adrogator* acquired the property and was not liable for debts. The Praetor gave a remedy, not by extending the fiction that there had always been *potestas* to the applicability of the praetorian liabilities, *de peculio*, etc.[6], which might have been useless since the *adrogator* could evade this by not creating a *peculium*, but by allowing an action against *adrogatus*, with the fiction that there had been no *capitis deminutio*. This of itself would not suffice, for *adrogatus* had no property, but the Edict went on to provide that, unless the action was defended[7], the creditor might enter into possession of the property which would have belonged to him if there had been no *adrogatio*, and sell it to satisfy his claim[8].

PASSING INTO *MANUS*. Where a woman *sui iuris* went into *manus* the resulting position was, *mutatis mutandis*, much the same as in *adrogatio*. There was the same praetorian action on previous contracts[9], and the same rule of absolute liability for inherited debts[10]. But it is not clear that there was at any time a power of noxal surrender in this case; certainly there was none in classical law[11].

quisitions, not being from the property of the *adrogator*, are *adventitia*, *castrensia* or *quasi-castrensia*, as the case may be.

1 The extinction as against *adrogatus* himself may be thought of as due to the *c. d.*, or, more probably, to a survival, a *filius* not having been capable of *obligatio* in very early law. Bonfante, *Corso*, 6. 24. 2 G. 3. 84. 3 4. 5. 2. 3. 4 G. 4. 77. 5 G. 3. 84. 6 It would not lie under the terms of the Edict, which gave it only where the contract was made by one under *potestas* (Lenel, *E.P.* 276). Thus Sabinus and Cassius denied it, but in later cl. law some jurists thought it admissible, 15. 1. 42. 7 Lenel, *E.P.* 117. 8 G. 3. 84 *in f.*; 4. 80. Early history, Desserteaux, *N.R.H.* 1912, 423. 9 G. *ib.* 10 G. 3. 84. 11 Inst. 4. 8. 7. In G. 4. 80, one passing into civil bondage seems to be put on the same level as a woman going into *manus*, for this purpose. But he could have had no property. The case seems unintelligible. For various interpretations Lenel, *E.P.* 422. The suggestion has been made (Desserteaux, *Capitis Deminutio*, 1. 276; 2. 1. 361 *sqq.*; *N.R.H.* 1912, 460) that the goods affected will be those which he has acquired for the *paterfamilias* since the entry

CESSIO IN IURE HEREDITATIS[1]. If a *legitimus heres*, before acceptance, made *cessio in iure* of the *hereditas* to another person that other became *heres* for all purposes[2]. If he purported to do it after entry he remained liable, *semel heres semper heres*. But the *cessio* transferred the goods of the *hereditas*, and debtors to it were released[3]. If a testamentary *heres* attempted to cede before entry, his act was a nullity. If after, it was as in the case of *legitimus*. If a *suus* attempted to cede, the Sabinians held the act a nullity; the Proculians held that it produced the same effect as attempted *cessio* by *legitimus* after entry. The whole notion was obsolete in later law; it was possible of course to transfer the various properties, and make agreements as to liabilities, but there was no question of transfer of the *hereditas*.

It will be noticed that the *universitas* transferred was not that of the party, but that of someone else in which he had an inchoate interest. We are not told the reason of the difference of treatment between the cases of testamentary and *legitimi heredes*, which look much alike, but from Ulpian's way of stating the case it would appear to be matter of principle. Perhaps *scriptus heres* was not thought of as having a right at all, till entry, while *legitimus* had an inchoate right under the statute. But the opposite view may be held, that *heres scriptus* being specially appointed by the testator could not be allowed, in effect, to accept so far as to exclude intestacy, and at the same time evade personal responsibility. As to the *suus*, the Proculian view seems the more logical, but since Ulpian does not mention the case it seems probable that the Sabinian view prevailed.

It is not obvious why debtors were released. If *cessio* was a mere act of conveyance[4], they ought not to be in any way affected; debts were not assignable, but that is no reason why they should be annulled. If it is thought of as a judgement, this ought not to affect them as they were not parties, and a judgement, in general, affected only parties to it[5]. It is hardly likely that it was contemplated as a kind of *derelictio*.

into bondage. But see D. 4. 5. 2. 2. It is difficult to bring these goods within the definition of "what would have been his if he had not entered into bondage," and it is an unreasonable fine on one who has received the *filiusfamilias* by noxal surrender, and has employed him in his business. The text is defective and it may be that the missing part excluded the person *in mancipio*. See Krueger, *ad* G. 4. 80; Buckland, *Main Institutions*, 69.

1 G. 2. 35–37; 3. 85–87; Ulp. 19. 12–15. Garaud, *R.H.* 1922, 141.

2 Jörs, *R.R.* 236, suggests that it provided a way by which the *proximus* could in effect renounce in favour of the next, by accepting and then ceding.

3 Perozzi, *Ist.* 2. 489, holds this result due to the fact that the Romans saw in the act a renunciation. This states the fact but hardly explains it.

4 As to nature of *cessio in iure*, *ante*, p. 234.

5 Esmein (*Mél. Gérardin*, 229) in a study of *c. i. i.* accounts for the rules in this and other cases by the view that it is litigation, and that in early law *res iudicata pro veritate est*. That is: the effect is absolute, not merely relative to the parties, not in the sense that the fact is proved, but that the parties may not dispute it even against outsiders.

Adsignatio liberti. This was the right of a patron to assign the succession of a living *libertus* to one or more among his issue, under a senatusconsult of about A.D. 45[1]. The assignee must be in the *potestas*, and if he passed from it, or died without issue while the patron was alive, the *adsignatio* failed[2]. It might be by will or otherwise[3]. It was revocable and it might be conditional or *ex die*, but there might be no charge on it[4]. The *sc.* was needed to make this *adsignatio* possible since there is no such thing as the succession to a living man[5], and if the *libertus* outlived the patron the succession to him when he died was no part of the patron's estate. The right of succession was in the *liberi patroni*, not by way of succession to him, but as an independent right conferred by the XII Tables[6]. This was a power therefore in the patron to transfer a *universitas* in which he had not even an inchoate interest, a *universitas* which was not his own. Thus it needed express authorisation; hence the senatusconsult, and the rule that he could impose no charge on it. All he could do was to exclude some *liberi*; he could not benefit anyone else[7].

CXLII. *Addictio bonorum libertatis conservandae causa.* This was a rule, due to M. Aurelius[8] but modified from time to time, under which, if liberty had been given by will or codicil, and no *heres* entered, so that creditors were about to sell the estate and the gifts would fail, the estate might be assigned to one of the freed slaves, or (later[9]) an outsider, who gave security to the creditors[10]. The estate vested in him "as if he were *bonorum possessor*"; the liberties directly given thereupon took effect and he must carry out the others[11]. It was in effect a transfer of the *hereditas*, like *cessio in iure hereditatis*. Ulpian speaks of the addictee as acquiring the property like a *bonorum possessor*[12], but that would give him only a praetorian title, and, in classical law, would not have enabled him to free slaves in whose favour there was a *fc.* of liberty, so as to make them *cives*. His title, resting on rescript and *addictio*, was civil[13], but, debts not being transferable, he had only the same rights against debtors to the estate as a *bonorum possessor* had. As to his liability to creditors, the better view on confused texts[14] is that at first he could be sued only by the person or persons to whom he had given security, but that, later, creditors could sue him by *utiles actiones*.

Publicatio. In various cases of condemnation for crime, in fact in all

1 Inst. 3. 8; D. 38. 4. 1. pr. 2 Inst. 3. 8. 2; D. 38. 4. 1. pr. Modestinus (D. 38. 4. 9) lays down the contrary view that there may be *adsignatio* to an *emancipatus*. 3 Inst. 3. 8. 3; D. 38. 4. 1. 3. 4 38. 4. 7; h. t. 13. 3. 5 There could be no sale of such a thing, *post*, § CLXIX. 6 *Ante*, p. 378. 7 No such difficulty as to Latins. Their property on their death was treated as if it had been *peculium* all the time, see G. 3. 56 *in f.* 8 40. 4. 50. 9 As to this and other details, *ante*, p. 84. 10 Inst. 3. 11. 1. 11 40. 5. 4. 5; Inst. 3. 11. 1. 12 40. 5. 4. 21. 13 *Familiae erciscundae* available where *addictio* was to more than one, 40. 5. 4. 23. 14 40. 5. 3, 4. 22.

cases of capital sentence, i.e. involving loss of citizenship, the property of the criminal vested in the State, with certain limitations and exemptions in favour of children and others[1]. Apparently there was an administrative enquiry, and only if the estate proved to be solvent did it vest in the fisc. If it was insolvent it was sold by the creditors and the *fiscus* took no account of the matter. If it was solvent it vested in the *fiscus*, which paid off the creditors and could claim from debtors to the estate[2]. When the matters had been adjusted, it was usual to sell the property *en bloc* to a buyer who resold in detail, *bonorum sector*[3]. He had an *interdictum sectorium* to obtain possession of the property[4], but there is not usually any question of *universitas*[5]. Our information as to *bonorum sectio* is however very scanty[6].

On total forfeiture the *publicatus* was free of his old debts, but if allowed to retain some of his property he remained *pro rata* liable[7]. In any case, if he was free, he was liable for his old delicts[8].

SUCCESSION UNDER THE *SC. CLAUDIANUM*. We have seen that women who cohabited with slaves might be enslaved and lose their property with their liberty[9]—*successio miserabilis*. We are not told what became of the property. The expression *successio miserabilis* suggests that it went to children, and this agrees with the concessions made to children in later law where a criminal's property was forfeited, but the *sc.* is older than the earliest known of these concessions[10], and the ordinary forfeiture for crime is to the State. But as the woman herself passed into private hands, it is commonly held that her property went to the person to whom she was enslaved, and that he was liable and entitled by means of *actiones utiles* in respect of her estate, and no doubt also to noxal actions. The whole institution was abolished by Justinian[11].

BONORUM VENDITIO[12]. The details of this system will be considered in connexion with its chief application, execution of a judgement[13]. Here it is enough to say that in cases of insolvency either *inter vivos* or at death, with rules varying somewhat in the two cases, the estate was sold under the authority of the Praetor by a *magister bonorum* acting on

1 Buckland, *Law of Slavery*, 406 *sqq*. *Sc. Claudianum*, below. 2 48. 20. 4, 10. pr.; 49. 14. 1. 1, 6, 11, 17. As to enforcement of rights of or against the fisc, Mitteis, *R.R.* 1. 364 *sqq*. As to ways in which property might pass to the fisc and possible variations of treatment, Desserteaux, *Mél. Cornil*, 1. 199; *Capitis Deminutio*, 3. 36. His view that in later law the right of the fisc was thought of in some cases as succession is not really supported by texts in the *Corpus* which use such expressions as *hereditas vacans*, but it appears in the *scholia* in the *Basilica*. 3 G. 4. 146. 4 *Ib*. 5 Possibly at one time the *bonorum sector* bought the *universitas* and was liable and entitled to *utiles actiones*. 6 Condemnation as *servus poenae* destroyed all obligations and they did not revive on pardon, 44. 7. 30. 7 *Ante*, p. 97. 8 *Post*, § CXCVI. 9 *Ante*, p. 70. 10 48. 20. 7. pr. The *sc.* is of A.D. 52. 11 Inst. 3. 12. 1. 12 Kniep, *Mél. Girard*, 1. 623 *sqq* 13 *Post*, § CCXIX.

behalf of the creditors. He sold it *en bloc* to a *bonorum emptor*, the sale being by a sort of auction, the goods being "*addicta*" to the person who bid, not the highest sum, but the highest dividend on the debts[1]. Our concern here is with the position of the *bonorum emptor* regarded as universal successor. Both Gaius and Justinian so describe him[2], but the case differs notably from those already considered. These were civil, but here the succession was purely praetorian, like *bonorum possessio*[3]. The *emptor* had the goods *in bonis*, and he or his transferee would become *dominus* only by *usucapio*. There are other and more striking points of difference. It was not in fact universal succession at all. The debtor underwent no *capitis deminutio*; he remained liable for his old debts, since he could still be sued for the unpaid fraction[4], under restrictions which do not here concern us[5]. Indeed it seems that if any creditor had not put in a claim under the *venditio* he could sue for the whole debt, though he would not stand to gain anything by his abstention. On such a state of the law, it is difficult to see that the *universitas* passed. What passed were the debtor's assets, and these were technically still his, till the period of *usucapio* had run.

Thus the debtor's *universitas* did not vest in *bonorum emptor*. He became bonitary owner of the goods, having also an *interdictum possessorium* for possession[6]. He could sue debtors by praetorian actions, with the Rutilian *formula*, in which the bankrupt's name was in the *intentio*, but the *condemnatio* was to pay to the *bonorum emptor*, in an ordinary case of bankruptcy[7], and by another praetorian type of action, *formula Serviana*, with a fiction "*si heres esset*" if the insolvent was dead[8]. He was not liable for the debts, but only for the proportion of them that he had promised, and this liability did not rest on succession, but on his contract with the *magister bonorum*. It would be the logical result that he could not be sued by the creditors at all, but was liable only to the *magister bonorum* with whom he contracted. It is indeed observable that Gaius in describing the actions deals only with those brought by him[9], his other text, very imperfect, carrying the matter no further[10]. But Theophilus says he could sue and be sued by *utiles actiones*[11], and Lenel cites several texts which in their original form seem to have dealt with action against the *bonorum emptor*, but are not quite conclusive on the point against whom the action was brought[12]. There seems however no sufficient reason to reject the statement of Theophilus and the argument from analogous cases.

1 G. 3. 78 *sqq.*; *post*, § CCXIX. 2 G. *ib.*; Inst. 3. 12. pr. 3 G. 3. 80. 4 G. 2. 155 and see Lenel, *E.P.* 430. 5 See *post*, § CCXIX, and Inst. 4. 6. 40. 6 G. 4. 145. 7 G. 4. 35, 86. As to obligation of *deductio*, *post*, § CCXXXVIII. 8 G. 4. 35. It is, however, nowhere expressly stated that the field of these *formulae* was so divided. 9 G. 4. 35, 66. 10 G. 3. 81. 11 *Ad* Inst. 3. 12. pr. 12 Lenel, *E.P.* 428.

It is clear however that the notion of universal succession is of little use in this case, or in the connected system of *bonorum cessio*, which is identical in principle, though the debtor who had voluntarily surrendered his estate to his creditors had some special protection in the case of subsequent proceedings against him[1].

Note on *consortium* and *societas*

In a recently discovered passage (3. 154a–b) Gaius[2] contrasts the consensual *societas* of classical law with an archaic form known as *ercto non cito*[3] which existed between *sui heredes* who had not divided the *hereditas* between them. Since Gaius speaks only of *sui heredes* it probably did not come into being when *extranei heredes*, e.g. brothers succeeding an uncle, abstained from dividing their *hereditas*. This *consortium* seems to have been automatic unless the joint heirs took steps to partition, as Gaius describes it as *naturalis* as well as *legitima*.

A single *consors* could mancipate property of the *consortium* and could manumit a slave of the *consortium* so as to make him the *libertus* of them all. It does not appear, as has been maintained[4], that Gaius is referring to a particular *consors* to whom the management of the *consortium* had been entrusted by the others and who was thus their representative. Each of the *consortes* had this power of alienation and manumission by virtue of his membership of the *consortium*. The original conception was of each *consors* as potential owner of the whole property and this has left traces in classical law, as in the rule that manumission *vindicta* by one of common owners vested the whole man in the other. A *consors* could not acquire proprietary or contractual rights for his colleagues or bind them by contractual obligations, and no doubt his power of alienation was limited by a *ius prohibendi* in any other *consors*.

Gaius goes on to say that an artificial form of *consortium* among persons who were not joint heirs could be created before the Praetor *certa legis actione*, which suggests a special form of one of the general *legis actiones*, probably *per sacramentum in rem*. The passage thus confirms the view that *societas omnium bonorum* was descended from the ancient *consortium* of *sui heredes*.

1 *Post*, § CCXIX. 2 De Zulueta, *J.R.S.* 1935, 19 *sqq.*, *Institutes of Gaius*, 2. 174 *sqq.*; Daube, *Camb. L.J.* 1938, 381 *sqq.* with reff. 3 For various conjectures as to the meaning of this term, De Zulueta, *locc. citt.* 4 Solazzi, Glosse a Gaio, II (*Per il XIV Cent. delle Pand.*, Pavia, 1934); *contra* Buckland, *L.Q.R.* 1942, 483 *sqq.*

CHAPTER X

THE LAW OF OBLIGATIONS. GENERAL NOTIONS. VERBAL CONTRACTS. CONTRACTS *LITERIS*

CXLIII. The Law of Obligations is, roughly speaking, the law of *iura in personam*, of rights and duties existing between two or more persons but having, *prima facie*, no bearing on their relations to other people[1]. It has already been pointed out[2] that, while *obligationes* are classed as *res incorporales*, and so form part of the *ius rerum*, there are not wanting signs of a view that they are not *res*, but a conception with a close affinity to the notion of *actio*. This makes them a connecting link between the two topics. Apart from the texts already cited it may be noted that the *Regulae* attributed to Ulpian, as we have them[3], stop at intestate succession, that both the Digest and the Code contain the rubric, *De obligationibus et actionibus*[4], and that the association is helped by the use of the word "*actio*" to mean "right of action" as in the maxim: *minus est actionem habere quam rem*[5].

Justinian's definition of *obligatio* is: "*Obligatio est iuris vinculum quo necessitate adstringimur alicuius solvendae rei secundum iura nostrae civitatis*[6]." The word "*vinculum*" expresses the tie between the *creditor*,

1 It is far from covering the whole field. Apart from the restriction in earlier classical law to civil claims (*post*, § CXLIV) and neglecting the analysis which sees in *iura in rem* only a mass of negative duties imposed on individuals, there are many miscellaneous duties which are never called *obligationes*, e.g. in *damnum infectum* (*post*, § CCXLV) and *operis novi nuntiatio* (*post*, § CCIII), etc. 2 *Ante*, p. 186. 3 The original work covered the whole field, 44. 7. 25. 4 D. 44. 7; C. 4. 10. But this may mean merely "Of civil and praetorian obligations," *post*, § CXLIV. 5 50. 17. 204. 6 Inst. 3. 13. pr.; D. 44. 7. 3. pr. (Paul) is not a definition but a differentiation of two things. Marchi, *Bull.* 1916, 1, thinks P. was distinguishing *nexum* from *mancipatio*. The text has no doubt been altered, but it

reus credendi, and the *debitor*, *reus debendi*. "*Alicuius solvendae rei*" must be understood as covering any render or service with a money value. The words "*secundum iura*," etc., mean merely that it must be such an obligation as the law would enforce[1].

Obligatio[2], like *vinculum*, implies a tying together, and the same point of view appears in other terms, e.g. *nexum*, one of the oldest forms of obligation, and *contractus*, a noun which denoted only certain forms of binding agreement[3], while the verb, *contrahere*, was wider: there were many ways other than contract in which a man could contract an obligation[4]. It does not follow that both parties must be alike bound. In delict and in *stricti iuris* contracts only one was *obligatus*. In all cases, an *obligatio* had two sides: the right and the duty. Conceived of as a right, it was a *res*, and that is the aspect considered when *obligatio* is mentioned among the cases of *res*. As it was treated as part of the *ius rerum*, we should expect this aspect to be brought out in the definition, but that emphasises only the duty. In the actual treatment it is primarily regarded as a right, and though this might make little difference, since the right of *A* is the duty of *B* stated in another way, still this conception of *obligatio* as a *res* did in fact affect the discussion. We are told how we could acquire an obligation, the right, by the act of a subordinate, but not, in the treatment of obligations, how such a person's act could impose an obligation, the duty, on us. In contract the omission is not surprising, as, at civil law, no such thing could happen[5], but that is not so in delict; noxal liability was recognised by the XII Tables. But all these matters are discussed in the law of actions, in the course of the explanation of special types of action.

Debitum and *obligatio* are not distinguished in classical texts, but it has been shewn that they are distinguishable, *debitum* (*Schuld*) signifying that a relation exists such that one "ought" to pay and the other to receive, *obligatio* (*Haftung*) signifying that a liability can be enforced[6].

seems a simple distinction between the subject matters of actions *in personam* and those of actions *in rem*, in place in his *Institutiones*. It seems unlikely that in such a book he would discuss as part of the law an institution which had been dead for centuries.

1 It has been suggested that *obligatio* in early law rested on transfer of property. *Debere*, on this view = *dehabere*, and in *credere* the *dare* is obvious.

2 The word *obligatio* is rare before Gaius. Cicero uses it but hardly in a juristic sense (*Ep. ad Brut.* 1. 18. 3). *Obligare* is as old as Plautus, and is used by Cicero in a juristic sense (*pro Caec.* 3. 7; *pro Mur.* 2. 3). The lawyers rarely use abstract terms: they speak of *obligationes*, of an *obligatio*, but not of the abstract conception, *obligatio*. In like manner it has been noted that for them the "nature" of a thing is its physical characteristics; in the sense of juridical characteristics, *natura contractus, actionis*, it is the later men who use it (Rotondi, *Scr. Giur.* 2. 159). But this is not absolute, G. 4. 33.

3 But see *post*, § CXLV.

4 G. 3. 91; cp. Inst. 3. 14. 1.

5 *Obligatio* is civil in earlier classical law, *post*, § CXLIV.

6 Literature, Jörs, *R.R.* 41 *sq.* See also Cornil, *Mél. Girard*, 1. 199; *A.D.R.* 74; Siber, *R.R.* 2. 161, etc.; *contra*, for Roman law, Duquesne, *N.R.H.* 1913, 125; Koschaker, *Z.S.S.* 1916, 348, reviewing Steiner, *Datio in solutum*; Segrè, *St. Bonfante*, 3. 501.

Thus in a bare pact there is *debitum* but no *obligatio*: in conditional promise there may be *obligatio*, but there is no *debitum*. Thus arises the possibility that the *debitum* may rest on one and the obligation on another. This suggests a state of things in which the person bound is not the person who incurred the debt: in fact there is evidence that this was at one time the normal situation. We are better informed on procedural relations than on any others for early law, and it is notable that we find the actual liability usually falling on someone other than the debtor. The *praes*, not the actual loser, is liable for the *lis et vindiciae* and the *sacramentum*. *Vades* are responsible if a party fails to appear. A *vindex* is responsible if proceedings in execution are wrongly opposed[1]. In contract the earliest promises of which we really know anything are *sponsiones*, guarantees of another's debt. This early history is beyond our scope, but it may be observed that it is now widely held that the notion of obligation, at least of contractual obligation, begins in a state of things in which an obligation can be made binding only by giving either a hostage for its performance, or a thing to be forfeited if there is failure in performance, the hostage, through the intermediate stage of allowing a man to be his own hostage, as in *manus iniectio pura*, being the practical source of the later law of obligation[2]. A corollary to this is the view that to be *obligatus* in early law meant more than to be liable for a debt: it meant to be pledged for a debt, to be a *persona obligata* in much the sense in which a pledge is a *res obligata*: to be in a definite state of subjection, either in relation to the other party or, as some hold, generally, being no longer like any other freeman[3]. Hence it follows that mere performance does not end the matter: there must be release from the bondage[4]. But all this is disputed: in any case it is obsolete long before the Empire.

The personal nature of *obligatio* was one of its most marked characteristics. This was perhaps evidenced to some extent by the fact that it could not be assigned, but few rights were assignable. More significant is the fact that it was, in general, impossible at any stage in Roman law to acquire, directly, a right of this character through a transaction by a third party[5]. The same rule had held at one time in *iura in rem*, but it had disappeared, for *iure gentium* transactions, in later classical law[6]. In contract it never did. If *A*'s *procurator* *B* bought a horse for him, the transfer to *B* vested the horse in *A*, in later law, but rights and liabilities under the contract were in *B*, and would have to be transferred

1 *Post*, §§ CCVIII, CCXI. 2 G. 4. 25. Mayr, *Z.S.S.* 1921, 198, as to *praestare* and *praes stare*. 3 Various shades of opinion, Beseler, *Beitr.* 4. 92; Perozzi, *Le Obligazioni*, 65; Marchi, *Storia dell' Obligazione*, 69; *S.M.W.* 353; Jörs, *R.R.* 42. 4 *Post*, § CXCIII. 5 Limitations and modifications, *post*, § CXLIX. 6 *Ante*, p. 278.

by the device which evaded the difficulty that such things could not be assigned[1].

Obligatio was so intensely personal that it seems that, at one time, it died with the party liable. This was always so in delict, but in very early law it seems to have been not less true in contract[2]. The earliest *stipulationes* of which we know anything are *sponsio* and *fidepromissio* and neither bound the *heres*. Long before the Empire, however, ordinary promises of *res*, certain or uncertain, bound or benefited the *heres*. An essentially personal service, e.g. to paint a portrait, could not be understood of the *heres* either way (apart from action on a breach committed before the death)[3].

Another kind of question brings out the personal character of *obligatio*. If a slave made a contract, e.g. of hire, and the master dealt negligently with the property, or *vice versa*, what were the resulting liabilities? *Obligatio* being personal, could *A*'s act be breach of *B*'s contract? In the first case put, the rule seems to have been that the master's *culpa* could not make him liable on the contract[4], though if he had damaged the thing he might be liable in delict, under the *l. Aquilia*. Any *dolus* would subject him to the *actio doli*, and here the law went further and allowed this *dolus* to come into account in any *bonae fidei* transaction, under the "*ex fide bona*" clause in the *formula*[5]. In *stricti iuris* contracts earlier law knew no remedy but the *actio doli*, but later law, perhaps later classical law, gave an *actio utilis* on the contract itself[6], this way of dealing with it shewing that it was outside the true scope of the contract. If a slave committed a delict in respect of property held by his master under contract, the older view was that this gave no action on contract, but only, in appropriate cases, a noxal action. But the view which prevailed was that if the master was not to blame even in choice of the man, he could be sued *ex contractu*, but could free himself by handing him over. This was not noxal surrender as it was not in delict, but it gave a similar result[7]. If the wrongdoing slave was the subject of the contract, the rule seems to have been that his act was

1 *Post*, § CLXXXIX. 2 *Post*, § CL. For the views that in very early law obligations perished with the party, see, e.g., Korošek, *Erbenhaftung*, with full references to literature. 3 As to *stipulatio faciendi* in general, *post*, § CLIV. 4 No text states such a liability. 5 13. 6. 3. 5; 15. 1. 36. In *fiducia* a special clause in the Edict brought into account *dolus* by the *paterfamilias* of the actual fiduciary, Lenel, *E.P.* 294. 6 45. 1. 49. pr. Not good authority. Demand seems to have been made under the liability *de peculio*, putting the master in personal "*mora*." 7 Principal texts, Coll. 12. 7. 7, 9; D. 9. 2. 27. 9, 11; 13. 6. 20, 21. 1; 18. 6. 12; 19. 2. 11. pr., 1; 19. 2. 25. 7; 47. 2. 54. 1. Levy, *Konkurrenz*, 2. 71, limits this for classical law to a slave himself the subject of the contract, and in such a relation to the injured person that there can be no noxal action. This involves an inacceptable explanation of Coll. 12. 7. 9. If my slave steals a thing which I hold under liability for *custodia*, the owner has no *actio furti* (*post*, § CXCVII) and there would be no such right of *pro noxae deditione*.

no breach of the contract, which he did not make, and thus if a hired slave stole from the hirer, there was no *actio ex conducto* but only a noxal action *ex delicto*[1]. This is obscured by the fact that in transactions descended from *fiducia*, some texts refuse a noxal action but give one on the contract with a right of release by surrender—*pro noxae deditione*[2]. This may be due to the fact that, *in fiducia*, the receiver, being owner, could have no noxal action, the texts having been written of *fiducia*, and representing a transfer to the new system of a rule developed in the old to which alone it was appropriate. For *commodatum*, Justinian, in an interpolated text, gives, reasonably, a noxal action[3].

CXLIV. Classification of Obligations. Justinian follows, in the main, the order and treatment of Gaius. But while Gaius says nothing of *obligationes honorariae*[4], Justinian states his "*summa divisio*" as into two classes, civil and praetorian, the former created by statute or recognised by civil law, the latter by the Praetor, "*ex sua iurisdictione*[5]." He then states a "*sequens divisio*" which is in fact that of Gaius, based on the nature of the fact creating the *obligatio*, amplified by the addition of the heads of quasi-contract and quasi-delict. This is the division followed in his treatment, and though he does deal with praetorian obligations in quasi-delict, he says little of them in contract, and nowhere marks them off as a class under the head of *obligatio*[6]. Thus, for our purpose, the important division is into four classes.

1. Contract[7], which can be loosely defined as actionable agreement[8]. This is not exact, as certain pacts gave actions but were not called *contractus*. What Gaius means is those agreements which in classical law gave a civil law action[9]. Justinian merely follows Gaius.

2. Quasi-Contract. This may be defined as an obligation which arises

1 Principal texts, 9. 4. 19. 2; 17. 1. 26. 7; 19. 2. 45. pr., 1, 60. 7; 25. 2. 21. 2; 47. 2. 62. 5–7. 2 13. 7. 31; 27. 2. 62. 1, 7. Cp. 21. 1. 23. 8, 58. pr.; 9. 4. 40; 30. 70. pr., 3. See Buckland, *Slavery*, 125. 3 13. 6. 22. 4 Gaius knows nothing of *obligatio honoraria*. For him, *obligatio* is a civil conception. He mentions obligations which are in fact purely praetorian (3. 192, 209), but these are offshoots of civil obligation. He says nothing of obligations "*quasi ex delicto*," and the only quasi-contract he mentions is civil (3. 91). He treats only of civil modes of discharge; his language in 3. 181 being significant. What he has to say of what are in fact praetorian obligations he says under the law of actions. He contemplates the Praetor as capable of giving *actiones*, but not of creating *obligationes*. It must be remembered that his main notions are based on some work earlier than Julian's consolidation of the Edict. Many writers hold that this limitation to civil cases held throughout the classical age, see Segrè, *St. Bonfante*, 3. 500 *sqq.*, with full references to literature. 5 Inst. 3. 13. 1. 6 G. does not here mention this *summa divisio*. Elsewhere (e.g. 4. 110) he speaks of actions given by the Praetor, and Paul (Coll. 2. 5. 4) speaks of *actio honoraria* or *civilis*, based on civil law or praetorian jurisdiction. 7 As to *natura contractus*, Rotondi, *Scr. Giur.* 2. 159; *post*, § CCXXVIII. 8 See, however, *post*, § CXLV. 9 *Fiducia* answered the definition, but was not called a contract; as to the reason, *post*, § CLI.

without agreement or wrong done, but it is much more analogous to contract than to delict. Its somewhat heterogeneous content will be discussed later.

3. Delict. Obligation arising from a wrong, which may or may not be connected with a contract. Not all delicts are treated in Gaius or the Institutes, but four important cases, all known to the civil law. For though *iniuria* is, as we know it, mainly praetorian, Gaius is careful to base it on the XII Tables[1], and *rapina* is a derivative of *furtum*.

4. Quasi-Delict. This is not in Gaius; the cases treated hereunder by Justinian are all praetorian; the principle of distinction from delict will be considered later[2].

Gaius admits that his division into two heads is inexact, and involves treating under *negotia* some things which are not *negotia*[3], and in the Digest he appears as classifying obligations under three heads, contract, delict and "*ex variis causarum figuris*[4]." There are long citations from his "*liber aureorum*[5]" which are the source of Justinian's passages dealing with quasi-contract and quasi-delict, and suggest that these are what Gaius means by "*variae causarum figurae*," but do not suggest that all obligations must come under one of these heads. But these texts are in all probability very freely interpolated[6].

These are not the only classifications. Modestinus says: "*obligamur aut re aut verbis aut simul utroque aut consensu aut lege aut iure honorario aut necessitate aut peccato*[7]." Here the first three are contract and the others presumably cover everything else. But the classification passes from a basis in the creative fact to one in the enforcing authority with resulting overlapping, and the text is not helpful. The classes "*lege*" and "*iure honorario*" are defined but not illustrated. There were in fact a great number of obligations which might come under these heads, in particular the latter[8].

There were other distinctions of some importance. Leaving out of account merely moral obligations, not recognised by law, not all which the law would enforce were equally enforceable. Most were enforceable by action, but in some cases the law did not allow an action but did allow subsidiary effects. Some claims could be enforced only by way of retention, not by action. Thus the defendant in a real action could resist the claim unless reimbursed for certain expenses[9], but could not recover them by action. There was the same right where a creditor sought to

1 G. 3. 223. 2 *Post*, § CCIV. 3 *Summa divisio*, 3. 88; 3. 91. 4 44. 7. 1. pr. 5 44. 7. 1, 4, 5. 6 See Mitteis, *R.Pr.* 1. 86. 7 44. 7. 52. ? interp.; as to 44. 7. 25. 1, Arangio Ruiz, *Mél. Cornil*, 1. 81 *sqq.* and reff., 85, n. 1. 8 Many appear under the head of actions: in this case, even more than elsewhere, for historical reasons, the matter is persistently looked at from the point of view of procedure. 9 *Post*, § CCXXVIII.

enforce a pledge against a *bona fide* holder[1]. The husband's right to deductions in returning *dos* was in later law also enforceable by *condictio*, but the existence of this latter right was still disputed in late classical law[2]. The holder in *commodatum* or deposit had this right of retention apparently before he acquired an *actio contraria*, and at the beginnings of the contract of pledge this right of retention of the *res* was, it seems, the only right conferred by it[3].

There is also a classification into *obligationes civiles*, actionable at law, and *naturales*, enforceable only indirectly[4]. The expression *obligatio civilis* is itself ambiguous. An obligation might be enforceable by a civil law action or by an action given by the magistrate. The former were *obligationes civiles*, in a narrower sense, the latter being *obligationes honorariae*[5]. Again, of civil obligations in this last sense, some were always such, having their origin in the old civil law; others, originally praetorian, acquired civil law actions only later. These are sometimes said to be "*iure civili comprobatae*[6]."

All these are classifications according to mode of origin: there are others of a different type. *Obligatio* might be unilateral, where one party only was bound, as in delict and *stricti iuris* contract, or bilateral, where there were duties on both sides, as in sale and many other cases, or, while primarily unilateral, they might in certain events create obligations both ways, as in deposit, *commodatum*, mandate, *tutela*, etc.—imperfectly bilateral[7]. Again they might be either to do or to give or to abstain. They might be principal or accessory, such as those of a surety, for a *certum* or an *incertum*, a distinction having important effects in procedure, *bonae fidei* or *stricti iuris*[8], with similarly important effects (a classification differing from the others in that it is not exhaustive; there were obligations which were neither). They might be divisible or indivisible, a distinction obvious in its nature but not so simple in its application, having its chief importance in connexion with performance (*solutio*), with which topic it will be considered[9]. They might be simple or alternative, e.g. to give *A* or *B*, a distinction also material in *solutio*[10].

The artificial nature of Justinian's classification should be noticed,

1 20. 1. 29. 2. Another case, 3. 5. 17.
2 25. 1. 5. 2, perhaps due to Justinian, Schulz, *Z.S.S.* 1913. 57 *sqq.*
3 *Post*, § CLXVI. On these rights of retention, Riccobono, *Dal dir. Rom. al d. mod.* Ch. XI, XII. See also *ante*, p. 213.
4 *Post*, § CLXXXIX.
5 Inst. 3. 13. 1.
6 Not in the sources but suggested by, e.g., Inst. 3. 13. 1, though the class here spoken of as *comprobatae* would cover all not based on statute, but recognised at civil law.
7 No Roman authority. It is of little value in any case, and, on the views now held by some writers as to some of these cases (e.g. *tutelae*, *post*, § CCXXXIV), of very narrow application.
8 This distinction applies properly to the remedy, rather than to the obligation.
9 *Post*, § CXCIII.
10 As to modalities, e.g. *dies* or *condicio*, *post*, § CXLVIII.

at the cost of some anticipation. He gives four sources of obligation. He gives four types of contract, omitting innominate contracts and actionable pacts, which, in view of the late development of the former and the praetorian character of the latter so far as they were known to classical law, Gaius might reasonably do, but hardly Justinian. He gives four contracts "*re*," four consensual contracts, though *pacta praetoria* and *legitima* are not really distinguishable under Justinian, four delicts, though in fact there were many others and two of these four, *furtum* and *rapina*, were really one, and four quasi-delicts. This symmetrical scheme obviously does not correspond with practical facts.

CXLV. CONTRACT. A contract was, subject to a small correction already indicated[1], an agreement enforceable by action at law. It is however maintained that in classical law *contractus* had a wider field, corresponding to that of *contrahere*, its original meaning being anything which can be called a *negotium*, including *condictio indebiti*[2]. Not every-one who accepts the idea gives it the same width; it is impossible to go into the various shades of opinion[3]. Others hold, and it seems the more acceptable view, that the word as a term of art is not ancient, that its technical meaning is civilly actionable agreement, and that the looser uses found are largely due to the compilers[4] and, so far as they are classical, are not technical.

Contract involved a concurrence of two wills as to future conduct of one or both of the parties. Such a concurrence, to be capable of proof, must be in some way expressed. The law might hold that any expression sufficed, that where agreement was proveable there was a contract. Roman law did not take this position; it took the view that an agreement was not enforceable unless there was some reason why it should be. At first, like other systems, it found this reason in Form. The oldest contracts of Roman law are formal contracts, owing their validity to the fact that they are expressed in a certain way, with the corollary that this form was the essential. If that was gone through it was immaterial whether real consent was present or not[5]. But of those of which we have any knowledge *nexum* alone answers strictly to this conception. Consent

1 *Ante*, p. 409. 2 G. 3. 91. Perozzi, *Le Obbligazioni*, 47 *sqq.* Cp., for our early law: "the fact is the covenant or agreement, or the offence, which two are the only ways of making obligations". West's *Symboleography*, Pt. 1, § 3, cited Wambaugh, *Cases on agency* (2), 2. 3 Steiner, *Datio in solutum*, 60, does not include *solutio indebiti*. Bonfante, *Scr. Giur.* 3. 135, includes only *negotia* involving a *vinculum*. De Francisci, *Synallagma*, 2. 329, sees a school dispute, the Sabinians adopting the wide view, the Proculians, in most fields but not in all, the narrower. 4 Pernice, *Z.S.S.* 1888, 195; Riccobono, *Dal dir. Rom. al d. mod.* 303 and App. II, has an exhaustive discussion with a full account of the literature. See also G. Segrè, *Rend. Acc. Lincei*, 1929, 49, and *St. Bonfante*, 3. 500. 5 Thus, as we shall see, it was only gradually and imperfectly that the law took account in these contracts of factors affecting the validity of consent.

is at any rate emphasised in *stipulatio* in classical and later law[1]. The contracts "*re*" mark a further advance; for a very limited number of transactions the principle was recognised that the agreement became a binding contract if the subject-matter was handed over for the concerted purpose. A further development[2] was the consensual contracts. For a small but commercially important group of contracts the principle was accepted that mere consent, however evidenced, should suffice. All these conceptions existed by the beginning of the Empire. This progress, resulting in the existence of distinct groups of contracts, makes it difficult to lay down any general theory of contract for Roman law. It may be easier for the modern Roman law in which formal contracts have ceased to play a part, but for the actual Roman law there are at least two theories of contract, that of the formal (or rather *stricti iuris*) contracts, and that of the *bonae fidei* contracts[3]. In stating the general principles of contract this distinction has constantly to be borne in mind.

A contract involves agreement, *consensus*[4], concurrence of two minds, existing at the moment when the contract is made. This moment is readily determined in *nexum* (assuming that this is to be treated as a contract), and almost equally readily in *stipulatio*, where the question and answer ordinarily occur together. Even here there might be difficulty. If the offer and acceptance were not at the same time (and essentially all contracts can be reduced to offer and acceptance) it would be hard to prove that the stipulator's intent still existed at the time of the promise. Accordingly it was held that they must be substantially continuous. Thus, says Ulpian, if the stipulator left the room before the answer was given, there was no *stipulatio*, unless indeed it was only for a moment, and he duly returned and got his answer[5]. If, after the question was asked, the *stipulator* attended to other business, a *promissio* later in the day was useless[6]. We have no information as to the literal contract. We do not know how the debtor expressed his assent, but in the recorded cases it seems to have been on the spot[7]. In the contracts "*re*" there was ordinarily little difficulty, since the acceptance of the thing was normally acceptance of the contract. But in the consensual contracts and especially in sale and hire, much business was done by correspondence. Questions must have arisen whether an acceptance was prompt enough, whether an offer was still open, and so forth, but they are not represented in the legal texts[8].

1 2. 14. 1. 3. 2 Historically perhaps earlier. 3 *Mutuum*, loan for consumption, is *stricti iuris*, but not formal, but many of its rules were laid down before it was conceived of as a contract at all, *post*, § CLXII. 4 On tacit consent, Perozzi, *Ist.* 1. 135. 5 45. 1. 1. 1. 6 45. 1. 137. pr.; 45. 2. 12. pr. 7 Cicero, *de Off.* 3. 14. 58. 8 There seems no evidence on the rule which must have existed that an offer could not be accepted after a reasonable lapse of time. There is no direct evidence, for contract, as

As the only possible evidence of a man's intent is external facts there has been some controversy on the question whether the law is really concerned with his intent, or whether it can be said that for legal purposes there is no difference between a man's intent and the external expression of it. The Romans do not discuss this abstract question, *ex professo*, but appear to have taken the view that where intent was material it was real intent, and to have drawn remarkable conclusions[1]. The controversy has played a part in the discussion of two practical questions[2]: first, the interpretation of what purports to be a contract[3], secondly the question how far, when the meaning has been made clear, the agreement propounded represents a real "will" of the parties.

In dealing with formal contracts, on the first point, *stipulatio* was taken as the type. Ambiguous stipulations are dealt with in several texts. Some of these must be disregarded in laying down a general rule, as they deal with creation of *dos*, always favourably treated[4], and others, though they appear in the Digest as applicable to all transactions, were written of legacy, also exceptionally treated[5], so that it is unsafe, even for Justinian's law, and impossible for classical law, to apply them generally. Ignoring these, the first rule was to look at the dealings apart from the formal words so as to gather the meaning[6]. If this did not help, the local usage of such words was considered[7]. If that failed, there was a rule that the words must be so construed as to make the transaction effective. Thus a stipulation for payment "on the Kalends of January" meant the Kalends of next January, otherwise the debt need never be paid[8]. If all these failed, words were construed in favour of the *promissor*, to lessen the obligation not to enlarge it[9]. But if the words were clear the *promissor* could not insist on an interpretation favourable to him, other than the plain meaning[10].

to the effect of death of a party on an unaccepted offer: the texts which can be adduced dealing with other types of transaction suggest that either death of a party, or death and notice of the death, caused the offer to lapse (e.g. 12. 1. 41; 39. 5. 2. 6; h. t. 19. 3; Regelsberger, *Pandekten*, 1. § 150; Windscheid, *Lehrbuch*, 2. § 307); Fritze, Dissertation, Keil 1896. Offer of reward, e.g., for restoring lost goods (19. 5. 15), Brini, *Bilateralità delle Pollicitationes*, *Mem. Acc. Bologna*, 1908, 29. They could give rise only to an innominate contract.

1 But see Ferrini, *Opere*, 3. 349. See also *post*, § CXLVI. 2 Also in the question at what moment a contract made by correspondence is complete. See Schuster, *German Civil Law*, 87, for the different solutions reached by modern systems. 3 Van Wetter, *Pandectes*, 1. 271. 4 23. 3. 2, 70; 50. 17. 85. pr., etc. 5 50. 17. 12, 56, etc. Windscheid, *Lehrb.* § 84. 6 2. 14. 4. 3; 50. 17. 34. 7 50. 17. 34, 114. 8 45. 1. 41. pr., 80; 50. 17. 67. 9 34. 5. 26; 44. 7. 47; 45. 1. 38. 18, 99. pr.; 50. 17. 34; illustrations, 2. 15. 5; 45. 1. 106. "*Benignior*" solution means no doubt the same thing, so far as generally applicable, but these texts (e.g. 34. 1. 20. 1; 50. 17. 56, 168. pr., 192. 1) were written of legacy and *dos* and "*benignior*" is a suspicious word. 50. 17. 96 was written of wills. 10 45. 1. 99. pr., 110. 1 (where the words are not ambiguous). The document is construed as a whole and general words may be limited by other provisions, 50. 16. 126.

The same question might arise in *bonae fidei* contracts, especially in the loosely constructed consensual contracts. The rules, discussed almost exclusively in connexion with Sale, were much the same. The course of negotiations (*quod actum est*) was of primary importance[1]. Usage was also to be considered[2]. Apart from this, ambiguities were construed against the party who formulated the proposals, as in *stipulatio*, with the difference in effect that, there, this was necessarily the *stipulator*; here it might be either party. But the texts commonly treat the vendor as the formulator[3], and where this is not said but the ambiguity is construed against him, the transaction is usually called a *venditio*, implying that the proposals emanate from him[4]. Some texts which seem to deal with ambiguities and to give a different result are merely assigning the recognised meaning to the expressions used[5]. There is, however, an exception. If the difficulty was created by the mistake or fraud of the vendor's slave, the vendor was not prejudiced. Thus where land was sold by description and the vendor's slave, in pointing out the boundaries, included other land, the land sold was what was covered by the description[6], an application of the principle that a slave could not, without authorisation, make his master's position worse.

CXLVI. Assuming the real meaning arrived at, the question now arose, how far this represented a real intent. Was there anything in the circumstances to shew that there was no real consent? Often the facts would shew that there was no intent to set up a legal relation[7]; apart from such cases, this is the question whether there had been any fraud (*dolus*), duress (*metus*), or mistake, and, if so, what was its effect?

Fraud. *Dolus*. This may have caused such mistake as vitiated the agreement even apart from fraud. In other cases the rule was clear. Consent induced by fraud was none the less consent. In *stricti iuris* transactions the fraud had, till the time of Cicero[8], no effect on the liability. Thereafter the *exceptio doli* could always be pleaded in reply to a claim on a contract induced by fraud, and there was an *actio doli* where the matter had been completed[9]. In *bonae fidei* contracts, the words "*ex fide bona*" in the *formula* of the action enabled the injured party to prove the fraud, if he was sued, and, conversely, to claim on account of it if he sued. The result was not the same. In the last group, the *iudex*, taking notice of the *dolus* could, in appropriate cases, diminish the

1 18. 1. 6. 1, 33, 40, 77, 80. 2. 2 21. 1. 31. 20. 3 2. 14. 39; 18. 1. 21; 19. 1. 21. 6; 50. 17. 172. pr. 4 8. 3. 30; 18. 1. 33, 77, 80; 50. 17. 172. 5 18. 1. 40. 1, 80. 2; 50. 16. 90, 126, 169, 205; cf. 8. 2. 17. 3. 6 18. 1. 18. 1. 7 44. 7. 3. 2, 54. 8 *de Off.* 3. 14. 58 *sqq.*, "*nondum enim C. Aquilius, collega et familaris meus, protulerat de dolo malo formulas.*" 9 4. 3. 1. 1, if there was no other action, but *condictio sine causa* would sometimes be available. As to *restitutio in integrum*, *post*, §§ CCXLIII *sq.*

condemnatio without absolving the defendant[1]. But in a *strictum iudicium*, if the *exceptio doli* was proved, the action was lost, and the right of action consumed. On the wording of the *exceptio doli*[2], the action was lost if any fraud was proved, even though on the facts it did not induce the contract, e.g. was a minor matter which would not have affected the decision of the party. But we are told that the *exceptio doli* lay on the same grounds as the *actio doli*, and that this action did not lie for small matters[3].

Duress. *Metus*. The duress contemplated is not mere threats of evil consequences, but an immediate menace of death or extreme physical injury to the party or his family[4]. In the older texts it is coupled with *vis*[5], and the line between physical compulsion, which would certainly make the act unreal, and such threats as these, is not readily drawn. It might easily be held that consent given under such pressure was no consent at all and the transaction therefore a nullity, but that does not seem to have been the attitude of the law.

The ancient formal transactions were valid at civil law, even if induced by *metus*; the Praetor, in historical times, gave the necessary relief. *Mancipatio, metus causa*, was valid, but the *res* remained "*in bonis*" of the victim[6]. This rule had however nothing to do with consent; it expressed the fact, already noted, that in the ancient formal transactions if the form were duly gone through, consent was immaterial[7].

A few texts speak generally of transactions affected by *metus* as being void[8]. Some of these are on manumissions: as there could be no setting aside of a manumission which had taken effect[9], the only way in which to do justice was to declare it void *ab initio*, so that these are not in point. The other texts are general and are commonly construed to mean only that relief was given in such cases. But this is not the natural interpretation of most of them, and one or two can be construed only as excluding *voluntas* and declaring absolute nullity[10]. Other texts however speak of consent thus obtained as nevertheless consent: "*quamvis si liberum esset noluissem, tamen coactus volui*[11]." The titles dealing with these matters contain a number of texts which treat the transaction as valid *iure civili*, subject to praetorian relief, *restitutio in integrum* in some form. But the title in the Digest dealing with relief for *metus*

1 E.g. 19. 1. 41. 2 *Post*, § CCXXIII. 3 4. 3. 9. 5; 44. 4. 2. pr. 4 4. 2. 3 *sqq*. 5 E.g. Cicero, *ad Quint. fr*. 1. 1. 7. 21; cf. D. 4. 2. 1. 6 G. 4. 117; P. 1. 7. 6–8. 7 The same consideration applies to fraud. 8 Chief texts on *metus* (outside D. 4. 2 and C. 2. 19) G. 4. 117; P. 1. 7. 4–10; Fr. D. 7; Cons. 9. 3; C. 8. 38. 5; D. 23. 2. 22; 29. 2. 6. 7; 40. 9. 9, 17; 44. 4. 4. 33, 34; 50. 17. 116. 9 4. 4. 9. 6; Fr. D. 7; D. 40. 9. 9, 17. 10 Cons. 1. 3 *sqq*.; 29. 2. 6. 7. Schulz, *Z.S.S*. 1922, 171, hardly disposes of these texts, and Beseler, *Z.S.S*. 1924, 363, accepts these texts as classical law for informal transactions but hardly disposes of the others. 11 4. 2. 21. 5.

nowhere discusses *bonae fidei* transactions, though that in the Code contains late legislation assuming praetorian relief in such cases[1].

It seems at first sight on this state of the texts that *bonae fidei* transactions affected by *metus* must have been void. But so long as the matter was in the contractual stage and there had been no performance, the ordinary machinery of the *bonae fidei iudicium* gave protection, and it seems better to accept what is now the dominant view that in this case also the *voluntas* was supposed to be present, though the Praetor would if necessary relieve. But the conflict in the texts cannot be ignored out of existence, and it must be supposed that there was an opinion other than that which prevailed[2].

Error. If assent was given, on the assumption of the existence of certain facts, and they were not as assumed, there may be said to have been consent, not to what was actually proposed but to something else. Thus, wherever mistake affected the contract, it did so on the ground that there was no consent and the agreement was void. But on the important question when mistake did so affect the contract, it is difficult to draw any rational conclusion from the texts.

In *stipulatio* a mere error in drawing up the usual *cautio* could be corrected. If what the parties had intended to stipulate was clear, the writing was overridden[3], and it may be assumed that the same rule applied elsewhere. But the question arises, where the words of the *stipulatio* were clear, how far a party might plead that they were not what he meant. We are told that error excluded consent[4], but that is not helpful till we know the limits of the rule. Where there was no doubt as to the identity of the subject-matter the contract is valid whatever mistake there may have been as to its qualities[5]. But where the parties were actually thinking of different things, as there was no consent, there was no contract[6]. Naturally this does not mean that a mere assertion of the error sufficed; it must be proved. Even so this is out of harmony with the principles of formal contracts, and it is sometimes explained as meaning that there was no contract even though the words were clear, if, on the facts, they were understood by the other party as used in another sense. But this involves a forced interpretation of explicit texts[7].

There seems to be no direct information as to the effect, in *stipulatio*,

1 C. 2. 19. 3, 4, 5. In all these cases the property has been handed over, so that it is relief against transfer of property, not contract. 2 Modern writers have produced many theories, shewing nullity on one state of facts and relief on another, but there is no agreement as to basis. Windscheid, *Lehrb.* § 80, n. 2; recent elaborate study, Betti, *Ist.* 1. ch. 13. 3 2. 14. 4. 3; 50. 17. 92; C. 4. 22. 1. 4 2. 14. 1. 3; C. 1. 18. 9. 5 4. 3. 38; 45. 1. 22, 32. 6 Inst. 3. 19. 23; D. 45. 1. 137. 1; 34. 5. 3. 7 Similar rule in wills where there is no question of the other party's understanding, 28. 5. 9. pr.; D. 30. 4. But here there is not the same difficulty. In wills, intent rules.

of error as to the identity of the other party, but from certain texts, in the law of theft, it appears that if *A* agreed to lend money to *X*, believing *X* to be *Y*, and stipulated for its return, the whole transaction was a nullity[1].

For contracts with *bonae fidei iudicia* the rules are mainly stated in connexion with Sale. At first sight the principles look different. The guiding rule was that fundamental error avoided the contract, but the only way to determine what was fundamental error, is to enumerate the forms of error which are declared to vitiate the contract. Error *in negotio* avoided it, e.g. where one party thought it a sale, the other a loan[2], a point which could hardly arise in formal contracts. Error as to identity of what was sold avoided the contract, if it was as to the principal thing, not where it affected only an accessory[3]. Error as to quantity or price avoided it if it was to the prejudice of the party under the error, but not otherwise[4]. Error as to the person with whom the contract was made does not seem to be discussed, but it was material in some cases and probably was so treated, e.g. where *A* intended to let a farm to *T*, a good farmer, but the person who presented himself was another *T*, not such. No doubt the rule was as in *stricti iuris* contracts[5].

There remains what is called *error in substantia*. The texts do not tell a consistent story, but the view generally held, giving on the whole the best account of the texts, is that error as to the qualities did not affect the contract, unless it was such that the thing differed so widely from what it was supposed to be as to be in a distinct commercial category, e.g. where it was supposed to be gold but was in fact copper or plated, vinegar instead of wine, an *ancilla* instead of a man[6]. Another opinion is that the distinction must be such as would have determined for or against the purchase[7]. Apart from the indefiniteness of this, it does not suit the texts, for many differences which might well have put off the buyer did not affect the contract if it was actually made, e.g. the article was of low carat gold instead of high carat[8]. But the explanation preferred above is a rationalisation of the texts: it is not formulated by

1 *Arg.* 47. 2. 43. pr.–3, 67. 4, 76. Cf. 12. 1. 32. 2 44. 7. 3. 1; 12. 1. 18. 1. Must be distinguished from mistake as to the legal effect of the transaction gone through. If a man buys by stipulation and counter-stipulation, is it any defence to shew that he meant it to be *emptio venditio*? See 2. 14. 7. 12 (interp.). 3 18. 1. 9. pr., 34. pr. 4 19. 2. 52. 5 See n. 1 and Savigny, *System*, 3, § 136. Lauria, *L' errore nei negozi giuridici*, 14 *sqq.*, on *error in persona*, repudiates, for R.L. the categories of *error* found in the text-books. He makes it clear, at least, that in many of the cases nullity can be shewn without reference to the conception of *error*. (The same can be said of the treatment of mistake in some text-books on English law.) The essential factor, for him, is *dissensus*, of which *error* is a factor. Exposition of this conception of *dissensus*, Betti, *Ist.* 1. 423. 6 18. 1. 9. 2, 11. 1, 41. 1. Authorities in Moyle, *Sale*, 55. 7 Windscheid, *Lehrb.* § 76, n. 9. 8 18. 1. 10. D. 18. 1. 14 *in f.* seems in conflict with general rule, but it is not clear what *inauratum* means.

the jurists, and probably was never definitely conceived by them. Further, it was, at best, the rule of later classical law; there was it is said an older view which refused to take mistake of this kind into account as affecting the validity of the contract[1]. Again, many texts raise the hypothesis in the form "*si aes pro auro veneat*," and it has been contended[2] that the texts are not dealing with mistake at all, but with representations, express or tacit, made by the vendor, innocently or not, and only lay down the rule that if, e.g., a thing is expressly sold as gold and is copper, there is no sale. On this view misdescription "*in substantia*" prevented a contract from arising but misdescription on a minor point merely gave a claim for compensation. But there are texts which cannot be dealt with in this way[3]. It must be noted that even though the mistake prevented a contract from arising, another legal relation might exist. Thus, if the thing had been delivered, the ownership might have passed: there would be a *condictio* on the one hand to recover the thing, and on the other for recovery of any price paid[4].

CXLVII. Capacity. Since contract depended on consent the parties must be capable of this. We have already considered *pupilli*, women under *tutela*, lunatics, *prodigi*, Latins and peregrines[5], but something must be said of persons in *potestas*. Males over 14 had full contracting power, but the right under their contract vested at once in the *paterfamilias*, except so far as the contract concerned the *peculium castrense*, or *quasi castrense*, as to which they were treated as *patresfamilias*[6]. Conversely at praetorian law the *paterfamilias* was liable under their contracts to varying extents (with the same exception[7]), as under those of slaves[8]. But they themselves were liable at civil law. Their *castrense peculium*, however, was not liable on contracts which concerned the *paterfamilias*, so that the point became important only when the *filius* became *sui iuris*. If this was by *emancipatio*, the civil liability was destroyed by the *capitis minutio*, and, in any case, if the son did not succeed to the father, the action might be unjust. The Praetor dealt with the matter by an Edict, providing that if the son had not succeeded to the father, then, however he had become *sui iuris*, an action would lie against him, subject to "*beneficium competentiae*", and only "*causa*

1 18. 1. 45, where, however, the goods were definitely sold as of a certain character. Mackintosh, *Sale* (2), 94, n. Lenel, *Riv. de Derecho privado*, 1924, 97, makes a case for the view that all the law of *error in substantia* is due to Justinian. 2 Leonhard, *Irrtum*, § 26, as part of a wider thesis. See also Vangerow, *Pandekten* (7), 3. 266. Recent writers find Stoic notions at the bottom of this conception of *error in substantia*. Sokolowski, *Philosophie in Privatr.*; Ehrlich, *St. Scialoja*, 2. 731. See also review of Leonhard, 2nd edn., by Henle in *Gött. Gel. Anzeigen*, 1908, 427 *sqq.* 3 E.g. 18. 1. 11, 14. 4 12. 1. 32; 12. 6. 7, 12, etc. Error on the part of a representative, *post*, § CLXXXIV. Eisele, *Nichtigkeit obligatorischer Verträge*. 5 *Ante*, pp. 92 *sqq.*, 96 *sqq.*, 158 *sq.*, 168 *sq.* 6 49. 17. 4. 1. 7 49. 17. 18. 5. 8 *Post*, § CLXXXIV.

cognita," a restriction which allowed the refusal of any action, or of an action *in solidum,* if the circumstances called for this[1]. Action might indeed be brought while he was still *alieni iuris,* but *actio iudicati* was deferred[2]. If he was under 14 at the time of the contract, it seems that he cannot have been liable any more than one under *tutela* would, and there is no question of *auctoritas* in this case. As to females the better view seems to be that the principles were as for males, with however a very different result. They were capable of acquiring by contract, but incapable of binding themselves, so long as the perpetual *tutela* of women lasted[3].

The contract must be possible. The general rule was that an agreement for an impossibility was void. Impossibility might be either physical or legal. Physical impossibility meant inconceivability, what was contrary to the nature of things, a promise to touch the sky with one's finger, a sale of a hippocentaur and so forth[4]. Legal impossibility is exemplified, e.g. by promise or sale of a *res sacra* or the *Forum*[5]. The mere fact that it was impossible to the party was immaterial. If *A* undertook to paint a portrait as good as one by Apelles or to sell land not his, both were in a sense impossible, but that was no defence; if he did not carry out his contract he would be liable[6].

A thing impossible in fact or in law might not be obviously such. Here the classical law, especially in legal impossibility, and only in *bonae fidei* contracts, especially sale, gradually admitted a modification of the strict rules. Where one actually free was sold, in good faith, as a slave, the later classical law gave an *actio ex empto,* for which Paul's reason is that it is difficult to tell a slave from a freeman[7]. Where *ager religiosus* was so sold, Ulpian says that there was an *actio in factum*[8]. This implies that there was no valid contract, whereas in the case of the freeman it is clear that the transaction was a real sale. In later law, but perhaps not till Justinian, this and other similar cases of legal impossibility were on a level with that of the freeman, and there was an *actio ex empto*[9]. If the buyer knew the facts he had of course no remedy. Conversely the fact that the vendor was aware of the facts would not bar the buyer, and it may be inferred from other rules of sale that an

1 14. 5. 2 *sqq.* 2 14. 5. 5. 3 Girard, *Man.* 497; *ante*, p. 134. 4 G. 3. 97; Inst. 3. 19. 1; D. 45. 1. 35. 5 18. 1. 4, 22; 45. 1. 83. 5, 103, etc. 6 45. 1. 137. 5. General notion of impossibility, *ante*, p. 297, and Rabel, *Mél. Gérardin*, 473 *sqq.* He discusses the history of the word itself (*impossibilis*) which he holds, citing Wölfflin, to be not earlier than about Trajan's time, the idea having been expressed by "not in the nature of things," etc. He points out also that the general formula, "*impossibilium nulla obligatio*" (50. 17. 185), is not *expressly* applied to *b. f.* contracts. 7 18. 1. 4–5. 8 11. 7. 8. 1. 9 18. 1. 4–6.

innocent vendor had only to return the price, while, if he was fraudulent, consequential losses might come into account[1].

In contracts *stricti iuris* none of these developments occurred. The promisee had no remedy except that resulting from *dolus*, the *actio doli*, or, if he had stipulated against *dolus*, an action on that *stipulatio*, which had the advantage of being perpetual[2]. But this gives a false impression. A *stipulatio* for land which was in fact a *res religiosa* would not usually be by way of gift; other transactions would be connected with it. Thus other property might have been transferred in return for the promise. In such a case this could be recovered by *condictio sine causa*, even though the other party was innocent[3].

Another type was that in which a thing sold had ceased to exist at the time of the contract. Here, whether the vendor knew this or not, there was no contract and any price paid could be recovered[4]. But there was nothing to prevent the sale of a future thing, though, in a sense, delivery was impossible. The question therefore arose: was it possible to sell or promise a thing existing, but at present incapable of sale, subject to the condition of its becoming saleable? In the case of a freeman this was forbidden; it is improper to contemplate his falling into slavery[5]. Elsewhere the same principle is applied to *stipulatio* and to *res sacrae*[6], *religiosae* and *publicae*: it may have been general.

All this deals with initial impossibility, but a contract might become impossible after it was made (*casus*). A thing sold or promised might cease to exist, become *religiosa*, or be expropriated by the State. Here there certainly was a contract. The general rule applied was that if this occurred without the act or fault of the person liable, and before he was "*in mora*" he was released from his liability[7]. But the contract was not necessarily destroyed *ab initio*. Thus in sale, though a vendor was released by accidental destruction of the thing sold, the buyer must still pay the price[8]. The rule in counter *promissiones* where one party was released "*casu*" is not clear: some texts suggest that the other party could resist action, or reclaim if he had performed, but this is not clear[9].

An agreement for something illegal or *contra bonos mores* is void[10], the latter being illustrated by agreements to produce or prevent marriage or divorce, or in respect of the *hereditas* of a living person[11]. According

1 *Arg.* 19. 1. 13. pr.–3; 18. 1. 45, etc. Damages, etc. generally, *post*, § CLXXII *in f.*
2 It is a civil action on *stipulatio*: *actio doli*, like most praetorian penal actions, was *annua*, *post*, § CCXXXIII.
3 12. 7. 1, 4; doubtless *exceptio doli* on a counter promise.
4 18. 1. 57. pr., *post*, § CLXIX.
5 18. 1. 34. 2.
6 45. 1. 83. 5. Clearly, there were disputes. Sale of *hereditas viventis*, *post*, § CLXIX.
7 Windscheid, *Lehrb.* § 264, n. 5.
8 *Post*, § CLXXI. The risk is with him.
9 See 12. 7. 1. 2 and cp. 12. 4. 3. 4; analogous case, *cond. ob rem dati*, *post*, § CLXXXVII.
10 45. 1. 26, 27; C. 8. 38. 4, etc.
11 C. 8. 38. 4.

to some texts the same is true of simple promises of money where there is a further illegal or immoral purpose or *causa*, whether this is expressed or not, and of promises of money under an illegal or immoral condition[1], but it seems probable that in classical law these were dealt with by the Praetor, by *denegatio actionis* or *exceptio doli*[2]: the distinction has become meaningless in Justinian's time[3].

CXLVIII. MODALITIES. A valid contract, satisfying the foregoing requirements, might be subject to restrictions created by the parties. Of these, two, i.e. *dies* and *condicio*, need some consideration.

Dies (*a quo*) may be either *certus* or *incertus*, e.g. "on the kalends of June" or "on the death of *X*": it must be a futurity which is certain to arise, otherwise there is a condition. *Dies* in this sense was perfectly admissible and the *obligatio* existed, though not yet enforceable[4]. Payment could ordinarily be made at once[5], and if before the day there was no *condictio indebiti*[6]. The creditor could in some cases require surety[7]. He could presumably claim in bankruptcy (*bonorum venditio*[8]).

Dies ad quem is on a very different footing. There was an overriding rule, "*ad diem deberi non posse*[9]," which gave rise to difficulties which will best be considered in connexion with stipulation. All that need be said here is that the effect was not to nullify the obligation. The *dies ad quem* was ignored at civil law, but, as this would clearly do injustice, artificial constructions of the transaction were adopted which were not the same in legacy and stipulation[10].

Dies might occur in all contracts of classical or later law. It does not seem that it could occur in *nexum*, as it certainly could not in *mancipatio*. It seems inconsistent with the nature of the contract *literis*, though a letter of Cicero's is supposed to indicate its admissibility[11].

Condicio is more important. As we have seen[12] a conditional obligation is one subject to an event both future and uncertain. There could be no condition in *nexum* or in the contract *literis*[13]. Justinian speaks of doubts as to the admissibility of condition in *societas*[14], and Gaius shews that

1 45. 1. 19. 97. 2, 134, etc. 2 12. 5. 8. 3 See on these points Siber, *St. Bonfante*, 4. 105 *sqq.*, but not all his allegations of interpolation are acceptable. It may be that, as the texts say, where the improper purpose or *causa* appeared on the face of the *stipulatio*, this was simply void (45. 1. 19, 61). See also, *post* § CLXXXVII. 4 G. 3. 124; Inst. 3. 15. 2; D. 45. 1. 46. pr. 5 46. 3. 70. This is *dies certus*. If it is uncertain, since this was normally "on the death of *X*," it may be that this rule would not apply as there might be obvious reasons for postponement, e.g. if *X* was the *paterfamilias*. Or where the date is fixed in the interest of the creditor, on which point the Gloss cites 31. 43. 2; 22. 1. 3. 3; 13. 5. 18. pr.; 33. 2. 6. 6 12. 6. 10. Pledge on such a debt could be enforced, 20. 1. 14. 7 5. 1. 41. 8 For other results see Girard, *Man.* 501. 9 Inst. 3. 15. 3, *post*, § CLIV. 10 45. 1. 16. 1; 33. 1. 4; *post*, § CLIV. 11 *Ad Fam.* 7. 23. 1. 12 *Ante*, p. 297. 13 Vat. Fr. 329. The tacit conditions mentioned in 50. 17. 77 might occur in formal transactions, 23. 3. 43. pr., 61 (interp.). 14 C. 4. 37. 6.

there had been similar doubts for the other bilateral consensual contracts[1]. It has been suggested that this doubt may have rested on the view that as the contract is based purely on consent, there could be no contract at all till the consent was operative. There seem to have been no doubts in contracts *re*. Thus in pledge and *mutuum* (loan for consumption) it might be agreed that the *possessio* or the ownership, as the case might be, was not to pass till a certain event. But it is not easy to apply the notion of condition to deposit and *commodatum*[2].

The first point in relation to conditions is the question of the attitude of the law to a conditional *obligatio* while the *condicio* was outstanding. Many rules resulted from the proposition that pending satisfaction there was as yet no complete *obligatio*. Money paid in that time could be recovered as *indebitum*, till actual satisfaction[3]. If a thing sold ceased to exist, by accident, *pendente condicione*, there was no contract: the loss fell on the vendor[4]. A contract to sell a man his own property was void, but if it was conditional and the *res* was not his when the condition was satisfied, it was good[5]. A conditional stipulation did not "novate" a pre-existing one till the condition occurred[6]. If either party died, leaving no successor, before the condition arose, there was no contract[7]. *Pendente condicione* there could be no *usucapio* of goods delivered under a conditional sale[8]. On the question whether an action, lost because brought while the *obligatio* was yet conditional, could be renewed, the texts conflict[9]. But the transaction was not a nullity, in the meantime. It could not be renounced (except where a right of renunciation was a tacit or express term in the contract[10]). The capacity to contract must have existed when the agreement was made[11]. There was a "*spes debitum iri*" which passed to and against representatives[12]. A conditional creditor could claim *bonorum separatio*[13].

1 G. 3. 146. 2 The only obvious condition is that a future event is to decide which of certain contracts, e.g. deposit, or *commodatum*, or mandate, it is to be. See 16. 3. 1. 12 *sqq*. There are however texts which seem to shew a real condition and others in which it is a mere *lex* or term, e.g. 16. 3. 1. 22, 33. The use of the word *condicio* is not decisive. 3 12. 6. 16. pr. 4 18. 6. 8. pr. 5 18. 1. 61. 6 Conversely a conditional *obligatio* is not novated by a new *stipulatio*, till the condition occurs; till then there is no *obligatio* to novate. *Post*, § CXCIV. 7 Bufnoir, *Conditions*, 271 *sqq*. 8 41. 4. 2. 2. 9 20. 1. 13. 5; 21. 1. 43. 9; Inst. 4. 6. 33, etc. Bufnoir, *op. cit.* 240 *sqq*. In case of *dies* the action could not be brought again in classical law, G. 4. 53 *sqq*. Cf. Inst. 4. 6. 33b; P. 1. 10. 1. Conflicts, *post*, p. 424. *Post*, § CCXXXVII. 10 In mandate and *societas* there is a tacit right of renunciation, *post*, §§ CLXXVIII *sq*. 11 45. 3. 26. Betti, *Ist*. 1. 558, notes that while absolute capacity must have existed at the time of contracting, those requirements which are merely relative to the specific transaction, e.g. that the buyer is not owner, need exist only when the condition is satisfied. 12 18. 6. 8. pr. 13 42. 6. 4. pr.; *ante*, § CX. The right, where *stipulans* was a son or slave vested in the *pf.* though the condition was not satisfied till he had passed from *potestas*. 45. 1. 78. *Contra*, under wills, 28. 5. 7; 36. 2. 5. 7. There seems to be no direct evidence for other contracts in the case of *filius familias*, but it is probable that the rule was as in *stipulatio*.

These conflicting points of view, both that there was and that there was not an *obligatio*, naturally led to conflicts[1]. The texts disagree on whether an action, lost because brought *pendente condicione*, was renewable[2], and on the right of a conditional creditor to get *missio in possessionem*[3]. If a debtor of a *res* was "*in mora*" when it ceased to exist, his obligation survived[4]. If, however, the obligation was novated, this was said to purge the *mora*, but the texts disagree on the question, whether a conditional *novatio* had the same effect[5]. If one who was liable "*pure*" promised the same thing conditionally, there would be *novatio* if the condition occurred, but there was disagreement on the questions whether the second *stipulatio* amounted to a pact not to sue on the original one while the condition was outstanding[6], and whether if payment was made in error there was *condictio indebiti*[7]. But all these questions are the subject of much controversy[8].

If, in an ordinary conditional contract, the condition failed the result was that there was *ab initio* no contract at all. When the condition was satisfied, if no intervening event had discharged the obligation, there was a simple contract. Some texts say that the effect was retrospective[9]. But though this proposition is in harmony with some of the rules[10], it is inconsistent with others[11], and the better view is that it is not really an expression of any actual principle of law[12]. In fact the various decisions, even where classical, were a compromise—the needs of life were more important than theory.

The doctrine that occurrence of a *condicio* is retrospective bears on a much discussed question. Was a conditional contract affected by the death of a party? If the effect is retrospective it should not be, and it clearly was not affected under Justinian[13]. If there was no retrospective effect, it might be contended that there is no obligation till the condition happens, and an obligation cannot begin in the *heres*. It does not quite follow, since there was some sort of obligation: the parties were bound

1 The distinction between *debitum* and *obligatio*, Schuld and Haftung, has been utilised to explain these; *ante*, p. 406. 2 *Ante*, p. 423. 3 42. 4. 6. pr., 7. 14, 14. 2. 4 *Post*, § CLXXXVIII. 5 45. 1. 56. 8; 46. 2. 31; 46. 3. 72. Bufnoir, *Conditions*, 250 *sqq.* 6 2. 14. 30. 2; 12. 6. 60. 1. 7 12. 6. 60. 1. 8 *Post*, § CXCIV. Vassali, *Bull.* 1914, 192 *sqq.*, holds that the texts, much interpolated, shew a tendency in the compilers to assimilate the effects of a conditional transaction to those of one *sub die*. 9 18. 6. 8. pr.; 20. 4. 11. 1. 10 E.g. a conditional contract by a slave remained with his master at making though he was transferred, while a conditional legacy, where there was no retrospection, passed with him. 45. 1. 78. pr.; 50. 17. 18. But the theory is not necessary to this. Further illustration, Bufnoir, *Conditions*, 294. 11 The sale is void where the *res* perishes between making and fulfilment of condition, and the creditor is not entitled to fruits accrued before condition satisfied, 18. 6. 8. pr. Bufnoir, *cit.* 308, considers the question of failure after the *res* has perished. See also Seckel-Levy, *Z.S.S.* 1927, 163 *sqq.* 12 Girard, *Man.* 507; Arangio Ruiz, *Ist.* 80; Haymann, *Z.S.S.* 1928, 350. 13 Inst. 3. 15. 4; D. 18. 6. 8.

though there was nothing due. It is widely held[1], with variations in detail, that Justinian's rule that the contract is not affected is post-classical, though there are strong dissentient opinions[2].

On the question what amounted to satisfaction it is to be noted that a condition could not be partly fulfilled—until it was completely fulfilled it was not fulfilled at all[3]—and that in some circumstances a condition was treated as satisfied where in fact it was not. This occurred where the satisfaction was prevented by one interested in the non-fulfilment[4]. The rule seems to have been that this must have been in bad faith, that it must have been with a view to prevention, but where there was a definite act of prevention the intent was *prima facie* presumed[5].

Conditions impossible in law or fact invalidated the transaction; they were not struck out, as in wills[6]. So with illegal or immoral conditions, i.e. such as gave the transaction an illegal or immoral tendency. A promise to a man if he remained a bachelor (in classical law), or if he committed a crime, was bad[7], but promise by a man if he did wrong was good[8]. A promise by a man if he did not commit a wrong was void, as also was a promise to a man on the same terms[9].

Where a condition became impossible after the contract was made, as where there was a promise to *X* if he married, or freed, *S*, and *S* died, the contract failed apart from cases of prevention[10].

The conditions hitherto discussed were suspensive conditions, in fact the only real conditions. There were also what are called resolutive conditions, i.e. conditions the arrival of which was to destroy the obligation. These, we are told, were not conditions on the contract, but on the *resolutio*[11], i.e. *ab initio* destruction. But just as *ad diem deberi non potest*, so, *ad condicionem deberi non potest*. At civil law, such a condition was ignored. A *stipulatio* for 10 "*nisi navis ex Asia venerit*" was an absolute

1 Vassali, *cit.* regards it as very late. Suman, *Saggi minimi*, 38, credits it to Justinian. Riccobono, *St. Perozzi*, 351 *sqq.*, argues strongly for the view that J.'s rule was that of praetorian law, and ousted the civil rule in the fourth century, as a result of universalisation of *cognitio extraordinaria*, which made formulary distinctions unimportant. Accepted by, *inter alios*, Koschaker, *Festschr. für Hanauschek*, 120; Bonfante, *Corso*, 1. 514; Bohaček, *Note esegetiche*, 1 *sqq.*; and apparently, Levy, *Z.S.S.* 1926, 420. For Sochol, *Z.S.S.* 1927, 168, the Proculians hold them not heritable, Sabinians *contra*: this view prevailed but J. adopted the other. 2 Beseler, *Z.S.S.* 1926, 89, and Haymann, *Z.S.S.* 1928, 350, hold them heritable in classical law. Arangio Ruiz, *Ist.* 80, holds that opinion was divided. 3 45. 1. 85. 6. Expression of principle that conditions are indivisible, which has other results, Bufnoir, *cit.* 73. *Stipulatio poenae*, Cuq, *Man.* 599. 4 50. 17. 161. 5 *Arg.* 35. 1. 24; 40. 7. 3. 16, 38. 6 14. 7. 31; 45. 1. 7, 137. 6; G. 3. 98; Inst. 3. 19. 11. 7 P. 3. 4b. 2; D. 45. 1. 123; see *ante*, p. 421. 8 45. 1. 121. 1; h.t. 19 is only an apparent exception. 9 2. 14. 7. 3; 12. 5. 2, 3, 8. The latter is blackmail. No objection to a promise if a third person does a wrong: it is insurance. Or if a third person does not, e.g. to buy a house if my ship is not captured by pirates. 10 35. 1. 94. pr.; 45. 1. 85. 7; *ante*, p. 339. 11 18. 1. 3; 18. 2. 2. pr. It is a *conventio*, not a *condicio*, 41. 4. 2. 3.

promise but the Praetor intervened and allowed an *exceptio*, if action was brought after the ship arrived[1]. If the money was claimed before, as it could be, for it was an unconditional promise, and the ship afterwards arrived, the money could be recovered under a sale[2], and, presumably, on the principles of *condictio sine causa*, in a case of *stipulatio*[3]. But consensual contracts were on a special footing in respect of resolutive conditions[4]. They might be dissolved by consent, and therefore by a conditional consent. Such cases were prominent in the law of sale[5], but could occur in the other consensual contracts. It is important, however, to note a distinction. A hire might be for five years and would end automatically. It might be till a certain event happened and this is sometimes wrongly called a resolutive condition. A true "resolutive condition" dissolved the contract *ab initio*; here it ended it[6].

CXLIX. Contract, being essentially a relation between certain parties, could in strictness produce no effect for or against those not parties to it. Hence the principle that a man cannot contract to benefit or bind a third party. Detailed rules based on this notion will be considered under the head of stipulation[7], but some remarks may be made here on the general principle. There was a maxim: "*inelegans visum est ab heredis persona incipere obligationem*[8]." This principle would exclude promises to bind or benefit the *heres* alone, and all promises "*post mortem*" of either party. This is not necessarily an application of our principle. The rights and obligations of a *heres* were inherited and there was a logical difficulty in regarding him as inheriting those which could never on their terms have attached to the deceased. This point of view is suggested by the above passage from Gaius who rests the rule on an *inelegantia*, and not on the rule against contracts for third persons, which he discusses separately[9]. Ulpian distinguishes the *heres* from other third persons[10], and Justinian, in abolishing this rule, does not speak of that about third parties, but describes the rules he is abolishing as independent *regulae*[11].

However this may be, there is no doubt of the existence of the more general rule. The acquisition by the *paterfamilias* of the rights under contracts by sons or slaves was not a real exception[12]. How far classical law did admit of exceptions is debated. In dealing with a contract definitely made in favour of a third person[13] we must first consider how

1 44. 7. 44. 2. As to similar rule in promise of annuity "*quoad vivam*," Inst. 3. 15. 3, *post*, § CLIV. 2 41. 3. 19. 3 12. 7. 1. 2. 4 Costa, *Storia*, 439, holds that, in informal contracts, resolutive conditions operated *ipso iure*. 5 *Post*, § CLXXIII. 6 Examples of resolutive conditions, *post*, § CLXXIII. 7 *Post*, § CLIV. 8 G. 3. 100. 9 G. 3. 103. 10 45. 1. 38. 1. 11 C. 4. 11. 1. Special mention of *heredes* in *stip. faciendi*, *post*, p. 440. 12 *Post*, § CLXXXIV. 13 Effect *in rem* of *pacta de non petendo*, *post*, § CXCV.

far if at all it gave a right of action to the third party. The texts have been studied by Eisele, who shews that in nearly all cases the right of action is due to interpolation[1]. But there were other cases. Where a *donatio* was made on the terms that after a time the thing was to be handed to a third party, Diocletian gave the third party an *actio utilis*[2], but Eisele shews that this was *condictio* for recovery, not an action on the contract; it was in effect *cessio legis*, implied transfer of action[3]. Again if an *actor municipii* or a *curator* or a *tutor* made a *constitutum*[4] for payment to the *municipium* or ward, these could sue, *utilitatis gratia*[5]. This is an exception, says Eisele, explicable by the fact that in procedure these particular representatives had a closer relation to their principal than other procurators, so that exceptional treatment is not surprising[6].

There were a few other cases in which a third party had an action on the principle of *cessio legis*, to be considered later[7], and a further case in which a *mandator* had an action on the contract of his agent[8]. On the other hand a third party might be liable to action under the *actiones institoria* and *exercitoria*[9], and a *mandator* might be sued[10]. There were also some exceptional cases under the law of partnership[11]. And where a depositee redeposited, the original depositor had *a. dep. utilis* against the third party[12]. Apart from such exceptions, the rule that a contract did not bind or entitle a third party still existed in Justinian's law[13].

If *A* stipulated with *B* that *B* should give money to *X* or, conversely, that *X* should do something, *X* could neither sue nor be sued. But could *A* sue if the thing was not done? In strictness he could not. In the first case *A* had no *interesse*[14]. In the second, *B* had not promised to

1 Eisele, *Beiträge*, 76 *sqq.* Deposit or *commodatum* by non-owner, on terms that it is to be returned to owner. Owner has *utilis actio*, C. 3. 42. 8. 1; *dos* given on terms that it is to go to grandchildren: they have *utilis actio*, C. 5. 14. 7; sale by pledgee on terms that debtor is still to have a right to redeem, debtor has *actio utilis ex vendito*, 13. 7. 13. pr.
2 Vat. Fr. 286 (=C. 8. 54. 3). 3 *Post*, § CLXXXIX. 4 *Post*, § CLXXXII.
5 13. 5. 5. 9. 6 Eisele remarks that it is an exception not to the present rule but to that of non-representation, but that is merely an application of the rule under discussion. We cannot contract to bind or benefit another, even though this was the intent of all parties. *Actio ut. de in rem verso* where the act is by a freeman, v. Tuhr, *Actio de in rem verso*, 298.
7 *Post*, § CLXXXIX. 8 *Post*, § CLXXXIV. The case of money of principal lent by agent, the principal having a *condictio* (e.g. 26. 9. 2) does not require this principle. The liability is created by the transfer of property, *post*, §§ CLXII, CLXXXVII. 9 *Post*, § CLXXXIV.
10 *Ib.* 11 *Post*, § CLXXVII. 12 Coll. 10. 7. 8. Bonfante, *Scr. Giur.* 3. 243, holds that an *a. utilis* was given to third party more easily than is supposed. He cites Appuleius, *de magia*, 91, and considers that Coll. 10. 7. 8 and Vat. Fr. 286 (=C. 8. 54. 3) represent the classical law. On C. 5. 14. 7, Siber, *R.R.* 2. 175. Riccobono, *Lineamenti della dottrina della representazione diretta*, shews that classical law had gone far in this direction especially by giving *exceptio doli* against *repetitio* where the transaction had taken effect. 13 45. 1. 83. pr.; 50. 17. 73. 4; Inst. 3. 19. 3 and 4. On texts giving "singular successors" a right of action on contract (39. 2. 24. 1a), Bonfante, *Corso*, 2. 1. 355. See also *post*, § CLXXXIX as to buyer and seller. In C. 4. 27. 3, where a *procurator* contracts and takes a pledge, Justinian allows the contractual rights to vest in the principal. 14 C. 4. 50. 6.

do anything. The difficulty was avoided by making a penal stipulation: *B* promised to pay a penalty to *A* if the thing was not done[1]. But the classical law went further; it was ready to construe a promise that *X* should do something as a promise that *B* would procure that he did, though, so far as can be seen, only in a few cases, connected with litigation[2]. In the first case, though the render was actually to be to *X* it might well be that *A* had an interest in it, and this would entitle him to sue, e.g. a *contutor* stipulating with his colleague, *rem salvam pupillo fore* (he had an *interesse*, as he would be liable), and a *stipulatio* for payment to the stipulator's *procurator*, or to his creditor[3]. One text adds several cases in which *A*, being under a contractual obligation to *X*, contracted with *B* that *B* should do the service to *X*[4], and shews that the necessary *interesse* existed wherever *A* was under a legal liability, and probably wherever there was a pecuniary interest, and that here there was no difference between *stricti iuris* and *bonae fidei* contracts. Whether an *interesse affectionis* was ever enough, outside slave law[5], is doubtful[6].

Some agreements actionable in later, and even in classical law, were never called contracts[7], exceptions to a principle which existed throughout the history of the law, i.e. that no action lay on mere pacts as such. This principle is expressed in well-known texts: "*Sed cum nulla subest causa propter* (or *praeter*) *conventionem, hic constat non posse constitui obligationem. Igitur nuda pactio obligationem non parit sed parit exceptionem.*" "*Ut debitor vel servus domino vel dominus servo intelligatur ex causa civili computandum est*[8]." These texts indicate the need of "*causa*," beyond the mere fact of agreement. But the word "*causa*" is a very unreliable instrument. Even where used to signify a basis of right its meaning varies. The *iusta causa traditionis* is not quite the same as the *iusta causa usucapionis*[9]. In Sacramentum, "*secundum suam causam*[10]," the word may mean all the facts of title, the conveyance as well as the facts leading up to it. It also means many things which have little to do with a basis of right. It means a lawsuit[11], the accessories of a thing recovered by action[12], cause; indeed the lexicons give a bewildering

1 Inst. 3. 19. 3, which points out that an express undertaking to see that *X* did it was enough to give *A* an action. Cuq, *Man.* 597. Later history of penal stipulation, Guarneri-Citati, *Bull.* 1922, 241. 2 The proper interpretation of the *stipulatio rem ratam habiturum*, *post*, § CCXXXIX. See also 45. 1. 81. pr., 83. pr. Girard (*Man.* 484) holds that the same construction was freely applied in *b. f.* contracts. There are no texts. 3 Inst. 3. 19. 20. 4 45. 1. 38. 21. 5 Buckland, *Slavery*, 69 *sqq.* No general inference can be drawn from these cases. 6 In 21. 2. 71 pecuniary interest is not wholly absent. 7 *Post*, § CLXXXII. 8 2. 14. 7. 4; 15. 1. 49. 2. 9 *Ante*, pp. 228, 246. If putative *causa* had sufficed in general in *usucapio*, they would have been much the same. 10 But, as to these words, *post*, § CCVIII. 11 1. 18. 10. 12 10. 2. 44. pr.

number of meanings and shades of meaning. Here it is taken to mean a pre-existing fact giving validity, with the resulting rule that an action arose on agreement coupled with *causa*.

The *causa* was a characteristic of the transaction. Usually it was the form employed. But, in the consensual contracts, there is the difficulty that they had no necessary form; there was mere *conventio*, and the main text expressly declares this to be insufficient. Maine surmounts the difficulty by finding the *causa* not in the individual transaction, but in the importance of such transactions as a class[1]. In the contracts "*re*," the "*causa*" was delivery. But if that was a sufficient *causa*, any agreement with delivery ought to have been binding. But gratuitous delivery of an article for a temporary purpose would not make a contract unless it was within one of the recognised cases. No doubt it would frequently come within the conception of mandate[2], but for that purpose delivery was indifferent. The whole notion gives undue importance to the word *causa* in the texts quoted. What the writer[3] means is that there can be no action on a mere pact as such—the agreement must be one which the law makes actionable. He is expressing a great difference between the Roman conception and that of our law. To the Romans an agreement was not actionable unless there was some reason why it should be. To modern English law an agreement is actionable unless there is a reason why it should not be. "*Causa*" thus means actionability and not something independent of actionability which produces that characteristic. *Pacta legitima*[4] had no *causa* except the fact that enactments made them actionable. It has been said that *causa* is *voluntas legis* added to *voluntas* of the parties[5].

CL. Before entering on the Contracts, as classified by Gaius and Justinian, something must be said of two cases which do not appear in the classification.

Nexum. This highly controversial matter will be briefly dealt with as *nexum* had long been obsolete in classical law[6]. Little is really known of it: it has been doubted whether there ever was such an institution. No text tells us that there was a contract called *nexum*, but we have so little juristic literature of the Republic that that is not surprising. But we have texts which speak of *nexum* as creative of obligation, of *nexum aes* and *nexi liberatio*[7], and many literary texts dealing with debtors who

1 *Ancient Law*, 333. 2 E.g. 16. 3. 1. 11 *sqq.*; 47. 2. 14. 17. 3 Text is to some extent interp. If delivery was a sufficient *causa*, *permutatio* (*post*, § CLXXXI) should have been a civil contract. 4 *Post*, § CLXXXIII. 5 Bonfante, *Scr. Giur.* 3. 134. 6 See, for full discussion of texts and literature, De Zulueta, *L.Q.R.* 1913, 137. Girard, *Man.* 508. 7 The chief juristic texts are definitions by Manilius and Q. M. Scaevola, quoted by Varro, *L.L.* 7. 105, Cincius and Gallus Aelius, quoted by Festus *s.vv. Nexum, Nuncupata pecunia*; G. 3. 173, 174 of inferential value.

were *nexi*[1], so that it may be taken as certain that there was such a transaction, *per aes et libram*, which in some way reduced debtors to a sort of slavery, that great hardships resulted and that a *l. Poetelia*[2], of somewhat before 300 B.C., practically ended this state of things, presumably by requiring an actual judgement before seizure. The effect was not to abolish *nexum*, but, by depriving it of its chief value, the power of seizure (executive force), to leave it with no advantages to counterbalance its clumsiness, so that it went out of use.

The problem is, how to formulate this transaction. The view propounded by Niebuhr[3] was that the transaction was essentially self *mancipatio*, to be operative only if the due payment of money lent was not made. But self mancipation is not known to have existed in Roman law (though its analogue is found in most early systems[4]) and conditional *mancipatio* is at least in historic times an impossibility. Another view, due to Huschke[5], speedily became dominant, and was to some extent confirmed by Studemund's new readings in Gaius. According to him *nexum* was a contract, made with copper and scales, with a *nuncupatio* declaring the debtor "*damnas*" if he failed to fulfil his obligation. This *damnatio*, in early law, whether in a statute or in a will or in a contract, entitled the injured party to seize the debtor by *manus iniectio*, without judgement, and carry him into confinement[5a]. There is no direct evidence of its application to anything but debts of *certa pecunia*.

This hypothesis involves many assumptions. There is no direct evidence for "executive" force in *nexum*, and Huschke's view basing this on its "publicistic" character, as carried out before five witnesses representing the Roman people, involves an unproved assumption[6]. No text speaks of seizure under *nexum* as based on *addictio*, essential to *manus iniectio* in historic times[7]. We are not told that the *l. Poetelia* abolished the executive force of *nexum*, but only that it released *nexi*, and *nexum* went out of use. But *nexi* were seized and imprisoned, and those who reject Huschke are driven to other explanations. Mitteis held[8], on the evidence of texts which suggest two stages, that there was a loan *per aes et libram* which would lead to a judgement, and the debtor mancipated himself to the creditor to avoid the terrible consequences of an unsatisfied judgement. But this two-fold proceeding *per aes et libram* hardly helps and is neither necessary on the texts nor consistent with all of them; Lenel rejects it[9], holding that the loan was not *per aes et libram*,

1 For reff. to the passages in Dion. Hal. see De Zulueta, *cit.* 138, n. 2. For those in Livy, Roby, *R.P.L.* 2. 297 *sqq.* On the exception of those who "*noxam meruissent,*" de Visscher, *Mél. Fournier*, 755 *sqq.* 2 Varro, *L.L.* 7. 105; Cicero, *de Rep.* 2. 34. 59. 3 *Röm. Gesch.* 1. 322 (ed. 1853). 4 *Ante*, p. 134. 5 *Das Nexum.* 5*a* But see *post*, p. 620. 6 *Ante*, p. 238. It is not necessary to his theory. 7 *Post*, § CCXI. 8 *Z.S.S.* 1901, 96 *sqq.*; 1904, 282; *Röm. Pr.* 1. 136 *sqq.* 9 *Z.S.S.* 1902, 84 *sqq.*

and so gets rid of one of the transactions *per aes et libram*. But as in fact texts speak of *aes nexum* and of the money as due *per aes et libram*, Mommsen[1] held that the process *per aes et libram* was part of the loan transaction but was a *mancipatio* to operate only if the loan was not paid. The difficulty about self mancipation remains, and there is no more direct evidence for this view than for Huschke's, so that his doctrine cannot be said to be overthrown[2].

CLI. *Fiducia*[3]. This was essentially an agreement appended to a conveyance of property, involving a direction or trust as to what was to be done with it[4]. The recorded cases are in connexion with *mancipatio*, but we are told that it might be used with *cessio in iure*[5]. On the other hand there is no evidence that it could be used with *traditio*.

The *fiducia* was not an integral part of the conveyance though the *mancipatio* contains a reference to the *fiducia*, but an agreement made separately, though at the same time. It had no necessary form. The instances we have[6] shew that it might contain a number of provisions. Its main purpose is to determine the ultimate destination of the property, but it might also contain subsidiary provisions, e.g., where it was by way of security, provisions as to sale, as to disposal of any surplus in the price, and so forth.

Fiducia was important in the time of Gaius and long after[7]. The question arises why it is not in the list of contracts. It was in fact not called a contract. It may be called a *pactum*[8], but it differed from the actionable pacts known in the time of Gaius in that it had a *bonae fidei iudicium*[9]. The reason for its non-appearance in the lists may be its parasitic character; it could occur only as an appendage to a conveyance.

Fiducia had many applications. In the law of persons it occurred in *coemptio fiduciae causa*, in *adoptio* and *emancipatio*, and in *tutela fiduciaria*[10]. Its applications in the law of things were still more numerous. Gaius divides them into two classes—*fiducia cum creditore* and *fiducia cum amico*[11]. The first, much the better known, is mortgage, and its rules will best be dealt with in treating the law of "real security[12]." Here it is enough to say that it was in operation till long after the close of the

1 *Z.S.S.* 1902, 348 *sqq.* 2 For other opinions, mostly involving small variations, De Zulueta, *cit.*, who holds that Huschke's doctrine, as slightly modified by more recent writers, while not proved, is not disproved, and is not open to the objections to all the doctrines based on self mancipation. 3 Manigk, P.-W. *s.v.*; Jacquelin, *De la Fiducie.* 4 Grosso, *Sulla fiducia a scopo di manumisso*, shews ground for holding that its primary purpose was *remancipatio*—all applications of it to anything else being derivative: they are agreements releasing, in various circumstances, from the duty to reconvey. 5 G. 2. 59. 6 Girard, *Textes*, 825 *sqq.* 7 C. Th. 15. 14. 9. 8 The name *pactum fiduciae* is not in the sources, but "*fiduciam contrahere*," "*fiducia contracta*," etc. are (G. 2. 60; Inst. 3. 2. 8 etc.). But as to the verb "*contrahere*" see *ante*, p. 406. 9 G. 4. 62. 10 *Ante*, pp. 119, 122, 131, 146, 166. 11 G. 2. 60. 12 *Post*, § CLXVI.

classical age and that many texts which, in the Digest, deal with *pignus* have been shewn to have dealt with *fiducia*[1].

Of *fiducia cum amico*, before the introduction of the *bonae fidei* contracts, deposit and, no doubt, *commodatum* and many forms of mandate, were cases. So too it was common to transfer slaves with a *fiducia* for manumission in order to evade restrictive legislation, till this evasion was prohibited[2], and also in order to give the donee of the slave the position of patron. It was also used for *donatio mortis causa*, with a resolutive instead of the more usual suspensive condition[3], and other applications are suggested. As to most of these cases it seems to have been out of use by the time of Gaius, but it existed for gifts "*ut manumittatur*" till the time of M. Aurelius[4], and apparently later[5]. In *donatio mortis causa* it lasted at any rate till the time of Papinian[6].

The rights under *fiducia*[7] were not always the same. Under the law of persons it had to do with the destiny of freemen or with liberty. It is plain that an *actio fiduciae*, a personal action for damages, would not serve here. Damages were useless if a man to whom a son had been mancipated in the process of *emancipatio* refused to manumit him. The *actio fiduciae* probably did not apply to such cases: fulfilment was enforced by the direct intervention of the Praetor, using his power of *coercitio*[8]. In the case of gift "*ut manumittatur*," no enforcement was needed after M. Aurelius provided that the freedom should take effect automatically at the appointed time[9]. In noxal surrender of a son we are told that the Praetor would compel the release of the man when he had worked out the damages, and that there was no *actio fiduciae* here, but it is not clear that there was a *fiducia*, though it is sometimes assumed[10].

In *fiducia cum creditore* or *amico* in the *ius rerum*, the remedy was the *actio fiduciae* (*condemnatio* involving *infamia*), with its *actio contraria*[11]. The *formula* is much disputed, as is the question whether the action existed under the *legis actio* system[12].

In *fiducia cum amico*, it was reasonable that the principal should have

1 This is puzzling: there must have been, in the time of the classical lawyers, plenty of literature on *pignus*. Either the compilers altered the law of *pignus* by applying to it the law of an obsolete institution, or the rules of *fiducia cum creditore* had in great measure been applied to *pignus*: the latter seems more probable. Buckland, *N.R.H.* 1917, 5 *sqq.*
2 See, e.g., 40. 9. 7. 1.
3 39. 6. 42. See Jacquelin, *cit.*, 359.
4 No *fiducia* in the case actually dealt with in the enactment; *ante*, § XXXI.
5 Vat. Fr. 334a.
6 39. 6. 42, originally a case of *mancipatio cum fiducia*.
7 As to good faith in *usureceptio*, *ante*, p. 245.
8 Jacquelin, *cit.* 103 *sqq.*; G. 1. 137a, "*cogere*."
9 *Ante*, p. 85.
10 Coll. 2. 3. 1. Jacquelin, *cit.* 237.
11 G. 4. 182; P. 2. 13; *post*, § CCXXXIV. The edict contained a clause making "*fraus*" of the *paterf.* material, where the *fiducia* was with a subordinate member of the family. See Lenel, *E.P.* 294.
12 See on this and on the possibility of an alternative *formula in factum* (which is not consistent with its existence under the *legis actio*), Pernice, *Labeo*, 3. 1. 122; Lenel, *E.P.* 291; Girard, *Man.* 556.

a right of withdrawal. We are told of this in some cases[1], and it no doubt existed in all. The effect of exercise of this right would be to make execution of the *fiducia* an actionable wrong, so far as this involved more than return, and to enable the principal to recover the property. The remedy would be a *condictio ob rem dati*, which appears in the texts as *condictio ex poenitentia*, a post-classical name, introduced to the texts by the compilers[2]. In the case of gift "*ut manumittatur,*" the revocability continued after *fiducia* had ceased to be used, and was then applied also where, as it seems, *fiducia* had never been applied, i.e. where the transaction was a genuine sale, but there was to be manumission after a certain term of service[3]. There seems to have been no right of revocation here in classical law[4]. And texts give a right of withdrawal where a man had given an owner money to free his slave, with a *condictio ex poenitentia*[5]. It is no doubt in connexion with such post-classical extensions that the name *c. ex poenitentia* was introduced.

CLII. Classification of Contracts. Justinian, following Gaius, classifies contracts as of four types: *re, verbis, literis* and *consensu*. Their characteristics will be considered in discussing the different classes, but one or two remarks may be made here. Gaius is our earliest authority for the classification[6] and though he may have invented it, it is generally thought, and probable, that he adopted a traditional classification[7]. The question remains, on what this traditional order, which does not look very rational, actually rests. Of the many views[8] the most probable is that it rests on the Edict. In the edictal scheme contract was placed under the rubric, "*de rebus creditis.*" *Mutuum*, loan for consumption, was the typical *creditum* and its remedies therefore came first. It was followed in the Edict by the other real contracts, as *stipulatio* for a *certum* and the contract *literis* need no separate treatment from a procedural point of view, their remedy being the same as that for *mutuum*. The *actio ex stipulatu*, which was the remedy for the promise of an *incertum*, is in another part of the Edict altogether. But in stating the law of contract the verbal and literal contracts must be dealt with, and they come next as being the oldest. Last come the consensual[9].

1 24. 1. 49, written of *fiducia*. 2 E.g. 12. 4. 3. 3. Gradenwitz, *Interpolationen*, 146 *sqq*. The pact does not seem usually to have contained an express provision for return, at least in case of *f. cum creditore*, *post*, § CLXVI. 3 E.g. 40. 8. 3. 4 Buckland, *Slavery*, 633; Lotmar, *Marc Aurels Erlass*, 320 *sqq*. 5 12. 4. 3. 2, 3. 6 G. 3. 89. 7 His *commentarii* are largely built up of existing materials. For an extremely iconoclastic view, Kniep, *Der Rechtsgelehrte Gaius*, 30 *sqq*. 8 Chronological, *mutuum* attracting the other real contracts; order that of relative simplicity; proceeds from those with the most obvious external sign; merely arbitrary, etc. 9 Accarias, *Précis*, 2. 19; Moyle, *Instt. Just.* ad 3. 13. 2.

The classification, though serviceable enough for the purpose in view, is not very scientific. The verbal contracts and the literal contract are forms: the real and consensual are not forms, but groups of informal bargain which the law would enforce. This suggests a division into formal and informal[1], but this would need subdivision, for *stipulatio* in classical law is a form or mould into which any transaction could be run, while the other formal contracts are, each, a form for one particular transaction[2]. A classification which would express more clearly the actual distinctions would be into *stricti iuris* and *bonae fidei*, or what is the same thing, unilateral and bilateral, contracts, the latter being either perfectly bilateral, sale, hire and *societas*, or imperfectly, *pignus*, deposit, *commodatum* and mandate. But it seems better to follow the order of the Institutes, with the exception of taking real contracts last but one, with the effect of bringing together the formal contracts.

THE VERBAL CONTRACTS. Of these the most important is:

STIPULATIO. This was a contract made by question and answer, originally in Latin, and, probably, only in the form "*Spondesne?*" "*Spondeo,*" afterwards marked off as the form confined, in private law, to *cives*[3]. Its source has been variously explained; perhaps the most probable view is that its first application was in procedural undertakings given for litigants[4]. It existed already at the time of the XII Tables[5], and was probably applied first to promises of *certa pecunia* and *certa res*, then to *incerta*, and finally to acts (*stipulatio faciendi*), but all this was complete before the Empire[6]. It had formerly been the practice to arrange for *facienda* by *stipulatio* for a penalty if the act were not done, a method which left many traces in the law[7], and indeed continued in use for some purposes throughout the Empire[8].

The parties must be present together[9], and as we have seen[10], the proceeding must be continuous. The law required no witnesses, though

1 Girard, *Man.* 508. 2 This criticism is relevant only for the classical law. There was a time when *stipulatio* was a form for only one type of transaction, like the contract *literis*, indeed narrower still, for it may have been first applied only to promises of security in litigation or promises of statutory penalties (see n. 4). *Dotis dictio* and *iurata promissio liberti* have this character still in the law of the Empire. Again the imperfectly bilateral contracts do not seem to have been bilateral at all at first: the *actio contraria* is a secondary development. 3 G. 3. 93. 4 Mitteis, *Aus Röm. und Bürg. Recht*, 109, developing from *sponsio* by surety to self *sponsio* (*ante*, p. 407). See *S.M.W.* 62. For suggested derivations of the word *stipulatio*, and theories of the origin of the contract into the service of which these etymologies have been pressed, Costa, *Storia*, 337, n. 2; Bekker, *Z.S.S.* 1909, 41. 5 The Antinoite fr. of Gaius, 4. 17 a, shew that the XII Tables allowed *iudicis postulatio* in cases of *stipulatio*, *post*, p. 616. 6 Girard holds (*Man.* 521) that *stipulatio faciendi* is as old as Cato (d: 149 B.C.) (*R.R.* 144. 2 and 146. 2). 7 E.g. pact and *stipulatio* in servitudes, *ante*, p. 265; *receptum arbitri*, *post*, § CLXXXIII. 8 See Cuq, *Man.* 598. 9 45. 1. 1. pr. 10 *Ante*, p. 413.

proof would be difficult without them, unless, as came to be the usual course, a memorandum of the transaction was drawn up[1].

The rules underwent relaxation. Before the Empire other words might be used, "*Dabisne?*" "*Promittisne?*" and so forth[2]. In classical law any language might be used, and in later law even different languages, all that was needed being substantial agreement between question and answer[3]. But a conditional acceptance, where there was no condition in the *stipulatio*, was void, as was one which introduced fresh terms. Ulpian seems to add that if the *stipulator* at once agreed to these fresh terms this was a valid new stipulation, but this is no doubt due to the compilers[4]. If there was substantial agreement the fact that the answer contained useless verbiage was immaterial—*supervacua non nocent*[5].

The rule that question and answer must substantially agree was subject to one peculiar exception. Gaius and Justinian tell us that where the *stipulatio* was for ten and the promise for five or *vice versa*, there was no contract for want of identity[6]. But in the Digest we are told that in such a case the contract was good for the smaller sum common to both. For Gaius five and ten are two different things. The other view treats them not as things, but as quantities. Even so this view may be due to Ulpian or to the compilers[7]. The matter is complicated by the fact that in an analogous case, that of a *stipulatio* for two things and a promise of one, or *vice versa*, the contract was good for that one, the words being construed as two stipulations of which one was completed[8]. But where the *stipulatio* was for one of two things, *A* or *B*, and was accepted for one of them, the same construction was not adopted[9], though the choice would be with the promisor[10]. But a *stipulatio* for quantities, ten or twenty, accepted for ten, was valid on the principle that they were quantities and the greater included the less[11].

It was usual to express the *stipulatio* in a written note or *cautio*. A rescript of Severus provided that if the *cautio* alleged a *stipulatio*, even though it was not itself in the form of question and answer, and even though it was defective in that it spoke of the *promissor* as having promised but did not say that the *stipulator* had stipulated, a *stipulatio*

1 The absence of a legal requirement of writing is in striking contrast with the rules of Attic law which required writing in nearly all cases of contract, etc., evidence perhaps of a different standard of commercial morality. Collinet, *Études Hist.* 1. 61. 2 G. 3. 92; P. 2. 3. 1. Illustrations from Plautus, Costa, *Dir. priv. nelle com. di Plauto*, 273. 3 G. 3. 93; D. 45. 1. 1 *passim*. Ulpian says that "*Dabisne?*" "*Quidni?*" is good, but a mere nod will not serve, as it must be verbal, 45. 1. 1. 2. 4 45. 1. 1. 3. 5 "*Dabisne?*" "*Arma virumque cano, dabo,*" was good, says Florentinus, 45. 1. 65. pr. 6 G. 3. 102; Inst. 3. 19. 5. 7 45. 1. 1. 4 (interp.). 8 45. 1. 1. 5, 83. 4; cf. h. t. 29. The texts appear to be genuine. 9 45. 1. 83. 2. 10 *Post*, § CXCIII. 11 45. 1. 83. 3.

was to be presumed[1], and Paul tells us that, at least where there was a complete allegation of a *stipulatio*, this presumption was conclusive[2]. Ulpian seems to modify this, by saying that on such facts a party might still prove that a mere pact was meant, i.e. it was a *presumptio iuris*, not *iuris et de iure*[3], but this is probably due to Justinian. Even if it is classical the rule remains that no further evidence could be required that the form had been gone through. In A.D. 472 a rescript of Leo provided that all stipulations, even though not in solemn words but in any words expressing the intent, should have full force[4]. (The enactment contains the obscure words "*legibus cognitae*" which cannot be connected with any word in the text but *stipulationes*[5].) This may be, like many rescripts[6], merely an enunciation of existing law, but it is generally held that it suppressed the need of question and answer or express allegation of question and answer altogether, all that was now needed being some clear evidence of verbal assent[7].

The history and extent of these changes is matter of controversy. Riccobono has recently expressed the view that practically all the relaxations are post-classical, that Leo confirmed them and also provided that any words, with or without interrogation, which shewed that a *stipulatio* was meant, would suffice, so that texts in the Digest which assert the need of question and answer are mere survivals[8]. But since, long before Ulpian, the Sabinians treated a *stipulatio* to pay *B* and a third party, as wholly valid in favour of *B*, and this applies the rule that surplusage is no error, grotesquely applied elsewhere, and the Proculians held it valid only for half[9], it does not seem clear that in the somewhat similar case of *stipulatio* and promise of different amounts, validation for the common element[10] would have shocked the men of Ulpian's time. Riccobono also holds, no doubt rightly, that the habit of putting all stipulations into writing (and the indifference to form in the writing) made question and answer less important, that Leo's enactment confirmed this laxity and that thus many of Justinian's texts on question and answer are mere survivals. He shews that the habit of reducing

1 C. 8. 37. 1. The case suggests that the courts were already in the habit of accepting a complete *cautio* as sufficient evidence. 2 P. 5. 7. 2. But Riccobono holds (*Z.S.S.* 1922, 272) that this is interp. and C. 8. 37. 1 altered. *Praesumptiones iuris*, i.e. those which must be accepted in absence of proof to the contrary, are rare in classical law, though not wholly absent as Ferrini holds (*Opere*, 3. 147). Many were created in post-classical times by generalising the jurists' interpretation of a particular document, and they are common under Justinian. Donatuti, *Le Praesumptiones iuris*. 3 2. 14. 7. 12. 4 C. 8. 37. 10. 5 The enactment is probably abridged. 6 *Ante*, p. 19. 7 Girard, *Man.* 498. 8 *Z.S.S.* 1914, 243; *ib.* 1922, 262; *Bull.* 1921, 29. (Eng.tr. *Stipulation and the Theory of Contract*, 1957); *contra* Nicholas, *L.Q.R.* 1953, 63, 233. 9 G. 3. 103: D. 45. 1. 65. pr.; *post*, p. 440. 10 *Ante*, p. 435. We may even admit Ulpian's "*Quidni?*", (45. 1. 1. 2, Arangio-Ruiz, *Ist.* 299) if we observe that in Roman forms it is normally the utterance of the party acquiring which is important, *post*, p. 673.

transactions into writing, and the well evidenced notarial practice of adding a stipulation clause at the end of the document whatever its nature, reduced the oral *stipulatio* in Justinian's time to small importance[1].

These changes, whatever their extent, or date, did not affect the rule that the parties must be present together. Justinian modified this by a provision that if the *stipulatio* was embodied in a *cautio* alleging presence, this was presumed, and could be rebutted only by clear proof that one or the other party was absent, for the whole of the day on which the *cautio* was made, from the place from which it was dated. And if the *stipulatio* purported to be made by a slave sent for the purpose the presence and ownership of the slave were conclusively presumed[2].

CLIII. *Stipulatio* was unilateral, the questioner, *stipulator*, being in no way bound, the *promissor* acquiring no right of action. Like all other unilateral contracts it was what Justinian calls *stricti iuris*, i.e. it gave rise to a *strictum iudicium*. On a promise of a *certum*[3] this seems to have been[4] a *condictio*, but where it was a promise of an *incertum* or an act[5], the remedy was an *actio ex stipulatu*, which differed from a *condictio*, in that it stated, in a *praescriptio*, the basis of the liability, as *condictio* did not[6]. There was, in later classical law, an action called, perhaps only later, *condictio incerti*[7], but it was not applied to this case, probably because of the existence of this special remedy, introduced when *stipulationes* for *incerta* were first recognised.

Stipulations may be classified as divisible or indivisible, a distinction which applies to all obligations and will arise for discussion when we are dealing with performance of obligation[8].

They are also classifiable as conventional and procedural[9]. The former are the ordinary contracts with which we are dealing[10]. The latter are those undertakings which could be required in litigation, and in other cases, e.g. *tutela* and legacy, on application to the Court. They are classed

1 On the question whether *stipulatio* under Justinian is a written contract, *post*, § CLXI *in f.* The oral *stipulatio* can hardly have been obsolete: there were certainly cases in which the matter was not written and the medieval jingle: *Re, verbis, scripto, consensu, traditione, Iunctura vestes sumere pacta solent* (Bracton, fol. 16 b), could hardly have arisen if verbal contracts were no more. 2 C. 8. 37. 14. 3 De Francisci, *St. Perozzi*, 327, calls attention to a divergence of opinion as to what was a *certum*. On one view "what is in that chest" is a *certum*, on another an *incertum* (45. 1. 75. 5; Theoph. *ad* Inst. 3. 15. pr.; 18. 1. 7. 1; 45. 1. 74; 12. 1. 6). He considers the stricter view to be that of the time of Gaius, superseded in the time of Ulpian, but still surviving in some byzantine commentators. 4 See, however, Naber, *Mnemosyne*, 1892, 109, who holds (see also Accarias, *Précis*, 2. 66) that in classical law the action on a *stip. certi* was *a. ex stipulatu certi*, citing P. 5. 5 *a*. 1, 5. 7. 4; D. 44. 7. 18, 45. 1. 51 etc. (But it was in any case an action *ex stipulatu*.) See also Perozzi, *Ist.* 2. 213. 5 Transmissibility of these, *post*, § CLIV. 6 *Post*, § CCXXI 7 *Post*, § CCXXX. 8 *Post*, § CXCIII. 9 45. 1. 5. pr.; Inst. 3. 18. 10 Special rules of *sponsalia*, *ante*, p. 112.

as Praetorian, Aedilician or Judicial, according to the authority under which they are taken, and *Communes* where they might be ordered by a magistrate or a *iudex*. As they belong mainly to procedure, we need not consider them here, except to say that in some cases a mere *stipulatio* of the party sufficed, while in others there must be *satisdatio*, security of some type. Like the English "contract of record" they were scarcely contracts at all, though they assumed that form: for in many cases they could be compelled, and we are told that praetorian *stipulationes* "*ex mente praetoris descendunt*[1]," so that they could not be varied at the will of the parties.

The general rules as to capacity have already been stated[2], but, as there were rules peculiar to *stipulatio*, the rules of capacity for this contract must be stated though this involves some repetition.

1. Since the contract was essentially verbal no one who was deaf or dumb could take part in it, nor therefore could an *infans*. The rule remained in Justinian's law[3], notwithstanding the validity given to *cautiones*. It could of course be evaded by utilising a slave.

2. Only *cives* could use the form "*Spondesne?*" "*Spondeo*[4]."

3. *Stipulatio*, or other contract, between *paterfamilias* and *filius*, or *dominus* and slave, gave no action[5].

4. *Furiosi* could take part in no contract, except in a lucid interval[6]. We are not told if this applied to imbeciles, and we have no direct information as to the effect of drunkenness. There is a text suggesting that one who made a promise in a fit of extreme anger was not bound if he withdrew it on cooling[7].

5. A *pupillus* could contract so as to benefit, but not, without *auctoritas*, so as to bind himself, subject however to liability for enrichment and other protections of the other party, already mentioned[8].

6. Persons *in mancipio* were incapable of binding themselves in the time of Gaius[9], but there was presumably a *naturalis obligatio*.

7. A slave's *stipulatio* enured to his *dominus* or another having rights in him according to rules already considered[10]: he himself acquired no rights. *Promissio* by a slave is rare: we are told that at civil law it was void, but there was praetorian *actio de peculio* on it[11], and it created a *naturalis obligatio* which survived manumission[12]. As it had not the force of a verbal contract, Gaius doubts if it could be guaranteed by *sponsio*

1 45. 1. 52. pr. 2 *Ante*, p. 419. 3 G. 3. 105; Inst. 3. 19. 7. Riccobono, *Z.S.S.* 1922, 386. 4 G. 3. 93. 5 G. 3. 104; Inst. 3. 19. 6; as to *naturalis obligatio*, *post*, § CLXXXIX. 6 G. 3. 106; Inst. 3. 19. 8; C. 4. 38. 2. 7 50. 17. 48. Not on contract. Horace's "*ira furor brevis est*" is hardly conclusive. 8 *Ante*, § LVI; *filii* and *filiae familias*, *ante*, p. 419. Women in *tutela*, *ante*, p. 167. 9 G. 3. 104. 10 *Ante*, pp. 65, 278. 11 G. 3. 119, 176; Inst. 3. 29. 3; *de peculio*, *post*, § CLXXXIV. 12 15. 1. 50. 2; *post*, § CLXXXIX.

or *fidepromissio*[1]. But where a stipulation was made by a slave (or son) the *paterfamilias* did not always acquire the same right as if he himself had stipulated. He got what was stipulated for, but no more. If a slave stipulated for a right of way, the *paterfamilias* acquired a right of way, but if the slave stipulated that he be allowed to cross a certain field, what the master acquired was permission for the slave to cross the field, not for himself to do so. It was literally construed, a rule obscurely expressed in the Institutes in the words "*cum factum in stipulatione continebitur, persona stipulantis continetur*[2]."

As to the slave there was a still further difficulty. He could stipulate using his master's name or his own, or a fellow-slave's, or none at all[3]. But if he used his own name, stipulated, that is, "*sibi*," and it was for a *ius* of any kind, the *stipulatio* was void, as a slave could not have a right. The later jurists evaded this by understanding the word expressive of a right in a *de facto* sense[4], but this was not possible in all cases, as where a slave stipulated for a *cessio in iure* to him, and where it was possible it gave a result different from what was intended. The difficulty could be avoided by not mentioning the slave in the *stipulatio*.

As the slave's capacity was derivative he could acquire by *stipulatio* only for a master who was himself *capax*, not indeed to contract, since he might be an infant or lunatic, but to acquire[5]. Thus, as a man could not acquire a servitude for land not his own, his slave's *stipulatio* for it was void[6]. The *stipulatio* of a slave of a *hereditas* was void, unless a *heres* ultimately entered[7]. Where there were also rights in the man other than ownership, the question for whom he acquired might sometimes be in suspense. Thus where a slave in usufruct stipulated for a thing, its destination would depend on the ownership of the *peculium* out of which it was paid for[8].

CLIV. Content or substance of *stipulatio*. Some of these matters have already been dealt with, but there remain several points for notice.

It was a fundamental rule[9] that a third person could not acquire rights or be subject to obligation under a *stipulatio*, the difficulty being commonly met by a penal *stipulatio*: "Do you promise me 10 if you do not give *B* 5?" But this gives *B* no claim. The Institutes deal with the case in which a third person was joined with the actual contracting party in the *stipulatio*. Two cases are considered.

1 G. 3. 119. In 3. 176 he says it is as if *a nullo*. But this is civil law and even so is too energetic: the rule *solutum non repetere* on a *naturalis obligatio*, such as this created (*post*, § CLXXXIX), was effective at civil law. 2 Inst. 3. 17. 2. Individuality of the slave material in many ways, Buckland, *Slavery*, 155. 3 Inst. 3. 17. 1. 4 45. 1. 38. 6–9, 130. 5 41. 3. 28; 27. 8. 1. 15. 6 45. 3. 17. 7 45. 1. 73. 1. 8 7. 1. 25. 1. So too where the dealing is by a slave of a *captivus* who may or may not return with *postliminium*, 45. 1. 73. 1; 45. 3. 18. 2. 9 *Ante*, p. 426.

A stipulation between *A* and *B* provided that *A* would pay 10 to *B* and *C*, or that *A* and *C* would pay 10 to *B*. On the Sabinian view, the mention of *C* was surplusage: the *stipulatio* was good for the whole amount between the actual parties. On the Proculian view it must be construed as two *stipulationes* for 5 each, of which that concerning *C* was void, as he was not a party, so that the *stipulatio* was valid for 5 only between *A* and *B*. This view prevailed and was confirmed by Justinian[1]. If the case was one of those in which the *stipulatio* for a third person was valid[2] because the *stipulator* had an *interesse*, then the part affecting the third party would be valid. He indeed could not sue, but the whole would be due to the contracting party.

In Sale, however (it is probably true for all *bonae fidei* transactions), we are told that the addition of the third party was *supervacuum* and the whole was due to the contracting party[3], a sort of *ius accrescendi*.

If *A* promised *B* that he would pay to *B* or *C* this was valid: *C* was *solutionis causa adiectus*[4]. It was convenient to arrange that payment might be made to the principal or to some one for him, e.g. an *argentarius* in the debtor's town. Only the actual party could sue, but the debt might be discharged in either way. The converse case of a promise by *A* that he or *C* would pay *B* was dealt with in the same way[5].

The rule of classical law avoiding contracts *post mortem* of a party, or those purporting to bind or benefit the *heres* alone, which seems, as we have said, to rest on a principle independent of that just discussed, and was abolished by Justinian[6], did not affect promises which, as events turned out, did in fact affect the *heres* alone: this might happen in any contract for a future performance[7]. And a promise for performance after the death of a third party was of course quite valid.

We have seen that a promise of personal service died with the party[8]. But there is some reason to think that at one time all "*facere*" was deemed personal in principle and died with the party who was to do the act, at least as to the future. But in the first century a view appeared and ultimately prevailed, that it could be extended to include the *heres* by express mention of him in the *stipulatio*. This was a concession, against

1 G. 3. 103; Inst. 3. 19. 4; D. 45. 1. 110. pr. Analogous to the case in which the question includes more than the answer, or *vice versa*, *ante*, p. 435. 2 *Ante*, p. 427. 3 18. 1. 64. Same result in 8. 4. 5, but servitudes are indivisible. 4 46. 3. 12. 1; Inst. 3. 19. 4; *post*, § CXCIII. He might be a mandatory or a creditor. See, however, Kaden, *Z.S.S.* 1927, 559. If no instructions he would be *negotiorum gestor*. 5 At least in later law, *Nov.* 115. 6. 6 *Ante*, p. 426. One for payment after *capitis deminutio* of a party was equally bad in classical law, G. 3. 101. 7 A man could validly stipulate for payment to his son in the family, as this was to himself (Inst. 3. 19. 4), and it has precisely the same effect. But he could also stipulate *post mortem filii*, as this was not himself, and if it was *post mortem suam* and *filio*, the son had in later law an *actio utilis* (23. 4. 23; 45. 1. 45. 2 interp.) even though not *heres*. 8 *Ante*, p. 408.

accepted principle. On this view the *altercationes* mentioned by Justinian (and ended by his declaring stipulations for *facienda* heritable[1]) were on the question not whether such stipulations were heritable but whether they were heritable if no mention was made of the *heres*[2].

A promise for performance so many days before the death of either party (e.g. *pridie quam moriar*) was void, the rule being abolished by Justinian[3]. The reason given by Gaius is that it cannot be told till after the death when the debt was due, so that it is in effect for payment after death, and thus bad. But a stipulation for payment at death is good, and Gaius observes that the distinction, which existed also in legacies, was unreasonable[4]. The "*pridie*" cases were within the objection to *stipulationes praepostere conceptae* ("*si navis ex Asia venerit, hodie dari spondes?*") (void till Justinian validated them, without the impossible part[5]), a rule clearly ancient though Gaius does not state it. The *stipulatio*, "*cum moriar*," was not. In holding it valid, the lawyers decided that a man is alive at the moment of his death: it is, as they say, "*novissimum vitae tempus*[6]."

The rule "*ad diem deberi non posse*" is rational: it seems absurd to contemplate a debt which I am to owe you up to a certain day, which must come. Yet it might be useful. A capitalist who invests his balances periodically might reasonably promise to lend a man money to complete a contemplated purchase, provided it was asked for before the date at which his balances were usually invested[7]. And the civil law itself recognised a liability of sureties which ended in a definite time[8]. On the general rule Paul gives the illustration "10 *dare spondesne usque ad kalendas Iulias?*" and says that the limitation was ignored at civil law, but that if the promise was sued on after the agreed time there was an *exceptio doli*, or *pacti conventi*[9], so that the arrangement could be safely made. One

1 C. 8. 37. 13. There was no difficulty for breaches before the death. As to *stipulationes* limited to life (45. 1. 56. 4), see below. 2 Korošek, *Erbenhaftung*, and Scherillo, *Trasmissibilità delle stip. faciendi*, whose view is that in the text. (Further inferences drawn by him, *St. Bonfante*, 4. 216, are not convincing.) 3 C. 8. 37. 11. 4 G. 2. 232; 3. 100. 5 Inst. 3. 19. 14; C. 6. 23. 25. Leo had already abolished it in relation to *dos*. Koschaker (*Z.S.S.* 1913, 427) holds this cannot be the ground and adopts that of Gaius (he does not say why), which fails to account for the rule in "*cum moriar*"; a distinction so undisputed probably had some reason. Paul gives the rule in "*cum moriar*," Vat. Fr. 98. The "*pridie*" and "*praepostera*" rules were abolished by the same enactment; the former seems to be merely a special case of the latter. 6 G. 2. 232; 3. 100 (cp. 28. 5. 5). Conclusive as to their point of view. It has been described as a "puérilité" of commentators (Accarias, *Précis*, 2. 96), but it is Roman. The discussion of these "limiting cases" has attracted logicians in all ages. Accarias gives a list of cases in which "*cum moriar*" or "*moriens*" are void (95, n. 3), e.g. a *stipulatio* for a usufruct "*cum moriar*," which is meaningless. 7 Any conditional promise where the condition must be determined by a certain time is on much the same footing, but it is not so treated. 8 *Post*, § CLVI. 9 44. 7. 44. 1.

case is prominent. A man might be willing to undertake a liability but not that this should burden his heir. He might therefore promise "*quoad vivam*" or "*quoad vivas.*" This was treated in the same way: civil law ignored the limit, but if action was brought after the death there was an *exceptio*[1]. The Institutes carry this further, and say that a promise of "10 *aureos annuos quoad vivam*" was essentially perpetual, the *exceptio* being available in the same way[2]. This is puzzling. We are told elsewhere that a *stipulatio* "*in singulos annos quoad in Italia fuero*" was good[3]. And *locatio* could be for a limited time[4]. It appears to be a mere blunder[5]. A legacy to a widow "*in annos singulos quoad vivat*" was good and was determined *ipso facto* by her death[6], but legacies were construed by intent. A legacy *in annos singulos*, with nothing about death, ended *ipso iure* by the death, being construed as a number of separate legacies of which all but the first were conditional on the legatee's being alive when they fell due, unless indeed it was left to a corporation, when it was perpetual[7]. But a *stipulatio*, "*in annos singulos*," was one *stipulatio*, unconditional, *incerta* and *perpetua*, not affected by the death of the promisee[8].

The rule applied not only to *dies certa* or *incerta*, "*usque ad kalendas Iulias*" and "*quoad vivam*," but also to cases of condition, such as "*nisi Titius consul fiat*," "*nisi navis ex Asia venerit*[9]."

Exceptio non numeratae pecuniae. Where the *stipulator* sued on a promise to repay a loan of money, which in fact had not been made, Gaius observes that this could be proved under an *exceptio doli*[10]. But it is hard to prove a negative, and at some time not later than A.D. 215 a better defence was introduced—the *exceptio non numeratae pecuniae*[11]. When an acknowledgement of loan was sued on, the defendant had this *exceptio*, under which the burden of proof was on the plaintiff, to prove the loan (contrary to the usual rule in *exceptiones*, in which the burden of proof was on the defendant), and making the *cautio* a poor security. Accordingly it was confined to this case and was available only for one year[12]. But since the creditor by waiting a year could make it useless, it was further provided that the alleged debtor could bring a *condictio* within the year for return of the *cautio*[13], and presumably the exceptional rule as to burden of proof applied here. It was laid down by Alexander

1 45. 1. 56. 4. 2 Inst. 3. 15. 3. 3 4. 6. 43. 4 *Post*, § CLXXIV. 5 Mitteis, *Röm. Pr.* 1. 193. 6 33. 1. 5. 7 33. 1. 4, 6. 8 45. 1. 16. 1. But the above cited 4. 6. 43 shews that the insertion of a limit varies this construction. 9 See *ante*, p. 425. 10 G. 4. 116. 11 C. 4. 30. 3. Even if *exceptio doli* was used the *lex* gave the same advantage, within the time allowed. The institution is held by some writers to be post-classical, Perozzi, *Ist.* 2. 215. Suman, *de non num. pec.*, confines it till late in the third century to written acknowledgements without *stip.* But see Stoll, *Z.S.S.* 1927, 516. See also Kroell, *Rôle de l'écrit*, 174. 12 *Herm. Wis.* 1. 1. 13 C. 4. 30. 4, 7. ?post-class., *a. ad exhib.* in classical law, Taubenschlag, *Röm. Prr. z. Z. Diocl.* 274.

that the creditor need not prove the money to have been paid in coin, but only that there was a real debt, even a pre-existing one[1].

The system underwent changes. Diocletian extended it[2] to five years. Justin provided that if it was for a past debt specifically stated in the *cautio*, the *exceptio* was not available without written proof to the *iudex* that the statement in the *cautio* was untrue: the creditor must then prove that there was a real debt[3]. Justinian limited it to two years, extended it to other loans for consumption, and to some analogous cases (but here only within a very short limit of time), to which it had already been sought to apply it, and provided that, at any time within the two years, it could be made perpetual by notice to the creditor, or in his absence to certain officials[4]. In a Novel he excluded the system altogether if the creditor was an *argentarius*[5]. There is nothing to exclude the *exceptio doli* after the time had expired, but the burden of proof would be the other way. The system had probably no operation under the *formula*, but at first applied only in certain *cognitiones* and was generalised under or after Diocletian[6].

CLV. We have been dealing with *stipulatio* regarded as the principal transaction, but have now to consider what may be called accessory *stipulationes*, cases in which the *stipulatio* is an appendage to another. The cases are *adstipulatio* and *adpromissio*, an important form of surety.

Adstipulatio. In two cases it was usual to reinforce the *stipulatio* between the actual parties by one made with the *promissor* by a mandatary, who stipulated for the same thing (*idem*[7]). If the *adstipulator* sued on his contract he would be liable under his mandate to account for the proceeds to the principal or his *heres*, as the case might be[8]. The cases were: (1) to provide against the fact that in the *legis actio* it was

1 C. 4. 30. 5. 2 *Herm. Wis.* 1. 1. 3 C. 4. 30. 13. An interpolated text in the Digest apparently based on this enactment (22. 3. 25. 4) applied the rule to any express acknowledgement, whether the debt was old or then created. 4 C. 4. 30. 14. Some texts (apart from 22. 3. 25. 4) of earlier date than Justinian seem to refer to this system of protest, and it is therefore held by Girard (*Man.* 536) that this power of protest and perpetuation was older and was merely reorganised by Justinian. But he treats it as new; of the texts, C. 4. 30. 9 has been altered (Krueger's edn. *ad h. l.*), C. 4. 30. 8. 1 and 2 look like additions (*sin vero, sin autem, legitimum tempus, minime* are all suggestive more of Justinian than of A.D. 228), and C. Th. 2. 27. 1. 4 is too vague to prove anything: it may refer only to *condictio*, and is not understood by the *interpretatio* to refer to perpetuation. "*Querella,*" "*querimonia*" seem to have been used generally to denote any of the steps. C. 4. 30. 4, 8, 9, 10. 5 *Nov.* 136. 6. 6 Pernice, *Z.S.S.* 1892, 273 *sqq.* Since there is no *mutuum* unless the money has been lent it is odd that, apart from promise, the defence should be by *exceptio*, which, in principle, admits a *prima facie* claim. In practice the rule is that such a *cautio* is not admissible as evidence, without the consent of the defendant, unless a certain time has passed, or, in Justinian's time, the acknowledgement is express (22. 3. 25. 4). In his time it may be excluded altogether by protest within the two years. 7 G. 3. 110. Practically all our information on the rules is from Gaius. 8 G. 3. 111, 117.

impossible to sue by representative[1]. If the principal was away when it became necessary to sue, the *adstipulator* would sue on his contract and account for the proceeds. This ceased to be necessary under the *formula*, and Gaius does not mention it[2]. (2) Where the principal *stipulatio* was "*post mortem*" and therefore void. The contract of the *adstipulator* being *post mortem* of a third party was good[3]. As Justinian validated *stipulationes post mortem stipulatoris*, the *adstipulator* did not appear at all in the law of the Digest.

So far, an *adstipulatio* was merely an ordinary *stipulatio* which happened to be associated with another. But that does not properly represent the matter: it was intimately bound up with the other, as the *adstipulatio* was for "*idem.*" It was practically a case of correality. Payment to, or action by, or *acceptilatio* to, either of the *stipulatores* extinguished the debt, and the second chapter of the *l. Aquilia* imposed a penalty on an *adstipulator* who released the debt. Gaius observes that this was not necessary, as the action on the mandate would suffice, but notes that the former had the advantage that it imposed a penalty[4]. The real reason for this remedy is that *adstipulatio* is older than mandate. We do not know how the principal then recovered from the *adstipulator* what he had received: not to hand it over may have been theft under the wide early conception of *furtum*[5]. *Adstipulatio* has another mark of antiquity in its intensely personal nature. The rights of the *adstipulator* did not pass to his *heres*[6], which may have been true of all early contractual rights[7]. Further, a slave or person *in mancipio* could not be *adstipulator*[8]. If one in *potestas* or *manus* was *adstipulator*, the right of action did not vest in the *paterfamilias*, as it ordinarily would. The *adstipulator* himself could not sue so long as he was in *potestas*, and lost his right by passing out of it in any way involving *capitis deminutio*, e.g. *emancipatio*[9]. Though these peculiarities have been associated with the conception of mandate, they seem rather to be survivals from extreme antiquity[10].

As *adstipulatio* was purely accessory to the main contract it could not be for more, though it might be for less, and it might be conditional or

1 *Post*, § CCXXXIX. 2 Not recorded, but see Girard, *Man.* 796. 3 G. 3. 117. *Ante*, p. 440. Not available in "*pridie mortis*," for the objection to this was the same whether it was the *stipulator* or a third party. 4 G. 3. 215, 216. 5 *Post*, § CXCVI. 6 G. 3. 114; 4. 113. 7 G. 3. 114. Corresponding rule in converse case of *sponsor* and *fidepromissor*, *post*, § CLVI. 8 G. 3. 114. 9 *Ib.* No doubt, though this is not stated, the right was extinguished by *cap. dem.* of an *adstipulator sui iuris*. 10 Where a son contracted under mandate, the right vested in the *paterfamilias*, 14. 1. 5. pr. So would contract by slave, but *adstipulatio* is null (G. 3. 114). The rule that it fails on death, like the liability of *sponsor* and *fidepromissor*, with which Gaius couples it, is not the same as the rule in mandate, whatever the true extent of that rule, *post*, § CLXXIX. For if I contract under a mandate my *heres* can sue on the contract. *Fideiussio*, a typical mandate, differs on all these points.

ex die where the principal *stipulatio* was *pura*, but not *vice versa*[1]. The *adstipulator* need not use the same words if the import was the same[2].

CLVI. *Adpromissio*. *Adpromissores*[3] were accessories on the side of the *promissor*, sureties, who undertook to pay if the principal debtor did not. They were *sponsores*, *fidepromissores* or *fideiussores*. The obligations were in all three cases created by *stipulatio*, the respective forms being given by Gaius as "*idem dari spondes?*" "*idem fidepromittis?*" "*id fide tua esse iubes?*" He adds that he will explain what is the proper name for those to whom the question put is "*idem dabis?*" "*idem promittis?*" "*idem facies?*" but so far as extant does not return to the matter[4]. Probably they were *fideiussores*.

Sponsio was the oldest. This and *fidepromissio* could be used to guarantee verbal contracts only, and their antiquity is shewn by the fact that the obligation did not pass to the *heredes*. *Fideiussio* on the other hand could be used to guarantee any kind of obligation (itself however always a *stipulatio*), and the obligation passed to the *heredes*. The first two are a parallel to *adstipulatio*. *Sponsio*, involving the word "*spondeo*," was confined to *cives*[5].

As *adpromissio* was accessory, it could not be for more than was undertaken by the principal although it might be for less, and it might be conditional or *ex die* where the principal's undertaking was not, but not *vice versa*[6]. An *adpromissio* for more than the debt was void[7]. If, though not for more than the debt, it was for more than the mandate imposed on the *adpromissor*, it was good as between him and the creditor, but he could recover from his principal only the smaller amount[8]. But, at least in *sponsio* and *fidepromissio*, the principal promise need not be absolutely good: it sufficed that there was a *stipulatio* between persons qualified to contract in that form. Thus a *sponsio* or *fidepromissio* was valid even though the principal promise was by a *pupillus* without *auctoritas* of his *tutor*, or was *post mortem*, in which case there was not even a *naturalis obligatio*, while if it was on behalf of a peregrine or slave who had used the form "*spondeo*" Gaius doubts if it was valid[9]. This may date from a time when the promise of the *sponsor* was not subsidiary but was in actual fact principal[10]. For *fideiussio* the rule seems to have been that the original undertaking, whatever its form, must have created at least a natural obligation[11]. Thus a *fideiussio* taken after the original promisor had been deported was void[12].

1 G. 3. 113, 126. 2 G. 3. 112. 3 The word *adpromissio* is in no text, *adpromissor* in no classical text. Solazzi, *Bull.* 1930, 1. 4 G. 3. 115, 116. See Girard, *Man.* 799, as to the form used by the *fideiussor*. 5 G. 3. 118–121. A peregrine *fidepromissor* bound his *heres* if this was the law of his *civitas*. 6 46. 1. 8. 7. 7 *Ib.* 8 17. 1. 33. 9 G. 3. 119. 10 Mitteis, *Aus R. und Bürg. R.* 120; Koschaker, *Z.S.S.* 1913, 427; *ante*, p. 407. 11 G. 3. 119a. 12 46. 1. 47. pr.; cp. 14. 6. 18. Origins of *fidepromissio* and *fideiussio*, Collinet, *Mem. Acc. Bologna* (*Sc.M.*), 1931.

On the same principle, if the primary debt ceased to exist, the *adpromissor* was released. But there are distinctions. It must be the debt that is destroyed, not merely the debtor. If the debtor is deported or dies without successors the *adpromissor* is still liable[1]. And the debt must be completely destroyed. The fact that a debtor without means was entitled to the "*beneficium competentiae*" did not protect the surety[2]. A pact not to sue him did not release the surety if it was framed *in personam*[3]. A minor's right of *restitutio in integrum* did not protect an *adpromissor* who contracted, knowing of the minority[4]. And a praetorian release did not ordinarily protect the surety unless he had a right to reimbursement by the debtor, in which case the latter's pact would be futile if the surety could be sued[5]. Where a surety had released the principal by making the render impossible, this, quite logically, ended the suretyship, but left a liability to an *actio doli*. Later law, however, gave an *actio utilis*[6].

On general principle, a surety who had been called on to pay had a claim against his principal as *mandator*. But he was usually sued because his principal could not or would not pay, for though he could be sued though no action had been brought against the principal, this was unusual and might be an actionable *iniuria* to the latter[7]. And as there was not necessarily any juristic relation between different sureties for the same debt there would not be, on general principle, any claim at all against co-sureties. These and some other matters were regulated by a series of enactments now to be considered.

Sponsio is much older than mandate and the *sponsor* was provided, by the *l. Publilia*, of early date, with a special remedy not applicable to *fidepromissor*, the *actio depensi*[8]. This was an action, if he was not reimbursed within six months, which at first took the form of *manus iniectio*, and, on the disappearance of the *legis actio* system, became in the ordinary way an action for double damages in case of denial[9].

A *l. Appuleia*, about 200 B.C., applying to *sponsores* and *fidepromissores*, created a sort of partnership between co-sureties, so that any

1 46. 3. 95. 1; 16. 3. 1. 14; C. 8. 40. 1. Buckland, *R.H.* 1928, 460, *R.H.* 1933, 116; *contra*, Siber, *Gedenkschr. f. Mitteis*, 11; Desserteaux, *Mél. Cornil*, 1, 183; *R.H.* 1929, 291.
2 44. 1. 7. pr.; *post*, p. 693.
3 2. 14. 22. As to *pacta in rem, in personam*, *post*, § CXCV.
4 4. 4. 13. pr.
5 2. 14. 21. 5, 32.
6 Cuq, *Man.* 647, cites the following texts, shewing the evolution of the rule: 4. 3. 19; 46. 3. 95. 1; 45. 1. 88; 46. 3. 38. 4; 22. 1. 32. 6. It seems that if action against principal was time-barred, absolutely, the surety was released, *Arg.* 46. 3. 38. 4.
7 47. 10. 19.
8 G. 3. 127; 4. 9; 4. 171; see also P. 1. 19. 1.
9 The name "*depensi*" indicating a weighing has been held to shew very early origin, and also (Girard, *Man.* 808) that the payment must have been under a judgement, the formal satisfaction of which was in early law a payment *per aes et libram*, G. 3. 174.

who had paid more than his share could recover from the others[1]. His remedy is not known.

A *l. Furia de sponsu*[2], a little later than the *l. Appuleia*, came further to the relief of *sponsores* and *fidepromissores* by providing that they should be released by the lapse of two years from the due day, and that they were not to be liable for more than the amount of the debt divided by the number of sureties still living at the due day. This law gives rise to questions. We are told that it applied only in Italy[3]. The *l. Appuleia* still governed transactions in the provinces, and Gaius doubts whether it still exists as an alternative in Italy. From a recently discovered fragment of Ulpian[4] it is clear that "in Italy" means a surety given in Italy: it was immaterial where the principal contract was made. Gaius also tells us that the *l. Furia* also gave *manus iniectio pro iudicato* against a creditor who exacted from a surety more than his share. This could occur where the surety sued was not aware of the number of the sureties: lay literature shews us that suretyship was freely undertaken as a compliment with no serious expectation of responsibility[5]. The provision was a way of compelling the creditor to inform the surety of the number of his colleagues. But it may shew that the limitation was not "*ipso iure*," that the *lex* being *minus quam perfecta*[6], *manus iniectio* was the only way of enforcing the limit in the *legis actio* system, an *exceptio* being used under the *formula*[7].

A *l. Cicereia*[8], a little later, handled the same matter in a better way. It required the creditor to declare openly beforehand the amount of the debt and the number of *sponsores* and *fidepromissores*: a surety could, within 30 days, have a *praeiudicium* to determine whether this had been done: if it had not, the surety was released. This reference to *praeiudicium* indicates that the *lex* is later than the *l. Aebutia*[9]. Gaius tells us that the law does not mention *fideiussores* but that it was usual to make the declaration in that case also[10]. Probably *fideiussores* were not in existence when the law was enacted.

The later legislation applied to all *adpromissores*.

A *l. Cornelia*, probably of Sulla, provided that no one might be surety

1 G. 3. 122. A *lex imperfecta*? (*ante*, p. 6). More probably it annulled the suretyship. Kuebler, 170. 2 G. 3. 121; 4. 22. As it assumes provinces it must be later than 240 B.C. when the first province was founded. It is odd that Gaius speaks of Italy as a province, "*ceteris provinciis*." The fact that the *l. Appuleia* applied also to provinces suggests that provinces existed when it was enacted. 3 G. 3. 121. 4 Girard, *Textes*, 495. 5 Cuq, *Man.* 642. 6 Girard, *Man.* 806, for discussion of points under this *lex*. Appleton, *Mél. Gérardin*, 1 *sqq.*, holds that the reduction was *ipso iure*, referring to the above *lex* of G. and to Ulp. D. 45. 1. 72. pr. 7 G. 3. 121 may be read as shewing *ipso iure* division. But the word *obligantur* is uncertain. The absence of reference to the *exceptio* may indicate that the praetorian remedies which applied also to *fideiussor* were utilised. 8 G. 3. 123. 9 Girard, *Man.* 800. 10 G. 3. 123.

for one man to one man in the same year for more than the value of 20,000 *sesterces*, the surety being void as to the excess. The rule does not seem to have applied to conditional debts and was excluded where the surety was for *dos*, or in litigation, or for claims under a will or for taxes. From Gaius it seems that the obligation was reduced *ipso iure*, so that if surety was undertaken for more, and the creditor sought to enforce it, there would be a *plus petitio*[1]. The rule has disappeared from Justinian's law: nothing indeed is known of it beyond what Gaius says[2].

The *Sc. Velleianum*[3], of about A.D. 46, forbade women to undertake liability for others, either by way of surety (cumulative *intercessio*) or by *novatio*[4] or other mode releasing the person primarily liable (privative *intercessio*). Edicts of Augustus and Claudius had forbidden *intercessio* on behalf of the husband, and the *sc.* points out that the Courts had generalised this prohibition, which practice it confirms[5].

The *intercessio* was void, but, as in all early *scc.*, the rule was, in form, a direction to the magistrates, so that it was enforced by *exceptio*[6]. But the *intercessio* was so completely void that payment under it gave *condictio indebiti*[7]. The *sc.* was interpreted widely. It barred not only surety or pledge or *novatio* for another, but also the undertaking of a primary obligation for the benefit of another[8]. If the *intercessio* was by *novatio*, the original *obligatio* must necessarily be destroyed, but was revived by an *actio restitutoria*[9]. If it was a primary obligation undertaken for another the Praetor gave an action against that other[10]. And the *sc.* applied where evasion was attempted by a mandate given by the woman to a third person to act as surety[11]. By the practice of the jurists[12] some cases were excepted from the rule. It did not apply if the creditor was a minor and the principal debtor was insolvent[13], or if it was to save the father from execution of a judgement[14], or if, though she appeared as surety, it was really the woman's own affair[15], or if it was to provide a *dos* for her daughter[16], or, by a rescript of Pius, if she had deceived the creditor[17]. Mere mistake on the part of the creditor did not exclude the

1 *Post*, § CCXXXVII. It has however been held that it gave rise to an *exceptio*, and also that there was merely an action for recovery, but there is no trace of such an *exceptio* or of the application to this case of the general *exceptio senatusconsulti* (*post*, § CCXXIII, Lenel, *E.P.* 513) or of the action for recovery, which seems to belong to an earlier stage of evolution. *Condictio indebiti* in case of error.
2 G. 3. 124, 125. Lenel, however, finds dubious traces of it in Paul and Ulpian, *E.P.* 215 (44. 7. 42; 45. 1. 73. 1; 50. 16. 34).
3 P. 2. 11. See Gide, *Condition de la femme* (2), 153 *sqq.*
4 *Post*, § CXCIV.
5 16. 1. 2. pr.
6 H. t. 6; 44. 1. 7. 1.
7 16. 1. 8. 3; C. 4. 29. 9.
8 16. 1. 2. 1, 2. 5.
9 H. t. 8. 7, 13. 2. The name "*restitutoria*" is said to be due to Justinian.
10 H. t. 8. 14. As to this (so-called) *a. institutoria*, Lenel, *E.P.* 287.
11 H. t. 30, 32. 3.
12 I.e., not by express provision of the *sc.* See, e.g., 16. 1. 19. 5.
13 4. 4. 12.
14 16. 1. 21. 1.
15 H. t. 21. pr.
16 C. 4. 29. 12.
17 16. 1. 2. 3, 30. Another exception P. 2. 11. 2.

sc. unless the transaction was a disguised one, so that, on the face of it, it did not appear to be *intercessio*[1].

Justinian made a series of changes by enactments of which the general effect seems to be this[2]. He allowed such surety generally for provision of *dos*, or where it was on behalf of a slave who was to be free on payment of money. It was to be binding in any case, if, after two years, the woman confirmed it, or was paid for undertaking it, or acknowledged in the instrument that she was so paid, which makes the rule useless at the cost of a falsehood. But in all cases there must be writing and three witnesses[3]. Finally he provided that no *intercessio* on behalf of the husband should be valid, however often confirmed.

In the enactment providing that a woman might be *tutor* to her children he required such a *tutor* to renounce the protection of the *sc.*[4] This suggests that there was a right of renunciation, and a text of Pomponius implies the same[5], while one of Ulpian, quoting Julian, implies the opposite[6]. Probably there was no such right, except so far as it was provided by the rules of Justinian above cited.

CLVII. We saw that *sponsores* and *fidepromissores* had a means of recovering from their co-sureties what they had been made to pay in excess of their share. The *l. Appuleia* did not apply to *fideiussores*, but, very early, probably under the Republic, practice introduced the *beneficium cedendarum actionum*, i.e. a surety could before payment, or, in general, issue joined, require the creditor to transfer to him, by way of *procuratio in rem suam*[7], all his rights and securities against the debtor or other sureties[8]. The demand must be accompanied by offer of full payment, and must be made before payment[9]. As the creditor was under no duty to the surety he need surrender only such rights as he had: the surety had no ground of complaint if, e.g., the creditor had previously abandoned a security he held[10]. There was in this system an obvious difficulty. If the creditor was paid, he had no longer any rights to cede, and though he ceded them before payment, the payment would destroy them. The difficulty was met by treating the surety who paid, not as discharging the debt, but as buying it[11]. This is simple if the transaction was without judicial process, or before joinder of issue (*litis contestatio*[12]), and we are told that it was enforced by *exceptio doli*[13], so that the action would be lost if the *cessio* was not made as demanded. But if there was doubt as to the amount of the debt and the creditor refused *cessio*

1 16. 1. 4, 11, 19. 5. 2 C. 4. 29. 22–25; *Nov.* 134. 8. 3 As the same enactment (C. h. t. 23) also contemplates valid cases not in writing, its meaning is doubtful and disputed. 4 *Nov.* 118. 5. See *ante*, p. 151. 5 16. 1. 32. 4. 6 14. 6. 11. 7 *Post*, § CLXXXIX. 8 46. 1. 17; 46. 3. 76. 9 C. 8. 40. 11. Must be demanded and received: it was never implied. 10 C. 8. 40. 17. 11 46. 1. 36. 12 *Post*, § CCXXXV. 13 21. 2. 65.

because the offer was not enough, and at the hearing this proved to be so, and the surety sued thereon amended his offer, there could be no effective *cessio*, as some at least of the actions were destroyed by the *litis contestatio*. If the creditor proved wrong he would lose his action, though a debt was due and he had acted in good faith. It seems that injustice must have been done to one or the other if there was a real dispute as to amount, which could not be settled *in iure*[1].

The remedy just discussed affected co-sureties only incidentally: it was designed to give the surety the benefit of securities held by the creditor. Hadrian reinforced it by the *beneficium divisionis*[2], similar to, but not identical with, the rule of the *l. Furia*. There was no relation between sureties (apart from special contract) giving one any rights against the others, but he provided that a *fideiussor* might not be sued for more than the debt divided by the number of sureties solvent when the action was brought[3]. The right was enforced by refusal of the action or by an *exceptio* "*si non et illi solvendo sint*[4]," and, if this was not claimed, his obligation being essentially *in solidum*, the defendant surety had no claim against the others, nor, if in error, a *condictio indebiti*[5]. The right to division was lost by denial of the debt, and Papinian says that it did not apply where the *fideiussor* was given by a *tutor* to his ward[6].

The right applied only between sureties for the same debt and the same debtor, to the same creditor, not, e.g., as between a surety and one who was surety for him, *fideiussor fideiussoris*[7]. But it was indifferent that they had become sureties at different times, or that one was only conditionally liable[8].

It is not clear at what stage the solvency was looked into. Probably it was usually *in iure*: here there is no difficulty. But the use of the *exceptio* shews that it might be at the hearing and there is the difficulty that if the defendant surety proved the solvency of one who was not sued, or had not been allowed for, the action was lost and *litis contestatio* had destroyed the right against the others. Attempts have been made to avoid the difficulty by appropriate formulation[9].

Many texts tell us that action against the principal releases sureties[10] (other than mandators[11]). This would indeed follow from the fact that

1 Girard, *Man.* 807.
2 G. 3. 121. Paul makes it the Praetor. P. 1. 20. 1.
3 46. 1. 51. 4. Thus insolvency of a surety increases the burden of the others if it exists when the action is brought, but not if it supervenes.
4 46. 1. 28; C. 8. 40. 10. 1.
5 46. 1. 26, 39, 49. 1. The rule was probably applied in practice to *sponsores* and *fidepromissores*, out of Italy, who could not avail themselves of the *l. Furia*.
6 46. 1. 10. 1; 46. 6. 12 (? interp.).
7 46. 1. 27. 4, 51. 2.
8 46. 1. 27. pr., 48. 1. *Contra*, Levy, *Sponsio*, 155 on insufficient grounds.
9 Girard, *Man.* 807.
10 Cicero, *ad Att.* 16. 15. 2. *P. Sent.* 2. 17. 16; C. 8. 40. 15. 1; C. 5. 57. 2 (*et solvente* interp.); D. 44. 2. 21. 4; 46. 8. 1.
11 C. 8. 40. 23.

the principal debt is destroyed by *litis contestatio*. But it is usually rested on the unity of the obligation, *consumptio litis*, and the conclusion drawn that action against one *fideiussor* released the principal and the other sureties[1]. But, the contracts being distinct, there is here no unity of *causa*, which seems to be necessary, and the evidence is weak[2]. It consists mainly of several texts mostly post-classical which speak of *electio* between the persons liable[3], which suggests, though it is short of proving, that others are released. Justinian says what seems to mean that in old law there had been no such bar and he does not know why the old rule was abandoned[4]. It is thus probable (for his rather contemptuous language suggests that he is not speaking of the classics) that the new rule was post-classical[5]. There would be no bar in any case in favour of other sureties if the action was only for a share, under the *beneficium divisionis*. Suing a surety first was convenient if the debtor was away or insolvent, but without such reason it was a reflection on the debtor's solvency, and Gaius says that to sue a surety when the debtor was "*paratus solvere*" was an actionable *iniuria*[6]. It became usual in later law for sureties to agree not to avail themselves of this extinction, so that if, when sued, they pleaded *res iudicata*, there would be a *replicatio pacti conventi*[7]. Another, more ingenious, way was to make the *fideiussio* in a different form, to promise, not the debt but "whatever the creditor cannot recover from the debtor," which, in later classical law, was interpreted to mean "whatever he has been unable to recover by action against the debtor" (*fideiussio indemnitatis*), so that the debtor must be sued first[8].

Justinian provided that in all cases where several were liable for the same debt, action against one should not *ipso facto* release the others[9], which ended the difficulty. Later, he provided that the debtor must be sued first, but that if he was away, and the sureties were on the spot time must be given them within which to produce him. If they did not, they could be sued, having a right to cession of actions. This is the so-called *beneficium ordinis vel excussionis*[10].

1 See, e.g., Levy, *Konkurrenz*, 1. 190. 2 Siber, *R.R.* 2. 297. Buckland, *Jur. Rev.*, 1941, 1. 3 *Lex Rom. Burg.* 14. 7; C. 8. 40. 5, 19, 23; D. 27. 7. 7. For the word *electio* not signifying release of the others, C. 8. 40. 23. 4 *Nov.* 4. pr. 5 D. 46. 3. 84, where sureties for a slave are not released by action against *dominus*, may be interp. to express J.'s change (Levy, *cit.* 374), but may refer to surety for the *obligatio naturalis* of the slave. 6 47. 10. 19. But for such an action there must be evidence of intent to insult, *post*, § CCII. 7 C. 8. 40. 5, 28. 1. 8 45. 1. 116; 46. 2. 6. pr. The older view seems to have been (Celsus, 12. 1. 42. pr.) that on such words the creditor could still sue the surety first, and the *iudex* must determine what could have been recovered from the debtor, but apt words would exclude this. The name *f. indemnitatis* is not Roman. It is called *fideiussio* only in one text, probably interp. (46. 2. 6. pr.). 9 C. 8. 40. 28. On this legislation, Wylie, *Solidarity and Correality*, 227; Schulz, *St. Bonfante*, 1. 357. 10 *Nov.* 4. Names not Roman. The *Nov.* goes into great detail.

These *adpromissores* were not the only forms of personal surety. Besides the *praes* and *vas*, who will be considered in connexion with procedure[1], there are the cases of *mandatum credendae pecuniae*[2], *constitutum*, and the *receptum* of bankers[3], which will be considered later.

CLVIII. Plurality of Principals. There might be more than one principal creditor or debtor in the transaction. This represents the main case of Solidarity, with its distinction between Correality and Simple Solidarity. These relations are not confined to *stipulatio*, but it is primarily in this relation that correality is presented to us[4].

In general, where there were several parties to a divisible contractual obligation, it was divided between them[5]: if it was intended that each should be liable or entitled to the whole, this must be expressed in the transaction. This is well shewn in *stipulatio*. If, of several parties on one side, it was intended that each was to be liable or entitled to the whole, the creditor uttered the *stipulatio* and the *promissores* all answered together, or conversely, each creditor asked and the debtor answered once for all[6]. If there were more than one on each side, each *stipulator* asked and the *promissores* answered together. Some such form as this was the only way in which to make it one *stipulatio*; any other method would decompose into separate stipulations. But this would not be necessarily so if the *stipulatio* was by written *cautio*. There we are told that even if the *cautio* shewed that there were two *stipulatores* or two *promissores*, they were not *correi* unless the *cautio* expressly made them such—each would be liable or entitled only to a *pars virilis*[7].

The ordinary divided *obligatio* does not here concern us, and there was a case where all were liable, each for the whole, which also does not concern us. Where several were liable for a penalty for a joint delict, e.g. if two persons engaged in a theft, each was liable for the whole penalty. This may be called solidarity, but it is not the case we are dealing with. Each was liable for the whole, and would continue so liable though another had paid[8], their liabilities being entirely independent. But this applied only to the liability for the penalty[9]. Thus in the case mentioned there would also be a *condictio furtiva* for the value of the thing. Each was liable for the whole but payment by one discharged the rest.

1 Doubtful if they had any application outside procedural securities, Cuq, *Man.* 643. The *Praes* gives real security. 2 *Post*, § CLXXX. Called by commentators *mandatum qualificatum*. 3 *Post*, §§ CLXXXII *sqq*. 4 Though the distinction between correal *obligatio* and surety is clear, it must be borne in mind that the cases overlap. It was not unusual for correal debtors to become sureties for each other, reciprocally. Cuq, *Mél. Cornil*, 1, 157; *post*, p. 455. 5 45. 2. 11. 1; 38. 1. 15. 1. 6 Inst. 3. 16. 7 45. 2. 11. 1, 2. In informal contracts, the intent to exclude division must be clearly stated, h. t. 9. pr., 1. 8 47. 4. 1. 19; 9. 2. 11. 2; C. 4. 8. 1. 9 See, however, as to *dolus* and *metus*, *post*, §§ CLIX, CCIII.

Our case is that in which each of two or more persons was liable or entitled to the whole, but it was due only once, so that if the sum was once paid the whole was ended. This was what is commonly called solidary obligation, a name coined from the Roman expression, *in solidum*, which has no technical force, but is applied when it is wished to emphasise the fact that a man is liable for the whole[1]. Cases of this sort are numerous and familiar, though not always readily associated with the notion under discussion. There are many other than the primary case of joint contract, e.g., sureties, *inter se* (subject to the legislative restrictions already noted), surety and principal, *adstipulator* and principal, common owners of a slave liable on his contracts or noxally on his delicts, *dominus* and free *institor*, each of whom is liable on the latter's contract[2]. So too contracts by a member of a firm of *argentarii* or of slave-dealers (*venaliciarii*), or by one of joint *exercitores* in the business, were treated as made solidarily by them all[3]. So too where *A* made a legacy to *B* of what *C* owed *B*, or where several made a solidary deposit[4], or where several were jointly liable to pay compensation for a wrongdoing, as opposed to paying a penalty[5]. There are many others[6]. The possibilities of joint contract are endless.

These cases break into two groups, the essential difference being that in classical law, in one group, the bringing of an action by, or against, one, barred, or released, all the others. In the other group, roughly speaking, only satisfaction ended the obligation. To the first group the name correality may be applied, though it seems usual in modern writers to confine it to those cases in which the correal relation was expressly created by the parties, the others being spoken of as correal in a wide sense. The second case is commonly called simple solidarity. Where the plurality was on the creditor's side, it is called active correality (or solidarity), in the other case it is said to be passive. We deal first with correality, confining ourselves to the typical case, *stipulatio*, remembering that the same relation could also arise in the *bonae fidei* contracts[7] and in *mutuum*[8] (we have no evidence for the literal contract) or where a legacy was charged specially on two *heredes*[9].

A correal obligation was in content like any other; all that we need consider are the modes and consequences of its ending. Like all obligations, it ended by performance, as against all parties. It was completely destroyed in classical law by the *novatio necessaria* involved in *litis*

1 Thus in *de peculio* the liability is limited, but in *quod iussu* it is *in solidum*. 14. 5. 1.
2 Or his owner, if he is *servus alienus*, 14. 3. 17. 1.
3 2. 14. 27. pr.; 14. 1. 1. 25; 21. 1. 44. 1.
4 45. 2. 9.
5 C. 4. 8. 1.
6 E.g. 45. 2. 9. pr.
7 45. 2. 9. pr.
8 46. 1. 71. pr. But *mutuum* was usually reinforced by a *stipulatio*. As to solidarity in *commodatum*, Sorrentino, *St. Scialoja*, 1. 645.
9 30. 8. 1, but there is some interpolation.

contestatio in an action on it, between any parties[1], and by many other events. Anything which completely destroyed it as to one debtor, without affecting his personality, i.e. as Paul puts it[2], destroyed the debt, but not the debtor, destroyed it altogether. Thus it was ended by *novatio*[3] or *acceptilatio*[4] between any parties, or by an oath tendered and taken, that there was no debt[5]. It was ended by destruction of the thing due without *culpa* or *mora*[6] of a party. If it was by *culpa* or after *mora*, it survived against the party concerned, but on the texts it was extinct against the others in case of *mora*, but survived in that of *culpa*[7]. But the others were not released or barred by deportation, or death without successors, of one of the parties, or by *confusio* between one debtor and one creditor[8]. Conversely if one debtor gave an acknowledgement to one creditor, with the effect of lengthening the period of prescription of the action, it was, under Justinian, equally lengthened against all the debtors, and in favour of all creditors[9]. A set off held by one was of no avail to the others[10].

Praetorian defences, which did not destroy the obligation altogether, give rise to some difficulty, to be considered later[11]. The effect of *pactum de constituto* on the other parties is doubtful[12].

Justinian put an end to the most striking of these modes of discharge, by enacting that where there was a plurality of debtors, *litis contestatio* against one should not discharge the others. He does not mention plurality of creditors[13], but the omission is probably mere accident. It is clear on the texts and on the facts of life that plurality of debtors is the common and practical case.

If one correal creditor had received all, or one debtor had paid all, was there a right or obligation of contribution? The answer (there is controversy) seems to be[14] that there was no such right so far as the relation was merely one of correality. It is indeed suggested that, at any rate in post-classical law, any debtor who paid the whole could claim *cessio actionum*, as a surety could[15]. But such little evidence as exists for this is lessened in force by the fact that it was not uncommon for

1 46. 1. 5. 2 46. 1. 71. 3 *Post*, § CXCIV. 4 *Post*, § CXCV. 5 12. 2. 28. 3; 45. 2. 2. Brugi, *Ist.* 281 *contra*. But his texts (12. 2. 42. 1; 44. 5. 1. 3) do not prove his point. 6 *Post*, § CLXXXVIII. 7 22. 1. 32. 4; 45. 2. 18; 50. 17. 173. 2. Distinction explained away by some writers as unreasonable. Various solutions, Girard, *Man.* 790. 8 45. 2. 19; 46. 1. 71. 9 C. 8. 39. 4. 10 45. 2. 10. 11 *Post*, § CXCV. 12 13. 5. 10. Demangeat, *Oblig. Solidaires*, 86. 13 C. 8. 40. 28. 2; probably more than one statute fused together, Wylie, *Solidarity*, 227. Elaborate legislation in the Novels, e.g. *Nov.* 99. Collinet, *Ét. Hist.* 1. 124. 14 35. 2. 62. pr.; 45. 2. 10. Taubenschlag, *Röm. Prr. z. Z. Diocl.* 248, holds that in C. 8. 39. 1, Diocl. is introducing a general right of regress. But he does not seem to be enacting anything new: the joint borrowers are no doubt *socii*. 15 C. 4. 65. 13; C. 8. 40. 11; D. 19. 2. 47 (? interp.).

correi to agree to become sureties for each other, *fideiussio mutua* or *alterna*[1]: the texts may well refer to this case. But this harsh looking rule means little. Men did not become *correi*, at any rate expressly, by chance, without previous negotiation, and there were two well-known ways in which this inconvenience could be avoided. They frequently became sureties for each other, which gave all the various rights discussed in connexion with *adpromissores*. Or they might be *socii*, permanently, as in those cases, *argentarii*, *venaliciarii*, etc., already mentioned, in which correality was created by law, or for the purpose of this transaction only, and there was contribution *inter socios*[2]. Correality did not destroy the right of "regress" where it existed. Thus there was no difficulty where, as ordinarily, the case was one of consent, or where, though it was imposed by law, there was *societas*. Where the facts did not involve consent, they commonly created a regress. A testator could impose this liability on his *heredes*[3], but the one who had paid had *familiae erciscundae*. A principal and his *institor* (or the owner of the *institor*) were correally liable, but the *institor*, if compelled to pay, had his remedy under his contract of mandate. The liabilities of common owners of a slave on his contracts and delicts were correal, but the matter could be adjusted in *communi dividundo*[4].

CLIX. Simple Solidarity. The main distinction between this and the preceding case was that here *litis contestatio* between parties did not affect other parties, while satisfaction did[5]. Beyond this we do not know very much. Nothing would discharge which did not in the case of correality, but it is not clear that the converse is true even apart from *litis contestatio*. It is sometimes said that *acceptilatio* would not discharge[6]. As joint *stipulatio* involved correality, and *acceptilatio* was release from *promissio*, it might seem that the point could not arise, but this is not so. The liability of *tutores* was solidary, not correal. Where a *tutor* gave security, an *acceptilatio* on the stipulation released him; the question arises whether it released his colleagues. As it was

1 45. 2. 11. pr. Beseler, *Z.S.S.* 1924, 387; Collinet, *Ét. Hist.* 1. 131 *sqq.*, who rejects the notion and explains the text otherwise.

2 Good evidence of frequency of *societas* among *correi*, 35. 2. 62. pr.; 45. 2. 10. Contribution *inter socios*, *post*, § CLXXVII. This *societas* modifies other rules of the institution. The right of regress would make a *pactum de non petendo* useless unless available to all; accordingly it was so available, 2. 14. 25. pr. For the same reason a *transactio* was similarly available, 4. 8. 34. pr. Any *socius* could use a set off of any other, 45. 2. 10. On *confusio* between one *debitor correus socius* and the creditor, the others might use it to the extent to which they would have been entitled to claim against the *correus* who had become *creditor*, 46. 1. 71. pr. Probably similar modifications if they became mutual sureties.

3 45. 2. 9. pr.

4 10. 3. 15; 11. 1. 20. pr.; 14. 3. 13. 2.

5 E.g. 26. 7. 18. 1.

6 Girard, *Man.* 795, citing Gérardin. The analogy of *transactio* is not convincing, 27. 3. 15. It is not clear that this destroyed correal liability, in all cases; and it is a praetorian defence, *acceptilatio* is civil.

tantamount to satisfaction, it seems that it should do so. The same point arises in connexion with *novatio* and oath, but we have no information.

The question then arises: when was an obligation simply solidary? The first point is that no clear case can be shewn of this type on the side of the creditor[1]; it was always "passive" solidarity. It arose in certain praetorian delicts, *metus*, *dolus*, in the *actio de rationibus distrahendis* against tutors and perhaps some other delicts. It arose also in some contractual and quasi-contractual cases, where the liability had resulted from a breach of duty in a common undertaking, from *culpa* or *dolus*. It appears from several of the texts and it is the only rational rule, that this applied only if the fault was common. Among the cases mentioned are *tutela* and most of the *bonae fidei* contracts, including mandate. It is not stated in *negotiorum gestio*, but common *gestio*, though it must have occurred, is rarely discussed[2].

There was in general, as in correality, no recourse. But in the case of *tutores*, any *tutor* sued, if not personally guilty of *dolus*, was treated like *fideiussor* and given the *b. divisionis* and *cessionis*, even, it is said, an *actio utilis* where he had not taken *cessio*[3]. An interpolated text gives an *actio utilis* in the case of joint liability for *deiecta et effusa*, and says nothing about the *beneficia*[4]. *Tutela* seems the only clear case[5]. In the opinion of some critics most of these cases of simple solidarity are due to Justinian, having been correal in classical law[6].

It remains to consider why some cases were correal and others solidary. One opinion rests on a subtle distinction. In both cases there was only one object, one thing due, but in correality there was also only one obligation, so that what ended it for one ended it altogether, while in solidarity the obligations were distinct, and what happened to one need not affect the others. But this view is not consistent with the facts[7]. The same obligation could not be both civil and merely praetorian, as in the obligations of employer and *institor* on a contract. It could not be both simple and conditional as correal obligations could[8]. And while some texts speak of unity of obligation[9], others speak of

1 The case of *dos* promised to *vir* and *legata* to *uxor* may be one (23. 3. 29; 30. 84. 6). It is not correal, since these texts shew that action by one did not bar the other. But it was not solidary: the *heres* could claim security from the wife suing, to indemnify him from action by the *vir*, so that payment did not in principle discharge it either. The parties are forced by indirect means to be satisfied with one payment. It is not "*eadem res.*"

2 Girard, *Man.* 793, for other cases.

3 27. 3. 1. 11–13, to some extent interp.

4 9. 3. 4.

5 The same rule has been suggested in deposit, 16. 3. 22. But here both *heredes* have committed *dolus*; they would not be liable for *culpa* (h. t. 10). The liability *pro parte* in one case is not due to solidary *obligatio*, but to the fact that each has committed *dolus* in respect of different property.

6 See Eisele, *Archiv. für C. P.* 77. 374 *sqq.*; Albertario, *Bull.* 1913, 106, who accepts interpolations very freely.

7 Hunter, *Rom. Law* (4), 561; Girard, *Man.* 787.

8 45. 2. 7; Inst. 3. 16. 2.

9 E.g. 45. 2. 3. 1.

distinct obligations[1]. Moreover, it is merely giving the rule as a reason for itself: it does not shew why those who combined in a contract of *stipulatio* created only one obligation, while those who combined in a wrong created more than one. The expression *correi* is very rare[2]. The usual name is *duo rei*[3], a name equally applicable to any case in which two are liable, and not suggestive of any fundamental distinction.

Accordingly a more simple explanation is now more generally adopted. Whether there was one obligation, or more, there was at any rate only one thing due. There was an ancient rule: *non bis in idem*, and it follows that the same thing might not be claimed twice. The rule in correality was not a special rule for that case, but an application of ordinary principle; it is the rule in solidarity which needs explanation. There is no essential difference between the cases, and the renewed action was *bis in idem*, for it was *eadem res*. It is therefore suggested that there was no logical basis; it was an illogical relaxation, gradually extended, expressing the idea that those who do wrong ought not to be released from their obligation to compensate, except by satisfaction. No doubt some applications are due to Justinian[4]. It may be remembered that a similar difficulty was in some cases dealt with by the Praetor. One who had sued *de peculio* could not sue again, though unsatisfied, but the Praetor gave relief, as he did where buyer and seller were both liable *de peculio* and one had been sued[5].

CLX. There were some other verbal contracts.

Dictio Dotis. This is one of the three ways in which *dos* could be created in classical law: *datur aut dicitur aut promittitur*[6]. But *dictio* must be by the woman or her paternal ancestor or by a debtor to her, under her authorisation[7]. It was a solemn declaration that a certain thing or sum should be *dos*, made without need of any previous question[8]. It is possible that in early law *dictio* necessarily preceded the marriage, but in classical law it might be later. It was obsolete under Justinian, but many texts in the Digest which now speak of *promissio* were written of *dictio*. Some of these preserve the form: "*Stichus* (or *centum* or *fundus Cornelianus*) *tibi doti erit*[9]." The other party must be present, but need not say or do anything[10]. Hence arise doubts whether it is properly regarded as a contract, at least for early law[11]. In any case it gave rise to a

1 E.g. 46. 1. 5. 2 34. 3. 3. 3. 3 45. 2 *passim*. 4 History of the doctrine obscure. It has been inferred from 43. 24. 15. 2, that the idea is later than Labeo, but any inference from so corrupt a text is uncertain. The starting-point is probably in *dolus* and *metus*, as to which, *post*, § CCIII. 5 15. 1. 11. 8, 32. 1, 30. 4. 6 Ulp. 6. 1; 11. 20. 7 Ulp. 6. 2. 8 Kuebler, 152 and reff. 9 E.g. 23. 3. 25. 10 G. 3. 96, *post*, p. 673. 11 Karlowa, *R.Rg.* 2. 579. For later law, Gai. *Ep.* 2. 9. 3. Other institutions, usually held to have been unilateral in the sense that the offer was irrevocable even before acceptance, are *Votum* and *Pollicitatio*. As to the latter, *contra*,

strictum iudicium, but if it took the form of release from debt (*quod mihi debes, tibi doti erit*) the debt was not *ipso iure* destroyed, but only *ope exceptionis*[1]. It seems to have been a "formal" transaction. It might be conditional[2], and, no doubt, *ex die*. It is mentioned in literary texts of the Republic[3] and by Gaius and Ulpian[4], and it appears in an enactment of A.D. 396[5]. It is supposed to have been abolished by an enactment of 428 which validated any informal promise or *pollicitatio* of *dos*[6], but as this did not abolish *promissio* it seems rather to indicate than to cause the disappearance of *dictio*.

Iusiurandum Liberti. Also a verbal contract, *uno loquente*, but both parties present[7]. Where a manumission was otherwise gratuitous and was voluntary (i.e. where the master was not under an obligation to free, as under a *fideicommissum*), it was permitted to require an undertaking to render certain services[8]—*operae*. The difficulty that no promise by a slave was binding after manumission, while the man, once freed, might refuse the undertaking, was surmounted by requiring him to take an oath before he was freed, which put him under a religious obligation to renew the undertaking after he was free. The renewed promise was also under oath, though a *stipulatio* would have served as well. In fact, though the *iusiurandum* survived into Justinian's time[9], *stipulatio* had long been more usual. This had indeed the advantage for the patron that presumably it would not necessarily be destroyed by his *capitis deminutio* as the *iusiurandum* was[10]. There are traces of an early opinion that the oath before manumission was actually binding[11], but there is no evidence

Brini, *Mem. Acc. Bologna*, 1908 (*Sc. m.*), 1 *sqq.*; Albertario, *La Pollicitatio* (rev. Stoll, *Z.S.S.* 1931, 488). *Votum* is a vow of a gift to some divinity in a certain event, as in modern Roman Catholic countries, but in Rome with legal as well as religious sanctions (Karlowa, *cit.*). Machinery unknown, but the form "*voti damnas*" suggests *manus iniectio*. It survives into classical law but though named in the D. (50. 12. 2), it is really obsolete (Brini, *cit.* 33). *Pollicitatio*, technically used, means, in classical law, an undertaking, to a municipality, of a gift, either *ob honorem*, i.e. in respect of an honour conferred or to be conferred or not *ob honorem*. In the first case it was binding before anything was done; in the other only when the work was actually begun, at least where it was an *opus*, perhaps not where it was a promise of money. As to this and the change under Justinian, when the distinction is drawn between those given for any "*causa*," which here means almost any recognisable motive for a gift, and others, with other resulting changes, Albertario, *cit.* The institution may have originated in Imperial enactments of the second century (50. 12. 1. pr., 5, 6. 2, 7, etc.) but some applications, *inter vivos*, may be older (Brini, *cit.*). Institutions of a somewhat similar kind in English law would apparently be regarded, when concerned with *obligatio*, as irrevocable offers which become contracts when accepted. The Romans do not analyse them. Modern German analysis seems to see in them a type of obligation independent of contract.

1 23. 3. 44. 1. 2 50. 16. 125. 3 Reff. in Costa, *Storia*, 14. 4 See p. 457, nn. 6, 7, 10. 5 C. Th. 3. 12. 3 = C. 5. 5. 6, where the reference to *dictio* is suppressed. 6 C. 5. 11. 6. 7 G. 3. 96; D. 42. 2. 6. 3, *post*, p. 673. 8 38. 1. 7. 4, 13. 9 38. 1. 7. pr. 10 G. 3. 83; Inst. 3. 10. 1, which makes the destruction occur always. But see D. 33. 2. 2. 11 40. 12. 44. pr.

that this was so in historical times. The *iusiurandum* was a formal verbal contract, capable of release by *acceptilatio*[1], and perhaps of guarantee by *sponsio*[2]. The oath was binding even though taken by an *impubes*[3]. It must be made immediately on the manumission, otherwise it could not be compelled, though if actually taken later, it would be valid[4]. It was of course *stricti iuris*. Since we naturally think of services as to be done rather than given, we should expect a formula in the form "*dare facere oportere*." But in fact the *iudicium operarum* actually had the *intentio* in the form of *condictio certi*[5]: *dare oportere*. As has recently been shewn, an *opera*—a day's work—was conceived of as a unit of value and thus as a *dandum*, not a *faciendum*[6].

CLXI. The Contract *Literis*[7]. *Nomina Transscriptitia*. *Expensilatio*. We know little of this, though it was evidently important. Our substantial sources are a brief account in Gaius, a very different account by Theophilus[8], one or two references in other legal texts, a number of allusions in lay literature[9], and a defective inscription[10], these last being not concerned to explain it. The account by Gaius is, shortly, as follows: The contract, called *nomina transscriptitia*, was made in two ways. It might be "*a re in personam*" in which what was due in some other way was transformed into this contract by recording it as having been paid to the debtor. It might be "*a persona in personam*," in which case what was due from *A* was entered up as due from *B*, *A* having "delegated" *B*. It is distinct from *nomina arcaria*, similar entries but of real payments, the liability arising not from the entry but from the actual loan. Peregrines had not this mode of bookkeeping, and the Proculians held that they could not be parties to this contract, but the Sabinians held that if it was *a re in personam* they might be debtors under it, though not creditors.

This tells us little of the nature of the contract. Elsewhere we are told that it could not be conditional[11], but it is inferred from a letter of Cicero that it did admit of *dies*, though the brief remark is not quite conclusive[12]. The debtor must consent to the entry[13], and no doubt he would normally make a corresponding entry in his own book, but this does not seem to have been essential[14]. As it was acknowledgement of a

1 46. 4. 13. pr. 2 38. 1. 8. 1 speaks only of *fideiussio*. 3 38. 1. 7. 5; *a. utilis*, 40. 12. 44. 2. 4 38. 1. 7. 2; 40. 12. 44. pr. (? interp.). 5 Lenel, *E.P.* 338. 6 Deschamps, *Mél. Gérardin*, 157 *sqq.* Biondi, *Iudicium operarum*, 3, shews ground for thinking it *C. certae pecuniae*, 38. 1. 4 (corrupt). The notion of a day-work as a sum of money is found in other systems. 7 G. 3. 128 *sqq.* 8 *Ad* Inst. 3. 21. 9 Costa, *Storia*, 342 *sqq.*, with a theory as to the early history. 10 Girard, *Textes*, 847. 11 Vat. Fr. 329. 12 *Ad fam.* 7. 23. 1. It may be that the entry would be made on the day chosen. 13 Gaius does not say this, but it is inevitable. 14 In the case in Cicero, *de Officiis*, 3. 14. 59, the transaction is completed by entries made while the buyer is

loan it was always for a sum certain, unilateral and *stricti iuris*, the action being the *actio certae pecuniae creditae*. The *exceptio non numeratae pecuniae* was available, but as the basis of that defence was that the alleged loan had not been made, and the basis of this contract was a fictitious loan, this seems, at first sight, to make the contract useless. But it was always a sort of novation or recast of an existing transaction, or a way of opening a credit for the debtor, and the *exceptio* would be for use where the previous transaction had never existed, or the business contemplated had not gone through[1].

All this leaves the actual mechanism of the contract obscure. What was the *transscriptio*? In what account book did the entry appear? That there were two entries and that one was based on the other appears from the name and the fact that a single transaction consists of *nomina* in the plural[2]. Romans kept a daybook or *adversaria*, on which the day's dealings were noted, and these were, it seems, copied into the *codex accepti et depensi* from time to time[3]. It has been conjectured that *transscriptio* means transfer from the daybook to the other, but both entries were in the same book or, at any rate, made at the same time. The conjectures that this book was a special one kept for this purpose, and that it was a ledger, containing a statement of debts incurred and rights acquired, are without evidence. The usual view is that it was the ordinary cashbook, *codex accepti et depensi*—the statement of moneys paid out and in. The loan being fictitious, the book would not balance, and it is supposed that there were two fictitious entries, one stating money received, the other, the *expensilatio*, on the other side. If it was *a persona in personam*, the former would be an entry that the money had been received from the other debtor; if *a re in personam*, it would be an entry of receipt of what was due under the earlier dealing. This would apply even though the previous dealing was not binding, e.g. a sale before the consensual contract existed. Where there was no previous dealing, but it was intended to open a credit, we do not know anything of the form[4].

The contract fell into disuse with the practice of keeping private books, and disappeared late in the classical age[5], having survived longest

paying a call; he can hardly have had his account books with him, and (Girard, *Man.* 531) the point would have been material to the defence in the *Pro Rosc. com.*

1 C. 4. 30. 5.

2 Cicero, *de Officiis*, 3. 14. 59, "*nomina facit: negotium conficit.*"

3 Cicero, *Pro Rosc. com.* 3. 8.

4 This account represents orthodox opinion. But the evidence is scanty and different views are possible. That of Heck (*Archiv. f. civ. Pr.* 116. 129), that there is no warrant for the conception of it as entries in an account book, that it was merely a formal document, does not explain G. 3. 131–133. That the whole story in Gaius is a figment of G. or his authority (de Ruggiero, *St. Perozzi*, 394) is incredible.

5 It survived to Papinian, Vat. Fr. 329. See Costa, *Storia*, 347.

among bankers, who of course still kept books[1]. Justinian observes that these *nomina* were not now in use, but that there was still a sort of written contract. He says that where a man had given a written acknowledgement of a loan, not in fact made, and the time for the *exceptio non numeratae pecuniae* was past he was bound by his writing, at least if there was no *stipulatio*[2]. But though the practical effect was much the same this seems to be a confusion[3]. The man was bound by the *mutuum* and had provided evidence which barred him from denying that there was a *mutuum*. On this view the document was not the contract, but only evidence, though in the circumstances it was conclusive evidence[4].

1 They kept their customers' books. 2 Inst. 3. 21. 3 See, however, Collinet, *Ét. Hist.* 1. 59 *sqq.* But see also the arguments assembled by Girard, *Man.* 533. The custom of embodying transactions in writing is borrowed from Oriental practice, and Gaius speaks of *chirographa*, which seem to have been sealed by one, and *syngraphae*, sealed by both, as essentially peregrine. Vinogradoff, *Hist. Jurispr.* 2. 239. But with the extension of *civitas* under Caracalla, such documents begin to play a more important part under Roman law. As to the varying forms and names Mitteis, *Rom. Pr.* 1. 290. 2; Wenger, P.-W., *s.v. Signum*, and *Z.S.S.* 1921, 611; Kroell, *Rôle de l'écrit.* They seem to be all, so far as Roman law is concerned, merely evidentiary. Justinian uses the word *chirographum* freely, but he seems to mean by it no more than *cautio*, a memorandum of a transaction, usually sealed by one or both parties. 4 It is contended by Riccobono, *Z.S.S.* 1922, 262 *sqq.*, with textual support, that under J. the written *stipulatio* is no longer merely evidentiary: it has absorbed the Greek notion, and is a written contract, not a mere means of proof. This is accepted, e.g., by Binder, *St. Brugi*, 339, and, with some divergences, by De Ruggiero, *St. Perozzi*, 371. The contrary view is maintained by Siegel, *Arch. f. Civilpr.* 1915, 6, also with textual support. Perhaps the right solution is that of Arangio-Ruiz, *Ist.* 79, that J.'s rules represent a "*regime in divenire*": it was for a later generation to develop a clear doctrine. Riccobono's further doctrine that every note of contract was a *stipulatio* is difficult to reconcile with the insistence by the Greek commentators on the *stipulatio* clause. See, e.g., the repeated affirmation in Gloss (27) ὁ δεῖνα ἐπηρώτησε (*Bas.* 11. 1. 7; *Heimb.* 1. 571) that it is the *stipulatio* clause which bases *a. ex stip.* on the document. It is indeed disputed that Greek law ever developed an abstract written contract. Brandileone, *Rend. Acc. Bologna* (*Sc. mor.*), 1920, 57.

CHAPTER XI

OBLIGATIO (*cont.*). CONTRACTS *RE*. CONTRACTS *CONSENSU*. INNOMINATE CONTRACTS

CLXII. The contracts "*re*." These (*Mutuum*, *Commodatum*, *Depositum* and *Pignus*) have as their common quality the fact that the binding element is the handing over of the subject-matter[1]. This cannot be regarded as a "Form" in the sense that the contract is formal, for we shall see that, in many cases where the thing was in the hands of the person who was to hold it under the contract, there was no actual delivery. Nor can the contract properly be said to be binding by part performance, for in *mutuum* the only person bound, and in *commodatum* and *pignus* the person primarily bound, were those who received a service by the handing over, while in deposit the person primarily bound was one to whom the handing over was not a service. And that way of putting the matter leads to the view that part performance made an agreement binding, a notion of much later development[2]. But these contracts did involve a new conception; certain bargains were made binding, not certain ways of making bargains.

Mutuum. Loan, not for use, but for consumption, the debtor being

1 Historically the class begins with *mutuum* and *solutio indebiti*, both involving transfer of ownership and the notion of unjust enrichment. Gaius gives only these cases. The extension of the notion to cases where ownership does not pass, and points other than return arise, makes it difficult to assign any more precise meaning to the word "*res*"; Brasiello, *St. Bonfante*, 2. 541. Perozzi, *Ist.* 2. 31, excludes the notion for classical law except where ownership is transferred.

2 Innominate contracts, *post*, § CLXXXI.

bound to return, not the same thing, but the same quantity of things of that kind and quality[1]. Thus it applied only to what the Romans called *res quae mutua vice funguntur*[2]. Money is the obvious case, but it applied equally to any things commonly dealt with by number, weight or measure—corn, wine, etc. It is conceivable that anything might be the subject of *mutuum* if the parties so agreed. The contract was unilateral, binding only the receiver. It was *stricti iuris*, the remedy in case of money being the *actio certae pecuniae creditae*; in other cases *condictio triticaria*[3]. Questions of quality would be material here: no doubt the *intentio* stated the grade or quality of the goods[4].

Mutuum was the oldest of these contracts and the only one which was *stricti iuris*. It was not very frequent, for it was usually coupled with a *stipulatio* for return (commonly with interest—*fenus*), and where it was so reinforced it was superseded by the *stipulatio*[5]. *Mutuum*, conceived of as a contract, is not, probably, of great antiquity. But the notion of an obligation to restore[6], where one man is wrongfully enriched by the receipt of sums of money which should rightfully be another's, the basis of the later system of *condictio* (*sine causa*[7]), is very ancient. Money handed over on an undertaking to return it is an obvious form of this, and gradually, in the course of evolution of legal analysis, takes shape as a specific contract[8].

A *mutuum* might have subsidiary agreements in it. There would usually be a day fixed for repayment, or a provision that the property was not to pass, and *mutuum* arise, till some future day[9]. There might be a *solutionis causa adiectus*, and a place fixed for payment, and there might be conditions[10]. There might even be resolutive conditions, e.g. that in certain events the money was to be a gift[11].

It was of the essence of *mutuum* that *dominium* was transferred from the lender to the borrower, but in the complex relations which arose in trade there would be some relaxation of this rule. Some cases which look like relaxations are not really such but are expressions of the various

1 G. 3. 90; Inst. 3. 14. pr. 2 *Res fungibiles* is not a Roman expression. 3 *Post*, § CCXXX. 4 12. 1. 3; Lenel, *E.P.* 240. 5 45. 1. 126. 2. If the *stip.* was void, but nevertheless novated (G. 3. 176, *post*, § CXCIV), there would be no action at all, 46. 2. 1. 1. The earlier transaction putting the money in the defendant's possession might not have been *mutuum* at all. Segrè, *St. Simoncelli*, 336 (abstracted *Z.S.S.* 1927, 514) arguing from 12. 1. 9. 3, 4; 44. 7. 52. 1, 3; 45. 1. 126. 2, holds that Justinian constructed out of all the types an *obligatio re et verbis*, in which the *stip.*, even though *animus novandi* was expressed, was always accessory, and the earlier transaction construed as *mutuum*, so that there would be *condictio* in any event. 6 Girard, *Man.* 539; Pernice, *Labeo*, 3. 1. 220. 7 *Post*, § CLXXXVII. 8 Early loans of money no doubt usually took the form of *nexum*, *ante*, p. 429. 9 12. 1. 8. 10 E.g. in *nauticum fenus*, where the obligation to return does not arise unless the voyage is safely completed; *post*, p. 466, a suspensive condition. See also 12. 1. 7, 10; 45. 1. 122. pr. 11 39. 5. 1. pr., 18. pr.

forms which *traditio* might take. If *A* asked *C* for a loan and *C* told him that *B* owed *C* money and that if *A* collected it from *B* he might have it as a loan, there was a *mutuum* so soon as *A* had collected the money. At first sight the actual money seems never to have been *C*'s, but in fact it passed to *C*, and was transferred from *C* to *A* by *traditio brevi manu*[1]. One case, at least, appears to go further. *A* asked *C* for a loan and *C* got his debtor *B* to promise to pay *A* instead of *C*; there was a *mutuum* to *A*. In the actual case there was an error which vitiated the transaction, but it seems to be the opinion of Celsus that there would be *mutuum* apart from this error[2]. It is not however clear that the *mutuum* is contemplated as arising at the moment of the promise. If it arises only on payment, there is nothing exceptional[3].

If ownership did not pass, there was no *mutuum*. It does not follow that there was no liability. If the lender failed to transfer ownership because he could not alienate, he had a *vindicatio*, or, if the property had been consumed in good faith, a *condictio*. If it had been consumed in bad faith he had either this or, if he preferred, an *actio ad exhibendum*[4]. If the failure was due to his not being owner the true owner had a *vindicatio*, and if the thing had been consumed in good faith, the lender (so to call him) had *condictio*, and the owner, who had no direct claim against a *bona fide possessor* who had ceased to possess, could demand cession of these actions. If the property had been consumed in bad faith, the owner had the *actio ad exhibendum*[5].

As the actual thing lent had not to be returned, but its equivalent in kind and quality, there was no question of negligence. Apart from special agreement, whatever happened to the property lent, an equivalent must be returned[6].

Mutuum, as a result, perhaps, of its origin, was gratuitous, but the Roman business man did not lend gratuitously. What the rule meant was that interest, if any, and there usually would be[7], must be agreed for by a separate contract. This would normally be a *stipulatio*[8], for a mere pact would not base an action, though a pact to pay interest created a *naturalis obligatio*, which pacts ordinarily did not[9]. Interest

1 D. 12. 1. 2. 4 (*contra*, 17. 1. 34 in analogous cases); h. t. 9. 8; 45. 1. 126. 2.
2 12. 1. 32.
3 See, however, Girard, *Man.* 543. He cites other texts in support of the view that the Romans were groping at the notion of handling book credits as if they were money. Arnò, *Fictio brevis manus*, calls attention to conflicts in the texts, sometimes set down to interpolation, but, as he holds, more probably, survivals of doctrinal conflict. For him the followers of Q. Mucius allowed this *fictio* fully; those of Servius accepted it only gradually and partially. He finds the same conflict in many analogous cases.
4 12. 1. 12, 13. 1.
5 12. 1. 11. 2.
6 C. 4. 2. 11.
7 Loan at interest is called *fenus*, but so far as the loan is concerned it is the contract of *mutuum*.
8 Exceptional cases in which pact sufficed, *post*, § CLXXXVIII.
9 See, however, *post*, § CLXXXIX; 46. 3. 5. 2; C. 4. 32. 3.

was limited and there were penalties for exceeding the lawful rate[1]. The maximum rate for money loans in the Empire was 12 per cent. Justinian fixed it at 6 per cent. for ordinary loans, 8 per cent. for business loans and 4 per cent. for loans by senators. Compound interest (*anatocismus*) was forbidden[2].

Where interest was contracted for by separate *stipulatio* it would be recovered by a distinct action. But as a pact could not be sued on, it seems to follow that the interest in those cases in which pact sufficed would be recovered in the same action. Thus, in loans of grain, the fact that the value had in any case to be estimated in the judgement permitted of the addition of the interest also[3]. But in money loans by *civitates* (another case in which pact sufficed) there was an obvious difficulty. The *actio certae pecuniae creditae*, being for *certa pecunia*, did not admit of any addition to the sum named in the *intentio*. It is to be supposed that the interest due was added to the amount of the loan in the *intentio* of the action.

CLXIII. *Sc. Macedonianum.* This enactment imposed an important restriction on loans. A *lex lata* under Claudius laid some restriction, the nature of which is unknown, on loans at interest to *filiifamilias*, payable at the death of the *paterfamilias*[4]. A little later, under Vespasian, this *sc.* (named, it seems, after the person whose malpractices led to its enactment[5]) provided, in the form, then usual in *scc.*, of a direction to the magistrates, that no action was to be given to one who lent money to a *filiusfamilias*, even though the *paterfamilias* had since died. The language suggests that this would lead to an enquiry (*cognitio*) by the Praetor and consequent *denegatio actionis*, but it is clear that the defence was raised by *exceptio*[6]. Suetonius speaks of it as applying to loans at interest, but it applied equally to gratuitous loans[7].

The rule affected only loans of money to the *filius*, not loans of other property, or other contracts, e.g. sale, even though interest was to be paid on the price, nor surety for a loan to a third person, or *expromissio* on loan to a third person[8]. But this was subject to the rule that the *sc.* applied if they were mere masks, i.e. frauds on the *sc.*, the real purpose of the transaction being a loan to a *filius*[9]. It did not apply where money promised to a *filiusfamilias* was lent to him after he was a *paterfamilias*[10], but, conversely, it did apply if the money, promised while he was *sui iuris*, was paid to him after he was adrogated. On the other hand if it

1 See, e.g., for later law, C. Th. 2. 33. 2. In classical law what was paid in excess was imputed to the debt, or as an alternative could be recovered, P. 2. 14. 2, 4. Appleton, C., *Rev. Gén.* 1920; Pais, *Ricerche*, 4. 33.
2 C. 4. 32. 26, 28; D. 12. 6. 26. 1. See also *post*, § CLXXXVIII.
3 C. 4. 32. 11, 23.
4 Tac. *Ann.* 11. 13.
5 14. 6. 1. pr.
6 14. 6. 7. 10; cf. P. 2. 10. 1.
7 Suetonius, *Vesp.* 11; D. 14. 6. 7. 9.
8 14. 6. 3. 3, 7. pr., 3, 13.
9 14. 6. 3. 3, 7. pr.–3.
10 14. 6. 3. 4, 4.

was essentially a loan to a *filiusfamilias*, the *sc.* applied even though return was stipulated[1], so that the *mutuum* was superseded.

The protection applied to all those *alieni iuris*, of either sex[2], and it protected the *paterfamilias* against an *actio de peculio*—indeed this was probably its primary purpose[3]. It also protected sureties for the *filius*, at any rate if, as was commonly the case, they had a right to fall back on him[4]. And the defence was available to and against *heredes*[5].

The lawyers developed rational limitations to the provision of the *sc.* It did not apply if the creditor had no reason to think the man a *filius*, or was deceived by him, or he was generally thought a *paterfamilias*[6]. It did not apply so far as the money was applied to the father's concerns[7], or was needed for, and applied to, reasonable expenses such as the father ordinarily paid[8], or if the father authorised it or, knowing of it, did not prohibit[9] it, or if it did not exceed the *peculium castrense* or *quasi castrense*, or, under Justinian, if the loan was to a *miles*[10]. It did not apply if the *filius* acknowledged it after he was *sui iuris*, by part payment, or ratification or novation[11].

The obligation was not absolutely void: there was a *naturalis obligatio* on the son and his sureties[12], but not on the father. As to the son the effects of this *obligatio* were small, while he was a *filius*, for, if he paid, his father could recover[13]. He could not ratify[14], while a *filius*, but he could give a surety[15]. When *sui iuris* he could do all these things, but it does not seem that apart from ratification the *obligatio* could be used as a set-off against him. If the surety paid, he could not recover or claim from the *filiusfamilias*[16].

Fenus Nauticum, Pecunia Traiectitia[17], was a complicated transaction. It was loan for the purposes of a voyage, usually to buy cargo, for the out or home journey, the money not to be repaid unless the ship arrived safely. For the period during which the risk was with the creditor, interest might be agreed on by mere pact and was without legal limit, till Justinian, after hesitation, fixed it at 12 per cent.[18] For the period before starting, and after arrival, legal limits applied[19]. A slave was

1 14. 6. 6. 2 At least when *filiae* became *capaces*, Levy, *Z.S.S.* 1930, 282. 3 14. 6. 9. 2; Inst. 4. 7. 7. 4 14. 6. 9. 3. 5 14. 6. 7. 6, 7. 10. 6 14. 6. 3. pr.–2, 19. 7 14. 6. 7. 12. 8 14. 6. 7. 13; Greg. Wis. 10. 1. 9 14. 6. 7. 15, 9. 3, 12, 16. The *initium* being the important thing, the classics doubted if ratification sufficed, or if application to father's concerns of money borrowed for himself barred the *sc.* Julian held in the second case that it did and Justinian made ratification suffice. 14. 6. 7. 12; C. 4. 28. 7. 10 14. 6. 1. 3; C. 4. 28. 7. 1. 11 At least, in *novatio*, if he did it knowingly, 14. 6. 7. 16, 9 (interp.), 20; C. 4. 28. 2. 12 12. 6. 40. But see *post*, § CLXXXIX. 13 Difficulties if the thing is consumed, 12. 1. 14; 14. 6. 9. 1. 14 *Arg.* 14. 6. 20. 15 14. 6. 9. 3. 16 14. 6. 9. 4. 17 Huvelin, *Droit Commercial Romain*, 196. 18 P. 2. 14. 3; C. 4. 32. 26. 2. 19 22. 2. 3, 4. pr. There are two contracts, an ordinary *mutuum* till the voyage begins, and a *fenus nauticum* to arise when

usually sent with the ship, and there were formal rules as to his demanding the money on arrival[1]. Stipulations were usual for payment of the slave[2] and as to delay in payment[3]. It might be agreed that the creditor should be released from the risk if the voyage did not end by a fixed time or unauthorised ports were visited or unauthorised cargo was carried[4]. Whether the remedy on this contract was the same as on ordinary *mutuum* is not said. It was imported from Greek law and, though sometimes called *mutuum*[5], is treated distinctly in the sources[6]. It has therefore been contended by different writers that it gave an *actio in factum*, that it was an innominate contract, and that there was a *condictio ex lege*[7].

CLXIV. *Depositum.* This and the remaining "real" contracts were of a different type. They were praetorian in origin, simplifications of *fiducia*. They gave *bonae fidei iudicia*, and were what is called imperfectly bilateral; they are fully developed only under the Empire.

Deposit was the handing over of a *res mobilis*, gratuitously, to the care of the depositee. There was no transfer of ownership or even of legal *possessio*. Thus even if the depositor was not owner, the contract was valid: depositee must hand the *res* back to him, unless it was claimed by the owner, even if the depositor was a thief[8]. There might be an agreement that it should be handed to a third person[9]. But if depositee was himself owner at the time of the deposit, there was no contract[10]. If the deposit was by an owner incapable of binding himself, e.g. an unauthorised *pupillus*, the depositee was bound, but not the *incapax*, but where a deposit was made to a *pupillus*, without authority, if he was old enough to be capable of *dolus*, and committed it, he was liable[11]. As depositor need not be owner, a redeposit by a depositee was a valid contract, and might not be a breach of duty[12]. The original depositor might sue his depositee, but if the redeposit was reasonable, could claim only cession of actions against the second depositee, against whom, however, he had, in late classical law, an *actio utilis*[13].

The depositee must restore the thing on demand, whether there was a fixed term or not, together with its "*causa,*" accessories, fruits, etc.[14] He might not use it; to do so was *furtum*[15]. But he was liable only for

the first is ended by the starting, a sort of combination of loan and marine insurance. It is the source of *respondentia* and bottomry of commercial law. The second contract is conditional on the starting.

1 22. 2. 2. 2 22. 2. 4. 1. 3 22. 2. 9. Obscure rules, fixing a limit on these two charges, 22. 2. 4. 1. 4 C. 4. 33. 4. 5 22. 2. 6; 45. 1. 122. 1; C. 4. 33. 5. 6 D. 22. 2; C. 4. 33. 7 Reff. Bertolini, *Obblig.* (*P. Sp.*) 204. 8 16. 3. 1. 39; 16. 3. 31. 1; 5. 1. 64; Coll. 10. 7. 1. 9 Who has, under J. an *actio utilis depositi*, C. 3. 42. 8. 1; cp. Coll. 10. 7. 8. 10 16. 3. 15. *Contra*, if he has become owner since, C. 4. 34. 11. 11 16. 3. 1. 14, 15. 12 16. 3. 16. 13 *Ib.*; Coll. 10. 7. 8. 14 16. 3. 1. 24. 15 G. 3. 196; P. 2. 12. 5.

dolus, not for *culpa*[1], so that if it had been lost by accident, or slight negligence, he was not liable, but gross negligence "*dolo aequiparatur*[2]." The restriction on liability is due to the fact that he did not profit: the contract was wholly in the interest of depositor. Special pacts might make him liable to any extent, even for *casus*, but a pact not to be liable for *dolus* was void[3]. And one who offered himself as depositee was liable for everything but *casus*[4]. If depositee lost possession in a way which freed him from liability, but afterwards regained it, he was now in his old position, even though the recovery was after an action had been begun[5]. The fact that the liability might be varied by pact, and that men do not adjust their transactions to textbook classifications, led to doubts whether a given transaction was or was not deposit. If there was reward it was *locatio*: the texts discuss many such cases[6].

The depositor, as he benefited, was liable for *dolus* and *culpa*, for expenses involved in the care of the thing and for harm caused by it, which care on his part would have avoided[7]. If the contract was for return at a place other than that of deposit, he must pay reasonable resulting charges. For recovery of expenses the depositee had besides the action a right of retention analogous to pledge, but while this right of retention, in other cases where it existed, gave an *actio furti* if the thing was stolen from the holder, this was not so here[8].

The action against depositee was the *actio depositi*. The original *formula* was *in factum*[9], but in classical law, though this still existed, there was an alternative *bonae fidei formula in ius* which appeared before it did in *commodatum* and pledge[10]. From *litis contestatio* the *res* was at his risk if he could have returned it[11]. *Condemnatio* involved *infamia*[12]. But the judgement freed him from further liability in respect of the thing, which, if still in his possession, became practically his[13]. Under Justinian there could be no set-off[14].

1 13. 6. 5. 2; 16. 3. 1. 47; Coll. 10. 2. 1, 7. 6. 2 *Culpa lata, post*, § cxc. 3 16. 3. 1. 6, 7; 2. 14. 7. 15, 27. 3. Where a holder commits *dolus* in respect of the thing, there is *condictio*, apart from *actio depositi*, 16. 3. 13. 1. Albertario, *Bull.* 1912, 15 *sqq.* holds that all such pacts varying the liability were void till Justinian, but there is a great difference between pact against liability for *dolus* and pact for release from liability for past *dolus*. 4 16. 3. 1. 35 (? interp.). 5 16. 3. 1. 47–3, 20. If he sell the thing and recover it and afterwards lose it without fault he is liable: *dolus* perpetuates the liability, Coll. 10. 7. 10. 6 E.g. 16. 3. 1. 9–13. 7 13. 7. 31; 16. 3. 5. pr., 23 = Coll. 10. 2. 5. 8 Coll. 10. 2. 6. Justinian may have abolished this *ius retentionis*. C. 4. 34. 11. 9 Perhaps replacing a delictal liability to double damages under the XII Tables. Coll. 10. 7. 11. As to differences in effect between the two *formulae*, Rotondi, *Scr. Giur.* 2. 47. 10 Lenel, *E.P.* 288 *sqq.* 11 16. 3. 12. 3. Modification in later classical law, Girard, *Man.* 1074. 12 Coll. 10. 2. 4; 10. 6. 1; G. 4. 60; D. 3. 2. 1. 13 41. 4. 3. Levy, *Z.S.S.* 1921, 476, holds that in classical law he did not get *dominium* or the Publician, only a *quasi* or *utilis Publiciana*. He cites 6. 1. 70; 6. 2. 7. 1; 25. 2. 22. pr.; 41. 3. 4. 13; 41. 4. 1, 2. 21; 47. 2. 85. Description of it as like sale is a loose analogy, not to be pressed. He discusses the later history of this and cognate cases. 14 C. 4. 34. 11. Earlier law not clear, P. 2. 12. 12.

The action against the depositor was the *actio depositi contraria*, a nomenclature which expresses the fact that the contract created liability primarily in the depositee: the contract was imperfectly bilateral. It was a *bonae fidei iudicium* and *condemnatio* did not involve infamy[1].

Three cases of Deposit have very special rules:

Depositum miserabile. Where a deposit was made in time of riot, fire, shipwreck or similar calamity, so that the depositor was unable to choose his man, the depositee was liable to double damages for denial or *dolus*, a survival of the general liability under the XII Tables[2]. The *heres* was equally liable for his own *dolus* or denial, but there is a curious rule that he was liable *in simplum* for his predecessor's *dolus*, but only for one year, actions on contract being usually perpetual[3].

Sequestratio. Deposit by two or more jointly. It arose usually from a dispute affecting the thing, often a lawsuit[4], and the deposit was to be returned only when the dispute was settled, and to the person in whose favour it was decided. But it might equally arise in any joint deposit if the thing was to be returned to one, on a certain condition[5]. Only one could have a right to it and he only when the condition arrived[6]. For the *sequester* to give it up before was a breach of contract[7], but he might in some cases, on application to the Praetor, give the parties notice to find another person, or, on the same application, deposit the thing in a temple[8]. Sequestration was at times ordered by a *iudex*, but in later law he might not order *sequestratio* of money claimed[9]. It applied to land as well as moveables and it usually, but, at least in late law not always, gave possessory rights to the *sequester*[10], which prevented any party from acquiring it by *usucapio*. If the *sequester* had not *possessio*, but only detention, *usucapio* might still be running for the benefit of the winner[11]. The action bore the special name *actio depositi sequestraria*[12].

Depositum irregulare[13]. Deposit of fungibles, usually money[14], and with a banker, on the terms that he was to return an equivalent on demand, so that the ownership passed to him[15]. It was very like *mutuum*:

1 3. 2. 1; 16. 3. 5. pr. *Post*, § CCXXXIV as to *actio contraria*. 2 Coll. 10. 2. 7; 10. 7. 3, 11. Inst. 4. 6. 26, making it *in duplum* only on denial, contrary to all other evidence, seems a mere slip; Rotondi, *Scr. Giur.* 2. 104. 3 16. 3. 1. 1–4; h. t. 18; perhaps a relaxation of the rule, resulting from the early conception of it as a delict, that it was not transmissible at all. Rotondi, *cit.* 2. 122, 378. 4 16. 3. 5; 50. 16. 110. 5 16. 3. 6. If he gave it to a third person, presumably any of them could claim. 6 *Arg.* 16. 3. 6. 7 C. 4. 34. 5. 8 16. 3. 5. 2. 9 2. 8. 7. 2; C. 4. 4. 1. 10 16. 3. 17. 1. Also a survival for practical reasons from the rule in *fiducia*, *ante*, § CLI. Ciapessoni, *Il precarista detentore*. 11 41. 2. 39. Karlowa, *R.Rg.* 2. 607. 12 16. 3. 12. 2. *Sequestratio* is mentioned by Plautus, but it is not clear that it has legal consequences. For Cicero it seems commonly to mean dishonest concealment, *pro Clu.* 26. 72; *in Verr.* 1. 12. 36; 2. 2. 44. 108. For the word and the history of the institution, see Muther, *Sequestration und Arrest.* 13 Not a Roman name. 14 As to corn see 19. 2. 31. 15 19. 2. 31; 16. 3. 7. 2, 3.

indeed it might be *mutuum*. It might be agreed, e.g., that money was to be a deposit but that at any time the depositee might turn it into a *mutuum*, and use it[1]. There is but a fine line between this and the transaction we are considering, the difference being one of intent. This transaction was deposit throughout (though its purpose was not merely that of ordinary deposit) and from this fact many results followed, e.g. *bonae fidei iudicium* and *actio contraria*, *infamia*, absence of set-off under Justinian, recoverability at any time, and interest from *mora*. Neither the *sc. Macedonianum* nor the *exceptio non numeratae pecuniae* applied[2]. It is suggested by some texts that the subject-matter was at the risk of the depositor till actual use[3], but this is doubtful[4]. Where the money was to be used, interest was due, recoverable in the *actio depositi* itself[5]. But this involved one disadvantage. If the banker became insolvent, depositors were entitled to payment before ordinary creditors, but not where they had received interest[6]. It seems likely that the whole institution is post-classical[7].

CLXV. *Commodatum*[8]. Loan for use, the thing being returned. It seems to have been originally called *datio ad utendum*[9]. The lender was *commodator* or *commodans*, the borrower, "*qui commodatum accipit*" or the like[10]. It was usually for a short agreed time[11], and for a specified purpose. If the time was not stated the purpose must be, or it would not be possible to fix a limit of time: it is held indeed by some writers that the purpose was always stated and that so far as land is concerned, this was the real difference between *commodatum* and *precarium*[12]. *Commodatum* was perhaps, at first, not applied to land, but this application appears in classical law[13]. As the same thing must be returned, it did not normally apply to things necessarily consumed in use, but if the things were lent "*ad pompam vel ostentationem*," fruits lent for ornament in a procession and so forth, this was a valid *commodatum*[14].

The essential of the contract was the delivery, as in deposit, a mere physical transfer, giving only detention[15]. Thus, as in deposit, there was

1 12. 1. 9. 9. 2 C. 4. 30. 14. 1. 3 12. 1. 10; 16. 3. 1. 34. 4 16. 3. 24, 26. 1. 5 16. 3. 28, 29. 1; C. 4. 34. 4. 6 16. 3. 7. 2. 7 The only pre-Justinian text, a late one, Coll. 10. 7. 9, says clearly that it is *mutuum* though called deposit. Some of the texts are interpolated. See however Collinet, *Ét. Hist.* 1. 114 *sqq.* and Costa, *Storia*, 366, who cite Papinian (16. 3. 24). But the only parts of this text which speak of restoring "*tantundem*" say that here it is not deposit. See the document in Girard, *Textes*, 863 and Rotondi, *cit.* 2. 63. Jörs, *R.R.* 155, gives *dep. irr.* a classical origin. 8 Ferrini, *Opere*, 3. 81. 9 13. 6. 1. 1. The edict says "*commodasse*," h. l. pr. 10 *Commodatarius* is not a Roman word. 11 13. 6. 5. pr. 12 Bertolini, *cit.* 266. 13 13. 6. 1. 1; 19. 5. 17. pr. There could not be *commodatum* to take the fruits. 19. 5. 16. 1. 14 13. 6. 3. 6, 4. Just as in this country exhibition fruits are sometimes lent for the decoration of a table. 15 6. 1. 9; 13. 6. 8.

a valid contract even where the lender was not owner, and what was said as to deposit by a thief applies here also[1]. It is usually said that there could not[2] be *commodatum* of a *res incorporalis*, but this means merely that if *A* gave *B*, gratuitously, the enjoyment of usufruct of land or a slave, this was not *commodatum* but *precarium*. *Commodatum* must be for a specific purpose, but there was nothing to prevent one who had a usufruct from giving a *commodatum* of the thing to another, as one could who had no right at all. The *commodatum* was valid though the act might be a breach of his duties as usufructuary.

The loan must be gratuitous: if it was not, and the reward was to be in money, it was *locatio rei*. If the payment took another form it was an innominate contract, *permutatio* or the like[3].

It was normally for the benefit of the borrower alone, but cases might occur in which it was for the benefit of both, e.g. where two were giving a dinner in the rooms of one of them, and the other lent him objects to decorate his rooms[4]. We are told that it might be solely for the benefit of the *commodator*, but the cases look like benefit of both, e.g. a man lends his bride ornaments to wear at the wedding or a Praetor who is giving public games lends the players some outfit, or, the text adds, some one lends them to the Praetor[5]. We shall see that these distinctions were of importance in relation to the liabilities of the parties.

The borrower might keep the thing for the agreed time, or, if none was agreed, for a time reasonable for the purpose of the loan[6], subject to the obvious limitation that the lender could at once reclaim it if the borrower was misusing it in breach of the contract[7]. In early classical law the owner could not, it seems, bring *vindicatio* against any but a *possessor*, but in later law the real action lay against any who held the thing[8]. If the owner and lender vindicated from the borrower, it is not clear whether the existence of the contract gave an *exceptio* or whether the borrower must return the thing and rely on his *actio commodati contraria*. The latter is probable, except, indeed, where he had a *ius retentionis* for expenses: in this case he had an *exceptio doli* in the *vindicatio*[9]. But the owner seems usually to have proceeded by *actio commodati*, in which he had not to prove title.

The borrower must return the thing at the proper time with its "*causa*," i.e. accessories, fruits, *fetus*, etc., and any profits he had derived

1 13. 6. 15, 16; 5. 1. 64. 2 See Bertolini, *cit.* 262. 3 Inst. 3. 14. 2; 3. 24. 2; D. 13. 6. 5. 12. As to money consideration in *locatio*, *post*, § CLXXIV. 4 13. 6. 18. pr. 5 13. 6. 5. 10. The last case seems to be for the benefit of both, as the lender will see the games; how it should be thought of as for his benefit alone is difficult to understand. 6 13. 6. 5. pr., 17. 3. 7 *Arg.* C. 4. 65. 3. 8 6. 1. 9. Siber, *Passivlegitimation*, 26. 9 47. 2. 15. 2, 60.

from unauthorised use of it[1]. If he lost it without liability he must transfer any rights of action.

Normally the borrower was liable for all damage to the thing or its accessories, due to his *culpa*, having to shew the care of a *bonus paterfamilias*[2], but there were exceptions extending and limiting this liability. If the loan was for the benefit of both, he was bound only to shew the care he did in his own affairs[3], and if for the benefit of *commodator* alone he was liable only for *dolus*[4]. Conversely, the liability might be larger. As any pacts might be added it was possible to agree for any degree of liability, e.g. *casus*, but here as elsewhere a pact excluding liability for *dolus* was void[5]. He was liable for all risks, even *vis maior*, after he was in *mora*[6], for all damage resulting from unauthorised use of the thing[7], and for "*fatum*," i.e. everything, if, when he might have saved the borrowed thing, he preferred his own[8]. If condemned he could claim cession of any actions the lender had against third parties, and, to security for its delivery if the *commodator* ever recovered it[9].

If the thing was stolen from the borrower he had, in classical law an *actio furti* against the thief, and the owner had not. This is explained by Gaius as due to the fact that the owner had no interest, since the borrower was responsible for the thing[10]. This implies liability even without negligence, if the thing was stolen, a liability, known as "*custodia*," to be considered later[11]. Under Justinian a new rule was introduced, for the case of *commodatum*. The *dominus* had the choice. If he sued the thief, the borrower was freed from further liability. If he brought *actio commodati*, the borrower might sue the thief. But if when the *dominus* brought the *actio commodati* he did not know that the thing had been stolen, he could change his mind, remit the *actio commodati* and sue the thief, unless the borrower satisfied him, in which case he in turn could sue[12].

The *commodator* must refund all extraordinary expenses and all but the simple everyday medical expenses, even though the thing became extinct[13]. He had to make good damage caused by defects in the thing of which he knew, and was liable generally for *dolus*[14], but with the

1 Inst. 3. 14. 2; D. 13. 6. 5. 10, 13. 1; 22. 1. 38. 10. Unauthorised use in bad faith was *furtum*, 13. 6. 5. 8. 2 13. 6. 5. 2; P. 2. 4. 3; Coll. 10. 2. 1. 3 13. 6. 18. pr. In early classical law perhaps only for *dolus*. "*Diligentia quam in suis rebus*," *post*, § CXC. 4 13. 6. 5. 10, applied perhaps originally to both cases. 5 13. 6. 5. 2, 17. pr. Liability for *casus* implied if agreement expressly for return at a stated value, h. t. 5. 3. 6 *Post*, § CLXXXVIII. 7 13. 6. 5. 7, 18. pr. 8 13. 6. 5. 4; P. 2. 4. 2. Exact meaning controverted. Bertolini, *cit.* 468. 9 13. 6. 13. pr., 5. 1, 17. 5; 42. 1. 12; *ante*, p. 282. 10 G. 3. 203 *sqq.* Details and limitations, *post*, § CXCVII. 11 *Post*, § CXCI. 12 C. 6. 2. 22. The change is slight, *post*, p. 580. 13 13. 6. 18. 2, 4; P. 2. 4. 1; Coll. 10. 2. 5. 14 13. 6. 18. 3.

limitation, found in many contexts, that if he lent a slave, his liability could not extend beyond the man's value[1]. If the lender benefited by the loan he would be no doubt liable for *culpa*. He was liable for loss resulting from his not allowing the borrower to enjoy the thing as agreed[2]. For *impensae*, and, according to one text, for any claim, the borrower had a *ius retentionis*, till allowance was made[3].

Commodatum by an unauthorised *pupillus* was binding on the borrower, but not on the pupil[4], though if he sued he could no doubt be met by *exceptio doli* in respect of expenses which had improved his property[5]. A *commodatum* to a *pupillus* did not bind him in strict law, but a rescript of Pius gave an *actio utilis* to the extent of his enrichment[6]. Apart from ratification there was no direct action even if the *commodatum* lasted after puberty, even for *culpa* after puberty[7].

If several took a *commodatum* in common, the texts conflict on the question whether the obligation was *in solidum* or *pro parte*, but the dominant opinion seems to be that it was solidary, unless the contrary appeared[8]. *Coheredes* of a *commodatarius* were of course liable, under the rule of the XII Tables, only *pro parte* for fault of the deceased[9]. Each *heres* was presumably liable in full for his own *culpa*, but we are not told how far he could be sued on the *culpa* of another *heres*.

The lender's action was *actio commodati*, with alternative *formulae* as in deposit. The *actio commodati contraria* was wanted where *retentio* was not available (that was the more convenient remedy), e.g., where on the facts no *actio commodati* lay, or the expenses might exceed the claim, or the *iudex* had refused to take them into account[10].

CLXVI. *PLEDGE.* In connexion with this it is convenient to give a short account of the evolution of real security, though it is only to a small extent part of the law of obligations. The essence of these transactions is the giving to a creditor some right, essentially a right *in rem*,[11] over property, by way of security for the debt. At first this was effected

1 47. 2. 62. 6. Mommsen inserts a passage. 2 13. 6. 17. 3. 3 13. 6. 18. 4. 4 13. 6. 1. 2, 3; 26. 8. 5. pr. 5 *Arg.* 18. 5. 7. 1 etc. 6 See n. 4. 7 13. 6. 1. 2. 8 H. t. 5. 15–7, 21. 1. It looks like indivisibility. 9 C. 2. 3. 26; D. 13. 6. 3. 3 (prob. interp.) says that *heres* who has the whole is liable *in solidum*. 10 13. 6. 18. 4. See *post*, § CCXXXIV, as to *actio contraria*. The distinction between deposit and *commodatum* and, e.g., *mandatum* would be less clear in practice than in texts. *A* asks *B* to take care of silver in his absence, but he may use it if his own silver falls short on a festal occasion. It is *commodatum* on such an occasion, otherwise *deposit*. If *A* and *B* are common owners and *A* asks *B* to take care of the thing with permission to use it, but to lose no opportunity of selling it, all three contracts seem to be present, perhaps *societas* as well. 16. 3. 1. 11 *sqq.* On *b. f.* character of the *formula* in *ius*, *post*, § CCXXIX.
11 *Pignus* is not part of the law of *iura in rem*. *Possessio* is not treated in classical law as a *res*. It appears, in the institutional books, under actions, so far as it appears at all. Though security should be treated as a separate head, repetition is saved by taking it incidentally, as in personal surety, *ante*, § CLVI.

by *fiducia*[1]: ownership was transferred to the creditor, who was to reconvey the property, if the debt was duly paid, and it was usual to agree as to the circumstances in which the creditor might sell it. The so-called *formula Baetica*[2] is a model form for such transactions. *Fiduciarius* was owner and thus had the rights of owner, any restrictions on them being matter only of contract between him and the debtor. If he sold before the debt was due, or in any way contrary to his undertaking, he was liable to the debtor, but the sale was good, and the buyer had a good title not subject to the *fiducia*. The debtor was deprived of the use of the thing, though it was not uncommon, at least in the case of land, for the creditor to leave it in his hands as a *precarium*[3].

The creditor might not profit by the thing, and thus what he received by way of produce or rent or the like, was set off, in first instance, against interest due, and any excess against the debt, any further excess, e.g. on sale, going to the debtor[4], with interest in case of *mora*. He must not damage the thing and must restore it if the debt was duly paid, being liable in later law for *culpa*[5]. If the debtor found a purchaser and was prepared to pay the debt the creditor must reconvey. An obvious means of oppression and fraud was checked by a rule that the creditor could not become owner, free from the *fiducia*, even through an intermediary. An agreement that the creditor should have no right to sell was void: he could still sell on giving notice. If he had improved the thing he was entitled to the cost, and as account of this was taken in the *actio fiduciae*, it was, in effect, added to the debt[6].

Fiducia was not superseded by the appearance of *pignus* and *hypotheca*: it had such advantages for the creditor that it was kept in use[7]. It lasted throughout the classical age, and only disappeared with *mancipatio*: it is possible that *mancipatio* and *cessio in iure* were kept in existence for some time because they could be used for *fiducia*[8].

The protection of possession by the Praetor paved the way for the introduction of another form of security, *Pignus*[9], in which *possessio*

1 *Ante*, § CLI. 2 Girard, *Textes*, 827. 3 2. 8. 15. 2, *ante*, p. 245. 4 P. 2. 13. 1, 2. 5 The liability was originally only for *dolus* (*post*, § CXC), perhaps till Modestinus (Rotondi, *Scr. Giur.* 2. 141). 6 P. 2. 13. 1–7; 4. 12. 6; D. 13. 7. 6. pr., 22. pr. Many texts in the Digest, there referred to *pignus*, were written of *fiducia*. Remedies, *ante*, p. 432; *post*, § CCXXXI. 7 *Fiducia* could not be attached to *traditio* (*ante*, § CLI) so that this form of security applied only to *res mancipi*. It is held by Manigk (Pauly-Wissowa s.v. *Fiducia*) that the rules were so affected by reaction of those of *pignus* that the fiduciary creditor had, in effect, only a limited ownership. 8 The documents in Girard, *Textes*, 827 *sqq*., shew that there might be various terms. In neither is it expressly said that the property is to be returned on payment. (*Ante*, p. 431.) 9 The word *pignus* is very ancient in lay literature (Champeaux, *Mél. Girard*, 1. 161) and there are legal consequences, but it is not the "real" contract of *pignus*. The thing is to be forfeited in a certain event: it is a sort of conditional *traditio*. Senn, *N.R.H.* 1913, 591.

passed to the creditor, *dominium* remaining with the debtor, already existing in the Republic. This protected the debtor from such wrongful sales as might occur in *fiducia*, but it still deprived him of the enjoyment of the thing, unless the creditor allowed him to hold it *precario*. The creditor's protection at first was only *possessio* protected by interdicts, with a right of sale, if this had been agreed, but not otherwise[1]. There were so far as we know no special interdicts, but the texts suggest that *uti possidetis*, *utrubi* and *unde vi* were available[2].

A further development was the agreement, ultimately called *hypotheca*, in which the right to take possession was vested in the creditor, but the thing was not actually handed over. There might be an agreement that possession should not be taken till the debt was due: in any case it was *hypotheca* till the thing was actually taken over. The binding force of this security was first recognised for rents. A tenant could validly agree that his "*res*" should be pledged for his rent, the expression covering all his property "*invecta et illata*," except in passage, and the crops, after he had acquired them by *perceptio*[3]. The landlord had an *interdictum Salvianum* to recover them from the debtor as soon as rent was due[4], without which right his agreed security would have been worthless. He had also an *actio Serviana* for their recovery from any one who held them[5], and the interdict was ultimately made effective against third persons[6]. Similar agreements were made by urban tenants, but the interdict may not have been here available: the *actio Serviana* was not. Early in the Empire, and perhaps before, this action was extended (texts call it *utilis* or *quasi Serviana*) to other cases of hypothec, probably first to urban landlords, later to all cases, when (or later) it acquired the name of *actio hypothecaria*[7], the pledge without actual transfer becoming very usual.

Between hypothec and *pignus* there was no essential legal difference, but there was the physical fact that in the former the thing was left with the debtor, so that it was possible to create successive charges on the same thing[8]. It was equally possible to create hypothecs on a thing

1 20. 1. 35. 2 41. 3. 16; 43. 17. 2, 3. 8; 43. 16. 1. 9. The allusion in the first text seems to be to *utrubi*. 3 20. 6. 14; 47. 2. 62. 8. 4 G. 4. 147. These pledges arose without express agreement in the later classical law, *post*, § CLXVIII. 5 Inst. 4. 6. 7. 6 43. 33. 1; C. 8. 9. 1. Girard holds (*Man.* 828) that it ultimately extended to all pledgees. G. 4. 147; Inst. 4. 15. 3 and Theoph. *ad* h. l.; C. 8. 9. 1, "*debitoremve.*" 7 *A. hypothecaria utilis* where *res aliena* pledged and pledgor becomes owner, C. 8. 15. 5 (? interp.). Lenel now holds that all the names except *a. Serviana* are interp.: classical law gave the same action in all cases. 8 It has been maintained that the words *hypotheca*, *hypothecaria* are always interp. (Mitteis, *Z.S.S.* 1910, 489). But *hypotheca* seems to be in origin merely a Greek name for *pignus* (Erman, *Mél. Girard*, 1. 419) used only in dealings with Greeks till Severus. Later jurists use it more freely and as synonymous with *pignus* (20. 1. 5. 1). E. does not shew how Ulpian comes by the distinction in 13. 7. 9. 2, which

already held by a pledgee, and the obligational rules were, *mutatis mutandis*, the same. We deal with the two institutions together.

The contractual aspect of the matter can be shortly dealt with. It was, at least in later law, a *bonae fidei* transaction. Each party was liable for *culpa levis*[1] and it is sometimes said that the creditor in possession was liable for *custodia*[2], but this is doubtful[3]. He must not use the thing or make profit out of it, what is so received being imputable against interest and debt[4], as were damages received, e.g. for theft of it, except where the debtor was the thief[5]. (To these rules *antichresis* was an exception. This was an agreement, introduced towards the end of the classical period, that the creditor should have the fruits in lieu of interest[6].) He must restore the pledge when the debt was paid[7]. He could claim reimbursement of expenses properly incurred in the care of the thing, and compensation for damage caused by the thing, if there had been *culpa* of the debtor[8]. If the thing did not belong to the debtor, or, more generally, was in such a legal position that the creditor was lawfully deprived of his security, the debtor was liable whether he knew of the defect or not[9]. The actions were the *actio pigneratitia* for the debtor and *contraria* for the creditor, with *formulae* both *in ius* and *in factum*[10]. But the debtor could not bring his action unless he had discharged the debt, or was ready to tender the amount when he asked for the *formula*[11]. The debtor's action was the same whether the transaction was *pignus* or hypothec, though there would be less occasion for it in the latter case[12].

CLXVII. The creditor's means of enforcing his security are the following:

1. Right of Sale. From early times a right of sale might be agreed on[13], but, after Gaius, though before Paul, things were reversed: there

is that in the text, but he regards it as older than Ulp. and merely a means of using both words. Apart from terminology, pledge by agreement is as old as the Empire. As to its source, Girard, *Man.* 816; Manigk, *Pfandrechtl. Untersuch.* 1; Ebrard, *Die Dig. fragm. ad form. hypoth.*; Jörs, *R.R.* 109.

1 13. 6. 5. 2; 13. 7. 13. 1; Inst. 3. 14. 4. 2 Heumann-Seckel, *Handlexicon*, s.v. *custodia*. Buckland, *N.R.H.* 1917, 5. 3 E.g. C. 4. 24. 5, 8, 9. 4 13. 7. 22. pr.; 47. 2. 55. pr.; 20. 1. 21. 2; C. 4. 24. 1. 5 13. 7. 22. pr.; 47. 2. 15. pr. 6 20. 1. 11. 1; 20. 2. 8. 7 13. 7. 9. 5; Inst. 3. 14. 4, with its *causa*. Not if there were other debts even though not expressly secured, C. 8. 26. 1 (Gordian). Effects, *S.M.W.* 348. Paul (*Sent.* 2. 5. 2) says that pledge does not cover *fetus* and *partus*. *Contra*, Paul, 20. 1. 29. 1; C. 8. 24. 1. It has been suggested that the text in the *Sent.* is defective and said that these were not covered by *p. antichresis*. 8 13. 7. 16. 1, 31. 9 13. 7. 9. pr.
10 As in *commodatum* and *depositum*, Lenel, *E.P.* 259, but later. See *post*, § CCXXXIV, as to the *actio contraria*. It is maintained by some writers (see Levy, *Z.S.S.* 1915, 1; Biondi, *Iudicia bonae fidei*, 233 *sqq.*) that in classical law there was only a *formula in factum*.
11 13. 7. 9. 5. 12 The *actio hypothecaria* is an action, not on *obligatio*, but for the enforcement of the possessory right, and applies equally to *pignus*. See above. 13 The earliest reff. (20. 1. 35; 47. 10. 15. 32) may have been written of *fiducia*.

was an implied right of sale when the debt was due unless it was expressly excluded[1]. It does not appear that the creditor need have actually taken possession before sale, and though he could not sell to himself, even *per interpositam personam*[2], the debtor could sell to him[3].

2. Foreclosure. In earlier classical law the creditor could not become owner by lapse of time, i.e. there was no foreclosure except under an agreement that the property should be his if the debt was not paid by a certain day—*lex commissoria*[4]. This was modified by a practice, introduced early in the third century, by which the creditor could apply to the court to have ownership conferred on him—*impetratio dominii*. There was an official valuation and, after notice and a year's delay, he received praetorian ownership, being compelled however, if he took the thing, to accept it in full discharge, though the valuation was less than the debt, and, if it was more than the debt, to pay the difference to the debtor[5]. Further, the debtor could it seems still redeem, before *usucapio* was complete[6]. The *lex commissoria* was forbidden under Constantine[7].

Justinian modified this system in several ways. Either he, or some other late authority, provided that where there was an agreement that the creditor should not sell he could still do so after notice given three times[8]. He provided that, subject to agreement, there could be no sale till two years after notice or judgement. If no purchaser was found a *iudex* would fix a time for payment. If payment was not made by that time a further decree was issued on application, declaring the creditor owner. The debtor could still redeem within two years by paying debt, interest and costs. On sale any excess must be paid to the debtor and if the price was less than the debt, the creditor could still claim the rest[9]. He also provided that if the thing had passed to a third person the creditor could not bring the *actio hypothecaria*, etc., against him till he had exhausted his personal remedies against debtor and sureties[10].

The normal subject of a pledge was a thing owned by the debtor. If it was not his, he could not create a pledge over[11] it, but one to operate when it became his would be valid[12]. It could in any case be ratified when it became his, and in later law was so validated, *ipso facto*[13]. Praetorian ownership sufficed and even a *bona fide possessor* could pledge so as to bind himself, those claiming under him, and those against whom he had the *actio Publiciana*[14].

1 G. 2. 64. If no agreement, triple notice to debtor, P. 2. 5. 1; C. 8. 27. 14. On *Cons.* 6. 8, which says that, if the creditor has sold the *fiducia* or pledge, the *heres* has no action unless it was begun by the deceased, Huschke, *ad* P. 2. 17. 15. 2 P. 2. 13. 4; C. 8. 27. 10. 3 20. 5. 12. pr.; Vat. Fr. 9. 4 20. 1. 16. 9, where the words "*iusto... aestimandam*" are interpolated. 5 Chief texts C. 8. 33. 1, 2; these enactments assume earlier legislation which is lost. 6 *Arg.* 41. 1. 63. 4. 7 C. 8. 34. 3. 8 13. 7. 4. 9 C. 8. 33. 3. 10 *Nov.* 4. 2. 11 13. 7. 2. 12 20. 1. 16. 7. 13 13. 7. 41. 14 13. 7. 29; 20. 1. 18.

There might be pledges of rights other than ownership[1]. A debt might be pledged, but there would be no question of possessory rights. This was made effective by notice to the debtor, who could not then validly pay the original creditor, and could be sued by the pledgee, by *actio utilis*[2]. There might also be subpledge, pledge of a pledge, which is contemplated as a second pledge of the thing itself, under powers implied in the original pledge[3]. There was also what is known in English law as a "floating charge," a hypothec of stock-in-trade on the terms that it was to apply to new stock as it came in and to cease to apply to stock disposed of in the way of business[4]. Usufruct, and no doubt *emphyteusis* and *superficies*, could be pledged, but as nothing could be pledged which could not be sold, *usus* and *habitatio* doubtless could not[5]. It was possible to create a potential usufruct by way of pledge, i.e. to authorise the creditor to sell a usufruct in the property if the debt was not paid[6], and this might apply equally to *usus* and *habitatio*. There is a further remarkable case. A right of way or water to be created could be pledged, though urban servitudes could not. The creditor, if a neighbouring owner, could use the servitude till the debt was paid, and, if it was not, he could sell the easement to any other neighbouring owner[7]. Apart from the creditor's right to enjoy the way, this is like the last case—a neighbour might be willing to buy a right of way. But the text assumes it existing in the hands of the creditor, and a servitude cannot shift from one *praedium* to another. It is sometimes explained as meaning that the debtor has a servitude over adjoining land, and pledges that, but this also involves the inadmissible transfer to third persons of rights over the servient land[8].

Pledge was indivisible: so long as any part of the debt was unpaid the whole thing was still pledged, and, where it had passed into several hands, any of the owners was liable to *actio hypothecaria* for the whole[9].

The pledge was ended if the creditor sold the thing or renounced his right[10]. It was also extinguished by satisfaction of the debt, though not by its prescription. If the thing was in the hands of a third person, and he, when sued by the creditor for it, paid him off, he was regarded as buying the debt, and was entitled to *cessio actionum*[11].

The texts shew, as might have been expected, that *pignus* was mainly used for moveables, and hypothec for land and *iura*.

1 Brugi, *Ist.* 262. 2 20. 1. 20; 13. 7. 18. pr.; 42. 1. 15. 8; C. 8. 16. 4. 3 13. 7. 40. 2; 20. 1. 13. 2; C. 8. 23. 1, 2. 4 20. 1. 34. pr. Excluded by the modern French and German Codes. Scialoja, *Proprietà*, 43. It is in substance an application of the principle of h. t. 16. 7. No question of a *universitas*. 5 20. 1. 9. 1, 11. 2, 3. 6 20. 1. 15. pr. 7 20. 1. 12. 8 Text sometimes said to be mainly Justinian, Pomponius having said the opposite. Perozzi, *Ist.* 1. 765. 9 13. 7. 8. 2, 11. 3; C. 8. 27. 6; 8. 31. 2. 10 13. 7. 9. 3, 8. 1; 50. 17. 158. Time bar in late law, *post*, § CCXXXIII. 11 20. 6. 12. 1; *post*, p. 479.

CLXVIII. So far we have discussed rules applying to both forms: we have now to consider points involving a hypothec.

The difference between *pignus* and hypothec was that in the latter the thing remained with the debtor. Thus the same thing could be hypothecated to a number of persons in succession, which did not necessarily, or usually, involve any fraud. This institution, which seems to belong to the late classical age[1], led to many special rules. It was *stellionatus* to give a hypothec without declaring existing charges, or to alienate without declaring charges[2]. But the principal rules had nothing to do with fraud. If there were several charges, it was necessary to determine their priorities. The rule was that apart from privileged hypothecs, to be dealt with shortly, the earlier in date had priority, even though a later charger had gained actual possession[3]. This was modified by Leo, who gave priority to any hypothec registered with the public authority or made formally before three witnesses[4].

The first hypothecary could effectively bring the *actio hypothecaria* against the debtor or third persons (apart from superior title) or later hypothecaries[5]. These had the same right, except against earlier hypothecaries[6]. It was only the first creditor who destroyed the pledge by selling the thing[7]: he might pay himself out of the price, giving any surplus to the later pledgees in order, and any ultimate surplus to the debtor[8]. But all pledgees had a right of sale: if a later one sold, the sale was not void, but the lien of prior creditors was not affected: they could recover the thing from the buyer[9]; later ones could not.

The order of priority might be modified by *successio in locum*, a principle under which a later charge could be put in the position of an earlier one. These cases were (1) where the money was applied to discharge of the earlier incumbrance, at least if advanced expressly for that purpose, and a pledge agreed for at the time of the loan[10], (2) under the *ius offerendae pecuniae*. A later charger could step into the shoes of an earlier, by tendering to him the sum due to him, the substantial difference being that here the dealing was direct between the two creditors[11].

Renunciation by one pledgee affected no one but himself, except that it caused the next in order to step into his shoes[12].

1 Herzen, *Mél. Gérardin*, 299, holds it not older than Marcellus. He explains otherwise 16. 1. 17. 1 and 20. 3. 3. In earlier law a second hypothec was presumably conditional on discharge of the first.
2 13. 7. 36. 1; 47. 20. 3. 1.
3 20. 4. 11. pr.
4 C. 8. 17. 11.
5 20. 4. 12. pr.
6 20. 4. 12. 7.
7 20. 4. 12. 7; 20. 5. 5. pr.; C. 4. 10. 6; C. 8. 19. 1.
8 13. 7. 42; 20. 4. 12. 5.
9 The practical result is that he could not effectively sell. Girard, *Man.* 830.
10 20. 3. 3; C. 8 18.
11 P. 2. 13. 8; D. 20. 4. 19; 20. 5. 5; C. 8. 17. 5, 10; C. 8. 18. 4, etc.
12 20. 6. 12.

These rules of priority were much affected by the creation of privileged hypothecs. Of these the clearest cases were those of the fisc for taxes (and, later, some other debts[1]), of a creditor who lent money, under hypothec, to secure the preservation of goods[2], of one who lent the purchase price of land[3], and, under Justinian, of a woman for her *dos*[4], over the husband's whole property. There were many privileged debts, i.e. taking priority of other insecured debts. Some of these were transformed into tacit hypothecs, and it is hard to say in what cases they gained priority here too. The fisc, at least for taxes, seems always to have had priority, but apart from this it is disputed how priorities were arranged between privileged hypothecs.

Hypothecs may be classified as general, over a whole mass of property, or special, over a specific thing. They might arise by law, or, as in the ordinary contractual case, by express agreement. Of the former class there were two types, and it will be seen that some of each of these classes are special and some general.

1. Those established by a Court. These were (*a*) *pignus praetorium*, resulting from various cases of *missio in possessionem*, hardly a pledge till Justinian gave *actio hypothecaria* on it[5]; (*b*) *pignoris captio* under judgement. In later law if a judgement was not satisfied, property of the debtor might be seized and ultimately sold to pay the creditor[6].

2. Tacit hypothecs imported by law into certain dealings without agreement. They might be general, e.g. of the fisc for all debts, dating at latest from Caracalla, covering all the debtor's goods, of wards over the goods of *tutores* and *curatores*, for debts in respect of their administration, said to date from Constantine[7], that of *furiosi* against *curatores*[8], of children over their parents' property in certain events, to secure rights to *dos* and certain successions[9], of widows for *dos*[10], of legatee for his legacy over all goods of deceased in the hands of the person liable[11]. Some of these and several others were introduced by Justinian. They might be special, e.g. of landlord for rent over crops of a farm, and, in an urban *praedium*, over *bona invecta et illata*[12], of one who had lent money for repairs, over the house[13], of *pupillus* over goods bought with his money by a third person[14], etc.

A special hypothec had no priority over an earlier general charge, but if the creditor was the same, he could not proceed under the general hypothec, at least if it was later, till it was clear that the other would not

1 49. 14. 28; C. 4. 46. 1; C. 12. 62. 3. 2 20. 4. 5, 6. 3 C. 8. 17. 7. Diocl. 4 C. 5. 12. 30. 5 C. 6. 54. 3; 8. 21. 2; D. 13. 7. 26. pr. Ramadier, *Missio in bona*, 131 *sqq*. 6 C. 8. 22. 7 C. 5. 37. 20. 8 C. 5. 70. 7. 9 C. 5. 9. 8; C. 6. 61. 6, etc. 10 *Ante*, p. 110. 11 C. 6. 43. 1. 12 20. 2. 3, 4, 7; 20. 6. 14. 13 20. 2. 1. 14 20. 4. 7. pr.; C. 7. 8. 6.

suffice[1]. It does not seem that *A* with a special hypothec had any priority over *B* with a general hypothec of the same date[2].

CLXIX. Consensual Contracts. Transactions in which the mere agreement was binding. They were all bilateral (mandate only imperfectly so) and of great commercial importance, a fact which accounts for the attribution of contractual force to mere agreement. They were *Emptio Venditio*, *Locatio Conductio*, *Societas* and *Mandatum*.

Emptio Venditio[3]. The most important of all contracts. It was essentially sale for a price, the double name expressing the fact that it was bilateral but the duties on the two sides were different. The only other contract which had this characteristic was hire and that also was called by a double name—*Locatio Conductio*.

Its primary essentials were consent, object sold, and price.

Consent. No form was needed: consent could be shewn in any way[4], but in classical and later times it was usual to embody agreements for sale, if of any importance, in written documents[5]. These were good evidence, but no more, till Justinian provided that, where it had been agreed to embody the bargain in such a document, the contract should not be binding till this had been completed[6]. But here another factor came in. It was usual, as in all countries, to give something, as it is said, to "bind the bargain," *arra*, earnest, either money or some article. In classical law it seems to have only an evidentiary purpose, though in any contract there might be agreement for withdrawal on forfeit of *arra*, and in early law a sort of forfeit was used to give force to transactions otherwise unenforceable[7]. In Eastern systems, however, a right to withdraw on forfeit of *arra* seems to have been a general rule[8]. In his enactment, Justinian provides that where there is agreement for writing, and *arra*, either party can withdraw before the writing is complete, forfeiting *arra* or its value. The statement of the enactment in the Institutes after saying what seems to mean that he is making no change in unwritten contracts adds what seems to mean that the right to withdraw on forfeit is to apply to all contracts, whether written or not. There is much dispute: perhaps the best view is that he did in fact give the right of withdrawal in all cases, the statement that he is making no change in

1 20. 4. 2; C. 8. 27. 9. 2 A general hypothec, even to the fisc, was postponed to an earlier special hypothec, 20. 4. 8. These tacit hypothecs, priorities and privileges explain the Roman preference for personal security, *S.M.W.* 352. 3 As to origin of the contract (originally "real," simplification of mutual stipulations, generalisation of dealings by State, peregrine practice taken over through the Edict of the *pr. peregrinus*) Girard, *Man.* 568; Arangio Ruiz, *Ist.* 309; Ferrini, *Opere*, 3. 49; Vincent, *Dr. des Ediles*, 233. 4 P. 2. 17. 13. 5 Instances, Girard, *Textes*, 849 *sqq.*; Bruns, 1. 329 *sqq.* 6 Inst. 3. 23. pr.; C. 4. 21. 17. Lays down the same rule for other transactions and instances exchange and gift. 7 *Ante*, p. 407. 8 See, e.g., Collinet, *Ét. Hist.*, 1. 89 *sqq.*; Cornil, *Z.S.S.* 1928, 70.

unwritten contracts meaning (notwithstanding the interjected remark about *arra*) only that he is adding no requirements for their validity. The change, great in law, would be small in practice, partly because practice already followed Eastern lines, and partly because, *arra* being normally more than half the price, it would rarely be worth either party's while to enforce the contract[1].

Object sold. There was no sale without an object sold and anything could be sold which could enter into the *patrimonium*[2], if it was a thing in which the buyer could have an *interesse*. Thus a sale to a man of what was already his was void, and if he did not know of the fact he could recover any price paid[3]. If it was in part his, the sale was good for the rest[4]. And a man might buy the interdictal possession of a thing which was his, if that was vested in another[5]. He might buy conditionally what was his, the sale being operative only if it had ceased to be his when the condition operated[6]. He could buy what would be his on the occurrence of a condition: he was in effect buying release from the condition[7]. If he bought without knowledge of the conditional right, and the condition was satisfied, he could claim the price of the thing as if he had been evicted: he had, so to speak, evicted himself[8].

There must be a real object: sale of a non-existent thing, e.g. a hippocentaur, was a nullity[9]. It must be still existing. This point is discussed in two much interpolated texts and the classical law is not certain. The texts say that if the thing had wholly ceased to exist, when the contract was made, the sale was void: this is no doubt classical. If it had partly ceased to exist, and both were in good faith, then if the major part still existed the sale was good, allowance being made for what was lost[10]. Thus where land was bought in view of the timber on it, and this was burnt at the time of the contract, there was no sale[11].

1 See Mitteis-Wilcken, *Grundz. d. Papyrusforsch. Juristisch. T.* 1. 294. The view stated is that of Carusi, *St. Bonfante*, 4. 505, who states and criticises other views. For Collinet, *cit.*, there is no contradiction, and Justinian's rule applies to imperfect written sales and to all unwritten. Senn, *N.R.H.* 1905, 1, makes the rule of forfeiture of *arra* apply to all sales, written or not, but it is not clear whether he excludes further action or not. For Cornil, *cit.*, 51, the aggrieved party in unwritten sales has the choice of forfeit or damages, in which, he holds, there is nothing new. For Popesco, *Fonction pénitentielle des arrhes*, the words "*sive in scriptis*," etc. in the Inst. mean "whether *arra* is mentioned in the writing or not." But see Volterra, *Riv. Ital. p. l. Sc. Giur.* 1927, 157 and Carusi, *cit.*, 556.
2 18. 1. 34. 1. As to sale of things in fact inalienable, *post*, p. 483. 3 18. 1. 16. pr.; C. 4. 38. 4. If ultimate object is delivery of a thing for a price, the maker providing the materials, it was settled, after disputes, that this is sale, not hire of services, G. 3. 147; Inst. 3. 24. 4. 4 18. 1. 18. pr. 5 18. 1. 34. 4. 6 h. t. 61. 7 *Arg.* 19. 1. 29. 8 *Ib.* 9 45. 1. 97. pr.; 18. 1. 8. 10 18. 1. 57. 11 18. 1. 58. Two slaves were bought at a lump price and one was already dead: the sale was void; the unity of price implied that the point was to get the two, h. t. 44.

If, in such cases, the vendor knew and the buyer did not, then, if anything was left, the vendor must pay the *interesse*[1].

A future thing might be sold, e.g. "my next year's crop[2]," and a distinction was drawn between *emptio rei speratae*, such as this, in which case there was no sale unless the thing sold came into existence, and *emptio spei*, e.g. a shilling for the next cast of the net, which was good though the net came up empty. The first case gave a result which often recurs. If there was no crop, there was no contract, but, if the vendor had prevented the crop from coming, he was liable *ex empto*, i.e. there was an *actio ex empto*, though there was no contract[3].

A *hereditas* might be sold, like anything else, but it must be one in existence. The sale of the *hereditas* of a living or imaginary person was void: it was not allowed to speculate on chances of succession[4]. Under Justinian persons likely to succeed to a person yet living could validly agree as to the ultimate sharing of the succession, if the person whose *hereditas* was in question assented. But this is not sale, and he expressly restates the rule that there can be no contracts affecting future *hereditates*[5]. It is to be noted that in sale of an inheritance there were debts as well as assets, and the same may be said of sale of a *peculium*.

The sale must be legally possible. A sale of what was not *in commercio*, a freeman or a *res sacra* or *religiosa*, was void, and it was not thought fitting to allow sale of a freeman "*si servus erit*[6]." But if the buyer of a man thought he was a slave, classical law held the contract valid, because it was difficult to tell a slave from a freeman, and the vendor was liable for eviction. The same rule was applied under Justinian to the other cases[7], but in classical law there seems to have been only an *actio in factum* for the innocent buyer of *res religiosa*[8], while another text, perhaps altered by Justinian, tells us that an innocent purchaser of *res sacra religiosa* or *publica* has an *actio ex empto* for his *interesse*, though "*emptio non teneat*[9]." If only a small part of the property was such, the contract stood, but there was an *actio ex empto* for compensation[10].

Not only must the thing be *in commercio*; it must be one with which

1 18. 1. 57. 1. The text discusses further cases, even the improbable one in which they are agreeing for the sale of a house which both of them know to have ceased to exist. Most of this is interpolated. 2 18. 1. 8. pr., 39. 1. 3 18. 1. 8. pr. 4 18. 4. 1, 7. If there was a *hereditas*, not belonging to vendor, then, apart from *dolus*, he must give its value. If no *hereditas* at all, price paid and expenses (18. 4. 8). It was permissible to sell any rights in an existing *hereditas*, whatever they might prove to be—*emptio spei*—but not if the *hereditas* was of a living man (h. t. 9–11). Vassali, *Miscell. crit. d. D. R.* 1: interpolations are freely adopted. Review, Koschaker, *Z.S.S.* 1915, 433. 5 C. 2. 3. 30. 6 18. 1. 34. 2. 7 18. 1. 4–6, 34. 1. Haymann, *Haftung des Verkäufers*, 154, holds that even the rule for the freeman is due to Justinian. See, however, G. Longo, *St. Bonfante*, 3. 365. 8 11. 7. 8. 1. For Lenel, *E.P.* 227, this is edictal. For Siber, *R.R.* 2. 173, it is grotesquely interp. 9 18. 1. 62. 1. Cp. Inst. 3. 23. 5. 10 18. 1. 22–24.

the party could deal. It must be *in commercio* to him. A guardian could not buy his ward's property or a provincial official property in the province[1]. It was forbidden to sell the materials of a house, and thus any sale was void[2]. It may be that the same was true wherever the law forbade alienation, e.g. of dotal land, or of *res litigiosae*: it is, however, consistent with the texts to say that there was an *actio ex empto* to a buyer in good faith[3]. The sale of fugitive slaves, who were *res furtivae*, was expressly forbidden, so that this was void[4]. Sale of other *res furtivae* to a buyer in good faith was a valid contract[5].

There was nothing to prevent the sale of a third person's property. It might be difficult to carry it out, but that was the vendor's fault. It is plain that such a sale might be in good faith, with full knowledge of the facts; the vendor might intend to acquire from the owner, or induce him to convey to the buyer[6].

A *res incorporalis* might be sold, e.g. a usufruct or *usus* to be created in favour of the buyer. The enjoyment of an existing usufruct might be sold, but not of *usus*, which was inalienable: the buyer was presumed to know the law[7]. So a right of way to be created might be sold[8], and *A* might sell to *B* a right of way over *C*'s land, if *B* had adjoining land, though it might be difficult to carry it out.

The sale need not be of a specific thing; it might be, e.g., of a choice and it might be of a *genus*, i.e. a thing of a kind, without specifying the particular thing. But a distinction must be drawn. We have instances of sales of *genera* in the sense of so much, or so many, out of a given quantity belonging to the vendor[9], but no instance of a sale of that kind not out of an existing mass. This fact, and *a priori* considerations, have led to a general opinion that such a transaction was not sale[10]. It must have occurred; it is found in *stipulatio* and legacy[11], and a *bonae fidei* contract might be expected to be at least as widely construed as a *stricti iuris* transaction[12]. The exclusion would not be peculiar to Roman law[13].

1 18. 1. 34. 7, 46, 62. pr. 2 18. 1. 52. *Sc. Hosidianum*, Bruns, 200. 3 23. 5. 4, etc. Reff., Moyle, *Sale*, 20. Analogy suggests an evolution like that in the case of *res sacrae*. Probably conditional sale was valid as in purchase of *res sua*. 4 18. 1. 35. 3. 5 18. 1. 34. 3. Some things were excluded for other reasons, e.g. poisons, except recognised medicines, h. t. 35. 2. 6 18. 1. 28. 7 7. 1. 12. 2; 7. 8. 8. 8 8. 1. 20, 18. 1. 80. 1; 19. 1. 3. 2. 9 18. 1. 35. 5. 10 Seckel-Levy, *Z.S.S.* 1927, 117. 11 30. 37. pr.; 45. 1. 54; Ulp. 24. 14. 12 Karlowa, *R.Rg.* 2. 616. See, however, Haymann, *Haftung des Verkäufers*, 1. 71; *Iherings Jahrbücher*, 1928, 105; Beseler, *Z.S.S.* 1930, 34. 13 In Manu the thing must be at hand, *Inst. of Manu*, Jones, *ed.* Grady, 178. In Mohammedan law the thing must be seen by the buyer, Carusi, *Diritto e Filologia*, 203. See also *Ecloga*, ch. 9 (trans. Freshfield). There was a similar rule in Talmudic law. Hammurabi does not, so far as extant, deal, *ex professo*, with sale but San Nicolò has shewn (*Beitr. z. Rechtsgesch. im Bereiche der Keilschriftlichen Rechtsquellen*, 216 *sqq.*) that throughout Asia Minor, over a vast period of time, sale of a *genus* was handled as something juristically distinct from an ordinary sale.

In a sale of an alternative, this or that, the vendor might choose, but, if one ceased to exist before delivery, he must give the other[1].

CLXX. Price. The price must be in money, fixed, and real. It must be in money, or it would be impossible to distinguish buyer from seller and their duties were different. The rule and the reason are given by Gaius as Proculian. The Sabinians held that it might be sale though the price was not in money, and Gaius tells us that Caelius Sabinus urged that if a thing was given, clearly as the price for a thing offered for sale, the difficulty would not arise. Justinian did not adopt this[2] and the Proculian view prevailed[3]. But the Code adopts an enactment of A.D. 238, which declares, on such facts, not that it was sale, but that there was an action "*ad exemplum ex empto actionis*[4]." The purpose of the rule was served if some of the price was in money, and this sufficed: it was a sale, though something was undertaken besides payment[5]. Where a money price was agreed, there was nothing to prevent a subsequent arrangement that something else should be rendered instead, a *datio in solutum*[6].

The price must be *certum*. An agreement to sell, with no price fixed, was not a sale[7], nor was one expressed as "at a fair price." The normal price was a fixed sum, but "the price at which I bought the other," "the rate fixed in the market to-day," did as well—*id certum est quod certum reddi potest*[8]. Although pacts might be added to a contract of sale, a later agreement that the price should be altered in a certain event was regarded as creating a substituted new contract in that event[9]. As to an agreement for sale at such a price as a third party should fix, Labeo and Cassius (of different schools) held that there was as yet no contract. Others held that there was. Justinian ruled that there was a contract conditional on the fixing of the price by the person named, but only if a specific person was named[10]. But there was no sale if the price was left to be fixed by one of the parties[11].

The price must be real, a rule intended to prevent evasion of rules on *donatio*[12], by making the transaction look like a sale. It was no sale if a price was named, with no intention to exact it[13]; it was *donatio*, governed by the rules of *donatio*. There was difficulty where the price

1 18. 1. 34. 6. Alternative obligations, *post*, § CXCIII. 2 G. 3. 141; Inst. 3. 23. 2. 3 Gaius is definite, though he speaks of dispute as still existing. See D. 18. 1. 1. 1; 19. 4. 1. 4 C. 4. 64. 1. The thing given had been handed over and there was a complete *permutatio*. The action was, it should seem, *praescriptis verbis*. *Post*, § CLXXXI. 5 18. 1. 79. 6 C. 4. 44. 9, *post*, § CXCIII. 7 Inst. 3. 23. 1. 8 18. 1. 7. 1, 2. The parties do not know it, but it is certain what it is. Sale for "100 and whatever more I may sell it for" is good: there is a *certum*, with a further contingent right. See also Vat. Fr. 9. But see *ante*, p. 437. 9 18. 1. 72. pr. 10 Inst. 3. 23. 1; D. 19. 2. 25. pr.; C. 4. 38. 15; G. 3. 140. 11 18. 1. 7. pr. 12 *Ante*, § XCI. 13 18. 1. 36; C. 4. 38. 3.

was absurdly low. Where it was derisory, "*nummo uno*" or the like, there was, no doubt, no sale, but a masked *donatio*, but this is not stated for sale, though it is for *locatio*[1]. Where the price was merely low, here it was sale, if the price was to be exacted, unless the parties were husband and wife, when it was more severely scrutinised. On Julian's view the whole was void in this case if the price was plainly too low. On another view, seemingly based on a rescript of Severus and Caracalla, if there was evidence that it was *donationis causa*, and not in good faith, it was void; otherwise it was *pro tanto* a *donatio*[2], and therefore *pro tanto* void.

There was no rule that the price must be adequate[3]; the court would not prevent people from making their own bargains. To this there was in later law one exception, the so-called *laesio enormis*. Two texts in the Code say that if land had been sold at less than half its value, the seller could have the sale rescinded unless the buyer would make up the price to the full value[4]. They are attributed to Diocletian, but both shew signs of interpolation. The rule is not known to the framers of later *leges* in the Theodosian Code[5], so that, in view also of the crudeness of the rule, it is likely that it is due to Justinian[6]. It does not appear to have applied to anything but land, and there is no reason to think that the buyer had an analogous right in the converse case[7].

CLXXI. Confining ourselves for the present to simple cases without subsidiary terms, we have now to consider the duties of the parties.

Duties of vendor. Sale was a *bonae fidei* contract in which both parties benefited. The vendor must abstain from *dolus*, and must take care of the thing till delivery, being liable for *culpa levis*[8], i.e. he must shew the care of a *bonus paterfamilias*. He was also bound to "*custodia*[9]." He was not liable for *casus*, apart from agreement or *mora*. Thus if, after the contract, the thing was damaged by accident, or wholly or partially ceased to exist, without his fault, he was bound only to deliver what was

1 19. 2. 20. 1, 46. 2 18. 1. 38; 24. 1. 5. 5, 7. 6, 31. 3, 4, 32. 25. 3 Temporary regulations of price, e.g. of corn (*L. Sempronia*), Moyle, *Sale*, 75. In certain cases sale was compulsory: here there was sometimes a fixed price. C. 6. 43. 3; 7. 7. 1. Buckland, *Slavery*, 577. 4 C. 4. 44. 2, 8. 5 C. Th. 3. 1. 1, 4, 7; cp. C. 4. 44. 15. 6 C. 4. 44. 8 speaks of *iustum pretium*. Albertario's view (*Bull.* 1921, 1) that, for classics, *iustum* means in accordance with law and, where it means "fair," is interpolated, is probable. But it seems to have been used occasionally to mean actual value as opposed to that reached by *iuramentum in litem*, Levy, *Z.S.S.* 1922, 534 and Senarclens, *Mél. Fournier*, 701. 7 Waiver, Moyle, *Sale*, 186. Rule much discussed, Windscheid, *Lehrb.* § 396. Some continental systems adopt it with modifications, e.g. Code Civil, §§ 1674 *sqq.*, but not the German Civil Code. 8 Buckland, *L.Q.R.* 1932, 217. 18. 1. 62. 2 says that if *res* are sold *in aversione*, though not yet *adsignatae*, the vendor is liable only for *dolus*. The Gloss cites in support 18. 6. 4. 1, which is no authority. It is presumably the whole mass. For views as to the meaning, Paris, *Custodia*, 289, 343; Haymann, *Z.S.S.* 1919, 267. 9 18. 6. 3; 19. 1. 31; 47. 2. 14. pr.; *post*, § CXCI.

left and the buyer must still pay the price; the risk was on him[1]. There is an implied agreement that the maxim *res perit domino* was not to apply. The rule is clear, but its supposed injustice has led to a great variety of explanations of it[2]. To account for the origin of the rule on logical grounds is not to justify or account for it when it had ceased to be logical. It may be a mere survival[3]. When sale and transfer occurred at the same moment, the risk was on the buyer and after they were separated it remained on him. There is no doubt that this sort of survival did occur; *fiducia* left its mark on the institutions derived from it, but there we can see that what was undesirable disappeared. This rule remained and seems to have raised no question. The fair inference is that it corresponded to commercial needs[4]. It could always be excluded by agreement. We shall see later that the rule as to total destruction did not apply if the sale was conditional, or was not "*perfecta*" in other ways. On a sale of fungibles, at so much a unit, the risk did not pass till the counting or weighing or measuring was complete, and this whether what was bought was the whole mass or part of it[5]. This required the presence or consent of the buyer. If he did not appear on the fixed day, or on reasonable notice, the vendor was no longer liable for *culpa*[6], but only for *dolus*, so that all risk passed to the buyer[7].

The fact that the goods belonged to a third person did not affect the law of *periculum*, unless the vendor fraudulently represented them as his own: if he did it is commonly held that the risks were with him[8]. And wherever the risk was with the buyer the vendor was bound to assign to him any rights of action he might have against a third party in respect of the goods[9], since the buyer, having as yet no actual right in the goods, would have no remedy of his own[10].

The next duty of the vendor was to deliver the goods, if the buyer had paid, or was ready to do so, or in some way had fulfilled or was ready to fulfil, his part. As the buyer took the risk of diminution, so he had the benefit of increase; he was entitled to the thing as it was on delivery.

1 18. 6. 8; 21. 2. 11; Inst. 3. 23. 3; Vat. Fr. 23=C. 4. 48. 5. 2 Dernburg, *Pand.* 2. § 90; Girard, *Man.* 581 *sqq.*; Bertolini, *cit.* 508. Haymann (*Z.S.S.* 1920, 44 *sqq.*) (followed by Konstaninovitch, *Periculum emptoris*) maintains that it is a Byzantine notion. Rejected by C. Appleton, *R.H.* 1926, 375; Seckel-Levy, *Z.S.S.* 1927, 116; and, in part, by Rabel, *ib.*, 1921, 543. Reply by H., *Z.S.S.* 1928, 314. *Periculum emptoris* is stated in Vat. Fr. 23 (Diocl.), and is for Arnò, *Nuovi studi su Cassio*, 19, an opinion of Proculus which did not prevail. 3 Girard, *loc. cit.* 4 Appleton (*Rev. Gén.* 1912, 518) finds some advantages in it. The same rule exists in English law, but here it is logical, as ownership passes, and where it does not, the risk does not. 5 18. 1. 35. 5, 7; 18. 6. 8. pr. 6 18. 6. 5, 18; and *culpa lata*?, *post*, § CXC. 7 Elaborate rules as to disposal of goods thus left on vendor's hands, 18. 6. 1. 3, 4, 2. 8 *Arg.* 18. 1. 35. 4; 19. 1. 30. 1; 21. 2. 21. pr. (? interp.): the inference is rather uncertain. 9 47. 2. 14. pr., 81. pr.; Inst. 3. 23. 3a. 10 47. 2. 14. 1.

Accessions and fruits since the sale was *perfecta* went to him[1]. If, on land sold, a tree had since blown down, it belonged to him[2]. Day to day earnings in the meantime of a slave sold, the price of *fructus*, ripe at the time of the contract, received later, and other acquisitions of the same type went to the buyer, at least under Justinian[3]. But where land sold was at the time actually let to a tenant we are told that any rent paid belonged to the vendor, apart from agreement[4]. These words, and the fact that other texts shew that such agreements were made[5], shew that this does not mean merely that the rents were his, with a duty to account for them: though this is what we should expect, since he was not to keep the *commoda* of the thing sold[6]. He kept them.

The duty of delivery may be shortly stated thus. The vendor must put the buyer into control of the thing; he must give him *vacua possessio*, and must guarantee him against defects of title, but was not bound to make him owner[7]. Why the rule was put in this way is uncertain[8]. It can hardly have been to facilitate dealings with peregrines, provincial land and things held *in bonis*; these were more appropriately met by special rules. In *permutatio*, probably common with peregrines, the rule was otherwise; ownership must be given[9]. Probably it was to relieve a vendor from the obligation, often troublesome, of proving a perfectly good title, until it was disputed by a third person[10]. The remedies for eviction and the *bonae fidei* nature of *actio ex empto*, make the distinction, apart from this point, one of form.

To give *vacua possessio* was to put the buyer into exclusive possession, not defeasible by interdict, and free from burdens interfering with it except such as had been agreed on[11]. The existence of praedial servitudes

1 18. 6. 7. pr.; C. 4. 49. 2. 2; Inst. 3. 23. 3. Haymann, *Archiv f. Cpr.* 130, 154, holds that in classical law the buyer was entitled to fruits only from delivery, apart from imputable delay. See also, Id., *Z.S.S.* 1919, 334. But see also Siber, *Z.S.S.* 1925, 157.
2 *Arg.* 18. 6. 9. Acquisitions from outside to *peculium* of slave sold *cum peculio*, children born to a sold *ancilla*, P. 2. 17. 7; D. 19. 1. 13. 13.
3 Vat. Fr. 15; P. 2. 17. 7.
4 19. 1. 13. 11.
5 E.g. 18. 1. 68. pr.
6 C. 4. 48. 1.
7 19. 1. 11. 2, 2. 1; 18. 1. 25. 1. In 12. 4. 16 Celsus seems to say that "*dedi tibi pecuniam ut mihi Stichum dares*" is not sale, but an innominate contract, i.e. that agreement to transfer *dominium* is inconsistent with sale: it is *ob rem datio*. (In 19. 5. 5. 1 the contrary is held, but the word is "*accipiam*" which is less technical.) The rule seems unreasonable, but the interpretation is widely accepted. Reff. Girard, *Man.* 585, Buckland, *Tijdschr.* 1935, 359, Thomas, *Studies in Sale in memory of de Zulueta*, 160, and Yale, *ibid.* 171. Probably the text is abridged and thereby generalised—the unnecessary words "*pro portione*" suggest this. Celsus, on a set of facts put before him, held that on the whole (*proclivior sum*) the parties meant an innominate contract. The point was important (*stip. duplae*, Aediles' Edict).
8 Ricca-Barberis, *St. Bonfante*, 2. 129 (with predecessors whom he cites), holds that classical law required transfer of ownership. But his disposal of the texts against him (18. 1. 25. 1; 19. 1. 11. 2, 30. 1; 19. 4. 1. pr.; C. 8. 44. 17) is not convincing.
9 *Post*, § CLXXXI.
10 Girard, *Man.* 584.
11 19. 1. 3, 11. 13; 21. 2. 1.

grounded no claim (as they did not prevent possession) unless they were known to the vendor and concealed, or the land was sold free of them, *optimus maximusque*[1]. Though the vendor was not bound to make the buyer owner, the rule gives a similar result; the simple way of satisfying the rule was to make him owner. There is a further point: the vendor had not to make the buyer owner, but had he not to do what in him lay to make him owner? If the owner of a *res mancipi* sold it, was he bound to mancipate it? This might be material, e.g. the buyer of a slave might wish to free him so as to make him a *civis*. Good faith seems to require that the vendor should transfer all the right he had so that the affirmative view is the most probable[2]. If the law was so the system is convenient; the vendor need not shew title, and could not be disturbed till the buyer was interfered with, and the latter was protected.

The obligation to guarantee the buyer against eviction, a very important part of his protection, has a long history[3]. Under the XII Tables there was an action, probably called *actio auctoritatis*[4], in all cases of *mancipatio*, by which a *mancipans* who failed to defend the right of his transferee (by successfully acting as *auctor* if he was sued[5]) was compelled to pay double the price, the action being barred by lapse of the time of *usucapio*[6]. The action remained in use throughout the classical law[7], but Justinian eliminated it from the texts. It had nothing to do with *emptio venditio* as a contract; it is far older than the contract. Where the thing, though a *res mancipi*, was not mancipated[8], or where it was a *res nec mancipi* of considerable value, it was usual from early times to exact a promise of double the price in case of eviction. In some places, and in cases of small value, the stipulation was merely "*habere licere*," for a simple indemnity. In time the rule appeared that, in sale, as it was not good faith not to give the usual undertakings, these promises or one of them could be required, and an *actio ex empto* brought to enforce this, and then that it would be implied, and damages recovered in *ex empto* as if it had actually been made[9], but it was usual to make the promise expressly, perhaps to avoid the doubt under which class the sale came. Later, but early in classical law, the rule appeared that apart from this implication the buyer had a right to an indemnity if he was in effect deprived of the value of his purchase by reason of a defect in title[10].

1 18. 1. 59; 19. 1. 1. 2 Girard cites P. 1. 13a. 4; G. 4. 131a; D. 19. 1. 11. 2 (*Man.* 586). 3 Our knowledge of this history is mainly the result of the researches of Girard, summarised, with reff. to the actual essays, *Man.* 588. The propositions in the text do no more than state his account in outline; more recent Italian studies summarised, *Z.S.S.* 1927, 520. 4 Essentially penal, De Francisci, *St. su l. az. penali*, 21. See *post*, § CCXXXIII. 5 As to his intervention, Jörs, *R.R.* 160. 6 It does not seem to have been possible to exclude the warranty in *mancipatio*, and thus when it was a gift an imaginary price, *nummus unus*, is stated. Girard, *Textes*, 830. 7 P. 2. 17. 1–3. 8 *Ante*, p. 191. 9 P. 2. 17. 2. 10 C. 8. 44. 6.

When this rule appeared, the *stipulatio habere licere* practically disappeared. There were thus two cases, that of the *stipulatio duplae*, express or implied, and that of simple compensation.

(*a*) *Stipulatio duplae*, where it was made or could be implied, i.e. in cases of considerable value (including no doubt all *res mancipi*) in those parts of the Empire where it was usual, which were the most important. The action would be on the *stipulatio* or *ex empto*, in effect for breach of the duty to make the promise. It was normally for double the price, as in the *actio auctoritatis*[1]. It lay only if there had been an actual eviction, i.e. judgement under which the buyer had given up the thing or paid the damages[2]. If he abandoned it without action, though he knew there was no defence, or if he compromised, he lost the right[3]. If after the judgement the claimant, instead of taking the *res*, gave it to him[4], or died leaving no successor, there was no claim under the rule. So if the thing ceased to exist before the eviction[5]. The right was lost if the buyer allowed judgement to go without notifying his vendor[6]. Eviction was not necessarily of the whole; *evictio partis* gave a right to a proportionate part[7], but as a part is not the thing, it was usual, perhaps necessary, to stipulate for the case of eviction of "*rem vel partem*[8]." A part might be physical or legal, e.g. a usufruct, but not praedial servitudes or accessories[9].

(*b*) Cases in which the *stipulatio* did not apply. Here what was recovered was not a fixed sum, but the amount of damage, an indemnity[10]. It might be less or more than the price, according as the thing had fallen or risen in value, though, in later law, it might not exceed double the price[11]. There need have been no actual eviction. It was enough if the title was bad, and the buyer held only by another title, e.g. the owner had given it to him[12]. Thus there need have been no action at all[13]. It applied also where only an accessory was lost[14]. And, if the *res aliena* was sold knowingly, and the buyer was in good faith, he could recover *ex empto* without waiting for actual eviction[15]. If he had improved the property, he could usually avail himself of the *ius retentionis*: where

1 21. 2 *passim*. See h. t. 56. pr. 2 21. 2. 16. 1, 21. 2. 3 21. 2. 24, 56. 1. 4 21. 2. 57. 1. 5 21. 2. 21. pr.; C. 8. 44. 26. 6 21. 2. 49; C. 8. 44. 8. It does not arise if the adverse judgement was wrong through error of *iudex*, 21. 2. 51. pr.; Vat. Fr. 8. 7 21. 2. 1; P. 2. 17. 4. 8 21. 2. 56. 2. See Girard, *Man.* 595. If no *stipulatio* was made presumably the complete form was implied. 9 21. 2. 43, 49, 16. pr. Much controversy as to *evictio partis*. Bertolini, *op. cit.* 543, and reff. It may be that the "*pars*" for which the insertion is necessary is an undivided part or a usufruct or the like. 10 21. 2. 8, 43, 44. 11 19. 1. 44 (interp.); 21. 2. 70; C. 7. 47. 1. 12 21. 2. 9; P. 2. 17. 8. 13 19. 1. 29. 14 21. 2. 8. 15 *Arg.* 19. 1. 11. 12. The buyer need not pay if a suit for eviction was pending, Vat. Fr. 12 = 18. 6. 19. 1. As to interp. of texts allowing vendor to sue if he gives security, Perozzi, *Ist.* 2. 279. See C. 8. 44. 24.

he could not, e.g. not having possession, he could recover in this action[1].

All these rights might be varied by agreement[2].

CLXXII. A further obligation was warranty against secret defects[3]. Here too there was evolution. Apart from the ancient *actio de modo agri*[4], the civil law probably knew no remedies for undisclosed defect[5] except that it was *dolus* not to declare known important defects[6], a poor protection, since it would be difficult to prove knowledge. The Edict of the Aediles[7] went further, but in a limited field. It dealt originally[8] only with sale of slaves, the slave-dealer having a very bad reputation. It provided, in classical law[9], that on such sale in open market the vendor must declare all of a long list of defects that the slave had, mental, moral or physical. He must further promise that no such defects (*morbus, vitium*) existed other than those declared; if he refused to do this an *actio redhibitoria*, to set the contract aside, lay for two months, and an action for damages, perhaps the *actio quanto minoris*, for six[10]. As in any case if serious defects appeared[11], or *dicta* or *promissa* made proved untrue, the *actio redhibitoria* was available under the Edict for six months to set the contract aside and the *actio quanto minoris*, for damages, for twelve[12], the promise probably represents an earlier phase in which there was no liability except on actual promise. The Edict also contains a general clause against *dolus*. A similar Edict was soon introduced for similar sales of any live stock, but it does not seem to have expressly required a promise, though in practice it was so understood[13], and the defects, *morbus* and *vitium*, were all physical[14]. The action did not arise unless the defect affected value[15], or if the buyer knew or ought to have known of it[16]. That the vendor did not know was immaterial[17]. The general

1 19. 1. 45. 1. 2 Vat. Fr. 17; D. 22. 1. 18. pr.; 19. 1. 11. 18. This last text seems to imply that if warranty was expressly excluded, there was no obligation to return the price (though Julian disagreed), the thing being treated as an *emptio spei*, the vendor being however liable in full if he knew he had no title. 3 Bechmann, *Kauf*, 1. 361 *sqq.*; Eck, *Festgabe für Geo. Beseler*, 161 *sqq.*; Vincent, *Dr. des Ediles*; de Senarclens, *N.R.H.* 1927, 385; Monier, *La garantie contre les vices cachés* (see review, Haymann, *Z.S.S.* 1931, 474). 4 P. 2. 17. 4. For double the proportionate part of price, where area less than vendor stated, Lenel, *E.P.* 194. 5 *Contra*, Monier, *cit.* 10 *sqq.* 6 18. 1. 43. 2. 7 Lenel, *E.P.* 554 *sqq.*; Biondi, *Actiones Arbitrariae*, 1. 119 *sqq.* 8 Aul. Gell. *N.A.* 4. 2. 1. *de modo agri* and Aedilician actions originally penal, de Francisci, *Azioni Penali*, 22, 25. 9 Original form, Aul. Gell. *loc. cit.* 10 21. 1. 28. 11 *Arg.* 21. 1. 4. pr., 6. 12 21. 1. 21, 43. 6, 48. 2; P. 2. 17. 5. 13 See the edict, Lenel, *E.P.* 565. 14 The edict contained other provisions. The date of the introduction of the edict as to *iumenta* is uncertain. Varro does not know of it, for he recommends buyers to get express warranties and speaks of customary stipulations, and "*prisca formula*" resembling the terms of the edict, *Res R.* 2. 2, 2. 5. Cicero speaks of the edict as to slaves (*de Off.* 3. 17. 71) in a way which suggests that the other edict did not yet exist. 15 21. 1. 10. 2, 12. 16 21. 1. 14. 10, 48. 4. 17 21. 1. 1. 2.

effect of the action was to end the transaction. The thing was returned, and the price repaid, with interest and compensation for damage[1]. The thing, with its accessories, and damages for any deterioration, and all acquisitions through it, must first be returned[2], so that the action did not lie if the buyer had put it out of his power to restore, though, in general, if the impossibility was not due to his *culpa*, he was still entitled[3].

A puzzling text which speaks of the *condemnatio* as *modo in duplum, modo in simplum*, and explains this so as to make the action always involve a penalty of single value[4] has been much discussed. It may be that it referred originally to a special provision of the Edict, for vendors in bad faith[5]. It may be that the text originally referred to the double liability on eviction, the two obligations having been commonly described together as *stipulatio duplae*, the double penalty on refusal to restore being in conformity with other legislation of the late Empire. On this view the last words mean only that restoring is equivalent to a *condemnatio*[6].

The other action, *quanto minoris*, was available for damages, wherever the *actio redhibitoria* was, and also after the six months had expired[7], and presumably where it was a minor defect. If it was brought where the defect was so great as to destroy the value of the thing, *redhibitio* might be ordered instead of damages[8]. Bringing of the action for one defect did not prevent its renewal, within the twelve months, for another[9].

The Edictal system as stated covered only a small range of cases. In the Digest the rules apply to all sales. Two texts attributed to Ulpian say this, and one of them attributes the view to Labeo, but both shew signs of interpolation[10]. The extension may have been gradual, first to sales of slaves and beasts not in open market, and then to all sales and to all sorts of defect. Some of this is, no doubt, due to Justinian. A text of Ulpian says that there may be *redhibitio* of land if it is pestilential[11]. But this, even if genuine, does not expressly refer to the *actio redhibitoria*, and may represent only what seems an early rule, that even in the *actio ex empto*, if the thing was not substantially what was bargained for (and

1 21. 1. 23. 7, 60; P. 2. 17. 11; 21. 1. 25. 9, 29. 2, 30. 1. On 21. 1. 44. pr. (*accessio* of slave to another thing sold), Haymann, *Haftung*, 74. 2 21. 1. 23. 1, 9, 25. pr., 31. 2, 3. 3 21. 1. 31. 11, 12. 4 21. 1. 45; cp. h. t. 23. 4 where however the allusion is probably only to the originally essentially penal character of the Aedilician actions. All other texts appear to assume a *cond. in simplum*. 5 Buckland, *Slavery*, 65; Monier, *cit.*, 69. 6 De Senarclens, *St. Bonfante*, 3. 93 (good account of literature). Most writers however hold that double *condemnatio* for contumacy is classical. See, besides the reff. of de Senarclens, Riccobono, *Dal Dir. Rom.* 351. 7 21. 1. 19. 6; C. 4. 58. 2; 44. 2. 25. 1. 8 21. 1. 43. 6, ? within the six months. 9 21. 1. 31. 16; 21. 2. 32. 1. 10 21. 1. 1. pr., 63. 11 21. 1. 49.

there was *dolus*?), it could be handed back in the *actio ex empto*[1]. But Diocletian, in the Code, expressly gives *actio redhibitoria* in the case of pestilential land[2]. Whether, in general, in classical law, the rights which could be enforced by *actio redhibitoria* could also be dealt with by *actio ex empto*, is very doubtful, but it is clear for Justinian's law as to serious defects, though perhaps the Aedilician limits of time applied[3].

The *actio quanto minoris* is not prominent in the texts. It cannot be proved that *redhibitoria* lay for serious and *quanto minoris* for minor defects, but it is likely that they were so employed, and that the *actio ex empto* absorbed the principles of *quanto minoris* before it did those of *redhibitoria*. The general effect of the texts dealing with measure of damages seems to be that where there was express warranty the vendor was liable for the whole *interesse*, but apart from this only for the difference between value and price, unless he knew of the defect[4].

The rights could be varied by agreement. Sales in which all warranty was excluded were called *venditiones simplariae*[5].

The chief duties of the vendee can be shortly stated. He must make the vendor owner of the price[6]. Only when he had done this did the property vest in him, at least in later law, even if the goods were delivered, apart from agreement for security or credit[7]. Interest was due if payment was delayed beyond the agreed time, at once, if the sale was for cash[8]. As he took profits from the sale, he must pay expenses[9] *bona fide* incurred by the vendor since then. He was liable for *culpa levis* in his dealings with the thing wherever the interest in it might under the rules revert to the vendor[10]. He was in general bound to collect the goods.

The obligations being concurrent, neither could compel the other to perform unless he had done, or tendered, his own part[11]. Otherwise there would be the so-called *exceptio non adimpleti contractus*. This does not seem really to be an *exceptio*, even implied, as an *exceptio* would be in a *bonae fidei iudicium*. The plaintiff must prove his performance, while in a true *exceptio* the burden of proof was normally on the

1 19. 1. 11. 3, 6. 4. Text does not require *dolus*; see Pernice, *Labeo*, 2. 1. 179. 2 C. 4. 58. 4. 3 19. 1. 11. 7, Neratius. See, *inter alios*, Partsch, *Z.S.S.* 1912, 600, reviewing Haymann, *Haftung des Verkäufers*, who holds (but the grounds seem insufficient) that there was no such subsumption in classical law, and no liability in *a. ex empto* for *dicta*. See also Arangio Ruiz, *Ist.* 312 and Monier, *cit.*, 161, 186. 4 18. 1. 45; 19. 1. 6. 4, 13. pr., 21. 2; P. 2. 17. 6, 11. See *post*, p. 494. Monier, *cit.*, holds that *a. q. m.* is a Byzantine notion constructed out of the action on *stipulatio* against *vitia*. See, however, Haymann, *Z.S.S.* 1931, 479. 5 21. 1. 48. 8. Perhaps also excluding liability for eviction, Esmein, *Mélanges*, 414. 6 19. 1. 11. 2; Inst. 2. 1. 41. 7 18. 1. 19; *ante*, pp. 230, 240. 8 19. 1. 13. 20; P. 2. 17. 9; Vat. Fr. 2. On Siber's view (*Z.S.S.* 1925, 146) that it was due only on *mora*, Appleton, *R.H.* 1927, 249 and Haymann, *Archiv f. Cpr.* 130, 129. 9 19. 1. 13. 22, necessary; in later law *utiles* also, Riccobono, *Dal Dir. Rom. al Dir. mod.* 393. 10 13. 6. 5. 2; 19. 5. 20. 1. 11 19. 1. 13. 8. On the *exceptio mercis non traditae* (where vendor claims the price, without delivering the goods) which seems useless, Cuq, *Man.* 472.

defendant[1]. Apart from the special actions just discussed, the remedy was *actio ex vendito* for vendor, *ex empto* for vendee, both *bonae fidei iudicia*[2].

The measure of damages, in particular the question how far remoteness of damage was taken into account, presents difficulties, most prominent in Sale. Some texts simply speak of "*id quod interest*" or the like and may be understood to mean that any loss however remote came into account[3], and are so understood by some writers, as representing the classical law. Others cut the right down in various ways, e.g. the damages must be such as arise "*circa ipsam rem*[4]," or large claims must be excluded of which the vendor could not have thought[5]. The most recent writer[6] holds that these limits are interpolated: classical law had no limit of remoteness. Though some of his allegations of interpolation seem well founded[7], his doctrine seems extreme[8]. The more probable view on the texts is that classical law had such a rule, but alterations in the texts prevent us from knowing exactly what it was. Such a limitation is notoriously difficult to state and differences of opinion are likely.

CLXXIII. The obligations could be varied by agreement, but a pact excluding responsibility for *dolus* was void here as always[9]. Modifying pacts are prominent in the texts. Many were mere subsidiary terms which appear only on account of difficulties of interpretation, but there were others. These amounted to conditions, and as they were of great practical importance they need discussion. We have already considered[10] the nature and effect of conditions, and the distinction between suspensive and the so-called resolutive conditions, cases in which a contingency is stated in which the agreement is to be inoperative: "*pura emptio quae sub condicione resolvitur*[11]," but some special points of importance in the law of Sale must be noted. The risk of destruction did not fall on the buyer till a suspensive condition was satisfied[12], but if the thing

1 No real authority for the name; some of the reff. to the thing deal with verbal contract; Girard, *Man.* 567. On 19 1. 50, Collinet, *St. Bonfante*, 3. 409. 2 G. 4. 62. 3 E.g. 21. 2. 70; C. 8. 44. 21. 2, etc. 4 19. 1. 21. 3. 5 19. 1. 43 *sqq.* 6 Haymann, *St. Bonfante*, 2. 443. 7 E.g. the ref. at the end of 19. 1. 44 to Justinian's rule (C. 7. 47. 1) limiting damages to double the price (but he rejects the whole *lex*) and the words "*nam pretium...consequitur*" in 19. 1. 21. 3 (but he rejects much more). 8 He rejects the doctrine of 18. 6. 20 (Hermog.) "*non omne omnino quod venditor mora non facta consequi potuit veluti si negotiator fuit, et pretio soluto ex mercibus plus quam ex usuris quaerere potuit.*" He holds that the text said "not only interest, *sed omne omnino quod venditor mora non facta quaerere potuit.*" This seems impossible: no judge could say what "*quaerere potuit.*" It conflicts with the rule that *lucrum cessans* must be capable of precise estimation (9. 2. 29. 3) which we get in other connexions. The same point arises in 19. 1. 21. 3 "*neque enim si potuit ex vino negotiari et lucrum facere id aestimandum erit.*" He rejects this since if the thing had risen in price this is just what he could recover. True, if "*ex vino negotiari*" meant "*vinum vendere.*" But it does not: what is quite properly rejected is further profits he might have made by trafficking with the price. 9 2. 14. 27. 3. As to agreement to give ownership (12. 4. 16) *ante*, p. 488. 10 *Ante*, p. 422. 11 18. 1. 3; 18. 3. 1, 2. 12 18. 6. 8. pr.

was merely deteriorated this did not release him, apart from *culpa* of vendor[1]. The price was not due, and there was not even a *naturalis obligatio*, so that price paid could be recovered if the condition failed[2]. The fact that the *res* belonged to the vendee was immaterial if it ceased so to belong before the condition was satisfied[3]. The buyer could not usucapt *pro emptore* while the condition was pending[4], and was not entitled to fruits for that time[5]. The case was different under a resolutive condition. Here the contract produced its normal effects, so long as the event did not occur. If it occurred before anything was done, the whole was void, and there is nothing to be said. But if performance had already begun, machinery was necessary for undoing it. There was a personal action, which seems to have differed in form in the different pacts, by which, in general, the buyer could recover price and expenses[6], and the vendor the thing (or its value), presumably with compensation for deterioration due to the buyer's fault, and profits, or their value[7]. This implies, what might be expected, that the event itself did not annul the transfer of property and its effects, but some texts seem to imply that the rescission had effect *in rem*, the property reverting *ipso facto*, and the cases must be taken separately.

Pactum de retrovendendo. The vendor was to have the right to buy the thing back at an agreed price, usually that at which it was sold. With it may be taken *pactum de retroemendo*, an undertaking to buy it back on similar terms in certain events. Texts disagree as to the action. One gives a choice between action on the contract and the *actio praescriptis verbis*[8]. Another gives *actio in factum*[9]. Perhaps classical law gave an action on the contract, the compilers adding *praescriptis verbis*, but classical law may have given only *actio in factum*, the others being post-classical, but earlier than Justinian, the text, of the third century, being, on that view, genuine. There was no effect *in rem* even under Justinian.

Pactum protimeseos, right of pre-emption. The vendor was to have the right to buy at the price offered by any other bidder. The Digest gives *actio ex vendito*[10]. There was no effect *in rem*[11].

Emptio ad gustum. Pactum displicentiae. These look somewhat alike. In sales of wine, and similar commodities, it was almost a matter of course[12] to make the sale depend on approval by the buyer, a limit of time being commonly fixed. The pact usually created, it seems[13], a

1 18. 6. 8. pr.; Vat. Fr. 16. 2 12. 6. 16. pr. 3 18. 1. 61. 4 18. 2. 4. pr.; 41. 4. 2. 2. 5 18. 2. 4. pr.; C. 4. 48. 1; 4. 49. 2. 6 18. 2. 16. 7 18. 2. 6. pr., 16. Bertolini, *op. cit.* 479 *sqq.* 8 C. 4. 54. 2. 9 19. 5. 12. 10 18. 1. 75. 11 Difficult to distinguish from pact not to resell which in classical law may have been void unless tempered in some way. 19. 1. 21. 5. 12 18. 6. 4. 1; Cato, *R.R.* 148. 13 18. 6. 4; Cato, *cit.*, where ownership has not passed. Contrary inference sometimes drawn from 18. 1. 34. 5 seems not justified.

suspensive condition and the risk, of destruction and of deterioration, was on the vendor till approval or the *dies praestitutus*[1]. The rejection must be within the time fixed, usually short, but if none was fixed it seems that rejection might be made at any time, so that the risks might be on the vendor indefinitely[2]. It should be noted that here the testing was a momentary matter, not a question of continuous trial.

Pactum displicentiae was an agreement that the buyer might reject the goods if, on trial, he found them unsatisfactory. His discretion seems to have been absolute[3]. It is applied mainly to things of which extended trial would be needed, e.g. slaves or horses or land[4]. Though it might be suspensive (*si placuerit, erit tibi emptus*[5]) it was usually resolutive, and as such is in more than one form, "*si displicuisset inemptus erit*[6]," or "*si displicuisset, reddatur,*" or "*redhibeatur*[7]," but it does not seem that any difference of rule resulted[8]. The disapproval must be within the agreed time. If none was fixed, it must be within 60 *dies utiles*[9]. The power of rejection makes the rule of *periculum* rather illusory, for if the thing was damaged by accident it would be rejected. If it was destroyed by accident the loss, on the principles of resolutive conditions[10], should fall on the buyer, but the rules applied seem to have been those of the *actio redhibitoria*[11], so that destruction without fault would not bar the right to reject[12]. All profit must be accounted for[13]. The remedy was an *actio ex empto* or one *in factum*[14]. No text gives any effect *in rem* and one expressly negatives it; a hypothec created by the buyer was not affected by his rejection of the thing[15].

Lex commissoria. An agreement that if the price was not paid by a certain time (it might perhaps be applied to other undertakings of the buyer), the vendor might declare the sale void. It was not void *ipso iure,* as this would enable the buyer to cry off, if he did not like his bargain, by not paying the price[16]. It might be suspensive or resolutive, but was presumed to be the latter, so that risks were normally on the

1 18. 6. 4; 18. 1. 34. 5. The agreement in 18. 6. 1 is of a different type. It is disputed whether the right to reject is absolute, or proof of non-merchantable character is needed. The reference to *periculum acoris et mucoris* (18. 6. 4. 1; see, however, Vangerow, *Pand.* 3. § 635) is not to be taken as excluding other risks or limiting the right of rejection. 2 18. 6. 4. 1. 3 This suggests that there was no contract till he had actually decided. C. 4. 38. 13; Cuq, *Man.* 124. 4 19. 5. 20; Vat. Fr. 14; C. 4. 58. 4. 5 Inst. 3. 23. 4; D. 19. 5. 20. 1. 6 18. 1. 3; 41. 4. 2. 5; 43. 24. 11. 13; Vat. Fr. 14; C. 4. 58. 4. 7 18. 5. 6; 19. 5. 20. pr.; 21. 1. 31. 22. 8 See, however, Windscheid, *Lehrb.* 2. § 387, n. 7. 9 21. 1. 31. 22, extended for cause. 10 *Ante*, p. 425. 11 *Ante*, § CLXXII. 12 See 19. 5. 20. 1, which seems to apply the ordinary rule for resolutive conditions. 13 13. 6. 13. 1; Vat. Fr. 14. 14 18. 5. 6. According to Landucci, *Azioni per far valere il p. displ.*, the Sabinians gave *empti*, the Proculians *in f.*, and the former prevailed. 15 20. 6. 3. The rules under these pacts are much controverted. Windscheid, *Lehrb.* 2. § 387; Girard, *Man.* 764; Moyle, *Sale*, 80, 174. 16 18. 3. 2, 3.

buyer[1]. It seems to have been the rule, subject to agreement, that if the clause came into operation, anything given as *arra* or part payment was forfeited, and, conversely, that if the forfeiture occurred the buyer need not account for profits[2]. The vendee must offer the price unless this was prevented by the vendor[3]. The vendor must exercise his right of rescission promptly, and having declared either way, could not alter his mind: any act implying that the contract was still on foot bound him[4].

The personal remedy was *actio ex vendito*[5], but it is a vexed question whether the rescission operated *in rem*, i.e. caused reversion of ownership, *ipso facto*. A text of Scaevola and one of Severus Alexander give vendor a *vindicatio*[6]. Another of the same Emperor, immediately preceding, expressly refuses it[7]. In the first cases the ownership may not have passed; an agreement that the vendor may cry off if the price is not paid by a certain time is not necessarily an agreement for credit[8]. The better view seems to be that rescission had no effect *in rem*, even under Justinian, but many views are held[9].

In diem addictio. An agreement that the vendor should be entitled to set the contract aside if a better offer was received by a certain time. It might be suspensive or resolutive, but was usually resolutive[10]. We need not consider what amounts to a better offer; it is however clear that it must be such: a vendor could not avoid the contract by saying another offer was better, if it was not[11]. But he need not avoid unless he liked[12], apart from special agreement that the buyer might claim release, if there was a better offer, in which case he was free whether the vendor took the other offer or not[13]. Where he did propose to accept another offer, he must give the first vendee a chance of improving his bid[14]. The personal remedy seems to have been an *actio ex vendito*. But in this case there is evidence for an effect *in rem*[15]. Here and in the *lex commissoria*, the only two in which any case can be made out, the price would not in the ordinary way be paid, so that, apart from the nature of the condition itself, the ownership might not have passed. It is possible that it is this

1 18. 3. 1. 2. Longo, *Bull.* 1921, 46 (accepted Rabel, *Z.S.S.* 1926, 467), holds that it was at first always suspensive: classical law early made it resolutive: it was a clause in definite form and only Justinian interprets the words one way or the other according to intent. But the formalism can hardly have been so intense that no cases occurred in which the exact force of the words was uncertain. 2 18. 3. 4. 1; cp. h. t. 5 and 6. 3 18. 3. 4. 4. 4 18. 3. 4. 2, 6. 2, 7; Vat. Fr. 4. 5 18. 3. 4. pr. 6 18. 3. 8; C. 4. 54. 4. 7 C. 4. 54. 3. 8 But see *ante*, pp. 230, 240. 9 Girard, *Man.* 767; Bertolini, *cit.* 484 *sqq.* 10 18. 2. 2; 41. 4. 2. 4. Senn (*N.R.H.* 1913, 275) holds that as it dates from Plautus it cannot at first have been a condition, since there was doubt as to the possibility of conditions till far later (G. 3. 146). See also Vernay, *Servius et son École*, 206 *sqq.* Longo, *cit.* 40, holds similar views here to those he has in respect of *l. commissoria*, but dates the resolutive view only from Julian. Above, n. 1; Viard, *Pactes adjoints*, 61. 11 18. 2. 4. 5. 12 18. 2. 9. 13 *Ib.* 14 18. 2. 7, 8. 15 18. 2. 4. 3; 20. 6. 3; 6. 1. 41. pr. (prob. interp.); 35. 2. 38. 2.

which gives rise to decisions which seem to give an effect *in rem* to the pact. For the cases in which the price had been paid, and a hypothec created by the buyer is declared to be void[1], this may, it is said, be due to the fact that though there had been *traditio* there had been no *mancipatio*, and the *traditio* was invalid, since, the condition having occurred, there was no *causa*[2]. But the general form of the texts in the *corpus iuris* indicates that at least in the case of *in diem addictio*, and perhaps in a wider field, Justinian inclined to recognise an effect *in rem*[3]. All possible opinions are held[4].

CLXXIV. *Locatio Conductio.* This was the contract of letting and hiring for a price, bilateral, and having a double name because the rights and duties of the parties were different, as in *emptio venditio.* The transaction had three forms: *locatio rei,* the letting of an object to be used and enjoyed; *locatio operis,* the letting out of a job, or contract; and *locatio operarum,* the letting out of services[5].

Locatio rei[6], letting out a thing by mere agreement, for hire. The letter is *locator,* the hirer *conductor,* but the names do not express that distinction (and in one of the other types the *conductor* is not the hirer), but are supposed to indicate what is evidenced in some other ways, both for this contract and for that of sale, an earlier phase in which the contract was completed only by handing over the *res*—a contract "*re*[7]." On some facts it was difficult to tell whether it was sale or hire. Gaius says that leases in perpetuity were hirings[8]; in later law they merged in *emphyteusis.* Where gladiators were hired at a certain sum for those who were returned and a much larger sum for those who were killed, this, he says, was hire of the first, sale of the others, a conditional sale, in fact, of all[9]. Where money was given to a goldsmith, to supply a ring made of his own gold, Cassius treated this as sale of the gold, hire of services, but it was finally held to be sale[10].

The rules as to consent, object and price being much as in sale[11], few

1 18. 2. 4. 3; 20. 6. 3. 2 Windscheid, *Lehrb.* 1. § 90, n. 1. A *traditio* which is put out of action *ex postfacto* seems unroman and in fact this is giving the rule as a reason for itself. 3 Girard, *Man., cit.* 4 *Ib.*; Windscheid, *cit.* Pringsheim, *Kauf mit fremdem Geld,* 123, for discussion of the various cases of *vindicatio utilis,* on the assumption that they are all Byzantine. Bonfante, *Corso,* 2. 2, 277, holds that in all these cases *ipso iure* reversion occurs under J. but not in classical law. Some of the texts are interp. Others referred originally to provincial land and *ager vectigalis,* where there was no question of *dominium.* He does not advert to a possible narrow efficacy of *vind. utilis, ante,* p. 254. For Arnò, *Fictio brevis manus,* 35, the followers of Q. Mucius allowed real effect; those of Servius denied it. 5 Express classification into two types probably medieval, Arangio Ruiz, *Ist.* 317: *l. operis* (19. 2. 13. 10, 26) is also treated as *l. rei* ("*servum docendum conduxit,*" h. t. 13. 3; "*vitulos pascendos conduxit,*" h. t. 9. 5). No distinction of principle. Brasiello, *Riv. It. p. l. Sc. Giur.* 2. 529. 6 Costa, *Locazione di cose.* 7 *Locare* and *conducere* both originally imply physical displacement. 8 G. 3. 145. 9 G. 3. 146. 10 G. 3. 147. Apparent exception, *post,* p. 505. 11 Inst. 3. 24. pr.–5; G. 3. 143; D. 19. 2. 46.

remarks are needed. Justinian's rule on the effect of agreement to reduce the contract to writing does not seem to have applied here. As to object, this was always a *res corporalis* in the sense that there was a physical thing. But a usufructuary could let the enjoyment of the usufruct[1], just as he could sell it. It might be a moveable or an immoveable[2], but not a consumable, except as in *commodatum*, where it was hired "*ad pompam vel ostentationem*[3]." The hirer of a house or part of it was called *inquilinus*, one of land, *colonus*[4]. The rules as to what *res* may be the subject of *locatio* were much as in sale. The rule about error in the case of *res sacrae* does not seem to apply, and the letting of the services (it is not contemplated as *locatio rei*) of a *liber homo bona fide serviens* was valid as a contract[5]. The rules prohibiting sale or alienation of certain things, such as dotal land, did not apply to *locatio*[6], since that was often the only way in which they could be utilised.

The rules on reality and certainty of price were as in sale, with two modifications. The rent of land might be fixed in produce[7]. This raises the question whether in classical law the "*merces*" or rent had to be in money, though Justinian is clear that it must[8]. There was not the same reason as in sale, since there was not the same difficulty in distinguishing the parts. Gaius discusses the case of something lent in return for something lent, and doubts whether this is *locatio* or not[9]. Here the difficulty did exist, but it does not seem that Gaius can have thought money essential. It has been therefore held that the rule is due to Justinian. Texts which appear genuine lay it down[10], and perhaps the better view is that it was of late classical law[11]. Again, the *merces* might take the form of a proportionate part of the crop[12], *locatio partiaria*. As Gaius tells us that the *merces* must be *certa*[13], this is an exception. It has indeed been contended that *locatio partiaria* was really *societas*[14], but the texts shew that while it had affinities with *societas* it was really *locatio*, though subject to special rules[15]: the facts might sometimes leave doubts whether it was *locatio* or *societas* or an innominate contract[16].

There was the same doubt where the *merces* was to be fixed by a third party, settled in the same way[17]. The price was not necessarily a lump

1 7. 1. 12. 2; even to the owner (7. 4. 29) notwithstanding 50. 17. 45. 2 See 19. 2. 19. 1, 2. 3 *Arg.* 13. 6. 3. 6. 4 In later law *colonus* usually means *colonus adscriptitius* (*ante*, p. 90), who cultivated under persons who hired large tracts, *conductores*. But the free *colonus* still existed, no doubt mainly near large towns. 5 See, e.g., 41. 1. 19, 23. 6 23. 4. 22. pr.; 23. 5. 4. 7 19. 2. 19. 3. 8 Inst. 3. 24. 2. 9 G. 3. 144; cf. Inst. *cit.* 10 16. 3. 1. 9; 19. 5. 5. 2. 11 Ferrini, *Archiv f. c. P.* 81. 1, holds it Byzantine, but see Longo, *Mél. Girard*, 2. 105. See, however, Cuq, *Man.* 483. 12 19. 2. 25. 6, the *métayer* tenancy of later times. Costa, *cit.* 22, thinks it interp. Ferrini, *Opere*, 3. 5, thinks *pars quota* essentially *certa*. 13 G. 3. 142. 14 See, however, Pernice, *Z.S.S.* 1882, 57. 15 E.g. 47. 2. 83. 1. 16 17. 2. 52. 2; C. 2. 3. 9. 17 Inst. 3. 24. 1; D. 19. 2. 25. pr.; C. 4. 38. 15. 3. Costa, *cit.* 17, thinks it void in classical law.

sum; it was usually a number of periodical payments[1], a point of some importance in dealing with the rights of the parties.

Obligations of Lessor. He must hand over the thing to the lessee with the accessories, if any, usual in such cases[2]. The *conductor* had not *dominium* or *possessio*, but only detention[3], which it was the duty of *locator* to maintain, so that he was responsible if *conductor* lost it either from a defect in title, or because *locator* had conferred some *ius in rem* on a third person[4], who would not be bound by the contract. In that sense he had to guarantee *conductor* against eviction, and thus, if he sold the thing, he commonly made an agreement with the vendee to respect the right of the *conductor*[5]. The term, in rural leases, was usually five years[6]. At its end, if the tenant still remained in possession, with consent of the *locator*, there was a tacit *relocatio* for one year, and so on[7]. But, of houses, and wherever there was no agreed term, any such *relocatio* might be ended at any time[8]. *Relocatio* depended on consent: there was none if at the expiry of the term the *locator* was insane[9].

The *locator*, like the vendor, need not be owner[10]. Indeed it was a very usual thing for the tenant to sublet (*sublocatio*), especially houses[11].

The *locator* must keep the thing in substantial repair throughout the tenancy, subject to agreement, except for damage due to negligence of the tenant, who was liable for *culpa levis*[12]. The lessor also was liable for *culpa levis* in relation to the thing, and must compensate for damage due to defects, not disclosed, of which he knew or ought to have known[13]. If the thing was in such a state that it did not serve for the ordinary uses of such things, he was responsible, not on the ground of negligence, but for not supplying what he contracted to supply[14]. But the Aediles' Edict had no application to *locatio conductio*[15].

He must refund to the *conductor* any expenses. This does not mean the ordinary expenses of husbandry, etc., but money spent, either *necessariae impensae*, or, as it seems, even *utiles*, in maintaining the thing, expenditure, that is, for the benefit of the permanent interest in the thing[16]. He must also pay taxes and other public charges[17].

CLXXV. Obligations of hirer. He must accept delivery and enter into possession. He must deal with the thing as a *bonus paterfamilias*,

1 19. 2. 15. 4, 24. 2. 2 19. 2. 15. 1, 19. 2. 3 19. 2. 39; G. 4. 153; C. 7. 30. 1. 4 19. 2. 15. 1, 2, 8, 25. 1. Change of view in classical law as to measure of damages where *locator* in good faith, Costa, *cit.* 35. 5 19. 2. 25. 1; *post*, p. 502. 6 Esmein, *Mélanges*, 219. 7 19. 2. 13. 11. 8 *Ib.* The case of lease in writing is excepted. Text obscure. Monro, *Locati conducti*, *ad* h. l. 9 19. 2. 14. 10 19. 2. 9. 11 19. 2. 7, 30. A whole block, *insula*, is hired and sublet in "flats." Rural holdings, *ante*, p. 499. 12 19. 2. 15. 1, 25. 2; P. 2. 18. 2; Inst. 3. 24. 5. 13 19. 2. 19. 1. 14 E.g., he supplies jars which will not hold water, 19. 1. 6. 4 *in f.* 15 21. 1. 63. 16 43. 10. 1. 3; 19. 2. 55. 1. For *utiles impensae* it is possible that he has only a *ius tollendi*, h. t. 19. 4. 17 39. 4. 7.

being liable for *culpa levis*[1]. He must keep agricultural land in proper cultivation, not abandoning it, as land out of cultivation lessens in value[2]. As to his liability for *culpa* of employees, slave or free[3], the texts are confused and interpolated. The better opinion seems to be that the dominant classical view was that where a slave committed *culpa* under his master's contract, the master was not liable, *ex contractu*[4], but there was another view, which prevailed under Justinian, that he was liable, but could release himself by surrendering the slave[5]. This of course assumes that he was not himself negligent in the choice of slaves to do the work[6]. For free employees, on the same assumption, he ought not to be liable beyond cession of any actions he might have against them, while they might be liable *ex delicto*. But texts of Ulpian and Alfenus make the *conductor* absolutely liable for *culpa* of outsiders, apparently on a sort of implied contract in the hiring[7].

The *conductor* must not change the character of the *res* or deal with it in unauthorised ways[8]. He must restore it at the end of the tenancy in its original condition, subject to ordinary wear and tear[9].

The risk of accidental destruction was on the *locator*[10], not in the sense that he had still to provide the thing, but that he could claim no rent where the tenant could not enjoy[11], unless the failure was the tenant's fault[12]. If it was due to any fault of lessor or to defect of title he was liable for the whole *interesse*[13]. This principle allowed the tenant at a fixed rent to claim a rebate if climatic or other conditions had been such that he had not been able to utilise the land properly, or his crops had been destroyed or much damaged[14]. Small damages, such as might be expected, the tenant bore, but anything more fell on the *locator*[15]. If such a rebate had been allowed, and later years proved profitable, the arrears which had been released must be paid[16], but if the bad year was the last, no account was taken of previous profitable years[17]. Where a man was entirely prevented from enjoying, the rent was not due even *naturaliter*, so that if paid it could be recovered[18]. If sureties had been taken for the

1 19. 2. 25. 4. 2 19. 2. 25. 3, 51, 55. 2; P. 2. 18. 2. 3 *Ante*, p. 408. 4 19. 2. 45. pr., 60. 7. 5 9. 2. 27. 11; Coll. 12. 7. 9. 6 9. 2. 27. 11; 13. 6. 11; 19. 2. 11. pr.; Coll. 12. 7. 7. 7 19. 2. 11. pr., 30. 2; same rule in *societas*, *post*, § CLXXVII. 8 Inst. 3. 24. 5; D. 19. 2. 25. 3. 9 19. 2. 11. 2. 10 If accessories received at a valuation, the risk of them is on *conductor*, 19. 2. 54. 2. As to the liability for *custodia*, i.e. responsibility if the thing is stolen, *post*, § CXCI. This possible liability, and the fact that fruits are the tenant's only when *percepti* (*ante*, p. 221) and are usually hypothecated to the landlord (*ante*, § CLXVIII), create difficulties in the law of theft where the crops are stolen, *post*, § CXCVII. 11 19. 2. 33, 60. pr., 9. 1. 12 P. 2. 18. 2. 13 19. 2. 9, 15. 1, 15. 8. Costa, *cit.* 35, holds that classical law made him liable for the whole *interesse*, even where it was not his fault. 14 19. 2. 15. 2, 3, 27, 34. 15 19. 2. 25. 6. 16 19. 2. 15. 4. 17 *Ib.* So the text is commonly understood, but it may mean the exact opposite, which would be a more rational rule. 18 19. 2. 19. 6.

rent, and, the term having expired, there was a *relocatio*, express or tacit, they were not liable, but any "real" security the tenant had given was still under the charge[1].

The tenant might not dispute his lessor's title, so that if he claimed the thing as his own, in which case the *locatio* would be void, he must still give it back and raise the question of title independently[2]. Zeno seems to have imposed a double penalty if he did not[3], but these rules did not affect the right of retainer for expenses[4].

Locatio conductio being terminable, we have to consider how it might end. As it was a *ius in personam*, it is sometimes said that it ended if the property was alienated to a person on whom the contract was not binding. But that is not so: the contract was still binding, but the lessor by conferring a *ius in rem* on a third person had made it impossible for him to fulfil it. For this he would be liable, and thus it was usual to agree that the transferee would respect the tenant's rights[5]. If this was done, the ejected tenant could no doubt get cession of the lessor's action, though this would not release the lessor[6]. If the transfer was not due to his act, e.g. he was a usufructuary and died, the term was ended, on the basis of a tacit agreement that it was subject to his survival. But if he had concealed the fact that he was a usufructuary, the term continued and his *heres* would be liable[7]. Conversely the tenant was not bound to a buyer. If he refused to continue, the lessor, having no *interesse*, had no action to cede to the vendee[8]. If he had agreed with vendee to keep the tenancy going this might give him an *interesse*, so that if the tenant gave up the land he could cede his action to the vendee. But the effective plan was to make the *colonus* a party to the arrangement.

Death of a party did not affect the contract unless expressly: we are told that if it was agreed that the tenancy should be as long as one party chose, the death of that party would end it[9]. Apart from this the main causes of determination were:

Expiration of the term, apart from renewal express or tacit[10].

Renunciation by either party, if there was no agreed term. Even if there was, in late law[11] the *locator* of a house might renounce if he had personal need of it or it wanted repair, without incurring any liability on the contract. But renunciation must be at a reasonable time: if a

1 19. 2. 13. 11. 2 C. 4. 65. 25. 3 C. 4. 65. 33. 4 19. 2. 61. pr. 5 19. 2. 25. 1. So if locator creates *iura in rem* in any other way, e.g. gift of usufruct (7. 1. 59. 1), or by a legacy (19. 2. 32). 6 Later history of rule, Meynial, *Mél. Gérardin*, 413, with special ref. to C. 4. 65. 9. The rule no doubt had no application to *colonus adscriptitius*, but there seems no ground for the view that the free cultivating tenant had wholly disappeared in later law. 7 19. 2. 9. 1. 8 19. 2. 32. 9 19. 2. 4. May have ended by death in early law, h. t. 60. 1. Vermond, *Possession*, 276. See Inst. 3. 24. 6; C. 4. 65. 10. 10 C. 4. 65. 11. 11 Perhaps late classical law.

tenant was ejected from land, apart from breach of contract on his part, except at the end of a year (so that he could save his crops), there would presumably be a claim for damages. Release from further liability for rent would not do justice. He might, e.g., have incurred heavy expenses, in reliance on his contract, in respect of a business to be carried on on the premises, all rendered useless by the landlord's re-entry. But the whole rests on a single text in the Code, perhaps interpolated[1].

Destruction of the subject-matter. If it was not imputable to either party there were no liabilities. If it was due to *dolus* or *culpa* of either, he was liable for the full *interesse*[2]. No doubt the rule of determination applied where the property was expropriated by the State[3].

Forfeiture, at discretion of *locator*, notwithstanding the existence of a term, for gross misuse, or non-payment of rent for (in an actual case stated) two years[4]. Conversely, the tenant might end the tenancy, notwithstanding the existence of a term, if the *locator* refused to allow enjoyment or made it impossible. The *locator* might not exclude him from one year on undertaking to give him another later on[5]. To give him the right the deprivation need not be total, but mere temporary interruption, not substantially affecting his enjoyment, did not entitle him to determine the lease[6]. The term was equally ended if the prevention was by a third person, but, here, if *locator* was in no way privy, there would be no other liability[7], while if it was with his concurrence or privity he would be liable in damages.

If the *locator* was not the owner and the title vested in the *conductor*, he was discharged from further liability[8].

Here, as in sale and *societas*, there had been doubts whether there could be conditions on the contract[9], mentioned by Gaius[10] in connexion with the question whether a given transaction was sale or hire.

The actions were: *locati* for the *locator* and *conducti* for the *conductor*[11]; *bonae fidei iudicia*[12], and any pact could be added to the bargain except a pact not to be liable for *dolus*[13].

CLXXVI. We must now consider the other forms of *locatio conductio*, *operis* or *operarum*. Before distinguishing these it must be noted that

1 C. 4. 65. 3. Costa, *cit.* 103, thinks it possibly genuine and due to some local custom. Zeno (C. 4. 65. 34) allows renunciation by either party without liability, within one year of the commencement of the tenancy, even where there was a fixed term, unless there was a pact not to take advantage of this right. Not applied to houses till much later. Cuq, *Man.* 485. Possibly aimed at oppression by *potentiores*. 2 19. 2. 9. 4, 19. 6, 30. pr.; C. 4. 65. 29. 3 19. 2. 33. 4 19. 2. 54. 1; C. 4. 65. 3. 5 19. 2. 24. 4, 60. pr. 6 19. 2. 24. 4. 7 19. 2. 25. 2. 8 19. 2. 9. 6. 9 *Ante*, p. 422. 10 G. 3. 146. See D. 19. 2. 20. 11 Lenel, *E.P.* 300. See, e.g., 19. 2. 9. 6, 10. 12 Here, as elsewhere, Justinian limited the damages to *dupli quantitas*, whatever, in this connexion, that may mean. C. 7. 47. 1. 13 2. 14. 27. 3.

not all service could be the subject of this contract: it must be such service as "*locari solet*[1]." This excludes all liberal arts: for these a direct wage was unseemly, but gradually, in one case after another, it became possible to recover an *honorarium* in respect of them, when they were, in some cases, regarded as mandate[2]. It is not always obvious what is a liberal art: the Roman and our points of view are not the same: painting pictures was not a liberal art[3]. Some other services were excluded from various historical causes. A *mensor* did not "locate" his services, perhaps from religious associations in early days[4]. It is sometimes held to have been the rule that the work must be on a material object: there is a text which does not treat as *locatio* a case of employment as a messenger[5]. But no such rule is stated, and it is hardly consistent with the fact that Cicero mentions among the illiberal or sordid arts those of attendants on fashionable people[6]. But it would usually be for work on a material thing[7].

Where a slave was the subject of the contract it is difficult to distinguish it from *locatio rei*. Usually an agreement by the master that a slave shall work for hire for a third person is called *locatio servi*[8]: while if a freeman contracts to do the same thing it is *locatio operarum*[9].

The contract of service for hire took two forms: *locatio operarum*, letting of services, as in *locatio rei*, the *locator* being the person who let the services and took the hire[10], and *locatio operis faciendi*, in which the names were inversely applied: the man who did the work being the *conductor* and taking the hire. The probable cause of this is that in the usual case something was handed over to be worked on. But the names are confused: in one text a party is called both *conductor* and *locator*[11]. The case of *locatio operarum* was in general that of a worker at a day wage, or of that type: the other has more responsibility in it.

Locatio operarum[12]. The general principles being the same only a few points need be mentioned. Both parties were liable for *culpa*, and it was *culpa* in the workman not to be competent for the work he undertook[13]. He must carry out his work, but if he was prevented from doing the work by some cause extrinsic to himself, he was still entitled to his wage, unless he had succeeded in getting other work[14]. The death of the employer,

1 19. 5. 5. 2. 2 *Post*, p. 515. Kuebler, *Privatr. Komp. der Tribunen*, on jurisdiction of Tribunes in *honoraria*. Some work, e.g. that of professor of philosophy or law, was too dignified even for this, 50. 13. 1. 4, 5. 3 19. 5. 5. 2. 4 11. 6. 1. pr. 5 12. 4. 5. pr., construction of a particular arrangement; text altered. 6 *de Off.* 1. 42. 150. For a beautifier, the material object must be the employer. 7 19. 2. 19. 10 may be read to shew that *comites* of a legate "located" their services, but it was mandate, 50. 13. 1. 8. 8 19. 2. 42, 43, 45. 1, 60. 7. 9 19. 2. 19. 9, 22. 2, 38. 10 P. 2. 18. 1. 11 19. 2. 22. 2; cf. 19. 3. 1. pr. 12 Deschamps, *Mél. Gérardin*, 157. 13 19. 2. 9. 5. 14. 19. 2.19. 9, 38 pr.

where the service was personal, was such a case; here (and probably in all cases) death of the server ended the contract[1].

Here, as in *locatio rei*, the *merces* accrued due from time to time, which has one noticeable result. If a slave let out his services, the contract was not affected by alienation of the slave, but the right to the wage for the period after the alienation was in the new master, though not the right to sue for it[2].

Locatio operis. This was the putting out of a piece of work on contract. Here what was contemplated was not services but a completed piece of work[3], a house to be built, a slave to be trained, a coat to be dyed, and so forth: practically it was always a piece of work with a physical subject-matter. We have seen that where a man was to make a thing out of his own materials, the contract was sale[4], but there was an exception. One who contracted to build a house, finding the materials, was *conductor operis*[5], perhaps because the site was part of the finished product so that he only provided part of the material, or because the result of his work merged in the land, and had no independent existence.

Work of this kind was not necessarily, or usually, done by the contractor himself, so that death of a party did not affect it[6]. The *conductor* (*redemptor*) must do the work properly, being liable for *culpa levis*, including *imperitia*, as in the last case[7]. The same questions arose as to liability for *culpa* of assistants as in *locatio rei*, and no doubt the answer was the same. The price fixed might be a lump sum or so much for each part of the work: the latter arrangement did not prevent the *locator* from claiming for bad work when the whole was completed, unless it was arranged that the work should be approved at each stage[8]. The work must be done in the agreed time, or, if none was fixed, a reasonable time[9].

It might be agreed that the work should be such as to satisfy the *locator* or a nominee. This means what ought to satisfy: the judgement must be that of a *bonus vir*. Approval obtained by fraud was void, i.e. there could still be a claim for fraudulently concealed defects after the work had been approved[10].

The employer must accept the work when completed, and if, as was usual, it was subject to approval, must approve within a reasonable time on demand[11]. This is important on the question of risks, on which the

1 There is little textual authority on *locatio operarum*. 2 19. 1. 13. 13. If instead of a sale it was the ending of a usufruct, the owner could sue on the outstanding part of the slave's own contract, for he could acquire through the slave when the contract was made, 45. 3. 18. 3. 3 50. 16. 5. 1. 4 Early disputes, *ante*, p. 498. 5 19. 2. 22. 2. 6 *Arg.* C. 8. 37. 15. 7 19. 2. 51. 1. 8 *Ib.* 9 19. 2. 13. 10, 58. 1. 10 19. 2. 24. pr., 51. 1. Albertario, *L'arbitrium boni viri del debitore*, 14, rejects this for cl. law. But the rule is rational. 11 Implied in 19. 2. 36. See Cato, *de agr*. 144. 2.

conclusions to be drawn from the texts[1] appear to be the following. Apart from special pact the risk was on the *locator* (i.e. he must pay the *merces*, whatever happens to the work) so far as it had been approved, or, he having delayed approval (*mora*), was such that it ought to have been approved, and this, at least *pro tanto*, if the approval was of a part. Further, it was at his risk if, though not approved, it was destroyed by *vis maior*, e.g. earthquake (on the principle that this loss would have happened if it had been approved or not, and the *conductor* was not bound to supply more than the *locator* would have had if he had done the work himself), and also if the destruction was due to defect in the material or basis supplied by the *locator*. Apart from this it was at the risk of the *conductor*, so that the *merces* would not be due if the work was destroyed. Thus, as it was primarily on him, the burden of proof that the case came under one of the other heads was on him.

Two special cases of *locatio conductio* need mention.

Locatio irregularis (so-called). This occurred where the *conductor* received property, to return not the same but an equivalent, as in *depositum irregulare*, e.g. where a goldsmith received gold to make a ring but might use other, of the same fineness, or a carrier received grain in bulk on his ship, having to deliver not to each consignee his own, but the right amount out of what was on the ship[2]. The important question is, whose was the risk? If the ownership was in the *conductor*, it ought logically to be his, and no doubt this was so for the goldsmith. But in the carrier's case it seems that it was a term in the contract that apart from *culpa* he was liable only for goods which arrived safely. We have, however, very little information[3].

Carriage by sea. *Lex Rhodia de iactu*[4]. There was a rule adopted from Rhodian sea law[5], that where goods were thrown overboard to save a ship in peril, and the ship was saved, the loss was shared between all those concerned. As this included the shipmaster and all who had goods aboard, the rule was enforced by the *actiones conducti* or *locati*. The owner of the sacrificed goods proceeded against the shipmaster and he in turn against the various freighters[6], a roundabout method which is supposed, though there is no evidence, to have been superseded by direct actions for contribution.

CLXXVII. *Societas*. Essentially the union of funds, skill, or labour, or a combination of them, for a common purpose which often had, but

1 19. 2. 36, 37, 59, 62. But see Monro, *Locati Conducti*, *ad* h. t. 36. Seckel-Levy, *Z.S.S.* 1927, 223, basing on 14. 2. 10. pr.; 19. 2. 59, 62, see a school dispute. But no authority later than Labeo is cited for the alleged Proculian view. 2 19. 2. 31; 34. 2. 34. pr. *in f.* 3 On the old *actio oneris aversi* which seems to have lain for failure to deliver the cargo, Huvelin, *Dr. Commercial Rn.* 184. 4 D. 14. 2; P. 2. 7. 5 Ashburner, *Rhodian Sea Law*; Dareste, *Ét. d'hist. de Dr.* 3. 93; Huvelin, *loc. cit.* 6 14. 2. 2. 2.

need not have, profit for its aim. Common ownership was not of itself *societas*[1]: the essence was joint exploitation. If two men jointly bought the land at the back of their houses in order to keep it clear of buildings this was *societas*[2]. The relation involved "*affectio societatis*[3]," and the existence of this set up specially confidential relations sometimes called "*fraternitas*[4]." It differed from English partnership in that it did not necessarily aim at profit, but still more in the fact that while in our law partners are, within limits, agents for each other, and bind each other by dealings with third persons, this aspect of the matter did not appear in Roman law in ordinary cases, since one man could not in general contract so as to affect another[5]. Thus the law dealt almost entirely with the relations of the *socii, inter se*[6].

There were several types of *societas*[7], the chief being:

1. *Societas unius rei*, i.e. in one transaction, which might or might not be commercial. The above instance is of this type, and uncommercial.

2. *Societas alicuius negotiationis*. This was probably the most usual form. It was the carrying on in common of some one kind of business[8]. A specially important case of this was *societas vectigalis*, partnership in taxfarming. As it had special rules[9] it will call for separate discussion.

3. *Societas omnium bonorum quae ex quaestu veniunt*. This was *societas* in all business transactions, and where there was a *societas* but no evidence as to its type, it was assumed to be of this kind[10]. All business profits must be brought in, and all business debts might be charged against the *societas*[11]. The texts shew, indeed it is obvious, that it might be difficult to say what was trade and what was private profit[12].

4. *Societas omnium bonorum*. All assets of the parties formed a common fund. There were special rules which will need statement[13].

The chief requirements of *societas* were the following:

Each must contribute something, funds, skill, or labour, or a combination: otherwise it was *donatio*[14]. Contributions might differ in kind

1 17. 2. 31. 2 17. 2. 52. 12, 13. 3 17. 2. 31. It is now held by many writers that "*affectio societatis*" is a post-classical notion, that this text is largely interpolated, and that *communio* without *societas* could not result from, e.g., a joint purchase. E.g., Perozzi, *Ist.* 2. 300. But refusal to accept "*affectus*" as classical, not merely here, but generally, seems unjustified, G. 2. 50; 3. 208; 4. 178; P. 5. 4. 1; Vat. Fr. 253a. 4 17. 2. 63. pr. ?survival of *consortium* of joint heirs, *ante*, p. 404. 5 *Ante*, p. 426. 6 Exceptional cases, *post*, § CLXXVIII. 7 G. 3. 148 gives only two types, *alicuius negotiationis*, and *omnium bonorum*. 8 17. 2. 52. 4, etc. 9 17. 2. 5; *post*, § CLXXVIII. 10 17. 2. 7. There usually would be evidence. 11 17. 2. 7, 8, etc. A legacy would not come in (h. t. 9) or household expenses. 12 E.g. 17. 2. 7. How if one lets his house furnished? 13 *Post*, § CLXXVIII. Apart from this case the classification is not important. It is not exhaustive. A man might have joint dealings in more than one transaction of a type, but not in all, in more than one type of business, but not in all. But see 17. 2. 52. 14. 14 G. 3. 149; D. 17. 2. 5. 1.

and amount[1]. The purpose must be lawful and possible: one of a band of robbers could not bring proceedings for division of the spoil[2]. All must consent, thus no *socius* could introduce a *socius* without consent of the others. It might be conditional[3], though Justinian tells us that this had been doubted[4]. The agreement might be for a transaction or transactions, for a term or for life (*perpetuum*)[5]. No form was necessary, and thus the consent might be tacit (*re*[6]).

Effects of *societas*. It was perfectly bilateral, and, the duties on each side being the same, it had only one name. It was *bonae fidei*, even in a special sense, having a "*fraternitas*" which led to special rules. The main points as to the relations of the parties are the following:

The agreed capital must be duly provided. In some cases the ownership was to be common, in others only the use (*societas quoad sortem*, *quoad usum*). In the former case the law of warranties was probably as in sale, but the Edict of the Aediles did not apply[7]. On the same principle the risks would be common, as if it were a sale, but if only the use was to be common, the rule was perhaps as in *locatio rei*: the risk was on the owner, and destruction, though it did not impose on him a duty to replace, gave him no right to contribution[8].

The shares might be unequal, at least if the contributions were[9], and, after dispute, it was settled that a man's share in the profits need not be the same as his share in the losses[10]. He might be wholly excluded from loss, which was not *donatio*, for his co-operation might be worth buying at that price[11], but he could not be excluded from profit: this was a *societas leonina*[12]. The shares might be fixed by an arbitrator, and if his decision was unfair the *societas* was not void, but the assignment might be corrected[13]. It might even be left to one of the parties, a result of *fraternitas*: the rule has no parallel in any other contract[14]. Here too an unfair allotment was corrected. If no shares were agreed, they were equal whatever the contributions: inequality, if wanted, must be agreed for[15]. Where one's share in loss differed from that in profits, the periods at which accounts were taken would be material[16]. It is commonly held that account was taken at the end of the partnership, with, no doubt, interim drawings, which would be inconvenient if the *societas* was for

1 17. 2. 6, 80. 2 17. 2. 3. 3, 57. 3 17. 2. 1. pr. 4 C. 4. 37. 6. 5 17. 2. 1. pr. 6 17. 2. 4. pr.; cp. Inst. 4. 1. pr. 7 As to when it was *quoad sortem* and when *quoad usum* (expressions not Roman) views differ. It is a matter of interpretation of the contract and of the nature of the contribution, 17. 2. 52. 3, 58. 1. 8 Little textual authority. 9 17. 2. 29. pr. 10 17. 2. 30; G. 3. 149; Inst. 3. 25. 2. 11 17. 2. 29. 1. 12 17. 2. 29. 2, from the well-known fable. More complex arrangements, h. t. 44, 52. 7. 13 17. 2. 75 *sqq.* 14 17. 2. 6; cf. 18. 1. 35. 1. 15 17. 2. 29. pr.; C. 4. 37. 3; G. 3. 150. 16 If *A* was to have half the gains and a quarter of the losses, and in the first six months the firm made £100 and in the second lost £100, on an annual account *A* gains and loses nothing, on a six-monthly he gains £25.

life or a long term. The difficulty did not arise if it was for a transaction or transactions. There are no texts.

Apart from agreement each shared in the administration, and might use the firm property, but the business might be left to a manager who might or might not be a *socius*[1]. Apparently any *socius* might veto an administrative proposal of any or all the others, so as to make persistence in it a wrong[2], but if the prohibition was unreasonable or dolose, he would be liable for any resulting loss. Contracts of a *socius* could, on general principle, bind and entitle only himself, subject to account, but he could alienate firm property, with authorisation, which might, no doubt, be tacit, e.g. in the case of ordinary stock in trade[3].

Socii were liable for *culpa levis*[4], and could not set off, against damage due to this, profit resulting from other activities[5]. They were liable, exceptionally, for the *culpa* of slaves or others employed by them in the business[6]. They must account for receipts on firm business[7] and could claim contribution for expenses properly incurred[8]. For firm property in their hands, if they were in *mora* or had used it, interest was due and the liability was not limited to this, but went to the full *interesse* of the *socii*[9]. Texts conflict as to the position of the *socius* if he had not used the money and was not in *mora*[10]. If one had sold firm property and received the price he must divide it, but might require security in respect of anything he might have to return, e.g. in *quanto minoris*, and if one of his *socii* was insolvent, this increased the liability of the others[11]. Thus they were in effect sureties *inter se*. There might be difficulties as to what expenses were chargeable. Thus where a stock in trade of slaves revolted, and a *socius* was hurt in quelling the outbreak, Labeo held that his doctor's bill could not be charged, but Julian rejected this[12].

The general remedy was the *actio pro socio*, a *bonae fidei iudicium*[13]. There might be other remedies. For any delict, there was the appropriate action *ex delicto*. More important was the *iudicium communi dividundo*, which, as it aimed at division, would ordinarily end the firm, but could be brought as a friendly suit to settle how a particular thing ought to be

1 17. 2. 24, 67. pr. 2 See 10. 3. 28 and *post*, § CLXXXVI. 3 17. 2. 44, 58. pr. Perozzi, *Mél. Girard*, 2. 355. In 17. 2. 68. 1 the allusion is to sale of his share. 4 P. 2. 16. 1; D. 17. 2. 36, 52. 2. In h. t. 72 Gaius limits this to the care he shews in his own affairs, and gives the reason that a man who takes a careless partner has himself to blame: this is no reason, for it would apply to any contract: it may be because it is *pro tanto* his own affair, or it may be an application of *ius fraternitatis*, but it is probably due to Justinian. *Post*, § CXC, and Inst. 3. 25. 9 where the passage recurs. 5 17. 2. 25, 26. 6 17. 2. 23. 1; cf. *ante*, p. 501. As to *custodia*, *post*, § CXCI. 7 17. 2. 8–11, 52. 5, 74. 8 P. 2. 16. 1; D. 17. 2. 27, 38. 1. 9 17. 2. 60. pr.; 22. 1. 1. 1, *ius fraternitatis*. 10 *Ib.* 11 17. 2. 38. pr., 67. pr. 12 17. 2. 60. 1, 61. 13 As to *actio pro socio* as destroying the relation, *post*, p. 512.

shared[1]. And there might be other contractual actions: a *socius* might have given another a mandate in firm business[2].

In general the *socii* were, as against third persons, so many individuals: a man who had contracted with one *socius* had no right or liability as against the others. If all took part in the contract all were liable or entitled *pro rata*[3], or, if they were *correi, in solidum.* And there were exceptional extensions. The *actiones institoria* and *exercitoria* lay *in solidum* against any of them[4]. If a *socius* was acting under a mandate of another or others, the *actiones utiles* which arose out of mandate would apply[5]. Some special types of *societas* created solidary liability[6]. And under Justinian, but probably not before, a creditor of one could sue the others by an extended *actio de in rem verso*, so far as he had profited[7].

A *socius* could not, by taking a partner, add him to the *societas.* If he took such a partner, and allowed him to deal with firm business, he was responsible for his acts, and could not get rid of liability by ceding his actions against him[8]. As between its parties the subpartnership was valid. An *actio pro socio* on it would not affect the main *societas*[9], but, so far as the subpartnership was formed merely in respect of the concerns of the principal firm, it necessarily ended if that did.

CLXXVIII. Termination of *societas.* The principal causes of termination were:

Death of a *socius*, with notice[10]. This resulted from the personal relation, and it was impossible to agree *ab initio* that the *heres* of a *socius* should come in[11]. What ended the *societas* for one ended it altogether: if the others continued, even if it had been agreed *ab initio* that they should, it was a new *societas*[12], into which the *heres* might of course be admitted as any other person could. But though the *heres* was not a *socius*, the rights and liabilities already existing descended on him, so that he might be a party to the *actio pro socio*[13]. He must complete what was half done and shew the same care as a *socius*[14]. The end of the *societas* was not of course the end of the business: what it meant in effect was that there must be an adjustment of accounts, and the estate of the deceased *socius* had nothing to do with future happenings[15].

1 17. 2. 38. 1. 2 As to how far one action bars another, *post*, § CCXLII. 3 Doubts as to principle of division: 14. 1. 4. pr.; 45. 2. 11. 1; 45. 3. 37. 4 14. 1. 1. 25; 14. 3. 14. 5 *Post*, § CLXXX. 6 *Post*, p. 512. 7 *Arg.* 17. 2. 82. Interpretation disputed, Von Tuhr, *De in rem verso*, 307. 8 17. 2. 19, 21, 23. 9 17. 2. 22. 10 17. 2. 4. 1, 63. 10, 65. 9, 10, etc. 11 17. 2. 35, 59; G. 3. 152; Inst. 3. 25. 5. 12 17. 2. 65. 9. 13 And he will probably still be a common owner. 14 17. 2. 35, 37, 40, 63. 8, 65. 9. Probably *a. in factum*, h. t. 35. The *a. pro socio* of h. t. 63. 8 is in respect of past happenings. 15 There was nothing to prevent all members of an existing firm from agreeing with a specific outsider, that on the death of a certain, or any, *socius*, a new firm should come into existence of which he should be a member, at least after the doubt about conditions was settled.

Renunciation. It could of course end by mutual *dissensus*, but the rule went much further. Any *socius* could, even in defiance of agreement to the contrary, end the *societas* altogether at any time by renouncing it[1]. But though he ended the firm, he might be liable for damages. If he did it fraudulently, e.g. to keep an impending acquisition for himself or avoid an impending loss, he must account, whether it was for a term or not: he freed his *socii* from him, it is said, but not himself from his *socii*[2]. So too if, without fraud, he insisted on doing it at a time disastrous to the firm[3]. If there was an agreement not to renounce, it might still be done, with the same liability for fraud or disastrous choice of time[4]. Hence Pomponius says that an agreement not to renounce is a nullity[5], but the texts suggest that apart from fraud or special circumstances he would in such a case be liable for damages if, e.g., the loss of his services or capital made it impossible for the firm to go on[6]. Similar rules appear to have applied where the *societas* was for a term[7]. But there were circumstances, such as gross misconduct by a *socius*, or long and necessary absence on public affairs, which completely justified renunciation even where there was a term or a contrary agreement[8]. Renunciation might be express or tacit: alienation of the share was the chief case of the latter[9]. This was a breach of an agreement not to divide and the rules of renunciation applied[10].

Capitis deminutio. In later law this meant *maxima* or *media*, i.e. enslavement or deportation, with loss of property[11]. For Gaius, *minima* sufficed, though the parties could agree to renew[12]. Where there had been a *c. d. minima* and the *societas* continued, there were complex questions as to the rights of action on events before and after the change. In fact *capitis deminutio* is of small importance in later law, as a separate head: for *bonorum venditio* or *amissio bonorum* in any form, of which *c. d.* is ordinarily only one case, ended a *societas*[13].

Lapse of agreed time, arrival of determining condition, completion of purpose and destruction of subject-matter need only mention[14].

1 17. 2. 4. 1, 63. 10, 64. 2 17. 2. 65. 3; G. 3. 151; Inst. 3. 25. 4. 3 17. 2. 65. 5. 4 17. 2. 65. 6. 5 17. 2. 14; cp. h. t. 17. 2. 6 *Arg.* 17. 2. 17. pr.; h. t. 65. 3–6. Monro, *Pro Socio, ad* h. t. 16. pr. 7 17. 2. 14, 65. 5, 6. 8 17. 2. 14, 16. pr. 9 17. 2. 16. 1, 17. pr. 10 17. 2. 16. 1. 11 17. 2. 4. 1. 12 G. 3. 153. D. 17. 2. 58. 2, 65. 11 suggest a tendency even in classical law to ignore the *c. d. minima.* 13 17. 2. 4. 1, 65. 1, 12; G. 3. 154. A *relegatus* did not suffer *c. d.*, but might suffer confiscation. What Modestinus means by "*egestas*" (17. 2. 4. 1) is not clear. If a *deportatus* was allowed to keep part of his property (*ante*, p. 97) the *societas* would nevertheless be ended, which justifies the appearance of *c. d.* as a mode of termination. 14 17. 2. 63. 10. Knowledge of occurrence of the condition, completion or destruction would presumably be necessary. From h. t. 65. 6, it seems that even if a time was fixed the *societas* did not determine *ipso factc* on expiry of the time, but there must be express withdrawal. Cp. 19. 2. 14.

Actio pro socio. The normal purpose of this action was contribution, but *litis contestatio* ended the *societas*, where it was brought as a general action on the contract[1], though it could be brought as a friendly suit to adjust particular points without affecting the contract as a whole[2]. In any case it novated the rights on the points brought into issue. It was *bonae fidei*[3], *directa* on both sides, and subject to "*beneficium competentiae*": the *socius* was not condemned beyond what he could pay, except where he had fraudulently made himself unable to pay. This rule applied at first, perhaps even in classical law, only to *societas omnium bonorum*[4], and it never applied where the action was against a *heres*. What was unpaid remained due and security was taken for it, since the action had novated the claim[5]. *Condemnatio* involved infamy[6], which indicates that liability originally was only for *dolus*. Paul says that *societas* is destroyed by *actio* where either an action is brought on it, or it is otherwise novated by *stipulatio*[7]. This odd statement is explained on the view that *actio* here is used in its widest sense to denote any juristic act[8].

As *socii* were commonly also joint owners, the *actio communi dividundo*[9] also was usually available between them for adjustment of liabilities in respect of the property. As it affected only property questions and adjustment, i.e. not debts and credits, it was narrower, but it contained *adiudicatio*, which *pro socio* did not. It did not necessarily end the *societas* under Justinian: classical law is uncertain[10].

We have now to consider some types of *societas* which have special rules:

Societas venaliciorum. Partnership of slavedealers, usually, we are told, rascals[11]. The Edict of the Aediles was introduced for them, and there was a rule that where one sold, the aedilician actions lay *in solidum* against any *socius* whose share was not less than that of any other[12].

Societas argentariorum. Banking firms. These, at the other extreme of commerce, were an important body, through whom was done most of the serious business. Their books were relied on as records, and they were bound to produce them in litigation concerning their clients[13]. Of the many special rules affecting them only two bear on *societas*: a contract by a firm of *argentarii* created a correal obligation both ways, whether so meant or not[14], and a contract *literis* by any one of them had the same effect[15].

1 17. 2. 65. pr. 2 17. 2. 65. 15, perhaps only in late law. 3 17. 2. 52. 1. 4 17. 2. 63. pr., 63. 2; 42. 1. 16. On the question whether it applied to other actions between them enforcing obligations which might have come into *pro socio*, Levet, *Beneficium Competentiae*, 57. 5 17. 2. 63. 4, 5; *post*, § CCXXXIV. 6 3. 2. 1; Inst. 4. 16. 2. 7 17. 2. 65. pr. 8 Girard, *Man.* 617. 9 *Post*, § CLXXXVI. 10 17. 2. 43. Perhaps interpolated. 11 21. 1. 37, 44. 1. 12 21. 1. 44. 1. 13 2. 13. 4, 6, 10. 14 2. 14. 9. pr.; 4. 8. 34. pr., etc. Probably applied to all money loans and promises. Similar rule for joint *excercitores*, *ante*, p. 510; *post*, § CLXXXIV. 15 *Rh. ad Her.* 2. 13. 19.

Societas vectigalis. This was a *societas* for taxfarming, and it seems that similar rules applied to other *societates* contracting with the State, e.g. for exploiting mines and quarries[1]. The contract with the State was usually for five years. The chief rules are the following:

1. Besides the *socii* there might be investors (*participes*) whose position is imperfectly known[2], and who are not traceable in late law.

2. Death of one did not end the firm as to the others, unless he was the manager or held the contract with the State[3]. This does not imply permanence: the *societas* would be only for the five-year contract.

3. It might be agreed, *ab initio*, that the *heres* of a deceased *socius* should become one[4]. Apart from this, he would, unlike the *heres* of an ordinary *socius*, take his share of the rights and liabilities after the death, though, like a *particeps*, he had no voice in management[5].

4. On some obscure texts[6], it is sometimes said that there was no right of renunciation.

5. On certain texts[7] it is suggested that such firms were corporate, i.e. the rights and duties attached to the corporate body and not to the individuals. But there are many views, e.g., that they were corporate, that they might be, but were not necessarily, that the rule in either form did not apply to them but to *sodalitates* among the workers, that this was the classical view, but that under Justinian, it applied to the *societates*, and finally that it applied not to *societates vectigales*, which usually had but a short existence, but to financial groups of a permanent character which found capital for them[8].

Societas omnium (*universorum*) *bonorum*. Partnership in all property and undertakings. It was not corporate. It was the oldest form of *societas*, probably descending from *consortium*, an early practice by which *heredes*, instead of dividing, kept the *hereditas* together and enjoyed it in common[9]. It did not necessarily cover future acquisitions. It had the exceptional effect, possibly originating in *consortium*, that all *res corporales* of a member vested, by the mere agreement, in the firm as a

1 3. 4. 1. pr. All called *societates publicanorum*, but *vectigalis* more strictly applied, 17. 2. 63. 8; 50. 16. 16. Kniep, *Societates publicanorum*. 2 Monro, *Pro Socio*, 79. 3 17. 2. 59 pr., 63. 8. The others were frequently "sleeping partners," providing capital but not service. The passage speaking of the case in which death dissolves the *societas* has been altered, but the rule is probably classical, Mitteis, *R.Pr.* 1. 413. 4 17. 2. 59. 5 17. 2. 63. 8. 6 17. 2. 63. 8, 65. 15. 7 3. 4. 1. pr.; 37. 1. 3. 4. 8 See Mitteis, *R.Pr.* 404. 9 G. 3. 154a, b, *ante*, p. 404; 10. 2. 39. 3; 17. 2. 52. 6, 52. 8. The origin suggests—as *consortium* affected only the *hereditas*, which in case of *sui* was all they had—that *s. o. b.* would also cover only present possessions. In fact many of the texts say nothing of future acquisitions, and of those which do, two suggest that it was exceptional, and of these one deals with one specific future acquisition and excludes the rest (17. 2. 3. 2); the other, h. t. 73, speaking of "*universarum fortunarum*," required a gloss, "*id est earum quoque rerum quae postea adquirentur*." Cases dealing only with present property were probably the most usual, a much more reasonable sort of partnership.

whole[1]. How the lawyers constructed this tacit transfer is not clear[2]. *Iura in personam*, being intransferable, must be accounted for to the firm[3]. Future acquisitions, if they came in, had to be transferred[4], but nothing acquired by wrong came in[5]. There were special rules for cases in which the interest was terminable or inalienable, e.g. *dos* and usufruct[6].

As the property belonged to the *societas*, that body bore expenses[7], but was not responsible for penalties for delict or losses in gambling or the like[8]. This does not mean that the creditor suffered, but that, if the *socius* paid out of firm property, the whole was charged against his share, and it is clear that in such *societates* there was money belonging to individuals[9]. Revenue was no doubt shared out. Even apart from this, if judgement was obtained on such a liability, and was not satisfied, creditors could proceed to *bonorum venditio*, which would end the *societas* and make the debtor's share available. There would usually be no need to proceed to this extreme: the amount would be paid out of the common fund and charged against the *socius* concerned.

The ordinary modes of ending the *societas* applied. Thus it might be renounced[10]. As in other cases the transactions were the transactions of the party himself: it was he who must sue and be sued[11].

CLXXIX. *Mandatum*, the undertaking, by request, of a gratuitous service for another. The appointer was called *mandator*: *mandatarius* is a convenient but unauthorised name for the other party. The service might be of any kind connected with *patrimonium*, provided it was lawful and possible[12]. It usually involved entry into legal relation with a third party, but this need not be so: we read of a mandate to a *fullo* who was going to do the work for nothing[13]. Mandate seems to have begun as an isolated friendly service[14], to act as *adstipulator*, or surety, or as representative in litigation, but in classical law it had a much wider scope. It might be general, the management of the principal's affairs, the holder of such a mandate being properly called a *procurator*, though in the late classical law this name is applied to mandataries for a single service[15], the earliest application of it in this sense being to a *procurator ad litem*. Mandate might be subject to *dies* or condition, and of course to a limit of time[16]. It might be express or tacit[17].

1 17. 2. 1. 1. 2 Tacit *traditio* (17. 2. 2) and the *constitutum possessorium* sometimes suggested are unsatisfactory: it appears to have applied to everything, not merely to what was actually possessed by a party. Some hold it post-classical; Riccobono, *Z.S.S.* 1913, 190; Siber, *R.R.* 2, 206. 3 17. 2. 3. pr. 4 17. 2. 73. 5 17. 2. 52. 17, 53. 6 Usufruct could not be transferred. 7 17. 2. 73. 8 17. 2. 52. 18. 9 *Ib.* 10 17. 2. 65. pr., 3. 11 See, e.g., 17. 2. 52. 18; 47. 2. 52. 18. 12 17. 1. 6. 3; G. 3. 157. 13 Inst. 3. 26. 13. 14 See, however, Karlowa, *R.Rg.* 2. 665. 15 Karlowa, *loc. cit.* P. 1. 3. 2; D. 3. 3. 1; *post*, § CLXXXV. 16 17. 1. 1. 3. No sign of doubts as to conditions. 17 17. 1. 53; 50. 17. 60.

Mandate was gratuitous[1]. No reward could be recovered in the action on mandate, but it was possible, where remuneration had been agreed, to recover it by a *cognitio extraordinaria*[2]. Thus its gratuitous character is rather unreal but not unimportant: a mandatary, sued on his mandate, could not set off a claim for *honorarium*, or defend on the ground that it had not been paid. It was no part of the contract.

The mandate must concern the *mandator*: he must have an *interesse*[3]. This rule leads to a classification of mandates according as they interest *mandator*, mandatary or a third party, or any combination of these. The classification would have had little meaning in the Republic, but as mandate grew commercialised the distinctions became more important[4]. Any of them was valid if there was an *interesse* of *mandator*, but a mandate in the interest merely of mandatary or a third party, or both, gave no *actio directa*[5]. We are told that mandate in the interest of mandatary alone was mere advice and no mandate[6], but we are also told[7] that if it was a thing he would not have done, but for the advice, there was an *actio contraria*. The words represent Justinian's law[8], but are probably interpolated, the classical law giving only an *actio doli* in case of fraud. The rule that it must not be in the interest of a third party alone is rather unreal. There might be an indirect interest, not apparent on the contract. Thus where *A* gave *B* a mandate to assume a liability for *X*, *X* might be indebted to *A* and this would save him from insolvency. And it is said that in such a mandate the *mandator* was interfering in the affairs of the third party, liable *ex negotio gesto*, and thus interested[9]. It was agreed in classical law[10] that a mandate to lend money to a particular third person was valid against the *mandator*, at any rate if it was at interest[11]. This form of mandate became an important form of surety[12], and does not appear to be confined to cases of loan at interest. In fact the doctrine that the *mandator* must have an interest rests mainly on a text of Ulpian[13] which requires it not for the existence of a valid mandate, but for an *actio mandati directa*. No one had an action who had no

1 17. 1. 1. 4; G. 3. 162; Inst. 3. 26. 13. 2 These cases of recognised *salaria, honoraria*, grew in number as time went on, and services of almost any kind were dealt with in this way (50. 13. 1). It is not, however, clear that the notion of mandate was correspondingly extended, i.e. that, e.g., an *actio mandati* lay if the service was faultily rendered. Gaius and, even more clearly, Justinian treat mandate as confined to cases which might have been *locatio* (G. 3. 162; Inst. 3. 26. 13). See 17. 1. 7; C. 4. 35. 1. The general language of 17. 1 6. pr. is of small weight. Doubtless the limits of mandate and *locatio operis* were not precisely defined. 3 17. 1. 8. 6. 4 Justinian's classification is much more elaborate than that of G. in his Inst., though it purports to come from him. G. 3. 155; D. 17. 1. 2. 5 *Ib.*; Inst. 3. 26. 1–5. 6 G. 3. 156; Inst. 3. 26. 6; D. 17. 1. 2. 6. 7 *Ib.*; 17. 1. 6. 5. 8 See also 17. 1. 16. 9 *Arg.* 17. 1. 2. 2. 10 G. 3. 156. Servius had disagreed. 11 *Ib.*; 17. 1. 2. 5. 12 *Post*, p. 519. 13 17. 1. 8. 6.

interesse. Ulpian denies the limitation elsewhere[1], and Gaius gives no hint of it in his full treatment of the matter[2].

The powers of the mandatary might be very varied: their extent must be judged by the terms of the mandate. In general he might do whatever was necessarily or reasonably involved in the mandate or ancillary to it, but even a general business manager, *procurator*, had not necessarily, on the texts, any power of alienation[3]. He could not of course in any case do things in which direct representation was impossible, e.g. convey his principal's property by *mancipatio*.

Subject to a right of renunciation, the mandatary must carry out what he undertook[4]. He might not profit, and must account for receipts and transfer proceeds in the proper form[5]. In the execution of the mandate he was liable in early law only for *dolus*[6]. This agrees with principle, as he did not profit. But in later classical law he was liable for *culpa levis*, both views appearing in the Digest[7]. The change may be due to the fact that his services were now only nominally gratuitous[8]. He was responsible not only for positive damage, but for damage resulting from neglect to perform[9]. He must not exceed his powers[10]. Where he did so in a divisible operation, e.g. lent, or became surety for, a larger sum than was authorised, he could recover *ex mandato* to the limit of the authority[11]. But there had been disagreement. Thus, where he sold for less or bought for more than the authorised price, the Sabinians gave him no claim, but the Proculian view prevailed, on which he could claim, if he bore the difference himself[12].

The *mandator*, liable for *culpa levis*[13], must accept performance, take over rights properly created on his behalf, and indemnify the mandatary in respect of liabilities[14] incurred, by payment or *transactio*, or taking them over by *novatio*, etc.[15] He must reimburse him for expenses properly incurred, with interest, for the mandatary as he must not profit, must

1 17. 1. 6. 4. See Donatuti, *Teoria del mandato*, 2. 11, 44, who discusses the view that *m. cred. pec.* and *mand.* to become surety were not, strictly, mandate at all. 2 G. 3. 155–162. There might be *a. contraria* without the direct action. 3 3. 3. 63. This needs "*administratio*." Bonfante, *Corso*, 2. 2. 156, holds that in classical law he had the power without express authorisation but J. altered the texts limiting it to perishables. Taubenschlag, *Röm. Prr. z. Z. Diocl.* 269, considers the limitation to have been begun by Diocl. See also the lit. summarised by Rabel, *Z.S.S.* 1926, 471. As to relation of *procuratio* and mandate, *post*, § CLXXXV. 4 Inst. 3. 26. 11. He can delegate, but not a *procuratio ad litem*, 17. 1. 8. 3; C. 2. 12. 11. 5 17. 1. 8. pr., 10. 3, 20. pr. 6 *Culpa lata*? *Post*, § CXC. 7 17. 1. 10. pr., 1., 29. pr.; 19. 5. 5. 4; 50. 17. 23. 8 It can hardly be due to the confidential nature of the transaction, for the rule appears only when *mandatum* is commercialised. 9 17. 1. 5. 1, 8. 10, 12. 10, etc. 10 See *Greg. Wis.* 1. 1; Inst. 3. 26. 8; D. 17. 1. 5; on P. 2. 15. 3a, *ante*, p. 277. 11 17. 1. 33. 12 G. 3. 161; P. 2. 15. 3; Inst. 3. 26. 8; D. 17. 1. 3. 2, 4. 13 47. 2. 62. 5. 14 17. 1. 12. 9, 15, 26. 6. 15 17. 1. 45. pr.–5.

not lose[1]. But there was an illiberal rule that losses which had nothing to do with the mandate were not chargeable even though they would not have occurred but for the mandate[2].

Mandate ended of course by completion, impossibility, arrival of term or condition, mutual waiver, and so forth, but also by:

Revocation or renunciation. This right resulted from the confidential aspect of mandate. So long as nothing had been done, the *mandator* could revoke with impunity, but if he did so when the mandatary had incurred expenses or liabilities he must take these over[3]. The mandatary's power of acting under his authority lasted till he had notice of the revocation[4], and persons dealing with him were entitled to treat him as mandatary, till they had notice[5]. He could renounce, *re integra*, so long as his renunciation did not prevent the principal from conveniently getting the thing done at all[6], or in any case if he was attacked by illness[7], or had hostile interests[8], or the principal was insolvent[9]. If, apart from this, he renounced after acting, he would still be, in a sense, within his rights, but was more likely to injure the *mandator*, and be liable for damages. He must therefore give prompt notice of any revocation[10], and he must not leave a transaction unfinished[11].

Death of either party, as it was a personal relation, with similar rules as to notice of death in the case of the *mandator*[12], the *heres* of a deceased mandatary being bound to attend to uncompleted matters[13]. Here however mandate for performance after the death of either party raises a certain difficulty. This is said to be void because an *obligatio* cannot begin in the *heres*[14], and so far as death of the mandatary is concerned, this is clearly stated[15] and nowhere denied. There is the further reason that the confidence one has in a man does not extend to his unknown *heres*. But, in mandate for performance after the death of the *mandator*, the personal reason does not apply and the rule is not stated by Gaius, though it is by Paul, in the Digest, with the reason that mandate ends by death of either party[16]. One text may imply that a mandate to conduct my funeral gives no *actio mandati*[17], but another gives it on a mandate to build my monument[18], not easily distinguished. Another gives it on a mandate to buy land for my *heres* after my death[19], and Gaius gives it for *adstipulatio* on a *stipulatio post mortem*[20]. In one text in which the

1 17. 1. 15; P. 2. 15. 2. 2 E.g. a man travelling under mandate is robbed by highwaymen, h. t. 26. 6. 3 17. 1. 15; G. 3. 159; Inst. 3. 26. 9. 4 17. 1. 15. 5 46. 3. 12. 2. 6 17. 1. 22. 11. 7 17. 1. 23; P. 2. 15. 1. 8 *Ib.* 9 17. 1. 24, 25; P. 2. 15. 1. 10 17. 1. 22. 11. 11 *Arg.* 17. 2. 40. 12 17. 1. 26. pr.; G. 3. 160 (*integro mandato*); Inst. 3. 26. 10. In C. 4. 35. 15 it is said "*mandatum re integra domini morte finitur,*" a more limited proposition. *Furor superveniens*, Beseler, *Z.S.S.* 1924, 389. 13 *Arg.* 17. 2. 40. 14 *Ante*, p. 426. 15 G. 3. 158 (he gives that reason); D. 17. 1. 27. 3. 16 46. 3. 108. 17 11. 7. 14. 2. 18 17. 1. 12. 17. 19 17. 1. 13. 20 G. 3. 117. But this is within the principle of 46. 3. 108.

mandate was operative after death of *mandator*, the reason is assigned that on the facts (the text was written of *fiducia*) the *mandator* might have an action in his life so that the obligation did not begin in the *heres*[1]. In another, corrupt, it is said similarly that mandatary might incur expense, with a right of reimbursement, before the death[2]. It is not clear why it should be possible to incur expense on a monument before the death, and not on other *funeraria*[3]. In fact, since on almost any mandate it was possible for money to be expended before the death, or, failing this, for the *mandator* to have some claim, the exceptional case practically negatives the rule, which Justinian abolished[4].

The actions resulting from mandate were *bonae fidei iudicia*. They were the *actio mandati*, against the mandatary, condemnation involving infamy[5], and *actio mandati contraria* for reimbursement[6].

CLXXX. We have now to consider some special aspects of *mandatum*.

The position of mandate among consensual contracts seems at first sight remarkable. It differed from the others in that it was gratuitous, and, on the view that it gave an *actio contraria*, only imperfectly bilateral, thus resembling the contracts *re*. It resembled them also in that either party could withdraw before anything was done. And the doubt about conditions which existed in the other consensual contracts is not suggested here. But it differed from contracts *re* in essential ways: there was here no question of delivery. The matter is not mended by regarding delivery as part performance, of which this is another case. The mere agreement created a definite obligation, which justifies the place of the contract. If *A* gave *B* a mandate, and *B* simply neglected it, to *A*'s loss, an *actio mandati* lay[7]. To avoid liability there must be express repudiation in such circumstances as not to upset *A*'s plans. The *mandator* could withdraw only by *revocatio*[8], which implies something to revoke. Agreements for a right of withdrawal were common in sale[9], but sale was none the less a consensual contract. There was a right of renunciation in *societas*[10]. A *quid pro quo* is not an essential of consensual contracts: it is merely one of the factors which made for recognition. Commercial importance was the real test: most commercially important contracts would have consideration, but not necessarily all.

1 17. 1. 27. 1. 2 17. 1. 12. 17. 3 For the *actio funeraria* for expenses properly incurred in conducting a funeral, Lenel, *E.P.* 229; *post*, § CLXXXVII. 4 C. 4. 11. 1; 8. 37. 11. 5 G. 4. 62; Inst. 4. 6. 28; D. 3. 2. 1, liability having originally been only for *dolus*. 6 17. 1. 41; not normally infaming, D. 3. 2. 1; but see 3. 2. 6. 5. It is however maintained that the *actio contraria* is post-classical: the *actio mandati* in classical law having an *intentio* raising the claims on both sides, "*quidquid ob eam rem alterum alteri d. f. oportet, ex f. b.*" Biondi, *Iudicia bonae fidei*, 61. Lenel, *E.P.* 296 suggests that *a. mandati contraria* was *in factum*. 7 17. 1. 6. 1. 8 Inst. 3. 26. 9. 9 *Ante*, p. 496. 10 *Ante*, p. 511.

Mandatum as agency. An agent is one who sets up relations between principal and third party, taking no rights and incurring no liabilities, but acting as a mere conduit. Roman law never reached this conception in contract, but approached it in connexion with mandate. The Praetor made an inroad on the principle that a contract affected only the actual parties, by giving an *actio institoria* against the principal who had appointed a man to manage a business and to contract in relation to it[1], a case of mandate. Papinian went further and allowed an "*actio ad exemplum institoriae*," where the mandate was only for an isolated transaction[2]: whether the third party must have known of the authorisation in this last case is not clear[3]. But there was no such principle the other way. One text indeed says that as the employer was liable he must also be entitled[4], but this is Justinian and probably does not really represent the law even for his time. The principal could not ordinarily sue on the contract unless he had taken an assignment of the action in the way shortly to be considered. In some urgent cases, however, the matter was carried further: the principal could bring the agent's action as an *actio utilis*, and in all such cases an action by the mandatary, after this, was met by an *exceptio doli*. This is stated only where there was no other way of protecting the principal's interests, e.g. the agent was insolvent[5]. It has been suggested on the analogy of *tutores*, that the same may have been true where the agent could not or could no longer be sued, so that there would be no injustice in depriving him of his actions, e.g. in unilateral transactions[6], and thus an *actio utilis* is given to the principal where a *stipulatio praetoria* has been given to a *procurator*[7]. But it is clear that the principal did not in general acquire the agent's rights of action[8]: the notion that, where there was a right to have the action transferred, an *actio utilis* lay without transfer, is unfounded[9]. Further, the mandatary could be sued on his own contract, so that his position was far short of that of a true agent: the last point is important, for though he was entitled to an indemnity from his principal, this might be illusory.

Mandatum as a contract of surety[10]. The mandate to lend money to

1 *Post*, § CLXXXIV. 2 14. 3. 19. pr. 3 In some texts this is not mentioned (14. 3. 19. pr.; 19. 1. 13. 25). In two it is, but in both (3. 5. 30. pr.; 17. 1. 10. 5) there is another point. The person seeking the action is one who did not make the authorised contract, but guaranteed it. A surety is entitled to know what other guarantees there are. 4 19. 1. 13. 25. 5 14. 3. 1, 2; 46. 5. 5. 6 26. 9. 2; 45. 1. 79. Girard, *Man.* 720. 7 46. 5. 5; 39. 2. 18. 16; Betti, *Ist.* 1. 586. See also *ante*, p. 426. 8 See, e.g., 45. 1. 126. 2. 9 *Post*, § CLXXXIX. 10 Bortulucci, *Bull.* 1914, 129; 1915, 191. The author shews that the rules of this institution involve no anomalies, but are applications of the ordinary principles of mandate. Elsewhere (*Il mandato di credito*) he maintains that it is thought of as surety only in post-classical times.

a certain person[1], *mandatum credendae pecuniae* (the so-called *mandatum qualificatum*) imposed on the *mandator* the duty to indemnify the mandatary. If the debtor did not pay, the *mandator* must, so that he was in effect surety to the mandatary, for the debtor. It differed from *adpromissio* in that it was created by independent contract before the principal debt, and in that the creditor, mandatary, owed duties under the mandate to the surety, the *mandator*, his principal. And the duty of *mandator* was not to pay a certain sum if the debtor did not, but to indemnify the mandatary, not quite the same thing. This led to practical differences in the rules, of which the chief were the following:

Action against the debtor did not release the *mandator*, since it was not *eadem res*[2].

Mandator, like *fideiussor*, could demand *cessio* of actions and securities against the debtor, etc., but he was better off. The *fideiussor* could claim only such as still existed[3], but as the mandatary was bound to look after the interests of *mandator*, the latter was released if the mandatary had abandoned any rights[4].

The *mandator* could withdraw before performance, while the *fideiussor* could not. The *ll. Cicereia* and *Cornelia*[5] are supposed not to have been applied to *mandatores*. The *beneficium divisionis* and the *beneficium ordinis* are applied[6].

The *mandator*, being the originator, might be liable in circumstances in which a *fideiussor* would not, e.g. where there was a mandate for a loan to a minor who got *restitutio in integrum*[7]. A *fideiussor* would not be liable if he did not know the debtor was a minor[8].

Mandatum as assignment of contract. *Obligatio*, being personal, could not be assigned. This principle was evaded by the use of mandate in the form of *procuratio ad litem*. The assignment was effected by making the assignee a mandatary to sue on the claim, not to be accountable for the proceeds—*procuratio in rem suam*. In its simple form this was imperfect: the debtor could still pay the assignor, the assignor might revoke the mandate, at least till *litis contestatio*[9], and death of either party revoked the mandate. All this was gradually remedied. If the mandate was revoked by death, or expressly, the mandatary was allowed an *actio utilis* in his own name, though, in the last case, perhaps not till Justinian[10].

1 If no one is specified it is mere advice. Even where it was to a specific person there had been dispute. G. 3. 156; Inst. 3. 26. 6. 2 P. 2. 17. 16. 3 *Ante*, p. 449. 4 46. 3. 95. 11. 5 *Ante*, p. 447. 6 C. 4. 18. 3; *Nov.* 4. 7 See 4. 4. 13. pr.; 17. 1. 12. 13. The case of *m. credendae pecuniae* must be distinguished from that of a mandate to become surety, given by the debtor in every case of *fideiussio*, and from mandate to become surety for a third person. 8 *Ante*, p. 445. 9 *Litis contestatio* has brought the principal's right into issue and novated it, *post*, §§ CCXXXV, CCXXXIX. 10 3. 3. 55; C. 4. 10. 1, perhaps only where the revocation was unjustified. Where the

Again, in one case in the third century, but perhaps generally only under Justinian, it was provided that after notice to the debtor or part payment by him to the assignee, the original creditor could no longer claim the money or release the debt, nor could the debtor validly pay it to him[1]. There was now an effective transfer of such assignable right as the creditor had. Anastasius introduced a modification which must have done some injustice. He provided[2] that any one who had so bought a debt could never recover more than he paid for it, whatever the amount of the debt[3].

CLXXXI. INNOMINATE CONTRACTS[4]. These contracts are commonly treated in connexion with the contracts *re*, apparently as representing a generalisation of these, considered as resting on part performance. But the resemblance is remote and the evolution much later. They represent a new principle, i.e. that in an agreement for mutual services performance on one side binds the other. The essence is the *quid pro quo*, absent in the contracts *re*. The service might be a transfer, an act, or an abstention, having no relation to delivery, which, the essence of the real contract, might or might not be a service.

There is controversy on the evolution of these contracts[5], but in its broad lines the story seems to be as follows. There were cases in which it was clear that there was a contract, but not so clear what contract it was: it might be looked on as, e.g., sale or hire. In many such cases the doubt was settled and the action on one or other of these contracts given[6], but in others Labeo is said to have allowed an action with a *formula in ius* expressing a civil duty (*oportere*) with words prefixed setting out the facts[7]. This may be called "*agere praescriptis verbis*," but it was not the specific "*actio praescriptis verbis*" which we get later. It is not clear what it was called—possibly *actio civilis incerti*[8]. But a more difficult case was that of transactions analogous to existing contracts, but not really within the definition of any. There was always the

transfer was by way of gift it was still avoided by death of mandatary before *litis contestatio*, till Justinian. C. 8. 53. 33.

1 C. 8. 41. 3. There must have been actual *procuratio*, a mere agreement to assign was not enough. 2 C. 4. 35. 22. Justinian legislates against evasions, h. t. 23. 3 Cido, *Novatio*, Pt 3; Girard, *Man.* 776 *sqq.*; Jörs, *R.R.* 140; *post*, § CLXXXIX. 4 So called by modern writers. The principal instances have names, but they do not belong to a named class, and have no specially named actions, 19. 5. 3. Exhaustive study, de Francisci, Συνάλλαγμα. 5 See the literature cited, Girard, *Man.* 624. See also Partsch, reviewing Francisci, *Z.S.S.* 1914, 335 *sqq.* 6 G. 3. 145, etc. 7 19. 5. 1. 1. The language of Gaius (n. 6) suggests that Labeo's method was little followed, and it has been maintained that the word "*civilis*" in the text is interpolated. 8 19. 5. 6. Neratius. Cp. 19. 1. 6. 1. For de Francisci, *cit.*, classical law gave in a few cases an *a. in f.* for the positive *interesse* as opposed to *a. doli* or *cond.* for recovery, but the various names for the *a. praesc. verb.* (see next page), like the action itself, are post-classical.

actio doli, if one party had done his part, and the other refused to do his[1], and if what had been done was the transfer of a *res* there was a *condictio ob rem dati* for restitution[2]. Neither of these remedies was enforcement. They undid what had been done, putting the parties, so far as might be, in the position in which they would have been if the agreement had never been made. What was needed was to put them, so far as might be, in the position in which they would have been had the bargain been completed.

The case of *aestimatum*, handing over a thing at an agreed price, for sale or return, was dealt with in the Edict. A civil action of the type just described was given and was called *actio aestimatoria* or *de aestimato*. There was a *formula* but no edict: it was a civil action, and the transaction was contemplated as one of the type in which the doubt was whether it was sale or hire[3]. Another text of the same writer which may seem to regard it as not under any contract and to give an *actio in factum* does not refer to *aestimatum* at all[4]. However this may be, other cases were protected only by the negative remedies above mentioned and an *actio in factum*, which is found very early[5] and no doubt by the time of Ulpian covered all such cases. But in some of these, as time went on, some jurists, at least, gave a civil action, *agere praescriptis verbis*, and while some of these cases were probably classical[6], it is now fairly clear that the general action for all such cases was the work of Byzantine lawyers, probably before the time of Justinian. The compilers sought to fuse these remedies, and their terminology presents an extraordinary confusion. They speak of *actio in factum, actio civilis incerti, actio praescriptis verbis, actio praescriptis verbis in factum, actio civilis in factum*, of which names none is certainly classical as applied to this action, though *actio praescriptis verbis, actio civilis incerti* and even *actio civilis in factum*[7] may be. No doubt there was gradual extension. In the hypothesis "*facio ut des,*" on the face of the texts, Paul did not admit the action, while Ulpian did[8].

The innominate contracts are usually grouped after Paul (or Tri-

1 19. 5. 5. 3. 2 12. 4. 16 and *passim*. 3 19. 3. 1. Buckland, *Mél. Cornil*, 1, 139 (repr. *L.Q.R.* 1927, 74) and *L.Q.R.* 1932, 495. Gradenwitz's suggested interpolation (*Interpolationen*, 109) does not affect this view. Beseler, however (*Beit.* 2. 161), regards the whole passage as an invention of the compilers. For Arangio Ruiz, *Ist.* 292, the action was an ordinary *a. in f.* 4 19. 5. 13. pr. Buckland, *Mél. Cornil*, 143; *L.Q.R. cit.* 77. See *post*, p. 523. 5 19. 5. 1. pr. Julian who must have handled the *actio de aestimato* gives an *actio in factum* in these cases, 2. 14. 7. 2. 6 2. 14. 7. 2. For Meylan, *Origine de l'a. p. v.* 10, the action is classical. For de Francisci, Συνάλλαγμα, 1. ch. 9, it is Byzantine. For Lenel, *E.P.* 301, *non liquet.* 7 See Audibert, *Mél. Gérardin*, 21. He thinks the last is Byzantine, *Mél. Fitting*, 1. 49. In C. 4. 64. 6 we get "*praescriptis verbis incerta civilis actio.*" See, however, de Francisci, *cit.* 2. ch. 1. 8 19. 5. 5. 3, 15. Attempts to determine the order of evolution can be little more than guesses.

bonian) under four classes: *do ut des, do ut facias, facio ut des, facio ut facias*[1], an imperfect scheme which ignores, in form, the possibility of a service consisting in an abstention. The bargains were of innumerable kinds, but only two or three were important.

Permutatio. Barter or exchange. When we remember that the classical lawyers disputed whether sale involved a money price, and whether it was distinct from *permutatio* or not, it will be clear that we can know little of *permutatio*, as such, before Justinian. The contract was made by the actual transfer of the ownership on one side[2]. Thereupon the risk in the thing undelivered passed to the party who had delivered, the holder being liable only for *culpa*[3]. As *dominium* must pass for the contract to arise, it passed though there had been as yet no performance on the other side[4], and, as the duties on each side were the same, one who had performed but had received only with a defective title, could proceed without waiting for actual eviction[5]. The law as to compensation for defects was apparently as in sale[6]. It was a *bonae fidei* transaction, but the rules as to *laesio enormis* did not apply. The action of the one who had performed, if the other failed, is variously stated as a civil action, an *actio in factum* and the *actio praescriptis verbis*[7], indicating the evolution just considered. There was also a *condictio ob rem dati* to recover the *res*, if the corresponding render had not been made, at least if the failure was imputable[8]. Under Justinian it was called "*condictio causa data causa non secuta*[9]," and appears to have lain only where the *actio praescriptis verbis* would[10]. Where one had delivered but, for some reason, ownership had not been transferred, there could be no *actio praescriptis verbis*, as there was as yet no contract[11], but there was presumably a *condictio* for recovery.

Aestimatum[12]. This was, essentially, an agreement under which a thing was handed over by the owner to another person on the terms that he was to restore it, or an agreed price, usually within a fixed time. There might be variations in detail. Thus the profit of the receiver might consist entirely in the difference between the price he had agreed to give if he did not return the thing, and that at which he sold, or there might be some sort of reward. He might keep the thing, or sell it (which was the real aim), or return it. It appears to be the only case in which the Edict gave an action with *praescripta verba*, not called *actio praescriptis verbis*, but *actio aestimatoria*, or *de aestimato*[13]. Nothing but the fact that the

1 19. 5. 5. pr. 2 19. 4. 1. 3. 3 19. 5. 5. 1. 4 C. 4. 64. 4. 5 *Arg.* 19. 4. 1. 1, 2; 2. 14. 7. 2. 6 19. 4. 2; 21. 1. 19. 5. For Naber, *Mnem.* 1894, 83, this text is interp. 7 19. 4. 1. 1; 19. 5. 5. 1; C. 4. 64. 4. 8 *Post*, § CLXXXVII. 9 19. 4. 1. 4; C. 4. 64. 4. 10 *Ib.* 11 19. 4. 1. 3. 12 Thaller, *Mél. Appleton*, 639. 13 *Ante*, p. 522. Lenel now doubts whether there was such an action in the Edict (*E.P.* 301). The fact that it has a special name which no other "*innom. cont.*" has, is strong

primary purpose was not purchase by the receiver differentiated it from sale, and it can be regarded as sale under a suspensive condition[1]. It is fairly clear that unless by express agreement the ownership did not pass by the delivery to the dealer, but it passed, presumably, on sale to a customer or on expiry of the time limited for return. There is difficulty on the subject of risks. In one text Ulpian puts the risk on the intermediary[2], and, in another, on whichever initiated the transaction, for which he cites Labeo and Pomponius[3], and, as Paul says the same[4], this must be taken to have been the law. If the point of priority was not clear, Ulpian makes the receiver liable for *culpa*, which leaves the risk with the principal[5]. The transaction was *bonae fidei*[6]; a text which gives an *actio in factum* is not really concerned with *aestimatum*[7].

Precarium[8]. This is commonly treated as an innominate contract, but we know little of it: it has been described as an enigma[9]. It seems to have begun in revocable gifts by patrons to *liberti* and *clientes*, of property which they might hold and enjoy, but not alienate. In classical law it had lost its connexion with *liberti*, but had not changed its character. It was a gratuitous grant of enjoyment of land or goods, revocable at will, even though a contrary agreement had been made[10]. It might be of a *res incorporalis*, such as a right of way[11]. Common applications were permissions by a creditor *in fiducia* or an unpaid vendor, to the debtor, to hold the property[12]. It differed from *commodatum*, in that it applied primarily to land, and gave a general use and enjoyment, with the fruits[13], and not, as *commodatum* usually did, only a particular use. The *precario tenens* ordinarily had *possessio*[14].

It was a liberality, not a mutual benefit, differing from gift only in the right to resume it at any time[15]. Thus the holder was not liable for *culpa* but only for *dolus*[16]. Conversely it does not appear that the grantor was liable for any expenses, even such as fell on a *commodator*, but in appropriate cases there was no doubt an *actio doli*. The appropriate remedy for recovery was the interdict *de precario*, and when this issued,

evidence for this and some evidence for civil character: had a Praetor invented it we might have expected to know his name. Buckland, *L.Q.R.* 1932, 495.

1 Thaller, *cit.* 651. 2 19. 3. 1. 3 19. 5. 17. 1. 4 P. 2. 4. 4. 5 19. 5. 17. 1. 6 19. 3. 1. pr. Allusion to *bonae fidei* character probably interpolated, but any civil action on such facts must have been *bonae fidei*. 7 19. 5. 13. Authority to sell at a certain price is not of itself *aestimatum*. Few texts refer certainly to *aestimatum*, i.e. to the transaction dealt with by *a. de aest.* (P. Sent. 2. 4. 4; Inst. 4. 6. 28; D. 19. 3; 19. 5. 17. 1). D. 19. 5. 13. pr. deals only, like others, with an analogous case, as is said, *Mél. Cornil*, 1, 145, misunderstood by Ehrhardt, *Iusta causa traditionis*, 106. 8 Relation to *locatio*, Scherillo, *Rend. Ist. Lomb.* 1929, 389. 9 Bertolini, *Obbl.* 1. 420. 10 43. 26. 2. 2. 11 43. 26. 3. 12 43. 26. 6. 4; h. t. 20. 13 43. 26. 8. 4. 14 41. 2. 10. 1; probably always in classical law. Ciapessoni, *Il precarista detentore.* 15 43. 26. 1. 2. 16 43. 26. 8. 3.

as the *precarium* ceased, the holder became liable for *culpa* and "*omnis causa*," unconsumed fruits and the like[1]. The aspect of it as a gift is brought out further by the fact that, as Paul and Ulpian tell us, there was no special civil action against the holder: the interdict was all the owner had[2]. Paul indeed seems to contradict this: he says there was a civil action as in *commodatum*[3], but this probably means only that there was a *condictio* for recovery, on general principle, as there was a *vindicatio.*

As it was a personal matter, it ended, in classical law, on the death of the holder. His *heres* did not hold *in precario,* and was not liable to the interdict *de precario*[4], nor was he responsible for *dolus* of his predecessor[5]. In later law it was regarded as continuing, so that he was liable *de precario*[6]. But the death of donor or even alienation by him did not end the *precarium,* though it could be at once stopped[7].

There is no sign of an innominate contract in this, but under Justinian two texts give an action apart from the interdict, one a "*condictio incerti, id est praescriptis verbis*[8]," the other[9] an *actio praescriptis verbis.* Both are interpolated. If we treat this action as the mark of an innominate contract we may say that under Justinian, *precarium* became one. But it was essentially different: the mutual element was wanting[10].

Transactio[11]. Essentially, compromise of a dispute at law, impending, existing or already decided, if an appeal of any kind was still admissible[12]. It was the abandonment of a claim in consideration of something given or promised, or of a defence in consideration of being allowed to retain something[13]. In the former, the usual case, there would be an Aquilian *stipulatio,* and an *acceptilatio* or a pact not to sue[14], the former extinguishing the claim altogether, the latter giving an *exceptio pacti.* It was the usual practice, either as alternative to the formal release, or in addition, to stipulate for a penalty upon disregard of the agreement[15]. The penalty was usually in substitution for the agreed compromise, but

1' 43. 26. 8. 4, 6. 2 43. 26. 14; 47. 2. 14. 11. 3 P. 5. 6. 10. 4 P. 5. 6. 12. This text coupled with D. 10. 3. 7. 5 suggests that the *heres* of *precario tenens*, holding over, was liable to the interdict *de clandestina possessione.* On this interdict, Lenel, *E.P.* 469, n. 3. But Paul's text may merely mean that "*uti possidetis*" is available as he holds "*clam, ab altero,*" 43. 26. 12. 1. It survives *adrogatio*, 43. 26. 16. 5 43. 26. 8. 8, except for what he has received. 6 *Ib.*; at any rate if he knew, 44. 3. 11; C. 8. 9. 2. See, however, Partsch, *L. T. Praescriptio*, 16. 7 43. 26. 8. 1, 2. 8 43. 26. 19. 2. 9 43. 26. 2. 2. 10 It is not easy to define the scope of the *actio praescriptis verbis* under Justinian. See C. 4. 54. 2 (prob. interp.); D. 19. 5. 17. 2 (interp.). A general servant, de Francisci, Συνάλλαγμα, 1. ch. 8; 2. ch. 1. *Donatio sub modo* might equally come in under J., for it then gave *actio p. v.*, de Francisci, *cit.* 1. 254. *Ante*, p. 254. 11 Bertolini, *Della Transazione.* 12 P. 1. 1. 5; D. 2. 15. 7. pr., 11; C. 2. 4. 2, 32. 13 C. 2. 4. 24, 38. 14 2. 15. 2. 15 P. 1. 1. 3; D. 2. 15. 15, 16; C. 2. 4. 37.

it might be provided that they were to be cumulative[1]. If the promise was only informal, there was in earlier classical law only an *actio doli*[2]: an enactment of Alexander purports to give an *actio praescriptis verbis*, but it is probably interpolated[3]. In legacy of *alimenta* or the like, as the class affected was likely to be improvident and easily influenced, no *transactio* was allowed without consent of the Praetor[4]. Where several were concerned, a *transactio* by one did not benefit another, unless he had a right of regress[5].

The texts on this matter present some difficulty, but this is largely due to the fact that "*pacisci*" is used sometimes to mean (its original sense) compromise, sometimes to mean release, and sometimes to mean any sort of *conventio*. It may be assumed that before any action was begun there might always be release or compromise. In general this was equally true while an action was pending[6]. In those actions which *infitiando crescunt* there could be no compromise[7]. But there could perfectly well be release, as is said in D. 2. 4. 7. 23 (Ulpian), where the insertion of a "*non*", which Wenger requires[8], seems unnecessary and based on failure to see the sense in which *pacisci* is used. It is a case of release. After judgement, *pacisci* in the sense of compromise is no longer possible in any case[9]. But even after judgement there is nothing to prevent a release, by *pacisci*, by way of gift[10]. A difficulty is created, however, by Cicero, *pro Rosc. com.* 11. 32 and 12. 36, where a compromise seems to be valid in an Aquilian action (which *crescit infitiatione*) though *lis contestata est*. It is possible that the rule had not then developed.

1 2. 15. 16; C. 2. 4. 17. 2 C. 2. 4. 4, 28. 3 C. 2. 4. 6. See the adjoining enactments of the same Emperor. But the rule is stated in an enactment of Diocletian, C. 2. 4. 33. 4 2. 15. 8. pr. 5 27. 3. 15; *ante*, p. 455. 6 P. 1. 1. 5. 7 P. 1. 19. 2. 8 *Actio iudicati*, 87. 9 Cons. 9. 1 (A.D. 365), 9. 11 (A.D. 222), 9. 14 (A.D. 259), 9. 26 (A.D. 225); C. 2. 4. 32; D. 12. 6. 23. 1; cf. D. 39. 5. 17. 10 D. 12. 15. 1; P. 1. 1. 5a, also preserved in Cons. 4. 6 and 7. 6.

CHAPTER XII

OBLIGATIO (*cont.*). *PACTA.* INCIDENTS OF CONTRACTUAL OBLIGATION. QUASI-CONTRACT. EXTINCTION OF OBLIGATION. DELICT

CLXXXII. PACTA. In the preceding chapter contracts were discussed: we have now to consider what efficacy was allowed to such informal bargains as did not come within this conception, i.e. *pacta*.

The XII Tables contained a rule that proceedings for personal injury were barred by pact[1], and pact continued to be a complete civil defence to an action on delict, in later law[2]. The Tables contained other rules on pacts, which however do not directly concern us here[3].

The Praetors generalised the rule of the XII Tables: a pact not to sue was a praetorian defence in any action, so that it could destroy an obligation, though it gave no action: *nuda pactio obligationem non parit*,

1 8. 2. Girard, *Textes*, 17; Bruns, 1. 29. 2 2. 14. 17. 1. The primary meaning of *pactum* is no doubt agreement not to sue, for a *quid pro quo*. But for classical law the distinctions it has been attempted to draw between *pactum, conventio, pactum conventum* are of doubtful solidity. Various views, Bonfante, *Scr. Giur.* 3. 142; de Francisci, Συνάλλαγμα, 2. 481; Manenti, *Pacta conventa*; Mitteis, *R.Pr.* 149. 3 E.g. pacts by way of compromise to avoid execution of judgement, pacts between members of a *sodalitas* as to its rules (XII T. 3. 5; 8. 27, see also 1. 6).

sed parit exceptionem[1]. The next step was to allow pacts to vary obligations. The recognition of so-called *pacta adiecta*, pacts added to contracts, was a gradual process and their effect in classical and later law varied with their nature and with that of the contract in connexion with which they were made. They might be either *continua* (*in continenti facta*), made at the same time as the contract, or *ex intervallo*, made later[2]. In an informal *bonae fidei* contract, a *pactum continuum* was in effect a term in the contract, and was thus enforceable by plaintiff or defendant[3]. In *stricti iuris* contracts there is some difficulty. In *mutuum*, as the contract rested on delivery, it is usually held that any term or condition was in effect a pact, the rule being as in *bonae fidei* contracts[4]. Of *stipulatio* all that can be said is that at least one text says that *pacta in continenti* are treated as part of the *stipulatio*[5], but no text applies this except to those *pro reo*[6], which would give an *exceptio* in classical law. In Justinian's law the distinction between *exceptio* and embodiment means little[7].

There is no evidence that *pacta ex intervallo* were effective except in defence, a basis for *exceptio pacti*[8]. But the nature of the consensual contract involved one great limitation on this proposition. Such a contract might, before performance, be set aside by *contrarius consensus*[9]. Similarly, the parties might agree to vary its terms, which would be in effect to discharge the old and substitute a new contract. And where a pact was made which substantially altered the contract it was so construed, whether it benefited one or the other[10]. But a pact, to be so treated, must affect essential terms, e.g. price; a pact touching merely subsidiary matters was not so treated and was good only as a defence[11]. It was a question of fact in each case to which class the pact belonged.

The classical lawyers speak of contract as having certain effects, as creating certain obligations. The Byzantines think of it as an entity having certain characteristics which they call the *natura contractus*, i.e. its legal consequences and the legal conditions of its existence[12]. This

1 2. 14. 7. 4; P. 2. 22. 2. Pacts must be lawful (Cons. 1. 7 *sqq.*; P. 1. 1. 4). An *exceptio pacti* might be met by a *replicatio* on a counter-pact revoking it, Cons. 4. 4.
2 It is not clear why Viard, *Les pactes adjoints*, p. 140, rejects for classical law this terminology which expresses a distinction fundamental on the (orthodox) view accepted by him. On pacts in *stip.*, *id.* ch. 1.
3 2. 14. 7. 5.
4 *Contra*, Grosso, *Efficacia dei patti*, 7. Here, as elsewhere, interest can usually be attached only by *stip.*; *post*, § CLXXXVIII.
5 E.g., 12. 1. 40.
6 2. 14. 4. 3; 12. 1. 40.
7 12. 1. 40 is one of the *leges damnatae*. See Riccobono, *Z.S.S.* 1922, 345, for discussion. The Greek commentators lay down the rule that the pact is good only by *exceptio* (*Bas.* 11. 1. 7, sch. 3; Heimb. 1. 563; *Bas.* 23. 1. 42, sch. 1, 4; Heimb. 2. 633, 635). Apart from the general terms of 12. 1. 40 and the unimportant *exceptio* point this seems to be Justinian's law.
8 2. 14. 7. 5. On the view of Siber (*Z.S.S.* 1921, 85) and others that the restriction is Byzantine, see Grosso, *cit.* 23 *sqq.*
9 *Post*, § CXCV.
10 2. 14. 7. 6; 18. 5. 2.
11 18. 1. 72. pr.
12 Rotondi, *Scr. Giur.* 2. 211. Cf. G. 4. 33 (*eiusdem naturae actiones*); Maschi, *La concezione naturalistica del diritto*, 97 *sqq.*

leads to a new way of speaking of the effects of pacts. We hear that they do or do not "*mutare naturam contractus,*" i.e. can be pleaded or not in the action, that they *augent*, or *minuunt*, *contractum*. It is not clear that the change affected the law of *pacta adiecta* as stated in the *Corpus Iuris*[1].

The next step was to give an action on pacts not connected with a contract (*pacta vestita*); the Praetor in several cases (*pacta praetoria*) gave an *actio in factum*. The chief were[2]:

Iusiurandum voluntarium. It was open to a party to any dispute, whether litigation or not, to offer to the other party the opportunity to take an oath as to the truth of his claims, or himself to tender such an oath if the other party would allow it[3]. The other party need not take the oath or accept it from the offeror[4]. But whoever did take the oath in such conditions had *exceptio iurisiurandi*[5] if sued, and if he had to sue to enforce his right, he could bring an *actio iurisiurandi*, an *actio in factum* in which he need prove only that the oath was offered and taken[6]. The institution was distinct from the *iusiurandum necessarium* which could be required in certain cases[7]. Thus it could not be offered back (*relatum*) so as to compel the offeror to take it[8].

Constitutum. An informal undertaking to pay an existing debt, the promisor's or another's, at a fixed time[9]. It might be to the original creditor or another person[10]. The action was the *actio de pecunia constituta*[11], an *actio in factum*, but akin to the *actio certae pecuniae creditae*: in particular there was (or might be) a penal *sponsio*, here of half the amount in dispute[12]. It covered debts of any origin, contract (or quasi) or delict[13], but was at first confined to money, as the *actio c. p. c.* was, and extended, first to other things fungible, and, under Justinian, to anything[14]. The undertaking might be of less than the debt, or of one of alternatives due[15], or (*datio in solutum*[16]) of something other than what was due, accepted instead. It was void as to any excess over the debt

1 Platon, *Pactes et Contrats en Dr. R. et Byz.* 2 One has been considered—*pactum hypothecae* (*ante*, p. 475). It differs from the others in that its special action (*actio hypothecaria*) is in effect an *actio in rem*. When ultimately the *actio pigneraticia*, which has a *formula in ius*, was given on hypothec, it ceased to be, properly speaking, a Praetorian pact. 3 12. 2. 1–3. 4 C. 4. 1. 1; D. 12. 2. 5. 4. 5 12. 2. 9. pr. Difficulty as to extent to which this *exceptio* could be used by others concerned, e.g. sureties, *correi*, etc. Beseler, *Beiträge*, 3. 115, 4. 174. 6 12. 2. 9. 1, 11. 1; 44. 5. 1. 3. Remission of the oath by the party who had offered it was equally effective, 12. 2. 5. 4, 6. The *a. in f. iurisiurandi* was infaming if the action it replaced was, 12. 2. 9. 2. But it was only *in simplum* whatever the action it replaced was (h. t. 30. pr.), *perpetua*, though that were temporary (h. t. 9. 3) and always lay against the *heres* (h. t. 9. 7); Levy, *Privatstrafe*, 31. 7 *Post*, § CCXV, as to this and the confusion in the texts. 8 12. 2. 17. pr. 9 Inst. 4. 6. 9. 10 13. 5. 5. 2. 11 Inst. 4. 6. 8. Called *actio constitutoria* in 13. 5. 20. 12 G. 4. 171; Inst. 4. 6. 8. Not of one third as in the other case. 13 13. 5. 1. 6, 29. 14 C. 4. 18. 2. 15 13. 5. 5. pr., 13, 25. 16 *Post*, § CXCIII; 13. 5. 1. 5.

and interest[1]. The time fixed might be earlier or later than the due day of the debt, and though in principle it needed a fixed time, it seems in classical law to have given an action at once if no time was stated[2], but Justinian here required a delay of ten days[3]. It might be a promise, not of payment, but of security[4]. There must be a real debt, civil, praetorian or even natural, simple or *ex die* or conditional[5], and thus the promise was void if the original claim could be met by an *exceptio*[6]. If the debt was conditional, the *constitutum* was under the same condition[7], but it was immaterial that the debt was limited in time, e.g. that there was only an *actio annua*, and the year expired before the time fixed in the *constitutum*[8].

In later law the action was purely contractual, but there are traces of an original penal character. The heavy penal wager is one. Also in some cases (unknown) it had been *annua*[9], and there may have been doubts whether it lay to and against the *heres*[10]. But for Ulpian it was *ad rem persequendam*[11], and the penal wager was gone in later law, while Justinian, whose changes accompanied a fusion with the *actio receptitia*, shortly to be dealt with, made it *perpetua* in all cases[12]. The texts are not explicit as to how far the action destroyed the old obligation[13]: it is generally held that it did not, apart from express intent. Where it did, as it was a praetorian defence, there would be an *exceptio*[14].

The usual case was *constitutum* between debtor and creditor, but there might be *constitutum debiti alieni*[15], in effect surety, differing in some respects from *fideiussio*. Thus, though it usually left the old debt standing, it might be made so as to operate as a praetorian novation. If it left the old *obligatio* standing, action against one did not release the other[16]. It had no form, and it had a *quid pro quo*, i.e. suspension of the action. Hence a *fideiussio* which failed for defect of form was not construed as *constitutum*[17]. There need be no present debtor, e.g. the debt may be of a *hereditas* on which no *heres* has yet entered[18]. As to the *ll. Cicereia* and *Cornelia* the position is as in *mandatum credendae pecuniae*[19]. The

1 13. 5. 1. 8, 11. 1. 2 13. 5. 3. 2, 4. 3 13. 5. 21. 1. (interp.). 4 13. 5. 5. 3, 14. 1, 2. 5 13. 5. 1. 7, 1. 8, 3. 2, 19. pr. For classical law the natural obligation would probably be only on obligations by slaves or within the family (*post*, § CLXXXIX). Philippin, *Le pacte de Constitut*, holds that it could not be on a natural *obligatio*. But in his two main texts (p. 62) 13. 5. 11. 1; 13. 5. 24 there was no sort of *obligatio* to interest apart from the *const.* itself. 6 13. 5. 3. 1. 7 13. 5. 19. pr. There had been doubts as to *constitutum* of postponed and conditional debts, C. 4. 18. 2. 1. 8 13. 5. 18. 1. Valid though original render now impossible, if the impossibility had left an obligation outstanding, e.g. had supervened after *mora*, 13. 5. 21. pr., 23. 9 C. 4. 18. 2. 1. 10 *Ib.*; h. t. 1. 11 13. 5. 18. 2. 12 C. 4. 18. 2. 1. 13 13. 5. 10, 18. 3, 28; 15. 3. 15; 50. 8. 5. 1. 14 Girard, *Man.* 643. 15 13. 5. 28; P. 2. 2. 1. 16 13. 5. 18. 3. 17 13. 5. 1. 4. 18 13. 5. 11. pr. 19 *Ante*, p. 520.

b. divisionis and *excussionis* are applied to it by Justinian[1], either of two *constituentes* having previously been liable *in solidum*.

It might be made by the debtor to a new creditor[2]. This seems always to have novated, in the sense that after it the debtor could not discharge himself from the new creditor by paying the old, even where the new promise was made to one of *correi credendi* in the old debt[3].

CLXXXIII. *Receptum.* This is a group of three cases having in common little but the name[4]. *Receptum argentarii* was a transaction like *constitutum*, with a special *actio in factum*[5], *actio receptitia*, confined to bankers[6], and thus always for a third person's debt. It seems to have been of later origin, and never to have had any penal wager. It applied even in classical law to any kind of subject-matter[7], and the banker was liable even though the original debt was non-existent[8]. Justinian abolished it, fusing the institution with *constitutum*[9].

Receptum nautae cauponis stabularii. There are puzzles about this: the better view seems to be that where the goods had been received by the *nauta*, etc., with a special agreement "*res salvas fore*," the receiver was liable if the things were lost, no matter by whom they were stolen[10]. Another provision, apart from this agreement, will be discussed later[11], but there is much controversy on the whole matter.

Receptum arbitri. If parties agreed to accept an *arbiter* in a dispute, and he accepted the responsibility, however informally, and the parties had undertaken to obey the decision[12], the Praetor would compel the arbitrator to act, apart from certain grounds of excuse[13]. This however was not by action, but by a fine on him, enforced by seizure of pledges and other administrative measures[14]. Any freeman, *consularis, libertus, infamis*, might be such an *arbiter*, but not a slave[15].

Praetorian *pacta*, though in a sense unilateral, had in general a *quid pro quo*. So soon as the agreement was made for *iusiurandum* there was an agreement to abandon a claim or defence if an oath was taken. In *constitutum* and *receptum argentarii* there was suspension of the action.

1 C. 4. 18. 3. *Nov.* 4. 3. 1. 2 13. 5. 5. 2. 3 13. 5. 8, 10. But texts are few and the matter is obscure. J. Willems, *Mél. Cornil*, 2. 615. See Cornil, *Mél. Fournier*, 114, for an account of the similarity in certain effects between *constitutum* and *novatio*. 4 Costa, *Storia*, 405, sees a common "*funzione assicuratrice*." This would cover a much wider class. 5 Lenel, *E.P.* 132. 6 Theoph. *ad* Inst. 4. 6. 8. 7 *Ib.* 8 C. 4. 18. 2. 1. Perpetual and binding *heres*?, Levy, *Privatstrafe*, 29. 9 Formal or informal? Much disputed. Lenel, *cit.*; Platon, *Les Banquiers*, 1. 43; who, with others, thinks it formal. Perozzi, *Ist.* 2. 236 (with others), assumes need in all cases for the word "*recipio*," not evidenced. For civil origin, Karlowa, *R.Rg.* 2. 760. 10 47. 5. 1. 4; D. 4. 9. Controversies in this matter, Lusignani, *Respons. per Custodia*, 1. 26. 11 *Post*, § CCIV. 12 4. 8. 11. 4. 13 4. 8. 9. 4 *sqq.*, 15. It must be noted that the Praetor does not force the arbitration on the parties, but only, at their demand, on the arbitrator. 14 4. 8. 3. 1, 7. 15 4. 8. 3. 3, 7.

In *receptum nautae* the *nauta* was paid. *Receptum arbitri* may be an exception but here no action was given.

Pacta legitima, a non-Roman name for a small group of pacts made enforceable by the Emperor.

Compromissum. The above agreement to submit to arbitration. If it was informal the decision of the arbitrator (who was not an *arbiter* in the technical sense) was in no way binding[1]. If the agreement was formal it was still true that the decision did not directly affect the old rights. But it was usual to embody in the *stipulatio* an agreement for a penalty, if the decision was not obeyed. This might be what the parties chose, money, or "*quanti ea res erit*," and a mere promise to obey the decision sufficed. In all such cases there was an action on the *stipulatio*[2]. If the promise was to renounce a claim if the decision was adverse, this was in later law a conditional *pactum de non petendo*[3]. A pact not to sue on some other claim gave a like result: in cases of this type the agreement might be informal[4]. Justinian provided, in 529, that the decision should be directly binding, if the submission was under oath authenticated by writing[5], and, in 530, that where there was no such oath, if the parties accepted the decision in writing, or allowed ten days to elapse without notice of rejection, it was to bind in the same way[6]. Later, he forbade the machinery by oath, but left the provision of 530[7].

Pactum dotis. In 428 Theodosius allowed actionable validity to a pact to give a *dos*[8].

Pactum donationis. Justinian allowed such validity to a pact to make a gift[9]: here there was no *quid pro quo*.

These new creations much lessened the field of unsanctioned agreements, *nuda pacta*, and the question has arisen how far such things existed under Justinian. The use of the *stipulatio* clause as common form in all sorts of documents must have made them almost obsolete in writing, though perhaps not altogether[10]. Apart from this it would seem that an agreement, written or oral, for mutual services, still wholly unfulfilled, must have been a nude pact. On oral pacts a medieval argument[11] is that where there is no other *causa* a *causa donationis* is presumed, so that any undertaking without consideration is a *pactum donationis*, and Justinian made *pacta donationis* binding. But the language of the texts shews that he meant cases in which there was an

1 C. 2. 55. 1. 2 4. 8. 27. 7, 28. 3 Rotondi, *Scr. Giur.* 1. 285, shews that agreement to arbitrate did not in classical law give an *ex. pacti* even after the referee had decided (4. 8. 2; Cons. 9. 17); the only remedy was action on the promised penalty unless there was an express *p. de non p.* 4. 8. 11. 3. D. 4. 8. 13. 1 is interp. But C. 2. 55. 5 shews that it is older than Justinian. 4 4. 8. 11. 3, on general principle. 5 C. 2. 55. 4. 6 C. 2. 55. 5. 7 *Nov.* 82. 11. 8 C. Th. 3. 13. 4; C. 5. 11. 6. 9 Inst. 2. 7. 2. The enactment referred to is probably the obscure C. 8. 53. 35. 5. 10 Riccobono, *Z.S.S.* 1922, 307 *sqq.*, 344 *sqq.*; *ante*, p. 436. 11 Riccobono, *cit.* 366.

animus donandi[1], not that wherever a man had given an undertaking a *donatio* was to be implied, whatever the middle ages may have made of the rule.

CLXXXIV. AGENCY IN CONTRACT. Roman law did not readily accept direct representation, i.e. the notion that a legal transaction by *A* on behalf of *B* should bind or benefit *B*, in no way affecting *A*. It reached it in procedure[2] and in *traditio*[3], but not, generally, in contract: the personal nature of *obligatio* forbade this. That does not exclude the use of messengers, and the like, and it might on the facts be hard to say whether an intermediary was a messenger and the contract the principal's, or a representative and the contract his, though, practically[4], assignable to the principal. Apart from this, the principal steps were:

1. At civil law the *paterfamilias* acquired the rights resulting from contracts by members of the *familia*. This is not representation, but rests on the ancient view of such persons as his, the results of their activity in this, as in other fields, therefore vesting in him[5]. But the slave's individuality was material in many ways. If a slave bought a *res litigiosa* it was on his state of knowledge, not the master's, that penal liability depended[6]. It was his knowledge which barred *actio redhibitoria*[7]. An evicted buyer from a slave must give notice to the slave himself[8].

2. The Edict made him liable on their *negotia* to varying extents[9].

(*a*) By the *actio de peculio et in rem verso*[10] he was liable to the extent of the *peculium* at the time of the judgement, and so far as his own estate had profited[11]. In estimating the *peculium* he might deduct anything due to himself or another member of the *familia*[12], and must add anything due from them, or him, or outsiders, to it and anything he had fraudulently removed from the *peculium*[13]. He could not deduct for anything due to other creditors: first come first served[14]. It lay on any contractual or quasi-contractual liability[15]. If the son or slave died or was freed or left the *familia*, in any way, the *paterfamilias*, if he still held the *peculium*, was liable for one year[16]. Any holder of a slave with

1 See 39. 5. 1. pr.; 12. 7. 1. 2 and *ante*, p. 532, n. 9. 2 *Post*, § CCXXXIX. 3 *Ante*, p. 277. 4 Not formally, *post*, § CLXXXIX, and *ante*, p. 407. 5 As to acquisition by fructuary and *b. f. possessor*, *ante*, p. 279. 6 44. 6. 2. 7 21. 1. 51. 8 21. 2. 39. 1; 41. 3. 4. 17. On the general case of *stipulatio* etc. by representative, *post*, p. 536. 9 Persons *in mancipio*, Desserteaux, *Capitis Deminutio*, 1. 284, who holds that the actions were available against his holder. 10 Details as to this and the other actions, Buckland, *Slavery*, 166 *sqq*. 11 15. 1. 30. pr.; 15. 3. 1. pr.; Inst. 4. 6. 10; G. 4. 69, 73, and for his personal *dolus*, *ante*, p. 408. For slaves in the *peculium* of a slave (*vicarii*) the *actio de peculio* was limited to *peculium vicarii*, 15. 1. 19. pr. 12 15. 1. 5. 4, 9. 3. 13 15. 1. 7. 6, 9. 4; 15. 2. 1. pr. 14 15. 1. 52. pr. 15 15. 1. 1. 2; P. 1. 4. 5. Even *condictio furtiva* (quasi-contractual, 15. 1. 3. 12), and *actio iudicati*, even though the original debt of the son was delictal, 15. 1. 3. 11. Cases in which it was barred, Buckland, *loc. cit.* 16 15. 2. 1. pr.; difficulties as to what is retention of the *peculium*, Buckland, *cit.* 227 *sqq*.

peculium, e.g. the man himself[1], was liable, though the debt were incurred when the man belonged to some one else[2]. The *de in rem verso* clause was of little use in classical and later law (except that it was perpetual though the slave was dead[3]), as money spent on the master's affairs would ordinarily create a debt to the *peculium* which came into account in the *actio de peculio*[4]. All this is not agency, as the action lay even if the *negotium* had been forbidden[5], and there was a liability in the actual contractor, natural in the case of a slave[6], civil in the case of a son, though he had a certain praetorian protection if he became *sui iuris*[7]. The principle seems to be that one who provides the slave with the means of obtaining credit ought to take the limited risk[8].

(*b*) *Actio tributoria.* If a son or slave traded with the *peculium* or part of it to the knowledge of the *paterfamilias*, the latter was liable so far as that part of the *peculium* would go[9], with no right to deduct for debts due to him or members of the *familia*, the mode of estimation being in other respects as in the last case[10]. The action itself was the last stage of an elaborate process. Any creditor might call on the master to divide the *peculium* concerned among the creditors, including the master (*vocatio in tributum*[11]). This was a kind of bankruptcy of the slave, the master being the administrator[12]: it was this *vocatio in tributum* which gave the action its name. This lay only if he acted with *dolus* in the liquidation[13]. It was in fact penal to the extent that he must hand over what he would have handed over apart from *dolus*[14], and the fund may have lessened in the meantime. But it was not treated as penal: Julian speaks of it as essentially *ad rem persequendam*[15]. It was *perpetua* even though the slave were dead[16], but it lay against the *heres* only to the extent of his receipts[17], i.e. out of the property concerned. Only creditors of the slave could claim: it does not appear that they need have known of the master's *scientia* or even existence[18].

(*c*) *Actio quod iussu.* On a *negotium* by his authority (not mere *scientia*) the *paterfamilias* was liable *in solidum*[19], the authority being revocable till the act was done[20]. This looks like representation, but it

1 Disputes, Buckland, *Slavery*, 232. 2 15. 1. 47. 6. 3 15. 3. 1. 1.
4 On the suggestion that *de in r. v.* lay only if the property had been handed over with a view to such application, Buckland, *op. cit.* 181 *sqq.* 5 15. 1. 29. 1.
6 15. 1. 50. 2. 7 14. 5. 2. pr.; Lenel, *E.P.* 278; *ante*, p. 141. 8 Fructuary or *b. f. possessor* liable *de peculio* etc. if debt within his field of acquisition, 15. 1. 2. The view that there could be no *actio d. i. r. v.* in classical law unless there was a *peculium* (Von Tuhr, *Actio d. i. r. v.*, 238; Solazzi, *St. Brugi*, 205) is not acceptable. See Perozzi, *Ist.* 1. 218; Buckland, *Slavery*, 184. 9 14. 4. 1. pr. 10 14. 4. 1. 2. 11 14. 4. 1. pr. Whether the *vocatio* is the act of creditor or of Praetor is not clear. 12 See 14. 4. 6.
13 14. 4. 3, 7. 2, 12. 14 14. 4. 7. 2. 15 14. 4. 8. 16 14. 4. 7. 5, 8. 17 14. 4. 9. 2. 18 The contrary is sometimes held on general principles of representation.
19 Inst. 4. 7. 1; P. 1. 4. 6. Ratification appears to be enough, 15. 4. 1. 6. See, however, 15. 3. 5. 2. 20 15. 4. 1. 2.

does not really rest on that idea as it was confined to the family, the legal unit, and the action did not exclude liability on the part of the actual contractor. As the authority is an inducement to contract, it would normally be communicated to the third party, and may have been necessary[1]. This action seems to be the least important of the group: it is treated very briefly[2].

Gaius describes this system of remedies as available only for dealings by slaves and *filiifamilias*. For women *in manu* and civil bondsmen he tells a different story[3], the difficulties of which have already been considered[4]. As to their contracts made while in the family we have no information[5].

3. Outside the family there were further developments in commerce.

(*a*) *Actio institoria*. Where a man employed another, his slave or *servus alienus* or freeman[6], to manage a business undertaking, to be *institor*, he was liable on the contracts connected with the business[7]. The liability might be excluded by public notice, or express notice to one about to contract[8]. The action was *perpetua* and lay both to and against *heredes*[9]. The third party must know that the contract was connected with the business[10]: whether he must know of the principal's connexion with the business does not appear on the texts. The basis of the action as stated by Paul and Ulpian, i.e. that as we get the *commoda* we ought to bear the *incommoda*[11], hardly suggests this requirement[12].

(*b*) *Actio exercitoria*. If a principal (*exercitor*) set up a man, slave or free, to manage a commercial ship (*magister navis*) he was liable in the same way[13], and, with some exceptions[14], the principles are the same[15].

1 Discussion and reff., Buckland, *Slavery*, 167. 2 As to development in classical law of a civil obligation (*condictio*) in this case, *post* § CCXXX. 3 G. 4. 80. 4 *Ante*, p. 399. 5 G. 3. 104 seems, in a different connexion, to put them on a level with slaves in this matter. Lenel (*E.P.* 276) makes the Edict on such cases deal only with those in "*potestas*": his evidences are from the Digest—which does not speak of the obsolete cases of *manus* and civil bondage. 6 P. 2. 8. 1, 2. 7 Inst. 4. 7. 2; D. 14. 3. 1; P. 2. 8. 1. The restriction led to great subtleties of interpretation, e.g., 14. 3. 5. 11 *sqq.* 8 14. 3. 11. 2, 5. 9 14. 3. 15, i.e., as to transactions before the death; as to transactions *iacente hereditate*, h. t. 5. 17, 17. 3. But the relation did not continue with the *heres* except expressly, 12. 1. 41. 10 14. 1. 7. 2. 11 14. 3. 1. pr.; P. 2. 8. 1. 12 Usually held necessary. See Buckland, *Slavery*, 172. 13 14. 1. 1. pr. 14 *Magister* might appoint a deputy (even against the will of the *exercitor*), whose contracts would bind the latter in the same way, less readily allowed to *institor* (14. 1. 1. 5). *Exercitores*, if more than one, were always liable *in solidum* (14. 1. 1. 25). Another text states a difference where the *exercitor*, i.e. the principal, is *alieni iuris*, as compared with that of an *institor alieni iuris*, but the cases are not parallel and it is difficult to see in what the difference consists (14. 1. 1. 20). See also p. 536, nn. 1, 2. Contracts by "*discipuli*" of an *institor* or *magister* bind him *in solidum* (P. 2. 8. 3). This is analogous to the *actio institoria* itself. See 14. 1. 1. 2. Difficulties where the *institor* or *magister* was a *filius* or slave of another *paterfamilias* and where the *exercitor* was such. See P. 2. 6. 1; D. 14. 3. 1, 11. 8; 14. 1. 5. 1, etc. 15 The same questions arise as to knowledge of the principal by the third party, and see 14. 1. 7. 1, 2.

Though these cases resemble agency, as they involve authority and are outside the family, they are not agency. The principal did not acquire rights under the contract, except, in late law, if there was no other way of avoiding loss, in the *institoria*[1], or by special *cognitio* in the *exercitoria*[2]. The actions would ordinarily have to be assigned. And *institor* and *magister* were liable[3], which is inconsistent with agency.

4. The furthest point reached as a general principle was in mandate, already discussed[4]. The *actio de in rem verso utilis*, by which in some cases, under Justinian, a third party with whom an unauthorised person had dealt could sue the interested party to the extent of his profit[5], had nothing to do with agency.

In relation to these contracts by subordinates and agents a question arises, rendered almost unanswerable by the state of the texts. The state of mind and knowledge of the parties is often material to rights and liabilities, in case, e.g., of error, of redhibition for defect, of *dolus*, of dealing in *res litigiosae*. The question is: whose state of mind is material, that of the principal or the actual contracting party? The texts, which have certainly been in many cases interpolated, tell a conflicting story. The point has been investigated by Schulz[6], who concludes that in classical law, where the representation was indirect, i.e. the contract did not directly bind or entitle the principal, e.g. contract by a mandatary, only the state of mind of the mandatary was material, but if it was direct, e.g. *stipulatio* by a slave, that of the principal alone was material, except where the slave was acting independently, there being differences of opinion among the jurists as to the drawing of this distinction. Sometimes the distinction is between contracts for the *peculium* and those *domini nomine*, i.e. on the master's account, sometimes between authorised and unauthorised, sometimes between general and special authorisation, but these distinctions greatly overlap. He holds that the compilers tend, but not consistently, to make the state of mind of both material in all cases[7].

CLXXXV. *Obligatio quasi ex Contractu.* Justinian's second head of *obligatio*, apparently based on the "*liber aureorum*" or "*rerum cottidianarum*" of Gaius, but probably interpolated[8]. He selects a few cases among the large class of obligations covered by the same conception, i.e. those having nothing delictal about them, and not contracts,

1 14. 3. 1–2. 2 14. 1. 1. 18. 3 14. 1. 1. 17; 14. 3. 7. 1. 4 *Ante*, p. 519. 5 See C. 4. 26. 7. 3. Von Tuhr, *Actio de i. r. v.* 293 *sqq.*; Taubenschlag, *Röm. Prr. z. Z. Diocl.* 278. 6 *Z.S.S.* 1912, 37. 7 There may have been differences of opinion; the solutions applied in defence are not always the same as those in claim, or those in contractual actions as those in delictal cases. 8 The description of them as *ex variis causarum figuris* (44. 7. 1. pr.; cp. h. t. 5) is probably genuine, Riccobono, *Dal Dir. Rom. al Dir. mod.* 274.

but analogous thereto. It seems impossible to find any principle to which those he mentions can be reduced, or which, admitting these, will exclude a number which he does not mention. The cases treated are:

Negotiorum Gestio[1]. This may be described as looking after another man's affairs, without his authority (which would be mandate[2]). The primary action was *negotiorum gestorum* against the *gestor*, who had the *actio negotiorum gestorum contraria* for reimbursement. They were *bonae fidei*, but as the Edict promised a praetorian action there must at one time have been an alternative formulation *in factum*[3].

The services rendered might be of any kind, repair of a house, becoming surety, buying or selling stock in trade[4], etc., but to entitle the *gestor* to the *actio contraria* it must be shewn not only that the act was a reasonable one, but that it was in the circumstances reasonable for the *gestor* to do it, and not leave it to the person concerned[5]. It must also have been done in the interest of the principal[6]: if it was also in the interest of the *gestor* he had the action only if he could have protected his own interest without the other. Thus one of common owners who repaired the house had not in classical law this action against his co-owner, but *communi dividundo*[7]. It must have been useful when it was done, or have been accepted as such by the principal[8]: the fact that later events destroyed its utility was immaterial[9]. On ratification the *gestor* might treat it as mandate if he preferred, but it did not become mandate *ipso facto*: it did not lead to *infamia* and was not affected by the death of the

1 3. 5; C. 2. 18. Partsch, *Neg. gestio.* 2 Frese, *Mél. Cornil*, 1. 327; *St. Bonfante*, 4. 399, holds that classical law knew nothing of this unauthorised intervention: the Ed. dealt only with *procurator*, whose remedy was *a. neg. gest.* Though he acted under mandate, it was not normal mandate and the remedy was not *a. mandati*. That there is mandate is clear (G. 4. 84) and D. 17. 1 must be completely recast if *procurator* is to be cut out. 3 G. 4. 62. Lenel, *E.P.* 101, who thinks (*Z.S.S.* 1914, 210) that the original *formula in factum* dealt only with absence of the principal; Partsch, *cit.* 10, who also holds (*cit.* 4) that the Edict was understood as giving the action both ways, the *act. contraria* being post-edictal. The *actio curationis* of 26. 8. 11 is interp. 4 3. 5. 3. 2, 21, 29, etc. 5 E.g. absence, h. t. 2; Inst. 3. 27. 1. 6 Riccobono, *Dal dir. Rom. cit.* § VI and *Riv. del Dir. Comm.* 1917 (abstract, *Z.S.S.* 1927, 541), holds that this is classical law, but the compilers make it into a subsidiary action to recover expenses, without reference to the purpose. Hence extended, e.g. in common ownership, to cases where classical law excluded it. The *b. possessor sine re* who pays debts or legacies of the estate has already been mentioned (*ante*, p. 393). Putative *heres* is not quite on the same footing, he does not owe the debt, etc. Classical texts say *heres* not released—payer has *c. indeb.* against creditor (12. 6. 19. 1). Others, probably altered, say *heres* is released and give payer a claim against him (3. 5. 44. 2; 3. 5. 48). Riccobono, *cit.* 250 *sqq.* G. Segrè, *St. Brugi*, 404. For Partsch (*cit.*) *animus negotii alieni agendi* is not classical. For Rabel, *St. Bonfante*, 4. 281, it is present imperfectly in classical law and not wholly gone under Justinian. 7 Unless he was protecting an interest of the other owner rather than a common interest. 3. 5. 39; 10. 3. 6. 2. As to 3. 5. 30. 7; 10. 3. 19. 2, Accarias, *Précis*, 2. 424. 8 3. 5. 8, 9. 1. 9 3. 5. 9. 1.

principal[1]. It must not have been prohibited by the principal[2], or done *donandi animo*[3], or in execution of a pious duty[4], or under mandate by, or legal duty to, the principal[5].

The direct action might lie where the *contraria* did not, e.g. where the act was forbidden[6], or where it was not a reasonable act of administration[7], or where it was done for the purposes of the *gestor*, though an interpolated text gives *actio contraria* even in this case, to the extent of the principal's enrichment[8]. It was immaterial that the *gestor* was mistaken as to the identity of the principal[9]. If it was the affair of the *gestor*, but he thought it another's, neither had the action[10]. If it was another's, but he thought it his own, he had no *actio contraria*, but if still in possession of the thing he had a right of retention like any other *bona fide possessor*[11]. Africanus in one text[12] gives the *actio negotiorum gestorum* to the person really interested, where circumstances barred other remedies, and in another a *condictio* to the extent of the enrichment[13]. This seems the better view, *gestio* not entering into the matter at all.

The *gestor* must carry out what he undertook, and account for proceeds, his position not being affected by death of the principal[14]. He was liable for *culpa levis* but, if the affair was urgent, only for *dolus*[15]. The risks were not on him, unless the loss resulted from his doing what the principal would not have done: here he was liable for *casus* but might set off profit resulting from the same administration[16]. The principal must take over liabilities duly incurred and refund "*utiles impensae*," though in the event they may have come to no good[17], the measure of damages being benefit at the time to the *dominus rei*, not cost to *gestor*[18].

Tutor and Ward, *Curator* and Ward. The obligations in these quasi-contractual relations have been considered in the law of persons[19]. In the case of the *tutor* there were special remedies, but in that of the *curator* the remedy was *actio negotiorum gestorum*[20].

1 Girard, *Man.* 665; Van Wetter, *Pand.* 4. 304. It may concur with mandate by a third party, 3. 5. 3. 11. Partsch, *op. cit.* 14, holds that the Edict did not give the action here, but that there was an *actio utilis* (3. 5. 20. 3; 3. 5. 27; 17. 1. 6. 1) and later jurists ignored the distinction (3. 5. 3. 11, 5. 6). 2 3. 5. 7. 3; 17. 1. 40. Disputes, C. 2. 18. 24. 3 3. 5. 43; 17. 1. 60. 1. 4 3. 5. 33; C. 2. 18. 5. 5 17. 1. 6. 1; C. 2. 18. 20. 6 See n. 2. 7 3. 5. 9. 1. 8 3. 5. 5. 5. 9 3. 5. 5. 1. 10 3. 5. 5. 6. 11 10. 3. 14. 1; 44. 4. 14. 12 3. 5. 48. Partsch, *op. cit.* 37, cites 5. 3. 50. 1; 5. 4. 10; 11. 7. 32. pr.; 11. 7. 14. 11, as proving that *a. n. g. contraria* lay on such facts. But the last two are under another edict and the others deal with carrying out the wishes of a testator, and the language of 5. 3. 50. 1 shews this as a determining factor. 13 12. 1. 23. 14 3. 5. 3. 7, 7. 1, 30. 2. 15 3. 5. 3. 9; P. 1. 4. 1; Inst. 3. 27. 1. 16 3. 5. 10. 17 3. 5. 2, 9. 1; 46. 7. 5. 6. 18 3. 5. 9. 1. 19 *Ante*, §§ LV, LXI. 20 Some texts make the remedy an *a. n. g. utilis* (C. 5. 37. 26. 1; C. 2. 18. 17; C. 5. 54. 2; C. 5. 51. 7). Others give *a. negotiorum gestorum* simply (26. 7. 5. 6; 27. 3. 13; 27. 3. 4. 3; C. 2. 30. 1; C. 4. 26. 1). The question which group represents the classical law is answered both ways, e.g. by Lenel (*Z.S.S.* 1914, 203 *sqq.*) in the sense that the description of the

Heir and Legatee. The general nature of the obligation has already been set forth[1]. According to Ulpian it had been disputed what degree of care must be shewn, but he and Paul make *heres* liable for *culpa levis*[2]. Africanus lays down the same rule for legacy and *fideicommissum*, with the corrective that if the person charged was getting nothing from the *hereditas* he was liable only for *dolus*. As the text says[3], this is applying the rule of *bonae fidei* contracts, correct for *fideicommissa*, but more questionable for legacy, since in classical law the personal remedy on legacy was *stricti iuris*, and the rules in *condictio sine causa* were different[4]. The obligation applied primarily to legacy *per damnationem*, but so far as legatee *per vindicationem* could use the personal action[5], the same rule would apply to him. In the real action the *heres* was liable, as it seems, only for active interference with legatee's rights.

CLXXXVI. COMMON OWNERSHIP. The relation arising where two or more own a thing in common, whether *socii* in the strict sense or not. The theoretical formulation of the relation between co-owners is controverted. Does each owner hold *dominium* of the whole, limited by the concurrence of the others? Or does he own only his own undivided part? Or a potential physical part not yet determined? Or is his right not ownership at all, but an analogous right? All these opinions, and others, are held. No text settles the matter and it is plain that the solution would have a repercussion on the mutual rights and duties[6].

The duties were like those in *societas*, but less in scope. The position might arise in many ways, e.g. joint purchase, legacy or inheritance. The remedy in the last case, i.e. the mode of enforcing the duties, primarily that of dividing, was the *iudicium familiae erciscundae*: in all other cases it was *communi dividundo*[7], but the rules were in general the same. The action was a *bonae fidei iudicium*[8], *duplex*, in the sense that its formula did not distinguish plaintiff and defendant: it was expressed to apply to all parties alike[9], though, in view of questions of proof, the claimant of the action was treated as plaintiff[10]. We have already dealt with the peculiar function of the *iudex*, that of *adiudicatio*, distribution of parts among the claimants[11]. In allotting, the *iudex* must follow the unanimous wish of

action as *utilis* is due to Justinian. This seems on the evidence the better view (see, however, Partsch, *op. cit.* 66 *sqq.*). The reason for the change is not very clear: Lenel holds that it was in order to differentiate this action from the ordinary *neg. gest.* It is also likely that some texts give the direct action where originally it was *utilis*. But the field of *a. n. g. utilis* is still obscure, Rabel, *St. Bonfante*, 4. 299.

1 *Ante*, pp. 316, 335, 348. 2 30. 47. 5; P. 3. 6. 9. 3 30. 108. 12. 4 *Post*, § CLXXXVII. 5 *Ante*, p. 335. 6 Reff., *ante*, p. 207, 404. Earlier literature, Windscheid, *Lehrb.* § 169*a*, nn. * and 5. Perozzi, *Ist.* 1. 747, suggests an oscillation between the first two opinions. 7 D. 10. 3. History and successive formulations, *post*, § CCXXII. 8 In later law, but as to classical law, see Riccobono, *Dal Dir. Rom.*, *cit.* 183; Cuq, *Man.* 553. 9 Lenel, *E.P.* 210. 10 10. 3. 2. 1. 11 *Ante*, p. 252.

the parties, but if that failed he must divide fairly, any inequality being adjusted by *condemnationes* for equalising payments[1]. The action need not cover all the property: a part might be divided without disturbing the rest[2], and it was possible for one or more of common owners to claim division without affecting the community among the others[3].

This division was the main, and at first the only, function of the action, but as we know it, any question arising out of the rights and duties of the common owners might be brought into account in the division[4]. Thus profits and expenses properly incurred must be shared[5], and damage by one of them, due to *culpa levis* (*in concreto*, at least in later law) must be allowed out of his share[6]. There was no *infamia*. No co-owner might erect a construction on the common property, without consent (or non-prohibition) of all: the only way to get over the difficulty was to divide[7]. The right of division was essential to the relation, and an agreement never to divide was void[8], but one not to divide for a certain time was valid, if the court thought it advantageous to common interests[9], and the effect seems to be not to allow division with resulting liability for any loss to the others, but refusal of division[10]. Apart from this there was no liability for loss resulting from division at a disadvantageous time, as in *pro socio*[11]. There was nothing to prevent a co-owner from disposing of his share so that another would take his place in the community[12], or from pledging it[13]. But he could not create a praedial servitude[14]. The relation was not affected by the death of a party[15].

The rights under the action applied only to matters accruing during the community. It was not available for expenses incurred before it began or after its end[16], and if a co-owner spent money, thinking he was sole owner, the principles of *bonae fidei possessio* applied: he had a right of retention, but no right of action, which here practically means that if another owner was the plaintiff it would be allowed, but not where he

1 10. 3. 3. 1, 6. 1, 21; Inst. 4. 17. 4, 5. 2 10. 3. 13. Thus the action can be repeated, not so *familiae erciscundae*. 10. 3. 4. 2; 10. 2. 20. 4. 3 10. 3. 8. pr. Exception, h. t. 19. 1. 4 10. 3. 3. pr. Berger, *Entwicklungsgesch. d. Teilungskl.* 95, assumes for earliest times a *condemnatio* for equalising payments. 5 10. 3. 4. 3, 11. 6 10. 2. 25. 16; 10. 3. 14, much debated text; Riccobono, *Dal Dir. Rom., cit.* is a commentary on it; Berger, *cit.* 211, review, Fehr, *Z.S.S.* 1912, 576. Probably (Riccobono, *cit.* 195; Bonfante, *Scr. Giur.* 3. 401) it was not till Justinian that the action could be brought for these contributions alone, leaving the community undisturbed. *Contra*, Fehr, *cit.* 7 10. 3. 28. The question whether absence of prohibition sufficed has been much discussed in Italy. See, e.g., Fadda, *St. Brugi*, 139; Bonfante, *Corso*, 2. 2. 15; Perozzi, *Mél. Girard*, 2. 355; *Ist.* 1. 747; Riccobono, *Essays in Legal History*, 1913, ed. *Vinogradoff*, 33. The answer really depends on the view taken of the true nature of co-ownership. 8 10. 3. 14. 2; C. 3. 37. 5. Bonfante, *Scr. Giur.* 3. 512, considers this not classical. 9 10 3. 14. 2. 10 *Ib.* 11 There is no *fraternitas*, but the *iudex* has a wide discretion. 12 10. 3. 6. 1, 14. 3, 24. 1. 13 10. 3. 6. 9. 14 8. 1. 2; 8. 3. 34. pr. 15 10. 3. 4. 3; cp. 17. 2. 65. 9. 16 10. 3. 4. 3; C. 3. 37. 3.

himself was[1]. Where he was mistaken as to the identity of the other owner, one text gives him the action, the error being immaterial, while another gives him only *actio utilis*. But, as in *negotiorum gestio*, he had not the action if he did the act for his own purposes[2]. There is a conflict also where the right held in common was less than ownership, but the dominant view is that if it was a "*ius*" in the strict sense, the direct action lay, but a common pledge gave only *actio utilis*[3]. As it was essentially for division it could not lie where there was nothing to divide[4]. Thus it was not available if the community had ceased, from destruction of the *res* or any other cause, but *actio utilis* lay for expenses during the community[5].

On the question of the juridical nature of common ownership depends the question how far the actions etc. which an owner had for the protection of his property[6] lay between co-owners. The better answer seems to be that most of them did not: adjustment must be made in *communi dividundo*[7].

MONEY PAID BY MISTAKE. *Condictio indebiti*[8]. Where a man made a payment in error, in discharge of an obligation which did not in fact exist, to one who received in good faith, he could recover by the *condictio indebiti*, a *stricti iuris actio in personam*. The case was, we are told, analogous to *mutuum*, except that the payment was in discharge, not creation, of an obligation. Thus it was recoverable from a *pupillus* (or in classical law, a woman) only where a *mutuum* would be[9]. But *mutuum* was always a transfer of fungibles, while here the render may have been of any kind possible in any obligation[10]. Thus the *condictio* might be either *certae pecuniae*, or *triticaria* or *incerti*.

There must have been no debt at time of payment. A debt valid at civil law, but defeasible by *exceptio peremptoria* was no debt[11]. Nor was a conditional debt so long as the condition was unsatisfied[12]. But one *ex die*, even *ex die incerto*, was an existing debt, and irrecoverable: it was only payment which was postponed[13]. And a *naturalis obligatio* excluded *condictio indebiti*[14]. A debt due to *X* was an *indebitum* if paid to *Y*,

1 10. 3. 14. pr., 1. The text goes on to give *a. neg. ges. utilis*, no doubt due to Justinian.
2 10. 3. 6. pr., 2, 29. 3 10. 3. 7. 8; 45. 3. 32; 10. 3. 10. 1, etc. See, however, Biondi, *Legit. nelle az. div.* 42, who cites the relevant texts. 4 C. 3. 38. 9. 5 10. 3. 11.
6 E.g. *damni infecti*, *operis novi nuntiatio*, noxal actions, *actio l. Aquiliae*, etc.
7 Riccobono, *Essays in Legal Hist.*, *cit.* 56; Perozzi, *Ist.* 1. 750, who cites the highly conflicting texts, 17. 2. 47. 1; 10. 2. 16. 5; Coll. 12. 7. 8; D. 9. 2. 27. 1; 11. 3. 9. pr., 14 2; 47. 10. 15. 36, 17. 9; 47. 2. 43. 12, 62. pr.; 9. 4. 8; 10. 1. 4. 6, 7; 33. 3. 4; 8. 5. 11, 14. 1. *Contra*, Biondi, *Iudicia bonae fidei*, 107. 8 D. 12. 6; C. 4. 5. 9 G. 3. 91; Inst. 3. 14. 1. 10 A security given may be recovered (12. 6. 31), and reimbursement for service rendered (12. 6. 26. 12). 11 Vat. Fr. 266, for exceptions, where the *exceptio* is of a penal character. Accarias, *Précis*, 2. 436. 12 12. 6. 16. pr.
13 12. 6. 10, 16. 1, 17. Possible basis of these distinctions on that between *debitum* and *obligatio*, Cornil, *Mél. Girard*, 1. 205. *Ante*, p. 406. 14 12. 6. 38. 1.

unless *Y* was *solutionis causa adiectus*, or in some way authorised to receive it[1]. Payment of a debt due from a third person was an *indebiti solutio*, unless it was paid in the name of the third person, in which case the necessary error did not exist[2]. To pay one thing when another was due was an *indebiti solutio*, unless it was by consent as a *datio in solutum*[3]. If there was no real debt a *datio in solutum* was *indebiti solutio*[4]. If, owing one of two things a debtor gave both, he could condict one, and, after doubts, Justinian gave him the choice[5].

There must have been a real and reasonable error. If the money was paid with knowledge that it was not due, this was a gift, even where the payer intended to recover it[6]. Though there is doubt on the texts it seems that it must have been an error of fact, not law, except for some specially protected persons[7]. Where the payer was in doubt whether it was due the classical rule seems to have been that he could not recover by this action, unless he paid on the understanding that he was to have it back, if it proved not due—this, says Ulpian, was a *negotium*. Justinian puts doubt on the same level as error[8].

The receiver must be in good faith, otherwise his act was *furtum* and the remedy *condictio furtiva*[9], with the practical difference that the risk in *condictio indebiti* was with payer[10], in the other case with receiver: *fur semper in mora est*. Restitution must be with *fructus*, *partus* and accessories[11], but expenses might be deducted[12], rules which created certain difficulties of procedure[13]. Interest could not be claimed[14].

The question arises whether the action was for enrichment or for what was given. Where it was money, what was paid could be recovered by *c. certae pecuniae*, whatever had happened to it[15]. Where it was a specific thing the receiver must return (apart from *dolus* or *culpa*) only his enrichment, allowing for expenses[16]. But where what was paid was fungibles other than money (*c. triticaria*) the matter is not clear. On the analogy with *mutuum* and the language of some texts[17], the better view is

1 12. 6. 22. pr.; C. 4. 5. 8. 2 12. 6. 44. 3 12. 6. 19. 3. Where payment was with another's property, by mistake, one text allows *condictio* of the possession, another gives the payer no right, even where there was no debt. 12. 6. 15. 1, 19. 2. Difficult cases, h. t. 26. 4–6, 13. 4 *Arg.* 12. 6. 23. 2, 26. 4. 5 C. 4. 5. 10; *post*, § CXCIII. They are at payer's risk. 6 12. 6. 1, 50; 22. 6. 6; 22. 6. 9. 2; 50. 17. 53. 7 22. 6. 9. pr.; C. 1. 18. 6; C. 1. 18. 10; C. 6. 50. 9; C. 4. 5. 5. Women and children and probably soldiers and rustics; 22. 6. 9. pr. Error of law seems to have been allowed where it was a point so difficult that it would not have been easy to get safe advice (22. 6. 9. 3). This would usually be "subsumption of facts under the rule" as Savigny puts it (*Syst.* 3, *Beil.* viii. v). On error of law in general, Sokolowski, *Mél. Cornil*, 2. 443 (not always convincing). 8 12. 6. 2. pr.: C. 4. 5. 11. 9 13. 1. 18, but see *post*, § CXCVI. 10 See n. 16. 11 12. 6. 15. pr. 12 12. 6. 26. 12. 13 Girard, *Man.* 659, similar difficulty, *ante*, p. 465. 14 C. 4. 5. 1. 15 Von Tuhr, *Aus Röm. und Bürg. R.* 301, on 46. 3. 66. 16 12. 6. 65. 5, 8. For Siber, *R.R.* 2. 219, the restriction to enrichment is due to Justinian. 17 12. 6. 7; 19. 5. 25; C. 4. 50. 6.

that the *quantitas* had to be restored, irrespective of its fate, which hardly seems to be negatived by a text which says that, corn being so delivered and consumed, the *pretium* must be restored[1].

The plaintiff must prove the payment and that the debt was not due[2] (except that if the receiver fraudulently denied the payment and this was proved, he must then prove that it was due, and the burden was in general on the payee, if the payer was a minor, a soldier, a woman, or a rustic[3]). It is a debated point whether having proved that it was not due he had still to prove that he thought it was due, or whether this was presumed, the creditor being allowed to prove that the payment was made in knowledge of the facts. The better view seems to be that he must prove the error, i.e. facts to account for the error, otherwise the rule that the error must be reasonable could hardly be applied[4].

There remains an important exception. If the debt was one of those denial of which involved double liability, payment in error could not be recovered as *indebitum*[5]. Such were claims under the *l. Aquilia,* judgement debt, *certa legata per damnationem* in classical law, and any legacy in favour of certain beneficiaries under Justinian[6]. The rule is clear: its reason is obscure. It has been suggested that otherwise the debt might be disputed without penalty. It would be paid and *condictio indebiti* then brought. If the payer lost he would be no worse off. But this was to take on himself the burden of proof which would otherwise be on the creditor. It would require proof of the facts which shewed that it was not due, and also proof that he did not know these facts. And the case supposed is one of doubt, and doubt was not enough in classical law[7]. A more probable suggestion is that it was a sort of compromise. By paying he avoided the risk involved in denial, and a compromise carried out ought not to be undone. But it was an odd compromise, under which he paid all that was claimed. There could in fact be no *transactio* in such a case[8].

In some cases there could not be said to be no debt, but the party was on the facts entitled to pay less, and had, in error, failed to make the deduction, e.g. *retentiones* omitted, Falcidian or Pegasian deductions not made, *cautio usufructuaria* not taken, *compensatio* not claimed. There are texts giving *cond. indebiti* in these cases, but it seems the better view that they are due to Justinian[9]. The different case of a putative *heres*

1 12. 6. 65. 6. But see Girard, *loc. cit.* 2 22. 3. 25. pr. 3 22. 3. 25. pr., 1. But the text is mainly due to Justinian. 4 See, however, Girard, *loc. cit.*: proof that it is not due ordinarily involves proof of the facts accounting for the error. 5 C. 4. 5. 4; Inst. 3. 27. 7. 6 G. 4. 9; P. 1. 19. 1; Inst. 4. 6. 19. 7 Even though, as is probable, the rule originated before distinction was drawn between fact and law in the matter, the fact that doubt is not error remains. 8 P. 1. 19. 2. Bertolini, *Transazione*, 364. 9 See for this view and the conflicting texts, Kipp, *Z.S.S.* 1921, 345; see also Pflüger, *Condictio und kein Ende.*

who pays legacies with his own money where there was no debt has already been considered[1].

CLXXXVII. This completes the list of quasi-contractual obligations as given by Justinian, but there were others, more or less analogous, some of which need mention. Analogous to *negotiorum gestio* are *curatio*, already dealt with, the *actio funeraria*, the creditor *missus in possessionem*, and the case of *protutela*.

The *actio funeraria* is an *actio in factum perpetua*[2], akin to *negotiorum gestorum*, by which one who had undertaken funeral arrangements without legal liability could recover the cost from the person actually liable[3]. The rules shew that this was to provide for absence or negligence of the *heres*[4]. The cost might not be excessive (since the *heres* paid the bill) even though the deceased had wished the excess[5]. Conversely the action did not lie if the thing was done so meanly as to be on the facts an insult to his memory[6]. It did not lie if the service was done out of piety without thought of repayment[7], or where there was no reason for intervention[8], or, in strictness, to one who thought he was *heres* and so was not acting for another[9]. Prohibition by the *heres* did not necessarily bar the claim, for he might be going to neglect the matter, and, e.g., a descendant not *heres* might reasonably think it ought to be done at the expense of the estate and so do it, not *donandi animo*[10]. The claim was a privileged debt, i.e. payable in preference to other unsecured debts, whether the claim was on the estate of the deceased or on that of the person liable[11].

Missus in possessionem. There were actions *in factum* to and against a creditor *missus in possessionem* for his duly incurred expenses and for profits received by him, and damage by his *dolus*[12]. There were many other cases of *missio in possessionem*[13], each with its own rules. In those cases in which the *missus* was not the interested party, the *actio negotiorum gestorum* and its *actio contraria* lay.

Analogous, but somewhat remotely, to common ownership was the case of disputed boundaries. The action, *finium regundorum*, was of the same double character, with an *adiudicatio*, but the quasi-contractual

1 *Ante*, p. 537. 2 11. 7. 31. 2; Lenel, *E.P.* 230. 3 11. 7. 12. 2. Payable out of the estate, h. t. 1, 14. 1. The Edict describes the person liable as "*is ad quem ea res pertinet.*" This is because, though primarily *heres* or *b. p.* is liable, there are other cases, e.g., on burial of a woman, the receiver of *dos* (11. 7. 20. 2) a deceased *filius* having no *heres*, the *pater* (P. 1. 21. 10). On this and other questions connected with this action, de Francisci, *La legitt. pass. n. az. funeraria* and other papers there cited; Levy, *Privatstr.* 33; Beseler, *Z.S.S.* 1924, 390. 4 E.g. 11. 7. 14. 13. 5 11. 7. 12. 5, 14. 6. 6 11. 7. 14. 10. Brini, *Rend. Acc. Ist. Bologna*, 1929 (*Sc. Mor.*), 80. 7 11. 7. 14. 7. 8 *Arg.* 11. 7. 14. 13. 9 11. 7. 14. 11, *ex causa*, 32, *utilis*. Possibly Byzantine, Biondi, *Compensazione*, 171. 10 11. 7. 14. 13, perhaps Justinian, Beseler, *Beitr.* 1. 65. 11 42. 5. 17. pr. 12 42. 5. 9. pr. *Heres* of *missus* liable only to extent of profit if it rested on *dolus*, h. l. 7, 8. 13 *Post*, § CCXLV.

points could not so readily arise. Still, where the judgement transferred part from one to the other, the loser was liable for *dolus* affecting the value of that part and for its fruits from *litis contestatio*[1]. Till then, if in good faith, he was in the position of a *bona fide possessor*[2]. It is limited in earlier law to the actual "*fines*" of a few feet between lands (not in cities[3]): these spaces the XII Tables excluded from *usucapio*. Whether in classical law the same remedy was applied to disputes affecting a wider area (*controversia de loco*) is disputed. Under Justinian it covers all such boundary cases[4].

Actio protutelae[5]. This action lay against one who had acted as *tutor* without due appointment. The obligations were similar to those of a *tutor*. Accounts were rendered in the same way[6]. The same care must be shewn[7]. Interest was due[8]. The Digest calls the action edictal, but it is probably a Byzantine invention, the case being essentially one of *negotiorum gestio* in classical law[9].

More important are the cases analogous to *condictio indebiti*[10], the primary application of the principle that a man was not to enrich himself at the cost of another. It cannot be said that there was any such general rule, but many cases were provided for by a *condictio sine causa*, using that name in its widest, perhaps the only classical, sense[11]. The chief cases were:

Condictio ob rem dati or *ob causam dati*[12], called under Justinian, *condictio causa data causa non secuta*[13]. Its main application was to the case which became the commonest type of innominate contract: a *res* was handed over for a return to be made. If that did not follow the *condictio* lay[14]. It had other applications, e.g. money given as *dos* where the marriage did not follow[15]. If the counter render became impossible without fault of the intended receiver, the dominant classical view was that *casus* released the receiver, so that the money or *res* could not be

1 10. 1. 4. 1, 2. 2 *Ib.* 3 Cicero, *Top.* 43. 4 Girard, *Man.* 672. 5 D. 27. 5; C. 5. 45. 6 C. 5. 45. 1. 7 27. 5. 4. 8 27. 5. 1. 8. 9 Pernice, *Z.S.S.* 1898, 163; Peters, *Z.S.S.* 1911, 263 *sqq.*; Partsch, *Negotiorum Gestio*, 62 *sqq.*, who makes it *n. g. utilis*. The name *protutelae* is no doubt a late coinage, but the texts suggest that it was in classical law a special action, designed primarily for the case of doubt if *gerens* was *tutor* or not, promised, not in the Edict on *negotiorum gestio*, but in the Edict on *tutela*, and called *actio negotiorum gestorum pro tutore* (P. 1. 4. 8). There seems no sufficient ground for thinking, with Partsch, that this name is interpolated. Any counter-claim of *gerens* was enforced by *actio n. g. contraria* (27. 5. 5) as was perhaps any such claim by a *tutor* (Partsch, *op. cit.* 47; *ante*, p. 164). 10 De Visscher, *La Condictio*, 82; Koschembar-Lyskowski, *Die Condictio*; Pflüger, *Condictio und kein Ende*; Betti, *Valore dommatica*, 55. 11 Even this name is not certainly classical. 12 C. 4. 6. Pomponius (D. 12. 6. 52) and Paul (h. t. 65. 2, 4) distinguish "*ob causam*" past and "*ob rem*" future. See h. t. 65. 3 and 12. 4. 1. 1, 2. Pflüger, *cit.*, holds all classical *condictio* to rest on *datio*, which involves his rejection of "*fieri*" in G. 4. 5 as a gloss. 13 12. 4 rubr. See C. 4. 6. 5, 6 where it is not treated as the name of the action. 14 19. 5. 5. 1. 15 C. 4. 6. 1. *Condictio* for recovery of *don. m. c.* is put by J. under this rubric, D. 12. 4. 12

recovered. But some classical jurists took the more equitable view that in cases of impossibility there should always be recovery and Justinian extended this doctrine by interpolations[1].

Condictio ob turpem causam, ob iniustam causam[2]. Available where money had been received for an immoral or illegal purpose or by some illegal or immoral action, the two cases being on the same footing. If the turpitude was on the side of the *dans* or of both, e.g. a thief gave money to prevent the giving of information[3], the money was irrecoverable, but it was otherwise if the receiver alone was a wrongdoer, e.g. money was paid under a promise induced by "*vis*[4]," or to prevent a crime[5], or to secure return of what ought to be returned without it[6]. Here it could be recovered whether the event in view of which it was given followed or not[7]. The risk was with the *turpis persona*[8].

Condictio furtiva[9]. This was quasi-contractual, since the *heres* was liable[10] and the action lay *de peculio* on theft by a slave[11]. The risk was on the thief and equally on his *heres*[12]. There was an analogous action, the *actio rerum amotarum*, available where one party to a marriage had taken property of the other, the notion of theft being excluded in such a case[13].

Condictio sine causa. Justinian gives this name to a group of cases, not all covered by the foregoing, in which a remedy was given for causeless enrichment[14]. There was no general principle: the cases mentioned in the title are those of promise without real *causa*, or *animus donandi*[15], of compensation paid by a *fullo* for lost goods which the owner had subsequently recovered[16], of money given for *dos* where the marriage did not follow[17]. The rules as to risk were no doubt as in *condictio indebiti*.

1 12. 4. 3. 3–5. pr.; 5. 4, 16; C. 4. 6. 10. See, Vangerow, *Pand.* 3, § 591. A *datio* where the thing has been damaged, or is subject to charges, does not liberate according to 46. 3. 33. 1. It is held, e.g. by Perozzi, *Ist.* 2. 408, that in classical law it discharged, with *actio doli* if the defect was due to the *dans*. Buckland, *Harvard L.R.* 1933, 1281. 2 In later law *turpis causa* seems to be purpose, *iniusta causa*, dishonest acquisition. 3 12. 5. 3, 4. 1; C. 4. 7. 5. 4 12. 5. 6, 7. 5 12. 5. 2. pr. 6 12. 5. 2. 1, 9. pr.; C. 4. 7. 6, 7. 7 12. 5. 5; C. 4. 7. 4, without interest. 8 C. 4. 7. 7. 9 *Post*, § CXCVIII, and Monro, *de furtis*, App. II. The line between this exceptional case where ownership has not passed, and *c. ex iniusta causa*, where it has, is blurred in the Digest. Pflüger, *Z.S.S.* 1911, 168 *sqq.* 10 13. 1. 5, 8. pr. 11 13. 1. 4, 19. 12 13. 1. 7. 2. 13 *Post*, § CXCVIII. An analogous *condictio* was suggested by some jurists where land was *vi possessum*. 13. 3. 2; 47. 2. 25. 1. 14 D. 12. 7; C. 4. 9. 15 12. 7. 1. 2. 16 12. 7. 2. 17 12. 7. 5. Other cases are mentioned, 7. 5. 5. 1; 19. 1. 11. 6; Inst. 2. 8. 2; C. 4. 9. 2. Koschembar-Lyskowski, *Condictio*, 1, §§ 4–11, sets out the various applications of the action including those here given and others. In many of them the case is one of what has become or been shewn to be an *indebitum* after the event, e.g. those in the text above, payment of one alternative without knowledge of right of choice (12. 6. 32. 3), paying without making the Falcidian deduction (35. 3. 1. 9: see *ante*, p. 342 and D. 35. 2. 1. 12, 31), payment of legacy or debt the *hereditas* being afterwards evicted (12. 6. 3). There are other cases, e.g. *condictio* given where there had been only a *ius retentionis*. See on these cases, *ante*, p. 543. Kipp, *Z.S.S.* 1921, 345. Effect on ownership of payment of

Condictio ex lege. This action seems to mean no more than the only text in the title says[1], that where a *lex* created an obligation and gave no special remedy, this *condictio* lay: it overlaps the previous cases, and is probably Byzantine.

Condictio ex poenitentia. This too seems to be Byzantine. In the system of *fiducia*, if one who had made a *fiducia cum amico* for any purpose changed his mind before it was carried out, he could recover the *res* by *actio fiduciae*[2]. When *fiducia* disappeared, this was replaced by a *condictio.* But the field of *fiducia cum amico* was narrow in the Empire. The only certain case is that of a slave transferred to be freed, and here there was not always a *fiducia.* The Digest gives *condictio ex poenitentia* in such cases and in transactions indirectly aiming at the same thing, e.g. gift of money to buy and free a slave, though the texts are not quite consistent[3]. It was given also where a man had undertaken a journey for reward paid beforehand: the text says there was a *locus poenitentiae* and implies that there was one in all such cases, i.e. in all innominate contracts[4] (for there is no *fiducia* here). The general proposition is certainly not true: there is no reason to suppose any general theory of *condictio ex poenitentia*[5].

In the second century the praetorian obligations enforced by the *actio quod iussu, institoria* and *exercitoria* appear to have been adopted into the civil law in the sense that a direct *condictio* was given as an alternative to these remedies, at least where the facts would have given a *condictio* had the slave been free and the actual contracting party was a member of the family[6]. In strictness this is a liability *ex contractu*, but it is not clear that it was so thought of: the point of view may well be an independent one. A man who sets his subordinate in the family in motion must accept the consequences. On this view it is quasi-contractual.

There remain a group of cases which can hardly be called analogous to those stated in the Institutes. Among these are:

Actio ad exhibendum. A proceeding calling for production preparatory to another action. It was often essential to a right of action that the other party be in possession of the subject of it, notably in *rei vindicatio*, to which this preliminary was primarily applicable[7]. But it was not confined to this[8]. It might be with a view to any real action, including

damages, *ante*, p. 468. If a *b. f. possessor* has disposed of the thing in good faith, and it has ceased to exist or been usucapted, it seems that there was a *condictio* for the price, *arg.* 3. 5. 48; 12. 1. 23; C. 4. 52. 1.

1 13. 2. 2 *Ante*, p. 431. 3 Buckland, *Slavery*, 632 *sqq.* 4 12. 4. 5. pr. 5 Gradenwitz, *Interpolationen*, 146. 6 Mitteis, *R.Pr.* 1. 227 (citing principal texts), Mayr, *Condictio*, 276. As to the so-called *condictio generalis*, *post*, § CCXXX. 7 10. 4. 1. As to the *formula* in the *actio ad exhibendum*, Lenel, *Z.S.S.* 1916, 116 *sqq.*; *E.P.* 223. 8 10. 4. 3. 1, "*cum multae sint causae.*"

hypothecaria[1], interdicts[2], *vindicatio in libertatem*[3], *actio furti*[4], *actio noxalis*[5], accusation of a slave for crime[6], examination of a slave by torture[7], and even in cases in which no litigation was directly in view, e.g. to facilitate the exercise of an option in *legatum optionis*[8]. Indeed it seems that any real economic interest, not otherwise protected, and not exceeding legal rights, would entitle to this action[9]. But further action was always contemplated[10]. It was available against any holder with the power of producing, whether *possessor* or mere *detentor*[11], and anyone who had *dolo malo* ceased to possess, e.g. by handing it to another[12], or by changing its character, e.g. by melting it down[13]. Where the claimant had an *interesse* both at *litis contestatio* and at judgement[14], holding by the defendant at time of judgement sufficed, though it began after *litis contestatio*, and conversely, if it was *bona fide* lost before judgement, the defendant was entitled to *absolutio*[15]. It was not available to or against a *heres* as such, though he might be liable or entitled on his own account[16].

The *obligatio* is quasi-contractual: there need have been no interference with right, and the plaintiff had not to prove that he was really owner. In fact, except in dolose abandonment of possession, which is not a primitive part of the scheme of the action, the obligation arose only on *litis contestatio*, much as in interdicts, a point which suggests a praetorian obligation. But as we know it the action is civil[17]. It was *in personam*[18] and the *formula* contained an *arbitrium* clause[19].

The obligation was to produce, satisfied by production, with the accessories[20], even in a damaged condition, though, if the damage was wilful or negligent, and the plaintiff proved to be entitled, there might be the ordinary remedies[21]. If, though technically in possession, the defendant was at the moment unable to produce, e.g. it was a slave *in fuga*, it was enough that he gave security for production when it became possible[22]. But the production must be "*in eadem causa.*" If the holder had usucapted since *litis contestatio* in the *actio ad exhibendum*, he would not be entitled to *absolutio* unless he was prepared to accept a *rei vindicatio* in which the *intentio* was dated back to *litis contestatio* in the *actio*

1 10. 4. 3. 3. 2 10. 4. 3. 5. 3 10. 4. 12. pr. 4 10. 4. 12. 2. 5 10. 4. 3. 7. 6 C. 3. 42. 2. 7 10. 4. 20. 8 10. 4. 3. 6; h. t. 10. 9 10. 4. 19. Cp. h. t. 5. 3–5, 18. H. t. 3. 9, which states the right very widely, is due to Justinian. Beseler, *Beitr.* 1. 1, 2. 128, maintains that in classical law it was a preliminary only to real action. For Lenel, *E.P.* 222, its original scope covered this and noxal actions, but it was occasionally used more widely in classical law. 10 10. 4. 3. 11. 11 10. 4. 3. 15–5. 12 10. 4. 5. 2, 14. 13 10. 4. 9. 3, 12. 3, but not where the *dolus* was his slave's without his privity. 14 10. 4. 7. 7. 15 10. 4. 7. 4, 5. 16 10. 4. 8, 12. 6. 17 19. 5. 16. 1. Lenel, *E.P.* 225. 18 10. 4. 3. 3. 19 Inst. 4. 6. 31. 20 10. 4. 9. 7, "*causa.*" 21 10. 4. 17; C. 3. 42. 7. Sabinus seems to have held that damage could come into account in *ad exhibendum*, 10. 4. 9. 3. 22 10. 4. 5. 6.

ad exhibendum (*dies repetita*)[1], and if delay in production had caused loss of a right, e.g. it was now too late to exercise an option[2], or for the slave whose production was claimed to enter on a *hereditas*[3], the defendant must make compensation.

As it seems impossible to find any positive basis for the classification, a large number of other cases might have found a place here. Such are the duties between patron and freedman[4], the obligation to give a *dos*[5], and the countless edictal liabilities. Many of these were negative, e.g. most of those enforced by interdict. But there were many others[6].

CLXXXVIII. We must now consider incidental rules of obligation, applicable mainly to contract and quasi-contract.

INTEREST. The rules as to rate of interest have been mentioned[7]: we have now to state the cases in which it was due. It might be due in any transaction by express agreement[8], a separate contract, ordinarily *stipulatio*[9]. But pact sufficed in *nauticum fenus*[10], in loans by cities[11], in later classical law in loans of fungibles other than money[12], and, under Justinian, in loans by bankers[13]. Further, in any *mutuum*, a pact for interest created an *obligatio naturalis*[14]. Where interest was due under these rules in a separate contract, the fact that from any cause the debt had ceased to be recoverable would not necessarily bar the claim for interest already due, except that none was due if the principal debt was void *ab initio*, and, under Justinian, if a debt was time-barred, a claim for interest was barred too[15]. Interest was due by law in some transactions, e.g. in sale, from the delivery of the goods[16], in debts to minors[17] and to the *Fiscus*[18], in some cases of *dos*[19], and in some charitable gifts[20]. A *socius* was entitled to interest on his money applied to firm purposes, and was conversely liable if he used money of the firm for his own purposes[21]. A mandatary or *negotiorum gestor* or *tutor* could claim for advances, and was liable for interest on money he held and neglected to invest, or used[22], and, as it seems, for money he ought to have got in, at least in late law[23]. Finally, interest was due from *mora* in all *bonae fidei* transactions, though it

1 10. 4. 9. 6. As to *diei repetitio*, *post*, § CCXLI. 2 10. 4. 10. 3 10. 4. 11. pr. 4 *Ante*, p. 88. 5 *Ante*, p. 107. 6 Restitutory interdicts require a positive act: some presuppose what is substantially a delict, but not all; see *post*, § CCXLVIII. But the obligations to give guarantees against possible damage of various kinds (*aquae pluviae arcendae*, *post*, § CCIII, *operis novi nuntiatio*, *post*, §§ CCIII, CCXLVI, *damni infecti*, *post*, § CCXLV, etc.) might be placed under this head, and the same may be said of the *actio metus* (*post*, § CCIII), and those on fraud on patron's rights (*ib.*) at least where the defendant is no party to the wrong. 7 *Ante*, p. 465. 8 19. 5. 24. 9 *Ib.*; P. 2. 14. 1. It might be a separate clause in the same *stipulatio*. 10 22. 2. 7. 11 22. 1. 30. 12 C. 4. 32. 11. 13 *Nov.* 136. 4. 14 C. 4. 32. 3; *post*, § CLXXXIX. 15 12. 6. 26; 22. 1. 7; C. 4. 32. 26. pr. 16 19. 1. 13. 20, *ante*, p. 493. 17 *Arg.* 40. 5. 26. 1. 18 22. 1. 17. 5. 19 C. 5. 12. 31. 20 C. 1. 3. 45. 4. 21 *Ante*, p. 509. 22 3. 5. 18. 4 37; 26. 7. 7. 8. 23 26. 7. 15.

ceased to run if the *mora* was purged by tender of what was due[1]. A similar rule applied in claims for *fideicommissa* and some forms of legacy; under Justinian, all forms[2].

Where the liability was not based on agreement, interest was recoverable only in the principal action, so that if payment was accepted without interest, or the debt was time-barred, the right to interest was lost[3].

Mora. Failure to discharge a legal duty on demand made at a proper time and place, sometimes called *mora ex persona*, as distinct from *mora ex re*, where "*dies interpellat pro homine*." But this latter expression is unwarranted. There was no *mora ex re*—in some cases, some effects of *mora* were produced where there was no formal *mora*, e.g. liability to interest on price from delivery of goods sold. The expression is suggested by a text which says that where there is no one from whom the demand can be made, there is *mora in re*[4]. But it is generally held that this case and that of a defendant who holds a thing by theft or similar delict, who is always in *mora*[5], were the only cases in which demand was not necessary[6].

The delay must be wrongful: there was no *mora* if the debtor was unable, through no fault of his own, to be at the place[7], or if he had reasonable grounds for doubting that the debt was due, provided, in this case, he was ready to litigate at once[8]. *Mora* or no *mora* was a question of fact rather than law: the *iudex* must decide it on all the facts[9]. The principal effects of *mora debitoris* were these:

1. The thing was at his risk (*perpetuatio obligationis*). This was modified, at least in later law, to the extent that he was not liable unless the destruction involved a loss to the creditor which would not have occurred if there had been no *mora*[10], not for an accident which would have happened equally if the *res* had been handed over, unless indeed (at least under Justinian) the creditor could shew that, if it had been delivered, he would have sold it, so that the loss would not have fallen on him[11]. The debtor in bad faith was liable for the highest value since the *mora*[12]. There was no liability if the loss was caused by the imputable fault of the other party[13].

1 22. 1. 1. pr. At local rates, *post*, § CCXXIX. 2 G. 2. 280; D. 30. 39. 1. 3 19. 1. 49. 1. 4 22. 1. 23. 1; cp. 22. 1. 32, 38. 1; 40. 5. 26. 1; Segrè, *St. Brugi*, 391. 5 13. 1. 8. 1. 6 *Contra* for cl. law, Siber, *R.R.* 2. 253, who holds that the requirement had many more exceptions; Gensmer, *Z.S.S.* 1924, 86, but in some of his cases the jurists are interpreting rescripts; Montel, *Mora del debitore* (rev. Felgentraeger, *Z.S.S.* 1931, 523. 7 12. 1. 5; 16. 3. 1. 22; 19. 1. 3. 9. Gensmer, *cit.*, on *culpa* as sometimes sufficient. 8 22. 1. 21, 24; 45. 1. 91. 3. 9 22. 1. 32. pr. On difficult questions where *mora* is material in *a. de pec.* etc., and as between principal and surety. Solazzi, *Riv. It. p. l. Sc. Giur.* 1919, 3; Riccobono, *Dal. dir. Rom.* 614; Brugi, *Ist.* 433. 10 4. 2. 14. 11; 10. 4. 12. 4; 16. 3. 14. 1 (all interp.). 11 6. 1. 15. 3 (prob. interp.). 12 13. 1. 8. 1. 13 As to history of matter and conflicting Mucian and Servian doctrine, Arnò, *Perpetuatio obligationis*.

2. He was responsible, but only in *bonae fidei* transactions[1], for fruits the creditor would have received[2], and for accessories.

3. He must pay interest in respect of money and other fungibles, in the same case, at local rates, not exceeding the legal maximum[3].

The creditor might be *in mora*, where he had not accepted a tender of performance made by the debtor, at a proper time and place, not a mere expression of willingness to perform, which might or might not be realisable[4]. The *mora* resulted from refusal, or absence at the agreed time and place, the fact of absence being notified in court by the debtor[5]. *Mora* of the creditor, like that of debtor, required fault. If refusal was due to reasonable doubt of the sufficiency of the tender, and he was prepared to litigate at once, he was not *in mora*[6]. The chief effects of his *mora* were:

1. The debtor was liable only for *dolus*[7] (even where liable for *culpa* before), and accordingly the *res* was at the risk of the creditor[8].

2. The creditor must pay any cost involved in care of the *res*[9].

3. Interest ceased to run if the money was deposited in custody of the court, but not otherwise, as the debtor still had the use of it[10].

Mora was purged, i.e. its consequences no longer operated and the original state of liability was restored, for the future, without prejudice to any rights of interest, etc., already accrued, if the party entitled renounced his right under the *mora*[11], or the debtor made a proper tender[12], or the defaulting creditor so presented himself to accept[13], or the debt was novated[14].

1 And in *fcc.* and some legacies—all under Just. 30. 39. 1; 22. 1. 3. 2 4. 2. 12. pr., 13. 3. 4. Even for such as would have been due to special activity if the creditor usually shewed this. 3 *Ante*, p. 465; sale, *ante*, p. 493. 4 46. 3. 39, 72. pr.; C. 8. 42. 9. 5 C. 4. 32. 6; D. 13. 5. 17; 46. 3. 72. pr.; C. 8. 27. 5. 6 46. 3. 72. pr.; 13. 5. 17. As to absence not due to his fault, 13. 5. 18. pr., which seems to mean that in such case there is no *mora* on either side. 7 17. 1. 37; 18. 6. 1. 3; 33. 6. 8. 8 See n. 7. 9 18. 6. 1. 3. 10 26. 7. 28; 22. 1. 1. 3, 7; C. 4. 24. 10; 4. 32. 19 (details of this *lex* due to J.). Stated only of money, but no doubt applying *mutatis mutandis* to other fungibles. It seems that in sale of specific things if the creditor refuses them, they are at his risk and the debtor, after notice, may throw them away (18. 6. 1. 3, 4, wine; h. t. 13, furniture). This it is denied in legacy of wine (33. 6. 8) and Gradenwitz, *Bull.* 1929, 53, holds that *effundere* merely meant discharge into a tank, which will, or may, much reduce its value. Classical law obscure. If tender was made *in iure* and refused, the Praetor would refuse the action (46. 3. 30). If tender was made out of court, and in other forms of *mora*, it does not seem that any penalties other than those in the text were incurred. See, however, Guarneri-Citati, *Contrib. alla doctrina della mora* (*Ann. Palermo*, 1925, 161; review by Ebrard, *Z.S.S.* 1927, 417) who holds that under J. refusal of tender at any stage barred any new action. 11 2. 14. 54. 12 18. 6. 18; both here *in mora*. 13 *Ib.* 14 13. 1. 17. Guarneri-Citati, *Contrib.*, *cit.* 11, holds that in classical law the *purgatio* was only by *exceptio* or *denegatio actionis*—in post-classical law, *ipso iure*. Accepted, Koschaker, *Festschr. für Hanausek*, 132, and Ebrard, *Z.S.S.* 1927, 422. Rejected, Bohaček, *Note Eseget.* 364. Guarneri-Citati, *cit.*, holds that in earlier classical law only tender purged, not *novatio*. But see Ebrard, *cit.* and reff. As to conditional novation, *post*, § CXCIV.

CLXXXIX. *Obligatio Naturalis.* Hitherto we have dealt only with civil and praetorian obligation. But in the Empire there was a new development. Any obligation contracted in accord with reason, though not in accord with accepted forms and requirements, might be given a modified validity. Not all such cases were so dealt with but there was a group, not numerous, and gradually formed, to which the conception of *obligatio naturalis* was applied. No action lay[1], but they could be made effective in other ways, not all to the same extent. The only rule clearly common to all was that payment made could not be recovered: a natural obligation always excluded *condictio indebiti*[2].

The whole conception is later than Labeo, but perhaps not much later[3], and it is generally held that its first application was recognition of an *obligatio naturalis* of a slave on his contract[4]. The chief cases were[5]:

(*a*) *Negotia* by a slave with his master or third persons. In general there was no question of a right in the former slave after freedom[6]: it is only from the point of view of liability that the question arose, except that his natural right against his master survived if he took his *peculium*[7], to the extent of barring *c. indebiti.* Subject to this, it arose, broadly speaking, on any transaction of the slave which would have been a valid contract if he had been free. Besides excluding *condictio indebiti* (*solutum non repeti*) it might be a basis for pledge, *fideiussio* or other surety, and perhaps novation[8], and, if on a verbal contract, it might be discharged by *acceptilatio*[9]. And it is doubtful whether judgement, apart from actual satisfaction, in *actio de peculio*, affected the liability[10].

(*b*) Transactions between *pater* and members of the same family. So long as the *filiusfamilias* was in the family the rules of *peculium* applied, but on release, if he took the *peculium*, he took with it any claim he had against the father, but only to the extent of *solutum non repeti*[11]. Where the liability was the other way no doubt the same rule applied as in the case of a slave. Where he contracted with an *extraneus* the *obligatio* was *civilis* and has already been considered[12].

1 It does not seem to have been available as set-off in classical law. 16. 2. 6 is shorn from a context in which the master is suing on a contract by a slave and the set-off is what is due from the slave, recoverable by *a. de pec.* 40. 7. 20. 2 must be read in the light of 15. 1. 49. 2. What may be set off is what is due from the *heres*, his master. It is a natural *obligatio* only because he is a slave and between master and slave this is ignored. In 46. 8. 8. 1 it is recovery of money paid. 2 46. 1. 16. 4. 3 Not clear that Javolenus (35. 1. 40. 3) and Seneca (*de ben.* 6. 4. 7) cited Girard, *Man.* 680, contemplate any legal liability, but it is clear in Neratius (12. 6. 41). See also Julian in 46. 1. 16. 4, etc. 4 Pernice, *Labeo*, 1. 150 *sqq.* 5 The cases are sometimes classified (Savigny, *Oblig.* §§ 9 *sqq.*), but this throws no light on the rules. 6 2. 14. 7. 18; 50. 17. 146. 7 12. 6. 64; apparently only to exclude *condictio indebiti.* 8 12. 6. 13. pr.; 44. 5. 1. 4; 46. 1. 35. 9 46. 4. 8. 4. 10 15. 1. 50. 2; 44. 2. 21. 4. 11 12. 6. 38; 4. 5. 2. 2. 12 *Ante*, p. 419.

(*c*) *Nudum pactum.* It is usually held that a nude pact did not create a natural obligation[1], but there were a few exceptions[2].

(*d*) *Sc. Macedonianum.* Action was barred on loan to a *filiusfamilias*, but there was a natural obligation. Payment could not be recovered[3], and there might be *novatio*, after he was *sui iuris*[4]. *Fideiussio* and hypothec seem not to have been void, but to have themselves created only a natural obligation[5]. It could not be used as set-off[6].

(*e*) *Pupilli* without *auctoritas* who had not profited. The texts conflict, but a natural obligation seems to have been admitted in later law; its extent is doubtful. It could not be used as set-off[7].

(*f*) Minors and interdicted *prodigi*. A minor who had obtained *restitutio in integrum*, one who in later law contracted without his curator's consent, and *prodigus* under interdict, were all probably bound by a *naturalis obligatio*, but its extent is not known[8].

(*g*) Civil bondsman and *filiafamilias*. These could not bind themselves in classical law: there may have been a natural obligation[9].

(*h*) Effect of *litis contestatio*. In many cases *litis contestatio* destroyed the old obligation, substituting for it the right under the action[10]. If this proceeded normally no question would arise, but it might not, and the question whether a natural obligation survived is material. If, e.g., judgement was not given within a certain time, it could not be given at all[11]. It is clear that there was a natural *obligatio* in this case with the usual effects[12]. Where the action was lost by *plus petitio* there was a natural obligation[13], as also where it was lost by error of the judge[14].

(*i*) *Capite minuti. Capitis deminutio* destroyed at civil law all contractual and quasi-contractual obligation. In *c. d. maxima* the present point did not arise; if the man was restored to his original position his obligation revived: if he was not he was free of all, even though pardoned. The same seems to be true of *c. d. media* if all the property was forfeited. If only part, he remained liable to action *pro parte*, and not beyond at

1 Girard, *Man.* 682, cites 45. 1. 1. 2; 46. 1. 56. pr. Riccobono, *Z.S.S.* 1922, 365 *sq.*, basing on the Gloss holds that under J. it did create one. See also Vašny, *St. Bonfante*, 4, 178. 2 Pacts for interest, no *c. indebiti*, 46. 3. 5. 2, hypothec good, 13. 7. 11. 3; pact promising master money for liberty, *expromissio* good, 16. 1. 13. pr.; as to C. 4. 14. 3, *ante*, p. 86; a slave's promise creates *obl. nat.* G. 3. 176 says it has not the force of a verbal obl. If so it is a pact and is another exception. And pact was always good as a defence. 3 12. 6. 40. pr.; 14. 6. 10. 4 C. 4. 28. 2. 5 14. 6. 9. 3, 4. 6 The fact that there was no *ob. naturalis* under the *Sc. Velleianum* shews how partial was the recognition of this kind of obligation. 12. 6. 40. pr. gives reasons. 7 12. 6. 41; 36. 2. 25. 1; 46. 3. 95. 4. 8 46. 3. 95. 3; C. 2. 23. 2; Bas. 26. 1. 25 (Heimbach, 3. 97). 9 G. 3. 104; *ante*, p. 134. 10 *Post*, § CCXXXV. 11 *Post*, § CCXXXII; G. 4. 104, 105. 12 46. 8. 8. 1. Machelard, *Obl. Naturelles*, 370. 13 20. 1. 27. Machelard, *cit.* 384. 14 See 12. 6. 28, 60. pr.

all[1]. In *c. d. minima* an *obligatio naturalis* survived, but in the most practical case, *adrogatio*, a better remedy was found[2].

More or less doubtful cases are those of a claim barred by lapse of time[3], a creditor deprived of his claim by way of penalty[4], and *confusio* between debtor and creditor[5], but these we need not here consider.

How far these cases are classical is doubtful. Opinion tends to hold all those not within the family as post-classical[6]. An extreme view makes the whole institution post-classical[7]. It would not follow that the solutions given are interpolated, but only that they would not turn on *naturalis obligatio*.

TRANSFER OF *OBLIGATIO*. As we have seen, *obligatio*, being of an intensely personal nature[8], was not thought of as transferable, but, in connexion with mandate[9], we saw how assignability was reached by an indirect method based on the conception of the assignee as a representative of the assignor, *procurator in rem suam*. We have also dealt with the automatic transfer of *obligatio* in various forms of universal succession[10], and in the case of guardianship, on the termination of the wardship[11].

A text in the Code allows *utilis actio* where a debt has been given as *dos* and assumes such an action where a debt has been sold[12]. Another

1 C. 8. 40. 1, *actiones utiles*, *ante*, p. 97. Desserteaux, *Mél. Cornil*, 1. 183, holds that for earlier classical law no *obl. nat.* survived *c. d. max* or *med.*, but there was gradual relaxation and in later law the debt practically still exists, sureties and the person in whom the property had vested being liable, so that whether the confiscation had involved *c. d.* or not there was always at any rate a *nat. obl. Ante*, p. 446. 2 *Ante*, p. 399; as to a woman passing into *manus*, G. 4. 80, *ante*, *ib.* 3 Machelard, *Obl. Nat.* 464; Windscheid, *Lehrb.* 2. § 289, n. 2; Girard, *Man.*, 683; *post*, § CXCII. Klingmüller, *Festschr. f. Dahn*, 55, denies any *nat. obl.* The fact that pledge is still good, C. 8. 30. 2, is due to the formulation of the *a. hypothecaria* in the Edict. 4 E.g., 12. 6. 19. pr. Machelard, *cit.* 512. 5 *Post*, § CXCII. 6 Pringsheim, *Z.S.S.* 1926, 350 and reff.; Perozzi, *Ist.* 2. 33, confines the notion for classical law to slave's transactions. The gradual extensions involve a new view of the meaning of the term. From *de facto* obligation it comes to mean something like moral obligation. Vašny, *St. Bonfante*, 4. 131, admits some other cases. 7 Siber, *Denkschr. f. Mitteis*, 1. But on his view that in classical law *obl. nat.* = *obl. iuris gentium*, see Pringsheim, *Z.S.S.* 1926, 350; Lauria, *Rev. It. p. l. Sc. Giur.* 1926, 149; Beseler, *Tijdschr.* 1928, 318; Arangio Ruiz, *Ist.* 375. The thesis assumes an absolute consistency among classical lawyers in the use of words, an improbable thing and especially so with such a word as *naturalis*, absence of movement of thought in the three classical centuries and Byzantine origin for whatever is not clearly classical. 8 *Ante*, p. 407. Even where the contract affected the enjoyment of land the benefit did not pass with the land. Where a man let a farm with agreements as to proper cultivation, and died leaving the land away from the *heres*, the legatee could not enforce the covenants, nor could the *heres* for lack of *interesse*. If a legatee of land ousted the tenant, his remedy was only against the *heres*. It was an obligation of the deceased (19. 2. 32). 9 *Ante*, p. 520. 10 *Ante*, §§ CX, CXLI *sq.* 11 *Ante*, p. 155. Texts record many cases in which *A*, under a liability to *B*, may release himself by transfer, in this form, of actions he has against third parties (e.g. 10. 2. 18. 5; 47. 2. 14. pr.). Many of these probably interpolated, Beseler, *Beitr.* 3. 172 *sqq.* 12 C. 4. 10. 2.

gives it on legacy of a debt[1]. Another, dealing with sale of debt, assumes a mandate[2]. The first text probably assumes a mandate. The second excludes mandate and its *actio utilis* is commonly thought to be due to Justinian.

There were cases, too numerous to be set out in detail, in which one in whom a right of action was vested was compellable to transfer it to another, by this indirect method (*cedere, mandare, transferre actionem*[3]). As familiar instances may be cited the vendor, who must cede, as part of the *commoda rei*, actions acquired in respect of the *res* since the sale[4], the creditor paid by a surety, in certain cases[5], the mandatary, who must cede all actions acquired in executing the mandate[6], the pledge creditor, who must cede actions he has acquired, as part of the *commoda rei*[7], and so forth.

Where this *cessio* could be claimed as of course, the actual claim and transfer might seem an idle form and the person entitled have been allowed to proceed as if he had had a transfer. Some steps were indeed taken in this direction, the action being however not one in which *cessio* was feigned (*actio ficticia*), but an *actio utilis suo nomine*, usually an *actio in factum*[8].

To this automatic transfer the name *cessio legis* has been given. The notion no doubt starts from the cases of a transfer which had become inoperative before it was acted on[9], but it gradually extended to cases where there had been no transfer. Thus as early as Pius such an action was allowed to a buyer of a *hereditas*[10], to *heres ab intestato* for legacies paid under a will afterwards upset[11], to *tutor* sued for negligence, against *contutores*[12]. So, if a depositee redeposited, the first depositor had *actio utilis* against the second depositee[13]. Caracalla gave a judgement creditor, where there was nothing to seize, an *actio utilis* against his debtor's debtor[14]. Where a gift was to be restored to a third person, Diocletian gave him an *actio utilis*[15]. Later law allowed it under agreement to sell, or legacy of, a debt[16]. Justinian gave the principal an *actio utilis ex empto* where a procurator had sold, and to a *fideicommissarius* who had paid off a pledge which should have fallen on the *heres*[17]. But these cases represent no general principle. It is clear on the texts that in general,

1 C. 6. 37. 18. 2 C. 8. 41. 1. 3 Schulz (*Z.S.S.* 1906, 82) in a careful study of the principles of forced *cessio* (he does not discuss *cessio legis*, feigned *cessio*) gives a list of over 60 texts dealing with such cases and the list is not exhaustive. 4 47. 2. 14. pr. 5 46. 1. 17; 46. 3. 76. 6 17. 1. 20. pr., 27. 5. 7 20. 1. 21. 2; 20. 5. 7. pr. 8 Cuq, *Man.* 634; Steiner, *Datio in solutum*, 127. 9 Mandate, *ante*, p. 520. 10 2. 14. 16. pr.; C. 4. 39. 5. 11 5. 2. 8. 16. 12 27. 3. 1. 13. 13 Coll. 10. 7. 8. 14 C. 4. 15. 2. Similar but wider right of the *fiscus*, h. t. 3, 4. 15 Vat. Fr. 286; C. 8. 54. 3. 16 C. 4. 15. 5; C. 4. 39. 7–9; C. 6. 37. 18. 17 19. 1. 13. 25; D. 30. 57.

where *cessio* had not been actually taken, there was no right to sue: surety is a well-known instance[1].

CXC. THE THEORY OF *CULPA*. *Dolus* or intentional damage is not perfectly easy to define, but as it was in itself a delict it will be considered later[2], and can here be left with the remark that in contract and quasi-contract it always created liability.

Culpa[3] was failure to observe the standard of conduct which the law required, varying in the different cases. In the texts we get degree of *culpa* represented in three ways: *culpa* (*culpa levis*), failure to shew *diligentia maxima*, failure to act as, in the circumstances, a *bonus paterfamilias* would act[4]; *culpa lata*, failure to shew any reasonable care, *non intelligere quod omnes intelligunt*[5]; *culpa levis* in another sense, called by moderns *culpa levis in concreto*, not to shew the same *diligentia* as the party ordinarily did in his own affairs[6]. The first two are objectively defined, but the last is taken from a different, a subjective point of view. It was not a distinct degree of *culpa*, for it might conceivably be greater or less than either of the others. A very punctilious man might fall short of his standard on occasion, while still shewing the care of a *bonus paterfamilias*, and a worthless man might satisfy this standard while shewing less care than a reasonable man would. But in fact this standard was not thought of as lower than that expressed by *culpa lata*[7].

The general effect of the texts on liability in particular cases may be stated in the following rather confusing propositions, omitting for the present the *stricti iuris* relations.

1. A party benefiting by the transaction was liable for *culpa levis*, e.g. both parties to sale, hire, pledge, and innominate contracts, the depositor, the commodatary and the principal in *negotiorum gestio*[8].

2. One who did not benefit was liable only for *dolus*, and, according to some texts, for *culpa lata*: *culpa lata dolo aequiparatur*[9].

3. In some cases a party was liable for *culpa levis in concreto*. In some of these, *tutela*, *heres* under *fideicommissum* and depositee[10], we

1 41. 2. 49. 2; C. 8. 40. 11; 45. 1. 126. 2; 14. 3. 1, etc. There could be no transfer of this sort by the debtor except by *novatio*, involving consent of creditor. There were of course cases in which a man took over a debt, and was really *procurator* (*cognitor*) *in rem suam*, e.g. 42. 1. 4. pr. But the creditor is not affected, though *litis contestatio* will produce *consumptio litis*, 46. 3. 23.
2 *Post*, § CCIII.
3 A wider sense in which it means any failure in duty, e.g. under the *l. Aquilia*, is not material here.
4 18. 6. 3: 13. 6. 18. pr. (*culpa levissima*, 9. 2. 44. pr.). It has recently been maintained (Kunkel, *Z.S.S.* 1925, 266, that the whole conception of *diligentia* and *diligens paterfamilias* is "subjective" and entirely unknown to classical law. See, hereon, Buckland, *St. Bonfante*, 2. 87.
5 50. 16. 213. 2.
6 10. 2. 25. 16, as opposed to *culpa levis in abstracto*.
7 E.g. 24. 3. 24. 5.
8 13. 6. 5. 2; 50. 17. 23; Coll. 10. 2. 1.
9 11. 6. 1. 1; 16. 3. 32; 36. 4. 5. 15; 50. 16. 226. The actual maxim is not Roman.
10 27. 3. 1. pr.: 36. 1. 23. 3; 16. 3. 32; Rotondi, *Scr. Giur.* 2. 100.

should expect liability for *dolus* only, and so some texts put it[1]. In others, common ownership, husband dealing with *dos*, *societas*[2], we should expect liability for *culpa levis*, and some texts lay this down[3].

4. In some cases in which on principle the liability was for *dolus*, and is so stated, other texts state a liability for *culpa levis*, e.g. mandate, *tutela* and *cura*[4].

5. The *negotiorum gestor*, though it was essential that the *gestio* should not be for his benefit, was liable for *culpa levis*[5].

6. The state of the texts makes it probable that the expressions *culpa lata*, *culpa levis*[6], were not used technically to denote degrees of *culpa* till the Byzantine age.

On this story, a record of historical changes, there are several remarks to be made.

(*a*) The line between *dolus* and *culpa* is not so sharp as it looks. In both of them external standards must be applied; the state of mind must be inferred from conduct. If a man's standard in business affecting another was plainly below what we expect in ordinary life, or of what he shewed in his own business, it may be called carelessness, but the suggestion of bad faith is obvious especially in the latter case. Slight carelessness is to be expected occasionally, and does not suggest bad faith. Thus, if damage occurred, *culpa levis* was presumed though of course it might be disproved, but the presumption of *dolus* (or *culpa lata*) was never made[7]; the facts relied on must be proved. We are told by Celsus that it is not good faith to shew in dealings affecting others less care than in one's own affairs, and the same text shews similarly that it is hard to distinguish between *culpa lata* and *culpa levis in concreto*: to shew in such matters less care than you do in your own is not reasonable conduct[8]. It has been suggested that the only difference between *culpa lata* and *culpa levis in concreto* is in the burden of proof. The former must be proved; the latter is *prima facie* presumed[9]. But this would still leave the conflicts in the texts.

(*b*) It has been shewn[10] that *culpa* originally meant active conduct—

1 26. 7. 7. 2; 30. 108. 12; 13. 6. 5. 2; 16. 3. 1. 10, etc. 2 10. 2. 25. 16; 17. 2. 72; 23. 3. 17. pr. 3 17. 2. 52. 2; 24. 3. 18. 1; 10. 3. 26. 4 17. 1. 10. pr.; Coll. 10. 2. 3; D. 50. 17. 23; 26. 7. 7. pr.; 27. 3. 1. pr.; 26. 7. 25. pr. Thus for *tutela* we get the liability stated in all three ways. 27. 3. 1. pr.; 26. 7. 7. pr., 41; C. 2. 18. 20. 5 3. 5. 3. 9; *ante*, p. 538. 6 Neither expression occurs in juristic texts before Justinian. Coll. 12. 5. 2 gives *lata neglegentia*, in a criminal matter. See p. 568, n. 4 and Kuebler, in Larner, *Rechtsidee und Staatsgedanke*, 63. 7 22. 3. 18. 1. 8 16. 3. 32, interp. in part. It is difficult to believe with Lenel, *Z.S.S.* 1917, 277, that the whole passage represents only Byzantine thought. The classical rule expressed seems to be that what purports to be negligence may be so gross as to raise an irresistible presumption of *dolus*. 9 C. 4. 24. 5. 10 Mitteis, *R.Pr.* 1. 322.

culpa in faciendo; negligent omission (*culpa in non faciendo*) being *neglegentia*, to which *diligentia* is the opposite[1].

(*c*) We are several times told[2] that *culpa lata* is on a level with *dolus* and this was clearly so for Justinian's time. But the whole conception of *culpa lata* is late[3]. Modestinus, in the *Collatio*, dealing with several contracts, evidently knows only one degree of *culpa*[4]. *Culpa lata* has little to do with contract; most of the allusions to it are in connexion with criminal law or quasi-contract (especially *heres* and *tutor*), or in the heterogeneous mass of praetorian liabilities[5]. The only direct allusions to it in relation to specific contracts are one or two on deposit[6], all suspicious, one in *precarium*, which also looks interpolated[7], one on mandate more than suspected[8], and one on the sale of a *hereditas* also doubtful[9]. Probably in classical law a gross failure in care was apt to be regarded as *dolus*, as Celsus suggests and Paul explicitly says[10].

(*d*) The cases in which one who did not benefit was liable for *culpa levis* were mostly late extensions of liability, dating, it may be, from the end of the second century[11]. They were cases of confidential relations and it is said that this was the cause of the increased liability[12].

(*e*) There was a group of contractual and quasi-contractual actions condemnation in which involved *infamia*. Such were *pro socio*, *fiduciae*, *mandati*, *depositi* and *tutelae*. In most of these cases texts give a liability for *culpa*, either *in abstracto* or *in concreto*: in some cases we find both. Mere negligence should hardly have such an effect. It has been suggested that *infamia* ensued only where the condemnation was for *dolus*[13], but no such limit is indicated. A better view[14] is that in earlier classical law these actions lay only for *dolus* and that the larger liability is either interpolated or a development of late classical law, some cases of what texts call lack of *diligentia* being readily construable as breaches of good faith[15].

1 E.g., 50. 17. 23. The distinction survives in *stipulatio*, *post*, p. 559. 2 44. 7. 1. 5, etc. 3 Mitteis, *cit.* 334, analyses the cases in which it is found. 4 Coll. 10. 2. 1. Lenel holds, with great probability (*Z.S.S.* 1917, 263 *sqq.*), that the expressions *culpa levis*, *lata*, used technically to express degrees of negligence, are post-classical. His article is a reply to Binding, who in *Normen* (2) 2. 711, and again *Z.S.S.* 1918, 1, maintains that these expressions are classical but that they denote originally—and in the Digest—not degrees of negligence, but two kinds of "*Schuld*" short of *dolus*, *levis* being negligence, *lata*, intentional conduct, without self-seeking fraudulent intent. It is difficult to reconcile the view that the terms do not, for Tribonian, represent degrees of negligence with, e.g., 21. 1. 31. 12; 17. 1. 29. pr. 5 Mitteis, *cit.* 334. 6 16. 3. 32; 44. 7. 1. 5; C. 4. 34. 1 = Coll. 10. 8, where *culpa lata* is not mentioned. 7 43. 26. 8. 6. Not contemplated as a contract. 8 17. 1. 29. pr. 9 18. 4. 2. 5. 10 16. 3. 32; 50. 16. 226 (? interp.). No doubt (Lenel, *cit.* 288), in the original not stated with such generality, but with reference to the facts of a case. 11 Mitteis, *cit.* 330. 12 See, however, *ante*, p. 516, as to mandate. 13 E.g. Bertolini, *Obblig.* (*Parte Sp.*) 785. 14 Mitteis, *cit.* 324. 15 In *tutela* it may possibly be due only to Justinian, but it is more probably late classic.

The transition to the rule of liability for *culpa* was a gradual one not complete till Severus.

(*f*) The cases of *diligentia quam suis rebus, culpa levis in concreto,* mentioned in the texts seem to be *fiducia, societas,* common ownership, *tutela,* husband as to *dos, fideicommissum* and deposit[1]. The last two are due to Justinian and do not even represent the law of his time as elsewhere stated, except so far as, in the actual case, the failure to act as carefully as in his own affairs was in fact *dolus*[2]. In *tutela* some of the later texts make a *tutor* liable for *culpa* simply, and it may be that the liability for *culpa levis in concreto* was a stage in the transition from liability merely for *dolus* to liability for *culpa*[3]. As to *fiducia* the rule is laid down generally[4]. In *societas* it seems to have been the settled rule from Gaius onwards[5]. In the other cases, *dos* and community, principle requires liability for *culpa,* and it may be[6] that the lessened liability expresses a view, late classic or Byzantine, that in an enduring relation the other standard is unfair. In all the cases in which the rule is well evidenced it is in part the defendant's own affair.

Among *stricti iuris* relations, in *mutuum* and the contract *literis* no question of *culpa* arose. In *stipulatio* to give a certain thing the promisor was liable only for *culpa in faciendo,* a survival of the old conception of *culpa*[7], and only for such as made delivery impossible, not, e.g., where his act had made the *res* less valuable but still deliverable[8]. Of course the *stipulatio* might be so framed as to express any liability the parties wished, and the texts usually consider not the liability on *stipulatio,* but that on the particular *stipulatio* under discussion; the actual words were material. Apart from this there seems to have been no remedy for negligence, or for active *culpa* which merely lessened the value of the thing. If there was *dolus, actio doli* lay[9], and gross negligence would readily be construed as *dolus.* In *stipulatio faciendi* the rule seems to be that the care of a *bonus paterfamilias* was required, but textual evidence is scanty[10]. In *c. sine causa* the rules were as in *stipulatio dandi*[11], while in *c. furtiva* all risks were on the person liable; *fur semper in mora est*[12].

1 The texts appear to be 16. 3. 32; 10. 2. 25. 16; 17. 2. 72; 18. 6. 3; 23. 3. 17. pr.; 24. 3. 24. 5; 27. 3. 1. pr.; 36. 1. 23. 3; 44. 7. 1. 4; Inst. 3. 25. 9. In 26. 7. 33 the restriction is only apparent. 2 16. 3. 32; 36. 1. 23. 3; cp. 30. 108. 12. 3 *Ante,* p. 156; Lusignani considers the rule in all cases interpolated, *Studi sulla responsibilità per custodia,* 2. 97. 4 Coll. 10. 2. 1. The reason assigned is that both benefit, true in *f. cum creditore,* perhaps the only case existing when the text was written, but not in *f. cum amico;* no doubt whichever benefited was liable for *culpa.* 5 17. 2. 72. 6 Mitteis, *cit.* 333. 7 P. 5. 7. 4; D. 45. 1. 91. pr., *sqq.* 8 4. 3. 7. 3. 9 *Ib.* 10 45. 1. 137. 2, 3. 11 See 12. 6. 65. 8; 39. 6. 39 (Girard, *Man.* 697, 698). 12 13. 1. 8, 16; as to legacy *ante,* p. 539.

CXCI. *Custodia.* This is a conception which gives much trouble. In many texts *custodia* (*custodire*) appears in its plain meaning of setting a watch or guard[1]. These cases are unimportant. But there are texts in which it is used to denote a certain obligation "*custodiam praestare*," meaning something more than to set a guard. This obligation, whatever it may have been, is stated more or less explicitly in a number of cases, e.g. commodatary[2], usufructuary[3], vendor[4], *nauta, caupo, stabularius* (at least in some cases[5]), etc. It seems to mean obligation to prevent theft and according to some writers, damage by third parties[6]. But the extent and history of this obligation are the subject of acute controversy. In some texts it appears as an absolute obligation to prevent the theft, i.e. responsibility to the owner if the thing is stolen, without reference to negligence[7], and this point of view seems to be represented by Gaius, who tells us that commodatary and *fullo* had *actio furti* on account of their responsibility if the thing was stolen, and the owner had none, as he had no *interesse*[8], and says nothing of negligence. In other texts it appears as *diligentia maxima* applied to the care of the thing against thieves[9], which is in keeping with the evolution of *culpa* from an original meaning confined to acts of commission, negligence leading to damage being separately named as *negligentia*, and avoidance of it as *diligentia*: the obligation to the same extent to prevent harmful intervention by third persons would be called the obligation "*custodiam praestare*." There are texts which, speaking of it as an absolute obligation, base it in some cases upon express agreement[10]. And while some texts which treat it as an absolute liability have evident signs of interpolation[11], some texts which speak of it as only an aspect of *diligentia* are open to the same suspicion[12].

Many interpretations are possible, and there are wide differences of opinion. On one view, in all the above cases, and in others (in which the existence of the obligation, apart from its extent, is very imperfectly evidenced), the classical law imposed an absolute liability, and Justinian, by systematic interpolation, cut this down to *diligentia in custodiendo*, not without leaving traces of the older doctrine. Another diametrically

1 E.g. Coll. 10. 7. 4; D. 6. 1. 21. 2 13. 6. 5. 5. 3 7. 9. 2. 4 18. 6. 3; 19. 1. 36, 47. 2. 14. pr. 5 4. 9. 1. 8; 47. 2. 14. 17 *inf.* 6 See Lusignani, *Responsibilità per Custodia*, 2. 49. Held by, e.g., Haymann, *Z.S.S.* 1919, 194; Perozzi, *Ist.* 2. 166; Collinet-Giffard, *Précis*, 2. 181; Vašny, *Custodia*, 108. The view seems inconsistent with 9. 2. 11. 9; 13. 6. 19; 19. 2. 41; 9. 2. 57. In favour, 9. 1. 4, by analogy. Some are made to support it by supposing alterations, e.g. 19. 2. 41; 19. 1. 36; 36. 4. 5. 22. Vašny *cit.* avoids the difficulty of 9. 2. 11. 9, which refuses the borrower the Aquilian action, by supposing the liability for *damnum* conditional on cession of the Aquilian, but neither the limitation nor the liability itself is evidenced. 7 E.g. 4. 9. 1. 8. 8 G. 3. 205–207. 9 E.g. 18. 1. 35. 4. 10 *Ib.*; 4. 9. 1. 8. 11 E.g. 13. 6. 5. 15. Lusignani, *cit.* 1. 62. 12 E.g. 18. 6. 3. See Berlin stereotype edition.

opposed opinion is that classical law knew no such obligation apart from *diligentia*, except as created by express undertaking, but Justinian has interpolated many texts so as to make the obligation absolute[1]. It is not obvious that the meaning must be the same in all cases, and it is clear that an absolute liability "*custodiam praestare*" might be imposed by special agreement and was so imposed almost as a matter of course in the case of carriers[2]. The same may have been true of *fullo* and *sarcinator*[3], and it is not unreasonable to impose such an obligation as a matter of law on a commodatary[4]. This would account for the language of Gaius who gives commodatary and *fullo* an *actio furti* in any case[5], which seems illogical unless there was a corresponding obligation to compensate the *dominus* in every case.

The whole question must be treated as yet unsolved, but Lusignani seems to have shewn[6] that no such absolute liability existed in classical law in the cases of vendor *conductor rei* and in general and that the extreme doctrine applying the absolute liability over a wide range of cases does not seem probable in itself or indicated by the texts[7]. So important a liability might be expected to be in the classical texts, but they repeatedly state *dolus* and *culpa* as limits for liability apart from special agreement[8]. *Custodia* as a form of liability occurs rarely, and never with a clear indication that it involves insurance against theft and damage[9].

CXCII. EXTINCTION OF OBLIGATION. The modes of extinction of *obligatio* may be classified as Involuntary or Voluntary, and as Civil or Praetorian. For clearness, the first classification will be adopted.

1 Lusignani, *cit.* 1. 1–23, for statement and criticism of various opinions as to the rule and its historical changes. 2 D. 4. 9. 3 The liability attached by English law to the trades of carrier and innkeeper, for loss of goods, without proof of privity or negligence, does not however apply to other trades. 4 See 13. 6. 5. 5. 5 G. 3. 205 *sqq.* 6 *Op. cit.* 7 See, however, for a far-reaching liability, Seckel, Heumann-Seckel, *Handlexicon*, s.v. *custodia*. Kuebler (*Berliner Festschrift für Gierke*, 2. 235 *sqq.*; *Z.S.S.* 1917, 73; *ib.* 39. 172) arrives at the following as the classical scheme. One who does not benefit is liable only for *dolus*. Where both benefit each is liable for *culpa*. One who alone benefits is liable for *custodia* also and in some cases for all risks. Haymann (*Z.S.S.* 1919, 167 *sqq.*) considers liability for *custodia* in the technical sense to have applied to commodatary, the worker for hire (*fullo, sarcinator*), and to *nautae caupones stabularii*. Vašny, *cit.*, finds it in borrower, *fullo*, *horrearius*, *nauta*, etc. and vendor, whose ownership he regards as immaterial to his *a. furti*. Arangio Ruiz, *Ist.* 349; *Responsab. contratt.* 67, has an interesting view of the matter. *Custodia*, as an absolute liability, represents a phase in the development of the notion of *culpa* as a basis of liability, the starting point having been liability for *dolus*. *Culpa* as a general basis of liability is rather late. He does not regard the absolute liability as proved in more than a few cases, and the notion of *culpa* affords it a moral justification. The scheme is attractive, but the generalisation of *culpa* must be earlier than he makes it. The dissertation of J. B. Pâris (*La responsabilité pour la custodia*) associates absolute liability with *actiones in factum*, so that it fades out as the remedies become *b. f. iudicia*. 8 P. 2. 16. 1; Coll. 10. 2, etc. 9 G. 3. 206, 207; P. 2. 4. 3.

The principal involuntary modes are:

(*a*) Supervening impossibility[1], of which destruction of the subject-matter is the typical case[2]. This did not discharge if, at the time of the destruction, the debtor was already *in mora*[3], or the destruction was by his act or with his privity, *dolo* or *culpa* (where he was liable for *culpa*), with knowledge that the obligation existed[4], or, in *stricti iuris* relations, if it occurred after *litis contestatio*[5]. The texts do not deal with other cases of supervening legal or physical impossibility, to which the same principles appear to apply[6].

(*b*) Death. Death of the creditor did not in general affect the obligation, except where it brought the rules of impossibility into play, but we have seen exceptions in *adstipulatio*[7], *societas* and mandate[8]. Here, death ended the contract, and till Justinian the *heres* of a woman with a claim for *dos* could not sue[9]. Death of the debtor was also ineffective, with exceptions and modifications already noted in *societas*, mandate, *sponsio* and *fidepromissio*[10]. And a *heres* was not liable in a real action except so far as he had himself possessed, not, for instance, where the deceased had ceased to possess but was still liable[11].

(*c*) *Capitis deminutio minima* of a creditor, as a rule, simply transferred his right to the person[12] into whose *potestas* he passed, but this belongs rather to the subject of succession otherwise than on death[13]. *Capitis deminutio minima* of the debtor extinguished his contractual and other non-penal obligations at civil law, subject to praetorian reliefs already dealt with in the same connexion[14].

(*d*) Prescription. Actions might be barred by lapse of time. The civil law admitted this only in a few cases, but many praetorian actions were limited to an *annus utilis*. The matter is one for the law of procedure[15]; here it is enough to say that leaving out of account surety, which was under special rules already considered[16], prescription began, in general, to run from the time when the action could have been brought[17], i.e. the first *dies utilis*, but it was delayed till puberty of the plaintiff[18], and, in late law, in other than *actiones perpetuae* (then limited to 30 years), till a minor plaintiff was of full age[19]. It was interrupted, and must begin again, if the debtor gave any acknowledgement[20], and it ceased to run on

1 Ferrini, *Opere*, 3. 370. 2 Applies only to specific things—*genera non pereunt*. 45. 1. 37, "*certos nummos*." 3 *Ante*, p. 550. 4 Inst. 3. 19. 2; D. 45. 1. 83. 5; *heres* and legatee, *ante*, p. 348. 5 16. 3. 12. 3. 6 Alternative obligations, *post*, p. 566. 7 *Ante*, p. 444. 8 *Ante*, pp. 510, 517. In *societas* and mandate not as to existing liabilities. 9 Ulp. 6. 7. 10 *Ante*, pp. 445, 510, 517. 11 6. 1. 42; see 10. 4. 12. 6. A rule of late law in *vindicatio*, *ante*, p. 258. 12 G. 3. 82 *sqq*. 13 *Ante*, §§ CXLI *sq*. 14 Penal liabilities not affected, 4. 5. 2. 3; *post*, § CXCVI. As to *capitis deminutio maxima* and *media*, *ante*, p. 553. Here, too, penal liabilities were not affected, 4. 5. 2. 3. 15 *Post*, § CCXXXIII. 16 *Ante*, § CLVI. 17 C. 7. 39. 3. 1. 18 C. 7. 39. 3. 1a; C. 7. 40. 2. 19 C. 2. 40. 5. 1. 20 C. 7. 39. 7. 5a.

litis contestatio, in classical law[1], and the institution of legal proceedings under Justinian[2]. It may have been suspended if from any cause the ordinary sittings of the courts were suspended. It is disputed whether its running, having once begun, was suspended if from any cause action became impossible[3], but if a debtor was absent and so could not be sued, interruption could be caused in later law by notice to a court[4].

The lapse of a principal action might destroy subsidiary claims, though they arose at a different time. Thus a surety was released if the debt was time-barred[5], and claims for interest were similarly barred to the extent already stated[6].

(*e*) *Compensatio*, to be discussed later[7].

(*f*) *Lex*. There were several cases, into which we need not go, in which the law deprived a man of his right by way of penalty, e.g. where a creditor seized the thing by force[8].

(*g*) *Duae lucrativae causae*. Two lucrative causes of acquisition could not exist in respect of the same thing and the same person[9]. If the *res*, being due on, e.g., legacy and gift, or two legacies, had been received under one, there was no claim even to the value under the other[10]. But both must be gratuitous and the *res* must have been received, not its value[11], and any difference might be claimed[12]. Thus if the legacy was simple and it was received by the gift, under some charge, the difference in value could be claimed[13]. The rule is often based on impossibility: the texts do not say this, and it is not more possible because he has paid for the *res*. It is replied that there was equitable relaxation; he was entitled to be reimbursed what it had cost him[14]. Some writers treat the rule as an interpretation of the donor's intent[15].

(*h*) *Confusio*. Where the right and liability vest in the same person[16], the case being regarded, though not quite consistently, as one of auto-

1 12. 2. 9. 3. 2 C. 7. 40. 2. 1. 3 I.e. whether the time was *utile*, *ratione cursus*, or only *ratione initii*. The latter view seems the better, the other being difficult to reconcile with the existence of *restitutio in integrum* where an action had become time-barred by absence (*post*, § CCXLIV). Girard, *Man*. 773 (citing Ubbelohde, *Berechnung des Tempus utile*); Dernburg, *Pandekten*, 1. § 90, and for a different view, Savigny, *System*, 4. 400. 4 C. 7. 40. 2. 5 *Ante*, p. 446. 6 *Ante*, p. 549; C. 4. 32. 26. pr. As to *naturalis obligatio* surviving *praescriptio*, *ante*, p. 554. 7 *Post*, § CCXXXVIII. 8 *Post*, § CXCIX. 9 44. 7. 17; Inst. 2. 20. 6. 10 Inst. 2. 20. 6. 11 30. 108. 4 is corrupt. It seems to make the second gift void, though the first has not yet operated. It deals primarily with *legatum debiti* (*alieni*). Schulz, *Z.S.S.* 1917, 176, dealing with the whole question of concurrent obligations. See also Beseler, *Beitr*. 4. 326. 12 Inst. 2. 20. 9. 13 45. 1. 83. 6. The Digest says, in words due to Justinian, that even if under one will he has the *res*, he can get it under the second if the testator so intended, 32. 21. 1. In the Inst. the contrary is stated, Inst. 2. 20. 6 *in f*. 14 Dernburg, *Pand*. 2. § 68. For Ferrini (*Opere*, 3. 385) the limitation of the rule to *lucrativae causae* is due to Julian. 15 This would justify 32. 21. 1 as against Inst. 2. 20. 6. Discussion of various views, Windscheid, *Lehrb*. 2. § 343a; cp. 50. 17. 139. 1. 16 46. 3. 107.

matic payment. A common case was that of one party being *heres* to the other, but it might also occur, e.g., by entry on *societas omnium bonorum*, or where a noxal creditor acquired the guilty slave. It was not really discharge since if the *hereditas* was sold as such the right revived[1], and if one correal debtor was *heres* to the party on the other side, the debt remained as against the others[2], and while *confusio* affecting the principal debtor released a surety, the converse was not true[3]. *Confusio* might occur on the side of debtors or creditors only, e.g. where one of joint debtors or creditors inherited from another. He retained the two rights, or two liabilities, though satisfaction of one discharged the other. But if they were not equally advantageous, e.g. one of them had a security, the less advantageous was extinct[4]. If a surety became *heres* to a debtor, or *vice versa*, the surety was avoided, though Proculus had held this true only of the first case[5].

It is to be noted that *compensatio, duae causae*, and *confusio* often resulted from voluntary acts, but they are cases in which it is an indirect, possibly undesired and uncontemplated, result of the act.

CXCIII. Voluntary modes of extinction. Besides the obvious cases of occurrence of *dies*, or some other event, which was to release on the terms of the contract, there were three important cases.

Solutio. Primitive *obligatio* implied subjection[6] and *solutio* meant release from this, a state of things reflected in the record in Gaius of the ancient form of release *per aes et libram*: "*me eo nomine a te solvo*[7]." Even in the Empire the word does not seem to be normally used for anything but payment in money; at any rate it seems never applied expressly to return of deposit, *commodatum* or pledge[8]. There are, however, texts applying it to render of other things than money[9] and, clearly, in later law it covers performance in general, doing what the liability requires[10]. By agreement something else might be substituted—*datio in solutum*—and, on the Sabinian view, which prevailed, this was an *ipso iure* discharge, the Proculian view being that it gave only an *exceptio*[11]. If the substituted thing was not properly done, e.g. if ownership in the substituted thing was not given, the classical view appears to have been that the original right revived[12] (with the result that the liability of sureties would also revive[13]), though some texts, probably

1 18. 4. 2. 18, 20. 1; cp. G. 4. 78. 2 46. 1. 71. pr. If there was a right of regress between the *correi*, e.g. *socii*, the debt was extinct to the extent to which reimbursement might be claimed under this right. 3 46. 1. 21. 3. 4 45. 2. 13; 46. 1. 5. 5 46. 3. 93. 2, 3. 6 *Ante*, p. 407. 7 G. 3. 174. 8 Steiner, *Datio in solutum*, 30. He finds it only in 16. 3. 1. 43 and h. t. 11, both interp. It is also in 46. 3. 35, where "*aut deposuerit*" is probably an addition. 9 41. 3. 46; 27. 1. 24; 12. 6. 63; 46. 3. 80. pr. etc. 10 50. 16. 176. 11 G. 3. 168; Inst. 3. 29. pr.; C. 8. 42. 17. 12 46. 3. 46. pr.; de Francisci, *Bull.* 1914, 311, citing Rabel. 13 Collinet-Giffard, *Précis*, 2. 196.

interpolated, give an *actio utilis ex empto* for the substituted thing[1]. But a performance defective in this way might be set right by *usucapio*[2].

Solutio must be of the whole debt, with accessories, etc., and must be at the agreed place[3], with elaborate rules as to place[4], if none was agreed. If there were several debts *solutio* was imputed to that named by the debtor[5]. If he named none the creditor might then and there impute it to debt already due, but must consult the interest of the debtor, choosing the most onerous[6]. Failing any distinction he might impute it to the oldest[7]. If he did not impute, the court would, on the same lines[8], and if no distinction could be drawn it was proportional payment of all the debts[9]. Payment might be by a third person, unauthorised[10], but it must be to the creditor, his authorised representative, or a *solutionis causa adiectus*[11]. Thus payment to a *negotiorum gestor* could be reclaimed by *condictio* till ratified[12]. Payment to a creditor of a creditor might discharge if it was a reasonable *negotii gestio*, but it operated only as *compensatio*, not as *solutio*[13]. Both parties must be *capaces*[14].

Payment extinguished the debt and released pledges and sureties[15], apart from cases in which payment was treated as purchase of the debt, where a surety paid (*beneficium cedendarum actionum*)[16].

Attempted payment put the creditor in *mora*[17]. If, after tender, the thing was deposited in a public place, e.g. a temple, with, under Justinian, the leave of a *iudex*, the debtor was released as by payment, though, till the creditor took the thing, he could revive the debt by taking it back[18]. If it could not be so deposited, e.g. live-stock, he might sell it for

1 13. 7. 24. pr.; 42. 4. 15; C. 8. 44. 4, etc. Steiner, *cit.*, 60 (full account of lit.) holds them all interp. See also review, Koschaker, *Z.S.S.* 1916, 348.

2 In money debt, if the debtor had nothing but land, and could not sell that, the creditor might be compelled, in late law, to take it at a valuation (*Nov.* 4. 3), and the court might in late law compel the creditor to accept payment by instalments, 12. 1. 21. The so-called *beneficium competentiae* (*post*, § CCXXXIV) gives a similar result.

3 13. 4. 9.

4 Solazzi, *Estinzione della Obbl.* c. 7.

5 46. 3. 1.

6 Siber, *Z.S.S.* 1925, 174, shews wavering (46. 3. 1–8) between contractual and unilateral view of *imputatio*. The choice of the creditor here mentioned is probably, as he says, Byzantine. Solazzi, *cit.* c. 9.

7 46. 3. 1 *in f.*; h. t. 2.

8 46. 3. 3. 1–5. pr.

9 46. 3. 8.

10 3. 5. 38; 46. 3. 72. 2. As to Labeo in 46. 3. 91, and "*invito beneficium non datur*" (50. 17. 69), see Kretschmar *Z.S.S.* 1917, 317 *sqq.*

11 3. 5. 38; 46. 3. 12. 1; 50. 17. 180. Texts disagree on the question whether payment can still be made to *sol. causa adiectus* who has suffered *capitis deminutio* or materially altered his position (45. 1. 56. 2; 46. 3. 38. pr., 95. 6). Desserteaux, *Mél. Girard*, 1. 353; *Capitis deminutio*, 2. 145 *sqq.*, thinks that it was a question of intent with a general presumption that the *facultas* was destroyed by fundamental economic change in the *status* of *adiectus*, whether *c. d.* or not, but he handles it throughout as a *facultas recipiendi* rather than a *facultas solvendi*.

12 46. 3. 12. 4.

13 44. 4. 6.

14 Pupils and minors, *ante*, pp. 159, 173.

15 Inst. 3. 29. pr.

16 *Ante*, p. 449. See also assignment, *ante*, p. 554, and *successio in locum*, *ante*, p. 479.

17 *Ante*, p. 550.

18 22. 1. 7, 41. 1; 46. 3. 39; C. 4. 32. 2, 6, 9, 12 and 19. As to allowance of *depositio* where actual payment was impracticable, Siber, *R.R.* 2. 277. Solazzi, *cit.* c. 10.

the benefit of the creditor, and, apparently he was in no way responsible if he let the thing go to waste, at any rate in sale[1].

In relation to *solutio*, the distinction between divisible and indivisible obligations is important. They might be indivisible by agreement or by nature. Thus an obligation to do a piece of work, to build a house or transfer an indivisible right, e.g. a praedial servitude, was indivisible: there could be no partial *solutio*[2]. So long as performance was incomplete the whole was due and could be sued for[3]. An alternative obligation was indivisible. If one who owed 100 or a house paid 50, he could still be sued for 50 or a house. If the action was limited to 50 or a half share in a house, the result might be the render of a half share in a house, which would not be what was contracted for[4]. Apart from this case indivisibility was important chiefly where there were several parties; it had the effect that, apart from express solidarity, each might be sued for the whole[5]. Where they were common owners or *socii* or *coheredes* (they would normally be one or another), adjustment would be made by *pro socio* or a divisory action. The same point might arise in *confusio*. If *A* and *B* were under an obligation to do a piece of work for *C*, and *A* became *C*'s *heres*, he could, in that capacity, claim performance from *B*, though in their mutual relations he would have to bear half the cost. But indivisibility presented many difficulties[6].

Alternative obligations[7], to give *A* or *B*, raised other questions. The transaction might shew which party was to choose[8], but if it did not, the choice was with the person liable, the promisor[9], vendor[10], *heres*[11], or the husband restoring *dos*[12]. But in legacy *per vindicationem* it was with legatee[13]. Payment of a part of one alternative was not even a partial discharge: the case was pendent. If that payment was completed the obligation was discharged: if the other payment was made, the part first paid could be recovered as *indebitum*[14]. *Acceptilatio* as to one alternative discharged the *obligatio*, and *acceptilatio* of part of one alternative discharged it *pro parte* if it was divisible: the rest could be satisfied

1 18. 6. 1. 3, 41; classicality disputed. *Ante*, p. 551. 2 45. 1. 2. 1, 72. pr. 3 8. 1. 17. 4 45. 1. 85. 4. 5 8. 1. 17; 10. 2. 25. 9. Bonfante, *Scr. Giur.* 3. 368, and Guarneri-Citati, *St. sulle obbl. indivis.* (abstracted, *Z.S.S.* 1927, 552), shew Justinian tending, sporadically, to assimilate them to *oblig. pro parte*, e.g. by allowing *solutio pro parte*. 6 Van Wetter, *Pandectes*, 3. § 337; Windscheid, *Lehrb.* 2. § 253 and literature there cited. 7 Vassali, *Misc. crit.* 3. 5, has interesting observations on alt. oblig. but with too much readiness to see material interpolations. 8 30. 8. 2, 84. 9, 11; 23. 3. 10. 6; 45. 1. 75. 8, etc. See Guarneri-Citati, *Mél. Cornil.* 1. 496 with good bibliography. 9 Inst. 4. 6. 33d; D. 13. 4. 2. 3; 45. 1. 75. 8. 10 18. 1. 25. pr., 34. 6. 11 30. 109. 1; 31. 15. 12 23. 3. 10. 6. A contract in which one alternative is contained in the other is not alternative; it is for the lesser. 31. 43. 3; 45. 1. 12. 13 *Ante*, p. 350. 14 12. 6. 26. 13, 14; 45. 1. 2. 1, 85. 4; 46. 3. 34. 10; 30. 8. 2, 34. 14; D. 31. 15.

by giving the proper proportion of either; here there was no possibility of being put off with part of each[1]. A pact not to sue for one alternative discharged the obligation, *iure exceptionis*, unless it was really a pact to limit the right of choice[2]. A choice by *promissor* and probably by promisee could be varied till actual completion[3]. The rule was different in legacy: a declaration by the person entitled to choose fixed his choice[4]. Thus a *promissor* who paid one alternative object, not knowing he had a choice, could recover by *condictio*, but a *heres* could not, nor could a legatee who had, in the same way, vindicated one[5]. If a *promissor* paid both, in mistake, he could in later law vindicate whichever he liked, at least where he had the original choice[6].

If one alternative was *ab initio* impossible, the other was alone *in obligatione*, so that if the first afterwards became possible, it was still a nullity[7]. If one became impossible without fault or *mora* after the *obligatio* arose, the other was simply due[8], but if, e.g. by declaration of the *heres*, the obligation had been fixed on one, impossibility affecting that one ended the obligation[9]. There is a suggestion in one of the texts for legacy and an uncertain inference from another for contract[10], that where one had become impossible, e.g. by death of the slave due, there was still the choice of giving the value of this, but most of the texts are explicit that the other must be given[11]. If both so died the obligation was at an end, but, as we saw, a buyer would still have to pay the price[12]. If one was tendered and perished while the creditor was *in mora*, the obligation was discharged[13]. If one died by fault of, or during *mora* of, the debtor he must give the other where he had the choice[14]. If both died, the first by accident, the second by his fault, he must give the value of the second[15]. If in the other order, the obligation was discharged, subject, at least in later law, to an *actio doli*[16].

Alternative obligation, in which both were *in obligatione* but only one was due, must be distinguished from *facultas solutionis* where the *facultas* was not *in obligatione* at all. *Solutionis causa adiectus* is a familiar instance[17], but there are others, e.g. in *laesio enormis*, the right of the buyer to avoid restoration by paying the difference[18], or the right of a third person, holder, to pay off a pledge instead of restoring the

1 46. 4. 17. 2 2. 14. 27. 6 (? interp.). 3 45. 1. 138. 1, 112. pr. 4 30. 84. 9; 31. 11. 1. 5 12. 6. 32. 3; 30. 84. 9; 31. 11. 1, 19. 6 There had been disputes, 12. 6. 32. pr.; C. 4. 5. 10. 7 45. 1. 128; 46. 3. 72. 4. 8 18. 1. 34. 6; 23. 3. 10. 6; 30. 47. 3; 31. 11. 1; 46. 3. 95. pr. 9 30. 84. 9; 31. 11. 1. 10 30. 47. 3; 46. 3. 95. 1, ? interp. Perozzi, *Ist.* 2. 125. 11 See 13. 4. 2. 3. 12 18. 1. 34. 6. 13 45. 1. 105. 14 46. 3. 95. pr. 15 *Arg.* 46. 3. 95. 1. 16 *Ib.* Killing of one of promised slaves, by *stipulator*, 9. 2. 55. Case of one or both being *in fuga* or *apud hostes*, 30. 47. 3. See, for lit., Van Wetter, *Pandectes*, 3. § 326. 17 *Ante*, pp. 440, 565. 18 *Ante*, p. 486.

thing to the creditor[1]. Such a discretion might arise in any contract; it was a question of interpretation whether it was *facultas* or alternative. In a *stipulatio*: "*Si S. non dederis*, 10 *dare spondes-ne?*" the render of *S.* is a *facultas*. The distinction was important in that if the *res in obligatione* was destroyed or otherwise ceased to be due, there was no liability to render what was *in facultate*, but impossibility of the *facultas* did not affect the obligation[2].

CXCIV. *Novatio.* Extinction of an obligation by the substitution of another for it. To bring the rules of *novatio* into play the new obligation must be by *stipulatio*, in the law as we know it, but, while it existed, the contract *literis* may have served the same purpose[3]. The notion of *novatio* is said to originate in the doctrine that there cannot be two distinct obligations for the same thing between the same parties any more than there can be two actions for *eadem res*. This principle is not well evidenced; the text mainly relied on merely says that of two stipulations for the same between the same, one is void[4], a much narrower proposition[5]. There are texts which admit the existence of two obligations for the same thing between the same parties, but these are treated as late equitable relaxations, though Ulpian regards it as an old settled rule[6]. However this may be, the rule of classical law was that, to effect a *novatio*, the new contract must involve some change[7], either in form, or parties or terms. The main rules were the following:

There must be an existing obligation: it might be merely natural[8], but some natural obligations could not be novated[9]. If the old bargain was void and the parties did not know this, there was an *exceptio* under the new, or *condictio* if it had been satisfied. If the *promissor* did know, the new contract was valid, but it was a *donatio*, not a *novatio*[10].

There must be a new obligation by formal contract. This need not be perfectly valid; it might novate and destroy the original obligation

1 20. 6. 12. 1. 2 44. 7. 44. 5. See, hereon, Siber, *R.R.* 2. 260. 3 See G. 3. 128–30; Cicero, *de Off.* 3. 14. 58–60. *Contra*, Perozzi, *Ist.* 2. 417. 4 45. 1. 18. This must be the second, otherwise it would be a novation. 5 Not a general overriding principle. It is merely that a contract is not superseded by another identical in all respects. There is nothing "*inelegans*" in itself in the existence between two persons of two obligations tending to the same thing (see n. 6). A civil and a praetorian obligation cannot be the same, but both may exist. Thus a man often has the choice of *actio ex empto* and *actio quanto minoris* (*ante*, p. 493). It is true that if owing a thing by sale I afterwards make a *promissio* of the same thing, the old *obligatio* is destroyed by *novatio*. But what if *animus novandi* was expressly excluded? What if, owing a thing by a promise for which there was a counter promise, I afterwards agree to sell it for a price? It seems that the old *obligatio* still exists at civil law, though there would be an *exceptio*. If a legacy to the creditor is advantageous, it is valid not only to the extent of the advantage, but absolutely, and the same is true of *legatum dotis* (*ante*, p. 351). 6 19. 1. 10; 44. 2. 14. 2; 50. 17. 159. See, however, Girard, *Man.* 738. 7 G. 3. 177; Inst. 3. 29. 3. 8 46. 2. 1 at least in late law. 9 *Ante*, § CLXXXIX. 10 12. 6. 62; 14. 6. 20.

though itself *inutilis*. One text suggests that it must set up an *obligatio*, either *civilis* or *naturalis*[1], but this was neither necessary nor sufficient. A promise by a slave did not novate, though it set up a *naturalis obligatio*[2]: it was not regarded as a verbal obligation at all. But a *stipulatio post mortem*, though void, destroyed the old obligation. Apparently any *stipulatio* sufficed if the parties were *capaces* of the form whether in the individual case it was valid or not[3].

The new promise must refer to the old debt, notwithstanding the change. A *stipulatio* for another thing in substitution was not a *novatio*, though it no doubt had the effect of a *pactum de non petendo* on the old promise. This rule was not abolished by Justinian, but was relaxed. The sum of money might be altered, the right, e.g. servitude, might be increased, but it does not appear that the debt could be wholly different[4].

There must be *animus novandi*. The texts have been so altered that the history of this matter is difficult to trace. Under Justinian it must be clear on the face of the transaction that *novatio* was meant[5]. The better view seems to be that in later classical law the intent must exist, i.e. be proveable[6], but Gaius does not mention intent[7]. Where a new stipulation was made for the same object, but with a change in some factor, *animus novandi* was presumed. It is obvious that it would be necessary in stipulating, e.g. with a new debtor, to make it clear that it was not intended merely to add a surety to the old *stipulatio*[8]. If there was no change the second *stipulatio* was ignored.

There must be change in form, parties or terms. As to form, the only possible one was substitution of *stipulatio* for some other debt, and here *novatio* was treated as a matter of course[9]. Till the relaxation by Justinian the only changes of terms we hear of are addition or removal of *dies*,

1 46. 2. 1. 1. 2 G. 3. 176, 179; Inst. 3. 29. 3. Gaius says that it is as if stipulated "*a nullo*." This is not the real reason, for the statement is incorrect: it creates a *naturalis obligatio*, apart from the edictal rules. In fact the statement, though it has been used for far-reaching conclusions, is obscure. There was no difficulty about taking a novatory promise, but as this releases the old, there must be authority, or, *in re peculii*, at least in later law, *administratio peculii*. P. 5. 8. 1; D. 46. 2. 20, 34. These texts say that a *procurator* could novate for us: this means only that his general authority is as good as an express mandate to a third party, implying our assent. The rights under his contract will not be directly acquired by us. 3 There are other cases, G. 3. 176. See, however, *S.M.W.* 485. 4 45. 1. 58, 56. 7, 91. 6; 46. 2. 1; C. 8. 41. 8. Steiner, *Datio in solutum*, 86, holds that under J. identity of object was no longer needed. His texts do not go so far. C. 8. 41. 8 is not in point. In D. 45. 1. 58 the new object is contained in the old. In 46. 2. 28 (which must be meant) the new object is "the value of" the old. And in C. 4. 2. 10, however the obscure final words are understood, there is no evidence of more than an implied *p. de non pet.* The texts shew increasing laxity, but no more. 5 C. 8. 41. 8. 6 46. 2. 2; Inst. 3. 29. 3a. Scialoja, *St. Perozzi*, 413, holds *animus novandi* essential in classical law. Jörs, *R.R.* 135, holds it presumed in classical law. Other views, Costa, *Storia*, 433. 7 G. 3. 176 *sqq.* 8 See 46. 2. 6. pr. 9 13. 5. 24; G. 3. 177.

condicio or surety[1]. As to surety Justinian speaks of *fideiussor* where Gaius says *sponsor*: it may be that for Gaius only change as to *sponsor* sufficed, and he notes that the Proculians did not admit that change as to surety was enough. As to conditions, a conditional *stipulatio* neither novated nor could be novated[2]. The story of the texts is that conditional *stipulatio* novated a simple one only when the condition was realised, so that it became identical with the old one. One might have expected this to nullify the second[3]. If the first was conditional and the second simple, there was *novatio* when the condition arrived so that there was a debt to novate[4]: here there is the same difficulty.

Much attention has lately been given to the question what, if any, was the effect on the old obligation of a conditional *stipulatio* for the same thing[5]. The better view seems to be that it had none at civil law but that it gave an *exceptio* while the condition was pending and if it failed, at any rate where it was between the same parties[6], that in earlier classical law it did not purge *mora* or prevent *mora* from arising after it, but that Marcellus[7] made it purge *mora, ope exceptionis,* if between the same parties. It may have been *ipso iure* in *condictio furtiva,* a reflex of the principle giving pact civil effect in delict[8].

It might be a change of parties. Change of creditors occurred where, with the assent of the creditor, the debtor promised the debt to a new creditor, in effect, assignment of a debt. Change of debtor occurred where a new debtor promised the same debt to the creditor: the assent of the original debtor was not needed; that of the creditor was evident. It might be by way of gift, but more often the new debtor was a debtor of the old one[9]. In transactions of this kind there was a special terminology. Where *A* owed *B* money and the debt was novated by *stipulatio* of *B* in which *C* promised to pay, *C* was usually indebted to *A*. It was substitution of the debtor's debtor. This *delegatio debitoris*[10] may be itself called a *novatio*, so that there are two novations, but it is usually thought of as a *solutio*: *qui delegat solvit*[11]. *C*'s debt to *A* was now novated and replaced by a debt to *B*. This was the strict meaning of *delegatio*, substitution of *A*'s debtor for himself in a debt of *A*'s. But the word was used loosely wherever *C* promised to pay *B* on behalf of *A*, whether *C* was a debtor to *A* or not[12]. The word *expromissor* is used for a debtor's

1 G. *ib.*; Inst. 3. 29. 3. 2 46. 2. 14. 3 *Ante*, p. 568. 4 46. 2. 14. 1. 5 G. 3. 177; D. 23. 3. 80. 6 12. 1. 36; G. 3. 179. 7 46. 3. 72. 1–3. 8 Koschaker, *Festschr. f. Hanausek*, 118. See also Kaden, *Z.S.S.* 1924, 164; Bohaček, *Note Esegetiche, Ann. Palermo*, 11, 341; Guarneri-Citati, *ib.* 161, whose views, differing on several points, are considered by Koschaker; Siber, *R.R.* 2. 282. 9 There may be more than one change. If *A* owes *B* 10 on sale, and with *B*'s consent *C* promises to pay this 10 in 10 days all three kinds of change have occurred. 10 46. 2. 11–12. 11 46. 1. 18; Seneca, *de Benef.* 6. 5. See, however, G. 3. 176. 12 *Ib.*; 23. 3. 5. 8.

debtor or any other person taking over a debt and to one promising his own debt even to his old creditor[1].

Novatio destroyed the old debt with all securities and liabilities; in particular it purged *mora*, so that, e.g., interest which had begun to run on account of this, ceased to run[2]. The new contract normally created a new *obligatio*, subject to what has been said, but the accessory elements of the old one did not apply to this, except so far as expressly preserved[3].

The effect of *litis contestatio* was akin to that of *novatio*[4], and it is here and there called novation[5]. But it was produced in effect without the consent of both parties, for though, in classical law, litigation still rested in form on consent, this was unreal, since it could be compelled, and the *novatio* is usually distinguished as *novatio necessaria*[6]. Its effects[7] were not quite the same. Thus it did not, of course, purge *mora* or destroy pledges[8], and, in general, the obligation could not differ from that which the action was brought to enforce[9].

CXCV. Release of the debt. The primary rule was that an obligation was to be discharged in the form in which it was made[10]. Performance was probably, as we have seen[11], not of itself necessarily a discharge in early law. Payment of money borrowed by way of *nexum* did not completely discharge the obligation without release *per aes et libram*, but this is due to the effect on the debtor's personal position, and not strictly to mere obligation, so that we cannot say that a promise to pay was not discharged, at one time, by payment but only by *acceptilatio* as well[12]. The extreme antiquity of the formal modes of discharge is, however, against the notion that they can have been invented as modes of gratuitous discharge[13]. But performance was a complete discharge, *ipso iure*, in classical law, and the rule requiring form applied only to voluntary release without satisfaction.

Release *per aes et libram*. A solemn weighing with copper and scales, *libripens* and five witnesses. Gaius gives the form for release from judgement[14]. The debtor recited the fact of judgement and declared himself released by copper and scales, the act emanating here, as elsewhere, from the person benefiting under the transaction. The form in Gaius is corrupt, and no doubt was suitably varied in different applications. It applied also to *nexum*, to legacy *per damnationem* of things estimated by weight or

1 23. 3. 36; 14. 6. 20; 39. 5. 19. 4; 12. 3. 4. 2 *Ante*, § CLXXXVIII. 3 13. 7. 11. 1. Validity of defences to old claim, 46. 2. 12; Girard, *Man.* 745. 4 G. 3. 180, 181, *post*, § CCXXXV. 5 Vat. Fr. 263; C. 7. 54. 3. 2. 6 Based on 46. 2. 29. 7 *Post*, § CCXXXV. 8 22. 1. 35. 9 See, however, as to noxal actions, *post*, § CCV. 10 46. 3. 80; 50. 17. 35, 100, 153; cp. G. 3. 170. 11 *Ante*, p. 407. Livy, 22. 10. 12 Eisele, *Beiträge*, 16. 13 *Contra*, Cornil, *A.D.R.* 91. 14 G. 3. 173 *sqq.*

number, and as some thought, of measurable things[1], and possibly to any form of *damnatio*[2]. The effect was to destroy the obligation completely.

Accepti relatio. Release of contract *literis* by some form of entry[3], probably an entry in the debtor's *codex* with the creditor's consent. Gaius does not mention it[4]. But a special form of it is *a priori* probable and the form *acceptum referre* is well evidenced[5].

Acceptilatio. The most important formal mode, as it released from the most important formal contract of classical and later law, *stipulatio*, as well as from *iusiurandum liberti*[6]. Of the form given by Gaius the essential words were "*habesne acceptum?*" "*habeo acceptum*[7]." Ulpian says that "*acceptum facis,*" "*facio*" served as well, and that as it was, like *stipulatio, iuris gentium*, it might be in Greek[8]. It could not be under express *dies* or *condicio*[9], though the obligation released might, and the *acceptilatio* would operate when the *dies* or *condicio* arrived[10]. It might cover more than one *stipulatio*, and, conversely, though this was doubted in the time of Gaius, it might, in later classical law, be a release of part of a promise, unless the promise was indivisible, in which case the *acceptilatio* of part was void[11]. It could not be by *procurator* in classical law[12], and while a slave could take an *acceptilatio* he could not give one[13].

The act proceeded from the party to be released. It effected extinction, like payment[14], releasing sureties and *correi*, and where given to a surety it released the principal, even if his contract was not *stipulatio*[15]. It might accompany performance and serve as a receipt.

Though it applied only to verbal contract it might be used in a wider field by first novating the contract. The *stipulatio Aquiliana* is an important illustration. It was a means of discharging any debts existing between two parties by novating them by a *stipulatio* and releasing this by *acceptilatio*. We have the form twice[16], not quite identically, and thus shewing that it might vary both in expression and inclusiveness. Both are very inclusive. As stated, it covered *iura in rem*, these being con-

1 G. 3. 175; perhaps because a judgement might have been at one time for a weight (i.e. of *aes rude*) and was later for a number (of coins) but never for a measure. 2 It is suggested that *sponsor* to have the *actio depensi* must have paid *per aes et libram*, the name of his action, and the repeated use by Gaius of the word "*dependere*" in speaking of him supports this. Eisele, *Studien*, 28 *sqq.*; not an application of the notion of discharge in the form in which the obligation was undertaken. 3 Vat. Fr. 329. *S.M.W.* 477. 4 G. 3. 170. 5 Lewis and Short, *Latin Dictionary*, s.v. Accipio, E. 6 46. 4. 13. pr. It is not shewn that it applied to *dotis dictio*, but it probably did. 7 G. 3. 169. 8 46. 4. 7, 8. 4. 9 46. 4. 4, 5; cp. h. t. 13. 6. Like other *actus legitimi*, it might be dependent on a tacit condition, h. t. 11. 3; 23. 3. 43. pr.; 50. 17. 77. 10 45. 1. 56. 8; 46. 4. 12. D. 46. 3. 16 makes the release date back; probably interp.; Bohaček, *Ann. Palermo*, 11. 379. 11 G. 3. 172; D. 46. 4. 9, 13. 1. 12 46. 4. 13. 10. H. t. 3 probably interp.; see also C. 8. 41. 4. 13 46. 4. 8. 1, 2, 11, 22. 14 46. 4. 5. 15 45. 2. 2; 46. 4. 13. 7, 12. An *acceptilatio* which failed as such might be a *pactum de non petendo*, 46. 4. 8. pr., 19. 16 46. 4. 18; Inst. 3. 29. 2.

templated as actionable liabilities[1]. It might cover only one group of debts or all. Neither form seems to cover delicts and possibly it was not usual to include these. Its use was not an act of charity; men do not usually abandon their claims for nothing. Where cross claims existed enquiry would shew that a balance was due one way. Matters were simplified by *stipulationes Aquilianae* and *acceptilationes* on the old debts and a new *stipulatio* for the balance[2]. No doubt it was often a compromise.

Consensual contracts could be discharged as from formation by *contrarius consensus*, provided nothing had yet been done. This was a full civil law discharge[3]. If something had been done, or some event had released one party, it would only be a *pactum de non petendo* available by way of *exceptio*[4]. It was disputed whether giving a surety was such part performance as barred civil discharge by *contrarius consensus*[5].

As contracts *re* essentially involved something done there was no discharge by *contrarius consensus*. Acceptance of return of the *res* would in effect destroy it for the future, *ex fide bona*, but not for the past, unless there was special agreement, amounting to *pactum de non petendo*[6].

Pactum de non petendo. Apart from delict, a praetorian defence. It was an informal agreement not to sue, express or tacit, i.e. inferred from conduct. It might apply to any debt or part of a debt and be subject to any limitations[7]. It might be consented to by messenger, or by a slave[8]. The defence was an *exceptio pacti*, which need not be expressed in *bonae fidei iudicia*, and might be met by *replicatio doli*, etc., and as a praetorian defence, gave a *condictio* if the debt was paid in mistake[9]. The pact might be either *in personam* or *in rem*[10]. *Pacta in rem* were pacts that no action should be brought, with no limitation as to the person affected. *Pacta in personam* were pacts that action should not be brought by or against particular persons. This was commonly shewn by naming the person: "*ne T* (*a T*) *peteret* (*peteretur*)," but this was not conclusive: it was to be decided, *ex mente*, the name being sometimes

1 46. 4. 18. Wlassak, *Z.S.S.* 1921, 394, credits all effects *in rem* to Just. Cornil, *Mél. Fournier*, 102, considers "*Quodve tu meum habes, tenes, possides,*" to refer only to *a. ad exh.*, *interd. quem fundum* and the like. It may in classical law have covered actions *in rem* actually pending; Segrè, *St. Bonfante*, 3, 5. 2 2. 15. 2; P. 1. 1. 3. 3 46. 4. 8. pr., 23; Inst. 3. 29. 4. See 18. 5. 5. pr.; sometimes held a Byzantine principle (Stoll, *Z.S.S.* 1924, 1). But see Boyer, *R.H.* 1930, 602. Release by one is, in such a case, mutual release. But see Siber, *Z.S.S.* 1921, 73. 4 2. 14. 58; C. 4. 45. 1, 2. But as they are all *bonae fidei*, this is much the same. The thing done must, apart from special agreement, be undone. 5 Papinian allows it. Paul on Julian's authority holds that the release is only by *exceptio*. 18. 5. 3; 46. 3. 95. 12. 6 Texts are wanting, see 13. 6. 17. 5. 7 2. 14. 7. 6, 17. 3, 27. 7, 41. 8 2. 14. 2, 28. 2. 9 12. 6. 32. 1; cp. h. t. 24. 10 2. 14. 17. 7–19.

inserted only to shew who made it, with no intention of limitation[1], and a pact was presumed to be *in rem*. It might be made to exclude particular persons who would otherwise be entitled to use it[2]. A pact *in personam* affected only him who made it, not even his *heres*[3]. One *in rem* affected anyone suing or sued for the same debt, if there was a right of regress, as otherwise the pact would be illusory[4]. A pact by one of several creditors could not be used against the others, even if it was *in rem*, unless there was regress[5]. A surety, as he could claim reimbursement, could use a pact made with his principal[6], but not *vice versa*, or one made with a co-surety, as the right of regress did not exist[7]. *Socii* had such a right, and thus the pact of one could be used by the others[8]. The rule, being due to the right of regress, did not apply where on the facts this was excluded. Thus a *fideiussor* who acted *donandi animo*, renouncing his right of regress, could not use his principal's pact[9], and conversely, if, though nominally a *fideiussor*, it was really his own affair, his nominal principal could use a pact made with him, for the formal positions were in fact reversed[10]. A pact made with a vendor was available to the buyer[11], since he had or might have a claim *ex empto*. A pact by or to the *possessor* of a *hereditas* did not in any way affect the true *heres*[12]. Correal debtors as such had no right of regress, and a pact not to sue one did not therefore affect the others[13].

A pact that a third party should not be sued was void, and was not confirmed though he afterwards became *heres* to the pactor[14]. Thus it was generally held that a pact by *reus* that a surety should not be sued was of no value, but Paul held that, as it was the principal who really benefited here, the purpose of the general rule required that the surety should be allowed to use the pact[15]. Pacts by *tutor* or *curator* that the ward should

1 2. 14. 7. 8. 2 2. 14. 17. 3, 22. 3 2. 14. 21. pr., 25. 1; 24. 3. 31. 1; 23. 4. 20. 2. 4 2. 14. 21. 5, 32. 5 2. 14. 27. pr.; see h. t. 28. 1. 6 2. 14. 21. 5, 32. 7 2. 14. 21. 5, 25. 2, 26. 8 2. 14. 14, 25. pr. Julian in 34. 3. 3. 3 seems to deny *socii* the pact. It has been maintained, on 2. 14. 19. 1–21. pr.; 24. 3. 31. 1; 23. 4. 20. 2, that a *heres* had not the right in classical law unless expressly mentioned. Cuq, *Man.* 625. But in all these texts the pact is expressly *in personam*. The distinction between *p. in r.* and *p. in personam* is, however, largely the work of the compilers. Rotondi, *Scr. Giur.* 2, 307, who seems to hold, what is difficult to accept, that the classics saw no difference between pact "*ne petam*" and one "*ne peteretur*." 9 2. 14. 32. 10 2. 14. 24. For Pringsheim *Z.S.S.* 1921, 292, these rules are Byzantine. 11 2. 14. 17. 5. Sabinus held that this applied even if it was *in personam*; no doubt the pact is treated as part of the *commoda rei*. He also allowed it in case of donee, but this, it would seem, must depend on the terms of the gift. 12 2. 14. 17. 6. 13 46. 3. 34. 11. *Ante*, p. 454. The rule in 2. 14. 25. pr. applies only to *socii*. 14 2. 14. 17. 4. Or that he should not sue, 2. 14. 17. 6. Sale gives exceptions, e.g. n. 11 above, and if a co-owner makes a pact not to divide for a time, this is good against a buyer of his share. 10. 3. 14. 3. 15 2. 14. 27. 1.

not be sued were available to the ward, an equitable relaxation, carrying out the principle that actions lying against the guardian could be brought against the ward at the end of the wardship[1].

Within the family the rules were different, since the subordinate acquired for the *paterfamilias*. A pact by son or slave[2] "*ne peteretur*" or "*ne a patre peteretur*" was good for the *paterfamilias*[3]. A son's pact "*ne a se peteretur*" was valid for him or the *pater* or his *heres* if sued on the son's obligation[4], but if the son was dead, as it was personal, it was useless[5], a rule more logical than reasonable: *de peculio* still lay for a year. A slave's pact "*ne ipse peteret*" was null[6]; he could never sue. But a slave's or son's pact not to sue, if *in rem*, was valid against the *pater*, *in re peculiari*, if he had *administratio peculii* and it was not *donandi animo*[6]. A son's personal pact not to sue might be good, as in some cases he could sue[7]. A pact by *paterfamilias* that the son should not be sued was not good for the son, but the father could use it if sued on the son's account, to which Paul or Tribonian adds the limitation, "*si in paciscendo id actum sit*" which destroys the rule[8].

Where the pact was not available the *exceptio doli* might sometimes be used as a "*subsidium*[9]," but the principle is obscure. A debtor had *exceptio doli* on a pact to his procurator or surety[10], provided that this was meant, and the same rule is applied as between co-sureties[11]. A father's pact that his son should not be sued gave the son *exceptio doli*, at any rate under Justinian[12]. A slave's pact "*ne a se peteretur*" gave the master an *exceptio doli*[13]. So, too, if a *filius* made such a pact with creditors of a *hereditas* on which he would enter after *emancipatio*, or a slave *heres* acted similarly, though the slave's pact was null, and the son's was lost by the *emancipatio*, they had *exceptio doli*, though this was doubtful in classical law, for the slave[14].

In delict, by virtue of words in the XII Tables, pact was a complete defence at civil law, and, as the Tables[15] use the same language as to coming to terms after *litis contestatio* on any claim, it is possible that the same rule applied there, but there is no sign of this in later law.

1 2. 14. 15, 28. 1; C. 2. 3. 22; not *vice versa*, *ante*, p. 156. 2 Or a *b. f. serviens*, and no doubt fructuary, within their field of acquisition. 3 2. 14. 17. 7–21. 1. 4 2. 14. 19. 1, 20. 5 2. 14. 21. pr. 6 2. 14. 28. 2. It never bars the father's right to sue on an *iniuria* to the son, his right being independent of the son's, h. t. 30. pr. 7 2. 14. 28. 2, 30. pr. 8 2. 14. 21. 2. 9 2. 14. 10. 2. 10 *Ib.*; h. t. 25. 2. 11 2. 14. 26. 12 2. 14. 21. 2. 13 2. 14. 21. 1. 14 2. 14. 7. 18, 19. Many of the texts have probably been altered: how far these rules are classical may be doubted. Koschaker, *Festschr. f. Hanausek*, 141. There has no doubt been generalisation by omission of circumstances. Analogous principles to those stated in the text were applied in case of *confusio*, *transactio* and set off, 4. 8. 34. pr.; 16. 2. 5, 9. 1; 45. 2. 10. 15 1. 7; 8. 2. Girard, *Textes*, 12, 17; Bruns, 1. 19, 29; *Cons*. 9. 1.

CXCVI. *Obligatio ex Delicto*[1]. This, the second of Gaius' two classes of obligation, involved essentially a wrong done, consisting in breach of a *ius in rem*, giving rise to an action for a penalty, distinct from that which also existed in many cases, for restoration. A mere pact was a complete defence at civil law[2]. As a penalty could not be imposed on one who did not know what he was doing, a *furiosus* was not liable in delict and an *impubes* only when he was *doli capax*[2a]. Action was in origin a legal substitute for self-help, which here meant revenge[3]. Revenge being personal, it did not lie against the wrongdoer's heir[4], but was unaffected by his *capitis deminutio*[5]; though his legal personality was changed, he was still the same man. Where two or more in concert committed a delict, each was liable to the whole penalty; satisfaction by one did not release the others[6]. This is perhaps because revenge would not be so subdivided.

Justinian's symmetrical arrangement, giving four delicts, is artificial. It treats rapine and theft as distinct delicts, whereas rapine is aggravated theft, and it omits wrongs, some of which we shall discuss, which, on any reasonable definition of the word, are delict for his time[7]. He considers them all to be of one class in that they all originate "*re, id est ex ipso maleficio*," where *res* is used in the sense of *factum*[8]. The four which he discusses, certainly the most important, are *Furtum*, *Rapina*, *Damnum iniuria datum* and *Iniuria*.

Furtum. Defined by Justinian as "*contrectatio rei fraudulosa vel ipsius rei vel etiam usus eius possessionisve*[9]." This omits certain essential elements. In the law as we know it[10], the subject-matter must have been a *res mobilis* or one which became *mobilis* by the theft, e.g. crops[11], though Sabinus is said to have held that there could be theft of land[12].

1 De Visscher, *R.H.* 1928, 335 (*Ét.* 257), holds that the conception of delictal liability as *obligatio* is of the Empire. 2 The XII Tables state this explicitly only for *membri ruptio*. 2. 14. 17. 1 states it also for *furtum*. P. 1. 19. 1, 2 seems to exclude it for *damnum*. Perozzi, *Ist.* 2. 368, doubts its generality. See, however, Girard, *Man.* 423. 2*a* 9. 2 5. 2; 47. 2. 23. 3 De Visscher, *St. Bonfante*, 3, 235 (*Ét.* 111), contrasts the *poena* and *vindicta* of personal injuries and the *noxa* of personal wrongs and thus accounts for differences in the surviving rules. 4 *Post*, p. 691. 5 *Ante*, p. 140. 6 47. 2. 21. 9; 9. 2. 11. 2; 47. 10. 34. Apparent exception in *dolus* and *metus*, *post*, § CCIII. 7 For G. *delictum* or *maleficium* is a civil delict. The word *crimen* is appropriate to public wrongs, Albertario, *St. Perozzi*, 221 and *Delictum e Crimen*. But the usage is not so constant as to require, as he claims, expulsion of any text conflicting, e.g. G. 1. 128, 2. 181 where it seems to mean misdeed of any kind, 3. 197, 208 where *crimen* must refer to *furtum* as a civil wrong, P. 5. 26. 2 where *delictum* is a crime; still less, pompous enactments of the late classical age. See Segrè, *St. Bonfante*, 3. 578. 8 44. 7. 4 (Gai.); Inst. 4. 1. pr. 9 Inst. 4. 1. 1. 10 There was much change in the conception of *furtum*, on the resulting confusion in D. 47. 2, Buckland, *Tijdschr.* 1930, 117. 11 47. 2. 25. pr. 12 Aul. Gell. 11. 18. 13. *Actio de tigno iuncto*, *ante*, p. 212.

It must have been with a view to profit, *lucrifaciendi gratia*[1], which is, however, as illustrated in the texts, a very unworkable requirement[2]. The *res* must be a *res in commercio* to which some one has a right. Thus there could be no *furtum* of ordinary *res nullius*, or of *res sacrae*, though here there were other remedies[3]. So there could be no *furtum* of *res hereditariae*: they belonged to no one at the moment[4]. As a by-product of the old law of *usucapio lucrativa pro herede* the rule actually was that there could be no theft of such things till they had actually been possessed by the *heres*[5]. But if, though the *hereditas* was vacant, there was some other right existing in the *res*, e.g. usufruct or pledge, which gave the holder a right of action for theft, this right was not affected, and in such a case the *heres* also had a right of action when he had entered[6].

Contrectatio means handling, and thus theft involved actual meddling with the thing. It did not necessarily involve taking the thing without consent from the owner's possession into the thief's. That is the obvious case, but there were others, e.g. inducing a debtor to pay to him by pretending that he was the creditor, or was the person authorised by him to collect the money[7], or even, according to most of the jurists, knowingly to receive payment of what was not due[8]. Still more striking are what were called in Justinian's law, *furtum usus* and *furtum possessionis*. That a borrower should be liable for theft for selling the thing is rational, but the law went further. There was *furtum usus* if a depositee used the thing, or a borrower, not thinking the owner would assent, used it for unauthorised purposes[9]. It was *furtum possessionis* for an owner to take the thing from one who had a *ius in rem* against him, usufructuary, pledgee or the like, or even from a *conductor* with a right of retention for expenses[10]. These were thefts, and though some classical texts assume that

1 47. 2. 1. 3. Not so stated in Inst. or in G. or in *P. Sent.*, but Sabinus speaks of it in Aul. Gell. 11. 18. 21. 2 It seems to mean little more than that wanton destruction is not theft whatever else it is. Monro, *de furtis*, 77, shews that the texts indicate an uncertain notion. See 47. 2. 55. 1. It is contended by Huvelin (*N.R.H.* 1918, 73 *sqq.*) that as a general requirement it is due to Justinian. See also Huvelin, *Furtum*, 1. 537, 783; Berger, *In tema di Derelizione*, 56. Sabinus, in Aul. Gell. *cit.* seems to mean by it no more than intention not to restore. 3 *Ante*, p. 184. 4 G. 3. 201; D. 47. 2. 69. For the remedy by *crimen expilatae hereditatis*, see 47. 19. 1. 5 G. 2. 52; 3. 201; P. 2. 31. 11; D. 47. 19. 2; C. 9. 32. 6. The analysis which sees in it an inroad on possession seems to be of the second century. Huvelin, *Furtum, cit.* 323, 564; Buckland, *L.Q.R.* 1927, 326. But as to very early law, Bonfante, *Scr. Giur.* 2. 683. A fructuary who has never enjoyed has the action, a rule turning on the original conception of usufruct. Buckland, *L.Q.R. cit.*; *ante*, p. 269. 6 41. 3. 35; 47. 2. 69–71. 7 47. 2. 43. pr., 1, 81. 6. The essential point is intent to pass the ownership to some one other than the actual receiver. If, however misled, the owner intended to pass the property to the actual receiver it is not *furtum* whatever else it may be. Buckland, *L.Q.R.* 1941, 467. 8 13. 1. 18. The language of this text and some others goes further than the principles expressed in those cited in the last note. 9 47. 2. 77. pr.; G. 3. 196, 7; Inst. 4. 1. 6, 7. 10 47. 2. 15. 1, 19. 5, 60; G. 3. 200; Inst. 4. 1. 10.

what was stolen must be a *res aliena*[1], the rules were classical, but the expressions, and notions, *furtum usus, possessionis,* probably were not[2]. The notion of theft as involving intent to deprive the owner of his whole interest is not the Roman conception.

The *contrectatio* must be *fraudulosa*; it must be against the interested person's will[3]. One who thought the owner consented was not a thief, nor was one who thought the owner did not consent, when in fact he did[4]. It was not theft to take a thing in good faith, even though the error was one of law, and it was immaterial how causeless the error was[5].

Persons other than the actual thief might be liable to the *actio furti*, i.e. those who have helped *ope et consilio*[6]. It is not easy to draw a clear line, but, roughly, *ope* means by physical help, and *consilio* by advice, not advice to steal, mere encouragement, but suggestions as to method[7]. If several were concerned in a theft, each was liable to the whole penalty; there was no release by payment by one of them[8].

There might be *furtum* with no *actio furti*. If a *filiusfamilias* stole from the *pater* no *actio furti* lay as there could be no action at all in such a case, but there was *furtum*, for accomplices were liable and the *res* was *furtiva*[9]. No *actio furti* lay where one party to a marriage stole from the other, because no infaming action lay in such a relation[10], but accomplices were liable, the *res* was *furtiva*[11], and there was a special action for the recovery of the property—*actio rerum amotarum*[12]. We are told that there was no *actio furti* for "*domestica furta,*" i.e. theft by *liberti* and free employees living with the patron[13]. Apparently the domestic authority sufficed for that[14].

CXCVII. Presumably it would usually be the owner[15] who sued for theft, but others might have a sufficient *interesse* to entitle them to

1 G. 3. 195; P. 2. 31. 1. 2 Probably thought of as *furtum* by wrongly taking the use or the possession. Discussion and reff., Monro, *de furtis*, App. 1. No text, literary or juristic, even under J. seems to mention a case of *f. usus* or *f. possessionis* as such. 47. 4. 1. 15 merely means that, for the writer, theft is an inroad on possession. See also Perozzi, *Ist.* 2. 325. 3 Inst. 4. 1. 1. 4 47. 2. 46. 7, 8. 5 47. 2. 46. 7, 84. Dispute in connexion with *servi corruptio*, *post*, § CCIII. 6 Inst. 4. 1. 11. Huvelin (*Furtum*, 1. 392 *sqq.*) with predecessors, holds that in early law the expression "*ope consilio*" had no relation to assistance to the thief but referred to the act of the principal, "*ope*" being his act, "*consilio*" his intent, G. 4. 37. 7 47. 2. 50. 3; Inst. 4. 1. 11. If it did benefit the thief but was not so intended Gaius doubts whether there is not an *actio in factum* for the *culpa*, below, n. 14. 8 C. 4. 8. 1. Theft by several slaves of the same master, *post*, § CCV. 9 5. 1. 4; 47. 2. 16, 17; Inst. 4. 1. 12. 10 25. 2. 1, 7; C. 6. 2. 22. 4; *post*, § CXCVIII. 11 25. 2. 29. 12 25. 2; C. 5. 21; *post*, p. 582. 13 47. 2. 90; 48. 19. 11. 1. 14 The earlier conception was wide. Sabinus laid little stress on the element of guilt. He makes a man liable for "*ope et consilio*" after the theft. He and Q. Mucius, older still, lay it down that any use by a *detentor* in excess of his right is *furtum*. He and others also hold that there may be *furtum* of land. Aul. Gell. 6. 15; 11. 18. 13, 23. 15 There might be *furtum* of free persons. Gaius (3. 199) speaks of those in *potestas* or *manus* and *iudicati* and *auctorati*. He does not mention those *in mancipio*. In

sue. Conversely the owner had no action if he had no *interesse*, i.e., where someone was responsible to him, so that he did not stand to lose by the theft. The types of *interesse* other than that of the owner were two.

(*a*) The positive *interesse* of one who had a *ius in rem* in the thing, including a *bona fide possessor*[1]. Usufructuary, *emphyteuta* and usuary are the other obvious cases[2]. These had the action by reason of what they lost[3], as also had the owner[4]. Although one or two texts create difficulty the better view seems to be that an ownership acquired after the theft, not by universal succession, did not give *actio furti* unless there was renewed *contrectatio*[5]. There might of course be a right to claim cession of actions[6].

(*b*) A negative *interesse* in those responsible to the owner if the thing was lost, which *interesse* barred any in the owner[7]. The penalty was kept; the owner had no claim to it, though there was in classical law some doubt in *commodatum*[8]. But there must be a real liability. If the victim of the theft was insolvent, and so had nothing to lose, the owner had the action and he had not, and if he became insolvent before the action it passed to the owner[9], though here, too, there were doubts in *commodatum*[10]. So, too, if the owner released his claim under the contract, he had the action and the other party had not[11].

Among those said to have this right are borrower, *conductor operis*, especially *fullo* and *sarcinator*, *conductor rei*[12], mandatary, *nauta*, *caupo* and *stabularius*[13]. But while in some cases it is said that they had the action if the theft was by their *culpa*[14], in others it appears that, subject to the limits already stated, they always had it, and, in some, this is based on the obligation *custodiam praestare*[15]. This raises the question already considered[16] as to the meaning and changes of meaning of this word. It should be noted that as *culpa levis* was always presumed, these

Justinian's law texts still speak of *actio furti* in respect of those in *potestas* (Inst. 4. 1. 9; D. 47. 2. 14. 13, 38) but it may be doubted if it was a living part of the law.

1 47. 2. 12. 1, 20. 1, 54. 4. 2 47. 2. 15, 46. 1–4. Pledge creditor and holder with *ius retentionis*, *post*, p. 580. 3 It is held by Schulz, *Z.S.S.* 1911, 23 *sqq.*, that no one but the owner had this positive *interesse* in classical law (except where the owner was the thief) all others mentioned being responsible to him for the thing, and having the action on that account and excluding him. But this seems in conflict with the sources. Buckland, *N.R.H.* 1917, 5 *sqq.* 4 47. 2. 46. 1. 5 47. 2. 41. 1, 46. pr., 47, 57. pr., 67. 1. 6 47. 2. 14. pr. 7 G. 3. 203; Inst. 4. 1. 13. 8 19. 2. 6; C. 6. 2. 22. 3a. 9 47. 2. 12. pr., 14. 17; G. 3. 205; Inst. 4. 1. 15. 10 C. 6. 2. 22. 1b. 11 47. 2. 54. 1, 91. pr. 12 If standing crops are stolen they are the landlord's property: he alone can bring *c. furtiva* (19. 2. 60. 5). But *colonus* at moneyrent can bring *furti* (47. 2. 26. 1), an exceptional rule due to his inchoate interest. Similar rule for the Aquilian (9. 2. 27. 14). On apparent conflicts (47. 2. 83. 1, 52. 8), Costa, *Locazione*, 95. 13 G. 3. 205 *sqq.*; Inst. 4. 1. 15, 16; D. 47. 2. 12. pr., 14. 2, 9, 12, 14, 17. 14 E.g. 47. 2. 14. 12. 15 E.g. 47. 2. 12. pr., 14. 2, 14. 17, etc. 16 *Ante*, § CXCI.

holders would always be *prima facie* liable for the loss without the need of appeal to the notion of absolute liability.

For *commodatum* the law was altered by Justinian. He provided that where a thing lent was stolen, the owner had the choice whether he would sue the thief, in which case all liability of the *commodatarius* was ended, or rely on his contract, leaving the *commodatarius* to sue the thief. But if he took this course not knowing of the theft, he could change his mind on discovering the facts[1]. The alteration of the law is not important.

A surety for the borrower, though he might have to pay, had not *actio furti*[2]. He is sued on his separate contract. Ulpian in one text[3] tells us on the authority of Julian and Celsus, that the *paterfamilias* of a borrower has not the action, and in another[4] that one whose *filius* has taken, as *fullo*, a thing to clean, which is stolen, has *furti* if the *peculium* is solvent. The conflict is noted and unsatisfactorily explained by the Gloss. The real explanation seems to be that the first text is from his "*ad Sabinum*" and gives civil law; the other, from his "*ad Edictum*" gives the praetorian law[5].

Two exceptional cases must be noted. We hear of an *interesse* based on the right of retention for expenses, the action being allowed to every one who had such a right, except depositee[6], but there is no evidence except where the thief was the owner. Also, a pledge creditor had the action, but its basis is obscure. Some texts base it on a liability for the thing[7]. Others make the creditor impute the damages to the debt[8], inconsistent with this basis[9]. Others give both him and the owner the action[10], also inconsistent with the *custodia* basis. Some allow pledgee to recover on a unit of the whole value, while others limit the unit to the amount of the debt[11]. He could not sue twice on two thefts if the amount due to him had been recovered on the first[12]. Yet he could hardly be less liable because the debt had been paid. No doubt there are differences of opinion, and changes of doctrine here, but the matter is controversial[13].

There was an overriding rule that the *interesse* must be *honestum*. While a *b. f. possessor* had the action, a *m. f. possessor* had not, because his *interesse* was not *honestum*, though the thing was at his risk[14]. For the same reason a depositee who has acted dolosely with the thing, e.g. by lending it, though he was liable had no *actio furti*[15]. But one who had an honest *interesse* did not lose it because he had been dishonest. If a

1 Inst. 4. 1. 16; C. 6. 2. 22. 2 47. 2. 14. 10, 86. 3 47. 2. 14. 10. 4 47. 2. 52. 9. 5 Buckland, *Tijdschr.* 1930, 138. 6 47. 2. 15. 2, 60; 47. 8. 2. 23; C. 4. 34. 11. 7 47. 2. 14. 16, suspicious. 8 13. 7. 22. pr.; 47. 2. 15. pr. 9 19. 2. 6. 10 Unless the thing is worth less than the debt, 47. 2. 12. 2, 14. 6, 46. 4. 11 47. 2. 14. 5–7, 15. pr., 88. 12 47. 2. 14. 6. 13 *Ante*, p. 579, n. 3. 14 47. 2. 12. 1. 15 G. 3. 207; Inst. 4. 1. 17; D. 47. 2. 14. 3. Servius had held that in some cases a thief might have *actio furti*, but this was not accepted; h. t. 14. 4, 77. 1.

thing was stolen from the owner, who had stolen it from a pledgee, he had the *actio furti* as owner[1]. A *fullo* was liable for *custodia*. If he lent the thing and it was stolen, we are told that he had the *actio furti*[2], though himself liable for theft for his loan. If *A* stole a man and he stole from *A*, *A* had *furti noxalis* against his owner[3]—a grotesque case, but correct in principle; *A*'s *interesse* in the thing was *honestum*; it did not matter that he had no *honestum interesse* in the thief[4].

CXCVIII. The actions resulting from theft are of two types:

(i) *Ad poenam persequendam*, the *actio furti* for a penalty. *Furtum manifestum*[5] was more severely dealt with than *furtum nec manifestum*. It occurred where the thief was caught in the act, as to the meaning of which expression there were different views. On one view it was during commission, on another, while still at the place, on another, generally however rejected, while still in possession of the thing[6]. The classical law as stated by Gaius seems to have accepted presence at the spot[7]. Justinian goes further and accepts a view of Sabinus stated by Paul, that it was still manifest if the thief, on the same day, had not yet deposited the thing in a safe place[8]. According to the Institutes "caught" meant "*visus vel deprehensus*," which seems to mean seen and identified[9], but the Digest requires capture or at least pursuit and capture of the goods thrown down by the thief[10]. A man was still committing *furtum* so long as he had the thing, but if it had ceased to be manifest it did not become so if he was afterwards caught with the goods[11]. To this there was an ancient exception. If a man's premises were solemnly searched "*lance licioque*," i.e. by a man wearing a loin cloth and bearing a dish, and the goods were found, this was manifest theft[12]. This rule, of the XII Tables and perhaps Greek[13], which is explained in many ways[14], seems to have been obsolete in classical law. Manifest theft was capitally punished under the XII Tables, while non-manifest involved only a twofold

1 P. 2. 31. 19. 2 47. 2. 48. 4. 3 47. 2. 68. 4. 4 Some texts conflict and say that one who acts dolosely with the *res* loses any *a. furti*. 4. 9. 4. pr.; 47. 2. 14. 8, 9.
5 On the early history of the notions *furtum m.* and *fur m.*, De Visscher, *Fur manifestus* (*Ét.* 137) 6 G. 3. 184, 185; Inst. 4. 1. 3; D. 47. 2. 3 *sqq.* 7 G. 3. 184.
8 47. 2. 4. 5; Inst. 4. 1. 3; P. 2. 31. 2. The limitation to the same day did not exist in the time of Gaius, who speaks of uncertainty. It is attributed to Paul in the Digest, where it may be interpolated. 9 Inst. 4. 1. 3. 10 47. 2. 7. 2, 3. 11 47. 2. 6.
12 G. 3. 192 *sqq.* 13 Aristophanes, *Nub.* 495, cited Gneist, *Syntagma, ad* G. 3. 192.
14 Gaius, *loc. cit.*, observes that the provision is ridiculous, as such search would be resisted by a thief and there was no penalty for this. He states and rejects explanations of the rule. See Danz, *Gesch. d. R.R.* § 155, n. 2; Gneist, *Syntagma, cit.*; Costa, *Storia*, 314; Karlowa, *R.Rg.* 2. 777 *sqq.*; Weiss, *Z.S.S.* 1922, 455. De Visscher, *Procédure d'Enquête lance et licio* (*Ét.* 217), holds the probable view that the institution of informal search is later than the XII Tables and that formal search gave the fourfold penalty only if theft was proved, otherwise threefold. He also accepts the view that it represents a primitive magical rite.

penalty[1], it may be on account of the element of doubt which surrounds non-manifest theft, but other explanations of the difference are offered[2]. The Praetor introduced a fourfold penalty for manifest theft, which gives the odd result that as the civil penalty for non-manifest theft was unaltered, that gave an *actio in ius*, and manifest an *actio in factum*[3].

The unit of which a multiple was taken was the *interesse* of the plaintiff. For *dominus* in possession, and in negative *interesse*, that was the value of the thing, for usufructuary it was that of the usufruct. If the thing had increased in value, the increased value was the unit; if it had diminished the thief did not benefit[4]. The unit covered extrinsic resulting losses, e.g. if a slave were stolen, the value of an inheritance to which he was instituted, and on which he could not be authorised to enter[5], and, where evidences of a debt were stolen, the amount of the debt, if the theft prevented recovery[6]. The action was *perpetua* and available to the *heredes* of the victim, but, like all actions *ex delicto*, not against the *heres* of the wrongdoer[7]. *Condemnatio* involved *infamia*[8]. Bringing the action did not bar proprietary actions which might lie[9].

(ii) *Ad rem persequendam*, to recover the property. The owner had the proprietary remedies against the thief or other holder. He had *vindicatio*, *actio ad exhibendum* and the possessory interdicts, and a thief, as a *mala fide possessor*, was liable whether he had transferred or not, in classical law by the *actio ad exhibendum*, in later law by the *vindicatio* itself[10]. A usufructuary had *vindicatio ususfructus*[11].

But there was also a remedy peculiar to cases of theft called *condictio furtiva* which, as we know it, was illogical, since it expressed a right on the part of the owner to have the ownership transferred to him: "*dare oportere*[12]." It was a quasi-contractual action, available against the thief or his *heres*, and, unlike the delictal obligation, extinguished, to the extent already mentioned, by *capitis deminutio*[13]. Since a thief was not owner he could not "*dare*"; and Gaius has no better explanation to give than that it was allowed "*odio furum*." Possibly it lay at first only where the thing had ceased to exist. It has been suggested that it was a generalisation of the *actio rerum amotarum* which lay on theft between husband and wife[14], which was much like it. Both were *perpetuae* and lay to and against

1 G. 3. 189. 2 See, e.g., Maine ,*Anc. Law*, 379. The fourfold penalty originally ransom, De Visscher, *Procédure d'Enquête*, *cit.* 3 G. 3. 189, 190; Lenel, *E.P.* 332. 4 47. 2. 50. pr. 5 47. 2. 27, 52. 28. 6 47. 2. 27. 2. For the puzzles involved, Monro, *de furtis*, 37. 7 47. 1. 1. pr.; Inst. 4. 12. pr., 1; G. 4. 112. 8 3. 2. 1. 9 13. 1. 7. 1. 10 6. 1. 27. 3; *ante*, pp. 258, 548. 11 7. 6. 5. 1. 12 G. 4. 4. Its anomalous nature, and the view of Sabinus that land could be stolen, are reflected in texts suggesting it where land is "*vi possessum*." 13. 3. 2; 47. 2. 25. 1. 13 *Ante*, p. 140. 14 Primarily for taking by wife, but also available in later classical law where the *vir* stole. Levet, *Bénéfice de competence*, 30. There must be divorce before action, 25. 2. 25.

the *heres*[1]. In both, as the defendant was always in *mora*, it lay though the thing had ceased to exist[2]. In both, increase must be paid and lessening in value was ignored[3], and in both, *fructus* and extrinsic profits came into account[4]. But *condictio furtiva* was available only to owner and pledge creditor[5], the other to a *bona fide possessor*[6].

It seems that in practice the owner relied usually on the *condictio* rather than on *vindicatio*, even though the defendant was the *heres*[7], since it dispensed with evidence as to the position or existence of the thing.

There were subsidiary actions connected with *furtum*. One on whose premises a search made resulted in the discovery of the goods was liable to a threefold penalty, *furtum conceptum*, a simplification, or secularisation, of the still older *furtum lance licioque conceptum* already mentioned[8]. Similarly one who placed stolen goods in another's house was liable to the same penalty[9] (*furtum oblatum*). Gaius says there was no penalty under the XII Tables for resisting search, but the Praetor gave an *actio in factum* for fourfold[10] (*furtum prohibitum*), and, further, an action for failure to produce stolen goods afterwards found on the premises (probably on formal search, *furtum non exhibitum*). The penalty is not stated[11]. These actions are classed by some of the jurists as varieties of *furtum*[12]. Justinian, observing that they had fallen into disuse (some of them lasted into the fifth century[13]), says that in all these cases there is a liability for *furtum nec manifestum*[14].

In modern systems theft is usually dealt with as a crime, not a wrong to be handled by an action for damages, and this was essentially the attitude of early Roman law. It is clear that this alternative was possible in the Empire; in fact, as thieves have, commonly, no money, the civil remedy would often be worthless. Ulpian tells us that criminal

1 25. 2. 6. 2, 3, 21. 5; 13. 1. 7. 2. Limitation in later law to enrichment of *heres*, (C. 5. 21. 3), Taubenschlag, *Röm. Prr. z. Z. Diocl.* 280. 2 25. 2. 3. 3, 17. 2; 13. 1. 8. pr. 3 25. 2. 29; 13. 1. 8. 1. 4 25. 2. 21. 3, 4; 13. 1. 3. 5 13. 1. 1, 12. 2. 6 25. 2. 17. 3, 20. Mommsen *Strafr.* 757. But the later development of *actio rerum amotarum*, after marriage without *manus* became usual, seems at least equally probable, the *condictio* being a civil action, the other an *actio in factum*. Lenel, *E.P.* 308. It may be that in origin this was a penal action, with a *condemnatio in duplum*; Pampaloni, *Sopra alcuni azioni attinenti al delitto di furto*; Zanzucchi, *Il divieto delle azioni famose* (both cited by Huvelin, *Furtum*, 1. 621), who hold that it was only under Justinian that the action became the quasi-contractual institution which we know. See also De Francisci, *Azioni penali*, 79 and, *contra*, Levy, *Privatstrafe*, 114. 7 13. 1. 7. 2. 8 G. 3. 186, 191; P. 2. 31. 3; *ante*, p. 581. 9 G. 3. 186, 187, 191; P. 2. 31. 3, "*ne apud se inveniretur*." G. attributes these provisions to the XII Tables but they are probably Praetorian; see Huvelin, *Furtum*, 1. 53. 10 G. 3. 188, 192. It is probable that Gaius is wrong in saying that the XII Tables gave no action for resisting search. 11 Inst. 4. 1. 4. Commonly supposed to have been fourfold. Not mentioned in any classical text. 12 G. 3. 183. 13 Gaius, *Ep.* 2. 11. 2. 14 Inst. 4. 1. 4.

proceedings were the more usual course[1], and Julian says that judgement in such proceedings barred any *actio furti*[2]. The converse is probably true.

CXCIX. *Rapina. Vi Bonorum Raptorum*[3]. Theft with violence, erected into a special delict in the troubled times of the Republic, and becoming a permanent part of the law. The action was *in factum* and condemnation involved infamy[4] and fourfold penalty, or rather, as this included the value of the thing, threefold and compensation. Being penal and praetorian, it was *annua*, but, as it covered compensation as well, *perpetua* as to the single value[5]. Some jurists doubted if it was purely penal and Justinian classes it as *mixta*[6], but it had the main characteristic of penal actions that it was not available against the *heres*[7]. As the act was normally *furtum*[8] there would be *condictio furtiva*. The principles were in general those of *furtum*[9]. Thus it applied only to *res mobiles in commercio* and owned. The *contrectatio* must be *fraudulosa*[10].

There are, however, signs of divergence. What could be recovered was a multiple of the *verum pretium*, not of the *interesse*, but one text says this of *furtum* also[11]. Though in general those who could bring it were the same, one text, probably due to Justinian, says that any sort of *interesse* sufficed in this case[12]; in classical law the rule was probably as *in furtum*[13]. One text suggests that mere encouragement made a man liable for *ope consilio*[14], which is consistent with the genesis of the action. The action was a bar to *actio furti* and any action *ad rem persequendam*[15]. Probably in classical law it was barred by *actio furti*, but under Justinian it was still available for any excess recoverable by it[16]. It is plain that, in manifest theft, *furti* would be the better remedy, but not in other cases. The action can hardly have been barred by *vindicatio*, at least as to threefold.

This delict involved bad faith, but violent enforcement of claims, even in good faith, needed repression. Such conduct had been criminal from the Republic[17], and Marcus Aurelius provided that one who seized property to satisfy a claim, without judicial process, should forfeit his

1 47. 2. 93. 2 47. 2. 57. 1, corrupt. 3 Edicts dealing with mob violence out of which it grew, Cuq, *Man.* 566; Niedermeyer, *St. Bonfante*, 2, 400. 4 Lenel, *E.P.* 395; D. 3. 2. 1. 5 G. 3. 209; Inst. 4. 2. pr. 6 G. 4. 8; Inst. 4. 6. 19. See, however, 47. 8. 2. 27. 7 47. 8. 2. 27, even to enrichment—*sufficere condictionem*. 8 47. 8. 1. It does not seem that *contrectatio* was necessary (47. 2. 81. 4; 47. 8. 2. 2); see the terms of the Edict: "*cuius dolo malo*," Lenel, *E.P.* 391. 9 47. 8. 2. 23. 10 47. 8. 1, 2. 18, 20; C. 9. 33. 1. 11 47. 2. 50. pr.; 47. 8. 2. 13. 12 47. 8. 2. 24, which gives it even to a depositee. 13 Gaius treats it as always being *furtum*, which seems to involve this. G. 3. 209. 14 47. 2. 81. 4. But the meaning of *dolus* here may be limited by 47. 8. 2. 2. 15 47. 8. 1. 16 *Ib.* 17 Mommsen, *Strafr.* 657; 4. 2. 12. 2, partly interp. In classical law violent seizure of pledges by the creditor came under the *l. Iulia de vi*, though not theft. P. 5. 26. 4; D. 47. 2. 56.

claim[1]. In A.D. 389 it was provided that one who seized property under a *bona fide* claim of right should, if the claim was well founded, forfeit his right, and if it was unfounded should give back the property and its value as well. This penalty applied to land as well as moveables[2]. The actions were no doubt ordinary proprietary actions, at any rate so far as the forfeiture of property was concerned. Whether, where the claim was well founded, the *heres* of the wrongdoer was equally liable does not appear: he could hardly have been liable to penalty in the other case.

CC. *DAMNUM INIURIA DATUM*[3]. Wrongful damage to property.

The law on this topic is mainly based on the *l. Aquilia,* of uncertain date, but earlier than the introduction of mandate[4]. It does not seem that, as the Institutes suggest, and the Digest says[5], it superseded earlier provisions as matter of law[6], but it was of overwhelming practical importance and seems to have swamped them. On the other hand there was praetorian legislation on the matter[7], apart from extensions of the *lex.* This law, however, with its extensions, was much the most important part of the scheme of remedies. The words *damnum iniuria datum* mean damage unlawfully caused, but we get the expression *actio damni iniuriae*[8].

The *l. Aquilia* contained, besides a penalty for *adstipulatores* who fraudulently released the debtor[9] (which does not here concern us) and a vaguely indicated procedure for *multa* as an alternative, in the case which does concern us[10], two important provisions for a civil remedy for damage to property. Its first chapter provided that anyone who unlawfully killed another's slave or beast within the class of *pecus,* i.e. such as feed in herds, was liable to pay the owner the highest value the thing had had within the previous year[11]. Its third chapter provided that anyone who unlawfully damaged another's property in respects not coming under the first chapter, by burning, breaking or destroying, was liable to pay him the value the thing had had within 30 days before[12].

The time was reckoned back, from the injury not from the death[13].

1 D. 4. 2. 13; 48. 7. 7. 2 C. 8. 4. 7; Inst. 4. 2. 1. 3 Ferrini, *Opere,* 5. 191; Pernice, *Sachbeschädigungen*; Grueber, *Lex Aquilia*; Monro, *ad legem Aquiliam*; Thayer, *Lex Aquilia. Actio de pastu pecoris,* an ordinary delictal action, not analogous to *de pauperie,* Fliniaux, *Mél. Cornil,* 1. 247; Lenel, *E.P.* 198. 4 It contains provisions for unfaithful *adstipulator,* not needed if *actio mandati* existed, G. 3. 215. 5 Inst. 4. 3. pr.; G. 3. 210; D. 9. 2. 1. pr. 6 Girard, *Textes,* 17 *sqq.* 7 4. 9. 5. 1; 39. 4. 1; 47. 9. 1, etc. 8 Inst. 4. 3. pr.; G. 3. 210; G. 4. 9; D. 9. 2. 32. pr., etc. We have also *damnum iniuria.* In Inst. 4. 4. pr. it may be *damnum iniuria* in apposition (Monro, *cit.* 43), though some editors insert "*datum.*" Buckland, *R.H.* 1927, 120. 9 *Ante,* p. 444. 10 Cic. *Brut.* 34. 131. 11 G. 3. 210, 214; Inst. 4. 3. pr.; D. 9. 2. 2. Inst., h. t. 1, give a list of the animals, all ordinary domestic beasts, treated as *pecus.* D. 9. 2. 2. 2 adds elephants and camels if tamed. 12 G. 3. 217; Inst. 4. 3. 13; D. 9. 2. 27. 5. For the view that ch. 3 originally dealt only with destruction of *ceterae res,* Jolowicz, *L.Q.R.* 1922, 220; review, Lenel, *Z.S.S.* 1922, 575. 13 9. 2. 21. 1. Julian.

The third chapter did not, like the first, say the highest (*plurimi*) value within the 30 days, but this was read in, in order to give the provision a meaning[1]. On these words a man who merely damaged the property had to pay the whole value, but, apart from the bad economics of such a rule[2], one text implies that what he had to pay was the difference between the highest value and the value after the damage[3].

The *actio legis Aquiliae* was delictal and penal with the ordinary consequences that it did not lie against the *heres*, except to the extent of his enrichment[4], was not extinguished by *capitis deminutio*[5], and made each of joint wrongdoers liable in full. It was penal as to the whole claim, not merely as to excess over the harm done[6]: as there often would be no such excess, it might, like the *actio doli*, be penal where what was paid was merely compensation. It was penal also in the sense that it was for double in case of denial[7], but this alone did not cause an action to be regarded as penal[8]. We are told that one who confessed the fact of killing could not afterwards deny liability, but might prove that the man was not dead or died from natural causes[9]. The action on confession (*actio confessoria*) is spoken of as lying where "*confiteatur occidisse*" but it seems clear that to avoid the double penalty there must be admission of liability, not merely of the fact[10].

The damage must be unlawful, but need not be wilful; negligence was enough[11]. But the negligence must be active; mere omission did not suffice[12]. Cases which look like exceptions, as of one who, having lit a fire, neglected to look after it, so that it spread to the next property[13], were cases in which an act was done with insufficient attention to consequences. The strongest case is that in which *A* lit a fire and *B* watched it negligently. *B* was liable[14]. But he was not a casual passer without privity; he was one who had done something to make himself responsible.

1 G. 3. 218. 2 No inducement to stop if some damage had been done, unless the deft. might take the *res*, which would operate as a compulsory sale and is not evidenced. 3 9. 2. 24. On the measure of damages where a thing promised is damaged or destroyed by the promisee (9. 2. 54, 55), Thayer, *cit.* 117. 4 G. 4. 112; D. 9. 2. 23. 8; *post*, § CCXXXIII. 5 4. 5. 2. 3. 6 *Arg.* 9. 2. 11. 1. Pernice, *Sachbeschädigungen*, 125; Collinet-Giffard, *Précis*, 2. 152. 7 9. 2. 23. 10; *post*, §§ CCXI, CCXII. 8 E.g. the action on *l. per damnationem*. 9 9. 2. 23. 11, 25. pr.; 42. 2. 4. The distinction drawn seems to rest on a confused notion of possibility. See Monro, *l. Aquilia*, App. 3. 10 9. 2. 23. 11 seems to imply that confession of the fact alone makes the action *confessoria*, but only, it seems, because it dispenses with proof of the *iniuria*. But in Coll. 12. 7. pr. the words are "*si fatebitur iniuria occisum esse*," and in D. 9. 2. 25. 2 (interp. Beseler, *Beiträge*, 1. 54) the principle is the same. It must be remembered that *culpa* sufficed and was presumed. 11 G. 3. 211; Inst. 4. 3. 3; D. 9. 2. 5. 1. 12 *Arg.* "*occidere*," etc. 13 9. 2. 27. 9 = Coll. 12. 7. 7. See also 9. 2. 8. pr.; Pernice, *cit.* 164 *sqq.*; Grueber, *l. Aquilia*, 208 *sqq.* 14 9. 2. 27. 9; Coll. 12. 7. 7.

In most of these cases the remedy was not the direct action but a Praetorian extension[1].

The negligence need not be extreme; slight negligence sufficed[2]. This rule raises the question, where there was a contract between the parties in which *culpa* did not create liability, e.g. deposit, whether damage caused by negligence created the Aquilian liability. There is no decisive text and both views are held[3]. The dominant opinion is that the liability existed[4].

Contributory negligence of the aggrieved person might be a defence. This is sometimes misleadingly called "*culpa*-compensation," which suggests both a quantitative relation between them, and the notion of damage to the defendant by the plaintiff, neither of which has anything to do with the matter. The Roman principle is causal. The *nexus* was broken if there intervened, between the *culpa* of the defendant and the damage, some other cause without which the damage would not have occurred[5]. Where a man wounded another not mortally, who died in consequence of being neglected, he was liable for the wounding but not for the death[6]. But if the original act was wilful it is generally held (there is no clear text) that intervening negligence of the injured person was no defence, though there was the same breach of causal *nexus*[7]. Where the intervening event was a wrongful act of a third person the texts present some difficulty, but their doctrine seems to be as follows[8]: Where a slave, wounded by *A* and then by *B*, died, if each act would certainly have killed, *A* had wounded, *B* had killed. If several wounded and it was clear which killed, he alone was liable for the killing. If it was not made out that one killed, more than another, all were liable for killing. If it was clear that *A*'s wound would have killed, but not clear whether *B*'s would or not, apart from *A*'s previous act, both were liable. But it is usually held that the texts cannot be reconciled[9].

CCI. The statute was at first very narrowly construed. At one time it seems that it was inferred from the etymology of the word "*occido*" that the act must have been done directly by the person of the wrongdoer or a weapon held by him. The early lawyers extended this to killing

1 Thayer, *cit.* 65, 88, 101, holds that there was liability for omission wherever there was a duty (to anyone?) to act. 2 9. 2. 44. pr. 3 Pernice, *cit.* 78 *sqq.*; Windscheid, *Lehrb.* § 455, n. 12 *in f.* 4 But this reduces the rule *in depositum* to an absurdity in a wide range of cases. A workman could contract out of Aquilian liability (9. 2. 27. 29). The implied terms of the contract of deposit seem to be on much the same footing. 5 9. 2. 11. pr.; 50. 17. 203. 6 9. 2. 30. 4, 52. pr. 7 On 9. 2. 9. 4 see Thayer, *cit.* 65. 8 The principal texts are 9. 2. 11. 2, 3, 15. 1, 51. 1. 9 Pernice, *op. cit.* 130; Windscheid, *Lehrb.* 2. § 258, n. 15; Beseler, *Beitr.* 3. 9, 4. 194. Necessity as a defence, 9. 2. 29. 3 (Grueber, *cit. ad l.*); h. t. 49. 1; 47. 9. 3. 7; self-defence, 9. 2. 4, 5. pr., 45. 4; protection of rights, 9. 2. 29. 1; consent (*volenti non fit iniuria*), 9. 2. 7. 4; 19. 2. 30. 2; 47. 10. 1. 5.

by, e.g., actually administering poison[1]. The rule so understood was expressed in the words that it must be "*corpori corpore*," by the wrongdoer's body to that of the injured thing[2]. Further, "*rumpere*" in the third chapter was interpreted to mean "*corrumpere*," so that it covered any form of material damage and the other words became unimportant[3]. And, in construing the words "highest value" the jurists included what is called "*damnum emergens*," loss due to extrinsic circumstances[4], and "*lucrum cessans*," profit which the fact prevented the owner from making[5]. The killing of one horse of a pair, of one of a troupe of actors[6], are instances of the first, as the loss was greater than the value of the thing as a single thing. The second is illustrated by loss of a *hereditas* on which the slave would have entered[7]. But it must be material loss: value of affection was not taken into account[8]. Though the statute applied only to *res mobiles*, its application was extended to land[9].

Even so extended, the statute was narrow; it was left to the Praetor to make further extensions, not of the action itself, but by providing analogous remedies for analogous cases. Such are the following:

(*a*) The *lex* applied only where the aggrieved person was the *dominus*[10]. The Praetor gave an *actio utilis*, or one *in factum*, to persons with lesser *iura in rem*, e.g. usufruct, the unit being the value of the interest, the owner having also an action for the value of his interest[11]. A *b. f. possessor* had the action for the full value, but if ultimately sued by the owner, must give up what he had recovered[12]. Under Justinian, probably not before, a pledgee had it if the debtor was insolvent, or if he had from any cause lost his personal claim against the debtor[13]. In these cases it lay even against the owner, as an *actio in factum*[14]. In general one with a mere *ius in personam* had not the extended action, but one text gives it to a *colonus* where weeds are sown in a cornfield[15].

(*b*) *Leges* did not apply to persons not *cives*, unless expressly, but an *actio ficticia* was given in this case as if they were *cives*[16].

(*c*) The *lex* covered only cases of property. Injury of a freeman was

1 9. 2. 7. 6, 9. pr. 2 Inst. 4. 3. 16. 3 G. 3. 217. 4 Inst. 4. 3. 10.
5 G. 3. 212; Inst. 4. 3. 10. Where a slave is killed there are alternative criminal proceedings.
6 9. 2. 22. 1. 7 9. 2. 23. pr.; Inst. 4. 3. 10. It must not be speculative, 9. 2. 29. 3.
8 9. 2. 33. pr. 9 9. 2. 27. 7–9; Coll. 12. 2. 7. 10 On the difficult texts where ownership changes by legacy, Thayer, *cit.* 73 (4. 2. 13. 3, 15 pr., 41. pr.). 11 9. 2. 11. 10.
12 5. 3. 55; 9. 2. 11. 8, 17. 13 9. 2. 30. 1, interp. De Medio, *St. Scialoja*, 1, 29.
14 9. 2. 12, 17. The genuineness of 17 may be doubted, as to *b. f. p.*, in view of 5. 3. 55.
15 9. 2. 27. 14 (cp. h. l. 20, which gives direct action to owner of grain with which sand has been mixed). In the present case the injury is to the crop, which will ultimately belong to *colonus*, indeed he hardly suffers injury till this has grown. No text authorises the view that a mere *ius in personam* gave the action (9. 2. 11. 9). Disputed whether 27. 14 is interp. or not, Debray, *N.R.H.* 1910, 643; Costa, *Locazione*, 92; Thayer, *cit.* 91. 16 G. 4. 37

thus not within it, for a man did not own his body. The Praetor gave an *actio utilis* to a freeman who, or whose *filiusfamilias*, had been injured[1], but not where a freeman was killed[2].

(*d*) The *lex* applied only where the damage was by the body to the body, *corpore corpori*. The Praetor gave an action, *utilis* or *in factum*, in cases not within this conception, where it was by but not to the body, as by dropping a ring into a river[3]. It might not be harmed, but in effect it was destroyed. So too where it was to, but not by, the body, as by putting poison where a slave was likely to take it, but not actually administering it[4]. So too where it was neither, as by opening a stable door so that animals escaped and were lost. It is easy to see that these lines might be difficult to draw. There is no great difference between mixing the seed in the bag, which gives the direct action, and sowing false seed which does not[5]. The line between actually administering poison and facilitating the taking might be rather fine.

In some cases an *actio utilis* was given; in others an *actio in factum*. Gaius makes it *utilis* wherever it was not *corpore*[6]: the Institutes say that if it was not *corpore* or *corpori* the action was *in factum*, which would make it *utilis* if it was *corpore* but not *corpori*[7]. But the texts in the Digest do not conform to any rule. Even the direct action is given in cases which seem to be more appropriate to one of the others[8], and as between these, no logical scheme is attainable, perhaps because the question was one of procedure[9], never very important, and practically obsolete under Justinian. In view of the words "*reddendo actiones in factum accommodatas legi Aquiliae, idque utilitas huius legis exigit*[10]," it is to be doubted whether any distinction is intended.

CCII. *Iniuria*. Insult, contumely. Justinian, following Paul, tells us of the many senses in which this word is used, with the Greek equivalent in each case[11]. It might mean unlawful action, as in the case just considered; it might mean any unlawful interference with right; it might mean an unjust judgement, but, as a special delict, it meant *contumelia*, insult or outrage, represented in Greek by ὕβρις.

The XII Tables contained provisions against a number of forms of insult, probably only assaults, usually subjecting them to a fixed money

1 9. 2. 7. pr., 13. pr. 2 *Arg.* 9. 1. 3; 9. 2. 7. pr.; 9. 3. 1. 5. De Medio, *cit.*, thinks the right of *liber homo* is due to Justinian. 3 19. 5. 23. 4 9. 2. 7. 6. 5 9. 2. 27. 14, 20. 6 G. 3. 219. 7 Inst. 4. 3. 16. Rotondi, *Scr. Giur.* 2. 444, thinks G.'s account exhaustive: where it was not *corpori* classical law gave *a. in f.* for damages, not related to the Aquilian, a subsidiary action for lack of other remedy, source of J.'s *a. in f. generalis*, as to which, Riccobono, *Dal dir. Rom.* 638, Thayer, *cit.* 61. 8 9. 2. 27. 19–21. 9 Disputed: it has been said that the *actio in factum* was not *in duplum contra infitiantem* and did not go to the highest value, but see Pernice, *cit.* 157; Grueber, *cit.* 199; Thayer, *cit.* 61. 10 19. 5. 11. 11 Inst. 4. 4. pr.; Coll. 2. 5. 1.

penalty[1]. This crude system, limited in scope and inflicting penalties which with changes in the value of money had become derisory in the later Republic[2], was then superseded in practice by a series of praetorian edicts[3]. The first, known later as "*edictum generale*" and probably designed to deal only with the acts contemplated by the XII Tables, provided in terms which, as we know them, cover any form of *iniuria*, that an *actio in factum* would lie, in which the plaintiff must specify the nature of the *iniuria* complained of and the amount claimed, the case to be tried by *recuperatores* who would fix the amount of the *condemnatio*[4]. The next dealt with *convicium*, public insult, and there followed other edicts extending the scope of the action[5]. These begin a profound change in the conception of the wrong, assisted by the very general form of the *edictum generale*, which lent itself to juristic interpretation, so that, in the law as we know it, the wrong consisted in outrage or insult or wanton interference with rights[6], any act, in short, which shewed contempt of the personality of the victim or was such as to lower him in the estimation of others, and was so intended[7]. All that was needed was that the act be insulting in kind and intention, and unjustified[8]. Not only the actual insulter was liable but any accomplice, even one who did no more than encourage the offender[9].

The evolution was somewhat interrupted by a *l. Cornelia de iniuriis* of the time of Sulla, which provided a criminal or quasi-criminal remedy for "*pulsare, verberare, vi domum introire*" (covering the whole field of the *iniuriae* dealt with in the XII Tables)[10], and apparently some other proceedings[11]. On one view, this legislation excluded these wrongs from the ordinary *actio aestimatoria iniuriarum*, till late in the classical age, when a rescript of Severus and Caracalla restored the right to bring a

1 Girard, *Textes*, 17, 18; Bruns, 1. 29, 30. Greek basis of this "*edictum generale*," De Visscher, *Ét.* 329. Various views as to early notions, Weiss, *Krv.* 1919, 34; C. Appleton, *Mél. Cornil*, 1. 51; De Francisci, *Az. penali*, 48. Haesert, *Bull. Ac. R. Belgique*, 1929, 235, finds a gradual supersession of the idea of order and *boni mores* by that of *contumelia*. 2 Aul. Gell. 20. 1. 13. 3 History, Girard, *Mél. Gérardin*, 255 *sqq.* 4 Aul. Gell. *ib.*; Coll. 2. 6. 1; Lenel, *E.P.* 399. 5 47. 10. 15. 2; *adtemptata pudicitia*, Inst. 4. 4. 1; *infamandi causa facta*, 47. 10. 15. 25, etc. Lenel, *E.P.* 397 *sqq.* 6 So early as Labeo the *generale edictum* was understood as wide enough to cover the special cases. 47. 10. 15. 3, 15. 26. See, e.g., 47. 10. 13. 7, 15. 31, 23, 27, etc. 7 The principles are not those of our law of defamation. Intent was the gist: it is immaterial to liability in our law, apart from privilege. It was wider (47. 10. 1. 2). In most cases publication to third persons was not needed, apart from *convicium*. The wrong was doing intentionally what was likely to injure a man's reputation or outrage his feelings. 8 G. 3. 220; Inst. 4. 4. 1; 47. 10. 3. 1, 4, 12, 13. 1, etc. Many *iniuriae* had other remedies. *Actio contraria iniuriarum* for wrongfully bringing the action, G. 4. 177 (*post*, § CCXVIII), and there were other remedies for this. 47. 10. 43; P. 5. 4. 11. 9 47. 10. 11. pr., 6. 10 3. 3. 42. 1; P. 5. 4. 8; 47. 10. 5. The reff. to the *lex* are cited Mommsen, *Strafr.* 785, n. 2. 11 See P. 5. 4. 8.

civil action in such cases[1]. But the view that the two remedies existed side by side is also held[2].

The action was in a special sense "*vindictam spirans*." It rested on outraged feelings, not on economic loss; hence some characteristic rules. Like other delictal actions it did not lie against the *heres* of the wrongdoer, but, contrary to the general rule, it was not available to the *heres* of the injured person[3]. It lay only within a year[4], and, as it rested on outraged feelings, not unless there was evidence of anger at the outset—*dissimulatione aboletur*[5]. As it had nothing to do with property, the penalty was measured according to the position of the parties, and the grossness of the outrage[6]. It was no defence that the defendant did not know the plaintiff, or mistook him for someone else[7], except that if the defendant had supposed the plaintiff a *paterfamilias* or a widow no action lay for the insult to the actual *paterfamilias* or *vir*[8]. But the truth of any statement charged was a complete defence[9].

The *iniuria* need not be directly to the person aggrieved; it is plain that *A* might be insulted by something done to *B*. But the important cases are of outrage to members of the family. An *iniuria* to a wife gave an action not only to her but to her husband[10]. An insult to a *filius* was an insult to the *paterfamilias* as well, who might sue for himself and for his son, though, as in certain circumstances the son might himself sue, there was a provision against two actions *nomine filii*[11]. Where a married *filiafamilias* was insulted there might be three actions, or more, her own, her husband's, her father's, and even her husband's father's[12]. A *sponsus* might have an action on an insult to his *sponsa*[13]. The penalty would not necessarily be the same in these cases: in each the personality of the plaintiff was considered[14]. And though insult to wife or child was insult to *paterfamilias*, the converse was not true[15]. The most remarkable case of indirect insult is that of *heredes*. An insult to the body or funeral was an insult to the *heres* if he had entered. If not, it was an insult to the *hereditas* and the *heres* on entry acquired it like other claims[16].

Iniuria to a slave was the subject of elaborate rules. For *verberatio*

1 Mommsen, *op. cit.* 804, n. 3; Girard, *Mél. Gérardin*, 258, 279 *sqq.*, basing on 47. 10. 7. 6, 37. 1. 2 Lenel, *E.P.* 397. The other view is difficult to reconcile with, e.g., G. 3. 220, who wrote long before Caracalla and treats assault as typical *iniuria* for the praetorian action. See also Strahan-Davidson, *Rom. Crim. Law*, 1. 219 *sqq.* 3 47. 10. 13. pr. "*lite* (*non*) *contestata.*" 4 C. 9. 35. 5. 5 47. 10. 11. 1; Inst. 4. 4. 12. As to transmissibility of this and other actions "*vindictam spirantes*," *post*, § CCXXXIII. 6 Inst. 4. 4. 7. 7 47. 10. 18. 3. 8 47. 10. 18. 4. But the fact that the offender did not know what the family relations of the person insulted were is no reply to an action by the *pater*, h. t. 1. 8. 9 47. 10. 18. pr. 10 47. 10. 1. 3. 11 *Ib.*; h. t. 17. 10–22. 12 47. 10. 1. 9; G. 3. 221; Inst. 4. 4. 2. 13 47. 10. 15. 24. 14 47. 10. 30. 1. 15 Inst. 4. 4. 2: exception, 47. 10. 11. 8. 16 47. 10. 1. 4, 6.

or inflicting torture, without justification, an action lay without proof of intent to insult the master[1]. This was *servi nomine*: "*hanc enim et servum sentire palam est*[2]." The master brought the action: how the penalties were assessed we do not know, or whether they were *in peculio*. Apart from this no action lay unless the *iniuria* was *atrox*; if it was, and was intended to insult the master, there was an *actio domini nomine*[3]. If no such intent was proved an action lay *servi nomine*, but it was still really on account of the master; such a thing did insult him, though the edict governing it said nothing of intent to insult the master[4]. It did not pass on alienation of the slave[5].

Of several masters all might have an action, and the damages would vary, not with their share, but with their position[6]. But in *iniuria* to a slave, apart from *verberatio*, etc., the action was not a matter of course: it was given *causa cognita*[7]. If there were less rights in the slave, e.g. usufruct, the fructuary might have an action, but the *iniuria* was *prima facie* presumed to be to the owner[8]. So too a *bona fide possessor* might have it, and, if the man was really free, both might have it[9].

A distinction between *atrox* and ordinary *iniuria* frequently recurs. As the question, which it was, was left to the Praetor, the distinction was perhaps not very exactly drawn. We are told that it might be *atrox ex re* (or *facto*) from its extreme nature, or *ex persona*, the person insulted being one to whom special respect was due (e.g. the patron, or a magistrate), or *ex loco*, where it was very public[10]. The chief results of *atrocitas* were that an action would lie on insult to a slave[11], and that the penalty was differently estimated. In general the plaintiff fixed his maximum claim by a *taxatio*, which the *iudex* could cut down. In *atrox iniuria* the Praetor fixed the maximum, usually at a higher rate, and the *iudex* did not interfere with it[12].

In an increasing number of cases there were criminal remedies for *iniuria*. In later law an *extraordinarium iudicium* for punishment was always an available alternative[13], used where the defendant was without means, and evidently sometimes in other cases of extreme insult. However the matter was tried condemnation involved *infamia*[14].

1 6. 1. 15. pr.; 47. 10. 15. 34. 2 47. 10. 15. 35. 3 *Ib*. This distinction between actions *domini* and *servi nomine* is unknown to Gaius, G. 3. 222. 4 47. 10. 15. 35; h. l. 44. 5 47. 10. 29. 6 Inst. 4. 4. 4. The action is *domini nomine*. In 47. 10. 16, Paul, quoting Pedius, gives the action in proportion to their shares. This may be *servi nomine*. ? Interp. Guarneri-Citati, *Misc. Eseg*. 70. 7 47. 10. 15. 34. 8 47. 10. 15. 45–48. Fructuary had no action on *iniuria* by *dominus*, or *vice versa*, or common owners of the slave against each other, 47. 10. 15. 36–38. 9 47. 10. 15. 48. 10 G. 3. 225; P. 5. 4. 10; Inst. 4. 4. 9; D. 47. 10. 7. 6–9 *sqq*. 11 47. 10. 15. 44. 12 G. 3. 224; Coll. 2. 2. 1. One condemned for *atrox iniuria* could not afterwards be a *decurio*, 47. 10. 40. 13 47. 10. 45; Inst. 4. 4. 10. 14 3. 2. 1. Concurrence with actions *ex contractu*, and other delictal remedies, *post*, § CCXLII.

CCIII. This ends the list of Delicts which the Institutes, following Gaius, expressly consider, but there were others which gave rise to what may for later law be called *actiones ex delicto*.

Metus. There was a complex praetorian machinery for relieving one who had been forced by threats to go through some legal transaction, or in later law, other damaging act[1], and to penalise the wrongdoer. There was an *actio quod metus causa* in default of restoration[2], an *exceptio metus* if a claim was made under the transaction[3], and *restitutio in integrum*[4], the nature of which varied with the nature of the right created[5]. The threats must be of death or bodily hurt, or wrongful enslavement, or a capital charge, or an attack on chastity, either to plaintiff or to a member of his family[6]. Mere money threats were not enough[7], and the fear must have been actual, and the imminence of the threat such that a normal man might reasonably have feared[8]. The action is not infaming. It lay, according to the texts, against not only the wrongdoer, but third persons, even innocent, who had profited, either immediately or indirectly[9]. The penalty was fourfold of the damage, including *damnum emergens*, etc., in the case of the wrongdoer, of their profit, in the case of others[10]. But the action was *arbitraria* in the sense that the *condemnatio* was incurred only if, where the *iudex* ordered restitution, the defendant failed to restore[11]. Here there was a difference between the positions of the wrongdoer and others. The former was necessarily *in mora*, and thus took the risk of *casus*[12], so that he might be unable to restore, and he might have parted with the proceeds[13], while a third party was liable only for his actual profit, which he could always restore and thus avoid the heavy *condemnatio*[14]. The action was available to *heredes*, but not against them, except to the extent of enrichment[15]. As in other delicts, where more than one person was engaged in the wrong, each was liable in full, but there was the exceptional rule that when one had made the wrong good, the others were released[16], a result of the principle that the action lay only "*si non res restituatur*[17]."

1 Accarias, *Précis*, 2. 931; *arg.* 4. 2. 9. 2. 2 4. 2. 14. 1. 3 4. 2. 9. 3. 4 4. 2. 1. All known in the Republic. Cicero, *de Off.* 1. 10. 32; *pro Flacco*, 21. 49; *In Verr.* 2. 3. 65. 152. The texts dealing with the different remedies are not clearly to be distinguished in the Digest. 5 *Post*, § CCXLIII. 6 4. 2. 3–6, 8. 3. 7 4. 2. 3. 1, 7. 1, 8. 1, 2; C. 2. 19. 4, 8. 8 4. 2. 5, 6. 9 4. 2. 14. 3 under J. But it is probable (Schulz, *Z.S.S.* 1922, 240; Beseler, *Beitr.* 1. 73, 4. 259) that under the Edict it lay only against the wrongdoer, while *r. i. i.* was *in rem*. S. holds that J. extended this effect to the action, practically suppressing the *r. i. i.* See Lenel, *E.P.* § 39. 10 4. 2. 14. 1, 7, 17, 18. 11 4. 2. 14. 3, 4. It may be that restitution barred the fourfold action in classical law only if it was before *litis contestatio*. See, e.g., Biondi, *Actiones arbitrariae*, 1. 42; Beseler, *Beitr.* 3. 155. 12 4. 2. 14. 1, interp. 13 4. 2. 14. 5, *in f.* 14 4. 2. 14. 5. 15 4. 2. 19; *post*, § CCXXXIII. 16 4. 2. 14. 15, 16. 1. No sufficient reason to hold with Albertario, *Bull.* 1913, 106 and Bonfante, *Scr. Giur.* 3. 217 that the rule of release in such circumstances is interp. See also, above, n. 11. 17 4. 2. 14. 1, 15.

The action being praetorian and penal was *annua*, but lay, *in simplum*, after the year, *causa cognita*, if there was no other remedy[1]. It seems that in early law it did not lie till the loss was completed, not, e.g., on an extorted promise, where there was only the *exceptio* or *restitutio*, but in classical law this limitation was extinct[2]. In other respects the remedies seem to have been nearly co-extensive. None was subordinate; the party could choose whichever suited the case, but there are difficulties as to the use of more than one. If the defendant accepted the *arbitrium*, and restored, there was no room for the other remedies, but if he had been condemned, there is doubt on the texts[3]. On the older view, the action was purely penal, so that if the injured party was sued, on, e.g., an extorted promise, he still had the *exceptio*. The harshness of this was avoided by including in the fourfold a release of the debt, i.e. condemning for threefold and a discharge: in later law the rule is clear that the fourfold barred any other remedy, and the transaction stood. Whether this is due to Justinian is disputed[4].

Dolus. The definition by Labeo, adopted by Ulpian, is "any craft or deceit employed for the circumvention or entrapping of another person[5]." It is sometimes added, for the purpose of this action, that it must have induced some act of the aggrieved party, as in *metus*, but there was no such restriction[6], though it was no doubt only in that case that there could be *restitutio in integrum*. Where this was applicable there would be no *actio doli*. Little is known of this *restitutio*; it seems to have been in Julian's Edict[7], but may have been applied only in matter of procedure[8]. The *actio doli* was conceived of as penal, and was thus available to[9] but not against *heredes*, except to the extent of enrichment[10], and was barred by an *annus utilis*[11]. It was *arbitraria*[12], and lay only if the damage had not been made good[13]. As elsewhere if more than one person was engaged in the wrong, each was liable for the whole, but here if one had made the wrong good, the others were released[14]. In these

1 4. 2. 14. 1, 2. 2 Karlowa, *R.Rg*. 2. 1065. 3 4. 2. 14. 9–11; Girard, *Man*. 449. 4 Text perhaps interp. 5 4. 3. 1. 2. But, at least in late law, it lies for wilful injury, with no requirement of preconcerted fraud, e.g. 4. 3. 34. Litten, *Festschr. f. Güterbock*, 257. 6 4. 3. 7. 6, 18. 5, etc. 7 4. 1. 7. 1. 8 Lenel, *E.P.* § 40; see Duquesne, *Mél. Fournier*, 185. The Digest aims at suppressing the *in int. rest*. 9 G. 4. 112; Inst. 4. 12. 1. 10 4. 3. 17, 26, where it is *perpetua* and not *famosa*, h. t. 28, 29. 11 44. 7. 35. Constantine requires it to be begun within an *annus continuus* (with some reliefs) and finished within two *annos continuos* (C. Th. 2. 15. 1). Justinian modifies this: it is enough that it be finished within two *annos continuos*, whenever begun (C. 2. 20. 8). It is possible that C. Th. 2. 15. 1 enacted the same thing, *tempus anni* being a corruption for *tempus biennii*, but see Gradenwitz, *Z.S.S.* 1913, 293. The *exceptio* is not similarly limited. 15. 1. 30. 6 probably interp.; Beseler, *Beitr*. 3. 86. 12 4. 3. 18. pr. 13 Satisfaction after *litis contestatio*, *ante*, p. 593, n. 11; satisfaction of judgement, Bonfante, *Scr. Giur*. 3. 218. 14 4. 3. 17. pr., 4. 3. 1. 8–4; the action lies only if there is no other remedy against him, or another, by which "*res servari poterit*"—not therefore if it is already *servata*. Buckland, *L.Q.R.* 1939, 222.

respects it resembled the *actio metus*, but it differed in that it lay only against the wrongdoer, not against third parties[1], was infaming[2] and was subsidiary, i.e. was not allowed if there was any other remedy, either against the wrongdoer or another[3] (even a *popularis actio*[4]), or where the *exceptio* sufficed[5]. Even where there had been another remedy but it was time-barred or released, there was no *actio doli*[6]. But if the other remedy was illusory, on account of insolvency of the potential defendant, the *actio doli* was allowed[7], as also in case of reasonable doubt as to the existence of another remedy[8]. The only certain exception is that it was alternative to *actio metus*[9], but there are texts suggesting that in later classical law it was sometimes alternative to other actions[10].

The action being purely praetorian, these points and other grounds of exclusion would be determined by the Praetor, and we are told that the action was given only *causa cognita*[11]. As it was infaming it was not allowed except in cases of some importance[12], and never to *liberi* or *liberti* against *pater* or *patronus*[13], or to any *humilis* against one of high rank[14]. Here an *actio in factum* was given which said nothing of *dolus* and was not infaming[15]. The same action was given in ordinary cases, after the *actio doli* was time-barred, to the extent of enrichment[16], and perhaps where it was barred by another remedy, itself time-barred.

Servi corruptio. A praetorian action with liability *in duplum*, for making a slave less valuable, by physical, mental or moral deterioration caused dolosely[17]. It did not lie for *culpa*, though for physical harm thus caused there was an Aquilian action[18]. The fact that he was already evil was no defence; it did not excuse making him worse[19]. The action was not available to or against a *bona fide possessor*[20], but since it lay as an *actio utilis* to anyone with a *ius in rem*, owner and fructuary might have it against each other[21]. It was *perpetua*[22] and noxal[23], but being delictal, was available to but not against the *heres*[24]. It was not extinguished by death, alienation or manumission of the slave[25]. The unit of which double was due included, besides the lessening in value, the amount of things stolen or damage done by the slave[26], and of any liability he might have

1 4. 3. 15. 3. 2 D. 3. 2. 1. 3 4. 3. 1. 1, h. t. 3, h. t. 4. 4 4. 3. 7. 2. 5 4. 3. 1. 4, 40. 6 4. 3. 1. 6, 7. 7 4. 3. 5, 6. 8 4. 3. 7. 3. 9 4. 2. 14. 13. 10 E.g. C. 2. 20. 1; D. 7. 4. 5. 3. Accarias, *Précis*, 2. 920. 11 4. 3. 1. 1. 12 4. 3. 9. 5, 10, 11. pr. 13 4. 3. 11. 14 4. 3. 11. 15 *Ib.*; h. t. 12. 16 4. 3. 28. 17 11. 3. 1. pr., 4, 5. 2. Concealing in flight, persuading to misconduct, idleness, crime, fraud or insolence, or wilfully causing injury to his body. 18 11. 3. 4. 19 11. 3. 1. 4; probably introduced for damage other than physical. Extension as *utilis* for *filii* (11. 3. 14. 1), post-classical. Lenel, *E.P.* 175. 20 11. 3. 1. 1. 21 11. 3. 9. 1; *utilis* for fructuary. 22 11. 3. 13; as a mere extension of a civil law principle. 23 11. 3. 5. 3. 24 11. 3. 13. 25 11. 3. 5. 4. 26 E.g., destruction of evidences of debt. 11. 3. 11. 1.

imposed on the owner, e.g. where he was induced to steal from, or damage the property of, a third person[1]. It was not barred by *actio furti*, e.g. where he stole "*ope consilio*" of a third party against whom *furti* had been accordingly brought, or by return of what he had stolen[2]. In later law the master might choose between this action and surrendering the slave, taking in return his original value[3].

Gaius discusses the case in which a third person tried to induce *A*'s slave to rob him, but the slave informed *A*, who, in order to trap the corrupter, told the slave to fall in with the plan. Gaius held, logically, that there was no liability for *servi corruptio*, as the slave was not corrupted, or for theft, as *A* consented. But Justinian, by a sort of rough justice, allowed both actions[4].

FRAUD ON CREDITORS. The classical law on this matter is obscure and controverted[5]. There seems to have been *restitutio in integrum*, with resulting rescissory action or *exceptio*, according to the nature of the transaction to be set aside, perhaps available only to the *curator bonorum*, and an *interdictum fraudatorium* available to any of the creditors, and there was probably an *actio in factum*. In the Digest the *restitutio* and the interdict do not appear, and the remedy is an *actio Pauliana*, a name which has been shewn[6] to be inserted by a glossator, after the first publication of the Digest. It lay where the debtor had impoverished himself to the detriment of his creditors, e.g. by alienations, by incurring liabilities or allowing rights to lapse[7], but not for failing to acquire[8] or for paying just debts[9]. There must be intent to defraud, but knowledge that creditors would suffer was enough and might be inferred from the circumstances[10]. The action required proof of insolvency and lay only where the creditors had taken possession: it was exercised for them by the *curator* or *magister*[11]. It lay against the debtor, who might have since acquired property, but even if he had not, in *terrorem* or as a sort of penalty[12]. But its chief field was against acquirers privy to the fraud[13], or even innocent, if the acquisition was gratuitous[14]. It was *fictitia*, the fiction being that the wrongful act had not taken place[15]. It was *arbitraria*[16], so that *condemnatio* was avoided by restitution, *in simplum*, *annua*, available to but not against *heredes*[17], and not noxal[18].

1 11. 3. 10, 14. 5–8. 2 11. 3. 11. 2, 12. 3 11. 3. 14. 9, interp. 4 G. 3. 198; Inst. 4. 1. 8. 5 Various views, Lenel, *E.P.* 435, 495; Solazzi, *Bull.* 1903, 127; Girard, *Man.* 452; Huvelin, *Furtum*, 467. 6 Collinet, *N.R.H.* 1919, 187. 7 42. 8. 1–5. 8 42. 8. 6. 2. 9 42. 8. 6. 7. 10 42. 8. 10. 2, 17. 1. 11 42. 8. 1. pr., 6. 7, 10. 1. 12 42. 8. 10. 24; h. t. 25. 7. 13 42. 8. 10. 1–4. 14 42. 8. 9, 25. 1. 15 Lenel, *cit.* 439. 16 42. 8. 10. 20. 17 42. 8. 1. pr., 11. It lay after the year and against *heredes* to extent of enrichment (h. t. 6. 14, h. t. 11) and was extended against innocent donees in the same way, h. t. 6. 11. 18 42. 8. 6. 12. It gave *de peculio*, etc. There is the same intermediate character in the next case to be considered.

FRAUD ON PATRON[1]. Provided against by two actions; *Fabiana*, where the *libertus* had left a will, *Calvisiana*, where he was intestate[2], having similar principles. The action was *in personam*, *perpetua*, *in factum*, and *arbitraria*[3]. It was available to and against the *heres*[4], and was quasi-contractual in other respects. Thus, if the act complained of was through a slave, the action was *de peculio*, etc.[5] It lay only after death of the *libertus*[6]. If the act was *inter vivos* the patron must shew not only that it lessened his gain, but that this was intended; if it was *mortis causa*, e.g. *donatio mortis causa* or legacy, the fact of injury sufficed[7]. It was brought against the receiver, whether in bad faith or not; *dolus* of the *libertus* sufficed[8]. The action covered *fructus* before and since *litis contestatio*[9]. As in fraud on creditors, it lay only for diminution, not for neglect to acquire[10]. It was specially aimed at gifts, and thus, where it was a sale or analogous transaction, the third party was allowed either to have the transaction set aside, receiving what he has given and restoring what he has received, or to have the bargain amended to fairness[11]. On a fair transaction the action did not lie at all, and the Edict provided that the Praetor would enquire into this[12]. It does not seem to have lain against later holders, or where the thing had ceased to exist[13], subject no doubt to the rule as to *mora*[14].

There are many other wrongs which can be called delicts in the sense of later law. Such are, e.g., acts dealt with by the interdicts *de vi*[15], and the various remedies for the safeguarding of rights between neighbours[16], the interdict *quod vi aut clam*[17], *damni infecti*[18], *operis novi nuntiatio*[19], and the *actio aquae pluviae arcendae*[20]. This is an old civil action for the case of work done on the defendant's land, varying the natural flow of water over the plaintiff's, to his damage, not wholly superseded by the more effective *operis novi nuntiatio*[21]. The owner is liable[22]. It must be work not reasonably incident to the ordinary cultivation of the land[23], and it must be recent, i.e. not so old that no one can say who did it or whether it was intentional or not[24]. It may even be neglect of work, e.g. where there is an established watercourse and the owner neglects to repair a dyke destroyed by storm[25]. If the work was done by *colonus* or *procurator*,

1 38. 5; *Frag. de formula Fabiana*; *Collectio libr. iur. antei*, 3, 299; Girard, *Textes*, 457; Baviera, *Fontes*, 521. 2 38. 5. 1. 6, 2, 3. pr.–3. 3 38. 5. 1. 26, 3. 2, 5. 1; *Fr. de i. F.* 1. 4 38. 5. 1. 26. 5 38. 5. 1. 22. Biondi, *Actiones arbitrariae*, 1. 165, holds that it was not considered as penal in classical law. 6 38. 5. 1. pr. 7 38. 5. 1. 1, 12, 27. 8 38. 5. 1. 4 9 38. 5. 1. 28, 2. 10 38. 5. 1. 6, 7. 11 38. 5. 1. 12, 13. 12 38. 5. 1. pr. 13 38. 5. 10. 14 *Ante*, p. 550. 15 *Post*, § CXLIX. 16 Bonfante, *Corso*, 2. chh. 14 *sqq.* 17 *Post*, § CCXLVIII. See Schulz, *Z.S.S.* 1922, 255, who shews the compilers making it quasi-contractual by giving it to some extent *in rem*. 18 *Post*, § CCXLV. 19 *Post*, § CCXLVIII. 20 Scialoja, *Proprietà*, 1, 368. 21 *Post*, § CCXLVI. 22 39. 3. 3, 4. 23 39. 3. 1. 3–7. 24 39. 3. 2. 3, 2. 8; 22. 3. 28. 25 39. 3. 2. 1, 2. 7.

without the owner's privity, the action lies only if the owner obstructs the neighbour in putting it right[1]. It does not lie if the complainant has acquiesced in the work[2]. For past damage the remedy is *quod vi aut clam*[3]. Our action lies against the *heres*[4], which is inconsistent with delictal character, and may be due to Justinian, who seems however also to have made it noxal[5].

Other essentially delictal actions are, e.g., *de rationibus distrahendis*[6], *de moribus*[7], that, under the XII Tables, *de arboribus succisis*[8], and its praetorian modification, *arborum furtim caesarum*[9], *de tigno iniuncto*[10], etc.

CCIV. *OBLIGATIO QUASI EX DELICTO.* This classification, which purports in the Digest to come from a work of Gaius[11], is probably interpolated, these obligations having been treated in classical law among "*variae causarum figurae*[12]." The Institutes give four cases.

Iudex qui litem suam facit. The main source is a text from Gaius, which recurs three times with small variations. An *actio in factum*[13] lay against a *iudex* who, from carelessness[14] or unfairness, gave a wrong decision, or, perhaps, neglected his duty in any way to the detriment of a party[15]. It was available also if he gave a judgement not authorised by the *formula*[16]. It was not available against the *heres*[17].

Res deiectae vel effusae: Where something was thrown from a dwelling on a way commonly used[18], to the damage of a passer or property, the householder was liable. The action was *in factum* for double the damage[19], but if there were several persons liable, satisfaction by one freed the others[20]. It was *perpetua* and available to but not against the *heres*[21]. *Culpa* need not be proved[22]. If a freeman was killed there was an *actio popularis annua*, for a penalty of fifty *solidi*[23]. If several wished to bring

1 39. 3. 4. 2, 3. 2 39. 3. 19, 20. 3 39. 3. 14. 2, 3. 4 39. 3. 6. 7. In classical law it probably lay against him only as owner. It lay both to and against a new owner, h. t. 6. 4, 14 (*potentiori*). In later law, *utilis* against *fructuarius*, h. t. 3. 4, 22. 2. 5 39. 3. 6. 7. Biondi, *Acts. noxales, cit.* Lenel, *E.P.* 377. 6 *Ante*, p. 163. 7 *Ante*, p. 109. 8 Girard, *Textes*, 19. 9 D. 47. 7; Huvelin, *Furtum*, 1. 67. 10 *Ante*, pp. 212, 215. 11 Actually "*quasi ex maleficio*," 44. 7. 5. 4, 5. As they are praetorian, G. does not mention them. 12 44. 7. 1. pr. 13 "*Vera aestimatio litis* (5. 1. 15. 1) or "*quantum aequum videbitur*" (50. 13. (6)? Lenel, *E.P.* 168, decides for the latter in classical law. 14 ? Only for *dolus* in classical law, Perozzi, *Ist.* 2. 387. 15 44. 7. 5. 4; 50. 13. 6; Inst. 4. 5. pr.; G. 4. 52. 16 G. 4. 52; D. 50. 13. 6. 17 5. 1. 16 (Julian, *contra*); or against *pater* where son a *iudex*: the son is liable to the extent of what was in his *peculium* when he gave judgement, 5. 1. 15, perhaps interp. Controversy whether there were two actions or one; Lenel, *E.P.* 168; de Francisci, *Az. penali*, 59. The account in text is of Justinian's law. Earlier story of the remedy, various views, de Francisci, *Synallagma*, 2. 129; Lenel, *E.P.* 167, 216. 18 9. 3. 1. pr.; Inst. 4. 5. 1. 19 9. 3. 1. pr., 4. Not noxally available for acts done by son or slave householder, but noxal if done by slave of householder, 9. 3. 1. pr. (son himself liable). 20 9. 3. 1. 10–4. 21 9. 3. 5. 5. 22 Talk of *culpa*, in h. t. 1. 4, 6. 2, proves nothing. In 1. 4 the requirement is negatived. In 6. 2 it means only responsibility. *Culpa*, it may be said, is conclusively presumed. 23 9. 3. 5. 5; Inst. 4. 5. 1.

it, persons interested in the deceased were preferred[1]. If a freeman was injured there was an *actio in factum*, for a penalty assessed by the *iudex*, *perpetua* so long as the injured man was alive, but not available to his *heres*[2].

Res suspensae. Things suspended from a building over a way in common use, to the danger of passers. There was an *actio popularis* for ten *solidi* against the occupier, not available against the *heres* (as such), and under similar principles to those as to *res deiectae*[3].

Nautae caupones stabularii. The principals of a ship, inn or public stable were responsible for theft or damage by those employed by them in the ship, etc. The action was *perpetua* and *in factum* in *duplum*, and was available to, but not against the *heres*[4]. As to inns, this extended to acts of permanent residents, but not of mere passing travellers[5]. If the offender was the defendant's slave the liability was noxal, and presumably ended by his death, but did not so end in other cases[6]. As it needed proof that the act was done by such a person, there might be an alternative action against him[7]. So far as theft was concerned it rested on a special edict[8], but there seems to have been no edict for *damnum*[9]; it may have been an extension of the *actio in factum* under the *lex Aquilia*[10]. An alternative remedy of different character and scope under the Edict, *de receptis*, has already been considered[11].

The common quality of these quasi-delicts is uncertain[12]. As to *caupo* (etc.) Justinian suggests that it is his fault for employing such people, and Ulpian notes that as he could not pick and choose among *viatores* he was not liable for them[13]. But this would make it delict, and moreover no amount of care would avoid the liability. It was in fact insurance. They were nearly all cases of vicarious liability, and even in the case of the *iudex* the name, an old one[14], shews that he was contemplated as taking over the liability for act of another.

CCV. We have now to consider the circumstances in which one might be responsible for another's delict. Apart from personal privity[15], there was what is called noxal liability for delicts committed by members

1 9. 3. 5. 5. 2 *Ib.* The text gives this action to others for an *annus utilis*. 3 Inst. 4. 5. 1, 2; D. 9. 3. 5. 6–13; 44. 7. 5. 5. Where damage is done an ordinary Aquilian action lies against the suspender, not against occupier as such, 9. 3. 5. 12. 4 47. 5; 44. 7. 5. 6; Inst. 4. 5. 3. 5 47. 5. 1. 6. 6 47. 5. 1. 5. 7 47. 5. 1. 3. 8 47. 5. 9 4. 9. 6, 7; 9. 4. 19. 2; Lenel, *E.P.* 205, who notes, and is disposed to reject for classical law, some subsidiary actions mentioned in the texts. 10 Lenel, *loc. cit.* 11 *Ante*, p. 531. 12 Moyle, *Instt. Iust.* 540; Girard, *Man.* 678, who considers any theoretical basis of the classification unattainable. 13 47. 5. 1. 6. 14 Girard, *Man.* 677, n. 1. 15 Connivance or failure to prevent, having the means, made the master fully liable (P. 2. 31. 28; D. 9. 4. 2, etc.). It was decided after discussion that this connivance did not affect the other liability of the slave himself if freed, or of a later owner. Even command did not, if the matter was serious (*facinus*) (9. 4. 2. 1; 47. 10. 17. 7, etc.).

of the *familia*, i.e. liability either to pay the damages or to hand over the offender. The XII Tables created it for *furtum*[1], the *l. Aquilia* for *damnum*[2], the Edict for *rapina, iniuria*[3] and other praetorian wrongs. The system did not apply to crime, contract, quasi-contract, or even quasi-delict except in the case of *deiectio*[4]. In *iniuria* the master could avoid noxal liability by handing over the slave to be thrashed, the *iudex*[5] determining the amount of chastisement[6], otherwise the noxal action went on. In *metus*, if the *dominus* had surrendered the slave noxally, he could still be sued for any enrichment[7]. In *dolus* the action was noxal only if the matter in which the *dolus* occurred was itself delictal[8]. But other texts make this point obscure[9].

The master's liability depended on his having *potestas*[10], which here meant power to produce the slave[11]. If, when sued, he would not defend, his proper course was to produce the man: the magistrate would authorise the plaintiff to seize him (*duci vel ferri iubere*) which released the master, though there might be minor rights in the man[12]. The transferee would usucapt, and, under Justinian, would be owner if the transferor was. If the master neither surrendered nor defended, he was liable *in solidum* with no right of surrender[13]. If the slave was absent, there was an *interrogatio* as to *potestas*. If this was admitted the action proceeded. If denied, and plaintiff proved the facts and *potestas*, there was *condemnatio* with no right of surrender[14]. If he was present the *interrogatio* was "*an*

1 G. 4. 76; D. 9. 4. 2. 1. 2 G. 4. 76. De Visscher, *Les actions noxales*, 27, holds that this was not expressly provided but inferred from the XII Tables. 3 G. 4. 76; Inst. 4. 8. 4. 4 9. 3. 1. pr. As it is *in duplum* it is better than the *actio e lege Aquilia*, also available where the slave is identified. 5 But it is probable that in classical law it was the Praetor, *in iure*. See de Visscher, *Tijdschr*. 1931, 39, *Ét*. 129. See *id*. 329 for the view, also probable, that the *verberatio* which appears here as a feature of the noxal procedure was originally distinct: a noxal action for *iniuria* by a slave supervened about the beginning of the Empire on the old system under which the slave was thrashed unless the master redeemed him. 6 47. 10. 17. 4–7. In later law it was usual to deal with it *extra ordinem*, by castigation under magisterial authority, h. t. 9. 3, 45. See Naber, *Mél. Gérardin*, 467, who thinks the passage interpolated. *Contra*, Lenel, *E.P.* 402. History, de Visscher, *R.H.* 1930, 189. 7 4. 2. 16. 1. 8 4. 3. 9. 4; 44. 7. 49. 9 4. 4. 24. 3; 10. 4. 16. Noxal actions are allowed in delict and not in contract, since it is not a liability in the master, but a right to ransom the slave from vengeance. In time payment and surrender come to be regarded as alternative, some texts treating payment as the primary duty (9. 4. 1; 42. 1. 6. 1; cp. 2. 10. 2; 9. 4. 2. pr.), a reversal of the original conception; Girard, *Mélanges*, 2, 353; de Visscher, *Les actions noxales*, holds that under the XII Tables there was merely a right of seizure and ransom, but no action: noxal actions are a creation of the pontiffs. 10 9. 4. 21. 2, 3. 11 50. 16. 215; Buckland, *Slavery*, 101, 106. 12 9. 4. 15, 21. pr. 9. 4. 32 requires an actual conveyance. For various views as to this requirement and the genuineness of this text, Biondi, *Bull.* 1928, 115; de Visscher, *R.H.* 1926, 322 and *Nature juridique de l'abandon noxal*; Pissard, *Ét. Girard*, 1. 244; Girard, *Man.* 725; Lenel, *E.P.* 162; *Z.S.S.* 1927, 13. The better view seems to be that, at any rate, if the matter went to judgement, there was a duty to convey. 13 9. 4. 21. 4, 22. 3. 14 2. 9. 2. 1; 9. 4. 21. 2.

eius sit," with similar consequences[1]. If the master was absent and the slave present, the slave might be "*ductus*," and the defendant was released[2]. But anyone interested, e.g. usufructuary, might defend on behalf of the master[3]. The *formula* of the action stated the right of surrender as alternative both in the *intentio* and in the *condemnatio*[4]. Till *condemnatio*, payment or surrender are alternatives (but the power of surrender has nothing to do with *arbitrium iudicis*[5]): after *condemnatio*, which was always primarily for money, the surrender became merely facultative[6]. It did not then release if there were minor rights outstanding[7], and the *actio iudicati* was for the money only[8]. One who would have had *potestas* but for his fraud was liable, under praetorian rules, as if he still had it[9].

Noxa caput sequitur. Liability followed the delinquent[10]: the person liable was the owner at the time of the action[11]. Thus, apart from fraud, death, alienation, manumission or abandonment of the slave before *litis contestatio* released the owner[12], though it might make someone else liable. There could be no noxal action between master and slave, and none would arise after transfer[13]. And if the guilty slave passed into the hands of the injured person the action was extinct and would not revive on alienation[14]. If, *dolus* apart, the slave was freed or transferred during the action, this was transferred[15], against himself or his new master.

It seems that in classical law death of the man after *litis contestatio* did not release, but that his dead body might be surrendered[16]. This was gone under Justinian, so that the death left the owner liable *in solidum*.

Holders of lesser *iura in rem* could not be sued noxally, but a similar result was produced by the rule that if the owner surrendered, they

1 Lenel, *E.P.* 161. 2 2. 9. 2. 1; 6. 2. 6; 9. 4. 39. 3. 3 9. 4. 26. 6. Lenel, *Z.S.S.* 1927, 16, puts *b. f. possessor* on the same footing, evidence hardly adequate. 4 Lenel, *Z.S.S.* 1927, 17. 5 *Formulae*, Lenel, *E.P.* 165, 330; Biondi, *Bull.* 1928, 99. 6 42. 1. 6. 1. It is only between *litis cont.* and *condemnatio* that it is alternative: till *l. c.* death of slave releases, as it would not a true alternative, 9. 4. 7. pr.; *ante*, p. 567. As to nature of the obligation before *l. c.*, Steiner, *Datio in solutum*, 102. 7 42. 1. 4. 8. 8 5. 3. 20. 5. 9 9. 4. 12, 22. 4; 47. 2. 42. 1. 10 47. 2. 18. The *caput* is that of the slave, de Visscher, *cit.* 15. 11 9. 4. 7. pr. 12 9. 4. 5. 1–7. pr., 14. pr. 13 47. 2. 17; G. 4. 78; Inst. 4. 8. 6. 14 47. 2. 18. School dispute, G. 4. 78. This worked unfairly where, e.g., *A* bought under mandate for *B* or held the slave in *fiducia*. Hence he can get an indemnity, not delictal damages, under the contract, unless the slave is surrendered to him (17. 1. 26. 7), also short of fairness, for he may have bought the slave under special instructions, so that his faults are in no way imputable to him, and the damage may exceed the man's value. It applies the rough rule that an owner ought not to be liable beyond the slave's value, to a case in which it is unfair. The rule has little importance under Justinian: a buyer under mandate would rarely be interim owner. Buckland, *Slavery*, 125. 15 9. 4. 15. Controversy as to this *translatio* and the nature of the transferred action, *post*, § CCXLI. 16 G. 4. 81; *Aut.* G. 82, 87, unless owner had wrongfully killed him; cp. Livy, 8. 39.

could not enforce their right without paying the damages; hence the rule that they might defend on behalf of an absent owner[1].

Where a wrong was committed by several of a man's slaves, he ought, on principle, to be fully liable for each, but the Praetor limited the penalty to what would be due if one freeman had done the act[2], a rule originating in theft and extended to many delicts, but not to all, since, in some cases, it was not to be thought of as one, but "*plura facta.*" This was so in *iniuria*, and, as some thought, in *damnum*[3]. The alternative was surrender of all the slaves concerned. But proceedings in respect of one of the slaves who had been freed or alienated did not release the *dominus* who still held the others[4].

There were special rules for *publicani*. They were liable to an action *in duplum* where goods were violently seized or damaged by their employees, slaves or free, but payment of what would be due from a single free man was enough[5]. The slaves concerned must be produced, and if the actual offender was identified there was an ordinary noxal action[6]. If he was not produced it was *in solidum*[7]. The twofold included the *res*, so that the injured person could, if the slave was identified, proceed if he preferred by an ordinary noxal action on *rapina* or *damnum*[8]. Another edict, with apparently similar rules, dealt with simple theft in such cases[9].

If a slave committed delicts against different people, the owner was liable in respect of all, but the rule, *noxa caput sequitur*, made the first surrender release him, so that the last of several plaintiffs kept the slave, since all the rest would in turn have been liable. But surrender to *B* after *litis contestatio* with *A* would not free the owner from *A*[10].

Special rules existed under the *l. Aquilia*. No text applies the notion of *potestas*. In general an owner was not liable noxally for a slave *in fuga*, as he had not *potestas*, and a *bona fide possessor* was liable because he had[11]. But in *damnum* an owner was liable for a *fugitivus*, and a *bona fide possessor* was not liable[12]. It has been acutely suggested that something in the *lex* made it impossible to apply the idea of *potestas*, probably an energetic reference to *herus* or *dominus* as the person liable[13].

1 7. 1. 17. 2; 9. 4. 18, 26. 6, 33. If the slave is in the hands of a fructuary there may have been *a. ad exhibendum* (10. 4. 3. 15) with *ductio* unless the fructuary defended.
2 9. 4. 31; 47. 6. 1.
3 2. 1. 9; 47. 6. 1. 2.
4 47. 6. 3. pr.
5 39. 4. 1. pr., 3. 3. *In simplum* after a year.
6 39. 4. 2, 3. pr., 2.
7 39. 4. 1. 6.
8 39. 4. 1. 3, 4.
9 Confused in the Digest. Of the two edicts, one (39. 4. 1. pr.) dealt with "*vi ademptio*," the allusion to *furtum* and *damnum* being interpolation or late interpretation. The second (h. t. 12. 1) dealt with *furtum*, *damnum* being an addition. Arangio Ruiz, *St. Perozzi*, 229; Lenel, *E.P.* 335, 387.
10 2. 9. 1. 1, 2: it is *dolus*. Delict in connexion with contract, *ante*, p. 408.
11 9. 4. 12; 47. 2. 17. 3; P. 2. 31. 37; *ante*, p. 601, n. 3.
12 9. 2. 27. 3.
13 Girard, *N.R.H.* 1887, 430 *sqq.*; *Man.* 723. Cp. 9. 2. 11. 6: it is only the *dominus* who has the action.

Under Justinian noxal liability applied only to slaves, but in classical law a son (no doubt, not a daughter) could be surrendered in the same way. The softening of manners and acquisition of proprietary rights by *filiifamilias* put an end to this. The holding was not fiduciary, but in later classical law the holder was compelled to free the man when he had worked out the damages[1]. The Institutes apply this also to slaves[2], but it is not so stated in the Digest or Code.

Pauperies. The XII Tables gave an analogous *actio in simplum* with a right of surrender, where damage was done by an animal in such circumstances that no man was to blame[3]. We know the rule only as it was in later law[4]. We are told that the action lay only where the violence was not natural to such beasts, and thus not where a wild beast was concerned[5]. But we also hear that if the wild beast had escaped, the old owner, being no longer owner, was no longer liable, which implies that the action would have lain had the beast still been in captivity[6]. The action was subject to the general principles of noxal actions. It could be brought by the *heres*, but not against him, *qua heres*, but only *qua* owner[7]. Anyone might bring it who had an *interesse* in the safety of the *res*[8]. If a free person was injured, the claim would cover cost of treatment, value of time, and profits lost[9]. The XII Tables dealt only with quadrupeds[10], but, later, an *actio utilis* was given in the case of other animals[11].

There was a further provision in the Edict of the Ediles, which seems to have been designed to provide a remedy in the case of wild animals, because there was none in *pauperies*. If a wild animal was kept by the wayside and damaged property, there was an action for double damages, and if a freeman was injured, at the discretion of the *iudex*. If a freeman was killed the penalty was 200 *solidi*[12]. Justinian declares this to be alternative to the *actio de pauperie*[13].

1 Coll. 2. 3. 1. He is *in mancipio*, but here, on the view which prevailed, one manumission destroyed the *potestas*. G. 4. 79; Inst. 4. 8. 7 (which says that at one time it was allowed for daughters). 2 Inst. 4. 8. 3. 3 9. 1. 1. pr., 3. On the view of Biondi, *Actiones noxales*, that *de pauperie* was not noxal in classical law, Lenel, *Z.S.S.* 1926, 2. Reply, *Bull.* 1920, 00. 4 By which time it has undergone changes. 9. 1; Inst. 4. 9; P. 1. 15. 5 Inst. 4. 9. pr.; D. 9. 1. 1. 7, 10. The carrying of disease was enough. *Lex Rom. Burg.* 10. 3. (P. 1. 15. 1b). 6 Inst. 4. 9. pr.; D. 9. 1. 1. 10, probably interp. Haymann, *Z.S.S.* 1921, 357 and Levy, *Konkurrenz*, 2. 1. 225, hold that both the limitation to domestic beasts and the rule that it must be *contra naturam* are Byzantine; *Contra*, Jörs, *R.R.* 178. 7 9. 1. 1. 17. Death of the animal before *l. c.* destroyed the claim (h. l. 13) but not death after *l. c.* (h. l. 14). 8 9. 1. 2. 9 9. 1. 3. 10 9. 1. 1. pr. 11 9. 1. 4. 12 Inst. 4. 9. 1; D. 21. 1. 42 (the amount is no doubt interp.). 13 Inst. 4. 9. 1. Nothing is known of the *l. Pesolania de cane*, P. 1. 15. 1.

CHAPTER XIII

THE LAW OF PROCEDURE. *LEGIS ACTIO. FORMULA. COGNITIO*

CCVI. The Law of Actions[1] may be described as the Law of Procedure, of Litigation, of Remedies. Before stating its elements, as it was in Roman Law, some preliminary observations must be made.

The subject covers two sets of rules, which may be called the law of actions, strictly so called, and the law of procedure. The former deals with distinctions between different types of remedy, e.g. *Actio*[2] and *Interdictum*, the classifications of these, according to their varieties, e.g. *actio in rem*, *in personam*, *interdictum prohibitorium*, *restitutorium*, *exhibitorium*, and so forth, and rules determining the remedy for each wrong. The latter branch deals with the steps to be taken in the course of the proceeding by the plaintiff who desires to bring the matter before the Court, and the steps to be taken by the defendant if he disputes the claim. It is difficult to separate these altogether in discussion, except

1 Bethmann-Hollweg, *C.P.*; Keller-Wach, *C.P.*; Wenger, *Inst. des Röm. Zivilprocessr.*; Bertolini, *Il processo civile*; Costa, *Profilo Storico del processo civile Romano*. 2 Occasionally used so as to cover any mode of procedure, e.g. G. 1. 8, where it includes *interdicta*. Albertario (*Contributo allo studia della procedura*) rightly notes that texts calling interdicts actions are often interp. But it is hardly possible to reject every such use of the word in classical law. See Lenel, *E.P.* 477. Any legal proceeding for enforcement of a right may be called action.

at the cost of repetition, but nearly all the long sixth title in the fourth book of the Institutes deals with the former topic.

The law of actions is the law of litigation, the law governing the submission of claims to a tribunal for settlement. But it must not be forgotten that legal remedies in Rome originated in self-help, and that early Roman Law did not regard litigation as essential to the conception of an "*actio*."

Both Gaius and Justinian start from the conception of the Law of Actions as the Law of Remedies, Adjective Law, but depart from this notion in the actual treatment. The substantive praetorian law (there was no civil law on the matter) as to liability of the *paterfamilias* on transactions by members of the *familia*, or business agents[1] (*institor, magister navis*), and the law, civil and praetorian, on his liability for wrongs committed by members of the *familia*[2] (noxal liability), both logically belonging to the law of obligations, are treated under actions, and practically all that we hear of purely possessory rights is said in connexion with interdicts[3]. This is justified by the consideration that the "right" of *possessio, per se*, consists of nothing but the right to these remedies: *possessio* has a purely procedural content[4]. The other cases constitute a difficulty in regarding the *ius rerum* as the law of rights with a money value, but in view of the close affinity between *obligatio* and *actio*, and of the fact that both these sets of rights are marked by a strongly specialised form of procedure, it is not surprising that they are attracted to this topic. The Romans possessed no such theory of representation as that which makes such a treatment unlikely in modern systems. And Gaius, whom Justinian follows, introduces these rules not as independent objects of discussion, but as illustrations of certain types of action considered from the point of view of procedure, so that, as his language shews[5], it is for convenience, and to avoid repetition, that he treats them in detail here, instead of treating their substantive characteristics under the law of obligations, where the matter properly belongs. The method adopted may be partly the result of the habit, observable in ordinary speech, of using the same word, action, to denote both the right of action and the procedural steps, a practice possibly explaining the affinity between action and obligation[6].

The co-ordination of the law of actions with the law of things and the law of persons as a third element in the classification, is the feature of the institutional arrangement which has met with the most hostile criticism. Some of this rests on misapprehension: it is impossible for instance to lay much stress on Austin's language, as he misunderstands

1 G. 4. 69 *sqq.*; Inst. 4. 7. 2 G. 4. 75 *sqq.*; Inst. 4. 8. 3 G. 4. 143 *sqq.*; Inst. 4. 15. 2 *sqq.* 4 *Ante*, § LXXII; *post*, § CCXLIX. 5 G. 4. 69. 6 D. 44. 7.

the Roman arrangement[1]. But the point that these rules of adjective law should be subordinated to, not co-ordinated with, the substantive rules is clearly sound. If, however, the view be accepted that the law of persons was a descriptive chapter and the law of things the statement of the modes of acquisition and loss of substantive rights, the actual position of the law of actions as an appendix to it is justified, and the treatment of it as a new *genus* is a logical error, without effect on the actual treatment. It has been shewn that in the effort to construct a triad the Romans were constantly led into errors of this kind[2]. In any case few will dispute Maine's proposition that the author of this arrangement, whoever he was, achieved a great feat of abstraction[3]. It is true that the institutional scheme is defective, that it would have been far better to base the arrangement absolutely on rights or on duties. But the Romans were only gradually reaching the clear-cut conception of a right which we possess, and in the conditions which existed, the arrangement under the heads of those persons who can be affected, the rights which the law will protect, and the means by which this is done, seems to merit Gibbon's remark that it is "no contemptible method[4]." A more logical method would have been a division simply into Substantive Law, the *ius rerum*, and Adjective Law, the *ius actionum*. The Law of Persons would have found its place as an introduction to the *ius rerum*, as in modern Codes[5], so that it is the law of persons, rather than the law of actions which is undeserving of a separate place. The effect of such a change would have been very small: the opening phrases of the first, second and fourth books of Gaius would have needed modification, but the rest of the matter might have stood as it is.

CCVII. Procedure was in a sense the most important part of the law. A state of things can be conceived, and has indeed existed in undeveloped communities, in which the only permanent law was that regulating the submission of disputes to a central authority: Cadi justice. In all early communities procedure is the most prominent part of the law. At first it may be regarded as State regulation of self-help, but in civilised communities this mode of redress tends to be superseded by a system in which the question is first decided by a Court of Law, and the remedy then put in force by it, or under its authority.

If both parties to a dispute were always agreed on facts and law, and ready to carry out their legal duties, there would be no need of a law

1 It is difficult to extract a consistent doctrine from Lect. XLIII and its notes (pp. 749–763, ed. 1875), or to see what part of the Law of Actions would be suitably placed as a subhead of the Law of Persons as conceived by Gaius or his authority. 2 Goudy, *Trichotomy in Roman Law, passim.* 3 *Early Law and Custom*, 367. 4 *Decline and Fall*, ch. XLIV (Bury, 4. 470). 5 *Code Civil, Livre* I; *Bürgerl. Gesetzbuch*, §§ 1–89.

of procedure. But this is not so, and rules of law do not enforce themselves. In any dispute, therefore, in which the parties have not been able to come to terms, the enforcement of the law depends, ordinarily, on the willingness of the party who conceives himself to have a right which has been infringed, to take the necessary steps to procure a decision by a court of law. It is for him to initiate proceedings. In Rome he would have to take certain formal steps, which varied historically, in order to bring the other party before the court, and he would have to decide, not always an easy matter, which of the possible remedies would meet his case. If what he complained of was that a right *in rem* which he claimed to have was disputed, to his injury, he would ordinarily bring an *actio in rem*, a *vindicatio*, the generic name of all actions to enforce such rights. If what he complained of was breach of a contractual or quasi-contractual obligation, or a delict, he would bring, normally, an *actio in personam*, of which there were, in the Roman Law, many kinds. The tribunal would decide the question, and in the ordinary course judgement was given for damages or penalty (or in some cases an order of restitution), or the defendant was absolved. But there might be proceedings open to him which, while they would usually in the long run take the form of an ordinary action, began in another way. Thus for interference with purely possessory rights (or where what was for the moment complained of was interference with possession) or with some family rights, or with what may be called public rights, e.g. the right to use a highway, the remedy in classical law took the form of an interdict, a complex procedure in which the first step was a formal order of the magistrate, disregard of which led to an action or actions of the ordinary type. There was another type of action, *praeiudicium*, which aimed merely at a declaration by the court, e.g. that so and so was a *libertus*, such a proceeding being usually the preliminary to another. There were of course many other complications.

In the long evolution of the Roman Law the forms of litigation naturally underwent great changes. But these were more fundamental than this way of stating the matter would suggest. They were so great and so well marked that the descent of one from the other is obscured: in each case it may almost be said that there is supersession rather than evolution. If we neglect primitive institutions[1] we have three systems succeeding in time, *legis actio*, *formula* and *cognitio extraordinaria*. These will be considered in detail, but the main differences may be usefully stated here. In the *legis actio* the matter was brought before the magis-

1 On the speculative question whether the *rex* himself decided in primitive law see (in favour) Wenger, *Zpr.* 50; Cornil, *A.D.R.* 121; (against) Binder, *Die Plebs*, 528. See also de Francisci, *Storia*, 1. 127; Koschaker, *Z.S.S.* 1930, 724.

trate by a fixed ritual, each party and the magistrate himself going through a series of acts and declarations, prescribed partly by statute, partly by priestly lawyers, interpreting the statute. These ceremonials completed, the matter was referred for trial and decision to another person or persons (*iudex*, *arbiter*), not an official but a private person, chosen from a list (*album iudicum*) the constitution of which was changed from time to time, but may be said to have been made up of the better class of *cives*. If the decision was against the defendant, it was enforced by seizure of him by the plaintiff, and, in the last resort, sale into slavery.

In the formulary system, dominant in classical law, there was still a preliminary hearing before the magistrate and reference to a *iudex*, but there were three great changes. The magistrate no longer recited words prescribed for him[1]; he controlled the proceedings. His right of *iurisdictio* enabled him to prescribe the form in which the issue should be submitted to the *iudex*, the *formula* (chosen indeed by the parties from models set forth by the magistrate, but subject to his approval), to refuse to issue it at all if he thought fit, and to allow the insertion in it of defences which he thought reasonable, though they were not material in civil law or admissible under the old regime. In such matters he now had great power. Further, the instruction to the *iudex*, the *formula*, was now written, a step almost inevitable, so soon as it became possible to submit the more complex issues and to give the wide discretionary powers which mark the new system. And, though the system of personal seizure survived through the formulary period, it was partly superseded by a more reasonable system, invented by the powerful magistrate, the Praetor, under which execution of judgement proceeded directly against the goods of the debtor—*bonorum venditio*, the whole estate being seized and sold, a process resembling the modern bankruptcy, but leaving the debtor still liable to pay out of later acquisitions any part of his debt which the sale of his property had left unsatisfied.

In the third system, *cognitio extraordinaria*, there was a fundamental change. There was no longer a reference to a second person for hearing. The magistrate, or his deputy, before whom the matter came from the beginning, himself heard and decided the case. There was thus no issue of a *formula*, though the claim and defence were still usually stated in writing. A still more rational system of enforcement had been devised. Instead of making bankruptcy the inevitable result of an unsatisfied judgement, the law authorised the seizure and sale of so much of the property of the debtor as would satisfy the judgement.

1 The automatic character of his action must not be exaggerated. He might refuse concurrence if the formal requirements were not complied with, and an individual magistrate might construe this rather widely. The automatic character of his action under the *legis actio* is not universally admitted, *post*, § CCXIV.

The words *actio* and *iudicium* bore many meanings and shades of meaning. Of the various meanings of the word *actio*, those which most concern us are three. It might mean a right of action[1]. It might mean the remedy as a whole, as in the sixth title of Book 4 of Justinian's Institutes[2]. It was sometimes used to express the proceeding by *legis actio* as opposed to *formula*, the latter being called *iudicium*[3], and this usage left a trace in later law in a tendency to confine the word to civil law actions[4]. In this old narrow sense the word had from another point of view a wider significance; as will appear in the discussion of *pignoris capio* and *manus iniectio*, *actio* did not necessarily imply litigation; it was a process for the enforcement of a right.

Of the meanings of the word *iudicium* some appear above. Thus it might mean procedure by *formula* or *cognitio* as opposed to *legis actio*, and, occasionally, in later law, a praetorian proceeding as opposed to civil. It is indeed held[5] that in classical law it meant the actual written *formula* itself, a signification which accentuates the distinction between the old oral and the new written process. *Iudicium* was also used to denote an action tried by a *iudex* as opposed to an *arbiter* or *arbitri*[6]. It is also used, but mainly in literary texts, to denote the second stage in the proceeding, as opposed to the procedure before the magistrate, *in iure*, but it has been shewn that the orthodox name for the later stage was proceedings *apud iudicem*[7]. In the *cognitio* system it means the whole hearing.

A distinction is drawn between *lis* and *iurgium*[8]. Cicero speaks of *iurgium* as a friendly dispute: *non lis inimicorum iurgium dicitur*[9]. Varro seems to say that they are the same thing[10]. Some legal texts suggest that as applied to legal process the name *iurgium* was specially applied to the divisory actions[11], which would accord with Cicero's language. The point is not important for classical law[12].

CCVIII. THE *LEGIS ACTIO*. This expression is not free from difficulty. Gaius tells us that these proceedings were so called either as having

1 "*Nihil aliud est actio quam ius quod sibi debeatur iudicio persequendi,*" 44. 7. 51. See also 50. 17. 204. 2 But the initial phrase is from the text printed in n. 1. 3 Wlassak, *Prozessgesetze*, 1. § 8. 4 See, e.g., the opening clauses in G. 4. 5 Wlassak, *loc. cit.* 6 *Post*, §§ CCX, CCXVII. 7 Wlassak, *cit.* 1. 27; *Iudicationsbefehl*, 285; Wenger, *cit.* 21, 181. But in G. 4. 103 *sqq.* the "*iudicium*" which expires in 18 months must be the proceeding before the *iudex*, otherwise the time would date from the beginning of the proceedings *in iure*. The Praetor did not "*praecipere*" the *formula* (105) but the proceeding. Cicero, *Part. Or.* 28. 99, cannot mean anything else. Wenger says (*Praetor und Formel*, 3) that Wlassak has explained this. No ref. is given: it may be to *Prozessgesetze*, 2. 12, which refers the words, inadmissibly, to the whole process. In Pliny, *Ep.* 5. 1. 6. 7, the "*iudicium*" seems clearly the hearing. 8 Cicero, *de Legg.* 2. 12. 29; Livy, 5. 13. 9 De Rep. 4 (*Nonius*, 431). 10 Varro, *L.L.* 7. 93. 11 E.g. Vat. Fr. 294; C. Th. 2. 26. 4; D. 10. 2. 57. 12 Suggested explanations, Karlowa, *C.P.* 5 *sqq.* Relation of *iurgium* to *arbitrium*, Düll, *Der Gütegedanke im R. Zivilprozess*, 12.

been introduced by *lex*, or as being framed strictly according to the words of a *lex*[1], so that they constituted a fixed ritual, a fact which he illustrates by the case of one who sued for injury to his vines and failed because he called them vines, the word in the *lex* being *arbores*. There appears to have been an appropriate *legis actio* for each wrong, the exact form for each case having been elaborated by the Pontiffs, as on the words of the *lex*. But though there were many *legis actiones*, of the words of which we know little, we are told by Gaius[2] that there were but five "*modi lege agendi*," five moulds into one or other of which every *legis actio* was cast, whatever the formal words: *sacramentum*, *iudicis arbitrive postulatio*, *condictio*, *manus iniectio* and *pignoris capio*.

SACRAMENTUM. This is described by Gaius[3] as *generalis*, which seems to mean that it was applicable where no other was prescribed[4]. Thus it might be used as an *actio in rem*, to enforce a *ius in rem*, e.g. ownership, or as an *actio in personam* to enforce *iura in personam*, *obligationes*, and, in the former case at least, it had an elaborate ritual.

The process in a real action began by a summons by the plaintiff to the defendant, the prescribed form of which (if any) we do not know, to appear in court—*in ius vocatio*[5]. As it was essential to the *legis actio*, as a mode of litigation, that both parties be present and play their part, obedience to the summons could be compelled. If the defendant disobeyed, the creditor proclaimed the fact (*antestamino*), seized him, and brought him before the court[6]. It is probable that some circumstances excused from obedience to the summons, e.g. *morbus sonticus* and *status dies cum hoste*, which would certainly cause postponement of the hearing before the *iudex*[7]. If the defendant evaded *in ius vocatio* by trickery or flight, the creditor might seize him—*manum inicere*[8], which probably means bring him by force before the magistrate's court[9].

The parties being before the court, the plaintiff formally made his claim. In a claim of ownership, he placed a hand on the object and said: "*Hunc ego (hominem) meum esse aio ex iure Quiritium, secundum suam causam sicut dixi. Ecce tibi vindictam imposui*[10]," at the same time

1 G. 4. 11. Added words not in the prescribed ritual vitiated the process, Vat. Fr. 318. See *post*, p. 673. 2 G. 4. 12. 3 G. 4. 13. 4 Karlowa, *op. cit.* 13, holds it to mean that *sacramentum* is available if no other is provided, which is not the same thing. See however von Mayr, *Mél. Girard*, 2. 171 *sqq.* 5 XII Tab. 1. 1. The principal authorities for the procedure are the XII Tables, as restored (Girard, *Textes*, 12; Bruns, 1. 17); G. 4. 11 *sqq.*; Cicero, *pro Murena*, 12. 26 *sqq.*; Val. Probus, *Notae iuris*, "*in legis actionibus*"; Aul. Gell. 20. 10. 6 "*Igitur em capito*," XII Tab. 1. 1. If he was ill the creditor must provide carriage, XII Tab. 1. 3. 7 See the reff. Bruns, 1. 20. 8 XII Tab. 1. 2. 9 The Praetor in Rome. As to Italy, Girard, *Org. Jud.* 1. 272. The view in the text is that of Bethmann-Hollweg, 1. 106. On another view it was a formal *manus iniectio* (Puchta, *Inst.* 2. § 160; Karlowa, *C.P.* 321), *post*, § CCXI. 10 "*Secundum...dixi*" is obscure. *Causa* = mode of acquisition has not been stated; the reference may be to *causa* in the sense of accessories, etc. Cp. 12. 1. 31. pr.

touching it with a wand (*festuca*). The other party now made a similar claim in the same form, this *vindicatio* and counter *vindicatio* being *manus consertio*. This done, the Praetor ordered them both to stand away: "*Mittite ambo hominem.*" Then the first party formally asked the other the ground of his claim: "*Postulo anne dicas qua ex causa vindicaveris.*" The other replied: "*Ius feci sicut vindictam imposui*[1]." Then the first party said: "*Quando tu iniuria vindicasti, sacramento*[2]" (50 or 500) "*te provoco,*" and the second replied: "*Et ego te.*" The *sacramentum* was a sum of 50 *asses* if the matter was worth less than 1000 or it was a question of liberty, in other cases 500[3]. The successful party recovered his *sacramentum*, but the loser's was forfeited to the State[4]. In historic times the money was not deposited, but security was taken[5], a third party, called a *praes*, pledged land (*praedium*) for the *sacramentum*[6]. Then the Praetor assigned interim possession to one party—*vindicias dicere*, normally, no doubt, to the present possessor[7]. Security was taken (by *praes*) for the thing and the interim profits, *litis et vindiciarum*, for the event of judgement against the holder[8]. The next step was the appointment of a *iudex*[9] of the qualified class to try the issue, originally at once, but after a *l. Pinaria* of uncertain date, after 30 days' delay[10], so that the parties had time to come to terms. At some time in the proceedings[11], there was a joint formal appeal to witnesses, a proclamation to bystanders: "*testes estote*[12]," said by Festus to be *litis contestatio*[13]. The *iudex* did not act at once; there was a delay to the third day, i.e. the next day but one, *dies perendinus*[14], on which the hearing began. He did not give a direct judgement, *condemnatio* or *absolutio*, but a *sententia* that the *sacramentum*

1 "*Ius feci*" is not easily translated but the general sense of the declarations is clear.

2 "To" *sacramentum* or "by" *sacramentum*? Karlowa, *C.P.* 16, takes the latter view but Gaius makes the whole *sacramentum* come later. On the meaning of *sacramentum*, Strachan-Davidson, *Problems of the Roman Crim. Law*, 1. 46 *sqq.*

3 Figures much later than the XII Tables, C. Appleton, *La monnaie Romaine*, 8; *L'Hypercritique*, 11.

4 G. 4. 13.

5 Originally deposited with the pontifices, "*ad pontem,*" Varro, *L.L.* 5. 180.

6 Varro, *L.L.* 6. 74; Festus, *s.v. Praes*; Cicero, *ad Att.* 12. 52; *Verr.* 2. 1. 150; *Phil.* 2. 78; *pro Rab. Post.* 4. 8. See Debray, *N.R.H.* 1910, 528 *sqq.*

7 Bethmann-Hollweg, *C.P.* 1. § 42; Girard, *Org. Jud.* 1. 74. In *causae liberales* the *vindiciae* are given *secundum libertatem*, 1. 2. 2. 24. C. Appleton, *Le Procès de Virginie*, 9; in claims against the people, in favour of them, Festus, s.v. *Vindiciae.*

8 G. 4. 16. Exact meaning of *vindiciae* disputed. Interim profits is the meaning suggested by this text, but the word seems to have covered all advantages of interim possession. Festus, s.v. *Vindiciae.*

9 How was the *iudex* seised of the case? He must have been "*iudicare iussus,*" we do not know how. Wlassak, *Judicationsbefehl*, ch. 1.

10 G. 4. 15.

11 Later analogy suggests the end of the *legis actio*, but it has been suggested that it was at the beginning. Girard, *Man.* 1036, and reff.

12 Festus, s.v. *Contestari.* The words may be a summoning of witnesses for the hearing, or, more probably, an appeal to bystanders to bear witness that the ceremonial has been properly performed.

13 As to this expression, *post*, §§ CCXV, CCXXXV.

14 G. 4. 15; Val. Probus, "*in legis actionibus*"; Festus, s.v. *Res comperindinata.*

of one of the parties was *iniustum*[1]. If the party justified was the interim possessor, the matter was at an end; if it was the other, the *praedes* were liable for the thing and its fruits, and one or the other would always forfeit the *sacramentum*[2].

Sacramentum brought to enforce an obligation was less dramatic. There was no *manus consertio*. The plaintiff said: "*Aio te mihi dare oportere* (*tantum*)[3]," and the defendant denied liability. There was then the *sacramentum*, but no question of *praedes litis et vindiciarum*[4]. The *iudex* gave his *sententia*, and if the claim was for a fixed sum, the way was clear for proceedings in execution. If the amount was uncertain, there was a further proceeding, *arbitrium litis aestimandae*, in which the arbiter determined the money value of the claim[5], and the case was then ripe for execution. Whether this *arbitrium* was applicable to claims *in rem* is disputed; no doubt the remedy against the *praedes* would be usually adopted[6].

This description assumes that the matter proceeded with no complications, but, apart from doubts due to lack of evidence, and the obscurity, and scattered nature, of what does exist, there were variations in the course of the proceedings which must be mentioned. *Manus consertio* is spoken of above as taking place in court, but there are traces of *manus consertio ex iure*, in case of land; the parties went to the land[7]. Even in historic times there was a pretence of this; the Praetor said: "*Ite viam*," and the parties left the court, "*Redite viam*," and they returned with a turf[8]. This use of a symbol was not confined to land; if what was being claimed was too large or too numerous an aggregate to be brought into court, part could be brought in to represent the whole[9].

It has been assumed above that the party appeared personally under *in ius vocatio*, but the *vindex* mentioned by Gaius[10] under the *formula*, who appeared also in *manus iniectio*, may have also acted in *sacramentum*. It is probable, however, that his intervention occurred only where there was some ground of excuse for non-appearance, e.g. *morbus sonticus*,

1 Cicero, *pro Caec.* 33. 97; *de Domo*, 29. 78. See however von Mayr, *Mél. Girard*, 2. 177, and reff. 2 The *praedes* are adapted from *praedes*, sureties for debtors to the State, and may therefore have been like them subject to executive seizure without legal process. But while the *praedes sacramenti* gave an undertaking to the Praetor, the others gave it to the adverse party (G. 4. 16). 3 Val. Probus, *loc. cit.* 4 Probus gives the form of challenge where the claim is denied. If admitted there would probably be *manus iniectio*. If it was neither admitted nor denied the plaintiff used a phrase beginning "*quando neque ais neque negas*" (Probus, *loc. cit.*), but the result we do not know. Various views, Karlowa, *C.P.* 112. 5 Val. Probus, *loc. cit.*: little is known of this, Keller-Wach, *C.P.* § 16; Wenger, *Zpr.* 136. 6 Various views, Girard, *Man.* 361, and *post*, p. 621. 7 Cicero, *pro Murena*, 12. 26; Aul. Gell. 20. 10. 8 Cicero, *pro Murena*, 12. 26. 9 G. 4. 17; a sheep for a flock, a tile for a building, perhaps an article to represent a *hereditas*. 10 G. 4. 46.

or the like. Many views are held[1] as to his function. It is fairly clear that he was not a representative by whom the procedure was continued, for there was no representation in the *legis actio*, but the weight of argument is in favour of the view that he pledged himself in some way for the future appearance of the party summoned. We know no details.

There was perhaps another way in which a third party might intervene. A text of Probus shews a litigant asking: "*Quando te in iure conspicio postulo anne far auctor?*[2]" This may mean that the party summoned might offer as a substitute the person through whom he claimed a right, but it is also possible that the phrase is part of the plaintiff's *nuncupatio* in the *actio auctoritatis*[3].

CCIX. The *legis actio* involved co-operation, and could not proceed if, after the *in ius vocatus* had been brought into court, he refused to take the further steps. There could be no decision. Probably in real actions the thing was simply left in the hands of the holder, and in personal actions the facts were treated as *confessio*, but it is also possible that in each case it entitled the claimant to detain the other party till he took the necessary steps[4]. The case was different *apud iudicem*; he waited till the middle of the appointed day and if either party had not by that time presented himself, judgement went in favour of the other[5].

The proceeding would not be completed in a day; even the *legis actio* might not, and there were the delay of 30 days for the appointment of a *iudex*, and the *diei perendinatio*, while the actual hearing might take many days. The question arises how the presence of the party summoned was secured for these adjournments. The *vadimonium* of the formulary system originated in the *legis actio*. In its later form security was given by verbal contract, but in the *legis actio* it was by a special undertaking by sureties called *vades*[6]. It is not quite clear in which of these various delays they were used: it seems that *vadimonium* was used in all adjournments of the *legis actio*[7], and for the transfer from *ius* to

1 Bertolini, *Il processo civile*, 1. 94, and reff. Wenger, *Zpr*. 92 and reff. 2 Val. Probus, *loc. cit.* 3 *Ante*, p. 489. See however Karlowa, *C.P.* 75, who cites, for the first opinion, Cicero, *pro Caec.* 19. 54, and *pro Mur.* 12. 26, which however are far from conclusive. As to possibility of *cognitor in iudicio*, *post*, § CCXXXIX. 4 See Girard, *Man.* 1032, n. 4; Bertolini, *op. cit.* 1. 98; Karlowa, *C.P.* 323. These writers are dealing with the necessary giving of *vadimonium* (and they cite Plautus, *Persa*, 2. 4. 18, the application of which is not certain). The same rule would no doubt apply to other failures to comply with procedural rules. See however as to *actio in personam*, *ante*, p. 612, n. 4. Wenger, *Zpr.* 102, holds that on admission of a real right, there was an *addictio* as in *c. in iure*. This is not evidenced. 5 XII Tab. 1. 8. Girard, *Textes*, 12; Bruns, 1. 19. 6 Fliniaux, *Vadimonium*, and review, Debray, *N.R.H.* 1910, 142, 521 *sqq*. D. considers the question whether the party also promised to appear. See also *ib.* 534 as to Varro (*L.L.* 6. 74) on *Sponsor*, *Praes* and *Vas*. Gaius, 4. 184 *sqq*. 7 G. *ib.*; Aul. Gell. 6. 1. 9.

hearing[1]. If postponement of the *iudicium* was needed (*ampliatio*), it was, as it seems, not to the next day but to *dies perendinus* and there might be more than one such *diffissio*[2]. But there was no *vadimonium* here; the fact that judgement went by default, if a party had not appeared by noon on the appointed day, would suffice[3].

Vadimonium was limited in amount; it might not exceed half the sum at issue or 100,000 sesterces, except in *actiones iudicati* and *depensi*; here it was for the full amount[4]. It had different forms, sometimes a mere promise, sometimes with surety, sometimes under oath[5]. It is uncertain how far the distinctions go back to the *legis actio*, but in actions for land *vadimonium* was *purum*, i.e. without security[6], and this no doubt applied to *legis actio*, since the immobility of land and the liability of the *praedes* gave sufficient security[7]. And, in some cases, in the *legis actio*[8], the *vades* gave security by way of *subvades*.

In historical times the reference was most commonly to a single *iudex*[9], who was sworn[10]. It has been held, mainly on the strength of the text of Pomponius which says that "*actiones apud collegium pontificum erant*," one of whom was annually appointed, "*ut praeesset privatis*[11]," that the pontiffs sat as *iudices* in early law, but this is not generally accepted[12]. On the other hand the *iudex* was not the only person to preside in a *iudicium*. In some cases the matter went to an *arbiter*, as is now usually held, where an expert was required[13], in others before three *arbitri*, i.e. in *finium regundorum*, and for the purpose of estimating the value of interim fruits (*vindiciae*) in *sacramentum*[14], which issue, however, may have been tried by *iudicis arbitrive postulatio*[15].

Where peregrines were concerned the case might go before *recuperatores*[16], but, as peregrines had in general no right to the *legis actio*, this was confined to those communities with which there existed special treaties. It is not certain that these cases were tried by *legis actio*, but,

1 G. 3. 224; 4. 15; *l. Rubria*, 21 *in f.* Girard, *Textes*, 76. 2 XII Tab. 2. 2. Apart from non-completion, there might be *diffissio* for *morbus sonticus*, etc. 3 These points are controverted, Bertolini, *cit.* 1. 96; Karlowa, *C.P.* §§ 41, 42; Fliniaux, *op. cit.* 1; Wenger, *Zpr.* 183. 4 G. 4. 186. 5 G. 4. 185. In some cases *recuperatores* were named at once with power to give judgement for amount of *vadimonium* if it was not observed. *Ib.* 6 D. 2. 8. 15. pr. dealing with later system, but probably equally applicable to earlier. 7 See however Keller-Wach, *C.P.* n. 543. 8 Aul. Gell. 16. 10. 8. 9 Details as to *iudices*, *post*, § CCXVII. 10 Cicero, *de Off.* 3. 10. 44. 11 1. 2. 2. 6, Karlowa, *C.P.* 23. The probable religious origin of *sacramentum* aids this opinion. 12 Girard, *Org. Judic.* 1. 58. The actions were with them in the sense that they were guardians of the forms. 13 Eisele, *Beiträge*, 1 *sqq.*, infers from etymology that an *arbiter* was originally one who had to investigate on the spot. 14 XII Tab. 12. 3; Cicero, *de Legg.* 1. 21. 55. Wlassak, *Processg.* 2. 293 *sqq.* 15 Girard, *Man.* 1050; but not mentioned in new Gaius fr., *post*, p. 617. 16 Early history of *recuperatores*, de Francisci, *Storia*, 1. 307.

probably, the treaty sometimes provided for this[1]. If the transaction had taken place on Roman soil the *recuperatores* were Romans; if elsewhere, of the nation of the peregrine[2]. The proceeding was to be speedy: recuperators must give their judgement within ten days[3].

Another possible tribunal was that of the *centumviri*. These seem to be of no great antiquity; the organisation with which we know them cannot be earlier than 240 B.C., when the tribes became 35 in number[4]. They were chosen from the tribes: the method is not known. They adjudicated in *hereditatis petitio*, in claims of *tutela*, and, apparently, in some other real actions[5]. Under Augustus the court was reorganised; the *decemviri stlitibus iudicandis* were incorporated with it and took precedence[6]. The court was increased to at least 180[7]. It sat in groups or sections (*consilia, hastae*), acting, it is supposed, sometimes together, sometimes separately, and, it seems, sometimes in pairs[8]. The court continued in existence throughout the classical age[9].

The *decemviri stlitibus iudicandis*[10] are more recent than the *centumviri*. Pomponius speaks of them as created after the appearance of the *Praetor Peregrinus*[11], but they are not traceable before the beginning of the seventh century[12]. They tried cases of liberty[13], and perhaps *civitas*. They ceased to exist as a separate court under Augustus[14].

Not every day was available for the proceedings *in iure*. The utterance of the formal words "*do, dico, addico*," besides being limited as to place[15], was confined to certain days[16]. Some days, *dies fasti*, were wholly available, others, *dies nefasti*, wholly excluded. Others were available if the *comitia* did not meet, and others were, for various reasons, available only partially, *dies intercisi*. Late in the Republic there were changes in the assignment, of which the chief was that market days, formerly

1 Girard, *Org. Judic.* 1. 83, 99 *sqq.*; Wlassak, *Processg.* 2. 299 *sqq.* 2 Dion. Hal. 6. 95. 3 *Ib.*; Girard, *cit.* 1. 102. See also *l. Colon. Genetivae*, 95, which gives 20 days (Girard, *Textes*, 97; Bruns, 1. 130). 4 Festus, s.v. *centumviralia iudicia.* Not found before 190 B.C. Girard, *Org. Judic.* 1. 23. 5 Cicero, *de Or.* 1. 38. 175; *pro Caec.* 18. 53. Dispute as to extent of their jurisdiction and as to extent to which it was exclusive. Pissard, *Les questions préjudicielles*, 51; Wlassak, *loc. cit.*; Daremberg et Saglio, s.v. *Centumviri*; Koschaker, *Z.S.S.* 1930, 679, reviewing Bozza, *Compet. dei Centumviri.* The meaning of *quadruplex, duplex iudicium* is not clear. Pliny, *Ep.* 1. 18. 3; 4. 24. 1; Quint. 11. 1. 78; 12. 5. 6. 6 Sueton. *Aug.* 36. 7 Pliny, *Ep.* 6. 33. 2. 8 Girard, *Man.* 1059. 9 Obsolete in time of Diocletian, Wlassak, P.-W. III. 1950. 10 Not to be confused with an earlier plebeian tribunal of *decemviri*, Girard, *Org. Judic.* 1. 83. 11 1. 2. 2. 29. 12 *C.I.L.* 1. 38; Mommsen, *Staatsr.* 2. 1. 605; *D.P.R.* 4. 314. Nap, *Tijdschr.* 1929, 83, dates them from 129 B.C. 13 Cicero, *pro Caec.* 33. 97. 14 The *tresviri capitales* (1. 2. 2. 30; Livy, 9. 46) elected in the sixth century by the centuries were police magistrates, but there is some evidence for a subordinate function in civil jurisdiction. Mommsen, *op. cit.* 2. 1. 599; *D.P.R.* 4. 307. As to a *l. Papiria*, giving them certain functions in *sacramentum* (Festus, s.v. *Sacramentum*), Girard, *Org. Judic.* 1. 178. 15 As to place or places, Girard, *cit.* 1. 183. 16 Bruns, 1. 41 *sqq.*

excluded, were made available unless they fell on a day expressly *nefastus*[1]. Even *dies fasti* might be rendered unavailable by a temporary closing of courts of justice (*iustitium*), effected by the authority of a magistrate, especially in times of tumult or national lamentation[2]. In the same way the *iudicium* might not take place except on lawful days. But while it seems clear that the mere fact that a day was *nefastus* would not necessarily bar proceedings, as there was no question of using the formal words, the whole question of the days available is obscure[3].

The word plaintiff, used in the foregoing account, does not properly express the relation of the parties; it is the language of a later system[4]. Each made a claim in real actions, and neither could win without proving his title; the burden of proof was not on one rather than on the other. But this was less important than it looks. In the absence of proof on either side, the party in possession, under the system of *vindiciae*, was left in possession, so that if the original *vindicans* made no case, the other remained in possession whether he had made a case or not[5].

The foregoing account is of *sacramentum* in its known form. Its name suggests religious origin; probably the *sacramentum* was originally an oath, supported by an expiatory offering, to be forfeited to the gods by the party whose oath was proved false[6]. It has also been held that the offering was not on account of falsity, but for removing the matter from the arbitrament of the gods[7]. The postponement under the *l. Pinaria* may be associated with secularisation of the proceeding; it was no longer necessary to settle at once the question before the gods[8].

Originally presided over by the *rex*, the proceeding passed to the consuls, on the founding of the Republic, and, by the *l. Licinia*, to the Praetor. The *praetor peregrinus* had jurisdiction where aliens were concerned, *praesides* in their provinces, and possibly in certain cases the curule aediles. Only those mentioned could act; inferior magistrates, e.g. municipal magistrates, had not ordinarily the *legis actio*[9].

CCX. *IUDICIS ARBITRIVE POSTULATIO*[10]. This process could be adopted as an alternative to *sacramentum* wherever it was specially authorised by statute. Gaius says that the XII Tables allowed it in claims based on stipulation and in actions for partition of an *hereditas* and a *l. Licinnia*

1 See Girard, *cit.* 1. 19, 60, 181. 2 Cuq, Daremberg et Saglio, s.v. *Iustitium.* 3 Girard, *op. cit.* 1. 87. 4 G. 4. 16. 17 avoids this language. 5 So, presumably, if both are *iniusta.* 6 See the reff., Bertolini, *cit.* 1. 115. 7 Ihering, *Evolution of the Aryan*, 359. 8 Eisele, *Beiträge*, 222. Von Mayr, *Mél. Girard*, 2. 171, traces it from *sacratio capitis*, through *sacratio bonorum*, to expiatory offering. He discusses other views. The notion of *sacramentum* as a bet, which neither wins, seems to ignore the probable origin. 9 1. 7. 4; cf. P. 2. 25. 4. 10 Gaius' account was omitted from the Verona palimpsest but has been discovered in a parchment fragment, PSI 1182, published by Arangio-Ruiz in 1933, now G. 4. 17a. Discussion by De Zulueta, *J.R.S.* 1936, 174 *sqq.*, *Institutes of Gaius*, 2. 238 *sqq.*

extended its scope to cover actions for partition of common property in general[1]. The plaintiff asserted his claim in formal words, saying, in an action on stipulation, "*Ex sponsione te mihi* (*tantum*) *sestertiorum dare oportere aio. Id postulo aias an neges.*" The defendant denied the debt and thereupon, instead of challenging *sacramento*, the plaintiff asked the Praetor forthwith for the issue to be tried. "*Quando tu negas, te praetor iudicem sive arbitrum postulo uti des.*" There would be *in ius vocatio* and *vadimonia*, if necessary, but apparently no thirty days' delay, as in *sacramentum* and *condictio*. Apart from divisory actions there would always be a money *condemnatio*[2]. The precise distinction between *iudex* and *arbiter* is much discussed[3]. An *arbiter* was probably an expert who decided questions involving the exercise of discretion, as in the partition actions, and where the claim was not for *certa pecunia*. The *iudex*, who alone would be required in claims for *certa pecunia*, which involved merely the question of liability, in later law certainly exercised the functions of *arbiter* also. It has been suggested that the combination of the two roles in one person was achieved in this *legis actio*[4].

The procedure of *iudicis postulatio* avoided both the technicalities of *sacramentum* and the forfeiture of a penal sum to the state. Gaius' account is purely historical, and the three cases he mentions may not be exhaustive of the scope of the action but merely examples. The illustration is of a *sponsio certae pecuniae*, but it was doubtless available in all forms of verbal contract. But it was not an *actio generalis*, like *sacramentum*, and was probably not used, for example, in the *actio finium regundorum*[5]. It did not therefore supersede *sacramentum*. Where there was a choice of action it presumably lay with the plaintiff.

CONDICTIO[6]. This process was also limited to cases allowed by statute. It was introduced by a *l. Silia* for enforcement of obligations for *certa pecunia* and extended later by a *l. Calpurnia* to claims for *certa res*[7]. The dates are not known: it is commonly held that they were nearly of the same date, about 250 B.C., but they may be later[8]. Since they defined the field of application of the action not, as in *iudicis postulatio*, by reference to specific causes of action, but by reference to the type of right claimed, the cause of action was not stated in *condictio*, and jurisprudence could, within limits, bring new causes of action within the sphere of the process. After *in ius vocatio*, the parties appeared *in iure*, and the plaintiff solemnly asserted his claim, "*Aio te mihi sestertiorum* (*tantum*) *dare oportere. Id*

1 G. 4. 17a; D. 4. 7. 12. 2 Bethmann-Hollweg, *C.P.* 1. 64. 3 Broggini, *Iudex Arbiterve*, 24 *sqq.*, 94 *sqq.*, 159 *sqq.* 4 E. Levy, *Z.S.S.* 1934, 305. 5 Buckland, *R.H.* 1936, 741 *sqq.* 6 Gaius' account has been completed by PSI 1182, now G. 4. 17b; De Zulueta, *J.R.S.* 1936, 182 *sqq.*, *Institutes*, 2. 241; for older views, Jobbé-Duval, *Proc. civile*, 63 *sqq.* 7 G. 4. 19. 8 Girard, *Man.* 1051; Nap, *Tijdschr.* 1929, 62, makes it 125 B.C.

postulo aias an neges." If the defendant denied the debt, the plaintiff gave him notice to appear thirty days later to receive a *iudex*. This giving of notice is the *condictio*, explained by Gaius as *denuntiatio*[1], from which the action takes its name. The interval between claim and nomination of the *iudex* in *sacramentum* and *condictio* provided an opportunity for the defendant to find out the precise ground on which he was being sued and to collect evidence.

In the later *actio certae creditae pecuniae*, the plaintiff could insist on a penal sum being staked on the result of the action—*sponsio* and *restipulatio tertiae partis*[2]. But the account in the new fragment of Gaius does not mention it and, as it is clearly called for by the context, this silence suggests that it formed no part of the *legis actio*. Probably, like other details of civil procedure which were formerly referred to this *legis actio*, such as *iusiurandum necessarium*[3], it was invented by the Praetor. We may get some hint of the scope of the *legis actio* from the later *condictiones* of the formulary system[4]. Apart from cases of *stipulatio certae pecuniae* and *certae rei* (in which it was alternative to *iudicis postulatio* and presumably also to *sacramentum*, although we know little about what that action covered), it was probably extended to cover *expensilatio*, *mutuum* and cases of unjust enrichment, to which latter *sacramentum* may not have applied at all. *Condictio* was perhaps also available to recover the penalties prescribed in certain cases by the XII Tables[5]. Gaius wonders why *condictio* was introduced, since one could enforce claims of *dari oportere* by the existing actions[6]. But its scope was wider than *iudicis postulatio* and it provided a simpler form than *sacramentum*, having also the advantage that it avoided the security for the *sacramentum* which must sometimes have been a denial of justice. Not every poor litigant could get a friend to risk 500 asses.

CCXI. These three actions were forms of litigation, reference of a dispute for settlement. We pass to two others which, at least primarily, had not this characteristic, but were modes of enforcement of a right, regulated self-help.

MANUS INIECTIO, essentially, seizure of a person against whom there was a claim, no doubt older than organised redress by way of litigation. As we know it, it was subject to rules of form, appearance before a magistrate, and limitation as to the cases in which it might be used. Gaius describes it as of three types: *iudicati*, *pro iudicato* and *pura*[7].

Manus iniectio iudicati. The process was as follows: after 30 days

1 G. 4. 18. 2 G. 4. 171. See reff. in Karlowa, *C.P.* 233; Lenel, *E.P.* 232. 3 By which the plaintiff was entitled to put the defendant to his oath as to the existence of the debt, *post*, § CCXV. 4 *Ante*, p. 545 *sqq.*; *post*, p. 682 *sqq.* 5 E.g. XII Tab. 8. 3.; but see De Zulueta, *J.R.S.* 1936, 183. 6 G. 4. 20. 7 G. 4. 21 *sqq.*

from the judgement[1] or other event justifying the seizure the claimant brought the party liable directly before the magistrate (*in ius ducit*) and said, "*quod tu mihi iudicatus*" (or *damnatus*) "*es sestertium* (*X milia*), *quandoc non solvisti, ob eam rem ego tibi sestertium X milium iudicati manum inicio*[2]." The defendant might not defend himself against the *manus iniectio* (*manum depellere*), but if he claimed that it was not justified, some one must appear on his behalf to prove this—a *vindex*. The effect of the intervention was that the defendant was released, and further proceedings were against the *vindex*[3]. The action of the *vindex* was not an appeal: there was no rehearing of the original dispute. He might shew that there had been no such fact basing the *manus iniectio* as was claimed or that the creditor had been satisfied or had come to terms. He may have been allowed to shew that the *iudex* had taken a bribe, a capital offence under the XII Tables[4], but he was not entitled to shew simply that the judgement was wrong.

We are not told how the proceedings against the *vindex* were framed, but, from the practice in the later *actio iudicati*[5], which seems to be modelled, substantially, on *manus iniectio*, it appears that it was referred to a *iudex*[6], and it seems that if the *vindex* failed he was condemned *in duplum*[7]. Apart from this intervention, or satisfaction of the claim (*iudicatum facere*), the *manum iniciens* might carry off the debtor (who, in historic times, was "*addictus*" to him by the magistrate[8]) and keep him for 60 days in a private prison, during which time they might come to terms[9]. There was as yet nothing definitive; the debtor was still free and a *civis*, and had not lost his property. The holder must produce him publicly on three successive market days[10] and proclaim the amount of the debt, presumably to facilitate redemption. At the expiration of this time "*capite poenas dabant aut trans Tiberim peregre venum ibant*[11]," which is understood to mean that the creditor might either kill him or sell him into foreign slavery. Another text says that, where several creditors had obtained *manus iniectio*, "*partis secanto: si plus minusve secuerint se*

1 XII Tab. 3. 1. 2 G. 4. 21. Gradenwitz, *Mél. Girard*, 1. 506, suggests divergence here from the original form. The account in the text is of the institution in historical times. 3 G. 4. 21. There were rules, not fully known, as to the financial standing of persons admissible as *vindices*, according to the position of the debtor; XII Tab. 1. 4. See also *l. Colon. Genetivae*, 61 (Girard, *Textes*, 91). 4 Aul. Gell. 20. 1. 7. 5 *Post*, § CCXIX. 6 It was referred from the magistrate to another tribunal in certain quasi-criminal cases of *manus iniectio pura*, which went before the *tresviri capitales*, Girard, *Org. Judic.* 1. 177. 7 Inferred from the double damages in cases known to have descended from *manus iniectio*, e.g. *actio depensi*, *ante*, p. 466. The proof drawn from the obscure *l. Colon. Genetivae*, 61, is disputed. Girard, *Man.* 1043; *Textes*, 91. 8 G. 3. 189; Aul. Gell. 20. 1. 44. See Karlowa, *C.P.* 158. 9 The XII Tables contain rules as to his treatment during this time (3. 3, 4). 10 Apparently the last three *nundinae* of the 60 days: we are told "*tertiis nundinis partis secanto.*" 11 Aul. Gell. 20. 1. 47; *ante*, p. 135.

fraude esto[1]." This was later understood to mean that the creditors might cut the debtor to pieces without responsibility if they cut more than their share, but it is spoken of as unheard of; there was no record of its ever having been done[2]. "*Capite poenas dare*" might mean merely enslavement, and since this would deprive him of his property it has been contended that "*partis secanto*" means merely division of the property, any inequality being capable of adjustment[3]. It is objected that a *civis* could not become a slave at Rome. But this lofty principle, which was not true of later law, is not well evidenced[4], and is difficult to reconcile with the dispute mentioned by Gaius, of an age, as the context shews, earlier than the Praetor's edict[5]. There is nothing inconsistent with the notions of a primitive people in the literal understanding of the rule. There is much controversy[6].

The *l. Poetelia*, of 326 B.C.[7], provided, *inter alia*, some amelioration of the position of the *addictus* for debt. Debtors were not to be chained or imprisoned or to pay with their persons, but rather with their goods, a statement of Livy[8] which seems to mean that the power of killing or selling was taken away, and to imply that they could work out the debt and, as a corollary, that the limit of 60 days disappeared[9].

The question remains: what were the cases of *manus iniectio iudicati*? Judgement, though the typical case, was not the original, for the system is, no doubt, older than judgements in the modern sense: it may be assumed that it applied to *nexum*[10], and to *legatum per damnationem* of a certain sum[11]. It applied also, even primarily, to a *confessus*[12]. Gaius speaks of its application to *iudicatus* and *damnatus*[13]. "*Damnatus*" appears to cover not only one condemned in a judgement, but one *damnatus* (*damnas esto*) by will, or by a contract, e.g. *nexum*, or perhaps by *lex*, e.g. *l. Aquilia*[14].

1 XII Tab. 3. 6; Aul. Gell. 20. 1. 48. The position of creditors who have not obtained judgement is not clear. 2 Aul. Gell. 20. 1. 52. 3 Karlowa, *C.P.* 163, 178; *secare* he compares with *bonorum sectio*. Radin, *Partis secanto*, makes it refer to property. What is sold is the right to dispose of the property and the last rule means that, if the buyer sells it for less or more than he gave, there is no claim either way. 4 It rests mainly on Cicero's rhetorical language, *pro Caecina*, 34. But see Mommsen, *Strafr.* 945. 5 G. 3. 189; did a *fur manifestus* become a slave immediately on *addictio*? See also Aul. Gell. 20. 1. 7, quoting Caecilius on the same rule of the XII Tabs.: "*in servitutem tradit.*" 6 See the much discussed view of Ihering, *Scherz und Ernst, Eine civilprozessualische Attrappe*, who treats it as a device compelling sale of the debtor to one of them. 7 Girard, *Man.* 515. 8 Livy, 8. 28; Varro, *L.L.* 7. 105. 9 Girard, *Man.* 1045. 10 *Ante*, p. 429. 11 The double liability of *infitians* indicating the origin in *m. ini.* applied only to the case of *legatum certi, ante*, p. 335; G. 4. 9. It is presumably *iudicati*, as G. does not mention it among later extensions. 12 XII Tab. 3. 1, but see for limitations, *post*, § CCXVI. 13 G. 4. 21. As to this distinction, see Karlowa, *C.P.* 58. 14 Double damages *contra infitiantem*, G. 3. 216. But there is no proof that the remedy under the *l. Aquilia* was ever *m. iniectio* (*post*, p. 622, n. 4) and the equation, *damnatio* = *m. iniectio* cannot be generalised.

There was probably *condemnatio* in *condictio* and in *iudicis postulatio*, though here and in *sacramentum in personam* for a *certum*, and in *sacramentum in rem* (if proceedings were taken against the actual party, and not against the *praedes*) the person liable was a *iudicatus*. The fact that both *sacramentum* and "*lis et vindiciae*" were recoverable from another person seems to put the actual party in a very favourable position, but, if the matter stood thus, it would be oppressive, for a poor man would hardly get *praedes* on such terms. It must be noted however that the case differs from that of a *vindex*, who certainly took over the liability[1], while in the case of the *praedes* no event had happened to release the party himself. It seems probable therefore that if the winner preferred he might, when the matter had been reduced to a *certum* by *arbitrium litis aestimandae*, proceed by *manus iniectio* against the original party[2]. The *praes* was apparently a *sponsor*, and, if he had satisfied the obligation, by *depensio*, had *manus iniectio* (*pro iudicato*) against his principal. It has been suggested on the evidence of a passage in Gaius[3] that the magistrate would take steps to seize for the winner the property in question, but this is improbable and not justified by the text.

CCXII. *Manus iniectio pro iudicato.* Gaius tells us that *leges* had extended the right of *manus iniectio* to certain cases, as if there had been a judgement, i.e. with the same incidents[4], of which the most important is that any defence must be raised by a *vindex*. The *l. Publilia* gave it to a *sponsor* not reimbursed within six months, perhaps only where the payment had been made *per aes et libram, depensio*[5]. The *l. Furia de sponsu* gave it against one who had exacted from *sponsor* or *fidepromissor*, under a judgement, more than his share of the debt. Perhaps here too *solutio per aes et libram* is assumed. He adds that there were other cases of the same kind[6]. In practice the function of the *vindex* was here different from that in *m. i. iudicati*. Nominally it was the same; he could not go behind the facts which justified the seizure. But in *m. i. iudicati* these were definite readily established facts which the *vindex* must disprove; here it was in effect ordinary litigation, begun in an unusual way. The *vindex* cannot have been under the burden of proof; it is, e.g., impossible that anyone, by merely charging me with having put filth on sacred ground, as in the Luceria case[7], could compel me to find some one who could prove that I had not done so, on pain of double liability in case of failure. It was in fact merely a device, which survived in the

1 "*Vindicem dabat qui pro se causam agere solebat,*" G. 4. 21. 2 Koschaker, *Z.S.S.* 1916, 358. See however Girard, *Man.* 361. 3 G. 4. 48. 4 G. 4. 23. 5 *Ante*, p. 446. 6 The only other clear case is a provision for the town of Luceria that for certain offences against public order, anyone might proceed for a fixed penalty by *manus iniectio pro iudicato* (Girard, *Textes*, 25). No doubt there were other cases of the same type. 7 See *post*, p. 624, n. 1.

later *actiones in duplum contra infitiantem* of later law, to shorten proceedings by penalising groundless defences.

Manus iniectio pura. This was a later development. Gaius[1] speaks of cases in which *leges* gave *m. i. pura*, in which the defendant had no need of a *vindex*, but could defend himself. As there had been a *manus iniectio*, he might be said to be his own *vindex*. It has been contended that there was no liability *in duplum*[2], but the institution would be meaningless without this: *manus iniectio* would be only another form of *in ius vocatio*. Gaius indicates differences between this and the other cases, but says nothing of a difference as to the liability. And as the *l. Vallia* turned nearly all *manus iniectio* into *m. i. pura*[3], it is difficult to understand how the cases should have survived into later law as actions with double liability on denial if they had not had this character in their last phase as *manus iniectiones*[4]. The conception of *m. i. pura* seems to be a clumsy device for securing double liability of *infitians* in certain cases. Gaius gives as instances the claim under the *l. Furia testamentaria* against one who took a legacy greater than 1000 *asses*, and that under the *l. Marcia* against usurers[5]. It is uncertain for other recorded cases whether it was *pro iudicato* or *pura*[6].

The conditions were altered by a *l. Vallia* of uncertain date, but probably not long before the *l. Aebutia*[7], which made all *manus iniectio* "*pura*" except under judgement and in the *actio depensi* of the *sponsor*[8]. It is clear from this and other known facts, that the *l. Poetelia*, notwithstanding the language of Livy[9], had not abolished execution on the person; it long survived the disappearance of the *legis actio*.

Manus iniectio differed from the *modi lege agendi* previously discussed in that it was not essentially litigation. It has been suggested that it is grouped with the others because by the intervention of a *vindex* it might result in litigation[10]. But this can hardly be the reason unless this litigation is itself a part of the *legis actio* totally unrecorded. Gaius says nothing of any formal words spoken by the *vindex*, or of the litigation.

1 G. 4. 23 *sqq.* *Nexum*, see *ante*, p. 429. 2 Mitteis, *Z.S.S.* 1901, 114. 3 Below.
4 The action on *l. per damnationem certe* and the Aquilian action were both *in duplum* and were perhaps *m. iniectiones purae* under this law. That they were *m. i.* is assumed from the expression of the liability as "*damnas esto*" (G. 2. 201; D. 9. 2. 2. 1) coupled with the later double liability and the word *damnatus* in *m. i.* All other recorded *m. i.* is on a *certum*: the Aquilian is not. On 12. 1. 9. 1, Naber, *Mnemosyne*, 1892, 182. See also G. 2. 213; Lenel, *E.P.* 202. It may be that to get this remedy the plaintiff had to assess the value beforehand, as he had to do in *furti nec manifesti* (12. 3. 9; Lenel, *E.P.* 329) which also gave double liability though it is not only *contra infitiantem*. 12. 1. 9. 1 may be a reminiscence of this.
5 The exact conditions are uncertain, G. 4. 23. 6 Girard, *Man.* 1046, n. 1.
7 Girard, *Man.* 1046. 8 G. 4. 25. 9 Livy, 8. 28. 10 Ihering, *Geist* (5), 1. 150 *sqq.* If the further proceeding against the *vindex* was a separate *legis actio*, presumably *sacramentum* at first, this view is necessarily excluded.

The sharp distinction between litigation and execution might have been expected in Gaius, but hardly in the ancients from whom the classification is derived. It appears to have been grouped with the other forms because it was, like them, a formal process prescribed under the *lex* for the enforcement of a right[1].

CCXIII. *Pignoris capio.* Essentially the seizure of property of the debtor in order to put pressure on him. It is primitive, dating from days before the *legis actio*, when it had in strictness no legal effect. Even after it had become a regulated *legis actio*, it no doubt continued to be applied beyond the legal sphere. If a man seized a chattel of his debtor, having no legal right to do so, the debtor could claim it, but only at the risk of immediate proceedings for the debt, and no doubt such extra-legal pledges often resulted from agreement. As a legal institution it is explained by Gaius[2] as follows: the creditor, where *pignoris capio* was allowed, seized property of the debtor to hold as a pledge, using formal prescribed words (*certa verba*), as in other *legis actiones*, but there was no appearance in court, the debtor himself need not be present, and it could be done on *dies nefasti*, when, in general, because the intervention of the magistrate was involved, *legis actio* was not possible.

Gaius tells us that it was allowed by custom where a soldier's stipend (*aes militare*), or the money needed to procure a horse for an *eques* (*aes equestre*), or fodder for the horse (*aes hordearium*), was not provided by the person liable, this charge being, at least in case of *aes hordearium*, imposed on certain persons as a tax[3]. The XII Tables allowed it against one who bought a beast for sacrifice and failed to pay the price, or hired a horse from one who meant to use the hire money to buy a sacrifice, and had not paid the hire. It was allowed by a provision of the censors to a *publicanus*, for unpaid taxes. Gaius does not suggest other cases, but it is sometimes held that these are only examples and that it was a much more general remedy[4]. This seems unlikely. Gaius indeed tells us[5] that in *damnum infectum*, though the praetorian remedy was usually adopted[6], it was possible to proceed by *legis actio* and it is suggested that this was *pignoris capio*, for which view there is little evidence[7]; the liability is of a very different type. There is another recorded case in the Empire[8], but that was seizure by persons exploiting under the State and had no relation to the *legis actio*. There is another somewhat earlier case in

1 This is substantially the definition of *legis actio* given by Ihering elsewhere (*op. cit.* (4), 2. 639; *Tr. Franç.* 3. 331). In the other passage he is considering not the character of *legis actio*, but the character of *modi lege agendi*. 2 G. 4. 26 *sqq.* 3 Mommsen, *Staatsr.* 3. 256; *D.P.R.* 6. 1. 290. 4 E.g. Lenel, *Essays in Legal Hist.* ed. Vinogradoff, 132. 5 G. 4. 31. Extra-legal seizure is irrelevant here. 6 *Post*, § CCXLV. 7 Karlowa, *C.P.* 216 *sqq.*, who gives the evidence. 8 *Lex Metalli Vipacensis*, 16, 35, 41, etc. Girard, *Textes*, 120; Bruns, 1. 289.

which *manus iniectio* and *pignoris capio* were allowed where filth was thrown in a certain area, which may have been a private case, i.e. *popularis*[1], but is not ancient or very closely connected with the old *legis actio*. On the whole the list given by Gaius seems probably to be exhaustive for early law[2].

The fact that some of these cases are based on *mores* and not on *lex* has suggested the view that in the expression *legis actio* the word *lex* is used in an extended sense, though there are different opinions as to what this meaning is[3]. But the forms are regulated by statute, and the fact that some applications are older than the statute does not seem to require this concession; *tutela legitima* is older than the statute.

What is the common quality of the recorded cases? They all, with the very doubtful exception of *damnum infectum*, affect the State or religious interests[4], and it is contended that as the State can do itself justice, these are cases in which the State had delegated the power of enforcement to the person more immediately concerned and responsible. The interests of religion were indeed only remotely affected, and neither State nor religion was concerned in *damnum infectum*. But apart from this doubtful case, they were all cases in which there was public interest, and in which there was no juristic relation between the parties. Those who were to provide the funds for the soldier were not responsible to him but to the State. The tax was not due to the *publicanus* but to the State. Informal sale and hire were not recognised as giving an action in early law. This indirect remedy was given where there was no action because the public interest was concerned[5].

The seizure of a pledge was in itself a poor remedy. It might indeed, if valuable and indispensable property was seized, put pressure on the defaulter, but one would expect further steps to be possible. Gaius tells us of none, and other sources give little help. There is no hint of sale. Whether the system was or was not a delegation of the magistrate's power of seizure, by way of *coercitio*, it was plainly modelled on it and would probably give the same right over the pledge, i.e. to destroy it, if the claim was not satisfied[6]. This right may have existed here, and, on the same analogy, may have been the only right. Sale in State cases would have suggested action in our case[7], but as the State did not sell, that analogy fails. It is, however, widely held that the further proceedings

1 *Sc. de pago Montano*, Girard, *Textes*, 130; Bruns, 1. 189. See also a more ancient provision for the town of Luceria giving *m. i.* on such facts; Girard, *Textes*, 25; Bruns, 1. 283.
2 As to a case under the *l. Quinctia*, see below, n. 5.
3 Mitteis, *R.Pr.* 1. 34.
4 Cuq, *Inst. Jur.* 1. 430; *Man.* 843.
5 *Pignoris capio* by officials under the *l. Quinctia* (Girard, *Textes*, 105; Bruns, 1. 114) is not the *l. a.* But here too there is no action.
6 Mommsen, *Strafr.* 53.
7 That is the way in which the State enforces its claims: action is for *privati*.

were an action[1], and that this explains the position of *pignoris capio* in this group. It would not be an action by the victim claiming that the seizure was wrong; that would be a *vindicatio*, probably *sacramentum*, and certainly a distinct *legis actio*. It must therefore have been an action to enforce redemption, perhaps, in view of the language of Gaius[2] and of analogous provisions of the so-called *l. Iulia municipalis*[3], for an amount larger than the original claim, but recoverable only after a certain lapse of time. But if this special machinery existed, Gaius, whose account is full, would certainly have thought it worth mentioning. He tells us of the *iudicium in sacramentum* and *condictio*. He tells us that there was dispute on the question whether *pignoris capio* was a *legis actio*; some refused so to regard it because it was not *in iure*, did not need presence of the adversary and could take place on *dies nefasti*, all impossible in the others[4]. He says that the general view was that it was a *legis actio*, because of the *certa verba* used. He does not advert to the existence of this *iudicium* which must, one would suppose, have involved appearance before the magistrate for the appointment of the *iudex*. Two texts are however cited to prove the existence of this action. One is a text of Cicero in which he calls the *publicanus* "*pignerator ac petitor*[5]." But another reading is "*aut petitor*," which makes some difference. And little importance attaches to a rhetorical utterance dealing with provincial procedure and made long after the introduction of *formulae*. The other text, of Gaius[6], is more important. He tells us that there was in later times an *actio fictitia* given to the *publicanus* containing "*talis fictio...ut quanta pecunia olim si pignus captum esset, id pignus is a quo captum erat luere deberet tantam pecuniam condemnetur*." The fiction is complex. The form given is, it seems, that of the *formula*, in *oratio obliqua*. He gives other illustrations of *formulae fictitiae in personam*, but this is the only one which says "*luere debere*" and not "*oportere*," a fact which suggests that the remedy it replaced was not an action. If the seizer had no action, but only means of putting pressure, this fiction seems exactly designed to give an action instead. If there had been an *actio* it is not easy to see why the expression "*dare oporteret*" was not used; the *formula* would have been much simpler[7].

CCXIV. DECAY OF THE *LEGIS ACTIO*. The rigid formalism and consequent inexpansibility of the *legis actio* was unsuited to the needs of advancing civilisation. Still less was it suited, since its forms and ceremonies were to a great extent secrets in the hands of patrician magistrates

1 Ihering, *Geist* (5), 1. 158 *sqq*. 2 G. 4. 32. 3 E.g. 43; Girard, *Textes*, 84; Bruns, 1. 104. 4 G. 4. 29. 5 *In Verr*. 2. 3. 11. 27. 6 G. 4. 32.
7 The text loses little significance in this connexion if we accept the view (Wlassak, *Judicationsbefehl*, 277) that the word *forma* does not mean the formula, but the *forma* of the censors issued for *publicani*.

and pontiffs, to the plebeians, steadily growing in strength. The opening of various magistracies to plebeians and the publication of the Calendar and other information by Cnaeus Flavius, about 300 B.C.[1], did something to help them, and when, half a century later, a plebeian *pontifex maximus* expounded the law publicly[2], all the value of the system, even to the patricians, was gone. Only its inconveniences were left, and it was superseded by the more rational Formulary System. Simplification had already begun within the *legis actio* itself, by the introduction of actions *per sponsionem*[3], a method of evading the real action by *sacramentum*[4]. One party, apparently the party in possession, promised a small sum to the other, if the thing claimed belonged to that other, having already given security for delivery of the *res* and the interim profits, by way of surety, replacing the old *praedes*, and therefore called *satisdatio pro praede litis et vindiciarum*[5]. Action was brought on the promise, probably by *condictio*[6], and the trial of the question whether the *summa sponsionis* was due would settle the property question[7]. Gaius[8] makes it clear that the action was in form *in personam*, a claim for the amount of the *sponsio*, but the decision rendered possible a claim against the sureties for the thing, so that it was in effect a decision on the *ius in rem*. Since the *sponsio* was, as we know it, *praeiudicialis*, not *poenalis*, i.e. not actually exacted[9], its amount would be indifferent. The action would normally be *condictio* after this action was introduced, but a certain *l. Crepereia* of unknown date shews that, if the case was one going before the *centumviri*, the claim would be by *sacramentum in personam*. The same statute also provided that the *sponsio*, in the same case, should be 125 sesterces[10]. The purpose of this provision may have been to secure that the resulting *sacramentum* should be on the lower scale, but it is obscure, and the fact that, on the money values of the late Republic, 125 sesterces were equivalent to 500 *asses*, i.e. the *sacramentum* in important cases, has given rise to other explanations[11].

1 Livy, 9. 46; D. 1. 2. 2. 7. 2 1. 2. 2. 35. 3 See Karlowa, *C.P.* 97. 4 Naber, *Mél. Girard*, 2. 309, states and rejects various opinions as to the reason for its introduction, himself concluding that it was in order to substitute a single issue—is the thing the plaintiff's?—for the duplex question which we saw to be essential to *sacramentum in rem*. 5 G. 4. 91, dealing, however, with the later system. 6 Jobbé-Duval, *Ét. de proc. civile*, 485 *sqq.*, holds that they were not tried by *legis actio*, but by a procedure not clearly defined, the *sponsio* forming the instruction to the *iudex*. He rests this mainly on Cicero, *Verr.* 2. 1. 45. 115, which he considers to distinguish between *l. actio* and procedure *per sponsionem*. Accepted, Cuq, *Man.* 296. But it seems only to distinguish between *lege agere in hereditatem* and the more circuitous process. He associates with this action the enigmatic "*deductio quae moribus fit*" (Cicero, *pro Tullio*, 8. 20; *pro Caec.* 1. 2, etc.) which has been assigned by different writers to *sacramentum in rem*, interdict *uti possidetis* and interdict *unde vi*. 7 Probably the action consumed the claim *in rem*, Bozza, *St. Bonfante*, 2. 628. 8 G. 4. 95, "*summam sponsionis petimus.*" 9 G. 4. 94. 10 G. 4. 95. 11 E.g. Naber, *loc. cit.*

The Praetor's interdict played, as we shall see, a very important part in the formulary system, but interdicts were already issued under the *legis actio* system. How far the Praetor could, at that time, thus create new obligations we need not here consider, but he could certainly issue orders requiring obedience to existing law and enforce them by his *coercitio*[1]. No doubt some of the interdicts of later law, giving the ordinary interdictal procedure, either to a person aggrieved, or, where the interest was public, to any citizen, are older than the formulary system. If so, their later character suggests that they were tried by *sponsiones*.

The recuperatory procedure already mentioned[2] was probably in some cases by *legis actio*, in others by a different method, since the treaties on which it rested may have varied in their terms. We know little of this other procedure[3], but it has been conjectured that the instructions to the *recuperatores* were written.

In the formulary system, dominant in the classical age, the main lines of the procedure were unchanged. The issue came before a magistrate, was formulated in his court (*in iure*), and referred to another tribunal, *iudex*, *arbiter*, etc., for settlement. But this similarity is accompanied by fundamental changes in the character of the proceedings. The most significant change is that instead of the "*certa verba*" of the *legis actio* there were "*concepta verba*[4]." The proceedings *in iure*, instead of consisting in the recitation of fixed traditional forms of words, now resulted in a statement of the issue in a *formula* or instruction to the *iudex*, based on one of a set of models provided by the Praetor in his Edict, and modified, so far as was necessary, to state the exact question, subject to the Praetor's approval. This control was only one expression of a great change which had occurred in his share in the control of litigation. He had now an extraordinarily free hand. He could create new actions by his Edict, thereby creating rights and liabilities not known to the civil law. He could admit defences not known to civil law and he could refuse actions where civil law allowed them[5].

Another important change was that the instructions to the *iudex* (*formula*) were put into writing, an almost inevitable result of the greater elasticity of the proceedings; without it, disputes as to the exact issue submitted would have been frequent.

The judgement was now, apart from the divisory actions, either a *condemnatio* for a sum of money or an *absolutio*[6]. Other minor points will be considered in dealing with the course of an action.

1 As to "*de glande legenda*," Pliny, *H.N.* 16. 5. 15. 2 *Ante*, p. 614. 3 Karlowa, *C.P.* 218 *sqq.*; Girard, *Org. Judic.* 1. 99 *sqq.* 4 G. 4. 30. 5 See, however, *post*, p. 629; for terminology, see *post*, p. 718; Buckland, *Tulane L.R.* 1939, 163 *sqq.* 6 As to non-existence of *absolutio* in early law, see a view of Huvelin, *Mél. Gérardin*, 344 *sqq.*

There remains the question of the history of these changes. Of their legislative history a few words must suffice. Gaius tells us that the *legis actio* was superseded by the effect of the *l. Aebutia*, and the *ll. Iuliae*[1]. The *l. Aebutia* is held by Girard to have been enacted between 149 and 126 B.C.[2] The *ll. Iuliae* appear to date from Augustus and are no doubt parts of the piece of legislation called the *l. Iulia Iudiciorum*[3]. Gaius does not tell us what part was played by each of these enactments, and many views are held[4]. According to one the *l. Aebutia* substituted the *formula* for the *legis actio per condictionem*, and did not affect the others, the work being completed by the *l. Iulia*[5]. According to another, more widely accepted, the *l. Aebutia* merely authorised the *formula*, so that suitors could proceed in either way while the *l. Iulia* swept away the *legis actio* altogether[6]. In any case, after its enactment the *legis actio* was gone, apart from fictitious litigation[7], except, as Gaius tells us[8], in the case of *damnum infectum* (in which, he observes, it was not used), and where the case was to go before the *centumviri*, in which case it must be tried by *sacramentum*. To this extent it survived to the time of Paul[9].

All this assumes the *formula* newly introduced by the *l. Aebutia* so far as *cives* are concerned. But it is maintained[10] that it was already in use for certain transactions, e.g. sale, in the time of *legis actio*, the *iudicia* being *honoraria* and made *legitima* by the *l. Aebutia*. The reasoning is necessarily *a priori* and rather inconclusive. The view that the consensual contract of sale cannot have been so late as that *lex* in view of the high development of civilisation loses force when we reflect that

1 G. 4. 30. 2 *Mél.* 1. 67 *sqq.*, 114 *sqq.*; *Man.* 1058. There is evidence that, at the earlier date, *legis actio* was the only mode, while at the later the magistrate had the power *denegare actionem*, a result of the *l. Aebutia*, but this origin is disputed, *post*, p. 629. Reply, Wlassak, *Judicationsbefehl*, 276. Similar approximate dating, on different grounds, Mitteis, *R.Pr.* 52. 3 Girard, *Z.S.S.* 1913, 295 *sqq.*; *Man.* 1058. He dates the *l. Iulia iudiciorum publicorum* in 17 B.C., and the other, *privatorum*, which abolished the *legis actio*, in the same or the next year, but this though probable is not so securely made out. He rejects the view (Wlassak, *Processg.* 1. 191 *sqq.*) based on the plural in G. 4. 30 that there were two *ll. Iuliae iud. privatorum*, one dealing with Rome and the other with the *municipia*, and shews the untenability of the view expressed by Mommsen (e.g. *Strafr.* 128) that these *ll. Iuliae* are identical with the *l. Iulia de vi*. 4 Collinet-Giffard, *Précis*, 1. 90. 5 Eisele, *Abhandl.* 68; Cuq, *Inst. jur.* 1. 714; *Man.* 852; Pflüger, *Z.S.S.* 1922, 153, who holds that in other actions the *formula* came to be used, but only by praetorian authority. The *l. Iulia* gave it here too a statutory basis, without however extending to it the civil law effect of *ipso iure consumptio*. 6 Wlassak, *Processg.* 1. §§9, 10; see however Hoetink, *Tijdschr.* 1929, 253; Jobbé-Duval, *Mél. Cornil*, 1, 517, thinks the *l. Aebutia* merely allowed a *formula* to be used with the *l. a.*, the parties agreeing on a written issue. This made the *l. a.* unimportant and the *l. Iulia* abolished it. This view harmonises with the way in which rules of the XII Tables were long evaded rather than repealed. 7 *Cessio in iure*, manumission *vindicta*, etc. 8 G. 4. 31. 9 P. 5. 16. 2; *ante*, p. 615. 10 Mitteis, *R.Pr.* 1. 44.

Greek law perhaps never reached it at all. But the hypothesis explains the known facts better than most of the other hypotheses.

The statement of the legislative provisions which caused the disappearance of the *legis actio* leaves open the question, whence come the new ideas of the new system? The disappearance of the dramatic element was prepared by the *legis actio per condictionem*, and thus this action has been described as not only the last development of the *legis actio*, but also the first step in the new system[1]. In fact, little distinguishes it from the early *formula*[2]. The source of the writing is obscure. It has been said that *recuperatores* received their instructions in writing[3], and this suggested it, but there is no evidence for the fact. It is also said that it may come from the practice in provincial jurisdiction[4], and it may also be considered a natural result of the more complex nature of the issue, and the increased prevalence of writing, but there is no certainty. The use of variable "*concepta verba*" instead of "*certa verba*" came no doubt from one of these sources, perhaps from the provincial procedure through the intervening stage of the *praetor peregrinus*[5]. This variability is one aspect of the changed position of the magistrate. He could now create actions, refuse actions, admit new defences and so forth. This power can hardly have been expressly conferred by the *l. Aebutia.* Probably it was a usurpation of the Praetor rendered possible by the power of issuing *formulae*, given by the statute. It was no doubt contemplated as an exercise of the *imperium*, favoured by public opinion, and therefore not checked by authority. These powers were, no doubt, not all exercised at the beginning. The *exceptio doli* did not exist till Cicero's time[6]. *Praescriptio pro reo* became an *exceptio* later still[7]. Whether any of the powers existed under the *legis actio* system is disputed. Girard holds that none of the powers in litigation which we regard as essentially praetorian (*missio in possessionem, interdicta*, etc.)

1 Keller-Wach, *C.P.* 95. 2 Naber, *Tijdschr.* 1918, 230. 3 Arangio Ruiz, *Ist.* 110. 4 Girard, *Man.* 1056. It is also suggested that the instructions in the *arbitrium litis aestimandae* were written. Huvelin, *Mél. Gérardin*, 333. See also Koschaker, *Z.S.S.* 1913, 434. Partsch, *Schriftformel* (48 *sqq.*), arguing from the form in which disputes between certain Greek communities were referred by the *pr. peregrinus*, under direction of the Senate, to arbitral courts for decision, concludes that something like the *formula* was in use in the court of *pr. peregrinus* before the *l. Aebutia* and, *a fortiori*, in the provinces. Naber, *cit.*, holds that it was used in *l. a. per cond.* and borrowed from the Greeks. 5 Girard, *ib.* An internal origin of the *formula* may seem in itself more probable. Some hypotheses start from this point of view. Keller (*loc. cit.*) traces it from the freer hand the magistrate had in *condictio*, the magistrate's instructions here being an anticipation of the *formula*. Huvelin (*Mél. Gérardin*, 319) traces it from the instructions to the *iudex* in the *arbitrium litis aestimandae*, the *formula* having begun in similar instructions without any previous trial by *sacramentum*. But the interpretation of his principal text (Cicero, *de Orat.* 1. 36. 166, 167) is not satisfactory. See also Arangio Ruiz, *Ist.* 110. 6 *De Off.* 3. 14. 60. 7 *Arg.* G. 4. 133.

existed under the *legis actio*, except so far as they enforced civil law rights[1], but a different view is elsewhere held[2]. The most doubtful case is *denegatio actionis*[3]. Of several recorded instances, one is older than the *l. Aebutia* and others may be. The first concerns *manumissio*, and is on the instructions of the Senate, both circumstances which lessen its weight, but hardly destroy it[4]. It is certain that in 177 B.C. the Senate could direct the Praetor as to the exercise of his *imperium*, but it is not so clear that it could order him to do what was wholly outside his competence. The other cases can be but little later than the *lex*, and if we have to choose between immediate exercise of this great power, without precedent, and the possibility that it was already, in the period immediately before the *l. Aebutia*, to some extent in operation, the latter seems to be the more probable[5].

The solution is simple if we accept the view that for certain purposes the *formula* was already in use *inter cives* before the *l. Aebutia*[6]. But the facts just mentioned involve a *legis actio*, and this implies a similar power in that case. It seems probable that the magistrate might *denegare legis actionem*, and there seems no evidence for the view that a civil suit would lie, after the magistracy was over, for exercises of the *imperium*, how ever unjust. Public proceedings, e.g. for malversation, are a different matter[7].

CCXV. COURSE OF AN ACTION UNDER THE FORMULARY SYSTEM[8]. The normal beginning was *in ius vocatio*[9], and the adversary, now describable in all cases as the defendant, must come or give a *vindex*[10]. The

1 Girard, *Mélanges*, 1. 75 *sqq.*, 126 *sqq.*, 169 *sqq.* 2 Not an arbitrary power, Levy-Bruhl, *Denegatio actionis*. Based on *lex* or edict except so far as, e.g. in immoral *stipulationes*, he has certain functions of the Censor. See, however, Wenger, *Praetor und Formel*, 50 *sqq.* 3 See the opposing views of Mitteis, Lenel, and Wlassak, cited and considered by Girard, *loc. cit.* 4 Livy, 41. 9. 5 See also Costa, *Profilo Storico*, 32, and Cornil, *Dr.R.* 92, for expressions of this view. 6 *Ante*, p. 628. 7 Mommsen, *Staatsr.* 1. 699, and Wenger, *Praetor und Formel*, 49, hold that an action lay, but neither gives any cases and W. is clear that none lay for a *denegatio actionis*, however unjust. For Betti, *Ist.* 1, §§ 11–13, the Praetor's *imperium* being a residuum of the royal absolutism, he not only defined actions, but gave actions and *rest. in int.* before the *l. Aebutia*. But the system of *stipulationes praetoriae* seems to imply a not very early date when he could not give actions but could force people to take steps rendering them liable to civil actions. There seems no trace of a praetorian action or *exceptio inter cives* till after the *formula* was introduced and *restitutio in int.* implies a praetorian action or defence. See, however, Jobbé-Duval, *Proc. civ.* 181. 8 The following account is of procedure at Rome. As to jurisdiction, *post*, § CCXX. 9 With a statement of the nature of the claim—an informal "*editio actionis*," required by the Edict. Lenel, *E.P.* § 9. Wenger, *Praetor und Formel*, § 1. *Litis denuntiatio*, *post*, § CCXXVI. 10 G. 4. 46; Lenel, *E.P.* 65. The *vindex*, if he fails to produce his man, is liable to *actio in factum* for "*quanti ea res erit*" (2. 8. 2. 5), an obscure saying not cleared up by h. t. 3 and 5. pr. Cuq (*Man.* 868) holds it to mean that he is liable whether the actual defendant was or not, though the *vindex* of the *l. a.* was liable only if the defendant would have been. The *vindex* of classical law has become *fideiussor iudicio sistendi causa* in the Digest.

Edict provided that if he did not appear, or give a *vindex*, an *actio in factum* for a penalty would be given against him, and it contained other auxiliary rules on the matter[1]. There was an *actio in factum* against the *vindex* who failed to produce his man, and *missio in possessionem* against the defaulter himself[2]. It seems that the old right of taking him by force before the magistrate if he would not come or give a *vindex* still remained[3]. There was however an alternative to *in ius vocatio*. *Vadimonium*, still used in case of postponement, might also be used to initiate proceedings[4]. *Vadimonium* was now by verbal contract[5], and, in the present case, as it was extra-judicial, and matter of agreement, there was no general rule requiring surety[6]. It was distinct from the undertaking of a *vindex*. That presupposes *in ius vocatio*; this replaces *in ius vocatio*. The Edict also provided[7] that if a defendant hid and so made *in ius vocatio* impossible, the creditor might be given possession of the goods of the *latitans* (*missio in possessionem*) with an ultimate right to sell them, *venditio bonorum*[8].

It is a debated question whether there could be more than one plaintiff or defendant, apart from divisory actions. The better view seems to be that while the same result can often be obtained without this, e.g. by grouped actions referred to the same *iudex* (the parties concerned could appoint a common *procurator*[9]) and was in effect produced where there were common owners and one of them sued or was sued for all in respect, e.g. of a servitude[10], there was nothing to prevent joint action or joint defence[11].

The parties being in court, the plaintiff stated the nature of his claim and evidence, *editio actionis*[12], and asked of the Praetor the *formula* he wanted, *postulatio, impetratio actionis*[13]. The possible variety of defences and answers thereto made the matter *in iure* much more complex than under the old system. Thus, in a claim on a loan of money, the defendant might wish to plead that he was a *filiusfamilias* at the time of the loan, *exceptio Sci. Macedoniani*[14], and the plaintiff might answer that he had represented himself as a *paterfamilias, replicatio doli*[15]. Such matters might take time. If the business could not be completed in the day there

1 Perhaps *m. in poss.* Beseler, *Beitr.* 3. 20. 2 Lenel, *E.P.* 70 *sqq.* 3 See, e.g., 50. 17. 103. 4 Cicero, *pro Quinctio*, 19. 61. Not stated in extant legal texts. 5 G. 4. 184. 6 G. 4. 185, *ante*, p. 613; Fliniaux, *Vadimonium*, 48 *sqq.*; *vadimonium in iniuria* (G. 3. 224; Coll. 2. 6. 1), *ib.* 57; as to circumstances barring action for *vadimonium desertum*, *ib.* 79. 7 See Lenel, *E.P.* 415. 8 42. 4. 7. 1 *sqq.* 9 3. 3. 31. 1. 10 10. 1. 4. 5. 11 Festus, *s.v. Contestari litem*; D. 16. 3. 1. 44; 10. 2. 48. Wenger, *Zpr.* 80; Costa, *Profilo Storico*, 11. *Contra*, Biondi, *Compensazione*, § 16. 12 See 2. 13. 1, where it is not clear what refers to this *editio* and what to that which accompanied *in ius vocatio*. Something of the sort there must have been. 13 Cicero, *in Verr.* 2. 3. 65. 152; C. 3. 9. 1; C. 2. 57, rubr. 14 *Ante*, p. 465. 15 *Post*, § CCXXIII. On the proceedings *in iure*, Wlassak, *Klassische Processformel*, §§ 1, 2.

would be *vadimonium*. Ultimately the issues would be embodied in a *formula*, approved by the Praetor. It was issued under his authority, but it was not his duty to see that it stated the dispute correctly; that was for the parties[1]. What he had ordinarily to see to was that it stated a real issue of fact and law, or, in some cases, of fact, satisfying himself, in this last case, that the facts alleged were such as to justify the issue of the *formula in factum*[2].

The next step was the appointment of a *iudex*, whose identity was arrived at by a method to be considered later[3]. This settled, the *formula* was issued and accepted by the defendant, the transaction amounting, according to the view now dominant, to a contract between the parties[4]. This is *litis contestatio* (the very important effects of which will be considered later[5]), possibly still accompanied by a joint appeal to witnesses, "*testes estote*[6]." There appears to have been an express authorisation or instruction by the Praetor to the chosen *iudex* to proceed in accordance with the *formula*, *iudicare iubere*[7]. The exact machinery of the issue of the *formula* is disputed. It may have been accepted by the defendant from the Praetor[8], or, more probably from the plaintiff, under the Praetor's authority[9], in written form, or dictated by the plaintiff and written down by the defendant[10].

Something must be said of important variations of the proceedings *in iure*. In certain actions, *actiones interrogatoriae*[11], the plaintiff, before asking for his *formula*, might question the defendant as to circumstances which affected, not the liability in general, but his personal liability. This might be done in noxal actions, with results already stated[12]. The

1 As to meaning of "*dare actionem*," Wenger, *Praetor und Formel*, § 2—*d. actionem* means allow an action. In § 3 *dare iudicium* is interpreted to mean "approves the *formula*" (but this does not necessarily mean *iudicium* = *formula*. To approve the *formula* is to allow the hearing). The *nominatio iudicis* is a distinct act, possibly later: when this is done comes *litis contestatio*. 2 In dealing with insufficiently advised suitors he might on occasion be much more helpful. 3 *Post*, p. 635. 4 Wlassak, *Anklage und Streitbefestigung*, 3–36; Wenger, P.-W., s.v. *Editio*; *Praetor und Formel*. Schlossmann, *Litis contestatio*, 124 and 188 *sqq*., rejects this, returning to the view that it is a quasi-contract, resting on the Praetor's authority. So Lotmar, reviewing Wlassak (reply by W., *Sitzungsberichte*, Wien, 1920, 185) and Koschaker, *Z.S.S.* 1919, 364. Beseler, *Z.S.S.* 1930, 442, calls W.'s view an "*unbewiesene und irrige dogma*." 5 *Post*, § CCXXXV. 6 Festus, s.v. "*contestari*." 7 Partsch, *Schriftformel*, 10; Wlassak, *Iudicationsbefehl*. The *iussum* is, he says, accompanied by a copy of the *formula*. It is a distinct act. So Lenel, *Z.S.S.* 1922, 567. *Contra*, Arangio Ruiz, *Ist*. 124. The right, or duty, *iudicare*, being created by the magistrate, could be revoked by him, 5. 1. 5. 8. 8 Keller, *Litis Contestatio*, held that the *formula* was accepted from the Praetor, not the other party and thus reached the quasi-contract theory, see n. 4. 9 Wlassak, *Kl. Prozessformel*, 104; Girard, *Man*. 1073. 10 Lenel, *Z.S.S.* 1894, 374. The conception of the *formula* as a contract has important consequences, especially as to *translatio iudicii*, *post*, § CCXLI. 11 Demelius, *Die Confessio*, 245. Lautner, *Festschr. f. Hanausek*, 52, denies that the name is classical. Discussion of main points. 12 *Ante*, p. 600.

interrogatio also occurred in actions against the *heres* of a debtor. The plaintiff asked whether and for what share the defendant was *heres*[1], an important point as the XII Tables divided the liabilities among the *heredes*. If he refused to answer or answered falsely that he was not *heres*, or as to his share, he was liable *in solidum*[2]. Apart from this the action proceeded as if any admission made was true, but as this praetorian action might make one liable who was not really *heres*, there is much dispute as to its exact formulation[3].

In some cases the plaintiff might offer an oath to the defendant (*iusiurandum necessarium*). If he took it the action was lost[4]. If he refused it he was condemned. If he offered it back (*referre iusiurandum*), the analogous alternative was before the plaintiff[5]. But instead of offering the oath back, he might offer the plaintiff a *iusiurandum calumniae*. If this was refused the action was refused—*denegatio actionis*[6]. If it was taken the defendant must then swear or *referre*. It appears the better view[7] that this machinery of *iusiurandum necessarium* applied only to *condictio certae pecuniae* and *rei*[8], *actio de constituto*, *actio operarum operae* being contemplated as specific *danda*, like sums of money[9], and *a. ex testamento* for a *certum*. There are, however, other cases of *iusiurandum in iure*. In noxal actions if the defendant denied *potestas*, the plaintiff had the alternative of an action *sine noxae deditione* or of offering an oath to the defendant. If he took it he was absolved. If he refused it he was condemned, with a right of surrender[10]. There seems to be no *relatio*. So also in the *actio rerum amotarum* an oath might be offered after a preliminary oath *de calumnia*[11], but there was no *relatio*.

In any action in which the mere fact of losing it did not involve the defendant in any liability beyond the *interesse*, i.e. there was no *sponsio poenalis*, or liability to condemnation beyond the *simplum*, the plaintiff might offer the defendant a *iusiurandum calumniae*, i.e. that he was

1 11. 1. 1. pr. Lenel, *E.P.* 145. 2 11. 1. 5, 11. 3, 4. If he falsely says he is *heres*, and is insolvent, so that plaintiff suffers, the action against the true *heres* will be restored. The interrogations in *damni infecti* (11. 1. 10, 20. 2; Cuq, *Man.* 873) seem to have a different character and effect. 3 For various reconstructions, Lenel, *E.P.* 146. On the quasi-contractual nature of the *obl.* created, Riccobono, *Dal Dir. R.* 296. *Contra*, Lautner, *Festschr. f. Hanausek*, 55. Of the chief text, 11. 1. 11. 9, nearly every word is declared by one or other of the various critics to be interp. Under J. the *interrogatio* appears to be by the magistrate. 4 12. 2. 7. 5 12. 2. 34. 6, 7. 6 12. 2. 34. 4. No *consumptio litis*. The *iusiurandum calumniae* has a wider field, *post*, § CCXVIII. 7 Girard, *Man.* 1065. 8 The evidence for its application to *condictio certae rei* is not good: it is contended by Biondi, *Giuramento decisorio*, c. 1, that it applied only where there was a penalty (*sponsio tertiae partis*) and that the effect of refusal was not condemnation but merely that the action, with its liability to the penalty, would proceed. Cornil, *Dr.R.* 476, confines it to *condictio certi*. For a wider field, Cuq, *Man.* 874. 9 38. 1. 4; Lenel, *E.P.* 339. Such *operae*, dayworks, seem to have acquired a definite fixed money value, as in the old English land law. 10 9. 4. 21. 4. 11 25. 2. 11–14.

defending in good faith. The defendant might offer a similar oath to the plaintiff. If this was taken the action proceeded. A plaintiff who refused could not proceed with the action, but he could bring another. A defendant who refused was probably treated as *indefensus*[1].

CCXVI. Instead of defending, the defendant might admit the claim[2]. If the liability was for *certa pecunia*, there was no difficulty; he was treated as *iudicatus*. *Confessus pro iudicato habetur*[3]. But in all other cases the better view is that he was not *iudicatus*, as all *condemnatio* was for a fixed sum and the formulary system had no *arbitrium litis aestimandae*[4]. One text[5] shews indeed that even if the claim was for an *incertum* there might be admission of liability for a certain sum, and if the sum satisfied the plaintiff, this would in classical law[6] be *confessio certi*. Apart from this modern opinion is divided. The view now perhaps dominant is mainly based on words in the *l. Rubria*[7] (not unreasonably regarded as reflecting Roman practice), which say that a *confessus incerti* was to be treated as *indefensus* unless he gave full security[8]. This is hard measure for one who admits liability but disputes the amount, but is justified as a survival of the rule of the *legis actio* in which *confessio* barred the right to defend in any case. But the sting is taken from it by the rule suggested by the closing words of the same chapter of the *l. Rubria* that, in a case of mere dispute as to amount, the defendant would not be treated as a *confessus* if he was still ready to defend[9]. If this is so, a mere acknowledgement of general liability in the case of an *incertum* has little legal effect. But opinions differ[10].

In an *actio in rem* the principle was the same: *confessio* did not make the party *pro iudicato*. The practical effect was different. It was as if there had been a "*pronuntiatio*[11]." The subsequent proceedings varied according as the *res* was moveable or land. In the former case the Praetor authorised the plaintiff to take it[12]. In the latter he issued an

1 G. 4. 171 *sqq*. On the distinct *iusiurandum voluntarium*, *ante*, § CLXXXII. Much controversy, Bertolini, *Proc. civ.* 1. 261. In the Digest (12. 2) the different cases of oath are inextricably confused owing to changes in the law. 2 Demelius, *Die Confessio*; Giffard, *Confessio in iure*. 3 P. 5. 5a. 2. With consequent liability to *a. iudicati*, 30. 71. 2. Püschel, *Confessus pro iudicato est*, 81 *sqq*.; Kaden, *Z.S.S.* 1925, 540, holds no such action necessary, not quite convincing. 4 *Ante*, p. 612. 5 42. 2. 6. 1. 6 For the practice in the earlier days of the *formula*, Giffard, *Confessio in iure*, 88. 7 Cap. XXII. Girard, *Textes*, 76; Bruns, 1. 99. It deals with Gallia Cisalpina and the name *Rubria* has no real authority. 8 We shall see shortly that in all cases of claim for a *certum*, anyone *indefensus*, in any of the ways in which this might occur, was treated as *iudicatus*, so that in all cases of *confessio*, *certi* or *incerti*, the defendant was treated as *indefensus*, but it was only in the former case that this was equivalent to *iudicatus*. 9 It is not the most obvious interpretation of the opening words of the chapter. 10 Lenel, *E.P.* 410, 413. 11 42. 2. 6. 2; *post*, p. 641. 12 2. 3. 1. 1, "*duci vel ferri iubere*." If claimant not really owner, still "*qui auctore praetore possidet iuste possidet*": he has the Publician and will usucapt. Pissard, *Études Girard*, 1. 255 and reff.

interdict "*quem fundum*" or one of its congeners[1]. Only if this was not obeyed or not properly met, did the defendant become *indefensus*[2].

An *indefensus* was one who did not take the steps necessary to defence; it was still a characteristic of the process that it needed cooperation of the parties. He was one "*qui se non defendit ut oportet*[3]." This might occur in many ways. He might refuse "*accipere iudicium*[4]," or to give security where this was required[5], or to answer interrogations lawfully put[6], or to make the *sponsio* in an *actio per sponsionem*[7]. He might "*latitare*[8]," and so forth[9]. The effect of this in other than real actions[10] was that the Praetor issued a decree of *missio in possessionem*, under which the plaintiff might enter into possession of the defendant's property and ultimately proceed to *bonorum venditio*. The process would be stayed if the defendant did what was required, and the *possessio* would be vacated[11]. But if the action was for a certain sum of money the *indefensus* in all these cases was *pro iudicato*[12].

It is evident that the function of the magistrate was very different from his part in the *legis actio* and details, later to be considered, will shew this still more clearly. He had to decide difficult points and exercise a wide discretion, so that it is not surprising that he habitually acted with a *consilium* of lawyers[13]. It should be noted that there might be agreement as to the material facts, but dispute as to the law. We shall see later that there were many matters which the Praetor did not refer to the *iudex*, but decided himself, a practice which tended to increase. Here it seems that if on the agreed facts the Praetor held that there was no case he could refuse the action, but if he held that there was a claim the admission of the facts would probably amount to a *confessio*, with practical effects, as we have seen, varying in different cases. But we are not fully informed.

CCXVII. *Iudex* and procedure before him[13a]. The *centumviri* and *decemviri* did not appear in the formulary system, but the other tribunals already mentioned recurred[14]. The usual case was reference to *iudex* or *arbiter*. Apart from consent[15] the *iudex* was chosen by a system of names offered by the plaintiff[16], till one was accepted. Any rejection was under

1 *Post*, § CCXLIX. 2 Giffard, *op. cit.* 135. 3 42. 4. 5. 3; G. 3. 78; *lex Rubria*, c. XXI; Lenel, *E.P.* 413. 4 46. 7. 18. 5 2. 3. 1. 1; *post*, § CCXL. 6 11. 1. 9. 4. 7 *L. Rubria*, c. XXI. 8 *Ante*, p. 631. None the less an *indefensus* if having given a *vindex* he fails to appear, 42. 4. 2. pr. 9 Absence without defence, exile, and death without *heres* gave the same right. History of edicts on *latitatio* and *absentia*, Fliniaux, *Études Girard*, 1. 43. 10 Dealt with as above stated. 11 42. 5. 33. 1. 12 *L. Rubria*, c. XXI. Girard, *Man.* 1067. As to proceeding by representative, *post*, p. 708. 13 Bethmann-Hollweg, *C.P.* 2. 136. 13*a* *Post*, p. 718. 14 The *tresviri capitales* may be neglected. 15 By consent of parties a *iudex* might perhaps be chosen not on the *album*. Girard, *Man.* 1071, citing 5. 1. 12. 2, not conclusive. There seems no evidence for choice by lot under the *formula*. 16 Cicero, *pro Rosc. com.* 15. 45.

oath of belief that the *iudex* proposed was not likely to be fair[1]. There is no known limit to the number of rejections, but it is supposed that one obviously refusing without reason was treated as *indefensus*. The *iudex* chosen could not refuse to serve and was sworn[2].

Both *iudex* and *arbiter* were drawn from the *album iudicum*[3]. There was no fundamental distinction; an *arbiter* was a *iudex*. *Arbitri* seem to have acted where there was a greater discretion, notably in *bonae fidei iudicia*[4], but *actiones arbitrariae* were not necessarily tried by *arbiter*. The *album* normally contained, in the Republic, all the qualified members of certain high classes of society, varied on political grounds from time to time[5]. Immediately before Caesar the list consisted of 3 *decuriae* of 300 each of senators, *equites* and *tribuni aerarii* (a large class, less wealthy than the *equites*). Caesar excluded these, but maintained 3 *decuriae*, the third consisting also of *equites*. Augustus added a fourth *decuria* of less wealthy persons for minor cases, and Caligula added a fifth of the same class. As these classes did not now include all the members of the groups[6] a list was issued annually under the control of the Emperor, but a name remained till the age of exemption from service[7], and the *equites* were always predominant among the *iudices*.

Recuperatores now tried also cases in which *cives* alone were concerned[8]. Their exact competence is not known, but it seems that, apart from the provinces and municipalities, their jurisdiction was mainly, though not exclusively, in actions with a certain delictal character[9]. They did not, in some cases, exclude the *unus iudex*[10], and it is not clear whether the choice was with the parties or the magistrate[11]. As we have seen[12], the main advantage of the recuperatory procedure was increased celerity, secured by a short limit of time within which the judgement must be delivered, and other rules[13].

The instructions to the *iudex* were in a *formula*, a complex structure to which we shall recur. It was in the general form "if you find such facts" or "such liability" in the defendant, or "if you find such a right to belong to the plaintiff," "give judgement in his favour; if you do not so find, absolve the defendant." Perhaps the 30 days' delay of the

1 Bethmann-Hollweg, *C.P.* 2. 455. 2 5. 1. 39; 50. 5. 13. 2; Cicero, *de Off.* 3. 10. 44. 3 Originally *arbitri*, being experts, were perhaps not required to be on the *album*. 4 Cicero, *de Off.* 3. 17. 70. 5 Mommsen, *Staatsr.* 3. 528 *sqq.*; *D.P.R.* 6. 2. 132. From the list of qualified persons prepared by the Praetor the quaestors made out a list for the year. 6 See, however, as to senators, *D.P.R.* 6. 2. 489, n. 1, where an opinion in the German text is modified. 7 Mommsen, *Staatsr.* 3. 537; *D.P.R.* 6. 2. 142. 8 G. 4. 46. 141, 185; Ulp. 1. 13a. 9 Girard, *Man.* 1071. 10 Wlassak, *Processg.* 2. 313 *sqq.* 11 *Sortitio*, Wenger, P.-W. *s.v. Reciperatio.* 12 *Ante*, p. 615. De Francisci, *Storia*, 1, 307. 13 Jurisdiction of *tribuni plebis*, in some civil cases, but *extra ordinem*, Wenger, *Zpr.* 52; Jobbé-Duval, *St. Bonfante*, 3. 196.

l. Pinaria did not survive in this system[1], but the practice as to *dies perendinus* and, in general, postponements, where needed, to the next day but one, remained in operation[2].

The parties were present but took no formal part in the proceedings. The case was handled by advocates (*patroni, oratores*[3]). It was usual, though not universal, to begin with speeches of the respective advocates[4], then to take the evidence, and then, after other speeches and discussion with the *iudex*, to pass to the judgement[5]. There were no strict rules of evidence. Hearsay was admissible, though recognised as less weighty than direct testimony. Documents were of course admitted, and even written statements, under oath or not, by persons not produced as witnesses[6]. The defendant could, even before the hearing, call on the plaintiff to produce the documents on which he relied and apparently, with the judge's consent, he could call for the plaintiff's accounts, though the latter was not going to put them in. There was no such right the other way[7]. There were however rules excluding certain witnesses. Neither the parties nor persons closely connected with them could be witnesses[8]. Slaves could not be witnesses, except in a few cases, especially transactions by them where there was no other evidence. Their examination was normally by torture. They could not give evidence against their master, or, from the middle of the second century of the Empire[9], for him. Most of the recorded exclusions belong to *publica iudicia*. There was no general limit on the number of witnesses, but according to the Digest the *iudex* might set one if he thought fit[10], and for some cases of recuperatory procedure it was provided that a limited number of witnesses, usually ten, might be formally summoned, *denuntiati*, and so placed under an obligation of attendance[11]. This does not shew that more could not be heard, and there was no *denuntiatio* and compulsion in ordinary cases; attendance of witnesses was voluntary. As the *iudex* must decide for himself, he was not bound by any piece of evidence. If the defendant confessed liability, the *iudex* need not believe him; such admissions are not always trustworthy[12]. If one party offered another

1 See however, Wenger, *Praetor und Formel*, 73.

2 Aul. Gell. 14. 2. 1.

3 Bertolini, *Processo civ.* 2. 295.

4 The old *causae coniectio* (G. 4. 15) is now of little value and may have disappeared though Sabinus (50. 17. 1) seems to mention it, allusively, as an existing thing.

5 See G. 4. 15, written of *legis actio* system but probably equally applicable here. Bethmann-Hollweg, *C.P.* 2. 586 *sqq.* In Cicero's speeches it is usually clear that the court is already in possession of the evidence.

6 Bethmann-Hollweg, *loc. cit.*

7 D. 2. 13; C. 2. 1; Lenel, *E.P.* 59.

8 22. 5. 6, 9, 10.

9 Buckland, *Slavery*, 86.

10 22. 5. 1. 2, probably interp. In later law, much legislation prescribing a minimum of evidence, e.g. C. 4. 20. 15. 6; C. 4. 20. 9, "*nemo iudicum unius testimonium in quacumque causa facile patiatur admitti,*" but this is said of *cognitiones*.

11 Bethmann-Hollweg, *op. cit.* 2. 598.

12 *Ib.* 595. Demelius (*Die Confessio*, 357 *sqq.*) says, on general principle, that the *iudex* must follow it if it was not withdrawn. But it does not seem that it could be withdrawn, Püschel, *cit.* 83.

an oath *in iudicio*, its taking or refusal probably did not bind the *iudex*, though it might affect his mind[1]. In doubtful cases the *iudex* might offer an oath; the effect of the result was for him to consider[2].

If both parties were absent on the appointed day, nothing happened: there might be a new hearing on a later day. If the plaintiff was away, as the *iudex* must absolve unless the plaintiff proved his case, the burden of proof being on him, the defendant was entitled to *absolutio*. If the defendant was absent, the plaintiff must perhaps still prove his case, as voluntary abstention might have other causes than knowledge that there was no defence, but it is generally held that *condemnatio* went as a matter of course as in *legis actio*[3]. But absence means non-appearance after a long period of waiting. It seems that the *iudex* ought not to give judgement in such a case till 4 o'clock, and then only after sending out a messenger to proclaim the need of attendance, otherwise he ran the risk of having made *litem suam*[4]. All this might be avoided if the absent party sent a messenger to justify his absence and asked for a postponement, or, in case of defendant, if a voluntary *defensor* appeared for him[5]. Apart from this, as there was no appeal, the only relief was by *restitutio in integrum*, given only on certain grounds[6].

Roman Law had no system of precedent[7]; a *iudex* was not bound by previous decisions, even though, as often happened, the same affair had been before another court, between different parties, or, *a fortiori*, where it was a similar case. But previous decisions were not without effect; they seem to have operated much as they do in modern continental courts[8].

The issue was fixed by *litis contestatio* and *formula*, and it was, *prima facie*, the business of the *iudex* to decide on the matter as it stood at *litis contestatio*, disregarding later happenings, a survival from *sacramentum*, in which it was strictly logical. The question whether a *sacramentum* was *iustum* or not could not be affected by later events. But the

1 22. 3. 25. 3, interp. Demelius, *op. cit.* 85 *sqq.* 2 C. 7. 45. 11 (interp.?). Wenger, *Zpr.* 191, and Biondi, *Giuramento*, c. II, hold that the oath offered and taken *in iudicio* was decisive and that the *iudex* had, in classical law, no power to tender an oath. As to presumptions conclusive or rebuttable, drawn from proof of certain facts at different epochs in the law, Cuq, *Man.* 898. 3 Girard, *Man.* 1100, n. 3 and reff.; Kipp, P.-W. s.v. *Eremodicium*; Bertolini, *Pro. civ.* 2. 131; Petot, *Défaut in iudicio*, 28; but the texts are inconclusive. Some sort of hearing there must have been, for the *iudex* had to fix the amount of the *condemnatio*. Cornil, *Dr.R.* 425, thinks him authorised, but apparently not bound, to find for the other. Chief texts: Cicero, *Verr.* 2. 2. 17. 41; Suet. *Calig.* 39; D. 4. 4. 7. 12–8; 5. 1. 73–75; 5. 2. 17. 1; 17. 2. 52. 18; 40. 12. 27. 2; 42. 8. 3. 1; 46. 7. 13. pr.; C. 3. 1. 13. 2. 4 Bethmann-Hollweg, *C.P.* 2. 603, 605. 5 3. 5. 30. 2; 46. 7. 5. 1. Bethmann-Hollweg, *loc. cit.* 6 *Post*, § CCXLIV. Procedure *per contumaciam* belongs to the system of *cognitiones*, *post*, § CCXXVI. 7 C. 7. 45. 13. 8 1. 3. 38. As to how far a *iudex* was bound by the opinion of patented jurists and by *decreta* of the Emperor, *ante*, pp. 19, 25.

rule operated unreasonably where the defendant had satisfied the plaintiff in the meantime. It was not applied in *bonae fidei iudicia*; all agreed that it was within the *officium iudicis* to absolve in such a case; it could not be said that a man ought, *ex fide bona*, to pay twice. All agreed that it did not apply in *actiones arbitrariae*, since the *iudex* was authorised to absolve if the thing was restored at his desire. The Sabinians held that it ought never to apply on such facts, *omnia iudicia absolutoria esse*[1], and this view prevailed; it is uncertain when[2]. Similar questions might arise as to accidental destruction of the thing. In contract and real actions these are considered elsewhere[3].

CCXVIII. *Officium Iudicis*[4]. We have spoken of the *iudex* as bound by the *formula*, but he had, in fact, much discretionary power, most of which was not excluded by the *formula*, but some of which seems at odds with it. Most of his special powers will best be considered in dealing with the different actions[5], but those of the second type must be considered here. In all *bonae fidei iudicia* he might allow certain kinds of set off. It might be said (Gaius says something like it[6]) that this is covered by the words *ex fide bona* in the *intentio*. But that would require him to take it into account, whereas he had absolute discretion[7]. Another illustration is provided by what Pomponius calls "*stipulationes iudiciales*[8]" which do not seem to be provided for in the *formula*, though they might be covered by the *clausula arbitraria*. He mentions "*de dolo*," and the case was, apparently, like that given by Gaius[9]. A defendant might have usucapted *pendente iudicio*, and might then have pledged or mancipated the *res*. Giving it back would not destroy the right of the third party. Accordingly *absolutio* was withheld till the defendant promised that he had not committed and would not commit *dolus*; if this was not made good, the facts would give a new claim[10].

According to the *formula* the *iudex* must condemn or absolve[11]. This does not provide for the case of inability to make up his mind, and in fact it seems to have been usual to have repeated hearings till he could decide[12]. It was however possible, by leave of the magistrate, for the

1 G. 4. 114. 2 Inst. 4. 12. 2. It makes "*si paret*" mean "*si parebit.*" In D. 45. 1. 84 Paul seems to express the Proculian doctrine, but it has been suggested that the claim is not on a promise to build, but on one for a penalty if this is not done by a certain time. 3 *Post*, § CCXXXVI. 4 Inst. 4. 17. 5 Many texts which speak of things done *officio iudicis* refer, not to the *unus iudex* of the *formula* but to the official *iudex* of the *cognitio*, 23. 2. 13; 3. 3. 73, etc. 6 G. 4. 63. 7 *Ib.* Convenience might determine his course. 8 45. 1. 5. pr. Used by Ulpian in another sense, 46. 5. 1. 1. 9 6. 1. 20. pr. 10 Other cases, Inst. 4. 17 *passim*. 11 In view of the effect of *l. cont.* it might be thought that not to condemn was to absolve, but the case would be still pending; there would be no *exc. r. iud.* Apart from the practical advantage of being able to point to a judgement, there may have been cases in early law in which *exc. rei in i. ded.* was not available (Eisele, *Beitr.* 15). 12 Aul. Gell. 14. 2. 11.

iudex to be released on his swearing "*rem non liquere*," in which case a new *iudex* was appointed[1], a case of *translatio iudicii*[2].

The *iudex*, who might have advisers[3] (*adsessores*), must give judgement openly, and orally, in the presence of the parties, at a time and place at which his court lawfully and usually sat[4]. There was no conditional judgement[5]; it must be *condemnatio* or *absolutio*[6]. The place of conditions on the judgement was taken, as we have seen, by requiring undertakings before it was given. The *condemnatio* was not a mere statement that the plaintiff was entitled; it must state how much was due[7], as there was no *arbitrium litis aestimandae*. The task might be hard, as the mode of calculation of damages, the date as at which they were to be assessed, and the relevant factors varied greatly. One case was specially provided for by edict. A promise for performance at one place might be sued on at another, where the defendant was. As payment here might be more costly to the promisor there was risk of *plus petitio*. It might indeed be worth less to the promisee. The Edict gave an action "*de eo quod certo loco*," in which the *iudex* was authorised to take these matters into account[8].

Having arrived at the amount due, the *iudex* ordered payment of that sum, allowing, if he liked, a certain time for payment[9]: apparently a judgement merely written or not properly delivered, or not stating the amount due, was a mere nullity[10].

Of several judges, e.g. *recuperatores*, all must be present: the majority decided[11]. If one had been allowed to swear, *rem non liquere*, he must be there[12]. If there was not an absolute majority either way, there must be *absolutio*, but Pius decided (or declared) that in *causae liberales* the decision in such a case must be for liberty, whichever way the action was framed[13]. If a majority was for *condemnatio*, but disagreed as to amount, the smallest was taken, says Julian; all were agreed to this extent[14].

The *iudex* must abide by the *formula*, but a decision not authorised by it was not a nullity. Gaius tells us that a *condemnatio* for more than the *certum* claimed, or one which went beyond a *taxatio* in the *condemnatio* was valid, though the *iudex* was liable for any loss caused, as one who "*litem suam fecit*[15]." A judgement once given could not be corrected; *semel enim male seu bene officio functus est*[16].

1 Aul. Gell. 14. 2. 25. 2 *Post*, § CCXLI. 3 2. 2. 2; Cicero, *Top.* 17. 65. Bethmann-Hollweg, *C.P.* 2. 621 *sqq.* 4 42. 1. 1, 5. 1, 47, 59; C. 7. 43. 4–8. 5 49. 4. 1. 5. 6 *Sententia*, in cl. texts, never means judgement: it is the opinion of the *iudex* on which he bases his judgement, Biondi, *St. Bonfante*, 4. 37. 7 G. 4. 48, 52. 8 *Post*, §§ CCXXIV, CCXXXVII. Evolution as to what might come into account, Dumas, *N.R.H.* 1910, 610. 9 42. 1. 4. 5. 10 C. 7. 43 *passim*; C. 7. 44. 1; D. 42. 1. 59. 11 42. 1. 39. 12 42. 1. 36, 37. 13 42. 1. 38. pr. Anticipated by *l. Petronia*, 40. 1. 24. 14 4. 8. 27. 3; 42. 1. 38. 1. 15 G. 4. 49–52. 16 42. 1. 55.

The duty of the *iudex* was not always merely to condemn or absolve. Of possible variations, to be considered later, the chief may be enumerated here. In some actions preliminary to other proceedings there was no *condemnatio*, but a question was submitted to the *iudex*, e.g. "*an Titius civis sit*" (*actiones praeiudiciales*). Here his judgement was a *pronuntiatio*, that *T*. was or was not a *civis*[1]. In real actions and some others the *iudex*, if he found for the plaintiff, might, before *condemnatio*, make a *pronuntiatio* to that effect, and, if he thought fit, order restoration of the *res*, and, only if this was disobeyed, issue a *condemnatio*—*actiones arbitrariae*[2]. In actions for division of property or adjustment of boundaries he had a power of *adiudicatio*, i.e. of issuing a decree vesting such divided shares as he thought fair among the parties, his act constituting a transfer of the ownership[3]. In noxal actions the defendant might be ordered either to pay the penalty or to surrender the wrongdoer, the result being somewhat like that in *actiones arbitrariae*, but essentially different: it was a *facultas solvendi* at the discretion of the defendant[4].

There was no appeal, and *absolutio* ended the matter, apart from *restitutio in integrum*[5] and *calumnia*. If he had not offered *iusiurandum calumniae* under rules already stated[6], the defendant, after *absolutio*, might bring a *iudicium calumniae*, in which, if he shewed that the proceedings were in bad faith, he recovered one-tenth of the claim, or, if it was a claim of liberty from slavery, one-third of the value of the man from the *assertor*[7]. Apart from bad faith, there was a *iudicium contrarium* for one-tenth in *iniuria*, and one-fifth in a small group of other cases[8]. There was an *actio in factum* (also called *calumniae*) against one who for reward brought an action in bad faith, for fourfold within a year, and in *simplum* after the year[9]. These *iudicia contraria* create the possibility that the plaintiff might be condemned. As the condemnation went as a matter of course if the action was lost, the two issues might be embodied in one *formula*, the part referring to the claim for *calumnia* being an appendix to the rest[10]. It has been contended that the *intentio* embodied the two issues as in the divisory actions[11], but the name *iudicium contrarium* does not suggest this. The same method may have been applied in other cases[12]. The defendant could stay further proceedings by satis

1 *Post*, p. 651. 2 *Post*, § CCXXIV. Herdlitcska, *Zur Lehre vom Zwischenurteil*, contends for a much wider field for *pronuntiatio*. 3 *Ante*, p. 252; *post*, § CCXXIV. 4 As to its character, *ante*, p. 601; *post*, § CCXXIV. 5 *Post*, § CCXLIII. 6 *Ante*, p. 633; G. 4. 174 *sqq*. 7 G. 4. 175. 8 G. 4. 177, 178. Abolished under Justinian: the *iusiurandum calumniae* was now exacted in all cases and by the court. C. 2. 58. 2. pr. Form, Lenel, *E.P.* 403. 9 Or, conversely, failed, corruptly, to take such steps, 3. 6. 1 (not *bona fide* compromises). See Lenel, *E.P.* 106. 10 See, e.g., Lenel, *E.P.* 314. 11 Partsch, *Neg. Gestio*, 55 *sqq*. *Post*, § CCXXXIV. 12 E.g. *ante*, p. 154.

fying the creditor. The obligation was now for a sum of money, and this might be discharged like any other. If it was not, further proceedings were in execution.

CCXIX. EXECUTION OF JUDGEMENT. Under the *formula*, as in the *legis actio*, it was for the plaintiff to take steps for the enforcement of his right. It was not now by *manus iniectio*, but by *actio iudicati*, a new method which was a praetorian copy of the older one[1], of which it retained the substantial characteristics, with different formalities. The defendant was brought before the magistrate after at least 30 days[2], as before, and an *actio iudicati* was demanded. The *formula* is not known, but it is clear that under *iudicia legitima*[3], immediately connected with the old system, it expressed a civil obligation, while in the others, *iudicia imperio continentia*, it was a praetorian *formula* of some kind, persons condemned in such actions not being *iudicati* in the sense of the old law[4]. If the validity of the judgement was disputed so that the matter went to a hearing, personal surety must be found, who gave *satisdatio*[5], thus resembling the *vindex*, and the liability would be, in general, for double damages[6] as under *manus iniectio*. No text expressly states the need of *actio iudicati*, but though it was formerly thought that it was wanted only where the judgement was disputed[7], its necessity in all cases is inferred from many texts[8], and none indicates that execution was possible without it. It has been suggested that the requirement was to guard against execution where there had been no judgement, the creditor, in case of dispute, having to prove the judgement, the defendant having to prove, if he could, that it was in some way defective. There are indications of a right in the defendant (not the plaintiff) to challenge the judgement without waiting for the plaintiff to proceed, *revocatio in duplum*[9]. There was no question of disputing the soundness of the decision; it was not appeal. The only grounds were objections to the formal validity of the judgement[10]. And as allowing this proceeding to go to a *iudicium* involved double liability in case of failure[11], it would not normally go so far; the defendant admitted liability and execution proceeded.

1 Girard, *Man.* 1108. Praetorian in construction (P. 1. 2. 4, "*datur*") it is really civil, G. 3. 180 (*oportere*); Wlassak, *Processg.* 1. 98.

2 G. 3. 78, *partim lege XII Tabularum, partim edicto praetoris*, i.e. for *iudicia imperio continentia*. *Iudex* can extend, but not shorten the time, 42. 1. 4. 5. This and many other rules shew that the procedure throughout aimed at getting the parties to come to terms; Düll, *Der Gütegedanke im R. Zivilpr.* 26, 124.

3 *Post*, § CCXXXII.

4 Lenel, *E.P.* 443 *sqq.*

5 G. 4. 102.

6 G. 4. 9.

7 Bethmann-Hollweg, *C.P.* 2. 635.

8 E.g. 20. 1. 13. 4; 42. 1. 6. 1; 44. 4. 9, etc.

9 Cicero, *pro Flac.* 21. 49. Other texts Lenel, *E.P.* 445. Obscurities, Biondi, *St. Bonfante*, 4. 93.

10 49. 8. 1. pr.

11 He could not avoid the risk by paying under the judgement and then bringing *c. indebiti*, 17. 1. 29. 5. Problematical ways in which judgement could be attacked without risk, Wenger, *A. Iudicati*, 43; *Zpr.* 220.

The abolition of *manus iniectio* was abolition of formalities; it did not greatly alter the right of the judgement creditor. Personal seizure remained; the creditor, authorised by the magistrate (*duci iubere*[1]), carried off the debtor and kept him in confinement, being bound to supply him with necessaries[2], and, probably, to let him work off the debt[3]. Literary texts speak of the debtor as *addictus*[4], but Gaius does not here use the word[5], and the right of destroying or selling into slavery which resulted from *addictio* in the *legis actio* no longer existed. The confinement put pressure on the debtor: perhaps it was mainly used for solvent debtors. It continued through the classical age, and later[6].

As, in the old system, the debtor's property did not pass to the holder during the detention, whatever happened at its end[7], so, too, the *ductio* gave no right to the property. Accordingly, the Praetor[8] introduced *bonorum venditio*, modelled on the mode by which the State recovered from its debtors[9]. Seizure of the man did not bar procedure under this Edict[10]. The proceedings were as follows. The Praetor, on the application of the creditor, issued a decree of *missio in possessionem*[11], under which the creditor might take possession for custody of the property and advertise the seizure (*proscribere*[12]). After 30 days the Praetor authorised him to summon a meeting of creditors, who appointed a *magister bonorum* to conduct the sale[13], at which point the debtor became *infamis*[14]. Interim care was provided for either by the creditors or some of them or a *curator bonorum*[15] appointed by them, any who administered being responsible to the others for *dolus* and entitled to refund of proper expenses from the fund[16]. The *magister* published the conditions, including an inventory of

1 P. 5. 26. 2. On the theoretical difficulty of connecting up judgement in *a. iudicati* with seizure and *m. i. p.*, i.e. what replaces the formal acts of early law, Wenger, *Praetor und Formel*, § 4. 2 Cuq, *Man.* 902. 3 Bethmann-Hollweg, *C.P.* 2. 665. Kleinadam, *Festschr. f. Dahn*, 2. 1. 4 Reff., Bethmann-Hollweg, *C.P.* 2. 662, nn. 4, 5. 5 G. 3. 199. 6 Lenel, *E.P.* 411. Woess, *Z.S.S.* 1922, 487. Personal seizure may however have been confined in cl. law to *iudicia legitima*: there is something exorbitant in giving this ancient civil remedy in *iudicia honoraria*. But, if so, this must have been later disregarded. 7 *Ante*, p. 619. 8 Gaius (4. 35) attributes it to Publius Rutilius, probably P. Rutilius Rufus, Praetor before 100 B.C.; Girard, *Man.* 1111. Our knowledge of the system is imperfect, largely derived from texts altered to express the later system of *distractio bonorum*. Degenkolb, *Magister und Curator*, holds that the general administration was with the *curator*, the *magister* having only such powers of administration as the individual *missi* (whose delegate he was) possessed, e.g. the right to sell specific things in case of necessity (42. 5. 8. 1) and no right of action except to enforce fulfilment of undertakings given by the *bonorum emptor*, other than the actual promise of a dividend, *ante*, p. 403. 9 Mommsen, *Staatsr.* 1. 178; *D.P.R.* 1. 203. 10 *Arg. l. Rubria*, c. XXII *inf.*; Girard, *Textes*, 77; Bruns, 1. 100. Wenger, *Zpr.* 223, thinks it was usual to employ both. Perozzi, *Ist.* 2. 76, makes the creditor elect. 11 See Cicero, *pro Quinct.* 8. 30. 12 G. 3. 79; D. 42. 4. 7. 1; i.e. put notices in prominent places. 13 G. 3. 79; details of powers of *missi*, Solazzi, *St. Scialoja*, 1. 663. 14 G. 4. 102; *l. Iul. Munic.* 117. 15 Interim administration, *post*, § CCXLV. 16 42. 5. 8, 9.

the goods and a list of debts[1]. After another delay he sold the goods, normally *en bloc*, to the highest bidder[2]. The bids were not of money, but of a dividend on the debts[3], and there were rules determining which was to be preferred of those offering the same dividend[4]. Secured creditors retained their rights, and privileged debts, of which there were many kinds, were paid first, in full, so far as the assets would go[5]. The necessary information on these points was no doubt part of the conditions announced by the *magister*. We do not know how debts due *ex die* or *sub condicione* were treated (probably they became due when they would, apart from the *venditio*[6]), or as to the proof necessary to allow a claim to rank in the schedule of debts; it certainly was not confined to judgement debts[7]. The position of creditors who have abstained from claiming in the *venditio* is obscure; they can hardly have had a claim against the *bonorum emptor* or the *magister*[8]. The purpose of the delays and notices was to give everyone a chance to come in, but there may well have been persons who never heard of the matter. No doubt they retained full rights against future acquisitions[9], as those who had claimed did in respect of the unsatisfied part of the debt[10].

As we have seen, this proceeding in execution was available not only against a *iudicatus*, but against *confessus* and *indefensus* to an extent already stated[11]. But the method had a wider field. It also occurred in cases which have nothing to do with litigation. It was at first not primarily for enforcement of judgement, but a means of pressure in a variety of conditions. It was in effect the Roman equivalent of bankruptcy proceedings. It lay against a debtor who hid or absconded, fraudulently (*fraudationis causa latitans*), unless he was prepared to defend an action, which stayed the proceedings[12]. It lay against a dead man's estate if there was no *heres*, and here the delays were cut down by

1 Cicero, *pro Quinc.* 15. 50. 2 G. 3. 79, supplemented by Theophilus, *ad* Inst. 3. 12. pr., not quite consistent. Hence different views as to details. Kniep, *Mél. Girard*, 1. 623, makes the "*proscribi*" come at the end of 30 days' possession, and amends the end of the text, in which the delays are imperfectly stated. 3 G. 2. 155, "*pro portione.*" 4 A large creditor to a smaller, a creditor to a relative, a relative to an outsider, 42. 5. 16. 5 42. 5. 24. 2; list of these priorities, Lenel, *E.P.* 429. Rotondi, *Scr. giur.* 3. 1, explains these preferences on the ground that there was no bidding above 20*s.* in the pound and the *emptor* kept any excess. 6 Paul says in one text that conditional creditors can get *m. i. p.*, in another that they cannot, but only those can who can sell (42. 4. 6. pr., 14. 2). Perhaps they could come in and claim but not initiate proceedings; perhaps the right is interp. Various opinions Ramadier, *Missio in possessionem*, 45 *sqq.* He suggests that conditional creditors could claim only where, as in case of *pupillus*, there would be long possession. 7 Regulated by Justinian, C. 7. 72. 10. 8 Cuq, *Man.* 904, suggests on 17. 1. 22. 10 and 42. 7. 5 that they had an *actio in factum* against one who had received a dividend, for a *pro rata* refund. But these texts are not concerned with *bonorum venditio*, *post*, § CCXXVII. 9 C. 7. 72. 10. 1 a. There has been no *capitis minutio*. 10 Rights of action under *venditio*, *ante*, § CXLII. 11 *Ante*, § CCXVI. 12 42. 4. 7. 1.

half, because, as Gaius says, "*de vivis curandum erat ne facile bonorum venditiones paterentur*[1]." It lay against one who had made voluntary surrender of his estate to his creditors (*cessio bonorum*). This was provided for by a *l. Iulia* at the beginning of the Empire and gave the debtor some advantages. He was not thereafter liable to personal seizure for what was unpaid of the debts, as an ordinary bankrupt was[2]. He was not liable for them at any time beyond his means[3], a protection given to other bankrupts only for a year[4], and he did not become *infamis*[5]. Conversely, where a debtor was a *pupillus* or was absent "*rei publicae causa, sine dolo malo,*" although there might be seizure, the Praetor would not authorise *venditio*[6].

Under a *sc.* of unknown date it was provided that in the case of *clarae personae* the creditors might choose whether they would proceed by *b. venditio*, of the whole estate, or have a *curator* appointed after the *m. in possessionem* to sell in detail so much of the goods as would satisfy the claim, *bonorum distractio*[7]. This avoided *infamia* and, limited as it was to persons of some distinction, was probably introduced for this reason rather than on economic grounds. The creditors, having chosen one course, could not fall back on the other[8]. This *curator bonorum* is distinct from the edictal *curator* appointed in some cases where there was a *missio*, not to be followed by immediate sale, whose business it was to administer in the meanwhile[9], as in the case of debtor *pupillus* or *absens reipublicae causa*, or apart from insolvency, e.g. where a *heres* was instituted conditionally, and other cases[10].

CCXX. The foregoing account assumes that proceedings under the judgement were against the debtor, but this was not always so. Often[11] the defendant had to give security, by way of surety (*iudicatum solvi* or *pro praede litis et vindiciarum*), and in such a case the plaintiff might, if he preferred, bring action against the sureties.

The appeal found early in the Empire does not seem to have applied

1 G. 3. 79. 2 G. 3. 78; C. 7. 71. 1. The advantages are such that the question arises why all insolvents did not do it. That it was allowed only in insolvency from misfortune is faintly suggested by Seneca, *de benef*. 7. 16. 3. Woess, *Z.S.S.* 1922, 505, who offers other reasons, cites also C. Th. 4. 20 rub. and 1. As to the possibility that Gratian altered the law by allowing it only where insolvency was accidental, not due to negligence, Levet, *Bénéfice de Compétence*, 191. Reasons for not taking this course, Bethmann-Hollweg, *C.P.* 2. 689. It is possible that there must have been an action. See 42. 3 and C. 7. 71 *passim*. 3 Inst. 4. 6. 40. 4 C. 7. 75. 6. And, for that time, protected against seizure, Woess, *cit.* 526. 5 C. 2. 11. 11. *Cessio* could be revoked before sale, D. 42. 3. 5. 6 42. 4. 3, 6; According to Wenger, *Zpr.* 229, a *curator* was appointed, who sold enough. 7 27. 10. 5. Other cases of *distractio bonorum*, Wenger, *Zpr.* 230. 8 27. 10. 9. It seems (Ramadier, *op. cit.* 144 *sqq.*) that this implies an extension to other cases, since the purpose of the original introduction would not have been served if the choice had been left to the creditors. Degenkolb, *Magister und Curator*, 16. 9 Lenel, *E.P.* 434. 10 42. 7 *passim*. 11 *Post*, § CCXL.

to the *formula*[1], but proceedings might be stopped in some ways which need mention. There might be *restitutio in integrum* on certain recognised grounds[2], varying in form, but in general undoing so far as possible the impeached transaction. But mistaken or even dishonest judgement was not a ground; the remedy, if any, was against the *iudex, qui litem suam fecit*[3]. If the judgement was obtained by fraud of the other party, there was no need of *actio doli* against him, as there was *restitutio*[4]. If a man became a *confessus certae pecuniae* under threats of violence, there was an *actio metus*[5] and there might be *restitutio*, but all this gave no relief against mere error. *Denegatio actionis iudicati*[6] was a form of *restitutio in integrum*; it was not a mode of appeal on error, but only shewed that there were circumstances in the case which made it unfair to treat the judgement as conclusive. There might also be *intercessio*. Though the act of a *iudex* could not be vetoed, any colleague of the Praetor could veto a decree of his, in furtherance of execution[7], but there is little trace of this and no sign that it was used to give relief in error.

The procedure above described was at Rome, and initiated before the Praetor. Something must be said on other jurisdictions[8]. In Rome there were, besides the Praetors, the curule aediles[9] with similar powers in matters within their competence. But though in the Empire much civil jurisdiction passed to other officials, the various *praefecti*, etc., it does not seem that the methods of the *formula*, the *ordo iudiciorum*, had any application in these cases.

In the provinces the *praeses* was the magistrate, the aedilician part being in his hands in imperial provinces, but in those of quaestors in the others[10]. The *praeses* held periodical assizes in the principal towns of his province (*conventus*)[11]. The law was essentially as at Rome, for *cives*, but there are indications that it was influenced by local usages and that the details of form in litigation were not quite the same as at Rome, or identical in all provinces[12].

In Italy, till the Social War, there were many regions, some Latin, some merely peregrine, which were governed from Rome, but under their own laws. Any litigation of *cives* resident in them would have to take place at Rome, with limitations not well known[13]. After the Social War, with its great extension of *civitas*, it remains true that the Roman

1 Wenger, *Zpr.* 201. 2 *Post*, § CCXLIII. 3 *Ante*, p. 598. 4 4. 3. 25. 5 On general principle. Cicero records a case where *recuperatores* had been coerced and others of less weight as precedents. Girard, *Man.* 1115, n. 4. 6 E.g. 9. 4. 14; 42. 1. 4. pr. 7 Mommsen, *Staatsr.* 1. 266; *D.P.R.* 1. 300. 8 Wenger, *Zpr.* 4; Bethmann-Hollweg, *C.P.* §§ 72 *sqq.*; de Francisci, *Storia*, 2. 1. 297. For the system up to Cicero's time, Greenidge, *Legal Procedure*, 18 *sqq.*; Girard, *Org. Judic.* 1. 272. In general, *actor sequitur rei forum*, Vat. Fr. 326. 9 G. 1. 6. 10 G. 1. 6. 11 Greenidge, *op. cit.* 129. 12 Greenidge, *op. cit.* 124. 13 Girard, *Org. Judic.* 1. 272.

courts were in principle the fit tribunals for litigation between Romans, wherever domiciled, but of this principle there were important derogations. In many towns there survived for a time the practice, belonging to the earlier state of things, of sending *praefecti iure dicundo* who held periodical assizes, exercising the jurisdiction of a Roman magistrate, in civil matters, but possibly with a limitation on amount. The generalisation of municipal institutions superseded these, and for classical law the system was that municipal magistrates had jurisdiction in matters below a certain amount[1], not necessarily the same in all places, but with power in more important cases to require *vadimonium* from a defendant for appearance at Rome[2]. They might not try certain types of action, the exclusions no doubt not being always the same[3]. And they had *iurisdictio* only, not *imperium*. Thus they usually had not the *legis actio*, as expressed in the fictitious litigation of manumission, etc., which, however, is not really *iurisdictio*[4], and they could not proceed to the steps by which the Praetor, under his *imperium*, facilitated execution and compelled the taking of the proper steps in litigation. They could not order *bonorum venditio* under judgement[5], though they could order personal seizure. Interdicts, *missio in possessionem*, *restitutio in integrum* were, in general, beyond their powers[6] and had to be referred to Rome, though there were exceptionally privileged places[7].

CCXXI. THE STRUCTURE OF THE *FORMULA*. The *formula* usually contained many parts. Its general construction is well known, but there are important details of which we are not informed[8], and there is much controversy. The various parts must be considered separately: they did not all occur in any one *formula*.

Nominatio iudicis. This necessary preliminary part always occurred. It ran "*T. iudex esto*," and even if the single judge was an *arbiter* he was called *iudex* at this point[9]. But *recuperatores* were called such here[10], and the same rule was perhaps applied where there were three *arbitri*[11], if any of these survived into the formulary system[12].

Praescriptio. This too was a preliminary part, as its name indicates. Gaius tells us that there had been two types[13]:

Praescriptio pro actore, i.e. to safeguard the plaintiff. If there was a stipulation for a number of payments and one or more, but not all, were

1 *L. Rubria*, cc. XXI, XXII; *Fr. Atestinum* (Girard, *Textes*, 79); P. 5. 5a. 1. 2 *L. Rubria, ib.* 3 Mommsen, *Staatsr.* 3. 815; *D.P.R.* 6. 2. 466. 4 P. 2. 25. 4. 5 50. 1. 26. 1. 6 *Ib.*; 2. 1. 4; G. 4. 139. Exceptions Jobbé-Duval, *St. Bonfante*, 3. 192. 7 The appointment of *Iuridici* for regions of Italy under Marcus Aurelius (Vat. Fr. 205; *Vita M. Ant. Phil.* 11. 6), following Hadrian, cuts down to some extent the jurisdiction of Roman magistrates. Functions, Wenger, *Zpr.* 53. Pius had abolished Hadrian's system, Mommsen, *Staatsr.* 2. 1084; *D.P.R.* 5. 391. 8 Lenel, *E.P.* x. 9 G. 4. 36; Bethmann-Hollweg, *C.P.* 2. 105. 10 G. 4. 46. 11 *Ante*, p. 614. 12 Wlassak, *Processg.* 2. 293; as to the person of "*esto*," Lenel, *E.P.* 113. 13 G. 4. 133

due, an action on the promise would bring the whole *obligatio* into issue, and the whole right of action would be consumed by *litis contestatio*[1]. To prevent this the scope of the action might be limited by inserting the words: "*Ea res agatur cuius rei dies fuit*[2]." Again, on a contract for sale of land, if action was brought for formal conveyance, to prevent this from barring further action for other liabilities under the contract, the plaintiff might insert the words: "*Ea res agatur de fundo mancipando*[3]." These allow of later action on the same transaction, but Gaius gives other instances, of a different type. Where a contract was made by a *filiusfamilias* or slave the right vested in the *paterfamilias*; there was a *praescriptio* stating that it was a contract made by the subordinate, perhaps only in cases of *condictio certae pecuniae*[4]. In action on a *stipulatio* for an *incertum*, Gaius tells us there was a *praescriptio loco demonstrationis*, but what he gives is merely a *demonstratio*[5]. But if an action on such a *stipulatio* was brought against a surety, there was a true *praescriptio*[6]. There is, however, much controversy about these *praescriptiones*[7].

Praescriptio pro reo[8], inserted on behalf of the defendant. It belongs to the early days of the *formula*[9]; in the time of Gaius the defences originally raised in this way were raised by *exceptio*, by which it seems to have been replaced in some cases as early as Cicero[10]. In the time of Gaius it was obsolete. The principal recorded cases are:

1. *Praescriptio praeiudicii*[11]. Some actions might not be brought if the decision would prejudice that of a more important issue. There appear to be three cases in which a *praescriptio*, or, later, *exceptio praeiudicii* was admitted[12]: (i) *Exceptio quod praeiudicium hereditati non fiat*, which bars any action for what could be recovered by *hereditatis petitio*[13]; (ii) *Exceptio extra quam si in reum capitis praeiudicium fiat*[14], not mentioned in legal texts[15]; (iii) *Exceptio quod praeiudicium fundo partive eius non fiat*, barring action for a right, based on ownership disputed between the parties, till the *vindicatio* had been brought[16].

1 *Post*, § CCXXXV. 2 G. 4. 131; Cicero, *de fin*. 2. 1. 3. 3 G. 4. 131 a. 4 G. 4. 134, 135. The imperfect text speaks of *intentio* in "*dare oportere*," which points to this limitation. 5 G. 4. 136. 6 G. 4. 137. 7 Partsch, reviewing Schlossmann, *Z.S.S.* 1907, 440 *sqq*. They resemble *demonstrationes*. 8 Pissard, *Questions Préjudicielles*. 9 G. 4. 133. 10 He speaks freely of *exceptiones*, e.g. *de Inv*. 2. 19. 57. It may be that the older *exceptiones* were originally *praescriptiones*. 11 Pissard, *cit*. ch. III. 12 But this does not exclude *denegatio actionis* in a wider field. 13 G. 4. 133. Many opinions as to the reason of this rule, see Pissard, *loc. cit*. 14 Cicero, *de Inv*. 2. 20. 59. 15 These shew a wider rule, that a civil suit must not be brought so as to prejudice a criminal trial (*post*, § CCXLII), probably enforced by *denegatio actionis*. 16 44. 1. 16, 18. There is a general rule that a *maior causa* must not be prejudiced by a *minor*, enforced by *denegatio actionis*. Pissard gives the recorded cases (pp. 148 *sqq*.). There is no certainty as to what is and what is not a *maior causa*, and P. holds that in later law the distinction is replaced by the principle that the "procès conditionnant" must be tried before the "procès conditionné" (p. 232), which is probably what is meant by *maior causa*.

2. *Praescriptio longi temporis* (which hands on the name to *praescriptio longissimi temporis*, which has nothing to do with the formulary system). In view of the late date of this institution (it cannot be traced earlier than the end of the second century)[1], it is probable that it never was a *praescriptio* in the formulary sense; the name is elsewhere applied to cases of *exceptio* which never were *praescriptiones*[2].

The *praescripta verba* at the beginning of some actions are not called *praescriptiones*, and it is not clear whether they were properly *praescriptiones* or *demonstrationes*. Since their earliest application was to cases of civil obligation, with uncertainty under what head they should come[3], they seem to have the character of *demonstrationes*.

Praescriptiones pro reo give rise to an important and difficult question. In their later form, as *exceptiones*, they had the effect that proof of the *exceptio* involved loss of the action, and this, by *consumptio litis*, commonly involved destruction of the claim. The question is whether this was equally true of the *praescriptio*, or whether the effect of proof of the *praescriptio* was to withdraw the issue, the *litis contestatio* being conditional on the failure of the point raised in the *praescriptio*. Both views are maintained by writers of authority[4].

Demonstratio. This is one of the four parts which Gaius speaks of as the "*partes formularum*" (*demonstratio, intentio, adiudicatio, condemnatio*[5]). This does not mean that they must occur, for though this may be true of *intentio*[6], it is certainly not so of the rest. The meaning seems to be that the *formulae* in which these parts were used would be meaningless without them, while the omission of an *exceptio* or *taxatio*, etc., would not vitiate the *formula*, but only alter its effect. This appears to be true even of *demonstratio*, for a *formula* which said that the *iudex* was to condemn to "whatever on this account (*ob eam rem*) proves to be due" had no force without a *demonstratio* to shew what the matter in question was. The *demonstratio* was not a statement of the issue, but of the nature of the matter in issue, a short statement of the transaction

1 Partsch, *Longi temporis praescriptio*, 109 *sqq*. 2 Bethmann-Hollweg, 2. 404; Pissard, *cit*. 122. 3 *Ante*, § CLXXXI. 4 Wenger, *Zpr*. 144; Wlassak, *Z.S.S.* 1912, 80 *sqq*.; Partsch, *Longi temporis praescriptio*, 70; Pissard, *cit*. 112 *sqq*. The chief arguments for the view are the form "*ea res agatur*," which expresses a limit on the submission, and is the same as in *pr. pro actore*, which had this limiting effect, a probable assumption that *pr. pro reo* descends from *denegatio actionis*, which excluded *l. cont*., and its close affinity with the *demonstratio* which operated in the suggested way (G. 4. 58). But it is pointed out that Gaius speaks of the change to *exceptio* as formal and does not hint at so great a change in effect, that not all *prs. pro actore* aim at limiting the submission, that "*ea res agatur*" need be no more than words introducing the question, without technical significance, and that *pr. pro reo* does not probably descend from *den. actionis*, but from *praeiudicia* separately submitted. It is not certain that all were treated alike. 5 G. 4. 39. 6 See, however, *post*, p. 652.

on which the claim rested, as a guide to the *iudex*. It need not state the wrong, but rather the facts which constitute the legal relation in connexion with which the wrong is alleged. This was simpler than embodying it all in the *intentio*, but not logically necessary. It was not necessarily a statement of admitted facts[1], though it often might be, but the fact that sale was alleged in a *demonstratio* did not dispense with the necessity of proving it, if disputed. It was not a critical part. Errors in it could be adjusted—*falsa demonstratione rem non perimi. Plus petitio* or *minus petitio* in it could be set right, in the sense that a new action could be brought, the *litis contestatio* not having been operative[2] (subject perhaps to limits which will be considered later[3]). Thus if the matter was wholly wrongly described in the *demonstratio* there was no valid *iudicium*; the *intentio* referred explicitly to the case in the *demonstratio*, and the real question had not been put in issue.

The *demonstratio* was used only in some personal actions, not in actions *in rem*, or in actions *in factum* (with some exceptions[4]), because here the *intentio* stated the material points. But on the question what actions *in personam*, i.e. on *obligatio*, needed it, there is difficulty. There is no sign of it in *condictio certae pecuniae*[5], though here the fact that the *intentio* did not state the *causa* seems to render some guide necessary, unless *iudex* is to have a roving commission to enquire into any transactions of that type which might have occurred between the parties[6]. It occurred in *actio ex stipulatu*, i.e. on a *stipulatio* for an *incertum*[7], but probably not in *actio ex testamento* on a legacy *per damnationem*, where the *intentio* stated the *causa*[8]. It occurred in divisory actions[9], and, apparently, in all *bonae fidei iudicia*[10]. It probably occurred in *condictio incerti* of which we know little[11]. There was no *demonstratio* in the *actio furti manifesti*, an *actio in factum*[12], nor was there, according to Gaius, in *furti nec manifesti*, if his *formula* is correct[13]. It may have occurred in some of the *formulae* under the *l. Aquilia*, and it appears to have occurred in the *actio iniuriarum*, though this was *in factum*, of a special type[14].

A *demonstratio* contained, after the statement of facts, the words

1 Criticism of a hypothesis of its origin in such a statement, Koschaker, reviewing Arangio Ruiz, *Z.S.S.* 1913, 433. 2 G. 4. 58. 3 *Post*, § CCXXXVI. 4 *Post*, p. 652; and § CCXXXI. 5 Lenel, *E.P.* 237. 6 Suggested by Cicero, *pro Rosc. com.* 4–6, 13–16. 7 G. 4. 136. 8 Lenel, *E.P.* 367. 9 Lenel, *E.P.* 207; Audibert, *Mél. Appleton*, 11 *sqq.* 10 G. 4. 47. 11 Lenel, *E.P.* 156. 12 Lenel, *E.P.* 332. 13 G. 4. 37. Lenel shews reason for doubting if it is complete. Somewhere the value seems to have been stated (50. 16. 192; cp. 12. 3. 9). See too Ulpian in 47. 2. 19. pr., "*demonstrari*." A *scholium* in the Basilica (*Bas.* XXII. VI. 9, *Sch.* 2; Heimbach, 2. 583) seems to put this in the *intentio*. It might be either there or in *taxatio* or *demonstratio*. Lenel rejects *intentio* and *taxatio*, on grounds that do not look very strong and holds that it is a *demonstratio*. 14 G. 4. 60; Coll. 2. 6. 4. *Post*, p. 652; and § CCXXXI.

"*qua de re agitur*" or the like, the logical basis of the rule that error in the *demonstratio* excluded the real issue from the *iudicium*[1].

CCXXII. *Intentio*[2]. The most important part of the *formula*. It defined the issue submitted to the *iudex*, and by it the claim stood or fell. Error in it might be fatal, for there was no power of amendment, except by *restitutio* in certain circumstances[3], and, the action being lost, the right was destroyed by *litis contestatio*[4]. It was accordingly drawn with great precision. A properly drawn *intentio* shewed whether the action was *in rem* or *in personam*, *in ius* or *in factum*, for *certum* or *incertum*, a *iudicium strictum* or *bonae fidei*, each type having its characteristic words. In the ordinary *formula* ending with a *condemnatio*, the *intentio* raised a hypothesis which was, in essence: "if you find such and such points proved." In an *actio praeiudicialis* it was in an entirely different form: it was a question submitted to the *iudex*, of which "*an Titius libertus Auli sit*" may be taken as the type[5], the answer of the *iudex* being a *pronuntiatio*. As its name shews it was commonly a preliminary to another proceeding. In actions *in rem* for ownership, the *intentio* ran[6]: "*si paret fundum Cornelianum quo de agitur, Auli Agerii ex iure Quiritium esse*[7]," with special forms for rights less than ownership (*ius itineris in f. C. Ai. Ai. esse*[8]) and further complications in *actiones ficticiae*, e.g. *actio Publiciana*[9]. Thus it simply alleged a right in the *res* and not a claim against the defendant, so that it did not contain the defendant's name. In actions *in personam* the *intentio* stated an

1 Cicero laughs at them as useless, as, apart from this, they seem to be, in view of the "*ob eam rem*" in the *intentio*. *Pro Murena*, 13. 28; *Brut.* 79. 275. 2 G. 4. 41. As to its presence in all *formulae*, *post*, p. 652. 3 *Post*, § CCXLIV. 4 *Post*, § CCXXXV. 5 G. 4. 44; Lenel, *E.P.* 311, 341. Gaius (*ib.*) tells us that *praeiudicia* are numerous. Those recorded seem to be (Pissard, *Questions Préjudicielles*, ch. VI) *An libertus sit* (G. *ib.*; *an ingenuus sit* is not recorded, but see Lenel, *E.P.* 341); *an liber sit* (Inst. 4. 6. 13), declared to be the only one of statutory origin (but see Lenel, *E.P.* 380, 383, who thinks it interp., and rejects the corresponding *an servus sit*); *utrum ex servitute in libertatem petatur an ex libertate in servitutem* (40. 12. 7. 5; C. 7. 16. 21); *de partu agnoscendo*, to compel a father to recognise a child (Inst. 4. 6. 13; C. 8. 46. 9); a corresponding one for a father claiming a child *an filius Agerii sit* (D. 6. 1. 1. 2); *quanta dos sit* (G. 4. 44, purpose uncertain); *an ex l. Cicereia praedictum sit* (G. 3. 123; *ante*, § CLVI); *an iure bona venierint* (42. 5. 30, M. Aur. and Verus, on the question whether the *bonorum venditio* was justified); *an ea res qua de agitur maior sit* 100 *sestertiis*, and another apparently connected with it (P. 5. 9. 1; purpose obscure—Lenel, see now *E.P.* 526). The list was probably longer in classical law: there may have been many in connexion with questions of Latinity and *civitas*. The *praeiudicia* in C. Th. 1. 2. 5 and in many *leges* in C. Th. 11. 30 and 36 appear to be the interlocutory decisions so prominent in the procedure by *cognitio* (*post*, § CCXXVI), but the *praeiudicium sanguinis* of C. Th. 16. 2. 19 may perhaps, as Gothofredus suggests (*ad h. l.*), refer to one of the *praeiudicia* affecting *status*. 6 G. 4. 3, 36. 7 *Aulus Agerius* (from *agere*) is the name given to the plaintiff in these model *formulae*. Similarly the defendant is called *Numerius Negidius* (from *negare*). 8 See Lenel, *E.P.* 193. They do not contain the words "*ex iure Quiritium*." 9 G. 4. 36; *ante*, § LXX.

obligation in the defendant "*dare oportere*[1]," "*dare facere oportere*[2]," "*damnum decidere oportere*[3]" (and possibly other forms[4]) according to the nature of the *obligatio*, as will later appear. In actions *in factum* it stated a hypothesis of fact according to the truth or falsity of which the *iudex* was to condemn or absolve[5].

If the claim was for a *certum* or it was a *vindicatio*, the *intentio* began with "*si paret*[6]," and stated the *certum*, or subject of the *vindicatio*. If it was for an *incertum* it began "*quicquid paret*[7]," referring to the statement in the *demonstratio* or *praescripta verba*[8]. In an *actio ex testamento* on a legacy the *intentio* stated the fact of the legacy[9], and in the *actio furti* it stated the thing stolen[10], though, as we have seen[11], there may have been a *demonstratio* as well. But details of formulation in delictal actions are uncertain.

A statement of the issue seems essential to all litigation and it is sometimes said that every *formula* had an *intentio*. But some cases have raised difficulty. In the divisory actions, in their earlier form, before there was any question of allowances, *praestationes*, there was nothing that could be called an *intentio* except the words "*quantum adiudicari oportet*," which Gaius quotes as part of the *adiudicatio*[12]. But the point here is hardly more than verbal, apart from certain historical inferences on the origin of the *formula* which are connected with it[13]. Another case is that of the *actio iniuriarum* and perhaps the other actions "*ex bono et aequo*[14]," where there was a *demonstratio* followed by "*quantum bonum aequum videbitur condemna*[15]," in which the *intentio* was so to speak merged in the *condemnatio*. Here too historical inferences are drawn from the form, which has been the subject of much controversy[16].

1 G. 4. 4. 2 G. 4. 2, 47, 60. The original meaning of *damnum decidere* is "come to terms." On this and "*pro fure*," de Visscher, *Ét.* 293. 3 G. 4. 37, 45. 4 Lenel finds "*praestare oportere*" in the divisory actions, and in *pro socio*; Mayr, *Z.S.S.* 1921, 195, only in the divisory actions. Others find it in the *de peculio* group, *E.P.* 208, 211, 269, 297. As to the divisory actions, Audibert, *Mél. Appleton*, 1. 5 Variations, *post*, § CCXXXI. 6 G. 4. 41. 7 G. 4. 41, 47. 8 *Ante*, pp. 521, 649. 9 G. 2. 213; Lenel, *E.P.* 368. 10 G. 4. 37. 11 *Ante*, p. 650. 12 G. 4. 42. 13 See Arangio Ruiz, *Le formule con demonstratio* and review by Koschaker, *Z.S.S.* 1913, 434; Audibert, *Mél. Girard*, 1. 48. It contains the word *oportet*, the mark of an *intentio*. It bears the same relation to the *adiudicatio* as the undoubted *intentio* which follows it does to the *condemnatio* for *praestationes*. And Gaius elsewhere includes, in his statement of a part of the *formula*, other connected parts, G. 4. 34, 136. 14 *Post*, § CCXXXI. 15 Lenel, *E.P.* 399. 16 Lenel, *loc. cit.*; Partsch, *Schriftformel*, 29 *sqq.*, 39 *sqq.*, Huvelin, *Mél. Gérardin*, 337 *sqq.*, and especially Audibert, *Mél. Girard*, 1. 35 *sqq.* As to *actio ad exhibendum*, Lenel, *Z.S.S.* 1916, 116; *E.P.* 220. De Visscher, *Formules in factum*, *N.R.H.* 1925, 193, *Ét.* 359 (followed by Perozzi, *Mél. Cornil*, 2. 199, who adds further arguments from the language of G. 4. 60, which assume that G. never speaks without exact precision and completeness as to which see n. 13 above) maintains that *as. in f.* had no *intentiones* and that G. 4. 60 which contradicts this is an interpolation, due to a change in conception

CCXXIII. *Exceptio*[1], a result of the *l. Aebutia*, and the Praetor's power of formulation. The question whether anything of the sort existed in the *legis actio* system, need not here be considered[2]. An *exceptio* was a defence which did not deny the *prima facie* validity of the claim, but alleged some circumstance which nevertheless barred it. It may be called a collateral defence, but in fact the nature and sources of *exceptiones* are so various that no general description is very informing. Though they were in form praetorian the defence they set up was not necessarily such. Some *exceptiones* gave effect to defences based on *leges*[3], or on *senatusconsulta*[4], or on imperial enactments[5]. The reason why the transaction was met in this way, instead of being declared simply void, in these civil cases, was not always the same. Under *senatusconsulta* it was probably because these *senatusconsulta* date from a time before the Senate had assumed the power of directly varying the civil law, and still acted by directions to magistrates[6]. As to *leges* many explanations are offered, more or less conjectural[7]. As to Hadrian's *beneficium divisionis* among sureties, which was in some cases enforced by *exceptio*, this may be because the *exceptio* was designed not exactly as a defence but as a means of forcing the creditor to modify his *intentio*, as in some applications of the *exceptio doli*[8]. But the great majority of *exceptiones* were praetorian both in form and character. Many have presented themselves in the course of the treatment of substantive law, e.g. *doli*, *metus*, *pacti conventi*, *rei venditae et traditae*, *iusti dominii*[9], etc. Some, e.g. *cognitoria*[10], *rei iudicatae vel in iudicium deductae*[11], will be considered later, but while it is impossible to enumerate them all a few must be mentioned here.

The so-called *exceptio senatusconsulti* was a general *exceptio* to cover all cases in which an *exceptio* was available on account of the provisions of a *lex* or *sc*. It was open to the parties to use either this general form[12], for any such provision, or to use an *exceptio* specifying the enactment,

of the *intentio* from "statement of the right brought into issue" to "l'énoncé des prétentions du demandeur, de ce qu'il doit prouver...ses conclusions." But see G. 4. 41, and Lenel, *Z.S.S.* 1928, 1.

1 G. 4. 115 *sqq.* 2 See Girard, *Mélanges*, 1, 75 *sqq.*, 148 *sqq.* and reff. 3 *Exc. l. Cinciae*, excessive gifts, *ante*, p. 254; *exc. l. Plaetoriae*, fraud on minors, *ante*, p. 170; perhaps under the *l. Furia testamentaria*, excessive legacies, some writers holding that there was an *exceptio* here, *ante*, p. 342. 4 E.g. *Sci. Macedoniani*, loans to *filiifamilias*, *ante*, p. 465; *Sci. Trebelliani*, where *heres* is sued after handing over a *hereditas* under *fideicommissum*, *ante*, p. 355; *Sci. Velleiani*, where a woman has become surety, *ante*, p. 448. 5 *Ante*, p. 450. 6 *Ante*, p. 14. 7 Krueger, *Röm. Rechtsq.* 21, n. 82. 8 E.g. *compensatio*, under M. Aurelius, *post*, § CCXXXVIII. It is *dolus* to persist in a claim after knowledge that it is unfounded. See 50. 17. 177. 1. 9 Some under procedure, e.g. *exc. iurisiurandi*, *praeiudicii*. 10 *Post*, § CCXXXIX. 11 *Post*, § CCXXXV. 12 Lenel, *E.P.* 513, "*si nihil in ea re contra legem vel senatusconsultum factum est.*"

exceptio senatusconsulti Velleiani, legis Cinciae, etc., or one merely alleging the facts which made the *exceptio* available[1].

The *exceptio litis dividuae* is usually supposed to have dealt with the case of one who, having a claim which admitted of subdivision, e.g. a single contract for the sale of two things, elected to sue on one part of it. If he then sued on the other part in the same magistracy, he was met by this *exceptio*[2]. In like manner, one who having several claims against one person brought one or more, but deferred others, so that, as Gaius says, they might go before different *iudices*, could not sue on these in the same magistracy, but would be met by the *exceptio rei residuae*[3]. But a rule that a man could not bring two or more claims against another in the same magistracy unless he brought them together seems absurd. "*Plures lites*" can hardly be confined to disputes in the same transaction[4], and, even so, the rule looks absurd. It cannot in reason apply if he did not know of the other claim at the time of the first action and the task of the *iudex* when this was pleaded must have been almost impossible. Probably the *exceptio* contemplates the situation where there are several *lites* in progress, but not yet *contestatae*, against the same man, and convenience requires that they should all be tried together. These rules seem to have disappeared from Justinian's legislation, except for a possible trace in one text[5]. The *exceptio rei litigiosae* was aimed at trafficking in property the subject of litigation[6].

Exceptiones are sometimes spoken of as equitable defences, and no doubt most of them can be so described. But there was nothing equitable about most of the *exceptiones* based on *lex* or senatusconsult or about some of praetorian origin, e.g. the obscure *exceptio annalis Italici contractus*, which seems to have limited action on pledges taken in Italy to one year[7], or the similar *exceptio* in the *actio de peculio annalis*[8], or the *exceptio rei iudicatae*[9]. The point is important in connexion with the rules as to statement of *exceptiones* in *bonae fidei iudicia*[10].

It is clear that an *exceptio doli* could sometimes replace other equitable exceptions, and we are told that it could replace any *exceptio*[11], i.e. where the existence of the defence was known to the other party. If so it must presumably have been expressed in *b. f. iudicia* or the rule that

1 *Post*, p. 657. 2 G. 4. 56, 122. 3 G. 4. 122. 4 Biondi, *Compensazione*, 51, holds that *l. d.* dealt with division of a single claim and *r. r.* with different claims arising out of the same transaction. This is he says the plain meaning of G. and the only possible meaning of *res residua*. But "*plures lites*" is not an obvious description of different claims on the same transaction. G. 4. 131a sees no difficulty in action for another breach of the contract though both occurred at once. In C. Th. 2. 18. 3 = C. 3. 1. 10, also cited, the matters, though arising out of the same transaction could not have been dealt with by one action in cl. law. Buckland, *R.H.* 1932, 301 *sqq.* 5 46. 8. 4. 6 *Post*, § CCXLIV. 7 C. 7. 40. 1; *Fr. Ulp. disputationum*, 3; Girard, *Textes*, 495; Lenel, *E.P.* 505; *Z.S.S.* 1906, 71. 8 *Ante*, p. 533. 9 *Post*, § CCXXXV. 10 *Post*, § CCXXIX. 11 44. 4. 2. 5.

only equitable defences were implied would be meaningless. It is not clear that this application (*ex. doli generalis*) is classical. But it is clear that the *exceptio* covered not only *dolus* in the transaction, but anything which made bringing the action inequitable[1].

The *exceptio* did not deny the *intentio*, but raised a counter-hypothesis, "unless something else is true." It was negative in form, introduced by *nisi, si non, si nihil* or the like, and thus directed the *iudex* not to condemn if the *exceptio* was proved. In the *exceptio* the defendant was *in loco actoris* and the burden of proof was on him[2]. The anomalous so-called *exceptio non numeratae pecuniae*, which imposed on the plaintiff the proof of the loan, and if the claim was on a *mutuum* was in fact a denial of the basis of claim altogether has already been considered[3].

To the proposition that a successful *exceptio* must, on the logic of the *formula*, destroy the action, there are two apparent, or suggested, exceptions. It has been maintained that, where the *exceptio doli* was used as a means of compelling allowance of a counter-claim, it caused no more than a reduction of the *condemnatio*[4]. Again, it is clear that where a man could not be condemned beyond his means, failure to allow for this would cause only reduction. We are told in the Digest that the means of raising this point was an "*exceptio quod facere potest*[5]." But the description of this as an *exceptio* dates from a time when the *formula* and the true *exceptio* have long been obsolete; in classical law it was in all probability a *taxatio*[6]. A text, attributed to Paul, which says that *exceptiones* sometimes merely reduced the *condemnatio*[7], is no doubt in its present form compilers' work, probably in reference to this case.

Just as an *intentio*, though proved, might be defeated by an *exceptio*, so an *exceptio*, though proved, might be met by a further reply, put in by the plaintiff—a *replicatio*[8]. As this raised a new hypothesis, on proof of which there was to be a *condemnatio*, it was introduced by "*aut si*" or the like[9]. Thus, if there was a breach of contract and an agreement not to sue induced by fraud, the *exceptio*, "*nisi inter eos convenerit ne peteretur*[10]," would be followed by a *replicatio*, "*aut si in eo pacto aliquid doli mali N. Negidii factum sit*," or the like. The matter did not necessarily end here. There might be a further reply by the defendant, called a *duplicatio*, or *triplicatio* (for the name *duplicatio* was sometimes applied to the *replicatio*[11]), though not in the case given, for to an *exceptio*

1 *S.M.W.* 705; Girard, *Man.* 1096; Cuq, *Man.* 867. Chief texts, 9. 2. 47; 44. 4. 2. 3–5, 8. pr., 12, 16; 44. 7. 44. 1; 45. 1. 36; 50. 17. 56. 2 44. 1. 1. 3 *Ante*, p. 442. Probably not known to the formulary system. 4 *Post*, § CCXXXVIII. 5 44. 1. 7. pr. 6 Girard, *Man.* 1098. 7 44. 1. 22, discussed later in connexion with *compensatio*, see n. 4. 8 G. 4. 126, 127; Vat. Fr. 294; D. 44. 1. 2. 1. 9 G. 4. 126a. In 4. 126 he introduces a *replicatio* with "*si non*," but "*aut si*" would give the meaning. 10 G. 4. 121, 126. 11 44. 1. 2. 3; Vat. Fr. 259; G. 4. 127.

or *replicatio doli*, no reply but disproof was admitted[1]. Proof of it was decisive. But it is doubtful how far these remoter cases arose in practice.

Exceptiones were classified in several ways. They might be *perpetuae* (*peremptoriae*) or *temporales* (*dilatoriae*)[2]. The former were always available and would bar the action whenever brought. Such were *exceptio doli, metus, pacti conventi in perpetuum, rei iudicatae vel in iudicium deductae, quod contra legem senatusconsultumve factum est*[3]. These are the illustrations given by Gaius[4]. The others were effective only for a certain time or under certain conditions, and might be avoided by delaying the action or bringing it in a manner not open to the objection. Of the first type he mentions *pacti conventi*, where the agreement not to sue was only for a certain time and the *exceptiones rei residuae* and *litis dividuae*[5]. Of the second type, which he speaks of as *ex persona*, as opposed to *ex tempore*, he mentions the *exceptio cognitoria*[6], avoided by bringing the action personally or choosing a fit *cognitor*. Even the *exceptio doli* in some applications had this character: it was the means by which allowance of *compensatio* could be compelled[7]. Gaius does not mention this; the rule of M. Aurelius for *stricta iudicia*[8] was introduced after he wrote[9]. But though the *exceptiones* are called *dilatoriae*, they were just as destructive to the action as the others. If successfully brought they destroyed the action[10]; they were *dilatoriae* in the sense that the threat of them would cause the plaintiff to delay or remould his action.

Gaius also classifies *exceptiones* as "*in edicto propositae*" and "*causa cognita datae*[11]." This implies that those given only after enquiry, and not on demand, were not set out in the Edict though there would be no difficulty in promising them conditionally, with such expressions as "*si qua mihi iusta causa videbitur*" or "*causa cognita*" which the Edict uses in other connexions[12]. But apart from the *exceptio iusti dominii* these *exceptiones causa cognita datae* seem to have been mostly *in factum conceptae*, an unfortunate name, since nearly all *exceptiones*, but *iusti dominii* and the *exceptio usufructus*[13] and the like, were *in factum*, in the sense that they alleged facts and not rights. Those, however, to which the name was specially applied were such as had no individual

1 44. 4. 4. 13. No *replicatio doli* was allowed to an *exceptio iurisiurandi*, 44. 1. 15. 2 G. 4. 120 *sqq.*; Inst. 4. 13. 8 *sqq.* 3 Lenel, *E.P.* 513, and *ante*, p. 653. 4 G. 4. 121. 5 G. 4. 122; *ante*, p. 654. *Ex. n. n. pecuniae* is not an instance, as it is not a true *exceptio*, *ante*, p. 655. 6 G. 4. 124. *Post* § CCXXXIX. 7 *Post*, § CCXXXVIII. 8 Inst. 4. 6. 30. 9 *Restitutio* of omitted *exceptiones*, *post*, § CCXLIV. 10 G. 4. 123; D. 44. 1. 3. 11 G. 4. 118. 12 2. 13. 6. 8; 4. 3. 1. 1, etc. 13 *Exceptio iusti dominii*, 17. 1. 57; as to this *exceptio*, Appleton, *Propr. Prét.* ch. XVI; *exceptio usufructus* not evidenced, but commonly held to have been the reply where a *dominus* vindicated from the fructuary.

name and were framed for the special case. Thus in actions by *parens* or patron or the *heres* of patron it was not permissible to use the *exceptio doli* or others of like character, and an *exceptio* would be framed setting out the facts complained of without the use of the objectionable word[1]. Again, where parties were agreed as to what was the act alleged to be dolose, and it was denied, the task of the *iudex* might be limited by alleging the fact instead of making a general allegation of fraud[2]. A somewhat similar case is provided, as we have seen, where an *exceptio* was based on an enactment[3].

Exceptiones are also classified as *rei cohaerentes* or *personae cohaerentes*[4]. The latter were not necessarily available to every party who might be sued on the transaction. Thus an *exceptio pacti conventi*, where there were several debtors, might be *in personam*, i.e. so expressed as to be available to only one of them[5]. Paul in the Digest gives as an example the *exceptio in id quod facere potest*[6], the so-called *beneficium competentiae*, not available to sureties of the debtor, but this was not an *exceptio* at all in classical law. The great majority were available to any defendants[7]. It does not follow that they were equally available against all plaintiffs. The *actio doli* lay, in general, only against the wrongdoer, the *actio metus* at least in late law against anyone who had profited[8]. This is reflected in the corresponding *exceptiones*, which can be distinguished from this point of view as *in personam* and *in rem*. The *exceptio doli* could not be brought against a plaintiff by reason of the *dolus* of one from whom he derived title, at any rate unless he held by gift[9], but the *exceptio metus* was not under the same restriction; like the action, it lay against those deriving title from the wrongdoer. Thus, like the action, it is said in the Digest to be "*in rem scripta*[10]."

The structure of the *formula* shews that the *exceptio* was not a part of its original design. The "*si paret*" of the *intentio* links directly with the "*condemna, si non paret absolve*" of the *condemnatio*. The *condemnatio* does not refer to the "*nisi*" of the *exceptio*, so that the *formula* directs the *iudex* not to condemn if the *exceptio* is proved, but does not tell him to absolve in that case. This is due to the conversion of *praescriptio pro reo* into *exceptio* after the structure of the *formula* was settled. In practice, the logical point was not taken: the *iudex* absolved.

We shall see later[11] that there were some types of action in which some *exceptiones* need not be expressly pleaded.

CCXXIV. *Condemnatio*. A direction to the *iudex* to condemn the

1 44. 4. 4. 16. 2 46. 2. 4. 3 *Ante*, p. 653. 4 44. 4. 4. 27; 44. 2. 7. 4; Inst. 4. 14. 4. 5 *Ante*, p. 573. 6 44. 1. 7. pr. *Post*, § CCXXXIV. 7 E.g. *doli*, *metus*, *Sci. Velleiani*, *Macedoniani*, etc. 44. 1. 7. 1. 8 *Ante*, p. 593. 9 44. 4. 4. 31. 10 44. 4. 4. 33. 11 *Post*, § CCXXIX.

defendant, if the conditions for condemnation are satisfied, if not, to absolve him[1]. For a *certum*, Gaius gives the form: "*Iudex Nm. Nm. Ao. Ao. sestertium x milia condemna, si non paret absolve*[2]." In the case of *incertum*, in an *actio in factum*, he gives: "*quanti ea res erit, tantam pecuniam iudex Nm. Nm. Ao. Ao. condemna, s. n. p. a.*[3]" For a *bonae fidei iudicium* he gives a form differing slightly but not essentially[4]. In real actions the form was as stated for an *actio in factum*[5]. In many cases it was for a multiple[6]. As the *interesse* taken into account was differently calculated in different actions, the words expressing this varied. In some actions it was estimated as at *litis contestatio*, in others, e.g. *condictio furtiva*, real actions and actions *in factum* (other than those *in bonum et aequum conceptae*), it was taken as at judgement, or even in some cases at the highest value in the meantime[7]. In these it was "*quanti ea res erit*" or the like, in the former class it was "*quanti ea res est*," as, e.g., in *condictio triticaria*[8]. The contrary rule in *condictio furtiva* is due to the fact that a thief was always *in mora*[9]. On principle, in *condictio incerti*, it should be "*est*." In the actions *in factum* "*in bonum et aequum conceptae*" it seems to run "*quantam pecuniam tibi bonum aequum videbitur*[10]."

The *condemnatio* was always for a sum of money, but, besides subsidiary clauses with special names, there were variations which must be mentioned. In some cases *condemnatio* produced, besides the pecuniary liability, *infamia* in the defendant[11]. This did not apply to an *actio contraria*[12], or to cases in which a *heres*, as such, was condemned: he was not condemned *suo nomine*. The same applied to a representative, for the same reason, and the principal was not *infamis* as he was not condemned

1 Importance of actual *absolutio*, *ante*, p. 639. It is held by Audibert, *Mél. Girard*, 1. 57, citing 42. 1. 3 and 50. 17. 37, that there was no direction to absolve in *formulae* which on his view had no *intentio* (*ante*, p. 652), and he rejects the view that the texts refer to cases in which the *absolutio* clause has been omitted by error. This doctrine is difficult to reconcile with the very general language of Gaius (4. 48 *sqq*.). That this language does not fit neatly into the *formula* in *actio iniuriarum* is true, but we have just seen a similar lack of coherence with the *exceptio*. The words "*s. n. p. a.*" do not fit neatly with an *intentio* in "*quidquid paret*," but they certainly occurred there, G. 4. 47; D. 19. 1. 1. pr.

2 G. 4. 43.

3 G. 4. 47. On the question whether the instruction to the *iudex* were in the second or third person, Wlassak, *Z.S.S.* 1912, 95; Lenel, *E.P.* 113. It seems to have been in the third person, but Gaius uses both forms (G. 4. 43, 45, 47, 50).

4 G. 4. 47.

5 G. 4. 51, which shews a similar form for any action on an *incertum*. *L. Rubria*, XX, gives an instance in action on a *stipulatio incerti*.

6 E.g. *actio furti*.

7 As in *condictio furtiva*.

8 13. 3. 4; *post*, § CCXXX.

9 G. 2. 79; D. 13. 1. 8. 1.

10 *Post*, § CCXXXI. See Lenel, *E.P.* 399. Variations and details, Cuq, *Man*. 857, n. 3.

11 *Furti*, *rapinae*, *doli*, *iniuriarum* (in all of which *transactio* is on the same level), *pro socio*, *tutelae*, *mandati*, *fiduciae*, *depositi*, and perhaps some others; Cuq, *cit*. 227; Greenidge, *Infamia*, 131.

12 3. 2. 1.

at all[1]. In noxal actions the *condemnatio* ran "*tantam pecuniam dare aut noxam dedere*," the surrender being a *facultas solvendi*[2].

Condemnatio occurred in all actions except *praeiudicia*, but probably it was not in the earlier form of the divisory actions, for the only function of the *iudex* was *adiudicare*[3], before allowances were taken into account. The same might still be true in the case of things which admitted of equal division, but, since allowance for expenses and damages had to be made, it is probable that in classical law there was always a *condemnatio*. But the formulation of these actions is much disputed[4].

The *condemnatio* might contain certain subsidiary clauses.

1. *Clausula arbitraria*. An authorisation to the *iudex* to order actual restitution, to his satisfaction, and to condemn only if this was disobeyed ("*nisi arbitratu tuo* (or '*iudicis*') *restituat*[5]," or the like), another negative condition on the *condemnatio*. If the order was disobeyed there was no direct enforcement, by *multa* or *missio in possessionem*, for it was an order, not of the Praetor, but of the *iudex*. But the machinery used was effective. The plaintiff might assess the value under oath of good faith (*iusiurandum in litem*[6]) and the condemnation was for that amount. Paul tells us that in such a case the assessment was not too carefully looked at from the point of view of perjury[7]. Still, there were restrictions. The *iudex* need not allow the assessment under oath; he might condemn on his own valuation[8]. According to the Digest, even if the oath was taken, he might ignore the estimate[9], and in some cases he might, beforehand, fix a maximum, a sort of *taxatio*[10]. The oath was never allowed unless disobedience was wilful[11], or the defendant had fraudulently made restoration impossible[12]; here it acted as a penalty.

It is difficult to say exactly what actions had this *arbitrium* clause[13]. Most of our information is from Justinian, and there are indications that he used the word *arbitraria* loosely. *Actiones in rem* (with a possible exception for praedial servitudes[14]) were *arbitrariae*, at any rate if tried by the *formula petitoria*[15]. Among personal actions there were *ad exhibendum, doli, metus*[16], *Fabiana*[17] (and, no doubt, *Calvisiana* and the

1 3. 2. 1; 3. 2. 6. 2; Greenidge, *Infamia*, 130. 2 *Ante*, p. 601. Lenel, *E.P.* 195. 3 Equalizing payments? 4 Lenel, *E.P.* 206 *sqq.*; Audibert, *Mél. Appleton*, 1. 5 4. 2. 14. 11; Inst. 4. 6. 31; G. 4. 114. Levy, *Z.S.S.* 1915, 1 *sqq.*, rejects "*arbitratu tuo*" in the *formula*. Power to order restitution is due to his being an *arbiter*. See, however, Lenel, *E.P.* 113; Wenger, *Zpr.* 140. 6 D. 12. 3. 7 12. 3. 11. 8 12. 3. 4. 2, 5. 1. 9 Or even absolve, 12. 3. 4. 3, 5. 2. First text probably interp., but this rule seems classical. 10 12. 3. 4. 2, perhaps not classical. See 6. 1. 68 and Girard, *Man.* 686, on possible historical development. 11 12. 3. 2, 4. 4, 5. 3. 12 42. 1. 41. 1. 13 Düll, *Der Gütegedanke im R. Zivilpr.*, sees the essence of *actiones arbitrariae* in the special aim at compromise, satisfaction of the creditor without *condemnatio*. 14 Lenel, *E.P.* 193; *contra*, G. Segrè, *Atti Acc. Torino*, 1930, 425. 15 6. 1. 35. 1. If embodied in the *formula per sponsionem* it must have been in a different form. 16 Inst 4. 6. 31. 17 *Fr. de f. Fab.* 1.

action called *Pauliana*[1]), *aquae pluviae arcendae*[2], *actio in factum* on an alienation *iudicii mutandi causa*[3], *actio redhibitoria*[4], and some cases under interdicts[5]. It is not clear that in all these cases there was *iusiurandum in litem*[6]. There are other doubtful cases. The *actio de eo quod certo loco* is the only action called *arbitraria* in classical texts[7], but it was not *arbitraria* in this sense at all. It was so called because it gave the *iudex* discretion to determine what allowance was to be made where what was due in one place was sued for at another[8]. In the noxal *actio iniuriarum* the master could evade condemnation by allowing the man to be castigated, *arbitratu iudicis*. But there was no *iusiurandum in litem* or order of the *iudex*; it was for the master to decide[9]. Ordinary noxal actions are sometimes so called in view of the language of some texts[10]. But there was no *iusiurandum*, surrender was not ordered by the *iudex* and was not alternative to *condemnatio*, but was a *facultas* embodied in the *condemnatio*[11]. In the *formula in ius* given by Gaius for deposit and *commodatum*, the letters N.R. occur after the word *condemnatio*, no doubt meaning "*nisi restituat*," but they are out of place and there seems to be no other trace of this clause in a *bonae fidei iudicium* in "*dare facere*," and they are usually rejected as an error. This is confirmed by the fact that Gaius does not insert the words in the corresponding *formula in factum*[12], though most *arbitrariae actiones in personam* are *in factum*. But the clause occurs in several actions for *incertum*, and Marcian and Ulpian, late in the classical age, tell us that there might be *iusiurandum in litem* in any *bonae fidei iudicium*[13], which however may not refer to this use of it. Texts speaking of *restitutio* as avoiding condemnation in deposit[14] are not conclusive—*omnia iudicia absolutoria sunt*, and this very rule makes the extension less probable. The language of these texts: "*condemnandum te nisi restituas*," "*condemnandum tamen si res non restituetur*," recalls the *arbitrium*, but the form may be due to Justinian. It may be that in post-classical times the notion was extended to such actions, the letters N.R. being an interpolated expression as are many other things in the MS.[15] But it does not appear that the *clausula arbitraria*

1 *Ante*, p. 596. 2 39. 3. 22. 1. 3 4. 7. 4. 6. 4 *Ante*, p. 491. 5 *Post*, § CCL. 6 On scope of *iusi. in l.*, Marchi, *St. Scialoja*, 1. 167; Levy, *Z.S.S.* 1921, 481. 7 Even they may be interp. They are Inst. 4. 6. 31, 33 c; D. 13. 4. 2. pr., 2. 8, 3, 4. 1, 5, 8, 10; 13. 5. 16. 1; C. 3. 18. 1. 8 This action has been much discussed. Beseler, *Das Ed. de eo q. c. loco*, who confines it to *certa pecunia*, the case of other *certae res* being met by mention of the place of payment in the *intentio*. Id. *Tijdschr.* 1928, 326; Girard, *Man.* 1103; May, *Mél. Girard*, 2. 151 *sqq.*; Lenel, *E.P.* 241. See also *post*, § CCXXXVII. 9 47. 10. 17. 4–6. 10 9. 4. 14. 1; Inst. 4. 17. pr. 1 (*arbitrium, officium iudicis*); Inst. 4. 6. 31. 11 42. 1. 6. 1. 12 G. 4. 47. 13 12. 3. 5. pr.; 13. 6. 3. 2 (? interp.). Ref. may be to oath offered by *iudex* for lack of evidence. 14 16. 3. 1. 21, h. t. 22. 15 Extreme view, Kniep, on Gaius, *passim*.

could be used for any purpose other than restitution[1], e.g. to compel specific performance of a bargain[2].

2. *Taxatio.* This was a limitation on the *condemnatio*, having more than one type. It might be a limitation to a fixed maximum sum, e.g. "*dumtaxat* 5 *millia*[3]." It is not easy to say where this was admitted. It is not found in real actions or the *actio ad exhibendum*, or, of course, where the claim was for *certa pecunia*, but Gaius seems to assume that it was always present in claims for an *incertum*[4]. It is recorded in *iniuria*, and in *furtum*[5], but not in the Aquilian action. It is found in the *actio ex empto*[6]. It may be that it might always occur in actions on consensual contracts. The language of Gaius would admit it in deposit and *commodatum*, but he does not put it in the *formula*, and Lenel therefore rejects it[7]. The omission is hardly conclusive; his purpose is to compare two *formulae* and he may well have omitted unessential parts identical in both. In the *actio ex stipulatu*, i.e. on a *stipulatio* for an *incertum*, it seems to have occurred, though we know it only in *damnum infectum*[8]. Beyond these cases we know nothing, but a plaintiff could always put in a *taxatio* if he chose[9].

Another type of *taxatio* was that expressing limitation of the *condemnatio* to the content of a particular fund, e.g. "*dumtaxat de peculio et in rem verso*[10]." It is probable that the limitation in certain cases to the extent of actual profit, "*quod ad eum pervenit*," was similarly expressed[11]. There was also the limitation called *beneficium competentiae*, probably expressed by a *taxatio*, "*dumtaxat in id quod facere potest*[12]," or the like. Where in *vindicatio* the defendant had *bona fide* ceased to possess, but was still liable for any "*causa*" in his possession[13], and on

1 Later law, *post*, § CCXXVII. "*Restituere*" is not in itself conclusive against its application here; in *vindicatio* there need have been no previous possession. 2 The propositions in the text represent the ordinarily accepted opinion, but this has been attacked. Biondi (*Actiones Arbitrariae*, 1; see also May, *Mél. Girard*, 2. 151) holds that the expression *actio arbitraria* was not known to the classical law as indicating a special type of action having a *cl. arbitraria*, and that though this clause did occur in some actions (see G. 4. 114) its appearance in the texts is in many cases, notably in *doli*, *metus*, and other penal actions, due to the compilers. See, however, Wenger, *Zpr.* 139 and reff. Lenel, *E.P.* 113, 179, etc., accepts the clause for many actions in which B. rejects it. 3 G. 4. 51. 4 *Ib.* 5 G. 3. 224; D. 50. 16. 192. As to *furtum*, it is not clear whether this was in the *condemnatio* or not. Lenel now holds that it was in a *demonstratio*, *E.P.* 329. See *ante*, § CCXXI. For *iniuria* Paul says (Coll. 2. 6. 1) that it must not be less than the *vadimonium*. Lenel (*Z.S.S.* 1927, 381) notes that this prevents plff. from fixing it low to lessen the $\frac{1}{10}$ for *calumnia* (G. 4. 177). Fliniaux, *Vadimonium*, 55, amends to "*non majorem*," following Huschke. 6 C. 4. 49. 4 (A.D. 290), but this dates from a time when the formulary system was practically obsolete. 7 G. 4. 47. Lenel, *E.P.* 154. 8 *L. Rubria*, c. XX; Lenel, *E.P.* 154. 9 E.g. Cicero, *pro Tull.* 3. 7. 10 *Ante*, p. 533. 11 E.g. *heres* liable on delict, *post*, § CCXXXIII. 12 *Post*, § CCXXXIV. 13 Gaius says there is no *taxatio* in a real action, but is referring to a fixed maximum, G. 4. 51.

similar facts in the *actio redhibitoria*, this may have been limited by *taxatio*, but the words "*quanti ea res erit*" may have sufficed.

3. *Adiudicatio*[1]. Already considered as a mode of acquisition[2]. The form in Gaius is "*Quantum adiudicari oportet, iudex Titio adiudicato*[3]," no doubt incomplete, and as the power must cover *adiudicatio* to more than one, probably corrupt. The word *Titio* has been conjecturally amended in various ways[4]. In *communi dividundo* and *familiae erciscundae* what was divided was previously common property, in *finium regundorum* there was or might be a complete transfer from one to the other.

4. *Deductio* in actions by *bonorum emptor*[5].

CCXXV. THE SYSTEM OF *COGNITIO EXTRAORDINARIA*[6]. The function of the magistrate in the formulary system, the *ordo iudiciorum*, was more independent than in the *legis actio*; we have noted the incidental matters, apart from control of the *formula*, with which he dealt[7], and we shall later have to discuss the specially magisterial remedies which he utilised[8]. In proceedings of this kind the line between judicial and administrative action was likely to be blurred, both being based on the *imperium*. In the system of procedure which superseded the *formula* in the third century, procedure "*extra ordinem*[9]," the outstanding change, apart from differences of detail, is that there was no longer any reference from Praetor to *iudex*; the *ordo iudiciorum* was gone and the whole matter was tried by the magistrate or his deputy. The other changes will shew that the basing of all litigation, and the steps in it, on consent, a conception which governed the earlier systems, was also gone; the magistrate controlled the whole procedure. As a contract between the parties *litis contestatio* cannot form part of the scheme of *cognitio*, in which the contract notion is gone. But the name persists, to mark a critical point in the proceedings, varied from time to time[10], its effects being modified by legislation. Little is heard of it in the fourth and fifth centuries, but Justinian restores it to prominence, while much reducing its practical importance. Hence it may be said[11] that civil procedure was superseded by administrative action. But it was still judicial. The magistrate must abide by the law. The hearing was a *iudicium*, but a *iudicium extraordinarium*. The main rules of procedure remained, from time to time modified by legislation. The system owed its origin and extension partly

1 G. 4. 39, 42. 2 *Ante*, p. 252. 3 G. 4. 42; *ante*, p. 652. 4 Lenel, *E.P.* 208. It can be saved by supposing a case in which it was agreed that the whole, being indivisible, should be allotted to *T.*, the other party or parties being compensated, or each party may have had a separate *formula*, differing only in the name in the *adiudicatio*. 5 *Post*, § CCXXXVIII. 6 Cornil, *Dr.R.* 461 *sqq.* 7 *Ante*, § CCXIV. 8 *Post*, ch. XV. 9 Hartmann-Ubbelohde, *Ordo Iudiciorum*, 416 *sqq.* 10 *Post*, § CCXXXV. 11 Girard, *Man.* 1135, "Tout cela est une conséquence de l'idée qu'il n'y a pas là justice civile mais acte de police." Pernice, *Festg. f. Geo. Beseler*, 51.

to its simplicity and convenience, and partly to the fact that, consonantly with imperial ideas, the method tended to centralise authority and to transfer, to the Emperor's official, power which had been in part vested in a *iudex* not so directly under the Emperor's control. The assimilation to administrative and police action which undoubtedly occurred was a natural result.

In the Republic it can hardly be said that the new system yet existed, for though the Praetor issued many orders in judicial matters, e.g. *restitutio in integrum, missio in possessionem*, interdicts, etc., the proceedings were initiated in the ordinary way, and further proceedings were usually[1] tried under the *ordo*[2]. But the founding of the Empire brought a change. On the introduction of *fideicommissa*, though the recorded story shews that they were regarded as civilly valid[3], Augustus ordered that those submitted to him should be enforced by the consul, and this "*paulatim conversum est in adsiduam jurisdictionem*[4]," soon transferred to a new officer, the *praetor fideicommissarius*[5]. Similarly, *honoraria* in mandate, not recoverable by ordinary action, could, from early in the Empire, be recovered by process *extra ordinem* before the Praetor[6]. The nomination of *tutores*, with the consideration of questions arising from it, excuses, etc., was vested in imperial officials from M. Aurelius onwards[7], and the removal of *tutores suspecti* was with the Praetor[8]. The obligation to provide *alimenta* for poor connexions, which appeared under Pius, was in the hands of the consuls[9], as was the enforcement of the obligation to provide a *dos*[10]. The *praefectus urbi* dealt with complaints by slaves against masters[11], and the Praetor with *fideicommissa* of liberty overdue[12].

Here there was no supersession of an existing jurisdiction, but that appeared in the second century. The first step seems to have been transfer to, or usurpation by, officials charged with functions affecting public order (*praefecti annonae, vigilum*) of jurisdiction in private suits arising out of matters within their field of authority[13]. *Causae liberales* were tried by *cognitio* at least from Pius onwards, and probably the same is

1 *Denegatio actionis* and "*duci iubere*" (*ante*, pp. 630, 634) are however his own acts. 2 *Causae cognitio dans le système formulaire*, Lévy-Bruhl. They are *cognitiones*, but not *extra ordinem*; Jobbé-Duval, *St. Bonfante*, 3. 169. 3 *Ante*, p. 353. 4 Inst. 2. 23. 1. 5 *Ante*, p. 353. 6 *Ante*, p. 515. Kuebler, *Privatrechtl. Komp. der Tribunen* (*Festschr. f. Hirschfeld*), 54. 7 *Ante*, §§ LIII, LIV. Not ordinary jurisdiction. 8 *Ante*, p. 160. 9 So Girard, *Man.* 676, arguing from the source of the Digest texts in which it is considered. C. 5. 25. 2–4 speaks of "*competens iudex*." 10 23. 2. 19. This obligation may be of later origin; *ante*, p. 107. 11 G. 1. 53; Coll. 3. 3. 1. 12 *Ante*, p. 84. *Causae fiscales* are hardly an instance; the State is doing justice in its own case. 13 Girard observes (*Man.* 1137) that this explains why these offices are held by lawyers; *Textes*, 910.

true of questions of *ingenuitas*[1]. In imperial provinces, and regions, like Egypt, specially appanages of the Emperor, the *cognitio* was generalised early in the Empire[2]. And in the provinces generally it superseded the *formula*, on one view, about the beginning of the third century, the surviving and, in part, doubtful cases being regarded as exceptional, and, on another, somewhat later, in view of these cases[3].

How and when the *ordo* disappeared in Rome is not clear. No legislation abolishing it for Rome is extant, and it is commonly supposed to have died out not long after the provincial supersession[4], a generation before the famous constitution of Diocletian (A.D. 294[5]), by which he ordered *praesides* of provinces not to give *iudices*, as they had been doing, but to try cases themselves, providing that, if business was too pressing, they might, except in some important cases[6], appoint *iudices* as deputies. It was just at this time that the system of *provinciae* was made to cover Italy also[7], the new system being probably in full operation before this enactment. The *iudices* to whom the enactment notes that *praesides* had been in the habit of sending cases, are called *iudices pedanei*, an obscure word which probably does not refer to the *unus iudex privatus*, but to delegates of a new type[8]. Thus the provision was that magistrates were not to treat jurisdiction as a function to be handed over as of course to someone else, but to regard it as their own duty, not delegate it, except when overburdened with work, and then not in all cases[9]. Naturally the pressure on the *praeses* of the new style of province, a relatively small region, would be less than that of the old.

1 35. 1. 50; 40. 12. 27. 1. *Addictio bonorum libertatis causa* and similar matters (*ante*, § CXLII) are so handled, but they are later than this instance. 2 For Egypt, Girard, *Textes*, 897. 3 Mitteis, *Reichsr. und Volksr.* 132; Partsch, *Schriftformel*, 111 *sqq.* Wlassak, *Röm. Provinzialpr.*, holds that the *formula* was used in imperial provinces, though not in "procuratorian" districts, but that, by Hadrian's time, the *praeses* may choose between *cognitio* and reference to a *iudex*, the *iudex* being however chosen by him, *iudex pedaneus*. Even here the *formula* has changed its character and becomes rather an official statement of the issue than an agreed issue between the parties. (See also Wlassak, *Judicationsbefehl*, 269.) In this form it lasted, on this view, in the provinces to the time of Diocletian (C. 4. 49. 4; 4. 52. 3; 8. 38. 3; Cons. 5. 7) and apparently till Constantius abolished *formulae* altogether (*post*, p. 665). Mitteis (*Z.S.S.* 1919, 360 *sqq.*) is not satisfied as to change in character of the *formula*. Wenger, *Zpr.* 251, holds that in this intermediate twofold *cognitio* the *l. contestatio* (and therefore the instrument) is still contractual. Boyé, *Dénonciation introductive*, 279 *sqq.*, regards Wlassak's view as an unsupported conjecture, involving the continuance, in one province under one magistrate, of two radically different systems. He accepts the probability of the use of the *formula* in imperial provinces governed by senatorial magistrates. 4 No trace of *ordo* in Rome after middle of third century, Mommsen, *Staatsr.* 3. 539; *D.P.R.* 6. 2. 144. 5 C. 3. 3. 2. 6 Hartmann-Ubbelohde, *Ordo Iudiciorum*, 604. 7 *Ante*, p. 50. 8 Hartmann-Ubbelohde, *cit.* 602 *sqq.* 9 C. 3. 3. 2. 1.

CCXXVI. Proceedings in a *cognitio* were begun, not by *in ius vocatio* or *vadimonium*, but till, at earliest, the fifth century, by *litis denuntiatio*[1], issued under the authority of the magistrate[2], apparently in writing, the request for it being in effect *postulatio actionis*[3]. This must be followed up by a statement of the case within four months[4], another four months being obtainable for cause[5]. But before Justinian[6] this was superseded by a summons issued by the magistrate on a statement submitted by the plaintiff (*libellus conventionis*[7]) and communicated to the defendant by an official, the claim fixing a day for appearance, not less than 10 (under Justinian 20) days later[8]. The official took security for appearance, before which the defendant must submit his statement of defence (*lib. contradictionis, responsionis*[9]). These new methods were of gradual introduction. The *lib. conventionis* was much later than the change of system; the case was stated in a *formula* of the old type till 342[10], when the *formula* was abolished, and the formal *impetratio actionis* existed till 428[11]. The administrative character of the process only gradually reflected itself in details of procedure.

If the plaintiff did not appear on the day fixed, the case was dismissed[12], but as there had been no *litis contestatio* it could be renewed. Under Justinian there was an elaborate machinery for this case, the results differing with the cause[13]. If the defendant failed to appear the sureties might be proceeded against, and, in the last resort, the magistrate, apart from his power of fining ("*multare*"), could compel appearance by

1 C. Th. 2. 4, *passim*. See Boyé, *cit.*, and Steinwenter, *Versaümnissverfahren*, for evidence of gradual evolution. 2 As to the magistrate having jurisdiction, *post*, p. 668. At first *denuntiatio* may have been a private act, like *in ius vocatio*, but early in the fourth century the intervention of authority was required, C. Th. 2. 4. 2. Costa, *Profilo storico*, 151. Protection for minors, C. Th. 2. 4. 1. Some cases in which *denuntiatio* not needed, C. Th. 2. 4. 3, 6. The question whether *litis denuntiatio* was ever used in the formulary system is disputed, Kipp, *Litis Denuntiatio*. Wlassak, *Röm. Provinzialprozess*, thinks it essentially provincial, a measure to unify the varying provincial practices. He also holds, p. 58, that it was never absolutely private: though at first the act of the party, there was always magisterial authorisation. Hypotheses on the source of this method and for the view that it began with the *praetor peregrinus*, Eisele, *Beiträge*, 268 *sqq*. 3 *Postulatio simplex*, Wenger, *Zpr*. 265, Fliniaux, *R.H.* 1930, 207, reject the view of Collinet and Andt who confine *postulatio* to the rescript process, *post*, p. 671. 4 Mitteis, *Grundzüge der Papyrusf*. 2. 1. 40; *Z.S.S.* 1906, 351, shews the four months to be a maximum. No procedure *in contumaciam* (see below) till the time has expired, but nothing to bar earlier action if parties and magistrate are ready. 5 C. Th. 2. 6. 1. Automatic extension of time in certain cases, h. t. 3 and 4; C. Th. 2. 7. 3. Further postponement for not more than two months by consent, C. Th. 11. 33. 1. 6 See *Nov*. 53. 3. Collinet, *Procès par libelle*. Steinwenter, *Festschr. f. Hanausek*, 36 *sqq*., shews it in use in Egypt, for cases exempt from *denuntiatio*, early in the fifth century. 7 Inst. 4. 6. 24. 8 *Nov*. 53. 3. 2. 9 C. Th. 1. 16. 10; 2. 14. 1; *Nov*. 53. 3. 10 C. 2. 57. 1. See however Partsch, *Schriftformel*, 120. 11 C. Th. 2. 3. 1; C. 2. 57. 2. 12 *Arg*. C. Th. 2. 6. 1. Cases of shortened period and others of provisional decree on less stringent proof, Wenger, *Zpr*. 314. 13 *Novv*. 112. 3, 115. 2.

force[1]. If the defendant evaded service of summons or other preliminary steps, there was a procedure *in contumaciam*, an elaborate system of notices to be served on him if he could be reached, and proclamations if he could not[2]. The effect varied in different cases and from time to time; Justinian legislated repeatedly on the matter[3].

On the appointed day there was a *cognitio*. The parties appeared and stated their cases and the facts on which they relied. The close of this stage was apparently *litis contestatio*[4], but with effects much modified[5]. A time so defined was unsatisfactory and Justinian provided, in effect, that *litis contestatio* was to occur when the parties had taken the oath against *calumnia*[6]. *Confessio* now led to immediate judgement whatever the nature of the claim[7]. The class of *actiones interrogatoriae* was gone, but interrogations became even more important. In any action, and on any point, either party might submit an *interrogatio* to the other, by leave of, and through, the *iudex*, as it seems, at any stage. The answer was evidence against the person who gave it[8], but it does not seem that it had any other effect. It could not be used against the asker, and there seems no satisfactory evidence that refusal to answer was penalised, as it was in the *actiones interrogatoriae*[9]. *Iusiurandum necessarium* had a wider scope. Instead of being confined to a small group of actions[10] it could be offered in any action with the same right of "*relatio*" and the same results of taking and of refusal as in the formulary system, and, at least under Justinian, after *litis contestatio*[11].

Much of the old terminology remained. We still hear of *exceptio*,

1 D. 2. 5. 2. 1; 2. 8. 2. 5. 2 C. Th. 12. 1. 23; C. 7. 43. 9, and h. t. *passim*. Steinwenter, *Versaümnissverfahren*. Earlier legislation, *Appendix legis Rom. Wisig.* 2. 2 (*Coll. libror. iuris anteiust.* 3. 260 *sqq.*). See also H. Krueger, *Z.S.S.* 1925, 73. 3 Details and reliefs, C. 7. 43 *passim*. See generally, Koschaker, *Z.S.S.* 1915, 444, reviewing Steinwenter, *Versäumnissverfahren*. Judgement without these final steps, if the defendant, warned by the *iudex*, wilfully abstains, C. 7. 43. 2. For Wlassak, *Röm. Provinzialpr.* 36 *sqq.*, the contumacy procedure is of provincial origin: it is there that first appears the conception essential to it that non-appearance is disobedience to the magistrate. Boyé, *Dénonciation*, 6. For Steinwenter, *cit.* 92, it is not Greek, but is a generalisation in the *cognitio* system of the method employed in *fideicommissa* of liberty (D. 40. 5. 26. 7, *ante*, p. 84) and in fiscal cases (49. 14. 42. 1). C. 7. 43. 8 is held to shew that it was available against plaintiff. See Wenger, *Zpr.* 273. 4 C. Th. 2. 4. 4; C. 3. 1. 14. 4; 3. 9. 1. *Preces* to the Emperor, followed by rescript, amounted to *l. c.*, C. Th. 1. 2. 10 = C. 1. 20. 1. Effects of *l. c.*, *post*, § CCXXXV. See C. 3. 1. 16. 5 The changes do not depend on change of procedure or coincide in time with it. 6 C. 2. 58. 1, 2. Refusal is ground for judgement, *ib.*; counsel had to take a similar oath, *ib. Nov.* 53. 3 makes *l. c.* occur at signature of the *libelli*, with rules for failure to sign. On *litis contestatio*, "*mota controversia*," "*lis inchoata*," Albertario, *Z.S.S.* 1914, 305 *sqq.*; Steinwenter, *Z.S.S.* 1930, 188. 7 C. 7. 59. 1. 8 11. 1. 1. 1 (interp.), 7, 21. 9 Texts in D. 11. 1 which seem to apply the old system (e.g. 8, 9. 3, 9. 7, 11. 4) actually refer only to the old *actiones interrogatoriae* and may be anachronisms. 10 *Ante*, p. 632. 11 Different forms of oath confused in D. 12. 2. See C. 4. 1. 1, 8, and *post*, p. 667.

replicatio, *litis contestatio*, interdict, but the terms have changed significance. When Justinian said that an *exceptio doli* was available he meant that *dolus* might be pleaded and would (in general) bar the claim; he did not mean that it was pleaded in the old way. A possessory interdict was, for him, a possessory action: the actual issue of an interdict was a thing of the past. But some *exceptiones* were now disposed of before *litis contestatio*, e.g. those dealing with capacity of parties, representatives, or the court[1], and also, perhaps, *exc. praeiudicialis*, and those alleging previous judgement or *transactio*, or bar by lapse of time[2]. Others were dealt with in the old way with two modifications. *Exceptiones peremptoriae* not claimed could be brought in at a later stage, without *restitutio in integrum*[3], and, as an indirect result of express legislation, some *exceptiones* no longer destroyed the action[4].

The principal changes in procedure after *litis contestatio* are the following. *Exceptiones* might be gone into, and an interlocutory judgement given on them, before the final decision[5]. There was much legislation on burden of proof. Oral evidence was distrusted, and there were many enactments affecting capacity to give evidence, and on the weight to be attached to it[6]. "*Testis unus, testis nullus*" was laid down as a general rule[7], and, apart from this, a minimum of evidence was required in some cases[8]. An outside witness was not to be heard in opposition to a document duly authenticated and witnessed[9]. Justinian excluded evidence by *humiles* not vouched for by persons of higher rank, unless under torture[10]. Hearsay was in general excluded[11]. Witnesses were summoned by the court, and could be compelled to give surety for their appearance, distinguished persons being exempt[12]. The questions were asked by the *iudex* and the answers recorded[13]. There was much legislation on the mode of proof of documents[14].

The distinction between *iusiurandum necessarium* and *voluntarium in iudicio* is much obscured. Justinian seems to have put any oath offered at any stage, by a party with approval of the *iudex*, or by the *iudex*, on the same level[15]. If it was refused in first instance judgement went against the offeree on the point, subject to appeal, and the *iudex* in appeal might confirm the judgement or, if he thought the oath should not have been

1 Cons. 6. 2; C. 2. 12. 13; C. 8. 35. 13. 2 Bethmann-Hollweg, *C.P.* 3. 265. 3 C. 8. 35. 8. So that there is little difference between *b. f. iudicia* and others, Brugi, *Ist.* 157. 4 *Compensatio*, *post*, § CCXXXVIII; *plus petitio*, *post*, § CCXXXVII. 5 C. Th. 11. 30. 37. 6 Bethmann-Hollweg, *C.P.* 3. 274. Reasons for preference for writing, Kroell, *Rôle de l'Écrit*, 134. 7 C. Th. 11. 39. 3. 1 = C. 4. 20. 9. 8 E.g. C. 4. 20. 15. 6, 18. 9 C. 4. 20. 1. Does not bar evidence that they are not genuine, P. 5. 15. 4. Recognition of presumptions in later law, Cuq, *Man.* 898; Donatuti, *Le praesumptiones iuris*. 10 *Nov.* 90. 1, a comprehensive enactment. 11 *Nov.* 90. 2. 12 C. 4. 20. 16, 19. 13 Bethmann-Hollweg, *C.P.* 3. 277. 14 *Ib.* 279 *sqq.* 15 C. 4. 1. 12. 1a. Justinian's legislation, Demelius, *Scheidseid und Beweiseid*, 123 *sqq.*

offered, and was reasonably refused, disregard it and go into the merits[1]. If it was taken when offered, or taken or refused on *relatio*, judgement went accordingly on the point, not necessarily the whole issue[2], with no appeal. Thus the party originally offering the oath had no appeal[3].

The case proceeded from day to day, adjournment being to a day fixed by the *iudex*[4]. Non-appearance was treated like non-appearance before *litis contestatio*. The administrative character of the process led to decreased publicity. *Cognitiones* were under cover, and in later law the ordinary public had access only by leave of the *iudex*[5]. The calendar of *dies fasti*, etc., disappeared in the Christian regime; the available days, changed from time to time, were the same for all stages of the process, and about the same in number as in the old system[6].

CCXXVII. Jurisdiction was vested in many officials[7]. In Rome, and later in Constantinople, the *praefectus urbi*, the *vicarius urbis*, and the *praefecti annonae* and *vigilum* had jurisdiction, in some cases limited to particular affairs: the old Praetor lost jurisdiction long before his name disappeared[8]. In a province the *praeses* sitting in his chief town was the ordinary judge[9]. Municipal magistrates had a limited jurisdiction, and, in the later Empire, many towns had also a *defensor civitatis*, with similar jurisdiction, concurrent with that of local magistrates[10]. All these were accustomed to act with assessors who gave opinions but had no share in the decision, and in the important courts the best available legal learning was used for this purpose[11].

It was a common practice to delegate the jurisdiction from initiation to decision to a deputy to whom the name *iudex pedaneus* was applied; the magistrates seem indeed to have tended to shift off the burden of civil jurisdiction. Diocletian, as we have seen, provided[12] against this, except under pressure of work. The Emperor Julian enacted, in A.D. 362,

1 C. 4. 1. 12. 2. 2 C. 4. 1. 12. 1a. 3 C. 4. 1. 12. 3. 4 C. 3. 11. 1, 3, 4. 5 Bethmann-Hollweg, *C.P.* 3. 189. *Contra*, Wenger, *Zpr.* 74, citing C. Th. 13. 9. 6 (=C. 11. 6. 5. pr.); 1. 12. 1; 1. 16. 9. But an enactment in C. Th. is evidence only for the time of enactment. Obsolete laws were retained. C. Th. 13. 9. 6 deals plainly with a specific type of case and is thus an argument against W. C. Th. 1. 16. 9 is so specific that its omission by J. is significant. The texts cited by B.-H. seem conclusive for Justinian. 6 2. 12 *passim*. Brugi, *Ist.* 62. Bethmann-Hollweg, *cit.* Temporary revival of the old system under Julian the Apostate. 7 Bethmann-Hollweg, *C.P.* 3. 35 *sqq.* 8 Boethius, *de Consol.* 3. 4, "*praetura, magna olim potestas, nunc inane nomen est.*" 9 Bethmann-Hollweg, *C.P.* 3. 45. 10 C. Th. 1. 29. 1, 6, 7. C. 1. 55. Special officials for cases affecting State finance, and for *milites*; a jurisdiction in the Bishop resting on consent (except in case of *clerici*), not appealable. C. Th. 1. 27. 1, 2; *Nov.* Val. 35; C. 1. 4. 7, 8. Cornil, *Dr.R.* 463. Wenger, *Zpr.* 333; Brugi, *Ist.* 62 as to this and agreed jurisdiction among Hebrews, and the law applicable. Busek, *La Jurisdiction ecclésiastique* (cited Jörs, *R.R.* 280) was not available to the writer. Emperor's jurisdiction, which has various forms, *post*, p. 671. 11 1. 22. 1; C. 1. 51. 11. *Actor sequitur rei forum*, C. Th. 2. 1. 4; *Nov.* Marc. 1. 6; C. 3. 13. 2. But an *actio in rem* may now be tried where the thing is. C. 3. 19. 3. 12 C. 3. 3. 2; *ante*, p. 664.

that there might be such delegation apart from pressure of work in matters of small importance[1]. The *iudices* so *dati* were not those of the old *album iudicum*, to try an issue submitted by the magistrate; the *album* was extinct, and they tried the whole matter as deputies. They were chosen from the advocates practising in the magistrates' courts[2]; in later law there were regular lists[3]. The growth of this system brought with it a certain share of the parties themselves in the selection of the *iudex*[4]. He was, under Justinian, expressly appointed for each case[5], and could exercise the magisterial power of compulsion, e.g. *missio in possessionem*, in case of contumacy[6]. His function ceased at judgement[7]; he had nothing to do with execution.

The judgement[8] was recited publicly at a formal sitting of the court[9], the parties being present, but like all other proceedings, it was set out in writing, from which it was read[10]. It was no longer necessarily for a sum of money, though whether it was for this or for the thing in dispute itself[11], it must still be certain and perhaps unconditional[12]. There might be interim judgements, e.g. on the admissibility of an *exceptio*[13], and these were issued in the same way. There would also be *pronuntiationes*[14] in *actiones praeiudiciales* and *arbitrariae*, and *adiudicationes* in the appropriate cases. While there was now no *taxatio* in the old sense, since that was an instruction to the *iudex*, who now heard the matter from the beginning, the rules imposing a limit on the *condemnatio* must still be observed[15]. Justinian added another, restricting damages in some cases to double the price[16].

In A.D. 529[17] Justinian laid down the rule that a *iudex* where he absolved the defendant could condemn the plaintiff for anything which proved to be due from him in the same transaction, observing that Papinian in his *Quaestiones* had held this admissible. Papinian may have

1 C. Th. 1. 16. 8=C. 3. 3. 5. 2 Bethmann-Hollweg, *C.P.* 3. 121 *sqq.* 3 C. 2. 6. 6. pr.; C. 2. 12. 27. 4 C. 3. 1. 14. 1. 5 Bethmann-Hollweg, *C.P.* 3. 125. 6 *Nov.* 53. 4. 1. 7 42. 1. 55. 8 Now called *sententia*, Biondi, *St. Bonfante*, 4, 45. 9 42. 1. 47. pr.; C. 7. 45. 6. 10 C. 7. 44. 1–3; C. Th. 4. 17. 1. It must be both, h. t. 2 and 4. 11 Inst. 4. 6. 32. This is enforcement of the actual render, specific performance. It applies to legacy (C. 6. 43. 1). There may perhaps even be enforcement of a promise to serve (C. 7. 45. 14) but here money *condemnatio* was usual (42. 1. 13. 1). In English law specific performance began under Wills. 12 49. 4. 1. 5; C. 7. 46. 3, 4. *Cond.* to "*whole debt with interest*," "*what you have received*," are invalid. The Inst. (4. 6. 32) say there must be such certainty as is possible, an obscure utterance. Some texts speak of a suspended *condemnatio* (e.g. 42. 1. 4. 5) and even of implied condition (9. 2. 40). There is nothing impossible in suspension or condition, the judgement being now a magisterial act, not limited to the terms of a *formula*. These texts are probably modified by Justinian. Vassali, *La Sentenza Condizionale*; Biondi, *St. Bonfante*, 4. 37. 13 *Ante*, p. 667. 14 *Ante*, p. 641. 15 *Beneficium competentiae, de peculio*, etc. 16 C. 7. 47. 1. 1. Costs, Costa, *Profilo storico*, 176. 17 C. 7. 45. 14.

held that *mutuae petitiones* could be implied in *bonae fidei iudicia*, but more probably was speaking of *cognitiones*[1].

If the defendant satisfied the judgement, the matter ended; if he did not, there was, apart from execution, a new institution, i.e. appeal[2]. This was to a higher court varying with the nature of the court of first instance[3], from a *iudex* to the magistrate who named him, from municipal magistrates to the Praetor at Rome, so long as his functions were real, or in some cases to the *iuridicus*, later to the *praeses*, from the *praeses* to the *praefectus praetorio*, and finally to the Emperor, except where the case had gone before the *praefectus praetorio*, who was unappealable except by act of grace[4]. There was no appeal to the Emperor except in matters of importance. In the late Empire a special appeal court of two delegates of the Emperor was appointed to try appeals to him[5]. Under Justinian there might not be more than two appeals on any one decision[6]. Notice of appeal must be given within very few days[7], and the appeal proceeded also with little delay, rules relaxed by Justinian. It might be on final judgement or on an interlocutory judgement, though some of these were unappealable in late law and practically all under Justinian[8]. The court either confirmed the decision, in which case the appellant incurred penalties to the court, and to the other party, or altered it; interlocutory judgements apart, it was not remitted for judgement to the court below[9].

Apart from appeal, a judgement might be void and no appeal necessary. This would be a good reply to proceedings in execution. Most of the cases are obvious, but we are told[10] that no appeal is necessary from a decision "*contra res prius iudicatas*," which does not mean contrary to precedent, but contrary to a decision already rendered in the same matter[11].

1 System further elaborated in the Novels. *Nov.* 96. 2. As to possible operation of the same idea in a narrow field (*iudicia contraria*), *ante*, p. 641. As to still wider application in classical law, *post*, § CCXXXIV.
2 C. Th. 11. 30 *sqq.* It may have been applied to *formula* in its last days, as a slight circumstance might decide the mode of trial, but there is no proof. Appeal must be distinguished from *relatio*.
3 Details, Bethmann-Hollweg, *C.P.* 3. 89, 325. Costa, *Profilo storico*, 178; Wenger, *Zpr.* 296.
4 C. Th. 11. 30. 16 = C. 7. 62. 19; *Nov.* Th. 13; C. 7. 42. 1. *Supplicatio* after he has become *privatus*.
5 C. 7. 62. 32.
6 C. 7. 70. 1. As to new evidence before the appeal court, Lauria, *Appellatio*, 7.
7 Bethmann-Hollweg, *C.P.* 3. 328.
8 C. Th. 11. 36. 18; *Nov.* Th. 17. 2. 2; C. 7. 45. 16. Bethmann-Hollweg, *C.P.* 3. 327. Justinian, having excluded such appeals generally, strikes out the relative provisions in the Theodosian code while reproducing the enactments so far as they deal with other matter. Gradenwitz, *Z.S.S.* 1917, 35, thinks such appeals excluded much earlier.
9 Bethmann-Hollweg, *C.P.* 337.
10 C. 7. 64. 1.
11 Wenger, *Zpr.* 298, also cites the more difficult case of "*contra sacras constitutiones*" which looks like a case for appeal, and Macer's illustration, 49. 8. 1. 2, does not help us. It seems to mean that a manifest error in law can be raised in any procedure under the judgement, without appeal. 49. 1. 19 says much the same. As to redress otherwise than by appeal under J., Biondi, *St. Bonfante*, 4. 95.

The Emperor, as magistrate, might sit in first instance[1] or on appeal, but his intervention was more usually in other ways. The most important was *consultatio* or *relatio*[2], the latter term seeming to mean the letter of reference and the former the accompanying *dossier*[3]. The process was used where an official, in doubt, before deciding, sent a *relatio* to the Emperor, the parties being informed, and any document they wished to send being included[4]. Enactments from time to time restricted his right to relieve himself of difficulty in this way. The answer, which was in the form of a rescript, usually gave a final judgement but might state a principle and remit the matter for actual judgement[5]. In later law the *relatio* went, sometimes, not to the Emperor himself but to his principal minister. This refers to *consultatio ante sententiam.* Officials were warned that it was to be so used, and not after judgement, to prevent suitors from appealing[6]. But *consultatio post sententiam* was common after Constantine, on the same method. It was mainly used in case of judgements of high officials not ordinarily appealable.

Another mode was *supplicatio,* petition to the Emperor by a private person, not allowed when the question was already before a court or had been decided and not properly appealed[7]. It was mainly used to bring matters before the Emperor or his delegate, in first instance, where for any reason it was unlikely that justice would be done, e.g. where the claimant was humble and the opponent a "*potentior,*" or where the claimant was of too high rank to go before the ordinary court, or the decision was of an unappealable magistrate. It might be decided by the rescript, but more often it was remitted, with a statement of principle[8], to a special judge. It was allowed if a *iudex* put obstacles in the way of appeal, and this seems to have paved the way to application of it by way of appeal from decisions not properly appealable.

If the final judgement was *absolutio* the matter ended, subject to *calumnia.* If it was *condemnatio,* no longer appealable, or confirmed on appeal, there might be execution of judgement. There must be a delay to give the defendant an opportunity of satisfying it[9]. When this had

1 Restrictions on bringing the matter before the Emperor in first instance, Cuq, *Man.* 817. 2 See Bethmann-Hollweg, *C.P.* 3. 90, 333–41; Andt, *La Procédure par Rescrit*; Wenger, *Zpr.* 307; Collinet, *Procès par Rescrit.* For the procedure, in particular the function of the *exsecutor*, Andt, *cit.* 90; Wenger, *cit.* 311; Collinet, *cit.* 4. 3 C. Th. 11. 29. 3 and 4; 11. 30. 1. 4 A party who sought to remove the matter from the ordinary procedure by seeking a *relatio* without bringing the other party into the matter by ordinary litigation lost his case and his right. C. Th. 11. 29. 6. 5 See *ante*, p. 19, as to rescripts as sources of law. Andt, *op. cit.*, shews that under *consultatio* there was normally a definite decision. The cases of remission are *supplicationes*, and the reply a *rescriptum ad preces*, a special way of beginning a suit. 6 C. Th. 11. 29. 2. 7 C. 1. 21 *passim*; h. t. 3 makes *infamis* one who brings a forbidden *supplicatio*. 8 Andt, *op. cit.* 17 *sqq.* 9 42. 1. 31. J. makes it four months. C. 7. 54. 2, 3.

expired execution proceeded. Personal seizure seems to have lasted into this system[1], but *bonorum venditio* to satisfy a judgement was certainly gone. The judgement being no longer a result reached by agreement between the parties the *actio iudicati* seems no longer appropriate. Execution is now the carrying out of a magistrate's order. There is no title on *actio iudicati* in the Digest or Code and the Institutes omit the allusions to it in Gaius, but it appears in the texts[2]. Most recent opinion regards it as still necessary[3]. But we hear nothing of a condemnation under it: in any case there is no double liability. As there were obvious circumstances in which execution would be improper, it seems likely that on the application for execution notice had to be given to the defendant who might make his point to the officials. If he did, there would be some sort of judicial process of which we know nothing. If he did not the matter probably never went beyond the officials. Appeals provided against the evils formerly met by allowing defence to *actio iudicati*, and the penalties of unsuccessful appeal replaced the double liability. If the judgement was for a specific thing the *officiales* seized the thing and gave it to the plaintiff[4]. If it was for money there was a delay, after which the *officiales* seized some part of the debtor's property (*pignus ex causa iudicati*) to satisfy the claim and charges. After two months, if the claims were not paid, the *pignus* was sold at auction by the *officiales*[5]. Creditors might bid. If the sale produced too little, there might be further seizure[6]. The creditor, if there was no buyer, might, if he would, take the goods in payment of the debt[7].

Though sale of a man's estate was no longer the effect of an unsatisfied judgement, it might still occur in any case of insolvency. This was *distractio bonorum*, already mentioned as a mode of execution of judgement against one of high rank[8], used in later law only where there were several unsatisfied judgements or clear and undisputed claims, or the insolvency was undisputed. There was *m. in possessionem*, and a *curator bonorum* was appointed to conduct the sale, after a delay, under Justinian very long[9]. Though he seized the whole, he did not sell in mass but in detail[10], and for a price, not a dividend. Thus there was no question of

1 Wenger, *Zpr.* 302; Woess, *Z.S.S.* 1922, 490. Detention was in a public prison
2 3. 3. 28; 15. 1. 3. 11; 42. 1. 4. pr.; C. 7. 54. 3. 1, etc.
3 Wenger, *Zpr.* 301; *Actio iudicati*, 223; Costa, *Profilo storico*, 203; Liebman, *St. Bonfante*, 3. 399; *contra*, Eisele, *Abhandl.* 182 *sqq.*; Biondi, *St .Bonfante*, 4, 89.
4 25. 5. 1. 2; 43. 4. 3. pr.; 6. 1. 68.
5 42. 1. 31; C. 8. 22. 2.
6 42. 1. 15. 2.
7 42. 1. 15. 3.
8 *Ante*, p. 645.
9 C. 7. 72. 10.
10 E.g. 42. 5. 9. 5, 6. The whole story of the various *curationes bonorum* is obscure and controverted. Degenkolb, *Magister und Curator*, 18 *sqq.* The *curator* appears to be normally appointed by the magistrate with consent of the creditors (42. 7. 2. pr.), but some texts speak of him as appointed by the creditors themselves, e.g. 17. 1. 22. 10; 42. 7. 5. These texts, which treat the *curator* as a simple mandatary of the appointing creditors, may refer to a private, extra-judicial arrangement. But see

any person taking the place of the debtor, or of rights and liabilities in the buyer. The proceeds were divided with the same privileges and priorities as in *bonorum venditio*, and where a debtor made voluntary *cessio* to his creditors the rules of *cessio bonorum* for the protection of the debtor still applied[1].

Note on Ritual Acts and Words[2]

It is not rare to see in modern books allusions to the "ritual dialogues" of Roman Law[3]. The truth is that ritual dialogue was unknown to the secular law (*secus* in sacral law[4], and in public law). The Roman principle, well known, was that the ritual words were spoken only by the person who is claiming or acquiring. The denial, the *confessio*, the assent, may be in any words. This is clear in *mancipatio* and its derivatives, in the contract *literis* (it was in the creditor's book that the entry was made), in *cessio in jure* and manumission *vindicta*. The new fragments of Gaius have made it clear for the whole field of *legis actio*. *Sacramentum in rem* is not an exception, though it has caused writers to speak of ritual dialogue. It is precisely because there both parties must claim that ritual words are assigned to them.

There seems to be no real exception. There is no good evidence for the view that a tutor giving *auctoritas* used the ritual words, *auctor fio*[5]. The texts cited[6] shew only an *interrogatio* and an assent. *Dictio dotis* looks like an exception to the principle, but it is not. The only persons who can use it are precisely those who have a legal claim to the *dos* on the expiration of the marriage, so that in saying *tibi doti erit*, thus defining the thing or sum of money as a *dos*, they are also establishing their eventual claim to the *dos* which they are undertaking to give. *Votum* is clearly sacral, as is also *iusiurandum liberti*. The remaining case is that of *stipulatio*. Gaius' account (3. 92, 93) shews that originally question and answer had exactly to correspond and certain words had to be used—a ritual dialogue. But the best view is that the institution is of religious origin, a secularisation of an ancient religious *sponsio*, involving sacrifices. This is not inconsistent with Mitteis' view[7] that it originated in suretyship, which would probably mark the first step in the secularisation process. It is thus parallel to *iusiurandum liberti*.

Degenkolb, *cit.* D. 17. 1. 22. 10 seems to deal with two hypotheses; if the *curator* having sold has not handed over the money, he is liable *ex mandato* to those who took part in the appointment, and *ex negotio gesto* to those who did not. But if he has completed his mandate he is under no liability to anybody, but the absent creditors may have a claim against the creditors under whose mandate the property was sold and who have received the price.

1 42. 3 *passim*; *ante*, p. 645. 2 Buckland, *Festschrift Koschaker*, I. 16 *sqq.* 3 Monier, *Manuel*, 2. § 71; Arangio-Ruiz, *Cours de Dr. Rom.* (*Les Actions*) 29, 36. 4 Cicero, *de div.* 2. 34. 5 Girard, *Man.* 229; Cuq, *Man.* 210. 6 Valerius Probus, 4. 7, cited by Cuq, gives formal words for the *interrogatio*, which is quite in order as the *interrogator* benefits, and none for the reply; but in any case the text deals with *l. actio* and not with *tutela*. 7 *Ante*, p. 434.

CHAPTER XIV

THE LAW OF PROCEDURE (*cont.*). INCIDENTAL RULES OF PROCEDURE

CCXXVIII. CLASSIFICATION OF ACTIONS. Actions can be classified from many points of view and the Institutes do this, though Gaius does not. The difference is not accidental. The tendency of the Byzantines to classification is helped by a change of point of view in looking at juristic conceptions[1]. The classics distinguished transactions (contracts, actions) by their forms. The later men, under the influence of philosophy[2], saw in them definite entities, having characteristics, content, etc., which they called the "*natura contractus, actionis*[3]," and they have a class of "general actions," e.g. *condictio generalis*, which we shall meet shortly, which have, strictly, no *natura*[4] at all, but borrow that of the special action appropriate to the particular case[5]. The main classifications are the following[6].

ACTIONS *IN REM, IN PERSONAM*[7]. This distinction, corresponding to our modern classification of rights *in rem* and *in personam*, was based not on what seems to us the primary distinction, that between the rights, but on what was to the Romans the primary distinction, that between the

1 Longo, *Bull.* 1905, 56; *St. Scialoja*, 1. 657; Rotondi, *Scr. Giur.* 2. 159; Collinet, *Études Hist.* 1. 192. 2 Collinet, *Ét., cit.* 198. 3 The expression occurs in Gaius (4. 33); with him it is a bold metaphor. 4 Collinet, *ib.*; *R.H.* 1930, 16.; de Visscher, *Condictio*, 135. 5 *Bas.* 23. 1. 9, *Sc.* 4 (Heimb. 2. 596). The actions called *generales* in one place or another seem to be *cond. generalis*; *a. de constituto*; *a. praescr. verbis*; *a. de pec.* and the others of that group; *a. iurisiurandi*; *hereditatis pet.* for the whole *hereditas*; *a. in factum generalis*; certain *b. f. iudicia* (17. 2. 38. pr.), *pro socio, tutelae, negotiorum gestorum*. The "generality" does not always rest on the same consideration and is vaguely conceived. 6 Inst. 4. 6. 1–31. 7 Albertario, *Riv. di dir. proc. civ.* 1928, 185, as to confusions due to change of attitude in later law.

remedies. It dates from days when men did not readily face abstractions. The *actio in rem* was an action for a physical thing, rather than the assertion of a right available against everyone, and it has been already noted that an *actio in personam* in its origin was thought of rather as a claim to a person[1]. But for classical and later law the two types may be regarded as means for the enforcement of, respectively, rights *in rem* and *in personam*.

The typical *actio in rem* was *vindicatio rei*, with its claim "*rem Auli Agerii esse ex iure Quiritium.*" This is the "*formula petitoria,*" which gradually superseded the other possible *formula*, "*per sponsionem,*" tried as a personal action on the *sponsio*[2], though the operation of the securities gave it such similar effects that it is spoken of as a form of real action[3]. The action covered all accessories and fruits from *litis contestatio*[4], but not earlier fruits, which so far as recoverable at all must be claimed by independent action[5]. But the defendant, from the time of Hadrian onwards, might claim by *exceptio*, *ius retentionis*, but not by action, an allowance for expenses to an extent which varied from time to time and according to his good or bad faith[6].

The ordinary *vindicatio* was of single things. But the Roman law allowed, in one case, that of a *grex*, the *vindicatio* as a unity of what was in fact a number of separate things. The point is that ownership of the flock did not necessarily involve ownership of all the individual animals. It was a unit, not a collection[7]. It has however been pointed out that some texts altered or misapplied by Justinian shew a tendency to treat it as a collection and to make the right to the *grex* depend on ownership of the individual cattle or at any rate most of them[8].

Ownership was not the only subject of actions *in rem*. *Hereditatis petitio*, though the right to a *hereditas* is not exactly *dominium*, seems to follow the same form: "*hereditatem* (or "*partem hereditatis*") *Titii Auli Agerii ex iure Quiritium esse*[9]." The actions for civil rights *in rem* less than ownership, e.g. usufruct or praedial servitude, are in the form "*ius usufructus Ai. Ai. esse,*" "*ius eundi, in fundum Cornelianum, Ai. Ai. esse*[10]." The scheme of remedies on such rights set forth in the sources

1 *Ante*, p. 564, "*se solvere.*" 2 *Ante*, p. 626. 3 E.g. G. 4. 91. Though one in possession does not need to vindicate, Just. tells us (Inst. 4. 6. 2) that there is *unus casus* in which possessor *actoris partes obtinet*. The old explanation is action by *dominus* against, e.g., depositee, but others are offered, Girard, *Man.* 365 and reff.; Henle, *Unus casus*, see Koschaker, *Z.S.S.* 1915, 440; Segrè, *St. Brugi*, 411; Siber, *R.R.* 2. 96 (but on 7. 9. 7. pr. But see p. 676, n. 4). 4 6. 1. 16, 17, 20. 5 13. 7. 22. 2. Pernice, *Labeo*, 2. 1. 350 *sq.*; as to *b. f. possessor*, *ante*, § LXXXII. 6 6. 1. 37, 48, 65; C. 3. 32. 5. *Ante*, § LXXVIII. As to a liability in classical law, extinct under Justinian, to pay twice their value in certain events, Petot, *Ét. Girard*, 1. 211, *fructus duplio*. 7 G. 4. 17; D. 6. 1. 1. 3, etc. 8 6. 1. 2, etc. See Bonfante, *Corso*, 2. 2. 300. 9 Lenel, *E.P.* 177. 10 *Ib.* 193.

provided an *actio confessoria*[1], the action claiming the right, and an *actio negatoria*, denying the right: "*ius illi non esse eundi*[2]," etc. The need for this action may not at first sight be clear. But it would not suffice to interfere with the enjoyment, leaving the claimant to bring action to enforce his right, since if he had been in actual enjoyment an interdict would be at his service by which he would usually be restored to enjoyment without proof of right, so that the owner of the land would be no better off[3]. The same might of course be said if the dispute were one of ownership, and yet there was no *actio negatoria* in that case; the plaintiff never put his case in the form of denial of the other party's right, but asserted his own. The principle was the same here; the plaintiff asserted his ownership free of this right. But, his ownership not being disputed, the mere allegation that the thing was his would be of no use to him. What he had to shew was that the alleged servitude did not exist. The negative form was a mere cloak to the fact that the owner was asserting his right as strictly as in *vindicatio*[4].

The name *actio confessoria* was applied in classical law to the Aquilian action for damage where the defendant had admitted the act; the adjective expresses the fact of *confessio*[5]. In the present case as denoting assertion of right it is found only in the Digest, and in extracts from only one *liber* of Ulpian's "*ad Edictum*[6]." It is possible that the name is Byzantine[7] and that the classical law spoke of *vindicatio ususfructus*, *actio de itinere*, and the like, though the name of the *actio negatoria*, is probably classical. There are traces of an *actio prohibitoria* in which the owner alleges "*ius sibi esse prohibendi Nm. Nm. ire*," etc.[8] Its purpose has been variously explained[9].

1 8. 5. 2, 4. 2. 2 8. 5. 2. pr. 3 D. 43. 19 *passim*. 4 7. 6. 5. 6; 8. 5. 2. pr. The former text contemplates *actio negatoria* in usufruct by an owner in possession, which looks like a voluntary acceptance of the burden of proof; see 22. 3. 2, "*ei incumbit probatio qui dicit non qui negat*." But the question of burden of proof is much disputed. Girard, *Man.* 374; Windscheid, *Lehrbuch*, § 198, nn. 15, 16. The natural thing would be to leave the fructuary to bring his claim. But many circumstances might make it desirable to "quiet the title," e.g. an alleged fructuary might be claiming from former tenants. This case suggests another point. If an owner brings a *vindicatio*, and the defence is that deft. has a usufruct, how is this raised? It is not a *plus petitio*, as, for this purpose at least, usufruct is not a part (at least where the usufruct is in a third party, 50. 16. 25). The answer is said to be an *exceptio ususfructus*, not well evidenced. 7. 9. 7. pr. (see also 8. 5. 16) (Keller-Wach, *C.P.* 185) deals with usufruct not validly created and the remedy there is analogous to *exceptio rei venditae et traditae*. An *exceptio* of that type would not serve the purpose if, e.g., the usufruct was derived, as it might be, from one from whom *vindicans* did not derive title, e.g. the present *vindicans* having usucapted since it was created. For a more general *exceptio ususfructus* the *exceptio pignoris* or *hypothecae* gives no analogy, for these are not civil law rights. 5 *Ante*, p. 586. 6 8. 5. 2, 4; 7. 6. 5; Ulp. *ad Ed.* 17. 7 Segrè, *Mél. Girard*, 2. 511 *sqq.* 8 7. 6. 5. pr.; 8. 5. 11; *Bas. Supp.* Zachariae, 112. 9 Discussion and reff., Segrè, *cit.* 527; Lenel, *E.P.* 190; Girard, *Man.* 373; Biondi, *Actio negativa*. It is difficult to hold with Beseler (*Beitr.* 179) and

Modelled on the civil *vindicatio* there were also praetorian actions *in rem*[1]. Such were the *actio Publiciana*[2], the *hereditatis petitio possessoria*[3], and certain *vindicationes utiles* already mentioned[4], all of which are stated as *actiones fictitiae.*

Actions *in rem* had the characteristic that the *intentio* alleged a right in the plaintiff and did not mention the defendant; it was not a question of a person, but of a *res.* This came to be regarded as the mark of an *actio in rem,* so that we get actions called "*actiones in personam in rem scriptae.*" Justinian[5] so describes the divisory actions, which were clearly *in personam.* The same may be true of *ad exhibendum*[6], which, as we know it, was certainly a civil action, but its formulation is uncertain[7]. Conversely, the *actio negatoria*[8] mentioned the name of the defendant, but this was not as defendant; it was as defining the extent of the right actually claimed; the claim was of ownership, free of a certain right *in rem,* i.e. a servitude vested in *B.* There might be others with such rights, but this was not in question.

Actions *in personam* were very numerous: each type of obligation had its own action. The *formula* stated the matter as an obligation in the defendant, apart from Rutilian *formulae*[9], the word expressing obligation being usually "*oportere.*" The nature of the obligation was expressed by technical words varying in the different cases. In contractual or quasi-contractual obligation for a certain sum or thing or quantity it was "*dare oportere*[10]." For an *incertum* it was "*dare facere oportere*[11]." In *condictio incerti* it may have been "*facere oportere*[12]." In the *actio furti* it was "*damnum decidere oportere*[13]." For the Aquilian the form is disputed[14]. In some actions it may have been "*praestare oportere,*" or "*dare facere praestare oportere.*" Lenel[15] finds this in the divisory actions and perhaps in *pro socio.* Others find it in *de peculio* and others of that group, but their formulation is uncertain. Of the divisory actions Justinian makes the odd statement that they seem to be both *in rem* and *in*

Arangio Ruiz (*Ist.* 229), who note interp., that it is Byzantine. The *scholion* (see n. 8) expressly attributes it to the Edict, and the Byzantines make little use of it and hardly seem to understand it. It may be (see Karlowa, *R.Rg.* 2. 469) that *a. negatoria* lay where there had been exercise of the alleged right and involved a claim for damages, *prohibitoria* where such an act was imminent. It would not be important.

1 On the view (Albertario, *Riv. di dir. proc. civ.* 1928, 185 *sqq.*) that the classics never applied the distinction, *in rem, in personam,* to praetorian actions, Segrè, *Rend. Acc. dei Lincei,* 1929, 31. 2 *Ante,* §§ LXXI, *sq.* 3 *Ante,* p. 390. 4 *Ante,* p. 258; as to *vindicatio* for provincial land, *ante,* p. 190. 5 Inst. 4. 6. 20. There are no doubt others. *Metus* is said to be one, but this is an *actio in factum,* and probably did not lie against third persons in cl. law, *ante,* p. 593. 6 Girard, *Man.* 1081. 7 Lenel, *E.P.* 220. 8 *Ante,* p. 676. 9 *Post,* p. 685. 10 G. 4. 4; 4. 18. *Actio operarum* claimed the services as "*danda,*" not "*facienda*" (*ante,* p. 459). 11 G. 4. 5; 4. 41. *Actio rei uxoriae, post,* p. 678. 12 Lenel, *E.P.* 157. 13 G. 4. 37. 14 See Lenel, *E.P.* 199. 15 *E.P.* 208, 211, 297; G. 4. 2; *Aut.* G. 108.

personam[1]. He confuses the claim with the ownership which it implied; in fact they were quasi-contractual actions *in personam*[2], to which the *adiudicatio* gave an air of being *in rem*. They were double in the sense that each party was plaintiff and defendant. The formulation has been much discussed. In their original form they dealt only with division, and the later incorporation of provision for allowances for expenses and other matters led to a specially complex formulation[3].

This account assumes the classification, actions *in rem*, *in personam*, to be confined to actions formulated *in ius*, whether as civil, or as praetorian, actions, the latter having a fiction or other device (*formula Rutiliana*[4], *diei repetitio*[5]). This is clearly the view of Gaius in his general definition[6], but Justinian, while retaining the language of Gaius[7], brings in actions *in factum*, stating many actions *in personam* and some *in rem*. Thus the *actio Serviana* and *actio hypothecaria* of the secured creditor[8] are called actions *in rem*, for though, as we have seen[9], *possessio* was not habitually thought of as a *ius in rem*, the pledge creditor had more than a mere possessory right, since his right was enforceable against a *vindicatio*[10].

CCXXIX. *IUDICIA STRICTA* (*ACTIONES STRICTI IURIS*), *IUDICIA BONAE FIDEI*[11]. The name *actio stricti iuris* seems to be due to Justinian[12]. The distinction is found in the *formula* and in the proceedings *apud iudicem* founded thereon: nearly all the results of the distinction were matter for the *iudex*[13]. It was expressed by the insertion, in the *intentio*, in *bonae fidei iudicia*, of the words *ex fide bona*—"*quidquid ob eam rem Nm. Nm. Ao. Ao. dare facere oportet ex fide bona*[14]." The name *bonae fidei iudicia* applied only to certain contractual and quasi-contractual actions formulated *in ius*. This is shewn by the various lists we possess coming from different dates, a fact reflected in the appearance of new, and disappearance of obsolete, cases[15]. They were the actions on consensual contracts, on *commodatum*, *pignus* and deposit (when formulated *in ius*), *fiducia*, *rei uxoriae*, *negotiorum gestorum*, *tutelae*, *familiae erciscundae*, *communi divi-*

1 Inst. 4. 6. 20. 2 They do not, however, presuppose the breach of any right. 3 Principal literature, Lenel, *E.P.* 206; Girard, *Man.* 667. 4 G. 4. 35. *Ante*, p. 403; *post*, p. 685. 5 *Post*, § CCXLI. 6 See G. 4. 2, 3. But the ambiguous terms in G. 4. 106, 107 are sometimes understood as bringing in *actiones in factum*. 7 Inst. 4. 6. 2, 15. 8 Inst. 4. 6. 31. 9 *Ante*, p. 203. 10 E.g. *actio prohibitoria*, *ante*, p. 676; *actio vectigalis*, Lenel, *E.P.* 186, etc. 11 G. 4. 62. 12 Inst. 4. 6. 28. Even *strictum iudicium* may not be classical; Pringsheim, *Z.S.S.* 1921, 649. There is no cl. evidence for any special name for actions *in ius*, *in personam*, not *bonae fidei*. 13 *Stricta iudicia* may descend from *sacramentum*, where the sole issue was whether the party had sworn falsely or not. This would explain the origin of the rule in *stricta iudicia* on the point, *omnia iudicia absolutoria*, *ante*, p. 639. 14 G. 4. 47. 15 Cicero, *de Off.* 3. 15. 61; 3. 17. 70; *de N. Deor.* 3. 30. 74; G. 4. 62; Inst. 4. 6. 28.

dundo[1], and the *actio praescriptis verbis*[2]. Justinian also gives *hereditatis petitio*, but this is a hasty analogy. By his time there had been so much legislation, on points affected by the distinction, that his proposition means in effect merely that in this action allowances for expenses and so forth might be claimed without an *exceptio doli*, a characteristic which, as his language shews, had suggested the same view to earlier lawyers[3]. Further he abolished the *actio rei uxoriae* and replaced it by an *actio ex stipulatu*, for restoration of *dos*[4], to which he gives the *bonae fidei* character of the old *actio rei uxoriae*, quite out of place in an *actio ex stipulatu*.

Although *iudicia bonae fidei*, in classical law, were always contractual, or quasi[5], we have no corresponding lists of *iudicia stricta* and it may be that all *formulae in ius*, in actions other than penal, were *strictae* or *bonae fidei*. This might be suggested by the fact that the rules of *rei vindicatio*, the typical real action, closely resembled those of *stricta iudicia*. But the important practical rule was that all actions on unilateral obligations on contract, or quasi, gave *stricta iudicia*, all other actions, formulated *in ius*, on contract or quasi, *bonae fidei*[6].

The following were the main practical differences:

(i) In *stricta iudicia* nothing could be considered which was not in the *formula*. It was this which made it difficult to admit that any event subsequent to *litis contestatio* could entitle the defendant to *absolutio*—*omnia iudicia absolutoria*[7]. But the most important result was that in *stricta iudicia* all collateral defences must be expressly stated by *exceptio*, otherwise they could not be considered. In the others, by virtue of the words "*ex fide bona*," the *iudex* could take some of them into account[8], though they were not expressly raised. How far this went is not clear. Facts which would have given rise to *exceptio doli*, *metus*, *pacti conventi*[9] could certainly be proved; in such actions they were within the *officium iudicis*. There are texts which speak of *exceptio doli*, *transactionis* and the like in *bonae fidei iudicia*, but these do not, mostly,

1 No information on *finium regundorum*. 2 This list, based on the Institutes, does not necessarily represent classical law. Biondi, *Iudicia bonae fidei*, 176 *sqq*., excludes the *actio rei uxoriae*, as to which *post*, p. 686, the divisory actions, the *actio pigneraticia*, as having in classical law only a *formula in factum* (see also Levy, *Z.S.S.* 1915, 1 *sqq*.), and the *actio praescriptis verbis*, as not then existing. His list is *empti venditi*, *locati conducti*, *negotiorum gestorum*, *mandati*, *depositi*, *fiduciae*, *pro socio*, *tutelae* and *commodati*. He gives this as the list of Gaius with the addition of *commodati*, which he considers to have appeared in that list at a point now illegible (G. 4. 62). Levy, *cit*., excludes it, by inference from G. 4. 62. But G. 4. 47 expressly gives it. 3 Inst. 4. 6. 28; cp. C. 3. 31. 12. 3. The dispute probably was only whether allowances could be claimed without *exceptio doli*. 4 Inst. 4. 6. 29; cp. C. 5. 13. 1. 5 As to delictal actions, *post*, p. 681 6 Monro, *de furtis*, App. II, as to *condictio furtiva*. 7 *Ante*, p. 639. 8 Vat. Fr. 94; D. 2. 14. 7. 5, 6; 10. 3. 14. 1. 9 *Ib*. See 50. 17. 116; 18. 5. 3. *Contra*, as to pact Grosso, *Efficacia dei patti nei b. f. iudicia*.

imply express *exceptio*, and those which do are commonly thought interpolated[1]. We are told of these *exceptiones* that "*bonae fidei iudiciis insunt.*" We know that large use was made of *exceptio doli* to introduce other defences[2], and that *exceptio doli* could be used as alternative to other *exceptiones*, e.g. *rei venditae et traditae*[3]. In Ulpian's time, if the text is genuine, the *exceptio doli* could replace any *exceptio in factum*[4], and we know that such *exceptiones* as that *e lege Cincia* could be replaced by an *exceptio in factum*[5], so that it is possible that almost any *exceptio* could be understood in *iudicia bonae fidei* if the plaintiff was aware of the existence of the defence. Indeed Ulpian's language seems to go beyond this. It is *dolus* to continue a claim, even though it was begun in good faith, on discovering the facts which exclude it[6]. Some of the extensions are no doubt classical, but it is by no means clear that what is laid down for the normal *exc. doli* is true for all these extensions. But apparently the *exceptio rei iudicatae* had always to be pleaded[7]. On these points *rei vindicatio* was on the same footing as *stricta iudicia*[8].

(ii) In *stricta iudicia* the literal meaning of words must be taken[9], while in *iudicia bonae fidei* account might be taken of terms usually implied, of customary interpretation of words, and so forth[10].

(iii) The rules of *compensatio* were different[11].

(iv) The rules of *pacta adiecta* were different[12].

(v) In *b. f. iudicia* interest was due from *mora*[13]. In *stricta iudicia* it could not be recovered at all, even from *litis contestatio*[14], unless specially agreed for[15]. Legacy was an exception[16]. Gaius says that Julian held, and others were coming to his view, that, in *sinendi modo*, interest was due from *mora*[17]. Paul applies this to all legacies[18]. They were certainly claimed by a *strictum iudicium*[19]. As the action on *l. sinendi modo* was for an *incertum*, "*quidquid dare facere oportet*[20]," there was no formal difficulty in including interest. It was no doubt a question of presumed intent, but, though Paul is quite general, it is difficult to apply the notion

1 E.g. 24. 3. 49. 1, compared with Vat. Fr. 94; Bethmann-Hollweg, *C.P.* 2. 284. 2 *Compensatio*, *post*, § CCXXXVIII; *accessio*, *ante*, p. 210; more widely under Justinian, Beseler *Beitr.* 1. 108. 3 Instances, Accarias, *Précis*, 2. 1074. 4 44. 4. 2. 5; Beseler (*Beitr.* 1. 107) thinks it due to Justinian. Biondi, *Iudicia Bonae fidei*, 3 *sqq.*, holds that *doli*, *pacti*, *metus* and *rei iudicatae* were so implied. 5 Vat. Fr. 310. 6 44. 4. 2. 5. Limitation at the end interp., Pernice, *Labeo*, 2. 1. 250. But it is not safe to infer from interchangeability in *iudicia stricta*, which in any case involves raising *in iure*, to equal treatment in *iudicia bonae fidei* which does not. 7 E.g. 44. 2. 22. Biondi, *cit.* 40, holds that this text refers to the *formula in factum*. 8 E.g. 44. 4. 4. 7. 9 Thus to prevent fraud not inconsistent with literal performance of the promise it was usual to add to stipulations a *clausula doli* (4. 3. 7. 3). But in this connexion the clause was unnecessary after the introduction of *a.* and *exc. doli*. 10 21. 1. 31. 20. 11 *Post*, § CCXXXVIII. 12 *Ante*, p. 528. 13 *Ante*, p. 550; Sale, *ante*, p. 493. 14 *Ante*, p. 549. 15 19. 5. 24. 16 In *fideicommissa* interest was due from *mora*, but these cases were not tried by *formula*, *ante*, p. 663. 17 G. 2. 280. 18 P. 3. 8. 4. 19 G. 2. 204. 20 G. 2. 213.

to a legacy of a certain sum, where the *intentio* would be for that sum. Under Justinian, the *formula* being gone, there was no procedural difficulty. In *rei vindicatio* there was no question of interest.

(vi) In *b. f. iudicia, fructus* were due from *mora*; in *stricta iudicia* from *litis contestatio*. This was laid down on equitable grounds by the Sabinians and accepted by the later classics[1]. As this could not apply to claims of *certa pecunia*, there was no procedural difficulty. In legacy[2] the history is as in the case of interest[3]. In *rei vindicatio* fruits were due from *litis contestatio*[4]. In *hereditatis petitio*, however, all existing fruits could be recovered in the same action, under the *sc. Iuventianum*[5], and the *mala fide possessor* of the *hereditas* must account for all fruits[6], even those which he has neglected to collect.

(vii) The distinction in reference to the rule "*omnia iudicia absolutoria*" has already been considered[7].

(viii) The mode of arriving at the amount of the *condemnatio* varied so much in different cases and circumstances that this is best dealt with under the obligations themselves. But Ulpian tells us that in *stricta iudicia* the *interesse* was to be valued as at *litis contestatio*, in *b. f. iudicia* as at judgement[8]. This is said in connexion with *iuramentum in litem*. The plaintiff in swearing the value might include considerations not existing at *litis contestatio*, and no doubt the *iudex* might do the same, and if the thing was less in value at judgement, from a cause not imputable to the debtor under the rules of his liability, this would benefit him. But this applied, in later law at least, in *stricta iudicia* also[9], and in *rei vindicatio*[10].

Delictal actions were not regarded as *stricta iudicia*. In *furtum* it must be remembered that there was an independent *actio ad rem persequendam*. If *vindicatio* was brought, the thief, a *mala fide* holder, was always in *mora*. If *condictio* was brought, this was quasi-contractual; its special rules have already been dealt with[11]. In *rapina* there was no other action, but this action was *in factum*, and the rules making *interesse* cover *lucrum cessans* and *damnum emergens* cover the principal points, as in the Aquilian, which was *in ius*. There could hardly be equitable *exceptiones* and pact was a complete defence. The *actio iniuriarum* was *in factum* and "*ex bono et aequo*," a class to be considered later[12].

1 22. 1. 38. 1, 7, etc. 2 And *fideicommissum*. 3 G. 2. 280; P. 3. 8. 4. 4 *Ante*, p. 675. A *mala fide possessor* was liable for all fruits, but in a different action, i.e. a *vindicatio* of the fruits. 5 5. 3. 20. 6, 6a. 6 5. 3. 20. 6c. 7 *Ante*, p. 639. 8 13. 6. 3. 2. 9 16. 3. 12. 3, 14. 1. 10 6. 1. 16. pr. In actions *in factum* (*post*, § CCXXXI) which are not under either of these heads, the damage was sometimes estimated as at *l. c.*, *quanti ea res est* (e.g. *constitutum*, Lenel, *E.P.* 251), and sometimes at judgement, *quanti ea res erit* (e.g. *metus* and *dolus*, Lenel, *E.P.* 112 *sq.*). 11 *Ante*, pp. 546, 550, 582. 12 *Post*, § CCXXXI.

CCXXX. *Condictio.* Most *stricta iudicia* (confining the term to actions *in personam*), but not all, were *condictiones*. The name is primarily used to denote an action of which the basic notion was readjustment of relations where one man was unjustly enriched at the expense of another, as in *condictio indebiti*[1]. The action on *stipulatio incerti* was not *condictio*, but *actio ex stipulatu*[2]; that on legacy *per damnationem* or *sinendi modo* was not *condictio*, but *actio ex testamento*[3]. Both these state the "*causa*" of the *obligatio* in the *formula*, but it was characteristic of *condictio* that it did not[4]. Thus the *intentio* of an action on money loan runs: "*si paret Nm. Nm. Ao. Ao. HS.* 10 *dare oportere.*" It is not clear how the *iudex* was informed of the exact issue; it was not by *praescriptio* or *demonstratio*, for Cicero shews[5] that the plaintiff could prove any *stricti iuris obligatio* of the amount claimed[6].

There was only one action called *condictio*; it was a general abstract action with many applications[7]. There is little doubt that in the formulary system the name *condictio* was first applied to claims of a certain sum under a *iure civili* obligation, i.e. in just the field of *condictio e lege Silia*. But this action is called *actio certae creditae pecuniae*[8], the name *condictio* for it not being found before the great jurists[9]. This suggests that *legis actio per condictionem* did not disappear till the *ll. Iuliae* when the new use became possible without confusion[10]. The fact that in this formulary *condictio* there could be a *sponsio* and *restipulatio* of one-third of the sum in dispute was formerly thought to indicate a link with the old *condictio* but the recent evidence suggests that there was no penalty in the latter[11].

The texts distinguish different cases of *condictio* by different names. One set turns on the "*causa*," the facts which gave rise to the action, e.g. *C. furtiva, indebiti*, etc. This grouping is unimportant from the present point of view; as the *intentio* said nothing about the *causa*, the names are mere convenient labels for use in treating the substantive law. The names *C. furtiva* (or *ex furtiva causa*) and *indebiti* are no doubt classical[12]. *C. ex lege*[13], *ex poenitentia*[14] and the oddly-named *C. causa data causa non secuta*[15] are not classical. *C. ob rem* (or *causam*) *dati*[16] (or *dato-*

1 Not a general principle, *ante*, p. 545. 2 Lenel, *E.P.* 151. But see *ante*, p. 437. 3 *Ib.* 367. 4 *Ib.* 237, *actio certae pecuniae creditae.* 5 *Pro Rosc. com.* 4, 5. 13–15. 6 *Ante*, § CCXXI. Perozzi, *Ist.* 2, 98, 263, holds that in cl. law the name *condictio* applied only to actions for restitution of property. Difficult to reconcile with Cicero, *Pro Rosc. com.* 4. 13, where a loan and a promise are subject to the same action. 7 De Visscher, *Condictio*, 44. The various "*causae condictionis*" of cl. law are mere applications of the general abstract action, which retains this character to the latest times. 8 G. 4. 13. 9 Cicero knows nothing of it. Terminology, Lenel, *E.P.* 232. 10 Wlassak, *Röm. Processg.* §§ 10 *sqq.* 11 G. 4. 171, 172; *Aut.* G. 96; *ante*, p. 618. 12 Not found in classical texts independent of Justinian. 13 13. 2, rub. 14 Gradenwitz, *Interpolationen*, 146. 15 D. 12. 4. The name is not easy to translate. It seems of little use in view of the *cond. ob rem* (or *causam*) *dati* which is classical. 16 12. 6. 65. pr.

rum) and *C. sine causa*[1] are probably classical. Though these names have their uses they obscure the fact that *condictio* was one action.

The other distinctions, according to the nature of what was claimed, are more important. From this point of view we get *C. certi*, *certae pecuniae*, *triticaria*, *incerti*, but not in any surviving classical texts. The names are rare even in the Digest, and all the texts shew signs of interpolation[2]. The classical terminology is thus uncertain. Some texts appear to confine the name *C. certi* to actions for *certa pecunia*[3], the *actio certae pecuniae creditae*. This fact, coupled with the language of Gaius[4], has led to the view that when the name *condictio* was first applied to these claims for a *certum* there were the two names, *C. certae pecuniae* and *C. certae rei*, which last acquired in later law the name *C. triticaria*[5]. But it is now generally agreed that the rubric in the Edict, "*si certum petetur*," covered both *certa res* and *certa pecunia*, which would thus both be varieties of *C. certi*. *Condictio* for *certa res* had two forms, for a specific thing and for a specific quantity, to which last alone the name *triticaria* can properly apply. But this name is almost certainly post-classical. The *formulae* for these cases were set out in the Edict[6]. The differences, "*dare, dare facere* (*facere*?) *oportere*," would require a model for each. Hence specific labels due either to the compilers or more probably to earlier post-classical writers; terminology did not necessarily stand still in the fourth and fifth centuries.

The so-called *C. incerti* presents difficulties. It is of late introduction, though not post-classical; the name is probably much later[7]. As a *stipulatio* for an *incertum* or a service gave *actio ex stipulatu*, stating its *causa*, and not a *condictio*, the field of this *condictio* was narrow. But the texts provide many illustrations[8]. A vendor transferring land omitted by error to reserve a servitude agreed on. *C. incerti* lay to have it created[9]. It lay for release from an *obligatio* undertaken in mistaken belief that there was a legal duty to undertake it[10], and to recover what had been given in *precario*[11]. Where by oversight a legacy had been paid without security for a possible Falcidian reduction, *C. incerti* lay to have this given[12]. As to formulation, Lenel holds[13] that, owing to its late introduction, no model appeared in the Edict. He thinks that, like *C. triticaria*, it stated in the *intentio* the specific render claimed; in the particular case of right to release he puts it as "*acceptum facere oportere*," not of

1 12. 7. As to narrow and wide significances of this name and on the scope of these *condictiones*, generally, *ante*, pp. 545 *sq*. 2 Girard, *Man*. 523. 3 12. 1. 9. 3; 46. 2. 12, both probably interp. Pernice, *Labeo*, 3. 211, n. 2. 4 G. 4. 50. 5 D. 13. 3. 6 Lenel, *E.P.* 231 *sqq*.; Pernice, *Labeo*, 3. 1. 203. 7 Lenel, *E.P.* 156, who (p. 157) rejects the view of de Visscher (*Condictio*) that "*certum*" was a characteristic of all *condictio*, the so-called *C. incerti* having been an *a. in f.* in cl. law. 8 Girard, *Man*. 654. 9 12. 6. 22. 1. 10 19. 1. 5. 1. 11 43. 26. 19. 2. 12 35. 3. 3. 10. 13 *E.P.* 156.

course stating the *causa*. On another view the render was stated in a *praescriptio*, the *intentio* being in "*dare facere oportere*[1]." But many of these *condictiones* are post-classical[2].

Gaius appears to make the name *condictio* applicable to all actions *in personam* with an *intentio* "*dari fierive oportere*[3]." This would cover all *iudicia stricta in personam*. A text attributed to Ulpian, but mainly compilers' work[4], speaks of *c. certi* as available wherever a *certum* is due on any kind of *obligatio*, and instances, *inter alia*, legacy, contract *re*, and even the Aquilian. To this action the name *condictio generalis* has been given[5]. A text in the Institutes[6] makes a *condictio* available as a substitute for any of the actions *in solidum* on a contract by slave or *filiusfamilias*. This has been supposed to refer to the same *condictio*, but it is wider, for, here, the claim would often be for an *incertum*. These texts involve a great widening of the notion of *condictio*. The *obligatio* might be civil or praetorian, certain or uncertain, on a claim *stricti iuris* or *bonae fidei* and even on delict. It is a single remedy under the name *condictio* for nearly all obligations, and the language of the Institutes does not suggest open innovation. But the nature and scope of the action are the subject of much controversy[7].

The name *iudicium*, applied to the classes "*stricta*" and "*bonae fidei*," does not exclude *arbitria*, for the two most characteristic *arbitria*, *communi dividundo* and *familiae erciscundae*, are in the list of *iudicia bonae fidei*. It has been suggested that all *actiones arbitrariae in personam* and *in ius* were *b. f. iudicia*, but the better view is that the insertion of the *arbitrium* clause had no bearing on the point, though it is likely that in later classical law the *arbitrium* clause might be added in appropriate cases in a number of *bonae fidei iudicia*[8].

While it is clear that in classical law the distinction was merely one of formulation, equitable defences being as admissible in the one group as in the other, subject to their being expressly raised, the disappearance of the *formula* with its strict rules of pleading rather confused this, but there seems to have been no real change in principle.

CCXXXI. ACTIO CIVILIS, ACTIO HONORARIA. The former gave

1 Bethmann-Hollweg, *C.P.* 2. 272. 2 Siber, *R.R.* 2. 215. 3 G. 4. 5. 4 12. 1. 9. pr., 1. 5 *Ante*, p. 674. Mayr, *Condictio*, 246, 276, holds, with Pernice and Mitteis, against Baron, that it is due to Justinian. Name due to Greek commentators. See also Platon, *Pactes et contrats*, 71 and de Visscher, *Condictio*, 126. 6 Inst. 4. 7. 8. Pflüger, *Z.S.S.* 1910, 168 *sqq.*, shews Justinian giving *condictio* where *vindicatio* is possible, apart from *furtum*. 7 Girard, *Man.* 649, 713. Inst. 4. 7. 8 expresses a tendency already existing in classical times to give *condictio* where a contract had been made with slave or *ff. iussu patrisfamilias*, the *iussum* being understood to cover general authorisation to trade, i.e. the field of *actio institoria*. 12. 1. 29; 14. 3. 17. 5; 17. 2. 84 (? interp.). The *iussum* is thought of as a civil source of obligation. 8 *Ante*, p. 659.

effect to a civil law claim, the latter to a right created by the magistrate[1]. Of the first class many were based on legislation, the XII Tables, *ll. Plaetoria, Silia, Calpurnia,* etc., but many were juristic creations. Thus the *formulae* on consensual contracts, and those *in ius* on *commodatum* and deposit, and others, were juristic. Of *actiones honorariae* nearly all were praetorian[2], but there were others; the *actiones redhibitoria* and *quanto minoris* were established by the Aediles[3].

The numerous *actiones honorariae* are found in all branches of the law. They were of three types:

Actiones fictitiae[4]. These were actions by which some existing action was extended to cases not within its terms, by a direction in the *intentio* that the *iudex* was to proceed as if a state of facts existed, which, if it did exist, would give the right. The *actio Publiciana* is a familiar instance. The *iudex* was directed to give judgement for the plaintiff if he would have been owner "*si anno* (*biennio*) *possedisset*[5]." Here the *iudex* had to assume a certain event whether it had occurred or not. In others an event which had happened was assumed not to have happened, e.g. where an action was allowed as if a party had not suffered *capitis deminutio*[6]. In some cases a *legis actio* was assumed as having occurred, e.g. in the *formula* given to the *publicanus*[7], where the fiction was in an unusual form[8]. In some cases the party was feigned to have a characteristic which in fact he had not, e.g. the actions to or against *bonorum possessor* with the fiction "*si heres esset*[9]," and the *actio furti* against a peregrine with a fiction "*si civis Romanus esset*[10]," needed because statutes did not apply to peregrines unless so expressed[11]. Sometimes a *formula* was given "*die repetita,*" i.e. referred back to an earlier date than the actual. Thus where in an *actio ad exhibendum* the *res* was usucapted during the action, and produced, the defendant was absolved only if he was prepared to accept a *vindicatio* dated back to a time before *usucapio* was complete[12]. The formulation was probably by fiction.

Rutilian *formulae,* one person being mentioned in the *intentio* and another in the *condemnatio.* The simplest instance is the *formula Rutiliana* in which *bonorum emptor*[13] alleged in the *intentio* a right of the debtor and the *condemnatio* directed condemnation to the *emptor,* or the claimant

1 P. 5. 6. 10; Vat. Fr. 47a; Coll. 2. 5. 5. 2 G. 4. 110–12. 3 *Ante,* p. 491. 4 G. 4. 32 *sqq.* 5 See G. 4. 36, where the words "*fingitur usucepisse*" state the matter inaccurately. If *usucapio* were presumed there would be nothing to try. What is feigned is lapse of time: the other requirements of *usucapio* must be proved. 6 E.g. *ante,* p. 399 (*adrogatio*). 7 G. 4. 32. *Manus iniectio* may have been feigned in some cases. 8 Possible inferences from the exceptional form, *ante,* p. 625. 9 G. 4. 34. 10 G. 4. 37. 11 More than one fiction might appear in a *formula,* e.g. where a *bonorum possessor* of a deceased pledgee brought an *a. utilis e l. Aquilia.* 12 See *post,* § ccxli. 13 *Ante,* p. 403; G. 4. 35.

alleged a claim against debtor and the *condemnatio* was of *emptor*. A possible case is that of action against a *paterfamilias* on contract by a subordinate, in which, on the dominant view[1], the *intentio* stated an obligation in the subordinate (with, if he was a slave, the fiction, "*si liber esset*") and the *condemnatio* was against the *paterfamilias*. But the formulation is disputed. A third case, needing separate consideration, is that in which a party proceeded by a representative[2].

Actions formulated *in factum*. All the foregoing were formulated *in ius*; their *intentio* stated, directly or with help of a fiction, a legal claim "*oportere*," "*ius ei esse*," etc. But in the present group the *intentio* merely alleged facts and the *iudex* was directed to condemn if he found those facts, otherwise to absolve. These actions placed great power in the hands of the Praetor and clearly needed careful and exact formulation. We have dealt with numbers of them, e.g. actions on praetorian delicts[3], on deposit, *commodatum* and *pignus*[4], on *pacta praetoria*[5], the *actio Serviana* of the landlord[6]. The most important question in regard to them is that of their position in respect of the points which differentiate *bonae fidei* and *stricta iudicia*. Since the *iudex* had to decide on certain facts and no other it seems that *exceptiones* must be inserted expressly. But there is a small group of actions *in factum* in which the *iudex* is directed to condemn in "*quantum bonum aequum videbitur*[7]." There do not seem to be many[8]: some may have become *b.f. iudicia* early in classical law[9]. In the matter of equitable *exceptiones* they were probably on the same footing as *bonae fidei iudicia*.

These types of action, designed by the magistrate, were *actiones honorariae*. But legislation is not always particular about such distinctions. We have seen that, while nothing could be more praetorian than *bonorum possessio*, the *l. Papia Poppaea* gave it in certain cases[10]. The resulting actions, praetorian in form, were based on a statute. So

1 Lenel, *E.P.* 282. 2 *Post*, § CCXXXIX. 3 *Ante*, § CCIII. 4 G. 4. 47. 5 *Ante*, p. 529. 6 *Ante*, p. 475. 7 Lenel, *E.P.* 169, 173, etc. 8 The recorded cases seem to be injury to freeman by *res deiectae* (9. 3. 1. pr.), *actio funeraria* (11. 7. 14. 6), *rei uxoriae* (4. 5. 8), damage by wild animal (21. 1. 42), *iniuriarum* (47. 10. 17. 2), *sepulchri violati* (47. 12. 3. pr.), *iudex qui litem suam facit* (50. 13. 6, ? interp.). Other possible cases, Girard, *Man.* 676, 1084. As to these actions, Grosso, *Riv. It. p. l. Sc. Giur.* 1928, 46. 9 Much controversy on formulation of *a. rei uxoriae* and *a. fiduciae*. As to the former (G. 4. 62, where its presence is clear, Capocci, *Bull.* 1928, 139), see Levy, *Z.S.S.* 1929, 472. It may have been *in f. ex bono et aequo* in Julian's Edict, but *in ius* and *bonae fidei* later. *A. fiduciae* is held by Lenel (*E.P.* 291) to have always been *in f. ex b. et ae.*, the class of *b. f. iudicia* not being confined to *formulae in ius*. Other views are cited by him. For Grosso (*Appunti sulla formula dell' actio fiduciae*) it was *in ius* containing the words *oportet*, but probably "*ex b. et aeq.*" and not "*ex b. f.*" As to existence of the action under the *l. actio*, Pernice, *Labeo*, 3. 122; Girard, *Man.* 556. 10 *Ante* p. 379.

too a statute might give an *actio fictitia*[1]. It adopts the praetorian remedy, but it is difficult to call the action an *actio honoraria*[2].

The expression *a. in factum* was not always used in the technical sense. We have seen[3] that it is by the assumption that the name was used loosely, to cover any action which specified the material facts, however formulated, that the texts dealing with praetorian extensions of the Aquilian action have been more or less harmonised, and also that among the bewildering variety of names given to the *actio praescriptis verbis*, some incorporate the element "*in factum*," though it is formulated *in ius*[4].

In connexion with *actiones honorariae* the expression *actio utilis* gives rise to difficulty. The only proposition which can safely be laid down by way of definition is that every *actio utilis* was an extension, on grounds of utility, of an existing action, and it is probable that it ordinarily contained in its *formula* some reference to the parent action. It was usually *honoraria* in the strict sense, praetorian both in form and origin. But the later jurists no doubt applied the name to an extended action created by juristic activity without the Edict, after the Praetor had ceased to be a source of law, and some are due to the compilers. An *actio utilis* might be of any of the three types of *actio honoraria*, and probably most *actiones fictitiae* might have been called *actiones utiles*, though there are many to which the name is not applied. On the other hand there was nothing *utilis*, nothing like extension of an existing action, in many *actiones in factum*. There were indeed cases in which an *actio in factum* was itself extended as *utilis* to new cases[5]. Thus the name does not fall in with the above scheme, but cuts across it in nearly all possible ways.

CCXXXII. *Iudicia Legitima. I. quae imperio continentur* (*imperio continentia*). *Iudicia legitima*, in classical law, were, according to Gaius, those brought within a mile of Rome before "*unus iudex*," all parties being *cives*[6]. All others were *imperio continentia*. This had nothing to do with other characteristics of the action. A purely praetorian action *in factum* gave a *iudicium legitimum* if it satisfied these requirements; an *actio ex stipulatu* did not, if it did not satisfy them[7]. As "*legitimus*" means statutory, Wlassak[8] concludes that *iudicia legitima* were those in which the *formula* was issued under the directions of a *lex*[9], so that *imperium* played no part in it, from the Roman point of view, and *legis actio* had nothing to do with the conception[10]. Thus, for the first introduction of *iudicia legitima*, the *lex* in question was the *l. Aebutia*,

1 *L. Rubria*, xx; Girard, *Textes*, 75. 2 An action might be in more than one class, e.g. Rutilian action by *bonorum emptor* on a claim giving an *actio fictitia*. 3 *Ante*, p. 589. Monro, *l. Aquilia*, App. 4. 4 *Ante*, p. 522. 5 13. 5. 19. 1. 6 G. 4. 104. 7 As to meanings of the word *iudicium*; *ante*, p. 609. 8 *Röm. Processgesetze*, 1. ch. I. 9 *Ib.* 37 *sqq.* 10 *Ib.* 54 *sqq.*

which authorised *formulae* generally, but did not command them in any case[1]. The limitation to *cives*, he holds, followed from the principle that a *lex* was essentially between *cives*, and the restriction to *unus iudex* merely expressed the fact that *unus iudex* was the normal civil tribunal; the collegiate courts being later and exceptional. The limitation to Rome was a mere result of the fact that the only tribunal, that of the Praetor, sat at Rome. The *ll. Iuliae* substituting *formula* for *legis actio* were nearly contemporary with the *l. Iulia municipalis*, by which a uniform system of procedure was laid down for municipalities, and Wlassak holds that thereafter a *iudicium* in a municipality might be *legitimum* if it satisfied the other requirements. Gaius' limitation[2] to Rome is to be explained by the fact that he was writing of Rome and disregarded the municipalities altogether.

Whatever be thought of this historical account[3] the distinction is important, since the effects differed in many ways. *Adiudicationes* in *iudicia imperio continentia* gave only praetorian rights[4]. A woman needed *auctoritas tutoris* to be a party to a *iudicium legitimum*[5]. A *tutor praetorius* was needed if such a *iudicium* arose between *tutor* and ward[6]. A *iudicium legitimum* was at once ended if a party suffered *capitis deminutio*[7]. The old obligation being destroyed this amounted to destruction of his right, to the advantage of the other; presumably there might be *restitutio in integrum* in appropriate cases. *Iudicia imperio continentia*, owing their force to the *imperium* of the magistrate, ended at once if that *imperium* ended[8]. *Iudicia legitima* were not so determined. The early law is not clear, but by the *l. Iulia iudiciaria* they were extinguished by the expiration of 18 months from *litis contestatio*[9]. This extinction of the remedy destroyed the right of the plaintiff, which had been novated by the *litis contestatio*, either *ipso iure* or by the *exceptio rei iudicatae vel in iudicium deductae*[10]. It seems that a *naturalis obligatio* survived: it survived judgement[11]. It does not appear that there was any *restitutio* unless it was obtainable on one of the recognised grounds[12]. In later classical law the rule in the provinces was perhaps different. Paul, citing Scaevola, says that expiry of the magistrate's *imperium* did not destroy the

1 *Röm. Processgesetze*, 1. ch. II, 103 *sqq.*; *ante*, p. 628. 2 G. 4. 104. Wlassak, *op. cit.* § 33; Wenger, *Zpr.* 20, 45. 3 Gaius would hardly have made so misleading a statement, especially in view of the fact that the frequency of his references to provincial law has led to the view that he was a provincial. Probably the conception had become fixed before the *ll. Iuliae*; proceedings in a municipality might have been thought of as *iudicia legitima*, but in fact were not. 4 *Ante*, p. 252. 5 *Ante*, p. 167. 6 *Ante*, G. 1. 184. 7 G. 3. 83. 8 G. 4. 104. 9 *Ib.* Nothing to do with limitation of actions: it is not a rule as to the maximum time which may elapse between the wrong and the proceedings. *Post*, § CCXXXIII. 10 *Post*, § CCXXXV. 11 *Ante*, p. 553. 12 *Actio doli* in appropriate cases, 4. 3. 18. 4.

iudicium[1]. But the text says "*iudices a praeside dati*"; the reference may be to delegation and *cognitio extraordinaria*, which had then practically superseded the *formula* in the provinces[2].

The distinction between *iudicia legitima* and others belongs to the *ordo*; it is gone in later law. As to the time which ended a *iudicium* in the later system, we learn that Theodosius enacted the rule that it must end within 30 years[3], not the 30 years which limit the right itself, but 30 years from *litis contestatio*. Justinian substituted three years from commencement of proceedings[4], but all that was now destroyed was the action; there was nothing to bar a new action on the facts[5].

CCXXXIII. Actio Perpetua, Actio Temporalis. In principle the civil law had no statute of limitations; a right of action once accrued was not lost by lapse of time. There were exceptions. Under the XII Tables[6] the action usually called *actio auctoritatis*[7] was barred by lapse of the period of *usucapio*. By the *l. Furia de Sponsu*, *sponsores* and *fidepromissores* were released, in Italy, by lapse of two years[8]. Complaint that the details required by the *l. Cicereia* had not been given must be raised within 30 days[9]. The *querela inofficiosi testamenti* must be brought within a limit of time which varied historically[10]. But praetorian actions break into two groups: some were *perpetuae*, some were *temporales* (*temporariae*[11]). The limit for temporary actions was nearly always an *annus utilis*, though the *actio redhibitoria* was limited to six months[12]. Whether this is an *annus* of *dies utiles* or an *annus continuus* beginning with the first *dies utilis* is disputed[13].

It is not easy to determine on principle what praetorian actions were *perpetuae* and what *temporales*. In general, those purely for compensation, or restoration, *actiones ad rem persequendam*, were *perpetuae*. But it cannot be safely said that other actions were temporary, though Paul adopts from Cassius this basis, making penal actions temporary[14]. But in the same text he states and adopts another criterion, i.e. the question whether the action was in furtherance of, or in opposition to, the civil law, and Gaius holds the same, observing that *furti manifesti*, though praetorian and penal, was *perpetua*, as it only replaced a civil law remedy[15]. The same is said of *arborum furtim caesarum*[16]. A difficulty in applying

1 5. 1. 49. 1. 2 *Ante*, p. 664. Carus (A.D. 282–3), C. 7. 64. 6, allows the *praeses* to fix a time within which judgement must be given: if not so given it is void. 3 C. Th. 4. 14. 1. 4 C. 3. 1. 13, March 530; the Code contains laws of slightly earlier dates which seem to refer to the system of Theodosius, C. 7. 39. 9; C. 7. 40. 1e. Shorter periods, varied from time to time, for causes affecting the *fiscus*. C. Th. 10. 1. 4, 13; C. 3. 1. 13. 1; C. 10. 1. 11. 5 Apart from *contumacia*: a final decision may be made against the contumacious party. 6 6. 3. Girard, *Textes*, 15. 7 *Ante*, p. 489. 8 G. 3. 121. 9 G. 3. 123. 10 *Ante*, p. 329. 11 G. 4. 110, 111. 12 *Ante*, p. 491, aedilician. 13 *Ante*, p. 563. 14 44. 7. 35. 15 G. 4. 111. 16 47. 7. 7. 6.

the first of these criteria is that it is not easy to say what was a penal action. The *actio doli* was penal, though only for restitution[1]. The *actio ex testamento* was not, though it might involve double liability[2]. The fact that *condemnatio* may exceed the defendant's profit is not decisive; this might happen in most actions. Perhaps as near as we can get is the proposition that an action was penal if its primary object was the repressing of a wrong and the stigmatising of the wrongdoer rather than a mere adjustment of property relations[3]. Thus the *actio doli,* though only for restitution, made the defendant *infamis*[4]. The name cannot be confined to delictal actions, since Gaius distinguishes these as a class of penal actions[5]. But no test explains the cases. The *actio iniuriarum* was praetorian, penal and *annua*[6], though it could not be said to be, as Paul puts it, "*contra ius civile*[7]." *Sepulchri violati* was praetorian and penal, but *perpetua*[8]. So was the *actio in duplum* for *res effusae*[9]. The *actio de peculio annalis* was praetorian and not penal[10]. In fact the matter was one of express legislation in which no invariable principle is traceable. There is the further complication that in some *actiones annuae* there survived an *actio in factum* to the extent of enrichment[11], and in some, the penalty being recoverable by an *actio annua*, there survived an *actio in simplum*[12].

In later law these principles were modified. Theodosius provided that all the so-called *actiones perpetuae* should be subject to a time limit, fixed at 30 years in ordinary cases, except for *pupilli*[13]. Further legislation fixed longer terms for specially privileged cases[14], and no limit applied to claims of the *fiscus* for taxes, from the collectors[15]. Further, Justinian provided that the time limit where it was less than 30 years was not to apply to minors[16].

ACTIO AD REM PERSEQUENDAM, AD POENAM PERSEQUENDAM[17]. This distinction has been incidentally considered above. A few supplementary remarks are needed. There was a class of actions both for a penalty and for the "*res*"—Justinian calls them "*mixtae*[18]." Such were the *actio vi bonorum raptorum, depositi miserabilis,* the Aquilian action, etc. Justinian adds as an example the *actio in duplum* for a legacy to a religious

1 Not available against *heres* except for enrichment, 4. 3. 26. 2 *Ante*, p. 348. 3 De Francisci, *Azioni penali*, § 1. 4 4. 3. 11. 1. 5 G. 4. 112. 6 G. 3. 224; Inst. 4. 4. 7; D. 47. 10. 13. pr.; C. 9. 35. 5. 7 44. 7. 35. 8 47. 12. 3. pr. 9 9. 3. 5. 5. 10 *Ante*, p. 533. 11 E.g. 42. 8. 10. 24, fraud on creditors. 12 E.g. 3. 6. 4, 5, *calumniae*; 39. 4. 1. pr., *publicanus qui vi ademit*; Inst. 4. 2. pr., *vi bonorum raptorum*. 13 C. Th. 4. 14. 1 = C. 7. 39. 3. Ascoli, *St. Scialoja*, 1. 475. Bringing proceedings interrupts prescription and J. enacts (C. 7. 39. 9) that if an action is begun and is abortive the new period is to be 40 years, a sort of reward to the man who has at least taken steps to the enforcement of his right. 14 E.g. C. 7. 39. 6, 7; *Nov.* 111. 15 C. 7. 39. 6. 16 C. 2. 40. 5. 1. Interruption and suspension of prescription, *ante*, p. 563. 17 Inst. 4. 6. 16 *sqq*. 18 Levy, *Privatstr.* 140; Berger, *Interdicta mixta, in f.*

house[1], but this is a mere extension, and limitation, of the rule for some legacies *per damnationem*[2], and in classical law *actiones in duplum contra infitiantem* were not on account of that alone treated as penal. *Actiones mixtae* were penal for ordinary purposes, and not available against the *heres*, though there might be an action to the extent of enrichment[3].

In general where several were liable to a penal action each was liable in full; if *A* and *B* had stolen, it was no defence to *A* that *B* had paid fourfold. We have seen a modification of this where a man was liable on delict of his subordinates[4]. But there were other cases in which payment of the penalty by one released all, e.g. *metus*[5], *res deiectae et effusae*[6], *servi corrupti*[7], *de rationibus distrahendis*[8], *dolus*[9], and no doubt others, though in some of the cases the restriction seems to be due to Justinian[10]. The rule represents hesitation and perhaps changes of view as to their character[11]. These cases must be distinguished from *condictio furtiva* subject to the same rule[12]: this was probably correal in classical law, since it was civil and *ad rem persequendam*, while these were praetorian and penal[13].

ACTIONS TRANSMISSIBLE OR NOT TO OR AGAINST THE *HERES*. The general principle was that actions *rei persequendae causa* were available both ways, while penal actions *ex delicto* were normally available to the *heres*, but not against the *heres* of the wrongdoer (unless they had reached *litis contestatio*) except to the extent of enrichment[14]. But there were many exceptional cases. The right of action of the *adstipulator* did not pass to the *heres*[15], nor did the *querela inofficiosi testamenti*[16] or the wife's claim in *actio rei uxoriae*[17]. Conversely the liability of *sponsor* and *fidepromissor* did not pass to their *heredes*[18].

As to penal actions, the *heres* was never liable for delict of the ancestor, though there was a gradual extension of the principle that he

1 Inst. 4. 6. 19. Mitteis, *Z.S.S.* 1916, 328 *sqq.* 2 *Ante*, p. 349. 3 4. 2. 16. 2; 44. 7. 35, etc.; see below. 4 *Ante*, p. 602. 5 4. 2. 14. 15. 6 9. 3. 1. 10–3. 7 11. 3. 14. 2 (? interp.). 8 26. 7. 55. 1. 9 4. 3. 17. In *dolus* and *metus* the rule appears to be classical, due to the doctrine that it is for reparation and this ends the matter, 4. 3. 2–4, *ante*, p. 593. 10 E.g. 11. 3. 14. 2. The rule makes them solidary. The case in 9. 3. 1. 10–3 looks as if it was correal in classical law; there is not necessarily any personal delict. 11 Girard, *Man.* 427. 12 C. 4. 8. 1. 13 Much recent literature as to nature and rules of penal actions. De Francisci, *Azioni penali*; Levy, *Privatstrafe* (for whom all praetorian *ac. in f.* were essentially penal in cl. law. Though they often had a reparatory function this does not make them *ad rem persequendam*. This function grows more prominent and modifies the rules, but fundamentally they are penal: it is only J. who obscures this); Riccobono, *Z.S.S.* 1927, 75. 14 Inst. 4. 12. 1. Riccobono, *cit.*, for extensions by fiction of *l. c.* where proceedings begun have not reached that stage before the death. 15 G. 3. 114. 16 *Ante*, p. 329. 17 Ulp. 6. 7. The fact that *heres* of fructuary could not sue for the usufruct does not turn on this principle: it is *interitus rei*. *Ad exhibendum* was not available either way though *heres* might be liable or entitled to it personally, 10. 4. 12. 6. 18 G. 3. 120.

could be sued to the extent of his enrichment by an action the nature of which is disputed[1]. The action against the *heres* of a municipal magistrate who failed by *dolus* or gross negligence to take proper security from a *tutor*[2] was no exception; it was quasi-contractual, available against him on ordinary rules. There were a few actions, specially *vindictam spirantes*, in which the *heres* could not sue on delict to his predecessor, e.g. *iniuriarum*[3], *de mortuo inferendo*[4], the action for unauthorised *in ius vocatio* of a *parens* or patron[5] and in a case of fraud, *calumniae causa*[6], *actio de moribus*[7] and, probably, *sepulchri violati*[8]. The rule applied to bringing the action, not to continuing one which had reached *litis contestatio*, or, in late law, had been actually begun[9].

CCXXXIV. *Actio directa, adiectitiae qualitatis.* The latter name is a modern invention to mark off a group of actions in which a *paterfamilias* or employer was made responsible for acts of subordinates. Such were *de peculio et in rem verso, tributoria, quod iussu, institoria, exercitoria, actio ad exemplum institoriae* in mandate, in all of which the name of the subordinate appeared in the *intentio* and that of the principal in the *condemnatio*. Such were the various noxal actions, in which the name of the *paterfamilias* appeared in the *intentio*[10]. The classification not being expressly stated by the Romans, views differ as to the cases properly coming under the class of *actiones adiectitiae qualitatis*. The *actio de pauperie* and the analogous aedilician action do not correspond to any direct action, but the former at least resembled a noxal action. Probably the class ought to cover the liabilities for employees of *nautae caupones* and *stabularii*[11], and the special liabilities of *publicani* for their servants[12], but the classification is unimportant[13].

1 Logically it would be *c. sine causa*, 47. 8. 2. 27. Girard, *Man.*, *loc. cit.* The notion is classical, its applications gradually widened. It is a settled general rule under Diocletian, *Hermog. Wisig.* 2. 1. Albertario (*Bull.* 1913, 112) seems to hold it nearly always due to Justinian, but is very ready to see interpolations. The introduction of the principle by Cassius is asserted by Venuleius (42. 8. 11), and though Pernice thinks this unlikely (*Labeo*, 2. 1. 199) there is much evidence of his activity as a magistrate apart from this, *ante*, p. 9. It is not clear why the whole story should be supposed untrue. Levy, *Privatstr.* 89, on the history. He holds that it was the ordinary delictal action with *condemnatio* limited to enrichment. De Francisci, *Az. pen.* 65, holds that this is so only in later law; in cl. law it was a *cond.* or an *a. in f.* See Rotondi, *Scr. Giur.* 2, 371, as to Byzantine extension (Inst. 4. 12. 1) to *dolus ex contractu*. 2 *Ante*, p. 164. 3 47. 10. 28. 4 11. 7. 9. 5 2. 4. 24. 6 3. 6. 4. 7 C. Th. 3. 13. 1; *ante*, p. 109. 8 De Francisci, *Az. pen.* 56. 9 C. 1. 20. 1. If a father sued on *iniuria* to the *filius, filii nomine*, and died after *l. c.* the action passed to the son as an individual, not to *heres* as such; 47. 10. 17. 22. 10 Lenel, *E.P.* 330. 11 *Ante*, p. 599. 12 *Ante*, p. 602. 13 The expression *actio directa* used to denote proceeding against the actual wrongdoer (G. 4. 77) is also used in other senses. *Actio directa* is opposed to *actio utilis*, e.g. under *l. Aquilia*, Inst. 4. 3. 16; opposed to *actio fictitia*, G. 4. 34; opposed to the *actio ad exhibendum* which is a preparation for it, 10. 4. 3. 13; opposed to one resulting from *restitutio in integrum*, 16. 1. 8. 13 (cp. C. 3. 32. 24), etc. *Directa* as opposed to *contraria*

ACTIO IN SIMPLUM, DUPLUM, TRIPLUM, QUADRUPLUM. There was no action for more than fourfold, though the Aquilian, which gave the highest value within a year before, might give more than four times the real *interesse*. *Actiones ad rem persequendam* were normally *in simplum*, though sometimes *in duplum contra infitiantem*, e.g. *actio ex testamento*[1]. Many penal actions were *in simplum*, e.g. *doli*, many *in duplum*, e.g. *furti nec manifesti*, *servi corrupti*, and the Aquilian action *contra infitiantem*. *Actiones in triplum* were few. Justinian mentions only a new one introduced by him for a case of *plus petitio*[2]. *Furti concepti* and *oblati* were obsolete. Fourfold actions were numerous, but *metus* differed from the others, e.g. *furti manifesti*, in that it was *arbitraria*; the penalty was incurred only if restitution was refused in the action[3].

ACTIONES QUIBUS IN SOLIDUM PERSEQUIMUR[4], *QUIBUS NON SEMPER IN SOLIDUM PERSEQUIMUR*. The latter class included various types. In some the *condemnatio* was confined to a certain fund, e.g. *de peculio et in rem verso*[5]. In the actions in which a *heres* was liable to the extent of enrichment there may have been a restrictive clause in the *condemnatio*, e.g. "*dumtaxat in id quod ad eum pervenit*[6]." Justinian includes those actions in which there was a set off[7], but this would include, potentially, nearly all actions. The *actio in factum* to the extent of enrichment surviving an *actio annua* would be another example[8]. A type distinct from these is found in actions in which the *condemnatio* was limited to the defendant's means: "*in id quod facere potest*," the so-called *beneficium competentiae*[9]. The chief cases were, the debtor who had suffered *bonorum venditio*, for one year[10], but with previous *cessio bonorum*, perpetual[11], action against patron or ascendant[12], actions against one who made a

does not seem to be usual. We find *principalis* (13. 6. 17. 1) and *recta* (h. t. 18. 4). It must be noted that there are indications in classical times of *formulae* in which the *intentio* was for mutual obligations (*alterum alteri d. f. oportere, ex f. b.*). See Cicero, *de Officiis*, 3. 17. 70; *Top*. 17. 66; G. 3. 155. These have been usually held to be distinct *formulae*, perhaps issued together, but it is maintained by Partsch (*Negotiorum Gestio*, 50 *sqq*.) that in classical law *iudicium contrarium* means a *formula* in which the *intentio* states the mutual obligation and that this was the method employed in *tutela* (*ante*, § LIX), *commodatum*, deposit, *pignus*, *fiducia*, but not mandate. The independent *actio contraria* is on this view Byzantine. P. also holds that it is only where the *formula* is of this independent type that *condemnatio* in the *iud. contrarium* does not involve infamy. Critical observations, Bortolucci, *Bull*. 1915, 192, n. 4. For a view accepting the *intentio* expressing mutual obligations in a somewhat different list of cases, including mandate, and excluding the name *iudicium contrarium* in such cases for classical law, see Biondi, *Iudicia bonae fidei*, 59. For Wenger, *Zpr*. 161, *non liquet*. Lenel, *E.P.* 319, rejects P.'s view.

1 *Ante*, p. 348. 2 Inst. 4. 6. 24. 3 *Ante*, p. 593. 4 Inst. 4. 6. 36. 5 *Ante*, p. 661. 6 If the action was *c. sine causa*, the limit would be probably in the *intentio*: if on the delict (*ante*, p. 692), some such *taxatio* as this would be needed. 7 Inst. 4. 6. 39. 8 *Ante*, p. 690. 9 Zanzucchi, *Bull*. 1916, 61 *sqq*.; Levet, *Bénéfice de Compétence*; Solazzi, *Estinz. della Obbl*. c. 13. 10 *Ante*, p. 645. 11 Inst. 4. 6. 40; D. 42. 3. 4. pr. 12 Even mother of children *volgo concepti*, 42. 1. 16; Inst. 4. 6. 38.

contract while *in potestate*, not *heres* for a substantial share to his *paterfamilias*[1], *pro socio*[2], action against a *miles*[3], action for *dos* against the wife or her *paterfamilias*[4], or for recovery of it from the husband[5] (in later law any action between husband and wife[6]), and action against donor for the gift[7]. The principle applied only to contract and quasi-contract and apart from *dolus*. In estimating the estate there was not always a deduction for debt to other persons (*occupantis potior est causa*)[8], though in some cases some debts were deducted[9], and a donor sued for the gift could deduct all debts, except those also due as gifts[10]. "*Quod facere potest*" was not the same in all cases; in general it was literally taken, but a donor was allowed to retain the necessaries of life[11], and this may have been generalised under Justinian[12]. As to *cessio bonorum* and *milites* it may be that the same rule applied in classical law[13].

The whole debt, having been brought into issue, was destroyed by *litis contestatio*. To protect the creditor, the *iudex* required the debtor to give security by verbal contract to pay the rest when he was able. We are told this of *pro socio*[14], and, for Justinian's law, of action for recovery of *dos*[15]. The language does not indicate a universal principle: it may be that in some cases, e.g. *donatio*, the right was exhausted.

This defence is said in some texts to have been raised by *exceptio*[16], but it is usually held that it was in effect a *taxatio*, raised by such words as "*dumtaxat in id quod facere potest*," in the *condemnatio*[17]. But it seems not to have been expressed in the *formula* at all in the *actio rei uxoriae*[18], which Lenel considers to have had an exceptional *formula in ius* expressing the duty as "*dotem reddere oportere*," the *condemnatio* being to "*quod aequius melius erit*," which, he thinks, covers this point[19].

Actiones Populares, Privatae. In ordinary cases there are, even before the litigation, an assignable plaintiff and defendant. But the Roman Law, like other systems, recognised cases in which, the facts being such as to affect public interests, any member of the public might sue, in some cases keeping the penalty[20], in others keeping none, or only

1 14. 5. 2. pr., 1, "*causa cognita.*" 2 Inst. 4. 6. 38; D. 42. 1. 16; cp. h. t. 22. 1, probably only in *s. omn. bon.* in cl. law, Levet, *cit.* 47. 3 42. 1. 18. 4 Conflict and gradual growth of doctrine, Arnò, *Arch. Giur.* 1926. 5 24. 3. 15. 2–17; 42. 1. 20. 6 42. 1. 20. 7 42. 1. 19. 1; Inst. 4. 6. 38. 8 42. 1. 19. 1, 61, other than judgement debts. See, however, Levet, *cit.* 157, 185, and Solazzi, *cit.* 9 *Socii*, 17. 2. 63. 3; *emancipatus*, 14. 5. 3. 10 42. 1. 19. 1. 11 *Ib.* 12 50. 17. 173. pr., Paul, a generalisation by Justinian of 42. 1. 19. 1, also Paul. The whole restriction may be of Just., Riccobono, *Cristianesimo e dir. priv.* 15. But the case of *donator* seems classical. 13 Zanzucchi, *cit.* But see Levet, *cit.* 209, whose exclusion of it for *donator* in cl. law (p. 198) is hardly successful. 14 17. 2. 63. 4. 15 C. 5. 13. 1. 7. 16 *Ante*, p. 655. 17 *Ib.* 18 24. 3. 12. 19 *E.P.* 307. 20 See p. 695, nn. 2–5.

a small part as a reward[1]. The former class, which was small, was the most important in private law. It included *sepulchri violati*[2], some cases of *res deiectae*[3], *res suspensae*[4], and *albi corruptio*[5]. The latter, a large class, is mostly concerned with local by-laws and the like.

These actions were all penal, and those specifically mentioned above were all praetorian, and, like most praetorian penal actions, *annuae.* But since no one had in general any special right to the action (though in *res deiectae* and *sepulchri violati* there were preferences in case of competition[6]) they could not exist as assets till *litis contestatio*. Thus there was no question of transmission to *heredes*, and, as penal, they were not available against *heredes*[7]. There could be no representation on the part of plaintiff, and thus no *cessio actionis*[8]. They could not be brought by *infames*[9], nor, except where relatives were preferred, by women or *pupilli*[10].

CCXXXV. We have now to consider in more detail important points in the course of an action as yet only incidentally treated.

Litis Contestatio. The point at which this occurred, and the conception of it as a contract between the parties, have already been considered[11]. We have now to state its main effects.

(i) Destruction of any obligation brought into issue. Here an important distinction must be drawn. In one class of actions, *legitima iudicia in personam*, formulated *in ius*, the old *obligatio* was destroyed "*ipso iure*," i.e. it no longer existed, so that if the action was renewed the *intentio* could not be proved; there was no *obligatio*[12]. In other actions, real or personal, *in factum* or *in ius*, *legitima* or *imperio continentia*, though the pre-existing right or obligation was destroyed, this was only *iure praetorio*, by the help of an *exceptio rei iudicatae vel in iudicium deductae*[13]. Gaius tells us[14] that in *legis actio* the destruction was always *ipso iure*, *exceptiones* not having been in use as under the *formula*. There is no reason to suppose that the bar had then any relation to the theory of *novatio necessaria*, a notion of a developed jurisprudence. It rested on the simpler notion, common to most systems of law, *non bis in idem*[15]—an

1 Karlowa, *R.Rg.* 2. 979. Instances, *l. mun. Tarent.* 4 (Girard, *Textes*, 65); *l. Col. Genetivae*, 73 (*ib.* 94). Cases in which it is fairly divided, as in our "*qui tam*" actions, occur, e.g. the penalty for breach of edictal rules as to opening of wills, 29. 5. 25. 2. The cases in which the penalty goes to the State are mostly statutory, and, where it is really *pro populo*, the name *actio popularis* is not expressly given. Sometimes only a local magistrate can bring the action; Karlowa, *R.Rg.* 2. 980 *sqq.* 2 47. 12. 3. pr. The *a. popularis* for a penalty lay where no one proceeded by the ordinary action available to those interested. 3 9. 3. 5. 5. 4 9. 3. 5. 13. 5 2. 1. 7. pr. 6 47. 12. 3. pr., 6; 9. 3. 5. 5; cp. 47. 23. 2, 3. 7 47. 23. 8. 8 47. 23. 5. 9 47. 23. 4. 10 47. 23. 6. 11 *Ante*, pp. 611, 632, 667. 12 G. 3. 180 *sq.*; 4. 106, 107. 13 *Ib.* 14 4. 108. 15 Eisele, *Abhandl.* 113. Guarneri-Citati, *Bull.* 1925, 163; Meylan, *Mél. Cornil*, 2. 83.

issue once decided must not be raised again. This must have been the governing principle in real actions, where there was no *obligatio*, and in actions *in factum*, in which no *obligatio* was expressly brought into issue. The question arises why in real actions the bar was only praetorian. The view that there was no bar in these cases in the *legis actio*, seems excluded by the general language of Gaius[1]. The system of *ipso iure* destruction was in fact applied only where the notion of *novatio* was possible, i.e. in *formulae in personam* and *in ius*, and of these, only to those to which it could have been thought of as applicable in early law, i.e. *legitima iudicia*[2]. It may be that in all cases in the early *formula* there was a *praescriptio*, and that it was only with the appearance of the *exceptio*, as we know it, that the sharp line appeared between *consumptio ipso iure* and *ope exceptionis*.

The *exceptio rei iudicatae vel in iudicium deductae* appears as one in Gaius[3], and it is widely[4] held that they were in fact but one. But since every case decided must have been *in iudicium deducta* the purpose of "*rei iudicatae*" is not plain. On the view that they were distinct it has been maintained[5] that, before the *l. Iulia*, since a *iudicium legitimum* was not barred by time, only the *exceptio rei in iud. ded.* was here available, as a judgement was the inevitable result. But in others there might be no judgement, as the expiry of the magistrate's *imperium* might destroy the *iudicium*. Here justice required that further action should be barred only by judgement. Hence the *exceptio rei iudicatae*; the two *exceptiones* thus referred to distinct classes of action, and one class of *iudicia legitima* supplied a third type, in which the bar was *ipso iure*, i.e. those *in personam, in ius*. When the *l. Iulia* introduced the risk of expiry by time (18 months) for *iudicia legitima*[6], on this view the *exceptio rei iudicatae* ought to have applied to both the types, and the other to have disappeared, but in fact we find both *exceptiones* (or both halves) applied in both cases. If we accept unity for the time of Julian, it does not follow that it was originally the same, and this view might explain the evolution, though the positive evidence is small. Of the retention of both halves and the placing of *rei iudicatae* first, though it is included in the other, Lenel's explanation[7] is that the parties used only the portion relevant

1 It has been suggested (*ante*, p. 628) that the *l. Aebutia* did not allow the *formula* in real actions, so that these would be on a different footing. But this is not generally accepted. If, as is sometimes held, *litis contestatio* in the *legis actio* was at its beginning, it is clear that the barring effect could not bear any relation to novatory effect, but must have been due to the independent rule *non bis in idem*, which barred repetition of a *legis actio*. See also Gradenwitz, *Aus Röm. und Bürg. R.* 392 *sqq.*, 402 *sqq.*, and Meylan, *cit.*
2 Meylan, *cit.*, finds its origin in *l. a. per condictionem*. 3 G. 4. 106, 107. 4 Lenel, *E.P.* 506. 5 Eisele, *Abhandl.* 1 *sqq.* 6 G. 4. 104. 7 Lenel, *E.P.*, *loc. cit.*

to the case, and as in most cases the previous litigation would have reached judgement, *rei iudicatae* was most common[1].

Modern writers distinguish from this normal function of the *exceptio rei iudicatae*, a "positive" function[2], i.e. not merely a bar to the same action between the same parties, playing the same parts, but as enforcing the principle, as between parties bound by the judgement, it must be assumed that the content of the judgement is true, not merely that there has been a judgement. This is based[3] on texts giving *exceptio rei iudicatae*, e.g. where a defendant *B* in *rei vindicatio* was defeated by *A* and afterwards vindicated[4], though the issue was not here the same. In the first case the question was whether the thing was *A*'s; in the second, whether it was *B*'s. The decision that it was *A*'s negatived the view that it was *B*'s and thus *A* could plead *res iudicata*[5]. Gaius uses similar language[6]: if in the first case judgement went for the defendant and he afterwards sued for some of the property in the hands of the plaintiff, the first suit proved nothing for the second; failure to prove that it was *A*'s was no proof that it was *B*'s. This merely expresses the true principle of the *exceptio*. But where the *exceptio rei iudicatae* was used by the loser in the previous action there was a *replicatio* "*rei secundum se* (plaintiff) *iudicatae*[7]."

We are told that there must be identity of *Res*, *Causa* and Person[8] but this needs defining. *Eadem res* means the same object[9]. It need not be the same *formula*—*actio in factum* on deposit would bar *actio in ius* on the same facts. It need not be the same action but the point must be the same[10]: *vindicatio* would not formally bar *condictio furtiva*[11]. The language twice quoted by Ulpian, from Julian[12], requires "*eadem quaestio*[13]," i.e. the question which it is now proposed to submit to the *iudex* must have been in substance already so submitted, so that a decision in the second case would necessarily be on a point already decided. As Paul put it[14]: "*singulis controversiis singulas actiones sufficere.*" The *causa*, i.e. the basis of claim, must be the same, but here a distinction is to be drawn. Real actions brought in and barred future action on all possible

1 If the case is decided for the plaintiff, in real actions, there is a *pronuntiatio* rather than a judgement: it has been suggested that here the *exceptio* would be "*rei secundum se pronuntiatae*," the texts which speak here of *res iudicata* being on this view interpolated. Little evidence is offered. Beseler, *Beitr.* 2. 139. See Mitteis, *Z.S.S.* 1912, 206 *sqq.*
2 See Levy, *Konkurrenz*, 1, 124; Leonhard, *Festsch. f. Dahn*, 2. 67; Wenger, *Zpr.* 207.
3 Keller-Wach, *C.P.* 363. Against the "positive" function, Eisele, *Z.S.S.* 1914, 326.
4 44. 2. 30. 1. 5 3. 3. 40. 2. 6 44. 2. 15. 7 44. 2. 9. 1. 8 44. 2. 27. Cp. h. t. 12–14.
9 In 44. 2. 12, 13 this appears as *idem corpus*, *idem ius*, *eadem quantitas*, but this last is not necessary, h. t. 7. pr. 10 44. 2. 3, 5, 8, 25. 1. 11 44. 2. 31; cp. 5. 3. 47; C. 3. 31. 3.
12 44. 2. 3, 7. 4. 13 Perhaps the word is interp. Beseler, *Beitr.* 2. 144; 4. 266. 14 44. 2. 6.

causae of the claim[1], except where the claim was expressly limited to a specific basis[2]. This did not bar action on a title accruing subsequently to the first action[3], or action against the same defendant on a subsequently accruing basis of liability[4]. But Paul, in a corrupt text, says that personal actions are different; each *causa* has its action[5]. This seems however to mean little more than that a claim for a debt will not bar a claim for another debt of the same amount. A claim misdescribed in the *demonstratio* can be brought again, for the real claim has not been in issue[6], and the practical result is the same if in the *intentio* a *causa* is stated which is not the real one. But there are difficulties in the case of *condictio*, where the *causa* is not stated[7].

As to *eadem res* and *eadem causa*, the main principles according to a recent work[8] are these. There is civil *consumptio* in either form only where there are the same *causa* and the same object. There is praetorian *consumptio*[9] (*denegatio actionis*) or judicial (*exceptio*, *cautio* against renewed action, etc.[10]), the latter the more usual, in many cases, wherever in fact the aim is compensation for the same harm[11]. It does not require, as it commonly does in the Digest, actual satisfaction. It arises in an increasing number of penal actions with the function of compensation. Where the same *factum* is two delicts there is commonly praetorian or judicial *consumptio*[12].

The parties must be the same. This means juristic identity[13]. The *exceptio* affected a successor, but not a predecessor, in title[14]. It covered a representative where the case had already been brought by or against the principal, and, subject to what will be said later, *vice versa*[15]. It is commonly held to cover the cases of principal and surety[16] (apart from *fideiussio indemnitatis*, where it was clearly not *eadem res*[17]), and that of

1 44. 2. 11. 1, 14. 2. 2 44. 2. 11. 2, 14. 2. 3 44. 2. 11. 4, 5, 25. pr. 4 44. 2. 9. pr., 17, 18. 5 44. 2. 14. 2. 6 *Ante*, p. 650. 7 *Ante*, p. 682. The question if, and, if so, how, the issue submitted to the *iudex* was limited in these cases, is very obscure. 8 Levy, *Konkurrenz der Aktionen*. See *post*, § CCXLII. 9 Wylie, *Solidarity and Correality*, maintains that satisfaction *consumptio* was known to cl. law in cases of joint contract, where though what was claimed was substantially the same there was some characteristic of the transaction, excluding absolute identity and thus excluding correality. 10 For Beseler, *Z.S.S.* 1924, 366, this *cautio* is Byzantine. 11 See, e.g., 17. 2. 38. 1, 43, the latter dealing with a case in which *pro socio* is brought for what could not come into *communi dividundo*. 12 *Post*, § CCXLII. On the general question it may be noted that the statement (Levy, *cit.* 1, 79) that *causa* and *res* are the same thing is a slightly misleading way of stating the fact that though the object was the same, it was not *eadem res* for this purpose unless the *causa* was also the same. The *causa* (p. 81) is the *negotium*, not the breach, the delict, not the damage. For L. (pp. 97 *sqq.*) the *causa* in a real action is the plaintiff's right, but the *causa actionis* must surely be a relation between the parties. 13 A claim by or against a man as *tutor* would not affect his rights or liabilities in his personal capacity. 14 44. 2. 4, 9. 2, 11. 9, 28. 15 44. 2. 11. 7. *Post*, § CCXXXIX. 16 But see *ante*, p. 451. 17 *Ante*, p. 451.

correi[1]. In later classical law there was an equitable extension in which identity of party is difficult to see. If the person primarily interested stood by and let judgement proceed when he could have intervened to protect his right, he was bound by the judgement, e.g. pledgee who knew that debtor was being sued for the thing, vendee in possession allowing vendor to be sued for the thing, husband allowing the wife or her father to be sued for a *res dotalis*[2]. Further it seems that if a will was upset at civil law, as *inofficiosum, ruptum* or *irritum*, so that legacies, etc., failed, the decision was binding on legatees, etc., though not on persons claiming the *hereditas* either independently of the will concerned, or not parties to the suit[3]. A remarkable extension existed in some questions of status. In claims for or against liberty, or *ingenuitas*, and some others, a decision was good not only against the actual party but against everyone[4], not in the sense that the man was conclusively held to be slave or free, etc., at the time of the judgement, but that any claim to the contrary must be independent of those then set up. This enlarged force of the judgement affected other rules. It applied only where there was a *iustus contradictor*[5]. There was machinery to deal with collusion[6], and the obscure rule as to repetition of *causae liberales*[7] was probably in some way connected with it.

Gaius puts *rei in iudicium deductae* and *rei iudicatae* on the same footing, as applying over the same field and, in general, this was so, at least in his time. The law of *compensatio* provided an exception. A *iudex* need not take *compensatio* into account. If he did, and allowed it, or rejected it as not properly due, future claim of it would be met by *exceptio rei iudicatae*. If he refused to consider it at all, it had not been in issue, and there was no *exceptio rei in iudicium deductae*[8].

CCXXXVI. The question how far the extinctive effect of *litis contestatio* was carried into the later system is disputed. There was no *ipso iure* destruction, since *legitima iudicia* had disappeared. Apart from this it may be thought to have survived to Justinian, since he abolished it for joint debtors[9], but it is not impossible that this choice among debtors equally liable (*electio*[10]) had already become an independent

1 *Ante*, p. 453. Here there is a sort of identity; they are a joint unity, but this is hardly so in surety. 2 42. 1. 63; 44. 2. 29. 1. 3 5. 2. 8. 16; 30. 50. 1. 4 1. 5. 25; 25. 3. 1. 16–3. pr.; 30. 50. 1. In this connexion we get the expression: *res iudicata pro veritate accipitur*, not of general application, Gradenwitz, *Aus Röm. und Bürg. R.* 410. Beseler, *Tijdschr.* 1928, 313, repudiates, for cl. law, any effect of *h. pet.* on legatees or *manumissi*. Esmein, *Mél. Gérardin*, 229, holds that in early law the effect of judgement was not relative but absolute and thus explains the rules of *cessio in iure*. 5 40. 16. 3; C. 7. 14. 1. 6 40. 16 *passim*. 7 Buckland, *Slavery*, 668. 8 16. 2. 7. 1. Beseler, *Beitr.* 4. 200, holds that rejection of the counterclaim as non-existent did not, in classical law, prevent it from being raised independently, the text being interp. *Post*, § CCXXXVIII. 9 C. 8. 40. 28. 10 C. 8. 40. 28. 1.

principle. There is no known enactment which abolishes the novatory effect for single debtors, and the *exceptio rei in iud. ded.* is not found in the *Corpus Iuris*, though there are traces of the old doctrine[1]. The procedure *in contumaciam* and the fact that a *iudicium* no longer perished in a short time had done away with the main applications of this *exceptio*. An enactment of uncertain date, but not later than Justinian, penalised the bringing of an action in one court if it was already pending in another[2], which suggests that, apart from penalty, such a thing was possible. It seems probable that under Justinian the extinctive effect of *litis contestatio* was practically gone[3]. It survived indeed as the basis of the law of *cessio actionum* by *procuratio*[4], but this had become a standing institution, independent of its theoretical basis.

The destructive effect of *litis contestatio* was not, even in classical law, so complete as might appear. The Edict contained rules for *restitutio* where through error in procedure, not involving great carelessness, an action had been lost[5]. There were cases in which an *actio de peculio* which had resulted in less than complete satisfaction could be renewed "*rescisso superiore iudicio*[6]." The law of *restitutio in integrum*[7] is indeed in great part a set of reliefs against the working of this principle. Where the loss was due to excessive claim there was some relief in the Edict and a full measure in later law[8]. Though there could be no change of parties after the novation, the magistrate could relieve even here in appropriate cases[9]. The rule *omnia iudicia absolutoria* is on the same lines. It is sometimes said that where an action was barred by *exceptio praeiudicii* (or the like[10]) there was relief on account of the injustice, but opinions differ[11].

(ii) Creation of a new obligation. The nature and content of this have been sufficiently indicated in dealing with judgement.

(iii) Any action which had reached *litis contestatio* was transmissible. Thus an *actio ex delicto* could be continued against the *heres*, or an *actio iniuriarum* continued by the *heres*[12].

(iv) Paul tells us that it made *actiones temporales* perpetual, which means only that if, e.g., an *actio annua* had reached *litis contestatio* it could continue to judgement though the year had expired[13].

1 E.g. 46. 2. 29. 2 C. 3. 1. 12. 2 (restored from the *Basilica*). See also C. 2. 2. 4. 3 Nothing can be inferred from C. 3. 10. 1 (*post*, p. 703), which seems to imply a power of renewing a claim: the point is raised, in the time of Zeno, before *litis contestatio*. 4 *Ante*, pp. 520, 554. 5 Lenel, *E.P.* 124 *sqq.* 6 15. 1. 30. 4, 32. pr., 47. 3; 15. 2. 1. 10. 7 *Post*, § CCXLIII. 8 *Post*, § CCXXXVII. But see n. 3. 9 5. 1. 57; Vat. Fr. 341. 10 *Ante*, p. 648. 11 Pissard, *Questions Préjudicielles*, 133. 12 *Ante*, p. 691. For "fictitious" extensions, Riccobono, *Z.S.S.* 1927, 75. 13 27. 7. 8. 1; 50. 17. 139. pr.

(v) There could be no change either in parties or *iudex*, subject to *translatio iudicii*[1].

(vi) The *res* became *litigiosa*, practically incapable of alienation[2].

(vii) *Usucapio* was not formally interrupted, but the practical effect was much the same[3]. *Praescriptio* seems to have been interrupted under Justinian by protest to an official, without litigation[4].

(viii) It fixed the subject-matter of the claim, but this rule had many limitations. The rule *omnia iudicia absolutoria*[5] modified the principle that the value was to be taken as at *l. contestatio*. It was ordinarily to be taken as at that time, but *stricta iudicia* and others differed as to inclusion of fruits and interest from that date[6]. If the object lessened in value through deterioration, or change in market prices, this did not in strictness affect the liability. But this applied in classical law only in cases of bad faith; a defendant in good faith was liable only if the deterioration was due to his fault[7]. Conversely, if the thing rose in value, this did not increase the liability unless the defendant was in bad faith, as in *c. furtiva* where the liability was for the highest value of the thing since the theft[8]. The effect of total destruction by *casus* was matter of school dispute; the view finally reached was that, apart from *dolus*, *culpa* or *mora*, it released the defendant[9]. But these rules can be applied safely only to real actions and *stricta iudicia*; in *bonae fidei iudicia* and actions *in factum* there was a multiplicity of distinctions according to circumstances, as to what could be recovered.

CCXXXVII. *Plus petitio. Minus petitio.* The rules on this topic express the logic of the *formula*. The *iudex* was to condemn only if the claim in the *intentio* was proved; in all other cases he was to absolve. If 10 were claimed and a debt of 9 was proved, *absolutio* followed. *Plus petitio* might occur in many ways[10]; *re*, claiming too much, *tempore*, claiming before it was due or while a condition was unsatisfied, *loco*, claiming at one place what was due at another, or *causa*, ignoring any alternative or option in the debtor[11]. In all such cases the action was lost in classical law, and, in general, finally lost, except for relief by praetorian *restitutio*, which Gaius mentions[12], and which Justinian tells us had been given to minors and in some cases of error[13]. In an action for an *incertum*, since the *intentio* said "*quidquid paret...dare facere oportere*," Gaius tells us there could be no *plus petitio*[14]. But this seems not clear except for excess in amount. If a claim was made *ante diem*, the action was appar-

1 Vat. Fr. 341; C. 3. 1. 16. *Post*, § CCXLI. 2 *Post*, § CCXLIV. 3 *Ante*, p. 243. 4 *Ante*, p. 250. 5 *Ante*, p. 639. 6 *Ante*, p. 680. 7 Girard, *Man.* 370, n. 1. 8 13. 1. 8. 1. 9 5. 3. 40. pr.; 6. 1. 15. 3. 10 In a rescript of Diocletian (Cons. 5. 7) it is said that it may be either *summa, loco, tempore, causa, qualitate, aestimatione.* 11 G. 4. 53d; Inst. 4. 6. 33d. 12 G. 4. 53. 13 Inst. 4. 6. 33. 14 G. 4. 54.

ently lost (though it is possible that the words "*quidquid*" and "*ex fide bona*" allowed the *iudex* to condemn for the present value of the claim) and finally lost, apart from *restitutio*. So if it was made *pendente condicione*, but here, at least on one view, the occurrence of the condition created a new obligation on which action could be brought[1]. If *A* or *B* was due at the defendant's choice, and *A* was claimed, this was a *plus petitio*[2] and might certainly occur in an action for an *incertum*, and the same is true if what was due in one place was claimed in another[3]. The special *actio* "*de eo quod certo loco*[4]" avoided the difficulty in this case, but it applied only to claims for *certa*[5]. It seems that there might be a risk of *plus petitio* in *incerta*. In *bonae fidei* cases[6] the *iudex* could make the necessary allowance.

An overstatement in the *demonstratio* was fatal to the action, but Gaius says "*nihil in iudicium deducitur*[7]": the action could be renewed (subject to the opinion of some jurists, that in infaming actions overclaim in the *demonstratio* was as fatal as in the *intentio*[8]). The effect is that if the *demonstratio* is not true there was no action; its truth is a condition not on *condemnatio* but on submission to the *iudex*. In actions *in factum* with an *intentio* "*si paret,*" Gaius, in a defective text[9], seems to say that overstatement in it was a *plus petitio*, but this probably does not apply to the actions "*ex bono et aequo.*" An overstatement in the *condemnatio* led only to *restitutio* as a matter of course[10].

It was not *plus petitio* to claim the wrong thing: the action was lost, but the real matter had not been in issue[11].

Minus petitio was claiming too little. This, in the *intentio*, bound the plaintiff in that action, but did not bar a new action, subject to the *exceptio litis dividuae*[12]. If in the *demonstratio*, Gaius holds, as in *plus petitio*, that "*nihil in iudicium deducitur,*" but adds that others, including Labeo, held the (more reasonable) view that it was lawful so to divide the claim, subject to the above *exceptio*[13]. *Minus petitio* in the *condemnatio* bound the plaintiff with no *restitutio* except for minority[14].

These classical rules resting on the *formula* were much changed in later law when this was gone. There was no longer any question of

1 *Ante*, p. 443. 2 G. 4. 53d; Inst. 4. 6. 33d. 3 G. 4. 53c; Inst. 4. 6. 33c. 4 *Ante*, p. 660. 5 Lenel, *E.P.* 241. 6 13. 4. 7. 7 G. 4. 58. 8 G. 4. 60. As to the use of this text in support of hypotheses on the origin of the *formula*, see Huvelin, *Mél. Gérardin*, 337; Audibert, *Mél. Girard*, 1. 62, and *ante*, § CCXIV. 9 G. 4. 60. De Visscher, *N.R.H.* 1925, 202, holds that this is not Gaius and that there could be no *p. p.* in them. The *initium* is not, for him, an *intentio* (*ante*, p. 652). But as he holds that it states the facts essential in the view of the Praetor to *condemnatio* (p. 223) and the action is certainly lost if some of these are not proved, the point seems little more than verbal. 10 G. 4. 57. 11 G. 4. 55; Inst. 4. 6. 35. 12 G. 4. 56; *ante*, p. 654. 13 G. 4. 58, 59. This seems to have prevailed, 13. 6. 17. 4. 14 G. 4. 57.

different parts of the statement, and Zeno provided[1] that in *plus petitio tempore* the plaintiff must wait twice the time by which he anticipated the true date, getting no interest for this time and paying all costs due to his wrongful claim. The *iudex* was to pay no attention to *minus petitio* but to condemn for what was due[2]. For other forms of *plus petitio* Justinian provided that the *iudex* was to ignore them and condemn for what was due, the plaintiff paying threefold the excess costs[3].

CCXXXVIII. *Compensatio*[4]. Set off. If *A* sued *B* on a promise of 10, the fact that *A* owed *B* something on some other transaction was irrelevant to the issue before the *iudex*. This liability could not be joined to the first, so as to permit the *iudex* to try both on one issue and strike a balance. The Roman habit[5] and the structure of the *formula* did not admit of the fusion of two issues. No doubt both might be submitted to the same judge, even at the same time, but they were distinct issues, *mutuae petitiones*[6]. To this exclusion there were even in early classical law some exceptions. Where a banker sued his customer he was required to allow what was called "*compensatio*" in the *intentio* of his action, claiming only the net balance due, after deducting anything actually due from him to the defendant, provided the debt was of the same kind[7] as that for which he was suing, commonly money[8]. If he failed to make this allowance, he lost his action, for *plus petitio*. The two debts being balanced, he had claimed more than was due. All mutual claims may have come into account and been consumed[9]. This rule did not turn on any logical distinction; it was one of convenience, resting on the confidential position of *argentarii* in commercial Rome. Most business was done through them. When the practice of private bookkeeping went out, the bankers were their customers' bookkeepers[10], a fact reflected in another edictal rule[11]: in any litigation the banker's books might be called for, though he was not a party. Our rule safeguarded illiterate persons against concealment by a banker who knew more of their affairs than they did themselves.

Another exceptional case was that of *bonorum emptor* in bankruptcy.

1 Or declared: his language does not suggest a new rule, Kipp, *Z.S.S.* 1921, 353.
2 C. 3. 10. 1.
3 C. 3. 10. 2. He adds (h. t. 3) that a plaintiff who has fraudulently got an acknowledgement from the debtor for more than is due, and submits this at the hearing, shall lose his action altogether. This is punishment for fraud, not a rule of procedure.
4 Appleton, *Histoire de la Compensation*; Biondi, *Compensazione*; Leonhard, *Mél. Girard*, 2. 85.
5 Pound, *J.R.S.* 1921, 275, observes that this attitude is not specially Roman, but is common to all early law. What seems Roman is the adherence to it at a stage of high development.
6 2. 1. 11. 1; 17. 1. 38. pr.; C. 4. 31. 6. Accarias, *Précis*, 2. 1104, and *ante*, p. 693.
7 Some held that it must be of the same quality, G. 4. 66.
8 G. 4. 64, 68.
9 Biondi, *cit.*, who seems to treat it as a matter of course. It seems unlikely: the injustice, where the debtor is ignorant, and happens not to raise a particular debt, is obvious.
10 See, e.g., 2. 13. 10. 1, 4. 1.
11 2. 13. 4 *sqq.*

If he sued a debtor to the bankrupt or deceased insolvent, he was required by the Edict[1] to allow for any debt due from the estate to the defendant. It need not be of the same kind or now payable; a debt due at a future day must be allowed for at its present value. But the *emptor* had no special knowledge of the relations between these parties and was not compelled to run the risk of *plus petitio*; the allowance was not by "*compensatio*" in the *intentio*, but by "*deductio*" in the *condemnatio*, where, as Gaius says, *periculum non intervenit*. Thus even though the claim was for a *certum*, "*incerti tamen condemnationem concipit*[2]." Apparently the *deductio* was inserted only on the defendant's request[3], but the omission of it could be set right by *restitutio in integrum*, as in any excessive *condemnatio*. This *deductio* did not rest on logical considerations, but on convenience and fairness. Apart from some such rule the debtor to the insolvent would have had to pay in full what he owed, getting only a dividend on what was due to him. Accordingly, if he paid without taking account of the counterclaim, he could recover[4].

Another exception was more important: it was general and rested on the logic of the *formula*. In all *b.f. iudicia* the *iudex* might, if he thought fit, allow, on grounds of good faith, any set off arising out of the same transaction, condemning for the balance. As the *intentio* claimed only what was due *ex fide bona*, there was no question of *plus petitio*, or any express reference to the set off[5].

The exclusion of all such matters in *stricta iudicia* remained[6] till a rescript of Marcus Aurelius of which Justinian tells us[7] that, by it, "*opposita doli mali exceptione, compensatio inducebatur*," in *stricta iudicia*. We know little of the system, since it was superseded under Justinian and unknown to Gaius. Since such *iudicia* were on unilateral transactions, the debt must have been in another transaction. It was perhaps confined

1 Lenel, *E.P.* 427. 2 G. 4. 66 *sqq.* 3 See G., *loc. cit.* The *argentarius* "*cogitur cum compensatione agere*" the *deductio* "*obicitur*" to the *emptor*. The view that *b. emptor* must deduct only in proportion to the dividend (Accarias, *Précis*, 1. 1319, as to which see Appleton, *Compensation*, 164) is revived by Biondi, *cit.*, 29, basing mainly on G. 4. 65, "*deducto quod bonorum emptor defraudatoris nomine debet*," which he says can mean only the dividend. But the text of G. is not to be construed as if it were a statute and the resulting rule is inacceptable. *A* and *B* have *contra* accounts of equal amount. At any moment they may be wiped out by a word. *A* now becomes insolvent and on this principle, *B* at once owes him something. See the analogous case, 16. 2. 9. pr. and Kreller, *Z.S.S.* 1929, 510. 4 I.e. claiming under his original right, 12. 6. 30. 5 G. 4. 47, 61–63. 6 It is sometimes said that the Praetor allowed at his discretion an *exceptio doli* where there was a counterclaim of the same kind. But P. 2. 5. 3 seems to refer only to the known cases, and this may be true of the texts in the D. In 44. 4. 4. 8 it is not a question of set off but of an implied *pactum*. See however, Jörs, *R.R.* 138; *S.M.W.* 492, and *post*, p. 705. 7 Inst. 4. 6. 30.

to debts of the same kind[1], but different views are held, as also on the question whether the rule extended in practice to *bonae fidei iudicia.* Probably these remained under the old rule, as Justinian states the rule for them and then that for *stricta iudicia* after M. Aurelius and suggests no reaction on the other case[2]. It is true that the *exceptio doli* was implied in *bonae fidei iudicia,* but it was not expressed and it is unlikely that the defendant should have been able, where there was such a counterclaim, to decide at any stage to upset the action, or not, without notice to the plaintiff. In *stricta iudicia* the difficulty did not arise; the *exceptio* must be demanded, and this would warn the plaintiff.

The ground on which the action was lost was not *plus petitio,* otherwise there would have been no need of *exceptio doli;* the mere failure to allow for the counterclaim would destroy the action, *ipso iure.* Moreover the right to sue later on the counterclaim was not affected by the fact that no account of it had been taken in this action[3], which could hardly be the case if it had been *ipso iure* in issue in the earlier action; there would have been an *exceptio rei iudicatae.*

It has been assumed above that failure to allow for the counterclaim, after insertion of the *exceptio,* involved loss of the action, but it has been maintained that the effect was merely to cause reduction of the *condemnatio* by the amount of the counterclaim[4]. The former solution is alone consistent with the general theory of the *exceptio.* The *iudex* was bound to absolve if an *exceptio* was proved[5], and this is the view most usually held in the present case. But the contrary view is supported on various grounds. It is said that it is unfair that a plaintiff should fail for not taking account of a set off of which he might not know the amount. But the claim of the *exceptio* was notice to him and the form for *argentarius*[6] was presumably available. Before allowing the *exceptio* the Praetor would require details of the counterclaim. It is said that Justinian shews no difference between the rules under the rescript of M. Aurelius and the old rules in *b. f. iudicia*[7], and Theophilus implies that there was none and that the action was not lost[8]. But in historical matters in which Gaius does not help, Theophilus is of little weight, and Justinian says that he is making a change and that in his system claims "*ipso iure minuunt,*" which suggests that this had not been so in *stricta iudicia,* to which the passage refers, though the novelty might be only in the words "*ipso iure.*" Again it is said that an *exceptio* did not necessarily upset an action. Several texts in the Digest say this, for the *exceptio doli* amongst others. But the *formula* had long been extinct and

1 P. 2. 5. 3. Very probably it was of narrow scope, Biondi, *cit.* 34, 43. 2 Inst. 4. 6. 30, 39. 3 16. 2. 7. 1. Girard, *Man.* 753. 4 E.g. Accarias, *Précis,* 2. 1108; Salkowski, *Inst.* (8), 441. 5 Apart from *replicatio,* not here in question. 6 G. 4. 64. 7 Inst. *loc. cit.* 8 Theoph. *ad Inst.* 4. 6. 30.

different rules were applied in the *cognitio*, so that the word *exceptio* and the rules stated for it in texts handled by the compilers are of little weight[1]. The case of the so-called *beneficium competentiae* is *prima facie* a strong one, but this was no doubt a *taxatio* in classical law[2]. But neither view is absolutely proved[3].

The law in *cognitiones* is not clear, but reduction may have become the rule there, in some cases (in view of the great power of the magistrate), and thus a model for Justinian[4]. He reorganised the matter, allowing *compensatio* of the same or different kinds (if it was so far "liquid" that it could be conveniently estimated in that suit) in all actions but deposit, and for recovery of land wrongfully occupied[5]. The rule applies to real as well as to personal actions, and under it "*actiones ipso iure minuunt.*" Thus the effect is reduction, but, for the rest, his rule is obscure. In real actions the judgement was for the *res* itself, and it is not clear how the allowance was made, possibly by way of *retentio* as in the case of chargeable expenses, or by set-off against *fructus*. In some cases indeed the *condemnatio* would have to be in money, e.g. where the defendant had destroyed the thing, or had *dolo malo* ceased to possess[6].

1 Most general statement 44. 1. 22. See also 16. 1. 17. 2, certainly, and 30. 85, probably, interp. 2 *Ante*, § CCXXIV. 3 Riccobono, *Dal Dir. Rom.* 392, holds that the *exceptio doli* necessarily led to loss of the action. Wenger, *Zpr.* 148, holds that it might diminish the *condemnatio*. But of the texts he cites 44. 1. 2. 2 is "too good to be true" for cl. law: it is designed to express the new doctrine. It contrasts sharply with Ulpian's "*quaedam exclusio*" (h. t. 2. pr.). In 24. 3. 17. 2 which he cites as a clear case, nothing is said of the effect of the *exceptio*. Arangio Ruiz, *L' exceptio in dimin. dalla condanna*, observes that the question of the *compensatio* must sometimes have needed discussion *apud iudicem* and cites texts which suggest that obedience to the principle was more formal than real. And, since the *exceptio* contemplates *dolus* after *l. c.* ("*factum sit neque fiat*"), it does not seem impossible that the *iudex* may have had power to dismiss the suit unless the plaintiff consented to a reduced judgement. 4 C. 4. 31. 12, commonly cited to shew a reform by Diocletian (e.g. Taubenschlag, *Rom. Prr. z. Z. Diocl.* 269), seems neither new nor significant. Where parties have struck a balance, payment of the rest of the larger debt frees pledges. 5 Inst. 4. 6. 30; C. 4. 31. 14. (As to counterclaim on a natural obligation, *ante*, p. 552.) The counterclaim must not be conditional or *in diem* (16. 2. 7. pr.) apart from days of grace under a judgement (h. t. 16. 1). It must be defendant's own claim in the same capacity (C. 4. 31. 9; D. 16. 2. 18. 1) and against the same person (16. 2. 16. pr.), except that a debt due to a *correus socius* of deft. can be pleaded as there is regress between them (45. 2. 10). For this reason a *fideiussor* can plead a set-off of his principal (16. 2. 5). A *tutor* suing as such could not be met by a debt due from him personally (16. 2. 23). It might be pending in another suit (h. t. 8). It must be clear: an alternative *obligatio* could not be pleaded, if the creditor had the choice, until he had chosen (16. 2. 22), but a debt due at another place could be pleaded with proper allowances (16. 2. 15). It might be raised in *actio iudicati*, though not mentioned in the original action (C. 4. 31. 2). It might be a claim *de peculio* and even here it was *in solidum* (16. 2. 9. pr.). The *iudex* need not take account of it: if he simply ignored it, it was not in issue and could still be sued on, but if the *iudex* examined and rejected it this was in effect a judgement, and any further claim was barred by *exceptio rei iudicatae* (16. 2. 7. 1). 6 The rule of Justinian that a plaintiff might be condemned (C. 7. 45. 14) might be understood to cover this case.

The words "*ipso iure*," much discussed, do not mean that the set-off operated as matter of course, for, as we have seen, the defendant need not use it and could sue on it independently, while if it had necessarily been in issue, there would have been an *exceptio rei iudicatae*. They may mean merely that it could come in without express mention in the *libellus conventionis*, with no question of *plus petitio* and its penalties[1]. Thus at no stage did Roman Law recognise a necessary *compensatio*, operating as matter of law, apart from act of the defendant. One case approaches this idea. In an action for recovery of *dos* we are told that "*necessariae impensae dotem ipso iure minuunt*[2]" while *impensae utiles*, if approved by the wife, can be brought into account by *exceptio doli*[3]. This may be ancient[4], but there is little evidence of that[5]; it seems to result from the conception of *dos* as a *universitas*, and, even so, *impensae* were not necessarily in issue, since if the husband did not deduct in the action for *dos*, he could condict afterwards[6], as could be done in other cases of counterclaim[7]. It must be remembered that the *actio rei uxoriae* was a *bonae fidei iudicium* in which no *exceptio doli* would need to be expressed. The case of *peculium*, *ipso iure* cut down by debts to *dominus*[8], is again a *pro tanto* recognition of it as a *universitas*. It no doubt originated as an interpretation of legacy of *peculium*[9].

1 Severus Alexander provided that where there was a liquid claim on each side there was "*ipso iure compensatio*" from the moment the two debts coexisted (C. 4. 31. 4). Girard (*Man*. 753, n. 3) observes that this rule, probably laid down by Septimius for a specific case (16. 2. 11, 12), and afterwards generalised (C. 4. 31. 5; C. 8. 42. 7), was merely an equitable rule to simplify the final calculation. See also Leonhard, *Mél. Girard*, 2. 97 *sqq*. But see also n. 9, below. 2 23. 4. 5. 2; Ulp. 6. 14 *sqq*.; *ante*, p. 109. 3 See hereon, Schulz, *Z.S.S.* 1913, 57 (reply, Riccobono, *Dal Dir. Rom.* 370); Bonfante, *Corso*, 1. 364; Beseler, *St. Bonfante*, 2. 77. 4 Ihering Geist (4), 3. 69; French transl. 4. 66. 5 But see Pernice, *Labeo*, 2. 1. 386: he does not carry it far back. See also Ulpian in 25. 1. 5, who hesitates as to the exact meaning of the rule. 6 25. 1. 5. 2. 7 *Ante*, § XL, and Schulz, *cit.* 8 19. 1. 30. pr. 9 See, e.g., 33. 8. 6. 1. *Argentarius*; *ante*, p. 703. Biondi, *cit.* 127, holds that Justinian's "*ipso iure*" means not indeed that the mere existence of the counterclaim extinguishes the debt, but that if it is raised and satisfies his requirements it operates by law—the *iudex* only declares it—and extinguishes the debt from the moment of coexistence. The rule (for him, new) that *mutuae petitiones* go to the same *iudex* (2. 1. 11. 1) is to facilitate the working of the system (p. 111). The "*ipso iure*" found in many texts on the point he attributes to Justinian (pp. 127 *sqq*.), but some of them seem clearly classical and to refer to *b. f. iudicia*. He observes however that often there is a new sense—mutual extinction antedated—and "*ipso iure*" is often substituted for *ope exceptionis*. But he hardly shews that this question of mutual extinction, cesser of interest and so forth did not arise under the old system in *b. f. iudicia*. He objects (p. 157), not without reason in their generality, to texts giving *c. indebiti* where there might have been *compensatio*, and shews the Byzantines speaking of *compensatio* where the classics spoke of *retentio, imputatio, confusio*. It is difficult to accept all his allegations of interpolation or to be sure that J.'s change is much more than a generalisation of what some had held for *b. f. iudicia*. See hereon, Kreller, *Z.S.S.* 1929, 515.

CCXXXIX. REPRESENTATION IN LITIGATION[1]. In the *legis actio* there was in general no representation: *nemo pro alio lege agere potest.* Justinian, who tells us this, mentions as, apparently, all the exceptions, a provision of the *l. Hostilia,* allowing *actio furti* on behalf of a captive or one absent on State affairs, or their ward, and three other cases which he calls *pro populo, pro libertate* and *pro tutela*[2]. The first is probably a reference to early *actiones populares* and has little real relation to representation; the second is *adsertio libertatis*[3], and the third is obscure. The most probable opinions are that it refers to the *crimen suspecti tutoris* which was open to anyone, was very ancient and heard by the magistrate[4], or to action on behalf of a ward, though this does not suit the name very well[5]. But the fact that representation was not possible in the *legis actio* does not prove impossibility in the actual hearing, which is no part of the *legis actio,* and a text in the *Ad Herennium,* quoting, apparently, an old *lex,* authorising aged and sick people to appoint *cognitores,* has led to the view that they were allowed at this stage in such exceptional cases[6]. It is also held, in view of, *inter alia,* the form of appointment of a *cognitor*[7], which is archaic, and follows closely the structure of other ancient forms, e.g. that of *manus iniectio,* that no restriction to special cases existed but that this *cognitor* was a general institution of the *legis actio*[8]. But this is not generally accepted[9]; in any case we know representation only in the later systems.

Apart from *tutores* and *curatores*[10], representatives were *cognitores* or *procuratores.* Not everyone could be a representative or appoint one. A *miles* could not be one for disciplinary reasons[11], or a woman because it was a *virile munus*[12]. The Edict contained provisions, imperfectly known[13], forbidding some persons, notably *infames* and *ignominiosi,* to appoint, or to be themselves appointed, representatives for this purpose, in some cases absolutely, in others without consent of the other party. It is clear that the point might be decided by the Praetor *in iure*[14]. But it might be settled *in iudicio,* and there were *exceptiones cognitoriae*[15], *procuratoriae,* by which such points were brought up. These are suitable only for objections made by the defendant; it seems that plaintiff's objection to a *cognitor* of his opponent must have been disposed of *in iure.*

1 G. 4. 82. 2 Inst. 4. 10. pr. 3 *Ante,* p. 73. 4 Girard, *Org. Judic.* 1. 70 and 75, n. 1, points out that this process was not a civil *legis actio.* 5 Bertolini, *Proc. Civ.* 1. 188, compares "*pro socio.*" For explanations Girard, *cit.*: Bertolini, *cit.*; Cuq, *Inst. Jurid.* 1. 408; Karlowa, *C.P.* 355. 6 *Rh. ad Her.* 2. 13. 20; Lenel, *Z.S.S.* 1883, 149. 7 G. 4. 83. 8 Eisele, *Beitr.* 91; *Stud.* 51; Frese, *Mél. Cornil,* 1. 327. 9 No direct evidence: the laxer rules of the formality (p. 709, n. 5) are against great antiquity: formlessness is not an essential of praetorian institutions. 10 *Post,* p. 710. 11 Inst. 4. 13. 11; C. 2. 12. 7, 9. 12 Inst. 4. 13. 11; C. 2. 12. 18. 13 P. 1. 2. 1; Vat. Fr. 320–324. Lenel, *E.P.* 89 *sqq.*; Debray, *N.R.H.* 1912, 370. 14 Vat. Fr. 322. 15 G. 4. 124; Inst. *cit.*

After the decay of the *formula* these questions seem to have been settled before *litis contestatio*[1]. Justinian abolished these *exceptiones*, at least so far as *infames* were concerned, as not being used[2], and in fact little is said in the *Corpus Iuris Civilis* on this matter, though it is clear that the disabilities or some of them still existed[3].

Representation appeared earlier in litigation than in substantive law, but at first it was short of what is called direct representation. The *cognitor* did not then "represent" in the modern sense: he was the actual party, who was condemned or absolved, and had or was liable to the *actio iudicati*[4]. But, at latest by the time of Cicero, judgement for or against a formally appointed *cognitor* affected the principal. It seems however that from the beginning he brought his principal's case into issue, so that, on the principle of "*non bis in idem,*" further action was barred.

Cognitores were appointed in the presence of the other party by "*certa et quasi solemnia verba.*" Gaius gives two forms, apparently as alternatives[5], but the difference between them ("*quod...peto, petis,*" "*quod...agere volo, agere vis*") may have to do with the type of action, or more probably with the place and time of appointment, and has played a part in the controversy as to origin[6]. There could be no condition on the appointment[7]. The *cognitor* need not be present, but if he was not, the appointment was not effective until he had accepted[8]. *Procuratores* were appointed informally[9] (so much so that one could act without appointment at all[10], *defensor*), but in any case he must be in existence by *litis contestatio*. The *formula* shewed in what capacity the party was acting, since the principal's name appeared in the *intentio*[11] and the representative's in the *condemnatio*[12]. The *formula* could not be altered; any further change must be by *translatio iudicii*[13].

These two kinds of agent did not in earlier classical law represent the

1 C. Th. 2. 12. 3 = C. 2. 12. 24. 2 Inst. *cit.* The *exceptio procuratoria* appears in the Digest, 3. 3. 57. 1; 17. 1. 29. 4, etc. 3 C. 2. 12. 6, 7, 9. 4 On behalf of defendant he is more like a *vindex* than a representative. 5 G. 4. 83. Added words did not vitiate the appointment, and it might be in Greek (Vat. Fr. 318, 319). 6 *Peto* is held by Wlassak to denote the moment of *litis contestatio*. This he thinks the original form, obsolete in classical law, see *Aut*. Gai. 91 (*Cognitur*, 44; *Mél. Girard*, 2. 637). But there is textual evidence for *peto* in the sense of action after *litis contestatio*, and Eisele holds (*Beitr*. 99) that this form was used where a *cognitor* was appointed *in iudicio*. But there is no evidence for such appointment. 7 Vat. Fr. 329. 8 G. 4. 83. 9 G. 4. 84, even conditionally, D. 3. 3. 3. For Frese, *Mél. Cornil*, 1. 327; *St. Bonfante*, 4. 399, cl. law knew no *procurator ad litem*. He was the ordinary *procurator*, general manager It follows that the *procurator* of G. 2. 39 and 2. 252 are glosses. The same must presumably be true of G. 4. 182. This view is difficult to accept. 10 E.g. G. 4. 84. Certain near connexions who acted without express appointment were on the same level as if appointed, 46. 7. 3. 3. For Frese, *cit.*, the *voluntarius procurator* is post-classical. 11 In the *formula* of a real action the principal would not appear at all in the case of *cognitio* for the defence. 12 G. 4. 86, 87. 13 *Post*, § CCXLI.

principal to the same extent. *Cognitor* for a plaintiff, duly appointed, with notice to the opponent, brought into issue the right of his principal, whose right of action was therefore consumed[1]. A *procurator* did not, so that the claim might possibly be renewed, a distinction reflected in the law as to the security which must be given. If the representative was on the defendant's side, since the plaintiff's right was necessarily in issue, security was always needed[2]. The *actio iudicati* must *prima facie* go to or against the person named in the *condemnatio*. But the Edict seems to have given it to or against the principal in the case of a *cognitor*[3], though this may have required a *translatio iudicii*[4]. It is said to have been allowed "*causa cognita*[5]," but that means only that if it was a case of *cognitio in rem suam* it was not so given.

In the case of *procurator* the *actio iudicati* was available under the Edict only to or against him[6]. But he was gradually assimilated to the *cognitor*, and in later classical law a *procurator* whose intervention was ratified, or whose principal was present, or who was appointed "*apud acta*," or had what Severus calls "*plena potestas agendi*," fully represented his principal, so that the latter's right was brought into issue, and the *actio iudicati*, with formal *translatio iudicii*, was available to and against him[7]. The *cognitor* had disappeared under Justinian, and the *procurator* whose powers were certain fully represented his principal[8]. But a mere volunteer, a *defensor*, or one of uncertain authorisation, was still in the old position and personally responsible.

The *tutor* also could represent his ward[9]. We know little of this matter in the *legis actio*. The rule of the *l. Hostilia* above mentioned[10] suggests that *tutores* could act at least in *furtum*, probably in all cases. It is likely in view of the early conception of *tutela*[11] that this was not thought of as representation; the rights were regarded as vested in the *tutor*. As to *curator furiosi* or *prodigi*, the XII Tables describe his power as *potestas* over the man and his *pecunia*[12]; he could alienate for him[13] and perhaps acquire. Pomponius says that the *curator furiosi* could not manumit for him[14], and this was a *legis actio*, but this is on the ground that manumission is not administration, so that there was probably no formal difficulty. However these questions are answered, the rules of classical law are fairly clear. Intervention by any of those guardians is

1 G. 4. 97, 98. 2 G. 4. 101. 3 Vat. Fr. 317, 331. 4 *Post*, § CCXLI. 5 Vat. Fr. *cit.* 6 No edict needed: his name is in the *condemnatio*, Lenel, *E.P.* 404. 7 C. 2. 12. 10; Vat. Fr. 317. 8 Inst. 4. 11. 4, 5. Disputes as to how far this is an advance on later classical law. See, e.g., Costa, *Profilo storico*, 127, who thinks (on Vat. Fr. 311, 317) that the wider extension is post-classical. Wenger, *Zpr.* 88, dates it from the time of Severus. 9 G. 4. 99. Apparently any acting *tutor*, within his field of operations. 46. 7. 3. 5; *ante*, § LVIII. 10 *Ante*, p. 708. 11 *Ante*, p. 142. 12 5. 7a. Girard, *Textes*, 14. 13 *Ante*, p. 168. 14 40. 1. 13.

treated as representation, and Gaius[1] shews that they were in most respects on the footing of an authorised *procurator*, and, in some[2], attained practical equality with *cognitor* before a *procurator* did.

The position of *curator minoris* is disputed. The Digest puts him on the same footing as *tutor*, but there has probably been much alteration of the texts. Possibly, at any rate till the third century, he had no such power; he could be appointed as *cognitor* or *procurator*, or act without appointment, as *defensor*, but that is a different matter[3].

Corporate bodies, incapable of acting for themselves, had, of necessity, representatives to act for them, called *actores*[4], appointed *ad hoc* in classical law, but, later, permanent, these being also called *syndici*[5]. There were rules as to the mode of appointment, applicable in all cases, and the appointment must also accord with their statutes[6], but a *procurator voluntarius* could act for them[7] as for ordinary persons[8].

CCXL. SECURITY IN LITIGATION. It is convenient to deal first with the case in which the principals were the parties, dealing afterwards with the complications which resulted from representation.

The plaintiff did not in general give security. The defendant, in classical law, gave, in real actions, security varying in form according as the action was *per formulam petitoriam* or *per sponsionem*. In the former case, which was a purely formulary creation, he gave security *iudicatum solvi*[9], an undertaking by surety, *satisdatio*, having three branches embodied in one *stipulatio*[10]; to satisfy the judgement if given against him, to defend, i.e. to take the necessary steps in order that the matter (which involves the cooperation of the parties) may proceed, and to commit (and to have committed in any earlier stage) no *dolus* in respect of the subject-matter (*clausula doli*)[11]. In actions *per sponsionem*, the security was *satisdatio pro praede litis et vindiciarum*[12], modelled on the old *praedes* of the *legis actio* of which this procedure is the descendant. As this mode is wholly obsolete under Justinian we are ill informed as to its content. The view most widely held is that of Lenel[13], that in different form it involved a promise of "*quanti ea res erit*" for the same hypotheses

1 G. 4. 101. 2 E.g. *de rato*, G. 4. 99. 3 Solazzi, *Minore Età*, 202 *sqq.*; Lenel, *Z.S.S.* 1914, 197 *sqq.*; *ante*, § LXII. 4 E.g. 2. 4. 10. 4. 5 3. 4. 1. 1. Dirksen, *Manuale*, s.v. *Syndicus*. 6 3. 4. 3. 7 3. 4. 1. 3. A duly appointed *actor* seems to have been in the position of a *cognitor*. See Ramadier, *Ét. Girard*, 1. 259 *sqq.* 8 "*Is qui liti se obtulit*" who appears in several texts, e.g. 7. 6. 5. 5; h. t. 6; 5. 3. 45; 6. 1 7, is not a representative. He is one who (commonly for purposes of fraud) accepts a *iudicium* in a real action in which he is not concerned. The D. gives the action against him, but the better view is that in cl. law he would be discharged as not possessing, but would be liable for *dolus*. Maria, *Ét. Girard*, 2. 237 and reff. and *ante*, p. 319. 9 G. 4. 91. 10 46. 7. 6. 11 Exact formulation disputed. For Lenel, it contained a promise of the amount of the judgement under the first head and "*quanti ea res erit*" under the others. Other views, *E.P.* 530 *sqq.*, and Duquesne, *Mél. Gérardin*, 197, *Mél. Fitting*, 1. 323, and Lenel's reply, *E.P.* 533. 12 G. 4. 91, 94. 13 *E.P.* 517 *sqq.*

as in the other case, i.e. for judgement (which, here, it must be remembered, was only for the amount of the *sponsio*, so that a *stipulatio* simply of the amount of the judgement would not have sufficed[1]), for failure to defend, and against fraud, past or future.

In actions *in personam* there was in general no security, but Gaius tells us that it was required in certain actions, i.e. *iudicati*, *depensi* and the old *actio de moribus*, and that it was also required in some cases by the Praetor where the defendant was suspect, as one who "*decoxerit*" (fraudulent bankrupt), one whose goods had already been seized for debt, and a defendant *heres* whom the Praetor thought suspect[2].

Under Justinian the system was much changed[3]. In real actions the judgement was normally for the thing itself, and it had become impossible for the defendant to transfer the *res litigiosa* in any way so as to bar the plaintiff's claim[4]. Moreover, the "real[5]" issue was involved with an increasing number of personal claims. Of the three actions *in personam* in which security was needed two, perhaps all, had disappeared[6]. Thus the need of security was gone in general where the parties were the principals. He tells us that there was no longer need for security in respect of the subject of the suit, but that the defendant must always give security for appearance[7]. But this is merely the modernised form of *vadimonium, cautio iudicio sisti*. He tells us that this was sometimes by oath, e.g. for those "*in sacro scrinio militantes*[8]" or by mere promise, as in case of *illustres*, or, in ordinary cases, by *satisdatio*, varying with the status of the parties[9].

The rules were more complex in the case of representation.

1. Representation on the side of the plaintiff. There was an important difference between *cognitor* and other representatives. In the time of Gaius the *cognitor* fully represented the principal and therefore gave no special security[10]. As other representatives, procurators and guardians, did not directly represent the principal it was possible for him to renew the action, his right not being in issue, and they must give security that the principal would ratify their action, *cautio de rato, rem ratam habiturum dominum*[11]. But complete representation was gradually extended to

1 "*si secundum me iudicatum erit, quanti ea res erit.*" 2 G. 4. 102. 3 Inst. 4. 11. 2. 4 *Post*, § CCXLIV. 5 Girard, *Man.* 372. 6 *Actio iudicati, ante*, p. 672. G. 4. 102 is not represented by anything in Inst. and D. 46. 7 says nothing of security after judgement. The cases of *heres suspectus* and defendant whose goods have been seized still remain. 42. 5. 31. pr., 33. 1. The edictal rule about *decoctor* is replaced by a rule that security can be required from a *suspecta persona* sued for a *res mobilis*, but not for land, probably only in real actions. 2. 8. 7. 2, 15. 7 Inst. 4. 11. 2. 8 C. 12. 19. 12. 9 D. 2. 6; D. 2. 11. 10 G. 4. 97. 11 G. 4. 98. There was also a *stipulatio amplius non peti*. It survived into Julian's edict (Lenel, *E.P.* 541; Debray, *N.R.H.* 1912, 5 *sqq.*), though of little value after the introduction of *de rato* with which it was usually coupled.

these. For *tutores* and *curatores* (*furiosi* and *prodigi*) the rule requiring *cautio de rato* was partially relaxed in the time of Gaius[1], and in the time of Severus this was required only from one whose powers were uncertain, e.g. one whose principal was not present and might have revoked the powers or one not authorised at all, *procurator voluntarius*[2]. This remained the law under Justinian except that *curator minoris* was now treated as a *tutor*. The promise was that the principal would ratify and would not renew the action, and that there had been and should be no *dolus*, the liability being for "*quanti ea res erit*[3]." It required *satisdatio*[4]. It was discharged by ratification[5], and was broken by renewed action by anyone who would have been barred by *res iudicata*, if the original action had been by the principal[6].

2. Representation on the side of the defendant. The general rule was that security *iudicatum solvi* must be given, since the plaintiff's right, being brought into issue, was destroyed. The rule dates from the state of things when representation even by *cognitor* was imperfect: it applied in all cases, whether the right was brought into issue or not: *omnimodo satisdari debet, quia nemo alienae rei sine satisdatione defensor idoneus intellegitur*[7]. The only distinction was that if the representative was a *cognitor* the principal gave it, in other cases the representative[8]. The principle remained under Justinian, though there were changes in detail. There were no *cognitores*. If the principal was present he gave security *iudicatum solvi*, or, if he preferred, could become surety for his representative, for all the clauses of *iudicatum solvi*, having in both cases to give also a hypothec[9] over his property and security *iudicio sisti*[10]. If the representative was *procurator voluntarius*, or the principal was not present, the representative gave security *iudicatum solvi*[11].

CCXLI. *Translatio Iudicii*. If, as is commonly held, *litis contestatio* was a *negotium* between the litigants[12], the terms being expressed in the *formula*, it follows, as is clear in fact, that no material change in the issue, e.g. insertion of an *exceptio*, or correction of *plus petitio*, could be made except by *r. in integrum*, involving a new *litis contestatio* and thus a new *negotium* and issue. Logically the same should be true of any change of persons. There are texts dealing with substitution of one person for another in the litigation, such a change being called *translatio iudicii*[13]. But as, under the libellary system, the strict rules of the *formula*

1 G. 4. 99. 2 C. 2. 12. 10; Vat. Fr. 317, 333. 3 Lenel, *E.P.* 541. 4 46. 8. 4, 8. pr., 23, etc. 5 46. 8. 12, 18. 6 46. 8. 1, 8. 1, 14, 22. 8. 7 G. 4. 101; Inst. 4. 11. 1. 8 G. 4. 101. 9 Inst. 4. 11. 4. Meaningless: the representative was not now liable to proceedings under the judgement. 10 Inst. 4. 11. 4. 11 Inst. 4. 11. 5. 12 *Ante*, p. 632. 13 3. 3. 27. pr.; 27. 7. 8. 1, etc.

no longer applied, traces of the institution are few and leave much uncertain; the matter is the subject of recent studies[1].

If the introduction of a new party called for a new *litis contestatio*, and *restitutio*, we must ask whether the transferred *iudicium* was a new one or the same transferred[2]. The texts do not settle this: the effects shewn in the texts are not those either of a wholly new *iudicium* or of a continuation of the old[3]; there is indeed no text which clearly says that *restitutio* was necessary in any of these cases. The rules applied do not help us much. Thus the question whether the procedural securities given for the old *iudicium* were valid for the new[4] is not decisive, since we are not certainly informed as to the wording of these securities.

The principal cases suggested by the texts are three.

(*a*) Those connected with representation. The Edict contained a provision[5] that a principal who had appointed a *cognitor*, could, on cause shewn, have the *iudicium* transferred to himself or another *cognitor*, and in practice a similar initiative was allowed to the *cognitor*[6]. No such rule applied to a *procurator*, but, here too, the *procurator* was assimilated to the *cognitor*, late in the classical age[7]. This *translatio iudicii cognitoria* is recorded, but we do not know the mechanism. In the case of *cognitor* of the plaintiff the security *iudicatum solvi* given by the defence was still valid[8]: in that of *procurator* it was not[9]. Hence Koschaker[10] holds that in the case of *cognitor* the transfer was effected officially with no new *litis contestatio* and no effect on the position of the parties, while in the other case there was a new *litis contestatio*, with *restitutio*. The old issue was destroyed and a new one created. He holds that the destructive effect of the old *litis contestatio* was avoided by a fiction "*ac si de ea re actum non esset.*" It is shewn by Duquesne that this does not fully meet the difficulty. If the action was *annalis* and the year expired while the first action was pending, or was one ended by death (e.g. *ex delicto*), and the defendant whose *procurator* was defending had died, the fiction would not suffice to prevent the operation of the rules barring the action. He takes a different view; for him there was *restitutio* in all *translatio iudicii*, and a new *litis contestatio*. The old *lis* was not necessarily completely destroyed. He suggests a fiction, evidenced in the texts, by means of which the new *litis contestatio* was dated the same day as the first, *litis contestatio repetita die*, which would avoid these difficulties[11]. But all the cases of *litis contestatio repetita die* which he finds are between the same parties. In none of them is a *litis contestatio* in the same civil action set

1 Koschaker, *Translatio Iudicii*; Duquesne, *Translatio Iudicii*. 2 Koschaker, 53 *sqq.*; Duquesne, 56 *sqq.* 3 Duquesne, *loc. cit.* 4 Koschaker, 72 *sqq.*; Duquesne, 59 *sqq.* 5 Vat. Fr. 341. 6 3. 3. 24. 7 See Duquesne, 161. 8 3. 3. 27. 1, written of *cognitor*. 9 20. 6. 1. 2. 10 *Op. cit.* 57 *sqq.*; 72 *sqq.* 11 *Op. cit.* 99.

aside. In all but one of them[1] it is in a purely praetorian procedure, so that his hypothesis is hardly proved[2].

(*b*) Succession. *Translatio iudicii successoria,* i.e. where a party dies *pendente lite,* and a *heres* takes his place. As a *heres* succeeds *ipso iure* to the rights and liabilities of the deceased at civil law and those under *litis contestatio* are not different from others, and the texts make it clear that the new *iudicium* was essentially the same as the old[3], all the incidents being retained, it might seem that there was here no *translatio* at all, though texts call it a *iudicium translatum*[4] and others indicate that there was a new *editio* and *acceptio iudicii*[5]. Koschaker holds[6] that there was no new *litis contestatio*: the *accipere iudicium* which is evidenced was a procedural contract, *sui generis,* which had the positive effects of *litis contestatio* without destroying the old[7]. Duquesne[8], pointing out that this is no more than a *litis contestatio* deprived arbitrarily of some of its effects, applies the same method as before, but some further refinement seems to be needed[9].

(*c*) Change of *Iudex*, dead, excused or removed. In this case everything is doubtful; but we hear that the *iudicium* must "*transferri*[10]." If the *iudex* was a party to the procedural contract, or a term in it, any change of *iudex* involved *translatio iudicii.* If he was appointed after *litis contestatio* the difficulty would not arise[11]; his personality would be no part of the procedural contract. Duquesne holds that he was appointed at *litis contestatio,* and that *mutatio iudicis* involves a new *litis contestatio* to which he applies the conception of *repetitio diei*[12]. Wlassak, holding that, though there is a new reference to the magistrate, this is not a new *litis contestatio* but a procedural contract, *sui generis,* supposes a *praescriptio*: "*ea res agatur de mutando iudice*" or the like, leaving the *iudicium* the same[13].

1 10. 4. 9. 6. *Absolutio* in *ad exhibendum* is refused in the circumstances unless deft. will accept a *vindicatio die repetita.* 2 The *intentio* is in the name of the principal, but if the new *cognitor* has been freed since *l. c.* in the first action, this requires him to have been appointed when he was *incapax.* 3 3. 2. 14; 47. 10. 28; 50. 16. 12; Duquesne, 165. 4 27. 7. 8. 1; C. 5. 53. 4. 5 E.g. 10. 2. 48. 6 *Op. cit.* 254. 7 Similar view for all cases of *translatio iudicii,* Wlassak, *Judicationsbefehl,* 61. 8 *Op. cit.* 167. 9 The formula suggested by D., who argues strongly for an *intentio* in the name of the deceased (p. 191), is not free from difficulties. It would require judgement even where it had already been given in a *iudicium legitimum,* or in a case in which the earlier *iudicium* had been extinguished by the expiration of 18 months. But it is possible on his framework to provide against this. 10 50. 5. 13. 3. 11 Lenel, *Z.S.S.* 1913, 337, cited Duquesne, 225. See also Partsch, *Schriftformel,* 32. 12 Duquesne, *loc. cit.* 13 *Judicationsbefehl,* 237 *sq.* D. 5. 1. 76. But if the name of the *iudex* is part of the procedural contract, this, however limited, is to vary the contract; this is explained by Wlassak's view of *translatio iudicii* in general (*ib.* 61) as not making a new *iudicium* but only altering it. But it is not easy to see why if it can be "*verändert*" in one respect, i.e. as to parties, it could not in any other.

The other cases of *translatio iudicii* are not helpful, as the point is involved with other issues so complex as to make it difficult to deduce any rule from them for *translatio iudicii* itself. Duquesne mentions three types of such cases. (i) Where a party underwent *capitis deminutio*[1]; (ii) noxal cases, e.g. where a slave the subject of a noxal action became *heres*, the ordinary successoral *translatio* being complicated by the change from noxal to direct action[2], or where the slave, a *statuliber*, became free during the action[3], or where a supposed slave was proved, during the action, to be free[4]; (iii) cases of transfer between *pater* and *filius*, e.g. an action by *pater*, suing *nomine filii* for an *iniuria* to the son, was transferred to the son[5], and a group of cases in which an action to which the son was a party was transferred to the *pater*[6].

CCXLII. Cumulation of actions[7]. One set of facts might give rise to more than one action. A defect in a thing sold might give the *actio ex empto* or the *redhibitoria*. A depositee who made away with the thing was liable *ex deposito*, and was also a *fur*. If a hirer of a slave wilfully killed him there might be action on the contract, the Aquilian action, and criminal proceedings. The same act might be two distinct delicts. Such a state of facts gave rise to questions as to the extent to which the possible actions were mutually exclusive or cumulative. The factors which create the difficulty in determining the rules may be roughly summarised. There were disputes and changes of doctrine among the classical jurists on some points. Many of the texts have clearly been altered by Justinian, and cannot readily be reconstructed. The recorded differences of opinion do not usually shew on what difference of principle they turn. And the statement that one action barred another is ambiguous. It might mean that *litis contestatio* barred, or judgement, or satisfaction. The bar might be civil or praetorian. In some cases the bar was partial; the second action might be brought, but only for excess over what was recoverable in the first. The matter has been the subject of much discussion. So far as both the actions are *ad rem persequendam*, it will suffice to refer to what has already been said[8], but something must be added as to cases of delict.

If the facts give an action *ad rem persequendam* and one *ad poenam persequendam*, distinctions must be drawn. If the delictal action is purely for a penalty (e.g. *furti*) the two claims are quite independent. If the delictal claim includes compensation (e.g. the Aquilian) though there was no procedural bar, there was praetorian or judicial relief against double

1 5. 2. 22. 3; Duquesne, 194. 2 3. 2. 14. 3 9. 4. 15. 4 40. 12. 24. 4. 5 47. 10. 17. 14, 22. 6 Duquesne, 207. 7 Levy, *Konkurrenz der Aktionen*. 8 *Ante*, § ccxxxv. As to the question from the point of view of *praeiudicium*, Pissard, *Les questions préjudicielles*, and *ante*, § ccxxi.

recovery on the lines already mentioned[1]. But under Justinian the delictal action could be brought after the contractual, for any excess recoverable.

Where the same act constituted two delicts the law is obscure, not for lack of authority: the texts are numerous, and some of them shew that the law was unsettled in classical times[2]. There are many possibilities. The two might conceivably be entirely independent. Each might bar the other, absolutely or by *exceptio*. Or there might be relief. The most acceptable account of an uncertain matter seems to be as follows[3]. If both the *causa*, the fact, and the aim of the action are the same, there is a complete bar. But this rarely happens: there is always some distinguishing feature. *Rapina* needs violence: *furtum* does not. *Quod vi aut clam* needs force or secrecy. *Arborum furtim caesarum* needs secrecy. The Aquilian needs neither. In such cases there is no bar, but there is an equitable notion that one act should involve only one penalty. Accordingly there was a praetorian or judicial bar, usually the latter. The methods are various. The Praetor might refuse the second action or give an *exceptio doli*. The *iudex* in the first action might refuse judgement unless the other was released. The *iudex* in the second action, where he has a free hand, e.g. has to decide *ex bono et aequo*, as in *iniuria*[4], might absolve if compensation had already been recovered. Where more was recoverable under the second a simple bar was unjust, and here the second action would be allowed only on renunciation of *actio iudicati* under the first. It is only Justinian who allows action for the excess, a method which ignores the "strict" character of most delictal actions. It is however plain that all were not agreed: some were for civil bar[5] on the ground of identity of *causa* and the maxim—one act, one penalty. Some were for absolute cumulation[6] and as the discussions are cut out we do not know the reasoning[7].

On concurrence of delictal and criminal liability the texts are con-

1 *Ante*, p. 698. 2 E.g. 44. 7. 32, 34. pr.; 47. 10. 7. 1. 3 Levy, *Konkurrenz*, 2. 1. 178. 4 44. 7. 34. pr. 5 *Ib.* 6 47. 7. 1, 11, where the civil and praetorian actions are confused. The cumulation in 44. 7. 60 and 50. 17. 130 is compilers' work, Levy, *cit.* 2. 1. 225. 7 It must be admitted that these results, rational as they are, involve so much reconstruction of texts that they cannot be called certain. Other opinions, Eisele, *Arch. f. Cp.* 1892. 327; Ferrini, *Dir. Pen. Rom.* 235 *sqq.*, cited Levy. Older views, vitiated by the fact that insufficient account is taken of compilers' changes, are, e.g., those of Mommsen, *Strafr.* 887, who thinks excess recoverable where they are remedies for distinct evils but not otherwise; Karlowa, *R.Rg.* 2. 985, who thinks them cumulative if based on different enactments, in early law, but where one or both was edictal, it was matter of the Praetor's intent, and that, in cl. law, the cumulation was met by one of the above devices; Pernice, *Sachbesch.* 132, who holds that, where the two wrongs involved only one state of facts, the second action lay for any excess, but, if the act produced two facts, each of which was a delict, they were absolutely independent, e.g. a *servus corruptus* stole.

fusing[1]. The law of Justinian was not the same as classical law, the mode of criminal prosecution having changed. The law may not have been the same for all cases of concurrence. An obscure text[2] suggests that where the delictal action aimed merely at compensation, as opposed to punishment of the offender, which was the aim of criminal proceedings, they were quite distinct, and a post-classical text draws a similar distinction[3]. According to Mommsen[4], so long as the old system of criminal procedure subsisted, the private action could not be brought while a criminal proceeding was pending or possible, but where the injury consisted in damage to property rights, as in *damnum* and theft, this rule did not apply: whichever was brought first, the other could be brought nevertheless. For later law he holds that no general rule can be laid down. Sometimes the possibility of criminal proceedings barred the others, often there was a choice[5]. But one text[6] gives a list of cases, all affecting property, in which civil proceedings could be brought, though a crime had been committed. The text cites these, including *damnum* and *furtum*, as cases in which, by the civil proceedings, a *praeiudicium* was created for the subsequent criminal proceedings, i.e. they were cumulative. We are also told[7] that the Aquilian action could be brought before criminal proceedings, but that no *praeiudicium* should result for the latter. It seems that the earlier case would in fact have decided the point or part of the point which would be in issue in the criminal proceedings, but that in those proceedings no account was to be taken of the earlier decision.[8]

Note on the Terminology of Actions

Where the Praetor is extending or modifying the field of an existing action, he uses the word *actio*. But where he gives a completely new action unknown to the civil law, he says "*iudicium dabo*" (e.g. *actio doli*, D. 4. 3. 1. 1).

It is usual to speak of the proceeding before the *iudex* as "*in iudicio*" as opposed to that before the Praetor, which is "*in iure*", but it has been shewn by Wlassak[9] that the phase is properly called "*apud iudicem*". The word "*iudicium*" is freely used to denote the whole process from *litis contestatio* to judgement (inclusive), thus including the last act *in iure*, but in some of the texts it is difficult to resist the impression that it is the hearing which the writer has in mind. Jurists' language is not as rigid as statutory language is, or should be, and this interpretation seems inevitable in e.g. G. 4. 109, where *imperio continebitur iudicium* is in the future tense, i.e. following *agatur* which refers to *litis contestatio*. *Agere* and *actio* refer properly to the moment of *litis contestatio*, but Gaius, 4. 95, can speak of *agere apud centumviros*. Strictly *actio* is appropriate for an *actio in personam* and *petitio* for *actio in rem*, whereas claims by the *cognitio* procedure, whether *in rem* or *in personam*, were described as *persecutio*. But at no time was terminology rigorous and *actio* tends to cover all.

1 See those cited by Monro, *l. Aquilia*, 5, and Coll. 12. 7. 2; D. 19. 5. 14. 1; 47. 2. 93; 47. 11. 5. 2 47. 10. 7. 1. 3 C. Th. 9. 20. 1 = C. 9. 31. 1. 4 *Loc. cit.* 5 47. 2. 57. 1. 6 48. 1. 4. 7 9. 2. 23. 9. 8 See C. 9. 31. 1. 2, "*per alteram quae supererit iudicatum liceat retractari.*" 9 Reff. in Wenger, *Institutes of R.L. of Civil Proc.* 190, n. 1.

CHAPTER XV

THE LAW OF PROCEDURE (*cont.*). PRAETORIAN REMEDIES

CCXLIII. *Restitutio in Integrum*, p. 719; CCXLIV. *Dolus*, 721; *Metus*, *ib.*; Minority, *ib.*; Absence, 722; Other cases, *ib.*; Scope of *Restitutio*, 723; CCXLV. *Missio in possessionem*, 724; Judgement and connected cases, *ib.*; Other cases affecting the whole estate of defendant, 725; Cases affecting a whole estate, not necessarily the whole estate of defendant, *ib.*; Cases affecting specific things, 727; CCXLVI. *Stipulationes praetoriae*, 728; CCXLVII. Interdicts, 729; CCXLVIII. Exhibitory, Restitutory, Prohibitory, 731; CCXLIX. Non-Possessory and Possessory, 732; *Adipiscendae, Retinendae Recuperandae Possessionis causa*, 733; CCL. Procedure under Single Interdicts, 736; CCLI. Procedure under Double Interdicts, 740; CCLII. Later history of Interdicts, 743.

CCXLIII. It has been necessary to speak incidentally of various praetorian methods of remedy and constraint other than ordinary actions. Some account of these devices follows[1].

Restitutio in Integrum[2]. An exercise of the Praetor's *imperium* by which, in effect, he caused to be treated as non-existent some event which had prejudiced a person's legal position[3]. It was in some respects the most significant of the specially praetorian remedies. *M. in possessionem* was in general a way of putting pressure on a party, and often had nothing final about it. *Stipulationes praetoriae* were mainly ancillary to the civil law, and Interdicts, though in origin they protected substantive final rights, and in some cases still had that character in classical law, were nevertheless, in these cases, in furtherance of, not in opposition to, the civil law, and in the chief field of their operation for private law, the protection of possession, they gave a provisional result[4]. But *restitutio in integrum* definitely destroyed rights existing at civil law, though they might be based on a statute, even the XII Tables[5].

Restitutio in integrum was given normally by decree of the Praetor, based on *imperium*[6] and issued on application after enquiry[7]. The application had in general to be made within an *annus utilis*, i.e. within a year, as it seems of *dies utiles*, from the time when the disability ceased[8],

1 Jobbé-Duval, *St. Bonfante*, 3. 165, brings out the point that they are essentially *iurisdictio*. 2 P. 1. 7; D. 4. 1. 3 4. 1. 1, 2, 7. 1. 4 *Post*, § CCXLVII. 5 See, e.g., 4. 1. 6 *in f.* Of course *actiones honorariae* and *exceptiones* might do the same. 6 50. 1. 26. 7 4. 1. 3. In some cases there was no decree: the *formula* sent to the *iudex* left him to decide whether the grounds for relief existed; Lauria, *St. Bonfante*, 2. 514. 8 "*Ex quo annus utilis currebat*," C. 2. 52. 7, which seems to imply that it was not an *annus continuus* from that date.

except in the case of *capitis minutio*, in which it was perpetual[1]. There was post-classical legislation on this time limit[2]: Justinian provided[3] that the limit should be four actual years from the beginning of the *annus utilis*, which in ordinary cases would be the cessation of the disability, though it seems that if a new disability supervened while the first existed the time did not begin to run while this endured, even for transactions affected only by the first disability[4].

To base a claim to *restitutio* there must be shewn an *interesse*, i.e. injury to a man's property rights resulting from a transaction, or an event, such as lapse of time, which has had legal consequences[5]. No rule specifies exactly what injuries to property sufficed, but there must have been such an injury. There was no *restitutio* from a marriage, since this could be undone at will[6], but there might be from a conveyance of *dos* which had been made[7]. A gift of liberty was irrevocable, and thus there was no *restitutio*, even where it was given under a *fideicommissum* in a codicil afterwards proved a *falsum*[8]. Conversely there was no *restitutio* where a minor had sold himself or let himself be sold as a slave and had suffered the penal enslavement which resulted, the reason assigned being that there was no *restitutio* from a *status mutatio*[9] (a proposition quite distinct from the rules we shall meet under which some of its effects could be set aside[10]). This implies that there was no *restitutio* from *adrogatio* or *adoptio*, and this seems to have been the law. No text allows revocation of an *adoptio* in this way, and indeed no property right seems to have been affected in classical law, but there is a text in which Ulpian holds somewhat hesitatingly that a minor who, having been adrogated, "*se circumventum dicat,*" could get *restitutio*[11]. We know that an *adrogatus impubes* could for good reason get the *adrogatio* ended by *emancipatio*[12], but this was a civil process and did not annul it *ab initio*. There is no evidence that an adult could get it set aside for, e.g., *dolus*, and the treatment of *adrogatio* of a *libertinus* "*per obreptionem*[13]" makes it likely that there was no such right.

Any property loss sufficed, either *damnum emergens* or *lucrum cessans*[14], and it might be either a realised loss, e.g. a transfer of property, or a liability incurred, an obligation undertaken or the like[15], a distinction reflected in the mode of relief.

1 4. 5. 2. 5. 2 C. Th. 2. 16. 2=C. 2. 52. 5. 3 C. 2. 52. 7. 4 C. 2. 52. 3. Changes in J.'s own legislation, Schulz (*St. Bonfante*, 1. 346), who makes much use of the argument that the compilers could not have left standing a text in direct conflict with the Code, if it had so stood in the first Code. This is to overrate both their carefulness and their competence. 5 4. 1. 1–4. 6 No effect on property. 7 4. 4. 9. 1. 8 40. 4. 47. pr.; 4. 4. 9. 6. Except by the Emperor, h. t. 10. See C. 2. 30. 2, P. 1. 9. 5a; Buckland, *Slavery*, 566 *sqq*. 9 4. 4. 9. 4. 10 Buckland, *Slavery*, 428. 11 4. 4. 3. 6. 12 *Ante*, p. 126. 13 *Ante*, p. 127. 14 4. 4. 44; 4. 6. 27. 15 4. 4. 41, 44.

Besides the *damnum* there must, however, be a *iusta causa*, some ground on which the relief was claimed. Of such grounds the Edict enumerates a considerable number.

CCXLIV. 1. *Dolus*[1]. The cases in which this was ground of *restitutio* have been considered under delict[2]. The compilers have to a great extent suppressed the discussions of it[3].

2. *Metus*. Also dealt with in the law of delict[4].

3. Minority[5]. A minor could claim *restitutio* where he had suffered damage and there was no other remedy[6], provided he applied within an *annus utilis* from attaining the age of 25[7], but not if he had voluntarily confirmed his action at any time after reaching that age[8]. *Restitutio* was not a matter of course; it must be shewn that the damage was due to his minority, i.e. to his inexperience[9], credulity or "*facilitas*," not merely where it turned out badly[10], or the contract was made by his predecessor in title[11]. It was not given to relieve him from consequences of his own wrongdoing[12], or, conversely, to enable him to enforce a penalty, as opposed[13] to damages, or where he pretended to be of full age[14]. It was for his own defect, not for fraud in the other party, which was not essential[15], and, further, the presence of guardians at the transaction, even where they carried it through themselves, did not necessarily bar the claim[16].

It might be given where he was a *filiusfamilias*, but only so far as he was interested, not, in general, for the benefit of the *paterfamilias*[17]. Thus, if he contracted at his father's order, the son, if sued after *emancipatio*, could apply for relief[18], though the father if sued *quod iussu* could not. A *filia* could get relief in a matter of *dos*, because of her interest[19].

1 The *actio doli* and *actio metus* are really a sort of *r. i. i.* This explains why they had not all the characteristics of penal actions; the restoration avoids any penalty, *ante*, p. 593. Hence too the purely subsidiary character of the *a. doli* (4. 3. 1. 1, 4 *sqq.*). Whether there was a special edict giving *r. i. i.* for *dolus* as for *metus* (4. 2. 1) is not clear. Two texts cited to shew it are late (4. 1. 7; 42. 1. 33), and rest on rescripts. See however Girard, *Man.* 450.
2 *Ante*, p. 594. 3 See however 4. 1. 1; 4. 1. 7. 4 *Ante*, p. 593. 5 Opinions as to difference of conditions giving rise to *exceptio* and *actio e lege Plaetoria*, and those for *exceptio doli* and *r. i. i.*, Debray, *Mél. Girard*, 1. 265. For Partsch, *Neg. gestio*, 83, all texts giving *r. i. i.* to *pupilli*, on transactions by the *tutor*, are interp. *Contra*, Solazzi, *Bull.* 1914, 296 *sqq.* 6 4. 4. 16. pr., 3. 7 4. 4. 1. 1; 4. 4. 19; C. 2. 24. 1. Events might make it impossible, see, e.g., 4. 4. 24. 2. 8 4. 4. 3. 2; C. 2. 45. 1, 2, it does not follow that in an appropriate case he would not have an *exceptio doli* as an adult would.
9 A minor may be relieved against another where only one was *captus*, 4. 4. 11. 6, Ulp. against Pomponius: the text also deals with the case where both are *capti*. If a minor contracted and gave security he could be *restitutus* in respect of both, 4. 4. 13. pr. 10 4. 4. 11. 3, 4, 44. The Praetor enquires: "*animadvertam*," 4. 4. 1. 1; "*causa cognita*," 4. 4. 16, 44.
11 4. 4. 1. 1. 12 4. 4. 9. 2. 13 4. 4. 37. pr. 14 C. 2. 42. 3, 4. 15 4. 4. 7. 7. C. 2. 21. 5. pr. 16 4. 4. 39. 1, 47; C. 2. 24. 1–5. 17 4. 4. 3. 4. 18 4. 4. 3. 4. The reference to action before *emancipatio* is in part at least interpolated. 19 4. 4. 3. 5.

If the son contracted not *iussu patris* and did not apply for relief, the father could do it for him on account of his liability *de peculio*[1], which, on principle, could not exceed that of the son.

4. Absence[2]. The Edict stated some cases of absence leading to loss of property or barring of a right by lapse of time, or loss of an action for non-appearance, and promised *restitutio* within an *annus utilis* from the time when the difficulty ceased[3]. The cases are, absence compelled by fear, or *bona fide* on State affairs, imprisonment, *de facto* slavery, *captivitas*, and some similar cases of absence of the other party, so that proceedings were impossible. It covered cases other than absence; a magistrate had been prevented by *intercessio* from acting, or had delayed matters so that the claim was time-barred, or the other party could not be *in ius vocatus*. It added that the same relief would be given in other similar cases[4]. The normal remedy was an *actio rescissoria*.

5. Error. This was not in general a cause of *restitutio*, but the Edict allowed it in certain procedural cases, some cases of *plus petitio*[5], and omission of an *exceptio peremptoria*[6].

6. Alienation *mutandi iudicii causa*[7]. Where one, in view of litigation, transferred the subject-matter to another, so as to change the conditions of the litigation, the Praetor gave *restitutio in integrum* and an *actio annalis in factum*, for the *interesse*, not available against the *heres*. Some cases in which this applied are *vindicatio* of property or servitude, e.g. where the thing was transferred to a "*potentior*," *aquae pluviae arcendae* and *operis novi nuntiatio*[8]. The *restitutio* is suppressed in the Digest, perhaps because *vindicatio* now lay against one who had *dolo malo* ceased to possess. The field of each remedy can hardly be determined[9].

1 4. 4. 27. pr. 2 Lenel, *E.P.* 120. 3 4. 6. 28. 3, 4. 4 4. 6. 26. 9–28. 1. 5 G. 4. 53; for adults only where the error was entirely excusable. Inst. 4. 6. 33. Another case, G. 4. 57. 6 G. 4. 125. See P. 1. 7. 2. Lenel (*E.P.* 124) cites 44. 2. 2, similar relief in a "*dilatoria*" case, of which Gaius doubts the possibility. 7 D. 4. 7. De Francisci, *Azioni pen.* 35. 8 C. 2. 54; D. 4. 7. 3, 4; "*quod vi aut clam*" also mentioned in h. t. 3. 9 The existence of this *r. i. i.* has been denied: discussion and statement of principal views, Pissard, *N.R.H.* 1910. 377 *sqq.*; Lenel, *E.P.* 125; Beseler, *Beiträge*, 2. 153 *sqq.*; Kretschmar, *Z.S.S.* 1919, 136; 1928, 556; Wenger, *Zpr.* 172. The machinery was apparently distinct from that dealing with alienation of a *res litigiosa*. By an edict of Augustus any sale of property the subject of pending litigation, by the plaintiff, was forbidden, an *exceptio* being given in any action by the buyer, who was also liable to a penalty, presumably only if he acted knowing the state of things (G. 4. 117a; *Fr. de i. fisci*, 8). The *exceptio*, which may have been *in factum* and stated in the Edict (Lenel, *E.P.* 513), did not prevent sale by a defendant, in possession. An enactment of 380 (C. 8. 36. 3) dealt with gift by will of such things by either party and provided, in effect, that the bequest should not be operative till the litigation was over. In 532 Justinian declared void all transfers by either party, a buyer with knowledge being bound to restore the property and pay an equivalent penalty to the *fiscus*; an innocent buyer could recover the price and one-third more (C. 8. 36. 5).

There were other *restitutiones* of less importance, e.g. where one had dealt in good faith with a *pupillus* under the *auctoritas* of one not in fact *tutor*[1], creditors of one who had been adrogated or had passed into *manus*[2], or had been emancipated[3], where a *heres* had entered *coactus* and the *fideicommissum* had failed to operate[4], and at least some cases of *translatio iudicii*[5].

The damage against which relief might be claimed being of many kinds, the relief itself varied. If a right of action, or of property, had been lost, the remedy was an *actio rescissoria*[6], with a fiction that the disqualifying event had not occurred. Where an obligation had been incurred, the remedy might be *exceptio*[7] or *denegatio actionis*[8]. Where the relief was against entry on a *hereditas*, it was by refusal of *actiones hereditariae*, both ways[9]. In some cases it was an *actio in factum* or *utilis* of some sort[10]. But all this is by ordinary procedural machinery. The Praetor's enquiry resulted in a decree of *restitutio*; the further steps under this, apart from *denegatio actionis*, were, in general, judicial, not praetorian *cognitiones*. In two texts, however, we are told that the Praetor himself, in the case of sale by a minor, could order the acts needed to effect the *restitutio*[11]. This does not appear in any other case.

The questions remain: against whom and in favour of whom might *restitutio* be granted? On the first point we have seen that the rules in *dolus* differ from those in *metus*[12]. Apart from this, it was available against the wrongdoer or the immediate beneficiary, or his universal successors, but not against ordinary acquirers from him[13], while minors could get *restitutio in rem*, i.e. against any holder, the defendant having a right to claim from his *auctor*[14]. It was excluded, however, against a patron or *pater* under Justinian[15] who says that the classics had doubted, and a decree was of no avail against persons not summoned to the *cognitio* of the Praetor: it was *res inter alios acta*[16]. On the second point it is laid down that the *heres* or other universal successor of one entitled to *restitutio* had the same right for the rest of the time left to the deceased, with a further provision that where the *heres* was himself a minor this time ran only from the moment when his minority ceased[17]. *Restitutio* against *dolus* or *metus* released sureties for the person affected[18], but

1 27. 6. 1, etc. 2 *Ante*, p. 398; Lenel, *E.P.* 117. 3 *Ante*, p. 141. 4 *Ante*, p. 356. 5 *Ante*, § CCXLI. 6 E.g. 4. 6. 28. 5. 7 E.g. 4. 2. 9. 3. 8 E.g. 4. 4. 27. 1. 9 4. 2. 21. 5. 10 E.g. 4. 5. 2. 1; 4. 7. 4. 5. The nature of these consequent steps leads Jobbé-Duval (*St. Bonfante*, 3. 185) to the probable view that it is later than the *l. Aebutia*. 11 See Girard, *Man.* 1130, n. 3, who attributes this to the word "*animadvertam.*" D. 4. 4. 13. 1 is explicit; h. t. 24. 4 less so; h. t. 41 has probably been altered. 12 *Ante*, p. 595. 13 4. 6. 21. 1. *Milites* have special privilege, 4. 6. 17. 14 4. 4. 13. 1, 15. 15 C. 2. 41. 2. 16 4. 4. 29. 2. 17 4. 1. 6; 4. 4. 19; Lenel, *E.P.* 129, doubting the authority of 4. 4. 19 on the last point. 18 4. 2. 14. 6; C. 2. 23. 2.

restitutio of a minor did not necessarily release his sureties since it may have been on account of his minority that sureties were taken[1]. They were, however, released if there was *dolus* or the like[2], and if the *restitutio* was against acceptance of a *hereditas*, any sureties were released whose liability was undertaken not for the man affected, personally, but for him in his capacity as *heres*[3].

There were cases of *restitutio* not provided for in the Edict, but resulting from juristic *interpretatio*. Where one had brought an *actio de peculio* and had not obtained full satisfaction, he could get *restitutio in integrum* though *litis contestatio* had consumed his right[4]. There are many other cases, some of them, no doubt, due to Justinian.

CCXLV. *Missio in Possessionem*[5]. This was ordered by *decretum* of a magistrate having *imperium*, and thus was not within the powers of a municipal magistrate[6]. Essentially it is giving to a party to a dispute, actual or potential, some amount of possessory right over property. Its purposes varied and thus its effects were not uniform. In some cases it covered the whole property of a person, in others a complex of property, e.g. a *hereditas*, not necessarily all the property of the person affected, in others a specific thing. It was provisional, but examination of some of the cases shews that in the long run it might have the effect of destroying civil law rights. The chief cases were:

M. in possessionem on a judgement, with the connected cases. In a certain sense, all *missio* is "*rei servandae causa*," but the name is specially applied to cases in this group, that of *iudicatus* or *condemnatus*, *latitans*, *indefensus*, deceased insolvent without a *heres*, one who has made *cessio bonorum*, and *qui capitali crimine damnatus est*[7]. The ultimate effects of this *missio* have been considered; it might result in *bonorum venditio*, but in some cases the decree led to the appointment of a *curator* and to a limited right of sale or no such right at all, as in the case of persons of senatorian rank or *pupilli indefensi*[8].

The decree gave a right to take possession, but did not effect the actual transfer of possession, in fact or in law. The creditors might take possession for custody, but, under the first decree, might not expel the debtor[9]. They might proceed to necessary acts of administration, such as letting the property, but if they had to bring an action they must

1 P. 1. 9. 6; D. 4. 4. 13. pr.; C. 2. 23. 1, 2. 2 C. 2. 23. 2. 3 29. 2. 89. The surety had no claim against the minor; 4. 4. 13. C. 2. 23, 1, which says the contrary, is probably interp., Guarneri-Citati, *Misc. Eseg.* 76. 4 Clearly classical. *Ante*, § ccxxxv. 5 Ramadier, *Missio in bona rei servandae causa*. Apart from the cases specially provided for by the Edict or legislature the magistrate might apparently give *m. i. p.* by virtue of his *imperium*, *causa cognita*, where circumstances required it. Older than *l. Aebutia*?, Jobbé-Duval, *cit.* 177. 6 2. 1. 4; 50. 1. 26. 7 Lenel, *E.P.* 421. 8 *Ante*, p. 645. 9 41. 2. 3. 23; *non possessionem sed custodiam rerum*.

appoint a *curator*[1]. They had an *actio in factum* against one who prevented them from getting control of items of the estate[2]. They were liable for *dolus*[3]. They had rights to contribution for proper expenses[4], the actions between the creditors being *in factum*[5]. The existence of a *curator* did not affect this except that where there was one, there was in general no obligation on the creditors themselves to administer[6].

M. in bona in the case of *adrogatus* and woman *in manu*[7].

M. in bona eius qui vindicem dedit[8].

M. in possessionem of *pupillus* whose *tutor* has failed to provide sustenance. It was *rei servandae causa,* giving a right to *possessio.* A *curator* was appointed with limited administration; he might sell what must be sold. It was post-edictal, created by Severus and Caracalla[9].

These cases cover the whole estate of the person affected; there was another group, mostly connected with succession, in which it was a whole estate, but not necessarily the whole estate of the other party.

M. in possessionem dotis conservandae causa. Little is known of this as it was rendered obsolete by Justinian's provision of a right of hypothec[10]. It was a decree giving the widow, not *possessio* with interdicts, but merely custody of her deceased husband's property to secure her *dos.* She had a right of administration, could take rents, and sell "*moventia,*" and must allow all receipts against *dos* and interest[11].

M. in possessionem ex Edicto Hadriani[12]. Where there was a will formally valid but alleged to be *ruptum* or *irritum*, or a substitute claimed to be entitled, the *scriptus heres* could claim, within a year[13], to be given possession of what was possessed by the deceased, pending the decision, provided the will had been formally proved. Justinian tells us that the aim was to secure the tax on inheritances. Nothing is known of the position of the *heres*, but, as he paid the tax, he must have had a power of administration. Justinian practically abolished it[14].

M. in possessionem ventris nomine. The Edict provided that, where a woman was shewn to be pregnant of a child, who, if born, would be *suus heres* of the deceased, the "*venter*" could have *missio in possessionem,*

1 42. 5. 14. pr. 2 43. 4. 1; de Francisci, *Azioni pen.* 77. 3 42. 5. 9. pr. 4 42. 5. 9. 4. 5 42. 5. 9. pr. 6 The *magister* had only to attend to the *venditio bonorum.* G. 3. 79. His appointment did not dispense the creditors from administering. A *curator* was appointed if an action was to be brought or defended and probably wherever the matter was likely to involve delay, as in the case of a pupil. Apparently also if it was necessary to sell individual assets (26. 10. 7. 2; 42. 5. 14. pr.). But there is obscurity about the various cases of *curatio bonorum.* It does not seem that the *missi* themselves, apart from *curator*, had any power of selling fruits. Ramadier, *op. cit.* 98 *sqq.* 7 *Ante*, p. 399. 8 *Ante*, p. 631. 9 26. 10. 7. 2; Inst. 1. 26. 9. 10 *Ante*, p. 110. 11 Lenel, *E.P.* 303, cites, as referring to it, 6. 1. 9; 44. 3. 15. 4; 46. 3. 48; 50. 1. 26. 1; C. 7. 72. 8. 12 C. 6. 33; Lenel, *E.P.* 363. 13 P. 3. 5. 16. 14 C. 6. 33. 3.

a *curator* being appointed[1]. There was an interdict[2]. The *curator* might be simply to the "*venter*," in which case the creditors had custody of the estate, or to the *bona* also, with the ordinary powers of administration[3]. The woman was entitled to maintenance out of the estate, with no duty to account even though no successor was born alive[4]; it was more important that the child should be secured than that the estate should reach the other person entitled without diminution[5]. This was real *possessio*; it was in fact *bonorum possessio*, but "*decretalis*[6]."

M. in possessionem ex Carboniano edicto. Also *bonorum possessio decretalis*[7]. Where it was alleged that an *impubes* set up as *heres* was not entitled, because he was, e.g., a supposititious child, he was given *b. possessio* under this edict, with the normal results provided *satisdatio* was given, the decision being ordinarily deferred till he was *pubes*[8]. By juristic inference from the last case he was entitled to maintenance in any event out of the estate, without account[9].

M. in possessionem curatoris furiosi heredis. Also *b. p. decretalis*[10]. Where a *furiosus* was made *heres*, neither he nor his *curator* could claim ordinary *b. possessio*[11], but, on application, he or his *curator*, or if neither of them applied, those entitled in his absence, could get possession with ordinary powers[12], until he became *capax* or died, when normal *b. p.* could be given accordingly. He was presumably entitled to maintenance in the meantime[13]. Justinian abolished the system, and provided that a *curator* could apply for ordinary *b. p.* for the *furiosus*, the grant becoming void if the *furiosus* died still insane or repudiated it on reaching sanity[14].

M. in possessionem si heres suspectus non satisdabit. The rules of *bonorum separatio* contemplated a *heres* clearly insolvent[15], but apart from this, if the creditors could shew that the solvency of the *heres* was doubtful, they might, *causa cognita*, claim security, and, failing this, *m. in possessionem* of the *hereditas*, and proceed in due course to *bonorum venditio*[16].

M. in possessionem, in *hereditatis petitio*, if the possessor evaded process. It was of the *hereditas* and thus differed from the ordinary *missio in possessionem* of a defendant "*latitans*"—that was over all his goods.

1 37. 9. 1. 2, 5. Rescript of Hadrian in case of dispute, h. t. 1. 14. 2 43. 4. 3. 2. 3 37. 9. 1. 17. 4 37. 9. 1. 19. 5 37. 9. 1. 2, 3, h. t. 3. 6 38. 15. 2. 2–4; *ante*, p. 398. *A. in f.* against the woman if she transferred possession to anyone else, *dolo malo* (25. 5. 1), de Francisci, *Azioni pen.* 32. 7 37. 10. 1. pr.; *ante*, p. 398. 8 In the interest of the child the Praetor might authorise immediate hearing, 37. 10. 3. 5. The child must also have obtained ordinary *b. p.* (37. 10. 3. 15–4), otherwise other claims could come in. Niedermeyer, *Z.S.S.* 1930, 78. 9 37. 10. 5. 2, 3. 10 37. 3. 1. 11 *Ib.* 12 37. 3. 1, *med.* 13 Arg. from preceding cases. 14 C. 5. 70. 7. Change slight in effect: no need of *decretum*, Girard, *Man.* 927. An inventory must be made. Similar provisions applied to other gifts by will, h. l. 7. Another possible case of *b. p. decretalis*, *ante*, p. 312. 15 *Ante*, p. 317. 16 42. 5. 31. pr.–3.

The present rule is due to Pius[1]. The *missus* took the fruits and kept them, thus putting pressure on the other party.

M. in possessionem where the question whether there would be a *heres* was "*diu incertum.*" The decree issued only "*causa cognita*": if necessary it might authorise the appointment of a creditor as *curator*[2].

M. in possessionem legatorum servandorum causa. If a legacy or *fideicommissum* was, by reason of condition, term or other cause, not immediately paid, the beneficiary might claim security from the *heres*, and if this was refused, *possessio* of the *hereditas*[3]. The main rules have been stated[4]. The chief effect was to impose on the legatee a duty to preserve the assets, and to give him a sort of pledge which prevented the *heres* from creating rights which should take priority of his[5]. He had an interdict, and[6], in later law, the possession might be enforced by officers of court[7]. A further right created by Caracalla, under which one whose claim was clear, and who had not received payment or security, could after six months' notice enter into possession of the goods of the *heres*, applied, till Justinian, only to fideicommissaries.

There remain cases of *missio in possessionem* of specific things.

M. in possessionem in rem of the fideicommissary. If the *heres* sold property of which there was a *fideicommissum* the fideicommissary could get *m. in possessionem* of it against a buyer with notice of the trust[8], and we are told that this would be enforced "*potestate praetoris,*" an officer of court actually carrying out the order[9]. The text is not above suspicion; in any case this was exceptional. Justinian abolished the institution calling it a "*tenebrosissimus error*"; we know little of its working[10].

M. in possessionem damni infecti causa[11], where damage to a man's property was threatened by the ruinous state of that of his neighbour. The original remedy was *legis actio*[12], but this was practically superseded by praetorian machinery[13]. On application, notice and other formalities[14], the Praetor would order security against the damage (*stipulatio praetoria*[15]): if this was not given, a decree "*in possessionem ire*" would issue[16]. This merely entitled the aggrieved person to go on the land without ejecting the owner[17]; apparently it might, by delegation, be issued by a municipal magistrate[18]. It did not confer *possessio*, but there was an *actio in factum* if it was resisted[19]. If the owner of the ruinous tenement persisted in refusing security or putting the matter right, a second decree

1 42. 4. 7. 19. 2 42. 4. 8; h. t. 9. pr., 3, 4. 3 36. 3. 1, 13; 36. 4 *passim.* 4 *Ante*, p. 348. 5 36. 4. 5. 22, 11. 1. 6 43. 4. 3. pr.; Lenel, *E.P.* 455. 7 36. 4. 5. 27. 8 P. 4. 1. 15. 9 43. 4. 3. pr. 10 C. 6. 43. 1; h. t. 3. 2. 11 Bonfante, *Corso*, 2. 1, ch. XVI; Scialoja, *Proprietà*, 388. 12 *Ante*, p. 623. 13 G. 4. 31. 14 39. 2. 4. 5. 15 G. 4. 31. 16 39. 2. 4. 1. 17 See 39. 2. 4. 4. 18 39. 2. 4. 3. 19 39. 2. 4. 2.

might be issued by a magistrate with *imperium*, giving the actual right of *possessio*[1]. This appears to have conferred praetorian ownership, excluding the old owner and ripening to civil ownership by *usucapio*[2], but there were provisions protecting the rights of third parties[3].

CCXLVI. *Stipulationes Praetoriae*[4]. Verbal contracts, not voluntary, but forced on a party to a dispute by the Praetor, and giving an ordinary action if the promise was not kept. Refusal to make the promise was dealt with differently in different cases; we have already seen the use of these stipulations in procedure and how refusal was dealt with[5]. Apart from procedure the principal cases are:

Damni infecti. As we have seen refusal led to *missio in possessionem*. It was in the discretion of the magistrate whether the undertaking should be by promise or by surety[6].

Operis novi nuntiatio. If work was being done or about to be done to land, such as to injure a neighbour's land, e.g. by causing a flow of water[7] or a smoke nuisance[8], or to interfere with his rights, e.g. light[9], the neighbour after notice on the spot might bring the owner before the Praetor[10]. If a *prima facie* case was shewn the Praetor ordered a *promissio*, normally by surety, not to do the act, the words being so framed that there was no liability if the work was lawful[11]. If the promise was refused there was an interdict[12] or in some cases an *actio in factum*[13].

Collatio bonorum vel dotis, already considered[14]. The promise was with

1 39. 2. 4. 4. 2 39. 2. 5. pr., 12. No doubt even the second decree will be nullified if the person liable falls into line before the *usucapio* is complete. *Arg.* h. t. 44. 1. 3 39. 2. 5, 10 *sq.* The security was against damage usually within a certain time and was renewable, h. t. 13. 15–15. 1. The interdict in 43. 4. 4. pr. is presumably available only after the second decree. *Arg.* 39. 2. 4. 2. 4 Lenel, *E.P.* 514. We are told that praetorian stipulations "*instar actionum habent*" (16. 2. 10. 3; 44. 7. 37), i.e. a man is entitled to these in certain circumstances, under the Edict, just as he may be entitled to an action; their content is determined by the Edict (or Praetor, 46. 5. 1. 10, 9), so that he is, if the circumstances entitling him arise, in much the same position as if he had applied for an action, the compulsory *stipulatio* providing the *intentio* for his action. Distinction between *stip. praetoria, iudicialis, communis, ante*, p. 438. Another classification, 46. 5. 1. 5 *Ante*, §§ CCXVI, CCXL. *Iudicatum solvi, pro pr. litis et v., de rato*, etc. 6 39. 2. 13. 1, 30, etc. In general, if on his own land, promise suffices, if *in alieno, satisdatio* needed, h. t. 7. pr., etc. An interpolated text makes the promise binding on alienees of the property, 39. 2. 24. 1 a. 7 *Actio aquae pluviae arcendae*, where the work is already done, *ante*, p. 597. Other remedies where the work has been done, 39. 1. 1. 8 *Arg.* 8. 5. 8. 6. 9 39. 1. 5. 9. Not positive servitudes, h. t. 14. 10 39. 1. 1, 5. 2. 11 Lenel, *E.P.* 549; D. 39. 1. 7, 8. 3. 12 39. 1. 20. pr. 13 39. 1. 20. 8. Machinery uncertain, the compilers having altered the texts. *Nuntiatus* could apply for remission of the notice (D. 43. 25). This seems normally to have been a *remissio* except so far as the *nuntians* had a right of prohibition (39. 1. 1. pr. or on giving security—here the *remissio* was complete, 43. 24. 7. 2), but the subsequent procedure is disputed. See for principal views and a hypothesis, Martin, *Études Girard*, 1. 123 *sqq.*, and for full account, especially of *remissio*, Bonfante, *Corso*, 2. 1, ch. XVII. See also Berger, P.-W. s.v. *Interdictum*, col. 1670. 14 *Ante*, p. 325.

surety[1]. If it was refused the remedy was refusal of *bonorum possessio* or of further proceedings under it[2].

Under the *l. Falcidia*[3]. If it was possible that a legacy would have to be cut down, a promise with surety, to refund proportionately, if necessary, could be exacted. If refused, action on the legacy was denied. Similar rules were in practice applied to *fideicommissa*[4].

Eviction of the *hereditas*. The Praetor might, *causa cognita*, require a promise, with surety[5], to restore a legacy if this occurred[6]. Refusal involved denial of action on the legacy[7], and if it was inadvertently paid, without security, there was *condictio* for the security[8].

Usufruct and similar rights[9]: the person entitled must give security for proper use, and for restoration on expiry of the right. The rules were similar to those in the last case[10].

Legatee against *heres*, etc. We have seen that security could be required, with surety[11]. Refusal involved *m. in possessionem*.

Rem salvam pupillo fore. This and the means of enforcement have been considered[12].

Satisdatio secundum mancipium, a problematical case[13].

CCXLVII. INTERDICTS[14]. These were in many ways the most important of the specially praetorian remedies and probably the oldest. An Interdict was an order of the magistrate issued on application and giving rise to further proceedings if disregarded. In early times it may have been enforced by the magistrate, but, as we know it, it was the initial step in an ordinary piece of litigation, with special formalities. It was in form praetorian and was, in most cases, set forth in the Edict, but the right which it protected was not necessarily praetorian. There were many rules of the civil law for breach of which no action was given, but enforcement was left to the *imperium* of the magistrate. This was the function of most of the interdicts which related to public interests, e.g. those for the protection of public ways and places[15]. Many private rights were similarly protected. The XII Tables contained a clause entitling a man to enter his neighbour's land to gather fruits which had fallen over the boundary. This was enforced by the interdict *de glande legenda*[16], and there were others[17]. How the order was at first enforced is unknown, but probably, from very early times, it was, as in later law, by *sponsiones*. These and, no doubt, many other interdicts, existed before the Praetor began to issue general edicts. This is a fact which must be borne in mind,

1 37. 6. 1. 9. 2 37. 6. 2. 8, 3. 3 *Ante*, p. 342. 4 35. 3. 1. pr., 3. 1, 6. 5 35. 3. 4. pr. 6 *Ib.*; h. t. 8. 7 *Arg.* 35. 2. 53. 8 35. 3. 3. 10. 9 *Ante*, p. 270. 10 See 7. 9. 7. 11 *Ante*, p. 727. 12 *Ante*, p. 152. 13 See Lenel, *E.P.* 546. 14 Ubbelohde, *Die Interdicte*; Berger, P.-W., s.v. *Interdictum*. 15 D. 43. 7–14. 16 43. 28; Girard, *Textes*, 17. 17 E.g. *de mortuo inferendo*, Lenel, *E.P.* 458; *si arbor...impendebit*, *ib.* 487, etc.

since it helps to explain some of the peculiarities of the interdict. The Praetor is issuing an order based on *imperium*: he is not *ius dicens*, and does not use the words "*do, dico, addico*." Hence an interdict might issue on a *dies nefastus* and the proceedings *in iure* were not confined to "*rerum actus*," i.e. the days available for judicial business, which exclude the time of public games and harvests[1].

The account in Gaius suggests that the interdict was a provisional remedy, i.e. that it and its dependent procedure did not finally settle the question at issue but merely determined which of two parties was to be plaintiff and which defendant in some litigation of the ordinary kind in contemplation. This is not far from the truth for possessory and quasi-possessory interdicts, and, in relation to two of these, *uti possidetis* and *utrubi*[2], it is evidently their purpose as they are known to us in the classical law. But it is not true of many other interdicts, of *de glande legenda*, or of the many interdicts which have nothing to do with possession. This has been well illustrated by a contrast[3]. If a man was actually enjoying a way over land and was interfered with by the owner, *X*, he could get the interdict *de itinere*, forbidding the interference and practically compelling *X*, if he wished to stop the enjoyment, to bring his *actio negatoria*[4], in which the question whether there really was a right of way would be finally settled[5]. Nothing could be more provisional. If however a man was enjoying a right of way and wished to repair the path, but was prevented from so doing, he could get an interdict forbidding the interference, but, to succeed under it, he must prove that he had a legal right to repair the way. There is nothing provisional about this[6]. The ordinary possessory interdicts, being fully described by Gaius, are better known to us than others, and, as they were provisional, it is easy to fall into the mistake of supposing that the provisional character is due to something inherent in interdicts. In fact it has nothing to do with their nature; the provisional character is in the right of possession. So soon as the Praetor had resolved that peaceable *de facto* enjoyment should not be interfered with except by legal process, he had created provisional rights, and the protection would have had the same provisional character whether it were by interdict, as it was in classical law, or by possessory action, without previous issue of an interdict, as it was under Justinian.

CCXLVIII. Interdicts were very numerous. Of many we know the form, at least approximately[7]. Of others we know only that they existed,

1 Wenger, *Zpr.* 237; Wlassak, P.-W. s.v. *Actus rerum*. 2 *Post*, § CCXLIX. 3 Accarias, *Précis*, 2. 1217. 4 *Ante*, p. 676. 5 43. 19. 1. 6 43. 19. 3. 11. For other such interdicts, Ubbelohde, *op. cit.* 1. 170. He holds that about half the known interdicts are definitive—among them many relating to private land. But in many of the cases the evidence is insufficient. 7 Lenel, *E.P.* 446 *sqq.*, where the known interdicts are collected.

and no doubt there were many more of which we know nothing. Interdicts can be classed in many ways[1] of which the most clear and exhaustive is into Exhibitory, Restitutory and Prohibitory[2].

Exhibitory interdicts. Orders to produce a person or thing the subject of dispute, ending with the word "*exhibeas*." Most of the few known interdicts of this type dealt with rights over persons. Thus the interdict "*quem liberum*," for the case in which a freeman was alleged to be wrongfully detained, ran: "*quem liberum dolo malo retines exhibeas*[3]." Similar were those for the production of children or freedmen alleged to be wrongly detained[4], and, though this was later than the Edict of Julian, one for a wife[5]. In the case of wife and children the production would be followed if necessary by another interdict of the prohibitory type, *de liberis ducendis, de uxore ducenda*[6], ordinary actions being unsuitable. For property the interdict was usually not needed, as the *actio ad exhibendum*[7] sufficed, but there was at least one interdict for production of property, i.e. that *de tabulis exhibendis* for the case of a will alleged to be wrongly suppressed[8]. There would be difficulty in the *actio ad exhibendum*, since till the contents of the will were known it was uncertain who had a right to it. If it was the will of a living man, the interdict did not apply, but the *actio ad exhibendum* did, because he was the owner[9].

Restitutory interdicts. These interdicts, which were numerous, were essentially orders to restore or undo something done contrary to law, ending with the word "*restituas*[10]." Many of them dealt with public rights such as those ordering an end to be put to interferences with *solum publicum, sacrum, sanctum*, public ways, rivers, etc., e.g. "*quod in flumine publico ripave eius immissum habeas si ob id aliter aqua fluit quam priore aestate fluxit, restituas*[11]." Others dealt with private rights, e.g. the interdict *de precario* for restoration of what was given *in precario*[12], the *interdictum fraudatorium* to set aside transactions in fraud of creditors[13], the interdict *quod vi aut clam*, which ran: "*quod vi aut clam factum est, qua de re agitur, id, si non plus quam annus est cum experiendi potestas est, restituas*[14]," and some possessory interdicts with which we shall deal later,

1 Berger, *cit.*, and *Z.S.S.* 1915, 176. 2 G. 4. 140–142; Inst. 4. 15. 1. 3 43. 29. 1. pr. 4 43. 30. 1. pr.; G. 4. 162; Inst. 4. 15. 1. 5 43. 30. 2. 6 43. 30. 2, 3. pr. 7 *Ante*, p. 547. 8 43. 5. 1. pr. 9 43. 5. 1. 10. 10 Ubbelohde, *cit.* 1. 195 *sqq.* 11 43. 12. 1. 19. *Interdicta popularia* (43. 8. 2. 34). Measure of damages, Ubbelohde, *cit.* 1. 47 *sqq.* 12 43. 26. 2. pr.; *ante*, p. 524. 13 42. 8. 10. pr.; *ante*, p. 596. 14 43. 24. See Lenel, *E.P.* 482. Available where anyone has done an act, secretly or by force (words construed very freely, e.g. a word of protest makes the act "*vi*," 43. 24. 1. 5 *sqq.*), by which harm is caused to the soil, or buildings or the like, permanently part of it. It is indifferent where the act was done (though most of the texts deal with acts done on the injured land) or that the act itself was lawful: the conditions in which it was done make it a wrong. The interdict is *annua*. As in the other cases in this group Justinian's treatment of the texts makes the matter somewhat obscure; *ante*, p. 596.

e.g. *quam hereditatem* and its congeners[1] (*quod legatorum*[2], *quorum bonorum*[3]) and *unde vi*[4].

Prohibitory interdicts, the most numerous class. These interdicts forbade some act and usually ended with "*veto*" or "*vim fieri veto*," where they prohibited interference with some act of enjoyment, but some of them, e.g. that forbidding interference with public rivers, had, according to Lenel, a different form. This interdict he states as: "*ne quid in flumine publico ripave eius facias, neve quid in flumine publico neve in ripa eius immittas quo statio iterve navigio deterior sit fiat*[5]." Many prohibitory interdicts dealt with interference with enjoyment of public ways and rivers, such as that last mentioned, the group of prohibitory interdicts dealing with *loca publica, sacra, sancta*, etc.[6] (which ran parallel with those ordering restitution in case of past interference and with others forbidding interference with persons repairing them[7]) and others[8]. Some dealt with similar interferences with private ways and the like[9], of which that *de itinere* may be taken as an example: "*quo itinere quo de agitur, hoc anno nec vi nec clam nec precario ab illo usus es quominus ita utaris vim fieri veto*[10]." Others enforced ancient rules affecting relations of adjoining owners[11]. Others ordered the handing over of a child (later a wife) unjustly detained[12]. Others dealt with rights of burial[13], others were part of the procedure under *operis novi nuntiatio*[14]. One dealt with interference with removal, by a tenant, of a slave not subject to lien for rent[15], and there were also many possessory interdicts which we shall have to consider. According to Gaius these prohibitory interdicts were called Interdicts, in a narrow sense, the other groups being also called *Decreta*[16].

Before passing to other classifications we must note that the peremptory form of interdicts masks two characteristics, which will be considered more in detail in connexion with the procedure under them. The interdict stated precisely the circumstances in which the duty arose, so that it was a conditional order, as can be seen by examining those set out above. Further, the peremptory form does not indicate any direct coercive process of the Praetor. The later proceedings, in case of dispute, were, after certain preliminaries, merely ordinary actions resulting in a *condemnatio* or *absolutio* with the usual characteristics.

CCXLIX. Interdicts are also classified as Non Possessory and

1 *Post*, p. 736. 2 *Ante*, p. 390. 3 *Ante*, p. 389. 4 43. 16. 1. pr. 5 43. 13. 1. pr.; Lenel, *E.P.* 460. 6 43. 6 *sqq*. 7 43. 11. 8 *de via publica*, 43. 10; *de cloacis*, 43. 23. 9 *De fonte*, 43. 22; *de fonte reficiendo*, 43. 22. 1. 10; *de itinere privato*, 43. 19; *de itinere privato reficiendo*, 43. 19. 3. 11; *de aqua*, 43. 20; *de rivis*, 43. 21, etc. 10 43. 19. 1. pr. 11 *De glande legenda*, 43. 28, *de arboribus caedendis*, for interference with one who cuts away trees overhanging his land, 43. 27. Both enforce rules in the XII Tables. 12 *De liberis ducendis, de uxore ducenda*, 43. 30. 2, 3. 13 *De mortuo inferendo, de sepulchro aedificando*, 43. 1. 2. 1. 14 *Ante*, p. 728. 15 *De migrando*, 43. 32. 16 G. 4. 140; Inst. 4. 15. 1.

Possessory. The latter are much the most important in private law, but the different types of non possessory interdicts already mentioned need a few remarks. Some were for the protection of private rights, not dependent on possession, of which class *de glande legenda* is an example. Others were so far private that they dealt with the prevention of the enjoyment by a particular person of a public right. Such was the interdict: "*ut via publica uti liceat*[1]." Others were simply for the protection of public rights, e.g. that for preventing interference with, or damage to, a public way. Of this interdict we are told that it aimed at *utilitas publica* and that it was *populare*, i.e. could be brought by anyone[2], but the mode of enforcement here was the same as in private interdicts.

Possessory interdicts might be Single or Double[3]: the nature of the distinction will appear in discussion of the procedure. They break into three groups, *adipiscendae*, *retinendae* and *recuperandae possessionis causa*[4] (with a group, mixed, or double, in another sense in that they might be either *adipiscendae* or *recuperandae possessionis causa*)[5]. They are the primary remedy for the provisional right of *possessio*[6]. Besides the true possessory interdicts there were others in modified form for the analogous protection necessary for the so-called quasi-possessory rights[7] arising in connexion with *res incorporales*, e.g. usufruct.

(i) *Adipiscendae possessionis causa.* These, as their name shews, were the machinery for obtaining possession, used by one entitled to it who had not yet possessed. The most important was the interdict *quorum bonorum* for the enforcement of *bonorum possessio*[8]. Closely connected with it was *quod legatorum*, by which *bonorum possessor* gained possession from one who held the property against his will on the pretext, true or not, of being a legatee under the will[9]. Others were:

Interdictum sectorium, the means by which the buyer of the estate of a debtor to the *fiscus*, usually in cases of forfeiture, could gain possession of what was in the hands of third persons[10].

Interdictum Salvianum, to enforce the landlord's hypothec for rent[11].

Interdictum possessorium. One of the remedies of the *bonorum emptor* in *bonorum venditio*. Little is known of it. The name is not official[12].

1 43. 1. 2. 1. 2 43. 8. 2. 2, 2. 34. 3 G. 4. 156, 160; Inst. 4. 15. 7. 4 G. 4. 143; Inst. 4. 15. 2. 5 43. 1. 2. 3 *in f.*; Vat. Fr. 92; *post*, p. 735. 6 *Ante*, § LXXII. 7 E.g. 43. 17. 4; 43. 18. As to terminology, *ante*, pp. 197, 261. 8 43. 2. 1; *ante*, p. 389. According to Lenel, it ran (*E.P.* 452): "*Quorum bonorum ex edicto meo illi possessio data est, quod de his bonis pro herede aut pro possessore possides, possideresve si nihil usucaptum esset quodque dolo malo fecisti uti desineres possidere, id illi restituas.*" 9 43. 3. 1. 2; Vat. Fr. 90. Some texts give this interdict to the *heres* as such (C. 8. 3. 1; D. 35. 2. 1. 11, 26. pr.; 46. 3. 40). It is now generally held that the texts are interpolated; *contra*, Lotmar, *Z.S.S.* 1910, 129. A legislative change after A.D. 200 is possible, on which view C. 8. 3. 1 would be genuine. See Lenel, *E.P.* 453; *Mél. Girard*, 2. 63; Perrot, *Ét. Girard*, 1. 171. 10 G. 4. 146. 11 *Ante*, p. 475. 12 G. 4. 145.

Interdictum fraudatorium. One of the means of setting aside acts in fraud of creditors[1]. There is no real authority for the name, and the compilers of the Digest have so confused the different remedies that little can be said of its rules[2].

(ii) *Retinendae possessionis causa*[3], so called as having the function of securing a possessor, whose title was disputed, in his actual holding, though in their working, as will shortly be seen, they might operate differently. There were two principal forms with variants, the double interdicts, *uti possidetis* and *utrubi*[4], the use of which, as we know them, was to determine which of two parties was to have possession, and the resulting advantageous position of defendant, in an impending real action, the burden of proof being on the plaintiff.

Uti possidetis, used in the case of land. In classical law it ran somewhat as follows: "*uti nunc eas aedes quibus de agitur nec vi nec clam nec precario alter ab altero possidetis quominus ita possideatis vim fieri veto*[5]." Thus the possession was adjudged to the actual possessor unless he had obtained it *vi clam* or *precario* from the other, in which case it was given to that other. In that case it did not, strictly, retain possession; no doubt the words producing this characteristic were not part of the primitive structure of the interdict.

Utrubi, used for moveables: "*utrubi hic homo quo de agitur maiore parte huiusce anni nec vi nec clam nec precario ab altero fuit, quominus is eum ducat vim fieri veto*[6]." Here the possession was adjudged to the party who had held it longer than the other in the past year, a difference of considerable importance[7]. The differences were gone under Justinian when both interdicts, i.e. the possessory actions which had taken their place, were governed by the rule of *uti possidetis*[8]. In reckoning the time that of predecessors in title was taken into account (*accessio possessionis*) probably by the Edict, as to *heres* and buyer, by *interpretatio* in other cases[9].

Besides these, there were accessory forms, such as *uti possidetis utile,* for usufruct[10] and no doubt *usus,* and the interdict *de superficiebus* modelled on *uti possidetis* for the case of *superficies*[11].

1 *Ante,* p. 596. 2 Lenel, *E.P.* 495. It is held by many writers that, notwithstanding G. 4. 144 *sqq.,* these interdicts are not properly called possessory. 3 G. 4. 148; Inst. 4. 15. 4. 4 *Ib.*; D. 43. 17; 43. 31. As to use of *uti possidetis* in later law against a mere trespasser who raises no counterclaim of right (43. 17. 3. 2–4), Girard, *Man.* 302. 5 43. 17. 1. pr.; G. 4. 160; Lenel, *E.P.* 470; Festus, s.v. *possessio.* 6 G. 4. 160; D. 43. 31. 1. pr. From the words "*hic homo*" it is inferred that the thing must be present. 7 G. 4. 151, 152. Important notably in connexion with the operation of *l. Cincia* on *donatio. Ante,* p. 254. 8 Inst. 4. 15. 4. 9 G. 4. 151; Lenel, *E.P.* 489. Many texts applying it to *usucapio* were originally written of *utrubi, ante,* p. 242. 10 43. 17. 4; Vat. Fr. 90. 11 43. 18. 1 pr.

(iii) *Recuperandae possessionis causa*[1]. These, as their name shews, were for recovery of possession of which one had been deprived.

De vi cottidiana[2]. One who had been turned out of possession, by force of an ordinary character (*non armata*) had this interdict to recover possession. It ran: "*unde in hoc anno tu illum vi deiecisti aut familia tua deiecit cum ille possideret quod nec vi nec clam nec precario a te possideret eo illum quaeque ille tunc ibi habuit restituas*[3]." This is very like *uti possidetis*, and would often be alternative to it. It was confined to dispossession from land by real force[4], and was brought by the person dispossessed against the dispossessor, a state of facts which would give *uti possidetis* too. It had the advantage that it covered not only the land but also "*quaeque ibi habuit*[5]," and, according to one view, the disadvantage that it created on recovery a new possession[6], while, it is said, that recovered by *uti possidetis* was regarded as the old possession[7]. And the limitation, "*hoc anno*," is not in *uti possidetis*.

De vi armata: "*unde tu illum vi hominibus coactis armatisve deiecisti aut familia tua deiecit, eo illum quaeque tunc ibi habuit restituas*[8]." There was no limitation to the year[9], at least till Justinian. The fact that the ejected person himself held *vi clam aut precario* from the ejector was no defence. In later law this clause disappeared altogether and the two interdicts were one, the interdict *unde vi*[10]. It is supposed that the interdicts *de vi* were older than *uti possidetis*, which would account for the overlapping[11].

De precario, the interdict by which an owner recovered from one to whom he had made a grant *in precario*[12]. It ran: "*Quod precario ab illo habes aut dolo malo fecisti ut desineres habere, qua de re agitur, id illi restituas*[13]."

Interdicta mixta (the name is not authoritative), also called *duplicia*[14]. They might have the effect of giving possession to one who had not possession before or of restoring possession to one who had had it before, so that they were *recuperandae* or *adipiscendae p. c.* according to the facts.

1 G. 4. 154; Inst. 4. 15. 6. 2 43. 16. 1. 3 Lenel, *E.P.* 465. 4 43. 16. 1. 3. Under Justinian a *naturalis possessor* has it, 43. 16. 1. 9, 10. But this probably means one not *in via usucapiendi*. 5 43. 16. 1. 33. 6 See 41. 3. 15. 2; 41. 4. 7, 4, shewing the possible effect on *usucapio*. 7 See however Appleton, *Propriété Prétorienne*, §§ 207, 208. 8 Lenel, *E.P.* 467. 9 See 43. 16. 3. 12; Lenel, *E.P.* 468. 10 43. 16. 1. pr. As to what is armed force, 43. 16. 3. 2 *sqq*. 11 The same may be true of an uncertainly evidenced interdict *de clandestina possessione*, Lenel, *E.P.* 469; Berger, P.-W. s.v. *Interdictum*, col. 1682. As to the so-called *interdictum momentariae possessionis* of later law and other late protections against violent dispossession, see Cuq, *Man.* 323. 12 43. 26; *ante*, p. 524. 13 Lenel, *E.P.* 486. 14 43. 1. 1. 1, 2. 3 *in f*. *Uti possidetis* and *utrubi* are *duplicia* in a sense much more important from the point of view of procedure. Berger, *Interdicta mixta*, shews that both names are Byzantine.

They were *quem fundum, quam hereditatem, quem usumfructum*, and perhaps *quam servitutem*[1]. Their use was this. In a real action the interim possessor must give security[2]. If he failed to do so this interdict issued, under which he would have to give it to the other if he in turn offered security. Lenel reconstructs it[3], hypothetically, as: "*quem fundum ille a te vindicare vult quem possides dolove malo fecisti quominus possideres si rem nolis defendere eoque nomine tibi satisdatum est aut per te stat quominus satisdetur restituas.*" The changes in the law of security in later law rendered these interdicts obsolete[4].

The same name might equally be given to other interdicts. Thus the interdict or interdicts "*ne vis fiat ei qui in possessionem missus est*" lay whether the holder refused to let possession be taken or ejected the *missus*[5], so that it was both *adipiscendae* and *recuperandae possessionis causa*[6].

CCL. The procedure under interdicts was somewhat complicated. The distinctions just stated do not for the most part greatly affect it, but we must bear in mind that between single and double interdicts, which is fundamental in the matter, and that between prohibitory and others which also has a certain bearing.

The procedure in single interdicts was simpler than that in double interdicts and will be first dealt with. Confining ourselves for the present to prohibitory interdicts we may take the case that *A* alleged that he had been in enjoyment of a certain right and that *B* had interfered with it. *A* would apply for an interdict and one would be issued to him, without discussion[7], in a form prohibiting any interference, but containing limiting words to shew that the prohibition did not apply unless the *de facto* enjoyment was such as the Praetor meant to protect. Thus in, e.g., *de itinere privato*, the form was: "I forbid force to be done by which *A* is prevented from enjoying that right of way which he has been

1 Ulp. Inst., Fr. 4 (Girard, *Textes*, 493); Vat. Fr. 92. 2 *Ante*, p. 711. 3 Lenel, *E.P.* 458. 4 *Ante*, p. 712. 5 43. 4. 1. 3; Lenel, *E.P.* 455, 469. *Ante*, p. 724 and Ubbelohde, *cit.* 1. 183 *sqq.* 6 Ulpian gives other classifications of interdicts. Some refer to the past, e.g. restitutory, others to the present, e.g. *uti possidetis*, 43. 1. 1. 2. Some are *annalia*, some *perpetua*, h. l. 4. Thus while most interdicts are *perpetua*, *unde vi* and others, having a penal character, are *annua*, e.g. 43. 4. 1. 8; 43. 16. 1. pr. Paul (43. 1. 2. 1) tells us that some are *divini iuris*, e.g. *ne quid in loco sacro fiat*, others *hominum causa*. Of the latter some are *publicae utilitatis*, others *privatae*. Of the last some are *iuris sui tuendi causa*, e.g. *de liberis exhibendis*, some *officii causa*, e.g. *de libero homine exhibendo*, others *rei familiaris causa*. Of these some raise the question of right, e.g. *de itinere reficiendo*. Others deal only with possession. He also tells us that some are noxal (perhaps interp., Biondi, *Act. noxales*, 78), e.g. *unde vi* and *quod vi aut clam*, h. t. 5 (Buckland, *Slavery*, 128); Ulpian also tells us that interdicts are *in rem scripta* but essentially *in personam* (h. t. 1. 3). The latter fact is obvious: the statement that they are *in rem scripta* seems to mean only that as standing forms in the Edict they cannot specify the person against whom they may be issued. 7 Some cases needed *causae cognitio*, e.g. 43. 13. 1. 6.

enjoying in the present year, his enjoyment not having been obtained from *B* by force or secretly or by permission[1]." The mention of a year had nothing to do with prescription. The question was not whether he had acquired the right by lapse of time, but whether there had been a peaceable enjoyment, so recent, and so full, as to raise a presumption of rightfulness such that the Praetor thought it ought not to be interfered with except by legal process.

If *A* was not interfered with the matter dropped. But if his right was really disputed, if *B* really intended to deny the right, and also thought that *A*'s enjoyment had not been such as satisfied all the requirements of the interdict, he would proceed to use some force in order to raise the question. The point was that if *B* acquiesced in the interdict, he would not be able to put a stop to *A*'s enjoyment except by bringing his *actio negatoria*, in which he would have the burden of proof[2]. If *B* used force and *A* proceeded under the interdict, and could not prove that he had been enjoying in the past year, to the necessary extent[3], or *B* proved that it was *vi clam aut precario* from him, *B* would win in the interdict and could disregard *A* altogether, obstructing his way, and leaving him either to abandon it or to bring an *actio confessoria*[4], in which he must prove his legal right to the servitude. If *A* proved the enjoyment and *B* failed to prove one of the defects, *A* would win in the interdict, and *B* must abandon his objections or bring his *actio negatoria*.

The force used by *B* would be merely formal, but enough to raise the issue, as it was disregard of the interdict. The parties went before the Praetor and the question was raised: had *B* disobeyed the interdict? The point, to be tried by a *iudex*, was raised in a noteworthy way, like that in real actions *per sponsionem*. *A* asked *B*: "Do you promise to pay me 10 if you have disobeyed the interdict[5]?" *B* answered: "I promise," and asked by way of *restipulatio*, "Do you promise me 10 if I have not disobeyed the interdict?" and *A* promised. The two stipulations were practically a bet. Each then proceeded to sue for the amount, i.e. two *formulae* for *c. certae pecuniae* were issued, one to *A*, one to *B*. Here three points must be noted:

(i) *B* had certainly disregarded the interdict; he may not have disobeyed it. If *A*'s enjoyment did not satisfy the requirements of the interdict, *B*'s acts were not a contravention of its terms, and *B* would win. He would be absolved in the *condictio* issued against him, while *A* would be condemned in the corresponding *condictio* brought by *B*.

1 43. 19. 1. pr. 2 Burden of proof in this case, *ante*, p. 676. 3 43. 19. 1. 4. On 30 days (43. 19. 1. 2), but this is probably due to Justinian. In classical law the *iudex* would require proof of substantial enjoyment within the last year. 4 *Ante*, p. 676. 5 G. 4. 165. This would not be the exact form, which might vary, *post*, p. 740.

(ii) *Exceptiones*[1]. The restrictive words in the interdicts themselves are called *exceptiones*[2], and apart from these it was possible for the Praetor to vary the words by introducing or omitting particular points to meet the equity of a particular case[3], and this may also be regarded as, in effect, inserting *exceptiones*. But as in any other actions, there might be *exceptiones* of the ordinary type in the resulting *formulae*[4] which would of course produce the same effect as elsewhere.

(iii) The whole duty being based on the Edict there was no liability except that which it stated. Each interdict was therefore drawn so as to express all the conditions on which the right which it protected was to depend[5], and the *iudex* had no need to look outside it to see exactly what had to be proved. Thus, in *quorum bonorum*, the claimant would not have to prove that he was entitled to keep the property, but, on the words of the interdict[6], he must shew that the goods were in the *bona* of the deceased, that he himself had a grant of *b. possessio*, that he was entitled to this grant at the time when he got it (*ex edicto*), and that they were now in the possession of the defendant, or would be but for his *dolus*. If he failed to prove any of these things there would be no duty "*restituere*" under the interdict[7]. Further the claimant would fail if the defendant shewed[8] that he held them under some claim other than *pro herede* or *pro possessore*. The importance of exact interpretation of a form of words is characteristic of the whole formulary system, and is shewn very clearly here. Interdicts were matter of careful drafting, to be reconsidered, if necessary, every year: the interdict "*unde vi*" is a good illustration. We have it in two forms, one from the time of Cicero, and one from Justinian, and we have traces of its form in classical law[9]. These forms differ materially.

If *A* failed in the action on the promise, he was condemned in the amount of the *sponsio*, and the matter was at an end. If, e.g., he had not been actually enjoying the servitude in the manner required by the interdict, and wished to make good his claim, he must bring *actio confessoria*. If, on the other hand, he won, a *formula* issued for a *iudicium secutorium*[10] for abstention from interference and damages in default. Whether there were damages for the force done between the issue of the interdict and the judgement is not clear. The form of the action is not known, and it has been suggested that in cases such as that of a right

1 See Ubbelohde, *cit.* 1. 457 *sqq.*, from whom the references are taken. 2 43. 19. 1. 11; 43. 24. 15. 5. 3 43. 13. 1. 6. 4 39. 1. 1. 10, *pacti conventi*; 43. 30. 1. 4, *rei iudicatae*; etc. 5 Even where, as in *de glande legenda*, the right was civil. 6 *Ante*, p. 733. 7 43. 2. 1. pr. 8 The burden of proof is on him, *Arg.* 5. 3. 13. pr. 9 *Pro Tull.* 19. 44; *pro Caec.* 19. 55; G. 4. 155; Vat. Fr. 93; D. 43. 16. 1. pr. 10 G. 4. 165. Name recorded only of the corresponding action in double interdicts, but as this has also a special name (*post*, § CCLI) it is likely that the name *secutorium* applied here as well.

of way the notion of restitution was inapplicable and that the *formula* was simply one for damages, while in those prohibitory interdicts which had to do with really possessory rights, such as those for the protection of *missi in possessionem*, it would be for restitution and only in default for damages[1]. There were no damages for the time before issue of the interdict; till then there was no duty. The view that there was no *arbitrium* for restitution in cases of interference with a right of way is connected with the opinion that there was no *arbitrium* in an ordinary *actio confessoria* in respect of them[2]. How the damages were assessed in such a case of interdict where no *restitutio* was ordered it is difficult to say[3].

If the interdict was not prohibitory, but restitutory or exhibitory, there was an alternative simpler process. After the formal act of disregard of the interdict, while the parties were in court, the defendant was entitled to refuse the *sponsiones* and demand an *arbiter*[4]. The effect would be that a *formula* would issue requiring restoration or production, as the case might be, with an *arbitrium* clause and a *condemnatio* in default of restitution. The substantial issue was the same as in the procedure *per sponsiones*, but raised in a different way. If the defendant left the court without calling for an *arbiter*, then and there, the system of *sponsiones* would be applied[5]. But the use of the *arbitrium* form did not make much difference in the law as we know it. It merely avoided the loss over the *sponsiones*[6], for even in cases tried by *sponsiones* an *arbitrium* clause would be inserted if the facts admitted of it[7]. Exactly why the alternative method was applied only in restitutory and exhibitory interdicts, which it may be remembered were the class also called *decreta*, is not clear[8]. It may perhaps be allied to the fact that they prescribe a positive act, and actual performance, such as was contemplated by the *arbitrium*, was more easily enforced here[9]. There are some prohibitory interdicts to which, as we have seen, it is possible that the *arbitrium* did not apply at all, and it may well be that it had no application at all to prohibitory interdicts in the earlier days of the interdict. The reason why the defendant preferred the *arbiter* is obvious: he avoided the risk of the *sponsiones* which, we are told, were not merely *praeiudiciales* but *poenales*, actually enforced[10]. The plaintiff ran the same risk, but does not appear to have had the same privilege.

1 If there was subsequent interference. *Arbitrium* in prohibitory interdicts generally, Lenel, *E.P.* 451. 2 Lenel, *E.P.* 193. 3 It does not seem that *iuramentum in litem* was admissible. 4 G. 4. 162 *sqq.* 5 G. 4. 164. 6 In early times the *sponsio* and the action on it may have been the last step, and the amount of the *sponsio* the real damages. The *sponsiones* gave civil actions and are older than the Praetor's power of creating actions. 7 G. 4. 165. 8 G. 4. 140. Gaius simply speaks of the *arbitraria formula* as a "*modestior via*," G. 4. 163. 9 In the ordinary possessory cases, where after issue of a prohibitory interdict there was an ouster, the *arbitrium* would obviously be applicable. 10 G. 4. 162, 168.

Two further observations must be made on single interdicts.

The issue in the *iudicium secutorium* was really decided in the litigation on the *sponsiones*, and the issue in each of the actions was the same. Thus it is probable that all the *formulae* were issued together.

It has been assumed in this account that the *sponsio* was on the question: has the interdict been disobeyed? But as the interdict failed if any one of its conditions was not satisfied, the task of the *iudex* might be considerably lighter. If, as would probably be often the case, only one of the points was really in dispute, the *sponsio* might be made to turn only on that point. Thus supposing the only doubt was whether the enjoyment had been by consent, the *sponsio* might be "Do you promise me 10 if I consented to your using the right of way?" Any other of the requirements might be embodied in the same way[1].

CCLI. The procedure in the double interdicts was more complex. There were essentially but two[2], *uti possidetis* and *utrubi*, with corresponding derivative forms for usufruct, *usus*, *superficies*[3], and, in later law, *emphyteusis*[4]. These interdicts were of a special character. As we know them in classical law, their purpose was to confirm one of two intending litigants in possession of the disputed property, so as to make him defendant in the coming real action, the burden of proof being therefore on the other, the plaintiff. The interdict was in terms addressed to both and directed whichever of them did not satisfy the conditions on which it protected actual enjoyment not to interfere with the other, if he did[5]. Thus there were practically two interdicts in one form of words. Hence the name, double interdicts, and complications in procedure. The conditions for *uti possidetis* were not quite the same as those for *utrubi*, as we have seen[6], but as there was no resulting difference in procedure it will suffice to deal with the former. Essentially it was an order to the following purpose: "I forbid force to be done by either of you whereby one of you is prevented from enjoying the land as he now does, not *clam vi aut precario* from the other."

If the parties meant to dispute the matter they used force against each other, a purely formal force (*vis ex conventu*[7]), but enough to be disregard of the interdict. They then made *sponsiones*[8] as before, with

1 In Cicero, *pro Caec.* 16. 45, the *sponsio* is on the question whether *vis* has been done "*contra edictum*," but these words bring in the whole interdict. 2 The "duplex" character attributed to *de aqua* (43. 20. 1. 26), where two persons both claim the right of use, and equally possible in many other cases, probably means merely that each will have an interdict. 3 43. 17. 4; 43. 18. 1. pr. 4 2. 8. 15. 1. 5 See the form, *ante*, p. 734. 6 *Ib.* 7 This expression, found in Cicero (*pro Caec.* 8. 22), does not seem technical: indeed it is not clear that as used by him it refers to this interdict. See Roby, *R.P.L.* 2. 514 *sqq.*; Ubbelohde, *Interdicte*, 1, 214 *sqq.* As to *deductio quae moribus fit*, Girard, *Man.* 1049. 8 G. 4. 166.

the important difference that, here, as either might have disobeyed the interdict there would be two bets involving four *stipulationes* and four *condictiones certae pecuniae*[1]. At this point another, rather accidental, complication steps in. The whole interdictal procedure would determine who was to be plaintiff, and who defendant, in a forthcoming real action. This was obviously an important issue. But the question arose, who was to keep the actual possession during trial of the interdict, a process which might take some time, since the facts necessary to its decision might not be easily got at. This not very important matter (no question of procedural importance was prejudiced by it) was simply dealt with. The opponents *X* and *Y* bid against each other for it. If *X* bid most it was given to him, and he then promised that if judgement in the interdict should eventually go for *Y*, he would give *Y* the amount of his bid. Hence a fifth *c. certae pecuniae*[2]. Sometimes this stipulation was omitted and when the possession was handed over to the highest bidder a *formula* for a *iudicium fructuarium* was given to the other, apparently for the value of the interim possession, i.e. the loss to him from not having had the interim possession, whatever that might amount to, in the event of his winning in the interdict. Apparently the lowest bidder might choose. If he chose the *iudicium fructuarium* the amount of the actual bid perhaps ceased to be of importance[3]. Some such alternative arrangement was convenient and even necessary in a case in which the interim possession was of uncertain value to one of the parties. He need not bid at all but would still retain the chance of recovering whatever the value of it might turn out to have been[4].

In addition to these *formulae* there would be the *iudicium secutorium*, called in this case *iudicium Cascellianum*[5], for the definitive transfer of the possession to the non-possessor if he should win in the interdict[6]. In this action he would recover not only the possession but also the interim fruits, so that, as Gaius tells us, the money recovered under the *iudicium fructuarium* or the *condictio fructuaria* was in effect a penalty[7].

Thus to each party were given two *condictiones certae pecuniae*, and to the party who did not get interim possession, either *condictio fructuaria*

1 G. 4. 166. 2 G. 4. 166 *sq.* 3 G. 4. 169. Exact content of this action not clear: it is consistent with the language of Gaius that, here too, what was recovered was the amount of the bid: "*de fructus licitatione agere.*" Possibly he might have *cond.* either for the amount of the bid or *incerti* for the value at his choice. For various views Ubbelohde, *Interdicte*, 2. 164 *sqq.*; Berger, *cit.* col. 1697. The text is imperfect and the crucial word "*similiter*" uncertain. 4 We are not told what happened if neither bid: presumably the thing remained with the holder and the *iudicium fructuarium* would lie, under which security had to be given, G. 4. 169. This also was called *iudicium secutorium*, G. 4. 169. 5 G. 4. 166; G. 4. 169. Cascellius was a magistrate of the age of Cicero, Roby, *Introd. to Digest*, CXXI. 6 It is issued to the litigant who has not interim possession: if the other wins in the *sponsio*, this *formula* is not wanted. 7 G. 4. 167.

or *iudicium fructuarium*, at his choice, and a final *iudicium secutorium* (*Cascellianum*). Here, as in single interdicts, the trial of one of the first *condictiones* determined all the questions material to the decision of all the actions, though questions of value, perhaps in the *iudicium fructuarium*, and certainly in the *iudicium Cascellianum*, would still remain open. All these *formulae* seem to have been issued together.

Here, too, disregard was not necessarily disobedience. Both parties disregarded the interdict, but it is clear that only one can have disobeyed it. Since one must have been in possession, for otherwise the proceedings would be absurd, it seems as if one must have disobeyed it, but there is difficulty. On the words of the interdict, it might seem on certain facts that neither had disobeyed. If, for instance, *X* held the property *precario* from *Y*, *Y* could not disobey, for the *possessio* by *X* was not within the terms of the interdict. And it is possible to contend that *X* cannot have disobeyed it, for *Y* did not possess at all. The matter is controverted, but it seems that in this case *X* had disobeyed the interdict. As against *X*, *Y* was still regarded as in possession[1].

The *sponsiones* were penal, actually enforced and their amount was not set off against the damages. Here arises the question: what determined the amount of the *sponsiones*? Could a plaintiff, sure of his case, fix them as he liked? Apparently the Edict contained a clause, only imperfectly known, which limited the *sponsiones* to an amount having some relation to the value of the right concerned, but exactly how we do not know. Possibly there was an oath[2].

These double interdicts were prohibitory, and thus the alternative method of *formula arbitraria*, without *sponsiones*, was not available. It is clear, however, that they were extremely well suited for an *arbitrium*, and that, as a matter of fact, the *formula* of the *iudicium Cascellianum* did contain such a clause[3]. This case therefore brings into strong relief the problem of the reason for the refusal of the *formula arbitraria* without *sponsiones* in prohibitory interdicts.

In the procedure of ordinary actions there was machinery by means of judgement in default, *actio in factum*, *missio in possessionem*, and the like[4], to deal with a defendant who disobeyed *in ius vocatio*, or failed to take the various steps involved in the defence of an action. As to what took the place of this in interdictal procedure our information, owing to the defective state of the MS. of Gaius, practically our sole authority, is unfortunately incomplete. In double interdicts, he tells us[5], when a

1 E.g. 41. 2. 17. pr.; 43. 17. 3. pr. This text adds that if two possess *in solidum*, but one holds *clam vi aut precario* from a third party, neither can win in the interdict against the other: both possess validly. Machelard, *Interdits*, 192 *sqq.*; Ubbelohde, *Besitzinterdicte*, 425. 2 Lenel, *E.P.* 472; Berger, *cit.* col. 1693. 3 G. 4. 166a *in f.* 4 *Ante*, § CCXVI. 5 G. 4. 170.

person against whom an interdict had been obtained refused to make the necessary *sponsiones*, or to take any of the other necessary procedural steps, there were *interdicta secundaria* by which he could be compelled to do so or, if he had possession, to abandon it to the other. We do not know if they applied also to single interdicts, or how they worked. Apparently, in the last resort, there must have been some direct intervention of the Praetor, perhaps *missio in possessionem* on the analogy of *stipulationes praetoriae*[1].

CCLII. We have seen that the issue of the interdict was followed by the issue of *formulae* in which the question was whether the duty declared in the interdict had been broken. The question arises, why, in view of this, the issue of the interdict was retained at all. The Praetor said, e.g. "I order you to remove the obstruction which you have put in the way which *A* was peaceably enjoying," an order which was followed, in a particular case, by steps leading up to a *formula* of which the gist was: "If it appears that *B* has obstructed a way of which *A* was in peaceable enjoyment, condemn him to pay or put it right." Instead the Edict might have said simply, "If anyone obstructs a way of which another is in peaceable enjoyment, I will give a *iudicium*," the nature of the necessary enjoyment being specified as it was in the interdict. By apt words the same issue might be raised in a more simple way without any departure from the provisional character of the proceeding. Why then was the issue of the interdict retained?

The answer seems to be historical. Interdicts existed before the standing Edict did[2], before the Praetor had begun directly to create actions, and they afforded an indirect means of doing so. The interdict was an order binding by virtue of the *imperium*[3], and before the Edict existed it could not be set out as a standing order: it had to be issued expressly in each case. After it had come to be stated in the perpetual Edict this ceased to be necessary; its preservation was a piece of conservatism. No doubt many of the known interdicts, or the germs of them, were incorporated as existing things into the Edict, and though there were many interdicts plainly later than the origin of the Edict[4], it is not surprising that the existing method was followed. Once embodied in the Edict as an integral part of it, and of the formulary system, their endurance was guaranteed so long as the formulary system lasted. With its disappearance they too were superseded. But the rights they had safeguarded were still protected. Instead of applying for an interdict,

1 See however Ubbelohde, *Interdicte*, 1. 295 *sqq.*, who thinks they operated like ordinary interdicts; Berger, *cit.* col. 1697. Saleilles (*Controversia possessionis*, §§ 64–66) thinks that the usual procedure was not to carry out the formalities under *uti possidetis*, but to utilise the *interdicta secundaria*.

2 Berger, *cit.* col. 1700.

3 G. 4. 139.

4 E.g. 43. 18.

the aggrieved person brought an action[1], in which the issue raised was the same as that in the *formula* issued in earlier days after disregard of the interdict. This is well exemplified in the case of *unde vi.* In the old system the interdict was issued in the form "*unde tu illum vi deiecisti* (etc.)...*vim fieri veto.*" In the Digest the rule was similar except that it was put in general impersonal form, and for the last three words were substituted the words "*iudicium dabo*[2]." The same development took place in all interdicts (though the words of the old interdictal form are used in most cases in the Digest[3]), and in relation to possessory interdicts, much the most important in private law, a system of possessory actions was developed, in which the issue was as in the old interdict, but the order itself was no longer issued[4].

We have seen that interdicts were not essentially provisional; possessory interdicts may be so described, but only because the right they protected was itself provisional: if it were not it would not be possession, but ownership. The true owner must always be able to recover from one who has no title but possession. Many considerations justify, and have produced in various legal systems, protection to a mere possessor: we need not here consider which of these were the cause of the Roman rules[5]. But there is one point which has led to controversy and may be mentioned. In the long run the mere possessor would have to yield to the owner. The *bonorum possessor sine re* might recover the thing from the *heres* by the interdict *quorum bonorum*, but he must ultimately give it up, if he was sued by *hereditatis petitio.* A bare possessor might win against the owner in *uti possidetis*, but the owner could regain his property by *vindicatio.* Why was he driven to this lengthy process? Why might not his ownership be pleaded in reply to, e.g., *uti possidetis*[6]? An *exceptio iusti dominii* would have served the purpose, and under such a plea he would have had to prove his title just as he would in *vindicatio.* The explanation may lie in a well-known characteristic of Roman procedure: *possessio* and *dominium* are distinct things[7], and the Romans did not like joining distinct issues in one *formula.* It was this for instance which made them so reluctant to admit set-off, *compensatio*, in *stricta iudicia*, and led them in classical times to drive the parties to *mutuae petitiones* even where the claims arose out of the same matter[8].

1 See rubric of D. 43. 1. 2 Lenel, *E.P.* 462; D. 43. 16. 1. pr. 3 E.g. D. 43. 2; 43. 6, etc. 4 E.g. 43. 16. 5 *Ante*, § LXXII. 6 Distinct from the question why possession was protected at all. It is maintained by Ubbelohde, *Besitzinterdicte*, 20, 97, 104, 430, etc., that *unde vi* (*cottidiana*) and *uti possidetis* were not available against an ousting *dominus*: i.e. that however the owner took it from the other he was not considered to have taken it *clam vi aut precario.* 7 41. 2. 12. 1: "*nihil commune habet proprietas cum possessione.*" 8 17. 1. 38. pr. See however *ante*, p. 693.

INDEX

(Figures in black type are principal references)